THE AMERICAN DEMOCRACY

THIRD EDITION ★★★ ELECTION EDITION

THE AMERICAN DEMOCRACY

THOMAS E. PATTERSON

Benjamin Bradlee Professor of Government and the Press
John F. Kennedy School of Government
Harvard University

Boston, Massachusetts Burr Ridge, Illinois Dubuque, Iowa
Madison, Wisconsin New York, New York San Francisco, California St. Louis, Missouri

McGraw-Hill

A Division of The ***McGraw-Hill*** *Companies*

THE AMERICAN DEMOCRACY

This book is printed on acid-free paper.

2 3 4 5 6 7 8 9 0 DOW DOW 9 0 9 8 7

ISBN 0-07-049128-3

This book was set in Palatino by GTS Graphics, Inc.
The editors were Lyn Uhl and David A. Damstra;
the designer was Joan E. O'Connor;
the production supervisor was Richard A. Ausburn.
The photo editor was Barbara Salz.
New drawings were done by Fine Line Illustrations, Inc.
R. R. Donnelley & Sons Company was printer and binder.

Cover photo credit:
Robert Shafer/Tony Stone Worldwide

Part opener credits:
Leif Skoogfors/Woodfin Camp
Jon Levy/Gamma Liaison
Jim Pickerell/FPG
James Schnepf/Gamma Liaison

Library of Congress Cataloging-in-Publication Data

ABOUT THE AUTHOR

Thomas E. Patterson is Benjamin Bradlee Professor of Government and the Press in the John F. Kennedy School of Government at Harvard University. He was previously distinguished professor of political science in the Maxwell School of Citizenship at Syracuse University. Raised in a small Minnesota town near the Iowa and South Dakota borders, he was educated at South Dakota State University and the University of Minnesota, where he received his Ph.D. in 1971.

He is the author of six books and dozens of articles, which focus primarily on the media and elections. His recent book, *Out of Order* (1994), received national attention when President Clinton said every politician and journalist should be required to read it. An earlier book, *The Mass Media Election* (1980), received a *Choice* award as Outstanding Academic Book, 1980–1981. Another of Patterson's books, *The Unseeing Eye* (1976), was recently selected by the American Association for Public Opinion Research as one of the fifty most influential books of the past half century in the field of public opinion.

His current research includes a five-country study of the news media's political role. His work has been funded by major grants from the National Science Foundation, the Ford Foundation, and the Markle Foundation.

TO MY CHILDREN,
ALEX
AND
LEIGH

CONTENTS IN BRIEF

CONTENTS

PART ONE FOUNDATIONS 1

SPEAKING TRUTH TO POWER

PART THREE GOVERNING INSTITUTIONS 321

APPENDIXES A-1

PREFACE FOR THE INSTRUCTOR

Anyone who writes an introductory American government text faces the challenge of bringing to life a vast amount of scholarship. Political scientists have developed a deep understanding of American government, but this knowledge exists as a set of more or less unrelated observations. When information is presented in this form in a text, fact is piled upon fact and list upon list, which is almost guaranteed to make politics a dull topic.

I have relied, instead, on a narrative form of presentation. Each chapter contains plenty of facts, but they are nearly always embedded in the context of a narrative theme. Research indicates that the narrative form is a superior method for teaching students a "soft" science such as politics. A narrative tells the reader why something is important and ties it to the rest of the discussion. Not only are narrative themes more likely to stick in the reader's mind than disconnected ideas, but they also combat the mental fatigue that invariably accompanies the reading of a lengthy textbook. When a text's material is compartmentalized, rather than integrated through narrative themes, the reader's experience is not unlike that of pouring through a recipe book. Lists of ingredients are less appetizing than food itself and a whole lot harder to ingest.

I have also written a tightly constructed book. My experience with teaching the introductory course suggests that many students find it difficult to grasp the essence of a chapter's argument if they read it a section at a time. Most chapters of this text can be read in an hour or less, and thus each reading assignment can reasonably consist of a full chapter.

A Broad Perspective

In writing this book, I rejected the impulse to impose a rigid framework on the analysis. The U.S. political system and scholarship on it are both remarkably pluralistic, and any attempt at orthodoxy distorts this reality. Accordingly, this text relies upon the several forms of analysis that have informed the work of political scientists, including the philosophical, historical, behavioral, legal, policy-analytic, and institutional. Each perspective has its strengths and its place in an explanation of American government.

Nevertheless, the book has a unifying core. The American political system is characterized by a few major tendencies, which are the key to understanding how the system operates. These tendencies include the following:

- An enduring set of political ideals that are the American people's common bond and a source of their political action.
- An extreme fragmentation of governing authority that is based on an elaborate system of checks and balances and that has far-reaching implications for the exercise of power and the making of public policy.
- A great many competing interests that are a result of the nation's great size, population diversity, and economic complexity.
- A strong emphasis on individual rights and judicial action that is a consequence of the nation's political traditions and social-economic experiences.
- A sharp separation of the political and economic spheres that has the effect of placing many economic issues outside the reach of political majorities.

These tendencies are introduced in the first chapter and are woven into subsequent chapters at various points. If students soon forget much of the information contained in this book, as they invariably will, they may at least retain an awareness of the deep underpinnings of the American political system.

INNOVATIONS IN THE THIRD EDITION

The response to the first two editions of this book was very positive. The text has been adopted for use at more than 400 American colleges and universities. Moreover, a sample survey conducted by the publisher indicates that the great majority of instructors who utilize the text one year also adopt it the next.

Although the first two editions were favorably received, I have chosen to revise the book substantially for this new edition. Students today are no less interested in politics than in previous years, but many of them are less accustomed to reading. Several instructors who use this text regularly suggested a reduction in the book's length. Accordingly, I set a goal of a 20 percent reduction in the text's length from the second edition, a reduction achieved without a loss of substantive content through a combination of editing and consolidation of several chapters.

The order in which subjects are discussed has not significantly changed from the second edition, but this new edition contains twenty-one chapters as compared with the twenty-seven chapters included in the last edition. Specifically, the separate chapters on limited and representative government in the second edition have been combined in this edition into a single chapter entitled "Constitutional Democracy." The second-edition chapter on economic rights has been eliminated and the information it contained has been integrated into this edition's chapters on equal rights and social welfare policy. The material from the second edition on vote choice has been distributed among the third-edition chapters on political participation and elections. Finally, the two chapters each on interest groups, the bureaucracy, and the judiciary in the second edition have been consolidated into a single chapter on each of these topics. The net result is that the third edition is closer in length to 600 pages than to the more than 750 pages of the second edition.

There is much that is new in the body of the text. The text has been thoroughly updated to include the latest scholarship and most recent political developments at home and abroad. The most substantial changes were occasioned by the Republican sweep of the 1994 midterm elections and the subsequent changes in Congress and national policy, but there are many other changes as well, including those relating to international trade and conflict.

The third edition also includes additional tables and figures. These have increased by nearly 50 percent, and emphasize the everyday realities of American life (for example, crime rates, trends in real wages, education spending and enrollments, women's status in the workplace, racial bias in the justice system, community activism, negativity in the news, and transfer payments to American families).

Finally, all chapters include two new boxes, one entitled *Your Turn* and the second entitled *States in the Nation*. These boxes are based on the same pedagogical philosophy that guided earlier editions. The boxed inserts in this text have the purpose of encouraging students to think more deeply and carefully about what they have read in the body of the text. The boxes are not mere fillers or diversions: they are part of a carefully considered instructional strategy. The text now presents five kinds of boxed inserts:

- *How the United States Compares*. Each chapter has a box that compares the United States with other countries on some aspect of politics emphasized in the chapter. American students invariably gain a clearer perspective and a deeper understanding of their own country's politics when they recognize how it resembles or differs from politics elsewhere.
- *States in the Nation*. The United States is one nation, but also consists of fifty states, which are alike in many ways but differ in important respects. These boxes compare the states along relevant dimensions, such as education spending, poverty levels, foreign trade (exports as a percentage of each state's economy), and party control of state government.
- *The Media and the People*. The world of everyday politics is largely beyond our direct observation. We depend on the media to inform us about this world, and these boxes—one in each chapter—are intended to give students a better understanding of the limits of this media-created reality.
- *Your Turn*. These boxes are intended to enable students to better understand both their own political views and those of other Americans. Each box asks for the reader's opinion on a political issue and then relates that response to the opinions of the American people as a whole. Included, for example, are questions on entitlement spending, UN peacekeeping operations, sexual harassment, term limits, and federal-state relations.

- *Critical Thinking.* Each chapter contains two boxes that ask students to analyze and integrate material presented in the chapter. The purpose is to encourage students to think critically and to make connections between concepts, research findings, and current issues of American politics.

As a final note, the third edition retains all previous appendixes, including a chapter-length discussion of state and local politics that is provided for the convenience of those instructors who include such a section in their national government course.

ANCILLARY PACKAGE

This text is accompanied by standard ancillary materials—an instructor's manual, a study guide, and a text bank. The test bank is available in printed form or on computer disk: IBM (5.25- and 3.5-inch disks) and Macintosh.

There are also special ancillaries (for example, videos) that are updated periodically; instructors can obtain information on these supplementary materials from their local McGraw-Hill sales representative or by calling Customer Service at 800-338-3987.

Students who use this text can also obtain a special subscription price on *The Washington Post National Weekly Edition.* Like many other instructors, I sometimes assign a source of information about current events as required or recommended reading in my undergraduate courses. The weekly edition of the *Post* is an effective option because it is devoted almost exclusively to politics and includes commentary and analysis by some of the country's best journalists, including David Broder, E. J. Dionne, Jr., George Will, and Meg Greenfield.

Your Suggestions Are Invited

Looking ahead, I invite from instructors and students any comments and criticisms that might inform future editions of the text. The strengths and weaknesses of a text are best discovered in its use, and I hope readers will share their experience with me. Professor Jerrold Schneider of the University of Delaware was kind enough to do so, and his suggestions are reflected in revisions I made on the role of parties in the congressional policymaking chapter. Professor Steve Mazurana of the University of Northern Colorado sent me his students' evaluations of *The American Democracy.* Their recommendations helped to improve several chapters of this new edition. If you have suggestions, please send them to me at the John F. Kennedy School of Government, Harvard University, Cambridge, MA 02138 (or contact me by E-mail: thomas_patterson@harvard.edu).

Thomas E. Patterson

PREFACE FOR THE STUDENT: A GUIDED TOUR OF THE AMERICAN DEMOCRACY

This book describes the American political system, which is one of the most interesting and most intricate in the world. The discussion is comprehensive; a lot of information is packed into each chapter. No student could possibly remember every tiny fact or observation that each chapter contains, but I believe that the main points of discussion are within your grasp if you are willing to reach for them. And once you have acquired these major points, then the smaller points will also be more readily understood.

The text has several features that will help you to understand the major points of discussion. Each chapter has, for example, an opening story that illustrates a central theme of the chapter. This story is followed immediately by a brief summary of the chapter's main ideas.

The "guided tour" below describes further how the organization and the special features of the book can help you in your effort to develop a basic understanding of the American political system.

Thomas E. Patterson

OPENING ILLUSTRATION

An illuminating narration of a compelling event introduces the chapter's main ideas.

CHAPTER 11

THE NEWS MEDIA: COMMUNICATING POLITICAL IMAGES

The press in America . . . determines what people will think and talk about—an authority that in other nations is reserved for tyrants, priests, parties and mandarins.

—Theodore H. White[1]

On the night of June 12, 1994, Nicole Brown Simpson and a friend, Ronald Goldman, were brutally murdered outside her home in the fashionable Brentwood area of Los Angeles. When her ex-husband, the former football star O. J. Simpson, was accused of the murders, every newspaper and television news program in the country gave the story prominent and repeated play. When replays of 911 calls revealed that O. J. Simpson had physically abused and intimidated his former wife after their 1992 divorce, a brief debate about the ravages of domestic violence ensued. The real issue of the Simpson news coverage, however, was the question of his guilt or innocence. Underlying the mountain of news coverage was the dramatic question: Could O. J. Simpson's good-guy public image have masked a more violent personality, one capable of murder?

Not all developments receive such intensive news coverage. Between 1983 and 1993, the birthrate among unwed women rose by more than 70 percent. According to U.S. Census Bureau statistics, 6.3 million children (27 percent of all children under the age of 18) lived in 1993 with a single parent who had never married, an increase from 3.7 million in 1983. Most of these families are mired in poverty (the average income is less than $10,000), and in many cases the children received no health care and have very little encouragement to perform well in school or stay out of trouble. The implications for society and public policy are enormous, yet this demographic trend is seldom mentioned in the news, let alone emblazoned in the headlines.

Although the news has been compared to a mirror held up to society, it is actually a highly selective portrayal of reality. The **news** is mainly an account of overt, obtruding events, particularly those which are *timely* (new or unfold

news The news media's version of reality, usually with an emphasis on timely, dramatic, and compelling events and developments.

293

"HOW THE UNITED STATES COMPARES" BOXES

Each chapter has a box that compares the United States with other countries in regard to a major political feature.

118 PART ONE ★ FOUNDATIONS

HOW THE UNITED STATES COMPARES

WOMEN'S EQUALITY

Although conflict between groups is universal, the nature of the conflict is often particularized. Racial conflict in the United States cannot readily be compared with, say, religious conflict in Northern Ireland. The one form of inequality common to all nations is that of gender: nowhere are women equal to men in law or in fact. But there are large differences between countries. A study by the Population Crisis Committee ranked the United States third overall in women's equality, behind only Sweden and Finland. The rankings were based on five areas—jobs, education, social relations, marriage and family, and health—where U.S. women had an 82.5 percent rating compared with men.

The inequality of women is also underlined by their lack of representation in public office. There is no country in which women comprise as many as half the members of the national legislature. The Scandinavian countries rank highest in terms of the percentage of female lawmakers. Other northern European countries have lower levels, but the levels are higher than that of the United States. Until the 1992 election, only 6 percent of U.S. House members were women. In 1992, as a consequence of reapportionment and the retirement of an unusually large number of incumbents, the number of women in the House nearly doubled. The following figures, estimated from several sources, indicate the approximate percentage of seats held by women in the largest chamber of each country's national legislature:

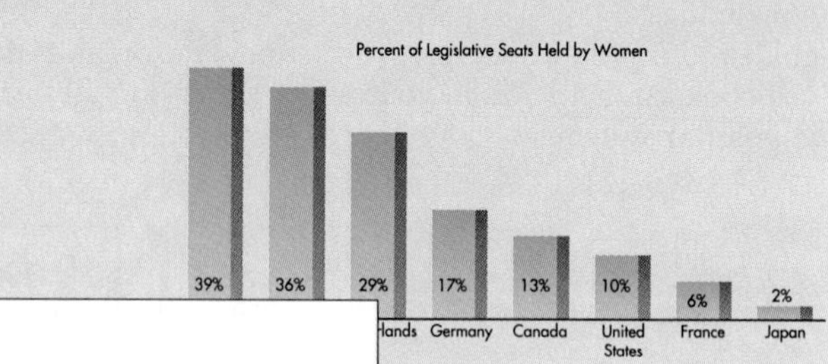

om political equality with men.[27] Women occupy ation's gubernatorial and congressional offices, and public offices are more likely than their male counre significant obstacles to political advancement.[28] vote is becoming increasingly potent. A few decades no difference in the partisan voting of men and pronounced "gender gap." It reached a record high elections when women voted nearly 10 percent more he gender gap is particularly pronounced when a e Democratic ticket. When Senators Feinstein and 92, each scored 14 percentage points higher among

CHAPTER 3 ★ CONSTITUTIONAL DEMOCRACY: PROMOTING LIBERTY AND SELF-GOVERNMENT 73

U.S. senators would be appointed by the legislatures of the states they represented. Because state legislators were popularly elected, the people would be choosing their senators indirectly. Every two years, a third of the senators would be appointed to six-year terms. The Senate was expected to check and balance the House, which, by virtue of the more frequent and direct election of its members, would presumably be more responsive to popular opinion.

Presidential selection was an issue of considerable debate at the Philadelphia convention. Direct election of the president was twice proposed and twice rejected because it linked executive power directly to popular majorities. The Framers finally chose to have the president selected by the votes of electors (the so-called Electoral College). Each state would have as many electors as it had members in Congress and could select them by any method it chose. The president would serve four years and be eligible for reelection.

The Framers decided that federal judges and justices would be appointed rather than elected. They would be nominated by the president and confirmed through approval by the Senate. Once confirmed, they would "hold their offices during good behavior." In effect, they would be allowed to hold office for life unless they committed a crime. The judiciary would be more of a "guardian" institution than a "representative" one.[20]

These differing methods of selecting national officeholders would not prevent a determined majority from achieving unbridled power, but control could not be attained easily or quickly. Unlike the House of Representatives, institutions such as the Senate, presidency, and judiciary would not yield to an impassioned majority in a single election. The delay would reduce the probability that government would degenerate into mob rule driven by momentary whims. The Framers believed that majority tyranny would be impulsive. Given time, the people would presumably come to their senses.

Modifying the Framers' Work: Toward a More Democratic Society

The Framers' conception of self-government was at odds with the one held by many Americans in 1787. The promise of self-government was one of the reasons that ordinary people had made great sacrifices during the American Revolution. This democratic spirit was reflected in the state constitutions. Every state but South Carolina held annual legislative elections, and several states also chose their governors through annual election by the people.[21]

In this context, the Constitution's provisions for popular rule were rather thin. Richard Henry Lee of Virginia criticized even the House of Representatives, which he said had "very little democracy in it" because each of its members would represent a large population and area.[22] Madison had claimed that this arrangement was necessary because otherwise representatives would be "unduly attached" to local interests and "too little fit to comprehend and pursue great and national objects." To Lee and others, such arguments were a mask for *elitism*—rule by a few who claimed to know the people's interests better than the people knew it themselves.[23] And it was not long after ratification of the Constitution that Americans sought a stronger voice in their own governing. The search has continued throughout the country's history: in no

★ CRITICAL THINKING

"Strong Democracy"? The possibilities for popular participation in government have always been more limited in national politics than local politics. Even at the time of the writing of the Constitution, the United States was too large to be governed except through representative institutions.

Proponents of popular rule have looked toward local communities as a place where people can participate more directly in government. In his book *Strong Democracy* (1984), Benjamin Barber argues that the Constitution's pessimistic view of human nature contributes to "thin" democracy in America. Barber says that voting is an important act but an inherently confining one. He prefers a "strong democracy" in which citizens are provided widespread opportunities for participation, including a greater say in policies that govern the workplace.

Where do you stand on the issue of popular control? What policy decisions, if any, would you shift from the national level to the local level, or from the private sector to the public sector, in order to increase the public's control over the policies that govern it?

"CRITICAL THINKING" BOXES

Boxes in the margins ask you to critically analyze and integrate material presented in the chapter.

Throughout their history Americans have embraced the same principles that were there at the nation's beginning, when they were put into words in the Declaration of Independence and the Constitution. Americans have quarreled over other matters, and over the practice of these principles, but they seem never to have questioned the principles themselves. As Clinton Rossiter concluded, "There has been in a doctrinal sense, only one America."[5]

This is a book about contemporary American politics, not U.S. history or culture. Yet American politics today cannot be understood apart from the nation's heritage. Government does not begin anew with each generation; it builds on the past. In the case of the United States, the most significant link between past and present lies in the nation's founding ideals. This chapter briefly examines the principles that have helped shape American politics since the country's earliest years.

The chapter also explains basic concepts, such as power and pluralism, that are important in the study of government and politics, and describes the underlying rules of the American governing system, such as constitutionalism and capitalism. The main points made in this chapter are the following:

- ★ *The American political culture centers on a set of core ideals—liberty, equality, self-government, individualism, diversity, and unity—that serve as the people's common bond.* These mythic principles have a substantial influence on what Americans will regard as reasonable and acceptable and on what they will try to achieve.
- ★ *Politics is the process that determines how a society will be governed.* The play of politics in the United States takes place in the context of democratic procedures, constitutionalism, and capitalism, and involves elements of majority, pluralist, and elite rule.
- ★ *Politics in the United States is characterized by a number of major patterns, including a highly fragmented governing system, a high degree of pluralism, an extraordinary emphasis on individual rights, and a pronounced separation of the ... spheres.*

: The Core Principles of ...ment

...on have a few great ideals that characterize their polit- ... Bryce observed, Americans are a special case.[6] Their ...eir national identity. Other people take their identity ...try that led them gradually to gather under one flag. ...was a France or a Japan, there were French and Japan- ...ip group united through blood.[7] Even today, it is kin- ...ere is no way to become Japanese, except to be born ... so for Americans. They are a multitude of immigrant ...itical tradition. The United States is a nation that was ...76 on a set of principles that became its people's com-

MAIN POINTS

The chapter's three or four main ideas are summarized in the opening pages.

try's individualistic culture and is a major reason for the lack of any large-scale government effort to reduce the economic and social gaps between Americans of varying racial and ethnic backgrounds. Nevertheless, a few policies—notably affirmative action and busing—have been implemented to achieve equality of result.

AFFIRMATIVE ACTION: WORKPLACE INTEGRATION

The difficulty of converting newly acquired legal rights into everyday realities is evident in the fact that, with passage of the 1964 Civil Rights Act, which prohibited discrimination in employment, it did not suddenly become easier for women and minorities to obtain jobs for which they were qualified. Many employers maintained a deliberate though unwritten preference for white male employees, while other employers adhered to established employment procedures that continued to keep women and minorities at a disadvantage; membership in many union locals, for example, was handed down from father to son. Moreover, the Civil Rights Act did not compel employers to show that their hiring practices were not discriminatory. Instead, the burden of proof was on the woman or minority group member who had been denied a particular job. It was costly and often difficult to prove in court that one's sex or race was the reason that one had not been hired. In addition, a victory in court affected only the individual in question; such case-by-case settlements were no remedy for a situation in which established hiring practices kept millions of women and minorities from competing equally for job opportunities.

A broader remedy was obviously required, and the result was the emergence during the late 1960s of affirmative action programs. **Affirmative action** is a deliberate effort to provide full and equal opportunities in employment, education, and other areas for women, minorities, and individuals belonging to other traditionally disadvantaged groups. Affirmative action requires corporations, universities, and other organizations to establish programs designed to ensure that all applicants are treated fairly. Affirmative action also places the burden of proof on the providers of opportunities; to some extent, they must be able to demonstrate that any disproportionate granting of opportunities to white males is not the result of discriminatory practices.

The Supreme Court's Position on Affirmative Action

Most issues that pit individuals against each other in a struggle over society's benefits eventually end up in the courts, and affirmative action is no exception. The policy was first tested before the Supreme Court in *University of California Regents* v. *Bakke* (1978). Alan Bakke, a white man, had twice been denied admission to a University of California medical school, even though his admission test scores were higher than several minority group students who had been accepted. Bakke sued, claiming the school had a "quota" system for minorities that discriminated against white males. The Court ruled in Bakke's favor but did not invalidate affirmative action per se. The Court said only that rigid racial quotas were an impermissible form of affirmative action in determining medical school admissions.[50]

★ STATES IN THE NATION

Annual Income Per Capita, by Race (in dollars): In all states, income levels of minorities are below that of whites.

STATE	WHITES	BLACKS	HISPANICS
Ala.	13,235	6,473	9,663
Alaska	19,903	12,816	11,885
Ariz.	14,964	9,688	7,374
Ark.	11,472	5,729	7,074
Calif.	19,028	11,578	8,504
Colo.	15,544	10,704	8,233
Conn.	21,466	11,695	9,786
Del.	17,263	9,683	10,066
D.C.	34,563	12,226	12,525
Fla.	16,052	7,550	10,582
Ga.	15,832	7,997	11,123
Hawaii	18,598	10,607	9,950
Idaho	11,723	8,785	6,303
Ill.	16,817	8,922	8,318
Ind.	13,553	8,739	9,221
Iowa	12,573	7,844	8,025
Kan.	13,817	8,445	8,007
Ky.	11,439	7,460	9,058
La.	12,956	5,687	10,188
Maine	13,019	10,089	9,946
Md.	19,789	12,343	13,198
Mass.	18,003	10,867	7,833
Mich.	15,071	9,195	9,298
Minn.	14,765	8,714	8,003
Miss.	12,183	5,194	8,621
Mo.	13,563	8,576	10,191
Mont.	11,634	7,657	6,021
Neb.	12,773	7,857	7,280
Nev.	16,241	9,366	9,348
N.H.	16,028	12,577	11,634
N.J.	20,406	11,542	10,761
N.Mex.	12,678	8,579	7,542
N.Y.	18,584	10,566	8,915
N.C.	14,450	7,926	9,544
N.Dak.	11,359	7,875	5,811
Ohio	14,049	8,702	9,248
Okla.	12,859	7,356	7,145
Oreg.	13,778	8,240	6,996
Pa.	14,688	9,140	7,489
R.I.	15,573	9,031	7,620
S.C.	14,115	6,800	10,723
S.Dak.	11,230	8,124	6,908
Tenn.	13,201	7,414	10,246
Texas	14,629	8,102	6,633
Utah	11,274	8,385	7,398
Vt.	13,597	8,991	11,501
Va.	17,361	9,439	12,220
Wash.	15,564	10,440	8,149
W.Va.	10,574	7,416	9,805
Wis.	13,793	7,021	7,050
Wyo.	12,629	8,490	7,967
National average	15,687	8,859	8,400

SOURCE: U.S. Bureau of Census, 1990 Census of Population and Housing

STATES IN THE NATION BOXES

Each chapter has a box that compares the fifty states on an aspect on politics.

MAJOR CONCEPTS

The introduction of a major concept is signaled by **bold type** and accompanied by a concise definition. These concepts are also listed at the end of the chapter and in bold type in the subject index.

CHAPTER 4 ★ CIVIL LIBERTIES: PROTECTING INDIVIDUAL RIGHTS 89

THE MEDIA AND THE PEOPLE

BALANCING THE RIGHTS OF THE PRESS AND THE ACCUSED

No right is absolute. All rights are balanced against other rights and the collective interests of society, which include an interest in protecting individual rights.

A classic example of rights in conflict occurs when the news media's interest in reporting a crime clashes with the rights of the accused. Lurid crimes are a staple of the news business. Few things seem to sell more newspapers or attract more news viewers than grisly stories of murder and mayhem. It is perhaps no surprise that America's first full-time reporter was hired to cover the crime beat. He was employed by the publisher Benjamin Day, who in the 1830s established the country's first mass-market newspaper, the *New York Sun*.

However, intense coverage of a crime can jeopardize the right of the accused to a fair trial. The gory details of a violent crime can inflame public opinion and make it difficult to empanel a jury of people who have not already prejudged the guilt of the accused. This problem received extraordinary attention in the celebrated trial of O.J. Simpson, who was accused of murdering his ex-wife Nicole Brown Simpson and her friend Ronald Goldman. The pretrial publicity was the most intense in the nation's history, and few people were without an opinion about O.J. Simpson's guilt or innocence. The presiding judge, Lance Ito, refused the media's demands for photographs and videotape of the slain bodies on the grounds that this material was so graphic (Nicole Brown Simpson was nearly decapitated in the knife attack) that it would prejudice public opinion. Jurors were sequestered and prohibited from reading, viewing, or listening to news coverage of the crime or trial. Yet Judge Ito permitted the trial to be televised.

In balancing the rights of the press and the accused, the courts have responded to the interests of both. On occasion, the Supreme Court has reversed convictions on grounds that intense or inflammatory news coverage had made a fair trial impossible. And courts at all levels have recommended that the press exercise self-discipline in the reporting of material that might bias a potential jury. Less often, judges have issued "gag orders" that forbid the press from reporting certain aspects of a crime. In *Nebraska Press Association* v. *Stuart* (1976), the Supreme Court overruled a Nebraska judge who had placed a sweeping gag order on the press. The Supreme Court acknowledged the power of the judiciary to restrain the press but concluded that any application of the power must be fully justified. The Supreme Court has also said that officials must also consider other options, such as moving the trial to another location, in any decision to restrict press coverage.

The unacceptability of **prior restraint**—governme
or publication before the fact—is basic to the current
sion. The Supreme Court has said that any attempt b
expression carries "a 'heavy presumption' against
News organizations and individuals are legally resp
what they report or say (for example, they can be sued
reputation is wrongly damaged by their words), bu
cannot stop them in advance from expressing their
some instances is news coverage of criminal proceedi
and The People). Another exception is the reporting
During the Persian Gulf war, U.S. journalists on stat
to work within limits placed on them by military auth
tion to the doctrine of prior restraint, the courts have
authority to ban uncensored publications by certain
ment employees, such as CIA agents, who have
national security activities.

"THE MEDIA AND THE PEOPLE" BOXES

Each chapter has a box that informs you about a major topic pertaining to the media.

SUMMARY

A short discussion, organized around the chapter's main points; summarizes each chapter's content.

258 PART TWO ★ MASS POLITICS

Summary

America's political parties are relatively weak organizations. They lack control over nominations, elections, and platforms. Candidates can bypass the party organization and win nomination through primary elections. Individual candidates also control most of the organization and money necessary to win elections and run largely on personal platforms.

Primary elections are the major reason for the organizational weakness of America's parties. Once the parties lost their hold on the nominating process, they became subordinate to candidates. More generally, the political parties have been undermined by election reforms, some of which were intended to weaken the party and others of which have unintentionally done so. Recently the state and national party organizations have expanded their capacity to provide candidates with modern campaign services and are again playing a prominent role in election campaigns. Nevertheless, party organizations at all levels have few ways of controlling the candidates who run under their banners. They assist candidates with campaign technology, workers, and funds but cannot compel candidates' loyalty to organizational goals.

America's parties are decentralized, fragmented organizations. The relationship among local, state, and national party organizations is marked by paths of common interest rather than lines of authority. The national party organization does not control the policies and activities of the state organizations, and they in turn do not control the local organizations. The fragmentation of parties prevents them from acting as cohesive national organizations. Traditionally the local organizations have controlled most of the party's work force because most elections are contested at the local level. Local parties, however, vary markedly in their vitality.

America's party organizations are flexible enough to allow diverse interests to coexist within them; they can also accommodate new ideas and leadership, since they are neither rigid nor closed. However, because America's parties cannot control their candidates or coordinate their policies at all levels, they are unable to present the voters with a coherent, detailed platform for governing. The national electorate as a whole is thus denied a clear choice among policy alternatives and has difficulty influencing national policy in a predictable and enduring way through elections.

Major Concepts

candidate-centered politics
nomination
party-centered politics
party organizations
primary election (direct primary)
service relationship

Suggested Readings

Allswang, John. *Bosses, Machines, and Urban Voters.* Baltimore: Johns Hopkins University Press, 1986. A penetrating study of the party machines that once flourished in America's cities.

Bennett, W. Lance. *The Governing Crisis: Media, Money, and Marketing in American Elections.* New York: St. Martin's Press, 1992. An assessment of the impact of candidate-centered campaigns on the governing process.

Ehrenhalt, Alan. *The United States of Ambition.* New York: Times Books, 1991. A provocative book that claims that self-starting politicians are the reason the U.S. government has a scarcity of sound leadership.

Herrnson, Paul S. *Party Campaigning in the 80's.* Cambridge, Mass.: Harvard University Press, 1988. An analysis that indicates political parties continue to have an important organizational role in the United States.

Kayden, Xander, and Eddie Mahe, Jr. *The Party Goes On.* New York: Basic Books, 1985. An assessment of how the two major parties have adapted to the political changes of recent decades.

Magleby, David B., and Candice J. Nelson, *The Money Chase: Congressional Campaign Finance Reform.* Washington, D.C.: The Brookings Institution, 1990. A careful study of the flow of money in federal elections.

Milkus, Sidney. *The President and the Parties: The Transformation of the American Party System since the New Deal.* New York: Oxford University Press, 1993. An assessment of the president's role in party conflict.

Schlesinger, Joseph. *Political Parties and the Winning of Office.* Ann Arbor: University of Michigan Press, 1991. An evaluation of the parties' role in elections.

KEY TERMS

A list of the chapter's major concepts facilitates review.

SUGGESTED READINGS

Annotated references encourage further pursuit of some of the best works of political science, both classic studies and recent research.

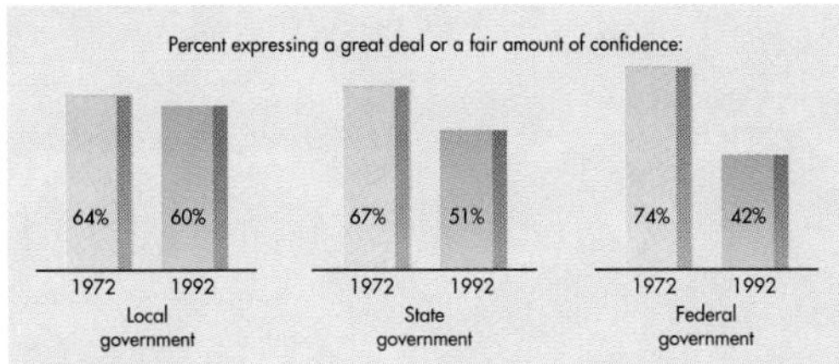

FIGURE 2-4
Changes in the Public's Confidence in the Federal, State, and Local Governments
The public's trust in government, particularly at the national level, has declined in recent decades.
Source: Surveys for the U.S. Advisory Commission on Intergovernmental Relations (ACIR) by the Opinion Research Corporation (1972) and the Gallup Organization (1992).

through specific public welfare programs funded with federal tax dollars."[41]

The second great wave of federal social programs—President Lyndon Johnson's Great Society—was also driven by public demands. Income and education levels had risen dramatically after the Second World War, and Americans wanted more and better services from government. When the states were slow to respond, Americans pressured federal officials to act.[42] The Great Society programs included federal initiatives in health care, education, public housing, nutrition, and other areas reserved previously to states and localities.

Public opinion is also behind the current rollback in federal authority. The Republican victory in 1994 was in large part a result of Americans' increased dissatisfaction with the federal government. Two decades ago, three-fourths of Americans expressed confidence in Washington's ability to govern effectively; today, less than half of the public holds this view (see Figure 2-4). Con-

FIGURES AND TABLES

Each chapter has figures and tables that relate to points made in the discussion.

YOUR TURN

SIZE OF GOVERNMENT

The Questions:

1. Would you say you favor smaller government with fewer services, or larger government with many services?

Smaller government, fewer services	Larger government, many services

2. Do you think that, in general, the federal government creates more problems than it solves, or do you think it solves more problems than it creates?

Creates more problems than it solves	Solves more problems than it creates

What Others Think: The first question appeared in a 1993 ABC News/Washington Post survey: 67 percent of the respondents said they favored a smaller government with fewer services while 30 percent expressed the opposite preference. The second question is from a 1993 CBS News/New York Times survey: 69 percent said they believe the federal government creates more problems than it solves while 22 percent concluded otherwise.

Comment: These questions address an issue that has persisted throughout the nation's history—what the size of government should be generally and the size of the federal government in particular. If you favor a smaller government and have a low level of trust in the federal government, you probably agree with current attempts to downsize Washington and shift policy responsibilities to the states.

YOUR TURN BOXES

Each chapter has a box that asks your opinion on a major political issure and then relates that opinion to the views of the American people as a whole.

ACKNOWLEDGMENTS

Early in the writing of the first edition of *The American Democracy,* I concluded that it would be enormously helpful if a way could be found to bring into each chapter the judgment of those political scientists who teach the introductory course year in and year out. These instructors are most able to provide the required insight into improving the pedagogical value of an introductory text. This recognition led us to initiate what is still today the most thorough review process ever undertaken for an American government text. In addition to the chapter reviews of a select number of expert scholars, we sent each chapter to a dozen or so faculty members at U.S. colleges and universities of all types—public and private, large and small, four-year and two-year. These political scientists, 213 of them in all, had well over a thousand years of combined experience in the teaching of the introductory course and provided various constructive ideas. They will go unnamed here, but my debt to these scholars remains undiminished by time. Reviewers are the lifeblood of a text, and their contribution lasts far beyond the edition they help strengthen.

I do want to thank by name the reviewers of the second and third editions. Their suggestions were detailed, lengthy, and extremely useful, and I am grateful that they took time from their own work to improve mine. My thanks to:

Danny M. Adkison, *Oklahoma State University*

James Chalmers, *Wayne State University*

Tom Chambers, *Golden West College*

Stephen Crescenzi, *Trenton State College*

Paige Cubbison, *Miami-Dade Community College*

Paul Dawson, *Oberlin College*

Larry Dodd, *University of Florida*

Steve Frank, *Saint Cloud State University*

Kristina Cline Gilbert, *Riverside Community College*

Hank Goldman, *Rio Hondo College*

Joel Grossman, *University of Wisconsin, Madison*

John Hale, *University of Oklahoma*

Steve Hatting, *University of Saint Thomas*

Michael Hawthorne, *Pembroke State University*

William Hudson, *Providence College*

Loch Johnson, *University of Georgia*

George Kaloudis, *River College*

Robert Kennedy, *Georgia Institute of Technology*

James D. King, *Memphis State University*

Samuel Krislov, *University of Minnesota*

Marston Leonard, *Hillsborough Community College*

Carl Lutrin, *California Polytechnic State University*

John McGowan, *Villanova University*

Michael Maggiotto, *Bowling Green State University*

Sandy Maisel, *Colby College*

Christopher Markwood, *Lamar University*

Michael D. Martinez, *University of Florida*

Bradley J. Miller, *Saginaw Valley State University*

Michael C. Munger, *University of North Carolina, Chapel Hill*

Garrison Nelson, *University of Vermont*

Patricia Pauly, *University of Kentucky*

William Pederson, *Louisiana State University, Shreveport*

Mark Peffley, *University of Kentucky*

James Perkins, *San Antonio College*

James Pfiffner, *George Mason University*

Donald Ranish, *Antelope Valley College*

Russell Renka, *Southeast Missouri State University*

Michael Rich, *Brown University*

David Rosenbloom, *The American University*

Donald Roy, *Ferris State University*

Nadia M. Rubaii-Barrett, *New Mexico State University*

Ronald Shaiko, *The American University*

Donald Songer, *University of South Carolina*

Lawrence Sullivan, *Adelphi University*

C. Stephen Tai, *University of Arkansas, Pine Bluff*

Carol Traut, *University of South Dakota*

Joseph K. Unekis, *Kansas State University*

David Uranga, *Pasadena City College*

Stephen L. Wasby, *State University of New York, Albany*

Gerald Wright, *Indiana University*

Norman Zucker, *Ursinus College*

Finally, I want to acknowledge those at McGraw-Hill and Syracuse University who contributed to the third edition. Peter Labella, my editor, deserves a special thanks. His sound judgment and personal commitment to this edition have improved the book from front to back. David Damstra also had a major impact; he carefully supervised the editorial production of the third edition, as he did for the two previous editions. Bert Lummus, Lyn Uhl, Mary Farrell, Karen Osborne, Robert Zolnerzak, Barbara Salz, Nancy Dyer, and Monica Freedman of McGraw-Hill also worked hard to bring this edition to life. At Syracuse University, I had the invaluable support of several graduate assistants and work-study students, including Lakshmi Srinivasan, Krisan Evenson, Jason Penfield, Tim Emmert, Tara Watson, and Amy Proux.

Thomas E. Patterson

THE AMERICAN DEMOCRACY

PHILAD
PASS AND
PHILAD

PART ONE

FOUNDATIONS

The United States has the world's oldest constitution still in force. France has had fourteen constitutions during the same period in which the United States has had one. The British statesman William Gladstone in 1878 declared the U.S. Constitution to be "the most wonderful work ever struck off at a given time by the brain and purpose of man."

A reason why this remarkable constitutional system has endured is that United States was founded on a set of ideals which continue to serve as a common bond for all Americans. If the practice of these ideals has changed greatly in the past two centuries, the principles themselves have not been challenged. Liberty, self-government, equality, individualism, diversity, and unity are as vital to Americans' welfare today as they were when the nation was founded. Chapter 1 discusses these ideals and their pervasive influence on the nation's politics.

The codification of these ideals in a constitution was itself a remarkable achievement. The writers of the Constitution had to design a government that could satisfy several different and somewhat competing ideals at the same time. The most pressing goal, which occasioned the writing of the Constitution in 1787, was to establish a government that was powerful enough to bind the separate states and their citizens in a single union. A second aim was to keep the nation's government from being so powerful as to threaten liberty. The desire for liberty had inspired the Revolution against England, and it did not make sense to overthrow one tyrannical government only to replace it with another. Finally, the Constitution would have to embody Americans' desire for self-government. This objective was not wholly compatible with the goal of nationhood, which required a transfer of power to a government that was more distant from the people than were the state governments. Nor was the objective of self-government entirely consistent with the goal of individual liberty, which required that there be limits on the power of the majority.

Chapters 2 and 3 in this section examine these constitutional questions and the way they were resolved by the writers of the Constitution. These chapters also discuss how constitutional practices have changed during the nation's two centuries and describe what they are today. A central theme of Chapters 2 and 3 is that basic constitutional issues are never fully settled. They are recurring sources of conflict, and each generation is forced to find new answers. Current debates over term limitations and federal-state relations are part of that ongoing process.

Constitutional government is, as Chapters 2 and 3 demonstrate, partly a matter of the structure of government. It is also a matter of individual freedom, of a system in which people have rights and liberties that are constitutionally protected from infringement by government. The concept of individual rights holds that each person should be free to pursue a life of his or her own choosing, as long as this freedom does not unduly restrict that of other people.

Although individual rights are rooted in principle, they are achieved through politics. No matter how "unalienable" Americans' rights have been said to be in theory, they have hardly been so in practice. No significant exercise or extension of any right has been achieved without a struggle. Chapter 4 discusses how civil liberties—specifically, the rights of free expression and due process of law—are protected both from and through political action. Chapter 5 examines the degree to which Americans' equality of rights and opportunities is affected by considerations of race, sex, and color.

★ ★ ★

CHAPTER 1

THE AMERICAN HERITAGE: SEEKING A MORE PERFECT UNION

One hears people say that it is inherent in the habits and nature of democracies to change feelings and thoughts at every moment. . . . But I have never seen anything like that happening in the great democracy on the other side of the ocean. What struck me most in the United States was the difficulty experienced in getting an idea, once conceived, out of the head of the majority.

Alexis de Tocqueville[1]

Shortly before midnight on November 5, 1996, Bill Clinton stood on the steps of the Old State House in Little Rock, Arkansas, and thanked the voters for electing him to a second presidential term. He then turned to the issue of national unity. "When we are divided," he declared, "we defeat ourselves." He promised a stronger future: "We've got a bridge to build." But the bridge, he said, would have to be wide enough to give everyone a chance to reach the other side. And the bridge could only be built if everyone lent a hand: "My fellow Americans, we have work to do."

President Clinton's words could have been addressed to any generation of Americans.[2] Threaded into his speech were references to time-honored American principles: democracy, freedom, equality, national purpose. The same ideals had filled the speeches of Ronald Reagan and John Kennedy, Franklin Roosevelt and Abraham Lincoln, Andrew Jackson and Thomas Jefferson.[3]

Of course, the practice of these ideals has changed greatly during the two centuries that the United States has been a nation. When the nation's founders proclaimed in 1776 that "all men are created equal," they did not have in mind racial minorities or women. And the assumption that Americans are one people with a common vision has always obscured deep divisions in society.[4] When Irish, Italian, and Polish immigrants reached this country's shores, they encountered nativist elements that scorned their folkways and attacked their religion. The Asians and Latinos who have come here more recently also have been made to feel less than fully welcome. The "English first" movement includes the not very subtle message that "true" Americans do not speak Spanish or Vietnamese or Cambodian.

Yet the American political experience has been remarkably enduring.

Throughout their history Americans have embraced the same principles that were there at the nation's beginning, when they were put into words in the Declaration of Independence and the Constitution. Americans have quarreled over other matters, and over the practice of these principles, but they seem never to have questioned the principles themselves. As Clinton Rossiter concluded, "There has been in a doctrinal sense, only one America."[5]

This is a book about contemporary American politics, not U.S. history or culture. Yet American politics today cannot be understood apart from the nation's heritage. Government does not begin anew with each generation; it builds on the past. In the case of the United States, the most significant link between past and present lies in the nation's founding ideals. This chapter briefly examines the principles that have helped shape American politics since the country's earliest years.

The chapter also explains basic concepts, such as power and pluralism, that are important in the study of government and politics, and describes the underlying rules of the American governing system, such as constitutionalism and capitalism. The main points made in this chapter are the following:

★ *The American political culture centers on a set of core ideals—liberty, equality, self-government, individualism, diversity, and unity—that serve as the people's common bond.* These mythic principles have a substantial influence on what Americans will regard as reasonable and acceptable and on what they will try to achieve.

★ *Politics is the process that determines how a society will be governed.* The play of politics in the United States takes place in the context of democratic procedures, constitutionalism, and capitalism, and involves elements of majority, pluralist, and elite rule.

★ *Politics in the United States is characterized by a number of major patterns, including a highly fragmented governing system, a high degree of pluralism, an extraordinary emphasis on individual rights, and a pronounced separation of the political and economic spheres.*

Political Culture: The Core Principles of American Government

The people of every nation have a few great ideals that characterize their political life, but, as James Bryce observed, Americans are a special case.[6] Their ideals are the basis of their national identity. Other people take their identity from the common ancestry that led them gradually to gather under one flag. Thus, long before there was a France or a Japan, there were French and Japanese people, each a kinship group united through blood.[7] Even today, it is kinship that links them. There is no way to become Japanese, except to be born of Japanese parents. Not so for Americans. They are a multitude of immigrant peoples linked by a political tradition. The United States is a nation that was founded abruptly in 1776 on a set of principles that became its people's common bond.[8]

U.S. politics is remarkable for its historical continuity, which is celebrated here in a ceremony at the Capitol in Washington D.C. (Joseph Sohm/Stock, Boston)

America's principles are habits of mind, a customary way of thinking about the world. They are part of what social scientists call **political culture,** a term that refers to the characteristic and deep-seated beliefs of a particular people.[9]

political culture The characteristic and deep-seated beliefs of a particular people.

The American political culture is said to include the following beliefs in idealized form:

- **Liberty** is the principle that individuals should be free to act and think as they choose, provided they do not infringe unreasonably on the freedom and well-being of others.
- **Self-government** is the principle that the people are the ultimate source of governing authority and that their general welfare is the only legitimate purpose of government.
- **Equality** holds that all individuals have moral worth, are entitled to fair treatment under the law, and should have equal opportunity for material gain and political influence.
- **Individualism** is a commitment to personal initiative, self-sufficiency, and material accumulation. This principle upholds the superiority of a private-enterprise economic system and includes the idea of the individual as the foundation of society.
- **Diversity** holds that individual differences should be respected and that these differences are a source of strength and a legitimate basis of self-interest.
- **Unity** is the principle that Americans are one people and form an indivisible union.

These ideals, taken together, are sometimes called "the American Creed." In practice, they mean different things to different people, and it is not useful to provide more complex definitions of these values at this point in the book. Few observers would argue, however, with the proposition that *a defining characteristic of the American political system is its enduring and powerful set of cultural ideals.* The Frenchman Alexis de Tocqueville was among the first to see that the main tendencies of American politics cannot be explained without taking into account the country's core beliefs. "Habits of the heart" was de Tocqueville's description of Americans' ideals.[10]

HOW THE UNITED STATES COMPARES

AMERICANS AS A POLITICAL PEOPLE

By some standards, Americans are not a very political people. The United States ranks near the bottom, for example, in voter turnout. Barely half of Americans go to the polls in a presidential election, compared with 70 to 90 percent of adults in most other democratic countries. In France, Italy, and Belgium, for example, turnout exceeds 80 percent.

In other ways, however, Americans are a highly political people. Americans have long believed in the exceptionalism of their political system. We have tended to believe that what works for us will also work for others and indeed that what works for us would be better for them than what they already have. In his book *World Politics and Personal Insecurity*, the political scientist Harold Lasswell wrote that "Americans who think about the problem of unifying the world tend to follow the precedent set in their own history." Presented after World War I with President Woodrow Wilson's plan for world peace based on American principles, the French premier Georges Clemenceau exclaimed, "This man Wilson with his Fourteen Points! The good Lord had only ten."

Given Americans' pride in their political system, it is not surprising that they attach great importance to political symbols. In Europe, national flags are not routinely displayed in public. In America, the flag is flown daily on government buildings and even on many private homes. The "Pledge of Allegiance" to the flag that is recited daily by American school children and the playing of the "Star Spangled Banner" at public events have no equivalents in European nations. A *Washington Post* survey indicated that a large majority of Americans believe it is unpatriotic to refuse to stand when their national anthem is played. A Gallup survey found that nearly 80 percent of Americans believe school children should be *required* to recite the "Pledge of Allegiance" each day.

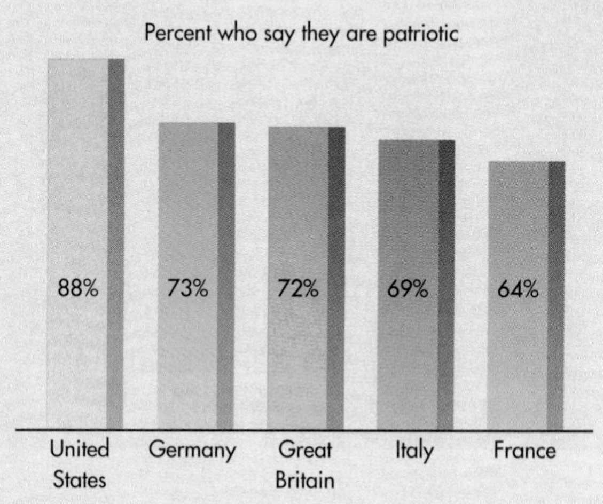

The distinctiveness of Americans' beliefs was evident in a five-nation Times-Mirror survey (1990–1991) that asked respondents whether they agreed with the statement, "I am very patriotic." As the accompanying graph shows, Americans ranked at the top; nearly 90 percent claimed to be highly patriotic. The disparity between the United States and Europe was particularly apparent among young adults. In Europe, young adults were substantially less likely to say they were patriotic than were older people. In the United States, the proportion of eighteen- to twenty-four-year-olds who said they were patriotic, 82 percent, was nearly as high as in other age groups.

SOURCE: Times-Mirror Center for the People and the Press survey, 1990–1991.

THE POWER OF IDEALS

The ideals held by Americans have had a strong impact on the nation's politics. Ideals serve to define the boundaries of action. They do not determine exactly what people will do, but they have a marked influence on what people will regard as reasonable and desirable. If people believe, as Americans do, that politics exists to promote liberty and equality, they will attempt to realize these values through their political actions. A nation's ideals cannot provide all the answers, but they are a source of many solutions. William James noted that human culture is largely "the resettlements of our ideas."[11] Through trial and error, a society—including American society—finds principles that work for it.

Why, for example, does the United States spend relatively less money on government programs for the poor and disadvantaged than do other fully industrialized democracies, including Germany, France, Switzerland, the Netherlands, Spain, Britain, Sweden, Italy, and Japan? Are Americans so much better off than these other people that we have less need for welfare programs? The answer is no. The United States ranks below several of these countries in per capita income and, of all these countries, has in both relative and absolute terms the greatest number of hungry, homeless, and poor people. The reason the United States spends less on social welfare lies chiefly in the emphasis that American culture places on *individualism*. We have resisted giving government a larger social welfare role because of our deep-seated cultural belief that able-bodied individuals should take responsibility for themselves and that success in life depends largely on personal effort (see Figure 1-1).

The distinctiveness of this cultural belief is evident in a Times-Mirror Center survey of opinions in Europe and the United States. When asked whether it is the responsibility of the government "to take care of very poor people who can't take care of themselves," only 23 percent of Americans said they completely agreed. The Germans were the closest to the Americans in their response to this question, but twice as many of them, 50 percent, said they believed that the state should take care of the very poor. More than 60 percent of the British, French, and Italians held the same opinion. Americans do not necessarily have less sympathy for the poor; rather, they place more emphasis on personal responsibility than Europeans do.[12]

Of course, social welfare policy is not simply an issue of cultural differences. The welfare issue, like all other issues, is part of the rough and tumble of everyday politics everywhere. There are always powerful interests aligned on both sides of important issues. In the United States, the Republican party, business groups, antitax groups, and others have resisted the expansion of the government's social welfare role, while liberal Democrats, unions, minority groups, and others have from time to time argued for greater intervention.

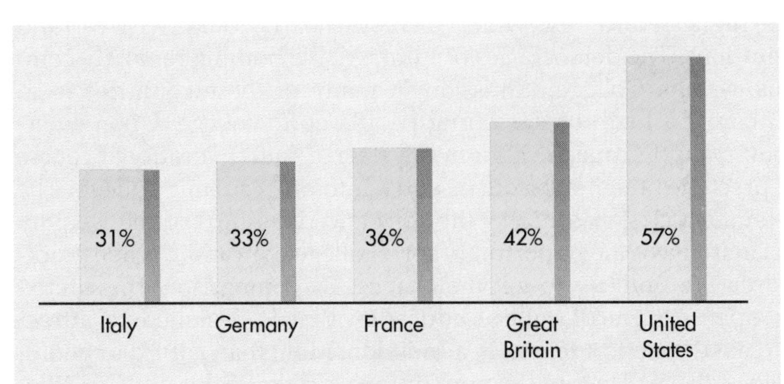

FIGURE 1-1 Opinions about the Source of Personal Success Expressed by Citizens of Major Democracies
Americans are more likely than Europeans to believe that their efforts are the key to personal success. Figures are the percentage of respondents who disagreed with the statement "Success in life is pretty much determined by forces outside our control." *Source: Times-Mirror Center for the People and the Press surveys, 1990–1991.*

The structure of U.S society helps promote the American Dream of success—for example, by encouraging young people to attend college. (Bob Daemmrich/ The Image Works)

Nevertheless, Americans' belief in individualism, which has no exact equivalent in European society, has played a defining role in shaping U.S. welfare policy.

Health policy is a similar story. Canada and the democracies of western Europe have government-run health care systems in which all citizens are entitled to free medical care. The United States has a privately based system that offers the most medically advanced care in the world; however, an estimated 40 million Americans are uninsured and have no way of paying for adequate medical care. President Bill Clinton's proposal to provide universal coverage through a combination of government and employer insurance plans was defeated in Congress in 1994, partly because the nation's individualistic culture made it difficult for Clinton to mobilize public support behind the idea of universal care.

The importance of individualism to American society is evident also in the emphasis on equal opportunity. If individuals are to be entrusted with their own health and welfare, they must be given a fair chance to succeed on their own. Nowhere is this philosophy more evident than in the country's elaborate system of higher education, which includes nearly 3,000 two-year and four-year institutions. The democracies of Europe have nothing remotely comparable to this system. College admission in many of these countries is so restricted that barely a tenth of the young people go to college. Upon entering high school, many European children are steered into a vocational course of study that precludes their subsequent entry into an academic college. The European system is a class-based one; the sons and daughters of the wealthy are almost certain to have the opportunity for a college education, while working-class children are unlikely to get the chance. By comparison, the United States has an open system of college education that is designed to attract nearly all who make the effort to obtain admission. More than a third of young Americans enter college. They are disproportionately the children of middle-class parents, but their ranks also include many from working-class homes.

Of course, the idea that success is within the reach of all Americans who strive for it is far from accurate. Mexican Americans in the Southwest, blacks in the inner cities, and poor whites in the depressed industrial belt of the Northeast and Midwest know all too well the limits on their lives. Homelessness, drugs, alcoholism, and family violence have shattered the American Dream for many. In some inner-city schools, the rates of pregnancy and illiteracy are higher than the graduation rate.

THE LIMITS OF IDEALS

Cultural beliefs originate in a country's political and social practices, but they are not perfect representatives of these practices. They are mythic ideas—symbolic positions taken by a people to justify and give meaning to their way of life.[13] Myths contain elements of truth, but they are far from the full truth.

High ideals do not come with a guarantee that a people will live up to them. The clearest proof of this failing in the American case is the human tragedy that began nearly four centuries ago and continues today. In 1619 the first black slaves were brought in chains to America. Slavery lasted 250 years. Slaves in the field worked from dawn to dark (from "can see, 'til can't"), whether in the heat of summer or the cold of winter. They could be bought and sold, and could be beaten, mutilated, and sexually abused with impunity. The Civil War changed the future of African Americans but did not ensure their equality. Slavery was followed by the Jim Crow era of legal segregation: black people in the South were forbidden by law to use the same schools, hospitals, restaurants, and restrooms as white people. For those who got uppish with their white superiors, there were beatings, firebombings, castrations, rapes, and worse—hundreds of African Americans were lynched by white vigilantes in the early 1900s. Today African Americans have equal rights under the law, but in fact they are far from equal. Compared with whites, blacks are three times as likely to live in poverty, twice as likely to be unable to find a job, twice as likely to die in infancy, seven times as likely to be sentenced to death if convicted of an interracial murder.[14] There have always been at least two Americas, one for whites and one for blacks.

Despite the lofty claim that "all men are created equal," equality has never been an American birthright. In 1892 Congress suspended Chinese immigration on the assumption that the Chinese were an inferior people. Calvin Coolidge in 1923 asked Congress for a permanent ban on Chinese immigration, saying that people "who do not want to be partakers of the American spirit ought not to settle in America."[15] Not until 1965 was discrimination against the Chinese and other Asian peoples effectively eliminated from U.S. immigration laws.

The discrimination against the Chinese is not among the stories that we like to tell about ourselves. Such lapses of historical memory can be found among all peoples, but the tendency to recast history is perhaps exaggerated in the case of Americans because our beliefs are so idealistic. How could a people that upholds the ideal of human equality have barred the Chinese, enslaved the blacks, stolen the Indians' lands, subordinated women, and interned the Japanese?

Cultural beliefs can even lull a people into a false sense of what they have accomplished. Some Americans think that by saying they believe in equality,

★ STATES IN THE NATION

Higher Education: America's emphasis on education extends to all states, which have large college systems relative to their populations.

STATE	FULL-TIME STUDENTS PER 1,000 POPULATION	NUMBER OF COLLEGES
Ala.	37	86
Alaska	20	8
Ariz.	32	40
Ark.	29	34
Calif.	28	322
Colo.	35	59
Conn.	25	47
Del.	37	10
D.C.	87	18
Fla.	22	105
Ga.	28	115
Hawaii	29	17
Idaho	36	11
Ill.	32	169
Ind.	34	78
Iowa	44	61
Kan.	38	49
Ky.	32	62
La.	34	33
Maine	26	31
Md.	25	56
Mass.	44	117
Mich.	30	102
Minn.	35	99
Miss.	36	46
Mo.	32	96
Mont.	36	19
Neb.	43	37
Nev.	15	9
N.H.	36	29
N.J.	22	62
N.Mex.	30	31
N.Y.	37	320
N.C.	34	122
N.Dak.	50	20
Ohio	32	165
Okla.	36	46
Oreg.	31	45
Pa.	33	220
R.I.	49	12
S.C.	30	60
S.Dak.	36	19
Tenn.	31	78
Texas	28	176
Utah	49	16
Vt.	43	22
Va.	31	86
Wash.	30	62
W.Va.	34	28
Wis.	37	64
Wyo.	36	9
National average	32	71

SOURCE: U.S. National Center for Education Statistics, *Digest of Education Statistics*, 1992.

Even as early Americans were expressing their commitment to the principle of equality, they were allowing slavery to persist. This is the only drawing known to have been made aboard a slave ship as it sailed to America. (National Maritime Museum, London)

they have achieved it. A 1988 Harris poll showed that two-thirds of white people believe that blacks "get equal pay for equal work." In fact, as U.S. Department of Labor statistics show, blacks in every occupational category are paid less than whites.

One reason America's ideals do not match reality is that they are general principles, not fixed rules of conduct. They derive from somewhat different experiences and philosophical traditions, and there are points at which they

This Thomas Nast cartoon from 1882 mocks restrictions on Chinese immigration, reflecting the fact that to some extent our cultural beliefs have always been myths. (Culver Pictures, Inc.)

conflict. Equality and diversity, for instance, emphasize fairness and a full opportunity for all to partake of society's benefits, whereas liberty and individualism emphasize personal freedom and threats posed to it by political power. Conflict between these sets of beliefs is inevitable. Both are commendable, but the advancement of one set comes only at some cost to the other. Take the issue of affirmative action. Proponents say that only through aggressive affirmative action programs will women and minorities receive the equal treatment in the job market to which they are entitled. Opponents say that aggressive affirmative action infringes unreasonably on the liberty of the employer and the initiative of the work force. Each side can say that it has America's ideals on its side, and no resort to logic can persuade either side that the opposing viewpoint should prevail.

Despite their inexact meanings, conflicting implications, and unfulfilled promise, the ideals of Americans have had a strong impact on the nation's politics. The United States would be a lesser nation today if not for the existence of its core values. All minority groups have gained, for example, from Americans' belief in equality. The idea that every individual has moral worth and is deserving of respect and fair treatment has given weight to demands for equality by those who have not attained it. As we will see in Chapter 5, no disadvantaged group—not blacks, Asians, Hispanics, Catholics, or Jews—has advanced toward equality without a struggle. Yet each group has drawn political strength from its appeal to America's image as a society of equal people. In such ways do cultural beliefs lend context and direction to a nation's politics.

★ CRITICAL THINKING

Cultural Beliefs as Myth and Reality

Cultural beliefs are mythical in that they are combinations of fact and wishful thinking. This mythical dimension can have far-reaching consequences. Consider the Harris poll in which two-thirds of white Americans said they believed that black Americans "get equal pay for equal work." The reality is otherwise: statistics indicate that, on average, blacks are paid less than whites in every job category. Does the mythical aspect of belief in equality allow white Americans to deceive themselves about how well off black Americans are? If not, what else might account for the misperception? To what degree do such misconceptions lessen the concern of white Americans with racial equality? Conversely, how does equality as myth promote progress in racial relations?

THE ORIGINS AND PERSISTENCE OF AMERICA'S IDEALS

In its two centuries as a nation, the United States has changed greatly. The first U.S. citizens lived a rural life near the Atlantic seaboard and were subject to the colonial ambitions of the great European powers. Today's Americans live in an urban society that spans an entire continent and is itself a world

The American ideal of equality has meant better employment opportunities for women in recent years. (Robert Rathe/ Stock, Boston)

THE MEDIA AND THE PEOPLE

LEARNING ABOUT THE AMERICAN WAY

The development of the American political culture was a result of the coincidence of western values and a New World that offered challenges and possibilities that were not found in the Old. One reason this culture has persisted is the country's natural advantages—in particular, its natural wealth and the protection its ocean barriers provide from potential enemies.

The maintenance of the American political culture also owes, however, to a learning process that social scientists call *political socialization* (which is discussed in detail in Chapter 8). Each generation teaches the next one and thereby contributes to the maintenance of the society's core beliefs. The socialization process starts in the family with exposure to the political views of one's parents and in the schools with the teaching of the country's history and traditions.

The mass media have become major agents of political socialization. The news and entertainment media highlight the values of the American political system with consistency and regularity. The messages are seldom delivered in a heavy-handed way, nor do they need to be. They reflect the beliefs of the audience, so that the media pass along and reinforce the culture's values almost automatically. The tendency is most apparent in the case of news about hostile nations. For decades, news about the Soviet Union was accompanied by explicit, and unflattering, comparisons of its values with ours.

All told, Americans get a thorough political education, as evidenced by the fact that some of our political catchphrases are so familiar that just about everyone can complete them:

"Government of, by, and for ________________."

"This land of the free and the home of __________."

"Life, liberty, and the pursuit of ______________."

"All men are created ___________________."

"One nation, under God, indivisible, with _______."

power. Yet the political life of the United States has been characterized by remarkable continuity because of the persistence of its founding ideals.

Most observers would agree that this continuity is the most remarkable feature of the country's governing experience. But where did these ideals come from and why do they persist? Although full answers to these questions would fill volumes, even partial answers are instructive.

A Free Country

Our popular history thrives on the illusion that freedom and justice were somehow invented in America in the late eighteenth century. In reality, the outlook of the first white American settlers was shaped by centuries of European life, which, in turn, had been molded by Greco-Roman and Judeo-Christian traditions. As Paul Gagnon has noted, "The first settlers did not sail into view out of a void, their minds as blank as the Atlantic Ocean. . . . Those who sailed west to America came in fact not to build a New World but to bring to life in a new setting what they treasured most from the Old World."[16]

America's special contribution was the enrichment of the freedom and dignity that the first settlers treasured most. The New World's vast wilderness and great distance from the mother country allowed a way of life that was unthinkable in the Old World.[17] Although British kings and Parliament tried to stretch their authority across the Atlantic Ocean, the great distance made it possible for the first white settlers to govern themselves more fully than even they had anticipated. They also found in America more liberty, equality, tol-

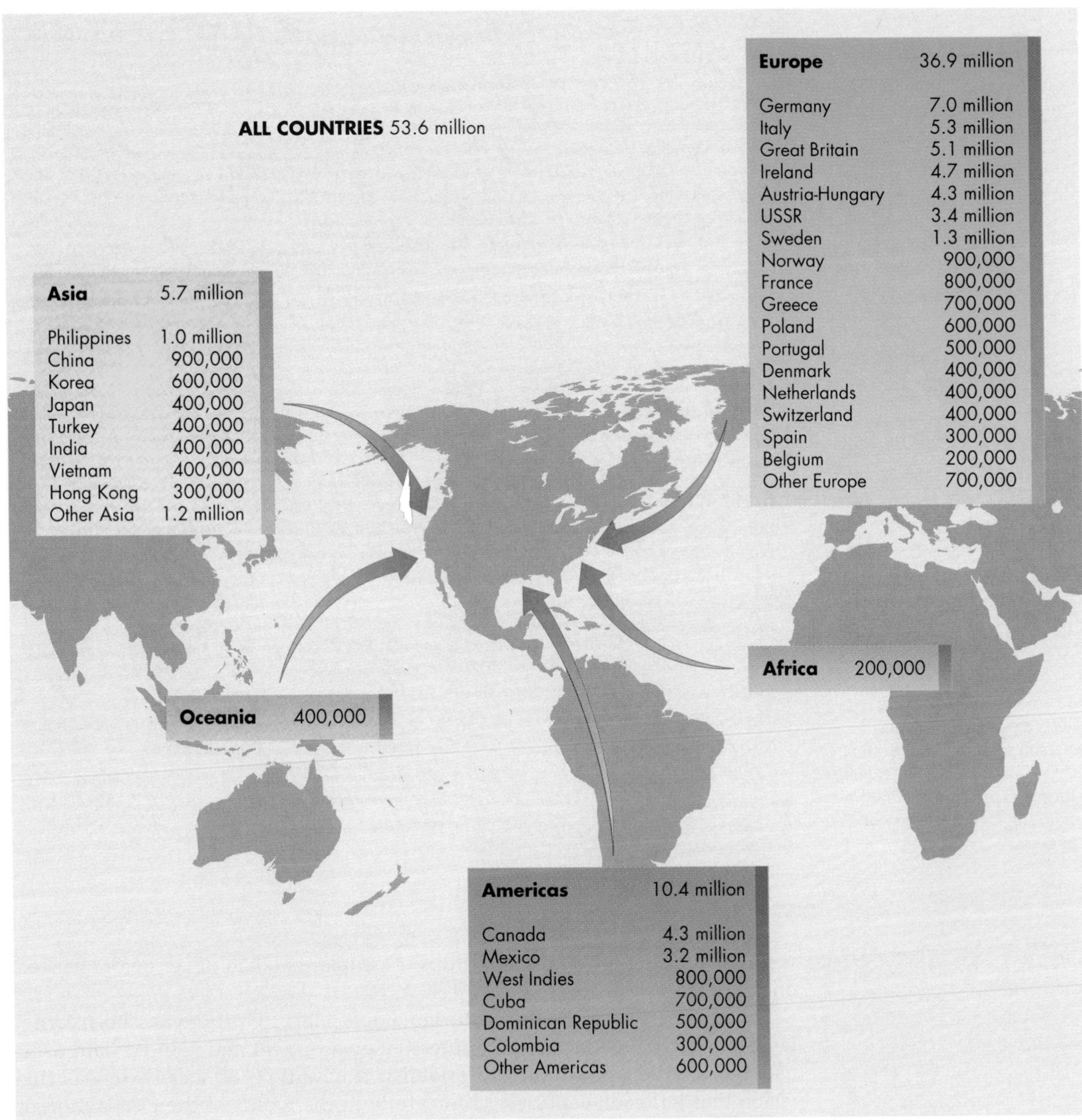

FIGURE 1-2 Total Immigration to the United States, 1820–1990, by Continent and Country of Origin
Source: U.S. Immigration and Naturalization Service.

erance, and opportunity than they had imagined. Europe's rigid aristocratic system was unenforceable in frontier America, where personal freedom was as close as the next area of unsettled wilderness.

Traditional ethnic and religious rivalries, while never far below the surface, were muted by the great task of settling America. Nationalities that warred constantly in Europe had to learn to coexist in America. Diversity became a watchword. Indeed, adherence to the "American Creed" was a virtual necessity in a country of mixed nationalities (see Figure 1-2). The nation's ideals

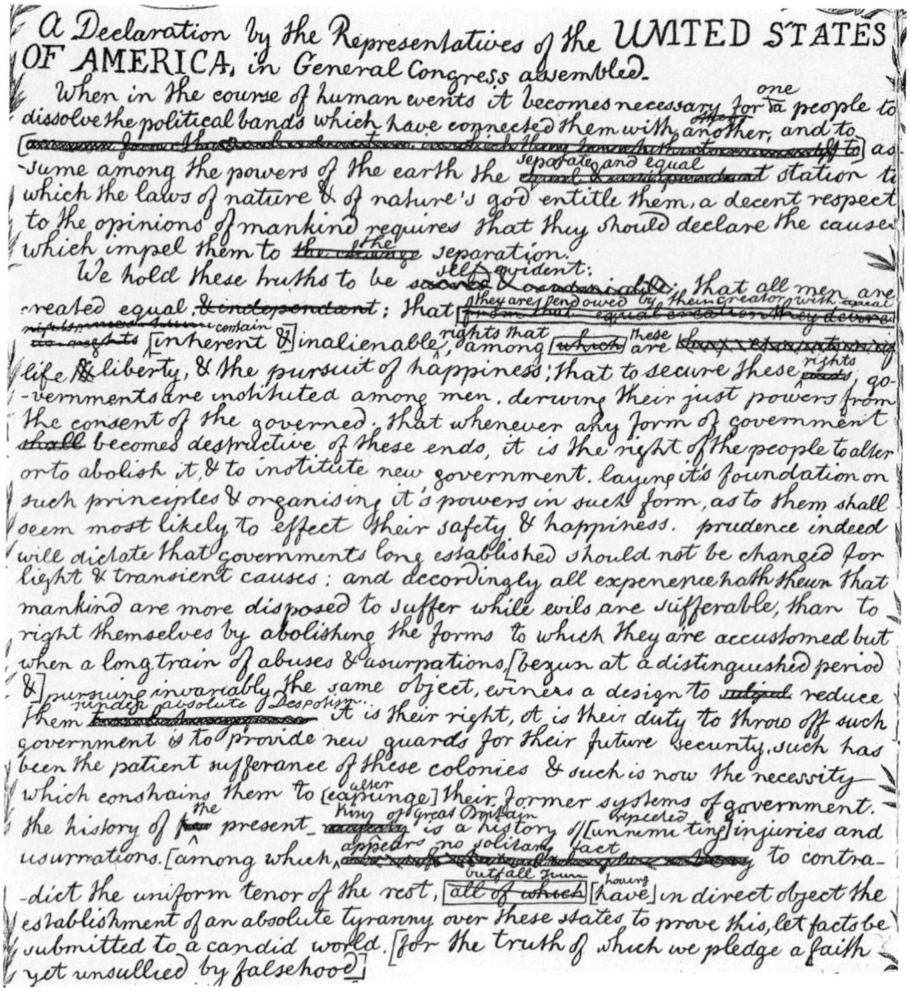

A Declaration by the Representatives of the UNITED STATES OF AMERICA, in General Congress assembled.

When in the course of human events it becomes necessary for one people to dissolve the political bands which have connected them with another, and to assume among the powers of the earth the separate and equal station to which the laws of nature & of nature's god entitle them, a decent respect to the opinions of mankind requires that they should declare the causes which impel them to the separation.

We hold these truths to be self-evident; that all men are created equal; that they are endowed by their creator with certain [inherent &] inalienable rights; that among these are life, & liberty, & the pursuit of happiness; that to secure these rights, governments are instituted among men, deriving their just powers from the consent of the governed; that whenever any form of government becomes destructive of these ends, it is the right of the people to alter or to abolish it, & to institute new government, laying it's foundation on such principles & organising it's powers in such form, as to them shall seem most likely to effect their safety & happiness. prudence indeed will dictate that governments long established should not be changed for light & transient causes: and accordingly all experience hath shewn that mankind are more disposed to suffer while evils are sufferable, than to right themselves by abolishing the forms to which they are accustomed. but when a long train of abuses & usurpations [begun at a distinguished period &] pursuing invariably the same object, evinces a design to reduce them under absolute Despotism, it is their right, it is their duty to throw off such government & to provide new guards for their future security. such has been the patient sufferance of these colonies; & such is now the necessity which constrains them to [expunge] their former systems of government. the history of the present king of Great Britain is a history of [unremitting] injuries and usurpations. [among which appears no solitary fact to contradict the uniform tenor of the rest, but all have] in direct object the establishment of an absolute tyranny over these states. to prove this, let facts be submitted to a candid world. [for the truth of which we pledge a faith yet unsullied by falsehood]

This is a portion of Thomas Jefferson's handwritten draft of the Declaration of Independence, a formal expression of America's governing ideals. (Library of Congress)

were the binding force among groups of people who had never before trusted one another.

The United States, as the historian Louis Hartz wrote, was "born free." Unencumbered by a legacy of oppressive government and age-old hatreds, it had the unique opportunity to establish a new type of society. It was this vision that Jefferson captured so forcefully in the words of the Declaration of Independence: "We hold these truths to be self-evident, that all men are created equal, that they are endowed by their Creator with certain unalienable rights, that among these are life, liberty, and the pursuit of happiness." The writing of the Constitution, eleven years after the Declaration, enabled them to strengthen their ideals by embodying them in the structure of their government (see Chapters 2 and 3). The country's elaborate system of checks and balances, for example, is designed to foster liberty by using power to offset power. In most countries final authority is vested in the national government alone, but in the United States it is also vested in state governments. In addition, at both the national and state levels, authority is divided among executive, legislative, and judicial branches. Many other democratic countries have no comparable fragmentation of power. *Extreme fragmentation of governing authority is a major characteristic of the American political system. This fact, as we will see in subsequent chapters, has profound implications for how politics is conducted, who wins out, and what policies result.*

A Rich Country

Although a proper constitution can promote a desired form of government, no constitution in and of itself can ensure the existence of such a government. Principles such as liberty and self-government tend to flourish only where wealth is reasonably abundant and widespread. In poor countries physical survival is a far more compelling issue than free speech or open elections.

Extreme poverty leads to a type of politics that restricts personal freedom, initiative, and influence, and contributes to intolerance and divisiveness. When Latin American countries achieved independence in the nineteenth century, they copied the U.S. Constitution but then fell under authoritarian rule. With their history of severe economic inequality based on the clash between the European and native cultures and on the rigid absolutism of the Spanish governing tradition, the Latin American countries were infertile ground for the implanting of democracy. Even today many of these nations are struggling to make democracy work against a background of entrenched privilege, abject poverty, and political violence.

The United States has the good fortune to be a rich land. Its vast fertile plains have made it a breadbasket of the world. It ranks among the top three countries worldwide in production of wheat, corn, potatoes, peanuts, cotton, eggs, cattle, and pigs. As for energy resources, the United States is first in uranium production, third in coal reserves, third in natural gas reserves, and sixth in petroleum reserves. In regard to nonfuel minerals, the United States ranks among the top five in copper, lead, sulfur, zinc, gold, iron ore, silver, and magnesium.[18] Americans are a fortunate people; their country's riches have enabled them to pursue a politics of high purpose.

The intimate connection between the nation's wealth and founding ideals is expressed in the so-called American Dream, which holds that anyone who works hard can succeed in America. The country's image as a land of opportunity has lured millions from abroad and buoyed the hopes of millions more already here. It is hardly surprising, then, that Americans have worried in recent years about the decline of the American Dream. Technological change and international competition have weakened the nation's industrial base with the result that wages and income have stagnated (see Figure 1-3). For the first time in history, young adults face the prospect of a standard of living below that of their parents.[19]

It is revealing, however, that individual Americans remain confident of their prospects for personal success. Although a majority of Americans today think the country is on the wrong track, an even larger majority do not see their personal lives in these terms (see Figure 1-4). They continue to believe that they will be rewarded by hard work. They are also confident that the nation's problems can be solved through individual initiative and enhanced opportu-

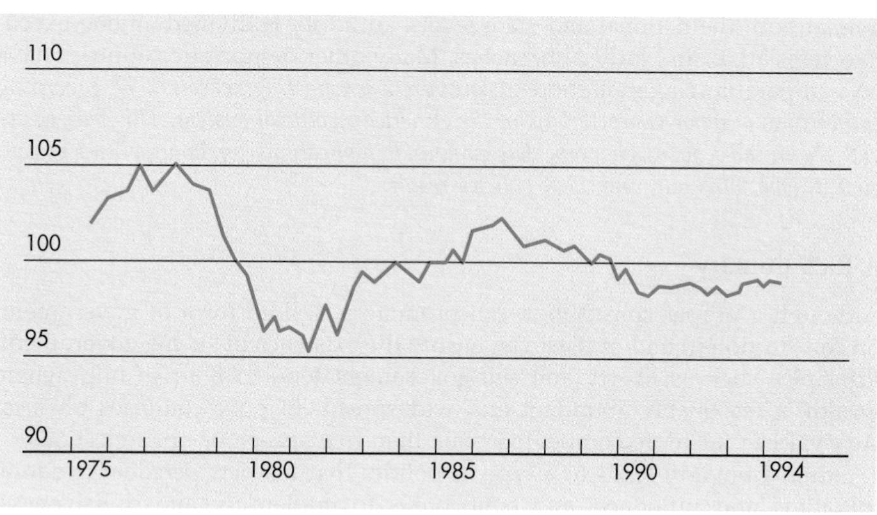

FIGURE 1-3 Trend in Real Wages of U.S. Work Force
Private wages and salaries, adjusted for inflation, have fallen during the past two decades, threatening the "American Dream." The second quarter of 1989 is used as the baseline ($n = 100$); numbers below that level represent a lower average level of real wages and salaries. *Source: Bureau of Labor Statistics.*

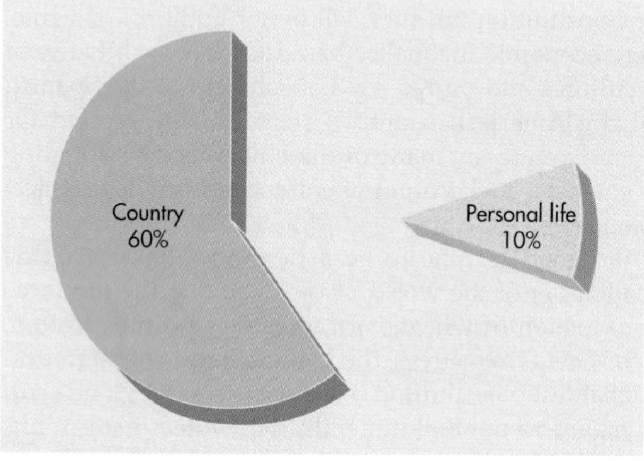

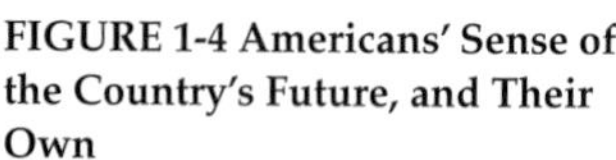

FIGURE 1-4 Americans' Sense of the Country's Future, and Their Own
The belief that things are on the "wrong track" drops sharply as the reference changes from the country to one's personal life. *Source: Survey by the Frank Luntz Research Companies, August 1994.*

nities. As most Americans see it, the way to renew the American Dream is to pursue it more vigorously.[20]

Politics: The Process of Deciding upon Society's Goals

Cultural ideals help shape what people expect from politics and how they conduct their politics. However, politics is more than the pursuit of shared ideals; it is also about getting one's own way. Commenting on the competitive nature of politics, Harold Lasswell described politics as the struggle over "who gets what, when, and how."[21]

CONFLICT AND CONSENSUS

Political conflict is rooted in two general conditions of society. One is scarcity. Society's resources are finite, but people's appetites are not. There is not enough wealth in even the richest of countries to satisfy everyone's desires.

Conflict over the distribution of resources is the inevitable result. This conflict is perhaps clearest on issues regarding how taxes will be spread among various income groups and who will be eligible for welfare benefits and how much those eligible will receive.

Differences in values are the other main source of political conflict. People see things in different ways. The right of abortion is freedom of choice to some and murder to others. People bring to politics a wide range of conflicting values—about abortion, about the environment, about the level of defense spending, about crime and punishment, about the poor, about the economy, about almost everything imaginable.

Politics in the United States is not the life and death struggle between opposing groups that typifies some countries, but there are many sources of contention. Perhaps no country has more competing interests than does the United States. Its settlement by people of many lands and religions, its enormous size and geographical diversity, and its economic complexity have made the United States a pluralistic nation. *This feature—competition for power among a great many interests of all kinds—is a major characteristic of American politics.*

It is a mistake to assume, however, that conflict is the sum of politics. At base, **government** is the effort of people to find agreeable ways of living together.[22] For government to work, people must have ways of advancing their collective interests as well as their separate ones. Government is not solely about winners and losers. It is also about problem solving. Public safety and national security are prime examples of people working together for an agreed-upon purpose.

government The effort of people to find agreeable ways of living together.

In the American case, public education has long been another area in which a conception of the common good has outweighed parochial concerns. Leon Sampson, a nineteenth-century American socialist, noted the stark difference between the philosophy of public education in the United States and that in Europe. "The European ruling classes," he said, "were open in their contempt for the proletariat. But in the United States equality, and even classlessness, the creation of wealth for all and political liberty were extolled in the public schools." Sampson concluded that American schools embodied a unique conception of equality: everyone was being trained in much the same way so that each person would have the opportunity to succeed. "It is," he said, "a socialist conception of capitalism."[23]

Of course, public education has never been a uniform experience for American children. Cities in the late nineteenth century neglected the education of many immigrant children, who were thereby placed at a permanent disadvantage. And southern schools for black children in the segregationist era were designed to keep them down, not lift them up. Today, whether an American child gets a good education depends to a significant extent on the wealth of the community in which he or she resides. The Supreme Court has concluded that government is obliged only to provide "an `adequate' education for all children," not "equality of education."[24] Nevertheless, compared with European democracies, the United States invests deeply in the education of its children and young adults (see Figure 1-5).

In sum, politics is a process that includes conflict *and* consensus, competition *and* cooperation. Accordingly, we shall define **politics** as, simply, the process through which a society makes its governing decisions.

politics The process through which society makes its governing decisions.

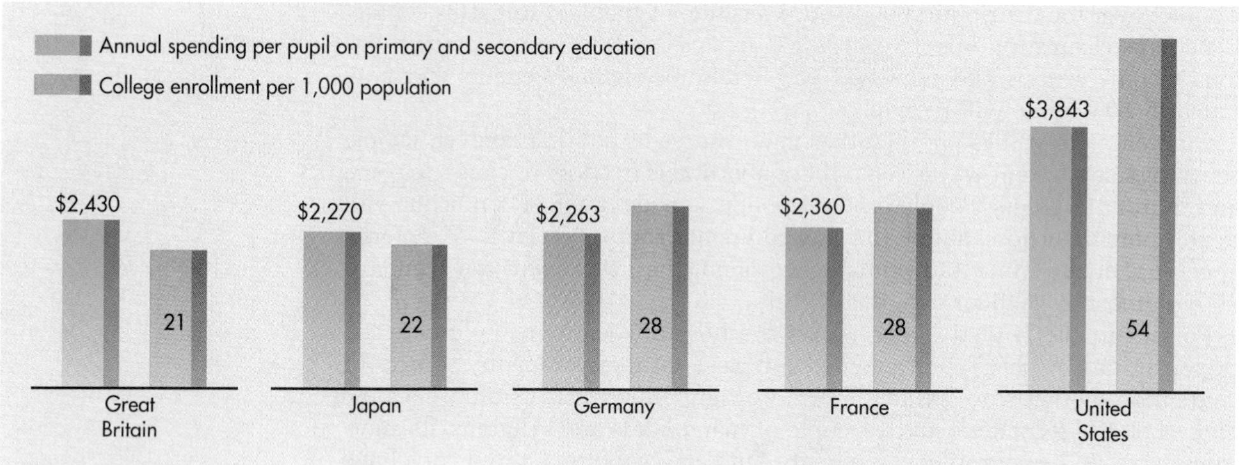

FIGURE 1-5 Spending on Primary and Secondary Education, and Levels of Enrollment, by Country Compared with European democracies, the United States spends more on education and makes a greater effort to provide the mass public with a college education. *Source: Organization for Economic Co-Operation and Development, 1992 (spending data), 1993 (enrollment data).*

power The ability of persons or institutions to control policy.

authority The recognized right of an official or institution to exercise power.

POWER, AUTHORITY, AND POLICY

Those who decide policy are said to have **power,** a term that refers to the ability of persons or institutions to control society's allocation of benefits and costs.[25] Power is perhaps the most basic concept of politics. Those who have sufficient power can decide how society will be governed. With so much at stake, it is not surprising that power is widely sought and often tightly held.

When power is exercised through the laws and institutions of government, the concept of authority applies. **Authority** can be defined as the recognized right of an individual, organization, or institution to make binding decisions. By this definition, government is not the only source of authority: parents have authority over their children; professors have authority over their students; firms have authority over their employees. However, government is a special case in that its authority is more encompassing in scope and more final in nature. Government's authority extends to all within its geographical boundaries. It can be used to redefine the authority of the parent, the professor, or the firm. Government's authority is also the most coercive. It includes the power to arrest and imprison, even to punish by death those who violate its rules.

policy Generally, any broad course of governmental action; more narrowly, a specific government program or initiative.

Governments exercise authority through policy. In its most general sense, policy refers to any broad course of action undertaken by government. U.S. **policy** toward Japan, for example, consists of a wide range of activities, from trade relations to diplomatic overtures. But policy is also used more narrowly to refer to specific programs or initiatives. The federal loan program for college students, for example, is a policy of government. The broad view of policy is the more evocative, because it acknowledges that government exercises authority by not making decisions as well as by making them. In choosing not to decide, a government accepts the existing situation, and the distribution of benefits and costs embedded in it.

THE RULES OF THE GAME

The play of politics takes place according to rules that the participants accept. The rules establish the process by which power is exercised, define the legitimate uses of power, and establish the basis for allocating costs and benefits among the participants. In the American case, the rules of the game of politics include democracy, constitutionalism, and capitalism.

Democracy

Democracy is a set of rules for determining who will exercise the authority of government. Democracy comes from the Greek words *demos,* which means "the people," and *kratis,* meaning "to rule." In simple terms, **democracy** is a form of government in which the people govern, either directly or through elected representatives.

democracy A form of government in which the people govern, either directly or through elected representatives.

Democratic government is based on the idea of the consent of the governed, which in practice has come to mean majority rule. The principle of majority rule, in turn, is based on the notion that the view of the many should prevail over the opinion of the few. The idea also reflects a kind of political equality in that the vote of each citizen counts equally, a principle expressed by the phrase "one person, one vote." In practice, democracy in America works primarily through elections. There are other, more direct forms of democracy, such as the town meeting and the initiative, but ours is a mainly representative system of government in which the people rule indirectly, through the officials they elect.

Democratic procedures, such as free and open elections, are not the same as democratic principles, such as self-government and equality. Rather, democratic procedures serve to promote democratic values. Elections are a means by which a people can achieve a greater degree of self-government and equality. Other rules for allocating governing authority, such as a hereditary monarchy, a theocracy, or a dictatorship, are not compatible with democratic principles. Democratic procedures are not, however, a guarantee that democratic values will flourish. Mexico is a case in point. Although Mexico in theory has a freely elected president and legislature, the system in practice is rigged. The outgoing president chooses the successor, who is then nominated by the dominant party, which has never lost a national election. Fraud in the counting of ballots has been widespread at times, and the Mexican legislature has acted as a rubber stamp for decisions made by the president.

Constitutionalism

For many Americans, "democracy" has the same meaning as "liberty"—the freedom to think, talk, and act as one chooses. However, the terms are not synonymous. The concept of democracy implies that the will of the majority should prevail over the wishes of the minority, whereas the concept of liberty implies that the minority has rights and liberties that cannot be taken away by the majority. The democratic model of government has long been accompanied by a fear of tyranny by the majority—the concern that a majority might ruthlessly impose its will on the minority. A more general concern about all government is the possibility of abuse of power. James Madison said that the possession of all power in the "same hands, whether of the many or the few, is the path to tyranny."[26]

Constitutionalism is a set of rules that restricts the lawful uses of power. In its original sense, constitutionalism in western society referred to a government based on laws and constitutional powers.[27] **Constitutionalism** has since

constitutionalism The idea that there are definable limits on the rightful power of a government over its citizens.

Free speech is a familiar aspect of constitutionalism. This anti–gun control rally took place in Austin, Texas. (Bob Daemmrich/The Image Works)

come to refer specifically to the idea that there are limits to the rightful power of government over citizens. In a constitutional system, officials govern according to law, and citizens have basic rights which government cannot take away or deny.[28] An example of constitutionalism in the United States is freedom of speech. Government is prohibited from interfering with the lawful exercise of free speech. No right is absolute, which means that some restrictions are permissible. For example, a person could be forcibly removed from the visitors' gallery overlooking the floor of the U.S. Senate for shouting at the lawmakers during debate. Nevertheless, free speech is broadly protected by the courts. During the war in the Persian Gulf, there were hundreds of demonstrations against U.S. policy without a single arrest and conviction for spoken words alone. There were instances where protesters were harassed by officials or other citizens, but those who opposed the war had the opportunity to express their views publicly.

The constitutional tradition in America is at least as strong as the democratic tradition. In fact, *a major characteristic of the American political system is its extraordinary emphasis on individual rights.* Issues that in other democratic countries would be resolved through elections and in legislatures are, in the United States, worked out through court action as well. As Tocqueville noted, there is hardly a political issue in America that does not sooner or later become a judicial issue.[29] Abortion rights, nuclear power, busing, toxic waste disposal, and welfare services are among the scores of issues that in recent years have been played out in part as questions of rights to be settled through judicial action.

This situation reflects the strong influence of cultural beliefs about liberty, individualism, equality, and diversity. Through claims to rights, Americans find protection against majorities and governmental authority, assert their individuality, and strive for equality, both as individuals and as groups.

Capitalism

Just as democracy and constitutionalism are each a set of rules governing the process by which society's costs and benefits are allocated, so too is capitalism. Societies have adopted alternative ways of organizing their economies. One way is socialism, which assigns government a large role in the ownership of the means of production, in regulating economic decisions, and in providing for the economic security of the individual. Under the form of socialism practiced in democratic countries, such as Sweden, the government does not attempt to manage the overall economy. In communist-style socialism, the government does take responsibility for overall management.

Capitalism is an alternative method for distributing economic costs and benefits. **Capitalism** holds that the government should interfere with the economy as little as possible. Free enterprise and self-reliance are the principles of capitalism. Firms are allowed to operate in a free and open marketplace, and individuals are expected to rely on their own initiative to establish their economic security.

capitalism An economic system based on the idea that government should interfere with economic transactions as little as possible. Free enterprise and self-reliance are the collective and individual principles that underpin capitalism.

As is the case with the rules of democracy and constitutionalism, the rules of capitalism are not neutral. If democracy responds to numbers and constitutionalism responds to rights, capitalism responds to wealth. Economic power is largely a function of accumulated wealth, whether in the hands of the individual or the firm. "Money talks" in a capitalist system, which means, among other things, that wealthier people will have by far the greater say in the distribution of costs and benefits through the economic system. This arrangement is not controversial in the United States: Americans strongly believe in the value of the free enterprise system (see Figure 1-6).

The United States does not have a purely capitalist system, in that the government plays a role in regulating and stimulating the economy (see Chapter 18).

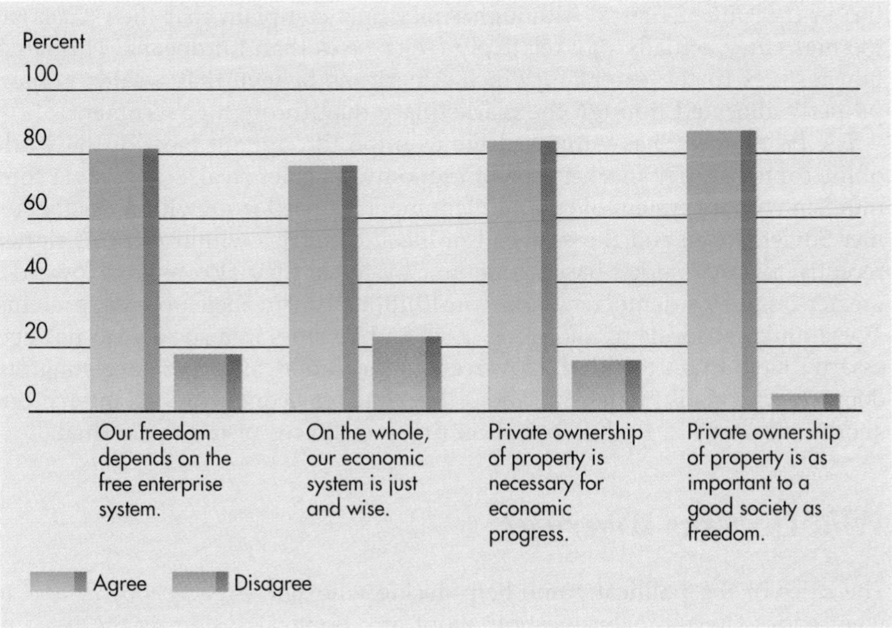

Percent
100
80
60
40
20
0
Our freedom depends on the free enterprise system.
On the whole, our economic system is just and wise.
Private ownership of property is necessary for economic progress.
Private ownership of property is as important to a good society as freedom.
Agree
Disagree

FIGURE 1-6 Opinions on Property and Capitalism
Americans strongly believe in the value of property rights and free enterprise. *Source: Adapted from Herbert McClosky and John Zaller, The American Ethos: Public Attitudes toward Capitalism and Democracy (Cambridge, Mass.: Harvard University Press, 1984), 133, 140 (Tables 5–1 and 5–3).*

Capitalism, the organizing principle of our economic system, emphasizes marketplace competition and self-initiative. As a result, economic wealth and power are very unequally distributed among Americans. This homeless man is on a sidewalk outside the White House. (Larry Downing/Woodfin Camp & Associates)

The term "mixed economy" is used to define this hybrid form of economic system, with its combination of socialist and capitalist elements. The United States has more elements of the capitalist model and fewer elements of the socialist model than do the countries of Europe. Because of their strong tradition of individualism, Americans tend to restrict the scope of governmental action in the area of the economy. *A major characteristic of the American system is a sharp distinction between what is political, and therefore to be decided in the public arena, and what is economic, and therefore to be settled in the private realm.*

For all practical purposes, this outlook places many kinds of choices, which in other countries are decided collectively, beyond the reach of political majorities in the United States. Although Americans complain that their taxes are too high, they actually pay relatively fewer taxes than Europeans. This situation testifies to the extent to which Americans believe that wealth is more properly allocated through the marketplace than through government.

The past decade has witnessed the triumph throughout most of the world of the capitalist, free market type of economy. Its chief rival, Soviet-style communism with its system of central planning, collapsed from within. As the former Soviet Union and the eastern European countries within its orbit shifted recently toward market-based economic systems, they also moved toward a greater degree of democracy and constitutionalism in their political systems. These different forms of allocating costs and benefits in a society do not necessarily have to go together. However, as the American experience suggests, democracy, constitutionalism, and a free market economy do reinforce one another in practice. Each is based on the free choices of free individuals.

Who Governs America?

The rules of the political game help decide who will exercise power and to what ends. The ultimate question about any political system is the issue of who governs. Is power widely shared and used for the benefit of the many? Or is power narrowly held and used to the advantage of the few? Although this entire book is in some respects an answer to these questions, it is useful here to consider what analysts have concluded about the American political system. Three broad theories predominate. None of them describes every aspect of American politics, but each has some validity.

RULE BY THE PEOPLE: MAJORITARIANISM

A basic principle of democracy, as discussed previously, is the idea of majority rule. **Majoritarianism** is the notion that the majority prevails not only in the counting of votes but also in the determination of public policy.

Majorities do sometimes rule in America. Their power is perhaps most evident in those states that offer voters the opportunity to decide directly on policy initiatives, which then become law if they receive a majority vote. The majority's influence is also felt indirectly through the decisions of elected representatives. When voters in the 1994 congressional elections expressed their dissatisfaction with "big government," President Clinton and members of Congress hurriedly initiated proposals to cut middle-class taxes. A more systematic assessment of the power of majorities is provided by Benjamin Page and Robert Shapiro's study of the relationship between majority opinions and more than 300 policy issues in the 1935–1979 period. On major issues particularly, they found that policy tended to change in the direction of change in majority opinion.[30]

Majorities do not always rule, however. There are many policy areas in which majority opinion is nonexistent or is ignored by policymakers. In these cases, other explanations of power and policy are necessary.

RULE BY GROUPS: PLURALISM

One of these explanations is provided by the theory of **pluralism,** which focuses on group activity and holds that many policies are effectively decided through power wielded by diverse (plural) interests.

Many policies are in fact more responsive to the interests of particular groups than to majority opinion. Agricultural subsidies, broadcast regulations, and corporate tax incentives are examples. In many cases, the general public has no real knowledge or opinion of issues that concern particular groups. For pluralists, the issue of whether interest-group politics serves the public good centers on whether a great many interests of a diverse nature achieve their goals. Pluralists contend that it is misleading to view society only in terms of majorities that may or may not form around given issues. They see society as primarily a collection of separate interests. Farmers, broadcasters, and multinational corporations have different needs and desires, and, according to the pluralist view, should have a large say in policies directly affecting them. Thus, as long as many groups have influence in their own area of interest, government is responding to the interests of most Americans. Pluralists such as Robert Dahl have argued that this is in fact the way the American political system operates most of the time.[31]

★ CRITICAL THINKING

Natural Advantages
In 1940 Senator Kenneth Wherry soberly exclaimed, "With God's help, we will lift Shanghai up and up, ever up, until it is just like Kansas City." Like many Americans before and since, Wherry assumed that our form of government could work as well nearly anywhere else in the world. In actuality, however, democracy has flourished only in societies where wealth is substantial and widely shared. Democracy has also worked best in physically secure countries and in those without a tradition of authoritarian rule.

Some analysts believe that the world is in an age when democracy will be extended throughout most of the globe. A main reason for this belief is the collapse of the Soviet empire.

What do you see as the likelihood of success of democracy elsewhere? What conditions will foster or inhibit the process of democratization? From what you know of the nondemocratic countries of Europe, Asia, Africa, and the Middle East, would you predict a democratic future for them? Why or why not?

majoritarianism The idea that the majority prevails not only in elections but also in determining policy.

pluralism A theory of American politics which holds that society's interests are substantially represented through the activities of groups.

YOUR TURN

AMERICA'S FUTURE, AND YOURS

The Questions:

1. Do you think the future generations of Americans will be better off, worse off, or about the same as people today?

   Better off | Worse off | About the same

2. As far as your personal future is concerned, are you optimistic or pessimistic about the opportunities for you to get ahead?

   Optimistic about personal opportunities | Pessimistic about personal opportunities

What Others Think: In a CBS News/New York Times poll conducted in 1992, only 25 percent of the respondents thought that future generations of Americans will be better off than people today. Larger proportions of respondents said future generations will be worse off (40 percent) or about the same (31 percent). These views are not mirrored, however, by Americans' thoughts about their own futures. A 1993 Roper survey indicated that 60 percent of Americans were optimistic about their personal opportunities to get ahead, whereas 33 percent were pessimistic.

Comment: These surveys reflect Americans' declining confidence in their nation's future and, to a lesser degree, their own. Thirty years ago, Americans had an almost unbounded belief in the so-called American Dream. While many people are still optimistic about the chances of personal success, they are concerned about their country's path. In a 1991 Gallup survey, only 37 percent expressed the unqualified belief that the United States is "the greatest country in the world," compared with 66 percent in a 1955 Gallup Poll. Americans' concerns today stem from fears of economic insecurity, governmental ineffectiveness, and declining moral values.

Some critics of pluralism question whether there is any real notion of the public good in a system that responds primarily to the demands of special interests (see Chapter 10). Other critics argue that pluralists wrongly assume that nearly all of society's interests are able to compete effectively through group politics. They see a system biased toward a small number of powerful groups. These critics are proponents of elite theory.

RULE BY A FEW: ELITISM

elitism The view that the United States is essentially run by a tiny elite (composed of wealthy or well-connected individuals) who control public policy through both direct and indirect means.

Elite theory offers a pessimistic view of the U.S. political system. **Elitism** holds that power in America is held by a small number of well-positioned, highly influential individuals who control policy for their own purposes. A leading proponent of elite theory was the sociologist C. Wright Mills, who argued that key policies are decided by an overlapping coalition of select leaders, including corporate executives, top military officers, and centrally placed public officials.[32] Other proponents of elite theory have defined the core group somewhat differently, but their contention is the same: America is essentially run, not by majorities or a plurality of groups, but by a small number of well-placed and privileged individuals.[33]

political system The various components of American government constitute a political system. The parts are separate, but they connect with each other, affecting how each performs.

Some elite theorists offer a conspiratorial view of the policy process. They see elites as operating behind the scenes and thus, even when there is the appearance of majority rule, actual power is wielded by a tiny group. In support of this contention, they note that key positions of political power are occupied by a relatively few people who often also have power in other realms, particularly industry.

Although some of the claims about a "power elite" are exaggerated, there

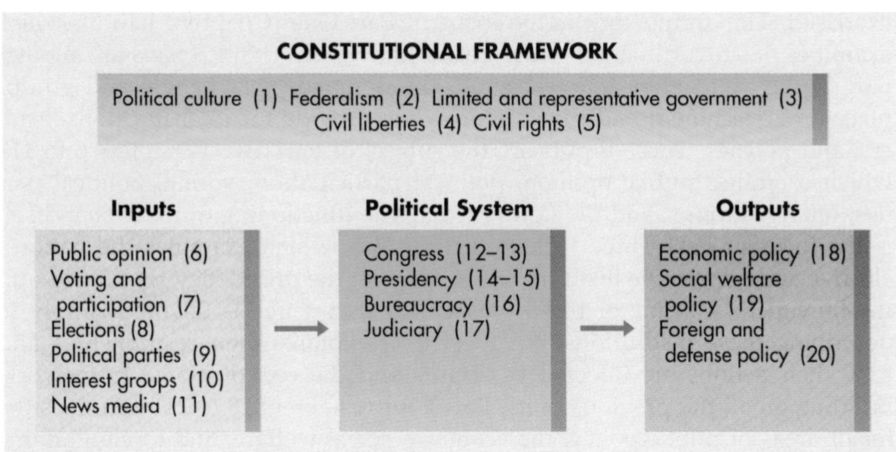

FIGURE 1-7 The American Political System
The book's chapters are organized within a political system's framework.

is no question that certain policy areas are controlled by a tiny circle of influential people. The nation's monetary policy, for example, is set by the decisions of the Federal Reserve Board, which meets in secrecy and is highly responsive to the concerns of bankers and financiers (see Chapter 18).

THIS BOOK'S VIEW OF POWER IN AMERICA

The perspective of this book is that each of these theories—majoritarianism, pluralism, and elitism—must be taken into account in any full explanation of politics and power in America. Some policies are decided by majority influence, whereas others reflect the influence of special interests and elites. The challenge is to distinguish the situations where each of these forms of influence predominate. Subsequent chapters will attempt that task.

The Concept of a Political System and the Book's Organization

As the foregoing discussion suggests, American government is based on a great many related parts, including the voters, institutions, interest groups, and the political culture. It is useful in some respects to regard these components as constituting a **political system.** The parts are separate but they connect with each other, affecting how each performs. The political scientist David Easton, who was a pioneer in this conception of politics, said that it makes little sense to study political relations piecemeal when they are, in reality, "interrelated."[34]

The complexity of government has kept political scientists from developing a dynamic explanatory model of the full political system, but the concept of politics as a system is useful for instructional purposes. The concept emphasizes the actual workings of government rather than its institutional structures alone. This approach characterizes this book, beginning with its organizational sequence.

As Figure 1-7 indicates, the political system operates against the backdrop of a constitutional framework that defines how power is to be obtained and exercised. This framework is the focus of Part One (Chapters 1 to 5), which examines the governmental structure and individual rights. *Inputs* are another part of the political system; these are the demands that people and groups place on government and the supports they provide for its institutions, leaders, and policies. These inputs are the subject of Part Two (Chapters 6 to 11), which examines public opinion, political participation, voting, political parties, interest groups, and the news media. The functioning of the system itself is the focus of Part Three (Chapters 12 to 17), which examines the nation's elective and appointive institutions—Congress, the presidency, the courts, and the bureaucracy. Some of the discussion in Part Three is devoted simply to describing these institutions, but most of it explores their relationships and how their actions are affected by inputs and the constitutional framework. Building on all the previous units, Part Four (Chapters 18 to 21) examines the major areas of public policy: the economy, social welfare, and foreign affairs. These are the system's *outputs:* its binding decisions on society.

The chapters are collectively designed to convey a reliable body of knowledge that will enable the reader to think broadly and systematically about the nature of the American political system. To assist in this process, this chapter has identified five encompassing tendencies of American politics that will be examined more closely in later chapters. The United States has:

- An enduring set of cultural ideals that are its people's common bond and a source of their political goals
- An extreme fragmentation of governing authority that is based on an elaborate system of checks and balances
- A great many competing interests that are the result of the nation's great size, population diversity, and economic complexity
- A strong emphasis on individual rights that is a consequence of the nation's political traditions
- A sharp separation of the political and economic spheres that has the effect of placing many economic issues outside the reach of political majorities

Underlying this book's concern with the broad patterns of the American political system is a question that must be asked of any democracy: What is the relationship of the people to their government? The answer to this question is the foundation not only of a reasonable assessment of the state of American democracy but also of good citizenship. Responsible citizenship depends finally on an informed perspective, on a recognition of how difficult it is to govern effectively and yet how important it is to try. It cannot be said too often that the issue of governing is the most difficult issue facing any society. Nor can it be said too often that governing is a quest, not a resolved issue. The Constitution's opening phrase, "We, the People," is a call to Americans to join that quest. E. E. Schattschneider said it clearly: "In the course of centuries, there has come a great deal of agreement about what democracy is, but nobody has a monopoly of it and the last word has not been spoken."[35]

Summary

The United States is a nation that was formed on a set of ideals that include liberty, equality, self-government, individualism, diversity, and unity. These ideals were rooted in the country's European heritage, and early America's vast open lands and abundant natural resources influenced their growth. They became Americans' common bond and today are the basis of their political culture. Although they are mythic, inexact, and conflicting, these ideals have had a powerful effect on what generation after generation of Americans has tried to achieve politically for themselves and others.

Politics is the process by which it is determined whose values will prevail in society. The basis of politics is conflict over scarce resources and competing values. Those who have power win out in this conflict and are able to control governing authority and policy choices. In the case of the United States, no one faction controls all power and policy. Majorities govern on some issues, while groups and elites each govern on other issues.

The play of politics in the United States takes place through rules of the game that include democracy, constitutionalism, and capitalism. Democracy is rule by the people, which, in practice, refers to a representative system of government in which the people rule through their elected officials. Constitutionalism refers to rules that limit the rightful power of government over citizens. Capitalism is an economic system based on a free market principle that allows the government only a limited role in determining how economic costs and benefits will be allocated.

Major Concepts

authority
capitalism
constitutionalism
democracy
diversity
elitism
equality
government
individualism
liberty
majoritarianism
pluralism
policy
political culture
political system
politics
power
self-government
unity

Suggested Readings

Dahl, Robert. *Democracy and Its Critics.* New Haven, Conn.: Yale University Press, 1989. An analysis of democratic politics by a leading advocate of pluralism.

Domhoff, William. *The Power Elite and the State: How Policy Is Made in America.* New York: Aldine de Gruyter, 1990. A critical assessment of American government by a leading proponent of elite theory.

Ellis, Richard J. *American Political Cultures.* New York: Oxford University Press, 1993. An assessment of the American political culture which concludes that individualism and egalitarianism are the main dimensions.

Fliegelman, Jay. *Declaring Independence: Jefferson, Natural Language, and the Culture of Performance.* Stanford, Calif.: Stanford University Press, 1993. An analysis of the role of language in the forging of a national identity at the founding of the American state.

Geertz, Clifford. *Myth, Symbol, and Culture.* New York: Norton, 1974. An analysis of the mythic and symbolic nature of cultural beliefs.

Hartz, Louis. *The Liberal Tradition in America.* New York: Harcourt, Brace, 1955. A classic assessment of the liberal tradition that underlies the American political system.

Merelman, Richard. *Making Something of Ourselves: On Culture and Politics in the United States.* Berkeley: University of California Press, 1984. An evaluation of culture and politics in the United States.

Norton, Anne. *Republic of Signs: Liberal Theory and American Popular Culture.* Chicago: University of Chicago Press, 1993. An insightful study of just how deeply American ideals have seeped into the country's symbols and language.

Pangle, Lorraine Smith, and Thomas L. Pangle. *The Learning of Liberty: The Educational Ideas of the American Founders.* Lawrence: University of Kansas Press, 1993. An intriguing exploration of the implications for education of America's founding ideals.

Shafer, Byron E., ed. *Is America Different? A New Look at American Exceptionalism.* New York: Oxford University Press, 1991. A series of essays on the issue of the unique nature of the American political culture.

CHAPTER 2

FEDERAL GOVERNMENT: FORGING A NATION

The question of the relation of the states to the federal government is the cardinal question of our Constitutional system. It cannot be settled by the opinion of one generation, because it is a question of growth, and each successive stage of our political and economic development gives it a new aspect, makes it a new question.

—Woodrow Wilson[1]

The Republican-controlled Senate moved quickly on legislation that would make it harder for Congress to impose mandates on state and local governments without also providing the funds to carry them out. The measure was the first bill introduced when the Senate convened, giving it the coveted designation as Senate bill S.1. It was part of the Republicans' Contract with America, which aimed to reduce the size and authority of the federal government.

The bill had strong backing from governors and mayors, who had borne the financial burden of federally mandated programs. States were required in their highway construction to use asphalt made with ground-up tires, even though this composition was more expensive than ordinary asphalt. Localities were required to test groundwater for a long list of chemicals and other contaminants, even if they had never shown up in the area's water supply. Pete Wilson, California's governor, even complained about Congress's "motor-voter" legislation, which required states to provide voter registration applications to car owners when they registered their autos. The total cost of such mandates to state and local governments was estimated at $3 billion annually. Senate bill S.1 would not eliminate existing mandates or prevent the enactment of new ones, but it would require Congress to fund any mandate that would cost states and localities more than $50 million annually.

Although the legislation was endorsed by the Clinton administration and cosponsored by a number of Democratic senators, it was opposed by other Democrats and by environmental, labor, and consumer groups. They feared that state and local governments would revert to the old practice of looking the other way while firms degraded the environment and exposed workers and consumers to hazardous risks. They doubted that mayors and governors, when faced with budgetary and corporate pressures, would keep their promise to maintain high environmental and safety standards in the absence of federally mandated requirements.

Senate bill S.1 is one of thousands of controversies that have occurred over the course of American history that have hinged on whether national or state authority should prevail. Americans possess what amounts to dual citizenship: they are citizens both of the United States and of the state in which they live. The American political system is a *federal system,* one in which constitutional authority is divided between a national government and state governments: each is assumed to derive its powers directly from the people and therefore to have sovereignty (final authority) over the policy responsibilities assigned to it. The federal system consists of nation *and* states, indivisible and yet separate.[2]

This initial chapter on American constitutionalism focuses on federalism. The nature of the relationship between the nation and the states was the question that dominated all others when the Constitution was written in 1787, and this chapter describes how the issue helped form the Constitution. The chapter's closing sections discuss how federalism has changed during the nation's history and conclude with a brief overview of contemporary federalism. The main points presented in the chapter are the following:

★ *The power of government must be equal to its responsibilities.* The Constitution was needed because the nation's preceding system (under the Articles of Confederation) was too weak to accomplish its expected goals, particularly those of a strong defense and an integrated economy. The Constitution created a stronger national government by granting it significant powers, particularly in the areas of taxation and the regulation of commerce.

★ *Federalism—the Constitution's division of governing authority between two levels, nation and states—was the result of political bargaining.* Federalism was not a theoretical principle, but a compromise made necessary in 1787 by the prior existence of the states.

★ *Federalism is not a fixed principle for allocating power between the national and state governments,* but a principle that has changed in response to changing political needs. Federalism has passed through several distinct stages during the nation's history.

★ *Contemporary federalism tilts toward national authority, reflecting the increased interdependence of American society.* However, there is a current trend toward reducing the scope of federal authority.

Before the Constitution: The Articles of Confederation

On June 12, 1776, as the thirteen American colonies braced for a full-scale revolutionary war against England, the Continental Congress appointed a committee composed of a member from each colony to decide the form of a central government. The task would be difficult. The colonies had always been governed separately, and their residents considered themselves Virginians, New Yorkers, or Pennsylvanians as much as they thought of themselves as Americans. Moreover, the American Revolution was sparked by grievances against the arbitrary policies of King George III of England, and Americans were in no mood to replace him with a powerful central authority of their own making.

These concerns led to the formation of a very weak national government that was subordinate to the states. Under its constitution, known as the Articles of Confederation, each state kept its "sovereignty, freedom, and independence." There was a national Congress, but its members were appointed and paid by their respective state governments. Each of the thirteen states had one vote in Congress, and the agreement of nine states was required to pass legislation. Moreover, any state could block constitutional change: the Articles of Confederation could be amended only by unanimous approval of the states.

The American union held together during the Revolutionary War out of necessity: the states had either to cooperate or to surrender to the British. But once the war ended, the states felt free to go their separate ways. Several states sent representatives abroad to negotiate trade agreements. Others negotiated directly with the Indian tribes. New Hampshire, with its 18-mile coastline, even established its own navy. In a melancholy letter to Thomas Jefferson, George Washington wondered whether the United States deserved to be called a nation.

A LACK OF NATIONAL POWER

Under the Articles of Confederation, Congress was denied the powers it needed if it was to achieve national goals. Although Congress had responsibility for defense of the states, it was not granted the power to tax, and so it had to rely on the states for the money to maintain an army and navy. During the first six years under the Articles, Congress asked the states for $12 million but received only $3 million—not even enough to pay the interest on Revolutionary War debts. Georgia and North Carolina contributed no money at all to the national treasury between 1781 and 1786. By 1786 the national government was so desperate for funds that it sold the navy's ships and had fewer than 1,000 soldiers in uniform—this at a time when England had an army in Canada and Spain occupied Florida.

Congress was also expected to shape a national economy, yet it was powerless to do so because the Articles forbade interference with the states' commerce policies. States imposed trade barriers among themselves. Connecticut placed a higher tariff on finished goods from Massachusetts than it did on the same goods shipped from England. New Jersey imposed a duty on foreign-made goods shipped from other states. New York responded by taxing goods from New Jersey shipped through New York ports.

The Articles of Confederation showed the fallacy of the adage "That government is best which governs least." The consequences of an overly weak authority were abundantly clear: public disorder, economic chaos, and inadequate defense.

County courthouses in Massachusetts in 1786 were the scenes of brawls between angry farmers and those who supported the state's attempts to foreclose on their property because of unpaid debts. The violence of Shays' Rebellion convinced many political leaders that the central government needed to be more powerful. (The Bettmann Archive)

A NATION IN DISARRAY

By 1784 the nation was unraveling. Congress was so weak that its members often did not bother to attend its sessions.[3] Finally, in late 1786, a revolt in western Massachusetts prompted leading Americans to conclude that the country's government had to be changed. A ragtag army of 2,000 farmers, armed with pitchforks, marched on county courthouses to prevent foreclosures on their land and cattle. Many of the farmers were veterans of the Revolutionary War; their leader, Daniel Shays, had been a captain in the Revolutionary army. They had been given assurances during the Revolution that their land, which lay fallow because they were away at war, would not be confiscated for reasons of unpaid debts and taxes.

Although many Americans sympathized with the farmers, Shays' Rebellion scared propertied interests, and they called upon the governor of Massachusetts to put down the revolt. He asked Congress for help, but it had no army to send.[4] He finally raised enough money to hire a militia that put down the rebellion, but Shays' Rebellion made it clear that a strengthening of national authority was necessary if the United States was to be saved. At the urging of the legislatures of several states, Congress authorized a constitutional convention to be held in late spring of 1787 in Philadelphia. Congress planned a limited convention: the delegates were to meet for "the sole and express purpose of revising the Articles of Confederation."

Negotiating toward a Constitution

The delegates to the Philadelphia constitutional convention ignored the instructions of Congress. They drafted a plan for an entirely new form of government. Prominent delegates (among them George Washington, Benjamin Franklin, and James Madison) were determined from the outset to establish an American nation built upon a strong central government. Recognizing what was likely to happen in Philadelphia, Patrick Henry, a fervent believer in state-level government, said that he "smelt a rat." When the convention adjourned, he realized that his fears were justified. "Who authorized them," he asked, "to speak the language of 'We, the People,' instead of 'We, the States'?"[5]

That question—"people or states?"—was the central one confronting the Philadelphia convention. If the national government was to be effective, as Pennsylvania's James Wilson argued, it had to be a government of the people, not of the states. The Confederation was inherently weak because the central government had no sure way short of war on a state to make it comply with the laws.

The process of writing the Constitution was a contentious one. All the delegates were men of means: they were for the most part lawyers, large landowners, and merchants. They shared a commitment to the interests of the propertied class, but they also had their differences. The Constitution is sometimes portrayed as the work of intellectual geniuses who put politics aside to create a document that would endure the test of time. In reality, the Framers of the Constitution fought like any other group of politicians, each promoting

The Constitution was written during the summer of 1787 in the East Room of the Old Pennsylvania State House, where the Declaration of Independence had been signed a decade earlier. The room was shuttered to keep eavesdroppers from listening in on the debate. Today, the building is a historical site. (Werner Krutein/Liaison International)

the ideas and values in which he believed. What set the Framers apart was the nature of the times in which they lived. They had experienced the American Revolution and the problems of nation building. They had thought long about and worked hard at the problems of government, and the Philadelphia convention gave them a unique opportunity to apply the constitutional lessons they had learned.

The Framers were astute politicians. After the Constitution was written, they decreed that it would take effect if ratified in special conventions by nine of the thirteen states. In establishing this process the Framers ignored their mandate from Congress, which required any change in the Articles to be confirmed by all the states. The Constitution would not have been adopted if Congress's procedure had been followed. North Carolina and Rhode Island were steadfastly opposed to the Constitution until it was clear that the other states would form a union without them, leaving them weak and isolated.

THE GREAT COMPROMISE: A TWO-CHAMBER CONGRESS

Debate at the constitutional convention of 1787 began over a plan put forward by the Virginia delegation, which was dominated by strong nationalists. The Virginia Plan (also called the large-state plan) called for a two-chamber Congress that would have supreme authority in all areas "in which the separate states are incompetent," particularly defense and interstate trade. The Virginia Plan also provided that the states would have numerical representation in Congress in proportion to their populations or tax contributions. Either way, representatives of the small states would be greatly outnumbered. Small states such as Delaware and Rhode Island would be allowed only one representative in the lower chamber, while large states such as Massachusetts and Virginia would have more than a dozen.

Not surprisingly, the Virginia Plan was roundly condemned by delegates from the smaller states. They rallied around a counterproposal made by New Jersey's William Paterson. The New Jersey Plan (also called the small-state plan) called for a stronger national government with the power to tax and to regulate commerce among the states; in most other respects, however, the Articles would remain in effect. Congress would have a single chamber in which each state, large or small, would have a single vote.

The debate over the New Jersey and Virginia plans dragged on for weeks before the delegates reached what is now known as the *Great Compromise.* It provided for a bicameral (two-chamber) Congress: the House of Representatives would be apportioned among the states on the basis of population and the Senate on the basis of an equal number of votes (two) for each state. The small states would never have agreed to join a union in which their vote was always weaker than that of large states,[6] a fact reflected in Article V of the Constitution: "No state, without its consent, shall be deprived of its equal suffrage in the Senate."

THE NORTH-SOUTH COMPROMISE: THE ISSUE OF SLAVERY

The separate interests of the states were also the basis for a second major compromise: a North-South bargain over economic issues. The South had a slave-based agricultural economy, and its delegates feared that the North, which

Southern delegates at the Constitutional Convention sought assurances that Congress would not bar the importation and sale of slaves and that their slave-based agricultural economy would be protected. The photo shows a Civil–War era building in Atlanta that was a site of slave auctions. (UPI/Bettmann)

had a stronger manufacturing sector, would gain a numerical majority in Congress and then proceed to enact unfair tax policies. If Congress levied high import tariffs on finished goods from foreign nations in order to protect domestic manufacturers and placed heavy export tariffs on agricultural goods, the burden of financing the new government would fall mainly on the South. Its delegates also worried that northern representatives in Congress might tax or even bar the importation of slaves.

After extended debate, a compromise was reached. Congress was to be prohibited by the Constitution from taxing exports but could tax imports. In addition, Congress would be prohibited from passing laws to end the slave trade until 1808. The South also gained a constitutional provision requiring each state to return runaway slaves to their state of origin. A final bargain was the infamous "Three-fifths Compromise": for purposes of both taxation and representation in Congress, five slaves were to be considered the equivalent of three white people; in effect, a slave was to be counted as three-fifths of a human being.

Although the Philadelphia convention has been criticized for the compromise over slavery, the issue of slavery was a powerful argument against a union. Northern states had no economic use for forced labor and had few slaves, whereas southern states had based their economies on large slave populations (see Table 2-1). John Rutledge of South Carolina asked during the convention debate whether the North regarded southerners as "fools." Southern

TABLE 2-1 U.S. Population and Percentage of African Americans, by State, 1790

State	*Total Population*	*African Americans (Percent)*
Connecticut	238,000	2.5%
Delaware	59,000	22.0
Georgia	83,000	36.1
Maryland	320,000	21.3
Massachusetts	476,000	1.3
New Hampshire	142,000	0.7
New Jersey	184,000	7.6
New York	340,000	7.6
North Carolina	394,000	26.9
Pennsylvania	434,000	2.3
Rhode Island	69,000	5.8
South Carolina	249,000	43.8
Virginia	748,000	40.9

SOURCE: U.S. Bureau of Census *Historical Statistics of the United States, Colonial Times to 1970,* Part I (Washington, D.C.: U.S. Government Printing Office, 1975), 24–36.

delegates declared that they would bolt the convention and form their own union rather than join one that prohibited slavery.

Federalism: National and State Sovereignty

federalism A governmental system in which authority is divided between two sovereign levels of government: national and regional.

sovereignty The ultimate authority to govern within a certain geographical area.

confederacy A governmental system in which sovereignty is vested entirely in subnational (state) governments.

unitary system A governmental system in which the national government alone has sovereign (ultimate) authority.

Viewed historically, the most important constitutional decision of the Philadelphia convention was one that underpinned all the deliberations but was not itself debated at great length. This decision was the establishment of **federalism,** which is a system in which **sovereignty,** or ultimate governing authority, is divided between a national government and regional (that is, state) governments. Because of federalism, the U.S. national government must act with due regard for the states, which are protected constitutionally from being abolished and from unwarranted interference in their policies.

Unlike many other features of the U.S. Constitution, the provisions for federalism had no basis in political theory. Indeed, federalism did not exist anywhere in the world before 1787. The United States had been governed as a **confederacy,** in which sovereignty was vested entirely in the state governments. Other countries had unitary systems of government. A **unitary system** vests sovereignty solely in the national government, which at its discretion has the authority to determine the structure and policies of the governments under it.

Within the U.S. federal system, there is a form of unitary government in the relationship between the states and their local governments. Although local units often have considerable autonomy, it is granted at the discretion of the state government, which can overturn local policy and in some circumstances can even abolish a local unit.

Federalism was an accommodation between the ideals of unity and diversity. The states already existed and had the loyalty of their people. When Virginia's George Mason said that he would never consent to a union that abolished the states, he was speaking for nearly all the delegates in Philadelphia. Americans would be governed as one people through their national government and as separate peoples through their respective state governments.

Alexander Hamilton (1757-1804), a strong nationalist was just thirty-two years old when he served as a delegate to the Constitutional Convention. (Courtesy of the New York Historical Society, NYC)

THE POWERS OF THE NATION

The Philadelphia convention met to decide the powers of the national government. Accordingly, the U.S. Constitution focuses primarily on the lawful authority of the national government, which is provided through *enumerated* and *implied powers.* Authority that is not in this way granted to the national government is left—or "reserved"—to the states. Thus the states have *reserved powers.*

Enumerated Powers

The primary goal of the writers of the Constitution was to establish a national government strong enough to forge a union that was secure in its defense and open in its commerce. The powers necessary to the achievement of this goal were granted to Congress, which would make the laws. The president would execute the laws, and the judiciary would rule upon them.

Congress's lawmaking powers are listed in Article I, section 8, of the Constitution. Seventeen in number, these **enumerated powers** (or **expressed powers**) include, for instance, the powers to tax, to establish an army and navy, to declare war, to regulate commerce among the states, to create a national

enumerated powers (expressed powers) The seventeen powers granted to the national government under Article I, section 8 of the Constitution. These powers include taxation and the regulation of commerce as well as the authority to provide for the national defense.

HOW THE UNITED STATES COMPARES

FEDERAL VS. UNITARY GOVERNMENTS

Federalism involves the division of sovereignty between a national government and subnational (such as state) governments. It was invented in 1787 in order to maintain the preexisting American states while establishing an effective central government. Since then a number of other countries have established a *federal* government, but most countries have a *unitary* government, in which all sovereignty is vested in a national government. In some cases, countries have developed hybrid versions. Great Britain's government is formally unitary, but Parliament has granted some autonomy to regions. Mexico's system is formally federal, but in actuality nearly all power is concentrated in the national government.

Country	*Form of Government*
Canada	Federal
France	Unitary
Germany	Federal
Great Britain	Modified unitary
Italy	Modified unitary
Japan	Unitary
Mexico	Modified federal
United States	Federal
Sweden	Unitary

currency, and to borrow money. In theory at least, these powers would enable the national government to achieve the common goals that the government of the Articles of Confederation had been unable to achieve. Congress's powers of commerce and currency, for example, would allow it to create a foundation for a viable national economy. The Constitution also prohibits the states from interfering with the national government's exercise of its lawful powers. Article I, section 10, forbids the states to make treaties with other nations, raise armies, wage war, print money, or make commercial agreements with other states without the approval of Congress.

The writers of the Constitution recognized that the lawful exercise of national authority would at times conflict with the actions of the states. In such instances, national law was intended to prevail. Article VI of the Constitution grants this dominance in the so-called **supremacy clause,** which provides that "the laws of the United States . . . shall be the supreme law of the land."

supremacy clause Article VI of the Constitution, which makes national law supreme over state law when the national government is acting within its constitutional limits.

Implied Powers

The Framers of the Constitution also recognized that an overly narrow definition of national authority would result in a government incapable of adapting to change. Under the Articles of Confederation, Congress was limited to those powers expressly granted to it, inhibiting its ability to respond effectively to the country's changing needs after the Revolutionary War. Concerned that the enumerated powers by themselves might be too restrictive of national authority, the Framers added the **"necessary and proper" clause,** or, as it later came to be known, the **elastic clause**. Article I, section 8, gives Congress the power "to make all laws which shall be necessary and proper for carrying into execution the foregoing [enumerated] powers." This grant gave the national government **implied powers:** the authority to take action that is not expressly authorized by the Constitution but that supports actions that are so authorized.

"necessary and proper" clause (elastic clause) The authority granted Congress in Article I, section 8 of the Constitution "to make all laws which shall be necessary and proper" for the implementation of its enumerated powers.

implied powers The federal government's constitutional authority (through the "necessary and proper" clause) to take action that is not expressly authorized by the Constitution but which supports actions that are so authorized.

The Authority of the States: Reserved Powers

The Framers' preference for a sovereign national government was not shared in 1787 by all Americans. Although Anti-Federalists (as opponents of the Constitution were called) recognized a need to strengthen defense and interstate commerce, they feared the consequences of a strong central government. The interests of the people of New Hampshire were not identical to those of Georgians or Pennsylvanians, and the Anti-Federalists argued that only state-centered government would protect and preserve this diversity.

The Federalists (supporters of the Constitution) responded by asserting that the national government would have no interest in submerging the states.[7] The national government would take responsibility for establishing a strong defense and for promoting a sound economy, while the states would retain nearly all other governing functions, including oversight of public morals, education, and safety. The national government, James Madison said, would neither want these responsibilities nor have the competence to fulfill them.[8]

This argument did not persuade the Anti-Federalists that their fears of an intrusive national government were unfounded. Even some of the Americans who were otherwise inclined to support the proposed constitution worried that it would lead to an overly powerful national government. The supremacy and "necessary and proper" clauses were particularly worrisome, since they provided a constitutional basis for future expansions of national authority. Such concerns led to demands for a constitutional amendment that would protect the states against encroachment by the national government. Ratified in 1791 as the Tenth Amendment to the Constitution, it reads: "The powers not delegated to the United States by the Constitution, nor prohibited by it to the States, are reserved to the States . . . " The states' powers under the U.S. Constitution are thus called **reserved powers.***

reserved powers The powers granted to the states under the Tenth Amendment to the Constitution.

Federalism in Historical Perspective

Since ratification of the Constitution two centuries ago, no aspect of it has provoked more frequent or bitter conflict than federalism. By establishing two levels of sovereign authority, the Constitution created competing centers of power and ambition, each of which was sure to claim disputed areas as belonging within its realm of authority.

Conflict between national and state authority was also ensured by the brevity of the Constitution. The Framers deliberately avoided detailed provisions, recognizing that brief phrases would give flexibility to the government they were creating. The document does not define what is meant by the "necessary and proper" clause, does not list any of the states' reserved powers, does not indicate whether the supremacy clause allows the states discretionary authority in areas where state and national responsibilities overlap, and does not indicate how *inter*state commerce (which the national government is empowered to regulate) differs from *intra*state commerce (which presumably is reserved for regulation by the states).

Not surprisingly, federalism has been a contentious and dynamic system, its development determined less by constitutional language than by the strength of contending interests and by the country's changing needs. Federalism can be viewed as having progressed through three historical eras, each of which has involved a different relationship between nation and states.

★ CRITICAL THINKING

National vs. State Powers
The Constitution establishes a system in which authority is divided between the nation and the states. What do you regard as the most important powers assigned to national government? (These powers are listed in Article I, section 8, of the Constitution, which is reprinted in the back of this book.) Are there any important powers—for example, in the areas of law enforcement and education—that you think should have been assigned to the federal government but were not? What would be different if, say, education policy were established largely by Washington rather than by states and localities?

*A federal system requires relationships not only between the national and state governments but also among the states themselves. The U.S. Constitution defines several state-to-state obligations. One provision is that states are not permitted to enter into commercial arrangements with other states except as approved by Congress. This provision is intended to prevent two or more states from joining together to gain unfair advantage over another state or states. The Constitution also requires each state to grant "full faith and credit" to the legal acts and judgments of other states. This means that such legal matters as marriages, wills, court settlements, and contracts rendered in one state are to be upheld by other states. Without the guarantee of full faith and credit, federalism would not work. For example, commerce would grind to a halt if firms incorporated in one state were not allowed to do business in another state or if a party could escape a legal obligation simply by crossing state lines.

THE MEDIA AND THE PEOPLE

ODD MAN OUT: STATES IN THE NEWS

Americans depend heavily on the news media for information about their political institutions. It is not true that the media entirely determine what citizens think of government, for that is far from the case. But it is no exaggeration to say that, for the large majority of people, the day-to-day operations of government are experienced mainly through the media.

What image of government do citizens get from the media? Although journalists often say they merely "tell it like it is," the news is actually a result of a whole series of selections. America's governments engage in thousands of activities each day, and only a few of these get covered by the press. A major influence on these selections is the "media market" for news organizations. The media market for television affiliates and most newspapers is the *local* community. Systems of high-speed transportation and communication now make national newspapers possible, but nearly all of the nation's 1,600 dailies target their news at a local audience. In contrast, the media market for the television networks is national in scope; the networks reach viewers throughout the country.

The unit of government that does not naturally coincide with media markets is the states. Media markets are defined by population centers, not state capitals. As a consequence, the state governments get much less attention from the press than either the national or local governments. News organizations naturally tailor their news-gathering practices to their markets. Thus, the television networks assign most of their correspondents to national stories while newspapers typically assign their reporters to local stories. State government is the odd man out, despite the fact that, on a daily basis, it is the unit of government that has the most direct impact on people's lives. Education, transportation, and public health policy are examples of areas that are governed more through state statutes than either federal laws or local ordinances.

AN INDESTRUCTIBLE UNION (c. 1789–1865)

The issue during the first era, which lasted from the Constitution's beginnings in 1789 through the end of the Civil War in 1865, was the Union's survival. Given the state-centered history of America before the Constitution, it was inevitable that the states would dispute national policies that they perceived as inimical to their separate interests.

The Nationalist View: *McCulloch* v. *Maryland*

A first dispute over federalism arose early in George Washington's presidency when his secretary of the treasury, Alexander Hamilton, proposed the creation of a national bank. Thomas Jefferson, Washington's secretary of state, opposed the bank on the grounds that its activities would benefit commercial interests and would harm small farmers, who in Jefferson's view were the backbone of the new nation. Jefferson rejected Hamilton's claim that because the government had constitutional authority to regulate currency, the "necessary and proper" clause allowed it to establish a national bank.

Hamilton's view prevailed when Congress in 1791 established the First Bank of the United States, granting it a twenty-year charter. Congress did not renew the charter when it lapsed in 1811, but, in 1816, established the Second Bank of the United States over the objections of state and local bankers. Responding to their complaints, several states, including Maryland, attempted to drive the Second Bank of the United States out of existence by levying taxes on its operations within their borders. Edwin McCulloch, who was head cashier of the U.S. Bank in Maryland, refused to pay the Maryland tax, and the resulting dispute reached the Supreme Court.

John Marshall, the chief justice of the Supreme Court, was, like Hamilton, a strong nationalist, and in *McCulloch* v. *Maryland* (1819) the Court ruled decisively in favor of national authority. It was reasonable, Marshall concluded, to infer that a government with powers to tax, borrow money, and regulate commerce could establish a bank in order to exercise those powers properly. Marshall's argument was a clear statement of *implied powers*—the idea that, through the "necessary and proper" clause, the national government's powers extend beyond a narrow reading of its enumerated powers.

Marshall also addressed the meaning of the Constitution's supremacy clause. The state of Maryland argued that it had the sovereign authority to tax the national bank even if the bank was a legal entity. The Supreme Court rejected Maryland's position, concluding that valid national law prevailed over conflicting state law. Because the national government had the power to create the bank, it could also protect the bank from actions by the states, such as taxation, that might destroy it.[9]

The *McCulloch* decision served as precedent for future assertions of national authority.[10] Marshall's opinion asserted that legitimate uses of national power took precedence over state authority and that the "necessary and proper" clause was a broad grant of national authority. This constitutional interpretation was of the utmost significance: as Justice Oliver Wendell Holmes, Jr., noted a century later, the Union could not have survived if each state had been allowed its own interpretation of national law.[11]

The States'-Rights View: The *Dred Scott* Decision

Although John Marshall's ruling in the *McCulloch* case helped strengthen national authority, the issue of slavery posed a growing threat to the Union's survival. A resurgence of cotton farming in the early nineteenth century revived the South's flagging dependence on slaves and heightened white southerners' fears that Congress might move to abolish slavery. Southerners consequently did what others have done throughout American history: they devised a constitutional argument to fit their political needs. John C. Calhoun of South Carolina argued that the Constitution had created "a government of states . . . not a government of individuals."[12] This line of reasoning led Calhoun to his famed "doctrine of nullification," which declared that each state had the constitutional right to nullify a national law.

John C. Calhoun (1782-1850) of South Carolina was a champion of states' rights. (Library of Congress)

In 1832 South Carolina invoked this doctrine, declaring "null and void" a tariff law that favored northern interests. President Andrew Jackson retorted that South Carolina's action was "incompatible with the existence of the Union," a position that was strengthened when Congress authorized Jackson to use military force against South Carolina. The state backed down when Congress agreed to amend the tariff act slightly.

States'-rights advocates gained an ally when Roger B. Taney, who held a state-centered view of federalism, became chief justice of the Supreme Court in 1836.[13] In 1857 the Taney Court issued its infamous *Dred Scott* decision.

Dred Scott (1795?-1858). (Library of Congress)

Dred Scott, a slave, had lived several years with his master in the free territory of Wisconsin, but was living in the slave state of Missouri when his master died. Scott applied for his freedom, citing a federal law—the Missouri Compromise of 1820—that made slavery illegal in a free state or free territory. Six justices, including Taney, concluded that slaves were "property" rather than "citizens." As property, a slave could never be made free solely by virtue of place of residence.[14]

The *Dred Scott* decision inflamed public opinion in the North and contributed to a sectional split in the majority Democratic party that enabled the Republican Abraham Lincoln to win the presidency in 1860 with only 40 percent of the popular vote. Lincoln had campaigned for the gradual, compensated abolition of slavery. By the time he assumed office, seven southern states had already seceded from the Union. In justifying his decision to wage civil war on these states, Lincoln said, "The Union is older than the states." In 1865 the superior strength of the Union army settled by force the question of whether national authority would be binding on the states.

DUAL FEDERALISM AND LAISSEZ-FAIRE CAPITALISM (c. 1865–1937)

Although the Civil War preserved the Union, a new challenge to federalism was surfacing. Constitutional doctrine held that certain policy areas, such as interstate commerce and defense, were the clear and exclusive province of national authority, while other policy areas, such as public health and intrastate commerce, belonged clearly and exclusively to the states. This doctrine, known as **dual federalism,** was based on the idea that a precise separation of national and state authority was both possible and desirable. "The power which one possesses," said the Supreme Court, "the other does not."[15]

dual federalism A doctrine based on the idea that a precise separation of national power and state power is both possible and desirable.

The Industrial Revolution, however, raised questions about the usefulness of dual federalism as a governing concept. The rapid growth of industry had given rise to large firms, which used their economic power to exploit markets and workers. Government was the only possible counterforce against their economic power. Which level of government—state or national—would regulate business?

Judicial Protection of Business

For the most part, the answer was that neither level of government would be permitted to do so. The Supreme Court was dominated by adherents of the doctrine of laissez-faire capitalism (which holds that business should be "allowed to act" without interference), and they interpreted the Constitution in ways that frustrated government's attempts to regulate business activity. In 1886, for example, the Court decided that corporations were "persons" within the meaning of the Fourteenth Amendment, and thus their property rights were protected from substantial regulation by the states.[16] The Fourteenth Amendment had been ratified after the Civil War to protect citizens (especially the newly freed slaves) from discriminatory actions by state governments.[17] It was not originally intended as protection for business.

commerce clause The clause of the Constitution (Article I, section 8) that empowers the federal government to regulate commerce among the states and with other nations.

The Court also weakened the national government's regulatory power by narrowly interpreting its commerce power. The Constitution's **commerce clause** says that Congress shall have the power "to regulate commerce" among the states but does not spell out the economic activities included in the grant of power. When the federal government invoked the Sherman Antitrust Act (1890) in an attempt to break up a monopoly on the manufacture of sugar, the Supreme Court blocked the action, claiming that interstate commerce covered only the "transportation" of goods, not their "manufacture."[18] Manufacturing was deemed part of intrastate commerce and thus, according to the dual federalism doctrine, subject to state regulation only. However, since the Court had previously decided that the states' regulatory powers were restricted by the Fourteenth Amendment, they were relatively powerless to control manufacturing activity.

Although the national government subsequently made some headway in business regulation, the Supreme Court remained an obstacle. An example is the case of *Hammer* v. *Dagenhart* (1918), which arose from a 1916 federal act that prohibited the interstate shipment of goods produced by child labor. The act was popular because factory owners were exploiting children, working them for long hours at low pay. Citing the Tenth Amendment, the Court invalidated the law, ruling that factory practices could be regulated only by the states.[19] However, in an earlier case, *Lochner* v. *New York* (1905), the Court had prevented a state from regulating labor practices, concluding that such action was a violation of firms' property rights.[20]

In effect, the Supreme Court had denied lawmaking majorities the authority to decide economic issues. Neither Congress nor the state legislatures were permitted to substantially regulate business. As the constitutional scholars Alfred Kelly and Winifred Harbison have concluded, "No more complete perversion of the principles of effective federal government can be imagined."[21]

National Authority Prevails

Judicial supremacy in the economic sphere ended abruptly in 1937. For nearly a decade, the United States had been mired in the Great Depression, which

Between 1865 and 1937, the Supreme Court's rulings severely restricted national power. Narrowly interpreting Congress's constitutional power to regulate commerce, the Court forbade Congress to regulate child labor and other aspects of manufacturing. (Library of Congress)

President Franklin D. Roosevelt's New Deal was designed to alleviate. The Supreme Court, however, had ruled much of the New Deal's economic recovery legislation to be unconstitutional. A constitutional crisis of historic proportions seemed inevitable until the Court suddenly reversed its position. In the process, American federalism was fundamentally and forever changed.

The Great Depression revealed clearly that Americans had become a national community with national economic needs. By the 1930s, more than half the population lived in cities (only 20 percent did so in 1860), and more than 10 million workers were employed by industry (only 1 million were so employed in 1860). Urban workers were typically dependent on landlords for their housing, on farmers and grocers for their food, and on corporations for their jobs. Farmers were more independent, but they, too, were increasingly a part of a larger economic network. Their income depended on market prices and shipping and equipment costs.[22]

This economic interdependence meant that no area of the economy was immune if things went wrong. When the Depression hit in 1929, its effects could not be contained. A decline in spending was followed by a drop in production, a loss of jobs, unpaid rents and grocery bills, and a shrinking market for foodstuffs, which led to a further decline in spending and so on, creating a relentless downward spiral. At the depths of the Great Depression one-fourth of the nation's work force was unemployed.

The states by tradition had responsibility for welfare, but they were near penniless because of declining tax revenues and the growing ranks of poor people. The New Deal programs offered a way out of the crisis; for example,

Hundreds of men wait in a food line for a sandwich and cup of coffee, the gift of a New York City newspaper. State and local governments could not cope with the enormous problems created by the Great Depression, so the federal government stepped in with its New Deal programs, greatly changing the nature of federal-state relations. (AP/Wide World Photos)

the National Industry Recovery Act (NIRA) of 1933 called for a massive public works program to create jobs and for coordinated action by major industries. However, the New Deal was opposed by economic conservatives (who accused Roosevelt of leading the nation down the road to communism) and by justices of the Supreme Court. In *Schechter* v. *United States* (1935) the Court invalidated the Recovery Act by a 5–4 vote, ruling that it usurped powers reserved to the states.[23]

Frustrated by the Court, Roosevelt in 1937 proposed his famed "Court-packing" plan. Roosevelt recommended that Congress enact legislation that would permit an additional justice to be appointed to the Court whenever a seated member passed the age of seventy. The number of justices would increase, and Roosevelt's appointees would presumably be more sympathetic to his programs. Roosevelt's scheme was resisted by Congress, but the controversy ended with "the switch in time that saved nine," when, for reasons that have never become fully clear, Justice Owen Roberts abandoned his opposition to Roosevelt's policies and thus gave the president a 5–4 majority on the Court.

Within months the Court upheld the 1935 National Labor Relations Act, which gave employees the right to organize and bargain collectively.[24] In passing the act, Congress had argued that labor-management disputes were disruptive of the national economy and therefore could be regulated through the commerce clause. The Supreme Court's decision upholding the act marked the end of the Court's interference in applications of the Constitution's commerce clause. In 1946 the Court openly acknowledged the change when it said that "we have nothing to do" with regulating commerce and asserted that Congress's commerce power is "as broad as the needs of the nation."[25] Thus the constitutional path was opened to a substantial increase in the national government's authority. The extent of national power was evident, for example, in the 1964 Civil Rights Act, which forbids racial discrimination by hotels and restaurants on the grounds that they provide lodging and food to travelers engaged in interstate commerce. When the law was challenged, the Supreme Court upheld it, concluding that "commerce" included public accommodations.[26]

The Supreme Court's decisions in regard to the federal government's taxing and spending powers followed a pattern similar to its commerce rulings. The Court placed restrictions on federal authority before lifting them in recognition of national needs.[27]

TOWARD NATIONAL CITIZENSHIP

As Americans became more interdependent economically, they were also growing together in other ways. Changes in transportation and communication made state boundaries seem less relevant. News and people traveled faster and farther than ever before, which raised the level of controversy that surrounded some state practices, particularly in the area of race relations. Was it right that black children in southern states were forbidden by law from attending the same public schools as white children?

The fact is, such practices were soon stopped. As will be discussed in Chapter 5, federal authority has compelled states and localities to eliminate government-sponsored discrimination and, in some cases, to create compen-

> **★ CRITICAL THINKING**
>
> **Congress vs. Supreme Court as Protector of the States**
> In a 1985 decision the Supreme Court said that the states should look primarily to Congress, and not to the Court, for relief from "undue burdens" placed on them by Washington. This position followed from earlier Supreme Court decisions that said, in effect, that the commerce and taxing powers of the federal government were defined more by national needs than by any constitutional provision.
>
> In your view, is the Supreme Court or Congress better equipped to safeguard America's federal system? Keep in mind that members of the Congress are elected by voters within the states they represent.
>
> Where do you place the 1994 congressional elections in your thinking on this issue? The voters in 1994 elected Republican majorities in both the House and Senate, and these lawmakers immediately began to cut away at federal programs and mandates with the aim of returning power to the states.

satory opportunities for minorities and women. In 1954, for example, the Supreme Court held that racial segregation in public schools was unconstitutional on grounds that it violated the Fourteenth Amendment.[28]

The idea that Americans are equal in their rights regardless of where they reside has also been applied in other areas. As Chapter 4 will discuss, states have been required to broaden individual rights of free expression and fair trial. An example is the Supreme Court's *Miranda* ruling, which requires police officers to inform crime suspects of their rights at the time of arrest.[29]

Of course, important differences remain in the rights and privileges of the residents of the separate states, as could be expected in a federal system. The death penalty, for example, is legal in some states but not others, and states differ greatly in terms of their services, such as the quality of their public schools. Nevertheless, national citizenship—the notion that Americans should be equal in their rights and opportunities, regardless of the state in which they live—is a more encompassing idea today than in the past.[30]

Federalism Today

Since the 1930s, the relation of the nation to the states has changed so fundamentally that dual federalism is no longer even a roughly accurate description of the American situation.[31] The national government operates in many policy areas that were once almost exclusively within the control of states and localities. The national government does not dominate these policy areas, but it does have a significant role. Much of this influence stems from social welfare policies that were enacted in the 1960s as part of President Lyndon Johnson's Great Society program, which included initiatives in health care, public housing, nutrition, welfare, urban development, and other areas reserved previously to states and localities.

An understanding of the nature of federalism today requires a recognition of two somewhat conflicting trends. The first is the long-term expansion of national authority that began in the 1930s and continued for decades. The second trend is very recent and involves a "devolution" (a passing down) of authority from the national government to the state and local levels. Devolution is in part a reaction to the decades-long increase in federal authority but has not completely reversed it. Stated differently, the national government's policy role has increased greatly since the 1930s even though that role has been reduced somewhat in the past few years.

We will start with an explanation of the first of these trends: the expansion of federal authority since the New Deal era.

INTERDEPENDENCY AND INTERGOVERMENTAL RELATIONS

Interdependency is a primary reason why national authority has increased dramatically in the twentieth century. Changes in transportation, commerce, and communication have brought Americans ever closer together. As a result, policy problems in one region of the country tend to affect other regions. Accordingly, national, state, and local officials have increasingly worked *together* to solve policy issues. This collaborative effort has been described as **cooperative federalism.**[32] The difference between dual federalism

cooperative federalism The situation in which the national, state, and local levels work together to solve problems.

Cooperative federalism brings federal and state government officials together to try to solve major problems. President Clinton is shown here addressing a meeting of state governors. (Paul Conklin/PhotoEdit)

and cooperative federalism has been likened to the difference between a layer cake, whose levels are distinct, and a marble cake, whose levels flow together.[33] Cooperative federalism is evident in public assistance programs such as Medicaid, which provides health care for the poor. Public assistance was traditionally a responsibility of the states, but during the Great Depression the national government also got involved. Today cooperative federalism prevails in Medicaid and many other public assistance programs, which are

- Jointly funded by the national and state governments
- Jointly administered, with the states and localities providing most of the direct service to recipients and a national agency providing general administration

Public education is primarily a state and local responsibility. As a result, the amount of money spent on public education varies widely. This modern classroom is typical of public schools in affluent suburbs. Well-equipped classrooms are much less common in poor rural areas and inner cities. (James Wilson/Woodfin Camp & Associates)

★ STATES IN THE NATION

Spending on Primary and Secondary Education: The states differ greatly in their annual public spending on education, a reflection of their substantial control over policy.

STATE	PER PUPIL EXPENDITURE	RANK
Ala.	$3,779	49
Alaska	9,290	2
Ariz.	4,140	44
Ark.	3,838	48
Calif.	4,608	37
Colo.	4,969	31
Conn.	8,188	4
Del.	6,420	12
D.C.	7,998	5
Fla.	5,303	27
Ga.	4,544	39
Hawaii	5,806	18
Idaho	4,025	47
Ill.	5,191	29
Ind.	5,641	20
Iowa	5,297	28
Kan.	5,459	25
Ky.	4,942	33
La.	4,352	43
Maine	6,162	15
Md.	6,447	11
Mass.	6,505	9
Mich.	6,402	13
Minn.	5,572	22
Miss.	3,390	50
Mo.	4,487	40
Mont.	5,348	26
Neb.	4,950	32
Nev.	4,976	30
N.H.	5,619	21
N.J.	9,712	1
N.Mex.	4,643	36
N.Y.	8,525	3
N.C.	4,810	35
N.Dak.	4,404	41
Ohio	5,963	16
Okla.	4,085	45
Oreg.	6,240	14
Pa.	7,748	6
R.I.	6,649	8
S.C.	4,573	38
S.Dak.	4,359	42
Tenn.	4,033	46
Texas	4,933	34
Utah	3,218	51
Vt.	7,172	7
Va.	5,517	24
Wash.	5,528	23
W.Va.	5,689	19
Wis.	6,500	10
Wyo.	5,932	17
National average	5,574	—

SOURCE: National Education Association, *Estimates of School Statistics,* 1993.

- Jointly determined, with both the state and national governments having a say in eligibility and benefit levels, and with federal regulations, such as those prohibiting discrimination, giving an element of uniformity to the various state and local efforts

Through its spending and regulatory activities, the federal government has encouraged the various states to pursue many of the same policies, such as assistance to poor families with dependent children.[34] This trend should not be misinterpreted to mean that the states are now powerless and indistinguishable. On the contrary, states and localities have substantial discretionary authority in many of the policy areas that touch Americans' lives most directly—among them public education, safety, health, and transportation. Public education, for example, remains largely a state and local function. Nearly 95 percent of the funding for primary and secondary schools is provided by states and localities, which also decide most policy issues, from teachers' qualifications to course requirements to the length of the school year. In terms of public expenditures, for example, Idaho, Mississippi, Oklahoma, and Utah spend much less on each pupil than do New York, Wisconsin, Delaware, and Wyoming (see box: States in the Nation). Yet differences in state policies are much less pronounced today than in the past.

GOVERNMENT REVENUES AND INTERGOVERNMENTAL RELATIONS

The interdependence of different sectors of modern American society is one of two factors that have compelled the federal government to assume a larger domestic policy role. The other is the federal government's superior ability to tax and borrow. States and localities are in an inherently competitive situation with regard to taxation. People and businesses faced with state or local tax increases can move to another state or locality where taxes are lower. Moreover, the federal government depends almost entirely on forms of taxation, such as personal and corporate income taxes, that automatically increase revenues as the economy expands. State and local governments depend more heavily than Washington on revenue sources, such as license fees and property taxes, that are comparatively inflexible. The overall result is that the federal government raises more tax revenues than do all fifty states and the thousands of local governments combined (see Figure 2-1). Finally, because it controls the American dollar, the federal government has a nearly unlimited ability to borrow money to cover its deficits. States and localities can go bankrupt and therefore cannot as easily find the credit to cover their budget deficits.

Fiscal Federalism

The federal government's revenue-raising advantage has helped make money the basis for many of the relations between the national government and the states and localities. **Fiscal federalism** refers to the expenditure of federal funds on programs run in part through state and local government.[35] The federal government provides some or all the money for a program, while the states and localities administer it.

The states possess the organizational resources to make fiscal federalism a workable arrangement. The national government could not run these programs on its own because it does not have enough local offices or employees to do the job. States and localities have those resources; they have nearly five times as many employees as the federal government. In fact, contrary to what many Americans might think, all the growth in public employment in the past decade has occurred at the state and local levels; their employment rolls have increased by more than 2 million workers, while the number of federal employees has actually declined during this period (see Figure 2-2).

The pattern of federal assistance to states and localities since 1955 is shown in Figure 2-3. Federal grants-in-aid increased tenfold during the last four decades. The sharpest rise came in the late 1960s and early 1970s as a result of President Johnson's programs. Even at the height of the New Deal in the 1930s, federal aid never accounted for more than 10 percent of state and local spending. With Johnson's Great Society, however, the figure rose above 20 percent and has remained in that range ever since. In other words, roughly one in every five dollars that local and state governments have spent in the past three decades was raised not by them, but by the federal government.

Cash grants to states and localities have extended Washington's influence over policy.[36] Through the funds it provides and the conditions it attaches to the use of those funds, Washington affects the policy choices of state and local governments. Presidents and members of Congress have used cash grants as inducements to state and local officials to establish programs they favor. State and local governments can reject a grant-in-aid, but if they accept it, they must spend it in the specified ways. And since most grants require states to contribute matching funds, the federal programs in effect determine how states will use some of their own tax dollars. Federal grants have also pressured state and local officials to accept broad national goals, such as the elimination of racial and other forms of discrimination. A building constructed with the help of federal funds, for example, must be accessible to handicapped persons.

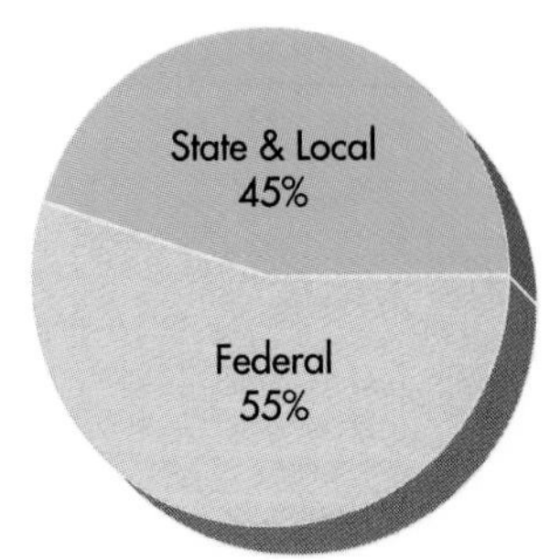

FIGURE 2-1
Federal, State, and Local Shares of Government Tax Revenue
The federal government raises more tax revenues than all state and local governments combined.
Source: U.S. Department of Commerce.

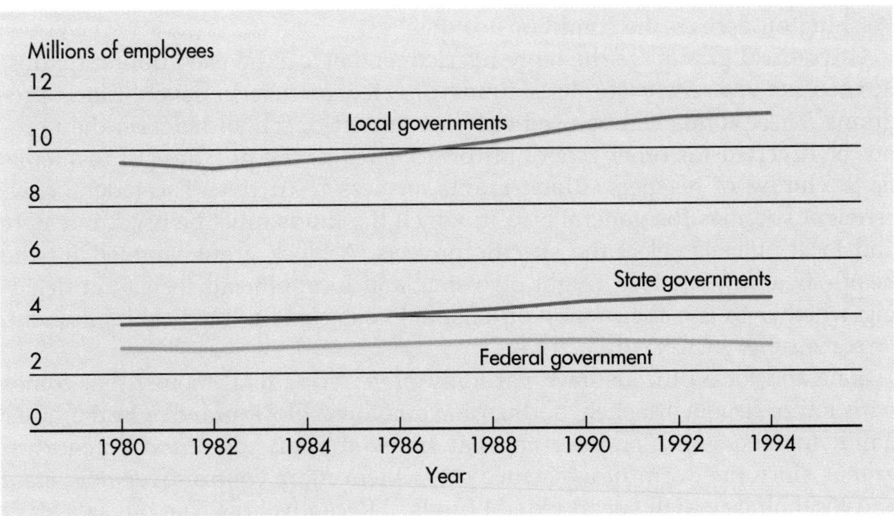

FIGURE 2-2
Employees of the Federal, State, and Local Governments
Levels of employment in state and local governments have increased in recent years, whereas the number of federal government employees has remained fairly constant.
Source: U.S. Advisory Commission on Intergovernmental Relations. Based on statistics compiled by the U.S. Bureau of the Census.

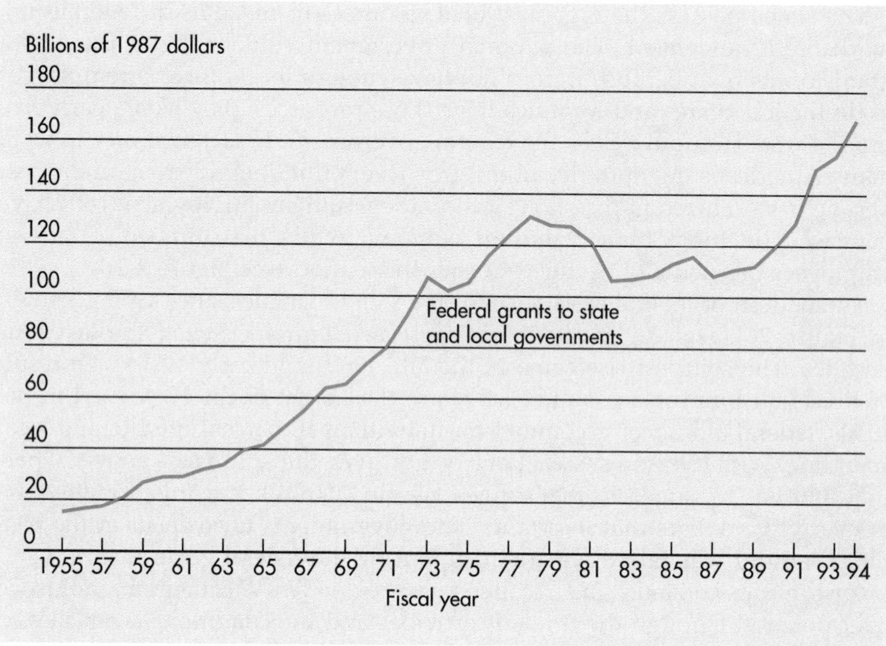

FIGURE 2-3
Federal Grants to State and Local Governments in Constant (1987) Dollars
Federal aid to states and localities has increased dramatically since the 1950s. *Source: Advisory Commission on Intergovernmental Relations, Significant Features of Fiscal Federalism, 1994 ed., vol. 2 (Washington, D.C.: ACIR, 1994), 30.*

State and local officials have often complained that federal grants contain too many restrictions and infringe too much on their authority, but they have been eager to get the money since it permits them to offer services they could not otherwise afford.[37] For example, a 1994 federal grant program enabled hard-pressed local governments to put more than 50,000 additional police officers on the streets.

CATEGORICAL AND BLOCK GRANTS

State and local governments receive two major types of assistance, categorical grants and block grants, which are differentiated by the extent to which Washington defines the conditions of their use.

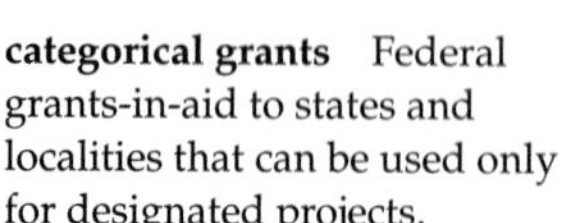

categorical grants Federal grants-in-aid to states and localities that can be used only for designated projects.

block grants Federal grants-in-aid that permit state and local officials to decide how the money will be spent within a general area, such as education or health.

Categorical grants are the more restrictive; they can be used only for a designated activity. An example is funds directed for use in school-lunch programs. These funds can be used only in support of school lunches; they cannot be diverted for other school purposes, such as the purchase of textbooks or the hiring of teachers. **Block grants** are less restrictive. The federal government specifies the general area in which the funds must be used, but state and local officials select the specific projects. A block grant targeted for the health area, for example, might give state and local officials leeway in deciding whether to use the money on hospital construction, medical equipment, or some other health care activity.

State and local officials have naturally preferred federal money that comes with fewer strings attached, so they have favored block grants. On the other hand, members of Congress have at times strongly preferred categorical grants, since this form of assistance gives them more control over how state and local officials will spend federal funds.[38] Recently, however, officials at all levels have looked to block grants as the key to a more workable form of federalism. This tendency is part of a larger trend—that of "devolution."

A NEW FEDERALISM: DEVOLUTION

Devolution is the idea that American federalism will be improved by a shift in authority from the federal government to the state and local governments. Devolution is reshaping American federalism and is attributable to both practical and political developments.

devolution The passing down of authority from the national government to the state and local governments.

Budgetary Pressures and Public Opinion

As a practical matter, the growth in federal assistance had run its course by the early 1980s. The federal government was facing huge budget deficits, and large new grants-in-aid to states and localities were not feasible. In fact, federal assistance actually decreased in terms of constant dollars (dollars adjusted to reflect the rate of inflation) during the 1980s.

By 1990, federal grant spending was again on the rise, but the reason was not the desire of Washington officials to expand assistance programs. Instead, a sharp rise in medical costs was driving the cost of the Medicaid grant program rapidly upward. It is an "entitlement program," which meant government could not deny the benefit to any eligible individual and thus could not simply place a cap on Medicaid spending. Thus, as the cost of medical care soared, so did the cost of health services for the poor. By 1990, Medicaid was absorbing two-fifths of all federal assistance dollars.

As budgetary pressures intensified, relations among national, state, and local officials became increasingly strained. An increase in unfunded mandates and cuts in some grant programs had forced states and localities to pay an increasingly larger share of the costs of joint programs. As they raised taxes or cut other services to meet the costs, taxpayer anger intensified. Some of the grant programs, such as AFDC, food stamps, and housing subsidies, had not been very popular before the budget crunch and now came under even heavier criticism.

By the early 1990s, American federalism was positioned for a major change. Two decades earlier, three-fourths of Americans had expressed confidence in Washington's ability to govern effectively. Less than half of the public now held this view, and most people were more inclined to entrust policy to the state and local governments (see Figure 2-4).

The Republican Revolution: Innovative Solutions or a Race to the Bottom?

When the Republican party scored a decisive victory in the 1994 congressional elections, Newt Gingrich declared that "1960s-style federalism is dead." The Contract with America, which Gingrich had written and which served as the GOP's campaign platform, called for sharp cutbacks in federally assisted welfare programs and for an end to welfare entitlements, which would further reduce grant spending. The Contract also proposed to lump dozens of categorical grants into a few block grants, thus giving states more control of how money would be spent.

That Republicans would lead the move to a more decentralized form of federalism was no surprise. Although both parties had initiated expansions of federal authority, Republicans had more often questioned the overall result. Republican presidents Richard Nixon, Ronald Reagan, and George Bush all advocated some version of a "new federalism" in which some areas of public policy for which the federal government had assumed responsibility would be returned to states and localities.[39]

The GOP's philosophical stance as the party of smaller government was behind these proposals, but so too was the fact that Democratic constituencies were the main beneficiaries of many federal grant programs. If the primary effect of fiscal federalism was to strengthen the nation's health, transportation, education, welfare, and public safety systems, a secondary effect was the distribution of a disproportionate share of the benefits to traditionally Democratic interests, including the cities, minorities, and the poor.

Upon taking control of Congress in 1995, Republican lawmakers moved quickly to reduce unfunded federal mandates on states and localities.[40] But their most significant legislative achievement came a year later, when they passed a sweeping welfare reform act (formally titled the Personal Responsibility and Work Opportunity Reconciliation Act of 1996). Its key element is the Temporary Assistance for Needy Families block grant (TANF), which ended the decades-old AFDC program that granted cash assistance to every poor family with children. TANF restricts a family's eligibility for federal assistance to five years and, after two years, a family head normally has to go to work or the benefits cease. Moreover, TANF gives states wide latitude in setting benefit levels, eligibility criteria, and other regulations affecting aid for poor families.

Advocates of TANF claimed that the states are "laboratories of democracy" and would find innovative ways to provide needy families with assistance and to move able-bodied recipients from welfare to work. Critics of TANF painted a darker picture, arguing that the states will engage in "a race to the bottom," competing with each other to slash programs to the bone in order to save money.

In truth, no one is quite sure what the long-term effects of TANF will be, or even whether devolution itself will prove to be a sound idea. What is clear, however, is that American federalism has reached a new stage, where answers to the nation's problems will be sought less in Washington than in the states and localities. (TANF and other aspects of the 1996 welfare reform legislation are discussed further in Chapter 19).

The Public's Influence: Setting the Boundaries of Federal–State Power

The ebb and flow in Washington's power in the twentieth century has coincided closely with public opinion. The American people have had a decisive voice in determining the relationship between the federal and state governments.

During the Great Depression, when it was clear that the states would be unable to help, Americans turned to Washington for relief. For people without jobs and money, the fine points of the Constitution were of little conse-

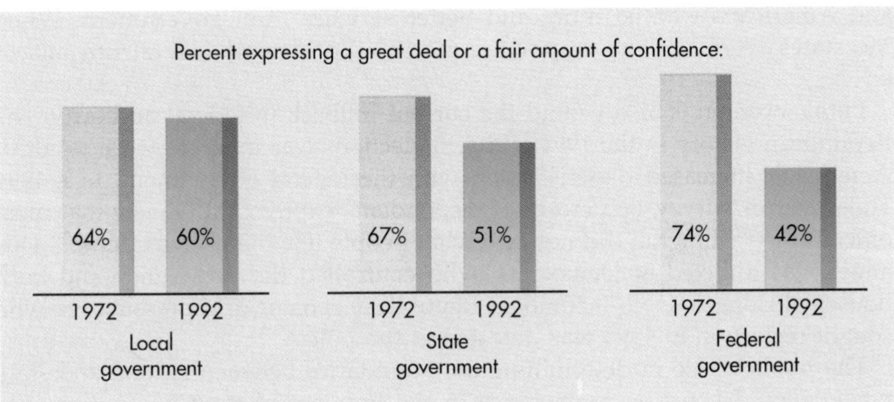

FIGURE 2-4
Changes in the Public's Confidence in the Federal, State, and Local Governments
The public's trust in government, particularly at the national level, has declined in recent decades.
Source: Surveys for the U.S. Advisory Commission on Intergovernment Relations (ACIR) by the Opinion Research Corporation (1972) and the Gallup Organization (1992).

quence. President Roosevelt's welfare and public jobs programs were a radical departure from the past but quickly gained widespread support. A 1936 Gallup Poll indicated, for example, that 61 percent of Americans supported Roosevelt's social security program, whereas only 27 percent opposed it. "The Social Security Act," Andrew Dobelstein noted, "reflected [the new public attitude] that the federal government had responsibility to promote the general welfare through specific public welfare programs funded with federal tax dollars."[41]

The second great wave of federal social programs—President Lyndon Johnson's Great Society—was also driven by public demands. Income and education levels had risen dramatically after the Second World War,

YOUR TURN

SIZE OF GOVERNMENT

The Questions:

1. Would you say you favor smaller government with fewer services, or larger government with many services?

Smaller government, fewer services	Larger government, many services

2. Do you think that, in general, the federal government creates more problems than it solves, or do you think it solves more problems than it creates?

Creates more problems than it solves	Solves more problems than it creates

What Others Think: The first question appeared in a 1993 ABC News/Washington Post survey: 67 percent of the respondents said they favored a smaller government with fewer services while 30 percent expressed the opposite preference. The second question is from a 1993 CBS News/New York Times survey: 69 percent said they believe the federal government creates more problems than it solves while 22 percent concluded otherwise.

Comment: These questions address an issue that has persisted throughout the nation's history—what the size of government should be generally and the size of the federal government in particular. If you favor a smaller government and have a low level of trust in the federal government, you probably agree with current attempts to downsize Washington and shift policy responsibilities to the states.

and Americans wanted more and better services from government. When the states were slow to respond, Americans pressured federal officials to act.[42]

Public opinion is also behind the current rollback in federal authority. The Republican victory in the 1994 midterm elections was in large part a result of Americans' increased dissatisfaction with the federal government. In a 1994 Times Mirror survey, 66 percent of respondents expressed the view that most officials in Washington did not care what people like themselves think.[43] This anger was directed at Democrats, who controlled the presidency and both houses of Congress. No incumbent Republican senator or representative who sought reelection in 1994 was defeated at the polls.

The public's role in determining the boundaries between federal and state power would come as no surprise to the Framers of the Constitution. For them, federalism was a pragmatic issue, one to be decided by Americans' needs rather than encrusted constitutional provisions. If, as Woodrow Wilson claimed, the relationship between the nation and the states is the cardinal issue of the U.S. constitutional system, it is also, as Wilson said, a question to be decided anew at each successive stage in the country's history.[44]

Summary

Perhaps the foremost characteristic of the American political system is its division of authority between a national government and the states. The first U.S. government, established by the Articles of Confederation, was essentially a union of the states.

In establishing the basis for a stronger national government, the U.S. Constitution also made provision for safeguarding state interests. The Great Compromise—whereby each state was equally represented in the Senate, as the smaller states demanded, and membership in the House of Representatives was apportioned by population, as the larger states insisted—was the breakthrough that enabled the delegates to the constitutional convention of 1787 to reach agreement. However, this agreement on the structure of Congress has been less historically significant than the Philadelphia convention's pragmatic decision to create a federal system in which sovereignty was vested in both national and state governments. The Constitution enumerates the general powers of the national government and grants it implied powers through the "necessary and proper" clause. Other powers are reserved to the states by the Tenth Amendment.

From 1789 to 1865, the nation's survival was at issue. The states found it convenient at times to argue that their sovereignty took precedence over national authority. In the end, it took the Civil War to cement the idea that the United States was a union of people, not of states. From 1865 to 1937, federalism reflected the doctrine that certain policy areas were the exclusive responsibility of the national government, while others belonged exclusively to the states. This constitutional position permitted the laissez-faire doctrine that big business was largely beyond governmental control. Federalism in a form recognizable today began to emerge in the late 1930s.

In the areas of commerce, taxation, spending, civil rights, and civil liberties, among others, the federal government now has an important role, one that is the inevitable consequence of the increasing complexity of American society and the interdependence of its people. National, state, and local officials now work closely together to solve the country's problems, a situation that is described as cooperative federalism. Grants-in-aid from Washington to the states and localities have been the chief instrument of national influence. States and localities have received billions in federal assistance; in accepting that money, they have also accepted both federal restrictions on its use and the national policy priorities that underlie the granting of the money.

As a result of the Republicans' sweeping victory in the 1994 congressional elections, the relationship between the nation and the states is again a priority issue. Power is shifting downward to the states, and a new balance in the ever-evolving system of U.S. federalism is taking place. This change, as has been true throughout U.S. history, has sprung from the demands of the American people.

Major Concepts

block grants
categorical grants
commerce clause
confederacy
cooperative federalism
devolution
dual federalism
enumerated powers (expressed powers)
federalism
fiscal federalism
implied powers
"necessary and proper" clause (elastic clause)
reserved powers
sovereignty
supremacy clause
unitary system

Suggested Readings

Anton, Thomas. *American Federalism and Public Policy: How the System Works.* New York: McGraw-Hill, 1989. An analysis of policy patterns of modern intergovernmental relations, including the role of private interests in federal programs.

Beer, Samuel H. *To Make a Nation: The Rediscovery of American Federalism.* Cambridge, Mass.: The Belknap Press of Harvard University Press, 1993. An innovative interpretive framework for understanding the impact of federalism and nationalism on the nation's development.

Federalist Papers. Many editions, including a one-volume paperback version edited by Isaac Kramnick (New York: Penguin, 1987). A series of essays written by Alexander Hamilton, James Madison, and John Jay under the pseudonym "Publius." The essays, published in a New York newspaper in 1787–1788, explained the Constitution and supported its ratification.

Ferrand, Max. *The Records of the Federal Convention of 1787.* New Haven, Conn.: Yale University Press, 1966. A four-volume work that includes all the important records of the Philadelphia convention.

Lowry, William R. *The Dimensions of Federalism: State Governments and Pollution Control Policies.* Durham, N.C.: Duke University Press, 1992. A case study of the way federalism actually works in practice.

Lunch, William H. *The Nationalization of American Politics.* Berkeley: University of California Press, 1987. An evaluation of the trend toward nationalization, including the ideological character it has assumed.

Maidment, Richard A. *The Judicial Response to the New Deal: The U.S. Supreme Court and Economic Regulation.* New York: Manchester University Press, 1992. An analysis of a major turning point in the constitutional interpretation of federalism.

Ostrom, Vincent. *The Meaning of American Federalism: Constituting a Self-Governing Society.* San Francisco: Institute for Contemporary Studies, 1991. An insightful assessment of federalism by a leading scholar in the field.

Storing, Herbert. *What the Anti-Federalists Were For.* Chicago: University of Chicago Press, 1981. An analysis of Anti-Federalist thought and its origins.

CHAPTER 3

CONSTITUTIONAL DEMOCRACY: PROMOTING LIBERTY AND SELF-GOVERNMENT

The people must be governed by a majority, with whom all power resides. But how is the sense of this majority to be obtained?

—Fisher Ames (1788)[1]

Who's in charge here? Newt Gingrich, who would become Speaker of the House when the new Congress convened in January, said he was. The GOP's ten-point "Contract with America" that Gingrich had helped formulate for the midterm elections was slated by the new Speaker to be voted on in the House within the first 100 days. He promised that it would prompt the most radical change in the direction of the federal government since Franklin D. Roosevelt's policies in 1933. "I will cooperate, but I won't compromise," said Gingrich.

The soon-to-be Senate majority leader, the Republican Robert Dole, took a somewhat different view of the voters' mandate. He saw no great ideological turn to the right in the Republicans' sweeping victory in the 1994 elections. He compared the Democratic rout to the Watergate elections of 1974 when the Republicans were "the bums." Dole said the polls did not show that voters were inspired to vote Republican by Gingrich's contract, and he expressed reservations about the contract's emphasis on supply-side economics and radical cutbacks in federal programs. He indicated his support for other parts of the contract but suggested that the whole package would be neither feasible nor desirable. "People are not looking for miracles," Dole said.

For his part, Democratic President Bill Clinton promised to work with the new Republican majorities in the House and Senate but claimed he would not be hostage to their agenda. Saying that the American people had elected him to bring about "responsible changes" in government, Clinton identified welfare reform and international trade as two areas where he and the Republicans might be able to find common ground. But he stated emphatically that

Like many leading Americans of the time, Thomas Jefferson admired the natural-rights philosophy of the English philosopher John Locke. Jefferson used some of Locke's phrases almost word for word in writing the Declaration of Independence. (The White House Historical association; photograph by the National Geographic Society)

he would use the veto to block any Republican initiative that conflicted with his own view of the national interest.

These varying claims to leadership of the American people can be traced back to the handiwork, two centuries earlier, of the writers of the Constitution. They created a government based on an elaborate system of checks and balances, which allows the majority's will to work through representative institutions but provides for substantial checks on this power. Among these checks is a division of power between the executive and legislative branches and, within the latter, a further division of power between the House and Senate. These divisions are reinforced by separate forms of election for the president, House, and Senate. As a result, U.S. elections frequently produce a divided outcome. Clinton claimed a mandate to represent the American people as a result of his election by them, but the GOP leaders of Congress claimed their own mandates as a result of the separate election of House and Senate members by the voters.

The situation is quite different in many other countries. Under other forms of democracy, elected officials are chosen in the same way in the same election, run on a common platform, and operate in political systems where executive and legislative power are combined in a single institution. As a result, to a degree not true of the United States, government elsewhere has a unified leadership.

limited government A government that is subject to strict limits on its lawful uses of powers, and hence on its ability to deprive people of their liberty.

self-government The principle that the people are the ultimate source and proper beneficiary of governing authority; in practice, a government based on majority rule.

The writers of the U.S. Constitution were intent on preventing a concentration of governing power. They wanted a government that, in addition to forging a union of the states, would satisfy two different and somewhat competing goals. It would be designed to protect liberty and, at the same time, to allow the majority to rule. The first objective was **limited government**—a government that is subject to strict limits on its lawful uses of power. The second objective was **self-government**—a government that is subject to the will of the people as expressed through the preferences of a majority. Self-government requires that the voters' preferences find their way into public policy in a substantial and timely way. However, limited government requires restraints on the majority as a way of protecting the rights and interests of the minority. These considerations resulted in a constitution that has provision for majority rule but also has built-in restrictions on the exercise of majority power.

This chapter describes how the principles of self- and limited government are embodied in the Constitution and explains the tension between them. The chapter also indicates how these principles have been modified in practice in the course of American history, before closing with a brief analysis of the contemporary situation. The main points of this chapter are the following:

- ★ *America during the colonial period developed traditions of limited government and self-government.* These traditions were rooted in governing practices, philosophy, and cultural values.
- ★ *The Constitution provides for limited government mainly by defining lawful powers and by dividing those powers among competing institutions.* The Constitution, with its Bill of Rights, also prohibits government from infringing on individual rights. Judicial review is an additional safeguard of limited government.
- ★ *The Constitution in its original form provided for self-government mainly*

through indirect systems of popular election of representatives. The Framers' theory of self-government was based on the notion that political power must be separated from immediate popular influences if sound policies are to result.

★ *The idea of popular government—in which the majority's desires have a more direct and immediate impact on governing officials—has gained strength since the nation's beginning.* Originally, the House of Representatives was the only institution subject to direct vote of the people. This mechanism has been extended to other institutions and, through primary elections, even to the nomination of candidates for public office.

The Roots of Limited Government

Early Americans' admiration for limited government was based partly on their English heritage. Other European nations of the eighteenth century implicitly acknowledged the divine right of their kings; England was an exception. British courts had developed a system of precedent known as "common law," which guaranteed trial by jury and due process of law as safeguards of life, liberty, and particularly property. These rights were defended by the courts and ordinarily respected by the king and Parliament.

The English philosopher John Locke (1632–1704) proclaimed that government must be restrained in its powers if it is to serve the common good. Locke's theory of individual rights and limited government, which had roots that reached back to the Greeks and Romans, became an inspiration to a generation of American leaders. Thomas Jefferson declared that Locke "was one of the three greatest men that ever lived, without exception."[2] In his *Two Treatises of Government* (1690) Locke advanced the liberal principle that people have **inalienable rights** (or **natural rights**), including those of life, liberty, and property. In Locke's view, such rights belonged to people in their natural state before governments were created. When people agreed to come together (or, in Locke's term, entered into a "social contract") in order to have the protection that only organized government could provide, their natural rights were neither taken from them by government nor surrendered by them to government. If the government protected their natural rights, they were obliged to obey it, but if the government failed to protect their rights, they could rightfully rebel against it.[3]

inalienable (natural) rights Those rights which persons theoretically possessed in the state of nature, prior to the formation of governments. These rights, including those of life, liberty, and property, are considered inherent, and as such are inalienable. Since government is established by people, government has the responsibility to preserve these rights.

Locke's ideas were part of the Enlightenment, an eighteenth-century European philosophical movement that sought to understand the proper order of nature and society. Locke's ideas dominated Enlightenment theories of government to the same degree that Sir Isaac Newton's ideas dominated Enlightenment theories of science. Locke's revolutionary ideas about rulers and natural rights had special appeal to American colonists because, among all people at this time, they had the freest governments and the most personal freedoms.[4]

COLONIAL AND STATE CONSTITUTIONS

The English tradition of limited government was reflected in the American colonial governments. In each colony there was a right to trial by jury and some freedom of expression.

The first formal constitution among the colonies, the Fundamental Orders of Connecticut, was written in 1639. It gave "freemen" the right to vote and commanded public officials to use their authority for "the public good." The Massachusetts Body of Liberties, drafted two years later, forbade arbitrary sentences by judges and guaranteed a citizen accused of a crime the right to challenge witnesses. Rhode Island's constitution of 1663 was an even bolder step toward limited government: it granted religious freedom for Christians and placed strict limits on the powers of the governor and the town representatives. In other colonies, however, officeholders had fewer restrictions on their authority and citizens had fewer rights. Religious freedom, for example, was not granted by all colonial governments.

When the American colonies declared their independence from England, they adopted state constitutions that defined the limits of government's scope and authority. The new states preferred written constitutions, since they had been governed by formal charters as colonies. In addition, Americans admired the contract theory of government, which was premised on a defined relationship between the people and those who exercised governing authority. By putting the nature of this relationship in writing, Americans believed they were placing limits on the rightful powers of government. No state chose to adopt the British model of an unwritten constitution. (The constitutional structure of Britain's government is defined by custom, common law, and legislative acts.)

THE DECLARATION OF INDEPENDENCE

The Revolutionary War was partly a rebellion against England's failure to respect its own tradition of limited government in the colonies. Many of the colonial charters had conferred upon Americans "the rights of Englishmen," but English kings and ministers showed less and less respect for this guarantee as time went on.

The period after the French and Indian War was the turning point. British and colonial soldiers had fought together to drive the French out of Canada and the western territories in 1763, but the British then imposed taxes that created great resentment in the colonies. Britain's seven-year war with France had created a severe financial crisis for the British government, which looked to the prosperous colonies for relief. Americans were forced to garrison English soldiers in their homes, and Parliament in 1765 levied a stamp tax on colonial newspapers and business documents, disrupting commerce and public communication. As the colonists were not represented in the British Parliament that had imposed the tax, the colonial pamphleteer James Otis declared that the Stamp Act violated the fundamental rights of the colonists as "British subjects and men." The colonists convened a special congress, which declared that the only laws binding on the colonies were those enacted by a legislature "chosen therein by themselves."

Although Parliament backed down and repealed the Stamp Act, it then passed the Townshend Act, which imposed taxes on all paper, glass, lead, and tea entering the colonies. In *Letters from a Farmer in Pennsylvania* (1767), John Dickinson claimed that the Townshend duties were punitive and destructive of the goodwill between Britain and its colonies. When other colonists joined

Drafting the Declaration of Independence, a painting by J. L. Ferris. Benjamin Franklin, John Adams, and Thomas Jefferson (standing) drafted the historic document. Jefferson was the principal author; he inserted the inspirational words about liberty, equality, and self-government. (The Bettmann Archive)

the protest, King George III sent additional British troops to America and interfered with colonial legislatures. These actions served only to arouse the colonists further. England then tried to placate the Americans by repealing the Townshend duties except for a nominal tea tax, which Britain retained in order to display its authority. The colonists viewed the tea tax as a petty insult, and in the "Boston Tea Party" of December 1773 a small band of patriots disguised as Indians boarded an English ship in Boston Harbor and dumped its cargo of tea overboard.

Three years later, sporadic acts of defiance had become a full-scale revolution. In a pamphlet called *Common Sense,* which sold 120,000 copies in its first three months, Thomas Paine had claimed that all of Europe—England, too—was rife with political oppression and that America was humanity's last hope of liberty. "Freedom has been hunted around the globe. . . . Receive the fugitive, and prepare in time an asylum for mankind." The idea was codified in the Declaration of Independence, which Thomas Jefferson prepared and Congress adopted on July 4, 1776. The Declaration honored the British tradition of specific rights by listing their violations by George III and based its argument for inalienable rights on Locke's philosophy. Even two centuries later, the words of the Declaration of Independence are eloquent testimony to Locke's vision of human liberty:

> We hold these truths to be self-evident, that all men are created equal, that they are endowed by their Creator with certain unalienable rights, that among these are life, liberty and the pursuit of happiness.

> That to secure these rights, governments are instituted among men, deriving their just powers from the consent of the governed.
>
> That whenever any form of government becomes destructive of these ends, it is the right of the people to alter or to abolish it, and to institute new government. . . .

★ CRITICAL THINKING

Why Is a Constitution Needed?

The Englishman James Bryce ranked America's written constitution, the world's first such document, as America's greatest contribution to the practice of government. The Constitution offered a new model of government in which a written document defining the state's lawful powers was a higher authority than the actions of any political leader.

The Framers' commitment to constitutionalism grew out of their recognition that, although government must have coercive power in order to function properly, this same power can be used by unscrupulous leaders to repress the very people they are supposed to serve.

Why do you think these two considerations—the coercive power of government and the corruptibility of human nature—lead almost inevitably to a belief in limited government and to the use of a constitution as a means to control the uses of power?

Constitutional Restraints on Political Power

The U.S. Constitution was written eleven years after the Declaration of Independence, with a different purpose. The Declaration was a call to revolution rather than a framework for government. Nevertheless, a concern for liberty was no less fundamental to the delegates at the constitutional convention in 1787 than it had been to leaders of the Revolution.

The challenge facing the Framers of the Constitution was how to control the coercive force of government. Government's unique characteristic is that it alone can legally arrest, imprison, and even kill people who break its rules.[5] Force is not the only basis of effective government, but government must have a final recourse to coercion if its authority is to prevail. Otherwise, persons could break the law with impunity, and society would degenerate to anarchy. The dilemma is that government itself can destroy civilized society by using its force to brutalize and intimidate its opponents. "It is a melancholy reflection," James Madison wrote to Thomas Jefferson shortly after the Constitution's ratification, "that liberty should be equally exposed to danger whether the government has too much or too little power."[6]

The men who wrote the Constitution sought to establish a government strong enough to enforce national interests, including defense and commerce among the states (see Chapter 2), but not so strong as to destroy liberty. Limited government was built into the Constitution through both grants and restrictions of political power.

GRANTS AND DENIALS OF POWER

grants of power The method of limiting the U.S. government by confining its scope of authority to those powers expressly granted in the Constitution.

denials of power A constitutional means of limiting governmental action by listing those powers that government is expressly prohibited from using.

The Framers chose to limit the national government in part by confining its scope to constitutional **grants of power.** For example, as we saw in Chapter 2, Congress's lawmaking authority is constitutionally confined to seventeen specified powers. Authority not granted to the government by the Constitution is in theory denied to it. In a period when other governments held broad discretionary powers, this was a remarkable restriction.

The Framers also used **denials of power** as a means to limit government, prohibiting certain practices that European rulers had routinely used to intimidate their political opponents. The French king, for example, could imprison a subject indefinitely without charge or trial. The U.S. Constitution prohibits such action: individuals have the right to be brought before a court under a writ of habeas corpus for a judgment as to the legality of their confinement. The Constitution also forbids Congress and the states from passing *ex post facto* laws, under which citizens can be prosecuted for acts that were legal at the time they were committed. Among its other denials of power, the Constitution prohibits religious tests as a qualification for office, and it forbids Congress and the states to enact bills of attainder (legislative trials).

USING POWER TO OFFSET POWER

Although the Framers believed that grants and denials of power could act as controls on government, they had no illusion that written words alone would restrain power. As a consequence, they sought to check power with power. The idea was to divide the authority of government, so that no single institution could exercise great power without the agreement of other institutions.[7]

The idea that a separation of powers was necessary to the preservation of liberty had been proposed decades earlier by the French theorist Montesquieu. His argument was widely accepted in America, and when the states drafted new constitutions after the start of the Revolutionary War, they built their governments around the concept of a separation of powers. Pennsylvania was an exception, and its experience only seemed to prove the necessity of separated powers. Unrestrained by an independent judiciary or executive, Pennsylvania's all-powerful legislature systematically deprived minority groups of their basic rights and freedoms: Quakers were disenfranchised for their religious beliefs, conscientious objectors to the Revolutionary War were prosecuted, and the right of trial by jury was eliminated.

James Madison is often called the "father of the Constitution" because he was instrumental in its writing and its ratification (through his contributions to the *Federalist Papers*). The portrait is by Gilbert Stuart. (Bowdoin College Museum of Art, Brunswick, Maine)

In *Federalist* No. 10, Madison asked why governments often act according to the interests of overbearing majorities rather than according to principles of justice. He attributed the cause to "the mischiefs of faction." People, he argued, are divided into opposing religious, geographical, ethnic, economic, and other factions. These divisions are natural and desirable, in that free people have a right to their personal opinions and interests. Yet factions can themselves be a source of oppressive government. If a faction gains full power, it will use government to advance itself at the expense of all others. (*Federalist* No. 10 is widely regarded as the finest political essay every written by an American. It is reprinted at the back of this book.)

Out of this concern came the Framers' special contribution to the doctrine of the separation of powers. They did not believe that it would be enough, as Montesquieu had suggested, to divide the government's authority strictly along institutional lines, granting all legislative power to the legislature, all judicial power to the courts, and all executive power to the presidency. This *total* separation would make it too easy for a single faction to exploit a particular kind of political power. A faction that controlled the legislature, for example, could enact laws ruinous to other interests. A better system of divided government would be one in which political power could be applied forcibly only when institutions agreed on its use. This would require a system of separated but *overlapping* powers. Since no one faction could easily gain control over all institutions, factions would have to work together, a process that would require each to moderate its demands and thus would serve many interests rather than one or a few.[8]

SEPARATED INSTITUTIONS SHARING POWER: CHECKS AND BALANCES

The Framers' concept of divided powers has been described by political scientist Richard Neustadt as the principle of **separated institutions sharing power.**[9] The separate branches are interlocked in such a way that an elabo-

separated institutions sharing power The principle that, as a way to limit government, its powers should be divided among separate branches, each of which also shares in the power of the others as a means of checking and balancing them. The result is that no one branch can exercise power decisively without the support or acquiescence of the others.

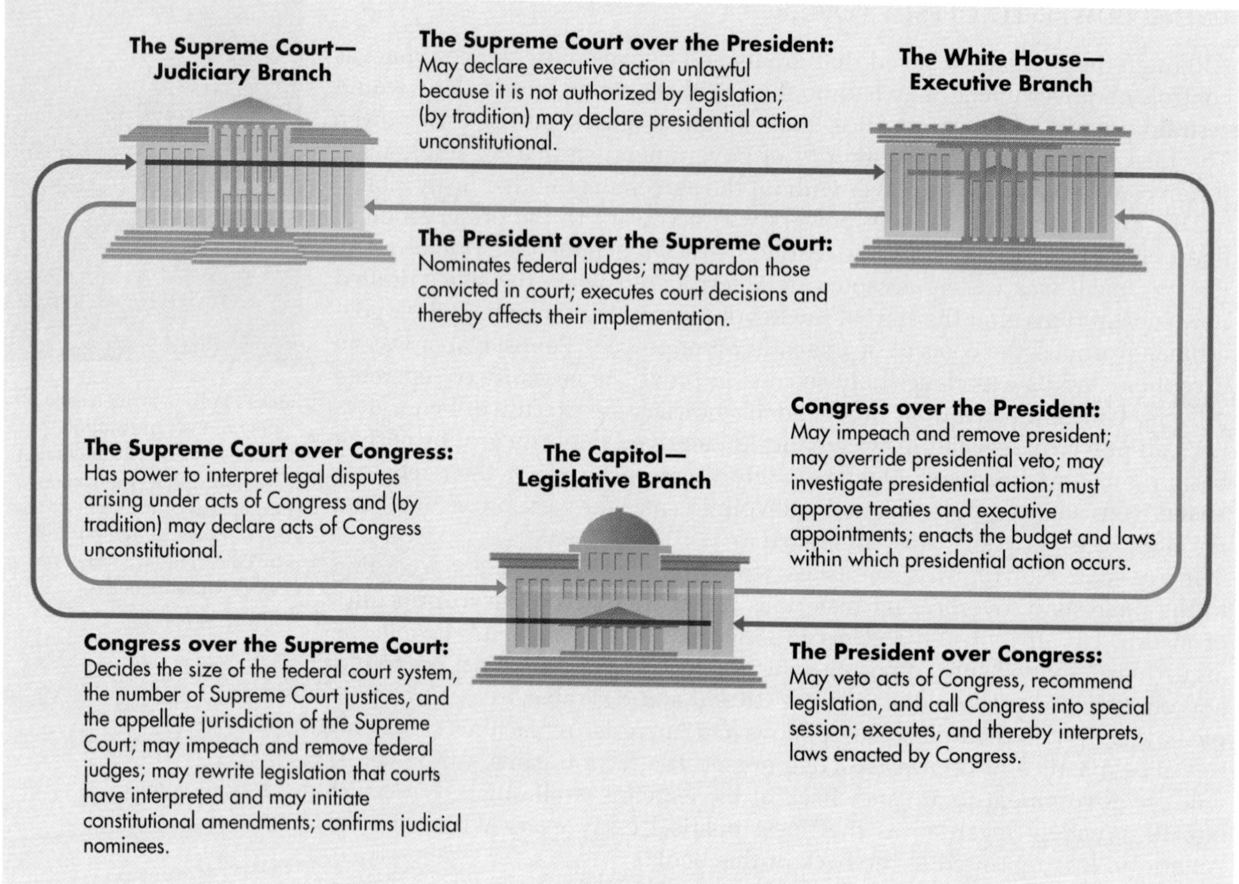

FIGURE 3-1 The System of Checks and Balances

checks and balances The elaborate system of divided spheres of authority provided by the U.S. Constitution as a means of controlling the power of government. The separation of powers among the branches of the national government, federalism, and the different methods of selecting national officers are all part of this system.

rate system of **checks and balances** is created (see Figure 3-1). No institution can act decisively without the support or acquiescence of the other institutions. Legislative, executive, and judicial powers in the American system are divided in such a way that they overlap; each of the three branches of government checks the others' powers and balances those powers with powers of its own.

Shared Legislative Powers

Under the Constitution, Congress has legislative authority, but that power is partly shared with the other branches and thus checked by them. The president can veto acts of Congress, recommend legislation, and call special sessions of Congress. The president also has the power to execute—and thereby to interpret—the laws made by Congress.

The Supreme Court has the power to interpret acts of Congress that are disputed in legal cases. By tradition, the Court also has the power of judicial review; it can declare laws of Congress void when it finds that they are not in accord with the Constitution.

Within Congress, there is a further check on legislative power: for legislation to be passed, a majority in each house of Congress is required. Thus the Senate and the House of Representatives can veto each other's actions.

Shared Executive Powers

Executive power is vested in the president but is constrained by legislative and judicial checks. The president's power to make treaties and appoint high-ranking officials, for example, is subject to Senate approval. In practical terms, Congress's greatest checks on executive action are its lawmaking and appropriations powers. The executive branch cannot act without laws that authorize its activities or without the money that pays for these programs.

The judiciary's major check on the presidency is its power to declare an action unlawful because it is not authorized by the legislation that the executive claims to be implementing.

Shared Judicial Powers

Judicial power rests with the Supreme Court and with lower federal courts, which are subject to checks by the other branches of the federal government.

THE MEDIA AND THE PEOPLE

CHECKS ON "THE FOURTH BRANCH OF GOVERNMENT"

The U.S. constitutional system is based on the concept of checks and balances—the notion that all power should be subject to formal limitations. When the Framers wrote the Constitution, this concept was applied to the three branches of government—the executive, the legislature, and the judiciary. The power of each would serve to check and balance the power of the other two.

The press has been called "the fourth branch of government." This term is a relatively new one. At the time the Constitution was written, the press was an adjunct of political authority (see Chapter 11). Not until the late 1800s did the press become an extraordinary political power in its own right. This development occurred when the press became a "mass medium." The spread of mass education and the invention of newsprint in the late 1800s made the newspaper a daily part of Americans' lives. The introduction of radio and television several decades later gave the media an even greater presence in American society.

The power of the press rests with its ability to influence what people think and talk about. The world of politics is beyond firsthand observation, so we depend on the press to bring this world within our reach. In deciding what to cover and what to ignore, the media exert a powerful influence over our images of politics. Some observers claim, in fact, that the media are the preeminent political power in today's society. At his Harvard commencement speech in 1978, the Russian writer Alexander Solzhenitsyn said: "The press has become the most powerful force in western countries. It has surpassed in power the executive, legislative, and judiciary."

Although most analysts would not go this far, none would deny that the media have considerable political power. Significantly, this power is exercised outside the system of constitutional checks and balances. The press, in fact, is protected from interference by other institutions. The First Amendment says that "Congress shall make no law . . . abridging the freedom of speech, or of the press." The dilemma is that the press is a private institution that is driven as much by its interest in profit as by its sense of public duty. Critics complain that the news media tend to present a relatively trivial and sensational view of politics (see Chapter 11).

Should the press be subject to checks and balances in the same way as the legislative, executive, and judicial branches? What form might these checks and balances take?

Congress is empowered to establish the size of the federal court system; to restrict the Supreme Court's appellate jurisdiction in some circumstances; and to impeach and remove federal judges from office. More important, Congress can rewrite legislation that the courts have misinterpreted and can initiate amendments when it disagrees with the courts' rulings on constitutional issues.

The president has the power to appoint federal judges with the consent of the Senate and to pardon persons convicted in the courts. The president is also responsible for executing court decisions, a function that provides opportunities to influence the way rulings are implemented.

FEDERALISM AS A FURTHER CHECK ON GOVERNMENT POWER

Theorists such as Locke and Montesquieu had not proposed a division of power between national and local authorities as a further means of protecting liberty. Nevertheless, the Framers came to look upon federalism (discussed in Chapter 2) as part of the systems of checks and balances established by the Constitution. Hamilton argued in *Federalist* No. 28 that the American people could shift their loyalties back and forth between the national and state governments in order to keep each under control. "If [the people's] rights are invaded by either," Hamilton wrote, "they can make use of the other as the instrument of redress." Madison wrote in *Federalist* No. 51 that a federal system is a superior form of limited government because power is divided between two distinct governments, as well as among their separate branches. "The different governments will control each other," he said, "at the same time that each will be controlled by itself."

THE BILL OF RIGHTS

Although the delegates to the Philadelphia convention discussed the possibility of placing a list of individual rights (such as freedom of speech and the right to a fair trial) in the Constitution, they ultimately decided that such a list was unnecessary because of the doctrine of expressed powers: government could not lawfully assume powers, such as the abridgment of human rights, that were not authorized by the Constitution. Moreover, the delegates concluded that a bill of rights was undesirable because government might feel free to disregard any right that was inadvertently left off the list or that emerged at some future time.

These considerations did not allay the fears of leading Americans who believed that no possible safeguard against tyrannical government should be omitted. "A bill of rights," Jefferson argued, "is what the people are entitled to against every government on earth, general or particular, and what no just government should refuse or rest on inference." Jefferson had included a bill of rights in the constitution he wrote for Virginia at the outbreak of the Revolutionary War, and all but four states had followed Virginia's example.

Opposition to the absence of a bill of rights in the federal constitution led to its addition. Madison himself introduced a series of amendments during the First Congress, ten of which were subsequently ratified by the states. These amendments, traditionally called the *Bill of Rights,* include such rights as free

LIMITS ON GOVERNMENT IN THE U.S. CONSTITUTION

Grants of power: powers granted to the national government by the Constitution; powers not granted it are denied it unless they are necessary and proper to the carrying out of granted powers.

Denials of power: powers expressly denied to the national and state governments by the Constitution.

Separated institutions sharing power: the division of the national government's power among three branches, each of which is to act as a check on the powers of the other two.

Bill of Rights: the first ten amendments to the Constitution, which specify rights of citizens that the national government must respect.

Federalism: the division of political authority between the national government and the states, enabling the people to appeal to one authority if their rights and interests are not respected by the other authority.

Judicial review: the power of the courts to declare governmental action null and void when it is found to violate the Constitution.

expression and due process for persons accused of crimes. (These rights, termed "civil liberties," are the subject of Chapter 4.)

The Bill of Rights is a precise expression of the concept of limited government. In consenting to be governed, the people agree to accept the authority of government in certain areas but not in others; the people's constitutional rights cannot lawfully be denied by governing officials.

JUDICIAL REVIEW

The writers of the Constitution both empowered and limited government. But who was to decide whether the government was operating within its constitutional powers? The Framers did not specifically entrust this power to a particular branch of government, although they did grant the Supreme Court the authority to decide on "all cases arising under this Constitution."

Most delegates to the Philadelphia convention apparently assumed that the Supreme Court would have the power of **judicial review:** the power of the courts to decide whether a governmental institution has acted within its constitutional powers and, if not, to declare its action null and void. There was precedent for judicial review in several states, and a form of it had existed during the colonial period. It is also noteworthy that the power of the courts to declare laws null and void was discussed and accepted at the ratifying conventions of at least eight of the thirteen states.[10] Still, because the Constitution did not explicitly provide for judicial review, it was a principle that had to be established in practice.

judicial review The power of courts to decide whether a governmental institution has acted within its constitutional powers and, if not, to declare its action null and void.

The opportunity arose with an incident that occurred after the election of 1800, in which John Adams lost his bid for a second presidential term after a bitter campaign against Jefferson. In the period between Jefferson's election and his inauguration, the Federalist-controlled Congress created fifty-nine additional lower-court judgeships, enabling Adams to appoint loyal Federalists to those positions before he left office. However, Adams's term expired before the secretary of state's office could deliver all of the judicial commis-

John Marshall forcefully expressed his nationalist views in important Supreme Court decisions during his thirty-four years as chief justice. (Stock Montage)

sions, which were subsequently withheld by Jefferson's secretary of state, James Madison. William Marbury was one of those denied a commission, and he asked the Supreme Court to issue a writ of *mandamus* (a court order requiring an official to take a specific action) ordering Madison to provide it.

Marbury v. *Madison* (1803), one of the most important judicial decisions in U.S. history, became the foundation for judicial review by the federal courts. Chief Justice John Marshall wrote the *Marbury* opinion. His ingenious decision asserted the power of judicial review without forcing the Court into a showdown with the executive or legislative branch. The Court ruled that Marbury had a legal right to his commission, thus implicitly criticizing Jefferson for failing in his constitutional duty to execute the laws faithfully. However, the Court said it could not issue Marbury a writ because the Constitution did not grant the Court this authority. Through the Judiciary Act of 1789 Congress had extended this authority to the Court, but Marshall argued that such a grant required a constitutional amendment. That being the case, Marshall concluded, the provision of the Judiciary Act that authorized the Supreme Court to issue writs of *mandamus* was unconstitutional.[11]

This decision established the Court's authority without placing it in jeopardy. The Court had invalidated an act of Congress, thereby asserting its power to interpret the Constitution. Congress could not retaliate for it had no way to force the Court to provide a writ that the justices refused to issue.

John Marshall served as chief justice for more than thirty years after *Marbury,* and the Court did not again invalidate an act of Congress. Nevertheless, *Marbury* had asserted the principle that the lawful powers of government are subject to judicial scrutiny. *Marbury* became a precedent for later Court rulings that clearly established the Supreme Court's position as the chief authority on the Constitution's grants of power and thus a critical actor in the preservation of limited government. The judiciaries of many countries lack this authority. The British high court, for example, cannot invalidate an act of Parliament.

Limited Government in Perspective

In the course of their history Americans have not always honored the principle of limited government. The greatest test of the nation's commitment to liberty came shortly after Reconstruction, when the question was whether former slaves would be granted a full measure of freedom. The answer was no. The North turned its back as the South's white majority systematically stripped black people of their constitutional rights, an injustice in which even the Supreme Court of the United States participated by its ruling in *Plessy* v. *Ferguson* (discussed in Chapter 5).

The history of racial oppression in the United States is a stark rebuttal to any simple claim that America is somehow superior to all other countries in the practice of liberty. Yet by the standards of a world in which brutal government is all too common, the United States has been relatively successful in restraining political power.[12] When Eldridge Cleaver, a founder of the Black Panther party in the 1960s, returned to the United States after a lengthy self-imposed exile, he admonished Americans for not living up to their nation's creed, but added, "With all its faults, the American political system is the freest in the world."[13]

The freedom that Americans enjoy cannot be attributed solely, or even primarily, to the Constitution. No document alone can ensure a limited government. In many parts of the world, politics is an unyielding struggle for survival between the many who are desperately poor and the very few who are rich. In contrast, the politics of the United States has been moderated by the country's natural abundance. In *Federalist* No. 10 James Madison anticipated that America's economic resources and opportunities would protect it from political extremism. Because property ownership was widespread, Madison foresaw that conflict would not degenerate into a war between those with property and those without it. Economic divisions would occur instead among differing property interests—landed, industrial, and commercial—each of which would be further divided, as in the case of small and large landholders. The net effect of this economic and social diversity, Madison concluded, would be a moderate level of political conflict that could be settled peacefully within a framework of limited government. The exercise of political power in all cases would require a compromise among competing interests, so that each of them would be compelled to respect the rights of the others.

Madison's prediction was reasonably accurate. In 1893 Friedrich Engels, the collaborator of Karl Marx, said that he saw no real chance of a wrenching class struggle in America because of its economic diversity and abundance.[14] And Engels was writing *before* the full fruits of the Industrial Revolution had produced for Americans a standard of living that was the envy of the world.

THE CONTRIBUTION OF DIVIDED POWERS

Although no constitutional arrangement could have checked political power had the United States lacked great wealth, the American experience indicates that constitutional provisions also contribute to limited government. Of all features of the U.S. constitutional system, none has been more important to the control of power than its allocation among separate branches. Throughout most of the country's history, each branch has guarded against abuses of power by the others, a system that has served to check the power of all three branches.

Few events more clearly illustrate this tendency than the Watergate affair, which first came to public attention when five burglars with links to President Richard Nixon's reelection campaign were apprehended inside the Democratic party's national headquarters. Nixon called the incident "bizarre," but the break-in was actually part of an orchestrated campaign of "dirty tricks" designed to ensure Nixon's reelection. Funded by illegal contributions and conducted through the CIA, IRS, FBI, Secret Service, and Nixon's own operatives (called the White House "plumbers"), the dirty-tricks campaign extended to wiretaps, tax audits, and burglaries of Nixon's political opponents (the "enemies list"), who included journalists and antiwar activists in addition to Democrats.

Although the Nixon White House managed for a time to obstruct justice (in one ploy, the president's assistants asked the CIA to tell the FBI to stop the

HOW THE UNITED STATES COMPARES

CHECKS AND BALANCES

All democracies place constitutional limits on the power of government. The concept of rule by law, for example, is characteristic of democratic governments but not of authoritarian regimes. Democracies differ, however, in the extent to which political power is restrained through constitutional mechanisms. The United States is an extreme case in that its government rests on an elaborate system of constitutional checks and balances. The system employs a separation of powers among the executive, legislative, and judicial branches. It also includes judicial review, the power of the courts to invalidate actions of the legislature or executive. These constitutional restrictions on power are not part of the governing structure of all democracies.

Country	*Separation of Powers?*	*Judicial Review?*
Belgium	No	No
Canada	No	Yes
France	Yes	No
Germany	No	Yes
Great Britain	No	No
Israel	No	Yes
Italy	No	Yes
Japan	No	Yes
Mexico	In theory only	Yes
United States	Yes	Yes

Watergate investigation on fictitious "national security" grounds), the facts of Nixon's dirty-tricks campaign gradually became known. The investigation was helped along, ironically, by Nixon's own words. During Senate hearings, a White House assistant revealed that Nixon had tape-recorded all his telephone calls and personal conversations in the Oval Office. At first Nixon refused to release transcripts of the tapes, but he then made public what he claimed were "all the relevant" ones. The House Judiciary Committee demanded additional tapes, as did the special prosecutor who had been appointed to investigate criminal aspects of the Watergate affair. In late July the Supreme Court of the United States (which included four justices appointed by Nixon) unanimously ordered the president to supply sixty-four additional tapes, which provided incriminating evidence against the president. Two weeks later, on August 9, 1974, Richard Nixon resigned from office, the first president in U.S. history to do so.

THE CONTRIBUTION OF JUDICIAL REVIEW

Judicial review has also been an important element in our system of limited government. Judicial review was essential if the judiciary was to be the constitutional equal of the other two branches and thus if it was to have legitimate authority to act against them when necessary. Neither elected branch has much to gain and might have much to lose by being rebuffed by the Supreme Court. Congress and the president have sometimes refrained from initiating policies of questionable constitutionality simply because they knew that the Supreme Court could invalidate their actions and thereby damage their prestige and undermine the legitimacy of their actions.[15]

Ironically perhaps, judicial review's greatest historical contribution to the protection of liberty has come in its application not to actions of Congress or the president but to those of the states. The states have the major responsibility for law enforcement and other policies where the interests of the majority and the rights of the individual most directly clash. Moreover, as Madison foresaw in *Federalist* No. 10, the smaller the unit of government, the more likely a single faction will gain full political power and use it to the disadvantage of others. The next chapter explains in detail the application of judicial review to local and state laws that involve issues of individual rights and liberties.

Representation in the Constitution

"We the People" is the opening line of the Constitution. It expresses the idea that, in the United States, the people will have the power to govern themselves. In a sense, there is no contradiction between this idea and the Constitution's provisions for limited government, since individual liberty is part of the process of self-government. In another sense, the contradiction is clear: restrictions on the power of the majority are a denial of its right to govern society as it chooses.

The Framers believed that the majority's power should be controlled.[16] In their judgment, a great risk of popular government was **tyranny of the majority.** Inflamed by an issue of the moment, the majority could become an irrational mob without any regard for others. To the Framers, the record of democracies left much to be desired. Said James Madison in *Federalist* No. 10: "It may be concluded . . . that such [uncontrolled] democracies have ever been spectacles of turbulence and contention; have ever been found incompatible with personal security or rights of property; and have in general been as short in their lives, as they have been violent in their deaths." There were even examples of democratic excess from the nation's brief history since the Revolution. In 1786, debtors had gained control of Rhode Island's legislature and made paper money a legal means of paying debts, even though existing contracts called for payment in gold. Creditors were then hunted down and held captive in public places so that debtors could come and pay them in full with worthless paper money. A Boston newspaper wrote that Rhode Island should be renamed *Rogue* Island.

tyranny of the majority The potential of a majority to monopolize power for its own gain and to the detriment of minority rights and interests.

democracy A form of government in which the people rule, either directly or through elected representatives.

republic Historically, the form of government in which representative officials met to decide on policy issues. These representatives were expected to serve the public interest but were not subject to the people's immediate control. Today, the term *republic* is used interchangeably with *democracy.*

DEMOCRACY VERSUS REPUBLIC

No form of self-government could eliminate completely the threat to liberty of majority tyranny, but the Framers believed that the danger would be greatly diminished by properly structured institutions.[17] Madison summarized the Framers' intent when he said in *Federalist* No. 10 that the Constitution was "a republican remedy" for the excesses historically associated with "democratic" rule. Today the terms **democracy, republic,** and **representative democracy** are used interchangeably to refer to a system of government in which ultimate political power rests with the majority through its capacity to choose representatives in free and open elections. To the writers of the Constitution, however, "democracy" and "republic" had different meanings. When the Framers complained about the risks of democracy, they were referring to "pure democ-

representative democracy A system in which the people participate in the decision-making process of government not directly but indirectly, through the election of officials to represent their interests.

racy," in which popular opinion was translated directly into public policy. In their use of the term "republic," the Framers were referring to representative government in which elected officials met in representative institutions to decide policy through extended debate and deliberation.[18]

The Framers' concept of a proper system of representation was similar to an idea put forth by the English theorist Edmund Burke (1729–1797). In his *Letter to the Sheriffs of Bristol*, Burke argued that representatives should act as public **trustees:** they are obliged to promote the interest of those who elected them, but the nature of this interest is for the representatives, not the voters, to decide. Burke was concerned about the ease with which society could degenerate into selfishness, and he thought it imperative for representatives not to surrender their judgment to popular whim.

trustees The idea of elected representatives as obligated to act in accordance with their own consciences as to what policies are in the best interests of the public.

LIMITED POPULAR RULE

The Constitution provided that all power would be exercised through representative institutions. There was no provision for any form of direct popular participation in the making of policy decisions. In view of the fact that the United States was much too large to be governed directly by the people in popular assemblies, a representative system was necessary. Moreover, the separation of powers meant that the majority's will, again by necessity, would be filtered through an institutional structure. The Framers went beyond what was necessary, however, and placed officials at a considerable distance from the people they represented (see Table 3-1).

The House of Representatives was the only institution that would be based on direct popular election—its members would be elected for two-year terms of office through vote of the people. Frequent and direct election of House members was intended to make government sensitive to the concerns of popular majorities. The Constitution specified, however, that the House could have no more than one representative for every 30,000 inhabitants. This provision was designed to ensure that each representative would represent a large area and population (keep in mind that the United States at the time was a sparsely populated, agrarian nation) and thus not be bound too closely to local concerns.[19]

TABLE 3-1 Methods of Choosing National Leaders Fearing the concentration of political power, the Framers devised alternative methods of selection and terms of service for national officials.

Office	*Method of Selection*	*Term of Service*
President	Electoral College	4 years
U.S. senator	State legislature	6 years (one-third of senators' terms expire every 2 years)
U.S. representative	Popular election	2 years
Federal judge	Nominated by president, approved by Senate	Indefinite (subject to "good behavior")

U.S. senators would be appointed by the legislatures of the states they represented. Because state legislators were popularly elected, the people would be choosing their senators indirectly. Every two years, a third of the senators would be appointed to six-year terms. The Senate was expected to check and balance the House, which, by virtue of the more frequent and direct election of its members, would presumably be more responsive to popular opinion.

Presidential selection was an issue of considerable debate at the Philadelphia convention. Direct election of the president was twice proposed and twice rejected because it linked executive power directly to popular majorities. The Framers finally chose to have the president selected by the votes of electors (the so-called Electoral College). Each state would have as many electors as it had members in Congress and could select them by any method it chose. The president would serve four years and be eligible for reelection.

The Framers decided that federal judges and justices would be appointed rather than elected. They would be nominated by the president and confirmed through approval by the Senate. Once confirmed, they would "hold their offices during good behavior." In effect, they would be allowed to hold office for life unless they committed a crime. The judiciary would be more of a "guardian" institution than a "representative" one.[20]

These differing methods of selecting national officeholders would not prevent a determined majority from achieving unbridled power, but control could not be attained easily or quickly. Unlike the House of Representatives, institutions such as the Senate, presidency, and judiciary would not yield to an impassioned majority in a single election. The delay would reduce the probability that government would degenerate into mob rule driven by momentary whims. The Framers believed that majority tyranny would be impulsive. Given time, the people would presumably come to their senses.

★ CRITICAL THINKING

"Strong Democracy"?
The possibilities for popular participation in government have always been more limited in national politics than local politics. Even at the time of the writing of the Constitution, the United States was too large to be governed except through representative institutions.

Proponents of popular rule have looked toward local communities as a place where people can participate more directly in government. In his book *Strong Democracy* (1984), Benjamin Barber argues that the Constitution's pessimistic view of human nature contributes to "thin" democracy in America. Barber says that voting is an important act but an inherently confining one. He prefers a "strong democracy" in which citizens are provided widespread opportunities for participation, including a greater say in policies that govern the workplace.

Where do you stand on the issue of popular control? What policy decisions, if any, would you shift from the national level to the local level, or from the private sector to the public sector, in order to increase the public's control over the policies that govern it?

Modifying the Framers' Work: Toward a More Democratic Society

The Framers' conception of self-government was at odds with the one held by many Americans in 1787. The promise of self-government was one of the reasons that ordinary people had made great sacrifices during the American Revolution. This democratic spirit was reflected in the state constitutions. Every state but South Carolina held annual legislative elections, and several states also chose their governors through annual election by the people.[21]

In this context, the Constitution's provisions for popular rule were rather thin. Richard Henry Lee of Virginia criticized even the House of Representatives, which he said had "very little democracy in it" because each of its members would represent a large population and area.[22] Madison had claimed that this arrangement was necessary because otherwise representatives would be "unduly attached" to local interests and "too little fit to comprehend and pursue great and national objects." To Lee and others, such arguments were a mask for *elitism*—rule by a few who claimed to know the people's interests better than the people knew it themselves.[23] And it was not long after ratification of the Constitution that Americans sought a stronger voice in their own governing. The search has continued throughout the country's history: in no

This 1793 cartoon depicts the Anti-Federalists as a "club" gathering to condemn the Federalist government. Jefferson stands with an auctioneer's gavel, wondering "whether 'tis nobler in the mind to knock down [that is, auction off] dry goods with this hammer or with this head to continue some means of knocking down a Government and on its ruins raise myself to Eminence and Fortune." (Historical Picture Service)

other constitutional area have Americans shown a greater willingness to experiment with new arrangements.

THE ERA OF JEFFERSONIAN DEMOCRACY

Thomas Jefferson, who otherwise admired the Constitution, was among the prominent Americans who questioned its provisions for self-government. To Jefferson, America was the hope of ordinary people everywhere for liberation from elite rule, and he reasoned that the American people might someday rebel against the small governing role assigned them by the Constitution.[24]

Ironically, it was Jefferson who may have spared the nation a bloody revolution over the issue of popular sovereignty. Under John Adams, the second president, the national government increasingly favored the nation's wealthy interests. Adams publicly suggested that the Constitution was designed for a governing elite, while Alexander Hamilton urged him to use force if necessary to suppress protests.[25] Jefferson asked whether Adams, with the aid of a strong army, planned soon to deprive ordinary Americans of their freedoms altogether. Jefferson challenged Adams in the next presidential election and, upon defeating him, hailed the victory as the "Revolution of 1800." (Jefferson and Adams became close friends through correspondence later in life. They died on the same day in 1826, and Jefferson asked on his deathbed whether Adams, who had been ill, still lived.)

Although Jefferson was a champion of the common people, he had no clear vision of how a popular government might work in practice. He believed that legislative majorities were the proper expression of the public's interest and accordingly was reluctant to use his presidency for this purpose.[26] Jefferson also had no illusions about a largely illiterate population's readiness for a significant governing role and feared the ruinous consequences of inciting the masses to contest the moneyed class. Jeffersonian democracy was thus mainly a revolution of the spirit; Jefferson taught Americans to look upon the national government as belonging to all, not just to the privileged few.[27]

THE ERA OF JACKSONIAN DEMOCRACY

Not until Andrew Jackson was elected in 1828 did the country have a powerful president who was willing and able to involve the public more fully in government. Jackson carried out the constitutional revolution that Jeffersonian democracy had foreshadowed.

Jackson recognized that the president was the only official who could legitimately claim to represent the people as a whole. Unlike the president, members of Congress were elected from separate states and districts rather than from the entire country. Yet the president's claim to popular leadership was diminished by the existence of the Electoral College, which also acted as a barrier to the public's influence on the office. Jackson first tried to persuade Congress to initiate a constitutional amendment that would abolish the electoral voting system. Failing this, Jackson persuaded the states to choose their presidential electors on the basis of popular voting. Jackson's reform, which is still in effect today, basically places the selection of a president in the voters' hands. The winner of the popular vote in each state is awarded its electoral votes; hence the candidate who wins the popular vote contest is also most likely to receive a majority of the electoral votes. Since Jackson's time, only twice has the loser of the popular vote won the presidency (Rutherford B. Hayes in 1876 and Benjamin Harrison in 1888).

Jackson also sought to put an end to the domination of wealthy families who controlled most high public offices, both elective and appointive. He persuaded states to abolish property ownership as a requirement for voting and promoted the rotation of public office (which his opponents derided as a mere "spoils system") as a means of keeping unelected officials in closer touch with the people.

Jacksonian democracy also brought with it the development of parties built on "grassroots" organization—that is, based on participation at the local level by ordinary citizens. The party's strength derived from its popular base, not, as had previously been the case, its network of elites. By the time he won a second term in 1832, Jackson's Democratic party had enlisted the participation of thousands of citizens. The election of 1832 also marked the introduction of the party nominating convention in presidential politics. Presidential nominations had earlier been controlled by party leaders in Congress and the state legislatures.

The development of grassroots political parties in the 1830s gave the people a powerful means of collective influence. Until then, each voter could only influence the selection of a single representative. With the advent of grassroots parties, a majority of individuals throughout the nation, united by affiliation with a political party, could choose a majority of representatives who shared the same policy goals. Majority opinion could thereby be more readily translated into public policy. So fundamental was the emergence of the grassroots party to the influence of the people that the historian James MacGregor Burns has called it America's "second constitution."[28]

Grassroots parties resulted in increased citizen participation in nineteenth-century elections. This painting depicts the fanfare surrounding Grover Cleveland's 1892 reelection campaign. (Chicago Historical Society)

THE PROGRESSIVE ERA

After the 1840s, the parties gradually drifted toward localism and favoritism. In the cities especially, they were taken over by powerful party bosses with an appetite for patronage. By the 1880s, some party bosses were in league with the robber barons to block government from regulating business trusts (see Chapter 2).[29]

Progressive movement An early 1900s reform movement that sought to make economic and political power more accountable by granting the public a more direct say in how it is governed.

delegates The idea of elected representatives as obligated to carry out the expressed wishes of the electorate.

The **Progressive movement** sought to reform the political system by reducing the power of corporations and party bosses and by giving the public a more direct role in governing. In its Declaration of Principles of 1911, the National Progressive League defined its goal as "the promotion of popular government." The Progressives rejected the Burkean idea (discussed earlier in this chapter) of representatives as trustees; they embraced instead the idea of representatives as **delegates**—officeholders who are obligated to respond directly to the expressed opinions of the people whom they represent.

The Progressive movement was made possible by changes in education and communication during the nation's first century. In 1787 the vast majority of Americans were illiterate, and many of those who could read could not afford the hand-printed newspapers of the time. During the nineteenth century, however, a broad-based public school system was created, and the invention of the high-speed printing press led to the "penny" newspaper. By the time of the Progressive movement, literacy was widespread in America, as was newspaper readership. Ordinary Americans believed themselves to be politically informed and wanted the greater influence that the Progressives promised.

As with other political reform movements, the Progressives were driven as much by political considerations as by a desire for reform. If the movement succeeded, the losers would be big business and Catholic-dominated urban machines. Most Progressives were small businesspeople, small townspeople, and Protestants.

Progressive Reforms

Two Progressive reforms gave voting majorities the direct power to decide policy at the state and local levels. One device was the *initiative,* which allows citizens through petition to place legislative measures on the ballot. A related measure was the *referendum,* which permits legislative bodies to submit proposals to the voters for approval or rejection. The Progressives also sought to give the public recourse against wayward state and local officials through the *recall,* in which citizens petition for the removal of an elected official before the scheduled completion of his or her term of office.

In terms of national politics, a significant Progressive reform was the direct election of U.S. senators, who, before the Seventeenth Amendment was ratified in 1913, had been chosen by state legislatures and were widely perceived as agents of big business (the Senate was nicknamed the "millionaires' club"). Earlier attempts to amend the Senate election procedure were blocked by the senators, who stood to lose their seats if they had to submit to direct vote by the people. Eventually, however, the Senate was persuaded to support an amendment by pressure from the Progressives and by revelations that corporate bribes had influenced the selection of several senators.

Of the many Progressive reforms, the most significant was the *primary election,* which gave rank-and-file voters a voice in the selection of party nominees. Party bosses would no longer have absolute control of nominations, which had been a chief source of their power. No greater blow to political parties can be imagined. When a party does not have the power to select its candidates, it cannot command their loyalty to its organizational and policy goals. Candidates will embrace or reject their party as it suits their needs. In other democracies, which have no primary elections, parties have retained control of the nominating process and therefore have remained strong. (Chapter 10 discusses party organization in detail.)

The Progressives had the support of two strong presidents, Theodore Roosevelt (1901–1909) and Woodrow Wilson (1913–1921), who shared the Progressives' opposition to business monopolies but also recognized the power inherent in a popular presidency. Roosevelt described the office as a "bully pulpit." Wilson, writing about the president's potential for national leadership, said: "His is the only national voice in public affairs. Let him once win the admiration and confidence of the country, and no other single voice will easily overpower him."[30] Roosevelt's and Wilson's conception of the president as national leader, legitimized through election by a majority of voters, helped change the presidency's image. In the view of the public, the president was superseding Congress as the chief instrument of democracy (see Chapter 14).

★ STATES IN THE NATION

Direct Democracy: The initiative and referendum are more common in midwestern and western states, where the Progressive movement was stronger.

STATE	INITIATIVE	REFERENDUM
Ala.	No	No
Alaska	Yes	Yes
Ariz.	Yes	Yes
Ark.	Yes	Yes
Calif.	Yes	Yes
Colo.	Yes	Yes
Conn.	No	Yes
Del.	No	No
Fla.	Yes	No
Ga.	No	No
Hawaii	No	No
Idaho	Yes	Yes
Ill.	Yes	Yes
Ind.	No	No
Iowa	No	Yes
Kan.	No	Yes
Ky.	No	Yes
La.	No	No
Maine	Yes	Yes
Md.	No	Yes
Mass.	Yes	Yes
Mich.	Yes	Yes
Minn.	No	No
Miss.	No	No
Mo.	Yes	Yes
Mont.	Yes	Yes
Neb.	Yes	Yes
Nev.	Yes	Yes
N.H.	No	No
N.J.	No	Yes
N. Mex.	No	Yes
N.Y.	No	Yes
N.C.	No	Yes
N.Dak.	Yes	Yes
Ohio	Yes	Yes
Okla.	Yes	Yes
Oreg.	Yes	Yes
Pa.	No	Yes
R.I.	No	Yes
S.C.	No	No
S.Dak.	Yes	Yes
Tenn.	No	No
Texas	No	No
Utah	Yes	Yes
Vt.	No	No
Va.	No	No
Wash.	Yes	Yes
W.V.	No	No
Wis.	No	Yes
Wyo.	Yes	Yes

SOURCE: Council of State Governments, *Book of the States, 1992–1993* (Lexington, Ky: Council of State Governments, 1992), 329, 340–41.

Beard's Economic Theory of the Constitution

The Progressive view that the original Constitution had erred in giving the majority too little power was expressed in the form of attacks on the Framers, the most notable of which was that of historian Charles S. Beard's *Economic Interpretation of the Constitution.*[31] Arguing that the Constitution grew out of wealthy Americans' fear of debtor rebellions, Beard claimed that its elaborate systems of power and representation were devices for keeping power in the

HOW THE NATIONAL POLITICAL SYSTEM WAS MADE MORE RESPONSIVE TO POPULAR MAJORITIES

EARLIER SITUATION	SUBSEQUENT DEVELOPMENT
Separation of powers, as a means of dividing authority and blunting passionate majorities.	Political parties, as a means of uniting authorities and linking them with popular majorities.
Indirect election of all national officials except House members, as a means of buffering officials from popular influence.	Direct election of U.S. senators and popular voting for president (linked to electoral votes), as a means of increasing popular control of officials.
Nomination of candidates for public office through political party organizations.	Primary elections, as a means of selecting party nominees.

hands of the rich. As evidence, Beard cited the Constitution's protections of property and referred to James Madison's secret notes on the Philadelphia convention, which showed that the delegates placed a high priority on property interests.

Beard's thesis was challenged by other historians, and he later acknowledged that he had not taken the Framers' full array of motives into account. Their concept of separation of powers, for example, was a time-honored governing principle that had previously been incorporated into state constitutions. Nevertheless, the Framers' system of representation was premised on a fear of unrestricted popular majorities and allowed the states to restrict suffrage. The Constitution required only that a state not impose stricter qualifications for voting in elections for the U.S. House of Representatives than were applied to elections for the larger house of the state legislature. The states allowed only propertied white males to vote, and it is likely that most of the Framers supported the limitation of suffrage to this class.

But it would be inaccurate to conclude that the Framers were opposed to a government by the people. They were intent on establishing a government that was subject to popular influence and yet would offer protection against a tyrannical majority. The Constitution was an attempt to strike a balance between representative government, which makes government more responsive to the will of the majority, and limited government, which restricts the power of the government and hence the majority. Today, such a government is called a **constitutional democracy.** It is democratic in its provisions for majority influence through popular elections and constitutional in its requirement that this power be exercised in accordance with law and with due respect for individual rights.

constitutional democracy A government that is democratic in its provisions for majority influence through elections, and constitutional in its provisions for minority rights and rule by law.

THE MODERN ERA: THE TERM-LIMITATION REFORM MOVEMENT

The debate over representation that began with the writing of the Constitution continues to the present day. An example is the widening debate over **term limitations,** or legal restrictions on the number of years that elected officials can remain in office.

term limitations A device that deals with the problem of entrenched leadership by prohibiting officials from serving more than a set number of years in a particular office.

Voters in Oklahoma were the first to act, deciding by a more than 2-to-1 margin in 1990 to limit state legislators to twelve years of service. California and Colorado voters followed suit in the same year. In the 1992 and 1994 elections, citizens in twenty-one states and the District of Columbia voted on term limits; in all these locations but one, term limits were adopted.

In 1995, however, the Supreme Court in *United States* v. *Thornton* dealt a serious setback to term-limit advocates. The U.S. Constitution specifies age, citizenship, and residency requirements for House and Senate office, and the Court held that additional limits on the holders of these federal offices would require a constitutional amendment. State and local offices are unaffected by the decision.

The term-limitation movement in many ways resembles the reform efforts of the past: it is based on the public's dissatisfaction with government, a belief that entrenched politicians are part of the problem, and a sense that the solution to these problems is to connect public officials more closely to the people they serve. The public's confidence in Congress, for example, has declined precipitously since the 1960s. By 1994, it had reached a record low: barely 20 percent said they trusted Congress to act in their interest. This attitude was the culmination of a series of scandals, from Watergate on, that rocked government and of chronic policy problems, such as rising budget deficits, that public officials seemed unwilling or unable to address adequately. At the same time, the American people have been subject to countless claims that officials are using the power of their office to stay in power. In campaigns, for example, incumbents have increasingly received large campaign contributions from interest groups that stand to benefit from keeping them in office. The net effect of these trends has been to convince many Americans that they have lost con-

Democracy is based on citizen participation, and the most fundamental way to participate is to vote. Residents of Columbus, Ohio, are shown voting in a midterm election. (David Burnett/Contact Press Images)

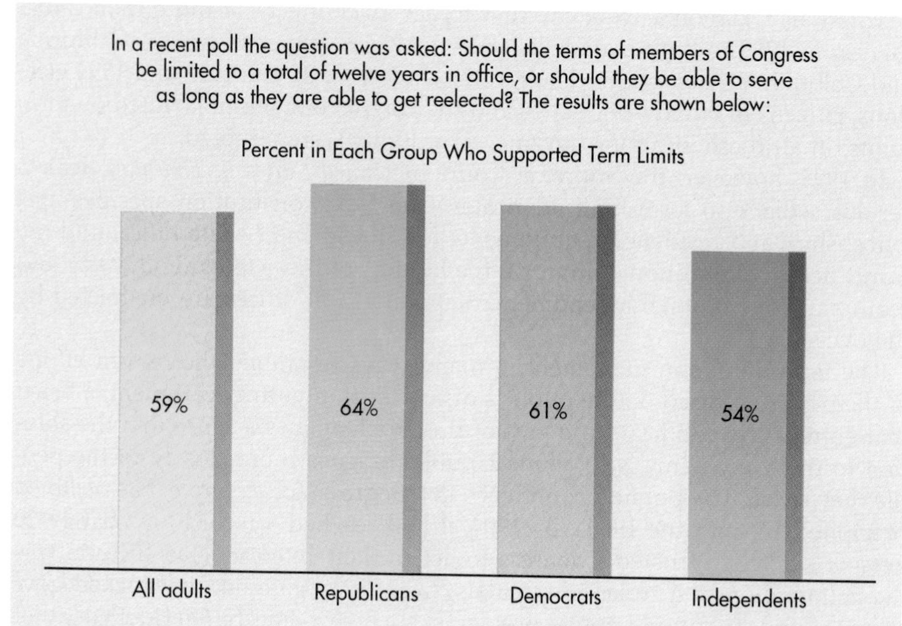

FIGURE 3-2 The Public's View of Term Limitations for Congress
A majority of Americans, regardles of party, favor term limitations for members of Congress. *Source: CBS/New York Times poll, September 8–11, 1994.*

trol of their elected representatives and that a restriction on the length of time that a person can hold public office is the best way for the citizenry to reassert its control (see Figure 3-2).

As was true of the reforms of the Jeffersonian, Jacksonian, and Progressive eras, the term-limitation reform has had its opponents. They have argued that the measure would force effective leaders out of office along with poor ones.

YOUR TURN

NATIONAL REFERENDA: GOOD IDEA OR BAD?

The Questions:

1. As things stand now, the president and Congress make the laws for the federal government. Some people have proposed that laws also be passed by national referendum, which would mean putting various proposals on the ballot so that people across the country could vote them up or down directly. Would you favor or oppose this idea?

   Favor   Oppose

2. Would you favor or oppose a constitutional amendment to require any federal tax increase to be voted on in a national referendum by the general public?

   Favor   Oppose

What Others Think: The first question was asked in a 1993 Los Angeles Times survey: the respondents favored a system of citizen legislation through national referenda by 65 to 25 percent. In response to the second question, which was asked in a 1992 Gordon Black survey, 72 percent of the respondents said they favored an amendment that would require a referendum on tax increases while 28 percent opposed it.

Comment: If you support the national referenda proposals, your views conform with the Progressive idea of direct democracy; if you oppose in principle the idea of national referenda, your opinions reflect the representational tradition of the writers of the Constitution.

They also argue that a legislature full of inexperienced representatives would be overwhelmed by the more experienced and knowledgeable lobbyists and bureaucrats with whom legislators have to contend. *The New York Times*, editorializing against term limits, argued: "If voters think a member of Congress should be shown the gate, let them say so on Election Day." The term-limitation issue, like similar reforms of the past, has also been a partisan one. Most of its supporters have been Republicans, who saw the reform as a way to break the Democrats' hold on Congress and state legislatures. GOP victories in the 1994 election dampened this motivation, but partisan considerations are always a part of institutional debates. The rules under which political power is won and lost always bestow some advantage on one side or the other, with the result that the rules themselves are a source of partisan conflict.

Summary

The Constitution was designed to provide for a limited government in which political power would be confined to its proper uses. Liberty was a basic value of America's political tradition and a reason for its revolt against British rule. The Framers wanted to ensure that the government they were creating would not itself be a threat to freedom. To this end, they confined the national government to expressly granted powers and also denied it certain specific powers. Other prohibitions on government were later added to the Constitution in the form of stated guarantees of individual liberties—the Bill of Rights. The most significant constitutional provision for limited government, however, was a separation of powers among the three branches. The powers given to each branch enable it to act as a check on the exercise of power by the others, an arrangement which, during the nation's history, has, in fact, served as a barrier to abuses of power.

The Constitution, however, made no mention of how the powers and limits of government were to be judged in practice. In its historic ruling in *Marbury* v. *Madison*, the Supreme Court assumed the authority to review the constitutionality of legislative and executive actions and to declare them unconstitutional and thus invalid.

The Framers of the Constitution respected the idea of self-government but distrusted popular majorities. They designed a government that they felt would temper popular opinion and slow its momentum, so that the public's "true interest" (which includes a regard for the rights and interests of the minority) would guide public policy. Different methods were established to select members of the House of Representatives and of the Senate, the president, and federal judges as a means of separating political power from momentary and unreflecting majorities.

Since the adoption of the Constitution, however, the public has gradually assumed more direct control of its representatives, particularly through measures affecting the way in which officeholders are chosen. Political parties, presidential voting (linked to the Electoral College), direct election of senators, and primary elections are among the devices aimed at strengthening the majority's influence. These developments are rooted in the idea, deeply held by ordinary Americans, that the people must have substantial direct control of their government if it is to serve their real interests.

Major Concepts

checks and balances
constitutional democracy
delegates
democracy (democratic government)
denials of power
grants of power
inalienable (natural) rights
judicial review
limited government
Progressive movement
representative democracy
republic
self-government
separated institutions sharing power
term limitations
trustees
tyranny of the majority

Suggested Readings

Beard, Charles S. *An Economic Interpretation of the Constitution.* New York: Macmillan, 1941. Argues that the Framers had selfish economic interests uppermost in mind when they wrote the Constitution.

Benjamin, Gerald, and Michael J. Malbin, eds. *Limiting Legislative Terms.* Washington, D.C.: Congressional Quarterly Press, 1992. A series of essays on the pros and cons of term limitations.

Ericson, David F. *The Shaping of American Liberalism: The Debates over Ratification, Nullification, and Slavery.* Chicago: University of Chicago Press, 1993. An analysis upholding the argument that issues of liberty have consistently been dominant in American ideology.

Kahn, Paul W. *Legitimacy and History: Self-Government in American Constitutional Theory.* New Haven, Conn.: Yale University Press, 1993. An analysis of how the principle of self-government has developed historically in the context of law and the judiciary.

Locke, John. *The Two Treatises of Government.* New York: Hafner, 1947. Published originally in 1690, Locke's work is a broad statement of the fundamental principles of limited government.

Marcus, George, and Russell Hanson, eds. *Reconsidering the Democratic Process.* State College: Pennsylvania State University Press, 1993. A series of essays on the state of democracy in modern America.

Mayhew, David. *Divided We Govern.* New Haven, Conn.: Yale University Press, 1991. An evaluation of the causes and consequences of the tendency toward divided control of U.S. government.

McDonald, Forrest. *We the People: The Economic Origins of the Constitution.* Chicago: University of Chicago Press, 1958. Argues against Beard's thesis that the Framers wrote the Constitution to suit their own economic needs.

Reid, John Phillip. *The Concept of Liberty in the Age of the American Revolution.* Chicago: University of Chicago Press, 1988. A study of the meaning of liberty to Americans in the late eighteenth century.

Tocqueville, Alexis de. *Democracy in America,* vols. 1 and 2, ed. J. P. Mayer. New York: Doubleday/Anchor, 1969. A classic analysis (originally published 1835–1840) of American democracy by an insightful French observer.

CHAPTER 4

CIVIL LIBERTIES: PROTECTING INDIVIDUAL RIGHTS

A bill of rights is what the people are entitled to against every government on earth, general or particular, and what no just government should refuse, or rest on inference.

—Thomas Jefferson[1]

Robert and Sarisse Creighton and their three children were asleep when FBI agents and local police broke into their home in the middle of the night. Brandishing guns, the officers searched the house for a relative of the Creightons who was suspected of bank robbery. When asked to show a search warrant, they said, "You watch too much TV." The suspect was not there, and the officers left as abruptly as they had entered. The Creightons sued the FBI agent in charge, Russell Anderson, for violating their Fourth Amendment right against unlawful search.

The Creightons won a temporary victory when the Eighth U.S. Court of Appeals, noting that individuals are constitutionally protected against warrantless searches unless officers have good reason ("probable cause") for a search and unless they have good reason ("exigent circumstances") for conducting that search without a warrant, concluded that Anderson had been derelict in his duty. In the judgment of the appellate court, Anderson should have sought a warrant from a judge, who would have decided whether a search of the Creightons' home was justified.

The Supreme Court of the United States overturned the lower court's ruling. The Court's majority opinion said: "We have recognized that it is inevitable that law enforcement officials will in some cases reasonably but mistakenly conclude that probable cause is present, and we have indicated that in such cases those officials . . . should not be held personally liable." Justice John Paul Stevens and two other justices sharply dissented. He accused the Court's majority of showing "remarkably little fidelity" to the Fourth Amendment.[2] Civil liberties groups claimed that the Court's decision gave police an open invitation to invade people's homes on the slightest pretext. However, the Court's decision was praised by law enforcement officials and conservatives, who contended that a ruling in the Creightons' favor would have made police hesitant to pursue suspects for fear of a lawsuit if a search failed to produce the person sought.

As this case illustrates, issues of individual rights are complex and political. No right is absolute. For example, the Fourth Amendment protects Americans not from *all* searches but from "*unreasonable* searches." The public would be unsafe if law officials could never search for evidence of a crime or pursue a suspect into a home. Yet the public would also be unsafe if police could frisk people at will or invade their homes with impunity. Such acts are characteristic of a police state, not of a free society. The challenge to a civil society is to establish a level of policy authority that balances the demands of public safety with those of individual freedom. The balance point, however, is always subject to dispute. Did FBI agent Anderson have sufficient cause for a warrantless search of the Creightons' home? Or was his evidence so weak that his forcible entry constituted an "unreasonable" search? Law enforcement officials and civil liberties groups had widely different opinions on these questions. Nor did the justices of the Supreme Court have a uniform view. Six of the justices sided with Anderson and three backed the Creightons' position.

civil liberties The fundamental individual rights of a free society, such as freedom of speech and the right to a jury trial, which in the United States are protected by the Bill of Rights.

Bill of Rights The first ten amendments to the Constitution, which set forth basic protections for individual rights to free expression, fair trial, and property.

This chapter examines issues of **civil liberties:** specific individual rights, such as freedom of speech and protection against self-incrimination, which are constitutionally protected against infringement by government. As we saw in Chapter 3, the Constitution's failure to enumerate individual freedoms led to demands for the **Bill of Rights.** Enacted in 1791, these first ten amendments to the Constitution specify certain rights of life, liberty, and property which the national government is obliged to respect. A later amendment, the Fourteenth, became the basis for extending these protections of individual rights to actions by state and local governments.

Issues of individual rights have become increasingly complex and important. The writers of the Constitution could not possibly have foreseen the United States of the late twentieth century, with its huge national government, enormous corporations, pervasive mass media, urban crowding, nuclear weapons, and the rest. These developments are potential threats to personal freedom, and the judiciary in recent decades has seen fit to expand the rights to which individuals are entitled. However, these rights are constantly being balanced against competing individual rights and society's collective interests. The Bill of Rights operates in an untidy world where people's highest aspirations collide with their worst passions, and it is at this juncture that issues of civil liberties arise. Should an admitted murderer be entitled to recant a confession? Should the press be allowed to print military secrets whose publication might jeopardize national security? Should prayer be allowed in the public schools? Should neo-Nazis be allowed to take their anti-Semitic message into predominantly Jewish neighborhoods? Such questions are among the subjects of this chapter, which focuses on the following major points:

★ *Freedom of expression is the most basic of democratic rights, but, like all rights, it is not unlimited.* Free expression recently has been strongly supported by the Supreme Court.

★ *"Due process of law" refers to legal protections (primarily procedural safeguards) that are designed to ensure that individual rights are respected by government.*

★ *During the last half century particularly, the civil liberties of individual Americans have been substantially broadened in law and given greater judicial protection from action by all levels of government.* Of special significance has been the Supreme Court's use of the Fourteenth Amendment to protect these individual rights from action by state and local governments.

★ *Individual rights are constantly being weighed against the demands of majorities and the collective needs of society.* All political institutions are involved in this process, as is public opinion, but the judiciary plays the central role in it and is the institution that is most partial to the protection of civil liberties.

Freedom of Expression

Freedom of political expression is the most basic of democratic rights. Unless citizens can openly express their political opinions, they cannot properly influence their government or act to protect their other rights. They also cannot hear what others have to say and thus cannot judge the merits of alternative views. And without free expression, elections are a sham, a mere showcase for those who control what is on people's lips and in their minds. As the Supreme Court concluded in 1984, "The freedom to speak one's mind is not only an aspect of individual liberty—and thus a good unto itself—but also is essential to the common quest for truth and the vitality of society as whole."[3]

It is for such reasons that the First Amendment provides the foundation for **freedom of expression**—the right of individual Americans to hold and communicate views of their choosing. For many reasons, such as a psychological need to conform to social pressure or a fear of harassment, Americans do not always choose to express themselves freely. Nevertheless, the First Amendment provides for freedom of expression by prohibiting laws that would abridge the freedoms of conscience, speech, press, assembly, and petition.

freedom of expression Americans' freedom to communicate their views, the foundation of which is the First Amendment rights of freedom of conscience, speech, press, assembly, and petition.

Freedom of expression, like other rights, is not absolute. It does not entitle individuals to say or do whatever they want, to whomever they want, whenever they want. Free expression can be denied, for example, if it endangers national security, wrongly damages the reputations of others, or deprives others of their basic freedoms. An individual's private thoughts are completely free, but words and actions may not be. For example, in 1991 when members of the militant antiabortion group Operation Rescue gathered in protest outside abortion clinics in Wichita, Kansas, they were acting within their constitutional right of free speech. When some of them forcibly restrained pregnant women from entering the clinic, however, they were no longer within their legal rights and were arrested.

In recent decades, free expression has received broad protection from the courts. Today, under most circumstances, Americans can freely verbalize their political views without fear of governmental interference or reprisal. In earlier times, however, Americans were less free to express their political views.

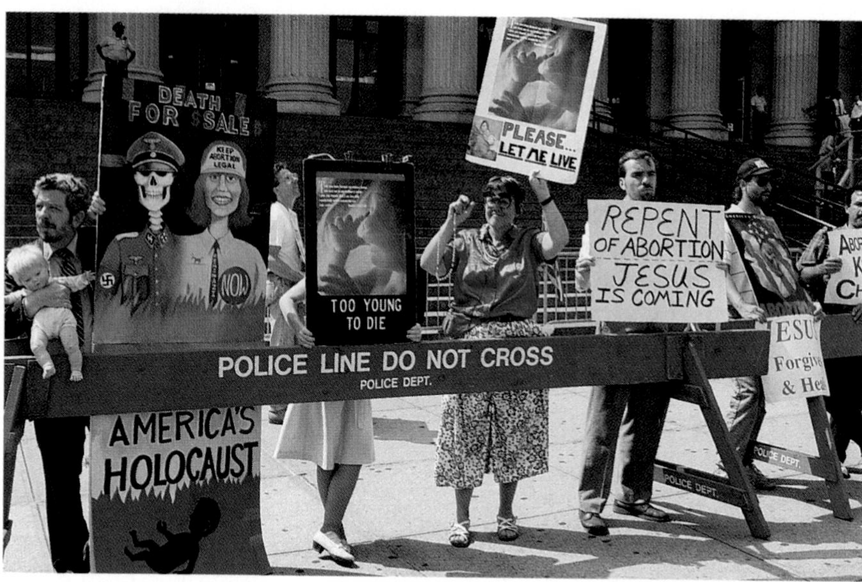

Exercising their right of free expression, antiabortion protestors gather outside a government building. (Robert Brenner/PhotoEdit)

THE EARLY PERIOD: THE UNCERTAIN STATUS OF THE RIGHT OF FREE EXPRESSION

The first legislative attempt by the U.S. government to restrict free expression was the Sedition Act of 1798, which made it a crime to print false or malicious newspaper stories about the president or other national officials. Thomas Jefferson called the Sedition Act an "alarming infraction" of the Constitution and, upon replacing John Adams as president in 1801, pardoned those who had been convicted under it. As the Supreme Court did not review the sedition cases, however, the judiciary's position on free expression remained an open question. The Court also did not rule on free speech during the Civil War era, when the government severely restricted individual rights.

In 1919 the Court finally ruled on a case challenging the national government's authority to restrict free expression. Two years earlier, Congress had passed the Espionage Act, which prohibited forms of dissent deemed to be harmful to the nation's effort in World War I. Nearly 2,000 Americans were convicted for such activities as interfering with draft registration and distributing antiwar leaflets. The Supreme Court upheld one of these convictions in *Schenck* v. *United States* (1919), ruling unanimously that the Espionage Act of 1917 was constitutional. In the opinion written by Justice Oliver Wendell Holmes, the Court said that Congress could restrict speech that was "of such a nature as to create a clear and present danger" to the nation's security. This **clear-and-present-danger test** also expressed the converse: government could not restrict political speech that did not pose any such danger.[4]

clear-and-present-danger test A test devised by the Supreme Court in 1919 in order to define the limits of free speech in the context of national security. According to the test, government cannot abridge political expression unless it presents a clear and present danger to the nation's security.

THE MODERN PERIOD: PROTECTING FREE EXPRESSION

Until the twentieth century, the tension between national security interests and free expression was not a pressing dilemma for the United States. The country's great size and ocean barriers provided protection from potential enemies, minimizing concerns of internal subversion. World War I, however, intruded upon America's isolation, and World War II brought it to an abrupt end. Since then, American's rights of free expression have been defined largely in the context of national security concerns.

Supreme Court justice Oliver Wendell Holmes, Jr. (1841–1935). (UPI/Bettmann)

Special Scrutiny

During the cold war that followed World War II, many Americans perceived the Soviet Union as bent on destroying the United States through internal subversion and global expansion. In this climate of opinion, the Supreme Court allowed government to put substantial limits on free expression. In *Dennis* v. *United States* (1951) the Court upheld the convictions of eleven members of the U.S. Communist party who had been prosecuted under the Smith Act of 1940, which made it illegal to advocate the forceful overthrow of the U.S. government.[5]

Fear of communist subversion began to subside in the mid-1950s, and the Court gradually modified its *Dennis* position.[6] On issues involving political expression (other types of expression, such as obscenity, are a different matter, as we shall see), the Court has generally followed the legal doctrine outlined by Justice Harlan Fiske Stone in 1938. Stone argued that courts have a special responsibility to protect the liberty conferred by First Amendment rights. If those in power can limit free expression, they can control what people know and think. The courts are therefore obligated to protect the broad right of citizens to criticize government and to participate without unreasonable government interference. Stone contended that laws restricting free expression require "more exacting [judicial] scrutiny . . . than most other types of legislation.[7]

Although the Supreme Court has not explicitly endorsed Stone's position, its decisions since the late 1950s have been consistent with his doctrine. The judiciary has held that government officials must show that national security is directly and substantially imperiled before they can lawfully prohibit citizens from voicing their political views. This demanding criterion was widely applied during the Vietnam war, when, despite the largest sustained protest movement in the country's history, not a single American was convicted solely for voicing objections to the government's Vietnam policy. (Some dissenters were found guilty on other grounds, such as inciting riots and disturbing the peace.)

The Supreme Court distinguished, however, between verbal speech and "symbolic speech." During the Vietnam period the Court upheld the conviction of David O'Brien for burning his draft registration card on the steps of the South Boston Courthouse, saying that the government can prohibit action that threatens a legitimate public interest as long as the main purpose in doing so is not to inhibit free expression. The Court held that the federal law prohibiting the destruction of draft cards was designed primarily to provide for the military's personnel needs.[8]

Yet the Supreme Court in 1989 protected the right of the burning of the American flag as a form of symbolic expression. The 5–4 ruling came in the

Civil rights attorney William Kunstler (*right*), with defendant Gregory Lee Johnson (*second from right*), addresses reporters outside the Supreme Court building. Kunstler defended Johnson in the celebrated case that ultimately established flag burning as a constitutionally protected form of political expression. (Bob Daugherty/ AP/Wide World Photos)

case of Gregory Lee Johnson, a member of the Communist Youth Brigade. In 1984 Johnson had set fire to a U.S. flag outside the hall in Dallas where the Republican National Convention was being held. The Supreme Court rejected the state of Texas's argument that flag burning is, in every instance, an imminent danger to public safety. A year later the Court struck down a new federal statute that made it a federal crime to burn or deface the flag.[9] "If there is a bedrock principle underlying the First Amendment," the Court ruled in the *Johnson* case, "it is that the Government may not prohibit the expression of an idea simply because society finds the idea itself offensive or disagreeable."[10]

The Supreme Court's flag-burning decisions were opposed in opinion polls by a large majority of Americans and were broadly attacked by leaders of both parties. Senate Majority Leader George Mitchell (D-Maine) said that the Court's ruling "cheapened the flag." By 97–3, the Senate supported a resolution by Mitchell and Senate Minority Leader Robert Dole (R-Kan.) that expressed "profound disappointment" in the Court's position. President George Bush said that, to him, flag burning was "dead wrong."

Press Freedom and Prior Restraint

Freedom of the press has also received strong judicial support in recent decades. In *New York Times Co.* v. *United States* (1971) the Court ruled that the *Times's* publication of the "Pentagon papers" (secret government documents revealing official deception about the success of the Vietnam war policy) could not be blocked by the Department of Justice, which claimed that publication would hurt the war effort. The documents had been illegally obtained by antiwar activists, who had turned them over to the *Times* for publication. The Court ruled that "any system of prior restraints" on the press is unconstitutional unless the government can clearly justify the restriction.[11]

THE MEDIA AND THE PEOPLE

BALANCING THE RIGHTS OF THE PRESS AND THE ACCUSED

No right is absolute. All rights are balanced against other rights and the collective interests of society, which include an interest in protecting individual rights.

A classic example of rights in conflict occurs when the news media's interest in reporting a crime clashes with the rights of the accused. Lurid crimes are a staple of the news business. Few things seem to sell more newspapers or attract more news viewers than grisly stories of murder and mayhem. It is perhaps no surprise that America's first full-time reporter was hired to cover the crime beat. He was employed by the publisher Benjamin Day, who in the 1830s established the country's first mass-market newspaper, the *New York Sun*.

However, intense coverage of a crime can jeopardize the right of the accused to a fair trial. The gory details of a violent crime can inflame public opinion and make it difficult to empanel a jury of people who have not already prejudged the guilt of the accused. This problem received extraordinary attention in the celebrated trial of O.J. Simpson, who was accused of murdering his ex-wife Nicole Brown Simpson and her friend Ronald Goldman. The pretrial publicity was the most intense in the nation's history, and few people were without an opinion about O.J. Simpson's guilt or innocence. The presiding judge, Lance Ito, refused the media's demands for photographs and videotape of the slain bodies on the grounds that this material was so graphic (Nicole Brown Simpson was nearly decapitated in the knife attack) that it would prejudice public opinion. Jurors were sequestered and prohibited from reading, viewing, or listening to news coverage of the crime or trial. Yet Judge Ito permitted the trial to be televised.

In balancing the rights of the press and the accused, the courts have responded to the interests of both. On occasion, the Supreme Court has reversed convictions on grounds that intense or inflammatory news coverage had made a fair trial impossible. And courts at all levels have recommended that the press exercise self-discipline in the reporting of material that might bias a potential jury. Less often, judges have issued "gag orders" that forbid the press from reporting certain aspects of a crime. In *Nebraska Press Association* v. *Stuart* (1976), the Supreme Court overruled a Nebraska judge who had placed a sweeping gag order on the press. The Supreme Court acknowledged the power of the judiciary to restrain the press but concluded that any application of the power must be fully justified. The Supreme Court has also said that officials must also consider other options, such as moving the trial to another location, in any decision to restrict press coverage.

The unacceptability of **prior restraint**—government prohibition of speech or publication before the fact—is basic to the current doctrine of free expression. The Supreme Court has said that any attempt by government to prevent expression carries "a 'heavy presumption' against its constitutionality."[12] News organizations and individuals are legally responsible after the fact for what they report or say (for example, they can be sued by an individual whose reputation is wrongly damaged by their words), but generally government cannot stop them in advance from expressing their views. An exception in some instances is news coverage of criminal proceedings (see box: The Media and The People). Another exception is the reporting of military operations. During the Persian Gulf war, U.S. journalists on station in Saudi Arabia had to work within limits placed on them by military authorities. In another exception to the doctrine of prior restraint, the courts have upheld the government's authority to ban uncensored publications by certain past and present government employees, such as CIA agents, who have taken part in classified national security activities.

prior restraint Government prohibition of speech or publication before the fact, which is presumed by the courts to be unconstitutional unless the justification for it is overwhelming.

U.S. journalists from the press pool film the allied land offensive during the Persian Gulf war. The military's restrictions on press coverage provoked a debate about whether such censorship is justified on national security grounds or is a violation of the constitutional right of press freedom. (P. Durand/Sygma)

FREE EXPRESSION AND STATE GOVERNMENTS

In 1790 Congress rejected a proposed amendment to the Constitution which would have applied the Bill of Rights to the states. Thus the freedoms guaranteed in the Bill of Rights were initially protected only from action by the national government, a constitutional arrangement that the Supreme Court upheld in 1833.[13] A century later, however, the Court began to protect individual rights from infringement by state governments. The vehicle for this change was the due-process clause of the Fourteenth Amendment to the Constitution.

The Fourteenth Amendment and Selective Incorporation

Ratified in 1868, the Fourteenth Amendment forbids a state to deprive any person of life, liberty, or property without due process of law. It was not until 1925 in *Gitlow* v. *New York,* however, that the Supreme Court decided that the Fourteenth Amendment applied to state action in the area of freedom of expression. Although the Court upheld Benjamin Gitlow's conviction for violating a New York law that prohibited advocacy of the violent overthrow of the U.S. government, the Court indicated that the states were not completely free to limit expression:

> For present purposes we may and do assume that freedom of speech and of the press—which are protected by the First Amendment from abridgement by Congress—are among the fundamental personal rights and "liberties" protected by the due process clause of the Fourteenth Amendment from impairment by the states.[14]

There is no indication that Congress intended the Fourteenth Amendment to protect First Amendment rights from state action. The Supreme Court justified this new interpretation by reference to **selective incorporation**—the absorption of certain provisions of the Bill of Rights, particularly freedom of speech and press, into the Fourteenth Amendment so that these rights would be protected from infringement by the states.

selective incorporation The absorption of certain provisions of the Bill of Rights (for example, freedom of speech) into the Fourteenth Amendment so that these rights are protected from infringement by the states.

Having developed a new interpretation of the Fourteenth Amendment, the Supreme Court proceeded during the next decade to overturn state laws that restricted expression in the areas of speech, press, religion, and assembly and petition.[15] The most famous of these judgments came in the case of *Near* v. *Minnesota* (1931). Jay Near was the publisher of a Minneapolis weekly newspaper that regularly made scurrilous attacks on blacks, Jews, Catholics, and labor union leaders. His paper was closed down on authority of a state law that banned "malicious, scandalous, or defamatory" publications. Near appealed the shutdown, and the Supreme Court ruled in his favor, saying that the Minnesota law was "the essence of censorship."[16]

Limiting the Authority of States to Restrict Expression

Since the 1930s, the Supreme Court has broadly protected freedom of expression from action by the states and by local governments, which derive their authority from the states. The Court has held that the states cannot restrict free expression except when such expression is almost certain to result in imminent lawlessness. A leading free speech case was *Brandenburg* v. *Ohio* (1969). The appellant was a Ku Klux Klan member who, in a speech delivered at a Klan rally, said that "revenge" might have to be taken if the national government "continues to suppress the white Caucasian race." He was convicted of advocating force under an Ohio law prohibiting "criminal syndicalism," but the Supreme Court reversed the conviction, saying the First Amendment prohibits a state from suppressing speech that advocates the unlawful use of force "except where such advocacy is directed to inciting or producing imminent lawless action, and is likely to produce such action.[17]

In a key case involving the right to assemble peaceably, the U.S. Supreme Court in 1977 upheld a lower-court ruling against local ordinances of Skokie, Illinois, which had been invoked to prevent a parade there by the American Nazi party. The Nazis had chosen Skokie for their assembly in order to dramatize their message of hate: the town had a large Jewish population, including many survivors of Nazi Germany's concentration camps. The American Nazis ultimately called off the parade, but not because they were compelled by law to do so. The Supreme Court has held that the right of free expression takes precedence over the mere *possibility* that a riot or some other evil might result from what is said. Before government can lawfully prevent a speech or rally, it must show that an evil is likely to result from the event and must also demonstrate that there is no alternative way (such as assigning police officers to control the crowd) to keep the evil from happening.[18]

The Court has broadly held that "hate speech" cannot be silenced. This ruling came in a unanimous 1992 opinion that struck down a St. Paul, Minnesota, ordinance making it a crime to engage in speech likely to arouse "anger or alarm" on the basis of "race, color, creed, religion or gender." The Court's majority said the First Amendment prohibits government from "silencing speech on the basis of its content."[19] This protection of violent *speech* does not, however, extend to violent *crimes*, such as assault, motivated by bias. A Wisconsin law that provided for increased sentences for such crimes was challenged as a violation of the First Amendment. In a unanimous 1993 opinion, the Court said that the law was aimed at "conduct unprotected by the First Amendment" rather than the defendant's thoughts or speech.[20]

The Supreme Court has recognized that freedom of speech and assembly may conflict with the routines of daily life. Accordingly, individuals do not have the right to hold a public rally in the middle of a busy intersection during rush hour, nor do they have the right to command immediate access to a public auditorium. The Court has held that public officials can regulate the time, place, and conditions of public assembly, provided that these regulations are reasonable and do not discriminate on the basis of the nature of these gatherings. In a 1992 case, the Court declared unconstitutional a local ordinance that imposed a fee of up to $1,000 to offset the costs of maintaining order at a public assembly; the more trouble expected, the higher the fee a group had to pay for permission to hold the assembly. The Court concluded that the First Amendment denies officials "unbridled discretion" in putting a price on speech "simply because it might offend a hostile mob."[21] Officials have an obligation to accommodate public gatherings and to treat all groups—including those that espouse unpopular views—in accordance with reasonable standards.

In general, the Supreme Court's position is that the First Amendment makes any government effort to regulate the *content* of a message highly suspect. In the flag-burning case, Texas was regulating the content of the message—contempt for the flag and the principles it represents. Texas could not have been regulating the act itself, for the government's own method of disposing of worn-out flags is also to burn them. But a content-neutral regulation (no public rally can be held in the middle of a busy intersection at rush hour) is acceptable as long as it is reasonable and does not discriminate against certain groups or ideas.

LIBEL AND SLANDER

The constitutional right of free expression is not a legal license to avoid responsibility for the consequences of what is said or written. If false information that greatly harms a person's reputation is published (libel) or spoken (slander), the injured party can sue for damages. The ease or difficulty of winning such suits has obvious implications for free expression. Individuals and organizations are less likely to express themselves openly if they stand a good chance of subsequently losing a libel or slander suit.

Libel is the more important issue for the political process because it affects the news media's ability to openly criticize governing officials. A leading decision in this area is *New York Times Co.* v. *Sullivan* (1964), in which the Court overruled an Alabama state court that had found the *Times* guilty of libel for printing an advertisement accusing Alabama officials of physically abusing black citizens during civil rights demonstrations. The Court ruled that libel of a public official requires proof of "actual malice," which was defined as a knowing or reckless disregard for the truth.[22] It is very difficult to prove that a publication acted with reckless or deliberate disregard for the truth; no federal official has won a libel judgment against a news organization in the three decades since the *Sullivan* ruling.

The *Sullivan* decision notwithstanding, the greatest protection against a libel judgment is truthfulness. The Court in a 1990 decision held that expressions of opinion deserve "full constitutional protection" against the charge of libel as long as they do not contain "a provably false factual connotation."[23] However, the press has less protection against a libel judgment when its target is a "private" person (an ordinary citizen) rather than a "public" official. The courts regard the communication of information about private individuals as less basic to the democratic process than information about public officials, and hence the press accordingly must take greater care in ascertaining the validity of claims about an ordinary citizen.

OBSCENITY

In 1990 the director of a Cincinnati museum, Dennis Barrie, was arrested on an obscenity charge for holding an exhibit that included homoerotic art by the photographer Robert Mapplethorpe. Although Barrie was acquitted in a jury trail, his arrest provoked a controversy that extended to Congress. Conservative Senator Jesse Helms (R-N.C.) attempted unsuccessfully to withdraw appropriations for the National Endowment for the Arts (NEA), which had partially underwritten the Mapplethorpe exhibit.

Obscenity is a form of expression that is not protected by the First Amendment. However, the Supreme Court has found it difficult to define which publicly disseminated sexual materials are obscene and which are not. The Court has struggled to develop a standard that gives predictability to the law without endangering First Amendment rights.

Museum visitors examine Robert Mapplethorpe's photographs in the Cincinnati exhibit that became the focus of a national controversy over the meaning of obscenity and government support for the arts. (Michael Keating/Gamma Liaison)

Chief Justice Warren Burger wrote in *Miller* v. *California* (1973) that because "what would offend the people of Maine or Mississippi might be found tolerable in Las Vegas or New York City," obscenity must be judged by "contemporary community standards."[24] In 1987 the Court ruled that sexual material could not be judged obscene simply because the "average" local resident might object to its content. Apparently "community standards" are to be judged in the context of a "reasonable person"—someone who would judge material on the merits of its content. To be obscene, sexual content must be of a particularly offensive type—still a rather vague criterion.[25]

The justices of the Supreme Court continue to have difficulty in reaching agreement on issues of obscenity, as a 1991 decision showed. The case involved an Indiana public decency law banning nude entertainment in barrooms and other public establishments. Five of the justices concluded that erotic nude dancing was not a protected form of expression. The other four justices disagreed and voted against the ban.[26]

The Supreme Court has distinguished between obscene materials in public places and in the home. A unanimous ruling in 1969 held that what adults read and watch in the privacy of their homes cannot be made a crime.[27] The Court created an exception to this rule in 1990 by upholding an Ohio law making it a crime to possess pornographic photographs of children.[28] The Court reasoned that purchase and distribution contributed to the spread of the crime of abusing minors through pornography.

Freedom of Religion

Free religious expression is the precursor of free political expression, at least within the English tradition of limited government. England's Glorious, or Bloodless, Revolution of 1689 centered on the issue of religion and resulted in the Act of Toleration, which gave members of all Protestant sects the right to worship freely and publicly. The English philosopher John Locke (1632–1704) extended this principle, arguing that legitimate government could not inhibit free expression, religious or otherwise. The First Amendment reflects this tradition, providing for freedom of religion along with freedom of speech, press, assembly, and petition.

In regard to religion, the First Amendment reads: "Congress shall make no law respecting an establishment of religion, or prohibiting the free exercise thereof." The prohibition on laws aimed at "establishment of religion" (the establishment clause) and its "free exercise" (the free-exercise clause) applies to states and localities through the Fourteenth Amendment.

THE ESTABLISHMENT CLAUSE

establishment clause The First Amendment provision that government may not favor one religion over another, or religion over no religion, and that prohibits Congress from passing laws respecting the establishment of religion.

The **establishment clause** has been interpreted by the courts to mean that government may not favor one religion over another or support religion over no religion. (This position contrasts with that of a country such as England, where Anglicanism is the official, or "established," state religion, though no religion is prohibited.) The Supreme Court's interpretation of the establishment clause has been described as maintaining a "wall of separation" between church and state, which includes a prohibition on nondenominational support for religion.[29] The Court has taken a pragmatic approach, however, permitting some establishment activities but disallowing others. The Court has permitted states to provide secular textbooks for use by church-affiliated schools,[30] for instance, but has forbidden states to pay part of the salaries of teachers in church-affiliated schools.[31] Such distinctions follow no strict logic but are based on judgments of whether government action involves *excessive* entanglement with religion."[32] In allowing public funds to be used by religious schools for secular textbooks but not for teachers' salaries, the courts have indicated that, whereas it is relatively easy to ascertain whether the content of a particular textbook promotes religion, it would be much harder to determine whether a particular teacher was promoting religion in the classroom.

The Court has developed a three-point test to determine whether a law providing aid to religion is constitutional: first, the main purpose of the aid must be secular and not religious; second, the main effect of the assistance must not be to promote one religion or religion per se; and third, the aid must not excessively involve the government in religion.[33] These restrictions do not, for example, allow substantial government grants to religious schools but do permit lesser contributions under some circumstances, such as the provision of secular textbooks and copies of standardized examinations.

In 1962, the Court held that the establishment clause prohibits the reciting of prayers in public schools.[34] A year later the Court struck down Bible readings in public schools.[35] Religion is a strong force in American life, and the Supreme Court's position on school prayer has evoked strong opposition, particularly from Protestant fundamentalists. An Alabama law attempted to cir-

YOUR TURN

RELIGION AND THE STATE

The Questions:

1. Should church and state be kept completely separate?

yes no

2. Should prayer be allowed in public schools?

yes no

3. Should schools be required to teach the biblical version of creation as well as Darwinian evolutionary science?

yes no

What Others Think: A 1994 U.S. News & World Report survey indicated that 53 percent of Americans think that church and state should be kept completely separate whereas 42 percent believe otherwise. Yet a large majority favor prayer in the public schools. A 1993 Time/CNN survey showed that 89 percent of the respondents who described themselves as "born-again Christians" and 70 percent of all others support prayer in the schools. In the same survey, 70 percent of born-again Christians and 52 percent of all others said they think schools should be required to teach creationism.

Comment: The Supreme Court's position on religion in the schools has never had broad public support. Opposition has been particularly intense in southern states where born-again Christians are concentrated. The disparity between Americans' opinions on church-state separation in the abstract and in specific contexts is also noteworthy. The pattern is a general one. For example, many Americans who support free speech in the abstract say they would deny a public forum to advocates of controversial views, such as racism, homosexuality, or atheism. Yet we know from experience that few people actually try to prevent such views from being expressed when public forums on these subjects are held in their communities.

cumvent the prayer ruling by permitting public schools to set aside one minute each day for silent prayer or meditation. In 1985 the Court declared the law unconstitutional, ruling that "government must pursue a course of complete neutrality toward religion.[36] Nevertheless, the Court's majority concluded that the law would have been acceptable if it merely set aside "a moment of silence." Presidents Reagan's and Bush's five appointees to the Court raised hopes among advocates of school prayer of a change of precedent, but the Court in 1992 reaffirmed the ban on state-sponsored prayer by extending it to include graduation ceremonies. A harbinger of a possible change in the court's position came in a 1995 decision that held that the University of Virginia had violated free-speech rights by withholding financial support from a Christian student magazine while subsidizing other student publications.[37]

THE FREE-EXERCISE CLAUSE

free-exercise clause A First Amendment provision that prohibits the government from interfering with the practice of religion or prohibiting the free exercise of religion.

The First and Fourteenth amendments also prohibit governmental interference with the "free exercise" of religion. The idea underlying the **free-exercise clause** is clear: Americans are free to hold any religious belief they choose.

Although people are free to believe what they want, they are not always free to act on their beliefs. The courts have allowed government interference in the exercise of religious beliefs when such interference is the secondary result of an overriding social goal. An example is the legal protection of children with life-threatening illnesses whose parents refuse to permit medical treatment on religious grounds. A court may order that such children be given medical assistance because the social good of saving their lives overrides their parents' free-exercise rights. And in 1986 the Supreme Court concluded that military regulations requiring standard headgear took precedence over an Orthodox Jewish serviceman's practice of wearing a yarmulke.[38] (Congress responded by enacting legislation that permitted yarmulkes.)

In some circumstances exceptions to certain laws have been permitted on free-exercise grounds. The Supreme Court ruled in 1972 that Wisconsin could not compel Amish parents to send their children to school beyond the eighth grade because this policy violates a centuries-old Amish religious practice of having children leave school and begin work at an early age.[39] In upholding free exercise in such cases, the Court may be said to have violated the establishment clause by granting preferred treatment to people who hold a particular religious belief. The Court has recognized the potential conflict between the free-exercise and establishment clauses and, as in other such situations, has tried to strike a reasonable balance between the competing claims.

When the free-exercise and establishment clauses cannot be balanced, the Supreme Court has been forced to make a choice. In 1987 the Court overturned a Louisiana law requiring that creationism (the Bible's account of how the world was created) be taught along with the theory of evolution in public school science courses. Creationism, the Court concluded, is a religious doctrine, not a scientific theory; thus its inclusion in public school curricula violates the establishment clause by promoting a religious belief. Creationists viewed the Court's decision as a violation of their right to the free exercise of religion; they argued that their children were being forced to study a theory of evolution that contradicts the biblical account of human origins.

Rights of Persons Accused of Crimes

Justice Felix Frankfurter once wrote that "the history of liberty has largely been the history of the observance of procedural guarantees."[40] No system of justice is foolproof; even in the most honest systems, innocent people have been wrongly accused, convicted, and punished with imprisonment or death. But the scrupulous application of procedural safeguards, such as a defendant's right to legal counsel, greatly increases the likelihood that true justice will result.

PROCEDURAL DUE PROCESS

procedural due process The constitutional requirement that government must follow proper legal procedures before a person can be legitimately punished for an alleged offense.

"Due process" refers to legal protections that have been established to preserve the rights of individuals. The most significant form of these protections is **procedural due process;** the term refers primarily to procedures that authorities must follow before a person can legitimately be punished for an offense.

The U.S. Constitution provides for several procedures designed to protect a person from wrongful arrest, conviction, and punishment. According to Article I, section 9, any person taken into police custody is entitled to seek a writ of habeas corpus, which requires law enforcement officials to bring him or her into court and state the legal reason for the detention. The Fifth and Fourteenth amendments provide generally that no person can be deprived of life, liberty, or property without due process of law. And specific procedural protections for the accused are spelled out in the Fourth, Fifth, Sixth, and Eighth amendments:

- *The Fourth Amendment* forbids the police to conduct searches and seizures unless they have probable cause to believe that a crime has been committed.
- *The Fifth Amendment* protects against double jeopardy (being prosecuted twice for the same offense); self-incrimination (being compelled to testify against oneself); indictment for a crime except through grand jury proceedings; and loss of life, liberty, and property without due process of law.
- *The Sixth Amendment* provides the right to have legal counsel, to confront witnesses, to receive a speedy trial, and to have a trial by jury in criminal proceedings.
- *The Eighth Amendment* protects against excessive bail or fines and prohibits the infliction of cruel and unusual punishment on those convicted of crimes.

These procedural protections have always been subject to interpretation. The Sixth Amendment, for example, provides the right to have legal counsel. But what if a person cannot afford a lawyer? For most of the nation's history, poor people had almost no choice but to act as their own attorneys. They had a right to counsel but could avail themselves of it only if they had the money to hire a lawyer or could find a public-spirited lawyer who would work for free. Today, if a person is accused of a serious crime and cannot afford a lawyer, the government must provide one. This change came about not through a constitutional amendment but through Supreme Court rulings that gave new meaning in practice to the Sixth Amendment.

SELECTIVE INCORPORATION OF PROCEDURAL RIGHTS

For most of the nation's history, the procedural protections in the Bill of Rights applied only to the actions of the national government. States in their criminal proceedings were not bound by them. There were limited exceptions, such as a 1932 Supreme Court ruling that a defendant charged in a state court with a crime carrying the death penalty had to be provided with an attorney.[41] The Court's general position, however, was that the states could decide for themselves what procedural rights their residents would have.

A noteworthy case was *Palko* v. *Connecticut* (1937). A Connecticut court had convicted Frank Palko of killing two policemen, and he was sentenced to life imprisonment. But Connecticut had a statute that permitted law enforcement authorities under certain conditions to appeal a sentence on the grounds that legal errors had been made at the trial. The authorities had wanted Palko to receive the death penalty, so they appealed the decision. Palko was tried again on the same charges and this time was sentenced to death. He appealed to the U.S. Supreme Court, claiming that Connecticut's second trial violated his right not to be tried twice for the same crime. The Fifth Amendment to the U.S. Constitution prohibits double jeopardy, and so do many state constitutions, but at the time Connecticut's did not. The Supreme Court refused to overturn Palko's second conviction, and he was executed.[42]

Justice Benjamin Cardozo wrote the Court's *Palko* opinion, which stated that the Fourteenth Amendment protects rights "fundamental" to liberty but not other rights provided in the Bill of Rights. Free expression is a "fundamental" right, since it is "the indispensable condition of nearly every other form of freedom." Some procedural due-process rights, such as protection against double jeopardy, are not in the same category, Cardozo claimed.

This view changed abruptly in the 1960s when the Supreme Court broadly required states to safeguard procedural rights. Changes in public education and communication made Americans more aware of their rights, and the civil rights movement dramatized the fact that rights were administered very unequally: the poor and minority group members had many fewer rights in practice than other Americans. In response, the Supreme Court in the 1960s "incorporated" Bill of Rights protections for the accused in state courts by ruling that these protections are covered by the Fourteenth Amendment's guarantee of due process of law (see Table 4-1).

This selective incorporation process began with *Mapp* v. *Ohio* (1961). Dollree Mapp's home had been entered by Cleveland police, who, though they failed to find what they were looking for, happened to discover some pornographic material. Mapp's conviction for its possession was overturned by the Supreme Court on the grounds that she had been subjected to unreasonable search and seizure.[43] The Court ruled that illegally obtained evidence could not be used in state courts.

Two years later, the Court's decision in *Gideon* v. *Wainwright* (1963) required the states to furnish attorneys for poor defendants in all felony cases. Clarence Gideon, an indigent drifter, had been convicted and sentenced to prison in Florida for breaking into a poolroom. He appealed on the grounds that he had been denied due process because he could not afford to pay an attorney. The

TABLE 4-1 Selective Incorporation Bill of Rights protections were extended through the Fourteenth Amendment to include action by the states

Supreme Court Case	*Year*	*Constitutional Right at Issue*
Gitlow v. *New York*	1925	First Amendment's applicability to free speech
Fiske v. *Kansas*	1927	Free speech
Powell v. *Alabama*	1932	Right to counsel in capital cases
Near v. *Minnesota*	1931	Free press
Hamilton v. Regents, U. of California	1934	Religious freedom
DeJonge v. *Oregon*	1937	Freedom of assembly and of petition
Mapp v. *Ohio*	1961	Unreasonable search and seizure
Robinson v. *California*	1962	Cruel and unusual punishment
Gideon v. *Wainwright*	1963	Right to counsel
Malloy v. *Hogan*	1964	Self-incrimination
Pointer v. *Texas*	1965	Right to confront witnesses
Miranda v. *Arizona*	1966	Self-incrimination
Klopfer v. *North Carolina*	1967	Speedy trial
Duncan v. *Louisiana*	1968	Jury trial in criminal cases
Benton v. *Maryland*	1969	Double jeopardy

Supreme Court agreed, thus extending the right to free legal counsel to impoverished defendants in state felony trials.[44]

During the 1960s the Court also ruled that defendants in state criminal proceedings cannot be compelled to testify against themselves[45]; have the rights to remain silent and to have legal counsel when arrested[46]; have the right to confront witnesses who testify against them[47]; must be granted a speedy trial[48]; have the right to a jury trial[49]; and cannot be subjected to double jeopardy.[50] The most famous of these cases is *Miranda* v. *Arizona* (1966), as a result of which police are required to inform suspects of their rights at the time of arrest. Ernesto Miranda had confessed during police interrogation to kidnapping and raping a young woman. His confession led to his conviction, which he successfully appealed to the Supreme Court on the grounds that he had not been informed of his rights to remain silent and to have legal counsel present during interrogation. Using other evidence of Miranda's crime, the state of Arizona then retried and convicted him again. He was paroled from prison in 1972 and four years later was stabbed to death in a bar fight. Ironically, Miranda's assailant was read his "Miranda rights" when police arrested him. By now the wording has become familiar: "You have the right to remain silent. . . . Anything you say can and will be used against you in a court of law. . . . You have the right to an attorney."

By 1969, when Chief Justice Earl Warren retired, nearly all the rights guaranteed by the Fourth through the Eighth amendments had been extended to defendants in state trial proceedings. Evidence indicates that local state law enforcement and judicial officials do not always uphold these rights fully,[51] but legal protections have been greatly expanded in the course of the century.

William Rehnquist was appointed chief justice of the Supreme Court by President Reagan in 1986. Rehnquist was a top Justice Department official in the Nixon administration before joining the Court in 1971 as an associate justice. (UPI/Bettmann)

WEAKENING THE EXCLUSIONARY RULE

As the Warren Court expanded defendants' rights during the 1960s, many law enforcement officials, politicians, and private citizens accused the Court of "coddling criminals" to such an extent that law-abiding people were not safe on the streets and in their homes. When Richard Nixon won the presidency after promising to restore "law and order" in the country, there were widespread expectations of a tougher policy on issues of crime. Although Nixon appointed four new justices to the Supreme Court, its positions on the rights of the accused did not undergo a sweeping transformation during the 1970s or early 1980s.

exclusionary rule The legal principle that government is prohibited from using in trials evidence that was obtained by unconstitutional means (for example, illegal search and seizure).

Since then, however, a shift in the Court's philosophy has been evident. The latest change can be seen in the application of the **exclusionary rule,** which bars the use in trials of evidence obtained in violation of the Fourth Amendment and hence protects people against "unreasonable searches and seizures" of their persons, homes, and belongings. The rule was formulated in a 1914 Supreme Court decision,[52] and its application was further expanded in federal cases. The *Mapp* decision extended the exclusionary rule to state trial proceedings as well. Subsequent decisions of the Supreme Court broadened its application to the point where almost any type of illegally obtained evidence was considered inadmissible in a criminal trial.

In the 1980s, the Supreme Court reversed the trend by placing restrictions on the rule's application, concluding that illegally obtained evidence can be

An officer frisks a teenage suspect against the hood of a police cruiser. The Supreme Court in recent years has relaxed the restrictions on search and seizure by police. (Blair Seitz/Photo Researchers)

admitted in trials if the procedural errors are small, inadvertent, or ultimately inconsequential. In a key 1984 decision, for example, the Court ruled that illegally obtained evidence can be used against a defendant if the prosecution can prove that it would have discovered the evidence anyway.[53]

Recent Supreme Court decisions have further weakened the exclusionary rule. In the 1960s, the Court developed the principle that police had to have a solid basis ("probable cause") for believing that an individual was involved in a specific crime before they could engage in search and seizure activity. This principle has been downgraded. In 1990, for example, the Supreme Court held that roadside checkpoints where police systematically stop drivers to check them for signs of intoxication do not violate their right to protection against unreasonable search.[54]

A more definitive statement of the Court's new position is *Whren* v. *United States* (1996), which unanimously upheld the conviction of an individual who had been found with packets of drugs in the front seat of his car after being stopped for a minor traffic infraction. The police had no evidence (no "probable cause") to believe that drugs were actually in the car but somehow suspected the driver was involved with drugs and used the traffic infraction as a pretext to stop and check him. The Supreme Court accepted defense arguments that the police had no clear evidence on which to base their suspicion; that the traffic infraction was not the real reason the individual was stopped; and that police usually do not stop a person for the infraction in question (turning a corner without signaling). But the Court concluded that the officers' motive was irrelevant, as long as an officer in some situations might reasonably stop a car for the infraction that occurred. Thus, the stop and search of the driver was deemed to meet the Fourth Amendment's reasonableness standard.[55]

The Supreme Court has also recently restricted habeas corpus appeals to federal courts by individuals who have been convicted of crimes in state courts. (Habeas corpus gives defendants access to federal courts in order to argue that their rights under the Constitution of the United States were violated when they were convicted in a state court.) A 1960s Supreme Court precedent had assured prisoners of the right to have their petitions heard in federal court unless they had "deliberately bypassed" the opportunity to make the appeal in state courts.[56]

This precedent was overturned in 1992, when the Court held that inmates can lose the right to a federal hearing even if a lawyer's mistake is the reason they failed to first present their appeal properly in state courts.[57] Another habeas corpus defeat for inmates occurred in 1993 when the Supreme Court held that federal courts cannot overturn a state conviction on the basis of constitutional error unless the prisoner can show that the error contributed to the conviction.[58] Previously, the burden of proof was on the state: it had to show that the error did not affect the outcome. Then, in *Felker* v. *Turpin* (1996), the Court upheld a recent federal law that severely restricts federal habeas corpus appeals by state prison inmates who have already filed one.[59]

The new limits are applauded by those, including Chief Justice William Rehnquist, who believe that multiple habeas corpus appeals clog the federal courts and delay the hearing of other cases of greater merit. On the other hand, civil libertarians argue that no procedure that can protect the innocent from wrongful conviction is too big a burden to place on the courts.

★ CRITICAL THINKING

When Should Procedural Error Result in a New Trial? Roger Coleman was convicted of rape and murder in a Virginia court and was sentenced to death. He sought to appeal the conviction on several grounds, including evidence that one of the jurors had told friends he wanted to sit on the jury in order to make sure Coleman was convicted.

Coleman had no money to hire legal counsel, and his appeal was prepared by voluntary attorneys who were not fully familiar with Virginia law. They filed the appeal a day after the deadline set by law. Prosecutors move to deny the appeal because it was late, and Virginia's highest court upheld the action. Coleman filed a habeas corpus petition to have the appeal heard in federal court. His petition eventually reached the Supreme Court, which turned it down, saying Coleman had forfeited his right to bring the petition because of the procedural error. The Court's ruling overturned a 1963 precedent which had held that state prisoners were entitled to seek federal habeas corpus petitions as long as they had not "deliberately bypassed" state courts. In its decision, the Supreme Court said it was fair to penalize Coleman because, unlike the situation at the trial stage, he had no right to an attorney at the appeal stage.

What reasoning would lead you to conclude that justice was served in Coleman's case? What reasoning would lead you to conclude otherwise?

★ STATES IN THE NATION

Rates of Violent Crime:
Urban and southern states have the highest crime rates.

STATE	RATE PER 100,000 PERSONS	RANK
Ala.	872	10
Alaska	660	20
Ariz.	671	19
Ark.	577	25
Calif.	1,120	4
Colo.	579	24
Conn.	495	32
Del.	621	23
D.C.	2,833	1
Fla.	1,207	2
Ga.	733	16
Hawaii	258	44
Idaho	281	41
Ill.	977	7
Ind.	508	31
Iowa	278	42
Kan.	511	29
Ky.	535	26
La.	985	6
Maine	131	48
Md.	1,000	5
Mass.	779	12
Mich.	770	13
Minn.	338	38
Miss.	412	34
Mo.	740	15
Mont.	170	47
Neb.	349	37
Nev.	697	17
N.H.	126	49
N.J.	626	21
N.Mex.	935	9
N.Y.	1,122	3
N.C.	681	18
N.Dak.	83	51
Ohio	526	28
Okla.	623	22
Oreg.	510	30
Pa.	427	33
R.I.	395	35
S.C.	944	8
S.Dak.	195	46
Tenn.	746	14
Texas	806	11
Utah	291	40
Vt.	109	50
Va.	375	36
Wash.	535	26
W.Va.	212	45
Wis.	276	43
Wyo.	320	39
National average	758	—

SOURCE: U.S. Federal Bureau of Investigation, 1992

However, no one claims that recent decisions mark a return to the lower procedural standards that prevailed before the 1960s. Many of the vital precedents set in that decade remain in effect, including the most important one of all: the principle that procedural protections guaranteed to the accused by the Bill of Rights must be observed by the states as well as by the federal government. In addition, the current Supreme Court has extended the procedural rights of the accused in a few areas. In 1991, for example, the Court reaffirmed and extended a 1986 ruling that black defendants are denied their rights when prosecuting attorneys use peremptory challenges (that is, rejections without explanation) to exclude black potential jurors, so that the trial is conducted with an all-white jury.[60] Gender imbalance can also be grounds for determining whether a defendant received a fair trial; recent rulings also include the decision that once a defendant asks for a lawyer, the police must halt their questioning until the lawyer arrives.[61]

CRIME AND PUNISHMENT

The theory and practice of procedural guarantees are often two quite different things, as Adrienne Cureton discovered on January 2, 1995. She is a plainclothes police officer who, with a uniformed partner, was called to the scene of a domestic dispute. When a struggle ensued, her partner radioed for help. When the officers arrived, Cureton and her partner had already handcuffed the homeowner. The officers barged in and mistook Cureton, an African American, for the other person involved in the dispute. They grabbed her by the collar, dragged her by the hair onto the porch, and clubbed her repeatedly with flashlights, despite her screams that she was a police officer.[62]

There are no reliable estimates of how often Americans' rights are violated in practice, but infringements of one sort or another are a daily occurrence in every major city. Minorities and poor people are the usual victims. African Americans in particular are substantially more likely than white people to believe that the police do not protect them adequately and to think that their rights will not be respected when they encounter the police. Two-thirds of black people say the criminal justice system is biased against them (see Figure 4-1).

Despite the uneven application of justice in America, watchdog groups such as Amnesty International give the United States fairly good marks in its treatment of the criminally accused (see box: How the United States Compares). Northern European countries are rated more highly, partly because their police are less likely to use force in dealing with suspects. Yet none of the European democracies has gone as far as the United States in establishing an elaborate set of legal procedures designed to protect the accused.

Another issue of justice in America is whether adherence to proper legal procedures produces reasonable outcomes. The Eighth Amendment prohibits "cruel and unusual punishment" for those convicted of crime, but judgments in this area are relatively subjective. Although the Supreme Court has ordered officials to relieve inmate overcrowding and to improve prison facilities in a few instances, it has concluded that inmates cannot sue over prison conditions unless prison officials show "deliberate indifference" to conditions.[63] The severity of a sentence can also be an Eighth Amendment issue. A divided Supreme Court in 1991 upheld a Michigan law that mandated life imprison-

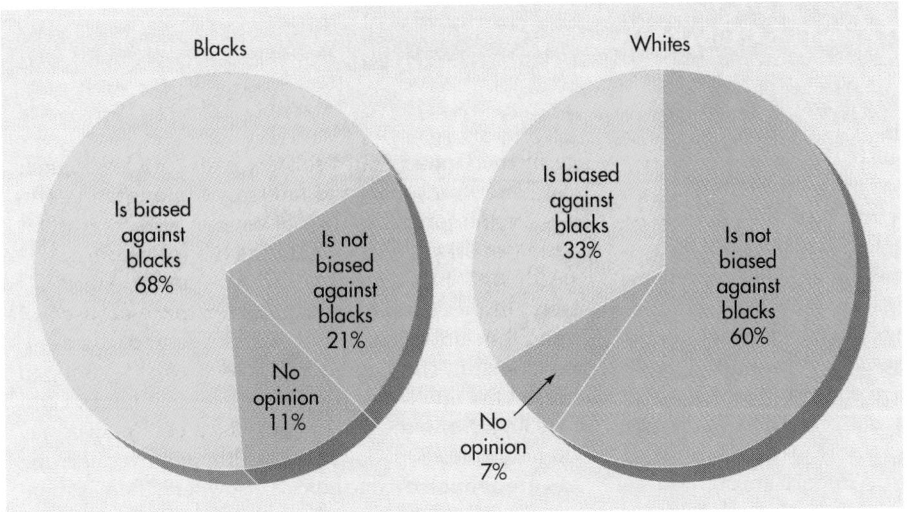

FIGURE 4-1 Opinions on Racial Bias in the Justice System
African Americans are much more likely than white Americans to believe that the justice system is biased against black people.
Source: Gallup Poll Monthly, April 1993.

ment without parole for a nonviolent first-offense conviction for possession of as little as 1.5 pounds of cocaine.[64] In general, the Court has shied away from decisions about what constitutes cruel and unusual punishment, preferring to leave them in the hands of legislative bodies.

In recent years, legislators in the United States have taken a tougher stance on crime. Congress and most states have mandated stiffer sentences, and the number of federal and state prisoners has more than doubled in the past decade. The U.S. prison population is the second largest in the world on a per capita basis (see box: How the United States Compares).

These actions reflect growing public concern with crime. Polls indicate that most Americans would like the courts to get even tougher with lawbreakers. Substantial majorities favor making parole more difficult, placing restrictions on bail, handing out more severe sentences, and limiting appeals for those convicted of crimes. One of the few issues that divides the public is the death penalty; although most Americans favor its extension, a substantial minority are opposed (see Figure 4-2).

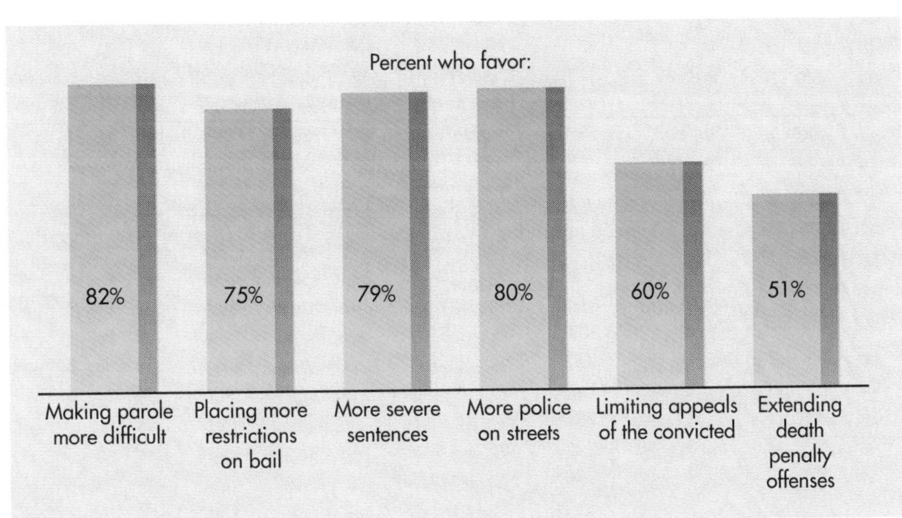

FIGURE 4-2 Opinions on Crime Issues
A majority of Americans favor tougher steps to deal with crime.
Source: The Gallup Poll Monthly, December 1993.

HOW THE UNITED STATES COMPARES

LAW AND ORDER

Individual rights are a cornerstone of the American governing system and receive strong protection from the courts. The government's ability to restrict free expression is severely limited, and the individual's right to a fair trail is protected through elaborate due-process guarantees.

According to Amnesty International, a watchdog group that monitors human rights achievements and violations around the world, the United States has a good record in terms of its constitutional protection of civil liberties. A number of countries in Asia, Africa, eastern Europe, the Middle East, and Latin America are accused by Amnesty International of "appalling human rights catastrophes" that include the execution, torture, and rape of persons accused of crime or regarded as opponents of the government. Amnesty International does not rank the United States as high as the countries of northern Europe in terms of respect for human rights. Among other things, Amnesty International faults police in the United States for "excessive force" in their treatment of prisoners and faults U.S. immigration officials for the forcible return of asylum seekers to their country of origin without granting them a hearing.

Although human rights groups admire America's elaborate procedural protections for those accused of crime, they are critical of its sentencing and incarceration policies. The United States is a world leader in terms of the number of people it places behind bars and in the length of sentences for various categories of crime. Defenders of U.S. policy say that although overall crime rates are about the same here as elsewhere, there is more violent crime in America. Critics reply that although the murder rate is high in the United States, it is also true that more than half of those in prison were convicted of nonviolent offenses, such as drug use or a crime against property. Whatever the reasons, the United States is second only to Russia in the proportion of its people who are in prisons.

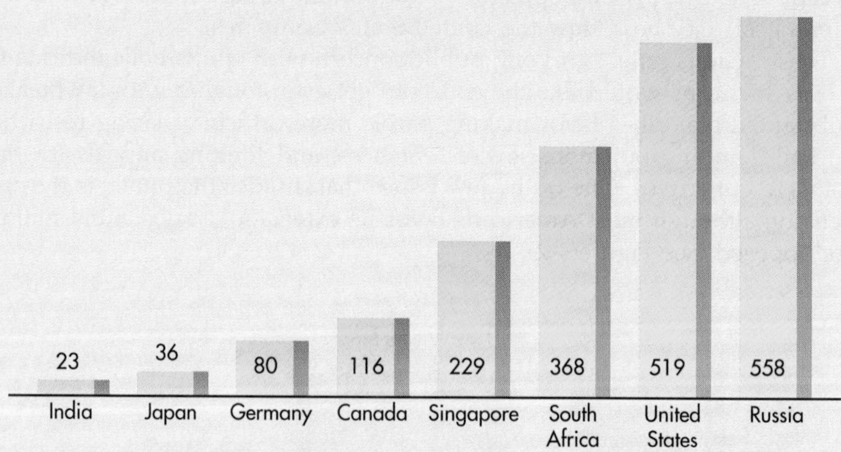

SOURCE: *Amnesty International Report*, 1993 (New York: The Sentencing Project, 1993), 1–5, 301–304, "Locking People Up around the World," *U.S. News & World Report*, September 19, 1994, p. 17.

The Right of Privacy

Until the 1960s, Americans' constitutional rights were confined largely to those enumerated in the Bill of Rights. This situation prevailed despite the Ninth Amendment, which reads: "The enumeration in the Constitution, of certain rights, shall not be construed to deny or disparage others retained by the people."

In 1965, however, the Supreme Court added to the list of individual rights, declaring that Americans have "a right of privacy." This judgment arose from the case of *Griswold* v. *Connecticut,* which challenged a state law prohibiting the use of birth control devices, even by married couples. The Supreme Court invalidated the statute, concluding that a state had no business interfering with a married couple's decision regarding contraception. The Court did not base its decision on the Ninth Amendment, but reasoned instead that an underlying right of privacy gave rise to such individual protections as the freedom from unreasonable search and seizure.[65]

The right of privacy was the basis for the Supreme Court's ruling in *Roe* v. *Wade* (1973), which gave women full freedom to choose abortion during the first three months of pregnancy.[66] In a 7–2 decision that overturned a Texas law prohibiting abortion except to save the life of the mother, the Supreme Court said that the right to privacy is "broad enough to encompass a woman's decision whether or not to terminate her pregnancy."

After *Roe,* antiabortion activists sought to reverse or weaken the Court's ruling. Attempts to pass a constitutional amendment that would ban abortions were unsuccessful, but those opposed to abortion succeeded in some of their efforts, such as their campaign to prohibit the use of government funds to pay

Abortion rights activists demonstrate outside the Supreme Court, while the justices inside hear arguments on Pennsylvania's controversial abortion law. By a 5–4 vote, the Court narrowly reaffirmed the principle that a woman has the right to choose an abortion during the early months of pregnancy. (Greg Gibson/AP/Wide World)

for abortions for poor women. Then, in *Webster* v. *Reproductive Health Services* (1989), the Supreme Court upheld a Missouri law that prohibits abortions in public hospitals and by public employees.[67] The ruling was in part a consequence of the efforts of antiabortion groups to influence Supreme Court appointments during the Reagan presidency. The Missouri law was upheld by a 5–4 majority and all three Reagan appointees on the Court (Justices O'Connor, Scalia, and Kennedy) voted with the majority.

The *Webster* decision was followed in 1992 by a judgment in the Pennsylvania abortion case *Planned Parenthood* v. *Casey*. Pennsylvania's law placed a 24-hour waiting period on women who sought an abortion, required doctors to counsel women on abortion and alternatives to abortion, required a minor to have a parent's consent or a judge's approval before having an abortion, and required a married woman to notify her husband before obtaining an abortion. The law was backed by the Bush administration, and antiabortion advocates saw the law as an opportunity for the Supreme Court to overturn the *Roe* precedent. In a decision that surprised many observers, the Court by a 5–4 margin reaffirmed the "essential holding" of *Roe* v. *Wade:* that a woman, because of the constitutional guarantee of privacy, has a right to abortion during the early months of pregnancy. The Court also ruled, however, that states can regulate abortion as long as they do not impose an "undue burden" on women seeking abortion. The Court concluded that the 24-hour waiting period, physician counseling, and the informed-consent requirement for minors were not undue burdens and were therefore constitutional. The spousal notification requirement, however, was judged to place a "substantial obstacle" in the path of women seeking abortion and was thereby declared unconstitutional.[68]

Abortion will certainly be a leading controversy for years to come. The American public is sharply divided on the issue (see Figure 4-3), and there are a great many deeply committed activists on both sides.[69] The Supreme Court is itself divided. The four justices who dissented in the Pennsylvania case expressed their willingness to overturn the *Roe* v. *Wade* decision. The likelihood of such an eventuality, however, diminished significantly with Democrat Bill Clinton's election as president. His first nominee to the Supreme Court, Ruth Bader Ginsberg, defended a woman's right of abortion during confirmation hearings. Ginsberg replaced Byron White, one of the four dissenting judges in the Pennsylvania case.

As with other rights, the right of choice of abortion is not only, or even primarily, played out in the courts. Abortion opponents have waged sit-ins and demonstrations outside clinics in an effort to stop the practice. Some of these protests have erupted in violent acts toward women and staff who tried to enter the clinics. In 1994, Congress made it unlawful to block the entrance to abortion clinics or otherwise prevent people from entering. The Freedom of Access to Clinic Entrances Act has been effective in reducing the violence outside abortion clinics but has not eliminated it, nor did it prevent gunmen in Massachusetts and Florida from killing abortion workers. Responsible voices within the antiabortion movement condemned the senseless murders, but few believe it could never happen again.

FIGURE 4-3
Opinions on the Abortion Issue
A majority of Americans support the legalization of abortion, but a majority also oppose the use of federal funds for abortions for women who cannot afford to pay for them. *Source: NBC/Wall Street Journal poll, April 17–20, 1993.*

The Courts and a Free Society

A free and democratic nation has a vital stake in maintaining individual freedoms. The United States was founded on the belief that individuals have an innate right to personal liberty—to speak their minds, to worship as they choose, to be free of police intimidation. The greatest threat to individual rights in a democratic society is a popular majority backed by elected leaders determined to carry out its will. Majorities have frequently preferred policies that would diminish the freedom of those who hold minority views, have unconventional lifestyles, or simply "look different" from the majority.

Americans are highly supportive of rights and freedoms expressed in abstract terms but are much less supportive—and in some cases antagonistic—when confronted with these same rights in concrete situations.[70] For example, although nearly all Americans say they support freedom of speech, many of them would deny it to particular groups. The gap between people's abstract and particular beliefs is even greater in the area of criminal rights. A Time/CNN survey indicated, for example, that half the American people would allow police to stop and search people for weapons if they merely fit a criminal profile (see Figure 4-4). Public support for such measures is even stronger after a highly publicized senseless act of violence, such as the 1995 terrorist bombing of the federal building in Oklahoma City. Although most citizens do not personally act out their opinions, their lukewarm respect for individual rights, particularly those of persons accused of crime, is a reason why there is so little public outrage over official violations of these rights.

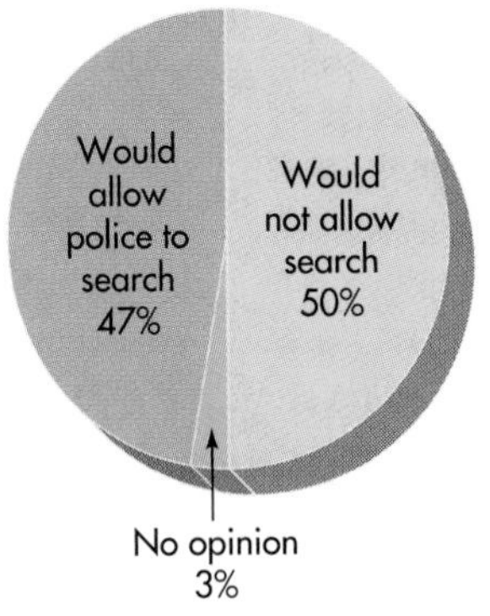

FIGURE 4-4 Opinions on Police Searches without Probable Cause
Americans are nearly as likely to say that they would allow police to search anyone who merely looked like a criminal as to say that they would prohibit such a search. *Source: Time/CNN survey by Yankelovich Partners, Inc., January 17–18, 1994.*

Greater support for individual rights exists among the political elite. Those who are most active politically, including officeholders and journalists, are more likely to express strong support for free expression and fair trial rights. They are also better positioned than the ordinary citizen to express their beliefs. However, they are not always willing to act. Often, the exercise of rights involves society's least savory characters—its murderers, rapists, drug dealers, and hate peddlers. Miscreants are hardly the type of person that engenders public support at any level.

The courts are not isolated from the public mood. They must balance society's need for safety and order against the rights of the individual. Nevertheless, the judicial branch can normally be expected to grant more consideration to the rights of the individual, however unpopular his or her views or actions, than will the general public or elected officials. How far the courts will go in protecting a person's rights depends on the facts of the case, the existing status of the law, prevailing social needs, and the personal views of the judges. Nevertheless, the courts regard the protection of individual rights as one of their most significant responsibilities, a perspective that is owed in no small measure to the Bill of Rights. It transformed the inalienable rights of life, liberty, and property into legal rights, thus putting them under judicial protection.[71]

Civil liberties are not blessings that government kindly bestows on the individual. Because of their constitutional nature, these rights are above government. In fact, it can be said that government exists to protect these rights. True,

★ CRITICAL THINKING

The Necessity of the Bill of Rights
The Bill of Rights was added to the Constitution despite the Framers' objection that it was unnecessary. Whose position—the Framers' or those who advocated the Bill of Rights—do you think history supports? Can you think of additional rights that you might have today if the Framers' position had prevailed? Can you think of rights that you might *not* have today if their view had prevailed?

government does not always act lawfully; the temptations of power and the pressures of the majority can at times lead governmental institutions to usurp individual rights. The courts are not immune to these influences and have the added pressure of the obligation to seek an accommodation between the claims of individuals and the collective interests of society (which, of course, include respect for civil liberties). While the courts have not always sided with individuals in their claims to rights, it is at least as noteworthy that they have not always sided with government in its claims against the individual.

The judiciary's importance to the preservation of civil liberties has increased as society has grown in complexity. Large, impersonal bureaucracies—public and private—are a defining characteristic of the modern age, and their power can easily dwarf the individual. Courts of law are an exception. The isolated citizen, who standing alone carries no weight with huge bureaucracies, is the center of attention in legal proceedings. Not surprisingly, then, individuals have increasingly turned to the courts for protection. In its recent terms more than a fourth of Supreme Court cases involved criminal law issues, a much higher proportion than even a few decades ago.

Courts alone cannot provide adequate protection for individual rights. A civil society rests also on enlightened representatives and a tolerant citizenry. If, for example, politicians and the public encourage police to infringe the rights of vaguely threatening minorities or nonconformists, the judiciary's protection of persons accused of crimes will not ensure justice. It may be said that the test of a truly civil society is not its treatment of popular ideas and of its best citizens but its willingness to tolerate ideas that the majority detests and to treat even its unpopular citizens with respect.

Summary

In their search for personal liberty, Americans added the Bill of Rights to the Constitution shortly after its ratification. These amendments guarantee certain political, procedural, and property rights against infringement by the national government. Freedom of expression is the most basic of democratic rights. People are not free unless they can freely express their views. Nevertheless, free expression may conflict with the nation's security needs during times of war and insurrection. The courts at times have allowed government to limit expression substantially for purposes of national security. In recent decades, however, the courts have protected a very wide range of free expression in the areas of speech, press, and religion.

The guarantees embodied in the Bill of Rights originally applied only to the national government. Under the principle of selective incorporation of these guarantees into the Fourteenth Amendment, the courts extended them to state governments, though the process was slow and uneven. In the 1920s and 1930s, First Amendment guarantees of freedom of expression were given protection from infringement by the states. The states continued to have wide discretion in criminal proceedings until the early 1960s, when most of the fair-trial rights in the Bill of Rights were given federal protection.

"Due process of law" refers to legal protections that have been established to preserve individual rights. The most significant form of these protections consists of procedures or methods (for example, the right of an accused person to have an attorney present during police interrogation) designed to ensure that an individual's rights are upheld. A major controversy in this area is the breadth of the exclusionary rule, which bars the use in trials of illegally obtained evidence. The right of privacy, particularly as it applies to the abortion issue, is also a source of controversy.

Civil liberties are not absolute but must be balanced against other considerations (such as national security or public safety) and against one another when different rights come into conflict. The judicial branch of government, particularly the Supreme Court, has taken on much of the responsibility for protecting and interpreting individual rights. The Court's positions have changed with time and conditions, but the Court has generally been more protective of and sensitive to civil liberties than have elected officials or popular majorities.

Major Concepts

Bill of Rights
civil liberties
clear-and-present-danger test
establishment clause
exclusionary rule
free-exercise clause
freedom of expression
prior restraint (of the press)
procedural due process
selective incorporation

Suggested Readings

Abraham, Henry. *Freedom and the Court*, 6th ed. New York: Oxford University Press, 1994. A general survey of judicial interpretations of civil liberties.

Blanchard, Margaret A. *Revolutionary Sparks: Freedom of Expression in Modern America.* New York: Oxford University Press, 1992. A historical study of twentieth-century freedom of expression.

Bodenhamer, David J. *Fair Trial: Rights of the Accused in American History.* New York: Oxford University Press, 1991. A comprehensive historical survey of the rights of the accused.

Daniels, Cynthia R. *At Women's Expense: State Power and the Politics of Fetal Rights.* Cambridge, Mass.: Harvard University Press, 1993. A look at the issue of fetal rights that goes beyond the issue of abortion alone.

Haiman, Franklyn S. *Speech and Law in a Free Society.* Chicago: University of Chicago Press, 1981. An assessment of the primacy of speech in a free society.

Lewis, Anthony. *Gideon's Trumpet.* New York: Random House, 1964. A summary of the case of Clarence Gideon and its effects on the right of persons accused of crime to legal counsel.

Mason, Alpheus T. *The Supreme Court: Palladium of Freedom.* Ann Arbor: University of Michigan Press, 1962. A classic assessment of the Supreme Court's role in protecting individual rights.

Murphy, Paul L. *The Shaping of the First Amendment: 1791 to the Present.* New York: Oxford University Press, 1991. A description of the development and application of First Amendment principles in American history.

Schwartz, Bernard. *The Great Rights of Mankind: A History of the American Bill of Rights.* New York: Oxford University Press, 1977. A historical overview of the Bill of Rights and its importance to limited government in the United States.

Sorauf, Frank J. *Wall of Separation: The Constitutional Politics of Church and State.* Princeton, N.J.: Princeton University Press, 1976. A well-written account of religious freedom as a constitutional issue.

CHAPTER 5

EQUAL RIGHTS: STRUGGLING TOWARD FAIRNESS

I have a dream that one day this nation will rise up and live out the true meaning of its creed: "We hold these truths to be self-evident: that all men are created equal."
—Martin Luther King, Jr.[1]

In 1991 the producers of ABC television's *Prime Time Live* put hidden cameras on two young men, equally well dressed and groomed, and then sent them on different routes to do the same things—search for an apartment, shop for a car, look at albums in a record store. The cameras recorded the reactions the two men received. One was greeted with smiles and was invited to buy, often at good prices. The other man was treated with suspicious looks, was sometimes made to wait, and was often asked to pay more. Why the difference? The explanation was simple: the young man who was routinely well received was white; the young man who was treated badly was an African American.

The Urban Institute had conducted a similar experiment a few months earlier. The experiment used pairs of specially trained white and black male college students who were the same in all respects—education, work experience, speech patterns, physical builds—except for their race. The students responded individually to nearly 500 classified job advertisements in Chicago and Washington, D.C. The black applicants got fewer interviews, had shorter interviews, and were given fewer job offers than the white applicants. An Urban Institute spokesperson said, "The level of reverse discrimination [favoring blacks over whites] that we found was limited, was certainly far lower than many might have been led to fear, and was swamped by the extent of discrimination against black job applicants."[2]

These two experiments suggest why some Americans are still struggling for equal rights. In theory, Americans are equal in their rights, but in reality, they are not now equal, nor have they ever been. African Americans, women, Hispanic Americans, the disabled, Jews, American Indians, Catholics, Asian

Americans, homosexuals, and members of nearly every other minority group have been victims of discrimination in fact and in law. The nation's creed—"all men are created equal"—has encouraged minorities to believe that they deserve equal justice and has given weight to their claims for fair treatment. But full equality is far from being a universal condition of American life. Inequality is built into almost every aspect of our society. To take but one example: African Americans with a correctable heart problem are three times less likely to receive the necessary surgery than are whites with the same problem.[3]

civil (equal) rights The right of every person to equal protection under the laws and equal access to society's opportunities and public facilities.

This chapter focuses on **equal rights,** or **civil rights**—terms that refer to the right of every person to equal protection under the laws and equal access to society's opportunities and public facilities. We saw in Chapter 5 that "civil liberties" refer to specific *individual* rights, such as freedom of speech, that are protected from infringement by government. "Equal rights" or "civil rights" have to do with whether individual members of differing *groups*—racial, sexual, and the like—are treated equally by government and, in some areas, by private parties. To oversimplify, civil liberties deal with issues of personal freedom, and civil rights deal with issues of equality.

Although the law refers to the rights of individuals first and to those of groups in a secondary and derivative way, this chapter concentrates on groups because the history of civil rights has been largely one of group claims to equality. The chapter emphasizes the following main points:

- ★ *Disadvantaged groups have had to struggle for equal rights.* African Americans, women, Native Americans, Hispanic Americans, and Asian Americans have all had to fight for their rights in order to come closer to equality with white males.
- ★ *Americans have attained substantial equality under the law.* They have, in legal terms, equal protection of the laws, equal access to accommodations and housing, and an equal right to vote. Discrimination by law against persons because of race, sex, religion, and ethnicity is now largely a thing of the past.
- ★ *Legal equality for all Americans has not resulted in de facto equality.* African Americans, women, Hispanic Americans, and other tradionally disadvantaged groups have a disproportionately small share of America's opportunities and benefits. Existing inequalities, discriminatory practices, and political pressures are still major barriers to their full equality. Affirmative action and busing are policies designed to help the disadvantaged achieve full equality.

The Struggle for Equality

Equality has always been the least fully developed of America's founding concepts. Not even Thomas Jefferson, who had a deep admiration for the "common man," believed that broad meaning could be given to the claim of the Declaration of Independence that "all men are created equal." To Jefferson, "equality" had a restricted, though significant, meaning: people are of equal moral worth and as such deserve equal treatment under the law.[4] Even then, Jefferson made a distinction between free men, who were entitled to legal equality, and slaves, who were not.

The history of America shows that disadvantaged groups have rarely achieved an additional degree of legal equality without a struggle. Equality is seldom bestowed by the more powerful on the less powerful. Resistance to granting disadvantaged groups a greater degree of equality is rooted in prejudice and privilege.[5]

Equality is a subject that loses urgency when it is considered apart from its historical context. The compelling need for the 1964 Civil Rights Act and other such laws, and the great triumph their passage represents, cannot be understood without an awareness of the long struggle that led up to them. We can establish this context by looking briefly at the efforts of African Americans, women, Native Americans, Hispanic Americans, and Asian Americans to achieve fuller equality.

★ CRITICAL THINKING

Why Are African Americans Not Gaining Ground? Although the lives of black Americans have improved in absolute terms since the mid-1960s, their lives have not improved much in comparison with those of white Americans. The job and income gaps have grown; the education gap is no longer narrowing; and the life expectancy of blacks has declined slightly while that of whites continues to increase.

Why are blacks going backward in some respects? Is it mainly that no major new policy initiatives have been made in their behalf in recent years and that some existing programs have been cut back? Or is it mainly that drug abuse, violence, and family disintegration have had a profoundly destructive impact on the black community? If both explanations apply, are they interconnected? Can anything but racism—historical and contemporary—be at the bottom of the whole problem?

In his controversial book *Losing Ground* (1984), Charles Murray argues that social welfare programs, such as Aid to Families with Dependent Children (AFDC), have actually hurt rather than helped African Americans. He contends that the programs create a dependency culture of unproductive Americans who live on welfare and pass along to their children a destructive lifestyle. What is your preliminary view of Murray's argument? (Chapter 19 will address this controversy more fully.)

AFRICAN AMERICANS

Of all America's problems, none has been as persistent as the white race's unwillingness to yield a fair share of society's benefits to members of the black race. The ancestors of most African Americans came to this country as slaves, after having been captured in Africa, shipped in chains across the Atlantic, and sold in open markets in Charleston and other southern seaports.

It took a civil war to bring slavery to an end, but the battle did not end institutionalized racism. When Reconstruction ended in 1877 with the withdrawal of federal troops from the South, whites in the region regained power and gradually reestablished racial segregation by enacting laws that prohibited black citizens from using the same public facilities as whites.[6] In *Plessy* v. *Ferguson* (1896), the Supreme Court endorsed these laws, ruling that "separate" facilities for the two races did not violate the Constitution as long as the facilities were "equal." "If one race be inferior to the other socially," the Court argued, "the Constitution of the United States cannot put them on the same plane."[7] The *Plessy* decision became a justification for the separate and *unequal* treatment of African Americans. Black children, for example, were forced into separate schools that rarely had libraries and had few teachers; they were given worn-out books that had been used previously in white schools.

Black leaders challenged these discriminatory state and local policies through legal action, but not until the late 1930s and 1940s did the Supreme Court begin to respond favorably to their demands. The Court began modestly by ruling that where no public facilities existed for African Americans, they must be allowed to use those reserved for whites.[8]

The *Brown* Decision

Substantial relief for African Americans was finally achieved in 1954 with *Brown* v. *Board of Education of Topeka,* arguably the most significant ruling in Supreme Court history. The case began when Linda Carol Brown, a black child in Topeka, Kansas, was denied admission to an all-white elementary school

Federal troops protect black students desegregating Little Rock Central High School after the Supreme Court's *Brown* ruling in 1954 that segregated public schools were unconstitutional. The ruling set off a wave of protests throughout the South. (Burt Glinn/Magnum)

that she passed every day on her way to her all-black school, which was twelve blocks farther away. The case was initiated on her behalf by the National Association for the Advancement of Colored People (NAACP) and was argued before the Supreme Court by Thurgood Marshall, who later became the Court's first black justice.[9] In its decision, the Court fully reversed its *Plessy* doctrine by declaring that racial segregation of public schools "generates [among black children] a feeling of inferiority as to their status in the community that may affect their hearts and minds in a way unlikely ever to be undone. . . . Separate educational facilities are inherently unequal."[10]

A 1954 Gallup Poll indicated that a sizable majority of southern whites opposed the *Brown* decision, and billboards were quickly erected along southern roadways that called for the impeachment of Chief Justice Earl Warren. In the so-called Southern Manifesto, southern congressmen urged their state governments to "resist forced integration by any lawful means." In 1957 rioting broke out when Governor Orval Faubus called out the Arkansas National Guard to block the entry of black children to the Little Rock public schools. To restore order and carry out the desegregation of the Little Rock schools, President Dwight D. Eisenhower used his power as the nation's commander in chief to place the Arkansas National Guard under federal control. For their part, northern whites were neither strongly for nor strongly against school desegregation. A Gallup Poll taken shortly after the *Brown* decision indicated that a slim majority of whites outside the South agreed with it.

The Black Civil Rights Movement

After *Brown*, the struggle of African Americans for their rights became a political movement. Perhaps no single event turned national public opinion so dramatically against segregation as a 1963 march led by Dr. Martin Luther King, Jr., in Birmingham, Alabama. An advocate of nonviolent protest, King had been leading peaceful demonstrations and marches for nearly eight years

Two police dogs attack a black civil rights activist (center left of picture) during the 1963 Birmingham demonstrations. Such images of hatred and violence shook many white Americans out of their complacency regarding race relations. (Charles Moore/ Black Star)

before that fateful day in Birmingham.[11] As the nation watched in disbelief on television, police officers led by Birmingham's sheriff, Eugene "Bull" Connor, attacked King and his followers with dogs, cattle prods, and firehoses.

The modern civil rights movement peaked with the triumphant March on Washington for Jobs and Freedom of August 2, 1963. Organized by Dr. King and other civil rights leaders, it attracted 250,000 marchers, one of the largest gatherings in the history of the nation's capital. "I have a dream," the Reverend King told the gathering, "that my four little children will one day live in a nation where they will not be judged by the color of their skin but by the content of their character."

A year later, after a months-long fight in Congress that was marked by every parliamentary obstacle that racial conservatives could muster, the Civil Rights Act of 1964 was enacted. As we'll discuss later in this chapter, the legislation provided African Americans and other minorities with equal access to public facilities and prohibited job discrimination. Even then, southern states resorted to legal maneuvering and other delaying tactics to blunt the new law's impact. The state of Virginia, for example, established a commission to pay the legal expenses of white citizens who were brought to court for violations of the federal act. Nevertheless, momentum was on the side of racial equality. The murder of two civil rights workers during a voter registration drive in Selma, Alabama, helped sustain the momentum.[12] President Lyndon Johnson, who had been a decisive force in the battle to pass the Civil Rights Act, called for new legislation that would end racial barriers to voting.[13] Congress's answer was the 1965 Voting Rights Act.

The Aftermath of the Civil Rights Movement

Although the most significant progress in history toward the legal equality of all Americans occurred during the 1960s, Dr. King's dream of a color-blind society has remained elusive.[14] By some indicators, the status of African Amer-

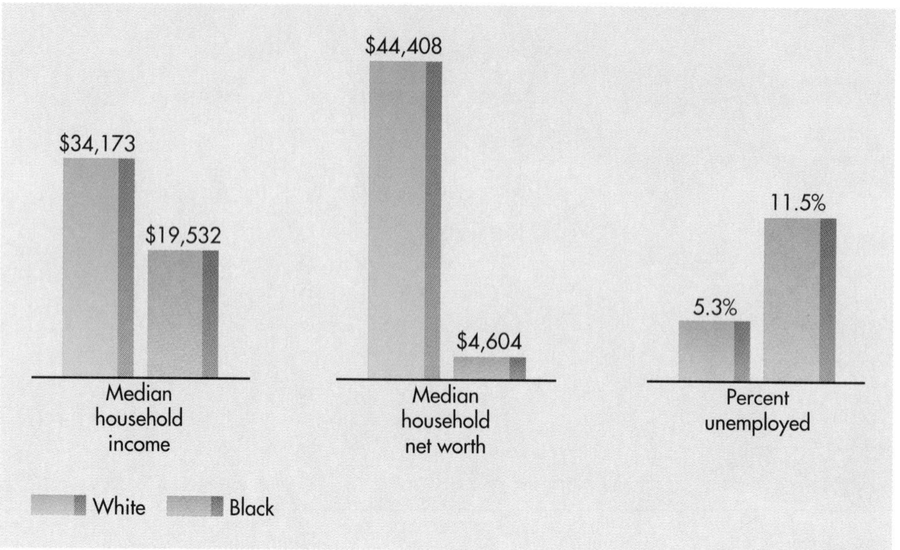

FIGURE 5-1 Indicators of the Economic Status of Whites and Blacks in the United States White Americans tend to be better off financially than black Americans. The prevalence of poverty among blacks is both a cause and an effect of persistent racial discrimination. *Source: U.S. Bureau of the Census, 1993.*

icans has actually deteriorated since Martin Luther King was assassinated in 1968. According to U.S. Department of Labor statistics, the unemployment rate for African Americans in the late 1960s was about 50 percent higher than the rate for whites; by the 1990s it was closer to 100 percent higher. During the same period, the gap in the incomes of black and white Americans has widened, not narrowed. The income of the average African American family is about 60 percent of the average white family's (see Figure 5-1).

Even the legal rights of African Americans do not, in practice, match the promise of the civil rights movement.[15] A 1993 Gallup Poll indicated, for example, that 68 percent of African Americans think that the American justice system is biased against black people. Well-publicized incidents provide support for this perception. In March 1991, an amateur photographer videotaped Los Angeles policemen kicking and clubbing Rodney King, a black man they had stopped along a roadway. Recorded transmissions on police radio indicated that King's beating was at least in part racially motivated. When the officers who led the beating were acquitted in state court, rioting erupted in Los Angeles' African American neighborhoods, leaving 52 dead and causing property damage exceeding $100 million. The subsequent conviction of the chief assailant on federal charges of violating King's civil rights helped quell, but did not completely dispel, the feeling of many African Americans that the nation has two standards of justice, one for whites and one for blacks.[16]

African Americans have made progress since the 1960s in winning election to public office. Although the percentage of black elected officials nationwide is still far below the proportion of African Americans in the population, it has risen sharply over recent decades.[17] As of 1994, there were more than 20 black members of Congress and 200 black mayors—including the mayors of some of the largest cities, such as Atlanta and Detroit. In 1989, Douglas Wilder of Virginia became the first African American to be elected governor in the South since post–Civil War Reconstruction.

WOMEN

The Rev. Martin Luther King, Jr., became the nation's conscience as he led the black civil rights movement from the Montgomery, Alabama, bus boycott in 1955 until his murder by a white supremacist in 1968. (Flip Schulke/Black Star)

The United States carried over from English common law a political disregard for women, forbidding them to vote, hold public office, and serve on juries.[18] Upon marriage, a woman essentially lost her identity as an individual and could not own and dispose of property without her husband's consent. Even the wife's body was not fully hers. A wife's adultery was ruled by the Supreme Court to be a violation of the husband's property rights![19]

The first women's rights convention in America was held in 1848 in Seneca Falls, New York, after Lucretia Mott and Elizabeth Cady Stanton had been barred from the main floor of an antislavery convention.[20] Thereafter, however, the struggle for women's rights became closely aligned with the abolitionist movement, but the passage of the post–Civil War constitutional amendments proved to be a setback for the women's movement. The Fifteenth Amendment, for example, said that the right to vote could not be abridged on account of race or color, but said nothing about sex.[21] After decades of struggle, the Nineteenth Amendment was finally adopted in 1920, forbidding denial of the right to vote "by the United States or by any state on account of sex."

Women's Legal and Political Gains

In 1923 women's leaders proposed another constitutional amendment, one that would guarantee equal rights for women. After numerous failed attempts to gain congressional approval, the Equal Rights Amendment (ERA) was passed by Congress in 1973 and went to the state legislatures for ratification. The ERA failed to gain the support of a legislative majority in the thirty-eight states needed for ratification. The proposed amendment was three states short when the deadline for ratification arrived in 1982.[22]

Although the ERA did not become part of the Constitution, it helped bring women's rights to the forefront at a time when developments in Congress and the courts were contributing significantly to the legal equality of the sexes.[23] Among the congressional initiatives that have helped women are the Equal Pay Act of 1963, which prohibits sex discrimination in salary and wages by some categories of employers; the Civil Rights Act of 1964, which prohibits sex discrimination in programs that receive federal funding; Title IX of the Education Amendment of 1972, which prohibits sex discrimination in education; the Equal Credit Act of 1974, as amended in 1976, which prohibits sex discrimination in the granting of financial credit; and the Civil Rights Act of 1991 and the Family Leave Act of 1993 (discussed later in the chapter).[24]

Women have made clear gains in the area of appointive and elective offices.[25] In 1981 President Reagan appointed the first woman to serve on the Supreme Court, Sandra Day O'Connor. When the Democratic party in 1984 chose Geraldine Ferraro as its vice-presidential nominee, it was the first time a woman ran on the national ticket of a major political party. The elections of Ann Richards in Texas (1990) and Christine Todd Whitman in New Jersey (1993) marked another milestone: for the first time, two large states had a woman as the incumbent governor.[26] In 1992, Barbara Boxer and Dianne Feinstein were elected to the U.S. Senate from California, the first time that women have held both Senate seats in a state. Despite such signs of progress, women

HOW THE UNITED STATES COMPARES

WOMEN'S EQUALITY

Although conflict between groups is universal, the nature of the conflict is often particularized. Racial conflict in the United States cannot readily be compared with, say, religious conflict in Northern Ireland. The one form of inequality common to all nations is that of gender: nowhere are women equal to men in law or in fact. But there are large differences between countries. A study by the Population Crisis Committee ranked the United States third overall in women's equality, behind only Sweden and Finland. The rankings were based on five areas—jobs, education, social relations, marriage and family, and health—where U.S. women had an 82.5 percent rating compared with men.

The inequality of women is also underlined by their lack of representation in public office. There is no country in which women comprise as many as half the members of the national legislature. The Scandinavian countries rank highest in terms of the percentage of female lawmakers. Other northern European countries have lower levels, but the levels are higher than that of the United States. Until the 1992 election, only 6 percent of U.S. House members were women. In 1992, as a consequence of reapportionment and the retirement of an unusually large number of incumbents, the number of women in the House nearly doubled. The following figures, estimated from several sources, indicate the approximate percentage of seats held by women in the largest chamber of each country's national legislature:

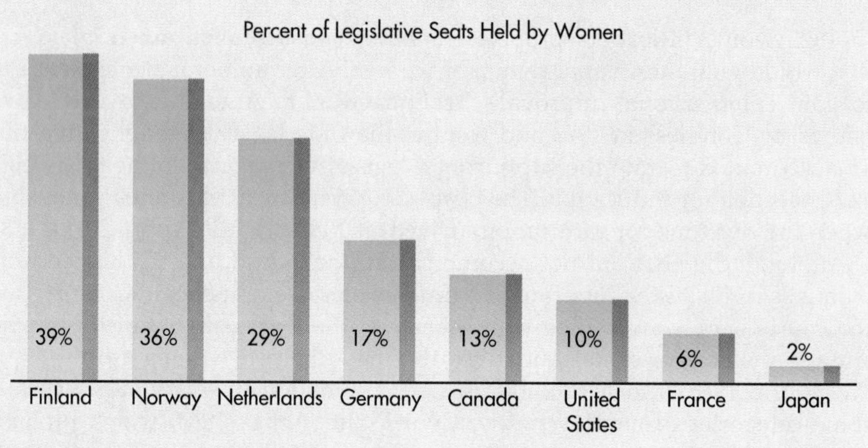

are still a long way from political equality with men.[27] Women occupy about 10 percent of the nation's gubernatorial and congressional offices, and women who hold lower public offices are more likely than their male counterparts to believe there are significant obstacles to political advancement.[28]

However, the women's vote is becoming increasingly powerful. A few decades ago, there was virtually no difference in the partisan voting of men and women. Today, there is a pronounced "gender gap."[29] Women are much more likely than men to vote for Democratic candidates. The tendency reached a record level in 1996 when Bill Clinton's support was about 15 percent higher among women than men. Indeed, Clinton and his Republican opponent, Bob Dole, ran virtually even among men. Clinton's margin of victory was attributable entirely to the women's vote.

TABLE 5-1 Preference for Male or Female Boss Both men and women say they would prefer to work for a man, although the preference for a woman as a boss has increased sharply in the past two decades.

"IF YOU WERE TAKING A NEW JOB AND HAD YOUR CHOICE OF A NEW BOSS, WOULD YOU PREFER TO WORK FOR A MAN OR A WOMAN?"

Year	*Gender*	*Prefer Male Boss*	*Prefer Female Boss*	*No Difference*	*No Opinion*
1993	Men	33%	16%	49%	2%
	Women	44	29	24	3
1982	Men	40	9	46	5
	Women	52	15	30	3
1975	Men	63	4	32	1
	Women	60	10	27	3

SOURCE: *The Gallup Poll Monthly*, September 1993, p. 20.

Job-Related Issues: Family Leave, Comparable Worth, and Sexual Harassment

In recent decades, increasing numbers of women have sought employment outside the home. Government statistics indicate that five in eight women worked outside the home in 1990 compared with only one in eight in 1950. Women have made gains in many traditionally male-dominated fields. For example, women now make up a third of the new lawyers who enter the job market each year. Women have gained acceptance as top managers; although both men and women say they would rather work for a male boss, this preference has declined sharply in recent years (see Table 5-1). The change in women's status is also reflected in education statistics (see Figure 5-2). In 1972,

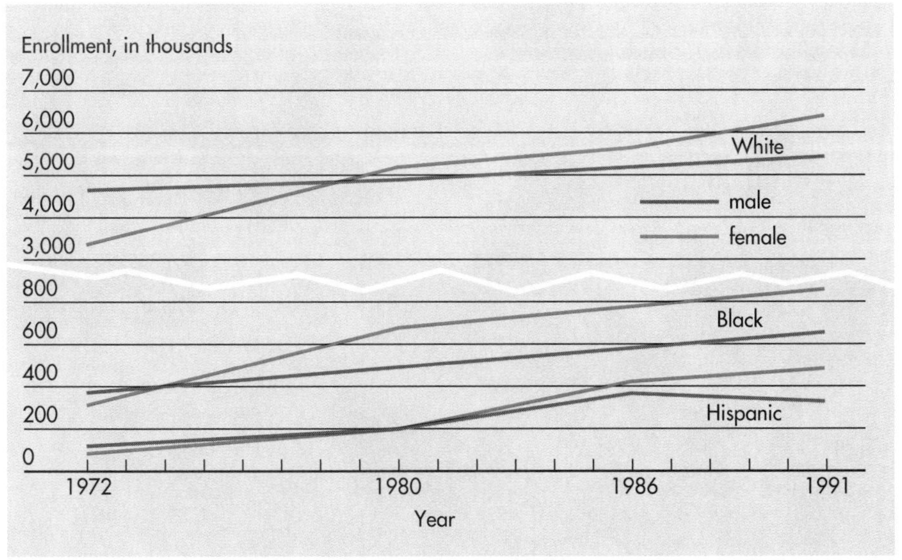

FIGURE 5-2 College Enrollment of Men and Women, by Race In 1972, more white, black, and Hispanic men than women enrolled in college. By 1991, the reverse was true. *Source: U.S. Bureau of the Census, Current Population Reports, series P- 20, no. 460.*

★ CRITICAL THINKING

Comparable Worth

Should women receive the same pay as men if their jobs, though different from those held by men, require similar levels of education and experience? At present, full-time female employees average only about three-fourths what full-time male employees earn, even though men and women do not differ greatly in their levels of education.

Establishment of the doctrine of comparable worth through legislative action is a goal of some women's groups. Opponents argue that salaries should be decided by market forces rather than by government policy.

Could a policy of comparable worth be accomplished on a large scale without disrupting the nation's economy? Can women achieve full equality without achieving income parity with men? Which of these considerations do you personally think is more important? Which is more likely to win out? What are other, longer-term ways of getting women's salaries to a higher level? What are the prospects for these remedies?

more white, black, and Hispanic men than women enrolled in college. By 1991, the reverse was true: more women than men of each race were enrolled.

The increase in the number of women in the workplace has created demands for the expansion of programs such as day care centers and parental leave. In 1993, Congress passed the Family and Medical Leave Act, which provides up to twelve weeks of unpaid leave for employees, male or female, to care for a new baby or a seriously ill family member. Upon return from leave, employees must ordinarily be restored to their original or equivalent positions with equivalent pay, benefits, and other employment terms.

Nevertheless, women are less than equal to men when it comes to job opportunities and benefits. Women hold a disproportionate number of the poorer-paying jobs. On average, women earn only about three-fourths as much as men. This situation has led to demands by women for equal pay for work that is of similar difficulty and responsibility and that requires similar levels of education and training—a concept called **comparable worth.** A comparable-worth policy would eliminate salary inequities resulting from the fact that some occupations are dominated by women and others by men. This view was the basis for a legal suit against the state of Washington brought by a group of female state employees, who won in a lower court but lost on appeal. Advocates of comparable worth did persuade the Minnesota and Iowa legislatures to enact new salary structures that may eventually provide employees of those states with equal pay, regardless of sex, for jobs requiring comparable training and skills.[30] In most states and at the national level, comparable-worth proposals have not gained appreciable legislative support. Opponents have argued that market forces alone should decide salaries in the private sector.[31]

Discrimination against women in the workplace includes sexual harassment. In 1980 Carolyn Kohlberer, who worked in a St. Paul, Minnesota, printing plant, complained to management after a male co-worker made lewd com-

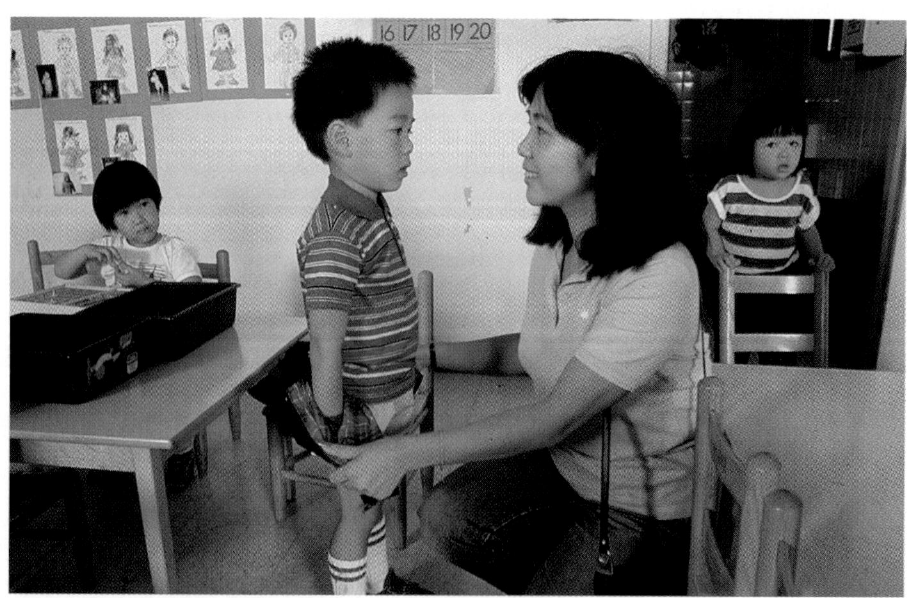

The majority of women with preschool children work outside the home, a situation that has created demands for government support of day care centers, parental leave, and other programs and services. (Jacques Chenet/Woodfin Camp & Associates)

Employees in certain job categories dominated by women—day care workers, secretaries, and so on—are paid less than those in male-dominated jobs with similar educational requirements and levels of responsibility. The concept of comparable worth is proposed as a remedy for such inequities. (Richard Kalvar/Magnum)

ments to her and another grabbed her breasts. When no action was taken, she sued and received a favorable settlement.[32] Ms. Kohlberer's treatment at work was not unlike that of thousands of other women, which has led to laws that prohibit sexual harassment. The legal standard for what constitutes sexual harassment is known as the "reasonable woman" standard. The question in each case is whether a reasonable woman would be offended by a supervisor's or co-worker's request for sexual favors, a display of sex-related pictures or objects, sexual language, or physical contact.[33] The issue received extraordinary national attention in 1991 in conjunction with the nomination of Clarence Thomas for a seat on the Supreme Court. University of Oklahoma law professor Anita Hill charged that Thomas had sexually harassed her when he was her supervisor a decade earlier at the Equal Employment Opportunity Commission.

NATIVE AMERICANS

When white settlers began arriving in America in large numbers during the seventeenth century, 8 to 10 million Native Americans were living in the territory that would become the United States. By 1900, the Native American population had plummeted to less than 1 million. Diseases brought by white settlers had taken a toll on the various Indian tribes, but so had wars and massacres. "The only good Indian is a dead Indian" is not just a hackneyed expression from cowboy movies. It was part of the strategy of westward expansion, as settlers and U.S. troops mercilessly drove the eastern Indians from their ancestral lands to the Great Plains and then took those lands too.

Today Native Americans number more than 1 million, of whom about half live on or close to reservations set aside for them by the federal government. Those who retain ties to a reservation are among America's most impoverished, illiterate, and jobless citizens. Native Americans are less than half as

YOUR TURN

SEXUAL HARASSMENT IN THE WORKPLACE

The Questions:
Consider this list of different situations. We're interested in knowing whether you think they are forms of sexual harassment—not just inappropriate or in bad taste—but sexual harassment. For each one, please indicate if you think it definitely is sexual harassment, if you are not sure if it is, or if you are definitely sure it is not.

1. If a male boss makes it clear to a female employee that she must go to bed with him for a promotion

   Definitely is | Not sure | Definitely is not

2. If a male boss asks very direct questions of a female employee about her personal sexual practices and preferences

   Definitely is | Not sure | Definitely is not

3. If a female boss asks very direct questions of a male employee about his personal sexual practices and preferences

   Definitely is | Not sure | Definitely is not

4. If a man once in a while asks a female employee of his to go out on a date, even though she has said no in the past

   Definitely is | Not sure | Definitely is not

5. If a male boss tells a female employee that she looks very attractive today

   Definitely is | Not sure | Definitely is not

What Others Think: These questions were asked in a 1991 Roper Organization survey. In all cases, women were more likely than men to believe a situation was an example of sexual harassment. However, the differences were small—about 5 percent on average. Over 90 percent of men and women regarded the first situation as an example of sexual harassment; in contrast, less than 5 percent of men and women viewed the last situation this way. Slightly more than half of all respondents regarded the second and third situations as examples of sexual harassment. Finally, 21 percent of the women respondents and 15 percent of the men regarded the occasional request for a date as a form of sexual harassment.

Comment: Sexual harassment is a serious problem in the workplace, but employers and employees in recent years have become more sensitive to the issue. The problem is primarily one of harassment of women by men, which is undoubtedly why women are more sensitive to the issue.

likely to attend college as other Americans, their life expectancy is more than ten years less than the national average, and their infant mortality rate is more than three times higher than that of white Americans.

The civil rights movement of the 1960s at first did not include Native Americans. Then, in the early 1970s, militant Native Americans occupied the Bureau of Indian Affairs in Washington, D.C., and later seized control of the village of Wounded Knee on a Sioux reservation in southwestern South Dakota, exchanging gunfire with U.S. marshals. These episodes brought attention to the grievances of Native Americans and may have contributed to the passage in 1974 of legislation that granted Native Americans on reservations a greater measure of control over federal programs that affected them. Native Americans had already benefited from the legislative climate created by the civil rights movement of the 1960s. In 1968 Congress had enacted the Indian Bill of Rights, which gives Native Americans on reservations constitutional guarantees that are similar to those held by other Americans.

The Senate Select Committee on Indian Affairs reviews legislation that affects Native Americans living on reservations, including the Taos Pueblo in New Mexico. (Paul Conklin)

In recent years Native Americans have filed suit to reclaim lost ancestral lands and have won a few settlements. But they stand no realistic chance of getting back even those lands that had been granted them by federal treaty but were later sold off or simply taken forcibly by federal authorities. Native Americans were not even official citizens of the United States until an act of Congress in 1924. This status came too late to be of much help; their traditional way of life had already been seriously eroded.

HISPANIC AMERICANS

The fastest-growing minority in the United States is that of Hispanic Americans, people with Spanish-speaking backgrounds. The 1990 census counted 22.4 million Hispanics living in the United States, an increase of 53 percent over the 1980 census; and it is projected that Hispanics will replace African Americans as the nation's largest racial or ethnic minority group soon after the year 2000. They have emigrated to the United States primarily from Mexico and the Caribbean islands, mainly Cuba and Puerto Rico. About half of all Hispanics in the United States were born in Mexico or claim a Mexican ancestry. Hispanics are concentrated in their states of entry; thus Florida, New York, and New Jersey have large numbers of Caribbean Hispanics, while California, Texas, Arizona, and New Mexico have many immigrants from Mexico. More than half the population of Los Angeles is of Hispanic—mostly Mexican—descent.

The term "Hispanic" can be misleading if it is construed to mean a group of people who all think alike (see Table 5-2). Hispanics cover a wide political spectrum, from the conservative Republican-leaning Cuban Americans of southern Florida to the liberal Democratic-leaning Puerto Ricans of the Northeast. Hispanic Americans share a common language, Spanish, but they are not monolithic in their politics.[34]

TABLE 5-2 Hispanics' Party Identification, by National Origin
Hispanics share a common language and ancestry, but differ sharply in their political leanings.

Party Identification	*Puerto Rican Americans*	*Mexican Americans*	*Cuban Americans*
Democratic	64%	60%	19%
Independent	22	24	17
Republican	14	16	64
	100%	100%	100%

SOURCE: *Latino National Political Survey*, reported in Rudolfo O. de la Garza, Angelo Falcon, F. Chris Garcia, and John A. Garcia, "Hispanic Americans in the Mainstream of U.S. Politics," *The Public Perspective*, July/August 1992, p. 19.

Illegal Aliens

Hispanic Americans have benefited from laws and court rulings aimed primarily at protecting other groups. Thus, although the Civil Rights Act of 1964 was largely a response to the condition of black people, its provisions against discrimination apply broadly to other groups as well. Hispanics have gained from the efforts of other groups, but they do not necessarily feel a common bond with those groups. In some communities, Hispanic Americans and African Americans in particular have had a tense relationship, reflecting competition over jobs and status.

Hispanics face some distinctive problems. The fact that many do not speak English led to a 1968 amendment to the 1964 Civil Rights Act that funds public school programs offering English instruction in the language of children for whom English is a second language. In addition, many Hispanics are illegal aliens and do not have the full rights of citizens. In *De Canas* v. *Bica* (1976), for example, the Supreme Court upheld a state law barring illegal aliens from employment.[35]

Hispanic Americans are growing in political and cultural influence as their numbers increase in California and other states. (Alon Reininger/Woodfin Camp & Associates)

In 1986 Congress passed landmark immigration and naturalization legislation, the Simpson-Mizzoli Act, which primarily affected Hispanics. The legislation provided that illegal aliens who could prove continuous residence in the United States for five years were eligible for citizenship. The act also mandated fines on employers who knowingly hired aliens without work permits, hoping the resulting lack of job openings would eliminate the main incentive for aliens to enter the country illegally. Hispanic American leaders had mixed reactions to the legislation, welcoming the provision granting citizenship to aliens of long-standing residence but worrying that the deportation of nonqualified aliens would result in the breakup of families. Some immigrants were also suspicious of the program, believing they would be arrested and deported when they applied for citizenship at the offices of the Immigration and Naturalization Service. Nevertheless, more than 2 million Hispanics applied for citizenship under the Immigration Reform and Control Act.

The issue of illegal aliens reached fever pitch in 1994 in reaction to California's Proposition 187—known to its supporters as the "save our state" initiative. Placed on the ballot through a citizen petition, it aimed to cut off public services to illegal immigrants, the great majority of whom were Mexicans. They would no longer receive state-funded food stamps, welfare, and medical care except in life-threatening circumstances, and they would no longer be eligible for public schooling at any level. State and local employees would be required to report illegal immigrants to the appropriate authorities, and the printing and sale of false citizenship papers would become a felony offense.[36] Governor Pete Wilson, a leading supporter of Proposition 187, said the state could not afford to "educate every child from here to Tierra del Fuego [Mexico]." There were 308,000 illegal aliens (10 percent of all students) in California's primary and secondary schools, and they were costing the state more than $1 billion annually.

Although a majority of Californians voted for Proposition 187,* it was opposed by most of the state's Mexican Americans. Many of them claimed the initiative was mainly a device for keeping new people from Mexico out of California. Surveys lent some support to the claim. A Field Institute poll indicated, for example, that a majority of white Californians would amend the U.S. Constitution to deny citizenship to children born on American soil to illegal aliens.

Growing Political Power

Hispanic Americans are an important political force in some states and communities, and their influence is likely to increase substantially in the future. Hispanics are projected to become the largest single population group in California in the next century. Like other immigrant groups, their political involvement can be expected to increase as they become more deeply rooted in the society and economy. At present, nearly half of all Hispanic adults are not registered to vote, which limits the group's political power.

More than 4,000 Hispanic Americans nationwide hold public office. In 1974

*At the time this book was printed, implementation of Proposition 187 was delayed pending review in the courts. Opponents obtained a restraining order on the grounds that the denial of a public education to children of illegal immigrants violated the Fourteenth Amendment's equal protection clause.

Arizona and New Mexico elected governors of Spanish-speaking background. New Mexico elected its second Hispanic governor in 1982. About twenty Hispanic Americans currently serve in the House of Representatives.

ASIAN AMERICANS

Chinese and Japanese laborers were the first Asians to come to the United States in large numbers. They were brought into western states during the late 1800s to work in mines and to build railroads. When the need for this labor declined, Congress in 1892 ordered a temporary halt to Chinese immigration. Over the next three decades, informal agreements kept all but a few Asians out of the country. In 1921 the United States ended its traditional policy of unlimited immigration and established immigration quotas based on country of origin. Western European countries were given large quotas and Asian countries tiny ones. About 150 Japanese a year were allowed to immigrate until 1930, when Congress excluded them entirely. Japan had protested a California law that prohibited persons of Japanese descent from buying property in the state. Rather than finess what was called "the California problem," Congress bluntly told Japan that its people were not wanted in the United States.[37]

This discrimination against Asians did not change substantially until 1965, when Congress enacted legislation that adjusted the immigration quotas to favor those who had previously been disadvantaged. This change in the law was a product of the 1960s civil rights movement, which, as we have indicated, sensitized national leaders to all forms of discrimination. About half a million people now emigrate to the United States each year, and a majority come from Asian and Latin American countries. By the year 2000, Asian Americans will number about 12 million, or between 4 and 5 percent of the total U.S. population. Most Asian Americans live on the West Coast, particularly in California.

Asian American children study U.S. history in a middle-school classroom. Many Asian American families emphasize academic achievement as a means of upward mobility. (Anthony Suau/Gamma-Liaison)

The rights of Asian Americans have been expanded primarily by court rulings and legislation, such as the Civil Rights Act of 1964, that were responses to the problems of other minorities. In a few instances, however, the rights of minorities have been defined by actions of Asian Americans. For example, in *Lau* v. *Nichols* (1974), a case involving Chinese Americans, the Supreme Court ruled that public schools with a large proportion of children for whom English is a second language must offer English instruction in the children's first language.[38]

Asian Americans are an upwardly mobile group. The values of most Asian cultures include a commitment to hard work, which, in the American context, has included an emphasis on academic achievement. For example, Asians make up a disproportionate share of the students at California's leading public universities, which base admission primarily on high school grades and standardized test scores. However, Asian Americans are still underrepresented in certain areas of the workplace. According to U.S. government figures, Asian Americans account for about 5 percent of professionals and technicians, nearly the same as their percentage of the population. Yet they hold less than 2 percent of managerial jobs; past and present discrimination has kept them from obtaining their fair share of top business positions.

OTHER GROUPS AND THEIR RIGHTS

Although civil rights efforts have been directed mainly at women and racial and ethnic minorities, other groups are also involved.

One such group are the nearly 15 million Americans (5 percent of the population) who have a physical disability so severe that they are unable to perform some critical function, such as hearing, seeing, or walking. A goal of the disabled is equal access to society's opportunities, which was facilitated by the 1990 Americans with Disabilities Act, granting the disabled the same employment and other protections enjoyed by other disadvantaged groups. In addition, the Education for All Handicapped Children Act of 1975 mandates that all children, however severe their disability, receive a free, appropriate education. Before the legislation, 4 million handicapped children were getting either no education or an inappropriate one (as in the case of a blind child who is not taught Braille).

The government has also acted to protect the elderly from discrimination. The Age Discrimination Act of 1975 and the Age Discrimination in Employment Act of 1967 prohibit discrimination against older workers in hiring for jobs in which age is not clearly a crucial factor in job performance. More recently, mandatory retirement ages for most jobs have been eliminated by law. Forced retirement for reasons of age is permissible only if justified by the nature of a particular job or the performance of a particular employee.

A group that until very recently had not received substantial legal protection is homosexuals. In *Bowers* v. *Hardwick* (1986), the Supreme Court upheld a state law banning sexual acts between consenting homosexual adults, ruling that the constitutional right of privacy does not extend to such acts. Gay rights also were dealt a setback when President Clinton's proposal to permit homosexuals to serve in the military was strongly opposed in Congress. The compromise policy that resulted is called "don't ask, don't tell." According to this informal policy, homosexuals in the military cannot be compelled to admit their sexual preference but can be dismissed from the armed services if they engage in verbal or behavioral displays of homosexuality.

However, gays gained a significant legal victory when the Supreme Court in *Romer* v. *Evans* (1996) struck down a Colorado constitutional amendment that nullified all existing and any new legal protections for homosexuals. In a 6–3 ruling, the Court said the Colorado law violated the Constitution's guarantee of equal protection since it subjects individuals to employment and other forms of discrimination simply because of their sexual preference. The Court concluded that the law had no reasonable purpose but was instead motivated by "animus" (hostility) toward homosexuals.

Equality under the Law

The catchphrase of nearly any group's claim to a more equal standing in American society has been "equality under the law." The importance that people attach to legal equality is understandable. When made into law, claims to equality assume a power that they do not otherwise possess. Once secure in their legal rights, people are in a stronger position to seek equality in other arenas, such as the economic sector. Once encoded in law, a claim to equality can also force officials to take positive action on behalf of a disadvantaged group.[39] Americans' claims to legal equality are contained in a great many laws, a few of which are particularly noteworthy.

EQUAL PROTECTION: THE FOURTEENTH AMENDMENT

equal protection clause A clause of the Fourteenth Amendment that forbids any state to deny equal protection of the laws to any individual within its jurisdiction.

reasonable-basis test A test applied by courts to laws that treat individuals unequally. Such a law may be deemed constitutional if its purpose is held to be "reasonably" related to a legitimate government interest.

strict-scrutiny test A test applied by courts to laws that attempt a racial or ethnic classification. In effect, the strict-scrutiny test eliminates race or ethnicity as a legal classification when it places minority group members at a disadvantage.

The Fourteenth Amendment, which was ratified in 1868, declares in part that no state shall "deny to any person within its jurisdiction the equal protection of the laws." Through this **equal protection clause,** the courts have protected such groups as African Americans and women from discrimination by state and local governments.

The Fourteenth Amendment's equal protection clause does not require government to treat all groups or classes of people the same way in all circumstances. In fact, laws routinely treat people unequally. By law, for example, twenty-one-year-olds can drink alcohol but twenty-year-olds cannot. The judiciary allows such inequalities because they are held to be "reasonably" related to a legitimate government interest. In applying this **reasonable-basis test,** the courts give the benefit of doubt to government. It need only show that a particular law has a sound rationale. For example, the courts have held that the goal of reducing fatalities from alcohol-related accidents involving young drivers is a valid reason for imposing a twenty-one-year minimum age requirement for the purchase of alcohol.

The reasonable-basis test does not apply, however, to racial or ethnic classifications, particularly when these categories serve to discriminate against minority group members. Any law that posits a racial or ethnic classification is subject to the **strict-scrutiny test,** under which such a law is unconstitutional in the absence of an overwhelmingly convincing argument that it is necessary. The strict-scrutiny test has virtually eliminated race and ethnicity as

Through protest demonstrations, students at Gallaudet College, which was founded to provide higher education for the hearing-impaired, succeeded in obtaining the appointment of the college's first hearing-impaired president. The students argued that the appointment of a president with normal hearing would be a severe setback in the effort of handicapped people to achieve rights. (Paul Conklin)

permissible classifications when the effect is to put members of a minority group at a disadvantage. The Supreme Court's position is that race and national origin are **suspect classifications**—that such classifications have invidious discrimination as their purpose and therefore any law containing such a classification is in all likelihood unconstitutional.

suspect classifications Legal classifications, such as race and national origin, that have invidious discrimination as their purpose and are therefore unconstitutional.

The strict-scrutiny test emerged after the 1954 *Brown* ruling and became a basis for invalidating laws that discriminated against black people. As other groups, especially women, began to organize and press for their rights in the late 1960s and early 1970s, the Supreme Court gave early signs that it might expand the scope of suspect classifications to include gender.[40] In the end, however, the Court announced in *Craig* v. *Boren* (1976) that sex classifications were permissible if they served "important governmental objectives" and were "substantially" related to the achievement of those objectives.[41] The Court thus placed sex distinctions in an "intermediate" (or "almost suspect") category, to be scrutinized more closely than some other classifications (for example, income levels) but, unlike racial classifications, justifiable in some instances. In *Rostker* v. *Goldberg* (1980), for example, the policy of male-only registration for the military draft was upheld on grounds that the exclusion of women from combat duty serves a legitimate and important purpose.[42]

The *intermediate-scrutiny test* is so inexact that some scholars question its validity as a legal principle. Nevertheless, when evaluating claims of sex discrimination, the judiciary applies a stricter level of scrutiny than is required by the reasonable-basis test. Rather than give government broad leeway to treat men and women differently, the Supreme Court has recently invalidated most of the laws it has reviewed that contain sex classifications. A leading case is *United States* v. *Virginia* (1996), in which the Supreme Court determined that the male-only admissions policy at Virginia Military Institute (VMI), a 157-year-old state-supported college, was unconstitutional. The state had developed an alternative program for women at another college, but the Court concluded it was no substitute for the unique education and other opportunities that attendance at VMI could provide. (The VMI decision also had the effect of ending the all-male admissions policy of the Citadel, a state-supported military college in South Carolina.)[43]

EQUAL ACCESS: THE CIVIL RIGHTS ACTS OF 1964 AND 1968

The Fourteenth Amendment applies only to action by government. It does not prohibit discrimination by private parties. As a result, for a long period in the nation's history, owners could legally bar black people from restaurants, hotels, and other accommodations, and employers could freely discriminate in their job practices. Since the 1960s private firms have had much less freedom to discriminate for reasons of race, sex, ethnicity, or religion.

Accommodations and Jobs

The Civil Rights Act of 1964 entitles all persons to equal access to restaurants, bars, theaters, hotels, gasoline stations, and similar establishments serving the general public. The legislation also bars discrimination in the hiring, promotion, and wages of employees of medium-sized and large firms. A few forms of job discrimination are still lawful under the Civil Rights Act of 1964. For example, an owner-operator of a small business can discriminate in hiring his or her co-workers, and a religious school can take the religion of a prospective teacher into account.

The Civil Rights Act of 1964 has nearly eliminated the most overt forms of discrimination in the area of public accommodations. Some restaurants and hotels may provide better service to white customers, but outright refusal to serve African Americans or other minority group members is rare. Such a refusal is a violation of the law and could easily be proved in many instances. It is harder to prove discrimination in job decisions; accordingly, the act has been less effective in rooting out employment discrimination—a subject that will be discussed in detail later in the chapter.

Housing

In 1968, Congress passed civil rights legislation designed to prohibit discrimination in housing. A building owner cannot refuse to sell or rent housing because of a person's race, religion, ethnicity, or sex. An exception is allowed for owners of small multifamily dwellings who reside on the premises.

Despite legal prohibitions on discrimination, housing in America remains highly segregated. Less than a third of all African Americans live in a neighborhood that is mostly white. One reason is the fact that the annual income of most black families is substantially below that of most white families. Another reason is the practice of banks. At one time, they contributed to hous-

Deacon John Hodge stands at the charred remains of Rising Star Baptist Church in Greensboro, Alabama. His church is one of more than two dozen predominately black churches that were torched by arsonists in 1996 alone. The burnings are an ugly reminder that racism—"America's curse," in the words of the sociologist Gunner Myrdal—is still the nation's most conspicuous shortcoming. (Karim-Shamsi-Basha/SABA)

ing segregation by "redlining"—refusing to grant mortgage loans in certain neighborhoods. This practice drove down the selling prices of homes in these neighborhoods, which led to an influx of African Americans and an exodus of whites. Redlining is prohibited by the 1968 Civil Rights Act, but many of the segregated neighborhoods that it helped to create still exist.

A 1991 study by the Federal Reserve Bank made it clear that race is still a factor in the lending practices of many banks (see Table 5-3). Although banks are bound by law not to discriminate in mortgage loans, the study indicated that, nationwide, black applicants were two-and-a-half times more likely than white applicants to be rejected. Even when high-income black applicants were compared with high-income white applicants, the difference persisted. Banks rejected more than twice as many well-paid black applicants. The rejection rate of Hispanic American and Asian American applicants also exceeded that of white applicants.[44]

EQUAL BALLOTS: THE VOTING RIGHTS ACT OF 1965, AS AMENDED

Free elections are perhaps the foremost symbol of American democracy, yet the right to vote has only recently become a reality for many Americans, particularly for African Americans.

The Nineteenth Amendment, which in 1920 gave women the right to vote, effectively ended resistance to women's suffrage; paradoxically, resistance to black suffrage was intensified by the Fifteenth Amendment, which in 1870 gave black persons the right to vote. Southern whites invented a series of devices, including whites-only primaries, poll taxes, and rigged literacy tests to keep African Americans from registering and voting.[45] For example, almost no votes were cast by African Americans between the years 1920 and 1946 in North Carolina.[46]

TABLE 5-3 Denial Rates for Home Purchase Loans (1990) Minority group applicants are much more likely to be denied a mortgage loan than are white applicants.

	PERCENTAGE REJECTED				
City	*Total*	*Asian*	*Black*	*Hispanic*	*White*
Atlanta	13.8%	11.1%	26.5%	13.6%	10.5%
Baltimore	8.6	7.3	15.6	10.1	7.5
Boston	12.9	15.4	34.9	21.2	11.0
Chicago	9.9	10.4	23.6	12.1	7.3
Dallas	12.5	9.3	25.6	19.8	10.7
Detroit	11.7	9.1	23.7	14.2	9.7
Houston	15.5	13.3	33.0	25.7	12.6
Los Angeles	14.7	13.2	19.8	16.3	12.8
Miami	18.0	16.9	22.9	17.8	16.0
Minneapolis	7.1	6.4	19.9	8.0	6.1
New York	18.7	17.3	29.4	25.3	15.0
Oakland	11.4	11.6	16.5	13.3	9.6
Philadelphia	11.3	12.1	25.0	21.0	8.3
Phoenix	16.4	12.8	30.0	25.2	14.4
Pittsburgh	13.3	12.2	31.0	13.9	12.0
St. Louis	14.0	9.0	31.8	13.5	12.1
San Diego	11.4	11.2	17.8	15.1	9.8
Seattle	11.8	11.6	18.3	16.8	10.7
Washington, D.C.	8.2	8.7	14.4	8.9	6.3

SOURCE: Federal Reserve Bank. Figures refer to 1–4 family homes purchased with conventional, FHA, FMHA, and VA mortgages. Refinancings are not included.

Barriers to black participation in elections began to crumble in the mid-1940s, when the Supreme Court declared that whites-only primary elections were unconstitutional.[47] Two decades later, through the Twenty-fourth Amendment, poll taxes were outlawed.

The major step toward equal voting rights for African Americans was passage of the Voting Rights Act of 1965, which forbids discrimination in voting and registration.[48] The legislation empowers federal agents to register voters and to oversee participation in elections. The Voting Rights Act, as interpreted by the courts, also eliminates literacy tests: local officials can no longer deny registration and voting for reasons of illiteracy. In fact, in communities where a language other than English is widely spoken, officials are now required by law to provide ballot materials in that language. If most civil rights legislation seldom has a significant and immediate impact on people's behavior, the Voting Rights Act is an exception. In the 1960 presidential election, voter turnout among African Americans was barely more than 20 percent nationwide. In 1968, three years after passage of the legislation, the turnout rate exceeded 40 percent. By 1972, turnout among African Americans was within 10 percent of the level for white Americans. In 1960, the gap had exceeded 40 percent (see Figure 5-3).

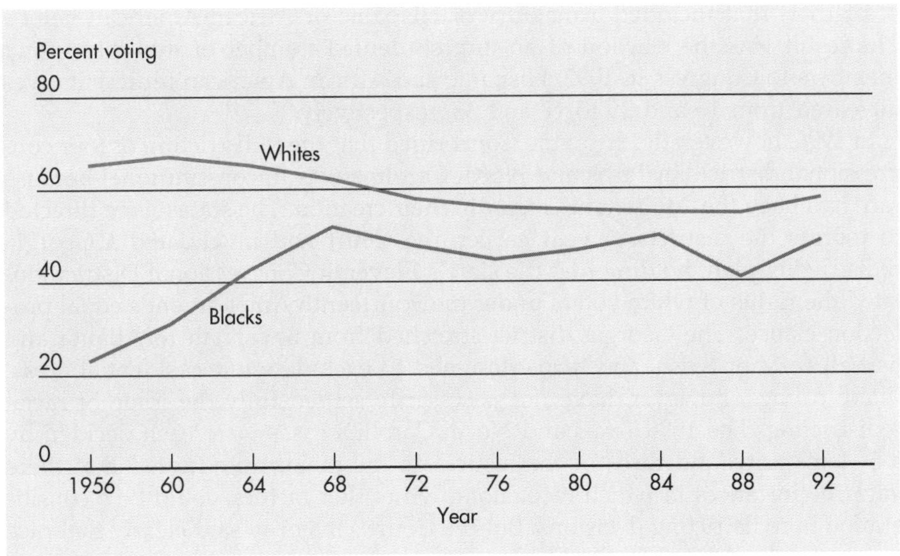

FIGURE 5-3 Voter Turnout in Presidential Campaigns among Black and White Americans, 1956–1992
Voter turnout among black Americans rose dramatically during the 1960s as legal obstacles to their voting were removed. *Source: Adapted from U.S. Bureau of the Census data.*

Congress renewed the Voting Rights Act in 1970, 1975, and 1982. The 1982 extension is noteworthy because it renews the act for twenty years and requires states and localities to clear with federal officials any electoral change that has the effect, intended or not, of reducing the voting power of a minority group. When congressional district boundaries were redrawn after the 1990 census (see Chapter 13), the 1982 extension became the basis for the creation

In 1992 Carol Mosely-Braun (D-Ill.) became the first African American woman elected to the U.S. Senate. She is shown here with First Lady Hillary Rodham Clinton during "Youth America Day" activities at the White House. (Brad Markel/Gamma-Liaison)

of districts that included a majority of Hispanic or African American voters. The result was the election of an unprecedented number of minority group members to Congress in 1992; Hispanic and African American representatives increased from 10 and 25 to 17 and 38, respectively.

In 1996, however, the Supreme Court ruled that the redistricting of four congressional districts in Texas and North Carolina was unconstitutional because race had been the "dominant" factor in their creation. The states were directed to redraw the districts. A year earlier, the Court had invalidated a Georgia redistricting plan, holding that the state's Eleventh Congressional District violated the rights of white voters under the Fourteenth Amendment's equal protection clause. The Georgia district stretched from Savannah to Atlanta and had all sorts of twists and turns designed to exclude white residential areas. These rulings, however, have not necessarily settled fully the issue of racial redistricting. The 1996 Texas and North Carolina cases were each decided by a 5–4 majority, and three of the justices in the majority indicated that there *might* be instances in which race, along with other factors, could be *a* consideration in redistricting decisions. But the Court's majority said clearly that race cannot be the *determining* factor.[49]

Equality of Result

The struggles of America's disadvantaged groups have resulted in significant progress toward equal rights, particularly during the past few decades. However, civil rights problems involve deeply rooted conditions, habits, and prejudices. For this reason, a new civil rights policy rarely produces a sudden and dramatic change in society. Despite their greater equality in law, America's traditionally disadvantaged groups are still substantially unequal in their daily lives. Consider, especially, the income disparity between white and minority families. The average Asian American family's income is three-fourths that of the average white family. For Hispanic American families, the average is two-thirds that of white families. The average falls to three-fifths for black families, and still lower for Native Americans.

***de facto* discrimination** Discrimination on the basis of race, sex, religion, ethnicity, and the like that results from social, economic, and cultural biases and conditions.

***de jure* discrimination** Discrimination on the basis of race, sex, religion, ethnicity, and the like that results from a law.

equality of result The objective of policies intended to reduce or eliminate the effects of discrimination so that members of traditionally disadvantaged groups will have the same benefits of society as do members of advantaged groups.

Such figures reflect ***de facto* discrimination,** which is discrimination that is a consequence of social, economic, and cultural biases and conditions. This type of discrimination is different from ***de jure* discrimination,** which is discrimination based on law, as in the case of segregation in southern public schools during the pre-*Brown* period. No law says that other Americans cannot have incomes as high as those of white males, but higher average incomes for white males are a fact of American life. *De facto* discrimination is difficult to root out because it is embedded not in the law but in the very structure of society. **Equality of result** is the aim of policies intended to reduce or eliminate *de facto* discriminatory effects so that members of traditionally disadvantaged groups may obtain the same benefits as members of traditionally advantaged groups. Such policies are inherently more controversial as many Americans believe that government's responsibility extends no further than the removal of legal barriers to equality. This attitude conforms with the country's individualistic culture and is a major reason for the lack of any large-scale government effort to reduce the economic and social gaps between Americans of varying racial and ethnic backgrounds. Nevertheless, a few policies—notably affirmative action and busing—have been implemented to achieve equality of result.

AFFIRMATIVE ACTION: WORKPLACE INTEGRATION

The difficulty of converting newly acquired legal rights into everyday realities is evident in the fact that, with passage of the 1964 Civil Rights Act, which prohibited discrimination in employment, it did not suddenly become easier for women and minorities to obtain jobs for which they were qualified. Many employers maintained a deliberate though unwritten preference for white male employees, while other employers adhered to established employment procedures that continued to keep women and minorities at a disadvantage; membership in many union locals, for example, was handed down from father to son. Moreover, the Civil Rights Act did not compel employers to show that their hiring practices were not discriminatory. Instead, the burden of proof was on the woman or minority group member who had been denied a particular job. It was costly and often difficult to prove in court that one's sex or race was the reason that one had not been hired. In addition, a victory in court affected only the individual in question; such case-by-case settlements were no remedy for a situation in which established hiring practices kept millions of women and minorities from competing equally for job opportunities.

A broader remedy was obviously required, and the result was the emergence during the late 1960s of affirmative action programs. **Affirmative action** is a deliberate effort to provide full and equal opportunities in employment, education, and other areas for women, minorities, and individuals belonging to other traditionally disadvantaged groups. Affirmative action requires corporations, universities, and other organizations to establish programs designed to ensure that all applicants are treated fairly. Affirmative action also places the burden of proof on the providers of opportunities; to some extent, they must be able to demonstrate that any disproportionate granting of opportunities to white males is not the result of discriminatory practices.

The Supreme Court's Position on Affirmative Action

Most issues that pit individuals against each other in a struggle over society's benefits eventually end up in the courts, and affirmative action is no exception. The policy was first tested before the Supreme Court in *University of California Regents* v. *Bakke* (1978). Alan Bakke, a white man, had twice been denied admission to a University of California medical school, even though his admission test scores were higher than several minority group students who had been accepted. Bakke sued, claiming the school had a "quota" system for minorities that discriminated against white males. The Court ruled in Bakke's favor but did not invalidate affirmative action per se. The Court said only that rigid racial quotas were an impermissible form of affirmative action in determining medical school admissions.[50]

★ STATES IN THE NATION

Annual Income Per Capita, by Race (in dollars): In all states, income levels of minorities are below that of whites.

STATE	WHITES	BLACKS	HISPANICS
Ala.	13,235	6,473	9,663
Alaska	19,903	12,816	11,885
Ariz.	14,964	9,688	7,374
Ark.	11,472	5,729	7,074
Calif.	19,028	11,578	8,504
Colo.	15,544	10,704	8,233
Conn.	21,466	11,695	9,786
Del.	17,263	9,683	10,066
D.C.	34,563	12,226	12,525
Fla.	16,052	7,550	10,582
Ga.	15,832	7,997	11,123
Hawaii	18,598	10,607	9,950
Idaho	11,723	8,785	6,303
Ill.	16,817	8,922	8,318
Ind.	13,553	8,739	9,221
Iowa	12,573	7,844	8,025
Kan.	13,817	8,445	8,007
Ky.	11,439	7,460	9,058
La.	12,956	5,687	10,188
Maine	13,019	10,089	9,946
Md.	19,789	12,343	13,198
Mass.	18,003	10,867	7,833
Mich.	15,071	9,195	9,298
Minn.	14,765	8,714	8,003
Miss.	12,183	5,194	8,621
Mo.	13,563	8,576	10,191
Mont.	11,634	7,657	6,021
Neb.	12,773	7,857	7,280
Nev.	16,241	9,366	9,348
N.H.	16,028	12,577	11,634
N.J.	20,406	11,542	10,761
N.Mex.	12,678	8,579	7,542
N.Y.	18,584	10,566	8,915
N.C.	14,450	7,926	9,544
N.Dak.	11,359	7,875	5,811
Ohio	14,049	8,702	9,248
Okla.	12,859	7,356	7,145
Oreg.	13,778	8,240	6,996
Pa.	14,688	9,140	7,489
R.I.	15,573	9,031	7,620
S.C.	14,115	6,800	10,723
S.Dak.	11,230	8,124	6,908
Tenn.	13,201	7,414	10,246
Texas	14,629	8,102	6,633
Utah	11,274	8,385	7,398
Vt.	13,597	8,991	11,501
Va.	17,361	9,439	12,220
Wash.	15,564	10,440	8,149
W.Va.	10,574	7,416	9,805
Wis.	13,793	7,021	7,050
Wyo.	12,629	8,490	7,967
National average	15,687	8,859	8,400

SOURCE: U.S. Bureau of Census, 1990 Census of Population and Housing

Bakke was followed by two rulings in favor of affirmative action programs, one of which—*Fullilove* v. *Klutnick* (1980)—upheld a quota system that required 10 percent of federal public works funds to be set aside for minority-owned firms.[51]

In the 1980s, the appointment of new, more conservative justices to the Supreme Court narrowed the scope of affirmative action policy. The Court held that preferential treatment of minorities could normally be justified only in cases where discrimination had been severe;[52] that affirmative action could be applied only in a way that did not infringe on the rights of white employees to keep their jobs (thus restricting the use of race as a basis for determining which employees would be terminated in the case of job layoffs;[53] that affirmative action programs may be approved only after close scrutiny by a court and that such programs can later be challenged by white workers who were not part of the original agreement;[54] and that, in some instances, minority group members must prove that racial imbalances in hiring or promotion have no valid business purpose (thus shifting the burden of proof in these instances from employer to employee).[55]

In a key 1995 decision, *Adarand* v. *Pena,* the Supreme Court sharply curtailed the federal government's affirmative-action authority. The case arose when Adarand Constructors filed suit over a federal contract that was awarded to a Hispanic-owned company even though Adarand had submitted a lower bid. The Court in a 5–4 ruling said that the government had to prove that a preference program for minorities was a response to specific past acts of discrimination, not just discrimination in a historic sense. This decision essentially reversed earlier precedents that allowed the federal government to give a preference to minority applicants. The Court said that Washington cannot set aside contracts for minority applicants unless, through costly and conclusive studies, it can demonstrate past discrimination particular to a situation, and even then, it must devise a program "narrowly tailored" to the situation.[56]

The Civil Rights Act of 1991

The Supreme Court's affirmative action decisions in the 1980s brought strong condemnations from civil rights and women's rights groups and led in 1990 to the passage in Congress of a civil rights bill that would have reversed several of the decisions. President Bush vetoed the measure, calling it a "quota" bill. He changed his mind a year later, after he was pressured to do so by moderate Republicans in Congress and after polls indicated that he was losing support among women and minority group leaders.

With the threat of a veto removed, Congress in late 1991 passed a civil rights bill that provides employment protections for women and minority group members. The legislation makes it easier for job discrimination victims (including sexual harassment victims) to sue for damages. The legislation also shifted the burden of proof back to employers in cases where they have relatively few women or minority group members among their employees. The employer must show in some circumstances why a lopsidedly white male work force is the result of a business necessity and not the result of systematic discrimination against women or minorities. As part of the compromise that led to passage of the legislation, it contains a provision that bans the adjustment of employment-related test results to boost the scores of minority group members (a practice called "race norming").

Differing Views of Affirmative Action

Few issues in recent years have provoked opinions as intense as those surrounding affirmative action. For its proponents, the statistics speak for themselves: on average, white males get more jobs, better pay, and more promotions than do members of other groups. In some occupations, most of them in the professions, well-qualified minority group members are in great demand. In most cases, however, white males have the edge. Civil rights groups have argued that affirmative action must be broadly and aggressively applied if the effects of past discrimination and lingering prejudice are to be overcome. If a union, business, university, fire department, or other organization has no or only a few women or minority group members, then it should be ordered by government to give them preferential treatment in hiring or admission. In such cases, some qualified white males may lose out, but this cost is an unavoidable necessity if discrimination against women and minorities is to be curtailed.[57]

Opponents of affirmative action say that the policy can end up favoring women and minorities over white males, an outcome that is called "reverse discrimination." Opposition to affirmative action is particularly strong when there is the reality or appearance of a quota system. Three-fourths of the respondents in a national survey said that programs giving preference to minorities in hiring and promotion are "unfair to qualified people who are not members of a minority," whereas only 10 percent said that such preference is "necessary to make up for a long history of discrimination."[58] Although explicit quotas are unlawful in most cases, the hiring and promotion practices of organizations are typically judged by the number or percentage of minorities and women included. As a result, implicit quotas or goals often become embedded in affirmative action efforts.

Opponents of affirmative action gained a major advantage with the Supreme Court's decision in *Adarand* v. *Pena*. Even supporters of affirmative action concluded that the ruling apparently marked the end of the era of extensive racial and gender preferences. By holding that affirmative action programs must be narrowly tailored and based on specific past acts of discrimination, the Court substantially restricted the ability of federal authorities to create lawful programs. Earlier, the Court had established the stricter standard of proof of discrimination for programs at the state and local levels.

Another blow to affirmative action programs is the California Civil Rights Initiative, which bans in California any public employment, education, or contracting program that is based on race or sex. Known as Proposition 209, the initiative was enacted by California voters in 1996 by a 54–46 percent margin. The measure received close national attention as a possible indicator of public attitudes on affirmative action. Support for Proposition 209 was particularly strong among white men, who have generally been the most consistent opponents of affirmative action policy.[59]

SOCIAL INTEGRATION: BUSING

In 1944 the Swedish sociologist Gunnar Myrdal gained fame for his book *An American Dilemma,* whose title referred to deep-rooted racism in a country that proclaimed itself to be the epitome of an equal society.[60] Since then, legal obstacles to the mixing of the races have been nearly eliminated. Public opinion has also changed significantly in the past half century. In the early 1940s a majority of white Americans believed that black children should not be allowed to go to school with white children; today only 5 percent of white Americans express this belief. There are also visible signs of black progress. In the past two decades, increasing numbers of African Americans have attended college, received undergraduate and graduate degrees, obtained jobs as professionals and managers, and moved into suburban neighborhoods.

However, the majority of black people still live largely apart from white people. The reality of American life today is racial segregation. More than two-thirds of African Americans live in neighborhoods that are all or mostly black; more than two-thirds of black children go to schools that are mostly black; two-fifths attend schools that are more than 90 percent black.

The *Swann* Decision

In 1971 the Supreme Court took the controversial step of requiring the busing of children in some circumstances. Affirming a lower-court decision, the Supreme Court held in *Swann* v. *Charlotte–Mecklenburg County Board of Education* that the busing of children from one neighborhood to another was a permissible way for courts to compel the integration of public schools where past years of official segregation had created residential patterns that had the effect of keeping the races in separate schools. Busing, the Court said, was allowed as a tool "in the interim period when remedial adjustments are being made to eliminate the dual school system."[61]

Few policies of recent times provoked so much controversy as the introduction of forced busing.[62] Angry demonstrations lasting weeks took place in Charlotte. When busing was ordered in Detroit and Boston, the protests turned violent. Unlike *Brown,* which affected mainly the South, *Swann* also applied to northern communities in which African Americans and whites lived apart as a result of economic and cultural differences as well as discriminatory real estate practices and local housing ordinances. In fact, the most segregated communities are in the Northeast and Midwest rather than the South. According to a segregation index created by researchers at the University of Michigan, there is less neighborhood integration in northern cities like Gary, Indiana, and Flint, Michigan, than in southern cities like Fayetteville, North Carolina, and Ft. Walton Beach, Florida (see Table 5-4).

The Course and Impact of Busing

A 1972 University of Michigan survey indicated that more than 80 percent of white Americans disapproved of forced busing. If opposition to busing is less intense today, it is no less one-sided. Recent polls indicate that upward of 75 percent of white Americans oppose the policy of busing.

TABLE 5-4 Segregation in U.S. Communities In communities with substantial white and African American populations, the degree of racial segregation tends to be higher in many northern localities than in southern ones.

Least Segregated Communities	*Segregation Index*	*Most Segregated Communities*	*Segregation Index*
Jacksonville, N.C.	31	Gary, Ind.	91
Lawton, Okla.	37	Detroit	89
Anchorage, Alaska	38	Chicago	87
Fayetteville, N.C.	41	Cleveland	86
Lawrence, Kan.	41	Buffalo, N.Y.	84
Clarksville, Tenn.	42	Flint, Mich.	84
Ft. Walton Beach, Fla.	43	Saginaw, Mich.	84

SOURCE: ISR, University of Michigan, 1994. Segregation index is based on the racial homogeneity of residential areas.

In large part because busing has been unpopular with the public, the policy has never been strongly supported by elected officials. The Democratic-controlled Congress on several occasions in the 1970s came close to forbidding the use of federal funds to assist busing any way. Richard Nixon was president when the *Swann* decision was announced, and he ordered the Justice Department to act slowly on busing cases; he hoped that opposition to busing would attract racially conservative whites to the Republican coalition. Under President Reagan a decade later, the Justice Department effectively ceased to pursue pro-busing lawsuits. The Reagan administration endorsed an antibusing initiative passed by voters in the state of Washington, but the

The controversy over court-ordered busing erupted into violence in many northern cities in the early 1970s. Ten school buses in Pontiac, Michigan, were destroyed by explosive devices planted by antibusing protestors. The interior of this bus was completely burned, leaving only bare metal and springs. (AP/Wide World)

THE MEDIA AND THE PEOPLE

THE NEWS IN BLACK AND WHITE

Because whites and blacks in America live apart to a significant degree, the portrayal of race relations in the news media is for many people the most important source of their understanding of the other race. Analyses of national media coverage of race relations by Robert Lichter and Linda Lichter, editors of *Media Monitor,* provide insights about this portrayal. The Lichters have found that the leading topic in stories about race relations is crime. Other major topics include election politics, education and employment issues.

News about race relations is dominated by controversy and "bad news." The media paint a picture not so much of a harmonious interracial society as of a country divided between black and white. Most stories are critical of the way in which African Americans are treated by whites. Stories tend to be weighted heavily toward those authorities who argue that racism is deeply embedded in American society, as opposed to those who claim that racism is an isolated phenomenon. Nearly all institutions of society, including business, government, and the schools, are cited as sources of the problem.

These patterns were evident in the news media's coverage of the Los Angeles rioting that followed the verdict of innocence in the trial of the policemen accused in the beating of Rodney King (see text). Television coverage was dominated by footage of burning buildings, looters, rioters, and interracial physical assaults (two-thirds of the footage of assaults came from repeated showings of the beating of truck driver Reginald Denny by black youths). There was substantially less coverage of the social and economic conditions of Los Angeles's African American community. The Los Angeles riots were not portrayed as a justified response to the verdict, but the rioting was blamed on black anger at the verdict and on government failures. Few of the voices heard in the news defended the rioters, but less than 10 percent characterized them as opportunists or criminals.

SOURCE: "The News in Black and White," *Media Monitor* 4 (February 1990), p. 1– 6; "The Rodney King Case, Part II," *Media Monitor* 7 (April 1993), 1–6.

Supreme Court ruled the law unconstitutional because it was based on racial categories and as such failed the strict-scrutiny test.[63]

Despite the controversy surrounding it, busing remains a part of national policy. Thousands of children throughout the nation are bused out of their neighborhoods for purposes of school integration. Busing has provided equality of result for some black children, but its effectiveness has been undercut by restrictions on it. In part because of the adverse reactions to busing, the Supreme Court has limited across-district busing to situations where it can be shown that school district boundaries were purposely drawn so as to segregate the races.[64] Since school districts in most states coincide with community boundaries, the effect of this position has been to insulate most suburban schools from integration plans. As a result, the burden of busing has fallen most heavily on poorer whites and African Americans in the inner cities.

In a key 1995 decision, *Missouri* v. *Jenkins,* the Supreme Court ruled that judges cannot order other taxpayers to finance improvements in inner-city schools in order to attract suburban white students to these schools. Kansas City had established magnet schools for this purpose, and the state of Missouri had objected to funding them. The case was decided by a 5–4 vote, and the dissenting justices argued that the ruling essentially overturned the precedent of allowing far-reaching measures to counteract the effects of historic discrimination.[65]

Persistent Discrimination: Superficial Differences, Deep Divisions

Discrimination has been called America's curse. In a country that is otherwise bountiful and generous, superficial differences—sex, skin color, country of origin—are sources of deep divisions and stark contrasts. To cite but one example: a black child born in the United States has more than twice the chance of dying before reaching his or her first birthday than a white child. The difference in the infant mortality rates of whites and African Americans reflects differences in their nutrition, medical care, and education—in other words, differences in their access to the most basic resources of a modern society.

As has been true throughout most of the nation's history, no greater challenge faces Americans than the rooting out of discrimination. The political scientist Jennifer Hochschild suggests that conflicting principles underlie the problem. We prize both diversity and equality, but diversity breeds inequality. Americans separate into groups, and they prize the traits of their particular group; white people do not encourage black people to move next door. We also prize both liberty and self-government. Busing enhances the liberty of black children but strikes against the wishes of the majority.[66]

Americans have no choice but to confront and resolve the contradictions. Inaction would mean that Americans had denied the *moral* imperative underlying their claim to a belief in equal opportunity. Inaction would mean that the United States had chosen to maintain two different societies, one for whites and one for minorities, the first superior and the second inferior.

Summary

During the past few decades, the United States has undergone a revolution in the legal status of its traditionally disadvantaged groups, including African Americans, women, Native Americans, Hispanic Americans, and Asian Americans. Such groups are now provided equal protection under the law in areas such as education, employment, and voting. Discrimination by race, sex, and ethnicity has not been eliminated from American life but is no longer substantially backed by the force of law.

Traditionally disadvantaged Americans have achieved fuller equality primarily as a result of their struggle for greater rights. The Supreme Court has been an important instrument of change for minority groups. Its ruling in *Brown* v. *Board of Education* (1954), which declared racial segregation in public schools to be an unconstitutional violation of the Fourteenth Amendment's equal protection clause, was a major breakthrough in equal rights. Through its busing, affirmative action, and other rulings, the Court has also mandated the active promotion of integration and equal opportunities.

However, as civil rights policy involves large issues of social values and the distribution of society's resources, questions of civil rights are politically explosive. For this reason, legislatures and executives as well as the courts have been deeply involved in such issues, siding at times with established groups and sometimes backing the claims of underprivileged groups. Thus Congress, with the support of President Lyndon Johnson, enacted the landmark Civil Rights Act of 1964; but Congress and recent presidents have been ambivalent about or hostile to busing for the purpose of integrating public schools.

In recent years affirmative action programs, designed to achieve equality of result for African Americans, women, Hispanic Americans, and other disadvantaged groups, have become a civil rights battleground. Affirmative action has had the strong support of civil rights groups and has won the qualified endorsement of the Supreme Court but has been opposed by those who claim that it unfairly discriminates against white males.

Major Concepts

affirmative action
comparable worth
de facto discrimination
de jure discrimination
equal protection clause
equal rights (civil rights)
equality of result
reasonable-basis test
strict-scrutiny test
suspect classifications

Suggested Readings

Barsh, Russel Lawrence, and James Youngbood Henderson. *The Road: Indian Tribes and Political Liberty.* Berkeley: University of California Press, 1979. An analysis of Native Americans' quest for their civil rights.

Bell, Derrick. *And We Are Not Saved: The Elusive Quest for Racial Justice.* New York: Basic Books, 1987. An analysis of the struggle, including the political and legal strategies, for racial justice.

de la Garza, Rudolfo O., Louis DeSipio, F. Chris Garcia, John Garcia, and Angelo Falcon. *Latino Voices: Mexican, Puerto Rican, and Cuban Perspectives on American Politics.* Boulder, Colo.: Westview Press, 1992. A study of the political opinions and behaviors of Hispanic Americans, based on a survey of more than 2,800 Latinos.

Evans, Sara M., and Barbara Nelson. *Wage Justice.* Chicago: University of Chicago Press, 1989. A study of Minnesota's comparable-worth policy that concludes the policy alone will not provide women with economic justice.

Faludi, Susan. *Backlash: The Undeclared War against American Women.* New York: Crown, 1991. A critical view of American society's treatment of women.

Kugler, Richard. *Simple Justice: The History of Brown v. Board of Education and Black America's Struggle for Equality.* New York: Random House, 1977. The best evaluation of the *Brown* case and its impact on school desegregation.

Kull, Andrew. *The Color-Blind Constitution.* Cambridge, Mass.: Harvard University Press, 1992. A constitutional analysis which argues that racial classifications are allowable, though sometimes regrettable, as long as they are reasonable.

Rinehart, Sue Tolleson. *Gender Consciousness and Politics.* New York: Routledge, 1992. An insightful evaluation of the impact of women's heightened political consciousness.

Rosenberg, Gerald N. *The Hollow Hope: Can Courts Bring about Social Change?* Chicago: University of Chicago Press, 1991. An analysis which concludes that civil rights goals achieved through the judiciary often have limited consequences.

Smith, Robert C., and Richard S. Hzer. *Race, Class, and Culture: A Study in Afro-American Mass Opinion.* Albany: State University of New York Press, 1992. A valuable evaluation of the political views and behaviors of black Americans.

Witt, Linda, Karen M. Paget, and Glenna Matthews. *Running as a Woman: Gender and Power in American Politics.* New York: Free Press, 1994. A careful analysis of the way women campaign, and how the process differs from the way men campaign.

PART TWO

MASS POLITICS

CLINTON
KANSAS
SPEAKING
TRUTH
TO
POWER

PART TWO

MASS POLITICS

"We, the people," are the opening words of the U.S. Constitution. The American political system is premised on the lofty idea that government is obliged to respond to the will of the people. This requirement is confounded, however, by the practical problem of self-government in a nation of more than 250 million people. All of us would like government to listen to our views. But if each of us was granted just one minute to address the Congress of the United States, 500 years would elapse before the last of us had spoken.

The role of the mass public is accordingly a challenging one. As citizens, we are asked to take time to participate in public affairs, yet only a tiny few among us get the opportunity to exert substantial direct influence over these affairs. Not surprisingly, Americans differ in their willingness to exercise their citizenship. Some people cannot be bothered with public affairs and others spend considerable time dealing with them. Most Americans fall between the two extremes, giving some time to politics but not immersing themselves in it. Nevertheless, the integrity of the American political system depends on popular influence. As the political scientist Harold Lasswell once wrote, the "open interplay" of the people and their government is "the distinguishing mark of popular rule."

This open interplay takes place through both individual and collective action. Citizens directly voice their opinions on public issues and participate directly in public affairs, primarily through voting. However, their influence is felt primarily when they join together in common purpose. This joining comes through intermediating organizations, the most important of which are political parties, interest groups, and the news media.

The chapters in this section explore these avenues of citizen politics. Chapter 6 examines the way Americans think politically and the effect of their opinions on government. Public opinion is an elusive but powerful influence in a democratic society. Chapter 7 discusses the nature and implications of citizens' participation in politics. This participation takes place through voting, group participation, social movements, and other forms of citizen activism. Chapter 8 focuses on elections and America's two-party system. In most democracies, voters can select between three or more major parties when they go to the polls. In the United States, there are only two major parties; this system substantially affects voters' choices and influence.

The remaining chapters in the section examine political intermediaries. Political party organizations are discussed in Chapter 9. Democratic government is almost inseparable from parties, which formed at the grass roots in the 1800s to provide a means by which citizens could act together as an effective majority. Interest groups, the subject of Chapter 10, are another vehicle of collective action. The interests they represent tend to be specialized ones, such as those of oil companies, women, or environmentalists. The news media, examined in Chapter 11, are a third linking organization. The present era is often described as the age of communications, a testimony to the political importance of newspapers, television, radio, and news magazines.

All democracies depend on public opinion, political participation, elections, parties, groups, and the media as means of popular influence, but the United States does so in relatively unique ways. For example, America's political parties are among the weakest in the world, while its interest groups and media are among the strongest. The reasons for the distinctive nature of American politics are many, and the consequences are significant. Political action enables Americans to make their voices heard, but the precise nature of this activity determines whose voice will be heard the loudest. ★ ★ ★

CHAPTER 6

PUBLIC OPINION AND POLITICAL SOCIALIZATION: SHAPING THE PEOPLE'S VOICE

To speak with precision of public opinion is a task not unlike coming to grips with the Holy Ghost.

—*V. O. Key, Jr.*[1]

When Iraqi tanks rolled into Kuwait in early August of 1990, most Americans were ill equipped to pass judgment on what was happening. They knew almost nothing about Iraq or Kuwait—what kind of leadership these countries had, what the conflict was all about, or what kind of relationship each country had with the United States at the time of the invasion. Within days, however, public opinion on the issue began to form. A Gallup Poll in early August indicated that 82 percent of Americans approved of President George Bush's decision to send troops to the Persian Gulf. Most Americans also said they would approve of the use of force to remove Iraq from Kuwait, although polls indicated they preferred a peaceful settlement of the crisis.

Bush's rhetoric soon become more militant; at one point he described Saddam Hussein, the Iraqi ruler, as "worse than Hitler." The American public grew increasingly pessimistic about the effectiveness of the economic embargo imposed on Iraq by the United Nations. Between early August and early October, according to ABC News/Washington Post polls, the percentage of Americans who thought the boycott would succeed dropped from 53 to 38. A militant mood crept over the country. When the United States attacked Iraqi troops by air on January 16, 1991, an ABC News/Washington Post poll indicated that 76 percent of Americans approved of the decision to go to war. Weeks later, a majority of Americans also expressed approval when a cease-fire was declared. Although earlier polls had shown that Americans believed the United States should continue fighting until Saddam Hussein had been deposed, the polls now indicated acceptance of Bush's announcement that the

Victory parades, such as this one in New York City, greeted U. S. troops when they returned from the Persian Gulf war. Public opinion in the United States strongly supported President Bush's response to the Gulf crisis. (T. L. Litt/Impact Visuals)

military objective had been met when the last Iraqi forces were driven out of Kuwait.

The unfolding of the Gulf crisis is a revealing example of the influence of public opinion on government. Public opinion rarely compels officials to take a particular action. Bush was not forced by public opinion to attack Iraqi forces, but, as he moved away from economic sanctions and toward the military option, public opinion supported the change. And when the war ended, public opinion would have allowed Bush to continue the military action if he had chosen to do so. Bush did not have a completely free hand. If the Gulf war had turned sour, the American public would have gradually withdrawn its support of the intervention as it had in the case of Vietnam. Bush also took several steps, which included obtaining United Nations and congressional approval for the military action, that helped secure public support for his actions. Americans would have been far less supportive had Bush acted alone. Nevertheless, Bush had considerable latitude in deciding the U.S. response to the Gulf crisis.

Public opinion has an important place in democratic societies because of the concept that government springs from the will of the people. However, public opinion is a far more elusive phenomenon than traditional discourse suggests. It is widely assumed that there is a clear-cut public opinion on current issues, but in fact, as the Gulf war illustrates, public opinion is seldom exact when it comes to questions of how to accomplish an agreed-upon goal.

This chapter discusses public opinion and its influence on the U.S. political system. A major theme is that public opinion is a powerful and yet inexact force in American politics. The policies of the U.S. government cannot be understood apart from public opinion; at the same time, public opinion is not a precise determinant of public policy. This apparent paradox is explained by the fact that self-government in a large and complex country requires a division of labor between the public and its representatives; the result is a government that is tied only loosely to its public and a public that ordinarily affects only the general direction of its government. The main points made in this chapter are the following:

- ★ *Public opinion consists of those views held by ordinary citizens which are openly expressed.* Public officials have many means of gauging public opinion but increasingly have relied on public opinion polls to make this determination.
- ★ *The process by which individuals acquire their political opinions is called political socialization.* This process begins during childhood, when, through family and school, Americans acquire many of their basic political values and beliefs. Socialization continues into adulthood, during which peers, political institutions and leaders, and the news media are major influences.
- ★ *Americans' political opinions are shaped by several frames of reference. Four of the most important are ideology, group attachments, partisanship, and political culture.* These frames of reference form the basis for political consensus and conflict among the general public.
- ★ *Public opinion has an important influence on government but ordinarily does not directly determine what officials will do.* Public opinion works primarily to impose limits and directions on the choices made by officials.

The Nature of Public Opinion

Public opinion is a relatively new concept in the history of political ideas. Not until democracy arose in the eighteenth century did the need arise to take full account of what the people were thinking on political issues. Although the predemocratic theorist Machiavelli warned that rulers who ignored the people's interests risked assassination, his notion of the public's influence was a far cry from the democratic idea of government as being of and for the people.[2] Public opinion today is central to the practice of democratic government.

DEFINING PUBLIC OPINION

Today, "public opinion" is a widely used term. It is typically applied in ways which suggest that the people have a common set of concerns. In fact, it is not very meaningful to lump all citizens together as if they constituted a single coherent public.[3] There is, to be sure, an occasional issue of such power and breadth that it captures the attention of nearly all citizens. The large majority of issues, however, attract the attention of some citizens but not others. The tendency is so pervasive that opinion analysts have described America as a nation of *many* publics.[4]

Hence, in defining "public opinion" we cannot assume that all citizens, or even a majority, are actively interested and have a preference about all aspects of political life. An opinion is a belief that a person holds about some exter-

public opinion Those opinions held by ordinary citizens that they express openly.

nal object. Such opinions become **public opinion** when they are expressed openly.[5] This expression need not be verbal. It could also take the form, for example, of a protest demonstration or a vote for one candidate over another. The crucial point is that a person's private thoughts on an issue become public opinion when expressed publicly.

People's willingness to express their opinions forcefully can affect the outcome of political conflict. Polls taken during the Vietnam war, for example, indicated that, until that last stage of the conflict, a majority of Americans supported the war effort. Yet, of the demonstrators who took to the streets to express their opinions, the vast majority opposed U.S. policy. The Nixon administration used the phrase "silent majority" to refer to those citizens who backed the war but were not publicly heard. In the end, they probably had less influence on Vietnam policy than the vocal demonstrators whom they far outnumbered.

WHAT ROLE SHOULD PUBLIC OPINION PLAY?

A fundamental principle of democracy is that the people's view ought to be the foundation of government. No true democrat, past or present, would reject the idea that a just government rests on the consent of the governed or that the people are in some sense the ultimate source of governing wisdom and strength.[6] Nevertheless, there has always been widespread disagreement about the exact role that public opinion should play in the formulation of public policy.

At one extreme are those who claim that it would be foolish to base policy decisions on whatever the people happen to think at the time. One such analyst, Robert Nisbet, says the idea that "public opinion must somehow govern, must therefore be incessantly studied, courted, flattered and drawn upon . . .

References to "American public opinion" can be misleading because American society consists of many publics, not just one. Americans may divide into publics on the basis of race, sex, age, occupations, and many other differences. (Robert Fox/Impact Visuals)

Public opinion includes contradictory elements. According to surveys, for example, most Americans say they want lower taxes but also say they want more public services. At a Boston rally, this demonstrator expresses his anger with President Clinton's tax-increase legislation while also demanding that government provide free health care. (Joel Stettenheim/Saba)

is the great heresy . . . of modern democracies." Nisbet claims that government has an obligation to respond only to the enduring and fundamental beliefs that citizens share as members of an ongoing political community. He labels these beliefs "public opinion" and distinguishes them from "popular opinion," which he defines as the transitory thoughts that citizens express on topical issues in the polls.[7] Nisbet's view stems from the classical liberal tradition that influenced the *Federalist Papers* (see Chapter 3). James Madison distinguished between the public's momentary passions and its enduring concerns, arguing that government is obliged to represent only the public's "true interest."[8]

In contrast, other analysts contend that almost any opinion held by ordinary citizens—whether stable or fleeting, reasoned or emotional—should be taken into account by government. George Gallup, who founded the public opinion polling industry in the United States, promoted this view. He believed that leaders should be closely in tune with the citizenry. "In a democracy," Gallup said, "the task of the leader is to decide how best to achieve the goals set by the people."[9] Gallup's view belongs to the tradition of the Jacksonian and Progressive movements (see Chapter 3), which were based on a strong faith in the judgment of ordinary citizens and a deep skepticism toward governing elites.

GOVERNMENT BY MAJORITY OPINION?

Most Americans today share Gallup's view: they want government to act in accordance with their views and are disenchanted when they believe it is ignoring public opinion. Indeed, the public has increasingly believed that government is out of touch with their interests. In a 1972 NORC poll, 74 percent of the respondents expressed confidence in the federal government's responsiveness; in a 1992 Gallup Poll, the confidence level was only 42 percent.

There are, however, several practical obstacles to government by public opinion in all instances. The most apparent reason is that people have differing opinions; in responding to one side of an issue, government is compelled to reject other preferences. Public opinion is also contradictory in many cases. Polls indicate, for example, that Americans would like better schools, health care, and other public services while they also favor a reduction in taxes. A significant increase in the quantity and quality of social services cannot be accomplished without additional taxes. Which opinion of the people should govern—its desire for more services or its desire for lower taxes?

There are also a great many issues where there is literally no concrete majority opinion. Agricultural conservation programs are a matter of intense concern to farmers, but of little interest to city dwellers. In such situations, a form of *pluralist* democracy usually prevails: government responds to the views of the intense minority. In still other cases, *elitist* opinion prevails. On the question of U.S. relations with Madagascar, for example, there is little likelihood of a popular constituency that knows or cares what the federal government does. In such instances, the policy opinions of an elite group of business and policy leaders ordinarily prevail.

Majority opinion, to the degree it governs policy, is normally confined to those few, broad issues that elicit widespread attention and concern. Although this situation may suggest a limited role for popular majorities, such issues, although few in number, typically have the most impact on society as a whole. Majority opinion can thus be viewed as playing a potentially significant role in policymaking. The key question is whether majority opinion actually does govern these critical issues. The final section of this chapter will offer a partial answer to this question.

HOW INFORMED IS PUBLIC OPINION?

A final limitation on the role of the public is its relatively low level of political information. Some citizens pay close attention to politics, but most do not, and some people pay hardly any attention at all. As a result, most people are poorly informed about politics. Fewer than half of adult Americans can readily recall both U.S. senators from their state. Their knowledge of geography is no better. On a map of the world, a majority of Americans cannot locate Vietnam, Sweden, or South Africa. A fifth of the citizenry cannot even find the United States.[10]

Most citizens would "flunk" a current affairs test. In 1993, a Times-Mirror survey asked a cross section of Americans five questions on people and events that were currently at the top of the news (the correct answers are in parentheses):

> Who is the president of Russia? (Boris Yeltsin)
>
> Do you happen to know the name of the country that is threatening to withdraw from the nuclear nonproliferation treaty? (North Korea)
>
> Who is Boutros Boutros-Ghali? (Secretary General of the U.N.)

> Do you happen to know the name of the ethnic group that has conquered much of Bosnia and has surrounded the city of Sarajevo? (Serbs)
>
> Do you happen to know the name of the group with whom the Israelis recently reached a peace accord? (Palestinians)

Only 6 percent of the respondents answered all five questions correctly and 9 percent knew four answers; 37 percent could answer none of the questions, and 21 percent answered only one question correctly. In other words, a majority of citizens knew little or nothing when asked relatively simple questions about world developments. (Citizens in six other countries were asked the same five questions; the results are summarized in the box: How the United States Compares.)

Although people with lower education levels are more likely to be uninformed, many college-educated people also lack basic information. A survey of Ivy League students found that a third could not identify the British prime minister, half could not name both U.S. senators from their state, and three-fourths could not identify Abraham Lincoln as the author of the phrase, "a government of the people, by the people, and for the people."[11]

The public's lack of information is not as significant a factor as might seem the case. Citizens do not necessarily have to be well informed about a situation to have a reasonable opinion about it. Opinions stem more from people's general beliefs, values, and policy orientations than from precise information about policy alternatives. Many people's opinions on the abortion issue, for example, derive from deep-seated religious beliefs. The fact that most individuals have only a foggy notion of the Supreme Court's role in the abortion dispute does not make these opinions any less relevant. Similarly, people can have a considered view of how the United States should respond to foreign aggression without a detailed knowledge of the globe or top foreign leaders.

Nevertheless, the public's lack of information restricts the role it can play in policy disputes. Public opinion can direct government toward certain goals, but it rarely provides a detailed guide to the way these goals are to be accomplished. The choice of one course of action over another requires knowledge of the likely consequences of the various alternatives. The average citizen rarely possesses such knowledge.

★ CRITICAL THINKING

Forming Opinions without Information

The level of the public's knowledge about some policy issues is shockingly low. How does this situation affect the public discussion of policy problems? What circumstances affect whether a citizen is likely to possess much factual information about a policy issue? Can you think of an issue about which a citizen could have a thoughtful opinion without having much information? How critical do you generally think it is that citizens have substantial information when forming their opinions on policy issues?

The Measurement of Public Opinion

Woodrow Wilson once said he had spent nearly all of his adult life in government and yet had never seen a "government." What Wilson was saying, in effect, was that government is a system of relationships. A government is not a building or a person; it is not tangible in the way that a car or a bottle of soda is. So it is with public opinion. No one has ever seen a "public opinion," and thus it cannot be measured directly. It must be assessed indirectly.

A time-honored method of interpreting public opinion is election returns. The vote is routinely interpreted by the press and politicians as an indicator of the public's mood—whether liberal or conservative, angry or satisfied, quiet or intense. When the Republicans piled up huge gains in the House and

HOW THE UNITED STATES COMPARES

CITIZENS' AWARENESS OF PUBLIC AFFAIRS

Americans' knowledge of public affairs is relatively low. Although most citizens say they follow the news regularly or often, they are not very attentive to what they see and hear. Even the simplest facts sometimes elude the average citizen's grasp. A 1994 Gallup Poll found, for example, that a third of Americans were unable to name the vice-president of the United States.

Low levels of public information are characteristic of most countries, but Americans rank lower than citizens of other western democracies by some indicators. In a seven-country survey conducted by the Times-Mirror Center for the People and the Press, Americans ranked next to last in terms of their ability to respond correctly to five questions about world leaders and events. Americans did their best on a question that asked them to name the president of Russia: 50 percent said Boris Yeltsin, but this was far lower than the 94 percent of Germans who named Yeltsin. Americans had the most difficulty with the question that asked them to name the country that was threatening to withdraw from the nuclear nonproliferation treaty: only 22 percent correctly said Korea or North Korea compared with 45 percent of Germans. In light of America's leading role in the world, its citizens might be expected to be uniquely well informed about international affairs. However, they are less knowledgeable in this area than Europeans, who live in closer proximity to other countries and who thus may be more attentive to world politics.

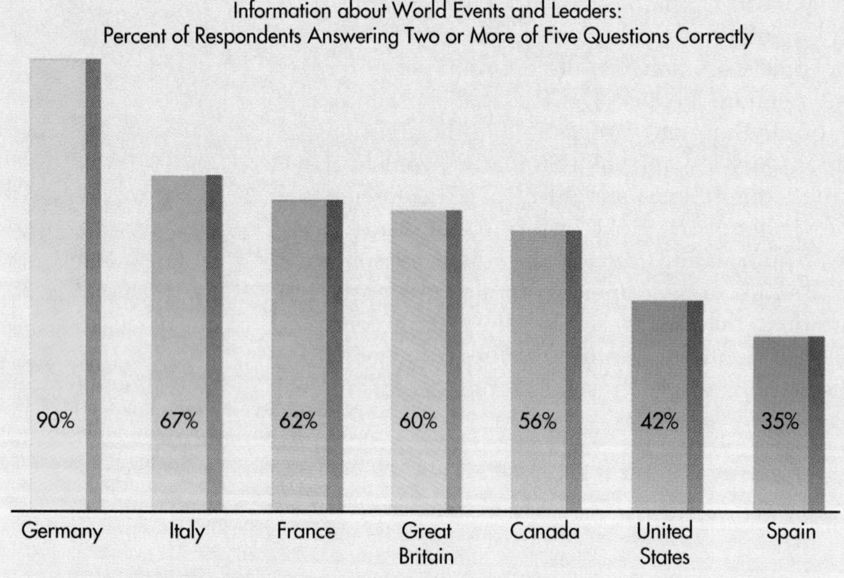

Senate in the 1994 congressional elections, pundits labeled it an angry backlash against government and the Democrats, who were in control of Congress and the presidency.

Letters to the editor in newspapers and the size of crowds at mass demonstrations are other means of judging public opinion. Yet another device is the activity of lobbyists, who bring the concerns of their constituents to government's attention.

All these indicators of public opinion are important and deserve the attention of those in power. These indicators, however, have shortcomings as a guide to what is on the minds of the people. Elections offer the people only a yes-or-no choice between candidates, and different voters will make the same choice for quite different reasons. The winning candidate may claim that the public has based its choice on a particular issue or inclination, but election returns almost always mask a much more complex reality. As for letter writers and demonstrators, they are not at all representative of the general population. Less than 1 percent of Americans participate each year in a mass demonstration, and fewer than 10 percent write to the president or a member of Congress. Studies have found that the views of letter writers and demonstrators are more intense and more extreme than those of other citizens.[12]

PUBLIC OPINION POLLS

In an earlier day, such things as elections and letters to the editor were the only means by which public officials could gauge what the public was thinking. Today, they can also rely on polls or surveys, which provide a more systematic method of estimating public sentiment.

In a **public opinion poll** a relatively few individuals—the **sample**—are interviewed in order to estimate the opinions of a whole **population,** such as the students of a college, the residents of a city, or the citizens of a country. If a sufficient number of individuals are chosen at random, their views will tend to be representative—that is, roughly the same as the views held by the population as a whole.

public opinion poll A device for measuring public opinion whereby a relatively small number of individuals (the sample) are interviewed for the purpose of estimating the opinions of a whole community (the population).

How is it possible to measure the thinking of a large population on the basis of a relatively small sample? How can interviews with, say, 1,000 Americans provide a reliable estimate of what 250 million are thinking? The answer is found in the theory of probability. Opinion sampling is based on the mathematical laws of probability, which can be illustrated by the hypothetical example of a huge jar filled with a million marbles, half of them red and half of them blue. If a blindfolded person reaches into the jar, the likelihood of selecting a marble of a given color is 50–50. And if 1,000 marbles are chosen in this random way, it is likely that about half of them will be red and half will be blue.

sample In a public opinion poll, the relatively small number of individuals who are interviewed for the purpose of estimating the opinions of an entire population.

population In a public opinion poll, the term *population* refers to the people (for example, the citizens of a nation) whose opinions are being estimated through interviews with a sample of these people.

The accuracy of a poll is usually expressed in terms of **sampling error,** which is a function of sample size. The larger the sample, the smaller the sampling error (see Table 6-1). Many people assume that a poll of the United States, with its 250 million people, must have a much larger sample to achieve the same level of accuracy as, say, a poll of Massachusetts or Arizona. In fact, the mathematics of polling are such that sample size is the critical factor. Thus, a sample of 1,000 people will have nearly the same level of accuracy whether the population is that of the nation, a state, or a large city. Again, a jar filled with marbles can illustrate the point. If half of them were blue and half were red, it would be predicted that the random selection of 1,000 marbles would yield about a 50–50 distribution by color, whether the jar held a million marbles, 10 million marbles, or 250 million.

sampling error A measure of the accuracy of a public opinion poll. The sampling error is mainly a function of sample size and is usually expressed in percentage terms.

A properly drawn sample of 1,000 individuals has a sampling error of plus or minus 3 percent, which is to say that the proportions of the various opinions expressed by the people in the sample are likely to be within 3 percent

TABLE 6-1 Approximate Sampling Error by Number of Opinion-Poll Respondents The larger a poll's sample, the smaller the error in estimating the opinions of the population from which the sample is taken.

Approximate Number of Respondents	*Approximate Sampling Error*
200	±7%
275	±6
375	±5
600	±4
1,075	±3
2,400	±2
9,600	±1

NOTE: Figures are based on a 95 percent confidence level. This means that for a given sample size (e.g., 600), the chances are 19 in 20 (95 percent) that the sample will produce results that are within the sampling error (e.g., ± 4 percent) of the results that would have been obtained if the whole population had been interviewed.

of those of the whole population. For example, if 55 percent of a sample of 1,000 respondents say that they intend to vote for the Republican candidate for president, then the chances are high that 52 to 58 percent (55 percent plus or minus 3 percent) of the whole population plan to vote for the Republican.

The impressive record of the Gallup Poll in predicting the outcomes of presidential elections indicates that the theoretical accuracy of polls can be matched in practice. For example, the Gallup Poll predicted a 44–37 percent victory for Bill Clinton over George Bush in 1992. The actual margin was 43–38. The Gallup Organization has erred badly only once: it stopped polling several weeks before the 1948 election and missed a late trend that carried Harry Truman to victory over Thomas E. Dewey.

SOURCES OF POLLING ERROR

probability sample A sample for a poll in which each individual in the population has a known probability of being selected randomly for inclusion in the sample.

Mathematical estimations of poll accuracy require a **probability sample**—a sample in which each individual in the population has a known probability of being selected at random for inclusion. In practice, pollsters can only approximate this ideal. Because pollsters rarely have a list of all individuals in a population from which to draw a random sample, they usually base their sample on telephones or locations. Random-digit telephone sampling is the most commonly used technique. Pollsters use computers to pick random telephone numbers, which are then dialed by interviewers to reach respondents. Because the computer is as likely to pick one telephone number as any other and because 95 percent of U.S. homes have a telephone, a sample selected in this way is usually assumed to be representative of the population.

Some polls are not based on probability sampling. For example, news reporters sometimes conduct "people-in-the-street" interviews to obtain individual responses to political questions. Although a reporter may imply that the views of those interviewed are representative of the general public's, the

George Gallup *(seated)* and his staff meet on the day after the election of 1948. Gallup's American Institute of Public Opinion had wrongly predicted that Republican Thomas E. Dewey would beat Democrat Harry Truman. The Gallup organization subsequently revised its polling procedures and has correctly predicted the outcome of every election since 1948. (AP/Wide World)

fallacy of this reasoning should be readily apparent. The sample will be biased by where and when the reporter chooses to conduct the interviews. For example, interviews conducted on a downtown street at the noon hour will include a disproportionate number of business employees who are taking their lunch breaks. Housewives, teachers, factory workers, not to mention farmers, are among the many groups that would be underrepresented in such a sample.

Polls can also be misleading if they include poorly worded questions. A 1992 Roper study received widespread attention when it indicated that more than a fifth of the American public had doubts about whether the Nazi extermination of the Jews actually happened. *The San Francisco Chronicle* described these individuals as "willfully stupid."[13] However, the poll was subsequently criticized for its use of a double-negative question: "Does it seem possible or does it seem impossible to you that the Nazi extermination of the Jews never happened?" Research has shown that double-negative questions confuse respondents. The Gallup organization did a follow-up poll in which half of the respondents were asked the original form of the Roper question and the other half were asked: "Do you doubt that the Holocaust actually happened or not?" In response to the straightforward question, only 9 percent of the respondents (as compared with 33 percent of those asked the double-negative version) expressed doubt about the Holocaust, a clear indication that the form of the Roper question had misled respondents.[14]

Despite these drawbacks, the poll or survey has become the most relied-upon method of measuring public opinion. More than 100 organizations are in the business of conducting public opinion polls. Some, like the Gallup Organization, conduct polls that are then released to the news media by syn-

THE MEDIA AND THE PEOPLE

THE USE OF POLLS BY THE PRESS

Public opinion polls are widely acknowledged to be the most accurate method of gauging what the public is thinking. Many polls are conducted by government and by candidates for public office. Others, such as the Gallup Poll, are produced by independent polling organizations. Recently, however, the news media have become a major source of public opinion polls.

Opinion polls are identified with "precision journalism," which aims to bridge what Walter Lippmann called the gap between "the news" and "the truth." Lippmann argued that the news should not be confused with the truth, claiming that the subjects of news coverage and the pressures of news delivery are obstacles to accurate reporting. It occurred to some, including Philip Meyer (then a reporter with Knight newspapers and now a journalism professor at the University of North Carolina), that news accuracy could be improved if the media had better in-house research. Meyer's influential book, *Precision Journalism* (1973), offered a blueprint for newsroom research, including the extensive use of polls. The first news organizations to develop a polling capacity were CBS News and *The New York Times,* which teamed up to sponsor their own poll. The New York Times/CBS News poll is now conducted about fifteen times annually. The ABC, CNN, and NBC television networks; *Washington Post* and *USA Today* newspapers; and *Time* and *Newsweek* magazines are among the other news organizations that commission their own polls.

Seldom does a major news event occur without one news organization or another conducting a poll about it. The media's reliance on polls is particularly pronounced during a presidential election campaign. In the early years of polling, from the 1930s through the 1950s, a leading newspaper, such as *The New York Times* or *Washington Post,* might have contained a dozen or so poll-based stories during the entire campaign. Today, a leading newspaper may run as many as a dozen poll-based stories in a week, many of them relying on the newspaper's own polls.

The media's emphasis on polls has been a subject of criticism. In campaigns, polls contribute to an emphasis on the horse-race aspects of the election at the expense of issue and leadership questions. Poll stories are also manufactured news. They are not reports on events that have actually happened but pseudo-events that the press has created. The media conduct the polls and then treat them as newsworthy developments.

dication. Most large news organizations also have their own in-house polls; one of the foremost of these is the CBS News/New York Times poll, which conducts about fifteen surveys annually for use in the *Times* and on CBS's newscasts (see box: The Media and the People). Finally, there are polling firms that specialize in conducting surveys for candidates and officeholders.

DESCRIBING POLL RESULTS

Polls provide information about public opinion, which must then be summarized if it is to be readily interpreted. It is not enough to interview hundreds or thousands of people; it is necessary also to describe their responses in a systematic way.

The most common way of describing poll results is in terms of *direction,* which is a measure of whether opinion on a particular question is favorable (positive) or unfavorable (negative). A 1993 Time/CNN poll asked respondents whether they would "favor or oppose building more prisons even if your taxes would be raised significantly." The direction of opinion favored the building of prisons; 60 percent supported this approach to crime and 35 opposed it.

Opinions can also be described in terms of *intensity,* which is a measure of the strength of a particular opinion. A person may, for example, favor the building of more prisons but not feel very strongly about it. Another person may hold the same opinion intensely and express anger that more criminals are not behind bars. A related dimension is *salience,* which is an indicator of how important people regard a particular issue or concern relative to other concerns. A recent NBC/Newsweek poll asked respondents how important they thought the crime problem was in their community. The issue had high salience for nearly a third of the respondents; others rated it less important than other issues, such as unemployment, education, or health care.

Stability is yet another characteristic of opinions. It refers to whether an opinion is relatively stable or changes over time. Majority opposition in the early 1970s to the death penalty, for example, proved to be unstable. By 1975, a majority was in favor of capital punishment, and support for it has risen further since then. A 1993 Harris survey, for instance, indicated that 67 percent of Americans favor "expanding the number of crimes to which the death penalty would apply."

These characteristics affect the degree of attention that particular opinions are likely to receive from government. Opinions of high salience or one-sided direction tend to get more attention than low-salience or divided ones. Similarly, officials are generally more responsive to intensely held or stable opinions than to weakly held or fleeting ones.

Political Socialization: How Americans Learn Their Politics

Analysts have long been interested in the process by which public opinion is formed. A century ago James Bryce proposed that opinion formation takes place in stages, beginning with the public's first impression of an issue, continuing through a period of public deliberation on the issue, and concluding with a public action—such as the enactment of legislation—that settles the issue.[15] We now know that the process of opinion formation is far more varied and haphazard than Bryce believed. Citizens arrive at their opinions by any number of routes, most of them quite casual and unreflective and many of them involving elaborate psychological defense mechanisms.

The learning process by which people acquire their opinions, beliefs, and values is called **political socialization.** For most Americans, the process starts in the family with exposure to the political views of the parents. The schools later contribute to the process, as do the mass media, friends, and other influences. Political socialization is thus a lifelong process.

political socialization The learning process by which people acquire their political opinions, beliefs, and values.

THE PROCESS OF SOCIALIZATION

The process of political socialization in the United States has several major characteristics. First, although socialization continues throughout life, most people's political outlook is substantially influenced by their childhood learning. The *primacy tendency* refers to the fact that what is learned first is often lodged most firmly in one's mind.[16] Most people do not reflect deeply on how they acquired their political preferences. Basic ideas about race, gender, and political party, for example, are often formed uncritically in childhood, much in the way that belief in a particular religion, typically the religion of one's parents, is acquired.

A second characteristic of political socialization is that it is cumulative. The *structuring tendency* refers to the tendency of earlier learning to structure later learning.[17] This tendency is less a function of age itself than of an accumulated attachment to particular ideas or values. Of course, the fact that the United States is a diverse and mobile society makes a basic change in a person's political views possible, especially when previous and current experiences are at odds with one another. However, individuals have psychological defense mechanisms that protect their ingrained beliefs; when faced with situations that might challenge their original views, they can readily muster reasons for clinging to them.

It is the unusual individual who can step away from the way in which he or she has learned to see the world and see it differently. Dramatic political transformation is uncommon and, when it has occurred on a large scale, it has nearly always been preceded by an extraordinary event that has shaken people out of their complacency. In such instances, it is usually younger adults who are more responsive. Their beliefs are less firmly rooted in past experiences and are therefore more easily changed. The *age-cohort tendency* holds that a significant break in the pattern of political socialization is almost always concentrated among younger citizens. Democratic President Franklin Roosevelt's New Deal initiatives, which sought to alleviate the economic hardship of the Great Depression, resulted in a substantial increase in Democratic loyalists among first-time voters, but not among habitual ones.

A final characteristic of political socialization in the United States is that it is relatively casual. It is not the rigid program of indoctrination that some societies impose on their people. Nevertheless, Americans receive a thorough political education. Their country's values are impressed upon them by every medium of communication: newspapers, daily conversations, television, movies, books.[18] This pattern can be described as the *saturation tendency.* One result is a level of national pride that few countries, if any, can match. When asked whether they are "proud to be an American," U.S. citizens of all backgrounds respond with a resounding yes (see Figure 6-1).

THE AGENTS OF POLITICAL SOCIALIZATION

As we have noted, the socialization process takes place through a variety of influences, including family, schools, peers, the mass media, and political leaders and events. It is helpful to consider briefly some ways in which these so-called *agents of socialization* affect the opinions that people have. Although these agents will be discussed separately, it should be kept in mind that, by and large, their influences overlap. Many of the same political values that people acquire at home and in school, for example, are emphasized regularly by the mass media and political leaders.[19]

The Family

The family is a powerful agent of socialization because children begin with no political attitudes of their own and are likely to accept uncritically those of their parents.[20] The family has a near-monopoly on the attention of the

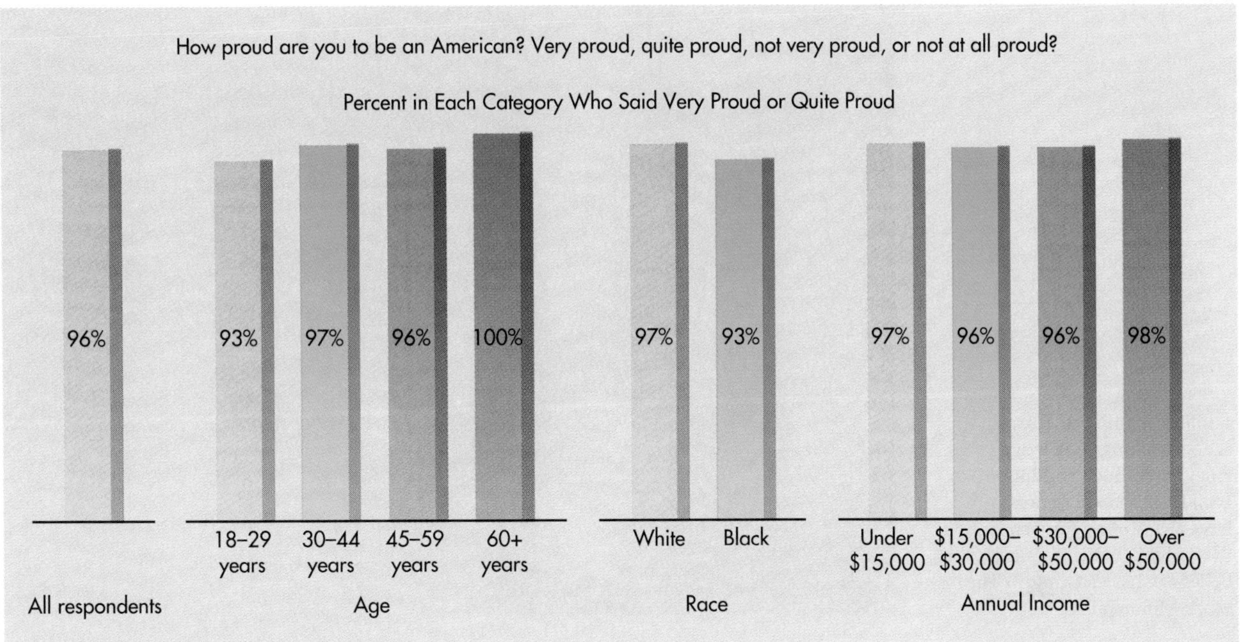

FIGURE 6-1 National Pride among Americans
Americans of all backgrounds and age levels express a strong attachment to the nation.
Source: Gallup survey, May 23–26, 1991.

young child, who also places great trust in what a parent says. By the time the child is a teenager and is not likely to listen to any advice a parent might offer, many of the beliefs and values that will stay with the child throughout life are already in place.

Some of these orientations are overtly political. Many adults are Republicans or Democrats today largely because they accepted their parents' party loyalty.[21] They now can give all sorts of reasons for preferring their party to the other. But the reasons come later in life; the loyalty comes first, during childhood. The family also contributes to basic orientations that, while not directly political, have political significance. For example, the American family tends to be more egalitarian than families in other nations, and American children often have a voice in family decisions. Such basic American values as equality, individualism, and personal freedom have their roots in patterns of family interaction.[22]

Opinions on specific issues of public policy are less substantially influenced by childhood experiences.[23] And, of course, a critical event, such as the Great Depression or the Vietnam war, may intervene to disrupt family influences.

The School

The school, like the family, has its major impact on children's basic political beliefs and values rather than on specific issues of policy. Teachers at the elementary level extol the exploits of national heroes and the superiority of the

Students in a North Carolina school reciting the Pledge of Allegiance. Such childhood socialization experiences can have a profound impact on an individual's basic political beliefs. (Charles Gupton/The Stock Montage)

country's economic and political systems.[24] While students in the middle and high school grades may encounter a more critical perspective in the classroom, they are more likely to receive a fabled version of the country's history and politics (see Chapter 1). U.S. schools are probably more instrumental in building support for the nation than the schools in other democracies. The pledge of allegiance, which is recited daily in many U.S. schools, has no equivalent in European countries.

There was a time when the schools contributed greatly to Americans' sense of social equality. Most American children, regardless of family income, attended public schools and studied a fairly standard curriculum. Today, because of the increase in private school enrollment and the sharp contrast between suburban and inner-city districts, the school plays a lesser role in maintaining a sense of equality.

America's colleges and universities also have a socializing effect. The sense of a citizen's obligations—to vote, to be active in community affairs, to take an interest in political news—is stronger among college-educated people than among people with less education. Support for individual rights, such as freedom of speech, is also stronger among this group. These tendencies are due in part to the direct effects of a college education; in the classroom and out, college students learn about and experience civic life. College-educated people are also likely to have more of the skills and contacts that promote political involvement, from which can flow consistent opinions. For example, freedom of expression, like other rights, is prized most highly by those citizens who make active use of it.

Peers

Members of peer groups—friends, neighbors, and co-workers—tend to have similar political views. Belonging to a peer group usually reinforces what a person already believes. One reason is that most people trust the views of their friends and associates. In addition, because members of a peer group share many of the same socializing experiences, they often think along the same lines, with the result that contradictory opinions are not often voiced within the group.

Many individuals are also unwilling to deviate too far from what their peers think. In her book *The Spiral of Silence,* Elisabeth Noelle-Neumann contends that most individuals want to conform and are reluctant to speak out against a dominant opinion, particularly when the issue contains a strong moral component.[25] The result can be the gradual eclipse of deviant opinions. There was a time in America when racist jokes and epithets were part of the everyday speech of many white Americans. The 1960s civil rights movement helped create a climate of opinion that made such expressions less acceptable. As racial slurs decreased in frequency, opinions about racial differences also became more moderate.

The Mass Media

The mass media are another powerful socializing agent. The media's influence, although diffuse and difficult to measure, is nonetheless substantial. While experts disagree, for example, on the extent to which violence on television contributes to the rising level of violence in American society, few hold it entirely blameless.

The media's socializing influence is also felt through its news coverage. Studies indicate that the way in which news stories are "framed" affects people's political perceptions.[26] For example, the public responds more favorably to presidential candidates when they are portrayed as leaders of a political coalition rather than as vote-seeking tacticians. In recent elections, the press

Vice-President Al Gore and Senator Robert Dole appear on NBC's interview show, *Meet the Press.* The news media are an important agent of political socialization. (AP/Wide World Photos)

has tended to frame candidates in the context of strategic manipulation, with the result that the public thinks less highly of the candidates than it did at an earlier time. (The media's influence is examined more fully in Chapter 11.)

Political Leaders and Institutions

People look to political leaders and institutions, particularly the presidency and the political party, as guides to opinion. The level of public approval of a nuclear arms limitation agreement with the USSR rose in 1987 after President Ronald Reagan endorsed the idea. In broader terms, political leaders play a significant role in shaping political debate and opinion through the symbols and slogans they use.[27]

However, the ability of a president to mold opinion has definable limits. Bill Clinton's proposal for a comprehensive change of the nation's health care system had majority support when it was announced in 1993. A year later, after a bitter partisan debate in Congress and fierce attack from the insurance lobby, his plan was opposed by most Americans. They still believed that health care reform was desirable, but they did not think Clinton's plan was the answer. Clinton's declining personal popularity contributed to the change of opinion. Research has found that a president's public support is a key factor in his ability to influence public opinion.[28] When people have doubts about a president's leadership, they are also reluctant to embrace his policy initiatives. (Chapters 8, 13, and 14 discuss further the impact of political leaders and institutions on public opinion.)

Frames of Reference: How Americans Think Politically

What are the frames of reference that guide Americans' opinions? The question is important in at least two respects. First, the ways in which citizens think politically provide clues about the likely effects of public opinion on government. What direction does public opinion take? Do the people want policies that are conservative, liberal, or something in between? A second reason for exploring how the people think politically is that a shared frame of reference can bring citizens together in the pursuit of a common goal. The opinions of millions of Americans would mean almost nothing if each person's views were different from those of all others. If enough people think the same way, however, they may be able to exert political power.

The subject of how Americans think politically fills entire books; here we outline four of the major frames of reference through which Americans evaluate political alternatives. The first tends to unite Americans; the other three give rise to differences of opinion among them.

CULTURAL THINKING: COMMON IDEAS

As we indicated in Chapter 1, Americans are unusual in their commitment to a set of ideals that nearly define the nature of the American political experience. Such principles as individualism, equality, and self-government have always meant somewhat different things to different people but nonetheless are a source of opinion consensus.[29] For example, most Americans reject government programs aimed at redistributing wealth from richer citizens to poorer ones. Such policies are common in western Europe but have had little appeal for Americans. Unlike Europe, which has had universal health care for nearly half a century, the United States retains a medical system in which access to health care depends significantly on the ability to pay for it. The major reason for the difference is Americans' deep-seated belief in individualism. A Times-Mirror survey found, for example, that only 23 percent of Americans, compared with 50 percent of Germans, 62 percent of the British, and 71 percent of the Spanish, agreed fully that "it is the responsibility of the government to take care of very poor people who can't take care of themselves."[30]

Americans' cultural ideals are a powerful, if inexact, influence on public opinion. They affect the way in which disputes are argued and affect what people regard as reasonable and desirable. Americans' ideals serve to define the general boundaries of acceptable political action and opinion.

IDEOLOGICAL THINKING: THE OUTLOOK FOR SOME

Commentators on public opinion in the United States often use such ideological words as "liberal" and "conservative" in describing how ordinary citizens think about political issues. In the early 1980s, for example, analysts spoke of "a conservative tide" that was supposedly sweeping the country and displacing the liberal trend that had dominated American politics for most of the preceding fifty years. Liberalism and conservatism are examples of an **ideology,** a consistent pattern of opinion on particular issues that stems from a basic underlying belief or beliefs.[31] An ideology is a relatively sophisticated pattern of thought. It requires that individuals have general beliefs that they can apply when responding to emerging issues. Their political opinions are thus highly structured and consistent; they form in predictable ways around basic beliefs.

ideology A consistent pattern of opinion on political issues that stems from a basic underlying belief or set of beliefs.

Ideological beliefs are concentrated among those who are most active politically. Studies indicate, for example, that delegates to national presidential nominating conventions are much more likely to think ideologically than either the rank-and-file voters within their party or the public as a whole.[32] Since activists are more visible than other citizens, they contribute to an impression that ideological belief systems are commonplace.

In fact, most Americans do not have a well-defined ideology. In an early study of ideology, Philip Converse concluded that the average citizen "fails to develop global views about politics."[33] Most people do not apply a broad framework when judging political issues, nor do they hold a highly consistent set of opinions. Converse concluded that only about 10 percent of citizens adhere to an ideology. Other scholars disputed this estimate and also questioned whether Converse's method of analysis was too restrictive.[34] All scholars agree, however, that only a minority of citizens—no more than one in three—readily understand and apply an ideological frame of reference to political issues.

Although most citizens do not have a "true" ideology, analysts have sometimes found it useful to apply ideological terms in describing tendencies in the way that ordinary citizens think about politics. The conventional approach

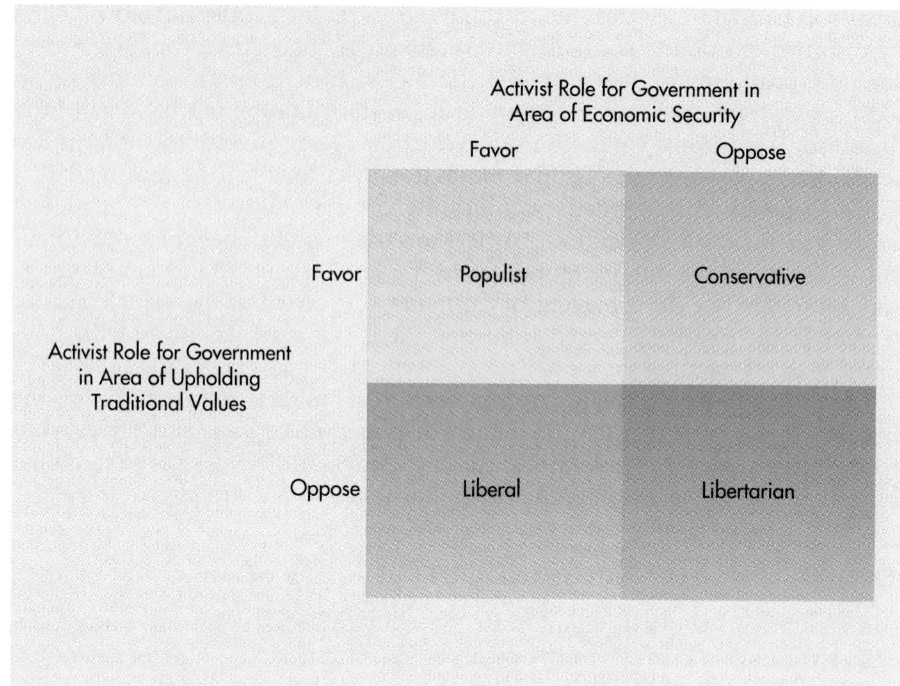

FIGURE 6-2 Types of Ideologies Americans can be classified as liberals, conservatives, populists, or libertarians, depending on their attitudes toward the government's role in the areas of economic security and social values.

has been to classify people as liberals or conservatives based on self-identification in response to a question of the following type: "Generally speaking, do you think of yourself as a conservative, a liberal, or a moderate?" Analysts have found, however, that many people are unable to say what is meant by "liberalism" and "conservatism."[35] Moreover, the terms are not entirely consistent in their relationship to government action. For example, whereas conservatism involves a rejection of government activism in the economic realm, it involves the use of government as a means of upholding traditional social values.

As a consequence, survey researchers have recently begun to measure ideological tendencies in the mass public through indirect means. They have asked respondents two questions: whether government should play a large role in determining the distribution of economic benefits in society and whether government should actively promote a particular set of social values. The yes-no responses to the two questions have been the basis for establishing four ideological types: conservatives, liberals, populists, and libertarians (see Figure 6-2).

conservatives Those who emphasize the marketplace as the means of distributing economic benefits but look to government to uphold traditional social values.

liberals Those who favor activist government as an instrument of economic security and equitable redistribution of resources but reject the notion that government should favor a particular set of social values.

Conservatives are defined as individuals who emphasize the marketplace as the means of distributing economic benefits but look to government to uphold traditional social values. In contrast, **liberals** favor activist government as an instrument of economic redistribution but reject the notion that government should favor a particular set of social values. True liberals and conservatives could be expected to differ, for instance, on the issues of homosexual rights (a social values question) and government-guaranteed health care (an economic distribution question). Liberals would view homosexuality as a private issue and believe that government should see to it that everyone has access to adequate medical care. Conservatives would oppose government-mandated access to health care and favor government policies that actively discourage homosexual lifestyles. **Populists** are defined as individuals who share with conservatives a concern for traditional values but, like liberals, favor an active role for government in providing economic security. **Libertarians** are opposed to government intervention in both the economic and social spheres.[36]

populists Those who favor activist government as a means of promoting both economic security and traditional values.

libertarians Those who oppose government as an instrument of traditional values and of economic security.

In sum, libertarians are the most committed to individual freedom, and populists are the most committed to government activism. Conservatives and liberals are committed to individual freedom in one area (the economic sphere for conservatives, the social sphere for liberals) but to government activism in the other (the social sphere for conservatives, the economic sphere for liberals). Of these ideological types, conservatives are the largest group. According to a 1994 Gallup Poll, for example, 30 percent of Americans are conservative, 16 percent are liberal, 20 percent are populist, and 22 percent are libertarian.[37]

GROUP THINKING: THE OUTLOOK OF MANY

Converse's study indicated that groups are a more important reference for Americans than is ideology; subsequent studies have confirmed his finding.[38]

YOUR TURN

IDEOLOGICAL IDENTIFICATION

The Questions:

1. Some people think the government is trying to do too many things that should be left to individuals and businesses. Others think that government should do more to solve our country's problems. Which view is closer to your own?

   Government doing too much

   Government should do more

2. Some people think that the government should promote traditional values in our society. Others think the government should not favor any particular set of values. Which view is closer to your own?

   Government should promote traditional values

   Government should not favor a particular values

What Others Think: These questions are used in combination to measure a person's ideology. Individuals are classified as *conservative* when they agree with the first statement of each question (opposition to government activism except in the promotion of traditional values). They are judged as *liberal* if they agree with the second statement of each question (support for government activism except in the promotion of a particular set of values). Individuals who oppose government activism in each area (agree with the first statement of the first question and the second statement of the second question) are defined as *libertarian.* The *populist* category consists of people who support activist government as a means of both solving problems and upholding traditional values (agree with the second statement of the first question and the first statement of the second question). According to a 1994 CNN/USA Today poll conducted by the Gallup Organization, 20 percent of Americans are populists, 22 percent are libertarians, 30 percent are conservatives, and 16 percent are liberals.

Comment: Most citizens do not have the structured and coherent belief system associated with a true ideology. However, most people do have opinions about traditional values and government activism, which can be used in assigning an ideology to them. You might consider whether the ideological category assigned to you by these questions conforms with the way you have characterized yourself in the past.

★ STATES IN THE NATION

Conservatism and Liberalism: The northeastern states have the highest concentration of citizens who identify themselves as liberals; the southern and mountain states have the most conservatives.

STATE	IDEOLOGICAL TENDENCY
Ala.	Conservative
Alaska	Moderate
Ariz.	Very conservative
Ark.	Conservative
Calif.	Liberal
Colo.	Moderate
Conn.	Liberal
Del.	Moderate
D.C.	Very liberal
Fla.	Conservative
Ga.	Conservative
Hawaii	Moderate
Idaho	Very conservative
Ill.	Moderate
Ind.	Conservative
Iowa	Moderate
Kan.	Moderate
Ky.	Moderate
La.	Very conservative
Maine	Conservative
Md.	Moderate
Mass.	Liberal
Mich.	Moderate
Minn.	Moderate
Miss.	Very conservative
Mo.	Moderate
Mont.	Conservative
Neb.	Conservative
Nev.	Conservative
N.H.	Conservative
N.J.	Liberal
N. Mex.	Conservative
N.Y.	Liberal
N.C.	Very conservative
N.Dak.	Very conservative
Ohio	Moderate
Okla.	Very conservative
Oreg.	Moderate
Pa.	Moderate
R.I.	Liberal
S.C.	Very conservative
S.Dak.	Very conservative
Tenn.	Conservative
Texas	Very conservative
Utah	Very conservative
Vt.	Moderate
Va.	Conservative
Wash.	Moderate
W.Va.	Liberal
Wis.	Moderate
Wyo.	Conservative

SOURCE: Adapted from Gerald C. Wright, Robert S. Erikson, and John P. McIver, "Public Opinion and Policy Liberalism in the American States," *American Journal of Political Science*, 31 (November 1987): 989.

Many Americans see politics through the lens of a group to which they belong or with which they identify. These individuals nearly always pay closer attention to issues that affect the group's interests than to more remote issues. Farmers, for example, are more likely to follow agricultural issues than they are labor-management issues. A group outlook is a source of both consensus and conflict. Farmers generally approve of government price supports for commodities; this opinion unites farmers but pits them against other groups, including consumers.

Because of the country's great size, settlement by various immigrant groups, and economic pluralism, Americans are a very diverse people. Later chapters will examine group tendencies more fully, but it is useful here to mention a few of the major group orientations.

Religion

Religious differences have always been a source of solidarity within a group and conflict with outsiders. At an earlier time, religion was a bitterly divisive force, as newly immigrant Catholics and Jews encountered widespread hostility and discrimination from entrenched Protestant groups. Today, Catholics, Protestants, and Jews share similar opinions on most policy issues.

Nevertheless, some important religious differences remain, although the opposing sides are not always the same. Fundamentalist Protestants and Roman Catholics oppose legalized abortion more strongly than do other Protestants and Jews. In contrast, on some welfare issues, such as food programs for the poor, Catholics and Jews are more supportive than are Protestants, especially those of fundamentalist beliefs. Such differences have at least a partial basis in religious beliefs. A belief in self-reliance, for example, is part of the so-called "Protestant ethic." Attitudes on abortion are tied to religious beliefs about whether human life begins at conception or at a later stage in the development of the fetus.

The most powerful religious force in contemporary American politics is the so-called religious right, which consists primarily of individuals who see themselves as born-again Christians and view the Bible as the infallible truth. Their views on such issues as homosexual rights, abortion, and school prayer differ significantly from those of the population as a whole. A Time/CNN survey found, for example, that born-again Christians are 37 percent more likely than other Americans to agree that "the Supreme Court and the Congress have gone too far in keeping religious and moral values like prayer out of our laws, schools, and many areas of our lives."

Class

Economic class has less influence on political opinion in the United States than in Europe, but it is nevertheless related to opinions on certain economic issues. For example, lower-income Americans are more supportive of social welfare programs, business regulation, and progressive taxation than are those in higher-income categories. An obstacle to class-based politics in the United States is that people with similar incomes, but differing occupations, do not share the same opinions. Support for collective bargaining, for example, is

Two coal miners, one a man and the other a woman, break for lunch. Economic class affects Americans' opinions. The political views of most union members, for example, are more liberal than those of most Americans. (Théodore Vogal/© Rapho/Photo Researchers)

substantially higher among factory workers than among small farmers, service workers, and those in the skilled crafts. The interplay of class and opinion will be examined more closely in Chapter 10, which discusses interest groups.

Region

Region has declined as a basis of political opinions. The increased mobility of the U.S. population has resulted in the relocation of millions of Americans from the Northeast and Midwest to the South and West. Their beliefs on issues such as social welfare tend to be more liberal than those of people who are native to these regions.

Nevertheless, regional differences are still evident in the areas of social welfare, civil rights, and national defense. Conservative opinions on these issues are more prevalent in the southern and mountain states than elsewhere (see box: States in the Nation).

Race

Race, as we saw in Chapter 5, is a significant source of opinion differences. Whites and African Americans differ on issues of integration: black people are more in favor of affirmative action, busing, and other measures designed to promote racial equality and integration. Racial groups also differ on many pocketbook issues, largely as a result of the differences in their economic situations: African Americans are more supportive of social welfare programs and government-backed job and training programs. The crime issue is another area where opinion differences are pronounced and predictable: African

Party loyalities are embedded in government's response to social and economic conditions. The loyalty of African Americans to the Democratic party is largely a consequence of its leadership on civil rights and social welfare issues. (Robert Fox/Impact Visuals)

Americans are less trusting of police and the judicial system. A Harris survey indicated, for example, that 51 percent of whites but only 17 percent of African Americans believe that the justice system treats people of the two races equally.[39]

Gender

Although male-female differences of opinion are small on most issues, gender does affect opinion on some questions. Perhaps surprisingly, these issues are not primarily those that touch directly on sexual equality. Opinion polls indicate that men and women are about equally supportive of affirmative action and do not hold significantly different opinions on abortion rights. But men and women do divide on issues involving physical coercion by the state. For example, in an ABC News/Washington Post survey on January 16, 1991, the night that the United States went to war with Iraq, 84 percent of men but only 68 percent of women said they approved of the action. Table 6-2 provides poll results that indicate the extent of male-female differences on several issues involving the use of physical force.

Men and women also differ, although less so, on social welfare issues. Women are more supportive of government spending for the poor and disadvantaged. This attitude may simply reflect the weaker economic position of women, but some analysts suggest that women have more compassion for society's underdogs. Whatever the reason for these variations, differences in men's and women's opinions are the basis for the *gender gap* that has typified voting in recent elections. Women are more likely than men to support the Democratic party, presumably as a result of its more active support of social

TABLE 6-2 Differences in Male-Female Opinion on Selected Issues Men are more likely than women to support policies that involve the use of force.

	PERCENT WHO AGREE	
Force-Related Issue	*Men*	*Women*
Describe self as a "hawk"—want to step up military effort in Vietnam (1968)	50%	32%
Favor death penalty for those convicted of murder (1988)	83	75
Approve of U.S. having gone to war with Iraq (1991)	84	68
Oppose a ban on possession of handguns (1993)	71	50

SOURCES: Gallup, April 4–9, 1968; Gallup, Sept. 25–Oct. 1, 1988; ABC News/Washington Post, Jan. 16, 1991; Gallup, Dec. 17–19, 1993.

welfare and civil rights programs. In the 1992 presidential election, for example, Bill Clinton's vote was 5 percentage points higher among women. The gap was particularly pronounced among younger women (there was a difference of 10 percent between men and women in the 18 to 29 age group). Women are also more likely than men to support Democratic congressional candidates.

PARTISAN THINKING: THE LINE THAT DIVIDES

In the everyday play of politics, no source of opinion more clearly divides Americans than that of their partisanship. Figure 6-3 provides examples, but they indicate only a few of the differences. On nearly every major issue of economic, social, and foreign policy, Republicans and Democrats have views that are at least somewhat different. In many cases, such as spending programs for the poor, the differences are substantial.

The term **party identification** refers to a person's ingrained sense of loyalty to a political party. Party identification is not formal membership in a party but instead an emotional attachment to a party—the feeling that "I am a Democrat" or "I am a Republican." Scholars and pollsters have typically measured party identification with a question of the following type: "Generally speaking, do you think of yourself as a Republican, a Democrat, an independent, or what?" About 70 percent of adults call themselves Democrats or Republicans. Of the 30 percent who prefer the label "independent," most say they lean slightly toward one party or the other.

party identification The personal sense of loyalty that an individual may feel toward a particular political party.

Early studies of party identification concluded that partisan attitudes were highly stable and seldom changed over the course of adult life.[40] Subsequent studies have shown that party loyalties are more fluid than originally believed; they can be influenced by the issues and candidates of the moment.[41] Nevertheless, most adults do not switch their party loyalties easily, and a substantial proportion never waver from an initial commitment to a party, which can often be traced to childhood influences. Partisanship affects opinions in the same way as other psychological commitments. Just as nationality colors

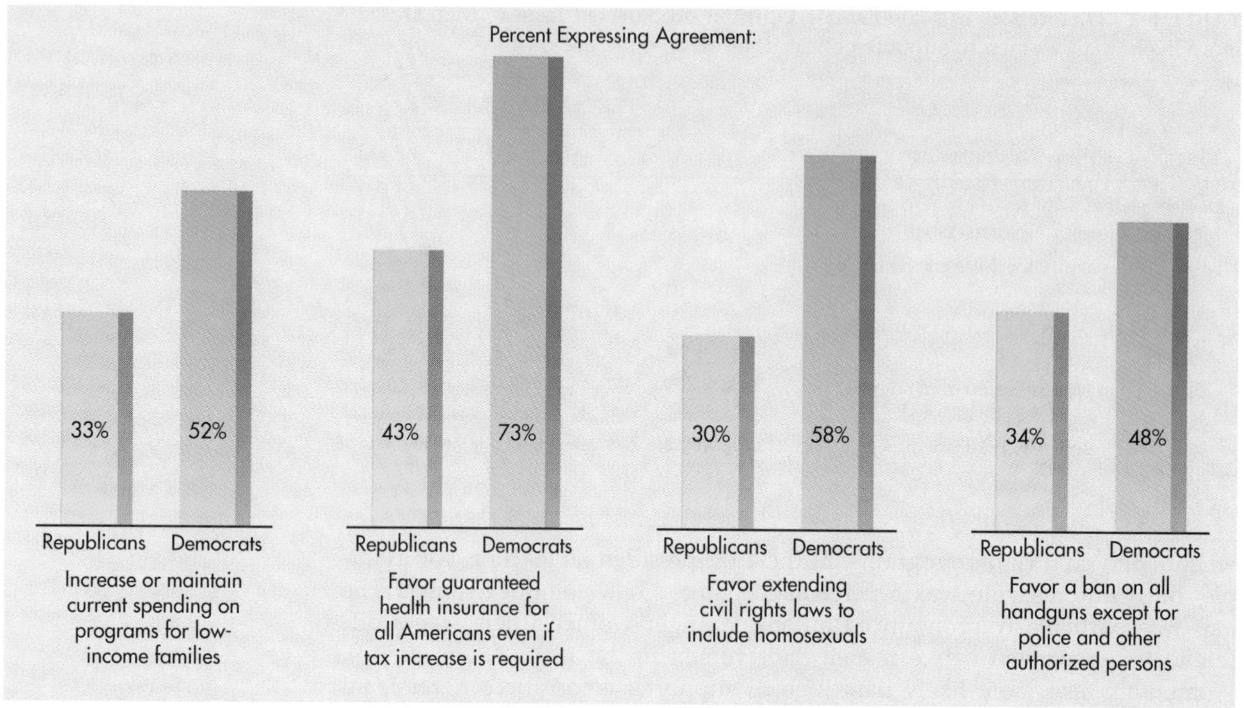

FIGURE 6-3 Partisanship and Issue Opinions
Republicans and Democrats differ significantly in their opinions on many policy issues. *Source: Gallup surveys, in order of questions: April 16–18, 1994; October 28–30, 1993; April 22–24, 1993; December 17–19, 1993.*

people's views of their country, partisanship tints people's political views.

For most people, however, partisanship is not simply a "blind" faith in the party of their choice. Some Republicans and Democrats know very little about their party's traditions, policies, or group commitments and unthinkably embrace the candidates and issues of their party. Party loyalties, however, are not randomly distributed across the population but are embedded in social and economic conditions. The fact that most African Americans are Democrats and most business executives are Republicans is not mere coincidence; their partisanship is rooted in their different life circumstances and the policy traditions of the Democratic and Republican parties.

Once acquired, partisanship affects how people perceive and interpret political developments. But it is not the only influence on their opinions, and it is subject to change when conditions make past loyalties less compelling. The civil rights issue, for example, helped to turn the "Solid South" into a Republican presidential stronghold after nearly a century of staunch support for the Democratic party. Conservative white southerners were comfortable with their Democratic loyalties until their party took the lead in Washington on issues of racial equality. Lyndon Johnson, whose presidency marked the peak of this leadership, lost the South when he ran for a second term in 1964. Johnson received 60 percent of the national vote but failed to carry the states of Alabama, Georgia, Louisiana, Mississippi, and South Carolina, which had never before supported a Republican nominee. Since 1964, these states have consistently backed the GOP in presidential elections.

Partisanship is obviously a strong force in American politics, but its influence is declining. This and other issues of partisanship are examined in depth at various points later in this book, particularly in Chapters 7, 8, 9, 13, and 15.

The Influence of Public Opinion on Policy

Yet unanswered in the discussion is the central question about public opinion: What impact does it have on government?

The fundamental principle of democracy is that the people's view ought to prevail on public issues. It is difficult, however, to put this principle into practice. In any society of appreciable size, it is simply not possible for the people directly to formulate public policies and programs. However, democracy can be said to exist when officials take the public's views into account when making policy decisions and when the people have recourse to free and fair elections when they believe their opinions are being ignored.[42]

Some analysts argue that the public's views do not count for enough; the elites, it is claimed, are so entrenched and remote they pay little attention to the preferences of ordinary citizens.[43] The most comprehensive study ever conducted of the relationship between public opinion and policy, however, concluded otherwise. In a study spanning fifty years of trends, Benjamin Page and Robert Shapiro found a substantial relationship between changes in public opinion and subsequent changes in public policy, particularly on highly visible issues. More often than not, policy changed in response to opinion rather than the reverse. In addition, the more important the issue, the more likely that policy adapted to changes in public opinion. Page and Shapiro concluded that U.S. officials are reasonably responsive to public opinion.[44]

Not all scholars have interpreted the evidence on public opinion and policy so favorably,[45] but there is little question that the public's views do have an impact. Public opinion is rarely powerful enough to force officials into a specific course of action, but public opinion does serve as a guiding force in public policy. There are many actions, for example, that officials dare *not* take for fear of public retribution. No politician who wants to stay in office is likely

★ CRITICAL THINKING

Should Leaders Govern According to Opinion Polls? These days, public officials and candidates for public office routinely use public opinion polls to keep track of what the people are thinking. Some observers argue that polls contribute to effective government by keeping political leaders from getting too far out of line with the public's thinking.

Other observers claim that poll results cannot substitute for leadership. Noting that the mass public is usually poorly informed about policy issues, Walter Lippmann concluded that leaders must take the responsibility for devising workable policies that the public, in the long run, will accept.

What is your view on the use of polls in governing? Should leaders rely heavily on public opinion polls in making their governing decisions? Or should leaders mainly apply their own judgments of the public interest?

Bags containing the bodies of American soldiers killed in the Vietnam war await shipment back to the United States. The large number of American casualties during the war helped to turn public opinion against U.S. involvement in Vietnam. (UPI/Bettmann Newsphotos)

to say, for example, that social security for the elderly should be abolished. And there are many actions that politicians willingly take in order to appeal to public opinion. In 1994, for example, Congress passed a $30-billion crime bill that authorized the building of more prisons, the placement of more police on the streets, and tough mandatory sentences for certain crimes. The legislation was enacted at a time when crime ranked first in the polls as America's major problem and despite predictions from criminal justice experts that it would not significantly deter crime.

Such examples, however, do not provide an answer to the question of whether government is *sufficiently* responsive to public opinion. This question, as was discussed earlier in the chapter, is a normative one, the answer to which rests on assumptions about the proper relationship between people's everyday opinions and what government does. The question is also complicated by the fact that politics includes a battle over the control of public opinion. People's views are neither fixed nor simply a product of personal circumstances. Public opinion is dynamic and can be changed, activated, and crystallized through political action.

In fact, one of the best indicators of the power of public opinion is the effort of political leaders to harness it in support of their goals. In American politics, popular demand for a policy is a powerful argument for it. For this reason and others, great effort is made to organize and represent public opinion through elections (Chapter 8), political parties (Chapter 9), interest groups (Chapter 10), the news media (Chapter 11), and political institutions (Chapters 12 to 17). Later chapters will also examine the direct impact of public opinion in particular policy areas: the economy (Chapter 18), social welfare (Chapter 19), and foreign affairs (Chapter 20).

Summary

Public opinion can be defined as those opinions held by ordinary citizens which are openly expressed. Public officials have many ways of assessing public opinion, such as the outcomes of elections, but have increasingly come to rely on public opinion polls. There are many possible sources of error in polls, and surveys sometimes present a misleading portrayal of the public's views. However, a properly conducted poll can provide an accurate indication of what the public is thinking and can dissuade political leaders from thinking that the views of the most vocal citizens (such as demonstrators and letter writers) are also the views of the broader public.

Individual opinions gain power to the degree that others share a similar view. Public opinion thus has the force of numbers. A major source of common opinions among Americans is their cultural beliefs, such as individualism, which result in a range of acceptable and unacceptable policy alternatives. Agreement can also stem from a shared ideology, although most citizens do not have a strong and consistent ideological attachment. In addition, individuals share opinions as a result of a shared party loyalty or a shared group circumstance, notably religion, class, region, race, or gender.

The process by which individuals acquire their political opinions is called political socialization. During childhood the family and schools are important sources of basic political attitudes, such as beliefs about the parties and the nature of the U.S. political and economic systems. Many of the basic orientations that Americans acquire during childhood remain with them in adulthood, but socialization is a continuing process. Major shifts in opinion during adulthood are usually the consequence of changing political conditions; for example, the Great Depression of the 1930s was the catalyst for wholesale changes in Americans' opinions on the government's economic role. There are also short-term fluctuations in opinion that result from new political issues, problems, and events. Individuals' opinions in these cases are affected by prior beliefs, peers, political leaders, and the news media. Events themselves are also a significant short-term influence on opinions.

Public opinion has a significant influence on government but seldom determines exactly what government will do in a particular instance. Public opinion serves to constrain the policy choices of officials. Some policy actions are beyond the range of possibility because the public will not accept change in existing policy or will not seriously consider policy that seems clearly at odds with basic American values. Evidence indicates that officials are reasonably attentive to public opinion on highly visible and controversial issues of public policy.

Major Concepts

conservatives
ideology
liberals
libertarians
party identification
political socialization
population
populists
probability sample
public opinion
public opinion poll
sample
sampling error

Suggested Readings

Asher, Herb. *Polling and the Public: What Every Citizen Should Know*, 2d ed. Washington, D.C.: Congressional Quarterly Press, 1991. A book that explains survey methods, analyses, and pitfalls in a way the ordinary citizen can understand.

Brace, Paul, and Barbara Hinckley. *Follow the Leader: Opinion Polls and Modern Presidents.* New York: Basic Books, 1992. An analysis that concludes that presidents follow public opinion closely, even too closely, in the making of decisions.

Dionne, E. J. *Why Americans Hate Politics.* New York: Simon & Schuster, 1991. An insightful account of the obstacles that rigid ideologies pose to the development of policies that the American public would prefer.

Jennings, M. Kent, and Richard Niemi. *Generations and Politics: A Panel Study of Young Adults and Their Parents.* Princeton, N.J.: 1981. A careful study of the relationship over time between the political beliefs of parents and their children.

Lippmann, Walter. *Public Opinion.* New York: Free Press, 1965. The classic analysis of public opinion (originally published in 1922).

McCloskey, Herbert, and John Zaller. *The American Ethos: Public Attitudes toward Capitalism and Democracy.* Cambridge, Mass.: Harvard University Press, 1984. A study of how American's ideals underpin capitalism and democracy and narrow the range of political choices.

Neuman, W. Russell, *The Paradox of Mass Politics: Knowledge and Opinion in the American Electorate.* Cambridge, Mass.: Harvard University Press, 1986. An assessment of how democracy works, given that most citizens are not particularly interested in or informed about policy and government.

Noelle-Neumann, Elisabeth. *The Spiral of Silence,* 2d ed. Chicago: University of Chicago Press, 1993. An intriguing theory of how public opinion is formed and muted.

Popkin, Samuel L. *The Reasoning Voter: Communication and Persuasion in Presidential Campaigns.* Chicago: University of Chicago Press, 1991. An intriguing analysis of how citizens form reasonable opinions despite their low level of information about politics.

Yankelovich, Daniel. *Coming to Public Judgment.* Syracuse, N.Y.: Syracuse University Press, 1991. A prescriptive book on how the public can be brought more fully into the policy process despite the complexity of modern issues.

CHAPTER 7

POLITICAL PARTICIPATION AND VOTING: EXPRESSING THE POPULAR WILL

We are concerned in public affairs, but immersed in our private ones.
—*Walter Lippman*[1]

It was the year of the angry voter. President Bill Clinton's ambitious health-care reform proposal had gone down to defeat in Congress after yearlong partisan wrangling and without so much as a vote being taken on the floor of either the House or the Senate. Legislation to build more prisons and toughen the penalties for crime had been enacted, but only after the bill nearly succumbed to parliamentary tricks. Promised reforms of lobbying and campaign spending never materialized. In a blistering editorial, *The New York Times* described the 103d Congress as the least productive and most fractious in memory.[2]

Americans were thoroughly disenchanted with Washington politics as they prepared to vote in the midterm congressional elections. Polls indicated that confidence in Congress had fallen to a record low: fewer than 20 percent of Americans said they trusted the institution to represent their interests. President Bill Clinton was also faulted. Americans criticized his governing style and were dismayed by the charges of personal misconduct that swirled constantly around him. His approval rating approached 40 percent, a near low for a president two years into his term.

On election day, the voters' anger produced a Republican victory of historic proportions. A net loss of 52 Democratic seats placed the House of Representatives in Republican hands for the first time since 1954. The Democrats also lost control of the Senate, which they had held for all but six years since 1954. Newt Gingrich, the House Republican leader, called the election "an American revolution," saying it was a final repudiation of the liberal policies that had marked the Democratic party since the presidency of Lyndon Johnson.

House Speaker-in-waiting Newt Gingrich and incoming Senate majority leader Robert Dole meet with reporters after House and Senate Republicans had caucused to select them as the party's congressional leaders. The Republicans' stunning victory in the 1994 midterm elections was achieved with a turnout of less than 40 percent of the nation's potential voters. (AP/Wide World Photos)

Although the Republicans' sweeping victory was the outstanding feature of the 1994 congressional elections, there was another feature worth noting: less than 40 percent of the adult population voted. Of the nearly 200 million Americans of voting age, roughly 125 million did not cast a ballot on election day. Despite the public's expression of anger at their elected representatives and despite a concerted get-out-the-vote campaign by the political parties, the media, and public service groups, the number of people who did not vote was far greater than the margin of the Republican victory. The GOP's congressional candidates outpolled their Democratic opponents by 4 percent of the total vote, a margin that seems substantial until we consider the fact that 15 times that number of adult Americans did not bother to vote in 1994. A CNN/USA Today poll showed that nonvoters preferred Democratic candidates by nearly a 10 percent margin. Had they voted in 1994, the Democrats, and not the Republicans, would have won a landslide victory.

political participation A sharing in activities designed to influence public policy and leadership, such as voting, joining political parties and interest groups, writing to elected officials, demonstrating for political causes, and giving money to political candidates.

Voting is a form of **political participation**—a sharing in activities designed to influence public policy and leadership. Political participation involves other activities in addition to voting, such as joining political parties and interest groups, writing to elected officials, demonstrating for political causes, and giving money to political candidates.

Democratic societies are distinguished by their emphasis on citizen participation. The concept of self-government rests on the idea that ordinary people have a right, even an obligation, to involve themselves in the affairs of state. A political system that claims to represent the public's interest is not necessarily a truly democratic system; citizens must also be given meaningful opportunities to participate in the process. From this perspective, the extent of political participation—how much and by whom—is a measure of how fully democratic a society is.[3]

The question of participation also extends to the reasons people are politically involved or not involved. It is one thing if political participation is like attendance at a rock concert, which is mostly a matter of individual taste and proximity, and quite another if participation is like attendance at an elite prep school, which is mostly a matter of social privilege. A democratic political system implies that society will not place substantial barriers in the way of those who want to participate. As we will see in this chapter, differences in the extent of political participation among Americans are explained by both individual and systemic factors, although the latter are more influential in the United States than in most other western democracies. One result is that the participation rate in U.S. elections is less than that of other countries, particularly among citizens of lower income and less education. The major points made in this chapter are the following:

- ★ *Voter turnout in U.S. elections is low in comparison with that of other democratic nations.* The reasons for this difference include the nature of U.S. election laws, particularly those pertaining to registration requirements and the scheduling of elections.
- ★ *Most citizens do not participate actively in politics in ways other than voting.* Only a small proportion of Americans can be classified as political activists.
- ★ *Most Americans make a sharp distinction between their personal lives and national life.* This attitude reduces their incentive to participate and contributes to a pattern of participation dominated by citizens with higher levels of income and education.

Voter Participation

At the nation's founding, **suffrage**—the right to vote—was restricted to property-owning males. Tom Paine ridiculed this policy in *Common Sense.* Observing that a man whose only item of property was a jackass would lose his right to vote if the jackass died, Paine asked, "Now tell me, which was the voter, the man or the jackass?" It was not until the 1820s that a majority of states had extended suffrage to propertyless white males, a change made possible by their continued demand for the vote and by the realization on the part of the wealthy that the nation's abundance and openness were natural protections against an assault on property rights by the voting poor.

suffrage The right to vote.

Women did not secure the vote until 1920, with the ratification of the Nineteenth Amendment. In the 1870s Susan B. Anthony tried to vote in her hometown of Rochester, New York, asserting that she had a right to do so as a U.S. citizen. The men who placed her under arrest charged her with "illegal voting" and insisted that her proper place was in the home. By 1920, men had run out of pretexts for keeping the vote from women. The best argument that the antisuffragists could muster was that women should not vote because they had no voting experience. Senator Wendell Phillips expressed the pro-suffrage view: "One of two things is true: either woman is like man—and if she is, then a ballot based on brains belongs to her as well as to him. Or she is different, and then man does not know how to vote for her as she herself does."[4]

After a hard-fought, decades-long campaign, American women finally won the right to vote in 1920. (Culver Pictures)

Black Americans had to wait nearly fifty years longer than women to be granted full suffrage. Blacks seemed to have won the right to vote with passage of the Fifteenth Amendment after the Civil War, but as we saw in Chapter 5, they were effectively disenfranchised in the South by a number of electoral tricks, including poll taxes, literacy tests, and whites-only primary elections. The poll tax was a fee of several dollars that had to be paid before one could register to vote. Since most blacks in the South were too poor to pay it, the poll tax barred them from voting. Not until the ratification of the Twenty-fourth Amendment in 1964 was the poll tax outlawed in federal elections. Supreme Court decisions and the Voting Rights Act of 1965 swept away other legal barriers to fuller participation of African Americans.

Today virtually any American—rich or poor, man or woman, black or white—who is determined to vote can legally and actually do so. Americans attach great importance to the power of their votes. They claim that voting is their greatest source of influence over political leadership and their strongest protection against an uncaring or corrupt government.[5] In view of this attitude and the historical struggle of various groups to gain voting rights, the surprising fact is that Americans are not active voters. Millions of them choose not to vote regularly, a tendency that sets them apart from citizens of most other western democracies.

FACTORS IN VOTER TURNOUT: THE UNITED STATES IN COMPARATIVE PERSPECTIVE

voter turnout The proportion of persons of voting age who actually vote in a given election.

Voter turnout is the proportion of persons of voting age who actually vote in a given election. Since 1920 the level of turnout in presidential elections has never exceeded 63 percent; thus a third or more of voting-age Americans have stayed away from the polls at each election (see Figure 7-1). The turnout level in recent presidential elections has averaged only slightly more than 50 percent. There was an upsurge in turnout to 55 percent in 1992, but the level then fell to 49 percent in 1996, the first time since 1924 that a majority of adults did not cast a presidential ballot. Turnout is even lower in the midterm congressional elections that take place between presidential elections. Midterm election turnout has not reached 50 percent since 1920, nor made it past the 40 percent mark since 1970. After a recent midterm election, the cartoonist Rigby showed an election clerk eagerly asking a stray cat that had wandered into a polling place, "Are you registered?"[6]

Nonvoting is far more prevalent in the United States than in nearly all other democracies (see box: How the United States Compares). In recent decades, turnout in major national elections has averaged less than 60 percent in the United States, compared with more than 90 percent in Belgium, more than 80 percent in France and Denmark, and more than 70 percent in Great Britain and Germany.[7] The disparity in turnout between the United States and other nations is not as great as these official voting rates indicate. Some nations calculate turnout solely on the basis of eligible adults, while the United States bases its figures on all adults, including noncitizens and other ineligible groups. Nevertheless, even when such statistical disparities are corrected, turnout in U.S. elections remains low in comparison with that of nearly every other western democracy.

Voting does not require vast amounts of time. It takes most people longer to go to a video store and select a movie than it takes to go to the neighborhood polling place and cast a ballot. Thus, the explanation for the relatively low turnout rate of Americans must entail considerations other than the time it takes to vote. The major factors that depress turnout in U.S. elections in comparison with other democracies include registration requirements, the frequency of elections, and the lack of clear-cut differences between the political parties.

FIGURE 7-1 Voter Turnout in Presidential Elections, 1896–1996 Voter turnout declined after registration was instituted at the turn of the century and has stayed low for most national elections ever since. *Source: U.S. Bureau of the Census.*

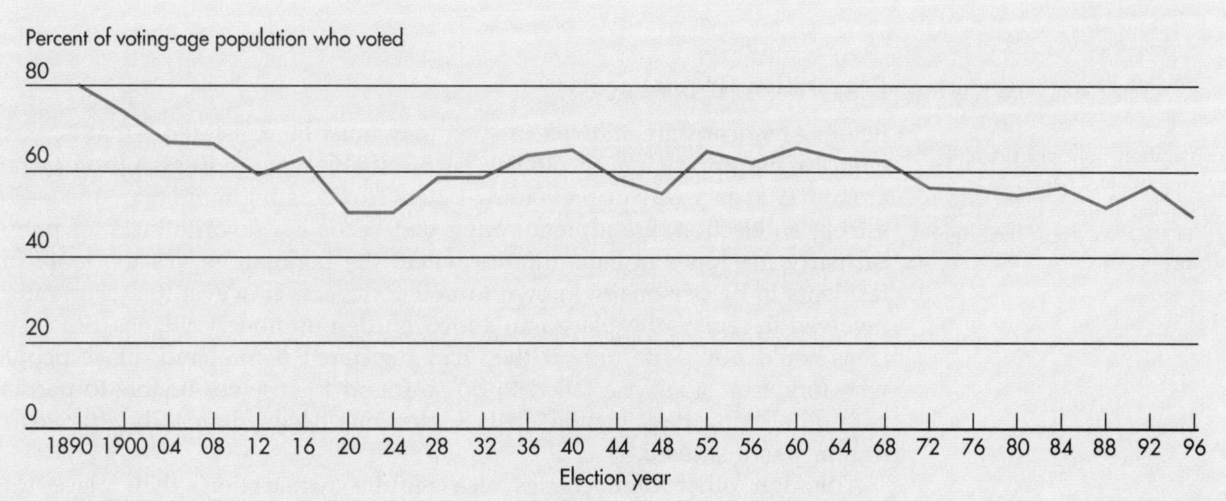

HOW THE UNITED STATES COMPARES

VOTER TURNOUT

The United States ranks near the bottom among the world's democracies in the percentage of eligible citizens who participate in national elections. One reason for the low voter turnout is that individual Americans are responsible for registering to vote, whereas in most other democracies, voters are automatically registered by government officials. In addition, unlike some other democracies, the United States does not encourage voting by holding elections on the weekend or imposing penalties, such as fines, on those who do not participate.

Another factor affecting the turnout rate in the United States is the absence of a major labor or socialist party, which would serve to bring lower-income citizens to the polls. In democracies where such parties exist, the turnout difference between upper- and lower-income groups is relatively small. In the United States, however, lower-income persons are much less likely to vote than higher-income persons.

Country	*Voter Turnout*	*Personal Registration?*	*Social Democrat, Socialist, or Labor Party?*
Belgium	92%	No	Yes
Italy	86	No	Yes
France	85	Yes	Yes
Denmark	83	No	Yes
Austria	82	No	Yes
Germany	78	No	Yes
Great Britain	78	No	Yes
Canada	69	No	No
Japan	67	No	Yes
United States	55	Yes	No

SOURCE: Foreign embassies, except data on United States, which is based on Federal Elections Commission information.

Registration Requirements

registration The practice of placing citizens' names on an official list of voters before they are eligible to exercise their right to vote.

Before Americans are allowed to vote, they must be registered—that is, their names must appear on an official list of eligible voters. **Registration** began around 1900 as a way of preventing voters from casting more than one ballot during an election. Fraudulent voting had become a favorite tactic of political party machines in communities where the population was too large for residents to be personally known to poll watchers. However, the extra effort involved in registering placed an added burden on honest citizens. Since citizens could now vote only if they had registered beforehand, those people who forgot or otherwise failed to do so found themselves unable to participate on election day. Turnout in U.S. elections declined steadily after registration was instituted.[8]

Although other democracies also require registration, they place this responsibility on government. In European nations, public officials have the duty to enroll citizens on registration lists. The United States—in keeping with its individualistic culture—is the only democracy in which registration is the individual's responsibility.[9] In addition, registration laws have traditionally been established by the state governments, and some states make it relatively difficult for citizens to qualify. Registration periods and locations are usually not highly publicized, and many citizens simply do not know when or where to register.[10] Eligibility can also be a problem. In most states, a citizen must establish legal residency by living in the same place for a minimum period, usually thirty days but sometimes as long as fifty days, before becoming eligible to register.

States with a tradition of lenient registration laws generally have a higher turnout than other states. Maine, Minnesota, and Oregon allow people to register at their polling place on election day, and these states rank high in voter turnout. Those states that have erected the most barriers are in the South, where restrictive registration was originally intended to prevent black people from voting. These historical differences continue to be reflected in state voter turnout levels (see box: States in the Nation).

One reason all states have not simplified their registration procedures is that many state and local officials, regardless of what they may say publicly, are not really interested in adding lots of new voters to the registration lists. Registration is not merely an administrative issue, but also a deeply political one. An increase or decrease in voter turnout can alter the outcome of elections. Poor and less educated voters are particularly discouraged by registration requirements. They are less likely to know when and where to register and, when they do, to have the time and transportation to get there. "The rich have the capacity to participate with or without assistance," Benjamin Ginsberg writes. "When assistance is given, it is primarily the poor who benefit."[11]

In 1993, in an effort to increase registration levels nationwide, Congress enacted a voting registration law known as "motor voter." Its supporters pre-

In Austin, Texas, a door-to-door drive simplifies voter registration. Many people fail to register to vote in states that impose more complex requirements and restrictions. (Bob Daemmrich/The Image Works)

★ STATES IN THE NATION

Turnout in the 1994 Congressional Elections: Southern states have a tradition of more restrictive suffrage; they tend even today to have low rates of voter turnout.

STATE	VOTER TURNOUT (PERCENT)	RANK
Ala.	38.0	31
Alaska	42.7	17
Ariz.	37.3	33
Ark.	39.4	27
Calif.	33.9	42
Colo.	41.0	24
Conn.	45.8	12
D.C.	37.2	34
Del.	39.6	26
Fla.	38.5	30
Ga.	29.9	48
Hawaii	41.0	23
Idaho	51.5	6
Ill.	35.3	40
Ind.	35.6	39
Iowa	46.7	11
Kan.	43.4	16
Ky.	27.4	49
La.	26.7	51
Maine	54.4	4
Md.	36.3	38
Mass.	47.5	10
Mich.	44.1	15
Minn.	52.6	5
Miss.	31.9	46
Mo.	45.5	14
Mont.	55.9	3
Neb.	48.1	8
Nev.	34.9	41
N.H.	36.8	37
N.J.	33.9	44
N. Mex.	38.9	28
N.Y.	37.1	35
N.C.	27.6	50
N.Dak.	50.1	7
Ohio	41.1	22
Okla.	41.6	19
Oreg.	41.2	21
Pa.	38.8	29
R.I.	45.6	13
S.C.	34.0	43
S.Dak.	59.7	1
Tenn.	37.7	32
Texas	33.4	45
Utah	41.7	18
Vt.	48.0	9
Va.	40.9	25
Wash.	36.7	36
W.Va.	30.1	47
Wis.	41.4	20
Wyo.	58.7	2
National average	37.8	—

SOURCE: Federal Election Commission.

dict that the legislation, so named because it requires states to permit people to register to vote when applying for a driver's license (it also requires states to provide registration through mail and at certain state welfare offices), will add as many as 50 million new voters to registration rolls by the end of the century. Other observers believe the figure will be much lower, inasmuch as state agencies cannot pressure driver's-license and welfare applicants into registering. Congressional Republicans made their support for the legislation contingent upon the inclusion of this provision. They had blocked the bill for several years, recognizing that a liberalized registration policy would mainly add lower-income Americans to the registration rolls, and hence benefit the Democrats.[12] Republican governors in California and a few other states refused to implement the new law, which led the Justice Department to file suit in 1995 to force compliance.

Frequency of Elections

Suppose you are a U.S. citizen who is determined to intelligently exercise the right to vote at every conceivable opportunity. Your job would not be easy. You would have to obtain information on a large number of candidates running for a wide variety of offices, from President of the United States to membership on the local school board.

The United States holds more elections than any other nation. No other democracy has elections for the lower chamber of its national legislature (the equivalent of the U.S. House of Representatives) as often as every two years, and none schedules elections for chief executive as often as every four years.[13] In addition, elections of state and local officials in the United States are often scheduled separately from national races. Two-thirds of the states elect their governors in nonpresidential election years,[14] and 60 percent of U.S. cities hold elections of municipal officials in odd-numbered years.[15]

This staggered scheduling reflects in some cases a deliberate effort by state and local officials to insulate their election races from the possible effects of other campaigns. During Franklin D. Roosevelt's four terms as president, for example, Republicans in several states, including New York and Connecticut, backed constitutional amendments that required gubernatorial races to be held in nonpresidential years. The purpose was to prevent other Democratic candidates from riding into office on Roosevelt's coattails.

The frequency of U.S. elections reduces turnout by increasing the effort required to participate in all of them.[16] Most European nations have less frequent elections, and the responsibility of voting is thus less burdensome. Many European nations also schedule their elections on Sundays or declare election day to be a national holiday, thus making it more convenient for working people to vote. In the United States, elections are traditionally held on Tuesdays, and most people must vote before or after work.

The contrast with European practice is especially marked in the case of primary elections. The United States is the only democratic nation in which party nominees are commonly chosen by voters through primary elections rather than by party leaders.[17] Consequently, Americans are asked to vote twice to fill a single office. Many voters skip the primaries, preferring to vote just once, in the general election. In statewide primaries, the average voter turnout is less than 30 percent, substantially lower than the turnout in general elections.

Party Differences

An additional explanation for low voter turnout in the United States has to do with voters' perception that there is not much difference between the major political parties. More than half of Americans claim that it does not make a big difference whether the Republicans or the Democrats gain control of government.[18] This belief is not entirely unfounded. The two major American political parties do not normally differ greatly in their policies. Each party depends on citizens of all economic interests and social backgrounds for support; consequently, neither party can afford to take an extreme position that would alienate any sizable segment of the electorate. For example, both parties share a commitment to the private enterprise system and to social security for the elderly (see Chapter 9).

Parties in Europe tend to divide more sharply over economic policies. There the choice between a conservative party and a socialist party may mean a choice between private and government ownership of major industries. Studies indicate that turnout is higher in nations whose political parties represent clear-cut alternatives, particularly when religious or class divisions are involved. Conversely, turnout is lower when, as in the United States, a nation's parties compete for the loyalty of voters of all religions and classes.[19] European parties, particularly those on the left, are also more closely tied to other organizations, such as labor unions, which assist in the mobilization of the electorate.[20]

WHY SOME AMERICANS VOTE AND OTHERS DO NOT

Even though turnout is lower in the United States than in other democracies, some Americans do vote in all or nearly all elections. But other Americans seldom or never vote. What accounts for such *individual* differences?

The factors that account for differences in public opinion (see Chapter 6) are not in all cases related to turnout differences. The turnout rates of men and women, for example, are similar. Among older women the voting rate is below that of men, but once age and educational differences are accounted for, sex is not related to turnout differences.[21] Race was once a very significant predictor of turnout but has become less important. African Americans still have a substantially lower turnout rate than whites, but the difference, which is about 10 percent in presidential elections, is far less than the 40 percent that existed even as recently as 1960 (see Chapter 5).

Large differences in voter turnout are associated with citizens' sense of civic involvement, age, education, and economic class.

Feelings of Civic Duty, Apathy, and Alienation

Regular voters are characterized by a strong sense of **civic duty**—that is, they regard participation in elections as one of the main responsibilities of citizenship. By election day in 1992, it was clear from the polls that Bill Clinton would handily defeat George Bush, yet regular voters were undeterred. Although they knew their votes would not sway the election, they voted anyway in order to fulfill their duty as citizens. This sense of duty is an attitude

civic duty The belief of an individual that civic and political participation is a responsibility of citizenship.

that most individuals acquire as part of their adolescent and childhood political socialization. When parents vote regularly and take an interest in politics, their children are likely to grow up viewing the vote as an important expression of their citizenship. Schools reinforce this belief by stressing the importance of the right to vote.

apathy A feeling of personal noninterest or unconcern with politics.

Many citizens do not have a strong sense of civic duty, and some of them display almost no interest in politics. **Apathy** is the term that describes a general lack of interest in or concern with politics. Just as some people would not attend the Super Bowl even if it were free and being played across the street, some people would not bother to vote even if a ballot were delivered to their door. As with civic duty, a sense of apathy is often the consequence of adolescent and childhood socialization. When parents disparage voting and other forms of political participation, their children are likely to hold a similar view when they reach voting age.

However, voter turnout is also affected by the degree to which people believe that their participation will make a difference. The level of turnout tends to increase when citizens have a high degree of trust in government and to fall when they are politically disillusioned.[22] Turnout in U.S. presidential elections dropped by 10 percentage points between 1958 and 1980, a period in which Americans' trust in Washington declined sharply under the onslaught of the Vietnam war, the Watergate scandal, economic stagnation, and other national problems (see Figure 7-2). After 1980, the public's confidence in the national government rose somewhat but at no time came close to reaching its earlier level. Trust in government began to fall again in 1988 and recently reached a record low of less than 20 percent.

alienation A feeling of personal powerlessness that includes the notion that government does not care about the opinions of people like oneself.

Alienation is the term that describes a sense of personal powerlessness that includes the notion that government does not care about the opinions of peo-

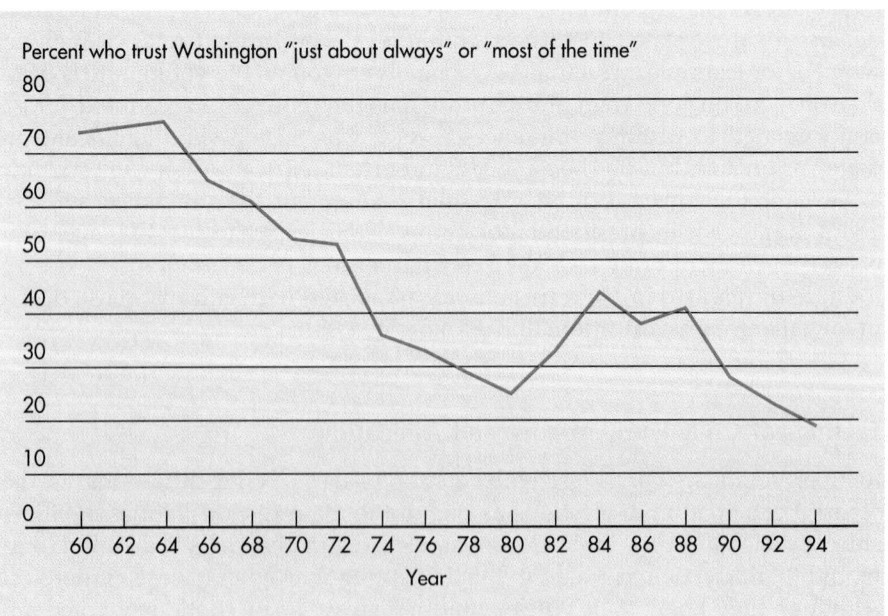

FIGURE 7-2 Confidence in the National Government
Americans' trust in Washington has declined sharply in recent decades; this growing sense of alienation has been paralleled by a decline in voter turnout. *Source: National Election Studies surveys, University of Michigan, except for the 1994 data, which are based on a New York Times/CBS survey.*

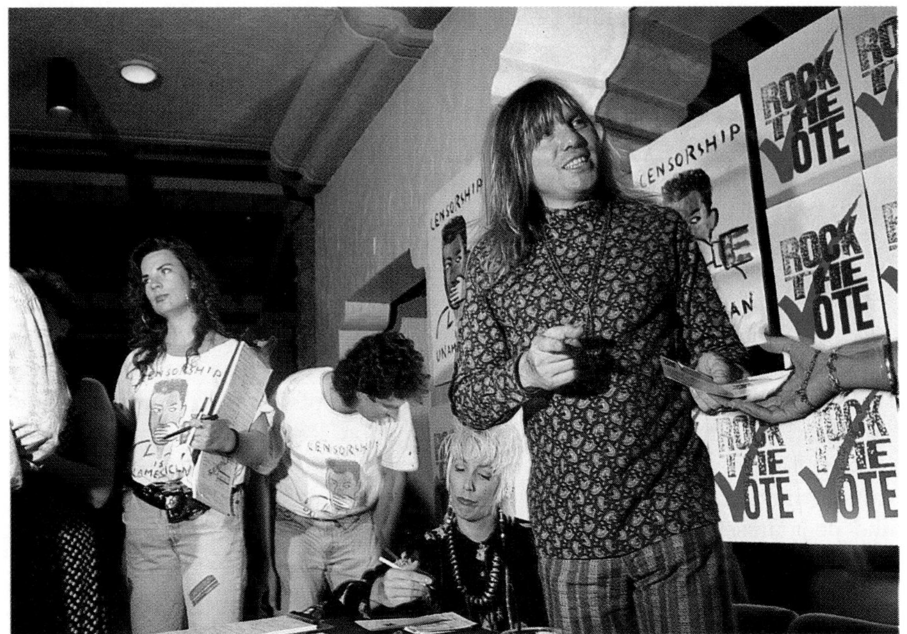

Young people have the lowest rate of voter turnout of any group. To increase their participation level, party and civic activists have developed novel approaches to registration, as in the case of this registration booth at a Hollywood Palace rock concert. (David Butow/ Black Star)

ple like oneself.[23] Alienation diminishes people's interest in political participation.[24] It might be thought foolish for people to withdraw from politics when they believe government is inept and uncaring. Yet, for some individuals, the vote is as much an affirmation of citizenship as it is an opportunity to influence the direction of government. Most people know that their single vote is unlikely to affect the outcome of an election. When disgusted with government, they may choose simply to retreat from politics. In a 1994 CBS News/New York Times poll, more than 60 percent of the respondents said there was not a single politician they admired. When people are so thoroughly disillusioned, it becomes understandable why some of them reject everything about politics, including the exercise of their right to vote.

Age

When viewers tuned in MTV at various times in the most recent presidential campaign, they might have thought at first that they had selected the wrong channel. Rather than a video of their favorite rock star, they saw the presidential candidates urging young people to vote.

The candidates had targeted the right audience for their get-out-the-vote message. Young adults are much less likely to vote than middle-aged citizens. Even senior citizens, despite the infirmities of old age, have a far higher turnout rate than voters under the age of thirty. Young people are less likely to have the political concern that can accompany such lifestyle characteristics as homeownership, a permanent career, and a family.[25] In fact, citizens under the age of thirty have a lower turnout rate than any demographic group of comparable size. Failure to vote among the young helps explain the overall drop in turnout in U.S. elections after 1960. The postwar "baby boom" resulted in an abnormally large number of young people eligible to vote after 1960, and the trend was exaggerated when the Twenty-sixth Amendment (ratified in 1971) lowered the voting age from twenty-one to eighteen.[26] The average age of the U.S. population is now increasing as a result of declining birthrates and lengthening life spans. The slight increase in turnout in the most recent presidential and congressional elections is probably attributable in part to this demographic trend.

Education

What does your college education mean? One thing it means is that you have a much higher probability of becoming an active citizen. The difference is striking. Persons with a college education are about 40 percent more likely to vote than persons with a grade school education. Researchers have concluded that education generates a greater interest in politics, a higher level of political information, a greater confidence that one can make a difference politically, and peer pressure to participate—all of which are related to the tendency to vote.[27]

Education, in fact, is the single best predictor of voter turnout. This fact led some analysts in the 1950s to conclude that increasing the overall level of education was the way to increase levels of turnout. Paradoxically, the overall education level of the American people has increased since then, but turnout has dropped. Political scientists have concluded that the positive effect of increased education levels has been more than offset by people's declining political loyalties and by their heightened sense of alienation.[28]

Economic Class

Turnout is also strongly related to economic status, as measured by income level (see Figure 7-3). Americans at the bottom of the economic ladder are

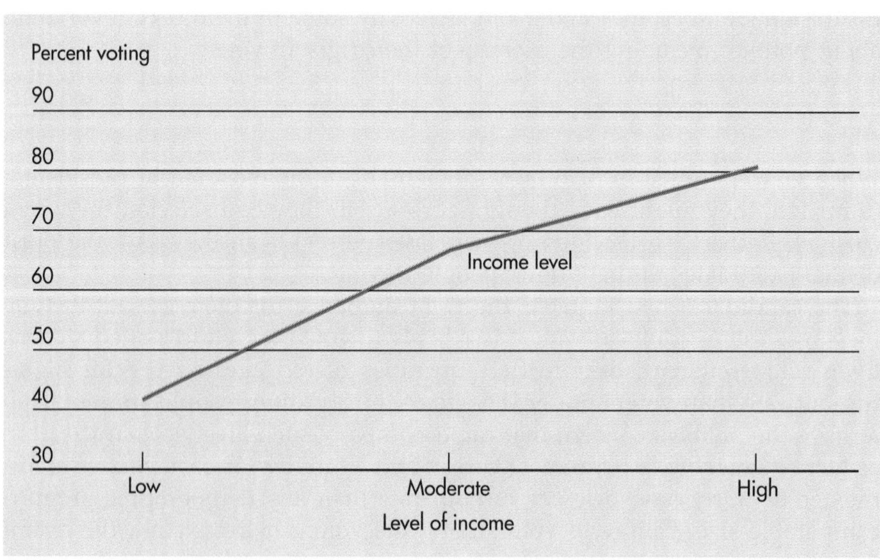

FIGURE 7-3 Voter Turnout and Level of Income
Americans of lower income are much less likely to vote. *Source: U.S. Bureau of the Census.*

about one-third less likely to vote in presidential elections as those at the top.[29] The difference is even larger in primaries and nonpresidential elections.[30]

In European democracies, economic status does not affect turnout to such a high degree. Europeans of lower income levels are encouraged to participate by class-based organizations and traditions—strong socialist parties, politically oriented trade unions, and class-based political ideologies.[31] In Britain, for example, the Labour party emerged with the growth of trade unionism and enrolled many manual laborers. Since 1918 the Labour party's membership card has carried a broad pledge "to secure for the workers by hand or by brain the full fruits of their industry." When the Labour party came to power in 1945, it made good on this promise to the working class by placing key industries under government ownership and adopting new social welfare programs. A major policy was government-paid medical care for all Britons, which was of particular benefit to lower-income people.

Although social class has declined in importance, European political traditions and institutions continue to encourage lower-class voter participation in ways that the U.S. political system does not.[32] The United States does not have, and never has had, a major socialist or labor party.[33] The Democratic party by and large represents poorer Americans, but their interests tend to be subordinated to the party's concern for the American middle class, which, because of its size and voting regularity, is the key to victory in U.S. elections.

Some analysts point out that once education level is controlled, income is a small factor in Americans' participation level. However, this observation does not adequately account for the absence of a lower-class political party in the U.S. system. The real test of the impact of income is whether poor people would turn out at a higher level if the party alternatives were different. Voting patterns during the Great Depression of the 1930s indicate that they would. In response to social security, public works projects, and other unprecedented class-based New Deal programs, turnout rose sharply among lower-income citizens.[34] Their voting rate stayed high through the 1950s because the New Deal agenda remained the focus of the domestic policy debate. As class-based appeals declined after 1960, turnout among those at the bottom of the economic ladder dropped by 25 percent from its 1960 level. Turnout at the top declined by only 4 percent. Today barely two-fifths of unemployed and working-class Americans vote even in a presidential election.[35]

THE IMPACT OF THE VOTE

Through their votes, the people choose the representatives who will govern in their name. But what is the relationship between the vote and the actions of government? What influence does the vote have on public policy? Fuller answers to these questions will be provided later in the book (see Chapters 8, 13, and 15), but it is useful to consider at least a partial response at this point.

Elections do *not* ordinarily produce a popular mandate for the policies advocated by the winning candidate. A mandate requires voters to consciously choose between candidates on the basis of the promises they make during the campaign. A difficulty with this interpretation of election results is that voters are not usually well informed about candidates' policy positions. In U.S.

Voters in New York City's Harlem turned out in record numbers during the Great Depression, a time when the Democratic party appealed directly to lower-income voters with its New Deal programs. (UPI/Bettmann Newsphotos)

House campaigns, less than half the voters can recall on their own the names of the two major-party nominees in their district and even fewer can identify these candidates' positions on major issues.[36] In presidential races, the voters are better informed, but most of them cannot readily recall more than a few of the differences in the candidates' platforms.

Several influences combine to limit the voters' awareness of issues. The candidates do not always make their positions altogether clear, either because they fear that taking a firm stand will lose them votes or because they do not have specific policies in mind. Many candidates have dodged the abortion issue in recent years by expressing personal opposition to it while at the same time promising to uphold a woman's right to choose as long as the courts permit it. Additionally, the news media concentrate their election coverage not on issues but on the strategic aspects of the candidates' pursuit of office (see Figure 7-4). By covering campaigns as if they were horse races, the media deemphasize substantive issues of policy, thereby making it more difficult for the voters to discover where the candidates stand.

Finally, voters can hardly be aware of issues if they are personally inattentive to politics. Most citizens do not follow campaigns closely and do not necessarily gain knowledge of even highly publicized issues.[37] In the 1994 congressional elections, voters cited excessive federal spending as a reason why they favored GOP candidates over their Democratic opponents. Polls indicated that nearly 60 percent of Americans believed the budget deficit had increased during the first two years of the Clinton presidency. In fact, because of budget-deficit legislation developed by Clinton and enacted by Congress, the deficit had fallen two straight years for the first time since the mid-1980s.

prospective voting A form of electoral judgment in which voters choose the candidate whose policy promises most closely match their own preferences.

There are, to be sure, some voters who are highly informed on the issues and cast their ballots on this basis. **Prospective voting** is a term used to describe this forward-looking type of voting. Prospective voting occurs when voters know the issue positions of the candidates and choose the candidate whose promises best match their own issue preferences.

A more prevalent form of voting is **retrospective voting,** which is the situation in which voters support the incumbent party or candidate when they are pleased with the performance, and reverse their position when they are displeased. George Bush's fate in 1988 and 1992 illustrates the importance that voters attach to past governmental performance. The nation's economy in 1988 was in the midst of the longest sustained upturn in a half-century, and opinion polls showed that a majority of Americans believed that the Republican party was more likely than the Democrats to keep the country prosperous. These conditions, more than any promise of future action or any personality traits of Bush, were the key to his victory. He had the support of more than 85 percent of the voters who had backed Reagan four years earlier.

retrospective voting A form of electoral judgment in which voters support the incumbent candidate or party when their policies are judged to have succeeded and oppose the candidate or party when their policies are judged to have failed.

In 1992, however, the U.S. economy was in its longest recession since World War II, and Bush was in political trouble. Three-fourths of the American public expressed concern about his handling of the economy, and their dissatisfaction was reflected in the outcome of the election. Bush lost by a substantial margin to Bill Clinton, who, despite widespread reservations about his personal character, represented the prospect of change. According to the National Election Studies survey, about 80 percent of the voters who supported Bush in 1988, but deserted him in 1992, believed that the economy was the nation's most important problem.

Retrospective voting is a somewhat weaker form of public control than prospective voting because it occurs after the fact: government has already acted, and nothing can change what has taken place. In 1988, Bush campaigned on a pledge of "no new taxes," a position he abandoned two years into his presidency when faced with the problem of rapidly increasing budget deficits. Americans were saddled with new taxes that many of them believed would never be levied during a Bush presidency. They could, and

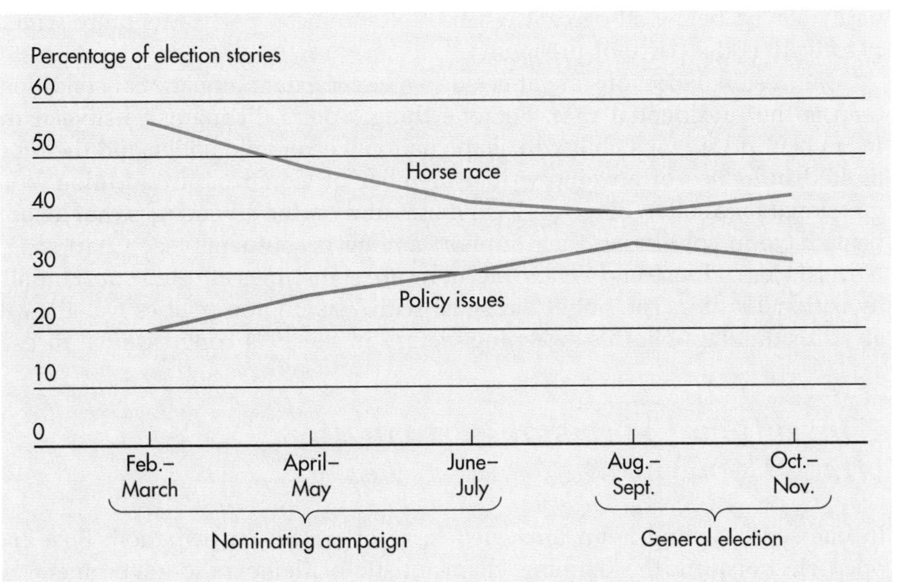

FIGURE 7-4 Dimensions of Election News Coverage Policy issues receive less attention from the news media than do the "horse-race" factors—the candidates' strategies, tactics, and positions in the contest. *Source: Figures based on author's content analysis of 1992 election coverage.*

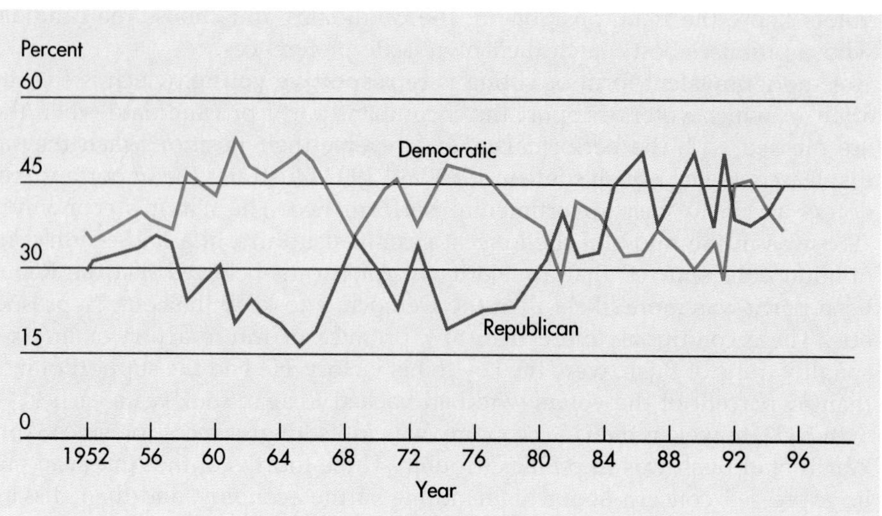

FIGURE 7-5 The Public's Perception of the Relative Ability of the Democratic and Republican Parties to Promote Prosperity.
Voters' support for a party's presidential candidate has typically been related to their opinion of the party's ability to mange the economy. *Source: Gallup Polls: Respondents were asked whether the Democratic or Republican party would do a "better job of keeping the country prosperous."*

did, deny Bush a second term of office, but this retrospective judgment on his first term did not alter what had transpired during his presidency. Nevertheless, retrospective voting can be an effective form of popular control over policy because it forces officeholders to anticipate the voters' likely response in later elections. "The fear of loss of popular support," the political scientist V. O. Key concluded, "powerfully disciplines the actions of government."[38]

Economic conditions are usually the key factor in the electorate's retrospective judgments.[39] When voters' confidence in the in-party's handling of the economy is high, so also is their support for its presidential candidate.[40] The Democratic party's share of the two-party presidential vote has normally stayed above 50 percent when a majority of the public perceive it as the party of prosperity (see Figure 7-5). Conversely, votes for the Democrats have ordinarily stayed below 50 percent when the Republican party was more widely perceived as the party of prosperity.[41]

Congressional elections are affected to a lesser extent by national conditions than is the presidential race. For one thing, voters distinguish between the incumbent president's ability to shape national economic policy and the more limited influence of any individual member of Congress. In addition, congressional races often hinge on local issues and on the advantages that incumbents have in solidifying their support among constituents (see Chapter 12). Nevertheless, House and Senate elections are sometimes affected substantially by national issues. The public's disgust with Washington politics was the catalyst for the Republican's sweeping victory in the 1994 congressional races.

Conventional Forms of Participation Other Than Voting

In one sense, voting is an unrivaled form of citizen participation. Free and open elections are the defining characteristic of democratic government, so voting is regarded as the most basic duty of citizens.[42] Voting is also the only form of citizen participation engaged in by a majority of adults in every democratic country.[43]

In another sense, however, voting is a restricted form of participation. Citizens have the opportunity to vote only at a particular time and place, and only on those predetermined items listed on a ballot. Voting takes up less than an hour a year for most citizens, and there is no guarantee that candidates will be able to keep the promises they made to the voters during the campaign. There are other forms of participation that offer a greater opportunity for personal influence or involvement. These may be divided into campaign activities, community activities, and attentiveness to the news.

CAMPAIGN ACTIVITIES

A citizen may engage in such campaign-related activities as working for a candidate or a party, attending election rallies or meetings, contributing money, and wearing a candidate's campaign button. The more demanding of these activities, such as doing volunteer work for a candidate or a party, require a lot more time and effort than voting. These activities are also less imbued with notions of civic duty than is voting.[44] Not surprisingly, the proportion of citizens who engage in these activities is relatively small. For example, about one in twenty adult Americans say they worked for a party or a candidate within the past year (see Figure 7-6).

Nevertheless, campaign participation is higher in the United States than in Europe. A five-country comparative study found that Americans ranked ahead of citizens of Germany, Austria, the Netherlands, and Great Britain in such activities as volunteering to work for a party or a candidate during an election campaign.[45]

One reason Americans, even though they vote at a lower rate than Euro-

★ CRITICAL THINKING

Is It Better to Vote Retrospectively Than Prospectively?

The civics-book model of voting suggests that a responsible voter is a person who chooses among the candidates on the basis of the positions they take on the issues of the campaign. V. O. Key, Jr., argued that this model has two basic drawbacks: it places extraordinary information demands on voters and requires them to accept at face value the promises that candidates make.

In Key's view, voters would be better advised to select their candidates retrospectively. They should consider the incumbent's past performance and, depending on whether they judge the performance to be effective, vote for or against the incumbent's party. The retrospective model places fewer information demands on voters and is based on the actual performance of government rather than on promises of future action.

Do you agree with Key's assessment? Are there particular times when prospective voting or retrospective voting is the more advisable basis of decision? Do you tend to judge parties and candidates on the basis of past performance or future promises?

Elections offer citizens an opportunity not only to vote but also to participate more actively in politics. These volunteers are placing telephone calls on behalf of Ross Perot's 1992 presidential candidacy. (Donna Bagby/Saba)

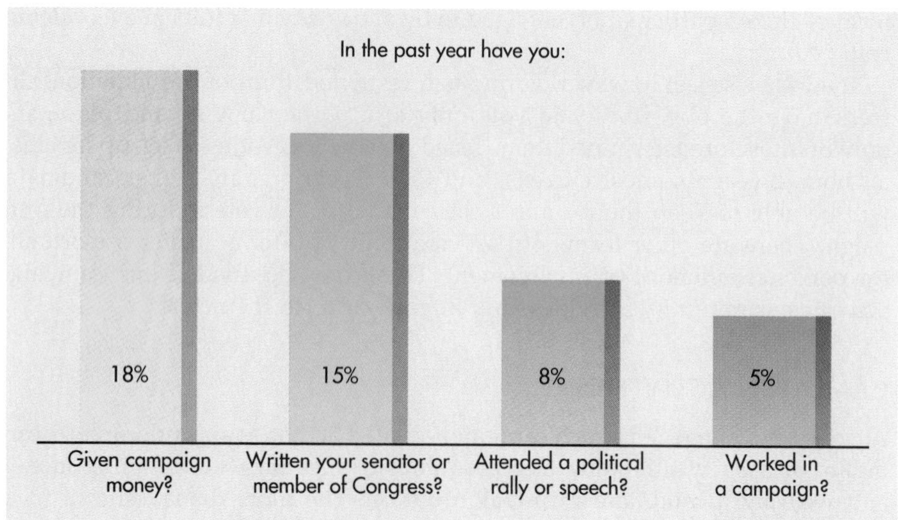

FIGURE 7-6 Political Activism Political activity other than voting involves only a minority of citizens. *Source: Roper surveys, 1993, except campaign money data, which is taken from a National Opinion Research Center survey, 1990.*

peans, are more likely than Europeans to work in a campaign is that they have more opportunities to do so.[46] Elections take place more often in the United States, and citizens can become involved in an election campaign by volunteering to work for either a party or a candidate (see Chapter 9). In Europe, campaigns are organized through the parties, and participation opportunities for those who are not party members are restricted. Moreover, the United States is a federal system, which results in campaigns for national, state, and local offices. A citizen who wishes to participate is almost certain to find an opportunity at one level of office or another. Most of the governments of

Parents vote on a resolution at a PTA meeting in Denver. Citizen participation in community groups such as the PTA is much higher than participation in party politics. (Chris Takagli/Impact Visuals)

Habitat for Humanity volunteers construct a home for a low-income family (former President Jimmy Carter is operating the circular saw). Americans are more likely than citizens of other democracies to take part in community activities. (Huemmer/Sipa Press)

Europe are unitary in form (see Chapter 2), which means that there are fewer elective offices and thus fewer campaigns in which to participate.

COMMUNITY ACTIVITIES

Many Americans participate in public affairs, not through campaigns and political parties, but through local organizations such as parent-teacher associations, neighborhood groups, Rotary clubs, church-affiliated groups, and hospital auxiliaries. Apart from their other purposes, these organizations also serve as a means to influence the public life of the community. Through such organizations, citizens can work to accomplish community goals and inform officials of their opinions on issues affecting the community.

The actual number of citizens who participate actively in a community group is difficult to estimate, but the number is surely in the tens of millions. The United States has a tradition of community participation that goes back to colonial days. Moreover, compared with local communities in Europe, those in the United States have more authority over policy issues, which is an added incentive to participation. Due to increased mobility and other factors, Americans may be less tied to their local communities than in the past and therefore less involved in community action. Nevertheless, a third of Americans claim that they frequently or sometimes participate in a group effort to solve a community problem, compared with about 15 percent in most European countries.[47] When it comes to donating money and time to a group, Americans have an even greater edge on Europeans (see Figure 7-7).

Increasingly, Americans are also involved in public affairs through membership in lobbying groups. This form of participation seldom consists of more

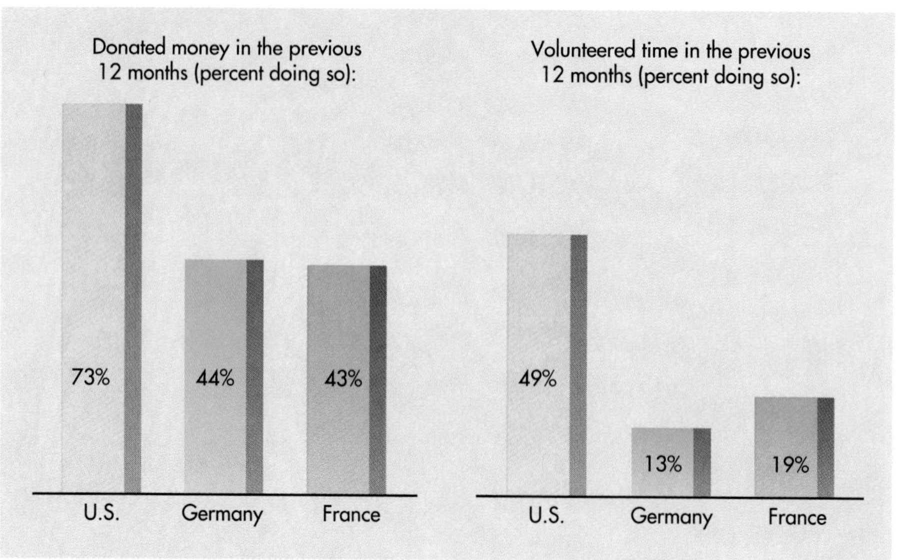

FIGURE 7-7 Conventional Participation in Three Countries Americans are more actively involved in volunteering time and donating money to groups and community causes than are the French or Germans. *Source: Helmut I. Anheier, Lester M. Salamon, and Edith Archambault, "Participating Citizens: U.S.–Europe Comparisons in Volunteer Action," The Public Perspective, March/April 1994, p. 17.*

than the contribution of annual dues that enable a national organization to pressure government officials or otherwise attempt to influence public policy. Examples of these groups are the National Organization for Women, Common Cause, the Christian Moral Government Fund, the Southern Poverty Law Center, the American Civil Liberties Union, and the National Conservative Political Action Committee. Chapter 10 discusses lobbying groups more fully.

FOLLOWING POLITICS IN THE NEWS

Campaign work and community participation are active forms of political involvement. There is also a passive form of participation: following politics by reading newspapers and newsmagazines and by listening to news reports on television or radio. It can safely be said that no act of political participation takes up more of people's time than does news consumption. The news is important to citizen participation: if people are to participate effectively and intelligently in politics, they must be aware of what is taking place in their communities, in their nation, and in the world.

News about politics is within easy reach of nearly all Americans. More than 95 percent of U.S. homes have a television set, and about 50 percent of Americans read a daily newspaper. However, the regular audience for news is much smaller than these figures suggest. If the regular audience for politics is defined as those who read a newspaper's political sections or watch television newscasts on a regular basis, then about a third of Americans qualify. Another third of the citizenry follow the news intermittently. The final third pay no appreciable attention to either television news or the newspaper.

For many citizens, news exposure is the only significant form of contact with the world of politics. Yet the role of the news audience is akin to that of spectators at a sporting event, not of the players. Marshall McLuhan characterized the modern world of mass communication as a "global village," suggesting that the media, particularly television, have effectively linked citizens everywhere.[48] Robert Entman is closer to the truth when he describes news-centered politics as "democracy without citizens."[49]

In a disturbing trend, many young people are ignoring the news. A 1990 survey conducted by the Times-Mirror Center for the People and the Press found that Americans under thirty years of age know less and care less about politics than any generation of the last half century and pay less attention to newspapers. They are inclined toward television usage, but, at that, do not pay much attention to television news. In fact, during the 1980s, the percentage of persons over fifty in the network news audience rose from 50 percent to 60 percent. A lot of young people apparently cannot be bothered with news about politics in any form.

In general, the U.S. news audience has been shrinking in size. Newspaper circulation has declined in recent decades from 70 percent of the population to 50 percent, and television news audiences have fallen by a similar amount. The major reason for the newspaper's drop appears to be television. Americans read less today, partly because they rely more heavily on television as an information and entertainment medium. The drop in the television news audience is largely a function of cable television, which has made it easier for people to ignore broadcast news. Through the 1970s, the television news audience included many "inadvertent" viewers; they watched the network news during the dinner hour because there was no other programming available to them. With cable, viewers have a wider variety of choices, from movies to sports to news. Many viewers, as high as 40 percent by some estimates, choose to ignore the news unless a sensational story, such as the O. J. Simpson trial, gets their attention. A 1994 Times-Mirror survey of citizens in eight democracies indicated that Americans are now about average in terms of television news exposure (see box; The Media and the People). Two decades ago, Americans were more likely than Europeans to watch television news regularly.

★ CRITICAL THINKING

What Kind of Citizens Will Young Adults Become?

Recent surveys indicate that young Americans differ significantly from older citizens in ways that suggest a decline in democracy. Today's Americans under thirty years of age pay less attention to politics than any generation of young people since polling began in the 1930s. Surveys by Peter D. Hart Research Associates found that fewer than 15 percent of those between the ages of fifteen and twenty-five believed that voting was an essential part of good citizenship. About half of them defined good citizenship in terms of caring personal relationships.

When respondents in the Hart surveys were asked how they would spend additional leisure time, not a single respondent mentioned civic or political participation. A significant minority even said that they could not imagine a circumstance in which they would be willing to fight for their country.

What do you make of these findings? Do the attitudes of young people today indicate that American democracy is imperiled? Why are today's young people less committed to public life than their parents and grandparents? What steps might be taken to instill in them a greater sense of civic duty?

THE MIDDLE-CLASS BIAS OF CONVENTIONAL PARTICIPATION

Citizens who work in campaigns, who take an active part in the community, or who pay close attention to the news have the same general characteristics as those who vote regularly. Compared with the population as a whole, they are older, have higher incomes, are more highly educated, are more likely to have a strong sense of civic duty, and are less likely to feel politically alienated or apathetic.

The class bias of conventional participation is particularly noteworthy.[50] Citizens of higher economic status are by far the most politically active individuals. They are most likely to possess the financial resources and communication skills that encourage participation and make it personally rewarding.[51] Among citizens who are most active in politics, three times as many have incomes in the top third as in the bottom third.[52] This tendency is predictable. Less advantaged Americans find it harder to contribute to organized activity even when they desire to do so. They often lack the money, information, contacts, and communication skills required to participate effectively. On the other hand, educated and affluent Americans possess the personal resources that enhance participation in public affairs.

THE MEDIA AND THE PEOPLE

WHERE AMERICANS GET THEIR NEWS, AND HOW MUCH THEY GET

Television is the medium through which Americans get most of their news about national affairs. In a 1994 Times-Mirror survey, 72 percent said they relied primarily on television news and only 15 percent cited the newspaper. Radio and magazines accounted for nearly all of the remaining 13 percent. These figures are somewhat misleading in that respondents were asked where they get "most" of their news, not how much news they actually get. People who say they get "most" of their news from television do not necessarily watch the news a lot. When people's news habits are measured by the frequency with which they read or watch the news, television's lead over the newspaper is less substantial. More than half of the adult population does not follow the news regularly. It is this group, the less attentive citizens, who provide television with its large majority. They watch a television news program every now and then but seldom or never read a newspaper.

The American news audience is shrinking. Newspaper circulation reached 70 percent of the public a few decades ago; today, the figure is about 50 percent. The television news audience has also declined. Until cable was widely available, Americans who wanted to watch television in the early evening had almost no alternative but to watch the news. The three major networks broadcast their nightly newscasts simultaneously and had a combined audience share of nearly 90 percent. With cable, viewers have a choice, not simply among networks, but between news and entertainment programming. News has been the loser in this situation; the networks' audience share during the evening news hour is barely 60 percent. To be sure, cable has also fostered a core of news "junkies" who immerse themselves in the Cable News Network (CNN), C-SPAN, and other news and public affairs programming. The more significant effect of cable, however, has been a substantial decrease in the number of Americans who follow television news regularly.

The change is evident when the size of news audiences in the United States is compared with those in Europe. In the 1970s, Americans ranked ahead of Europeans in terms of their news exposure. They have since lost their lead, as a 1994 Times-Mirror poll indicated:

	RANK IN TERMS OF SIZE OF THE . . .	
Country	*Newspaper Audience*	*Television News Audience*
France	5th	5th
Germany	1st	2nd
Italy	4th	1st
Spain	6th	6th
Great Britain	2nd	3rd
United States	3rd	4th

SOURCE: Times Mirror Center for The People and The Press, "Mixed Message about Press Freedom on Both Sides of Atlantic," March 16, 1994, pp. 30–31.

It is a mistake, however, to assume that virtually all middle-class Americans are politically involved. The proportion of the citizenry who participate beyond the act of voting or occasional attendance at a community forum is relatively small. Involvement in partisan politics is particularly uncommon. The political scientist W. Russell Neuman concludes: "Roughly speaking, only one in twenty Americans can confidently be described as actively involved. . . . Such activities as attending campaign meetings [and] contributing to political organizations . . . are, all things considered, rare phenomena."[53]

There is a class bias to political participation. Political fundraisers, such as the one being held here in a middle-class home, are almost unheard of in poor neighborhoods. (Cindy Reiman/ Impact Visuals)

Unconventional Activism: Social Movements and Protest Politics

Before mass elections became prevalent, the public often resorted to revolts and disorders as a way of expressing dissatisfaction with government. Tax and food riots were common forms of popular protest. The advent of elections allowed the masses to communicate their views in an institutionalized and less disruptive way. Elections are double-edged, however. Although they are commonly viewed as a means by which the people control the government, *elections are also a means by which the government controls the people.*[54] Since they have been freely chosen by the people to rule, representatives can claim that their policies reflect the popular will. It is difficult for people to claim they are justified in rioting against government policy that has been enacted by representatives they themselves placed in office.

Voting in elections is also limited to the choices that are offered. In the U.S. two-party system, the meaningfulness of the vote depends to some degree on whether the citizen accepts the alternatives offered by the Republican and Democratic parties. If neither choice is acceptable, voting becomes a hollow act, even a counterproductive one in that it lends legitimacy to the victorious party. An alternative for those who are dissatisfied with the status quo is participation in a social movement. **Social movements,** or **political movements,** as they are sometimes called, refer to broad efforts to achieve change by citizens who feel that government is not properly responsive to their interests.[55] Their efforts are sometimes channeled through traditional forms of participa-

social (political) movements Active and sustained efforts to achieve social and political change by groups of people who feel that government has not been properly responsive to their concerns.

The son of Mexican immigrants, Cesar Chavez organized a social movement in the early 1960s to fight for better pay and working conditions for migrant farm workers and to protest discrimination against Hispanics. Chavez (left) is shown here with Walter Reuther (center), president of the United Auto Workers, during a march protesting the low wages of grape pickers. (UPI/Bettmann)

tion, such as political lobbying, but citizens can also take to the streets in protest against government. Through demonstrations, picket lines, and marches, protesters dramatize their opposition to official policies.

Social movements do not always succeed, but they sometimes assist otherwise politically weak persons to force government to respond to their desires. For example, the timing and scope of the landmark 1964 Civil Rights Act and 1965 Voting Rights Act can be explained only as a response by Congress to the pressure created by the civil rights movement. The movement was in great part nonviolent, but it existed outside established channels—civil disobedience was one of its techniques—and it challenged existing power structures. Another effective social movement in the 1960s was the farm workers' movement, whose protests led to landmark legislation and court decisions that improved the working and living conditions of migrant workers.[56]

Protest can pose a serious threat to established authority, and government at times has responded violently to dissent.[57] In May 1970, during demonstrations against the Vietnam war, several unarmed students at Kent State University and Jackson State College were shot to death and others were wounded by national guardsmen who had been sent onto the campuses to restore order. The majority of the general public sides with authorities in such situations. In a *Newsweek* poll, 58 percent of respondents blamed the Kent State killings on the student demonstrators, while only 11 percent blamed the guardsmen.

Most citizens apparently believe that the proper way to express disagreement over public policy is through voting and not through protesting, despite the First Amendment's guarantee of the right "peaceably to assemble." In a 1972 University of Michigan survey, only 15 percent of those interviewed expressed approval of the Vietnam protests. Only 1 to 2 percent of the American public took to the streets in protest at any time during the 1960s and 1970s. Public opinion about demonstrations against the Gulf war was also negative, although less so than for protests against the Vietnam war, perhaps because U.S. involvement in the Gulf was shorter and more successful. A Gallup poll in early 1991 indicated that by a 2-to-1 margin Americans believed it was "a bad thing for Americans to be demonstrating against the war when U.S. troops are fighting overseas." This view was particularly pronounced among women, older persons, Republicans, and persons with lower education levels (see Table 7-1).

Recent American history would be very different had not the civil rights, women's rights, Vietnam protest, and other major social movements pressed their claims on government. Social movements have been the most effective way for groups outside the political mainstream to make significant claims on society. A successful social movement often evolves into conventional forms of politics. After the 1960s, for example, African Americans shifted from protest politics to activities such as lobbying and voter registration drives.

Protest politics in America goes back to the Boston Tea Party and earlier, but it has taken on new forms in recent years. Protest was traditionally a desperate act that began, often spontaneously, when a group had lost hope that it could succeed through more conventional methods. Today, however, protest is usually a calculated act—a means of bringing added attention and impetus to a cause[58] These tactical protests often involve a great deal of planning, including, in some instances, the busing of thousands of people to Washington for a rally staged for television. Civil rights, environmental, agricultural, and pro- and antiabortion groups are among those that have staged tactical protests in Washington within the past few years.

Citizens who participate in social movements tend to be younger than non-

TABLE 7-1 Opinions about Peace Demonstrations during the Gulf War, 1991
Most Americans believed that protests against the war were a "bad thing."

	ARE CURRENT DEMONSTRATIONS . . . ?		
	A Bad Thing	*Not a Bad Thing*	*No Opinion*
All respondents	63%	34%	3%
Male	58	40	2
Female	67	28	5
18–29 years	57	40	3
30–49 years	58	39	3
50 years and over	72	23	5
College grads	47	47	6
Some college	59	37	4
High school grads	68	30	2
Not high school grads	76	20	4
Republicans	71	26	3
Democrats	61	35	4
Independents	57	40	3

SOURCE: Gallup Poll, January 23–26, 1991.

participants, which is a reversal of the situation with voting. In fact, age is the best predictor of protest activity.[59] Participants in social movements also tend to emphasize nonmaterial values more than do nonparticipants. Social movements often develop in response to real or perceived injustices and thus attract idealists.[60]

Participation and the Potential for Influence

Although Americans claim that political participation is important, most of them do not practice what they preach. As we have seen, most citizens take little interest in participation except to vote, and a significant minority cannot even be persuaded that voting is worth their while. Americans are obviously not completely apathetic: many millions of them give their time, effort, and money to political causes, and roughly 100 million go to the polls in presidential elections.

Yet sustained political activism does not engage a large proportion of the public. Moreover, many of those who do participate are drawn to politics by a habitual sense of civic duty rather than by an intense concern with current issues. The emphasis that American culture places on individualism tends to discourage a sense of urgency about political participation. "In the United States, the country of individualism *par excellence,*" William Watts and Lloyd Free write, "there is a sharp distinction in people's minds between their own personal lives and national life."[61] Although wars and severe recessions can lead the American public to rely on government, most people under most conditions expect to solve their own problems. This is not to say that Americans have a disdain for collective action. In their communities particularly, citizens frequently take part in collective efforts to support a local hospital, improve the neighborhood, and the like. But Americans tend not to see their material well-being as greatly dependent on involvement in politics of the traditional kind.[62]

This tendency contributes to a class bias in American politics. For one thing, it helps maintain a relatively sharp distinction between that which is properly public (political) and that which is properly private (economic). The private component, which includes most economic relationships, is largely beyond the realm of political debate and action. Americans, says political scientist Robert Lane, have a preference for market justice rather than political justice.[63] They prefer to see benefits distributed primarily through the economic marketplace rather than through the policies of government. The nation's health care system is an example. Unlike the systems of Europe, which provide government-paid coverage for everyone, access to medical care in the United States is to some degree based on a person's ability to pay for it. There are about 38 million Americans who do not have access to adequate health care because they cannot afford health insurance.

America's individualistic culture also contributes to a class bias by its effect on the participation level of lower-income groups. As we have seen, citizens of lower economic status are substantially less involved politically than those of higher status. The difference is much greater in the United States than else-

YOUR TURN

POLITICAL AND COMMUNITY ACTIVISM

The Questions:

In the past year, have you:

Worked informally in a community?	Yes	No
Worked in a campaign or given money to one?	Yes	No
Taken part in a protest?	Yes	No
Attended a public meeting on town or school affairs?	Yes	No
Signed a petition?	Yes	No
Written your member of Congress or senator?	Yes	No
Attended a political rally or speech?	Yes	No

What Others Think: In a 1990 National Opinion Research Center poll, 29 percent of the respondents indicated they had worked informally in a community, which was higher than the number who indicated they had taken part in a protest (4 percent) or had worked in a campaign (5 percent) or given money (18 percent). In a 1993 Roper Center survey, 32 percent of the respondents said they had signed a petition, while 16 percent indicated they had attended a public meeting, 15 percent said they had written a member of Congress, and 8 percent claimed to have attended a political rally.

Comment: These surveys undoubtedly convey an inflated view of the level of activism in America; research has shown that respondents tend to overreport their participation in politics. Activism is characteristic of only a minority of citizens. If you answered yes to two or more of the questions, you have an activist tendency that is likely to persist throughout your adult life.

where. In other western democracies, the government assists poorer citizens in participating by assuming the burden of registering voters and by fostering class-based political organizations. By comparison, the poor in the United States must arrange their own registration and must choose between two political parties that are attuned primarily to middle-class interests.

During the 1950s and 1960s, many political scientists argued that the low turnout rate of lower-income Americans was largely immaterial because their preferences in regard to policies and candidates were not greatly different from those of other citizens. This viewpoint continues to have its advocates[64] but is less persuasive today.[65] As the income gap between lower- and upper-income Americans has widened in recent decades, so has the gap in their political opinions. As Walter Dean Burnham notes, "It is no longer possible to assume a quiet consensus, a happy apathy."[66]

The relatively low participation rate of the poor tends to reduce the influence of their opinions on public policy. Studies indicate that representatives are more responsive to the demands of participants than to those of nonparticipants,[67] although it must be kept in mind that participants do not always promote only their own interests. It would be a mistake, however, to conclude that large numbers of people regularly support policies that would mainly benefit others. A turning point in the defeat of President Bill Clinton's health care reform proposal came when middle-class Americans decided that it might increase the cost and reduce the quality of their own medical care. According to Time/CNN polls, support for the Clinton plan dropped from 57 to 31 percent in favor to 49 to 37 percent opposed between September 1993

Students at a California state university demonstrate against Proposition 209. The initiative proposed to end all racial, ethnic, and gender preferences in the awarding of university admissions, jobs, and government contracts in the state. The initiative passed by a 54–46 percent vote margin in 1996. (Kim Kulish/Saba)

and July 1994. Although this decline reflected a loss of support among all groups, the drop was particularly acute among higher-income groups. By mid-1994, those Americans with incomes over $20,000 were opposed to the Clinton plan by a 3-to-2 ratio. In contrast, a majority of those individuals with incomes under $20,000 still favored the plan. They would have been the principal beneficiaries of the Clinton plan, which called for universal health care insurance. On the other hand, most middle-class voters already had health insurance, either through an individual policy or an employment-related group policy.

In sum, the pattern of individual political participation in the United States parallels the distribution of influence that prevails in the private sector. Those who have the most power through participation in the marketplace also have the most power through participation in the political arena. However, the issue of individual participation is only one piece of the larger puzzle of who rules America and for what purposes. Subsequent chapters will provide additional pieces.

Summary

Political participation is involvement in activities designed to influence public policy and leadership. A main issue of democratic government is the question of who participates in politics and how fully they participate.

Voting is the most widespread form of active political participation among Americans. Yet voter turnout is significantly lower in the United States than in other democratic nations. The requirement that Americans must personally register in order to establish their eligibility to vote is one reason for lower turnout among Americans; other democracies place the burden of registration on government officials rather than on the individual citizen. The fact that the United States holds frequent elections also discourages some citizens from voting regularly. Finally, the major American political parties, unlike many of those in Europe, do not clearly represent the interests of opposing economic classes; thus the policy stakes in American elections are correspondingly lower. Some Americans do not vote because they think that policy will not change greatly regardless of which party gains power.

Prospective voting is one way the people can exert influence on policy through their participation. It is the most demanding approach to voting: voters must develop their own policy preferences and then educate themselves about the candidates' positions. Most voters are not well-enough informed about the issues to respond in this way. Retrospective voting demands less from voters: they need only decide whether the government has been performing well in terms of the goals and values they hold. The evidence suggests that the electorate is, in fact, reasonably sensitive to past governmental performance, particularly in relation to economic prosperity.

Only a minority of citizens engage in the more demanding forms of political activity, such as work on community affairs or on behalf of a candidate during a political campaign. The proportion of Americans who engage in these more demanding forms of activity exceeds the proportion of Europeans who do so. Nevertheless, only about one in every four Americans will take an active part in a political organization at some point in their lives. Most political activists are individuals of higher income and education; they have the skills and material resources to participate effectively and tend to take greater interest in politics. More than in any other western democracy, political participation in the United States is related to socioeconomic status.

Social movements are broad efforts to achieve change by citizens who feel that government is not properly responsive to their interests. These efforts sometimes take place outside established channels; demonstrations, picket lines, and marches are common means of protest. Protesters are younger and more idealistic on average than other citizens, but they are a very small proportion of the population. In addition, protest activities do not have much public support, despite the country's tradition of free expression.

Overall, Americans are only moderately involved in politics. They are concerned with political affairs but mostly immersed in their private pursuits, a reflection in part of our culture's emphasis on individualism. The lower level of participation among low-income citizens has particular significance in that it works to reduce their influence on public policy and leadership.

Major Concepts

alienation
apathy
civic duty
political participation
prospective voting
registration
retrospective voting
social (political) movements
suffrage
voter turnout

Suggested Readings

Barber, Benjamin. *Strong Democracy: Participatory Politics for a New Age.* Berkeley: University of California Press, 1984. A provocative assessment of citizenship in the modern age.

Conway, M. Margaret. *Political Participation in the United States,* 2d ed. Washington, D.C.: Congressional Quarterly Press, 1991. An up-to-date analysis of political participation patterns.

Crotty, William J., ed. *Political Participation and American Democracy.* New York: Greenwood Press, 1991. A series of essays on aspects of participation and their implications for American democracy.

Entman, Robert. *Democracy without Citizens: Media and the Decay of American Politics.* New York: Oxford University Press, 1989. A critical evaluation of citizen involvement in the context of news about politics and public affairs.

Key, V. O., Jr. *The Responsible Electorate.* Cambridge, Mass.: Belknap Press of Harvard University Press, 1966. The classic analysis of voting as a response to government's performance.

Neuman, W. Russell, Marion R. Just, and Ann N. Crigler. *Common Knowledge: News and the Construction of Meaning.* Chicago: University of Chicago Press, 1992. An assessment of how citizens interpret and use the news they receive.

Piven, Frances Fox, and Richard A. Cloward. *Why Ameri-*

cans Don't Vote. New York: Pantheon, 1988. An analysis of nonvoting which focuses on registration requirements and calls for simplified procedures.

Rosenstone, Steven J., and John Mark Hansen. *Mobilization, Participation, and Democracy in America.* New York: Macmillan, 1993. A careful analysis of participation in America based mainly on national surveys.

Tate, Katherine. *From Protest to Politics: The New Black Voters in American Elections,* enlarged ed. Cambridge, Mass.: Harvard University Press, 1994. A study of the transformation of a social movement into a conventional form of political participation.

Woliver, Laura R. *From Outrage to Action: The Politics of Grass-Roots Dissent.* Urbana: University of Illinois Press, 1993. A valuable case study of the impact of grass-roots protest.

CHAPTER 8

ELECTIONS AND THE TWO-PARTY SYSTEM: DEFINING THE VOTERS' CHOICE

Political parties created democracy and . . . modern democracy is unthinkable save in terms of the parties.

—*E. E. Schattschneider*[1]

Halfway across the country and two weeks apart, they faced off, each offering their own plan for a better America.

The Republicans met first, in San Diego. Their 1996 platform included a 15-percent across-the-board cut in personal income taxes, a constitutional ban on abortions, a balanced federal budget, parental choice of schools, business deregulation, and the assignment of a broad range of federal programs to state and local governments. The Republicans chose former Senate majority leader Bob Dole as their presidential nominee and named Jack Kemp, a former U.S. representative and cabinet secretary, as his running mate.

The Democrats met in Chicago, the same city where twenty-eight years earlier a Democratic national convention had been torn apart by the dispute over Vietnam war policy. This time, however, the Democrats were fully united. Bill Clinton's nomination was uncontested, the first time since Franklin Roosevelt in 1936 that an incumbent Democratic president seeking reelection had not faced opposition within his own party. The Democrats also unanimously chose Al Gore to run again for the vice-presidency. The Democrats' lengthy platform included tax benefits for low- and middle-income families, restrictions on handguns, protection of social security, reproductive freedom for women, and pledges to strengthen the nation's environmental, educational, and health systems.

The political parties, as their nominees and platforms illustrate, are in the business of offering the voting public a choice. Each party seeks to define itself in a way that will attract majority support.

Competition between political parties is the foundation of the public's influence through elections. The party is the one institution that aims to develop broad policy and leadership choices and then presents them to the public to accept or reject. Although many Americans distrust political parties and question their value, the fact is that democracy would be nearly impossible in practice without them.

Of course, parties are not the only means by which the public can exert influence. Interest groups such as the AFL-CIO and the American Medical Association provide individuals with the opportunity to act collectively. However, most such groups articulate the narrow and specific demands of a *minority* interest in society. In the United States, with its individualistic culture and tradition of freedom of association, group activity is more fragmented than in many other nations. Major political parties function in a different way. The party's goal is to create a *majority* by bringing together individuals with diverse interests. A **political party** is an ongoing coalition of interests joined together to try to get their candidates for public office elected under a common label.[2] Parties serve to pull diverse interests together and in the process offer the public competitive policy and leadership alternatives.

political party An ongoing coalition of interests joined together to try to get their candidates for public office elected under a common label.

In the American case, this competition takes place between two major parties, the Republicans and the Democrats. Because these parties have dominated U.S. elections for so long and are the only parties with any realistic chance of acquiring political control, Americans nearly take their **two-party system** for granted. However, most democracies have a **multiparty system,** in which three or more parties have the capacity to gain control of government separately or in coalition. Even democracies that have what is essentially a two-party system typically have important smaller parties as well. For example, Great Britain's Labour and Conservative parties have dominated that nation's politics since early in this century, but they have had competition from the Liberal party and, more recently, the Liberal Democrats.

two-party system A system in which only two political parties have a real chance of acquiring control of the government.

multiparty system A system in which three or more political parties have the capacity to gain control of government separately or in coalition.

America's two-party system has important consequences for the nation's politics. Neither major party can win an election by drawing its votes from only a small sector of the population; as a result, the two parties tend to appeal to many of the same interests. The policy traditions and tendencies of the Republican and Democratic parties do not differ sharply and consistently. For example, each party is committed to social security for the elderly and to substantial expenditures for national defense. Parties in European multiparty systems tend to be more programmatic. Each party has its distinctive platform and voting bloc. Of course, once in power, European parties are forced to adjust their programs to the prevailing realities. France's Socialist party, for example, won power in 1981 by attacking the center-right parties for failing to protect working-class and middle-class citizens from downward economic mobility *(déclassement),* but the nation's weak economy forced the Socialists to retain many of the pro-business policies of the previous government.[3] Nevertheless, European multiparty systems usually offer voters a more clear-cut set of choices than does the American two-party system.

To critics, the American parties' failure to take sharply different policy positions means that they offer the public "no genuine alternatives." To their admirers, however, America's major parties provide political stability and yet are different enough to give voters "a real choice." This chapter investigates America's two-party system and the type of choice it actually provides the public. It argues that the Republican and Democratic parties do offer a real and significant choice, but only at particular times and on particular issues. The main points discussed in this chapter are the following:

★ *Party competition is the mechanism that enables voting majorities to have a substantial influence on the direction of government.* This competition peaks during periods of realignment but at all times is a vital aspect of democratic government.

★ *Throughout most of the nation's history, political competition has centered on two parties.* This two-party tendency is explained primarily by the nature of America's electoral system. Minor parties exist in the United States but have been unable to compete successfully for governing power.

★ *The Republican and Democratic coalitions are very broad.* Each includes a substantial proportion of nearly every economic, ethnic, religious, and regional grouping in the country.

★ *To win an electoral majority, each of the two major parties must appeal to a diverse set of interests; this necessity normally leads them to advocate moderate and somewhat overlapping policies and to avoid taking detailed positions on controversial issues.* Only during periods of stress are America's parties likely to present the electorate with starkly different policy alternatives.

Party Competition and Collective Action

Elections offer Americans their best opportunity to influence the broad directions of the national government. Even though the act of the individual voter is not noticeable, the combined choices of millions of voters determine who will occupy the White House and sit in Congress.

Political parties give elections their force and direction. This contribution can be stated more broadly in terms of the party system's major function: the organization of political conflict.[4] The parties transform conflict over society's goals into electoral competition in which the losers accept the winners' right to make policy decisions. In this **party competition,** which is at the core of the democratic process, the parties form coalitions of interests, articulate policy and leadership positions, and compete for electoral dominance. In the process, political parties give citizens a choice among various leaders and policies.

party competition A process in which conflict over society's goals is transformed by political parties into electoral competition in which the winner gains the power to govern.

It is not always a choice that Americans find satisfying. In a 1994 Times-Mirror survey, 66 percent of the respondents expressed the view that most candidates, once in office, do not much care what people like themselves think. Such views are not groundless, but party competition is basic to democratic government. Parties give weight to the preferences of ordinary people. Because they have the strength of numbers, citizens have the potential for great influence in a democracy, but that potential cannot be realized unless they have a way to express a collective judgment. Parties are *the* way. When Americans go to the polls to elect a president or member of Congress, they can choose the Republican or Democratic alternative. This choice channels a great many different opinions into just two and in the process enables people

★ CRITICAL THINKING

The Advantages of Political Parties

The United States has the world's oldest representative government; it also has the world's oldest political parties. Is this just a coincidence? If you believe that it is, then why have political parties emerged in *every* democracy? Can you think of an effective alternative means—such as interest groups or the mass media—by which citizens can acquire collective influence? What are the advantages and disadvantages of parties in comparison with these alternative means of bringing citizens together?

to act together. In electing a party, the voters choose its programs over those of the opposing party.

The history of democratic government is virtually synonomous with the history of parties. When the countries of eastern Europe gained their freedom a few years ago, one of their first steps toward democracy was the legalization of parties. When the United States was founded two centuries ago, the formation of parties was also a first step toward the erection of its democracy. In case after case, democracies have found that they cannot do without parties and for the simplest of reasons: it is the competition between parties that gives popular majorities a chance to determine how they will be governed.

ORIGINS OF THE AMERICAN PARTY SYSTEM

Parties had not yet been invented when George Washington took office in 1789. Factions were known, however, and they were widely despised. Washington warned the nation of the "baneful effects" of factions. The term "faction" connoted a self-interested group bent on getting its own way at the expense of all others. While America's first leaders were therefore wary of any organized form of advocacy, they soon recognized the need to organize those who held similar political views.[5] Out of this recognition came the world's first parties. James Madison at first had likened parties to factions, but his misgivings gave way to an admiration; he saw that they were the only effective way for like-minded people to jointly promote their vision of America.

The First Parties

Political parties in the United States originated in the rivalry within George Washington's administration between Thomas Jefferson and Alexander Hamilton: as we saw in Chapter 3, Jefferson defended states' rights and small landholders, while Hamilton promoted a strong national government and wealthy interests. When Hamilton's ideas prevailed in Congress, Jefferson and his followers formed a political party, the Republicans (see Figure 8-1). By adopting this label, which was associated with popular government, the Jeffersonians sought to portray themselves as the rightful heirs to the American Revolution's legacy of self-government and political equality.

Hamilton responded by organizing his supporters into a formal party—the Federalists—and in the process created America's first competitive party system. The Federalists took their name from the faction that had supported ratification of the Constitution, thereby implying that they were the Constitution's true defenders. However, the Federalists' preoccupation with commercial and wealthy interests fueled Jefferson's claim that the Federalists were bent on establishing a government for the rich and wellborn. After Adams's defeat by Jefferson in the election of 1800, the Federalists and their philosophy never again held sway.

During the so-called Era of Good Feeling, when James Monroe ran unopposed in 1820 for a second presidential term, it appeared as if the nation might exist without parties. Monroe told Andrew Jackson that free government could survive without parties. Yet by the end of Monroe's second term, differences among America's interests had split the Republican party into the

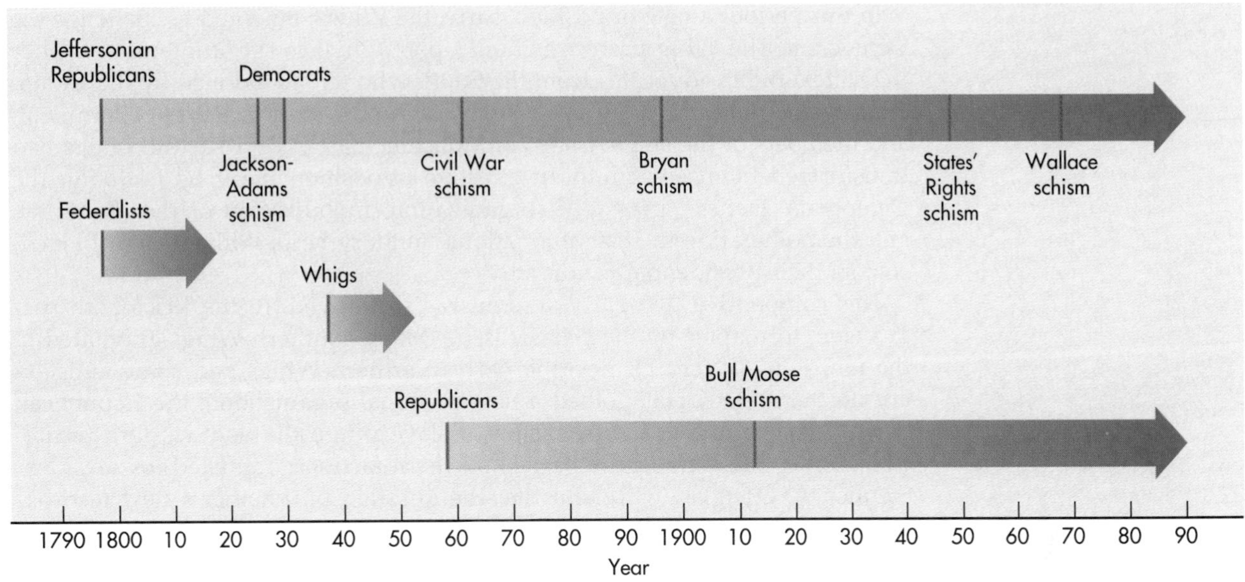

FIGURE 8-1 A Graphic History of America's Major Parties

National Republicans, led by John Quincy Adams, and the Democratic Republicans (later shortened to Democrats), led by Andrew Jackson. The National Republicans resembled the earlier Federalists in their support of commercial interests and a larger role for the national government, while the Democrats viewed themselves as Jefferson's rightful successors, since they favored small landholders and states' rights.

Andrew Jackson and Grassroots Parties

The idea of a government without party competition is utopian. The alternative is likely to be, not government for the common good, but government for and by a small elite. For all its shortcomings, competition between parties is the only system that can regularly mobilize collective influence on behalf of the many who are individually powerless against those few who have extraordinary wealth and prestige.[6]

This realization led Andrew Jackson during the 1820s to assert the principle of the "grassroots" party. Whereas Jefferson's party had been well organized only at the leadership level, Jackson sought a party that was built from the bottom up. Jackson's Democratic party consisted of committees and clubs at the national, state, and local levels, with membership open to all eligible voters. These organizational activities, along with more liberal suffrage laws, contributed to a nearly fourfold rise in voter turnout during the 1830s.[7]

By mobilizing the mass citizenry through party action, Jackson sought to break the hold of the Virginia and Massachusetts aristocracy on the presidency, opening the way to a government that was more directly responsive to ordinary citizens. At the peak of Jacksonian democracy in the 1830s, Alexis de Tocqueville wrote: "The People reign in the American political world as the Deity does in the universe."[8] Although Tocqueville exaggerated the people's true power, he caught the spirit of popular government that was behind the development of popularly based parties under Andrew Jackson.

In this period, a new opposition party, the Whigs, emerged to challenge the Democrats. The Whig party was built upon a diverse set of interests, including states'-rights advocates from the South who felt abandoned by the Democrats, former National Republicans who favored a strong central government, and members of the single-issue Anti-Masonic party.[9] By 1840, the Whigs had transformed themselves into an effective opposition party by imitating the Democrats' tactics—grassroots organization, mobilization of the electorate, and the nomination in 1840 of a national military hero, William Henry Harrison, as their presidential candidate.[10]

This competitive two-party system was short-lived. In the 1850s both parties were torn apart by the slavery issue. Many southern Whigs gravitated to the more pro-slavery Democratic party. Northern Whigs and some antislavery northern Democrats joined a new sectional organization, the Republican party, which opposed the extension of slavery into the new western territories. In 1860 the Democratic party's northern faction nominated for president Stephen A. Douglas, who held that the question of whether a new territory permitted slavery was for a majority of its voters to decide, while the southern faction nominated John C. Breckinridge, who called for the legalization of slavery in all territories. The Democratic vote in the fall election was split sharply along regional lines between these two candidates—with the result that the Republican nominee, Abraham Lincoln, was able to win the presidency with only 40 percent of the popular vote. The Republicans had eclipsed the Whigs and become America's other major party. However, the U.S. party system essentially collapsed in 1860, for the only time in the nation's history.[11] The issues of slavery and union were too basic and serious to be settled through peaceful competition between political parties.

REPUBLICANS VS. DEMOCRATS: REALIGNMENTS AND THE ENDURING PARTY SYSTEM

After the Civil War, the nation settled into the pattern of competition between the Republican and Democratic parties that has prevailed ever since. The durability of these two parties is due not to their ideological consistency but to their remarkable capacity to adapt during periods of crisis. By abandoning at these crucial times their old ways of doing things, the Republican and Democratic parties have essentially remade themselves—with new bases of support, new policies, and new public philosophies.

These periods of great political change are known as "realignments." A **party realignment** involves four basic elements:

party realignment An election or set of elections in which the electorate responds strongly to an extraordinarily powerful issue that has disrupted the established political order. A realignment has a lasting impact on public policy, popular support for the parties, and the composition of the party coalitions.

1. The disruption of the existing political order because of the emergence of one or more unusually powerful and divisive issues
2. An election contest in which the voters shift their support strongly in favor of one party
3. A major change in policy through the action of the stronger party
4. An enduring change in the party coalitions, which works to the lasting advantage of the dominant party.

Realignments are relatively rare. A simple change of power from one party to the other does not constitute a realignment, which is defined instead by the fullness and longevity of its effects. A realignment affects not just one election, but later elections as well. By this standard, there have been three realignments since the 1850s, and some observers believe the United States is now in the midst of a fourth.

Abraham Lincoln said that this portrait of him by Mathew Brady, which he used in his campaign literature, contributed to his election to the presidency as a Republican in 1860. (Library of Congress)

The Civil War Realignment

The Civil War resulted in a realignment along sectional lines. The Republicans were the dominant party in the larger and more populous North and were therefore also the nation's majority party. The Democratic party was left with a stronghold in what became known as "the Solid South." During the next three decades the Republicans controlled the presidency except for Grover Cleveland's two terms, and they held a majority in one or both houses of Congress for all but four of those years. Cleveland's initial victory in 1884 was made possible only by a split in Republican ranks. The GOP denied nomination to its own incumbent, Chester A. Arthur, and turned instead to James G. Blaine ("the Man from Maine"), who, it appears, had the support neither of progressive Republicans nor of his own running mate, John A. Logan.

The 1890s Realignment

The election of 1896 resulted in a further realignment of the Republican-Democratic party system. Three years earlier, an economic panic following a bank collapse had resulted in a severe depression. The Democrat Cleveland was president when the panic occurred, and that circumstance worked to the advantage of the Republicans. They gained strength in the East particularly because of fear of cheap credit, a policy advocated by the Democrats' 1896 presidential nominee, William Jennings Bryan. During the four decades between the 1890s realignment and the next one in the 1930s, the Republicans held the presidency except for Woodrow Wilson's two terms and had a majority in Congress for all but six years. As was the case with Cleveland, Wilson could not have won except for dissension within Republican ranks. In the election of 1912, the Republican vote for incumbent William Howard Taft was split by the Bull Moose party candidacy of Theodore Roosevelt, which enabled Wilson to win with less than 45 percent of the total vote.

The Great Depression and the 1930s Realignment

The Great Depression of the 1930s triggered a thoroughgoing realignment of the American party system. The Republican Herbert Hoover was president when the stock market crashed in 1929, and many Americans blamed Hoover, his party, and its business allies for the economic catastrophe that followed. The Democrats became the country's majority party, and their political and policy agenda favored a significant social and economic role for the national government. Franklin D. Roosevelt's presidency was characterized by unprecedented policy initiatives in the areas of business regulation and social welfare (see Chapters 2, 15, and 16). His election in 1932 began a thirty-six-year period of Democratic presidencies that was interrupted only by Dwight D. Eisenhower's two terms in the 1950s. During this period, the Democrats

The new order begins: Franklin D. Roosevelt rides to his inauguration with outgoing president Herbert Hoover after the realigning election of 1932. (UPI/Bettmann Newsphotos)

also dominated Congress, losing control only of the House in the periods 1947–1948 and 1953–1954.

The lasting impact of realignments is largely due to their effect on party identification (see Chapter 6). In the 1930s by responding to people's demands for jobs and welfare assistance, the Democratic party cemented its image as the party of the common people. The Republican party was widely perceived as the party of business and rich people. The Democratic party's image was more appealing to first-time voters; they came to identify with the Democratic party by a 2-to-1 margin.[12] These new partisans helped establish the Democrats as the nation's majority party, enabling it to dominate national politics for decades. Even in recent elections, Americans who reached voting age during the Depression era were more supportive of the Democratic party than people who reached voting age earlier or later (see Figure 8-2).

The real power behind the 1930s realignment and all other realignments can be found in public opinion. Although the electorate does not actually decide the particulars of new programs through its vote in such elections, it does decisively reject an existing policy direction and express a demand for new policies appropriate to the nation's problems. This new direction defines the nation's politics for years to come.

Of course, the effects of a realignment do not last forever. The issues that gave rise to the realignment gradually weaken and are replaced with newer ones. By the late 1960s, when the Democratic party was divided over Vietnam and civil rights, the political impact of the New Deal realignment was clearly waning.[13] The Republicans gained control of the presidency and, except for Jimmy Carter's single term, held it through the 1992 election. The GOP also made deep inroads in the once solid Democratic South.[14] The Republicans did not, however, establish themselves as the nation's new majority party. Democrats held control of the House of Representatives throughout the 1968–1994 period and had a majority in the Senate for all but six years in this span. When Bill Clinton took office in 1993, the Democrats controlled all three national institutions—the presidency, House, and Senate.

A NEW REALIGNMENT?

The Republican party's sweeping victory in the 1994 midterm elections has prompted some analysts to conclude that a new realignment is under way. Other analysts are more cautious. They note that major Republican breakthroughs in the 1946, 1952, 1968, and 1980 elections did not translate into permanent gains. Still other analysts suggest that the 1994 elections were a continuation of a recent trend toward electoral volatility—a voting public that shifts its loyalties from one party to the other.

In truth, it will probably be several years before it is known whether the 1994 elections signified a historic juncture in the party system. Nevertheless, the reasons why a realignment may or may not be in the offing are worthy of attention. Let's begin with a major obstacle to a full-scale realignment—the public's lukewarm attachment to parties.

Dealignment: The Weakening of Party Ties

A few decades ago, parties had a strong hold on people's thinking. *Party identification* (see Chapter 6) was far and away the most important single influence on voting choice. About 80 percent of adults claimed to identify with the Republican or Democratic party, and nearly half of them professed a strong attachment to their party of choice. Reflecting these loyalties, most voters cast a "straight ticket," supporting only candidates of their party in an election. By the early 1970s, party loyalties had weakened substantially. The proportion of voters who described themselves as independents had increased (see Figure 8-3), and most partisans claimed only a weak attachment to the party of their choice. This trend, as might be expected, was coupled with widespread **split-ticket voting** (see Figure 8-4), where the voter picks candidates of both parties for different offices when casting a ballot.

split-ticket voting The pattern of voting in which the individual voter in a given election casts a ballot for one or more candidates of each major party. This pattern is the opposite of straight-ticket voting, in which the voter supports only candidates of one party in a particular election.

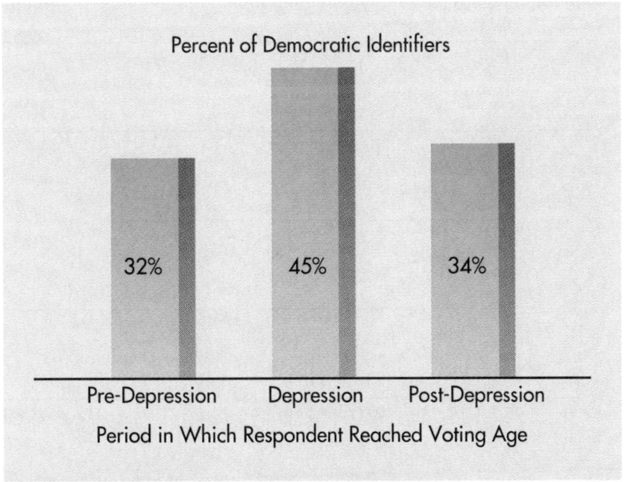

FIGURE 8-2 The Enduring Effects of Partisan Realignment Even today, Americans who reached voting age during the Depression era are more likely to support the Democratic party than those who reached voting age either earlier or later. *Source: Estimated by author from various polls.*

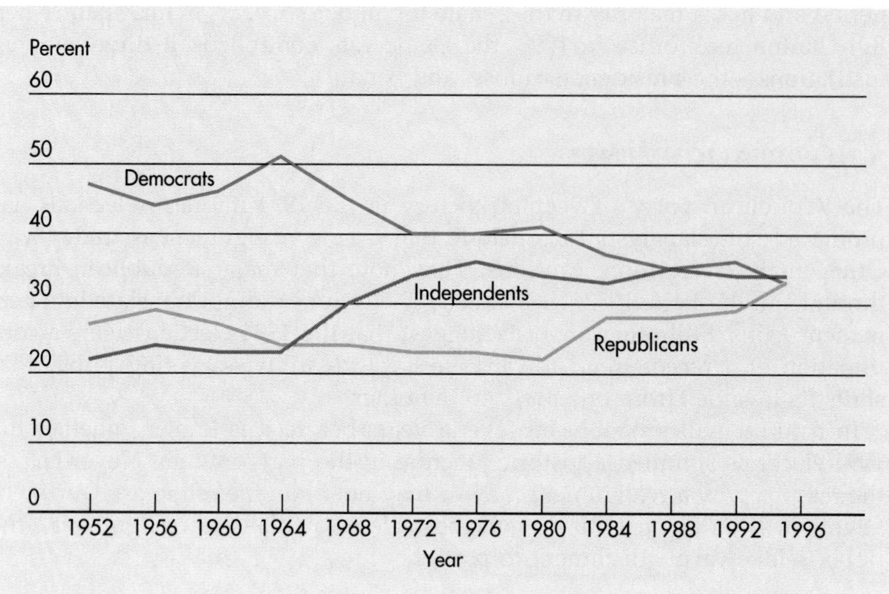

FIGURE 8-3
Partisan Identification
Party loyalties weakened in the late 1960s, and the proportion of independents increased. *Source: National Election Studies, 1952–1992; various surveys, 1993–1995.*

dealignment A situation in which voters' partisan loyalties have been substantially and permanently weakened.

The trend away from party identification has been termed a party **dealignment,** a partial but enduring weakening of partisan loyalties.[15] A dealignment is characterized by greater responsiveness of the electorate to short-term influence, such as the candidates and issues of the moment, than to the long-term influence of party identification. Declining partisanship has meant less stability in vote choices. In the 1940s and 1950s, when voters' party loyalties were stronger than they are today, presidential campaigns changed few people's minds. About 80 percent of the voters made their choice early in the campaign and stayed with it. Even the late deciders were not entirely open to persua-

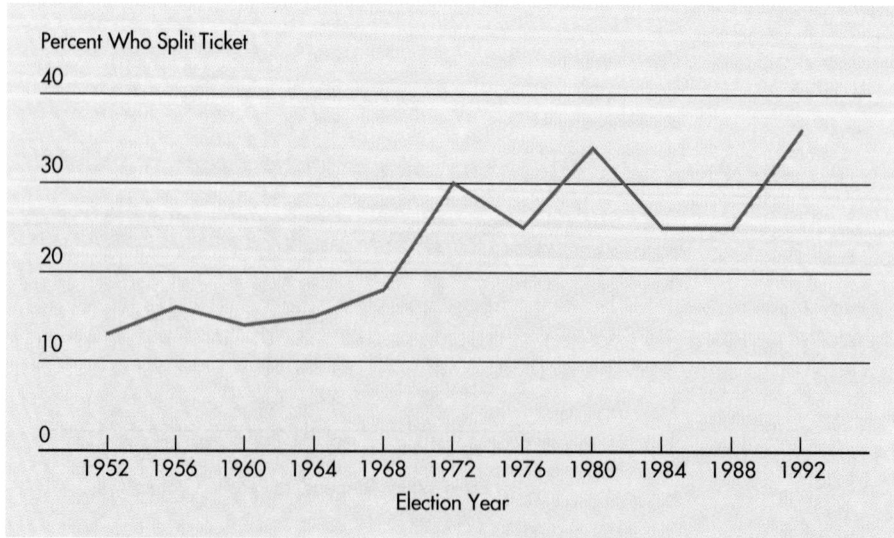

FIGURE 8-4 Split-Ticket Voting in Presidential and House Races The proportion of voters who split their ballot in presidential and House races has increased substantially in recent decades as a result of the decline in the strength of partisan loyalties. *Source: National Election Studies.*

sion; the large majority ended up supporting the candidate of their party.[16] Today's voters are more easily influenced by a campaign's issues, events, and candidates. The 1992 Clinton-Bush-Perot contest is an extreme example. Clinton trailed both of his opponents in June, but he shot ahead by more than 20 percentage points when Perot dropped from the race temporarily at the time of the Democratic National Convention and never fell behind again.

The decline of partisanship began in the 1960s, when divisive issues emerged and started to shake existing loyalties. The civil rights issue, for example, was unsettling not only to many southern Democrats but also to some white northern Democrats, particularly blue-collar workers and members of ethnic groups, who felt that black Americans were making rapid gains at their expense.[17] The Vietnam war and the Watergate scandal also created widespread alienation. Americans' trust in their elected representatives dropped sharply, as did their faith in political parties. The erosion of partisanship later rebounded somewhat, but has stayed at a substantially lower level than a few decades ago. Partisanship today is a far cry from what it once was.

If the decline of partisanship was attributable solely to the impact of divisive issues, such as the Vietnam war, then it could be expected to return to the earlier high level as new issues draw people back to the parties. In the judgment of some analysts, however, partisanship has declined in part for reasons that have nothing to do with the issues of the moment. For example, Americans today are better educated and more independent, and accordingly are more inclined to believe they can and should judge the candidates for themselves rather than on the basis of party. The decline in parties has paralleled the decline in authority of all traditional institutions, from the family to the churches. Why should parties be any different?

If the dealigning thesis is correct, the Republicans' 1994 victory is not the beginning of a period of prolonged success of the type the Democrats had from the 1930s on. Indeed, the GOP lost ground in 1996; the Democrats retained the presidency and gained nearly a dozen seats in the House of Representatives. According to the dealignment thesis, deep partisan loyalties are not likely to develop in today's world, and so the predicted scenario is a continuation of shifting support where the Republicans prevail at some times and the Democrats at other times. Some analysts even suggest that voters' weak partisanship may eventually enable a strong third party to emerge.

Republican Resurgence: On the Right Side of the Issues

The opposing thesis that the 1994 midterm elections herald a new era of Republican dominance is based partly on the scale of the GOP's victory. The party picked up fifty-two House seats and, in the process, took control of the House of Representatives for the first time in four decades. The Republicans also acquired control of the Senate, gaining eight seats on Election Day and picking up a ninth the next day when Alabama Senator Richard Shelby switched parties. The Republican victory also included control of an additional twelve governorships and seventeen state Senate or House chambers. Not since the 1952 election had voters so thoroughly repudiated the party in power. The election was so one-sided that no Republican governor or member of Congress lost a bid for reelection.

★ STATES IN THE NATION

Party Control of State Government: After their sweeping victory in the 1994 elections, the Republicans took control of many state governments.

STATE	GOVERNOR	STATE SENATE	STATE HOUSE
Ala.	Rep.	Dem.	Dem.
Alaska	Dem.	Rep.	Rep.
Ariz.	Rep.	Rep.	Rep.
Ark.	Dem.	Dem.	Dem.
Calif.	Rep.	Dem.	Rep.
Colo.	Dem.	Rep.	Rep.
Conn.	Rep.	Rep.	Dem.
Del.	Dem.	Dem.	Rep.
Fla.	Dem.	Rep.	Dem.
Ga.	Dem.	Dem.	Dem.
Hawaii	Dem.	Dem.	Dem.
Idaho	Rep.	Rep.	Rep.
Ill.	Rep.	Rep.	Rep.
Ind.	Dem.	Rep.	Rep.
Iowa	Rep.	Dem.	Rep.
Kan.	Rep.	Rep.	Rep.
Ky.	Dem.	Dem.	Dem.
La.	Dem.	Dem.	Dem.
Maine	Ind.	Rep.	Dem.
Md.	Dem.	Dem.	Dem.
Mass.	Rep.	Dem.	Dem.
Mich.	Rep.	Rep.	Rep.
Minn.	Rep.	Dem.	Dem.
Miss.	Rep.	Dem.	Dem.
Mo.	Dem.	Dem.	Dem.
Mont.	Rep.	Rep.	Rep.
Neb.	Dem.	*	*
Nev.	Dem.	Rep.	Split
N.H.	Rep.	Rep.	Rep.
N.J.	Rep.	Rep.	Rep.
N.Mex.	Rep.	Dem.	Dem.
N.Y.	Rep.	Rep.	Dem.
N.C.	Dem.	Dem.	Rep.
N.Dak.	Rep.	Rep.	Rep.
Ohio	Rep.	Rep.	Rep.
Okla.	Rep.	Dem.	Dem.
Oreg.	Dem.	Rep.	Rep.
Pa.	Rep.	Rep.	Rep.
R.I.	Rep.	Dem.	Dem.
S.C.	Rep.	Dem.	Rep.
S.Dak.	Rep.	Rep.	Rep.
Tenn.	Rep.	Dem.	Dem.
Texas	Rep.	Dem.	Dem.
Utah	Rep.	Rep.	Rep.
Vt.	Dem.	Rep.	Dem.
Va.	Rep.	Dem.	Dem.
Wash.	Dem.	Dem.	Rep.
W.Va.	Dem.	Dem.	Dem.
Wis.	Rep.	Rep.	Rep.
Wyo.	Rep.	Rep.	Rep.
Total:			
Rep.	30	25	25
Dem.	19	24	23
Ind.	1	0	0

*Nebraska has a unicameral, nonpartisan legislature.
SOURCE: National Conference of State Legislatures.

THE MEDIA AND THE PEOPLE

MEDIA BIAS: DEMOCRATIC OR REPUBLICAN?

For years, conservatives have argued that the media are biased in favor of the Democratic party. In *The News Twisters,* Edith Efron charged that the television networks in 1968 "actively opposed the Republican candidate, Richard Nixon." She tracked the amount of television good press and bad press received by Nixon and his opponents, Hubert Humphrey and George Wallace, and concluded that "network coverage tends to be strongly biased in favor of the Democratic-liberal-left axis of opinion, and strongly biased against the Republican-conservative-right axis of opinion."

Studies have shown that most journalists are liberal and Democratic in their personal beliefs. A 1992 survey found that journalists identified three-to-one with the Democratic party.

No scholarly study, however, has definitely linked journalists' partisan views to a substantial and systematic bias in favor of Democratic candidates. Efron, a conservative columnist, did her own content analysis rather than use trained coders, which is the accepted method. Studies employing the latter method (for example, those of Doris Graber, Michael Robinson, and C. Richard Hofstetter) have concluded that partisan bias plays a relatively small part in election news. These studies did detect one kind of bias, however, which results from journalistic values: good or bad press stems from bias inherent in storymaking situations. In 1992, for example, the Republican George Bush got negative coverage from the press because the prevailing story line was an incumbent president whose reelection bid was in trouble. This news theme was unfavorable and so, therefore, were the "facts" that reporters used to support it. But in 1988, it was the Democratic nominee, Michael Dukakis, who got the worst of the bad news. Dukakis was losing in the polls and the "facts" selected to explain his plight were accordingly negative ones.

It can be argued that even if the media system once had a Democratic bias, it now has a Republican one. This argument would include the role of talk radio. A substantial portion of Americans now say they get most of their information from this medium, and 70 percent of all talk-show hosts are outspoken conservatives. For its part, the mainstream press has become increasingly negative in its coverage of government and politicians (see Chapter 11). Although this negativism is aimed at both parties, its effect may favor the Republicans by heightening the public's distrust of government. In the 1994 midterm elections, this distrust worked strongly in the favor of the GOP, the party of smaller government.

SOURCES: Thomas E. Patterson, *Out of Order* (New York: Vintage, 1994), 104–111; Edith Efron, *The News Twisters* (Los Angeles: Nash, 1971), 47; David H. Weaver and G. Cleveland Wilhoit, "The American Journalist in the 1990s," Indiana University School of Journalism Research Paper, Bloomington, November 1992, p. 7.

The 1994 Republican victory also has two other characteristics of a realigning election. A first is that the victory was built on deep public dissatisfaction with politics as usual. Voter anger was the defining characteristic of the 1994 elections. The voters believed that their representatives in Washington were indifferent to their needs and controlled by special interests. Voters were also increasingly skeptical of the government's ability to solve problems, to rise above partisan bickering, or to deliver on its promises. Underlying these concerns were worrisome economic changes, including stagnant wages and salaries. The annual income of the average middle-class family, adjusted for inflation, had not increased since the 1970s. People were also concerned about disruptive social changes, including a perception of rising crime and declining moral values. The Democrats were an inviting target for voters who believed "big government" was wasting their hard-earned tax dollars and was fostering moral and economic irresponsibility through its welfare programs.

The other characteristic the 1994 election shares with a realignment is its impact on national policy. When Republicans took control of Congress, they

Representative Newt Gingrich holds a Rush Limbaugh book while meeting with reporters a day after the GOP's victory in the 1994 elections. The Republican campaign was defined by the Contract with America, a platform devised by Gingrich and based on the party's commitment to reducing the size of the federal government. (Chris Brown/Saba)

initiated major changes in both the way the government does business and the scope of its programs. The Republicans voted to eliminate three House committees and twenty-five subcommittees, prune 600 employees from the committees' staffs, halt closed-door committee meetings, and eliminate special-interest caucuses. They then moved to restore powers to the states and to cut federal spending and taxes. Their initiatives were reinforced with the themes of small government and individual responsibility, which resonated with a public tired of what it perceived as a remote and extravagant federal government. Even before the new Republican majority was sworn in, most Americans had concluded that the GOP, rather than the Democratic party, was better able to handle the nation's problems (see Table 8-1).

So what will the 1994 elections mean eventually? Will they be like the 1946

TABLE 8-1 Opinions of the Two Parties, before and after the 1994 Elections
The public expressed strong confidence in the Republican party after its sweeping victory in the 1994 elections.

Which party would do a better job on:	LATE 1993		LATE 1994	
	Republican	*Democrat*	*Republican*	*Democrat*
Unemployment	34%	49%	48%	41%
Health care	32	53	46	41
Taxes	46	37	57	30
Economy	42	41	54	33
Budget deficit	37	41	52	31
Crime	36	47	52	29
Welfare reform	36	47	55	35

SOURCE: USA Today/CNN surveys by the Gallup Organization, December 19, 1993, and November 29, 1994.

★ CRITICAL THINKING

What If the United States Had Proportional Representation?

Politics is a game played under certain rules. These rules are often regarded as neutral in their effect: they define how the game is played and won but do not themselves influence the outcome. However, this view is naive. The rules can and do affect who wins and who loses.

A clear example is electoral systems. The United States has a single-member-district system in which the election winners are those candidates who get the most votes in a district. Most European countries, by comparison, have proportional representation systems, in which seats in the national legislature are distributed according to each party's share of the popular vote. The European system makes it possible for smaller parties to win legislative seats. In contrast, the American system discourages smaller parties. A party that receives 15 percent of the national vote might win no seats in Congress.

Which system—the proportional or the single-member district—do you prefer? Why? Is one system inherently better suited to the United States than the other? Why?

midterm elections, when the out-party gained fifty-five House seats only to lose the presidential election and seventy-five House seats two years later? Or will they be like the 1930 midterm elections, when the out-party swept the congressional races and then solidified its position as the country's next majority party by winning the presidency two years later?

A full answer lies ahead. Although the 1996 election was a setback for the GOP, some observers attribute the party's losses to an overzealous Republican majority in Congress. This majority aggressively sought to trim Medicare and other popular federal programs, which cost the party the backing of moderate voters in 1996. These analysts believe the GOP's philosophy of smaller government has a lasting appeal that will enable the party to regain its momentum once its leadership moderates its positions. Other analysts see the situation differently. They argue that Americans' desire for smaller government coexists with their interest in government programs associated with the Democratic party, such as social security, health care assistance, and environmental protection. From this perspective, neither the Republican nor Democratic party's philosophy fully corresponds with majority opinion, and thus neither party can expect to dominate national elections on a regular basis.

Electoral and Party Systems

The history of the United States is a story of the competition between two parties: Federalists vs. Republicans, Whigs vs. Democrats, and Republicans vs. Democrats. Every now and then, as in the case of Ross Perot's 1992 and 1996 candidacies, a third choice joins the fray, but two-party competition has been the rule. Why two parties? Most democracies have a multiparty system in which three or more parties compete regularly for power. Why does the United States have only two major parties? Another question: What role do minor parties or independent candidates such as Perot play in the American system? This section addresses these questions.

THE SINGLE-MEMBER-DISTRICT SYSTEM OF ELECTION

A major reason for the persistence of America's two-party system is the fact that the nation chooses its officials through plurality voting in **single-member districts.**[18] Each constituency elects a single candidate to a particular office, such as U.S. senator or representative; only the party that gets the most votes (a plurality) in a district wins the office. This system discourages minor parties. Assume, for example, that a minor party received exactly 20 percent of the vote in each of the nation's 435 congressional races. Even though one in five voters nationwide backed the minor party, it would not win any seats in Congress because none of its candidates placed first in any of the 435 single-member-district races. The winning candidate in each case would be the major-party candidate who received the larger proportion of the remaining 80 percent of the vote.

proportional representation A form of representation in which seats in the legislature are allocated proportionally according to each political party's share of the popular vote. This system enables smaller parties to compete successfully for seats.

By comparison, most European democracies use some form of **proportional representation,** in which seats in the legislature are allocated according to a party's share of the popular vote. This type of electoral system provides

HOW THE UNITED STATES COMPARES

PARTY SYSTEMS

For nearly 160 years, electoral competition in the Untied States has centered on the Republican and Democratic parties. By comparison, most democracies have a multiparty system, in which three or more parties receive substantial support from voters. The difference is significant. In a two-party system, the parties tend to have overlapping coalitions and programs, because each party must appeal to the middle-of-the-road voters who provide the margin of victory. In multiparty systems, particularly those with four or more strong parties, the parties tend to separate themselves, as each tries to secure the enduring loyalty of voters who have a particular viewpoint.

Whether a country has a two-party or a multiparty system depends on several factors, but particularly the nature of its electoral system. The United States has a single-member plurality district system in which only the top vote getter in a district gets elected. This system is biased against smaller parties; even if they have some support in a great many races, they win nothing unless one of their candidates places first in an electoral district. By comparison, proportional representation systems enable smaller parties to compete; each party gets legislative seats in proportion to its share of the total vote. All the countries in the chart that have four or more parties also have a proportional representation system of election.

NUMBER OF COMPETITIVE PARTIES

Two	*Three*	*Four or More*
New Zealand	Canada	Belgium
United States	Great Britain	Denmark
		France
		Germany
		Italy
		Netherlands
		Sweden

smaller parties an incentive to organize and compete for power. In the 1994 German elections, the Green and Free Democratic parties each won slightly more than 5 percent of the national vote and each received about 5 percent of the seats in the Bundestag, the German parliament. If these parties had been competing under the rules of the American electoral system, however, they would not have won any seats and would have had no chance of exercising a share of legislative power.

The adverse effect of electoral laws on U.S. minor parties is evident also in the election of the president. A presidential race is a winner-take-all contest, and only a strong party has any chance of gaining the office. The presidency can be won with less than a majority of the popular vote, as was the case in 1992, when Democrat Bill Clinton was elected with only a 43 percent plurality. In that election Ross Perot won 19 percent of the national vote, but his relatively strong showing gave him no share of executive power. By comparison, in France there must be a runoff election between the two candidates who receive the most votes if neither receives a majority—50 percent or more—of the vote. Minor parties that fare poorly in the first election can bargain with the final contenders, trading support in the runoff election for policy concessions or cabinet positions in the new government. In this way, the French system—unlike the American one—provides an incentive for smaller parties to compete.

The Republican and Democratic parties have institutionalized their hold on the U.S. party system with policies that are designed to promote their candidates. In the 1970s, for example, Congress established a system of public funding for presidential elections. Each major-party candidate receives a substantial sum of money ($62 million in 1996) with which to conduct a general election campaign. Minor-party or independent candidates get funding only if they receive at least 5 percent of the vote, which means that, unless they obtained that level of support in the previous election, they do not receive funds, if at all, until after the election. Moreover, they receive funds only in an amount equal to the ratio of their total vote to the average total vote of the two major-party candidates. Thus, in 1980, independent candidate John Anderson received $4.2 million after he won 7 percent of the presidential vote, compared to the $29 million awarded the Republican nominee Ronald Reagan and the Democratic nominee Jimmy Carter. Anderson ran his campaign on borrowed money and would have received no public funding if his vote total had dropped below the 5 percent level. In 1992, the billionaire Ross Perot campaigned on his own money, which made him ineligible for public funding (a candidate loses eligibility if he or she spends more than $50,000 in personal funds on the general election campaign). However, because he received 19 percent of the vote in 1992, Perot was eligible for and accepted public funding in 1996. He received $29 million. This amount was slightly less than half as much as Clinton or Dole received and reflected the fact that in 1992 Perot got slightly less than half of the average vote of the Republican and Democratic candidates.

MINOR PARTIES

Although the U.S. electoral system discourages the formation of third parties, the nation has always had minor parties—more than a thousand during the nation's history.[19] Most of them have been short-lived, and only a few have had a lasting impact. Only one minor party, the Republican party, has ever achieved majority status.

Minor parties in the United States have formed largely to advocate positions that their followers believe are not being adequately represented by either of the two major parties. This is both the strength and weakness of minor parties. Their followers are motivated by issue positions that are vital to them but less attractive to other voters. To increase its following, a minor party must broaden its platform; in so doing, however, it risks alienating its original supporters. Yet if it remains small, it cannot win elections and may eventually wither away.

In addition to providing a haven for those with atypical political views, minor parties increase the Republican and Democratic parties' responsiveness. A major party is always somewhat captive to its past, which is the source of many of its ideas and most of its followers. When conditions change, major parties are often slow to respond, which can enable a minor party to capitalize on the emerging issues. If it should gain a relatively large following, which has happened a few times in history, the major parties are forced to pay attention to the problems that are driving people to look elsewhere for leadership. The best example recently is Ross Perot's 1992 candidacy, which was fueled by the widespread perception that Washington had lost touch with the interests of the middle class. Both major parties saw the advantage they would gain if they could draw Perot's backers to their side in future elections. In 1994, the

Republicans succeeded in doing so, at least temporarily. Exit polls indicated that more than 60 percent of the Perot supporters voted Republican in the midterm elections.

Viewed historically, minor parties have formed in response to the emergence of a single controversial issue, out of a commitment to a certain ideology, or as a result of a rift within one of the major parties.

Single-Issue Parties

Some minor parties form around a single issue of overriding concern to their supporters, such as the present-day Right-to-Life party, which was formed to oppose the legalization of abortion. Some single-issue parties have seen their policy goals enacted into law. The Prohibition party contributed to the ratification in 1919 of the Eighteenth Amendment, which prohibited the manufacture, sale, and transportation of alcoholic beverages (but was repealed in 1933). Single-issue parties usually disband when their issue is favorably resolved or fades in importance.[20]

Ideological Parties

Other minor parties are characterized by their ideological commitment, or belief in a broad and radical philosophical position, such as redistribution of economic resources. Modern-day ideological parties include the Citizens party, the Socialist Workers party, and the Libertarian party, each of which operates on the fringe of American politics.

One of the strongest ideological parties in the nation's history was the Populist party. Its candidate in the 1892 presidential election, James B. Weaver, gained 8.5 percent of the national vote and won twenty-two electoral votes in six western states. The party, which is classified as a "protest party" by some scholars, began as an agrarian protest movement in response to an economic depression and the anger of small farmers over low commodity prices, tight

In 1896 the Populist party—a strong ideological party—nominated William Jennings Bryan as its presidential candidate. Bryan was also the Democratic nominee in that election. This Puck cartoon shows the Democratic party being swallowed by a Bryan-headed Populist snake. (Library of Congress)

credit, and the high rates charged by railroad monopolies to transport farm goods.[21] The Populists' ideological platform called for government ownership of the railroads, a graduated income tax, low tariffs on imports, and elimination of the gold standard. The Populist party in 1896 endorsed the Democratic presidential nominee, William Jennings Bryan, and its support probably hurt the Democrats nationally.[22] Large numbers of "Gold Democrats" left their party in fear of the inflationary consequences of Bryan's advocacy of the free coinage of silver.[23]

Perot's 1992 campaign resembled that of an ideological party, even though he ran as an independent candidate rather than as a party nominee. Perot's campaign was based not on a single issue but on broad public dissatisfaction with the ethical standards and performance record of established policymakers, Republicans and Democrats alike. Perot's 19 percent of the vote was second only to Theodore Roosevelt's 1912 percentage among presidential candidates who were not major-party nominees.

Factional Parties

The Republican and Democratic parties are relatively adept at managing internal conflict. Although each party's support is diverse, the differences among its varying interests can normally be reconciled. However, there have been times when factional conflict within the major parties has led to the formation of minor parties.

The most successful of these factional parties at the polls was Theodore Roosevelt's Bull Moose party. In 1908 Roosevelt, after having served eight years as president, declined to seek a third term and handpicked William Howard Taft for the Republican nomination. When Taft as president showed neither

Texan Ross Perot at a 1992 presidential rally in Dallas's Reunion Arena. Perot received 19 percent of the popular vote, the highest total for an independent or minor party candidate since Theodore Roosevelt's 27 percent in 1912. (Bob Daemmrich/The Image Works)

Roosevelt's enthusiasm for a strong presidency nor his commitment to the goals of the Progressive movement, Roosevelt decided to challenge Taft for the 1912 Republican nomination. Progressive Republicans backed Roosevelt, but Taft won the nomination with the support of conservative Republicans and the Republican National Committee. Roosevelt led a Progressive walkout to form the Bull Moose party (a reference to Roosevelt's claim that he was "as strong as a bull moose"). Roosevelt won 27 percent of the presidential vote to Taft's 25 percent, but the split within Republican ranks enabled the Democratic nominee, Woodrow Wilson, to win the presidency.

The most prophetic of the factional parties, however, may have been the States' Rights party of 1948 and George Wallace's American Independent party of 1968. Each of these parties was formed by southern Democrats who were angered by northern Democrats' willingness to use federal authority to bring about racial desegregation. The States' Rights platform asserted that the Truman administration was "totalitarian" in its disregard for states' authority in deciding racial issues. Wallace railed against "knee-jerk liberals" and "pointy-headed bureaucrats" who presumed to know what was best for everyone else. These factional campaigns foreshadowed the end of the Democratic Solid South.

Policy Formulation and Coalition Formation in the Two-Party System

The overriding goal of a major American party is to gain control of government by getting its candidates elected to office. In this effort, the party takes policy positions and organizes a coalition that it hopes will provide voters with a choice they want. The nature of this choice is constrained, however, by the nation's two-party system. Because there are only two major American parties, their policies and bases of support differ from what could be expected if numerous parties were in competition. To gain control of the government, the Republicans or Democrats must attract a majority of the electorate; the need to gain wide support usually leads both parties to advocate moderate policies and to avoid taking highly specific positions on controversial issues. American parties, Clinton Rossiter said, are "creatures of compromise."[24]

Rossiter's characterization describes American parties with reasonable accuracy during some periods. In other periods, however, the parties have pursued policies that have sharply divided Americans and offered them a clear choice. A complete description of the alternatives provided by the major American parties must include their actions in periods both of stability and of change, as the following discussion indicates.

SEEKING THE POLITICAL CENTER—SOMETIMES

Some critics contend that the two parties do not offer a real alternative.[25] In truth, the U.S. two-party system does not produce the range of alternatives offered by Europe's multiparty systems. In those systems, the various parties of the left (liberal), right (conservative), and center (moderate) typically offer voters sharply defined choices. For nearly a century, for example, Europe has

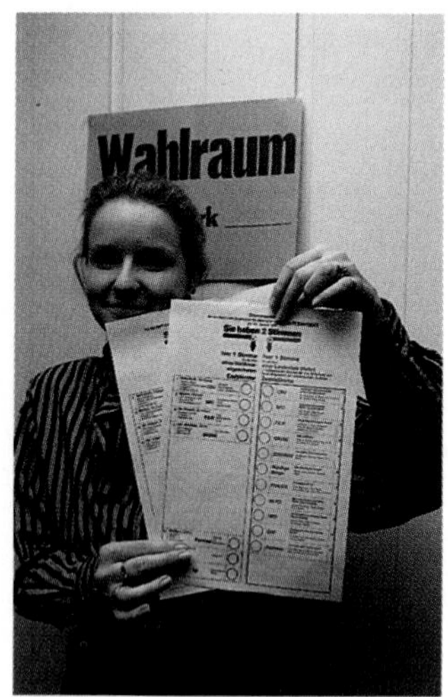

Germany's electoral system allocates legislative seats on the basis both of single-district voting and of the overall proportion of votes a party receives. This system requires that the German voter cast two ballots in legislative races: one to choose among the candidates in the particular district and one to choose among the parties. Shown here is a ballot from a German election. The left-hand column lists the candidates for the legislative seat in a district, and the right-hand column lists the parties. (Note the relatively large number of parties on the ballot.) (Photoreporters, Inc.)

had major socialist parties, whereas the U.S. party system has never offered socialism as a serious alternative.

The two major American parties tend to stay close to the center of the political spectrum.[26] Republican and Democratic candidates usually try to develop stands that will have broad appeal or at least will not alienate significant blocs of voters. Any time a party makes a pronounced shift toward either extreme, the middle is left open for the opposing party. Barry Goldwater, the Republican presidential nominee in 1964, proposed the elimination of mandatory social security and said he would consider the tactical use of small nuclear weapons in such wars as the Vietnam conflict—extreme positions that cost him many votes.

Political activists within the parties provide a centrifugal influence. Democratic activists are more liberal than other Democrats, and Republican activists are more conservative than other Republicans (see Table 8-2)—and either one can lead their parties away from the center. The conservative views of Republican convention delegates in 1992 contributed to an uncompromising antiabortion plank in the GOP platform, which contributed to George Bush's weak showing among women voters in the November election.[27] Nevertheless, many activists and most candidates are more pragmatic than ideological in their choice of issues. They normally try to avoid positions that will alienate moderate voters. They seek victory and do not knowingly embrace positions that will ruin all chances of achieving it.

Nonetheless, the Republican and Democratic parties do offer somewhat different alternatives and, at times, a clear choice. When Roosevelt was elected president in 1932, Johnson in 1964, and Reagan in 1980, the parties were relatively far apart in their priorities and programs. Roosevelt's New Deal, for example, was an extreme alternative within the American political tradition and caused a decisive split along party lines. In such periods of unrest as the 1930s, 1960s, and 1980s, the Democratic and Republican parties have clearly promoted different interests within society. The lesson of these periods is that the center of the American political spectrum can be moved. Candidates risk a crushing defeat by straying too far from established ideas during times of general satisfaction with government, but they may do so with some chance for victory during a turbulent period. Then, if conditions improve, the American public may show their support for the ascendant party's initiatives, thereby contributing to the creation of a new political center.

The 1994 midterm elections are an instructive example. The Republican victory was fueled by voter anger that was directed at Washington and that

TABLE 8-2 Ideology of Voters and National Convention Delegates, by Party
Party activists are substantially more ideological in their political beliefs than ordinary citizens.

	Democratic Delegates	*Democratic Voters*	*All Voters*	*Republican Voters*	*Republican Delegates*
Liberal	47%	28%	19%	12%	1%
Conservative	5%	23%	31%	45%	63%

SOURCE: CBS News/New York Times surveys, 1992.

Because they compete in a two-party system, America's major political parties are broad and diverse in their coalitions and leadership. The Republican senators pictured here span a wide ideological range. North Carolina's Jesse Helms (center) is one of the Senate's most conservative Republicans of recent decades, while Oregon's Mark Hatfield (right) is one of the most liberal. Virginia's John Warner (left) is a Republican moderate. (John Duricks/Wide World Photos)

vented itself on the Democratic party, which at the time controlled both the executive and legislative branches. The Republican's Contract with America was not a significant factor in the voters' judgment; less than a third of the voters claimed even to have heard of it, much less to know its contents. After the election, however, the contract became the guidepost to the GOP's efforts to reduce the cost and authority of the federal government, which did have substantial popular support. The public's views led many Democratic office-holders also to embrace cutbacks in federal power, thus shifting the entire party system toward the right.

PARTY COALITIONS

The groups and interests that support a party are collectively referred to as the **party coalition.** In multiparty systems, each party is supported by a relatively narrow range of interests. European parties tend to divide along class lines, with the center and right parties drawing most of their votes from the middle and upper classes and the left parties drawing theirs from the working class. By comparison, America's two-party system requires each party to accommodate a wide range of interests in order to gain the voting plurality necessary to win elections.[28] The Republican and Democratic coalitions are therefore very broad. Each includes a substantial proportion of voters of nearly every ethnic, religious, regional, and economic grouping (see Table 8-3). There are only a few sizable groups that are tightly aligned with a party. African Americans are the clearest example; they vote about 90 percent Democratic in national elections.

party coalition The groups and interests that support a political party.

Although the Republican and Democratic coalitions overlap, they are hardly identical. Each party likes to appear to be all things to all Americans, but in fact each builds its coalition through a process of both unification and division. If a party did not stand for something—if it never took sides—it would lose all support.

TABLE 8-3 Components of the Republican and Democratic Coalitions Both parties include voters of all backgrounds, although their coalitions are based more heavily on certain groups.

Democratic Coalition	*Republican Coalition*
Blacks (+40%)	Whites (+5%)
Hispanics (+20%)	White men (+7%)
Women (+3%)	White southerners (+8%)
Income under $15,000 (+13%)	Incomes over $75,000 (+10%)
Union households (+11%)	Employed (+2%)
Jews (+18%)	
Catholics (+3%)	

SOURCE: National Election Studies. Figures are estimates based on percent deviation of group's vote from overall two-party vote in 1976–1992 presidential elections.

Since the 1930s, the major policy differences between the Republicans and the Democrats have involved the national government's role in solving social and economic problems. Each party has supported government action to promote economic security and social equality, but the Democrats have consistently favored a greater degree of governmental involvement. To some extent, the national Democratic party's coalition reflects this tradition: it draws support disproportionately from society's "underdogs"—blacks, union members, the poor, city dwellers, Jews, and other "minorities."[29] Of course, many formerly underprivileged groups that are now part of the middle class have remained loyal to the Democratic party, which also includes a significant proportion of the nation's better-educated and higher-income voters.

In contrast, the Republican coalition consists mainly of white, middle-class Protestants. However, the GOP has recently made inroads among such traditionally Democratic groups as Catholics, Hispanics, and blue-collar workers. Once-loyal Democrats have defected for a number of reasons, including racial issues, concerns about the cost of big government, and fears about a decline in moral standards. They have been attracted by the Republican message of less government, lower taxes, and traditional values.

Regionally, the Democrats are strongest in the Northeast while the Republicans are strongest in the South and Mountain states (see box: States in the Nation, p. 217). A few decades ago, regional differences reflected tradition nearly as much as political attitudes. The Democratic party held sway over the South, despite the generally conservative views of its voters. In New England, Republicans were the majority even though their social views were more liberal than those of Republicans in most other areas. Since then, changes in society and communication have reduced regional anomalies and made issues a clearer basis of the divisions between the parties. In presidential politics, and increasingly also at the congressional level, the Democratic party now fares better in New England than in the South, while the opposite is true of the GOP.

There is a self-limiting feature to the national party coalitions. The larger party can dominate the other only by building a broader coalition, but this

The religious right is a major force within the Republican party. The Rev. Pat Robertson (right of center, front row) and the Rev. Jerry Falwell (center of second row) are shown here at the 1992 Republican National Convention. Rush Limbaugh and Marilyn Quayle, the wife of Vice-President Dan Quayle, are among those seated near Robertson and Falwell. (Joe Traver/Gamma-Liaison)

broader base can ultimately be its undoing: the party cannot continue indefinitely to satisfy all the groups in its coalition.[30] As a party attracts more interest groups, the likelihood of conflict among them increases. The Democratic party, for example, could not possibly have met the demands of both black Americans and white southerners over the long term. Perhaps the surprising aspect of the Democrats' New Deal coalition was not its eventual decline but its longevity—its survival for almost fifty years. If the Republican party should gain a clear-cut majority status, it too can be expected to have problems in managing its coalition. Indeed, a source of internal division may already exist in the growing number of fundamentalist Christians within the GOP (see Table 8-4). Their strong views on school prayer, abortion, and other social issues are not shared by many traditional Republicans. Shortly after the

TABLE 8-4 Presidential Voting Pattern of White Born-Again Christians White Americans who call themselves "born-again" Christians have voted solidly Republican in recent presidential elections.

	REPUBLICAN PERCENT OF TWO-PARTY VOTE	
	All Voters	*White Born-Again Christians*
Reagan–Carter (1980)	55	66
Reagan–Mondale (1984)	59	78
Bush–Dukakis (1988)	54	81
Bush–Clinton (1992)	47	73

SOURCE: For all voters: Federal Elections Commission; for born-again Christians: CBS News/New York Times polls, 1980–1988; Voter Research & Survey poll for ABC/CBS/NBC, and CNN, 1992.

1994 election, House Speaker-to-be Newt Gingrich started a debate on school prayer that proved divisive among Republicans, and he quickly shifted focus to the economic issues on which most Republicans agree.

Popular Influence and America's Two-Party System

"It is the competition of political organizations that provides the people with the opportunity to make a choice," E. E. Schattschneider once wrote. "Without this opportunity popular sovereignty amounts to nothing."[31] Thus the competitive nature of America's two major parties is a central issue in any evaluation of the nation's politics. Do the parties in fact give the public a meaningful choice?

Critics who contend that public policy in America is controlled by a wealthy elite argue that the two parties do not offer a real alternative.[32] These critics emphasize the tendency of Republican and Democratic policies to converge.[33] For nearly a century, for example, Europe has had major socialist parties, whereas the U.S. party system has never offered socialism as a serious alternative. Each U.S. major party has embraced private enterprise to a degree not found elsewhere. Of course, the American public has shared this attachment to private initiative, although from time to time polls have indicated public support for social welfare alternatives. In the two decades following World War II, for example, the American public, by a bare majority and apparently without much intensity, indicated a preference for a comprehensive system of government-paid health care. President Truman did propose legislation for such a health care system in the late 1940s, but the plan never came close to receiving the necessary congressional approval.

Noting such examples, leftist critics argue that America's major parties are tools of upper-class interests. Ironically, the Republican and Democratic par-

Members of France's Green party demonstrate outside the Paris Opera House. As a result of proportional representation, most European democracies have multiparty systems that, in most cases, include an environmental (green) party. (Maillac/Rea/Saba)

YOUR TURN

SUPPORT FOR THE TWO-PARTY SYSTEM

The Questions:

For a long time, we have had a two-party system where all presidents and almost all members of Congress and governors have been either Republicans or Democrats. Overall, do you think the two-party system has served this country well or not?

Has served country well	Has not served country well

Which of the following would you prefer?

A continuation of the two-party system of Democrats and Republicans	Elections in which candidates run as individuals without party labels	The growth of one or more new parties to challenge the Democrats and Republicans

What Others Think: According to a 1992 Harris poll, most Americans (61 percent) think the two-party system has served the country well. Nevertheless, they also believe that the system is no longer serving the country well and should be scrapped, although they disagree on the alternative. Only 29 percent expressed support for a continuation of the two-party system, 38 percent said they preferred elections without party labels, and 30 percent indicated a desire for new parties that would challenge the Democrats and Republicans. A negative opinion of the two-party system is more characteristic of younger voters than older ones. Among survey respondents of eighteen to twenty-nine years of age, nearly half thought the two-party system has not served the country well and more than three-fourths preferred an alternative to the present system.

Comment: Although many Americans would prefer politics without parties, a political system without parties would be more chaotic than the present one. All modern democracies have found that parties are an essential component of stable and sustained political competition. Americans' desire for third-party alternatives also has an idealistic dimension. The single-member plurality district system of elections makes it difficult for a third party to flourish in the United States. The development of a stable multiparty system would likely require a change to an electoral system based on proportional representation, which would be difficult to implement in a political system where the president, representatives, and senators are separately elected and where electoral apportionment is based on the states.

ties have not been spared by critics on the right, either. After all, it was George Wallace, a conservative, who made the slogan "Not a dime's worth of difference between them" the basis for a third-party campaign. Wallace contended that the Republican and Democratic parties were both overly solicitous of the opinions of minorities and liberals. Indeed, until Ronald Reagan's election in 1980, most of the attacks on the parties from political circles (as opposed to academic circles) came from the right, not the left.

Nonetheless, as we have explained in this chapter, the Republican and Democratic parties do offer somewhat different alternatives and, at times, a clear choice. When the parties have later converged again, that trend was always in large part a reflection of a change in the public's attitudes.

The continuous adjustment of America's two parties to the mood of the electorate reflects their competition for power. Each party has a realistic chance of winning a national election and thus has an incentive to respond to changes in public opinion. Viewed differently, a competitive opposition party is the public's best protection against an unresponsive government; the out-party provides the electorate with an alternative. Even in its weakened position after the Roosevelt years, the Republican party was strong enough to provide an alternative when the public's dissatisfaction with the Democrats rose, as in

1952, 1968, and 1980 at the presidential level and in 1946, 1952, and 1980 at the congressional level. And the GOP made a strong breakthrough in 1994 as a direct result of the public's anger with the performance of government.

In sum, America's parties do offer the public a real choice, even if the alternatives are not so sharply defined as those in some other democratic nations. Without political parties the American public would be in a weak position to influence the broad direction of public policy through elections.

Summary

Political parties give elections their force and direction. Through competition for the people's votes, parties give voters an opportunity to influence the policies of government. The people's voice is particularly decisive during realigning periods when the parties search for responses that will satisfy the public's desire for change. The policies that emerge typically define the nation's politics for years to come.

In the United States, party competition takes place within the confines of a two-party system; only the Democratic and Republican parties have any chance of winning control of government. Most other democracies have a multiparty system. The fact that the United States has only two major parties is explained by several factors: an electoral system—characterized by single-member districts—that makes it difficult for third parties to compete for power; each party's willingness to accept political leaders of differing views; and a political culture that stresses compromise and negotiation rather than ideological rigidity. America's two major parties are also maintained by laws and customs that support their domination of elections.

Because the United States has only two major parties, each of which seeks to gain majority support, they normally tend to avoid controversial or extreme political positions. The parties typically pursue moderate and somewhat overlapping policies. Their appeals are designed to win the support of a diverse electorate with moderate opinions. This form of party competition is reflected in the Republican and Democratic coalitions. Although the two parties' coalitions are not identical, they do overlap significantly: each party includes large numbers of individuals who represent nearly every significant interest in the society. Nonetheless, the Democratic and Republican parties sometimes do offer sharply contrasting policy alternatives, particularly in times of political unrest. It is at such times that the public has its best opportunity to make a decisive difference through its vote.

Major Concepts

dealignment
multiparty system
party coalition
party competition
party realignment
political party
proportional representation
single-member districts
split-ticket voting
two-party system

Suggested Readings

Burnham, Walter Dean. *Critical Elections and the Mainsprings of American Politics.* New York: Norton, 1970. The classic analysis of how long-term stability in the electoral process is punctuated periodically by major change.

Duverger, Maurice. *Political Parties.* New York: Wiley, 1954. A classic analysis of types of party systems, their origins, and their effects.

Keith, Bruce E., David B. Magleby, Candice J. Nelson, Elizabeth Orr, Mark C. Westlye, and Raymond E. Wolfinger. *The Myth of the Independent Voter.* Berkeley: University of California Press, 1992. An analysis which asserts that independent voters are actually not very "independent" in their voting patterns.

Lijphardt, Arend. *Electoral Systems and Party Systems: A Study of Twenty-Seven Democracies, 1945–1990.* New York: Oxford University Press, 1994. A comprehensive study of the relationship between electoral systems and party systems.

Mazmanian, Daniel A. *Third Parties in Presidential Elections.* Washington, D.C.: Brookings Institution, 1984. An assessment of the influence of America's third-party movements, including George Wallace's 1968 campaign.

Milkis, Sidney M. *The President and the Parties: The Transformation of the American Party System since the New Deal.* New York: Oxford University Press, 1993. A careful assessment of how presidential politics has affected the party system.

Pomper, Gerald M. *Passions and Interests: Political Party Concepts of American Democracy.* Lawrence: University of Kansas Press, 1992. A broad theoretical analysis of American political parties.

Rosenstone, Steven J., Roy L. Behr, and Edward H. Lazarus. *Third Parties in America.* Princeton, N.J.: Princeton University Press, 1984. An analysis of America's third parties and their impact on the two-party system.

CHAPTER 9

POLITICAL PARTIES: CONTESTING ELECTIONS

By the standards of political parties of most Western democracies, the American party organizations are comparatively weak and insubstantial.

—Frank J. Sorauf[1]

He was variously called the "stealth candidate," the "phantom candidate," and the "noncandidate." He gave few public speeches, rarely met the press, and seldom took to the streets to talk with voters. He won nomination to the U.S. Senate in California's Republican primary but had few ties to the Republican party organization. He had his own campaign organization, which was funded with $25 million of his own money. Nearly all of it was spent on an advertising blitz that carried his image to every corner of the state.

Michael Huffington had moved to California five years earlier, bringing with him a $70-million personal fortune acquired as a Texas oil business heir. He had no substantial experience in party politics, but he had money and ambition. Despite grumblings that he was a carpetbagger, Huffington won a seat in the U.S. House of Representatives in 1992. The campaign cost him $5 million. In Washington, Huffington soon made it known that he had no intention of staying in the House. He focused his energy on preparations for a campaign in 1994 against incumbent U.S. Senator Dianne Feinstein. He selected the image of an outsider committed to ridding society of its politics. "I'm in this," he said, "to get government out of the way of human decency." In his campaign ads, he appeared not in front of the Capitol where he worked but on a remote California mountaintop.[2] The strategy nearly worked; Huffington lost the election by less than 1 percent of the vote.

Huffington's campaign is an extreme example of the tendency in American politics toward candidate-centered politics. Earlier in the century, the political parties were in control of U.S. elections, but individual candidates gradually took command. By the 1960s, the presidential nominating convention was the

U.S. Senate candidate Michael Huffington and his wife at a campaign gathering on election day. Huffington spent about $25 million of his own money on the campaign and lost by less than 1 percent to incumbent Senator Dianne Feinstein. (David Butow/Black Star)

party-centered politics Election campaigns and other political processes in which political parties, not individual candidates, hold most of the initiative and influence.

candidate-centered politics Election campaigns and other political processes in which candidates, not political parties, have most of the initiative and influence.

party organizations The party organizational units at national, state, and local levels; their influence has decreased over time due to many factors.

last party stronghold in national politics. When party leaders relinquished control of convention delegates after the 1968 election, the transition from **party-centered politics** to **candidate-centered politics** was virtually complete. The reality of today's national elections is that candidates have most of the initiative and most of the power. Candidates for the presidency and for Congress raise their own funds, form their own campaign organizations, and choose for themselves the issues on which they will run. Parties still play an important part in these elections, but their role is secondary to that of the candidates.

The public's ambivalence about political parties is a main reason for the transition. The individualistic nature of the nation's political culture creates resentment of any concentration of power, including that of the political parties.[3] Americans have sought to control parties through restrictive laws (such as those requiring primary elections) that no other democracy has adopted. As a result, U.S. **party organizations** are among the weakest in the world and U.S. candidates are among the most independent. Americans prefer a relatively direct form of democracy—one in which their relationships with candidates are not substantially mediated by party organizations.

Each U.S. party is really three parties in one. There is, first, the *party in the electorate,* which consists of the voters who identify with it (Chapter 6). Second, there is the *party in office,* which consists of those officials elected under its label (Chapters 8 and 12 to 15). And third, there is the *party as organization* staffed and led by activists, which is the subject of this chapter. The following points are emphasized in this chapter:

★ *The ability of America's party organizations to control nominations, campaigns, and platforms has declined substantially.* Although the parties continue to play an important role, elections are now controlled largely by the candidates, each of whom is relatively free to go his or her own way.

- ★ *U.S. party organizations are decentralized and fragmented. The national organization is a loose collection of state organizations, which in turn are loose associations of autonomous local organizations.* This feature of U.S. parties can be traced to federalism and the nation's diversity, which have made it difficult for the parties to act as instruments of national power.
- ★ *Party organizations, particularly at the state and national levels, have recently made a comeback of sorts by adapting to the money and media demands of modern campaigns.* However, their new relationship with candidates is more of a service relationship than a power relationship.
- ★ *Candidates' relative freedom to run campaigns of their own making lends flexibility to U.S. politics but diminishes the electorate's capacity to influence national policy in a predictable direction.* The choice of a candidate made by voters in any one constituency has no strong relationship to the choices of voters in other constituencies.

Elections and the Decline of Party Control

Party organizations engage in a variety of activities, including public education. But the raison d'être of the party organization is the contesting of elections. Parties recruit candidates, conduct campaigns, and formulate platforms. Other organizations, including interest groups, also do some or all these things (see Chapter 10). But parties alone owe their existence to the pursuit of electoral success.

Ironically, U.S. party organizations do not dominate any aspect of campaigns, not even the selection of the candidates who run under their banners. Candidates who are not recruited by the party often run, and sometimes win. They become the party's choice, whether the organization likes it or not. Even candidates who have the party's enthusiastic backing are usually more concerned with marketing themselves than with promoting the party.[4] As William Crotty has noted:

> It is a politics of every candidate for himself, each with an individual campaign organization loyal only to the candidate and disbanded after the election. It is an antiparty politics of fragmentation and transitory candidate organizations. It is a politics with no core, no sense of collective effort. And, it should be added, it is a politics that has captured the political world.[5]

In the nineteenth and early twentieth centuries, the situation was different. The party organizations were in control of nominations, elections, and platforms. The story of how and why they lost their commanding position is basic to an understanding of the parties' present role and influence.

CONTROL OF NOMINATIONS

Nomination refers to the selection of the individual who will run as the party's candidate in the general election. The legendary William Marcy ("Boss") Tweed of New York City's Tammany Hall machine once remarked, "I don't care who does the electing just so I can do the nominating."[6] Tweed

nomination The designation of a particular individual to run as a political party's candidate (its "nominee") in the general election.

★ CRITICAL THINKING

Parties in the American Political Culture
The modern political party originated in America and is a cornerstone of democratic government. Yet Americans have never fully accepted parties. What do you think accounts for this reluctance? What is your own opinion of parties? On what is your opinion based?

was stating the obvious. His Democratic machine so thoroughly dominated New York City elections in the late nineteenth century that his hand-picked nominees were virtually guaranteed election. Even in constituencies where the parties are competitive, the nominating decision is a critical choice because it narrows a large field of potential candidates down to the final two, one Republican and one Democrat.

Party-Controlled Nominations

Until the early twentieth century, nominations were the responsibility of party organizations. In smaller communities where voters had personal knowledge of potential candidates, the parties often had no practical alternative but to nominate popular individuals who wanted to run. In the cities, however, the party organizations were in a commanding position. Party label was the prime influence on urban voters, so it was essential for candidates to have party backing. To receive nomination, an individual had to be loyal to the party organization, a requirement that included a willingness to share with it the spoils of office—government jobs and contracts.

Political spoils enabled party organizations to acquire campaign workers and funds but also enabled unscrupulous party leaders to extort money from those seeking political favors. When Richard Croker, a Tammany leader, was asked his opinion of the unrestricted coinage of silver, the major political issue of the 1890s, he replied, "I'm in favor of all kinds of money—the more the better."[7]

The party machines took contributions from business interests in return for favors from City Hall and then used this money to woo the ethnic voters whose support enabled them to control city government. At the time, party machines were the closest things that the United States had to full-service welfare agencies. Jim Pendergast's Kansas City machine handed out more than government jobs. When the party faithful were penniless in winter, the Pendergast machine delivered fuel to their homes. Hundreds of families had turkey and trimmings at the free dinners that "Big Jim" staged each Christmas.[8]

The power of the machines, most of which were Democratic organizations, made them targets of the reform-minded Progressives, who were mainly native-born Protestant Republicans. By destroying the machines, which relied on the support of working-class Catholic immigrants, the Progressives could reform the system while also weakening their partisan and religious foes. The Progressives argued for *party democracy,* claiming that party organizations should be run by the same principle that governed elections: power should rest with rank-and-file voters rather than the bosses. To accomplish this goal, the Progressives sought legislation that would narrow the authority of party leaders. In many states, restrictive laws were passed requiring the parties to choose their organizational leaders by secret ballot, to print public notices of their meetings, and to make all major policy decisions in public session.

primary election (direct primary) A form of election in which voters choose a party's nominees for public office. In most primaries, eligibility to vote is limited to voters who are registered members of the party.

Primary Elections

The most serious blow struck by the Progressives against the power of the party bosses was the introduction of the **primary election** (or **direct primary**) as a method of choosing party nominees. In place of the older system of party-designated nominees, the primary system placed nominations in the hands of voters. In an 1897 speech, Robert M. La Follette, Sr., the Progressive movement's acknowledged leader, advised, "Go back to the first principles of democracy: go back to the people. Substitute for both the caucus and convention a primary election."[9] The first primary election law was enacted in 1903 by Mississippi. Within a decade, most states had adopted primaries as the means of choosing nominees for at least some offices.

Senator Robert M. La Follette, Sr., of Wisconsin pushed for Progressive reforms, including the use of primary elections to select party nominees. La Follette is shown here near the end of his lengthy political career, speaking on radio as the Progressive party's 1924 presidential nominee. (Culver)

The introduction of the primary was an "escape from one-partyism." The primary provided the voters with a real choice in locations where elections were regularly dominated by one party. This was true not only of machine-controlled cities but also of states in the South, where the Democrats exercised absolute dominance. According to V. O. Key, "primary competition tended to be substituted for general election competition; competition within parties for competition between parties."[10]

Today all states have primary elections for contested nominations for U.S. Senate and House seats (in Alabama, Georgia, South Carolina, and Virginia, the parties can nominate through the convention method if they choose to do so). Nearly forty states use primaries to select their delegates to the presidential nominating conventions. The other states use the caucus method, in which voters assemble at local sites to discuss the candidates before expressing their preference for one of them. (The presidential selection process is discussed further in Chapter 14.)

Primary elections take a number of different forms. Most states conduct "closed" primaries, in which participation is limited to voters registered or declared at the polls as members of the party whose primary is being held. Other states use "open" primaries, a form that allows independents and voters of either party to vote in a party's primary, although voters are prohibited by law from participating in both parties' primaries simultaneously. Alaska and Washington have a third form of primary, known as the "blanket" primary. These states provide a single primary ballot listing both the Republican and Democratic candidates by office. Each voter can cast only one vote per office, but can select a candidate of either party. Louisiana has a variation on this form in which all candidates are listed on the ballot but are not identified by party.

In most states, the winner of a primary election is the candidate who receives the largest number of votes, even if not a majority. In some border and southern states, however, there is a provision for a runoff primary if no candidate receives a majority of the vote (or, in North Carolina, 40 percent of the vote) in the regular primary. Slightly more than half the states have a "sore-loser" law that prevents a candidate who loses a primary from running as an independent or third-party candidate in the general election.

Primaries have not completely eclipsed the party organizations. Many politicians begin their careers as party volunteers; in this capacity they gain the attention of party leaders, who help them win their first elective office. Having established their political career, they then move up the ladder on their own initiative. Additionally, many party organizations actively try to influence the outcome of primary elections by putting forward their preferred candidate. Nevertheless, *primaries are the severest impediment imaginable to the strength of the party organizations.* Primaries enable candidates to seek office on their own and, once elected (whether with or without the party's help), to build an independent electoral base that effectively places them beyond the party's control.[11]

Some states have passed laws limiting party activities during primary election campaigns to help ensure that nominations will not be controlled by organizational leaders. California and Oregon, for example, prohibit party organizations from endorsing candidates in primary elections. Other states, including New York and Colorado, allow parties to endorse candidates for nomination but require them also to list on the primary ballot any candidate who gets the support of a certain proportion of the delegates at the state convention (25 percent in New York). New York's parties are also prohibited by law from giving financial support to primary election candidates. The decline of party influence in New York is reflected in the fact that in a number of statewide races, the party-endorsed candidate has lost the primary election. The most recent case of such a defeat was in the 1994 race for the Democratic nomination for attorney general. Studies indicate, however, that party-endorsed candidates usually win contested statewide races.[12]

The absence of primaries in Europe is one of the main reasons the parties there have remained strong. They control nominations, and European candidates must operate within the party organizations. A popular leader will be given fairly wide latitude by the party, but it is the parties, not the candidates,

HOW THE UNITED STATES COMPARES

PRIMARY ELECTIONS AND STRONG PARTIES

Primary elections are a defining characteristic of U.S. political campaigns. Primaries were invented in the United States and are used in elections to a wide variety of offices, from president of the United States to city council members. A small number of other countries, including Venezuela, hold primaries for a few offices, but most democracies select their nominees through party organizations.

Nominations are a key element in establishing a party's strength. When a party controls its nominations, it is in a strong position relative to its candidates. Ambitious politicians must work through the party in order to gain office. This situation enables the party to demand loyalty to its platform and also enables it to control other electoral resources, including money and workers. In contrast, primary elections weaken the party. Aspiring politicians can seek nomination directly through a primary, thereby circumventing the party organization. And once elected, incumbents are usually beyond the party's control. Their direct ties to the voters make it difficult for the party to unseat them. From their strong position, candidates are also able to control campaign resources; about 90 percent of campaign funds in U.S. elections are raised directly by the candidates. Not surprisingly, U.S. candidates run on platforms of their own choosing; although most of them are loyal to the party's traditions, they have wide latitude in deciding where they stand on any particular issue.

Country	*Method of Choosing Nominees*	*Strength of Party Organizations*
Canada	Party organizations	Moderate
France	Party organizations	Strong
Germany	Party organizations	Strong
Great Britain	Party organizations	Strong
Italy	Party organizations	Strong
Japan	Party organizations	Strong
Mexico	Party organizations	Strong
United States	Primary elections	Weak

which dominate elections. The European philosophy of "party democracy" is different from that of the United States. Rather than impose external restrictions on party decisions, European democracies allow the parties to regulate their own affairs, counting on the threat of electoral defeat to keep them in line. By most accounts, European party organizations are no less honest than their U.S. counterparts and are considerably stronger.[13]

Ironically, primaries may have prolonged the life of the major U.S. parties. The political scientist Leon Epstein argues that primaries have enabled the Republican and Democratic parties to maintain their dominance of elections by providing disgruntled voters an opportunity within the two-party system to initiate change. Without this alternative, they might in a period of discontent have turned to a third party.[14]

CONTROL OF ELECTION CAMPAIGNS

Workers, money, and media have always been the key resources in campaigns, but their relative importance has changed over time, as has their control by parties and candidates.

Party Workers

From their grassroots inception in the Jacksonian era, U.S. parties have depended on a relatively small number of active members. The parties have never had the large dues-paying memberships that characterize some European socialist and labor parties. Even the party machines in their heyday did not attempt to enroll the party electorate as active members. The machine's lowest organizational echelon was the precinct-level unit. Each precinct had several hundred voters but only two party workers, a precinct captain and his assistant.

Patronage was the traditional source of party workers. To get or keep government employment, individuals had to work for the party during election campaigns. Instituted during Andrew Jackson's presidency, this "spoils system" was a perennial target of reformers, and when antiparty sentiment intensified around 1900, the Progressives demanded that merit-based hiring be expanded. As government jobs shifted from the patronage to the merit system, the party organizations lost some of their vigor. Today, because government has expanded in size, thousands of patronage jobs still exist. Their occupants help staff the parties, but many of them are more loyal to the politician for whom they work than to a party organization.

The parties also get help from volunteers. Volunteers are an important resource, but they are less reliable than patronage employees as campaign workers. Volunteers are more often interested in debating issues than in distributing leaflets, and they cannot be compelled to perform tedious campaign tasks or to work a set number of hours during a campaign.[15] Moreover, volunteers are often more concerned about a particular candidate or issue than about the party's cohesiveness.[16] In 1994 religious-rights activists took over the Minnesota Republican convention and endorsed for governor one of their own people, Allen Quist, even though the party already controlled the governorship. The GOP incumbent, Arne Carlson, subsequently beat Quist in a primary and then won reelection, but the insurgency caused a rift within the Minnesota Republican party.

Money and Media

Campaigns for higher office have changed radically during the twentieth century. The "old politics," which emphasized party rallies and door-to-door canvassing, was based on a large supply of workers. The "new politics" centers on the media and depends on money—lots of it. The cost of a U.S. Senate campaign usually exceeds a million dollars and can run as high as $25 million, depending on the state and the closeness of the race. House campaigns cost much less, but the expenditure of $1 million, if exceptional, is no longer unthinkable. A presidential campaign can cost more than $50 million in the general election stage and upward of $20 million in the primaries.

Candidates for major offices spend a lot more money on televised political advertising and other media activities than on grassroots organizing. All the recent presidential nominees expended about half their total budget on political advertising; other media operations, including news conferences and press releases, consumed a major share of the remaining money. In congressional races, particularly for the House, the emphasis on mass communication varies substantially. House candidates in New York City, for example, do not rely heavily on television advertising because the voters of each district are only a small part of the large and expensive New York media market. Nevertheless, on average, media operations, news and advertising together, account for about 60 percent of the spending on congressional races.[17]

The organization of the modern campaign reflects the "new politics." The key operatives are campaign consultants, pollsters, media producers, and direct mail fund-raising specialists, all of whom operate outside the formal party organizations. They are "hired guns" who work for candidates who can afford their hefty fees. Candidates are receptive to whatever grassroots support the parties can provide, but they do not depend on this help to anywhere near the degree that they rely on their media operations. Televised advertising in particular enables candidates to communicate directly and easily with the electorate, thereby reducing the importance of grassroots party efforts.

The flow of money in the modern campaign also reflects the candidates' dominance. At the turn of the century, when party machines were at their peak, most campaign funds passed through the hands of the party organizations. Today most of the funds go directly to the candidates. About 80 percent of their money is obtained through direct solicitation of individual contributors and interest groups (see Chapters 10 and 13).

Because of the high cost of American campaigns, candidates spend an inordinate amount of time raising funds. The "money chase" is relentless.[18] It has been estimated that a U.S. senator must raise $10,000 a week on average throughout the entire six-year term in order to obtain the amount of funds necessary to run a competitive reelection campaign. More than a few members of Congress have concluded that their office is not worth the personal price they must pay to keep it. Representative Mike Kopetski had worked as a staff member of the Senate Watergate Committee and served in the Oregon legislature before being elected to the House. In 1994, after only two terms in office, and despite gaining a prized seat on the Ways and Means Committee, Kopetski announced he would not run again. He expressed a love for public service, but it had become for him an intolerable grind. He was expected to fly back to Oregon almost every weekend for appearances and fund-raisers, to spend endless hours talking with donors and lobbyists, and to answer the 500 letters he received each week from constituents, in the hope that they would support him the next time around. "I just want to live the rest of my life," he said in explaining his decision to leave the Congress.[19]

In European democracies, parties continue to dominate campaign resources. British parties, for example, hire and assign the campaign manager for each of their candidates for the House of Commons. The entire cost of running the 650 races that constitute a British national election is about $40 million, which is what a single statewide race in California can cost. Further, European nations allot free television time for campaign messages, which is granted directly to the parties rather than the candidates (see box: The Media and the People). Such differences reflect the fact that European elections are party-centered. European candidates do not have the freedom to organize and run on their own, and this constraint has kept them from taking control of campaign media and money.

The media can do a more thorough job of promoting candidates than party organizations ever could. Ann Richards is shown here taping a radio commercial during one of her campaigns for the Texas governorship. (Bob Daemmrich/Stock, Boston)

CONTROL OF PARTY PLATFORMS

Beginning in the 1830s and for more than a century thereafter, U.S. parties had control of the national platforms adopted at the presidential nominating conventions held every four years. Each state party sent a delegation to the national convention, and most of the delegates were high-ranking organizational and elected party officials. The first real business at each convention was the formulation of the policy proposals that made up the platform, and

In 1994 Bill Clinton picked Tennessee Senator Al Gore, Jr., to be his running mate. After the convention they began a whirlwind bus tour of the Midwest, stopping in cities, small towns, and even cornfields to talk to voters. (Tomas Muscionico/Contact Press Image)

THE MEDIA AND THE PEOPLE

POLITICAL PARTIES AND TELEVISION CAMPAIGNING

The Republican and Democratic parties are weak organizationally. They do not have full control over the nomination of candidates and are not the centers of campaign organization. For the most part, candidates in the United States set up their own campaigns, raise their own funds, and determine their own platforms. This pattern is unusual. In most other democracies, party organizations choose the nominees, devise platforms on which candidates must run, and coordinate campaign activities. The United States is atypical for many reasons, among them a cultural bias against political parties and a federal system and demographic diversity that make party unity difficult to achieve.

The candidate-centered nature of U.S. elections is evident even in the use of television. In most democracies, televised campaigning on behalf of candidates takes place through the parties, which receive free air time to make their appeals to voters. U.S. parties do not receive unrestricted free time but instead may buy advertising time. The candidates, however, have nearly all the money, so it is they who buy and control the advertising time. Some democracies prohibit parties and politicians from buying television time to advertise their appeals.

Country	*Paid TV Ads Allowed?*	*Unrestricted Free TV Time Provided?*
Canada	Yes	Yes
France	No	Yes
Germany	Yes	Yes
Great Britain	No	Yes
Italy	No	Yes
Japan	Yes	Yes
Mexico	Yes	Yes
United States	Yes	No

the delegates took the platform seriously as a statement of their common interests and commitments. (Ticket balancing—the practice of choosing a vice-presidential nominee from a different region and wing of the party than the presidential choice—served the same purpose.)

Today the national convention is controlled by the candidate who has accumulated a majority of delegates in the state primaries and caucuses preceding it. Accordingly, the platform is tailored to the policy positions of the nominee-to-be. In an attempt to foster party unity, recent nominees have worked out platform compromises with their opponents and have even made concessions to their own delegates. Nominees, however, insist that major planks in the platform conform to their views and that controversial minor planks be omitted.

National platforms have never been officially binding on presidential candidates, much less on candidates for the House and Senate, who have traditionally embraced, ignored, or rejected platform planks as it suited their purposes. However, the transition from party-centered to nominee-centered conventions has reduced the applicability of the national platform to congressional campaigns. When the parties' organizational and elected leaders, including members of Congress, had control of the platform, they aimed to persuade the delegates to approve planks on which they could campaign. Today candidates for Congress pretty much ignore the national platform, running instead on platforms of their own devising.

In European democracies, a party's candidates are expected to campaign on the national platform and, if elected as a governing majority, to support its planks, which are formulated in conjunction with organizational leaders, particularly in the case of labor and socialist parties. In Great Britain's Labour party, for example, the national platform is prepared by an executive committee dominated by organizational leaders but also including elected party representatives.

Party Organizations Today

The influence of U.S. parties has declined relative to that of candidates, but parties are not about to die out. Political activists need a stable organization through which they can work together, and parties meet that need. Moreover, certain activities, such as voter registration drives, benefit all of a party's candidates and are therefore more efficiently conducted through the party organization. Indeed, parties have staged a comeback of sorts.[20] National and state party organizations in particular have developed the capacity to assist candidates with polling, research, and media production, which are costly but essential ingredients of a successful modern campaign.

Structurally, U.S. parties are loose associations of national, state, and local organizations (see Figure 9-1). The national parties cannot dictate the decisions of the state organizations, which in turn do not control the activities of local organizations. However, there is communication between the levels, which

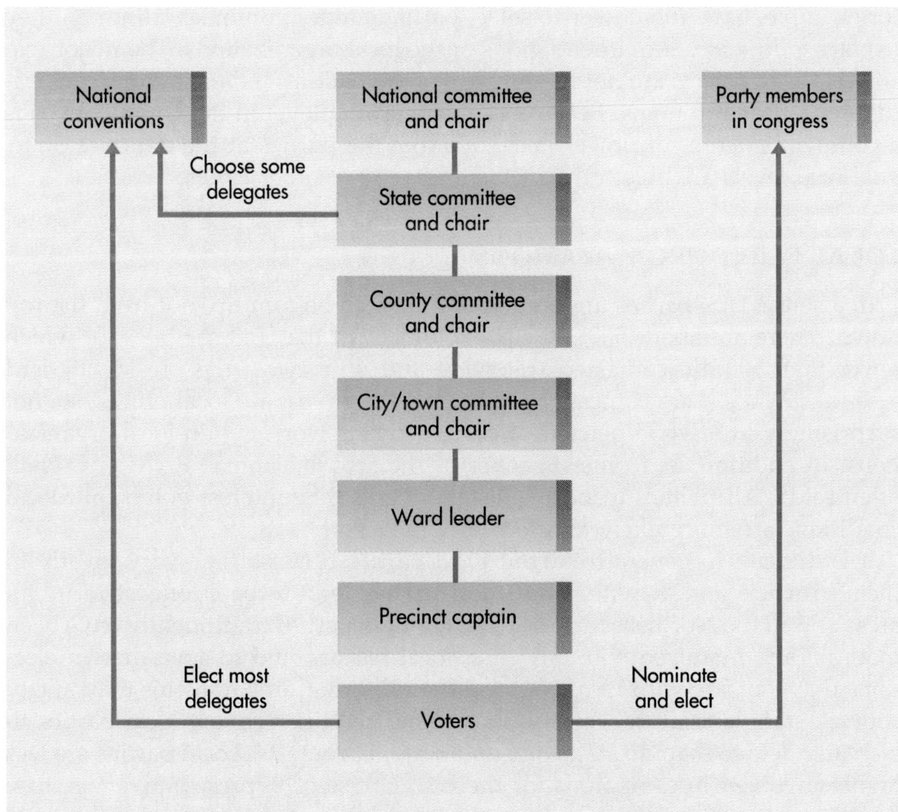

FIGURE 9-1 Organization of the Political Party
U.S. parties today are loosely structured alliances of national, state, and local organizations.

A century ago party bosses so dominated the electoral process in some cities that they were regularly accused of stuffing the ballot boxes and pillaging the public treasury. This 1875 cartoon shows New York City Boss Tweed being released from jail after a new jury found him not guilty of embezzlement. Tweed's organization was widely believed to have rigged the trial. (Historical Picture Service/Stock Mortage)

have a common interest in strengthening the party's position.[21] By comparison, European parties tend to be hierarchical: national parties in Great Britain, for example, have the power to select parliamentary nominees, although they usually follow the recommendations of the local organizations. The major reason that U.S. parties are not hierarchical is the nation's federal system and tradition of local autonomy. Because each governing level in the United States is a competing center of power and ambition, the parties at the national, state, and local levels are able to reject the authority of other levels.

LOCAL PARTY ORGANIZATIONS

In a sense, U.S. parties are organized from the bottom up, not from the top down. There are about 500,000 elective offices in the United States, of which fewer than 500 are contested statewide and only two—the presidency and vice-presidency—are contested nationally. All the rest are local offices, so, not surprisingly, at least 95 percent of party activists work within local organizations. In addition, as former Speaker of the House Thomas P. "Tip" O'Neill often said, "All politics is local." Distant events may interest voters, but local conditions are more likely to affect how they vote.

It is difficult to generalize about local parties because they vary greatly in their structure and activities. But local parties tend to be strongest in urban areas and in the Northeast and Midwest, where parties traditionally have been more highly organized.[22] In any case, local parties tend to specialize in elections that coincide with local electoral boundaries. Campaigns for mayor, city council, state legislature, county offices, and the like activate local parties to a greater degree than do statewide and national contests. Local parties are less highly involved in campaigns for the U.S. House of Representatives because most congressional districts overlap the boundaries of several local party organizations, and they are not accustomed to working together closely. Nevertheless, parties are active in congressional campaigns and, according to Paul Herrnson, have adapted successfully to the change toward candidate-centered politics.[23]

The Decline of the Big-City Machines

For many Americans, local party organizations are synonymous with the party machines that once flourished in the nation's cities. Well-staffed and tightly disciplined, the machines were welfare agencies for the poor, vehicles of upward mobility for newly arrived immigrant groups, and brokers of public jobs, contracts, and policies for those willing to meet the price. But above all, the machines could win elections.

The party machines were powerful, but they should not be viewed as representative of party politics in America. Their reign was relatively short: machines flourished during the latter half of the nineteenth century and within a few decades were in retreat in the face of economic and political changes. Moreover, the party machines were located primarily in the big cities of the Northeast and Midwest. Many southern and western cities did not have machinelike parties, and smaller communities rarely had highly organized parties.

Today only a few local parties, including the Democratic organizations in Albany, Philadelphia, and Chicago, bear any resemblance to the old-time machines. Of these organizations the most famous is Chicago's, which is today much less formidable than it was under the first Mayor Daley (his son was elected as Chicago's mayor in 1989) but is still a force to be reckoned with. The Daley machine was built on more than 30,000 patronage jobs in Cook County and Chicago government. Each of Chicago's 3,500 precincts (voting districts) had a precinct captain, nearly all of whom held a government job. Each captain's responsibility was to get to know the precinct's voters and gain their support. The precinct captains reported to fifty ward leaders, who also held patronage positions and were the link between City Hall and the voters, offering them services in exchange for support at the polls.[24] During his

Chicago mayor Richard Daley (at microphones) was the last of the big-city party machine bosses. He "ruled" Chicago during his 20-year, six-term reign. (UPI/Bettmann Newsphotos)

TABLE 9-1 Activities of County-Level Party Organizations Most county-level parties are actively involved in campaigns.

	PERCENTAGE OF ORGANIZATIONS REPORTING ACTIVITY	
	Republicans	*Democrats*
Opens campaign headquarters	69	67
Organizes telephone campaigns	78	76
Distributes posters or lawn signs	81	83
Sends mailings to voters	75	66
Conducts voter registration drives	78	79
Organizes door-to-door canvassing	69	67
Utilizes public opinion surveys	26	22
Purchases billboard space	10	10

SOURCE: Adapted from James L. Gibson, John P. Frendreis, and Laura Verez, "Party Dynamics in the 1980s," *American Journal of Political Science* 33 (February 1989): 73–74.

twenty-year reign (1956–1976) as boss of Chicago's Democratic machine, Richard J. Daley gained a national reputation as a political kingmaker. His support was critical to John F. Kennedy's drive for the 1960 Democratic presidential nomination. He may even have "stolen" the general election for Kennedy. Daley delayed reporting some of Chicago's returns until the vote totals from downstate Illinois were nearly complete, buying himself time to calculate how many Chicago votes were needed to swing the state in Kennedy's favor. Kennedy narrowly won Illinois, the result, some observers have claimed, of ballot box stuffing by the Daley machine. It is a fact that without Illinois' votes, Kennedy would have lost the election to Richard Nixon.

Nonmachine Local Organizations

In most urban areas the party organizations are important but bear no resemblance to a machine. They do not have enough workers to staff even a majority of precincts on an ongoing basis. They are fully active only during campaigns, when they open campaign headquarters, conduct voter registration drives, distribute posters or lawn signs, send mailings or deliver leaflets to voters, and help get out the vote (see Table 9-1).[25]

These activities can make a difference in a close race.[26] Further, the party organizations in most cities play a role in the nomination of candidates for local office. Although presidential and congressional races are typically candidate-centered, local races, such as those for city council and state or county legislature, are still party-centered in many places. Nominees often come from party ranks or are solicited by party leaders to enter politics. Sometimes the party's backing of a candidate will discourage others from waging a primary fight, and even if the nomination is contested, the party's efforts on behalf of one of the candidates can be decisive.

In other localities the party's role is less substantial. In some rural areas, the parties barely exist, if at all. In most suburbs, wards, and smaller communities, the parties exist organizationally but have little money and few workers. The individual candidates carry the burden. As one candidate in such a locality remarked, "I cannot count on the party to do what it should—like [encourage] registration, hand out literature, arrange coffees and meetings, and turn out the vote. The party should also at least provide poll watchers, but often [does not]."[27]

Party organizational strength at the local level may have increased slightly in recent years.[28] Today's party activists include many well-educated people who have strong communication and organizational skills, and they have used these skills to good advantage in their party work. Local organizations have recently also received some organizational support from the state and national levels, which they have used to adapt to today's poll- and media-oriented campaigns.

STATE PARTY ORGANIZATIONS

At the state level, each party is headed by a central committee made up of members of local party organizations and local and state officeholders. These state central committees do not meet regularly, and they provide only general policy guidance for the state organizations. They range in size from about twenty committee members in Iowa to more than 1,000 in California.[29] Day-to-day operations are directed by a *chairperson,* who is a full-time, paid employee of the state party. In some instances, the chairperson acts chiefly as an administrator of the party's activities. In other cases, the chairperson plays an active leadership role, helping to set policy and influence candidate recruitment. The central committee appoints the chairperson but often defers to the recommendation of the party's leading politician, usually the governor or a U.S. senator.[30]

In recent decades the state parties have expanded their budgets and staffs considerably. A few decades ago, half the state party organizations had no permanent staff whatsoever. The state party often operated out of the chairperson's home. Today, all state parties have a headquarters office; they have a budget that exceeds $500,000 on average and a staff of ten or more employees.[31] The increase in state party organization is due partly to improvements in communication technology, such as computer-assisted direct mail, which have made it easier for political organizations of all kinds, parties included, to raise funds.

But the expansion of state parties is due primarily to changes in the nature of elections. Statewide campaigns are vastly more sophisticated than in the past, and the state party organizations have responded to the change by developing the capacity to help candidates with their issue research, fund-raising, polling, media use, and campaign management. (These activities are discussed in detail later in this chapter.)

State party organizations concentrate on statewide races, including those for governor and U.S. senator,[32] and most of them are also involved in state legislative races. They play a lesser role in campaigns for national or local office, and in most states they do not endorse candidates in statewide primary contests. In some states, the state legislative parties also play an active campaign role. In New York, for example, Republican and Democratic campaign committees in the legislature raise funds and provide services to their party's legislative candidates. Their contribution is a substantial one. The Democratic Assembly Campaign Committee, for example, gave $48,743 to Syracuse-area candidate Joe Nicoletti when he first won a legislative seat in 1991.

NATIONAL PARTY ORGANIZATIONS

The national party organizations are structured much like those at the state level: they have a national committee, a national party chairperson, and a support staff (see Figure 9-2). Although in theory the national parties are run by their committees, the Democratic National Committee (DNC) with more than 400 members and the Republican National Committee (RNC) with more than 150 members are too cumbersome to act as deliberative bodies except on occasion. The national committees meet only a couple of times a year, and they usually ratify decisions made by a smaller core of party leaders.

The National Committees

The RNC and DNC include members chosen by each of the state parties, and the DNC also has members chosen at large and from constituent groups, such

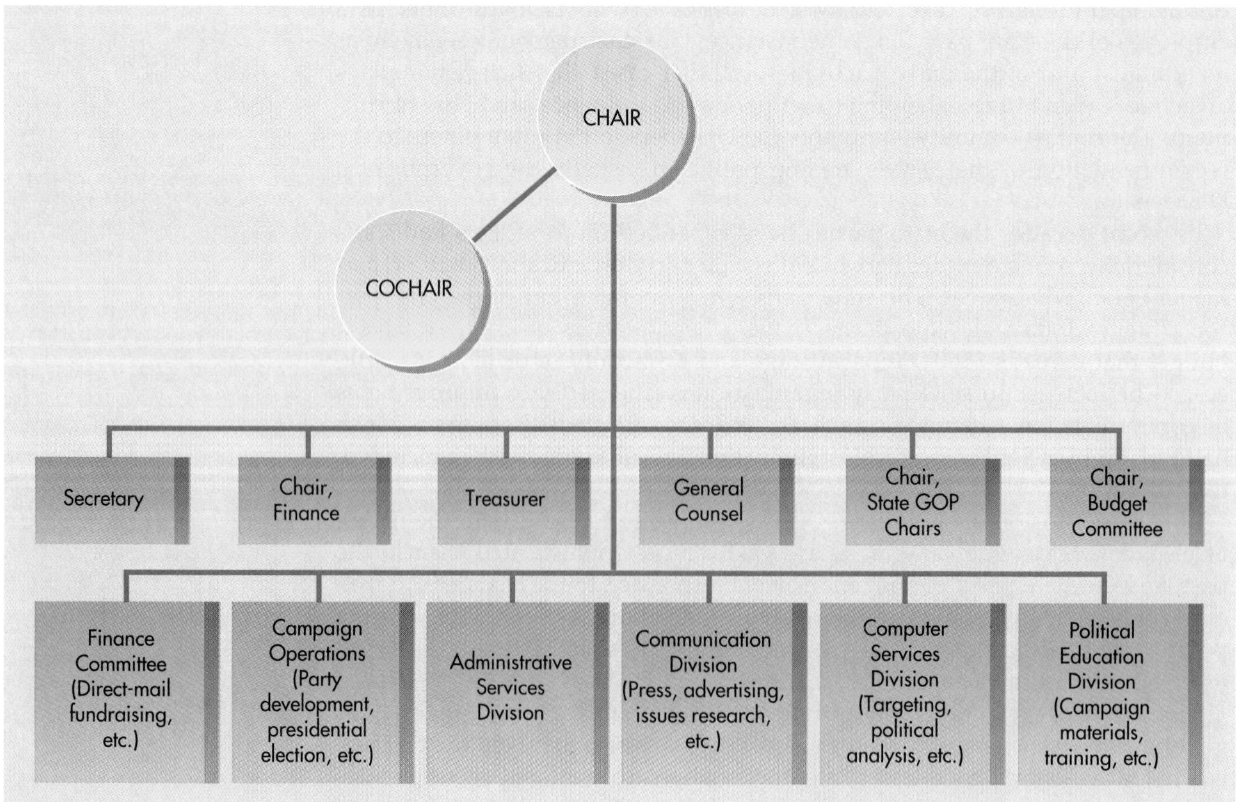

FIGURE 9-2 Organization Chart of the Republican National Committee *Source: Republican National Committee, 1994.*

In organizing their campaigns, candidates for major office depend more heavily on professional consultants than on party leaders. One of these consultants is James Carville, who ran the Clinton campaign's "war room" in 1992. Carville used the slogan "It's the economy, stupid" as a means of keeping the campaign effort focused on the nation's economic problems. (Spencer Tiery/AP/Wide World Photos)

as the Young Democrats and the Democratic Mayors Conference. The Democratic party is more diverse than the GOP and has been more concerned with the issue of fair representation of the party's various factions, including organized labor, women, and racial minorities.[33] There was a period when these constituent groups had a specified number of positions on the DNC. This policy was abandoned in the mid-1980s at the initiative of DNC Chairman Paul Kirk, who believed it gave the impression that the Democrats were a party of special interests.[34]

Whatever their demographic representation, neither the DNC nor the RNC is ideologically representative of the party as a whole. Democrats on the DNC are more liberal as a whole than rank-and-file Democrats, and Republicans on the RNC are more conservative than rank-and-file Republicans.[35] This pattern reflects the tendency of the political activist to be more ideological than the average citizen, which can make it difficult for national parties to craft policies that appeal to the broad electorate.

The national party administers the quadrennial presidential nominating convention. This is a major responsibility but ordinarily carries no real power. Influence at the national conventions is vested in the delegates, who are chosen in the states they represent, although the national party organizations are legally empowered to tell state organizations how to choose and certify their national convention delegates.[36]

When it comes to electoral activity, the national party organizations concentrate their efforts on campaigns for national office—the Senate, House, and presidential races. Both the RNC and DNC raise campaign funds and distribute them directly to candidates. However, the national committees also find it advantageous in some circumstances to contribute to the activities of

★ STATES IN THE NATION

National Party Contributions: The RNC and DNC give funds to state and local parties, particularly when key offices are at stake.

STATE	1994 CONTRIBUTIONS, IN THOUSANDS RNC	DNC
Ala.	$ 432	$ 134
Alaska	68	22
Ariz.	218	165
Ark.	93	68
Calif.	556	703
Colo.	85	182
Conn.	218	31
Del.	112	19
D. C.	—	—
Fla.	730	518
Ga.	265	251
Hawaii	476	19
Idaho	134	25
Ill.	85	115
Ind.	135	41
Iowa	211	396
Kan.	109	18
Ky.	111	6
La.	28	33
Maine	136	122
Md.	120	19
Mass.	69	354
Mich.	154	387
Minn.	102	268
Miss.	20	32
Mo.	93	41
Mont.	50	69
Neb.	69	8
Nev.	165	19
N.H.	76	71
N.J.	389	598
N. Mex.	93	72
N.Y.	1,255	352
N.C.	46	85
N.Dak.	31	82
Ohio	405	118
Okla.	193	15
Oreg.	111	48
Pa.	419	416
R.I.	72	12
S.C.	34	28
S.Dak.	30	8
Tenn.	206	140
Texas	215	562
Utah	30	23
Vt.	81	40
Va.	116	428
Wash.	176	338
W.V.	0	6
Wis.	141	38
Wyo.	59	37

SOURCE: Federal Elections Commission, 1994.

state and local party organizations. Most of this support is targeted at state and local races of national importance. Thus, in the 1993–1994 election cycle, the RNC and DNC gave large amounts of money to party organizations in California, New York, and Florida, where important gubernatorial contests were underway. In contrast, states such as South Dakota, Utah, and Vermont received only small amounts of money from the RNC and DNC during this period (see box: States in the Nation).

The National Chairperson

The national party's day-to-day operations are directed by a national chairperson chosen by the national committee. When a party controls the White House, the president's choice for chairperson is accepted by the committee. In the past, the chairperson was expected to run the party's presidential campaign and coordinate patronage appointments. These responsibilities have since been assigned elsewhere, depriving chairpersons of a major source of power.

The influence of the national chairperson today is highly variable. When a party controls the presidency, its national organization is, in effect, run from the White House. "It's a tough, tough job to be the National Chairman when you have the White House," said Richard Richards, who was an RNC chair during the Reagan presidency. "Every clerk and secretary in the White House thinks they can do your job better than you can."[37]

Several recent out-party chairpersons, however, have played major roles within their party. In 1992 Democratic chairman Ron Brown persuaded a number of state parties to move their presidential primaries ahead in order to settle the race early. The change enabled Bill Clinton to target his campaign at George Bush two months ahead of time. Brown was also instrumental in organizing the Democratic national convention in a way that played down the intraparty factionalism that had hurt the Democrats during past conventions. On the Republican side, a key chairman was William Brock, who headed the GOP after the Watergate scandal and helped revitalize it. Brock initiated a massive fund-raising effort that, by 1982, had raised $130 million and expanded the party's mailing list to include more than 1 million names.

The House and Senate Campaign Committees

Even more important than the DNC and RNC to the funding of elections are the Democratic and Republican campaign committees in the House and Senate: the Democratic Congressional Campaign Committee (DCCC), National Republican Congressional Committee (NRCC), Democratic Senatorial Campaign Committee (DSCC), and National Republican Senatorial Committee (NRSC). These committees account for more than 75 percent of the party funds provided to congressional candidates.[38] This money is not, as might be assumed, provided only to incumbents or even to all incumbents. The House and Senate committees target their funds on close races, whether or not an incumbent is involved.

A NEW PARTY ROLE: SERVICING CANDIDATE-CENTERED CAMPAIGNS

Recognizing the fact that campaigns have become candidate-centered, the national and state parties have assumed a service role, helping candidates conduct their personal campaigns. The GOP's William Brock was an important figure in this development; he saw that a revamped national organization could play a vital role in the age of technology-based campaigns. The Republican national organization developed campaign management "colleges" for candidates and their staffs, compiled massive amounts of electoral data, sent field representatives to assist state and local party leaders, and established a media production division.

The RNC operates out of a large building in Washington, D.C., and is run like a corporation, which is perhaps not surprising in view of the party's business roots.[39] The range of services it provides is impressive. For example, the RNC tapes and catalogues C-SPAN's coverage of congressional debate and can instantly retrieve the statement of any speaker on any issue. Republican challengers use this video material to create "attack" ads directed at the policy stands of Democratic incumbents. Republican incumbents use footage that shows them speaking out forcefully on issues of concern to their constituents. The DNC also works out of a building in the nation's capital, but its operations are less substantial and less well organized.[40] The DNC's later entry into the era of modern campaigning and its less affluent constituencies have kept it behind the RNC.[41]

The national party organizations, including the congressional campaign committees, play an important role in campaign finance. Although candidates for Congress get most of their money from other sources, the amount they receive from the parties is not trivial by any means. A party can legally give $10,000 directly to a House candidate or $17,500 to a Senate candidate. The party can also make larger contributions in the form of "coordinated expenditures," which are made by the party on behalf of a candidate. The party can, for example, conduct opinion polls or produce media advertising for a candidate. In House races, the legal limit (which is adjusted annually for inflation) on coordinated expenditures is about $25,000. In Senate races, the limit is about 5 cents for each adult citizen in the state. In populous California, coordinated expenditures in a Senate race can legally exceed a million dollars.

The total campaign expenditures of the three Democratic and three Republican national committees are shown in Figure 9-3. Among them, they spent more than $250 million in every recent election cycle except 1989–1990. The Republican party has consistently outspent the Democrats, although the gap has narrowed somewhat in the last decade. The GOP has more support among business groups and upper-income Americans, which accounts for its fund-raising advantage over the Democrats. Modern campaigns, as David Adamany notes, are based on a "cash economy," and the Democrats are relatively cash-poor.[42]

In their dealings with candidates, the national and state parties have more of a **service relationship** than a power relationship.[43] The parties may acquire

service relationship The situation where party organizations assist candidates for office, but have no power to require them to accept or campaign on the party's main policy positions.

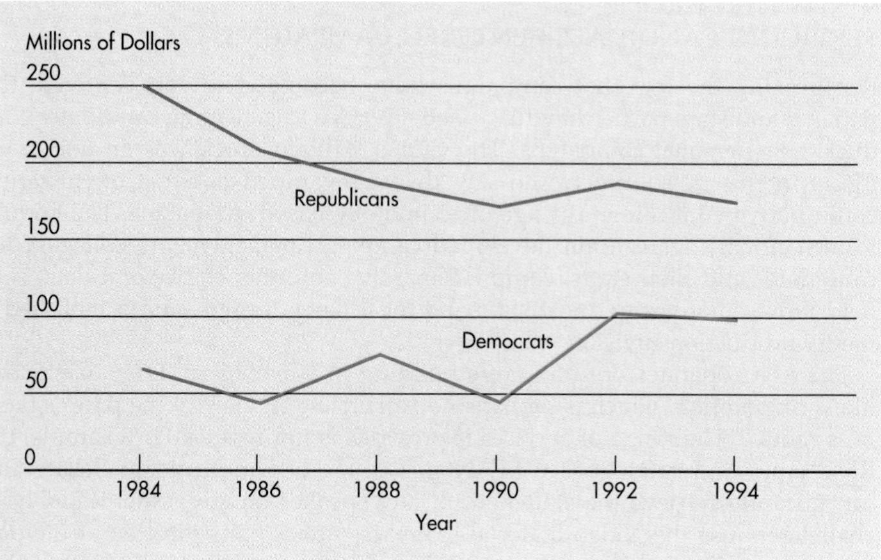

FIGURE 9-3 National Party Expenditures, 1984–1994
Over the years the Republican party has significantly outspent the Democratic party, although the gap has narrowed in recent elections. The figures include spending by the DNC, RNC, DCCC, NRCC, DSCC, and NRSC. *Source: Federal Elections Commission.*

some additional loyalty from officeholders as a result of the contributions they make to their campaigns. Nevertheless, the parties offer help to virtually any candidate with a chance of victory. Faced with the choice of losing an office outright, a party will normally assist even the campaign of a party maverick. Without the ability to control the nominating process, the party has little choice but to embrace all candidates who run under its banner. At a minimum, this approach increases the likelihood that the party will gain a legislative majority and thus control the committees and top leadership positions in the House or Senate.

Party Organizations and the Public's Influence

Strong political parties give the public its greatest potential for influence. When a party is cohesive and disciplined enough to adopt a common national platform which is accepted by all its candidates, the electorate has its best opportunity to decide the policies by which the nation will be governed. Voters in all constituencies have a common choice and thus can act collectively.

Because European parties are strong national organizations, they can offer this type of choice to their electorates. U.S. parties do not provide it. The Contract with America upon which Republican congressional candidates ran in 1994 was somewhat of an exception and might become a model that could revolutionize the way U.S. candidates conduct their campaigns. In general, however, U.S. candidates of the same party in different constituencies stand for different things, which deprives the electorate of an opportunity to elect a lawmaking majority pledged to a common set of policies. Of course, U.S. elections produce governing majorities, and it is safe to assume that most elected officials of a particular party share certain ideas. There are common bonds among elected representatives of the same party even when they run and win on their own.[44] But this is a far cry from a system in which voters everywhere have the same choice.

THE ADVANTAGES AND DISADVANTAGES OF CANDIDATE-CENTERED CAMPAIGNS

Candidate-centered campaigns have some advantages. First, they provide flexibility and new blood to electoral politics. When political conditions and issues change, self-directed candidates quickly adjust, bringing new ideas into the political arena. Strong party organizations are rigid by comparison. Until recently, for example, the British Labour party was controlled by old-line activists who refused to concede that changes in the British economy called for changes in the party's trade unionist and economic policies. The result was a series of humiliating defeats to the Conservative party.

Second, candidate-centered campaigns encourage national officeholders to be responsive to local interests. In building personal followings among their state and district constituents, members of Congress respond to local needs. Nearly every significant domestic program enacted by Congress is adjusted to accommodate the interests of states and localities that would otherwise be hurt by the policy. Members of Congress are not obliged to support the legislative position of their party's majority, and they often extract favors for their constituents as the price of their support. Where strong national parties exist, overarching national interests take precedence over local concerns. In both France and Britain, for example, the pleas of representatives of underdeveloped regions typically go unheeded by their party's majority.

As campaigns have become increasingly candidate-centered, competition over policy issues has focused on the president. On broad national issues, presidential initiatives have come to serve as a basis for party competition. Although this situation offers the electorate a choice, presidential-based politics is inferior to party politics in at least two respects. First, whatever the president's policy preferences, they overshadow other ideas and define national

YOUR TURN

PARTY AND REPRESENTATION

The Question:

Do political parties or interest groups better represent your political views? [Parties] [Groups]

What Others Think: This question was asked in an Advisory Commission on Intergovernmental Relations survey, and groups emerged as the choice of most people: 45 percent of the respondents said that groups better represent their interests, while 34 percent chose parties.

Comment: Americans' antipathy toward parties has deep roots, which is a reason why many of them believe that interest groups are better at representing their interests. The conflict that takes place between parties leads many people to regard partisan bickering as the most substantial effect of party competition. Yet this competition is basic to the public's influence on government. Interest groups are also an object of the public's mistrust, as Chapter 10 will indicate. At the conclusion of that chapter, you might want to reconsider the issue of whether parties or groups better represent your interests.

debate. A party agenda, in contrast, is formulated by a broader spectrum of leadership and thus provides a more fully representative set of views. Second, presidential politics lacks permanence. When a president loses power or leaves office, his agenda is eclipsed. In party politics, policy tradition and philosophy provide a source of enduring guidance.

Candidate-centered politics is also characterized by the prominent influence of special interests. In a party-based system, power can rest on sheer numbers, and so heavy emphasis is placed on appeals to the mass electorate. In a candidate-based system, by contrast, superior campaign funding is prized. In U.S. elections, money increasingly has come from special interests; their financial contributions are now three times that of the parties. (Chapter 10 discusses the role of interest groups more fully.)

Finally, candidate-centered campaigns can easily degenerate into personality contests. When the emphasis is on the individual candidate, rather than broad party differences, there is a tendency to focus on individual traits. Candidates try to portray themselves as virtuous and their opponents as deeply flawed characters. If not all campaigns are of the "holier than thou" variety, many of them are. In recent elections in New York, Virginia, Massachusetts, Maryland, and other states, a candidate's sex life dominated the campaign. U.S. Senator Charles Robb's reelection campaign in 1994 was greatly weakened by accusations of marital infidelity; Robb won only because his opponent, Oliver North, carried an even more negative image because of his role in the Iran-Contra scandal. Some observers characterize the modern campaign as the era of "attack politics," where negative appeals based on personality and narrow issues are the main thrust.

THE PARADOX OF MODERN U.S. ELECTIONS

Wistful longings for a return to the party politics of yesteryear have a touch of both unreality and amnesia. The party organizations are never going to regain their former level of influence, and perhaps that is just as well since they were far from perfect in the first place. After all, it was abusive practices by party leaders that led to the introduction of primary elections—America's drastic cure for the mischiefs of party.

Yet, and this is the central point, the electorate's opportunity to have a broad and consistent influence on national policy has been weakened by the decline of parties. The connection between electing and governing has been blurred. The problem is apparent from surveys that have asked Americans for their evaluations of Congress as a whole and of their own member of Congress in particular (see Figure 9-4). The public has a very low opinion of the performance of Congress; yet a relatively high proportion of citizens say their own member of Congress is doing a good job in Washington. This attitude prevails in so many districts that the net result in recent elections has usually been the reelection of a high proportion of incumbents.

The 1994 elections were an exception to the normal pattern. The public's disgust with the Democratic-controlled Congress and its lack of confidence in the Clinton administration combined to give the Republicans a major victory. This type of periodic upheaval is not trivial by any means, but it provides the

★ CRITICAL THINKING

The Public's Influence on Representatives
Members of Congress now win election largely through their own efforts rather than through political parties. In this situation, does the influence that constituents have on their particular representative in Congress have any necessary relation to the larger question of whether the public as a whole has influence over Congress as a whole? In answering, bear in mind that each member of Congress is but one of 435 House members or 100 senators.

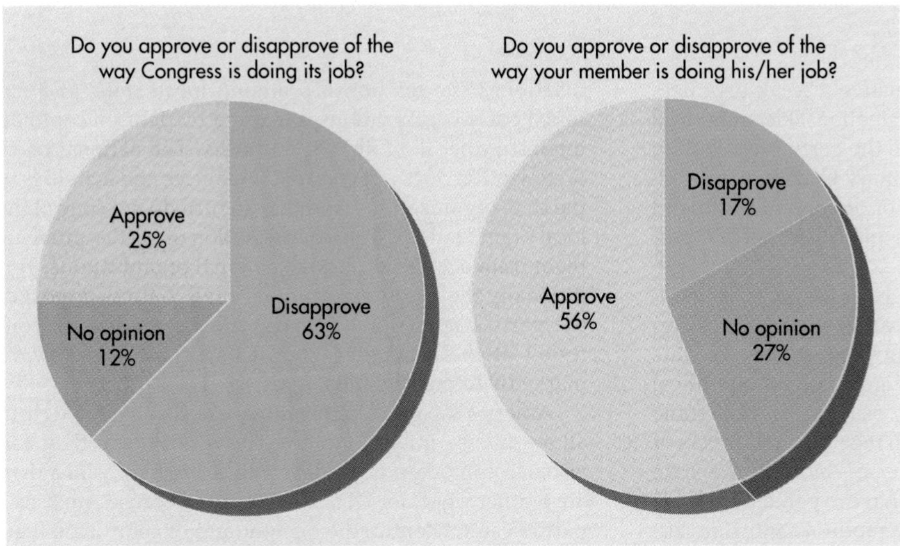

FIGURE 9-4 The Public's Rating of Congress and of Their Own Members of Congress, 1994 Americans have a higher regard for their own congressional representative than for Congress as a whole. *Source: CBS News/New York Times poll, September 8–11, 1994.*

public with less control than a system in which sustained party competition is the *regular* basis for the public's judgment. The prevalent belief that it is better to vote "for the person, not the party" conforms with Americans' trust in individualism but makes little sense as a guideline for collective action. Because of the power of incumbency, the Democratic party had controlled one or both houses of Congress since the early 1950s. This dominance is a sign of an unresponsive electoral system; no party in a democratic society should hold power for that long. This is the great paradox of modern U.S. elections. They appear to strengthen the public's hold on leaders by making the candidate-voter relationship in any given constituency a more direct one; yet they actually weaken that hold by making it more difficult for voters in different constituencies to act together.

Of course, as we have noted, the two parties differ in their policy tendencies and constituency interests, and so party labels do provide the voters in different constituencies some opportunity for collective action. Yet the history of democratic societies indicates that the potential for popular influence cannot be fully realized without strongly defined alternatives.[45] Grassroots parties—"the people's constitution," in the historian James MacGregor Burns's phrase—were established in the early nineteenth century to enable the mass public to assert its collective voice more effectively. Americans either never learned this history lesson very well or have forgotten it. The public today has no real appreciation of the value of strong parties and would welcome a further weakening of party power. A majority of Americans in a recent poll indicated they think the country would be better off without parties.[46] Most candidates also have no desire for truly strong parties. Although they eagerly accept the parties' help during campaigns, they would not welcome any change that made them subordinate to the parties. Parties survived the shift to candidate-centered campaigns and will persist, but their heyday has passed.

Summary

America's political parties are relatively weak organizations. They lack control over nominations, elections, and platforms. Candidates can bypass the party organization and win nomination through primary elections. Individual candidates also control most of the organization and money necessary to win elections and run largely on personal platforms.

Primary elections are the major reason for the organizational weakness of America's parties. Once the parties lost their hold on the nominating process, they became subordinate to candidates. More generally, the political parties have been undermined by election reforms, some of which were intended to weaken the party and others of which have unintentionally done so. Recently the state and national party organizations have expanded their capacity to provide candidates with modern campaign services and are again playing a prominent role in election campaigns. Nevertheless, party organizations at all levels have few ways of controlling the candidates who run under their banners. They assist candidates with campaign technology, workers, and funds but cannot compel candidates' loyalty to organizational goals.

America's parties are decentralized, fragmented organizations. The relationship among local, state, and national party organizations is marked by paths of common interest rather than lines of authority. The national party organization does not control the policies and activities of the state organizations, and they in turn do not control the local organizations. The fragmentation of parties prevents them from acting as cohesive national organizations. Traditionally the local organizations have controlled most of the party's work force because most elections are contested at the local level. Local parties, however, vary markedly in their vitality.

America's party organizations are flexible enough to allow diverse interests to coexist within them; they can also accommodate new ideas and leadership, since they are neither rigid nor closed. However, because America's parties cannot control their candidates or coordinate their policies at all levels, they are unable to present the voters with a coherent, detailed platform for governing. The national electorate as a whole is thus denied a clear choice among policy alternatives and has difficulty influencing national policy in a predictable and enduring way through elections.

Major Concepts

candidate-centered politics
nomination
party-centered politics
party organizations
primary election (direct primary)
service relationship

Suggested Readings

Allswang, John. *Bosses, Machines, and Urban Voters.* Baltimore: Johns Hopkins University Press, 1986. A penetrating study of the party machines that once flourished in America's cities.

Bennett, W. Lance. *The Governing Crisis: Media, Money, and Marketing in American Elections.* New York: St. Martin's Press, 1992. An assessment of the impact of candidate-centered campaigns on the governing process.

Ehrenhalt, Alan. *The United States of Ambition.* New York: Times Books, 1991. A provocative book that claims that self-starting politicians are the reason the U.S. government has a scarcity of sound leadership.

Herrnson, Paul S. *Party Campaigning in the 80's.* Cambridge, Mass.: Harvard University Press, 1988. An analysis that indicates political parties continue to have an important organizational role in the United States.

Kayden, Xander, and Eddie Mahe, Jr. *The Party Goes On.* New York: Basic Books, 1985. An assessment of how the two major parties have adapted to the political changes of recent decades.

Magleby, David B., and Candice J. Nelson, *The Money Chase: Congressional Campaign Finance Reform.* Washington, D.C.: The Brookings Institution, 1990. A careful study of the flow of money in federal elections.

Milkus, Sidney. *The President and the Parties: The Transformation of the American Party System since the New Deal.* New York: Oxford University Press, 1993. An assessment of the president's role in party conflict.

Schlesinger, Joseph. *Political Parties and the Winning of Office.* Ann Arbor: University of Michigan Press, 1991. An evaluation of the parties' role in elections.

CHAPTER 10

INTEREST GROUPS: ORGANIZING FOR INFLUENCE

A troubling dilemma lies at the core of the American political system. In an open and free society in which people have the right to express their political views, petition their government, and organize on behalf of causes, . . . people will pursue their self-interest even though the policies they advocate may hurt others, and may not be in the best interest of the nation.

—*Jeffrey M. Berry*[1]

They began their attack before the ink was dry on the Clinton administration's health care reform bill. The opening salvo came from the insurance companies, which argued that legislative restrictions on insurance premiums and eligibility criteria would cripple the health care industry. The National Federation of Independent Business soon joined the attack, warning that thousands of small businesses would go broke if employers were forced by law to insure their workers. For their part, health maintenance organizations (HMOs) objected to the plan's proposed caps on health spending, claiming that the Clinton plan would undermine the quality of Americans' medical care. By the time the groups opposed to health care reform had completed their mass advertising campaign, they had spent $40 million, more than four times the amount spent by advocates of health care reform.

During the yearlong lobbying effort, public support for Clinton's proposal declined from 75 percent to 40 percent, dooming the plan to defeat in Congress. Some observers concluded that the public had been bamboozled. Peter Hart, who conducted polls on the health care issue for NBC and *The Wall Street Journal*, said: "The worst of the process worked. Yes, there was a dialogue, but it was so influenced and affected by the special interest groups that the public didn't get a true and honest debate. What they learned is everything they had to fear—and very little about what they could hope for." Other observers argued that the campaign had enabled Americans to better understand what they actually wanted from health care reform. "What they say in all the polls is, 'We want an alternative plan, less threatening, less bureaucratic, but still a major plan,'" said Bob Blendon, a Harvard health care expert.[2]

The campaign against the Clinton health care plan suggests why interest groups are both admired and feared. Insurance companies, HMOs, and small businesses have legitimate interests that can be furthered or harmed by public policy. It is entirely appropriate for them to actively promote their interests. The same can be said of farmers, consumers, minorities, college students—indeed, of nearly every interest in society. Without groups to articulate and promote the various interests in society, policymakers and the general public would be less aware and less responsive to their concerns.

Indeed, the *pluralist* theory of American politics (see Chapter 1) holds that society's interests are most effectively represented through the efforts of groups. An extreme statement of this view is Arthur F. Bentley's claim in 1908 that society is "nothing other than the complex of groups that compose it."[3] Although modern pluralists make far less sweeping claims, they do contend that the group process, on balance, is open to a great range of interests, nearly all of which benefit from organized activity in one significant way or another.

Yet groups can wield too much power. If a group gets its way at an unreasonable cost to the rest of society, the public interest is harmed. When Clinton's health bill was submitted to Congress, polls indicated that most Americans believed the nation's medical care system needed a major overhaul. Nearly 40 million Americans were uninsured, millions of other had gaps in their coverage, and the cost of health care was increasing faster than the rate of inflation. These unfortunate conditions still remained when the Clinton bill went down to defeat a year later. It was also the case that the public's desire for health care reform was still there. Did the insurance, small business, and medical lobbies, in pursuit of their own narrow interests, derail a much-needed change in health care, whether in the form of the Clinton bill or one of the various alternatives proposed by members of Congress? Was the health care debate a harrowing example of how millions of dollars in special-interest lobbying can confuse and exhaust the citizenry?

Opinions on these questions differ widely, but there is no doubt that the special interest in some cases wrongly prevails over the general interest. Indeed, most observers are of the opinion that groups have achieved too much influence over public policy in recent decades. Some analysts describe the situation as the triumph of **single-issue politics:** separate groups organized around nearly every conceivable policy issue, with each group pressing its demands and influence to the utmost, at whatever cost to the broader society.

single-issue politics The situation in which separate groups are organized around nearly every conceivable policy issue and press their demands and influence to the utmost.

An **interest group** can be defined as a set of individuals who organize to promote a shared political interest. Also called a "faction" or "pressure group" or "special interest," an interest group is characterized by its formalized organization and by its pursuit of policy goals that stem from its members' shared interest. Thus a bridge club or an amateur softball team is not an interest group because it does not seek to influence the political process. Organizations such as the Association of Wheat Growers, Common Cause, the National Organization for Women, the World Wildlife Fund, the National Rifle Association, and the Anti-Defamation League of B'nai B'rith are interest groups because, despite their differences, they all meet the definition's two criteria: each is an organized entity and each seeks to further its members' interests through political action.

interest group A set of individuals who are organized to promote a shared political interest.

Interest groups promote public policies, encourage the political participa-

THE MEDIA AND THE PEOPLE

GROUPS IN THE NEWS

Although some journalists describe the news as a mirror held up to society, the news is actually a highly selective portrayal of reality. There are no objective standards for choosing a few news stories daily out of the thousands of events that occur each day. The choices are based on conventions. Journalists look for that which is new, interesting, and important. They also tend to tell their stories through the actions of familiar figures. News coverage of the U.S. Congress, for example, is not spread evenly across the institution's 535 members. Instead a few highly visible legislators—such as Newt Gingrich and Edward Kennedy—dominate news of the institution.

The same tendencies hold for coverage of interest groups. There are tens of thousands of interest groups in the United States, but the news brings to light only a few of them. A group is unlikely to receive news coverage unless it is embroiled in a controversy. Journalists are drawn to conflict because it provides a more dramatic form of news. A result is that group activity appears more conflictual than it actually is. Although groups sometimes fight for narrow advantage, they also work together. Furthermore, most of group activity involves service to members, which is rarely presented in the news.

News about groups is also biased toward mainstream groups that are readily recognizable to the general public. Journalists work within severe time and space constraints, which leads them to concentrate on groups that do not have to be explained in detail to the news audience. For example, the insurance, medical, and business lobbies received 80 percent of the news coverage of groups during the recent health care debate. Much of this coverage was negative in tone; these lobbies were not only heard, but also criticized. The arguments of other groups with an interest in health issues were simply not heard very often, as the following chart indicates:

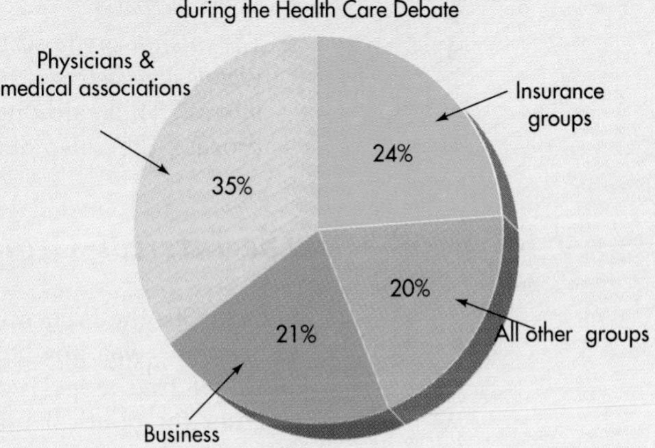

SOURCE: "Diagnosing Health Care Reform, " *Media Monitor*, May/June 1994, p. 2.

tion of their members, support candidates for public office, and work to influence policymakers. Interest groups are thus similar to political parties in certain respects, but the two types of organizations differ in important ways. Major political parties address a broad range of issues so as to appeal to diverse blocs of voters. Parties exist to contest elections. They change their policy positions as the voters' preferences change; for the party, winning is almost everything. In comparison, interest groups focus on specific issues of immediate concern to their members; farm groups, for example, concentrate on agricultural policy. A group may involve itself in elections, but its purpose is to influence elected officials.

This chapter examines the degree to which various interests in American society are represented by organized groups, the process by which interest groups exert influence, and the costs and benefits of group politics in regard to the public good. The main points made in the chapter are the following:

★ *Although nearly all interests in American society are organized to some degree, those associated with economic activity, particularly business enterprises, are by far the most thoroughly organized.* Their advantage rests on their superior financial resources and on the fact that they offer potential members private goods (such as wages and jobs).

★ *Groups that do not have economic activity as their primary function often have organizational problems.* They pursue public or collective goods (such as a safer environment) that are available even to individuals who are not group members, and so individuals may choose not to pay the costs of membership.

★ *Lobbying and electioneering are the traditional means by which groups communicate with and influence political leaders.* Recent developments, including "grassroots lobbying" and PACs, have given added visibility to groups' activities.

★ *The interest-group system overrepresents business interests and higher-income groups and fosters policies that serve a group's interest more than the public interest.* Thus, although groups are an essential part of the democratic process, they also distort that process.

The Interest-Group System

In the 1830s the Frenchman Alexis de Tocqueville wrote that the "principle of association" was nowhere more evident than in America.[4] The country's tradition of free association has always made it easy for Americans to join together for political purposes, and their diverse interests have given them reason to seek influence through specialized groups. Few nations have as many separate economic, ethnic, religious, social, and geographic interests as the United States. Moreover, because of federalism and separation of powers, numerous political institutions at all levels of government are available for groups to lobby. Not surprisingly, manufacturing, labor, agriculture, and other leading interests have not only national organizations but also separate state and local lobbies. Groups spent $29 million in 1990 to lobby New York's state government alone. The top spender was Philip Morris, which spent $566,223 in a successful effort to defeat a proposed statewide ban on the sale of cigarettes in vending machines.

The extraordinary number of groups in the United States does not indicate, however, that the nation's various interests are equally well organized. Organizations develop when people with shared interests have the opportunity and the incentive to join together. Some individuals have the skills, money, contacts, or time to participate effectively in group politics, but others do not. Some groups are inherently more attractive to potential members than others and thus find it easier to build large or devoted followings. Organizations also differ in their access to financial resources and thus differ also in their capacity for political action.

Therefore, a first consideration in regard to group politics in America is the issue of how thoroughly various interests are organized. Group politics is the politics of organization. Interests that are highly organized stand a good chance of having their views heard by policymakers. Poorly organized interests run the risk of being ignored.

ECONOMIC GROUPS

No interests are more fully or effectively organized than those that have economic activity as their primary purpose. An indication of their advantage is the fact that their Washington lobbyists outnumber those of other groups by more than 2 to 1.

Economic groups include corporations, labor unions, farm groups, and professional associations. They exist primarily for economic purposes: to make profits, provide jobs, improve pay, or protect an occupation. For the sake of discussion, such organizations will be called **economic groups,** although it is important to recognize that their political goals can include policies that transcend the narrow economic interests of their members. Thus the AFL-CIO concentrates on labor objectives, but it also takes positions on broader issues of foreign and domestic policy.

economic groups Interest groups that are organized primarily for economic reasons, but which engage in political activity in order to seek favorable policies from government.

An Organizational Edge

One reason for the large number of economic groups is their immediate access to abundant financial resources. Political activity does not come cheap. If a group is to make its views known, it normally must have a headquarters, an expert staff, and communication facilities. Economic groups can obtain the requisite money and expertise from their economic activities. Corporations have the greatest natural advantage: corporate funds can be used in support of lobbying activities. When the Persian Gulf war resulted in skyrocketing gasoline prices, the nation's oil giants spent some of their windfall profits on television and print advertising aimed at mitigating the popular perception that they were exploiting the crisis. They blamed government, saying that federal restrictions on oil exploration in the past, combined with the shortage of Middle Eastern oil, were pushing up gas prices at a rate beyond their control.

Many economic groups offer prospective members a powerful incentive to join: **private goods** (or **individual goods**), which are the benefits that a group can grant directly to the individual member. For example, workers in the state of Michigan cannot hold automobile assembly jobs unless they belong to the United Auto Workers (UAW). Economic groups are highly organized in part because they serve the individual economic needs of potential members. The predominance of economic interests was predicted in *Federalist* No. 10, in which James Madison declared that property is "the most common and durable source of factions." Stated differently, nothing seems to matter quite so much to people as their pocketbooks and livelihoods.

private (individual) goods Benefits that a group (most often an economic group) can grant directly and exclusively to individual members of the group.

Types of Economic Groups.

Most economic groups are of four general types: business groups, labor groups, agricultural groups, and professional groups.

Business Groups. Writing in 1929, E. Pendleton Herring noted, "Of the many organized groups maintaining offices in [Washington], there are no interests more fully, more comprehensively, and more efficiently represented than those of American industry."[5] Although corporations do not dominate the group system to the same degree as they did in the past, Herring's general conclusion still holds: more than half of all groups formally registered to lobby Congress are business organizations. Nearly all large corporations and many smaller ones are politically active. They concentrate their activities on policies that touch directly on business interests, such as tax, tariff, and regulatory decisions.

Business firms are also represented through associations. Some of these associations, such as the U.S. Chamber of Commerce, which represents more than 180,000 medium-sized and small businesses,[6] seek to advance the general interests of business and to articulate a business perspective on broad policy issues.[7] Other business associations, such as the American Petroleum Institute, are confined to a single trade or industry. Because each trade association represents a single industry, it can promote the interests of member corporations even when these interests conflict with those of business generally. Thus, while the Chamber of Commerce promotes a free trade policy, some trade associations seek protective tariffs because their member firms want barriers against foreign competition.[8]

Business interests have the advantage of what the economist Mancur Olson, Jr., calls "the size factor."[9] Although large groups can claim that government should pay more attention to them because they represent more people, small groups are more cohesive. Everyone is a consumer, but most consumers do not see any benefit in belonging to a consumer advocacy group. On the other hand, since business firms in a particular industry are few in number, they are likely to recognize the significance of their individual contribution to a collective effort. When the "Big Three" U.S. automakers—General Motors, Ford, and Chrysler—fought federally mandated safety and mileage-efficiency standards, the defection of any one of them would likely have meant defeat. But they stayed together and won concessions from the government; in the process, each automaker saved hundreds of millions of dollars in design and production costs on new autos. In one instance, the automakers gained a multiyear delay in the installation of air bags in all new cars. Their gain came at an unknown cost to consumers, whose newly purchased automobiles were less safe than they could have been.

Labor Groups. Since the 1930s, organized labor has been politically active on a large scale. Its goal has been to promote policies that benefit workers in general and union members in particular. Although some independent unions, such as the United Mine Workers, lobby actively, the dominant labor group is the AFL-CIO, which maintains its national headquarters in Washington, D.C. The AFL-CIO has more than 12 million members in its 100 affiliated unions, which include the International Brotherhood of Electrical Workers, the Sheet Metal Workers, the Communication Workers of America, and, as of 1987, the giant International Brotherhood of Teamsters.

At one time about a third of the U.S. work force was unionized, but less than one-sixth of all workers currently belong to unions. Skilled and unskilled

This 1873 lithograph illustrates the benefits of membership in the National Grange, an agricultural interest group. (Library of Congress)

laborers have been the core of organized labor, and their numbers are decreasing while professionals, technicians, and service workers are increasing in number. Professionals have shown little interest in union organization, perhaps because they identify with management or see themselves as economically secure. Service workers and technicians are also more difficult for unions to organize than traditional laborers because they work closely with managers and, often, in small offices.

Nevertheless, unions have made some inroads in recent decades in their efforts to organize service and public employees. Teachers, postal workers, police, firefighters, and social workers are among the public employee groups that have become increasingly unionized. Today, the nation's largest unions are those that represent service and public employees rather than skilled and unskilled laborers (see Table 10-1).

Agricultural Groups. Farm organizations represent another large economic lobby. The American Farm Bureau Federation is the largest of the farm groups, with roughly 3 million members. The National Farmers Union, the National Grange, and the National Farmers Organization are smaller farm lobbies. Agricultural groups do not always agree on policy issues. For instance, the Farm Bureau sides with agribusiness and owners of large farms, while the Farmers Union promotes the interests of smaller "family" farms.

There are also numerous specialty farm associations, including the Association of Wheat Growers, the American Soybean Association, and Associated

TABLE 10-1 The Largest Labor Unions, 1950s and 1990s The largest labor unions today represent service and public employees; in the past the largest unions represented skilled and unskilled workers.

1950s	*1990s*
1. United Auto Workers	1. National Education Association
2. United Steel Workers	2. International Brotherhood of Teamsters
3. International Brotherhood of Teamsters	3. American Federation of State, County, & Municipal Employees
4. United Brotherhood of Carpenters & Joiners	4. United Food and Commercial Workers International
5. International Association of Machinists	5. Service Employees International

SOURCE: U.S. Department of Labor.

Milk Producers. Each association acts as a separate lobby to try to obtain policies beneficial to its members' narrow agricultural interests.

Professional Groups. Most professions have lobbying associations. Perhaps the most powerful of these groups is the American Medical Association (AMA), which, with more than 250,000 members, represents about half of the nation's physicians. The AMA has consistently opposed any government policy that would limit physicians' autonomy. Other professional groups are the American Bar Association and the American Association of University Professors, each of which maintains a lobbying office in Washington.

CITIZENS' GROUPS

citizens' (noneconomic) groups Organized interests formed by individuals drawn together by opportunities to promote a cause in which they believe but which does not provide them significant individual economic benefits.

collective (public) goods Benefits that are offered by groups (usually citizens' groups) as an incentive for membership, but that are nondivisible (e.g., a clean environment) and therefore are available to nonmembers as well as members of the particular group.

Although economic interests are the best organized and most prominent groups, they do not have a monopoly on group activity. There are a great number and variety of other organized interests, which we shall refer to collectively as **citizens' groups** (or **noneconomic groups**). The members of groups in this category are drawn together for reasons other than their occupation. Sometimes they join because of a *solidarity incentive*—the opportunity for social contact. More often, they are motivated by a *purposive incentive*—the desire to promote a cause in which they believe.[10] Whether a group's goal is to protect the environment, reduce the threat of nuclear war, return prayer to the public schools, feed the poor at home or abroad, outlaw or retain legal abortion, or whatever, there are citizens who are willing to participate simply because they believe the policy goal is a worthy one.[11] Purposive incentives are powerful enough that nearly every conceivable interest within American society has a group that claims to represent it.

In comparison with economic groups, citizens' groups have a harder time acquiring the resources necessary for organization (see Table 10-2). These groups do not generate profits or fees as a result of economic activity. Moreover, the incentives they offer prospective members are not exclusive. Unlike the private or individual goods provided by many economic groups, most noneconomic groups offer **collective goods** (or **public goods**) as an incentive for membership. Collective goods are, by definition, benefits that must be shared; they cannot be allotted on an individual basis. The air we breathe is an example of a collective good; it is available to one and all. Broadcast signals are another example. They are accessible to anyone with a properly operating radio or television.

The Free-Rider Problem

This characteristic of collective goods creates what is called the **free-rider problem:** individuals can receive the good even when they do not contribute to the group's effort. Take the case of an environmental group that successfully lobbies Congress for tougher air pollution laws. The collective good produced by the legislation—cleaner air—is available to group members and nonmembers alike. Public broadcasting is another example. Although its programs are funded in part through viewers' donations, those who do not contribute can also watch the programs. The noncontributors are free riders: they receive the benefit without paying any of the costs of providing it. About 90 percent of those who regularly view or listen to public broadcasting do not contribute to their local station.

free-rider problem The situation in which the benefits offered by a group to its members are also available to nonmembers. The incentive to join the group and to promote its cause is reduced because nonmembers (free riders) receive the benefits (e.g., a cleaner environment) without having to pay any of the group's costs.

As the economist Olson notes, it is not rational, in a purely economic sense, for individuals to contribute to a citizens' group because they can obtain the benefits of its efforts without making a contribution. Participation in such groups is not rational in another sense as well: the contribution of an individual is so small that it does not affect the group's success in any significant way.[12] If your $25 contribution will not make any real difference to the quality of your local public broadcasting station, then why bother to give it the money?

TABLE 10-2 Advantages and Disadvantages Held by Economic and Citizens' Groups Compared with economic groups, citizens' groups have fewer advantages and more disadvantages.

Economic Groups	*Citizens' Groups*
Advantages	*Advantages*
Economic activity provides the organization with resources necessary for political action.	Members are likely to support leaders' political efforts because they joined the group in order to influence policy.
Individuals are encouraged to join the group because of economic benefits they individually receive (e.g., wages).	*Disadvantages*
	The group has to raise funds especially for its political activities.
In the case of firms within an industry, their small number encourages organization because the contribution of each firm is significant.	Potential members may choose not to join the group because their individual contribution may be too small to affect the group one way or another.
Disadvantages	
Persons within the group may not support leaders' political efforts because they did not join the group for political reasons.	Potential members may choose not to join the group because they get collective benefits even if they do not join (the free-rider problem).

Of course, many people join such groups irrespective of such considerations. Nevertheless, the free-rider problem is a reason why citizens' groups are less highly organized than economic ones. Recognizing the problem, many citizens' groups have created individual benefits, akin to those offered by economic groups, to make membership more attractive. They may, for example, provide their members with an organizational newsletter or arrange social gatherings.

Attracting Members

Despite their organizational difficulties, citizens' groups have increased in both number and membership in recent decades. The computer is a prime reason for the growth. In the past, a fledgling organization had to enlist potential members almost on a one-by-one basis. Today, however, group organizers can buy mailing lists and flood the mails with thousands of computer-generated "personal" letters asking recipients to join the group. For some citizens, an annual membership fee of $25 or $50 represents no great sacrifice and offers the personal satisfaction of contributing to a cause in which they believe. Direct mail, however, does not guarantee organizational vitality. Often, the response rate is so weak (less than 1 percent) that it does not even pay for the mailing's cost. When the return exceeds the cost, however, the group gains both money and members in a relatively easy and painless way.

Citizens' groups benefit when their "cause" attracts widespread attention. Greenpeace U.S.A. is one of the largest environmental groups, partly because of its starkly emotional appeals and high-profile tactics, including the interdiction of whaling fleets on the high seas. When French agents blew up the Greenpeace flagship, *Rainbow Warrior,* in New Zealand in 1985, the U.S. branch of Greenpeace responded immediately with a direct mail campaign, which got an astonishing 10 percent response rate. Today, Greenpeace U.S.A. has an operating budget in excess of $20 million and a membership of more than 1.5 million.[13]

Leadership can be a critical factor in the organizational success of citizens' groups. The political scientist Robert Salisbury argues that a resourceful leader is often the difference between a group that attracts a wide following and one that fails.[14] The Reverend Jerry Falwell and Ralph Nader are examples of leaders who had a decisive influence on the success of their groups. Falwell used his televised ministry and an astute sense of politics to mobilize the Christian right's resentment of social change. Falwell's Moral Majority became an organizational vehicle for a more conservative approach in areas such as abortion and public education. Falwell's activities turned a vague sense of discontent into a political movement that is a major force in today's politics.[15]

Nader first came to national attention in 1965, when his book *Unsafe at Any Speed* exposed the poor safety record of General Motors' Corvair automobile. Nader's adroit use of the media and his keen sense of emerging issues helped create for him an image as the country's foremost consumer advocate. His Public Citizen group works primarily on consumers' issues, including pollution control, auto safety, and pure food and drugs. Nader also heads Congress Watch, which publicizes alleged abuses of the public trust by members of Congress. In addition, Nader played an instrumental role in the formation of

Environmental activists protest against ocean dumping from a sailboat in New York harbor. Greenpeace U.S.A. is one of the country's most visible and influential interest groups. (Jim Sulley/The Image Works)

statewide, campus-based watchdog groups, such as the New York Public Interest Research Group (NYPIRG).

Types of Citizens' Groups

Most citizens' groups are of three general types: public interest groups, single-issue groups, and ideological groups.

Public Interest Groups. Public interest groups are those that claim to represent the broad interests of society as a whole. Despite their label, public interest groups are not led by people elected by the public at large, and the issues they target are ones of their own choosing, not the public's. Nevertheless, there is a basis for distinguishing such groups from economic groups: the latter seek direct material benefits for their members, while the former seek benefits that are less tangible and more broadly shared. For example, the National Association of Manufacturers, an economic group, seeks policies favorable to large corporations, while the League of Women Voters, a public interest group, seeks policies—such as simplified voter registration—that can benefit the public in general.

The League of Women Voters has existed for decades, but more than half of the currently active public interest groups were established after 1960. One of these newer organizations is Common Cause, which has more than 250,000 members. Their annual dues help support a seventy-person national staff of lobbyists, attorneys, and public relations experts. Founded by John Gardner, a former cabinet secretary, Common Cause, which describes itself as "a national citizens' lobby," concentrates on political reform in such areas as campaign finance. It has been the principal advocate of public funding of congressional campaigns; its ongoing "People vs. PACs" campaign is aimed at reducing the influence of interest groups on elections.

Single-Issue Groups. A single-issue group is organized to influence policy in just one area. Notable current examples are the various right-to-life and pro-choice groups that have formed around the issue of abortion. The number of single-issue groups has risen sharply in the past two decades, and they now lobby on almost every conceivable issue, from nuclear arms to day care centers to drug abuse. Single-issue groups with a national membership are the most prominent, but a vast number of single-issue groups are organized and operate autonomously on the local level.

Environmental groups are sometimes classified as public interest groups, but they may also be considered single-issue organizations in that most of them seek to influence public policy in a specific area, such as pollution reduction, wilderness preservation, or wildlife protection. The Sierra Club is one of the oldest of such groups; it was formed in the 1890s to promote the preservation of scenic areas. Also prominent are the National Audubon Society, the Wilderness Society, the Environmental Defense Fund, Greenpeace U.S.A., and the Izaak Walton League. Between 1960 and 1970, membership in environmental groups tripled in response to increased public concern about the quality of the environment.[16] Since then, membership in environmental groups has continued to grow.

Ideological Groups. Single-issue groups have a narrowly focused policy agenda. Other groups take a broader view, usually from the perspective of a general philosophical or moral stance. These groups have been labeled ideological groups. An example is the Christian Moral Government Fund, which was organized to restore "Christian values" to American life and politics.[17] Americans for Democratic Action (ADA) is another example of an ideological group; the ADA supports liberal positions on a wide range of social, economic, and foreign policy issues. Ideological groups on both the left and right have increased substantially in numbers since the 1960s.

Groups such as the National Organization for Women (NOW) and the National Association for the Advancement of Colored People (NAACP) can also be generally classified as ideological groups. Their aim is to promote the broad interests of a particular demographic segment of society. The NAACP was formed in 1909 to promote the political interests of racial minorities, primarily through initiating lawsuits on their behalf.

A SPECIAL CATEGORY OF INTEREST GROUP: GOVERNMENTS

While the vast majority of organized interests in the United States represent private concerns, a growing number of interest groups represent governments, both foreign and subnational.

Ralph Reed of the Christian Coalition, an interest group, is a leading conservative activist and theoretician. (Donna Binder/Impact Visuals)

The U.S. federal government makes policies that directly affect the economic development, political stability, and security of nations throughout the world. Arms sales, foreign aid, immigration, and import restrictions and other trade practices have a great impact on foreign nations. For this reason, most foreign nations supplement the political efforts made through their embassies with the services of paid lobbying agents in Washington. Although lobbying by foreign governments is subject to some restrictions, most governments have managed to circumvent these vague regulations. In addition to sending their own agents to Washington, many countries hire American lobbyists to assist their efforts. Roughly 1,000 registered agents represent foreign nations' interests in Washington.[18]

States, cities, and other governmental units within the United States also lobby heavily. While most major cities across the United States and two-thirds of the states have at least one Washington lobbyist, cooperative lobbying is perhaps more important. The intergovernmental lobby includes such groups as the Council of State Governments, the National Governors Conference, the National Association of Counties, the National League of Cities, and the U.S. Conference of Mayors. These organizations are, in essence, the trade associations of subnational governments. They represent the broad interests of cities and states while still allowing individual member cities and states to lobby for their particular interests. A second component of the intergovernmental lobby consists of organizations representing the concerns of bureaucratic specialists at the subnational level—for example, highway engineers, county welfare directors, and housing and redevelopment officials.

The interests of subnational governments vary greatly. The problems of frostbelt states differ from those of sunbelt states; cities in the industrial Northeast face problems that are almost unknown in cities of the Southwest. These differences impose limits on the effectiveness of the intergovernmental lobby. Nonetheless, its presence in Washington has demonstrably influenced many major policy decisions that affect state and local governments.[19]

YOUR TURN

INTEREST-GROUP INFLUENCE: GOOD OR BAD?

The Questions:

Indicate whether you think each of the following groups has primarily a *good influence* or a *bad influence* on the way things are going in this country:

Business groups	good influence	bad influence
Labor unions	good influence	bad influence
Environmentalists	good influence	bad influence
Women's movement	good influence	bad influence

What Others Think: The questions were asked in a 1994 Times-Mirror survey of citizens in the United States and seven other western democracies. Among U.S. respondents, business groups were judged by a 44 to 37 percent margin to have a good rather than bad influence. The public's view of labor unions was similar (42 to 37 percent positive), although many of the respondents who had a positive opinion of unions had a negative opinion of business, and vice versa. Environmentalists (67 to 21 percent) and the women's movement (59 to 28 percent) were judged more positively than either business or labor. These patterns also characterized public opinion in most of the other democracies in the study.

Comment: Unless you are in the conservative minority who view environmentalists and the women's movement negatively, the best indicator of your political leanings is probably your response to the business and labor questions. A pro-business and anti-labor response would place you on the conservative side of the political spectrum while the opposite pattern would place you on the liberal side. A pro-business and pro-labor response would indicate that you support interest-group politics while a negative response on both items would suggest you take a dim view of interest groups.

Inside Lobbying: Seeking Influence through Official Contacts

Modern government provides a supportive environment in which interest groups can seek to achieve their policy goals. First, modern government is involved in so many issues—business regulation, income maintenance, urban renewal, cancer research, and energy development, to name only a few—that

The U.S. Conference of Mayors represents the interests of cities in cooperative lobbying of the White House and Congress. Shown here is Mayor William Althaus of York, Pennsylvania, who at the time was president of the conference. (Janet Durrans/ AP/Wide World)

Lobbyists discuss pending legislation with members of the U.S. House of Representatives. Access to public officials and the capacity to provide them with useful information are crucial to effective inside lobbying. (Dennis Brack/Black Star)

hardly any interest in society could fail to benefit significantly from having influence over federal policies or programs. Moreover, most of what government does is decided without much publicity and with the participation of a relatively small group of officials. These conditions, as E. E. Schattschneider noted, are conducive to group influence.[20]

Second, modern government is oriented toward action. Officials are inclined to look for policy solutions to problems rather than to let problems linger. For example, when severe flooding along the Mississippi and Missouri rivers caused a steep decline in farm production and income in these parts of the country in 1993, Washington did not leave farmers to sink or swim on their own but quickly mobilized to assist them through government programs.

A group's ability to gain the government's support depends on any number of factors, including its size, its financial strength, and the nature of its policy demands.[21] Groups seek support through **lobbying,** a term that refers broadly to efforts of groups to influence public policy through contact with public officials. According to Norman Ornstein and Shirley Elder, the two main lobbying strategies may be labeled as "inside lobbying" and "outside lobbying."[22] Each strategy involves communication between public officials and group lobbyists, but the strategies differ as to what is communicated, who does the communicating, and who receives the communication. Let's begin by discussing **inside lobbying,** which is based on group efforts to develop and maintain close ("inside") contacts with policymakers. (Outside lobbying will be described in the next section.)

lobbying The process by which interest-group members or lobbyists attempt to influence public policy through contacts with public officials.

inside lobbying Direct communication between organized interests and policymakers, which is based on the assumed value of close ("inside") contacts with policymakers.

ACQUIRING ACCESS TO OFFICIALS

Inside lobbying is designed to give a group direct access to officials in order to influence their decisions. Access is a critical first step. Unless a group can get the attention of officials, it has no chance of persuading them to support its position.

Five U.S. senators got into trouble for accepting large campaign contributions from Charles Keating and then acting on behalf of Keating's beleaguered savings and loan. The "Keating Five" and their lawyers are shown at hearings of the Senate Ethics Committee, defending themselves against charges of influence peddling. (Brad Markel/Gamma Liaison)

Lobbying once depended significantly on tangible inducements, sometimes including indirect or even outright bribes. This old form of lobbying survives today. Through personal and family contributions, Charles H. Keating, Jr., owner of Lincoln Savings and Loan, contributed hundreds of thousands of dollars to the campaigns of five U.S. senators, each of whom interceded on his behalf with the Federal Home Loan Bank Board, which was investigating Lincoln's finances. When asked whether his contributions helped him, Keating said, "I certainly hope so." The investigation of Lincoln Savings lagged for two years, costing taxpayers an estimated $1.3 billion.

But modern lobbying generally involves more subtle and sophisticated methods than providing money or personal favors to officials. It focuses on supplying officials with information and indications of group strength which will persuade them to adopt the group's perspective.[23] As one lobbyist explained: "To a large extent, the three B's—booze, bribes, and broads—have disappeared. . . . Today, a good lobbyist must have the ability to draw up factual information—a lot of it—in a short period of time for people on [Capitol] Hill who want it. . . . Nowadays, taking someone to a football game or a goose hunt just doesn't quite make it."[24]

A group's chances of success are enhanced if it has effective lobbyists working on its behalf. Some of the best lobbyists are longtime Washington lawyers from prestigious firms who have built effective working relationships with top officials.[25] Former members of Congress are also in great demand as lobbyists. They have the unique right to go directly onto the floor of the House or Senate to speak with current members. Former members usually represent groups with which they had close ties while they were in office. Representatives Richard Ichord (D-Mo.) and Bob Wilson (R-Calif.) stepped from senior posts on the House Armed Services Committee to jobs with a lobbying firm that represented most of the nation's major defense contractors.[26]

Money is the essential ingredient of inside lobbying efforts. The American Petroleum Institute, for example, with its abundant financial resources, can afford a downtown Washington office staffed by lobbyists, petroleum experts, and public relations specialists who help the oil companies to maintain access to and influence with legislative and executive leaders.[27] Many groups spend $1 million or more annually on lobbying. Other groups survive with much less, but it is hard to run a first-rate lobbying campaign on less than $100,000 a year. Given the costs of maintaining a Washington lobby, the domination by corporations and trade associations is understandable. They have the money to retain high-priced lobbyists, while many other interests do not. The best that some groups can manage is to buy a small share of a lobbyist's time.

PERSUASION THROUGH CONTACT AND INFORMATION

The medium of exchange for most inside lobbying activity is information. Lobbyists supply officials with information and indications of group strength that will persuade them to adopt the interest group's perspective. Few policymakers today would support a group's claim simply because it asks them to. For a group to win out, it must make a strong case for its objectives. This effort could conceivably be targeted at legislative, executive, or judicial officials.

HOW THE UNITED STATES COMPARES

THE PREVALENCE OF LOBBYING

With its federal system and separate branches of government, the United States is a lobbyist's dream. If unsuccessful with legislators, the lobbyist can turn to executives or the courts. If thwarted at the state level, the lobbyist can turn to the national level of government. By comparison, the governments of most other democractic nations are not organized in ways that facilitate group access and influence. Great Britain's unitary government and parliamentary system, for example, result in a concentration of power in the majority party. Britain's prime minister and cabinet ministers are, at one and the same time, the majority-party leaders, the legislative leaders, and the executive heads. Their support is a great asset for a group but is correspondingly hard to achieve. A group may find it difficult even to get their attention. Not surprisingly, interests in Britain tend to organize nationally and to work through the political parties. Groups in the United States are more likely to function independently of parties and to organize at both the national and state levels.

U.S. lobbying groups are unparalleled in their number, in their spending, and in their impact (through PACs) on election campaigns. In fact, lobbyists of the traditional American type are found in only a few countries. Interest groups are important in all democracies, but the United States, Canada, and Britain are among the few countries in which groups hire lobbyists to intercede with officials on their behalf.

In all western democracies, interest groups seem to be gaining strength while political parties grow weaker. An explanation is that people's interests have become more focused and less ideological. Some traditional interest groups, such as labor, are on the wane in all democracies, while environmental groups and single-issue groups are on the increase.

SOURCE: Clive S. Thomas, "Interest Groups in Post-Industrial Democracies," *Newsletter of Political Organizations and Parties*, 9, no. 1, 1991, p. 8.

Lobbying Congress

The benefits of a close relationship with members of Congress are substantial. With support in Congress, a group can obtain the legislative help it needs to achieve its policy goals. By the same token, members of Congress also gain from working closely with lobbyists. The volume of legislation facing Congress is enormous, and members rely on trusted lobbyists to identify bills that deserve their attention and support. Some members of Congress even involve lobbyists directly in their legislative work. One congressional aide explained:

> My boss demands a speech and a statement for the *Congressional Record* for every bill we introduce or co-sponsor—and we have a lot of bills. I just can't do it all myself. The better lobbyists, when they have a proposal they are pushing, bring it to me along with a couple of speeches, a *Record* insert, and a fact sheet.[28]

As would be expected, lobbyists work primarily with members of Congress who share their views.[29] Union lobbyists work most closely with pro-labor legislators, just as business lobbyists focus mainly on pro-business legislators.

Lobbyists' effectiveness with members of Congress depends in part on their reputation for fair play. An effective lobbyist knows when and how to compromise. The goal, as one lobbyist put it, is "solution searching": finding a position that is beneficial to the group without conceding more than is necessary.[30] Lobbyists are also expected to play it straight with members of Congress. Said one congressman: "If any [lobbyist] gives me false or misleading information, that's it—I'll never see him again."[31] Arm-twisting is another unacceptable practice. A group that throws its weight around is likely to get a chilly response from members of Congress. During the debate over the North American Free Trade Agreement (NAFTA) in 1993, the AFL-CIO threatened retaliation against congressional Democrats who supported the legislation. The backlash was so intense that the union backed down on its threat. The safe lobbying strategy is the aboveboard approach: provide information, rely on longtime allies among members of Congress, and push steadily but not too aggressively for legislative goals.

Lobbying Executive Agencies

As the scope of the federal government has expanded, lobbying of the executive branch has increased in importance. Bureaucrats make key administrative decisions and develop policy initiatives that the legislative branch later makes into law. By working closely with government agencies, groups can influence policy decisions at the implementation and initiation stages. In return, groups assist government agencies by providing information and lending support when their programs are reviewed by Congress and the president.[32]

Nowhere is the link between groups and the bureaucracy more evident than in the regulatory agencies that oversee the nation's business sectors. For example, the Federal Communications Commission (FCC), which regulates the nation's broadcasters, uses information provided by broadcast organizations to decide many of the policies governing their activities. The FCC is some-

The broadcast industry is regulated by the Federal Communications Commission (FCC), which at times has been a "captive agency." Over the years, broadcasters have obtained a great many favorable decisions from the FCC. (Stephen Ferry/Gamma Liaison)

times cited as an example of agency "capture." The capture theory suggests that regulatory agencies pass through a series of phases that constitute a "life cycle." Early in an agency's existence, it regulates an industry on the public's behalf, but as the agency matures, its vigor declines until at best it protects the status quo and at worst it falls captive to the very industry it is supposed to regulate.[33] In the 1950s, the commercial networks successfully lobbied the FCC in a campaign against the establishment of a strong public sector television system. For example, public stations were assigned UHF frequencies, while commercial stations held the more powerful VHF frequencies, which were also the only ones that most television sets of the 1950s were programmed to receive. Without access to a large audience, public television was in a weak position to request additional funding from Congress. Without more funds, it had to struggle to develop the type of programming that would attract a larger audience. The consequences of this vicious circle linger today. Compared with Europe, where public broadcasting was established early and on a solid footing, the U.S. system is very weak. European public broadcasting networks, such as BBC-1 and BBC-2 in Britain and ARD and ZDF in Germany, have large audiences for both their news and entertainment programming. In the United States, the Public Broadcasting System (PBS) has only a thirtieth of the audience of the commercial broadcast networks (ABC, CBS, NBC, and Fox).

Research has shown that the capture theory describes only some agencies—and then only some of the time.[34] Agencies selectively cooperate with or oppose interest groups, depending on which strategy better suits agency purposes.[35] Agency officials are aware that they can lose support in Congress, which controls agency funding and program authorization, if they show too much favoritism toward an interest group. Public disclosure of favoritism can also irreparably damage an official's reputation. Agricultural secretary Mike

Espy resigned in 1994 when it became known that he had ordered a delay in the implementation of tougher food-quality standards for the poultry industry, after having accepted the use of a corporate jet, lodging, and football tickets from Tyson Foods Inc., one of the nation's leading poultry producers.

Although instances of favoritism occur, the U.S. bureaucracy ranks high in comparison with other national bureaucracies in terms of its efficiency and honesty.[36] Its dealings with lobbying groups are important to effective administration, which includes an understanding of the impact of programs on affected interests. From the viewpoint of the interest group, the bureaucracy's need for information is a lobbying opportunity.

Lobbying the Courts

Recent broad rulings by the courts in areas such as education and civil rights have made interest groups recognize that the judiciary, too, can help them reach their goals.[37] Interest groups have several judicial lobbying options, including efforts to influence the selection of federal judges. "Right-to-life" groups pressured the Reagan and Bush administrations to make opposition to abortion a prerequisite for nomination to the federal bench. The Clinton administration faced the opposite type of pressure from pro-choice groups on its judicial nominations.

Amicus curiae ("friend of the court") briefs are another method of judicial lobbying. An *amicus* brief is a written document in which a group brings its position on a particular case to a court's attention. For example, in the landmark affirmative action case *Regents of the University of California* v. *Bakke* (1978), fifty-eight *amicus* briefs representing the positions of more than one-hundred organizations were filed with the Supreme Court at its invitation.

Groups typically try to influence public policy through the courts by filing lawsuits. For some organizations, such as the National Association for the Advancement of Colored People (NAACP) and the American Civil Liberties Union (ACLU), legal action is the primary means of lobbying government. The NAACP, for example, has emphasized legal action since its founding in 1909 because it recognizes that minorities often lack influence with elected officials. The NAACP financed the 1954 *Brown* case, in which the Supreme Court declared that racial segregation of public schools is unconstitutional. Had the NAACP tried to achieve the same result by lobbying state legislators in the South, it almost certainly would have failed.

As interest groups increasingly resort to legal action, they often find themselves facing one another in court. Such environmental litigation groups as the Sierra Club Legal Defense Club, the Environmental Defense Fund, and the Natural Resources Defense Council have frequently sued oil, timber, and mining corporations.

WEBS OF INFLUENCE: GROUPS IN THE POLICY PROCESS

Lobbying efforts provide an incomplete picture of how groups obtain influence. To get a fuller picture, it is necessary to also consider two policy processes, iron triangles and issue networks, in which many groups are enmeshed.

Iron Triangles

An **iron triangle** consists of a small and informal but relatively stable set of bureaucrats, legislators, and lobbyists who seek to develop policies beneficial to a particular interest.[38] The three "corners" of one such triangle are the Department of Veterans Affairs (bureaucrats), the veterans' affairs committees of Congress (legislators), and veterans' groups such as the American Legion and the Veterans of Foreign Wars (lobbyists), which together determine many of the policies affecting veterans. Of course, the support of others, including the president and a majority in Congress, is needed to enact new programs to benefit veterans. However, they often defer to the policy views voiced by the veterans' triangle, whose members best understand the programs, problems, and policy needs of veterans.

iron triangle A small and informal but relatively stable group of well-positioned legislators, executives, and lobbyists who seek to promote policies beneficial to a particular interest.

A group in an iron triangle has an inside track to those legislators and bureaucrats who are in the strongest position to promote its cause. And because it can offer something of value to each of them in return, the relationship tends to be ironclad. The group provides lobbying support for the agency's funding and programs, and gives campaign contributions to its congressional allies. Agricultural groups, for example, contributed $12 million to congressional campaigns in the 1993–1994 election cycle. Most of the money was given to incumbents and, of these contributions, most went to the campaigns of members of the House and Senate agriculture committees. Figure 10-1 summarizes the benefits that flow to each member of an iron triangle.

Issue Networks

Iron triangles represent the pattern of influence only in certain policy areas and are less dominant than in the past. A more common pattern of influence today is the **issue network,** which is an informal grouping of officials, lobbyists, and policy specialists (the "network") who are brought together by their shared interest and expertise in a particular policy area (the "issue").

issue network An informal and relatively open network of public officials and lobbyists who have a common interest and expertise in a given area and who are brought together by a proposed policy in that area. Unlike an iron triangle, an issue network disbands after the issue is resolved.

Issue networks are a result of the increasing complexity and interconnect-

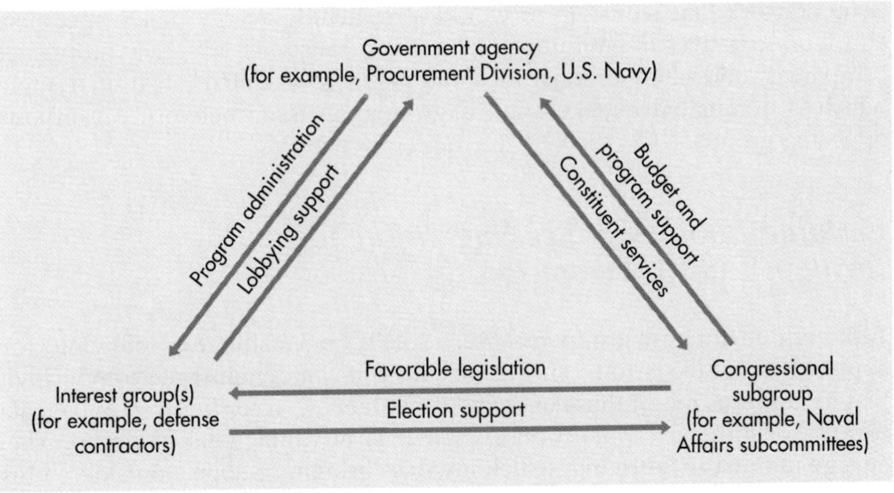

FIGURE 10-1 How an Iron Triangle Benefits Its Participants An iron triangle works to the advantage of each of its participants—an interest group, a congressional subgroup, and a government agency.

Many nuclear power issues are technical in nature, and issue networks tend to form when policy questions of this type arise. (Lowell Georgia/ Photo Researchers)

edness of policy problems. The complexity of modern issues often makes it essential that a participant have specialized knowledge of the issue at hand in order to join in the debate. Thus, unlike iron triangles, where one's position is everything, an issue network is built around policy expertise. On any given issue, the participants might come from a variety of executive agencies, congressional committees, interest groups, and institutions, such as universities or "think tanks." And, unlike iron triangles, issue networks are less stable and less clearly defined. As the issue develops, new participants may join the debate and old ones drop out. Once the issue is resolved, the network disbands.[39]

An example of an issue network is the set of participants who would come together if Congress proposed a major change in the requirements for constructing nuclear power plants. In early times this issue might have been settled by an iron triangle consisting of the Nuclear Regulatory Commission, the nuclear power industry, and the energy committees in Congress. Today, the issue network that would form would also include energy policy specialists and representatives of environmental groups, consumer advocacy groups, oil companies, and labor unions, to name just a few. Unlike an iron triangle, which is dominated by like-minded groups, an issue network can involve opposing groups.

Outside Lobbying: Seeking Influence through Public Pressure

outside lobbying A form of lobbying in which an interest group seeks to use public pressure as a means of influencing officials.

Although an interest group may rely solely on Washington lobbying, this approach is not likely to be successful unless it can demonstrate convincingly that its concerns reflect those of a vital constituency. Accordingly, groups make use of constituency connections when it is advantageous to do so. They engage in **outside lobbying,** which involves bringing public ("outside") pressure to bear on policymakers.[40] The "outside" approach typically takes the form of either *constituency advocacy* or *electoral action* (see Table 10-3).

TABLE 10-3 Tactics Used in Inside and Outside Lobbying Strategies Inside and outside lobbying are based on different tactics.

Inside Lobbying	*Outside Lobbying*
Developing contacts with legislators and executives	Encouraging group members to write or phone their representatives in Congress
Providing information and policy proposals to key officials	Seeking favorable coverage by news media
Forming coalitions with other groups	Encouraging members to support particular candidates in elections
	Targeting group resources on key election races
	Making PAC contributions to candidates

CONSTITUENCY ADVOCACY: GRASSROOTS LOBBYING

Some groups depend heavily on **grassroots lobbying**—that is, pressure designed to convince government officials that a group's policy position has broad public support.[41] To mobilize constituents, groups can mount advertising and public relations campaigns through the media. They can also encourage their members to write or call their elected representatives, or even see their representatives personally.

grassroots lobbying A form of lobbying designed to persuade officials that a group's policy position has strong constituent support.

Few groups have used grassroots lobbying more effectively than Mothers Against Drunk Driving (MADD). The group was formed by Candy Lightner, who lost a family member in a traffic accident caused by a drunk driver. She

Grassroots lobbying brought 2,000 farmers to Washington in 1978. The trucks and tractors circling the White House and Capitol were visible reminders to federal officials that agricultural workers were experiencing hard times (Arthur Grace/Sygma)

taught others who had suffered a similar loss to view themselves as a political lobby, and MADD's intense grassroots campaign resulted in a federal law that withholds highway funds from states with a legal drinking age under twenty-one. Through appearances on television news shows, letters to key members of Congress, and personal appeals to President Ronald Reagan, MADD won a campaign that at first appeared unlikely to succeed because of opposition by powerful restaurant and liquor lobbies. Since then, MADD, which now has a membership in excess of 2.5 million, has pressured state legislatures and local law enforcement officials to toughen penalties for people convicted of driving while intoxicated.

As with other forms of lobbying, the precise impact of grassroots campaigns is usually difficult to assess. Some members of Congress downplay its influence, but all congressional offices monitor letters and phone calls from constituents as a way of tracking their views. Most members receive hundreds of letters and phone calls each week from constituents, not counting fax messages, computer-generated mail, and organized grassroots postcard campaigns.

ELECTORAL ACTION: VOTES AND PACs

"Reward your friends and punish your enemies" is a political adage that loosely describes how interest groups view election campaigns. As part of an "outside" strategy, organized groups work to elect their supporters and defeat their opponents. The possibility of electoral opposition from a powerful group can keep an officeholder from openly obstructing its goals. Opposition from the National Rifle Association (NRA) is a major reason the United States has lagged behind other western societies in its handgun control laws, although polls show that most Americans favor such laws. The NRA's power has weakened as gun-related crime has increased, but the NRA ranks among the top ten groups in terms of campaign spending and boasts staunch supporters in every congressional district who are willing to work to defeat candidates who favor tougher gun control laws. The NRA even has a "test" that it sometimes offers candidates. Allen O'Donnell, a Nebraska college professor, received an A-minus on his NRA test, while his primary election opponent got an A and received the NRA's support. O'Donnell lost the primary.[42]

The principal way in which interest groups try to gain influence through elections is by contributing money to candidates' campaigns. As one lobbyist said, "Talking to politicians is fine, but with a little money they hear you better."[43] Money does not literally "buy" votes in Congress, but it does buy access. Members of Congress listen to the groups that underwrite their campaigns.

PAC Spending

political action committee (PAC) The organization through which an interest group raises and distributes funds for election purposes. By law, the funds must be raised through voluntary contributions.

The vehicle for group contributions is the **political action committee (PAC).** Through its PAC, a group can raise money for election campaigns by soliciting voluntary contributions from members or employees, but it cannot give organizational funds (such as corporate profits or union dues) to candidates. A PAC is not limited by law in the number of candidates to whom it can con-

Former White House Press Secretary James Brady, who was shot and partially paralyzed during the 1981 assassination attempt on President Reagan, celebrates a hard-fought victory over the National Rifle Association, a powerful gun lobby. Despite the NRA's opposition, the Senate had just passed a bill requiring a five-day waiting period for handgun purchases. (Wide World Photos)

tribute, but is legally limited in the amount it can contribute to any single candidate for federal office. As of 1995, the ceiling was $10,000 per candidate—$5,000 in the primary campaign and $5,000 in the general election campaign. These limits do not apply to state and local elections, which are governed by state law (see box: States in the Nation).

PACs mushroomed in the 1970s as a result of favorable changes in campaign finance laws (see Figure 10-2). There are now more than 4,000 PACs,

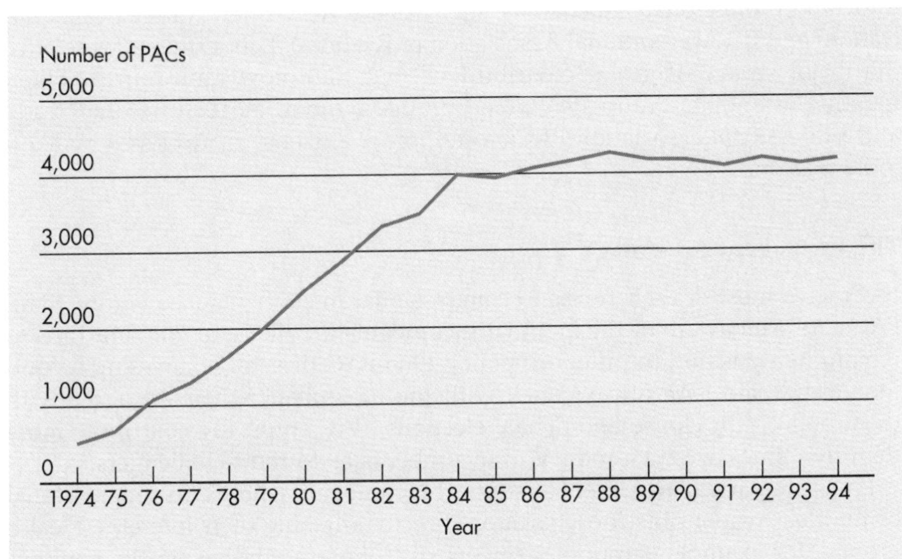

FIGURE 10-2 Growth in the Number of PACs, 1974–1994 The number of PACs began to increase sharply after campaign finance reforms were enacted in the early 1970s. *Source: Federal Elections Commission.*

★ STATES IN THE NATION

Limits on PAC Spending: Elections for state offices are regulated by the states, which in some cases limit PAC contributions.

STATE	LIMIT ON EACH PAC's CONTRIBUTION
Ala.	unlimited
Alaska	$1,000
Ariz.	$3,200*
Ark.	$1,000
Calif.	$5,000
Colo.	unlimited
Conn.	variable
Del.	$1,200*
D. C.	$600
Fla.	$500
Ga.	$2,500*
Hawaii	$2,000
Idaho	unlimited
Ill.	unlimited
Ind.	unlimited
Iowa	unlimited
Kan.	$2,000*
Ky.	$500
La.	$5,000*
Maine	$5,000
Md.	$6,000
Mass.	$1,000
Mich.	$3,400*
Minn.	$2,000*
Miss.	unlimited
Mo.	unlimited
Mont.	$8,000*
Neb.	unlimited
Nev.	$20,000
N.H.	$1,000
N.C.	$5,000*
N. Mex.	unlimited
N.Y.	$150,000*
N.C.	$4,000
N.Dak.	unlimited
Ohio	unlimited
Okla.	$5,000*
Oreg.	unlimited
Pa.	unlimited
R.I.	$1,000
S.C.	$3,500*
S.Dak.	unlimited
Tenn.	unlimited
Texas	unlimited
Utah	unlimited
Vt.	$3,000
Va.	unlimited
Wash.	$1,000*
W.V.	$1,000
Wis.	variable
Wyo.	unlimited

SOURCE: Federal Elections Commission, "Campaign Finance Law 94," Chart 2A.

*These states have variable limits, depending on the office being sought. In these cases, the dollar amount is the highest allowable for an office, usually governor.

TABLE 10-4 Number and Percentage of Political Action Committees (PACs) in Five Categories Most PACs represent business: corporations and trade associations make up 63% of the total.

Category	*Number*	*Percentage*
Corporate	1,877	45%
Noneconomic	1,145	28
Trade/membership association	770	18
Labor	347	8
Agriculture	56	1
All categories	4,195	100%

SOURCE: Federal Election Commission figures, 1994.

and PAC contributions account for nearly a third of total contributions to congressional campaigns. Because PAC money can be raised earlier and more quickly than money from individual contributors, PACs have become a critical factor in getting congressional campaigns off the ground. Their role is less significant in presidential campaigns, which are larger in scale and publicly funded in part and therefore depend on a wider range of funding sources than do congressional campaigns.

More than 40 percent of all PACs are associated with corporations (see Table 10-4). Examples include the Ford Motor Company Civic Action Fund, the Sun Oil Company Political Action Committee (Sunpac), and the Coca-Cola PAC. The next largest group of PACs consists of those linked to citizens' groups (that is, public interest, single-issue, and ideological groups), such as the liberal People for the American Way and the conservative NCPAC (National Conservative Political Action Committee). Ranking third are PACs tied to trade and professional associations, such as AMPAC (American Medical Association) and R-PAC (National Association of Realtors). Labor unions were once the major source of group contributions, but they now rank fourth. Taken together, economic-group PACs (corporations, labor, agriculture, and trade and professional association PACs) outnumber citizens' group PACs by a 70-to-30 margin.

The Incumbent Advantage

PACs give most of their funds to congressional incumbents (see Figure 10-3). PACs are well aware of the fact that incumbents are likely to win and thus to remain in a position to influence policy. One PAC director, expressing a common view, said "We always stick with the incumbent when we agree with them both."[44] In House and Senate elections, PACs typically contribute more than five times as much money to incumbents as to their challengers.

PACs are particularly likely to support incumbents who sit on congressional committees responsible for legislation directly affecting their interests. Health groups, for example, support members of Congress who sit on the committees (for example, the House Ways and Means Committee) that control most

As this 1889 cartoon by Joseph Koppler shows, at the end of the last century big business attempted to run the show in Congress through its enormous (and unregulated) campaign contributions. (The New York Historical Society, New York City)

of the health care bills. During the 1991–1992 election cycle, with a legislative battle over health care in the offing, health-related PACs gave members of these committees an average of $51,668 in campaign funds, nearly 70 percent more than they gave nonmembers. The American Medical Association alone gave over $750,000 to members of health-related committees. These legislators, said a spokesman for Syntex, a pharmaceutical company, "are players on our set of issues." Representative Alex McMillan (R-N.C.) received $68,250 from health groups for his 1992 campaign, largely because he had recently gained a seat on the House Energy and Commerce's subcommittee on health.[45]

The tendency of PACs to back incumbents has to some extent blurred longstanding partisan divisions in campaign funding. Business interests are the

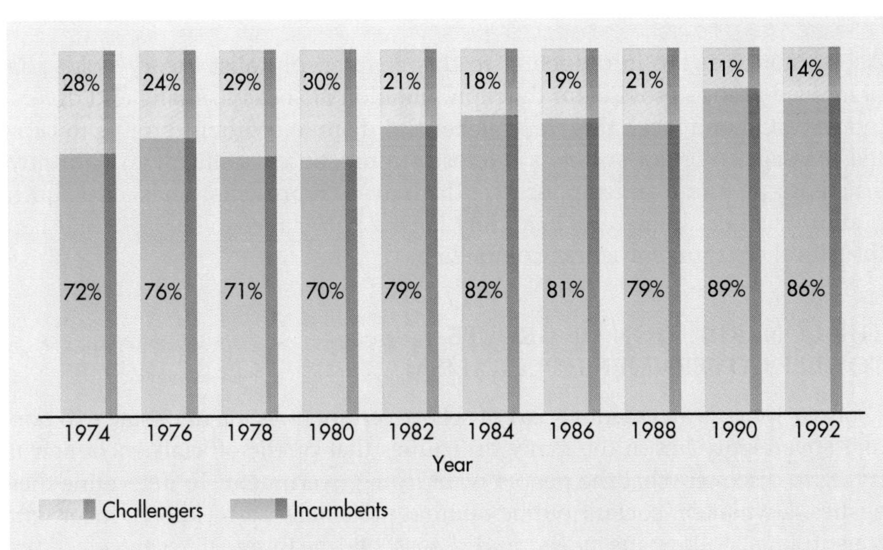

FIGURE 10-3 Allocation of PAC Contributions between Incumbents and Challengers in Congressional Races That Included an Incumbent, 1972–1992
In allocating campaign contributions, PACs favor incumbent members of Congress over their challengers by a wide margin. *Source: Federal Elections Commission.*

★ CRITICAL THINKING

Should PACs Be Abolished?
Interest groups play an increasingly large role in U.S. elections. PACs now provide about a third of all funds contributed to congressional candidates.

Much of the criticism of PACs has been directed at their tendency to back incumbents, particularly those in positions of influence over the policies affecting the group. Supporters of PACs say that interest groups should have a large role in campaigns and contend that PACs give like-minded people an opportunity to increase their voice by pooling their contributions.

Do you think PACs are a problem? If so, should PACs be abolished or simply regulated more closely? If you were to limit the role of PACs, what restrictions would you place on them?

most pragmatic. Although they generally favor Republican candidates, and strongly supported them in 1994 when it became clear the GOP could sweep the congressional elections, business groups are usually reluctant to anger Democratic incumbents. The result is that Democratic incumbents, particularly in House races, have received substantial support over the years from business-related PACs.[46] Other PACs, especially those organized to promote a particular public policy or ideology, are less pragmatic. The Christian Moral Government Fund, for example, backs only candidates who take conservative stands on issues such as school prayer and abortion.

Should PACs Be Abolished?

PACs are admired by those who believe that a campaign finance system based on pooled contributions by individuals is superior to one in which candidates rely on a few wealthy donors.[47] The advocates of PACs also claim that groups have a right to be heard, which includes the right to express themselves with money.

Critics argue, however, that PACs give interest groups altogether too much influence over public officials.[48] The opposition to PACs has increased in the last few years, as citizens have come to associate the influence of interest groups with what they see as an unresponsive federal government. Although members of Congress deny that they are unduly influenced by PAC contributions, there has been a growing sentiment within Congress to place restrictions on PACs. Agreement on the changes, however, has been difficult to achieve because of differences between Democrats and Republicans in the way they would reform the process and also because some incumbents are unwilling to support any change that would significantly alter the advantage they have under the present system. The controversy over PACs is not likely to subside, however, and Congress can be expected to take action on the issue in the foreseeable future.

The Group System: Indispensable but Flawed

As we noted in the introduction to this chapter, pluralist theory holds that organized groups provide for the representation of society's many and diverse interests. On one level, this claim is beyond dispute. Without groups to carry the message, most of society's interests would find it difficult to gain government's attention and support. Yet the issue of representation is also a question of whether all interests in society have a fair chance to succeed, and here the pluralist argument is less compelling.

THE CONTRIBUTION OF GROUPS TO SELF-GOVERNMENT: PLURALISM

Group activity is an essential part of self-government. A major obstacle to popular sovereignty lies in the many difficulties that public officials encounter in trying to discover what the people want from government. To determine their wishes, lawmakers consult public opinion polls, talk with experts, meet with constituents, follow the news, and assess the meaning of recent elections.

Organized groups are an additional means of determining popular sentiment, as they provide policymakers with a better picture of the policy concerns of various interests in society.[49] On any given issue, the policy positions that are likely to be expressed most clearly and intensely are those held by organized interests.

No group illustrates this better than the American Association of Retired Persons (AARP). With more than 30 million members and a staff of 1,600 employees, AARP has been a powerful lobby on issues affecting the elderly. Pressure from the AARP is a major reason that the social security system is nearly off limits whenever proposals to reduce the federal budget are discussed. The AARP was directly responsible for killing a catastrophic health insurance plan for the elderly for which senior citizens would have had to pay a surcharge. The legislation was enacted by Congress but rescinded a year later because of the AARP's opposition to the way it would be financed. Congress also reversed itself after the AARP objected to legislation that would have required increased payments from higher-income social security recipients who require nursing home care. AARP members are so responsive to policies affecting them that they generate more mail to Congress than any other group.[50]

The American Association of Retired Persons (AARP) is the largest citizens' group. The AARP's membership benefits include a periodic magazine, *Modern Maturity.* (Felicia Martinez/Photo Edit)

Some pluralists even question whether such terms as "the common good" and "the collective interest" are very useful. If people disagree on society's goals and priorities, as they always do, how can it be said that people have a "common" or "collective" concern? As an alternative, *pluralist theory* (see Chapter 1) would substitute the sum of people's varied (that is, plural) interests as a rough approximation of society's collective interest. The logic of this proposition is that, because society has so many interests, the common good is ultimately served by a process that enables a great many interests to gain favorable policies. Thus if manufacturing interests prevail on one issue, environmentalists on another, farmers on a third, minorities on a fourth, and so on until a wide range of particular interests are served, the collective interest of society will have been promoted.[51]

FLAWS IN THE PLURALIST ARGUMENT

Although pluralist theory offers some compelling arguments, it also has questionable aspects. In a direct attack on pluralism, Theodore Lowi argues that there is no concept of society's collective interest in a system that allows special interests to determine for themselves which policy benefits they receive, regardless of how many interests are served.[52] The fact that a great number and variety of interests receive a slice of the pie is beside the point if each group decides for itself what its slice is going to be. When each group makes its own choice, the basis of decision in each case is not majority (collective) rule but minority (special-interest) rule.

Interest-Group Liberalism

Lowi's concern is based on the ability of various groups to come close to monopolizing power in their special areas. The policies that result favor the interests not of a majority but of a series of minorities. The iron triangle is the clearest example, with a particular group working in tandem with legislators

Sometimes the interests of a group clearly diverge from majority opinion, as when the National Association of Auto Dealers lobbied successfully against legislation that would have required auto dealers to inform customers about any defects in used cars. (R. Sidney/ The Image Works)

and bureaucrats who have a stake in promoting the group's interest. Of course, the policy proposals that emerge from an iron triangle must still gain the acceptance of other officials, and this necessity serves as a restraint. But the sheer volume of modern legislation prevents most such policies from being studied closely and thus from acquiring the support of a true deliberative majority.

It is seldom safe to assume that what a popular majority favors is what a special-interest group wants. Consider the case of the federal law that required auto dealers to list the known defects of used cars on window stickers. The law was repealed after an extensive lobbying campaign financed by contributions of more than $1 million by the National Association of Automobile Dealers to the reelection campaigns of nearly 200 members of the U.S. House of Representatives.[53] Although an overwhelming majority of the general public would surely have favored retention of the law, the car dealers' view prevailed.

interest-group liberalism The tendency of public officials to support the policy demands of self-interested groups (as opposed to judging policy demands according to whether or not they serve a larger conception of "the public interest").

Lowi uses the term **interest-group liberalism** to describe the tendency of officials to support the policy demands of the interest group or groups that have a special stake in a policy. Interest-group liberalism constitutes a partial abdication by government of its authority over policy. In practical terms, it is the group, as much as the government, that decides policy. The adverse effects include a weakening of majoritarian institutions and an inefficient use of society's resources: groups get what they want, whether or not their priorities match those of society as a whole.

Economic Bias

Another flaw in the pluralist argument resides in its claim that the group system is representative. Pluralists recognize that better-organized interests have more influence but argue that the group process is relatively open and fluid and that few interests are at a serious disadvantage. These claims contain an element of truth but are far from the complete truth.

As we have seen, organization is a political resource that is distributed unequally across society. Economic interests, particularly corporations, are the most highly organized, and some analysts argue that group politics works almost entirely to the advantage of business.[54]. This generalization is less valid today. In fact, many of the public interest groups formed in the 1960s and early 1970s were deliberately created to check and balance the influence of existing groups, particularly corporate lobbies.[55]

Big government has also brought the group political system into closer balance. Groups form not only to influence policy but also in response to it. When new programs were created in the 1960s for the benefit of less advantaged interests in society, these interests tended to mobilize to protect their newly acquired benefits. The National Welfare Rights Organization was formed during the 1960s after new welfare programs were established.[56] Many of the newer interest groups have had a significant impact in areas such as civil rights, the environment, social welfare programs for the elderly and the poor, public morality, national security, and business regulation.

Nevertheless, interests differ significantly in their level of organization and degree of influence through group activity. Well over half of all lobbying groups in Washington are still business-related. The interest-group system is decidedly biased toward America's economically oriented groups, particularly its corporations.

The group system is also slanted toward upper-middle-class interests.[57] Studies indicate that individuals of higher socioeconomic status are dispro-

★ CRITICAL THINKING

Special and General Interests
Is the sum of special interests nearly the same as the general interest? An answer to this question requires a judgment about the degree to which people's interests are more separate than general. An answer also requires a judgment about the degree to which government's response to special interests limits its ability to respond to general needs.

Many citizens' groups lack the financial resources to publicize their needs, so they must rely on dramatic protest to attract media attention to their cause. These disabled Americans are demonstrating in front of the White House to urge passage of the Americans with Disabilities Act. (Johnson/Gamma Liaison)

portionately represented among group members and even more so among group leaders. These tendencies are predictable. Educated and affluent Americans have the skills and money that give organizational form to special-interest politics. Less advantaged Americans lack the money, information, contacts, and communication skills to participate even when they desire to do so. The poor, minorities, women, and the young are greatly underrepresented in the group politics system. A lack of organization does not ensure an interest's failure, just as the existence of organization does not guarantee success. However, organized interests are obviously in a better position to make their views known.

The battle over the Clinton health care proposal is a case in point. In addition to their $40 million mass advertising campaigns, the insurance, business, and medical lobbies sponsored letter-writing campaigns designed to get people with adequate medical coverage to write to their member of Congress urging the defeat of the Clinton proposal. More than a million such letters poured into the offices of Congress. The number of letters sent by lower-income people without health insurance coverage, but who would have been covered if the reform legislation had been adopted, was tiny by comparison.

The business and class bias of the group system is especially significant because the most highly organized interests are, in a sense, those least in need of political clout. Corporations and affluent groups already benefit the most from the distribution of society's material resources.

A MADISONIAN DILEMMA

James Madison recognized the dilemma inherent in group activity. Although he worried that government would fall under the control of a dominant interest, whether of the majority or of the minority, he realized that a free society is obliged to permit the advocacy of self-interest. Unless people can promote the separate opinions that stem from differences in their talents, needs, values, and possessions, they do not have liberty.

Ironically, Madison's constitutional solution to the problem of factions has become part of the problem. The American system of checks and balances, with a separation of powers at its core, was designed primarily to block control by a *majority* faction. Madison did not believe that a minority posed a significant threat, because "if a faction consists of less than a majority, relief is supplied by the republican principle, which enables the majority to defeat its [that is, the minority faction's] sinister views by regular vote." Madison's solution to this problem has more or less worked as planned with regard to majority factions. Throughout the nation's history, majorities have been frustrated in their efforts to gain full power by America's elaborate system of divided government.

This same system, however, has made it relatively easy for minority factions—or, as they are called today, special-interest groups—to get their way. Madison did not anticipate that divided government would lead to the delegation of authority in particular policy areas to small sets of officials. And because these officials are also likely to benefit from actions beneficial to the group, they are inclined to serve its purpose. Only by great effort—more effort than any official can muster for each and every policy decision—can society's broad interest be imposed on decisions made in these small policy realms. Chapters 11 and 13 will discuss this problem further.

Summary

A political interest group is composed of a set of individuals organized to promote a shared political concern. Most interest groups owe their existence to factors other than politics. They form for economic reasons, such as the pursuit of profit, and maintain themselves by making profits (in the case of corporations) or by providing their members with private goods, such as jobs and wages. Such interest groups include corporations, trade associations, labor unions, farm organizations, and professional associations. Collectively, economic groups are by far the largest set of organized interests. The group system tends to favor interests that are already economically and socially advantaged.

Other groups do not have the same organizational advantages as economic groups. They depend on voluntary contributions from potential members who may lack interest and resources or who recognize that they will get the collective good from a group's activity even if they do not participate (the free-rider problem). These noneconomic groups include public interest, single-issue, and ideological groups. Their numbers have increased dramatically since the 1960s despite their organizational problems.

Organized interests seek influence largely by lobbying public officials and contributing to election campaigns. Using an "inside strategy," lobbyists develop direct contacts with legislators, government bureaucrats, and members of the judiciary in order to persuade them to accept their group's perspective on policy. Groups also use an "outside strategy," seeking to mobilize public support for their goals. This strategy relies in part on grassroots lobbying—encouraging group members and the public to communicate their policy views to officials. "Outside" lobbying also includes efforts to elect officeholders who will support group aims. Through political action committees (PACs), organized groups now provide nearly a third of all contributions received by congressional candidates.

The policies that emerge from the group system bring benefits to many of society's interests, and in some instances these benefits also serve the general interest. But when groups can essentially dictate policies, the common good is not served. The majority's interest is subordinated to group (minority) interests. In most instances, the minority consists of individuals who already have a substantial share of society's benefits. As E. E. Schattschneider noted, the group system has "a strong upper-class bias."

Major Concepts

citizens' (noneconomic) groups
collective (public) goods
economic groups
free-rider problem
grassroots lobbying
inside lobbying
interest group
interest-group liberalism
iron triangle
issue network
lobbying
outside lobbying
political action committee (PAC)
private (individual) goods
single-issue politics

Suggested Readings

Birnbaum, Jeffrey H., and Alan S. Murray. *Showdown at Gucci Gulch.* New York: Random House, 1987. A case study of the limits of group influence in passage of the Tax Reform Act of 1986.

Chubb, John E. *Interest Groups and the Bureaucracy: The Politics of Energy.* Stanford, Calif.: Stanford University Press, 1983. A refutation of the common idea that the bureaucracy is captive to groups.

Cigler, Allan J., and Burdett A. Loomis, eds. *Interest Group Politics,* 4th ed. Washington, D.C.: Congressional Quarterly Press, 1994. A set of original essays on the impact of interest groups in the political process.

Hansen, John Mark. *Gaining Access: Congress and the Farm Lobby, 1919–1981.* Chicago: University of Chicago Press, 1991. A case study of the farm lobby's influence on Congress.

Lowi, Theodore J. *The End of Liberalism,* 2d ed. New York: Norton, 1979. A thorough critique of interest groups' influence on American politics.

Olson, Mancur, Jr. *The Logic of Collective Action,* rev. ed. Cambridge, Mass.: Harvard University Press, 1971. A pioneering analysis of why some interests are more fully and easily organized than others.

Rothenberg, Lawrence S., *Linking Citizens to Government: Interest Group Politics at Common Cause.* New York: Cambridge University Press, 1992. A careful case study of a leading lobbying group.

Schattschneider, E. E. *The Semisovereign People: A Realist's View of Democracy in America.* New York: Holt, Rinehart and Winston, 1960. A classic analysis of bias in the interest-group system and a critique of pluralist democracy.

Sorauf, Frank J. *Inside Campaign Finance: Myths and Realities.* New Haven, Conn.: Yale University Press, 1992. An award-winning book that describes the structure of campaign finance, including the role of PACs.

Walker, Jack L., Jr. *Mobilizing Interest Groups in America: Patrons, Professions, and Social Movements.* Ann Arbor: University of Michigan Press, 1991. An insightful analysis of how interest groups form and how they flourish or fail.

CHAPTER 11

THE NEWS MEDIA: COMMUNICATING POLITICAL IMAGES

The press in America . . . determines what people will think and talk about—an authority that in other nations is reserved for tyrants, priests, parties and mandarins.

—*Theodore H. White*[1]

On the night of June 12, 1994, Nicole Brown Simpson and a friend, Ronald Goldman, were brutally murdered outside her home in the fashionable Brentwood area of Los Angeles. When her ex-husband, the former football star O. J. Simpson, was accused of the murders, every newspaper and television news program in the country gave the story prominent and repeated play. When replays of 911 calls revealed that O. J. Simpson had physically abused and intimidated his former wife after their 1992 divorce, a brief debate about the ravages of domestic violence ensued. The real issue of the Simpson news coverage, however, was the question of his guilt or innocence. Underlying the mountain of news coverage was the dramatic question: Could O. J. Simpson's good-guy public image have masked a more violent personality, one capable of murder?

Not all developments receive such intensive news coverage. Between 1983 and 1993, the birthrate among unwed women rose by more than 70 percent. According to U.S. Census Bureau statistics, 6.3 million children (27 percent of all children under the age of 18) lived in 1993 with a single parent who had never married, an increase from 3.7 million in 1983. Most of these families are mired in poverty (the average income is less than $10,000), and in many cases the children received no health care and have very little encouragement to perform well in school or stay out of trouble. The implications for society and public policy are enormous, yet this demographic trend is seldom mentioned in the news, let alone emblazoned in the headlines.

Although the news has been compared to a mirror held up to society, it is actually a highly selective portrayal of reality. The **news** is mainly an account of overt, obtruding events, particularly those which are *timely* (new or unfold-

news The news media's version of reality, usually with an emphasis on timely, dramatic, and compelling events and developments.

Robert Shapiro, one of O. J. Simpson's lawyers, arrives at the Los Angeles courthouse. The Simpson trial was one of the most heavily covered news events in U.S. history. (Gilles Mingasson/Gamma Liaison)

ing developments rather than old or static ones), *dramatic* (striking developments rather than commonplace ones), and *compelling* (developments that arouse people's concerns and emotions as opposed to remote ones.)[2] These characteristics of the news have a number of origins, not the least of which is that the news is a business. News organizations must have revenue in order to survive, and this requires that they attract and hold an audience. As a result, the news product is designed to fascinate as well as to inform. Thus the Simpson story became headline news the instant the murders were discovered, and it remained newsworthy while the legal process surrounding the crime unfolded. The rising birthrate among unwed women is not considered particularly newsworthy, because it is a slow and steady process, dramatic only in its long-term implications. The columnist George Will notes that a development requires a defining event before it can become big news.[3] Without such an event, reporters have no peg on which to hang their stories.

press (news media) Those print and broadcast organizations that are in the news-reporting business.

News organizations and journalists, of either the print media (newspapers and magazines) or the broadcast media (radio and television), are referred to collectively as the **press** or the **news media**. The press is an increasingly important political actor. Its heightened influence is attributable in part to changes within the media. New technology, from television to cable to satellites, has dramatically increased the reach and speed of communication. In addition, the press has filled some of the void created by the decline in political parties and other political institutions.

Like political parties and interest groups, the press is a key link between the public and its leaders. In some ways, the press is better positioned than parties or groups to influence the public. On a daily basis, Americans connect to politics more through the news that is produced by the media than through the activities of parties or groups. In addition, although most Americans do

THE MEDIA AND THE PEOPLE

PUBLIC CONFIDENCE IN THE PRESS

What Alexander Hamilton said of judges is also true of journalists: their authority rests on the public's confidence in their judgment. Journalists' words are not backed by the power of the sword or of the purse. Their pronouncements have force to the degree that the public is willing to trust what they say.

Americans have a mixed view of the performance of journalists. The major complaints are that journalists are insensitive to people's privacy, that they are interested primarily in scandal and sleaze, and that they are biased in their coverage of issues and politicians. At the same time, however, the American public gives the press somewhat high marks in terms of its credibility and accuracy. A 1994 Freedom Forum survey found that two-thirds of Americans believe they would lack a reliable basis for judging politicians and issues if it were not for the news media.

Americans' confidence in journalists has waned in recent years. Journalists are perceived as being more honest than politicians but less so than other professional groups, including college professors, physicians, and engineers. Only a fourth of the public believes that journalists have high ethical standards. This level marks a decline from two decades ago, when a third of the public held this opinion. The trend in journalism toward a bolder and more judgmental form of reporting (discussed later in the chapter) has diminished the public's respect for the press.

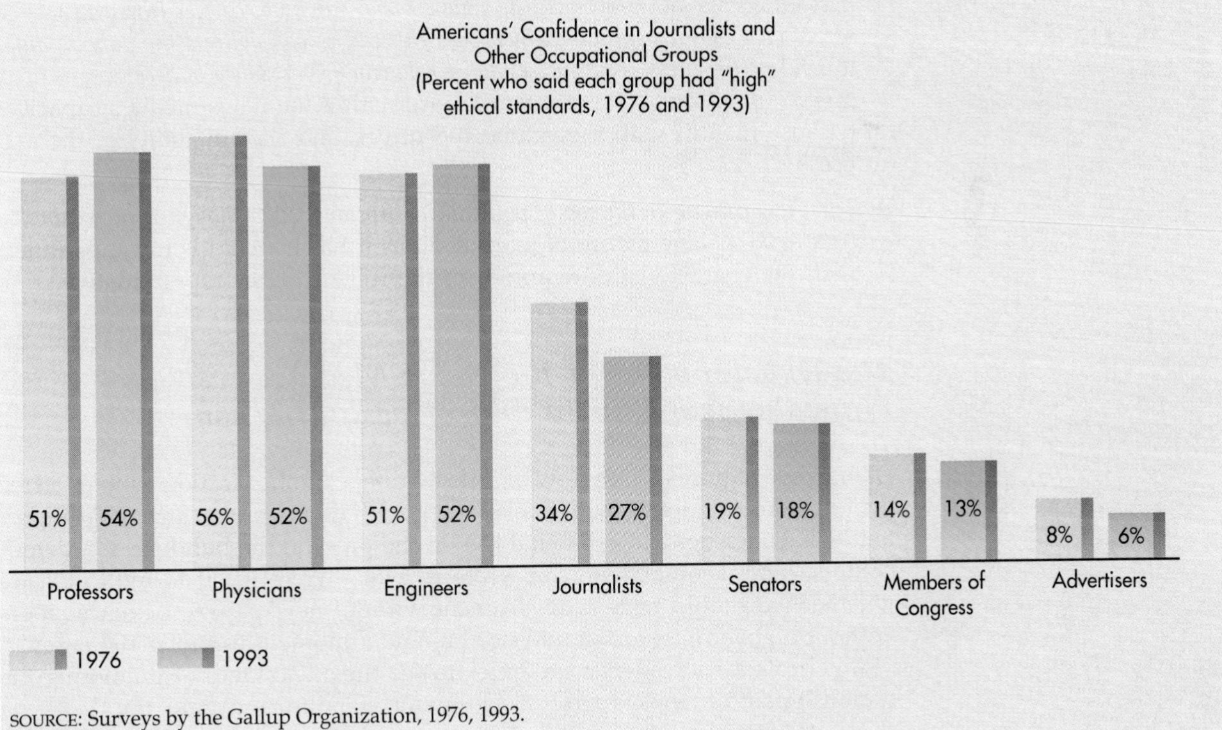

SOURCE: Surveys by the Gallup Organization, 1976, 1993.

not have a particularly high regard for the press, they have a more favorable view of it than of their political representatives (see box: The Media and the People).

This chapter argues, however, that the news media are a very different kind of intermediary than either parties or interest groups and that problems arise when the press is asked to perform the same functions as these organizations. The chapter begins with a review of the media's historical development and the current trends in news reporting, and concludes with an analysis of the roles the press can and cannot perform adequately in the American political system. The main ideas represented in this chapter are the following:

- ★ *The American press was initially tied to the nation's political party system (the partisan press) but gradually developed an independent position (the objective press).* In the process, the news shifted from a political orientation, which emphasizes political values and ideas, to a journalistic orientation, which stresses newsworthy information and evaluations.
- ★ *Although the United States has thousands of separate news organizations, they present a common version of the news which reflects journalists' shared view of what the news is.* Freedom of the press in the United States does not result in a robust marketplace of ideas.
- ★ *In fulfilling its responsibility to provide public information, the news media effectively perform three significant roles—those of signaler (the press brings relevant events and problems into public view), common carrier (the press serves as a channel through which political leaders can address the public), and watchdog (the press scrutinizes official behavior for evidence of deceitful, careless, or corrupt acts).* These roles are within the news media's capacity because they fit with the values, incentives, and accountability of the press.
- ★ *The press cannot do the job of political institutions, even though it increasingly tries to do so.* The nature of journalism as it has evolved is incompatible with the characteristics required for the role of public representative.

The Development of the News Media: From Partisanship to Objective Journalism

Democracy requires a free flow of information. Communication enables a free people to keep in touch with one another, with their leaders, and with important events. Recognizing the vital role of the press in the building of a democratic society, Thomas Jefferson wrote in 1787, "Were it left to me to decide whether we should have a government without newspapers, or newspapers without a government, I should not hesitate a moment to prefer the latter."[4]

America's early leaders were quick to see the advantages of promoting the establishment of newspapers. At Alexander Hamilton's urging, the *Gazette of the United States* was founded by John Fenno to promote the policies of George Washington's administration. Hamilton was secretary of the treasury and supported Fenno's paper by granting it the Treasury Department's printing contracts. Jefferson, who was secretary of state and Hamilton's adversary, complained that the newspaper's content was "pure Toryism." Jefferson persuaded Philip Freneau to start the *National Gazette* as the opposition Republican party's publication and supported it by granting Freneau authority to print State Department documents. When Jefferson resigned his post as secretary of state in 1793, Freneau lost his financial base and was forced to close down his newspaper.

Early newspapers were printed on hand presses, a process that limited production and kept the cost of each copy beyond the reach of ordinary citizens—most of which were illiterate anyway. Leading papers such as the *Gazette of the United States* had fewer than 1,500 subscribers and could not have survived without party support. Not surprisingly, the "news" they printed was a form of party propaganda.[5] In this era of the **partisan press,** publishers openly took sides on partisan issues. Their employees were expected to follow the party line. President James K. Polk once persuaded a leading publisher to fire an editor who was critical of Polk's policies.[6]

partisan press Newspapers and other communication media that openly support a political party and whose news in significant part follows the party line.

FROM A PARTISAN PRESS TO AN "OBJECTIVE" ONE

Technological changes helped bring about the gradual decline of America's partisan press. After the invention of the telegraph in 1837, editors could receive timely information on developments in Washington and the state capital, and they had less reason to fill their pages with partisan harangues.[7] Another major innovation was the rotary press (invented in 1815), a breakthrough that enabled commercially minded publishers to print their newspapers rapidly and cheaply and thus to increase their profit potential.[8] The *New York Sun* was the first paper to pass on the benefit of high-speed printing to subscribers by reducing the price of a daily copy from 6 cents to a penny. The *Sun's* circulation rose to 5,000 in four months and to 10,000 in less than a year.[9] Increased circulation and revenues gave newspapers independence from government and parties, a change that some political leaders welcomed. "The freedom and independence of the press," a congressional committee concluded in 1873, "is best maintained by the people, and their subscriptions are a more legitimate means of support than the patronage of the federal government."[10]

By the late nineteenth century, several American newspapers were printing 100,000 or more copies a day, and their large circulation enabled them to charge high prices for advertising. The period marked the height of newspapers' power and the nadir in their sense of public responsibility.[11] A new style of reporting—"yellow journalism"—had emerged as a way of boosting circulation.[12] The "yellow" press—so called because some of these newspapers were printed on cheap yellow paper—emphasized "a shrieking, gaudy, sensation-loving, devil-may-care kind of journalism which lured the reader by any possible means."[13] A circulation battle between William Randolph Hearst's *New York Journal* and Joseph Pulitzer's *New York World* is believed to have contributed to the outbreak of the Spanish-American War through sensational (and largely inaccurate) reports on the cruelty of Spanish rule in Cuba. A young Frederic Remington (who later became a noted painter and sculptor), working as a news artist for Hearst, planned to return home because Cuba appeared calm and safe; but Hearst cabled back, "Please remain. You furnish the pictures and I'll furnish the war."[14]

The excesses of yellow journalism led some publishers to consider ways of

$50,000 REWARD.—WHO DESTROYED THE MAINE?—$50,000 REWARD.

EDITION FOR GREATER NEW YORK

NEW YORK JOURNAL

AND ADVERTISER.

NEW YORK, THURSDAY, FEBRUARY 17, 1898.—16 PAGES. PRICE ONE CENT

[D]ESTRUCTION OF THE WAR SHIP MAINE WAS THE WORK OF AN ENEMY.

$50,000!

$50,000 REWARD! For the Detection of the Perpetrator of the Maine Outrage!

Assistant Secretary Roosevelt Convinced the Explosion of the War Ship Was Not an Accident.

The Journal Offers $50,000 Reward for the Conviction of the Criminals Who Sent 258 American Sailors to Their Death. Naval Officers Unanimous That the Ship Was Destroyed on Purpose.

$50,000!

$50,000 REWARD! For the Detection of the Perpetrator of the Maine Outrage!

NAVAL OFFICERS THINK THE MAINE WAS DESTROYED BY A SPANISH MINE.

[H]idden Mine or a Sunken Torpedo Believed to Have Been the Weapon Used Against the American Man-of-War---Officers and Men Tell Thrilling Stories of Being Blown Into the Air Amid a Mass of Shattered Steel and Exploding Shells---Survivors Brought to Key West Scout the Idea of Accident---Spanish Officials Protest Too Much---Our Cabinet Orders a Searching Inquiry---Journal Sends Divers to Havana to Report Upon the Condition of the Wreck. Was the Vessel Anchored Over a Mine?

BY CAPTAIN E. L. ZALINSKI, U. S. A.

(Captain Zalinski is the inventor of the famous dynamite gun, which would be the principal factor in our coast defence in case of war.)

Assistant Secretary of the Navy Theodore Roosevelt says he is convinced that the destruction of the Maine in Havana Harbor was not an accident.

The Journal offers a reward of $50,000 for exclusive evidence that will convict the person, persons or Government criminally responsible for the de[stru]ction of the American battle ship and the death of 258 of its crew.

The suspicion that the Maine was deliberately blown up grows stronger every hour. Not a single fact to the contrary has been produced.

Captain Sigsbee, of the Maine, and Consul-General Lee both urge that public opinion be suspended until they have completed their investigation. [Th]ey are taking the course of tactful men who are convinced that there has been treachery.

Washington reports very late that Captain Sigsbee had feared some such event as a hidden mine. The English cipher code was used all day yesterday by naval officers in cabling instead of the usual American code.

Yellow journalism was charcterized by its sensationalism. William Randolph Hearst's *New York Journal* whipped up public support for a war in Cuba with Spain through inflammatory reporting on the sinking of the battleship *Maine* in Havana Harbor in 1898. (Historical Pictures Service.)

reporting the news more responsibly. One step was to separate the newspaper's advertising department from its news department, thus reducing the influence of advertisers on news content. A second development was a new model of reporting called **objective journalism,** which was based on the reporting of "facts" rather than opinions and was "fair" in that it presented both sides of partisan debate.[15]

objective journalism A model of news reporting which is based on the communication of "facts" rather than opinions and which is "fair" in that it presents all sides of partisan debate.

A chief advocate of this new form of journalism was Adolph Ochs of *The New York Times*. Ochs bought the *Times* in 1896, when its circulation was 9,000; four years later, its readership had grown to 82,000. Ochs told his reporters that he "wanted as little partisanship as possible . . . as few judgments as possible."[16] The *Times*'s approach to reporting appealed particularly to educated readers, and by the early twentieth century it had acquired a reputation as the country's best newspaper.

Objective reporting was also promoted through newly formed journalism schools. Among the first of these professional schools were those at Columbia University and the University of Missouri. The Columbia School of Journalism opened in 1912 with a $2 million grant from Pulitzer.

Objective journalism is still a mainstay of daily news coverage. Although most publishers favor one partisan viewpoint or another editorially, the Democratic and Republican parties are usually accorded equal treatment on the news pages. Newspapers' partisanship has traditionally been most evident in their endorsements of candidates during election campaigns, but even this form of advocacy has diminished. One-fourth of America's daily newspapers no longer endorse candidates, and others do so without any consistent regard for the candidates' party affiliations.[17]

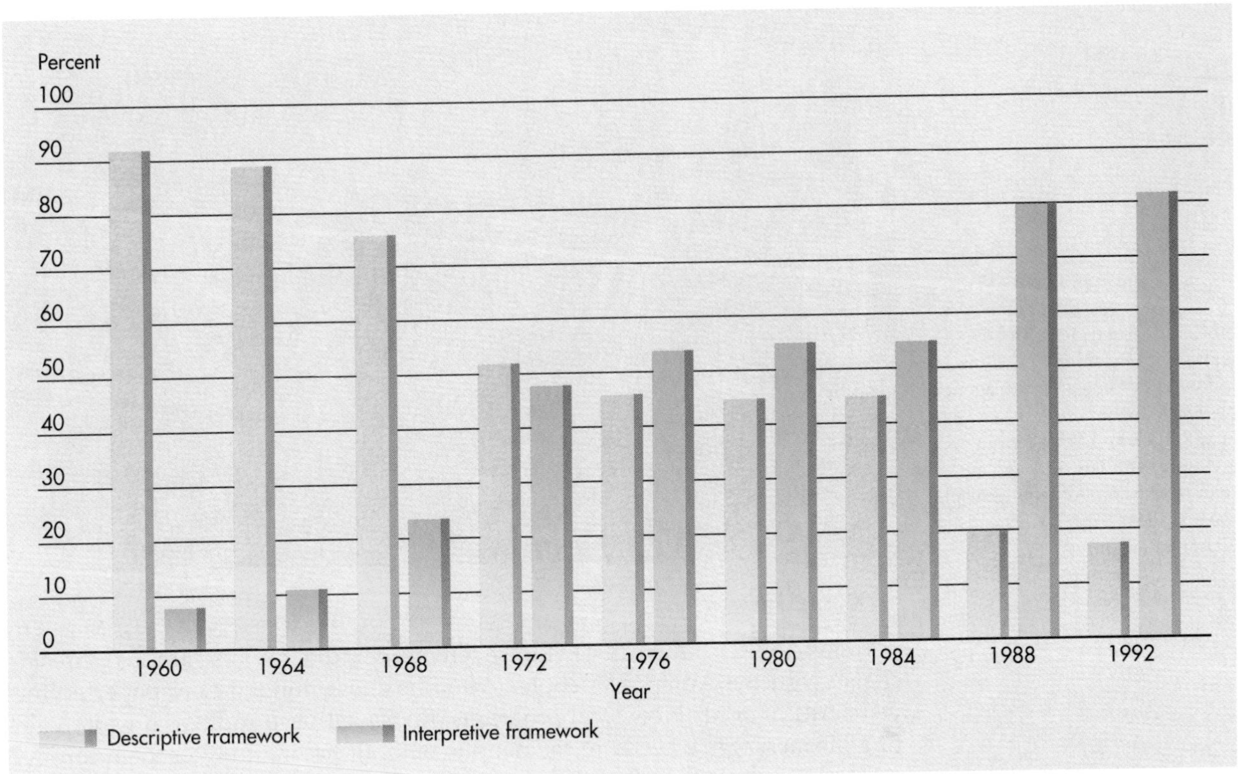

FIGURE 11-1 The Changing Framework of News Reporting, 1960–1992 (*The New York Times*) In the 1960s the vast majority of news reports were descriptive in nature; today, the vast majority are interpretive in nature. *Source: Thomas E. Patterson, Out of Order (New York: Vintage, 1994), 82.*

In another sense, however, the influence of objective journalism on newspaper reporting has declined. Unable to compete with television as a source of fast-breaking news, newspapers have gradually responded with stories that are designed to explain events rather than simply report them. The objective model rests on **descriptive reporting,** in which the reporter's task is to tell *what* has taken place. The reporter is guided by the five W's: *who* said *what* to *whom, when,* and *why.* Descriptive reporting is still an everyday aspect of news coverage but has given way in substantial degree to **interpretive reporting,** in which the reporter's job is to explain developments, providing an account of *why* something has occurred. Interpretive reporting gives journalists substantially more leeway in what they say; they are not confined to what they or others directly observe. As a result, newspaper coverage has become increasingly conjectural, as Figure 11-1 illustrates. From 1960 to 1992, the proportion of interpretive reports on the front page of *The New York Times* increased tenfold, from 8 percent to 80 percent.

descriptive reporting The style of reporting that aims to describe *what* is taking place or has occurred.

interpretive reporting The style of reporting that aims to explain *why* something is taking place or has occurred.

THE DEVELOPMENT OF THE BROADCAST MEDIA

Radio and Television: The Truly National Media

Until the early twentieth century, the print media were the only form of mass communication. Within a few decades, however, there were hundreds of radio stations throughout the nation, many of which were linked in national networks, such as the Red and Blue networks of the National Broadcasting Cor-

NBC anchorman Tom Brokaw walks with President Bill Clinton, followed by Secret Service agents. Network anchors such as Brokaw, Dan Rather, and Peter Jennings are more familiar to Americans than nearly any politician except the president. (Dirck Halstead/Gamma Liaison)

poration (NBC). Franklin D. Roosevelt used radio for his famous "fireside chats" with the American people. When business-minded newspaper editors were critical of his New Deal programs, Roosevelt used radio as a way of getting his messages directly to the people, without having to filter them through editors and reporters. Broadcasting was also revolutionary in a second way: it was the first truly national mass medium. Newspapers had local circulation bases, whereas radio could reach millions of Americans across the country simultaneously.

Television followed radio, and by the late 1950s more than 90 percent of American homes had a television set. The political potential of television was evident as early as 1952, when 17 million homes tuned in to the national Republican and Democratic party conventions.[18] However, television newscasts of the 1950s were brief, lasting no more than fifteen minutes, and relied on news gathered by other organizations, particularly the Associated Press and other wire services. In the early 1960s, the three commercial networks—CBS, NBC, and ABC—expanded their evening newscasts to thirty minutes, and their audience ratings increased.[19] Simultaneously, they increased the size and funding of their news divisions, and television soon became the principal news medium of national politics.

Today, television provides a twenty-four-hour forum of political news and information. The advent of the Cable News Network (CNN) and C-SPAN in the late 1970s brought Americans round-the-clock communication. Television talk shows, such as *Larry King Live,* have broadened the range of choices available to politically interested viewers. A parallel development is the growth in the number of radio talk shows. Nearly a fifth of the American public claims to listen regularly to a radio talk show, most of which are conservative in orientation. The undisputed king of the radio talk-show circuit is Rush Limbaugh, who is widely renowned for his blistering attacks on liberal politicians and policies.

Even more so than their newspaper counterparts, television journalists rely on an interpretive style of reporting. The reason is that television journalists use a narrative or storytelling mode in order to appeal to an audience accustomed to entertainment programming. "Facts" alone do not tell a story; they have to be interpreted in a way that makes them into a story. Reuven Frank, a network executive and pioneer in television journalism, once told his correspondents: "Every news story should, without any sacrifice of probity or responsibility, display the attributes of fiction, of drama. It should have structure and conflict, problem and denouement, rising action and falling action, a beginning, a middle and an end."[20]

Conservative Rush Limbaugh is the best-known, most influential, and most controversial of the radio talk-show hosts. (© 1995 Time Inc.)

Government Licensing and Regulation of Broadcasters

At first the government did not carefully regulate broadcasting. The result was chaos. Nearby stations often used the same or adjacent radio frequencies, interfering with each other's transmissions. Finally, in 1934, Congress passed the Communications Act, which requires that broadcasters be licensed and meet certain performance standards. Congress established the Federal Communications Commission (FCC) to administer the act through regulations pertaining to such matters as signal strength, advertising rates and access, and political coverage.

The principle of scarcity justifies the licensing and regulation of broadcast media. Because the number of available broadcasting frequencies is limited, those few individuals who are granted a broadcasting license are expected to serve the public interest in addition to their own. In principle, licensing is a means of controlling broadcasting. If a station fails to comply with federal broadcast regulations, the FCC can withdraw its license. However, the FCC seldom even threatens to revoke a license, for fear of being accused of restricting freedom of the press. A broadcast station can apply for renewal of its license by postcard and is virtually guaranteed FCC approval, which covers seven years for radio and five for television.

Because broadcast frequencies are a scarce resource, licensees are required by law to be somewhat evenhanded during election campaigns. Section 315 of the Communications Act imposes on broadcasters an "equal-time" restriction, which means that they cannot sell or give air time to a political candidate without granting equal opportunities to the other candidates running for the same office. (Election debates are an exception; broadcasters can sponsor them and limit participation to nominees of the Republican and Democratic parties only.)

At an earlier time, broadcasters were also bound by the "fairness doctrine," an FCC regulation that compelled broadcasters to air opposing opinions on major public issues. In 1987, broadcasters, on the grounds that the fairness doctrine infringed on press freedom, persuaded the FCC to rescind it.

Freedom and Conformity in the U.S. News Media

Some democracies impose significant legal restraints on the press. The news media in Britain are barred from reporting on anything that the government

YOUR TURN

PRESS FREEDOM: ABSOLUTE OR RESTRICTED?

The Questions:

Do you favor or oppose restrictions on the press:

To protect military secrets? Yes No

To curb racial or ethnic insults? Yes No

To restrict portrayals of explicit sex? Yes No

To restrict portrayals of unnecessary violence? Yes No

What Others Think: In the abstract, most Americans say they favor a free press. In a 1994 Times Mirror poll, for example, 65 percent of the respondents said they opposed "putting restrictions on what newspapers and TV news programs can report." This majority became a minority, however, when respondents were offered specific reasons for restricting press freedom: 69 percent said they favored government restrictions on press freedom in order "to protect military secrets"; 49 percent favored it "to curb racial or ethnic insults"; 59 percent favored it "to restrict portrayals of explicit sex"; and 52 percent favored it "to restrict portrayals of unnecessary violence."

Comment: If you answered no to all four questions, you are nearly an absolutist on the issue of press freedom. An affirmative response on all or most of the questions would indicate that you are willing to curtail press freedom somewhat in order to promote certain social values. An affirmative response only to the issue of military secrets would place your view roughly in line with that of the Supreme Court, which has upheld some restrictions on the press in the area of national security.

has labeled an "official secret," and the nation's tough libel laws inhibit the press from publishing unsubstantiated personal attacks.

In the United States, as we saw in Chapter 4, the First Amendment gives the press substantial protection. The courts have consistently upheld the right of U.S. newspapers to report on politics as they choose. Broadcasters, as the equal-time restriction indicates, have less freedom under the law, but they are subject to much less government control than those in Europe. In the case of both U.S. newspapers and broadcasters, the government cannot block publication of a news story unless it can convincingly demonstrate in court that the information would jeopardize national security. U.S. libel laws also strongly favor the press. A public figure who is attacked in a news story cannot collect libel damages unless he or she can demonstrate convincingly that the news organization was false in its accusations and knowingly or recklessly careless in its search for the truth.

Moreover, the U.S. government provides the news media with indirect economic support. Newspapers and magazines have a special postal rate that helps them keep their circulation costs low, and broadcasters pay only a few dollars annually in license fees. Such policies have contributed to the development of a truly enormous news industry in the United States: 1,600 daily newspapers, 7,500 weeklies, 10,000 radio stations, 5 national television news networks, 1,000 local television stations, and 6,000 cable television systems.[21]

The audience reach of leading news organizations is substantial. Each weekday evening, more than 20 million Americans tune into a network newscast. *Time* and *Newsweek* magazines reach over 3 million readers each week. *U.S. News & World Report*'s weekly circulation exceeds 2 million copies. *The New York Times, The Wall Street Journal, USA Today,* and the *Los Angeles Times* have daily circulations exceeding 1 million readers. Another three-dozen newspapers have circulations in excess of 250,000 readers. The average daily circulation of America's newspapers is roughly 40 million; on Sunday, newspaper circulation jumps to 60 million.[22]

In view of the great number and the freedom of news organizations in the United States, it might be expected that there would be great variation in the national news that Americans receive. And certainly the argument for a free press hinges on the expectation that it will result in a robust "marketplace of ideas." Press freedom is intended to produce full and open debate, in which all significant opinions on leading issues are widely disseminated and thoroughly voiced so that the public can weigh the competing arguments and choose among them on their merits.

The fact that press freedom is justified in terms of a free marketplace of ideas does not mean that those who control the media have the creation of such a marketplace in mind when they produce the news. The news is not a compilation of ideas. Rather, it is a set of stories, and not a very diverse one at that—most Americans receive a relatively uniform version of the news.

Each day, newspapers and broadcast stations from coast to coast are likely to highlight the same national news stories and to interpret them in similar ways. Any number of terms—pack journalism, groupthink, media concentration, the decline of the critical press—have been used to describe the fact that news reporting is fairly homogeneous. The basic reason the news is pretty much the same everywhere is that America's reporters, unlike their counterparts in some European democracies, do not take sides in partisan disputes. They do sometimes differ on which facts, events, and issues are more important than others, but these polite disagreements are a far cry from the disputes and diversity that characterized the nineteenth-century partisan press.

Of course, today's news organizations differ in the way they tell a given story. Broadcast news tends to be, in effect, headline news with pictures. A

★ STATES IN THE NATION

Newspaper Readership

STATE	PER CAPITA DAILY CIRCULATION	RANK
Ala.	.182	43
Alaska	.200	34
Ariz.	.193	39
Ark.	.196	38
Calif.	.206	29
Colo.	.291	7
Conn.	.252	10
Del.	.220	24
D. C.	1.550	1
Fla.	.231	17
Ga.	.159	49
Hawaii	.208	27
Idaho	.198	37
Ill.	.222	22
Ind.	.262	9
Iowa	.250	11
Kan.	.205	32
Ky.	.176	46
La.	.175	47
Maine	.211	25
Md.	.132	51
Mass.	.319	4
Mich.	.232	16
Minn.	.212	26
Miss.	.153	50
Mo.	.200	35
Mont.	.228	19
Neb.	.294	6
Nev.	.190	41
N.H.	.207	28
N.J.	.205	31
N. Mex.	.191	40
N.Y.	.384	3
N.C.	.203	33
N.Dak.	.295	5
Ohio	.244	13
Okla.	.206	30
Oreg.	.227	20
Pa.	.250	12
R.I.	.282	8
S.C.	.183	42
S.Dak.	.236	14
Tenn.	.179	44
Texas	.176	45
Utah	.160	48
Vt.	.224	21
Va.	.402	2
Wash.	.229	18
W.Va.	.234	15
Wis.	.220	23
Wyo.	.198	36

SOURCE: *Editor and Publisher International Yearbook, Annual, 1992.*

The audience reach of the U.S. news media is truly substantial. More than 20 million Americans each evening watch a network newscast and about half the adult population reads a daily paper. (M. Richards/PhotoEdit)

thirty-minute network news broadcast typically presents a dozen or so stories in the twenty-two minutes allotted to news content (the other eight minutes being devoted to commercials). Newspapers have the space to present news developments in greater depth; some, like *The New York Times* (which labels itself "the newspaper of record"), provide substantial detail. The reporting styles of news organizations also vary. Although most of them present the news in an understated way, others tend toward sensationalism. For example, when Jeffrey Dahmer, a convicted murder who had cannibalized his victims, was himself murdered in a Wisconsin prison in 1994, the *New York Post* gave its whole front page to the headline: "Death of a Monster." *The New York Times,* in contrast, gave the story a standard-size front-page headline, "Jeffrey Dahmer, Multiple Killer, Is Bludgeoned to Death in Prison." Such differences in approach, however, do not disguise the fact that most news organizations tell their audiences the same stories each day.

DOMINATION OF NEWS PRODUCTION

Another reason for the lack of diversity in national news reporting is that a few news organizations generate most of it. The quintessential case of concentrated news production is radio, with its "canned" network-provided news; almost no local radio station in the country produces its own national news reports.

The Associated Press (AP) is the major producer of news stories. It has 300 full-time reporters stationed throughout the country and the world to gather news stories, which are relayed by satellite to subscribing newspapers and

CNN is one of five major networks that dominate news coverage of national and international events. During the Persian Gulf war the whole world relied on the reports of CNN correspondent Peter Arnett, the only American reporter sending news out of the capital of Iraq at the time of the allied bombing. (Sygma)

broadcast stations. More than 95 percent of the nation's dailies are serviced by AP, and some also subscribe to other wire services, such as Reuters and the New York Times.[23] Smaller dailies lack the resources to gather news outside their own localities and thus depend almost completely on wire service reports for their national and international coverage.[24] They may give these reports a local or partisan slant, but most of what they say is a rehash of wire service dispatches.

Television news production is similarly dominated by just a few organizations. The five major networks—ABC, CBS, NBC, PBS, and CNN—generate most of the news coverage of national and international politics. For news of the nation and the world, local stations depend on video transmissions fed to them by the networks. The Persian Gulf war provided a dramatic example. When the allied bombing of Baghdad began on January 16, 1991, CNN had a correspondent in the Iraqi capital who single-handedly provided much of the world with its only news about what the war looked like from inside Iraq. It was reported that even senior Iraqi military staff were watching CNN for information about what the allies were doing.

NEWS VALUES AND IMPERATIVES

Competitive pressures also lead the producers of news to report the same stories. No major news organization wants to miss an important story that others are reporting.[25] The pressure *not* to be different is substantial. "Even at the best newspapers," Timothy Crouse notes, "the editor always gauges his own reporters' stories against the expectations that the stories [of other news organizations] have aroused."[26]

The networks, wire services, and a few elite dailies, including *The New York Times,* the *Washington Post, The Wall Street Journal, Los Angeles Times,* and *Chicago Tribune,* establish a national standard of story selection. Whenever one of them uncovers an important story, the others jump on the bandwagon. The chief trendsetter among news-gathering organizations is *The New York Times,* which has been described as "the bulletin board" for other major newspapers, newsmagazines, and television networks.[27] Herbert Gans notes, "When editors and producers are uncertain about a selection decision, they will check whether, where, and how the *Times* has covered the story; and story selectors see to it that many of the *Times*'s front-page stories find their way into television programs and magazines."[28]

The imperatives of the fast pace of daily journalism also tend to make the news homogeneous.[29] Journalists have the task each day of filling a newspaper or broadcast with stories. Their job is to produce an edition every twenty-four hours. Thus editors assign reporters to such beats as the White House and Congress, which can be relied on for a steady supply of news. On these beats the reporters of various news organizations see and hear the same things, exchange views on what is important, and, not surprisingly, produce similar news stories.

Finally, shared professional values guide journalists in their search for news.[30] Reporters are on the lookout for aspects of situations that lend themselves to interesting news stories—novel, colorful, and compelling developments.[31] Long practice at storytelling leads journalists to develop a common understanding of what the news is.[32] After the White House press corps has listened to a presidential speech, for example, nearly all the journalists in attendance are in agreement on what was most newsworthy about the speech, often only a single statement within it.

The News Media as Link: Roles the Press Can and Cannot Perform

When the objective model of reporting came to dominate American news coverage, the relationship between the press and the public was fundamentally altered. The nineteenth-century partisan press gave its readers overt cues as to how to evaluate political issues and leaders. In the presidential election campaign of 1896, the *San Francisco Call* devoted 1,075 column-inches of photographs to the Republican ticket of McKinley-Hobart and only 11 inches to the Democrats, Bryan and Sewell.[33] Many European newspapers still function in this way, guiding their readers by applying partisan or ideological values to current events. The *Daily Telegraph,* for example, is an unofficial but fiercely loyal mouthpiece of Britain's Conservative party (see box: How the United States Compares).

In contrast, U.S. news organizations do not routinely and consistently take sides in partisan conflict. Their main task is to report and analyze events. The media are thus very different from political parties and interest groups, the other major links between the public and its leaders. The media are driven by the search for interesting and revealing stories; parties and interest groups exist to articulate particular political opinions and values.

This distinction provides a basis for determining what roles the media can and cannot be expected to perform. The press is capable of fulfilling only those public responsibilities that are compatible with journalistic values: the signaler role, the common-carrier role, and the watchdog role. The media are less successful in their attempts to perform a fourth, politically oriented role: that of public representative.

THE SIGNALER ROLE

signaler role The accepted responsibility of the media to alert the public to important developments as soon as possible after they happen or are discovered.

As journalists see it, one of their responsibilities is to play the **signaler role,** alerting the public to important developments as soon as possible after they happen: a state visit to Washington by a foreign leader, a bill that has just been passed by Congress, a change in the nation's unemployment level, a demand by dairy farmers for higher milk prices, a terrorist bombing in a foreign capital.

The signaler role is one that the American media perform relatively well. The press is poised to converge on any fast-breaking major news event anywhere in the nation and nearly anywhere in the world. For instance, as the United States prepared to intervene forcefully in Haiti in 1994, dozens of U.S. journalists went to that trouble-ridden Caribbean nation to report from the scene. The NBC and CBS networks even sent their news anchors, Tom Brokaw and Dan Rather, despite a possible risk to their personal safety.

The media are particularly well suited to signal developments from Washington. More than half of all reported national news emanates from the

HOW THE UNITED STATES COMPARES

PARTISAN NEUTRALITY AS A NEWS VALUE

In the nineteenth century, the United States had a partisan press. Journalists were partisan actors and news was a blend of reporting and advocacy. Facts and opinions were freely intermixed in news stories. This type of reporting gradually gave way to a model of journalism that emphasizes the "facts" and covers the two parties more or less equally. American journalists, through both print and television, seek impartiality in their daily news reporting. For example, a political scandal, whether it involves a Democrat or Republican, is a big story for any major U.S. news organization.

European news organizations are less committed to partisan neutrality. Many European newspapers are aligned with a party, and although they focus on events, their coverage has a partisan component. In Great Britain, for example, the *Daily Telegraph* often serves as a voice of the Conservative party, while the *Guardian* favors the liberal side. Broadcasters in most European countries are politically neutral by law and practice, but there are exceptions, as in the case of the French and Italian broadcasters.

The difference between the U.S. and European media is evident in a five-country survey which asked journalists whether they agreed with the following directive: "Journalists should make sure they are not perceived as trying to influence the outcome of the conflict between political parties over the issues." Compared with their counterparts in Great Britain, Germany, Sweden, and Italy, U.S. journalists were more likely to express agreement with the statement.

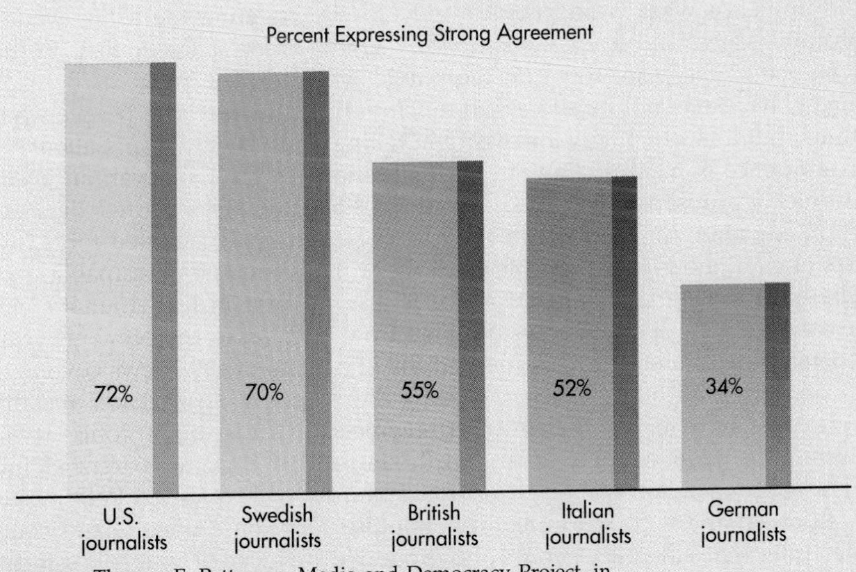

Journalists Should Not Try to Influence the Outcome of Partisan Conflict (Percent expressing strong agreement)

SOURCE: Thomas E. Patterson, Media and Democracy Project, in progress.

nation's capital, most of it from the White House and Congress. Altogether, more than 10,000 people in Washington work in the news business. The key players are the leading correspondents of the television networks and major newspapers, the heads of the Washington news bureaus, and a few top editors.[34]

The press, in its capacity as signaler, has the power to focus the public's

Through their signaler role, the news media alert the public to important developments in the nation and the world. Pictured here is CBS News anchorman Dan Rather, reporting live from Port Au Prince as U.S. military troops arrive in Haiti in 1994. (Haviv/SABA)

agenda setting The power of the media through news coverage to focus the public's attention and concern on particular events, problems, issues, personalities, etc.

attention. The term **agenda setting** has been used to describe the media's ability to influence what is on people's minds.[35] By covering the same events, problems, issues, and leaders—simply by giving them space or time in the news—the media place them on the public agenda.[36] The press, as Bernard Cohen notes, "may not be successful much of the time in telling people what to think, but it is stunningly successful in telling them what to think about."[37] This influence is most obvious in such situations as the Gulf war, an event that quickly aroused widespread attention. When the allies started their air raid on Baghdad, the broadcast networks began an unprecedented forty-two hours of continuous coverage. News of the war was almost inescapable.

The press's agenda-setting influence is also evident in less dramatic circumstances. In 1993, crime news doubled from its level in the previous year. On network television, crime accounted for 12 percent of 1993 news coverage, overshadowing all other issues, including the economy, health care, and the Bosnian crisis.[38] This emphasis was triggered by several high-profile cases, including the arrest of serial killer Joel Rifkin in New York, the parent-killing trial of the Menendez brothers, the kidnap-murder of 12-year-old Polly Klaas in California, and a crazed gunman's shooting spree on a Long Island commuter train that killed six people and wounded nineteen. The media's focus on crime continued into 1994, fed by new cases, such as the Simpson murder. The media's crime coverage had a dramatic impact on the public's agenda. At no time in the previous decade had more than 10 percent of Americans named crime as the nation's most important problem. Opinion polls in 1994, however, indicated that crime had become the public's leading concern (see Figure 11-2). The only feasible explanation for this heightened concern is the media's saturation coverage of the crime issue: Justice Department statistics indicate that the actual level of crime in America decreased by 2 percent in the 1993–1994 period.

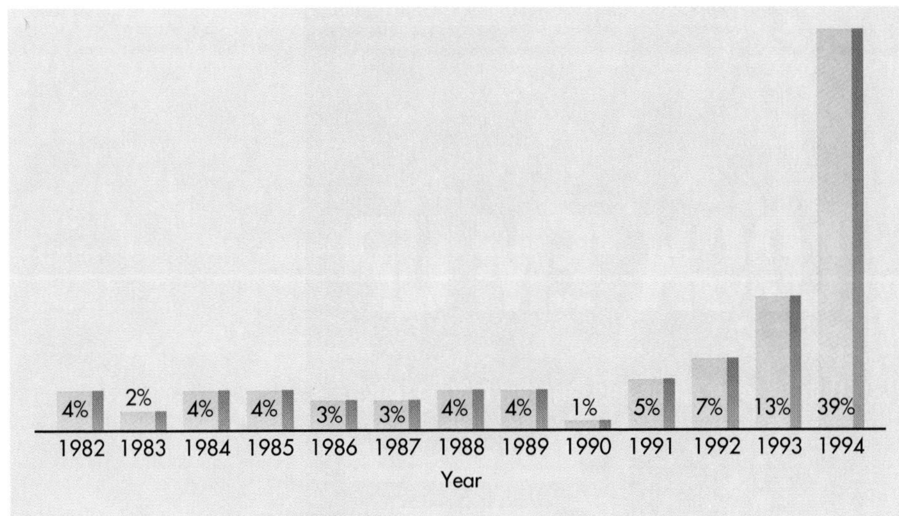

FIGURE 11-2 Percentage of Americans Who Said Crime Was the Nation's Most Important Problem, 1982-1994
As the news media's emphasis on crime intensified in 1993–1994, the public's concern with the issue rose dramatically, even though statistics indicated the national crime rate had actually declined slightly. *Source: Gallup Poll Monthly, August 1994.*

THE COMMON-CARRIER ROLE

Journalists base many of their news stories on the words of political leaders. The press thus plays what is labeled a **common-carrier role,** serving as an open channel through which political leaders and the public can communicate. "It is my job," a reporter explained, "to report the position of the politician whether I believe it or not."[39]

common-carrier role The media's function as an open channel through which political leaders can communicate with the public.

The value of the media's common-carrier role to the public is obvious. Citizens cannot very well support or oppose their leaders' plans and actions if they do not know what they are. The importance of the press's function as a common carrier is also apparent from the viewpoint of political leaders. If leaders are to gain the public's attention, they must have news exposure. Not surprisingly, leaders go out of their way to build relationships with reporters: they brief them on important plans, grant them access to confidential matters, and provide them working space in Congress, the White House, and other government offices.[40]

The press reciprocates the interest of political leaders in developing a close relationship.[41] Journalists are always on the lookout for fresh stories, and political leaders are their prime source. Franklin D. Roosevelt, an early master of the art of media manipulation, held twice-weekly press conferences in the Oval Office to release information about his upcoming programs. Reporters called these sessions "the best show in town" and eagerly sought to participate, even though Roosevelt's ground rules were strict. When he gave reporters confidential information, he expected it not to appear in the next day's headlines.[42]

The press today is less deferential to political leaders. Even though the president and prominent members of Congress can expect their major announcements to be reported, the press has increasingly pursued its own agenda. The celebrity status of the modern journalist is a reason. There have been well-known journalists in every era, but television has greatly increased the number of reporters whose names and faces are widely known to the public.

Heavy news coverage of the crime issue in 1993 and 1994 was followed by a sharp rise in the public's concern with crime, even though FBI statistics indicated the crime rate had actually decreased during this period. (© 1994 Time Inc.)

Indeed, television anchors such as Brokaw, Rather, and Peter Jennings are more familiar to Americans than most politicians. It is one thing for nameless, faceless journalists to defer to politicians, and another thing for well-known television correspondents and by-line reporters to do the same. Journalists have become accustomed to not only covering newsmakers, but making news of their own.

The Vietnam war and Watergate contributed to this development. The deceptions perpetrated by the Johnson and Nixon administrations convinced the press that the tendency to build the news around the words of the politicians was a mistake. "We didn't want [them] to dictate our agenda," was how one journalist expressed it.[43]

An indicator of the change is the journalist's prominence in the news. Whereas they were once the relatively passive voice behind the news, they are now nearly as active and visible as the newsmakers they cover. In no respect is this more evident than in the "shrinking sound bite" in television election coverage (see Figure 11-3). In 1968, when presidential candidates appeared in a television news story, they talked without interruption for an average of more than 40 seconds; by the 1992 campaign, the average had dropped below 10 seconds.[44] The voiceless candidate has become the norm: for every minute that the presidential candidates spoke on the evening news during coverage of the 1992 campaign, the journalists who were covering them talked six minutes.[45] Newspaper coverage has followed the same pat-

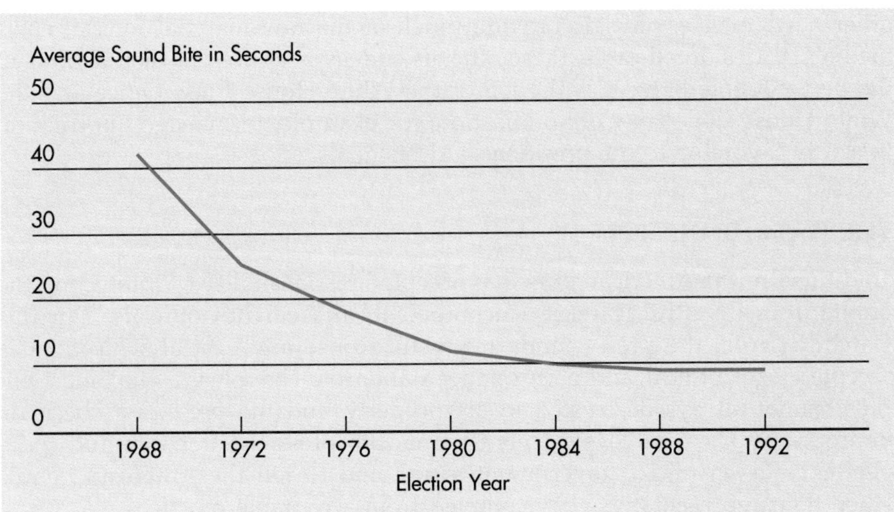

FIGURE 11-3 The Shrinking "Sound Bite" of Television Election Coverage
The average length of time that presidential candidates are shown speaking without interruption on television newscasts has declined sharply in recent elections. *Source: Adapted from Daniel C. Hallin, "Sound Bite News: Television Coverage of Elections 1968–1988," Journal of Communication 42 (Spring 1992): 6. The 1992 data are from "Clinton's the One," Media Monitor (Center for Media and Public Affairs, Washington, D.C.), November 1992, 2.*

tern. In 1960, the average continuous quote or paraphrase of a presidential candidate's words in a front-page *New York Times* story was fourteen lines. By 1992 the average had fallen to six lines.[46] On television and in the newspaper, the politician's views are now often subsumed in a narrative devoted primarily to expounding the reporter's views.

Nevertheless, public officials still retain the edge in many of their relations with the press. National news is mainly about the actions of political leaders and institutions, which is reflected in the hundreds of reporters who station themselves regularly at the Capitol and the White House, waiting for the latest word from top officials.[47] Through press conferences, press releases, and

The president's views are always sought after by the press. Here, President Clinton addresses a phalanx of reporters armed with cameras, microphones, and recorders. (Jim Bourg/Reuters/Bettmann)

★ CRITICAL THINKING

The News Media's Rights and Responsibilities
The news media have a favored position in law. They are the only private institution that enjoys special constitutional protection. Does the First Amendment's guarantee of freedom of the press place a special obligation on the media to behave responsibly? The media have become an increasingly powerful force in American politics. Is there a corresponding need for new checks on the power of the media? If so, what form should these checks take?

watchdog role The accepted responsibility of the media to protect the public from deceitful, careless, incompetent, and corrupt officials by standing ready to expose any official who violates accepted legal, ethical, or performance standards.

other news events, officials provide much of the raw material for the news media's stories. In all cases, these officials endeavor to present their actions in the best possible light. It is the job of the White House Press Office and the White House Office of Communication, for example, to manage information in a way favorable to the president and his goals.

THE WATCHDOG ROLE

Traditionally, the American press has accepted responsibility for protecting the public from deceitful, careless, incompetent, and corrupt officials.[48] In this **watchdog role,** the press stands ready to expose any official who violates accepted legal, ethical, and performance standards. The role is a vital one. Officials cannot always be trusted to act properly, and the press is a check on impropriety. The First Amendment grants the press the freedom and independence to scrutinize government action and to tell the American people when their representatives have strayed from acceptable practices.

The most notable exercise of the watchdog role in recent decades took place during the Watergate scandal. Bob Woodward and Carl Bernstein of the *Washington Post* spent months uncovering evidence that high-ranking officials in the Nixon White House were lying about their role in the burglary of the Democratic National Committee's headquarters and in the subsequent cover-up. Virtually all the nation's media picked up on the *Post*'s revelations. Nixon was forced to resign, as was his attorney general, John Mitchell. The Watergate episode is a dramatic reminder that a vigilant press is one of society's best safeguards against abuses of political power.

There is an inherent tension between the watchdog role and the common-carrier role. The watchdog role demands that the journalist maintain a skeptical view of political leaders and keep them at a distance. The common-carrier role requires the journalist to maintain close ties with political leaders. In the period before Watergate, the common-carrier role was clearly the dominant orientation. It perhaps still is, but journalists have become increasingly critical of political leaders and institutions.

Some of this criticism focuses on scandals, such as the Iran-Contra affair (President Reagan) and the Whitewater affair (President Clinton). Most of the criticism, however, is leveled at day-to-day politics. During Clinton's first year in office, for example, his television coverage was about 60 percent negative; Congress's coverage in the same period was even less favorable in tone. Some of this criticism was voiced through partisan opponents, but the expressed views of journalists were also more negative than positive.[49] A broader view of the trend toward negative news is provided by Figure 11-4, which shows the good news–bad news distribution for the 1960–1992 presidential nominees. The change is dramatic. Of all evaluative references to John Kennedy and Richard Nixon in 1960, only 25 percent were negative. In 1992, more than 60 percent of reporters' evaluative references to Clinton and Bush were negative.

Critics argue that the press has gone too far in its search for bad news, claiming that its incessant criticism weakens the leadership capacity of public officials and institutions.[50] Supporters of the press say that it is doing its job properly, that the public is better served by highly skeptical media than overly compliant ones.[51]

The public has an ambivalent view of the news media's skepticism.[52] As

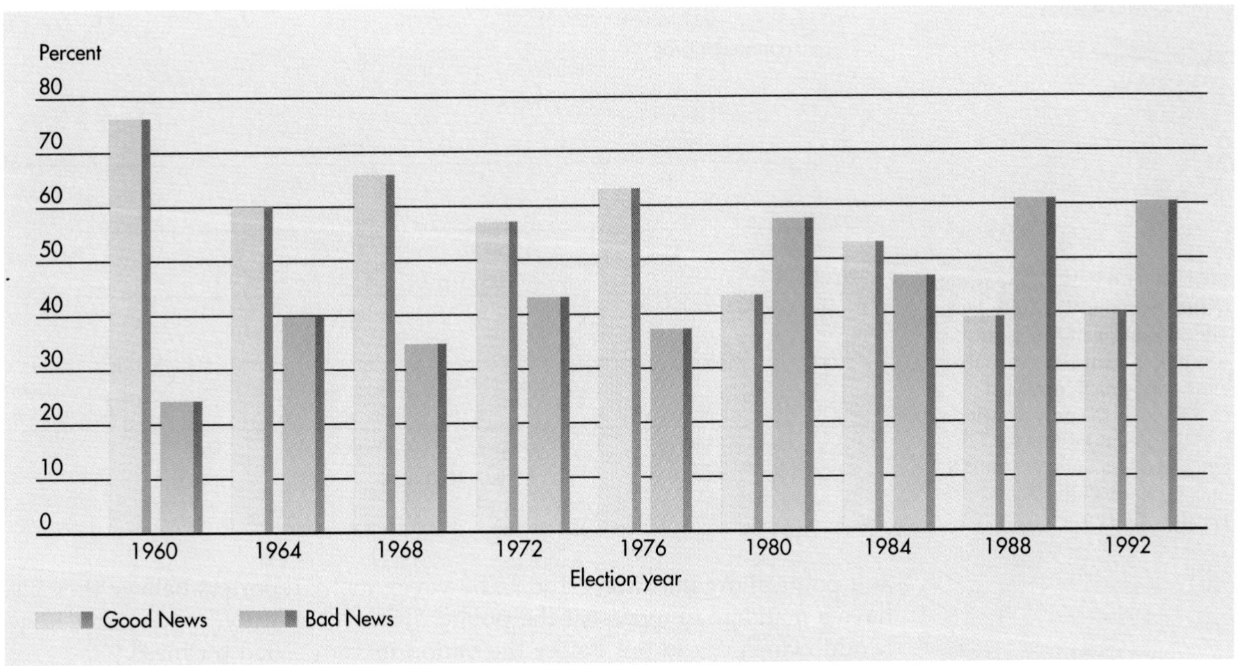

FIGURE 11-4 "Bad News" Coverage of Presidential Candidates Compared to "Good News" Coverage, 1960–1992
In the 1960s, candidates received largely favorable news coverage; today, their coverage is mostly negative. *Source: Thomas E. Patterson, Out of Order (New York: Vintage, 1994), 20.*

Figure 11-5 indicates, two-thirds of Americans believe press criticism is a key factor in keeping politicians from abusing public office. Yet two-thirds also say that the press gets in the way of efforts to solve society's problems. The press's skepticism is thus seen as both an obstacle to effective governance and a form of protection against wayward politicians.

THE PUBLIC REPRESENTATIVE ROLE

Traditionally, the **public representative role**—that of spokesperson for and advocate of the public—has belonged to political leaders, political institutions,

public representative role A role whereby the media attempt to act as the public's representatives.

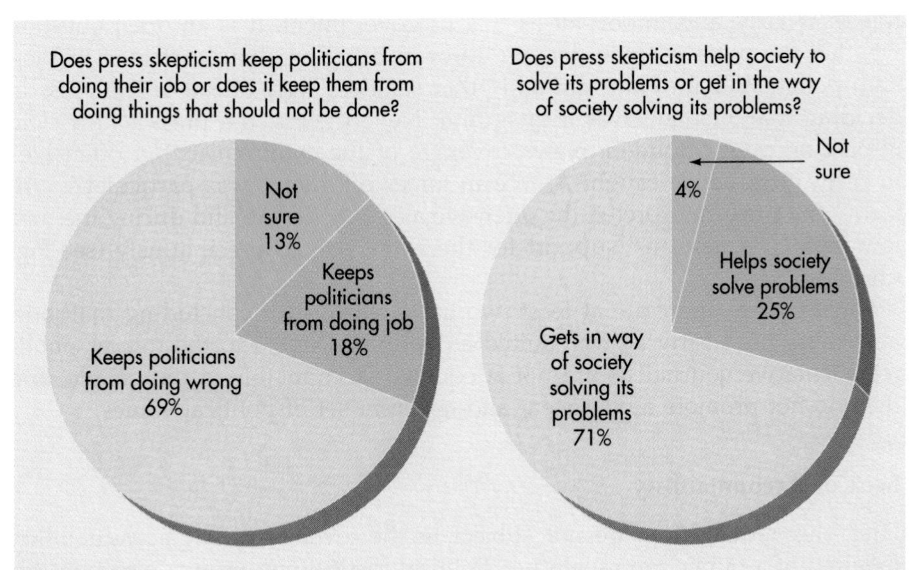

FIGURE 11-5 The Public's View of the Press's Skepticism
Americans believe that the media's skepticism offers protection against politicians' wrongdoing, but they also believe that this skepticism stands in the way of effective governance. *Source: Times-Mirror surveys, April and July 1994.*

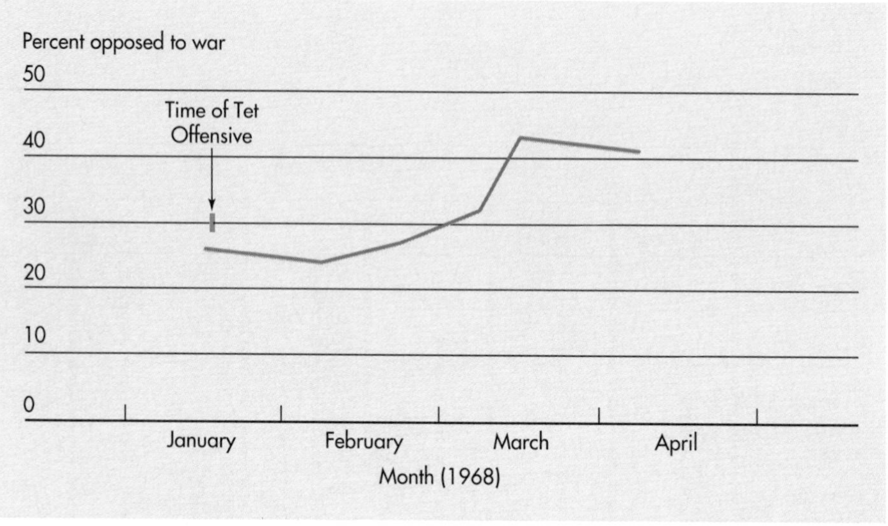

FIGURE 11-6 Public Opposition to the Vietnam War, Early 1968 The proportion of Americans wanting to reduce the military effort in Vietnam increased sharply after the press concluded that the communists' "Tet Offensive" was a defeat for U.S. forces. *Source: Gallup Polls, January–April 1968.*

and political organizations. Today, however, many reporters believe they also have a mandate to represent the public. "[Our] chief duty," newscaster Roger Mudd claims, "is to put before the nation its unfinished business."[53]

Although the press has to some degree always acted as a stand-in for the people, the desire of journalists to play the role of public advocate has increased significantly since the 1960s.[54] As journalists' status rose, they became more assertive, a tendency sharpened by the trend toward interpretive reporting. Vietnam and Watergate also contributed to the change; these events convinced many journalists that their judgments were superior to those of political leaders. James Reston, of *The New York Times*, said of Vietnam: "Maybe the historians will agree that the reporters and cameras were decisive in the end. They brought the issue of the war to the people, before the Congress and the courts, and forced the withdrawal of American power from Vietnam."[55]

The press has a role to play in determining society's choices. At times, its role is as large and important as that of government. It is an open question whether the press was the decisive force in bringing about a change in Vietnam policy. William Fulbright and other senators were ahead of the press in deciding that Vietnam was a quagmire. Nevertheless, the press had a clear impact on public opinion. News coverage of the communist "Tet offensive" in early 1968, which caught American forces off guard, was particularly critical.[56] The press interpreted the offensive as a U.S. defeat, and during the next few months Americans' support for the war declined precipitously (see Figure 11-6).

Nevertheless, there are at least two basic reasons for concluding that journalists are not nearly as well suited as political leaders to the role of public representative: journalists are not adequately accountable to the people, and they do not promote a consistent and coherent set of political values.

Lack of Accountability

First, the news media are not subject to the level of public accountability required of a public representative. Political institutions are made responsible to the public by a formal mechanism of accountability—elections. The vote gives officeholders a reason to act in the majority's interest, and it offers citizens an opportunity to boot from office anyone they feel has failed them. Thousands of elected officials have lost their jobs this way. The public has no comparable hold over the press. Journalists are neither chosen by the people nor removable by them. Irate citizens can stop watching a news program or buying a newspaper that angers them, but no major daily newspaper or television station has gone out of business as a result.

Indeed, the press actively resists public scrutiny of its activities. Whereas most government meetings and documents are open by law to the public, the press restricts access to its editorial meetings and source materials. The press has even opposed formal efforts at self-regulation. In 1973, with the sponsorship of several major foundations, a National News Council was established for the purpose of handling complaints about the news practices of the major U.S. newspapers and broadcast networks. Similar councils have been important in some European countries in correcting press abuses, but the U.S. council was a bust. It rarely found fault with news coverage, and a number of leading news organizations, including *The New York Times,* refused to participate in its activities, even though its members were working journalists (in Europe, journalists comprise only a portion of the membership). The National News Council was disbanded in 1984.

"News from Nowhere"

A second obstacle to journalists' attempts to play the role of public representative is that representation requires a point of view. Politics is essentially the mobilization of bias—that is, it involves the representation of particular values and interests. Political parties and interest groups, as we saw in Chapters

Although the news media exercise power through their capacity to communicate with the American people, they lack the accountability and incentives to adequately serve as the public's representatives. The news media are in the business of reporting stories rather than the business of organizing and representing public opinion. (Elizabeth Zuckerman/PhotoEdit)

★ CRITICAL THINKING

An Uninformed Public—Are the Media at Fault?
Survey after survey has demonstrated that the general public is not well informed about politics and public affairs. Some analysts place much of the blame on the press, which, they say, is more concerned with entertaining its audience than informing it. The news is also negative in tone: bad news takes precedence over good news. Critics conclude that these news tendencies lead the public to devalue news of politics.

Other observers place the blame for the public's low level of information squarely on the public itself. They point out that there is almost no vital piece of information about a policy issue that is not reported by the media at one time or another. These observers say that the problem is the public's failure to pay close attention to the news.

In your opinion, is the press or the public primarily to blame for the citizenry's low level of political awareness? What changes in news coverage might improve the public's understanding of politics?

8 through 10, exist to represent particular interests in society. But what political interests do the media represent? CBS News executive Richard Salant once said that his reporters covered stories "from nobody's point of view."[57] What he was saying in effect was that journalists do not consistently represent the political concerns of any segment of society. They respond to news opportunities, not to political interests. Above all, they prize good stories; the first fact of journalistic life is that the reporter must have a story to tell.[58] "It's like the pull of gravity," the *Boston Globe*'s Christine Chinlund says, "If you don't write, you don't exist for that day."[59]

The O. J. Simpson story is a prime example. His trial received more news coverage in 1994–1995 than any public policy issue, foreign or domestic. Judged by the media's priorities, Simpson's fate was more important than health care, unemployment, Haiti, drug abuse, education, and every other national problem. Murray Edelman said there is a "Gresham's law" of news prominence: "Dramatic incidents involving individuals in the limelight displace attention from the larger [issues]."

Presidential elections provide another illustration of the narrow view of the press. The candidates' blunders and gaffes tend to generate as many headlines as their stands on domestic and foreign policy.[60] Early in the 1992 Democratic campaign, for example, Nebraska Senator Bob Kerrey told an off-color joke at a political roast in New Hampshire. Kerrey whispered the joke in private, but his words were caught by a television boom mike aimed his way. Kerrey's blunder, first reported in the *San Francisco Examiner*, quickly became a national story.[61] At the same time, the press mostly ignored Bill Clinton's first major statement on the economy. Announced as such and delivered in Washington at Georgetown University, his speech called for "a new covenant for economic change." He proposed a comprehensive plan for revitalizing the economy: expansion of the earned income tax credit for the poor, more affordable FHA mortgages, a highway bill that would create thousands of construction jobs, tax incentives to discourage companies from moving overseas, a more fully funded Head Start program, job training and education programs for workers, apprenticeship programs for high school graduates, an innovative college loan program, and health care reform.[62] Yet Clinton's Georgetown speech was not reported at all by some news outlets.[63] The *Washington Post* described it in a single story on page four. In contrast, Kerrey's joke was the subject of four *Post* stories and an editorial ("Take My Joke, Please.")

Voters are not mindless recipients of media messages. Just because the press highlights something, or portrays the campaign in a particular way, does not mean that the voters will always see things in precisely the same way.[64] Nevertheless, in their research on the media's influence, the political scientists Shanto Iyengar and Donald Kinder found that the media have a substantial capacity to "frame" political choices. "By priming certain aspects of national life while ignoring others, [the news] sets the terms by which political judgments are rendered and political choices made."[65] By focusing on candidates' blunders rather than on their policies, the news media "depoliticize" issues, treating them more as tokens in a contest for personal advantage than as objects of serious debate.[66]

Lurking behind the press's inability to keep policy problems and issues in focus is its commitment to impartiality. American journalists do not easily deal with the value judgment that is at the heart of an issue, since such a judgment would require them to take sides. Martin Walker, the Washington bureau chief of the London newspaper *The Guardian* said: "European journalists are puzzled by this idea of objectivity, this intellectual apartheid."[67] Whether puzzling or not, the rules of American journalism require reporters to steer clear of political positions. If they sometimes overstep the boundary in practice, a commitment to impartiality still exercises a severe constraint on their decisions. It is a reason why journalists define issues in terms of controversy rather than substance.

The restless search of the press for the riveting story works against its intention to provide citizens a clear understanding of their stake in policy choices. It is a difficult job to formulate society's problems in a way that allows citizens to understand and act upon them. The news media cannot do the job consistently well. The journalist Walter Lippmann put it plainly when he said:

> The press is no substitute for [political] institutions. It is like the beam of a searchlight that moves restlessly about, bringing one episode and then another out of darkness into vision. Men cannot do the work of the world by this light alone. They cannot govern society by episodes, incidents, and interruptions.[68]

Vital, but Limited

Lippmann's point was not that news organizations are somehow inferior to political organizations but that each has a different role and responsibility in society. Democracy cannot operate effectively without a free press that acts effectively in its signaler, common-carrier, and watchdog roles. To keep in touch with one another and with the government, citizens must have access to timely and uncensored news about public affairs. In other words, the media must do their job well if democratic government is to succeed. However, the media cannot also be asked to do the job of political institutions. For reasons already noted, the task is beyond the media's capacity.

As previous chapters have emphasized, the problem of citizen influence is the problem of organizing the public so that people can act together effectively. The news media merely appear to solve this problem. The fact that millions of people each day receive the same news about their government does not mold them into an organized community. The news creates a pseudo-community: citizens feel they are part of a functioning whole until they try to act upon their news awareness. The futility of media-centered democracy was dramatized in the movie *Network* when its central character, a television anchorman, became enraged at the nation's political leadership and urged his viewers to go to their windows and yell, "I'm mad as hell and I'm not going to take it anymore!" Citizens heeded his instructions, but the main effect was to raise the network's ratings. It was not clear what officials in Washington were expected to do about several million people leaning out their windows and shouting a vague slogan at the top of their lungs. The film vividly illustrated the fact that the news can raise public consciousness as a prelude to organization, but the news itself cannot organize the public in any meaningful way. When public opinion on an issue is already formed, the media can serve as a channel for the expression of that opinion. But when society's choices are in their formative stage, the media are not an adequate guide to the action that should be taken.

Summary

In the nation's first century, the press was allied closely with the political parties and helped the parties mobilize public opinion. Gradually the press freed itself from this relationship and developed a form of reporting, known as objective journalism, that emphasizes the fair and accurate reporting of newsworthy developments. The foundation of modern American news rests on the presentation and evaluation of significant events, not on the advocacy of partisan ideas. The nation's news organizations do not differ greatly in their reporting; broadcast stations and newspapers throughout the country emphasize many of the same events, issues, and personalities, following the lead of the major broadcast networks, a few elite newspapers, and the wire services.

The press performs four basic roles in a free society. In their signaler role, journalists communicate information to the public about events and problems that they consider important, relevant, and therefore newsworthy. The press also serves as a common carrier, in that it provides political leaders with a channel for addressing the public. Third, the press acts as a public protector or watchdog by exposing deceitful, careless, or corrupt officials. The American media can and, to a significant degree, do perform these roles adequately.

The press is less well suited, however, to the other role it plays, that of public representative. This role requires a consistent political viewpoint and public accountability, neither of which the press possesses. The media cannot be a substitute for effective political institutions. The press's strength lies ultimately in its capacity to inform the public, not in its attempts to serve as their representative.

Major Concepts

agenda setting
common-carrier role
descriptive reporting
interpretive reporting
news
objective journalism
partisan press
press (news media)
public representative role
signaler role
watchdog role

Suggested Readings

Altheide, David L., and Robert P. Snow. *Media Worlds in the Postjournalism Era.* New York: Aldine–De Gruyter, 1991. An analysis of the mass media and culture, including the conditions that lead journalists to present a version of reality that serves the media's own ends.

Bagdikian, Ben H. *The Media Monolopy,* 4th ed. Boston: Beacon Press, 1992. An examination of the growing power of the press, including tendencies toward monopolies of ownership and news production.

Gans, Herbert J. *Deciding What's News.* New York: Vintage Books, 1980. A study of journalists' news values, focusing on major organizations, including CBS News and *Time* magazine.

Graber, Doris A. *Mass Media and American Politics,* 4th ed. Washington: D.C.: Congressional Quarterly Press, 1993. A leading text on the subject of media and politics.

Iyengar, Shanto, and Donald R. Kinder. *News That Matters.* Chicago: University of Chicago Press, 1987. An assessment of the impact of television news on the public's perceptions of politics.

Maltese, John Anthony. *Spin Control: The White House Office of Communications and the Management of Presidential News.* Chapel Hill: University of North Carolina Press, 1994. An assessment of how presidents attempt to manage news coverage.

Patterson, Thomas E. *Out of Order.* New York: Vintage Books, 1994. An analysis of how election news coverage has changed in recent decades.

Sabato, Larry J. *Feeding Frenzy: How Attack Journalism Has Transformed American Politics.* New York: The Free Press, 1991. An argument that recent tendencies in journalism are warping the democratic process.

Summers, Mark Wahlgren. *The Press Gang: Newspapers and Politics, 1863–1878.* Chapel Hill: University of North Carolina Press, 1994. A vivid portrayal of the press's transformation from partisan values to journalistic ones.

Weaver, Paul H. *News and the Culture of Lying.* New York: The Free Press, 1994. A critical assessment of the news media's tendency toward overstatement and thus to the creation of an artificial view of politics.

PART THREE

GOVERNING INSTITUTIONS

PART THREE

GOVERNING INSTITUTIONS

American democracy, it is sometimes said, is government by the people. So it is, but in a figurative sense. Direct democracy is a practical impossibility in a nation of the size and complexity of the United States. Americans are governed largely through institutions. There is no practical alternative in the realm of national politics.

As we indicated in previous chapters, a debate has long raged over the proper relationship between a people and its representatives. One view holds that the representatives must follow the expressed opinion of the constituency. Another view, first elaborated more than two centuries ago by the English theorist Edmund Burke, holds that the representative is obligated to exercise detached judgment in making policy decisions. The debate is essentially an issue of how best to serve the people's interests. The notion that representatives should take instructions from their constituents is based on the assumption that if they do not, they will promote their narrow and ultimately self-serving interests. In contrast, Burke's idea that representatives should follow their consciences is based on the assumption that if they listen too closely to those who elected them, they will serve parochial interests rather than the national or general interest.

The governing system of the United States, mostly by design but partly by accident, embodies elements of both these concepts of representation. The presidency is a truly national office that inclines its incumbent to take a national view of issues, while Congress is both a national institution and a body that is subject to powerful constituency influence. Chapters 12 and 13 show how the election, organization, and policymaking of Congress reflect both national and local influences. Chapters 14 and 15 reveal how the president's election, role, and power are affected by the office's national political base. Collectively, these chapters indicate how national and local factors come together in relations between the executive and legislative branches and between these two branches and their constituents, the American people.

However, the issue of how Americans are governed is not determined solely by the actions of elected representatives. Americans' daily lives are also affected by the decisions of unelected bureaucrats and appointed judges. Given the right context, they can be as influential as their congressional and executive counterparts. Indeed, some bureaucratic rulings and judicial decisions have been as far-reaching as many of those made by elective institutions.

Chapter 16 examines the federal bureaucracy, which is undoubtedly the least appreciated and most widely misunderstood of the nation's institutions. Chapter 17 considers the judiciary, which is also misunderstood but is more widely respected than the bureaucracy. The discussion of both the bureaucracy and the judiciary concentrates on the nature of these institutions, their historical development, their roles in modern politics, the recruitment of their officials, their impact on public policy, and their accountability to the public they serve.

★ ★ ★

CHAPTER 12

CONGRESSIONAL ELECTION AND ORGANIZATION: SHARING THE POWER

Whether . . . safe or marginal, cautious or audacious, congressmen must constantly engage in activities relating to reelection.

—*David Mayhew*[1]

As Speaker of the House of Representatives, Democrat Thomas S. Foley was the chamber's most powerful member. He was a skilled lawmaker who had used his influence to protect his district's interests. It was Foley's political clout that had saved the local Fairchild Air Force Base from closure during Pentagon cutbacks. He had every reason to expect the voters of his eastern Washington district to return him to the House for a sixteenth term. Instead, Foley became the first Speaker of the House since 1862 to be ousted at the polls. Although he outspent his opponent by 3 to 1, the voters of his district discarded him in favor of a political neophyte, Republican George Nethercutt, Jr. Said a voter who had supported Foley in the past, "I just feel that 30 years is plenty for one person to hold office. I just think it is time to move on."[2]

The voters in the 1994 midterm elections forced a lot of Democrats "to move on." In the process, they did more than send lawmakers like Foley into retirement. The Republicans gained control of the House and Senate and, with that, the opportunity to organize each chamber. Even those Democrats who won reelection were bumped from top leadership positions and coveted committee memberships. A thorough shake-up of Congress occurred, as is always the case when control shifts from one party to the other.

This chapter explains the nature of congressional election and organization, and the relationship between them. In the next chapter we will examine congressional policymaking. The following points are emphasized in this first of two chapters on Congress:

- ★ *Congressional elections tend to have a strong local orientation and to favor incumbents.* Congressional office provides incumbents with substantial resources (free publicity, staff, and legislative influence) that give them (particularly House members) a major advantage in election campaigns. However, incumbency also has some liabilities, which contribute to turnover in congressional membership.
- ★ *Congress is organized in part along political party lines; its collective leadership is provided by party leaders of the House of Representatives and the Senate.* These leaders do not have great formal powers. Their authority rests mainly on shared partisan values and on the fact that they have been entrusted with leadership responsibility by other senators or representatives of their party.
- ★ *The work of Congress is done mainly through its committees and subcommittees, each of which has its leader (a chairperson) and its policy jurisdiction.* The committee system of Congress allows a broad sharing of power and leadership, which serves the power and reelection needs of Congress's members but fragments the institution.

Congress as a Career: Election to Congress

In the nation's first century, service in the Congress was not a career for most of its members. Before 1900 at least a third and sometimes as many as half of the seats in Congress changed hands at each election. Most members left voluntarily. Because travel was slow and arduous, serving in the nation's capital required them to spend months away from their families. And because the national government was not the center of power and politics that it is today, many politicians preferred to serve in state capitals.

Like all other members of Congress, Senator Dianne Feinstein of California tries to win reelection by serving the interests of her constituents. Here, Feinstein talks to the press about proposed military base closings in California. She pledged support for the California communities and workers adversely affected by cutbacks in defense spending. (Wide World Photos)

TABLE 12-1 House and Senate Incumbents Reelected and Not Seeking Reelection, 1956–1996 Congressional incumbents who seek reelection have a very high rate of success.

	HOUSE INCUMBENTS		SENATE INCUMBENTS	
	Percent Not Seeking Reelection	*Percent Reelected of Those Seeking Reelection*	*Percent Not Seeking Reelection*	*Percent Reelected of Those Seeking Reelection*
1956	5%	95%	18%	86%
1958	8	90	18	64
1960	6	93	15	97
1962	6	92	12	83
1964	8	87	6	85
1966	5	88	9	88
1968	5	97	18	71
1970	7	95	12	77
1972	9	94	18	74
1974	10	88	21	85
1976	11	96	24	64
1978	11	94	30	60
1980	8	91	15	55
1982	9	90	9	93
1984	6	96	12	90
1986	10	98	18	75
1988	6	98	21	85
1990	6	96	17	97
1992	15	88	20	86
1994	12	91	26	92
1996	12	94	41	95

SOURCE: *Congressional Quarterly Weekly* Report, various dates.

The modern Congress is very different. Most of its members are professional politicians, and a seat in the U.S. Senate or House is as far as most of them can expect to go in politics. The pay (about $135,000 a year) is reasonably good, and the prestige of their office is substantial, particularly if they serve in the Senate. An extended stay in Congress is what most of its members aspire to attain.

Incumbents have a good chance of being reelected (see Table 12-1). They are not a sure bet to win again, but the odds are on their side. In the last decade, the reelection rate of House incumbents seeking another term has exceeded 90 percent, as has the reelection rate of Senate incumbents. In 1996, which was the most recent of these elections, 94 percent of House incumbents and 95 percent of Senate incumbents seeking another term were reelected.

These figures overestimate somewhat an incumbent's chances of reelection. Some incumbents retire from Congress when faced with a campaign they fear

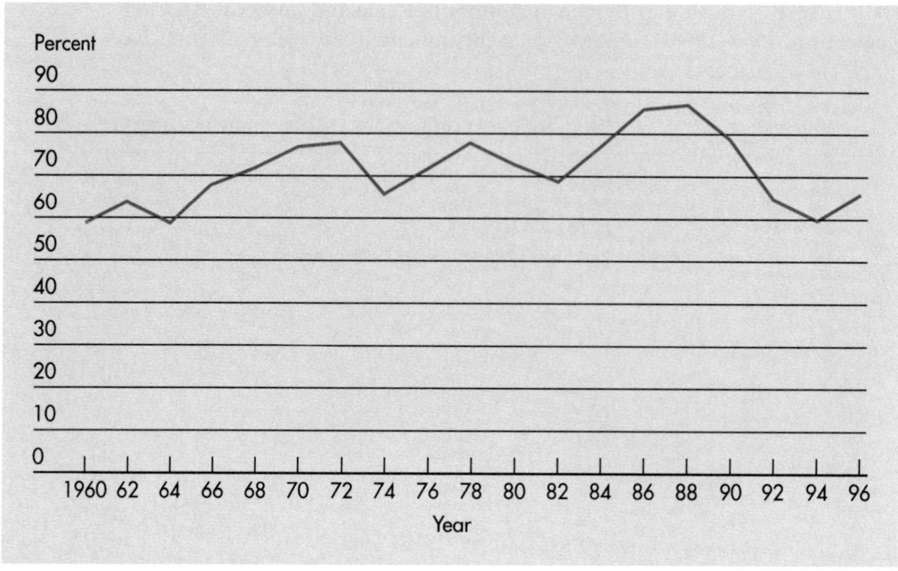

FIGURE 12-1 Percentage of House Incumbents Who Were Reelected by 60 Percent or More of the Vote, 1960–1996
The number of House incumbents who won reelection easily increased substantially after the early 1960s but has recently decreased. *Source: Congressional Quarterly Weekly Report, various dates.*

they will lose. Moreover, incumbents must stand for reelection again and again if they intend to make Congress a career; a single loss will halt or interrupt this goal. Over the period of a few elections, a substantial number of congressional seats can change hands. The 1992 and 1994 congressional elections are an extreme example: The turnover in House membership in these two elections was a combined 188 seats, the highest total of any two consecutive elections since World War II.

On balance, however, incumbents have a clear edge over their opponents, as their margin of victory indicates. In recent elections, most House incumbents (see Figure 12-1) and nearly half of Senate incumbents seeking reelection have received 60 percent or more of the vote. Even when voters are convinced that Congress as an institution is performing badly, they reelect a large majority of its members. One reason is that many congressional districts and a few states are so lopsidedly Democratic or Republican that the candidate of the weaker party has no realistic chance of victory. All incumbents, however, gain important election advantages from the office they hold, a subject to which we now turn.

USING INCUMBENCY TO STAY IN CONGRESS

Getting reelected is a high priority for members of Congress.[3] They may be more interested in issues of public policy than in reelection activities, but they must stay in Congress if they are to realize their policy goals. In Lawrence Dodd's phrase, members of Congress strive for **electoral mastery**—a strong base of popular support that will free them from constant worry over reelection and allow them to pursue other goals.[4] Some members of Congress acquire electoral mastery the easy way—through election in a constituency that lopsidedly favors their party. Most members have to make use of the advantages of their office in order to attain electoral mastery.

electoral mastery A strong base of popular support that frees a congressional incumbent from constant worry over reelection.

Pork, Favors, and Publicity

Members of Congress promote their reelection prospects by serving their **constituency**—the body of citizens eligible to vote in their state or district. Members of Congress pay close attention to constituency opinions when casting their votes on legislation, and they work hard to get their share of **pork barrel projects,** a term that refers to legislation that funds a special project for a particular locale, such as a new roadway or hospital. ("Pork" was the term for political graft or corruption in the late nineteenth century; when legislators adopted the practice of placing numerous items of pork into a single bill, people began to say, "Now the pork is all in one barrel.") Although pork barrel politics is often ridiculed by the public and has declined recently as a result of cutbacks in federal spending, the voters themselves are a main reason it continues. Constituents may disagree on issues of national policy, but they ordinarily do not object when federal money is spent on a project in their area.

Members of Congress also boost their reelection chances by catering to their constituents' individual needs, a practice known as the **service strategy.**[5] When constituents seek information about a government program, express an

constituency The individuals who live within the geographical area represented by an elected official. More narrowly, the body of citizens eligible to vote for a particular representative.

pork barrel projects Laws whose tangible benefits are targeted at a particular legislator's constituency.

service strategy Use of personal staff by members of Congress to perform services for constituents in order to gain their support in future elections.

YOUR TURN

SATISFACTION WITH CONGRESS

The Questions:

1. Do you approve or disapprove of the way Congress is doing its job?

   Approve | Disapprove

2. How about the representative in Congress from your district? Do you approve or disapprove of the way your representative is handling his or her job?

   Approve | Disapprove

3. Should the terms of members of Congress be limited to a total of twelve years in office, or should they be able to serve as long as they are able to get reelected?

   Limited to 12 years | Serve as long as reelected

What Others Think: These three questions were asked in a September 1994 CBS News/New York Times poll. Among respondents, 63 percent expressed dissatisfaction with the way Congress was handling its job, while only 17 percent disapproved of the job their representative was doing (although 27 percent claimed not to know whether their representative was doing a good job). On the term-limits issue, 59 percent expressed support for a twelve-year limitation, while 33 percent said representatives should be allowed to serve as long as they are able to get reelected.

Comment: Through the resources of their office, members of Congress build personal reputations as individuals who are attentive to their constituents' needs. On the other hand, the reputation of the institution itself depends primarily on national conditions and its handling of major legislative issues. The result, often, is that Americans have a favorable opinion of their own representative but an unfavorable one of the institution. It is the latter opinion that has given impetus to the term-limitation movement. The flurry of legislative activity that accompanied the Republican takeover in 1995 led to an increase in Congress's approval rating over the level of 1994, when the CBS News/New York Times survey was conducted. What remains to be seen is whether the change will be sustained. There was a similar increase in congressional approval during the early 1980s, but it soon faded.

opinion about pending legislation, or want help in obtaining a federal benefit, their representative usually responds. A representative or senator can often prod the bureaucracy to respond more quickly to a citizen who is encountering a delay or other obstacle in applying for social security or other federal benefits.[6] Congressional observers disagree on exactly how many votes can be won through these small favors,[7] but there is no doubt that constituency service helps—particularly in House races, where the incumbent's attentiveness to local people and problems is often a major campaign issue.

The service strategy is made possible by the staff resources provided to members of Congress. Each House member receives an office suite and an office allowance of around $500,000 a year, which supports a personal staff of about twenty full-time employees. Senators have larger budgets whose size depends on the population of the state they represent. Senators' personal staffs average about forty employees. Members of Congress are also provided office space in their state or district and, in the case of senators, a mobile office as well. The personal staffs of members of Congress spend the bulk of their time not on legislative matters but on constituency relations.

Congressional staffs also churn out newsletters and press releases designed to publicize the member for whom they work.[8] Television and radio materials are part of the publicity effort; members have free use of broadcast facilities located in the Capitol building. Members also promote their image through personal appearances in their home states and districts. At public expense, each House member is allowed about thirty visits to his or her district each year and each senator can take about forty trips home.

Finally, each member of Congress is permitted several free mailings annually to constituent households, a privilege known as the *frank*. The average House member sends out more than a million pieces of frank mail in an election year (although members are barred from sending franked mail within sixty days of the election).[9] Some congressional offices are quite shameless in their use of the frank. Certain House members, for example, routinely send congratulatory letters to all graduating high school seniors in their districts, an effort that is designed to impress these newly eligible voters and their parents. The letters are individually signed—by a machine that duplicates the member's signature.

Campaign Spending

Incumbents have a decided advantage when it comes to raising campaign funds. The cost of running for Congress has risen sharply in recent decades as campaign techniques, such as televised advertising and polling, have become increasingly sophisticated and costly (see Figure 12-2). Today, a successful Senate campaign usually costs several million dollars even in a small state, and a successful House campaign will often cost $300,000 to $500,000. The price of victory can go much higher. The 1990 North Carolina contest between Senator Jesse Helms and Charlotte Mayor Harvey Gantt was one of the most expensive Senate races in history, with Helms outspending Gantt $13.4 million to $7.8 million, for a combined total of $21.2 million.

As in the case of the Helms-Gantt race, incumbents are usually better-

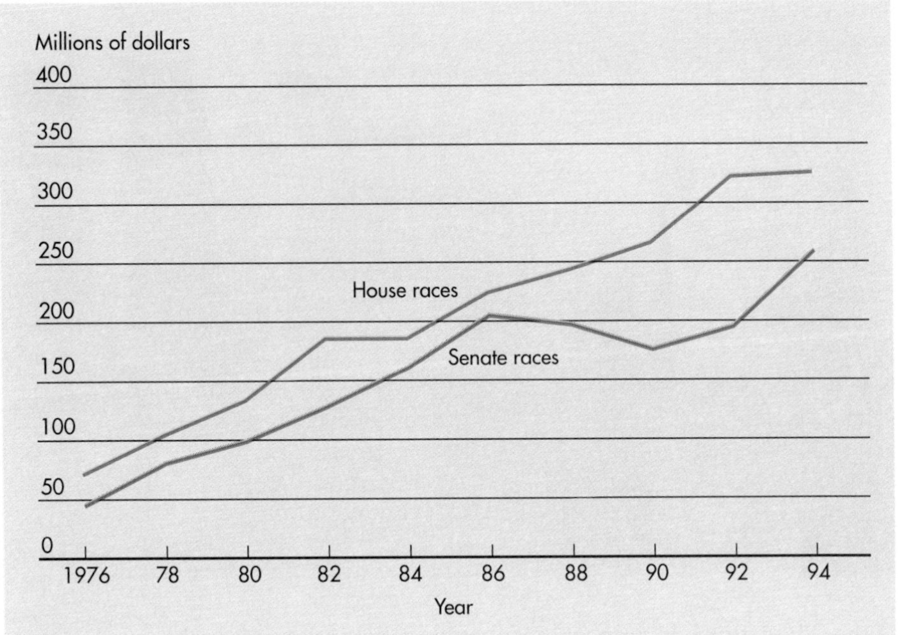

FIGURE 12-2 Congressional Campaign Expenditures, 1972–1994
The cost of running for congressional office has risen sharply as campaign techniques—television advertising, opinion polling, and so on—have become more elaborate and sophisticated.
Source: Federal Election Commission.

funded than their challengers. The political scientist Paul Herrnson concludes that the most successful candidates essentially run two campaigns: one in Washington where they appeal for campaign funds and one in the state or district where they appeal for votes.[10] Incumbents have a decided advantage in the first of these campaigns, which usually begins far in advance of the second. Incumbents' fund-raising advantage starts with their past campaigns and constituent service, which enables them to create mailing lists of potential contributors. Individual contributions, most of which are $100 or less, account for more than 40 percent of all campaign funds and are obtained mainly through direct mail solicitation. Incumbents also have an edge, when they need it, with the party campaign committees (see Chapter 9). These committees, though not the main contributors to congressional campaigns, do make sizable and timely contributions that can make a difference in close races.

Incumbents fare even better with political action committees (PACs, discussed in detail in Chapter 10), which contribute about 30 percent of campaign funds. Incumbents are well positioned to help PACs achieve their legislative goals; in recent elections, incumbents have received more than 5 times as much money in PAC contributions as their opponents. More than half the U.S. senators seeking reelection in 1994 received $1 million or more from PACs, and more than a dozen House members received half a million dollars or more. Many PACs are hesitant to oppose an incumbent unless it is clear that the candidate is vulnerable. "Anytime you go against an incumbent, you take a minute and think long and hard about what your rationale is," said Desiree Anderson, director of the Realtors PAC.[11]

Though money has been called "the mother's milk of politics," money does not always decide an election; in most elections it is not even the main factor. The political scientist Gary Jacobson has demonstrated that money is no

Senator Phil Gramm of Texas greets a supporter on the way to a fund-raising event during his 1990 reelection campaign. Like most incumbents, Gramm was able to raise more money than his opponent. (Najlah Feanny/SABA)

higher than third in importance, ranking behind partisanship and incumbency.[12] Nevertheless, the flow of money in congressional campaigns is significant both in itself and as an indicator of the other crucial factors, particularly the advantages of incumbency. A *Congressional Quarterly* study found that only 10 percent of incumbents said they had encountered trouble raising enough money to conduct an effective campaign, compared with 70 percent of challengers.[13]

Many challengers are able to raise only enough money for a token campaign. "Spending is particularly important for non-incumbents," political scientist Barbara Hinckley notes. "It significantly increases recognition and affects the vote."[14] Challengers who spend heavily have at least a chance of victory; those who spend little are almost certain to lose. In contrast, incumbents normally spend heavily only when they face a serious challenger.[15]

Senate races tend to attract well-funded challengers, but incumbents still derive a financial advantage from a variety of funding sources, including individual contributors, PACs, and political party sources. In recent years Senate incumbents have filled large campaign "war chests" well in advance of their

CONSTITUTIONAL QUALIFICATIONS FOR SERVING IN CONGRESS

Representatives: "No personal shall be a Representative who shall not have attained to the age of twenty-five years, and been seven years a citizen of the United States, and who shall not, when elected, be an inhabitant of that State in which he shall be chosen" (Article I, section 2).

Senators: "No personal shall be a Senator who shall not have attained to the age of thirty years, and been nine years a citizen of the United States, and who shall not, when elected, be an inhabitant of the State for which he shall be chosen" (Article I, section 3).

reelection campaigns, partly in order to discourage potentially strong challengers from running against them. A year before his 1994 Senate race, Daniel Patrick Moynihan (D-N.Y.) had already raised several million dollars; faced with the prospect of a tough campaign against a strong incumbent, the Republicans nominated a weak candidate and Moynihan won easily.

A race without an incumbent—called an **open-seat election**—usually brings out a strong candidate from each party and involves heavy spending, especially when party competition in the state or district is strong. In 1994, for example, the major-party candidates spent on average about a million dollars between them in open-seat House races.[16]

open-seat election An election in which there is no incumbent in the race.

Open-seat contests can be critically important to shifts in power in Congress. The Republican victory in the 1994 midterm elections was achieved primarily through success in open-seat races. There were fifty-two open House seats and nine open Senate seats in 1994, and the GOP won 80 percent of these races. Without these victories, the Republicans would not have gained control of either the House or Senate. The large majority of Democratic incumbents who sought another term in 1994 were reelected.

Gerrymandering: An Advantage for House Incumbents

Every ten years, after each population census, the 435 seats in the House of Representatives are reapportioned among the states in proportion to their population. States that have gained population since the last census may acquire additional seats, while those which have lost population may lose seats. After the 1990 census, California, Texas, and Florida were among the states that gained seats in the House. New York, Illinois, and Michigan were among those which lost seats.

The responsibility for redrawing House election district boundaries after a reapportionment—a process called **redistricting**—rests with the state governments. States are required by law to make their House districts as nearly equal in population as possible.[17] In establishing this principle in the early 1960s, the Supreme Court reasoned that districts of varying size give voters in smaller districts a larger voice in government, thus violating the "one person, one vote" principle of democratic government. Before this ruling, states commonly attempted to influence House elections through **malapportionment,** a situation in which election districts have greatly unequal populations.

redistricting The process of altering election districts in order to make them as nearly equal in population as possible. Redistricting takes place every ten years, after each population census.

malapportionment The situation in which election districts have greatly unequal populations, usually as a result of a deliberate attempt to manipulate political power.

Redistricting is a threat to House incumbents. Turnover in House elections is typically higher after a new census than in previous elections. The newly redrawn districts include voters who are unfamiliar with the incumbent, thereby diminishing a major advantage that incumbents have over their challengers. Moreover, when a state loses congressional seats, there are more incumbents than districts; thus incumbents may have to compete against one another in either a primary or general election. This situation occurred in New York after the 1990 census.

The effect of redistricting on House turnover would be greater if not for **gerrymandering**—the deliberate redrawing of an election district's boundaries to give a particular party or candidate an advantage. The Supreme Court has ruled that legislative redistricting for partisan political advantage is unconsti-

gerrymandering The deliberate redrawing of an election district's boundaries to give a particular party or candidate an advantage.

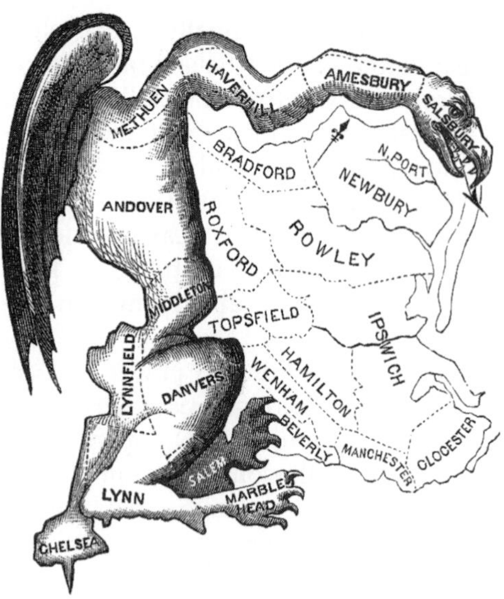

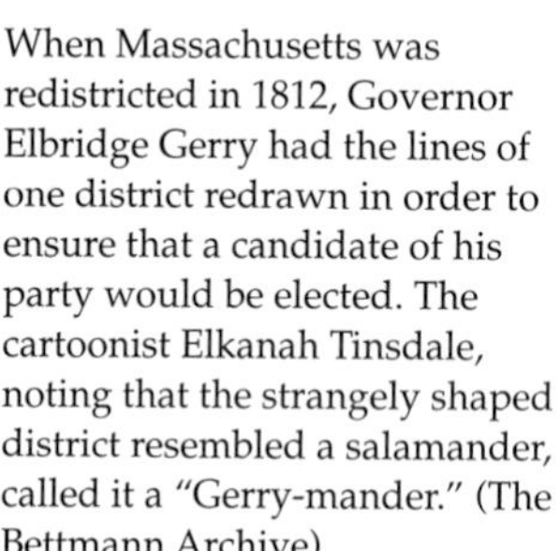
When Massachusetts was redistricted in 1812, Governor Elbridge Gerry had the lines of one district redrawn in order to ensure that a candidate of his party would be elected. The cartoonist Elkanah Tinsdale, noting that the strangely shaped district resembled a salamander, called it a "Gerry-mander." (The Bettmann Archive)

tutional but has left open the question of what exactly constitutes redistricting of this type.[18] Because of the Court's position, majorities in state legislatures, whether Republican or Democratic, were cautious when redistricting after the 1990 census, but they tended naturally to draw district boundaries in a way that would not hurt candidates of their party.

The state legislatures also tended to protect House incumbents of both parties by creating heavily Republican districts around Republican incumbents and heavily Democratic districts around Democratic incumbents. Incumbents of both parties get protected for both practical and political reasons. Incumbents complain loudly and may initiate court action if they feel they have been unfavorably singled out in a partisan redistricting plan. A more important reason is that an incumbent member of Congress is always a formidable opponent. It is risky for a party to jeopardize the reelection chances of its potential winners by forcing them into a race with an incumbent of the opposite party. A safer strategy is to concede the race by stacking the district with voters of the incumbent's party, which means that other districts will have fewer of these partisan voters.

Of course, gerrymandering is not a tool that can be applied to U.S. Senate races. The electoral district for such races is defined not by population but by geography: it consists of the entire state, and each state—large or small—elects two senators.

THE PITFALLS OF INCUMBENCY

Incumbency is not without its pitfalls. The potential problems include troublesome issues, personal misconduct, variation in turnout, and strong challengers.[19]

Troublesome Issues

Disruptive issues are a potential threat to incumbents. Although most elections are not waged against the backdrop of strong issues, those which are tend to produce the largest turnover in Congress. In the 1986–1990 period, when voters were relatively satisfied with national conditions, less than 5 percent of congressional incumbents lost their races. In the 1992–1994 period, when the public was angry over economic and social conditions and believed Congress was performing badly, the number of incumbents who were defeated exceeded 10 percent.

Personal Misconduct

Members of Congress can also fall prey to scandal. Life in Washington can be fast-paced, glamorous, and expensive, and some members of Congress get caught up in influence peddling, sex scandals, and other forms of misconduct. The "Keating Five" are a case in point. Five senators—Alan Cranston (D-Calif.), Dennis DeConcini (D-Ariz.), John Glenn (D-Ohio), John McCain (R-Ariz.), and Donald Riegle, Jr. (D-Mich.)—intervened in 1987 with federal thrift regulators investigating Lincoln Savings and Loan Association, a failing thrift institution owned by Charles Keating. Keating had contributed almost a third of a million dollars to the senators' campaigns and had given another $1 million to political organizations at their request. In 1991 the Senate Select Committee faulted four of the senators for poor judgment and cited the fifth, Senator Cranston, for a more serious breach of ethics. Cranston, a four-term senator who was in poor health, resigned his position as majority whip and announced he would not seek reelection in 1992. Glenn and McCain were subsequently reelected, while Riegle and DeConcini chose not to run again when their terms expired in 1994.

In most election years, ethical issues are probably the biggest threat to incumbents. More than 60 percent of House incumbents who lost their bid for reelection in the 1988–1992 period were shadowed by ethical questions. "The first thing to being reelected is to stay away from scandal, even minor scandal," says the political scientist John Hibbing.[20] Even the top leaders are not immune, as evidenced by the experience of former House Ways and Means Committee Chairman Dan Rostenkowski. Accused of gross misuse of congressional funds, he lost his House seat in 1994, despite having won by 20 percentage points two years earlier and outspending his 1994 opponent by more than 10 to 1.

Midterm Elections: A Special Problem for Incumbents of the President's Party

Historically, the party holding the presidency loses seats in the midterm congressional elections, particularly in the House of Representatives (see Figure 12-3). The 1994 midterm elections, when the Democrats had Bill Clinton in the White House and lost fifty-two House and eight Senate seats, produced higher losses than normal, but the president's party nearly always suffers a net loss. This tendency is not a function of the president's personal popularity. Although the losses tend to be greater when the president's public approval is low, the pattern holds even when confidence in the president is high. The pattern is a consequence of the change in the electorate between the presidential and midterm elections. Turnout is about 50 percent higher in presi-

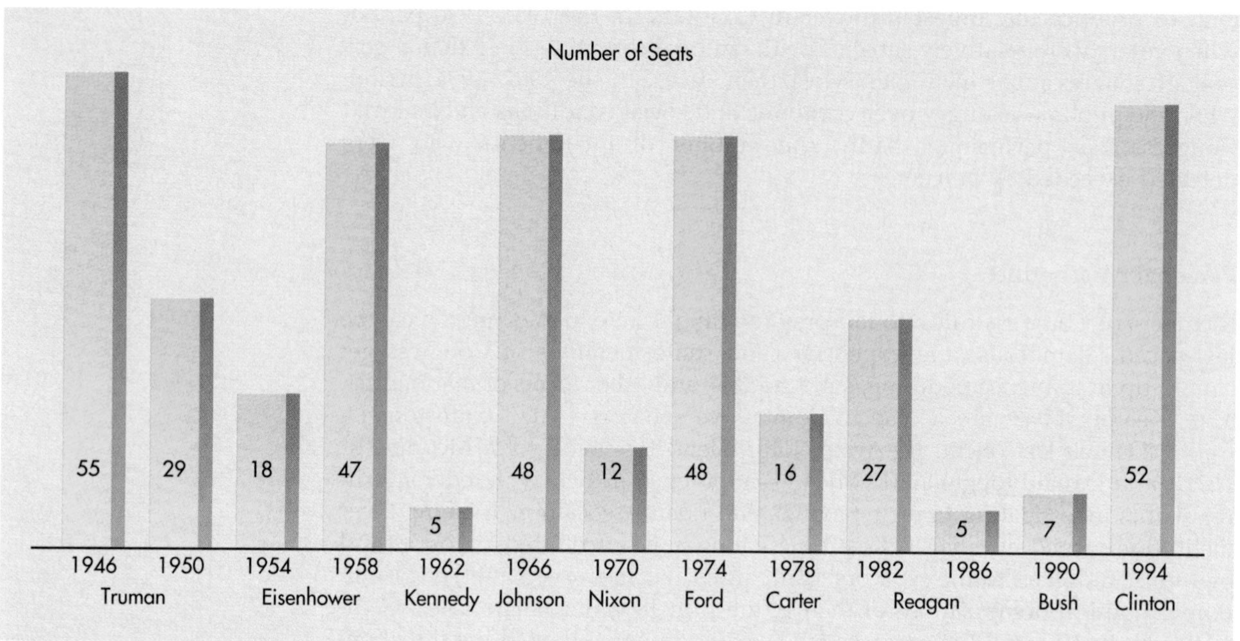

FIGURE 12-3 Net House Seats Lost by Presidential Party in Midterm Elections, 1946–1994 Historically, the party holding the White House has lost seats in the midterm elections.

dential election years, and the people who are drawn to the polls only in these years tend to have weaker party loyalties and are therefore more responsive to the issues of the moment. In any given election year, these issues usually favor one party, which contributes to the success of its congressional candidates as well as its presidential nominee. Most of the party's congressional candidates who win narrowly owe their margin of victory to the voters who participate only in presidential elections. When the midterm elections come along, these voters are absent and the in-party's candidates in closely competitive states and districts are vulnerable. Unless they can make inroads among midterm voters who backed their opponent in the previous race, they stand a good chance of losing. Since many of these voters are strong partisans, they are not easily swayed, and the typical result is the midterm defeat of a number of incumbents from the president's party.

Strong Challengers: A Special Problem for Senators

Finally, incumbents are vulnerable to strong challengers. Senators are particularly likely to face formidable opponents: after the presidency, the Senate is the top rung of the political ladder. Governors and House members are frequent challengers for Senate seats, and they have the electoral base, reputation, and experience to compete effectively.[21] Moreover, the U.S. Senate lures wealthy challengers. Michael Huffington spent more than $20 million of his own money in California's 1994 Senate race and nearly defeated incumbent Dianne Feinstein. The willingness of strong challengers to take on Senate incumbents is a major reason that Senate campaigns have remained somewhat competitive in recent decades.

House incumbents have less reason to fear strong challengers. A House seat is often not attractive enough to induce prominent local politicians, such as mayors or state legislators, to risk their political careers in a challenge to an incumbent. Political scientists Linda Fowler and Robert McClure speak of "the unseen candidates"—potentially strong House challengers who end up deciding that the costs of a campaign outweigh the benefits.[22] This situation leaves the field open to weak opponents with little or no governmental or political experience.[23] Potential candidates for Congress, however, are not unmindful of political developments, and when favorable conditions exist, they are more inclined to run. The GOP anticipated that it would gain seats in 1994, which brought a stronger-than-normal group of Republican challengers into the campaign and further increased the party's chances of success.

Nevertheless, the advantage in congressional campaigns rests with incumbents. As a result, the Congress is not as responsive as most national legislatures to political change. The Republicans gained a decisive victory in 1994 on the strength of the voters' anger at Washington, but a similar public mood in 1980 failed to translate into GOP control of the House of Representatives. In nearly every other western democracy, the conditions underlying the 1980 election would have produced a change in power. Democracy depends on periodic shifts in power between the parties to bring public policy into closer alignment with public opinion. In their research, Keith Poole and Howard Rosenthal found that changes in congressional voting patterns occur almost entirely around the replacement of defeated or retiring lawmakers with new members.[24]

WHO ARE THE WINNERS IN CONGRESSIONAL ELECTIONS?

Although members of the House and Senate are elected to represent their constituents, the average representative is very different from the average American in virtually every respect.[25]

Members of Congress are drawn heavily from the legal profession. Although only 1 in every 350 Americans is a lawyer, about 1 in 3 members of Congress has studied law. Attorneys are attracted to politics in part by Congress's role in lawmaking and by the public visibility that a campaign for office helps build, which can make a private law practice more successful. Along with lawyers, professionals such as business executives, educators, bankers, and journalists account for more than 90 percent of congressional membership.[26] Blue-collar workers, clerical employees, and homemakers are seldom elected to Congress. Farmers and ranchers are not as rare; a fair number of House members from rural districts have agricultural backgrounds.

Members of Congress are highly educated relative to the public they serve. About two-thirds have attended graduate or professional school. Fewer than 3 percent of Congress's members have had no schooling beyond high school, compared with 55 percent of the general population.

Finally, members of Congress are disproportionately white and male. Minority group members and women each account for only about 10 percent of the Congress. This proportion, however, is twice that of a decade ago. The 1992 elections were particularly important to the change; reapportionment and the retirement of an unusually high number of incumbents contributed to the election to Congress of more than thirty additional women and minority group members. Safe incumbency is a major obstacle to the election to Congress of more women and minorities. They have been no more successful than other challengers in dislodging congressional incumbents. In elections to state and local office, where incumbency is less important, women and minority candidates have made greater inroads.

Congressional Leadership

The way in which Congress works is related to the way in which its members win election. Because of their independent power base in their state or district, members of Congress have substantial independence within the institution they serve. The Speaker of the House and the other top leaders in Congress are crucial to its operation, but, unlike their counterparts in European legislatures, they cannot demand the loyalty of the members they lead. Speaker Newt Gingrich's extraordinary success in pushing the Contract with America through the House in 1995 was based less on the formal powers of his office than on the galvanizing force of the ideas the contract contained. Gingrich is the most powerful congressional leader of recent times, and House Republicans in 1995 took steps to strengthen the power of the chamber's top party and committee leaders. But there is an inherent tension in Congress between the institution's need for strong leadership at the top and the individual members' need to exercise power on behalf of constituents. The result is an institution where power is widely dispersed.

PARTY LEADERS IN CONGRESS

The House and Senate are organized along party lines. When members of Congress are sworn in at the start of a new two-year session, they auto-

The U.S. Capitol in Washington, D.C., with the House wing in the foreground. The Senate meets in the wing at the right of the central rotunda (under the dome). The offices of the House and Senate party leaders—Speaker, vice-president, majority and minority leaders and whips—are located in the Capitol building. Other members of Congress have their offices in nearby buildings. (Vanessa Vick/Photo Researchers)

TABLE 12-2 Number of Democrats and Republicans in House of Representatives and Senate, 1973–1998

	75–76	77–78	79–80	81–82	83–84	85–86	87–88	89–90	91–92	93–94	95–96	97-98
House												
Democrats	290*	293	276	243*	269*	253*	258*	262*	268*	259	205*	209*
Republicans	145	142	159	192	166	182	177	173	167	176	230	226
Senate												
Democrats	61*	61	59	47	45	47	54*	55*	56*	56	46*	45*
Republicans	39	39	41	53	55	53	46	45	44	44	54	55

*Chamber not controlled by the president's party. House Democrat total for 1991–1998 includes an independent member who caucuses with the Democratic members.

matically join either the Democratic or Republican caucus in their chamber. These caucuses then select **party leaders** to represent the party's interests in the full chamber and to provide some central direction to the body's deliberations.

party leaders Members of the House and Senate who are chosen by the Democratic or Republican caucus in each chamber to represent the party's interests in that chamber and who give some central direction to the chamber's deliberations.

The House Leadership

The main party leaders in the House are the Speaker, majority leader, majority whip, minority leader, and minority whip. The Constitution provides only for the post of Speaker, who is to be chosen by a vote of the entire House. In practice, this means that the Speaker is selected by the majority party's members, since only they have enough votes to choose one of their own. (Table 12-2 shows the party composition of Congress during the past two decades.)

The Speaker is often said to be the second most powerful official in Washington, after the president. The Speaker has the right to speak first on legislation during House debate and has the power to recognize members—that is, give them permission to speak from the floor. Since the House places a time limit on floor debate, not everyone has a chance to speak on a bill, and the Speaker can sometimes influence legislation simply by exercising the power to decide who will speak and when.[27] The Speaker also chooses the chairperson and majority-party members of the powerful House Rules Committee, which controls the scheduling of bills for debate.[28] Legislation the Speaker wants passed is likely to reach the floor under conditions favorable to its enactment; for example, the Speaker may ask the Rules Committee to delay sending a bill to the floor until there is enough support for its passage. The Speaker has other ways of directing the work of the House. The Speaker assigns bills to committees, can place time limits on the reporting of bills out of committees, and assigns members to conference committees. (The importance of these powers over committee action will become apparent later in this chapter and in the next.)

The Speaker is active in developing the party's position on issues and in persuading party members in the House to follow his lead.[29] The Speaker

Congressional leaders meet with President Clinton at the White House in 1995. Speaker of the House Newt Gingrich (left) and Senate majority leader Robert Dole (right) are seated next to Clinton. Seated next to Dole is Richard Gephardt, House minority leader. The Senate minority leader, Thomas Daschle, sits along side Gingrich. (Wide World Photos)

chairs the Steering Committee, which has ongoing responsibility for developing and promoting the majority party's legislative program. Although the Speaker cannot compel party members to support this program, they look to him for leadership. The Speaker can draw upon shared partisan views and has a few rewards on hand for cooperative party members; the Speaker can, for instance, help them obtain public spending projects for their districts and favorable committee assignments for themselves.

The Speaker is assisted by the House majority leader, who is elected by the majority party's members. The majority leader acts as the party's floor leader, organizing the debate on bills and working to line up legislative support. Typically, the majority leader is an experienced and skilled legislator.[30]

The majority-party whip has the important job of soliciting votes from party members and of informing them when critical votes are scheduled. Whips have been known to track down members who are out of town and persuade them to rush back to Washington for an important vote. As voting is getting under way on the House floor, the whip will sometimes position himself where he can be seen by party members and let them know how the leadership wants them to vote by giving a thumbs-up or thumbs-down signal.

The minority party has its own leaders in the House. The House minority leader heads the party's caucus and policy committee and plays the leading role in developing the party's legislative positions. If the president is also of the minority party, the minority leader will work closely with the president on legislative issues. The minority leader is assisted by a minority whip, who is responsible for lining up party members' support on legislation and informing them when votes are scheduled.

To a significant degree, the power of all party leaders in the House rests on the trust placed in them by the members of their party. They do not have strong formal powers, but they are expected to lead. If they are adept at promoting ideas and building coalitions, they will be able to exercise considerable power within their chamber.

The Senate Leadership

In the Senate, the most important party leadership position is that of the majority leader, who heads the majority-party caucus. The majority leader's role is much like that of the Speaker of the House, in that he formulates the majority's legislative policies and strategies and seeks to develop influential relationships with colleagues. Like the Speaker, the Senate majority leader chairs the party's policy committee and acts as the party's voice in the chamber.[31] The majority leader works closely with the president in developing legislative programs if they are of the same party. When Howard Baker was the Senate majority leader, he said that part of his job was to act as President Reagan's "point man" in the Senate.[32] For example, when the Reagan administration in 1981 sought congressional approval for the sale of AWACS surveillance planes to Saudi Arabia, Baker advised the White House not to press for a vote in order to give undecided senators enough time to study the effect of the sale on the security of Israel. Reagan agreed to hold off, and the sale was

HOW THE UNITED STATES COMPARES

LEGISLATIVE LEADERSHIP AND AUTHORITY

The U.S. House and Senate are separate and coequal chambers, each with its own leadership and rules. This type of legislative structure is not found in most democracies. Although many other democracies have a bicameral legislature like the U.S. Congress, nearly all power is vested in just one of the two chambers. In the British Parliament, for example, the House of Commons is far more powerful than the House of Lords; the latter can delay legislation but cannot kill it. In such a situation legislative power is more concentrated and easier to exercise. Thus in Great Britain the party that controls the House of Commons decides legislative policy. In the United States a party must control both the House of Representatives and the Senate if it is to exercise such power.

The U.S. Congress is fragmented in other ways as well: it has elected leaders with limited formal powers, a network of relatively independent and powerful committees, and members who are free to follow or ignore other members of their party. Most Democrats and Republicans vote with a majority of their party on major bills, but it is not uncommon for a fourth or more of a party's legislators to vote against their party's position on important legislative issues. In contrast, European legislatures have a centralized power structure: top leaders have substantial authority, the committees are weak, and the parties are unified. European legislators are expected to support their party unless granted permission to vote otherwise on a particular bill. Legislative leadership is much easier to exercise in Europe's hierarchical parliaments than in America's "stratarchical" Congress.

Country	*Form of Legislature*
Canada	One house dominant
France	One house dominant
Germany	One house dominant (except on regional issues)
Great Britain	One house dominant
Israel	One house only
Italy	Two equal houses
Japan	One house dominant
Mexico	Two equal houses
United States	Two equal houses

★ STATES IN THE NATION

House and Senate Committee Chairs: When the GOP took control of Congress in 1995, it also acquired all committee chair positions, affecting which states are represented in these key positions.

STATE	COMMITTEE CHAIRS 1993–1994	1995–1996
Ala.	0	0
Alaska	0	3
Ariz.	1	2
Ark.	2	0
Calif.	5	1
Colo.	0	0
Conn.	0	1
Del.	1	1
D.C.	0	0
Fla.	1	0
Ga.	1	0
Hawaii	1	0
Idaho	0	0
Ill.	0	1
Ind.	1	1
Iowa	0	1
Kan.	1	3
Ky.	2	1
La.	1	1
Maine	0	1
Md.	0	0
Mass.	3	0
Mich.	4	0
Minn.	1	0
Miss.	1	0
Mo.	1	1
Mont.	1	0
Neb.	0	0
Nev.	1	0
N.H.	0	0
N.J.	0	0
N.Mex.	0	1
N.Y.	2	3
N.C.	1	1
N.Dak.	0	0
Ohio	1	1
Okla.	0	0
Oreg.	0	2
Pa.	0	5
R.I.	1	1
S.C.	1	2
S.Dak.	0	1
Tenn.	1	0
Texas	3	2
Utah	0	1
Vt.	1	0
Va.	0	1
Wash.	0	0
W.Va.	2	0
Wis.	0	0
Wyo.	0	1

seniority A member of Congress's consecutive years of service on a particular committee.

eventually approved.[33] Democratic majority leader George Mitchell played a similarly key role in coaxing several of President Clinton's top bills through the Senate in 1993 and 1994.

Unlike the Speaker of the House, the Senate majority leader is not the chamber's presiding officer. The Constitution assigns this responsibility to the vice-president of the United States. However, since the vice-president is allowed to vote in the Senate only to break a tie, the vice-president seldom presides over Senate debates. The Senate has a president *pro tempore,* who, in the absence of the vice-president, has the right to preside over the Senate. President *pro tempore* is largely an honorary position that by tradition is usually held by the majority party's senior member. The presiding official has limited power, since each senator has the right to speak at any length on bills under consideration.

The Senate's tradition of unlimited debate stems mainly from its relatively small size (only 100 members, compared with the House's 435 members). Moreover, senators like to view themselves as the equals of all others in their chamber and are thus reluctant to take orders from their leadership.[34] For such reasons, the Senate majority leader's position is weaker than that of the Speaker of the House. One former Senate majority leader, Robert Byrd, jokingly called himself a "slave," saying that he served his fellow Democrats' needs without commanding their votes.[35] The Senate majority leader's actual power depends significantly on his leadership skills.[36] Lacking strong formal powers, the majority leader must convince party members that their interests coincide with his.

Like the House, the Senate has a majority whip; however, this position is less important in the Senate because that body's members are less subject to persuasive tactics. Nevertheless, the Senate majority whip sees to it that members know when important votes are scheduled and ensures that the party's strongest advocates on a legislative measure are present for the debate. "The leadership must have the right members at the right place at the right time," said Senator Byrd.[37]

Finally, the Senate has a minority leader and minority whip, whose roles are comparable to those performed by their counterparts in the House. As befits "a chamber of equals," the majority leadership in the Senate usually consults the minority leadership on the scheduling of legislation.

COMMITTEE CHAIRPERSONS: THE SENIORITY PRINCIPLE

Party leaders are not the only important leaders in Congress. Most of the work of Congress takes place in the meetings of its thirty-five standing (permanent) committees and their numerous subcommittees, each of which is headed by a chairperson. A committee chair schedules committee meetings, determines the order in which committee bills are considered, presides over committee discussions, directs the committee's majority staff, and can choose to lead the debate when a committee bill reaches the floor of the chamber for a vote by the full membership. (The process by which a bill becomes a law is discussed in Chapter 13.)

Committee chairs are always members of the majority party, and they usually have the most **seniority**—the most consecutive years of service on a particular committee. Party loyalty is seldom a criterion in the choice of a chair. When Senate Appropriations Chairman Mark Hatfield voted against the balanced budget amendment in 1995, the only Republican to do so, he retained his position despite calls for his dismissal.

The seniority principle was virtually absolute until the House Democratic majority decided in the early 1970s that committee chairs would henceforth be chosen by secret ballot.[38] Abuses by some committee chairs led to the change. Virginia's Howard Smith, who chaired the House Rules Committee in the 1950s and 1960s and was staunchly opposed to racial change, would sometimes leave Washington for his Virginia farm when civil rights legislation reached his committee. Because the Rules Committee could not meet unless he called it into session, Smith's absence was sometimes enough to persuade the full committee to "table" a bill, or set it aside. A committee chair now has less discretionary power; for example, a majority of the committee members can vote to convene meetings in the chair's absence.

Although the seniority principle is no longer absolute, the congressional majorities usually abide by it. Exceptions took place in 1995 when, at Speaker Gingrich's request, House Republicans bypassed some veteran members, most notably Representative Carlos Moorhead of California, who was the most senior Republican on both the Judiciary and Commerce committees. Gingrich wanted a more forceful individual than Moorhead as chair of these major committees.

The seniority system continues in use in Congress because it has several important advantages: it reduces the number of bitter power struggles that would occur if the chair were decided by open competition, provides experienced and knowledgeable committee leadership, and enables members to look forward to the reward of a position as chair after years of committee service.[39] Seniority gives ambitious members of Congress a reason to work on the business of their committees. If committee leadership were subject to control by party leaders or the president, members would have an incentive to curry favor with this leadership rather than devote their efforts to mastery of a committee's work. As it is, however, an ambitious member of Congress will pay attention to the committee's business because, through the seniority system, he or she might someday put this expertise to use as chairperson or ranking minority member of the committee.[40]

Congressional organization and leadership extend into subcommittees, which are smaller units within each committee formed to conduct specific aspects of the committee's business. Altogether there are about 200 subcommittees in the House and Senate, each with a chairperson who decides its order of business, presides over its meetings, and coordinates its staff. In both chambers, a subcommittee chair is often the most senior member on the panel, but seniority is not as important in these appointments as it is in the designation of committee chairs.

OLIGARCHY OR DEMOCRACY: WHICH PRINCIPLE SHOULD GOVERN?

In 1995, House Republicans gave committee chairs the power to select the chairs of their subcommittees and to appoint all majority-party staff members,

★ CRITICAL THINKING

National Office, Local Orientation: Good or Bad? Whereas legislators in most other democracies are preoccupied with national affairs, members of the U.S. Congress divide their attention between national and local concerns. Membership in Congress provides U.S. senators and representatives with the large personal budgets and staffs they need to retain the support of constituents in the home state or district—support that they must have if they are to be reelected. Incumbency also makes it relatively easy for members of Congress to raise money for their reelection campaigns—typically half a million dollars or more for representatives and several million dollars for senators.

In contrast, members of the Canadian House of Commons concentrate on national issues because their chances of reelection depend heavily on their party's nationwide popularity. Members of the House of Commons have only a small amount of staff help, and most of them spend only small amounts of money on their reelection campaigns.

What are the relative advantages and disadvantages of the American system? In serving their constituencies, do members of Congress also serve the interests of the country as a whole better than they would if they were preoccupied with national-level problems? Does the existence of a president in the U.S. system (Canada has no separate executive branch) lessen your concern about the local orientation of most members of Congress?

including those who work for the subcommittees. The changes were designed to give committee chairs more control over legislation. "If you're going to ask someone to lead, you've got to give him some leverage," said Republican Whip Tom DeLay. "This notion that we've got to have 100 and some odd [subcommittee] fiefdoms is over."[41]

The changes reversed House reforms of the 1970s that were designed to weaken the hold that chairs had on their committees. Selection of subcommittee chairs was removed from the committee chair and placed in the hands of the majority-party members of each committee.[42] Other actions were also taken to give House subcommittees a substantial degree of independence from their committee and its chair. (The Senate in the 1970s also granted more autonomy to its subcommittees, but the changes were less consequential because the Senate relies less heavily on subcommittees in its work.)

The reforms of the 1970s were premised on the idea that Congress should be "more democratic" in its organization.[43] By granting more authority to each subcommittee and by freeing its chairperson from control by the committee chair, power and leadership in Congress were more widely dispersed. The reforms also happened to serve the personal reelection and power needs of individual members. They would no longer have to wait many years to acquire the seniority that would place them in a position of institutional authority.

Although "more democratic" internally, the postreform Congress may have been less democratic externally. In order to get Congress to respond to majority sentiment on broad national issues, top leaders had to work against the separate agendas of committee and subcommittee leaders. Delay was common, and concessions were often necessary to get their support. The Republican reforms of 1995 were designed to strengthen the House's capacity to act as a *majoritarian* institution. Committee and subcommittee leaders would still wield considerable power, but they would also be tied more closely to leaders at the next level. To guard against entrenched power in the top leadership positions, House Republicans instituted term limits: four terms for the Speaker and three terms for committee chairs.

The opposing conceptions of Congress embedded in the 1970s and 1995 reforms have played themselves out many times in the history of Congress. The institution is at once a place for conducting the nation's business and for promoting constituency interests. At times, the position of top leaders has been strengthened. At other times, the position of rank-and-file members has been enhanced. At all times, there has been an attempt to create a workable balance of the two. The result is an institution very different from European parliaments, where power is thoroughly concentrated at the top (an arrangement reflected even in the name for rank-and-file members—"backbenchers"). The distinguishing feature of congressional leadership is its dispersion across the membership, with some provision for added power at the top.

The Committee System

When Congress first met in 1789, it had no committees. However, committees formed within a few years in the House, and the first Senate committees were

TABLE 12-3 The Standing Committees of Congress

House of Representatives	*Senate*
Agriculture	Agriculture, Nutrition, and Forestry
Appropriations	Appropriations
Banking and Financial Services	Armed Services
Budget	Banking, Housing, and Urban Affairs
Commerce	Budget
Economic and Educational Opportunities	Commerce, Science, and Transportation
Government Reform and Oversight	Energy and Natural Resources
House Oversight	Environment and Public Works
International Relations	Finance
Judiciary	Foreign Relations
National Security	Governmental Affairs
Resources	Judiciary
Rules	Labor and Human Resources
Science	Rules and Administration
Small Business	Small Business
Standards of Official Conduct	Veterans' Affairs
Transportation and Infrastructure	
Veterans' Affairs	
Ways and Means	

established in 1816. At present there are nineteen standing committees in the House and sixteen in the Senate (see Table 12-3). A **standing committee** is a permanent committee with responsibility for a particular area of public policy. Both the House and the Senate, for example, have a standing committee that specializes in handling foreign policy issues. Other important standing committees are those which deal with agriculture, commerce, the national budget, the interior (natural resources and public lands), defense, government spending, labor, the judiciary, and taxation. House committees, which average about thirty-five to forty members each, are about twice the size of the Senate committees. Each standing committee has legislative authority in that it can draft and rewrite proposed legislation and can recommend to the full chamber the passage or defeat of the legislation it considers.

standing committee A permanent congressional committee with responsibility for a particular area of public policy. An example is the Senate Foreign Relations Committee.

Each standing committee in Congress has its own staff, which, altogether, totals about 1,000 employees in the Senate and 1,300 in the House. Unlike the members' personal staffs, which concentrate on constituency relations, the committee staffs perform an almost entirely legislative function. They help draft legislation, prepare reports, organize hearings, and participate in altering bills within committee.

In addition to its standing committees, Congress also has a number of *select committees,* which are created to perform specific tasks and are disbanded after they have done so; *joint committees,* composed of members of both houses, which perform advisory or coordinating functions for the House and the Senate; and *conference committees,* which are joint committees formed temporarily to work out differences in House and Senate versions of a particular bill. The role of conference committees is discussed more fully later in the chapter.

Congress could not possibly handle its work load without the help of its committee system. About 10,000 bills are introduced during each two-year session of Congress; the sheer volume of this legislation would paralyze the institution if it did not have a division of labor. Yet the very existence of committees and subcommittees helps fragment Congress: each of these units is relatively secure in its power, jurisdiction, and membership.[44]

COMMITTEE POWER

At times, particularly when bills dealing with major issues are introduced, the full membership of Congress takes decisive action. On most bills, however, the full chamber merely votes to confirm or modify decisions made previously by committees and subcommittees. When a committee recommends passage of a bill, the measure has about a 90 percent chance of being approved by the full House or Senate, although about a third of these bills are amended on the floor.[45] Moreover, committees are the burial ground of most legislation introduced in Congress. Only about 10 percent of the bills that committees consider reach the floor for a vote; the others are "killed" when committees decide that they do not warrant further consideration and table them. The full House or Senate can overrule these committee rejections but seldom does so.

In the House particularly, most of the detailed legislative work—hearings, debates, and basic reworking of bills—is done by the subcommittees rather than by the full committees.[46] Unless a subcommittee's members are seriously divided or have highly unrepresentative views, their general response to a bill

With their staff members looking on, Senators Edward Kennedy (D-Mass.) and Nancy Kassenbaum (R-Kansas) of the Labor and Human Resources Committee discuss the start of health care reform hearings in 1994. The Labor and Human Resources Committee has jurisdiction over health issues in the Senate. (Wide World Photos)

usually prevails when it is considered by the full committee.[47] Senate subcommittees, in contrast, serve more as advisory bodies to the full committees than as separate working bodies within the committees.[48]

Although the power of committees and subcommittees should not be underestimated, statistics on their influence can be misleading. The fact that committee recommendations are followed about 90 percent of the time does not mean that committees hold 90 percent of the power in Congress. In making their decisions, committees are mindful that their positions can be reversed by the full chamber, just as subcommittees recognize that the full committee can overrule their actions. Consequently, committee and subcommittee decisions are made in anticipation of the probable responses of other members of Congress. Committee and subcommittee members must always ask whether their colleagues are likely to accept their recommendations.

COMMITTEE JURISDICTION

The 1946 Legislative Reorganization Act requires each bill introduced in Congress to be referred to the proper committee. An agricultural bill introduced in the Senate must be assigned to the Senate Agriculture Committee, a bill dealing with foreign affairs must be sent to the Senate Foreign Relations Committee, and so on. This requirement is a major source of each committee's power. Even if its members are known to oppose certain types of legislation, bills clearly within its **jurisdiction**—the policy area in which it is authorized to act—must be sent to it for deliberation.

jurisdiction (of a congressional committee) The policy area in which a particular congressional committee is authorized to act.

However, House and Senate leaders do have some discretion when they assign certain bills to committee. Although the House Commerce Committee has primary jurisdiction over commerce policy, for example, many other House committees have some responsibility for economic policy, so that the Speaker has a choice when some bills dealing with economics are to be assigned. Sometimes a bill may be broad enough to be reasonably assigned to any of several committees. In 1963 Senate majority leader Mike Mansfield sent a comprehensive civil rights bill to the Senate Commerce Committee, most of whose members were liberal northerners. He purposely avoided the Senate Judiciary Committee, which normally handles civil rights measures, because it was dominated by southerners who were likely to oppose the bill. Mansfield's justification for referring the bill to the Commerce Committee was that the proposed legislation would prohibit the disruptive effects that racial discrimination in public restaurants, hotels, and transportation facilities has on interstate commerce.

House subcommittees have secure jurisdictions like those of the committees: bills must be referred to the appropriate subcommittees within two weeks of their arrival in committee. The Senate has a similar policy. Thus responsibility in Congress is thoroughly divided, with each subcommittee having formal authority over a small area of public policy.[49] The House International Relations Committee, for instance, has five subcommittees: International Economic Policy and Trade, International Operations and Human Rights, Asia and the Pacific, Western Hemisphere, and Africa. Each subcommittee has about a dozen members, and these few individuals do most of the

THE MEDIA AND THE PEOPLE

C-SPAN (CABLE SATELLITE PUBLIC AFFAIRS NETWORK)

For years, television was barred from Congress except for special joint sessions, such as the president's annual State of the Union message. Congressional leaders objected to television on grounds that some members would grandstand, playing to the voters rather than engaging in serious debate.

In 1977, the House agreed to televise floor debate for a seven-month test period on a closed-circuit system. The test was followed by a vote to institute gavel-to-gavel coverage of House proceedings. Two years later, the House began to transmit its proceedings to the outside world through C-SPAN, which is carried by about 90 percent of the nation's cable systems. Television broadcasters were authorized to use the televised material for news purposes.

The Senate refused for nearly a decade to follow the House's lead. The Senate prides itself on being a more deliberative body than the House, and a majority of senators were convinced for a time that televised floor debates would disrupt the chamber's proceedings. In 1986, the Senate changed its position, in part because its members recognized that the House had gained a legislative advantage from its use of television. Like the House, the Senate operates the cameras and allows broadcasters to use the telecast material as they see fit.

The worst fears about the effect of television on Congress have not materialized. Most analysts conclude that the quality of Senate and House debate has not been substantially affected by the presence of television cameras. In fact, observers believe that C-SPAN has helped spark public interest in the legislative process. Although C-SPAN does not have a particularly large audience, roughly 4 million people pay at least some attention to it and a few hundred thousand avid citizens watch it closely. After heated floor debate on a major issue, congressional phone lines are often jammed with calls from opinionated C-SPAN viewers.

C-SPAN has had one noticeable effect on the behavior of members of Congress: an increase in the number of speeches made under special orders—a period at the end of each session when members can speak on any issue. The demand for the opportunity to give these speeches has been so heavy that the House and Senate have established limits on their length. In the 1980s Newt Gingrich and other Republicans used special-order speeches as an opportunity to reach C-SPAN viewers with attacks on the Democrats. Thomas P. "Tip" O'Neill, the Democratic Speaker of the House, ordered the cameras to occasionally pan the House floor during these speeches to show viewers that the orator was addressing a nearly empty chamber.

work and have the major voice in the disposition of most bills in their policy domain.

COMMITTEE MEMBERSHIP

Each committee includes Republicans and Democrats, but the majority party holds the majority of seats on each committee and subcommittee. The ratio of Democrats to Republicans on each committee is approximately the same as the ratio in the full House or Senate, but there is no fixed rule on this matter, and the majority party sets the proportions as it chooses (mindful that at the next election it could become the chamber's minority). Members of the House typically serve on only two committees. Senators often serve on four, although they can sit on only two major committees, such as Foreign Relations and Finance. There are also limits on subcommittee assignments; no House member, for example, can serve on more than five subcommittees.

Each standing committee has a fixed number of members, and a committee must have a vacancy before a new member can be appointed. These vacancies usually occur at the start of a new congressional session, when the committee positions of members who have retired or been defeated for reelection are reallocated. On nearly all committees, members retain their seats unless they decide to relinquish them or are forced to do so by changes in party ratios or committee size. The biggest change in committee memberships comes when a party loses control of the House or Senate; many Democrats had to relinquish committee assignments when the Republicans took control of Congress in 1995.

Each party has a special committee in the House and Senate which has responsibility for deciding who will fill vacancies on standing committees. Several factors influence these decisions, including the preferences of the legislators themselves. About 80 percent of newly elected members of Congress receive a committee assignment that they have requested.[50] New members usually ask for assignment to a committee on which they can serve their constituents' interests and at the same time increase their reelection prospects.[51] For example, when Phil Gramm was first elected to the Senate from Texas, a state that depends heavily on the defense industry, he requested and received a position on the Armed Services Committee.

Members of Congress also prefer membership on one of the most important committees, such as Foreign Relations or Finance in the Senate and Ways and Means or Appropriations in the House. Such factors as members' intelligence, experience, party loyalty, ideology, region, length of congressional service, and work habits weigh heavily in the determination of appointments to these prestigious committees. In both the House and the Senate, however, the choice rests with the special party committees established for the purpose of deciding standing-committee assignments.[52] House Republicans broke with tradition in 1995 by assigning an unusually high number of freshmen legislators to the top committees. Many of the coveted spots went to members who had defeated Democratic incumbents and were expected to face tough reelection races in 1996. The assignments also strengthened Speaker Gingrich's position, since many of the new members felt they owed their election and therefore also their allegiance to Gingrich.

Subcommittee assignments are handled differently. The members of each party on a committee decide who among them will serve on each of its subcommittees. The members' preferences, seniority, and personal backgrounds and the interests of their constituencies are key influences on subcommittee assignments.

★ CRITICAL THINKING

Do Committees Serve Their Constituencies or the Country?

The membership of congressional committees is not representative of Congress as a whole. The agriculture committees, for example, are filled with farm-state senators and representatives. This kind of arrangement obviously serves the interests of members of Congress and their specific constituencies. But does it also serve the interests of the country as a whole? Why, or why not?

Institutional Support for the Work of Congress

The range and complexity of the policy issues that Congress must confront have greatly increased in this century. As an initial response to policy complexity, Congress gave the president additional staff and authority (see Chapter 14). This approach gradually placed Congress at a substantial disadvantage to the president. The withholding of crucial information about the progress of the Vietnam war by presidents Johnson and Nixon persuaded many members of Congress that they could not maintain their institution as a coequal branch unless it had a larger and more expert staff. Accordingly, Congress increased its committee staffs and expanded its legislative bureaucracy, which consists of four agencies: the General Accounting Office, the Congressional Research Service, the Congressional Budget Office, and the Office of Technology Assessment.

The General Accounting Office (GAO), with about 5,000 employees, is the largest congressional agency. Formed in 1921, it has the primary responsibility of overseeing executive agencies' spending of money that has been appropriated by Congress.[53] The GAO has made news by bringing abuses by defense contractors to Congress's attention. (In one notorious instance, the GAO reported that the government was paying more than $1,000 apiece for wrenches available in hardware stores for less than $10.) Congress has recently broadened the GAO's responsibilities to include program evaluations, such as a major study on the need to reform government-paid health programs.

Created in 1914, the Congressional Research Service (CRS) is the oldest congressional agency and is part of the Library of Congress. (The CRS was originally the LRS—Legislative Reference Service.) The CRS is a nonpartisan reference agency. If a member of Congress wants historical or statistical information for a speech or bill, the CRS will provide it. It also prepares reports on pending legislative issues, although it makes no recommendations as to what action Congress should take. Finally, the CRS provides members with status reports and summaries of all bills currently under consideration in Congress. The 1,000-member staff of the CRS sometimes complains that it is too much Congress's errand boy (responding, for example, to a member's request for information with which to reply to a constituent's letter) and not enough of a research institute.

The Congressional Budget Office (CBO) is the newest agency, created by the Congressional Budget and Impoundment Control Act of 1974. The main role of the CBO's 200 employees is to provide Congress with projections of the nation's economic situation and of government expenditures and revenues.[54] The Office of Management and Budget (OMB) furnishes similar projections to the president, who incorporates them into the annual budget submitted to Congress. The CBO's figures enable Congress to scrutinize the president's budget proposals more thoroughly.

The Office of Technology Assessment (OTA), established in 1972, assesses technology policies and evaluates policy proposals in such areas as oil exploration and communications. Most of the work of the OTA's 200 employees could be done by other agencies, and some members of Congress have proposed that it be abolished.

In some ways, congressional agencies have strengthened Congress's ability to act as a collective body. Before the CBO was formed, for example, Congress lacked the authoritative information that is needed to challenge the president's budget proposals. Congress is still at a disadvantage, but the CBO's budget estimates give the House and Senate Budget committees (also formed in 1974) a basis for an institutional response.

In other ways, however, congressional agencies contribute to the fragmentation of Congress. These agencies are set up to serve all members of Congress, not just the top leadership. The party leaders obtain information from the congressional agencies that they can use in developing major proposals and in contesting the judgments of the executive branch. But these agencies are designed mainly to provide information directly to individual members, committees, and subcommittees. They use much of this information to advance their separate agendas.

The next chapter examines further how conflicts between the institutional needs of Congress and the individual needs of representatives and senators affect the role that Congress plays in national policy.

Summary

Members of Congress, once elected, are likely to be reelected. Members of Congress have large staffs and can pursue a "service strategy" of responding to the needs of individual constituents. They also can secure pork barrel projects for their state or district and thus demonstrate their concern for constituents. House members gain a greater advantage from these activities than do senators, whose larger constituencies make it harder for them to build close personal relations with voters and whose office is more likely to attract a strong challenger. Incumbency does have some disadvantages. Members of Congress must take positions on controversial issues, may blunder into a political scandal or indiscretion, or face strong challengers; any of these conditions can reduce their reelection chances. By and large, however, the advantages of incumbency far outweigh the disadvantages, particularly for House members. Incumbents' advantages extend into their reelection campaigns. Their influential positions in Congress make it easier for them to raise campaign funds.

Congress is a fragmented institution. It has no single leader; the House and Senate have separate leaders, neither of whom can presume to speak for the other chamber. The principal party leaders of Congress are the Speaker of the House and the Senate majority leader. These party leaders derive their influence less from their formal authority than from their having been entrusted by other members of their party with the tasks of formulating policy positions and coordinating party strategy. Individual party members can choose to follow or ignore their leader's requests.

The committee system is a network of about 35 committees and 200 subcommittees, each with its separate chairperson. Although the seniority principle is not absolute, the chair of a committee is usually the member from the majority party who has the longest continuous service on the committee.

It is in the committees that most of the work of Congress is conducted. Each standing committee of the House and Senate has jurisdiction over congressional policy in a particular area (such as agriculture or foreign relations), as does each of its subcommittees. In most cases, the full House and Senate accept committee recommendations about passage of bills, although amendments to bills are quite common and committees are careful to take other members of Congress into account when making legislative decisions.

Congress is supported by four agencies of its own: the General Accounting Office, which oversees executive spending and performance; the Congressional Research Service, which serves as a reference agency for congressional members; the Congressional Budget Office, which provides budget and economic estimates; and the Office of Technology Assessment, which evaluates technology policies.

Major Concepts

constituency
electoral mastery
gerrymandering
jurisdiction
malapportionment
open-seat election
party leaders
pork barrel projects
redistricting
seniority
service strategy
standing committee

Suggested Readings

Cain, Bruce, John Ferejohn, and Morris P. Fiorina. *The Personal Vote.* Cambridge, Mass.: Harvard University Press, 1987. A careful analysis of the relationship between constituency service and electoral independence.

Fenno, Richard F., Jr. *Home Style: House Members in Their Districts.* Boston: Little, Brown, 1978. The classic analysis of the varying relationships between House members and their constituents.

Fiorina, Morris P. *Congress: Keystone of the Washington Establishment,* 2d ed. New Haven, Conn.: Yale University Press, 1989. An analysis of how incumbent members of Congress use their office to win reelection.

Fowler, Linda L. *Candidates, Congress, and the American Democracy.* Ann Arbor: University of Michigan Press, 1994. An insightful analysis of congressional recruitment and its impact on representation.

Herrnson, Paul S. *Congressional Elections: Campaigning at Home and in Washington.* Washington, D.C.: Congressional Quarterly Press, 1995. A thorough study of the changing nature of congressional campaigns.

Jacobson, Gary C. *The Electoral Origins of Divided Government.* Boulder, Colo.: Westview Press, 1990. A study that challenges some aspects of the thesis that House elections are largely insulated from electoral change.

Malbin, Michael J. *Unelected Representatives: Congressional Staff and the Future of Representation.* New York: Basic Books, 1980. A careful assessment of the impact of congressional staffs on the legislative process.

Smith, Steven S., and Christopher J. Deering. *Committees in Congress,* 2d ed. Washington, D.C.: Congressional Quarterly Press, 1990. A comprehensive look at the House and Senate committee systems.

Swain, Carol M. *Black Faces, Black Interests: The Representation of African Americans in Congress.* Cambridge, Mass.: Harvard University Press, 1993. A critical assessment of the role of race in elections and representation.

Witt, Linda, Karen M. Paget, and Glenna Matthews. *Running as a Woman: Gender and Power in American Politics.* New York: Free Press, 1993. A comprehensive study of the problems faced by women candidates.

CHAPTER 13

CONGRESSIONAL POLICYMAKING: BALANCING NATIONAL GOALS AND LOCAL INTERESTS

There are really two Congresses, not just one. Often these two Congresses are widely separated; the tightly knit, complex world of Capitol Hill is a long way from the world of [the member's district or state]—not only in miles, but in perspective and outlook as well.
—Roger Davidson and Walter Oleszek[1]

In 1993 Congress enacted the North American Free Trade Agreement (NAFTA), which lowers trade barriers between the United States, Canada, and Mexico. NAFTA is North America's response to the European Union, which provides for free trade among the countries of western Europe as a means of integrating and strengthening their economies.

Initially, NAFTA appeared to be heading for defeat in Congress. Although the legislation had the support of the Clinton administration and most of the congressional leadership, its likely impact on the nation's economy was subject to dispute. Economic projections indicated that NAFTA was likely to benefit the nation as a whole but would also result in job and business losses in some areas. This prospect convinced a majority in Congress to withhold their support from the legislation; they did not want to vote for a bill that in the end might hurt the local economies of the states and districts they represented. Intense bargaining ensued between the legislation's supporters and those members of Congress who were willing to consider a vote for NAFTA in return for concessions that would protect their constituents. One such deal exempted citrus growers from a restrictive provision of the trade agreement, which was enough to persuade several Florida legislators to vote for it. In the end, the votes to assure NAFTA's passage were obtained, but at a substantial cost to the free trade principle that underlay the legislation.

The story of the NAFTA vote illustrates the dual nature of Congress: it is both a lawmaking institution for the country and a representative assembly for states and districts.[2] Members of Congress have both an individual duty to serve the interests of their separate constituencies and a collective duty to protect the interests of the country as a whole. Attention to constituency interests is the common denominator of a national institution in which each member must please the voters back home in order to win reelection. Congressional elections have been described as "local events with national consequences."[3] However, as the 1994 campaign illustrated, congressional elections can also be national events with national consequences. The voters' anger at Washington overrode local concerns, producing a Republican victory with potentially far-reaching consequences for national politics and policy.

The role of Congress in national policymaking is examined in this chapter. Because Congress is a large, complex organization whose members vary widely in their concerns and positions, the observations made in this chapter are necessarily broad. Nevertheless, there are discernible patterns to the policy actions of Congress and its members. One of the most significant is the pattern that emerged in deliberations over NAFTA—the adjustment of broad national goals to more specific local concerns.

This chapter describes the patterns of congressional policymaking in the context of Congress's three major functions: lawmaking, representation, and oversight. The main points made in the chapter are the following:

- ★ *Congress is limited by the lack of direction and organization usually necessary for the development of comprehensive national policies.* Congress looks to the president to initiate most broad policy programs but exerts a substantial influence on the timing and content of those programs.
- ★ *Congress is well organized to handle policies of relatively narrow scope.* Such policies are usually worked out by small sets of legislators, bureaucrats, and interest groups.
- ★ *Individual members of Congress are extraordinarily responsive to local interests and concerns, although they also respond to national interests.* These responses often take place within the context of party tendencies.
- ★ *Congress oversees the bureaucracy's administration of its laws, but this oversight function is of less concern to members of Congress than is lawmaking or representation.*
- ★ *Congress is admired by those who favor negotiation, deliberation, and the rewarding of many interests, particularly those with a local constituency base. Critics of Congress say that it hinders majority rule, fosters policy delay, and caters to special interests.*

The Lawmaking Function of Congress

lawmaking function The authority (of a legislature) to make the laws necessary to carry out the government's powers.

The Framers of the Constitution expected Congress to be the leading branch of the national government. It was to the legislature—the embodiment of representative government—that the people were expected to look for policy leadership. Moreover, Congress was granted the **lawmaking function**—the authority to make the laws necessary to carry out the powers granted to the national government. During most of the nineteenth century, Congress, not the president, was clearly the dominant national institution.[4] Aside from a few strong leaders such as Jackson and Lincoln, presidents did not play a major legislative role. In fact, Congress frequently made it clear that presidential advice was not wanted. Then, as national and international forces combined to place greater leadership and policy demands on the federal government, the president became a vital part of the national legislative process.

Today Congress and the president substantially share the lawmaking function. However, their roles differ greatly. The president's major contribution is made on the small number of broad legislative measures that arise each year in response to overarching national problems, although Congress also plays a large part in the disposition of such bills. In addition, Congress has the lead—and in many cases nearly the full say—on the narrower legislation that constitutes the great majority of the roughly 10,000 bills introduced during a two-year congressional session.

An understanding of Congress's lawmaking role requires an awareness of how laws are made. Lawmaking is an elaborate process that reflects the organizational complexity of Congress and the diffusion of power within it.

HOW A BILL BECOMES LAW

The basic steps in enacting a law are summarized in Figure 13-1. The first step in the legislative process is the creation of a bill. A **bill** is a proposed legislative act. Many bills are prepared by executive agencies, interest groups, or other outside parties, but members of Congress also draft bills and only they can formally submit a bill for consideration by their chamber. If a bill is passed by both the House and Senate and signed by the president, it becomes a **law** and thereby takes effect.

bill A proposed law (legislative act) within Congress or another legislature.

law (as enacted by Congress) A legislative proposal, or bill, that is passed by both the House and Senate and is either signed or not vetoed by the president.

From Committee Hearings to Floor Debate

Once a bill is introduced by a member of the House or Senate, it is given a number and a title. Ordinarily, the bill is then sent to the appropriate committee, which assigns it to one of its subcommittees. Most bills that reach a subcommittee are set aside on the grounds that they are not worthwhile. If a bill seems to have merit, the subcommittee will schedule hearings on it. This is a critical stage in a bill's development. The subcommittee invites testimony on the proposed legislation by lobbyists, administrators, and experts who inform members about the policy in question, provide an indication of the support the bill has, and may disclose weaknesses in the proposal. After the hearings, if the subcommittee still feels that the legislation is warranted, members recommend the bill to the full committee, which can hold additional hearings. The full committee may decide to kill the bill by taking no action on it but usually agrees with the subcommittee's recommendation, although it often alters specific provisions. In the House, both the full committee and a subcommittee can "mark up," or revise, a bill; in the Senate, markup is usually reserved for the full committee.

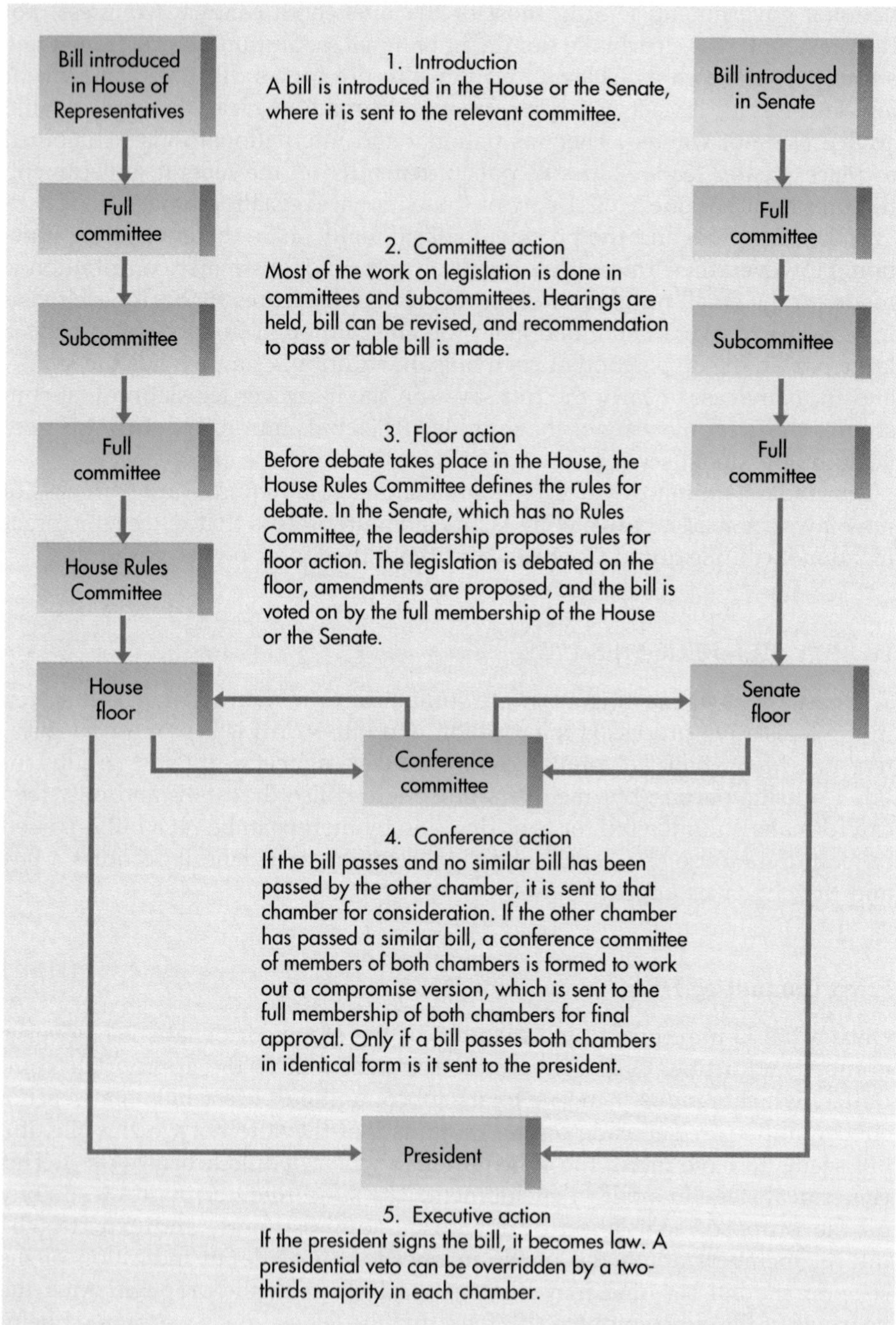

FIGURE 13-1 How a Bill Becomes a Law
Although the legislative process can be short-circuited in many ways, this diagram describes the most typical way in which a bill becomes law.

Once a bill is reported out of committee, it needs to be scheduled for floor debate by the full chamber. In the House, the Rules Committee has the power to determine when the bill will be voted on, how long the debate on the bill will last, and whether the bill will receive a "closed rule" (no amendments permitted), an "open rule" (members can propose amendments relevant to any of the bill's sections), or something in between (for example, only certain sections of the bill will be subject to amendment). The Rules Committee has this scheduling power because the House is too large to operate effectively without strict rules for the handling of legislation by the full chamber. The rules are also a means by which the majority party controls legislation. House Democrats employed closed rules to prevent Republicans from proposing amendments to major bills, a tactic House Republicans said they would forego when they took control in 1995. However, they immediately used closed rules to block amendments to Contract with America legislation, saying their pact with the voters required them to keep the proposals intact.

Most House bills of importance are scheduled for floor action under the Union Calendar, which sets the order of debate for finance and economic bills, and the House Calendar, which covers nonfinancial and noneconomic bills. There are also separate calendars for noncontroversial bills and private bills. On certain days, noncontroversial and private bills can be called up for a floor vote without action by the Rules Committee. (Private bills grant privileges or payments to individuals; for example, a private bill might allow a particular person to settle in the United States even though he or she does not meet the immigration requirements. In contrast, public bills deal with programs and broad categories of people and are what is normally meant by "legislation.")

The House and Senate require that a quorum (a majority of members) be present to conduct business on the floor. In order to expedite business, the House often adjourns to the Committee of the Whole. This committee consists of all House members and meets on the floor of the House but requires a quo-

Members of the Senate Budget Committee discuss the nation's budget. Most of the legislative work in Congress takes place in committees, which also decide the fate of most bills. (Wide World Photos)

rum of only 100 members and has relatively informal procedures. Once agreement is reached in the Committee of the Whole, the House will reconvene and proceed to vote on the legislation at hand.

cloture A parliamentary maneuver which, if a three-fifths majority votes for it, limits Senate debate to 100 hours and has the effect of defeating a filibuster.

filibuster A procedural tactic in the U.S. Senate whereby a minority of legislators prevent a bill from coming to a vote by holding the floor and talking until the majority gives in and the bill is withdrawn from consideration.

The Senate has no Rules Committee, relying instead on the majority leader to schedule its bills. All Senate bills are subject to unlimited debate unless a three-fifths majority of the full Senate votes for **cloture,** which limits debate to 100 hours. Cloture is a way of thwarting a Senate **filibuster,** a procedural tactic whereby a minority of senators prevent a bill from coming to a vote by holding the floor and talking until other senators give in and the bill is withdrawn from consideration. Filibustering is a Senate tradition that dates to the mid-1800s, and cloture was rarely invoked until recently. Cloture has become more common because filibustering itself has become more common. Two-thirds of the filibusters in the nation's history have taken place since the 1960s (see Figure 13-2), and Senate majorities have invoked cloture dozens of times in this period in order to force legislation to a vote. A number of senators attempted unsuccessfully in 1995 to get the Senate to adopt a rule that would have banned filibustering entirely.

The Senate also differs from the House in that its members can propose *any* amendment to *any* bill. Unlike House amendments, those in the Senate do not have to be germane to a bill's content. For example, a senator may propose an antiabortion amendment to a bill dealing with defense expenditures. Such amendments are called *riders* and are frequently introduced.

From Floor Debate to Enactment into Law

To become law, a bill must be passed in identical form by both the House and the Senate. About 10 percent of all proposals that are approved by both cham-

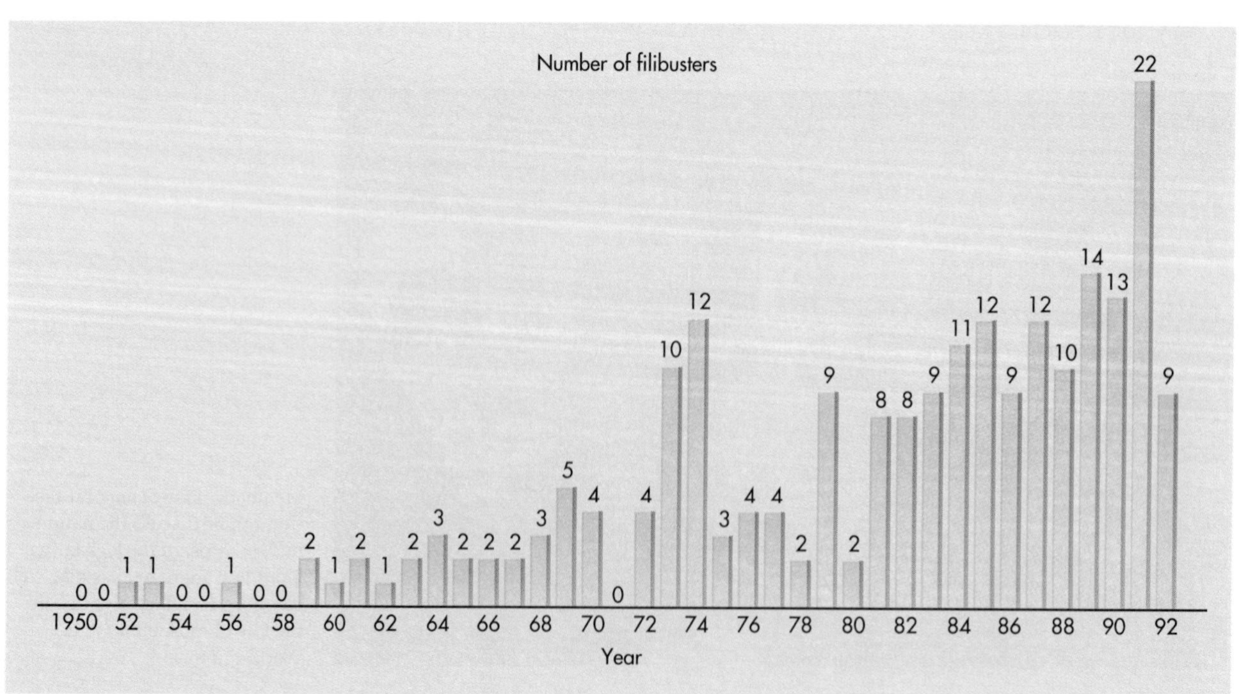

FIGURE 13-2 Senate Filibusters The use of the filibuster as a Senate tactic has increased substantially in recent decades. *Source: Democratic Study Group.*

Sam Nunn of the Armed Services Committee is one of the Senate's leading experts on national security issues. The committee system enables members of Congress to specialize in particular areas of public policy. (Gamma Liaison)

bers—the proportion is larger for major bills—differ in important respects in their House and Senate versions and are referred to a **conference committee** to resolve their differences. Slight differences in House and Senate versions of a bill are normally worked out informally, without a conference. Each conference committee is formed temporarily to handle a particular bill; its members are usually appointed from the House and Senate standing committees that worked on the bill originally. The conference committee's job is to bargain over the differences in the House and Senate versions and to develop a compromise version. It then goes to the House and Senate floors, where it can be passed, defeated, or returned to conference, but not amended. Nongermane amendments, however, can be voted on separately, so that each chamber has an opportunity to reject part of a conference committee's proposed version of a bill while accepting another part.

conference committee A temporary committee that is formed to bargain over the differences in the House and Senate versions of a bill. The committee's members are usually appointed from the House and Senate standing committees that originally worked on the bill.

After identical versions of a bill have passed both houses, the bill goes to the president for signature or veto. If the president signs the bill, it immediately becomes law. If the president exercises the *veto,* a refusal to sign a bill, it is sent back to its originating chamber with the president's reasons for the veto. Congress can *override* a veto by vote of a two-thirds majority of each chamber; the bill then becomes law. If the president fails to sign a bill within ten days (Sundays excepted) and Congress has remained in session, the bill automatically becomes law anyway. If the president fails to sign a bill within ten days and Congress has adjourned for the term, the bill does not become law. This last situation is called a *pocket veto* and forces Congress in its next session to start from the beginning; the bill must again pass both chambers and is again subject to presidential veto.

A program or project enacted into law may require an appropriation of funds. For instance, if Congress authorizes the U.S. Navy to build a new aircraft carrier, the carrier cannot be built unless Congress also appropriates the

★ STATES IN THE NATION

Representation in Congress: Each state has exactly the same Senate representation, but House representation varies widely.

	PERCENTAGE OF SEATS	
STATE	SENATE	HOUSE
Ala.	2.0%	1.6%
Alaska	2.0	0.2
Ariz.	2.0	1.4
Ark.	2.0	0.9
Calif.	2.0	12.4
Colo.	2.0	1.4
Conn.	2.0	1.4
Del.	2.0	0.2
Fla.	2.0	5.3
Ga.	2.0	2.5
Hawaii	2.0	0.5
Idaho	2.0	0.5
Ill.	2.0	4.6
Ind.	2.0	2.3
Iowa	2.0	1.2
Kan.	2.0	0.9
Ky.	2.0	1.4
La.	2.0	1.6
Maine	2.0	0.5
Md.	2.0	1.8
Mass.	2.0	2.3
Mich.	2.0	3.7
Minn.	2.0	1.8
Miss.	2.0	1.2
Mo.	2.0	2.1
Mont.	2.0	0.2
Neb.	2.0	0.7
Nev.	2.0	0.5
N.H.	2.0	0.5
N.J.	2.0	3.0
N.Mex.	2.0	0.7
N.Y.	2.0	7.1
N.C.	2.0	2.8
N.Dak.	2.0	0.2
Ohio	2.0	4.4
Okla.	2.0	1.4
Oreg.	2.0	1.2
Pa.	2.0	4.8
R.I.	2.0	0.5
S.C.	2.0	1.4
S.Dak.	2.0	0.2
Tenn.	2.0	2.1
Texas	2.0	6.9
Utah	2.0	0.7
Vt.	2.0	0.2
Va.	2.0	2.5
Wash.	2.0	2.1
W.Va.	2.0	0.7
Wis.	2.0	2.1
Wyo.	2.0	0.2

necessary funds. *This funding legislation must go through the same steps as the earlier authorizing legislation:* passage of identical appropriations bills in both houses, subject to presidential veto. Should the appropriations bill be defeated, as such bills occasionally are, the authorizing law is effectively negated.

On spending bills, the president has a line-item veto, which can be used to veto specific items in a bill without having to veto the entire bill. The veto kills an item unless the House and Senate by majority vote choose to restore it. The president then has the option of vetoing it again, in which case a two-thirds vote of the House and Senate is required to override the veto.

CONGRESS IN RESPONSE: BROAD POLICY ISSUES

The formal process by which a bill becomes law suggests that Congress and the president play legislative roles that are largely independent of each other. This impression is misleading. In practice, the lawmaking roles of Congress and the president are intertwined. Moreover, whether Congress or the president takes the lead depends on the type of policy at issue.

Some of the policy questions addressed by the national government transcend local or group boundaries. A sluggish economy, for example, affects Americans of all regions and of most occupational groups. Such issues normally call for a broad and well-coordinated policy response. Congress is not well suited to this task. Its strengths are deliberation and compromise. When a policy question requires comprehensive planning, the leadership usually comes from the president, with Congress playing a responsive role.

Fragmentation as a Policymaking Limitation

Fragmentation makes it difficult for Congress to routinely take the lead in developing policies that address broad national problems.[5] Congress is not one house but two, each with its own authority and constituency base. Neither the House nor Senate can act decisively without the other chamber's approval, and they are hardly two versions of the same thing. California and North Dakota have exactly the same representation in the Senate, but California has fifty-four House seats compared to North Dakota's one (see box: States in the Nation).

The committee system of Congress is likewise not designed to handle broad national issues. Such issues transcend committee jurisdictions, and neither the House nor the Senate has any institutionalized way for its committees to work together to originate major bills.[6]

The reelection needs of members of Congress are a further obstacle to its initiation of national solutions to national problems. It is difficult for senators or representatives to look beyond the special needs of their own districts or states. The energy crisis of the 1970s, for example, raised the issue of taxing the windfall profits that oil producers had made from higher oil prices. Members of Congress from oil-producing states such as Texas had a very different position on this issue than members from other states.[7]

To be sure, Congress sometimes does take the lead on large issues.[8] Except during Roosevelt's New Deal, Congress has been a chief source of major labor legislation, including the Taft-Hartley Act of 1947 (which legalized state right-to-work laws), the Landrum-Griffin Act of 1959 (which holds union officials to sound administrative and democratic practices), and plant-closing legislation in 1988 (which requires companies to notify workers sixty days before a plant closing or mass layoff). Congress also developed the Water Pollution Control Act of 1964, the Clean Air Act of 1963, and other environmental legislation.[9] Congress took the lead in the 1980s on tax simplification. Several proposals, including the Kemp-Roth and Bradley-Gephardt bills, became the foundation for the Tax Reform Act of 1986, a comprehensive overhaul of the personal and corporate tax codes. Federal aid to education, nuclear energy, and urban development are other areas in which Congress has at times played a leading role.[10]

A full assessment of Congress's lawmaking capacity must also take into account the Republicans' Contract with America. It included far-reaching proposals that could signal a new era of congressional leadership of national policy. It must be noted, however, that most of the contract's provisions were relatively simple ones directed at changing the rules by which the federal government operates: a balanced-budget amendment, the line-item veto, term limits, restrictions on unfunded federal mandates, and so on. These measures required Congress to make a choice but did not require it to engage in comprehensive planning. It is one thing to propose a balanced-budget amendment and quite another to develop an exhaustive master plan of the tax increases and spending cuts that would actually produce a balanced budget. The Contract with America demonstrated Congress's capacity for significant action, but not its capacity for sustained, broad-based planning. With its separate

Newt Gingrich and 300 Republican congressional candidates stand in front of the Capitol to dramatize their Contract with America. After their stunning victory in the 1994 elections, they launched an aggressive attempt to reduce the scope of the federal government, illustrating that, in some instances, Congress can take the lead on broad national issues. (Reuters/Bettmann Newsphotos)

THE MEDIA AND THE PEOPLE

CONGRESS IN THE NEWS

Speaker of the House Thomas P. "Tip" O'Neill once complained that if there was only one thing he could accomplish, it would be to persuade the news media that Congress is a coequal branch of government along with the president. O'Neill retired without achieving his goal. A Ph.D. dissertation by political scientist Richard Davis found that the presidency receives more than half again as much news coverage as Congress does. The tendency toward "presidentialization" of the news is more pronounced on national television than in newspapers but is characteristic of both mediums.

Davis also found that when Congress does get coverage from the media, it is often presented in the context of executive-legislative relations rather than as a powerful institution in its own right. In fact, two-thirds of all news about Congress is also about the president, whereas only a third of presidential news makes any reference to Congress. Even the president's leisure activities are considered newsworthy by reporters—a situation that grates on members of Congress, who believe that their institution cannot exercise its proper constitutional role as long as the media fail to report it coequally.

Of course, there are interludes when Congress is the center of media attention. When Republicans took control of Congress in 1995 and began action on their Contract with America, the press devoted most of its coverage to Congress. In the first month, President Clinton was the forgotten player; Congress received more than 5 times as much television news time. House Speaker Newt Gingrich alone got more coverage than Clinton. However, Congress tends to slip from the spotlight when it is not engaged in the passage of major legislation. Much of the work of Congress is institutional in nature and the press is less interested and adept in reporting on institutions than on people, a situation which in the long run works to the advantage of the president.

chambers and many voices, Congress is not an easy place in which to develop comprehensive programs and carry them through to passage. "Congress," Arthur Maass notes, "is limited by the lack of resources and organization typically needed for these tasks."[11]

Presidential Leadership, Congressional Response

In general, Congress depends on the president to initiate broad policy proposals, and for good reason: the president is strong in ways that Congress cannot match.

First, whereas Congress's authority is fragmented, the president is a singular authority.[12] The president seeks the advice of others within the executive branch, but ultimately the decision belongs to the chief executive. The decision may not be easy: some national problems are difficult to understand fully, let alone to manage effectively.[13] Runaway inflation admittedly bewildered President Carter, who proposed program after program—five in all—in a frantic effort to control it. Nevertheless, the president does not have to have a majority consensus within the executive branch in order to act. As sole chief executive, the president can unilaterally choose a course of action and direct assistants to prepare a legislative proposal for implementing it. Accordingly, the presidency is capable of a degree of policy planning and coordination that is far beyond the normal capacity of Congress. "It is the difference," one member of Congress said, "between an organization headed by one powerful man and a many-headed organization."[14]

Another advantage that presidents enjoy is a national political base, which focuses public attention on their actions and lends a national perspective to their choices. The president must take regional and state concerns into account, but these concerns do not affect the president's decisions as much as they influence those of members of Congress. In a way, the president's situation is the reverse of that of a member of Congress: the president cannot ignore state and local interests but must concentrate on national ones in order to retain power.

Presidential leadership means that Congress will pay attention to the White House, not that it will accept whatever the president proposes. President Clinton was in no position after the 1994 elections to demand much of anything from the Republican-controlled Congress. But even when Congress is in the hands of the opposite party, it often welcomes presidential initiatives as a starting point for its own deliberations. Frequently Congress will delay action on a problem until the president submits a plan. In the 1980s, for example, several attempts in Congress to strengthen air pollution standards were defeated by the opposition of industry and President Reagan. New legislation was finally enacted in 1990 after President Bush had proposed clean-air measures that strengthened the hand of proenvironmental forces. Congress went further than the administration desired, but Bush's plan provided the impetus that was needed to move the legislation along.

Organizational changes have improved Congress's ability to evaluate and modify presidential proposals. For example, as we mentioned in Chapter 12, the Congressional Budget Office (CBO) was created as part of the Budget and Impoundment Control Act of 1974, which also established the House and Senate budget committees. These committees initially had the task of proposing spending ceilings that, when approved by the full Congress, determined the size of the federal budget, both overall and within major categories, such as

President Bill Clinton speaks about the Mexican financial crisis during an address at the Treasury Department, as Treasury secretary Robert Rubin (center) and U.S. Trade representative Mickey Kantor listen. Despite the backing of Republican congressional leaders Newt Gingrich and Robert Dole, Clinton's proposed bailout plan for Mexico failed to gain quick approval in Congress, which forced Clinton to pursue another approach. In Congress, it is ordinarily easier for opponents to block legislation than it is for proponents to obtain quick passage of a bill. (Wide World Photos)

TABLE 13-1 Budget Ceilings Through 1993, there were separate caps on discretionary spending in the domestic, international, and defense areas; since 1994 there has been a single cap on discretionary spending.

	YEAR AND BUDGET OUTLAY (BILLIONS)						
	1991	*1992*	*1993*	*1994*	*1995*	*1996*	*1997*
Domestic spending	$200.5	$215.6	$230.7				
International spending	20.3	19.8	20.6				
Defense spending	330.8	310.3	298.9				
Total spending	$551.6	$545.7	$550.2	$542.6	$540.5	$547.5	$547.9

SOURCE: Office of Management and Budget.

defense and interior.[15] However, the federal government's fiscal problems have since prompted changes in the federal budgetary process that lessen the role of the budget committees. Under this process, the budget committees help set priorities (but not the overall level of expenditures) within the domestic, international, and military spending categories. Overall spending is capped according to a set of rules that are designed to trim the nation's chronic budget deficit and that limit Congress's budget options (entitlement spending, described in Chapter 19, is not included in the cap). The effect of these rules on budget ceilings is indicated in Table 13-1.

The budgetary process is itself revealing of the divergent policy roles of the president and Congress. The process begins in the executive branch when, in conjunction with the executive agencies, the president through the Office of Management and Budget compiles a proposed federal budget. Hundreds of agencies and thousands of programs are covered by the budget, and the president decides on a preliminary basis how much each will receive (see Chapters 14 and 15). This budget is submitted in January to Congress, which assigns it to committees (see Figure 13-3). They rework the president's budgetary proposals, usually in negotiation with the executive. The end of June is the official timetable for the completion of Congress's work on the budget, although it typically extends beyond this date. After the budget has been passed by the House and Senate and signed by the president, it takes effect on October 1, which is the start of the federal government's fiscal year.

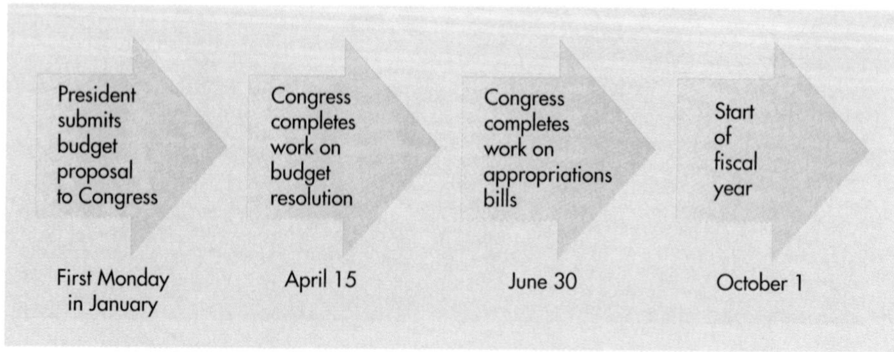

FIGURE 13-3 Annual Congressional Budget Schedule (Simplified)
Congress has about six months in which to modify the president's proposed budget.

Although Congress does not have the capacity to initiate the budget, it can have a decisive influence on the final version. Most of the budget is targeted for ongoing activities that cannot be eliminated: neither Congress nor the president would choose to close the national parks, mothball the Navy, or do anything else like that. The real choices in the budget are narrower, and once the budgetary process has reached the point where these choices are at issue, Congress can and does play a significant role. In 1995, congressional Republicans went beyond President Clinton's proposed $60 billion tax cut and $84 billion spending cut in forging a final budget. In sum, Congress can contest the president's priorities and establish priorities of its own, but it needs the president's budget recommendations as a place to begin its own work.

Of course, the same factors that make it difficult for Congress to initiate broad policy also make it difficult to persuade Congress to accept presidential initiatives. There is no permanent congressional majority waiting eagerly to line up behind the president's programs. As we will discuss in Chapter 15, Congress has rejected outright roughly half of all major presidential proposals in recent decades and has modified others substantially. Congressional majorities must constantly be created because each member has his or her own reelection base and does not have to take orders from any congressional leader. Much talk and bargaining precede the passage of comprehensive legislation, which also normally requires the stimulus of an urgent, major problem.[16] Even then, Congress may not be able to act swiftly or decisively enough. In 1995 the value of the Mexican peso suddenly plummeted, which posed an immediate threat to U.S. trade with Mexico. President Clinton quickly proposed a $40 billion loan guarantee package as a means of stabilizing the Mexican economy. Although the proposal had the backing of Republican leaders Gingrich and Dole, the bill was held up in Congress by members who were concerned with their constituents' response to a Mexican bailout. It was soon clear that Congress would not act fast enough to prevent a collapse of the Mexican economy. At this point, Clinton resorted to an alternative assistance package that was based on powers granted the president by Depression-era legislation and that did not require congressional approval.

Determined opposition from a sizable minority will often defeat a presidential initiative because so many tactics for blocking legislation are available in Congress.[17] A bill must pass through two legislative chambers that differ from each other in size, constituency, and term of office and even, at times, in majority party.[18] Inaction or rejection by either chamber is sufficient to kill a bill. If a bill can be stopped at any one of several points—House or Senate committee, House or Senate floor, authorization step or appropriations step—it usually *is* stopped, unless its backers reach a compromise with its opponents. On one occasion, Senator Dole compared Congress to a wet noodle: "If it doesn't want to move, it's not going to move."[19]

CONGRESS IN THE LEAD: NARROW POLICY ISSUES

Only a small proportion of the bills addressed by Congress deal with broad national issues of widespread interest. The rest cover smaller problems of less general interest. The leading role in the disposition of these bills falls not on

Congress is particularly adept at handling issues that are narrow in scope and that coincide with the jurisdiction of a particular committee. Price supports for agricultural products are an example. (Inga Spence/Picture Cube)

the president but on Congress and, in most cases, on a relatively small number of its members.

Congress's standing committees and their subcommittees decide most legislative issues.[20] Interest groups and bureaucratic agencies with a stake in a particular policy issue tend to concentrate their persuasive efforts on the committee that is responsible for formulating legislation in that policy area. Hearings on proposed legislation are held by a committee or subcommittee, not by the full membership of Congress. The testimony introduced at the hearings is published, but transcripts of congressional hearings run to over a million pages annually, far more than any member of Congress could read. Members of Congress consequently have little choice but to trust the judgment of committees and subcommittees.

Of course, committees and subcommittees do not operate in a vacuum.[21] Other members of Congress look for signs of trouble, as when a committee's vote divides sharply along party or ideological lines. In such a case the committee's recommendation on a bill is more likely to be debated, amended, or defeated on the floor. Committees also develop reputations for fair play. A committee that regularly seeks excessive benefits for a special interest can expect all its bills to start receiving close scrutiny on the floor. Some committees, such as the House Ways and Means Committee, pride themselves on drafting legislation that the full chamber will find acceptable. A question in each case is whether the committee has done its job in weighing the needs of a special interest against the general interest. For example, most members of Congress are not opposed in principle to special tax incentives for individuals and firms engaged in risky ventures, but they do not always feel that these entrepreneurs should be given tax breaks at the expense of other taxpayers.

Big government and social complexity have increased the pressure on committees to weigh the effects of their decisions on other policy areas and to respond to the views of people outside the committee. As we saw in Chapter

10, *iron triangles* (small, stable sets of bureaucrats, lobbyists, and legislators with a shared policy commitment) have given way in large part to *issue networks* (relatively open and fluid networks of bureaucrats, lobbyists, legislators, and policy specialists who are linked by a shared policy expertise, not by a common policy goal). Unlike iron triangles, issue networks cut across committee boundaries, with the result that members of a committee now operate less independently than they once did. Major environmental issues, for example, will draw the close attention of representatives and senators from most states and several committees.

Another congressional subgroup of importance is the *caucus,* which is an informal group of legislators with a shared interest who meet to exchange information and coordinate a legislative strategy designed to foster that interest. As we noted in Chapter 12, the traditional caucuses are composed of the party members in each chamber—the House and Senate Republican and Democratic caucuses. For our purposes in this chapter, the relevant caucuses are the newer ones that have been formed around constituent interests.[22] Some of these caucuses are regional; for example, there is a Northeast-Midwest Caucus as well as a Sunbelt Caucus. The black, Hispanic, and women's caucuses consist of members of Congress who belong to these demographic groups. Many caucuses have formed around constituency interests of members of Congress; the textile, steel, automotive, and agricultural caucuses are examples. (These caucuses are not official bodies of the Congress and are restricted in the use of congressional resources to support their activities.)

Whether the major influence on a particular bill comes from a subcommittee, committee, iron triangle, issue network, or caucus, the crucial point in each case is that a subset of Congress's members is essentially making national policy on behalf of the whole institution. Woodrow Wilson described Congress

There are dozens of informal caucuses in Congress which aim to represent the concerns of a particular constituency. In 1995, the House Republican majority eliminated funding for the activities of these caucuses. Here U.S. representatives Kwesi Mfune (D-Md.) and Jose Serrano (D-N.Y.), chairmen of the House black and Hispanic caucuses, hold a press conference to criticize the new policy. (Jay Mallin/Impact Visuals)

★ CRITICAL THINKING

Representation of National and Local Interests
Members of Congress are representatives both of the nation and of particular states and districts. These representative roles often complement each other but sometimes conflict. When should a representative place the needs of the nation ahead of the needs of his or her particular state or district? When should local needs dominate? Try to place your answers in the context of a specific issue, such as energy, trade, or defense-spending policy.

as a system of "little legislatures," referring to its dependence on subsets of members to do its work. Many of the bills that these "little legislatures" formulate will pass the full House or Senate with little or no alteration by other members. Because the legislative issues with which subsets of legislators deal are often narrow and technical, other members of Congress may neither know enough nor care enough to examine bills closely as long as they believe that the specialists are doing an acceptable job.

Congress's ability to lead on narrow issues is a substantial strength. In other democracies, the complexity of modern policymaking has led to a clear-cut subordination of the legislature to the executive. The legislature serves as an arena of debate and acts as a check on executive power but is in reality not a fully independent body. By comparison, the U.S. Congress has retained a significant lawmaking role, in part because of its constitutional separation from the executive, but also in part because its committee system gives it an independent source of policy leadership and expertise. The fragmented structure of Congress has, paradoxically, protected it from capture by the executive while at the same time making it dependent on the executive for leadership on most issues of overarching national concern.[23]

The Representation Function of Congress

In the process of making laws, the members of Congress represent various interests within American society, giving them voice and attention in the national legislature. Congress, with its individually elected, constituent-based membership and its decentralized system of power and work, has been characterized as a representative body par excellence. It expresses the concerns of countless interests, from those which would protect a local landmark from the wrecking ball to those which would devise a new banking system in the wake of the savings and loan scandal. The various members of Congress spread their time and energy across a wide range of interests. Congress is superb as a forum of expression for diverse interests.[24]

representation function The responsibility of a legislature to represent various interests in society.

The proper approach to the **representation function** has been debated since the nation's founding.[25] The writers of the Constitution tied members of Congress to their home states and districts, so that the interests of these entities would be represented in national politics. The diversity of America was to be reflected in its Congress, which would also respond to broad national concerns. A recurrent issue has been whether the primary focus of a representative should be the interests of the nation as a whole or those of his or her own constituency.[26] These interests always overlap to some degree but rarely coincide exactly. Policies that are of maximum benefit to the full society are not always equally advantageous to particular localities and can even cause harm to some constituencies. To the writers of the Constitution, the higher duty was to the nation. James Madison said in *Federalist* No. 10 that members of Congress should be those persons "least likely to sacrifice" the national interest to "local prejudice."

The local-national distinction was discussed in Chapter 3 in terms of the trustee and delegate models of representation. The trustee model holds that elected representatives are obligated to act in accordance with their own judgment as to what policies are in the best interests of society. The delegate model claims that elected representatives are obligated to carry out the expressed wishes of those who elected them to office. The choice is not a simple one, even for a legislator who is inclined toward either the delegate or trustee orientation. To be fully effective, a member of Congress must be reelected time and again, a necessity that compels him or her to pay attention to local demands. Yet, as part of the nation's legislative body, no member can easily put aside his or her judgment as to the nation's needs. In making the choice, most members of Congress, it appears, tend toward a local orientation, albeit one that is modified by both overarching and partisan concerns, as the following discussion explains.

REPRESENTATION OF STATES AND DISTRICTS: CONSTITUENCY POLITICS

Many members of Congress say that they are in Washington primarily to serve the interests of the state or district that elected them.[27] As natural as this claim may appear, it is noteworthy that members of the British House of Commons or the French National Assembly would not be likely to say the same thing: they consider their chief responsibility to be service to the nation, not to their localities. The unitary governments and strong parties of Britain and France give their politics a national orientation. The federal system and weak parties of the United States force members of Congress to take responsibility for their own reelection campaigns and to be wary of antagonizing local interests.[28] They are particularly reluctant to oppose local sentiment on issues of intense concern.[29] Support for gun control legislation, for example, has always been much lower among members of Congress from rural areas where sporting guns are part of the fabric of everyday life.

The committee system of Congress also promotes representation of local rather than national interests.[30] Although recent studies of committees indicate that the views of committee members are not radically different from the views of the full House or Senate membership,[31] committee membership is hardly random. Many senators and representatives sit on committees and subcommittees with policy jurisdictions that coincide with state or district interests. For example, farm-state legislators dominate the membership of the House and Senate Agriculture committees, and westerners dominate the Interior committees (which deal with federal lands and natural resources, most of which are concentrated in the West).

Constituency interests are also advanced by **logrolling,** the practice of trading one's vote with another member so that each gets what he or she most wants. The term dates to the early nineteenth century, when a settler would ask neighbors for help in rolling logs off land being cleared for farming, with the understanding that the settler would reciprocate when the neighbors were cutting trees. In Congress, logrolling occurs most often in committees where constituency interests vary. It has not been uncommon, for example, for agriculture committee members from livestock-producing states of the North to trade votes with committee members from the South where crops such as cotton, tobacco, and peanuts are grown.

logrolling The trading of votes between legislators so that each gets what he or she most wants.

Members of Congress are highly sensitive to local opinion on issues of keen interest to their constituents. Here Representative Charles Schumer of New York City promotes handgun control in an appearance at the National Press Club in Washington. Support for gun control is much higher among representatives from urban areas than among those from rural areas, where gun ownership is widespread. (The individual seated at left in the picture is former White House assistant James Brady, who was crtitically wounded during a handgun attack on President Reagan in 1981.) (Cynthia Johnson/Gamma Liaison)

Nevertheless, representation of constituency interests has its limits. A representative's constituents have little interest in most issues that come before Congress and even less information about them.[32] Whether the government should appropriate a few million dollars in foreign aid for Bolivia or should alter patent requirements for copying machines is not the sort of issue that local people are likely to know or care about. Moreover, members of Congress often have no choice but to go against the wishes of a significant portion of their constituency. The interests of small and large farmers in an agricultural state, for example, can differ considerably.

REPRESENTATION OF INTERESTS: GROUP POLITICS

Congress is almost ideally designed to represent interest groups. Its committees and subcommittees have legislative responsibility for policies that touch directly on particular groups, and members of Congress are receptive to lobbying efforts.

At one time, the representation of groups was nearly synonymous with the representation of constituents. The relationship of a farm-state senator to agricultural interests is an example. Such relationships are still important, but, as society has become increasingly complex and interdependent, interests have cut across constituency boundaries. The representation of groups has accordingly taken on new dimensions. One indicator is the emergence in recent decades of "outside lobbying"—pressure from the grassroots (see Chapter 10). Some of this pressure comes from the member's constituents, but much of it comes from networks of like-minded people who have a shared goal, not by virtue of living in the same state or district, but by virtue of shared values. Environmental issues, for example, typically transcend election districts.

Recent studies indicate that lobbying and PAC money result in "representation" for groups.[33] Indeed, research by Richard Hall and Frank Wayman suggests that, in some policy areas, committee members are more responsive to organized interests than to the views of unorganized voters within their districts.[34]

REPRESENTATION OF THE NATION: PARTY POLITICS

When a clear-cut and vital national interest is at stake, members of Congress can be expected to respond to that interest. The difficulty of using the common good as a routine basis for thinking about representation, however, is that Americans often disagree on what constitutes the common good and what government should do to further it.

In Congress, conflicts over national goals occur primarily along party lines. Republicans and Democrats have different perspectives on national issues because their parties differ philosophically and politically.[35] When President Clinton tackled the issue of budget-deficit reduction in 1993, for example, he chose to raise the level of taxes of persons with high incomes. His plan had strong support from congressional Democrats but was opposed by congressional Republicans, who wanted to achieve the reduction through deep cuts in federal domestic spending. Democrats and Republicans agreed that deficit reduction was vital to the national interest, but they disagreed on which groups in society should bear most of the costs.

Partisanship is the main source of cohesion and division within Congress. There are real and substantial differences between members of the two parties, such that they often end up on the opposite sides of broad national issues. Historically, nearly every major wave of national legislation has been driven by party ideology and enacted along party lines. Party is also the primary basis of ongoing conflict in Congress; on roll-call votes, a majority of Democrats often vote against a majority of Republicans (see Figure 13-4). The inci-

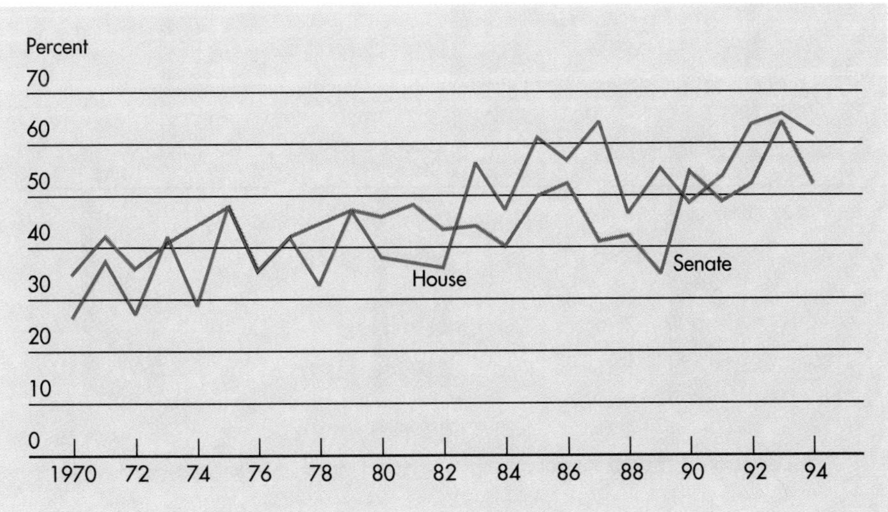

FIGURE 13-4 Percentage of Roll-Call Votes in House and Senate in Which a Majority of Democrats Voted against a Majority of Republicans, 1970–1994
Democrats and Republicans in Congress are often on opposite sides of issues; party-line voting has increased in recent years.

dence of party-line voting is occasionally very high; in the 1993–1994 term, for example, the average Senate and House Democrat voted with the Democratic majority more than 80 percent of the time, and the average Senate and House Republican voted with the Republican majority more than 80 percent of the time.[36] Divisions along party lines are common in committee voting as well.

Party differences are evident in the liberal or conservative pattern of individual members' voting records (see Figure 13-5). On major economic legislative issues during the 1993–1994 congressional sessions, for example, Senate Democrats had an average liberal score of 68 and Senate Republicans had an average conservative score of 75 (on percentile scales of 0–99). There were only three Republican senators (John Chaffee of Rhode Island, Mark Hatfield of Oregon, and James Jeffords of Vermont) who had scores that placed them on the more liberal side of the Senate. On the conservative side, there were only three Democrats (Richard Shelby and Howell Heflin, both of Alabama, and Sam Nunn of Georgia), and one of them (Shelby) switched to the GOP the day after the 1994 election.[37]

Partisanship also affects the president's relationship with Congress. Presidents serve as legislative leaders not so much for the whole Congress as for members of their own party. More than half the time, opposition and support for presidential initiatives divide along party lines (see Chapter 15).

In short, any accounting of representation in Congress that minimizes the influence of party is faulty. If constituency interests drive the thinking of many members of Congress, so also do partisan values. In fact, constituent and partisan influences are often difficult to separate in practice. In the case of conflicting interests within their constituency, members of Congress naturally side with those which align with their party. When local business and labor groups take opposing sides on issues before Congress, for example, Republican members are more likely than Democrats to back business's position.

★ CRITICAL THINKING

Party Unity and Fragmentation in Congress
The best predictor of the way individual members of Congress will respond to legislation is their party affiliation, Republican or Democratic. In view of this fact, do you think it makes sense for voters in congressional elections to "vote for the person, not the party"? Why, or why not? Then consider this question: Can anything but party unity overcome the fragmentation that besets Congress? Take the Republicans' Contract with America into account in your answer.

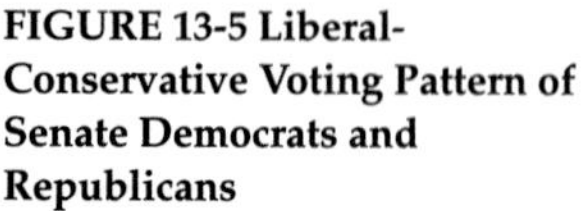

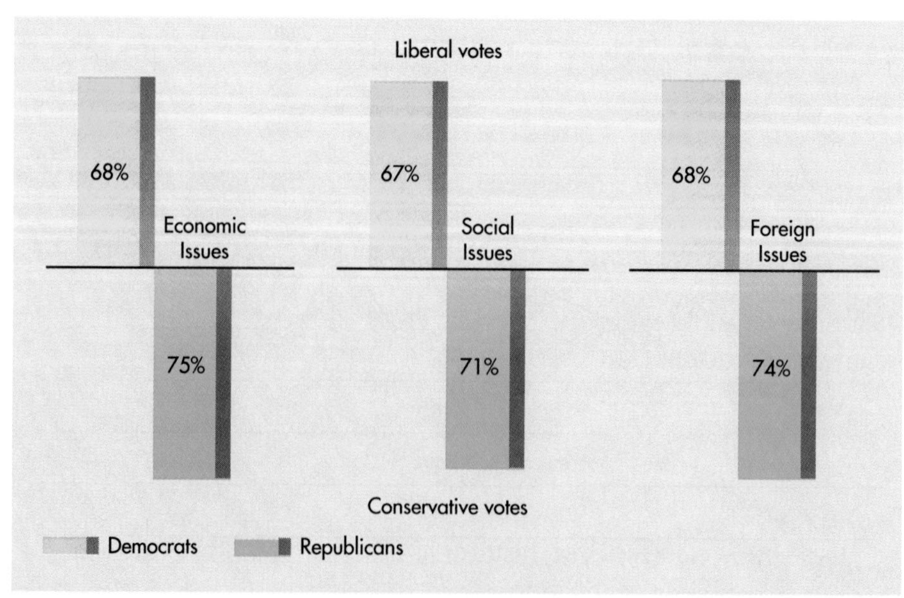

FIGURE 13-5 Liberal-Conservative Voting Pattern of Senate Democrats and Republicans
Democrats and Republicans in Congress are on opposite sides of the fence ideologically. *Source: Adapted from Richard E. Cohen and William Schneider, "Epitaph for an Era," National Journal, January 14, 1995, 83. Scores based on fifty-two Senate roll-call votes in 1994; each "yea" and "nay" vote was judged to be a liberal or conservative response, and the averages for all Senate Republicans and Democrats on all votes were then calculated.*

The Oversight Function of Congress

Although Congress enacts the laws governing the nation and appropriates the money to implement them, the administration of these laws is entrusted to the executive branch. Congress has the responsibility to see that the executive carries out the laws faithfully and spends the money properly, a supervisory activity that is referred to as the **oversight function** of Congress.

oversight function A supervisory activity of Congress that centers on its constitutional responsibility to see that the executive carries out the laws faithfully and spends appropriations properly.

THE PROCESS OF LEGISLATIVE OVERSIGHT

Oversight is carried out largely through the committee system of Congress and is facilitated by the parallel structure of the committees and the executive bureaucracy: the House International Relations and Senate Foreign Relations committees oversee the work of the State Department, the House and Senate Agriculture committees look after the Department of Agriculture, and so on. The Legislative Reorganization Act of 1970 spells out each committee's responsibility for overseeing its parallel agency:

> Each standing committee shall review and study, on a continuing basis, the application, administration, and execution of those laws, or parts of laws, the subject matter of which is within the jurisdiction of that committee.

However, oversight is easier to mandate than to carry out. If congressional committees were to try to monitor all the federal bureaucracy's activities, they would have no time or energy to do anything else. Most members of Congress are more interested in working out new laws and looking after constituents than in laboriously keeping track of the bureaucracy. Although Congress is required by law to maintain "continuous watchfulness" over programs, committees have little incentive to take a hard look at programs that they have enacted or upon which their constituent groups depend. Oversight normally is not pursued aggressively unless members of Congress are annoyed with an agency, have discovered that a legislative authorization is being grossly abused, or are reviewing a program for possible major changes.[38]

If a committee believes that an agency has mishandled a program, it can investigate the matter.[39] Congress's investigative power is not listed in the Constitution, but the judiciary has not challenged the power, and Congress has used it extensively. The Watergate, Iran-Contra, and Whitewater affairs prompted congressional investigations, which have also been used to focus attention on national problems such as crime, poverty, and health care.

When serious abuses by an agency are suspected, a committee is likely to hold hearings. Except in cases involving "executive privilege" (the right to withhold confidential information affecting national security), executive branch officials are compelled to testify at these hearings. If they refuse, they can be cited for contempt of Congress, which is a criminal offense. In 1990, in response to allegations that former Secretary of Housing and Urban Development (HUD) Samuel R. Pierce, Jr., and other HUD officials had granted illegal loans and otherwise conspired to defraud the government, a House sub-

Exercising its oversight function, the Senate Banking Committee held hearings in 1994 into the alleged involvement of President Clinton in the Whitewater scandal. Here Treasury department official Roger Altman testifies before the committee. Altman resigned his position after he was accused by senators of both parties of withholding information from the committee. (Terry Ashe/Gamma Liaison)

committee concluded that Pierce had channeled government funds to friends and lied to Congress about his actions. The subcommittee recommended that the special prosecutor investigating the HUD scandal explore the charge of perjury and bring Pierce to account if the allegation was substantiated. The investigative work of Congress and the special prosecutor helped bring about administrative and personnel changes within HUD.

Most federal programs must have their funding renewed every year, a requirement that gives Congress crucial leverage in its ongoing oversight function. If an agency has acted improperly, Congress may reduce the agency's appropriation or tighten the restrictions on the way its funds can be spent. A major difficulty is that the House and Senate Appropriations committees must review nearly the entire federal budget, a task that limits the amount of attention they can give any particular program.[40] Some programs are also reviewed for renewal each year by the House and Senate committees that authorized them. These committees, however, are busy with new legislation and are not greatly interested in conducting annual reviews of existing programs. They prefer to wait until administrative problems surface and then respond with investigations.[41]

LEGISLATIVE DEVICES FOR RESTRAINING THE BUREAUCRACY

Oversight conducted after the bureaucracy has acted has an obvious drawback: if a program has been administered improperly, some damage has already been done. For this reason, Congress in recent years has developed ways of limiting the bureaucracy's discretion in advance. One method is to include detailed instructions in appropriations bills. Department of Defense appropriations, for example, now often specify cost-accounting procedures that bureaucrats must use. Such instructions serve to limit bureaucrats' flexi-

HOW THE UNITED STATES COMPARES

NATIONAL LEGISLATURES: GOOD INFLUENCE OR BAD?

The past quarter century has been a difficult period for western democracies. Although they have seen the triumph of democratic capitalism over communist socialism abroad, they have faced disruptive social and economic forces at home. Perhaps at no time in history has social and economic change occurred at such a rapid pace, straining the capacity of governments to respond. Traditional institutions, from political parties to families, have weakened dramatically, and the global marketplace, postindustrial dislocation, and the surge of women into the work force have radically altered economic relationships. The comfortable policies of the past have been inadequate to the new challenges.

In any period of disruptive change, the public tends to express its anxieties through dissatisfaction with governing institutions. The public response is exaggerated in modern times by the expectation that government should be able to resolve society's problems. Although history suggests that adaptation to major social and economic change is slow and costly, there is a tendency today to believe that it can occur quickly and painlessly if government will only do its job properly. When the adaptation is neither quick nor painless, the predictable response is to blame government. In the case of the United States, this response can be seen, for example, in the tendency toward one-term presidencies. Whereas presidents were once nearly assured of a second term, reelection is no longer a certainty. Congress has also been a target of the public's anger; confidence in the institution has declined substantially from the level of three or four decades ago. Citizens elsewhere are also not very happy with their national legislatures, as indicated by a 1994 Times-Mirror Center survey that asked respondents in several western democracies whether their national legislature has been mainly a good influence or bad influence on the way things are going in the country:

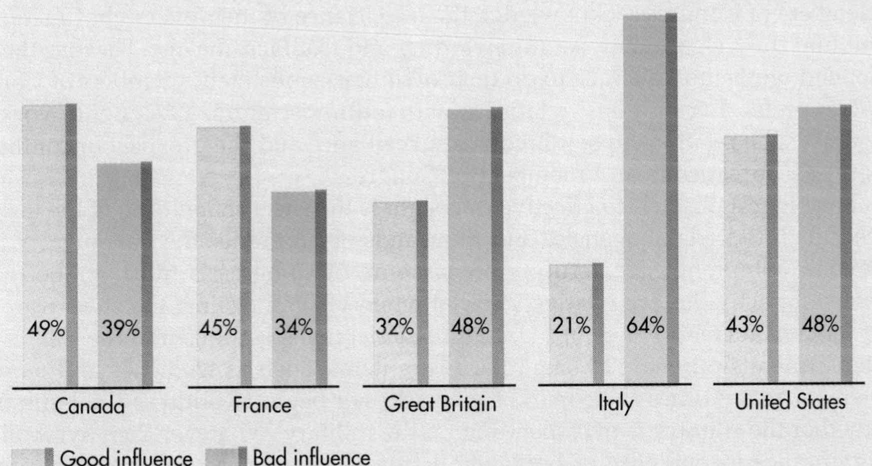

SOURCE: "Mixed Message about Press Freedom on Both Sides of the Atlantic," Times-Mirror Center for the People and the Press, Washington, D.C., March 16, 1994, p. 55. Respondents who voluntarily said the legislature was both a good and a bad influence accounted for about 10 percent of the samples and were apportioned equally between the two categories.

bility when they spend funds on programs and provide a firmer basis for holding them accountable if they disregard the intent of Congress.

Another oversight device is the "sunset law," which fixes a date on which a program will end (or "fade into the sunset") unless it is renewed by Congress.[42] Such laws are a response to the fact that any program, once established, tends to be perpetuated by the bureaucrats who run it and by the interests that gain from it. Sunset provisions help prevent a program from outliving its usefulness because, once its expiration date is reached, Congress can reestablish it only by passing a new law.

The "legislative veto" is a more intrusive and controversial oversight tool.[43] It requires that an executive agency have the approval of Congress before it can take a specified action. The Department of Defense, for example, cannot close a military facility unless Congress permits it to do so. Legislative vetoes are under challenge as an unconstitutional infringement on executive authority, and their future is unclear. (Congress's oversight tools are discussed more fully in Chapter 16.)

As indicated in Chapter 12, Congress has come to rely heavily on the General Accounting Office (GAO) to oversee executive agencies' spending and, more recently, their program performance. Some of the more blatant misuses of federal funds, particularly in the Department of Defense, have been uncovered by the GAO and then referred to the appropriate committees of Congress.

OBSTACLES TO OVERSIGHT

Members of Congress acknowledge the importance of their oversight function but find the task a somewhat unrewarding and troublesome one. Because they depend on the bureaucracy to do their own work effectively, members of Congress prefer harmonious relations with administrators. Oversight works against such relationships; it involves surveillance and the prospect of conflict between bureaucrats and members of Congress.

The biggest obstacle to effective oversight is the sheer magnitude of the task. With its hundreds of agencies and thousands of programs, the bureaucracy is beyond comprehensive scrutiny. Even some of Congress's most publicized oversight activities are relatively trivial when viewed against the sheer scope of the bureaucracy. For example, congressional investigations into the Defense Department's purchase of small hardware items, such as wrenches and hammers, at many times their market value do not begin to address the issue of whether the country is overspending on the military. Whatever their symbolic significance as evidence of bureaucratic waste, overpriced hand tools represent pocket change in a defense budget of billions of dollars. The real oversight question is whether the defense budget as a whole provides cost-effective national security. It is a question that Congress has neither the capacity nor the determination to investigate fully.

Oversight is a useful political tool for a party when it has a congressional majority but does not control the presidency. Through oversight, Congress can pressure the administration to alter its policies. In 1982, in response to allegations that the Environmental Protection Agency (EPA) was permitting some corporations to circumvent laws regulating the disposal of toxic wastes, Congress scheduled hearings on the question. When the EPA's top administrators claimed they had President Reagan's backing and refused to provide requested information, Congress issued subpoenas. When it was rebuffed again, Congress forced the resignation of the EPA administrator, Anne Burford, and pursued the prosecution of another agency official, Rita Lavelle, who was convicted and sentenced to a six-month prison term. As a result of the investigation, the EPA brought its activities more closely into line with existing laws.

Congress: Too Much Pluralism?

The congressional debate in 1995 on the line-item veto revealed a lot about the institution. A line-item veto was needed, proponents said, because Congess lacked the discipline to say no to constituent and special interests. The spiraling national debt could be slowed by a curb on pork barrel spending, but Congress seemed unable to exercise this restraint on its own. Supporters of the veto were willing to surrender part of their institution's power of the purse to the president, who would be able to veto those provisions of an appropriations bill that seemed unnecessary or excessive without killing the entire bill. The discipline to bring pork barreling under control would come from outside the Congress rather than from within.

As the example illustrates, Congress is an institution torn between service to the nation and to the separate constituencies within it. Its members have

YOUR TURN

DIVIDED GOVERNMENT

The Question:

In general, do you think it is better for the same political party to control both the Congress and the presidency so that they can work together more closely, or do you think it is better to have different political parties controlling the Congress and the presidency, to prevent either one from going too far?

Better for different parties to control Congress and presidency	Better for same party to control Congress and presidency

What Others Think: This particular question was asked in a 1990 NBC News/Wall Street Journal poll; 23 percent of the respondents said it is better to have one party in control, 67 percent said divided control was preferable, and 10 percent were unsure. Similar questions at other times have produced somewhat different results. In 1993, for example, when Congress and the presidency were controlled by the same party, public support for divided government was less substantial (in 1990, the Republicans held the presidency, and the Democrats controlled the Congress).

Comment: Since the late 1960s, the United States has had divided government more often than not, and some analysts suggest that Americans actually prefer it to the situation where one party controls both the presidency and the Congress. Divided government is a substantial check on executive and legislative power but can also result in deadlock and delay. Divided government also clouds the question of accountability: when people are dissatisfied with Washington, who should they blame—the president or Congress? When control of both institutions is in the hands of one party, accountability is a clearer issue. For this and other reasons, most political scientists argue that divided control is inferior to the situation where one party holds both the presidency and the Congress.

responsibility for the nation's laws. Yet they depend for reelection on the voters of their states and districts and are highly responsive to constituency interests. This focus is facilitated by the committee system, which is organized around particular interests. Agriculture, labor, education, banking, and commerce are among the interests represented through this system. It is hard to conceive of a national legislature structured to respond to special interests more closely than does the Congress of the United States. It is even harder to conceive of a national legislature that gives as much real power to these interests through committees as does the Congress.

Critics of Congress argue that it is too pluralistic and not sufficiently majoritarian. This criticism is quieted from time to time by a strong majoritarian thrust in Congress, as in the case of the Great Society programs of the 1960s or the more recent Contract with America. But these periods are atypical. Congress is ordinarily more responsive to a plurality of interests.

Pluralists argue that Congress should be responsive to constituent interests. The United States has in the presidency a majoritarian institution, and Congress is where the nation's diversity finds representation. From the pluralist perspective, Congress adds a necessary balance to the nation's politics. To its critics, on the other hand, Congress is so responsive to particular interests that it cannot ordinarily deal adequately with national policy needs. The welfare system would be an example. Since the early 1970s, liberals and conservatives

Congress is an institution where national and constituency interests often collide. Here demonstrators disrupt a luncheon where House Speaker Newt Gingrich was scheduled to speak. Waving empty cafeteria trays, the demonstrators protested changes in school lunch programs as part of the GOP's plan to reduce the budget deficit. The protest forced the cancellation of Gingrich's speech. (Wide World Photos)

alike have contended that the welfare system requires a drastic overhaul. Until recently, however, Congress had done little more than tinker with welfare reform.

The fact is, Congress cannot at once be an institution that is highly responsive to overarching national problems and also highly responsive to local and particular concerns. In a real sense, the strengths of Congress are also its weaknesses. The features of Congress that make it responsive to constituent interests are the very same ones that make it difficult for Congress to act as a strong instrument of the majority. In a large and diverse nation, there is merit in an institution that is sensitive to the local and the particular. The enduring question is whether Congress leans too far in that direction.

Summary

The major function of Congress is to enact legislation. Congress is not well suited to the development of broad and carefully coordinated policy programs. Its divided chambers, fragmented leadership, and committee structure, as well as the concern of its members with state and district interests, make it difficult for Congress to routinely initiate solutions to broad national problems. Congress often looks to the president for such proposals but has strong influence on the timing and content of major national programs.

Congress is more adept at handling legislation dealing with problems of narrow interest. Legislation of this sort is decided mainly in congressional committees, where interested legislators, bureaucrats, and groups concentrate their efforts on issues of mutual concern. Narrowly focused bills emerging from committees usually win the support of the full House or Senate. Committee recommendations are always subject to checks on the floor, and larger policy groups—issue networks and caucuses—have increasingly intruded on the committee process. Nevertheless, most narrow policy issues are settled primarily by subgroups of legislators rather than by the full Congress, although the success of these subgroups in the long run can depend on their responsiveness to broader interests.

A second function of Congress is the representation of various interests. Members of Congress are highly sensitive to the state or district on which they depend for reelection. As a result, interest groups that are important to a member's state or district are strongly represented in Congress. Members of Congress do respond to overriding national interests, but for many of them, local concerns generally come first. National representation tends to work through party representation, particularly on issues that have traditionally divided the Democratic and Republican parties and their constituencies.

Congress's third function is oversight, the supervision and investigation of the way the bureaucracy is implementing legislatively mandated programs. Oversight is usually less rewarding than lawmaking or representation and receives correspondingly less attention from members of Congress.

Congress is a slow and deliberative institution. It is also a powerful one; the process by which a bill becomes law is such that legislative proposals can be defeated or stymied rather easily. Congress is admired by those who believe that broad national legislation should reflect a wide range of interests, including local ones; that policies developed through a lengthy process of compromise and negotiation are likely to be sound; and that minorities should be able to obtain selective benefits and should have ways of blunting the impulses of the majority. Critics of the congressional process argue that, too often, it serves special interests, blunts majority opinion, and impedes a timely response to pressing national needs.

Major Concepts

bill
cloture
conference committee
filibuster
law
lawmaking function
logrolling
oversight function
representation function

Suggested Readings

Fenno, Richard F., Jr. *Home Style: House Members in Their Districts.* Boston: Little, Brown, 1978. A penetrating analysis of the varying relationships between House members and their constituents.

Harris, Fred R. *Deadlock or Decision: The U.S. Senate and the Rise of National Politics.* New York: Oxford University Press, 1993. An insightful study of the changing nature of the U.S. Senate.

Johnson, Loch K. *A Season of Inquiry.* Chicago: Dorsey Press, 1988. An insightful study of congressional oversight of intelligence activities.

Kingdon, John W. *Congressmen's Voting Decisions.* New York: Harper & Row, 1981. A study of congressional voting based in part on surveys of members of Congress.

Palazzolo, Daniel J. *The Speaker and the Budget: Leadership in the Post-Reform House of Representatives.* Pittsburgh, Pa.: University of Pittsburgh Press, 1992. An extensive analysis of the role of the Speaker in the budgetary process.

Reid, T. R. *Congressional Odyssey.* San Francisco: Freeman, 1980. A lively and insightful study of the passage of a Senate bill.

Rosen, Bernard. *Holding Government Bureaucracies Accountable,* 2d ed. New York: Praeger, 1989. An assessment of Congress's oversight function.

Smith, Steven S. *The American Congress.* Boston: Houghton Mifflin, 1995. A comprehensive text on Congress and its members.

Thomas, Sue. *How Women Legislate.* New York: Oxford University Press, 1994. A well-researched study that indicates women legislators pursue different policy agendas than men.

CHAPTER 14

PRESIDENTIAL OFFICE AND ELECTION: LEADING THE NATION

[The president's] is the only voice in national affairs. Let him once win the admiration and confidence of the people, and no other single voice will easily overpower him.

—Woodrow Wilson[1]

In 1994 Bill Clinton demonstrated why the presidency has been described as "both the most dynamic and most dangerous of our political institutions."[2] Ignoring complaints from Congress that it had a legitimate voice in the decision, Clinton prepared to invade Haiti, whose military generals had taken power in a coup that unseated the nation's constitutionally elected president. The generals brutalized and murdered their opponents and caused a tide of refugees to depart for the United States on ramshackle boats. Many of those fleeing were lost at sea. When an embargo imposed by the United Nations failed to persuade the Haitian generals to leave office, Clinton readied an invasion force. Casualties were anticipated, and there were fears that the United States would get bogged down in the running of Haiti for years to come. Critics also questioned whether the United States had any business invading a country simply because it had one of the world's many brutal regimes.

Although the worst could have happened in Haiti, it did not. Within the hour that U.S. combat troops were scheduled to invade the island, the generals agreed to leave office. No lives were lost when the troops landed, and within months most of the U.S. forces in Haiti were on their way home. A potential disaster had become a policy success.

The characterization of the presidency as "both the most dynamic and most dangerous" of U.S. political institutions stems from the leeway inherent in the office's constitutional authority.[3] As the sole head of the executive branch, the president is able to act more quickly and decisively than the Congress; this advantage is offset by ambiguity about the proper limits of presidential power. The writers of the Constitution sought to establish an independent presidency but also wanted to constrain the powers of the office. The Framers knew what they wanted from a president—national leadership, statesmanship in foreign affairs, command in time of war or insurgency, enforcement of the laws—but could devise only general phrases to describe the president's constitutional authority. Compared with Article I, which enumerates Congress's specific powers, Article II of the Constitution contains relatively vague statements on the president's powers.

The Constitution vests executive authority in a single chief executive. The Framers debated briefly the possibility of a three-person executive (one president each from the northern, middle, and southern states) but rejected the idea on the grounds that a joint office would be sapped of its energy by constant infighting. The Framers worried that a single executive might become too powerful but believed that adequate protection against such a threat was provided by the separation of powers and the president's selection by electors. The president would represent the people but would not be chosen directly by them. This arrangement would protect the chief executive against excessive public demands and at the same time deny the president the reserve of power that direct public election could confer.

The Framers did not anticipate that the president would someday be chosen through popular election. The Framers also did not foresee all the leadership implications of the president's national office. Senators and representatives are chosen by voters within a single state or district, a limitation that diminishes the claim of any one of them to national leadership. Moreover, since the House and the Senate are separate bodies, no member of Congress can speak for the whole institution. The president, in contrast, is a nationally elected official and the sole chief executive. These features of the office enabled presidents, as the executive demands on government increased during the twentieth century, to assume powers and leadership that helped transform the presidency into a permanently more powerful office.

This chapter explains why the presidency has become a stronger office than the Framers envisioned. The chapter also examines the presidential selection process and the staffing of the modern presidency, both of which contribute to the president's prominence in the American political system. The main ideas of the chapter are these:

- ★ *Public expectations, national crises, and changing national and world conditions have required the presidency to become a strong office.* Underlying this development is the public support that the president acquires from being the only nationally elected official.
- ★ *The modern presidential election campaign is a marathon affair in which self-selected candidates must plan for a strong start in the nominating contests and center their general election strategies on media, issues, and a baseline of support.* The lengthy campaign process serves to heighten the public's sense that the presidency is at the center of the U.S. political system.
- ★ *The modern presidency could not operate without a large staff of assistants, experts, and high-level managers, but the sheer size of this staff makes it impossible for the president to exercise complete control over it.*

Foundations of the Modern Presidency

Over the course of American history, each of the president's constitutional powers has been extended in practice beyond the Framers' intention. For example, the Constitution grants the president command of the nation's military, but only Congress can declare war. In *Federalist* No. 69 Alexander Hamilton wrote that a surprise attack on the United States was the only justification for war by presidential action. President Thomas Jefferson disputed even this exception, claiming that he could respond to invasion with only defensive action unless Congress declared war. Since Jefferson, however, the nation's presidents have sent troops into military action abroad more than 200 times. Of the twelve wars included in that figure, only five were declared by Congress.[4] Each of America's most recent wars—the Korean, Vietnam, and Persian Gulf wars—was undeclared.

The Constitution also empowers the president to act as diplomatic leader with the authority to receive ambassadors and the power to initiate diplomatic relations with other nations. The president is further empowered to appoint U.S. ambassadors and to negotiate treaties with other countries, subject to approval by the Senate. The Framers anticipated that Congress would have responsibility for developing foreign policy, while the president's job would be to oversee its implementation.[5] However, the president has become the principal architect of U.S. foreign policy and has even acquired the power to make treatylike arrangements with other nations, in the form of executive agreements. In 1937 the Supreme Court ruled that such agreements, signed and approved only by the president, have the same legal status as treaties, which require approval by a two-thirds vote of the Senate.[6] Since World War II, presidents have negotiated more than 10,000 executive agreements, as compared with fewer than 1,000 treaties ratified by the Senate.[7]

The Constitution also vests "executive power" in the president. This includes the responsibility to execute the laws faithfully and to appoint major administrators, such as heads of the various departments of the executive branch. In *Federalist* No. 76 Hamilton indicated that the president's real authority as chief executive was to be found in this appointive capacity. Presidents have indeed exercised substantial power through their appointments, but they have found their administrative authority—the power to execute the laws—to be of even greater value, because it enables them to determine how laws will be interpreted and applied. President Ronald Reagan used his executive power to *prohibit* the use of federal funds by family-planning clinics that offered abortion counseling. President Bill Clinton exerted the same power to *permit* the use of federal funds for this purpose. The *same* act of Congress was the basis for each of these actions.

Finally, the Constitution provides the president with legislative authority, including use of the veto and the opportunity to recommend proposals to Congress. The Framers expected this authority to be used in a limited and largely negative way. George Washington acted as the Framers anticipated: he proposed only three legislative measures and vetoed only two acts of Congress. Modern presidents have a different, more activist view of their legislative role. They routinely submit legislative proposals to Congress and often

THE PRESIDENT'S CONSTITUTIONAL AUTHORITY

Commander in chief. Article II, section 2: "The President shall be commander in chief of the Army and Navy of the United States, and of the militia of the several states."

Chief executive. Article II, section 2: "He may require the opinion, in writing, of the principal officer in each of the executive departments, upon any subject relating to the duties of their respective offices, and he shall have power to grant reprieves and pardons for offences against the United States, except in cases of impeachment."

Article II, section 2: "He shall have power, by and with the advice and consent of the Senate, to make treaties, provided two thirds of the senators present concur; and he shall nominate, and by and with the advice and consent of the Senate, shall appoint ambassadors, other public ministers and consuls, judges of the Supreme Court, and all other officers of the United States, whose appointments are not herein otherwise provided for, and which shall be established by law."

Article II, section 2: "The President shall have power to fill up all vacancies that may happen during the recess of the Senate, by granting commissions which shall expire at the end of their next session."

Article II, section 3: "He shall take care that the laws be faithfully executed, and shall commission all the officers of the United States."

Chief diplomat. Article II, section 2: "He shall have power, and with the advice and consent of the Senate, to make treaties, provided two thirds of the senators present concur."

Article II, section 3: "He shall receive ambassadors and other public ministers."

Legislative promoter. Article II, section 3: "He shall from time to time give to the Congress information of the state of the Union, and recommend to their consideration such measures as he shall judge necessary and expedient; he may, on extraordinary occasions, convene both houses, or either of them, and in case of disagreement between them, with respect to the time of adjournment, he may adjourn them to such time as he shall think proper."

veto legislation they find disagreeable. The champion of the veto was Franklin D. Roosevelt, who during his twelve years in office rejected 635 acts of Congress.

The presidency is a more powerful office than the Framers envisioned for many reasons, but two features of the office in particular—national election and singular authority—have enabled presidents to make use of changing demands on government to claim the position of national leader.

AN EMERGING TRADITION OF STRONG PRESIDENTS

The first president to assert forcefully a claim to popular leadership was Andrew Jackson, who had been swept into office in 1828 on a tide of public support that broke the hold that the upper classes had had on the presidency until then. Jackson used his popular backing to challenge Congress's claim to national policy leadership, contending that he was "the people's tribune."

Whig theory A theory that prevailed in the nineteenth century and held that the presidency was a limited or restrained office whose occupant was confined to expressly granted constitutional authority.

Jackson's view of the presidency, however, was not shared by most of his successors during the nineteenth century, because national conditions did not routinely call for strong presidential leadership. The prevailing conception of the presidency was the **Whig theory.** In this view, the presidency was a limited or constrained office whose occupant was confined to the exercise of expressly granted constitutional authority. The president had no implicit powers for dealing with national problems but was primarily an administrator, charged with carrying out the expressed will of Congress. "My duty," said

President James Buchanan, a Whig adherent, "is to execute the laws . . . and not my individual opinions."[8]

Theodore Roosevelt rejected the Whig tradition when he took office in 1901; he attacked the business trusts, pursued an aggressive foreign policy, and pressured Congress to adopt progressive domestic policies. Roosevelt embraced the **stewardship theory,** which calls for a strong, assertive presidential role that is confined only at points specifically prohibited by law, not by undefined inherent restrictions.[9] As "steward of the people," Roosevelt said, he was obliged "to do anything that the needs of the Nation demanded unless such action was forbidden by the Constitution or by the laws."[10]

stewardship theory A theory that argues for a strong, assertive presidential role, with presidential authority limited only at points specifically prohibited by law.

Roosevelt's image of a strong presidency was shared by Woodrow Wilson, but his other immediate successors reverted to the Whig notion of the limited presidency.[11] Herbert Hoover's restrained conception of the presidency prevented him from taking decisive action even during the economic devastation that followed the Wall Street crash of 1929. Hoover argued that he lacked the constitutional authority to establish public relief programs for jobless and penniless Americans.

Hoover's successor, Franklin D. Roosevelt, shared the stewardship theory of his distant cousin Theodore Roosevelt, and FDR's New Deal signaled the end of the limited presidency. Today the presidency is an inherently strong office.[12] The modern presidency becomes a more substantial office in the hands of a persuasive leader such as Lyndon Johnson or Ronald Reagan, but even a less forceful person such as Jimmy Carter or George Bush is now expected to act assertively. This expectation not only is the legacy of former strong presidents but also is the result of the need for presidential leadership in periods of national crisis and of changes that have occurred in the federal government's national and international policy responsibilities.

THE NEED FOR PRESIDENTIAL LEADERSHIP IN NATIONAL CRISES

National crises have enabled presidents to assume powers beyond those provided in the Constitution. Emergencies usually demand speed of action and singleness of purpose. Congress—a large, divided, and often unwieldly institution—is poorly suited to such a response. In contrast, the president, as sole head of the executive branch, can act quickly and decisively. Abraham Lincoln's response to the outbreak of the Civil War is a notable example. Acting on his own authority, Lincoln called up the militia, blockaded southern ports, increased the size of the Army and Navy, ordered conscription, suspended the writ of habeas corpus, and placed part of the nation under martial law. Some of these actions (for example, suspension of the writ of habeas corpus) are not clearly assigned to the president by the Constitution. Nevertheless, when Congress convened in 1861, after Lincoln's war orders had already taken effect, it acknowledged the validity of his actions by passing a law stating that his directives had the same authority "as if they had been issued and done under the previous express authority and direction of the Congress of the United States."[13]

★ CRITICAL THINKING

The Increase in Presidential Power

It has been said that constitutionality bends to necessity. How does the axiom help explain the increased power and responsibility that the president has acquired during the twentieth century? Is the axiom strictly accurate, given that the provisions for presidential authority in Article II of the Constitution are relatively vague in any case?

Similarly, Congress formally endorsed Franklin Roosevelt's directive, issued in the wake of the Japanese attack on Pearl Harbor in 1941, that ordered the

Japanese-Americans assemble for evacuation from San Francisco to inland detention camps in April 1942. President Franklin Roosevelt ordered this drastic program in the crisis atmosphere that followed the Japanese attack on Pearl Harbor. His order was upheld by the Supreme Court as a lawful exercise of the president's authority as commander in chief. (Library of Congress)

evacuation of 135,000 Japanese Americans living on the West Coast. Fearing subversive activities among these Japanese Americans, Roosevelt instructed federal authorities to seize their property and relocate them in detention camps farther inland until the war's end. Japanese Americans challenged the legality of Roosevelt's order, but the Supreme Court upheld their forced evacuation from coastal areas (although it voided their involuntary detention).[14]

In such instances the other branches of government have had little choice but to accept presidential claims to extraordinary powers. Constitutionality has given way to perceived necessity in times of crisis. Lincoln's critics called him a dictator, but a congressional majority affirmed that his extraconstitutional actions had been necessary to save the Union.

National crises have had a lasting impact on the conduct of the executive office. Modern presidents are expected to be powerful in part because some of their predecessors assumed extraordinary powers in critical times. Lincoln, Roosevelt, and other strong presidents left a legacy for later presidents. Every strong president has seen the power of the office as flowing from a special relationship with the American people. As Harry S Truman noted in his memoirs, "I believe that the power of the President should be used in the interest of the people and in order to do that the President must use whatever power the Constitution does not expressly deny him."[15]

THE NEED FOR PRESIDENTIAL LEADERSHIP OF AN ACTIVIST GOVERNMENT

During most of the nineteenth century the United States did not need a strong president. The federal government's policymaking role was small, as was its bureaucracy. Moreover, the nation's major issues were of a sectional nature (especially the North-South split over slavery) and thus suited to action by Congress, which represented state and local interests. The U.S. government's role in world affairs was also small.

Today the situation has greatly changed. The federal government has such broad national and international responsibilities that strong leadership from presidents is essential.

Foreign Policy Leadership

The president has always been the foreign policy leader of the United States, but during the nation's first century that role was a rather undemanding one. The United States avoided getting entangled in the turbulent politics of Europe, and though it was involved in foreign trade, its major preoccupation was its internal development. By the end of the nineteenth century, however, the nation was seeking to expand the world market for its goods, and the size and growing industrial power of the United States was attracting more attention from other nations. President Theodore Roosevelt advocated an American economic empire, looking south toward Latin America and west toward Hawaii, the Philippines, and China (the "Open Door" policy) for new markets. However, the United States' tradition of isolationism remained a powerful influence on national policy. The United States fought in World War I but immediately thereafter demobilized its armed forces. Over President Woodrow Wilson's objections, Congress then voted against the entry of the United States into the League of Nations.

World War II fundamentally changed the nation's international role and the president's role in foreign policy. In 1945 the United States emerged as a global

Harry S Truman's presidency was characterized by bold foreign policy initiatives. He authorized the use of nuclear weapons against Japan in 1945, created the Marshall Plan as the basis for the economic reconstruction of postwar Europe, and sent U.S. troops to fight in Korea in 1950. Truman is shown here greeting British Prime Minister Winston Churchill at a Washington airport in early 1952. (UPI/Bettmann Newsphotos)

superpower, a giant in world trade, and the recognized leader of the non-communist world. The United States today has a military presence in nearly every part of the globe and an unprecedented interest in trade balances, energy supplies, and other international issues affecting the nation's economy.[16]

The effects of these developments on America's political institutions have been largely one-sided. Because of the president's constitutional authority as chief diplomat and military commander and because of the special demands of foreign policy leadership, the president, not Congress, has taken the lead in addressing the United States' increased responsibilities in the world. (The special demands of foreign policy and how they work to the president's advantage are discussed more fully in Chapter 15.)

Domestic Policy Leadership

The change in the president's domestic leadership has also been substantial. Throughout most of the nineteenth century Congress jealously guarded its constitutional powers, making it clear that domestic policy was its business. James Bryce wrote in the 1880s that Congress paid no more attention to the president's views on legislation than it did to the editorial positions of prominent newspaper publishers.[17]

By the early twentieth century, however, the national government was taking on regulatory and policy responsibilities imposed by the nation's transition from an agrarian to an industrial society, and stronger presidential leadership was becoming necessary. In 1921 Congress conceded that it lacked the centralized authority to coordinate the growing national budget and enacted the Budget and Accounting Act, which provided for an executive budget.[18] Federal departments and agencies would no longer submit their annual budget requests directly to Congress. The president would oversee the initiation of the budget, developing the various agencies' requests into a comprehensive budgetary proposal, which would then be submitted to Congress as a baseline for its deliberations.

During the Great Depression of the 1930s, Franklin D. Roosevelt's New Deal responded to the public's demand for economic relief with a broad program that involved a level of policy planning and coordination that was beyond the capacity of Congress. In addition to initiating public works projects and social welfare programs aimed at providing immediate relief, the New Deal made the government a partner in nearly every aspect of the nation's economy. If economic regulation was to work, unified and continuous policy leadership was needed, and only the president could provide it. Later Congress institutionalized the president's economic role with the Employment Act of 1946, which assigns to the federal government an ongoing responsibility "to use all practicable means . . . to promote maximum employment, production, and purchasing power."

Roosevelt's power, like that of the strong presidents before him, rested on the support of the American people.[19] In the early 1930s the nation was in such desperate condition that Americans would have supported almost anything Roosevelt did. "If he burned down the Capitol," said the humorist Will Rogers, "we would cheer and say 'Well, we at least got a fire started.' "[20]

Presidential authority has continued to grow since Roosevelt's time. In response to pressures from the public, the national government's role in such areas as education, health, welfare, safety, and protection of the environment has expanded greatly, which in turn has created additional demands for presidential leadership.[21] Big government, with its emphasis on comprehensive planning and program coordination, favors executive authority at the expense of legislative authority. *All* democracies have seen a shift in power from their legislature to their executive. In Britain, for example, the prime minister has taken on responsibilities that once belonged to the cabinet or the parliament.

The president's preeminence as domestic policy leader does not mean that Congress no longer plays a significant role.[22] As we saw in Chapter 13, major policy initiatives do emanate from Congress, which also modifies or rejects many presidential proposals.[23] Moreover, Congress tends to seek the president's leadership only on particular types of legislative measures—principally those which address truly national issues from a national perspective.[24] (The president's domestic policy role is discussed further in Chapter 15.)

Choosing the President

As the president's policy and leadership responsibilities changed during the nation's history, so too did the process of electing presidents. The changes do not parallel each other exactly, but they are related politically and philosophically. As the presidency drew ever closer to the people, their role in selecting the president grew ever more important.

THE DEVELOPMENT OF THE PRESIDENTIAL SELECTION SYSTEM

The process by which the United States selects its chief executive has evolved through four cumulative systems (summarized in Table 14-1 and described below), each of which resulted from popular reforms that were aimed chiefly at granting the American people a larger say in choosing the president.[25] The justification for each of the reforms was **legitimacy,** the idea that the selection of the president should be based on the expressed will of the people.[26]

legitimacy (of election) The idea that the selection of officeholders should be based on the expressed will of the people.

The First and Second Systems: Electors and Party Conventions

The delegates to the constitutional convention of 1787 were steadfastly opposed to popular election of the president. They feared that popular election would make the office too centralized and too powerful, which would undermine the principles of federalism and separation of powers. The Framers devised a novel system, which came to be called the Electoral College. Under the Constitution, the president is chosen by a vote of electors who are appointed by the states. Each state is entitled to as many electors as it has members of Congress. The candidate who receives the majority of electoral votes is elected president.

In the first two presidential elections, the electors unanimously selected George Washington, the only presidential candidate in history to receive the

TABLE 14-1 The Four Systems of Presidential Selection

Selection System	*Period*	*Features*
1. Original	1788–1828	Party nominees are chosen in congressional caucuses. Electoral College members act somewhat independently in their presidential voting.
2. Party convention	1832–1900	Party nominees are chosen in national party conventions by delegates selected by state and local party organizations. Electoral College members cast their ballots for the popular-vote winner in their respective states.
3. Party convention, primary	1904–1968	As in system 2, except that a *minority* of national convention delegates are chosen through primary elections (the majority still being chosen by party organizations).
4. Party primary, open caucus	1972–present	As in system 2, except that a *majority* of national convention delegates are chosen through primary elections.

votes of all electors. Nevertheless, the Framers anticipated that in some elections no candidate would gain the electoral majority required by the Constitution, in which case the House of Representatives (with each state having one vote) would select the president from among the top five vote getters (later changed to the top three by the Twelfth Amendment). The House soon did decide an election, choosing Thomas Jefferson in 1800.

Jefferson's election by the House resulted from a development that the Framers had not foreseen. In its original form, the Constitution provided that each elector would cast two ballots. The candidate who placed first, provided that he received the votes of a majority of electors, became president, and the second-place candidate became vice-president. The Framers had not anticipated the emergence of political parties and the formation of party tickets. In 1800 Jefferson teamed with vice-presidential candidate Aaron Burr on the Republican party's ticket, and each elector who voted for Jefferson also voted for Burr. This led to a tie and nearly a constitutional crisis when Burr tried to persuade the Federalists in Congress to elect him as president. Jefferson finally prevailed on the thirty-sixth House ballot. After he took office, the Twelfth Amendment was enacted to prevent ties in the Electoral College; the amendment provides that each elector shall cast one ballot for a presidential candidate and one ballot for a vice-presidential candidate.

In the 1790s, party members in Congress assumed the power to name a presidential nominee. Their choice was not binding on the electors, who could vote as they pleased; but the need for party unity and the prestige of the Congress led some electors to follow the recommendation of their party's congressional caucus, earning it the title of "King Caucus."[27]

In choosing the nation's first presidents, electors often acted somewhat independently, exercising their own judgment in casting their votes. This pattern changed after the election in 1828 of Andrew Jackson, who believed the people's will had been denied four years earlier when he placed first in the popular voting but failed to gain an electoral majority. Jackson could not persuade Congress to support a constitutional amendment which would have eliminated the Electoral College but did obtain the next-best alternative: he persuaded the states to tie their electoral vote to the popular vote. U.S. elections are regulated primarily by state law, and state legislatures are empowered by the Constitution to determine the method of selection of their state's electors. Under Jackson's reform, which is still in effect today, the party whose candidate wins the popular vote is entitled under state law to designate its electors. Thus the popular vote directly affects the electoral vote, and one candidate is likely to win both forms of the presidential vote. Since Jackson's time, only Rutherford B. Hayes (in 1876) and Benjamin Harrison (in 1888) have won the presidency after having lost the popular vote.

Jackson also eliminated King Caucus. In 1832 he convened a national party convention to nominate the Democratic presidential candidate. The parties had their strength at the grassroots, among the people, whereas Congress was dominated by the wealthy interests against which Jackson was fighting. Since Jackson's time, presidential nominees have been formally chosen at national party conventions.

The Third and Fourth Systems: Primaries and Open Races

The system of presidential selection that Jackson had created remained intact until the early twentieth century, when the Progressives initiated primary elections as a way of wresting control over presidential nominations from party

John F. Kennedy was the first president whose nomination clearly derived from victories in the primaries. As a Catholic and a junior senator, Kennedy had no chance of winning the Democratic presidential nomination in 1960 unless his primary campaign was successful. Kennedy is shown campaigning in West Virginia, a heavily Protestant state whose primary he won. (AP/Wide World)

bosses (see Chapter 3). However, most states either stayed with the older system of party selection or adopted nonbinding primaries. As a result, party leaders continued to control a majority of the convention delegates who selected the presidential nominees.

Through 1968, a strong showing in the primaries enabled a candidate to demonstrate popular support but did not guarantee nomination. In 1952, for example, Senator Estes Kefauver beat President Harry Truman in New Hampshire's opening primary and went on to win twelve of the thirteen primaries he entered; however, Kefauver was denied nomination by party leaders, who believed that his views were inconsistent with the party's traditions.

open party caucuses Meetings at which a party's candidates for nomination are voted upon and which are open to all of the party's rank-and-file voters who want to attend.

In 1968, the Democratic nomination went to Vice-President Hubert Humphrey, who had not entered a single primary and was closely identified with the Johnson administration's Vietnam war policy. After Humphrey narrowly lost the 1968 general election to Richard Nixon, reform-minded Democrats forced changes in the nominating process. The new rules gave rank-and-file party voters more control by requiring that states choose their delegates through either primary elections or **open party caucuses** (meetings open to any registered party voter who wants to attend). Although the Democrats initiated the change, the Republicans were also affected by it. Most states that adopted a presidential primary in order to comply with the Democrats' new rules also required Republicans to select their convention delegates through a primary. Today it is the voters in state primaries and open caucuses who play the decisive role in the selection of the Democratic and Republican presidential nominees.

YOUR TURN

A NATIONAL PRESIDENTIAL PRIMARY

The Question:

It has been suggested that presidential candidates be chosen by the voters in a nationwide primary election rather than by political party conventions as at present. Would you favor or oppose this?

Favor Oppose

What Others Think: This question has been asked in Gallup Polls a number of times since the 1960s, and the results have been the same each time: a large majority of Americans would prefer a national primary as the method of selecting presidential nominees.

Comment: The history of the U.S. presidential election system is the story of a process in which the relationship between candidates and voters has become ever more direct. The adoption of a national primary would be the culmination of this trend. Nominations would essentially be decided by plebiscite. Advocates of a national primary have put forth some convincing arguments: it would reduce the length of the campaign significantly, diminish the importance of campaign skills as an influence on presidential choice, simplify the process, and increase the level of popular participation. Despite these advantages, political scientists have cautioned against the adoption of a national primary. They see such a contest as potentially dangerous and effectively marking the end of the party's role in the campaign. A national primary would work to the advantage of candidates who possess the name recognition or large amount of money required for a nationwide campaign. Although such aspirants would in most cases be highly respected public officials, they could also be political mavericks or celebrities without any significant political experience. The public might be particularly responsive to such candidates during periods of crisis.

The modern presidential selection process is a long and grinding process that bears almost no resemblance to the way in which other democratic countries select their chief executives. When Helmut Kohl gained a fourth term as Germany's chancellor in 1994, the campaign lasted just a few weeks. The typical campaign for prime minister of Great Britain lasts about three weeks. By comparison, a U.S. presidential campaign officially spans nine months and actually starts much earlier. The main reason the U.S. campaign lasts so long is that the voters choose the nominees as well as the final winner. No European democracy uses primary elections as a means of choosing its nominees for public office.

In sum, the presidential election system has changed from an elite-dominated process to one that is based on popular support. This arrangement has strengthened the president by providing the chief executive with the reserve of power that popular election confers upon democratic leadership.

THE CAMPAIGN FOR NOMINATION

The recent changes in the nominating process have made the race for the presidency more wide open than ever before.[28] Recent nominating campaigns, except those in which an incumbent president is seeking reelection, have typically attracted about a half-dozen or more contenders. Most of them are not well known to the nation's voters before the campaign, and few have a significant record of national accomplishment. Among the active Democratic candidates when the 1992 campaign began, for example, not one had a national reputation. Less than 10 percent of the public claimed to know anything about Bill Clinton other than his name.

Media and Momentum

A key to success in the nominating campaign is **momentum**—a strong showing in the early contests which leads to a buildup of public support in subsequent ones. If candidates start off poorly, reporters will lose interest in covering them, contributors will deny them funding, political leaders will not endorse them, and voters will not give further thought to supporting them.

momentum A strong showing by a candidate in early presidential nominating contests, which leads to a buildup of public support for the candidate.

For these reasons, presidential contenders now give extraordinary attention to the early contests, particularly the first caucuses in Iowa and the first primary in New Hampshire.[29] A win in either state can result in a media bonanza for the winner. After narrowly winning New Hampshire's 1976 Democratic primary, for example, Jimmy Carter appeared on the covers of *Time* and *Newsweek* and received 2,600 lines of coverage within those issues, compared with 300 lines for all five of his Democratic challengers combined. Within a week of his New Hampshire triumph, Carter's national recognition level jumped from 20 percent to 80 percent, and his support among Democratic voters tripled. In the same week, all of Carter's opponents either stood still or dropped in the polls.[30]

Voting in primaries is not affected by partisan loyalties, since all candidates are of the same party. Without partisanship as an anchor, vote swings in response to momentum can be substantial. After Michael Dukakis won the New Hampshire primary in 1988, his nationwide support among Democratic

Presidential nominating campaigns often attract a large number of contenders, who initially concentrate their efforts on New Hampshire's primary, the first in the nation. A GOP fundraiser in Manchester, New Hampshire, in 1995 attracted eight potential Republican candidates (from the left): commentator Pat Buchanan, Senator Phil Gramm, Senator Arlen Specter, Senate majority leader Robert Dole, former governor Lamar Alexander, U.S. Representative Bob Dornan, former ambassador Alan Keyes, and Senator Richard Luger. (Reuters/Bettmann)

voters in polls doubled. Most New Hampshire winners have, like Dukakis, gained significant public support after the primary. Clinton is an exception to the proposition that, to win the presidency, a candidate first has to win New Hampshire's primary. Clinton led in the New Hampshire polls until Gennifer Flowers claimed an adulterous affair with him. Clinton finished second in the primary but came back strongly on Super Tuesday (so-called since a large number of states, most of them in the South, hold their primaries on this single day) because of regional strength and superior financing.

Money has become a critical factor in the nominating races. This is so because many states have moved their primaries and caucuses to the early phase of the nominating period in an effort to increase their influence on the outcome. In the first month alone of the 1996 campaign, twenty-four state contests were scheduled. To compete effectively in so many contests in such a short period, candidates need money, lots of it. Dan Quayle and Jack Kemp were two of the potential challengers for the 1996 Republican nomination who decided not to run because of the money demands. By contrast, Robert Dole, Phil Gramm, Pete Wilson, and Lamar Alexander spent months on end in 1995 seeking the estimated $20 million that strategists believed would be necessary to run a strong campaign.

Although money and momentum help explain nominating outcomes, they do not account for initial success or enduring appeal. Why does one candidate start strongly or maintain strength while another does not? There is no single answer, but a candidate must have strength of one kind or another to prevail. Issues can be important: the main reason George McGovern won the Democratic nomination in 1972 was that his anti-Vietnam stance attracted a stable and committed voting bloc. Critical events can also matter: the inter-

★ CRITICAL THINKING

The New Elite in the Nomination Process

The process of choosing presidential nominees has greatly changed in the past few decades. Among other things, the old elite of party leaders—governors, mayors, members of Congress, and party chairs—has given way to a new elite of journalists and the candidates' hired consultants—pollsters, media specialists, and the like. What are the implications of this shift? In regard to this change alone, is the new system an improvement over the old?

national crisis that resulted when Iranian militants took control of the U.S. embassy in Teheran in late 1979 gave President Carter's popularity a temporary boost that enabled him to turn back Senator Edward Kennedy's challenge for the 1980 Democratic nomination. Public familiarity is another factor: George Bush's successful drive to the 1988 Republican nomination owed mainly to support built up during his vice-presidency. In short, political influences of varying kinds have a strong impact on nominating races. Presidential nominations are not decided strictly by momentum, money, and superior strategy. Since 1968 the preprimary poll leader in contested nominations has won about half the time.

Candidates in primary elections are assisted by the Federal Election Campaign Act of 1974 (as amended in 1979). This act provides for federal "matching funds" to be given to any candidate who raises at least $5,000 in individual contributions of up to $250 in each of twenty states. Candidates who accept matching funds must agree to limit their expenditures to a set amount, which is adjusted each election year to account for inflation. In 1996 the spending limit for each candidate for the nominating phase of the campaign was nearly $30 million.

The National Party Conventions

After the state primaries and caucuses have been held, the national party conventions occur. These were once tumultuous affairs during which lengthy, heated bargaining took place before a presidential nominee was chosen. An extreme case was the Democratic convention of 1924, at which delegates took 103 ballots and ended up nominating an unknown "dark horse," John W. Davis. Today's conventions are relatively tame; not since 1952 has a nomination gone past the first ballot. The leading candidate has usually acquired enough delegates in the primaries and caucuses to lock up the nomination before the convention even begins. Nevertheless, the party convention is a major event. It brings together the delegates elected in state caucuses and primaries, who then vote to approve a party platform and to nominate the party's presidential and vice-presidential candidates.

Some recent conventions have been the scene of major disputes. The strategies and issues of nominating campaigns can so alienate the losers that they cannot accept defeat gracefully. In 1968, when the Vietnam war was at issue, Democratic contender Eugene McCarthy at first refused to support the party's nominee, Hubert Humphrey, even though they were both from Minnesota and had been personal friends. However, national conventions are ordinarily occasions for cementing party unity and building bridges to party voters. As many as 150 million Americans watch part of the proceedings on national television, and for many of them it is a time of decision. About a fifth of voters solidify their presidential choice during the conventions, and most of them decide to back the nominee of their preferred party.[31]

All recent nominees have received a "bounce" in the polls from their party's convention. In 1992, Clinton was deadlocked in the polls going into the convention but came out with a big lead; Perot's abrupt (though temporary) withdrawal from the race and a show of party unity at the convention combined to give Clinton a 27-point lead over Bush. The 1992 Republican National Con-

★ STATES IN THE NATION

Candidates for Presidential Nomination by State of Origin (1960–1996)

STATE	NUMBER OF CANDIDATES
Ala.	1
Alaska	0
Ariz.	3
Ark.	1
Calif.	7
Colo.	1
Conn.	0
Del.	2
D.C.	0
Fla.	1
Ga.	1
Hawaii	0
Idaho	1
Ill.	5
Ind.	2
Iowa	1
Kan.	1
Ky.	0
La.	0
Maine	1
Md.	1
Mass.	5
Mich.	2
Minn.	3
Miss.	0
Mo.	2
Mont.	0
Neb.	1
Nev.	0
N.H.	0
N.J.	0
N.Mex.	0
N.Y.	5
N.C.	1
N.Dak.	0
Ohio	2
Okla.	1
Oreg.	0
Pa.	2
R.I.	0
S.C.	1
S.Dak.	1
Tenn.	3
Texas	5
Utah	0
Vt.	0
Va.	3
Wash.	1
W.Va.	0
Wis.	0
Wyo.	0

SOURCE: Compiled by author; excludes candidates who were not taken seriously, did not campaign actively, or were on the ballot only in their home state. Candidates who ran more than once are counted only once.

Although the national conventions are not the tumultuous and decisive events they once were, they do offer the political parties a showcase for their candidates and platforms. Shown here is a scene from the 1996 Republican convention, which selected Bob Dole and Jack Kemp as the party's presidential and vice-presidential nominees. (Joe Traver/Liaison)

vention was a more heated gathering that focused on social issues such as abortion and illegitimacy, and it had a polarizing effect on the electorate. Bush gained 8 points during the convention week, but lost most of this gain after only a few days. Clinton's bounce in 1992 was the highest ever recorded by polls, while Bush's net gain was among the lowest. In 1996, Clinton and his Republican opponent, Bob Dole, had offsetting bounces, which worked to Clinton's advantage since he had held the lead heading into the party conventions.

The party conventions choose the vice-presidential nominees as well as those for president. By tradition, the vice-presidential selection rests with the presidential nominee. Critics have argued that the vice-presidential nomination should be decided in open competition, since the vice-president stands a good chance of becoming president someday. The chief argument for keeping the existing system is that the president needs a vice-president in whom he has complete confidence.

THE CAMPAIGN FOR ELECTION

The winner in the November general election is almost certain to be either the Republican or the Democratic nominee. A minor-party or independent candidate, such as George Wallace in 1968, John Anderson in 1980, or Ross Perot in 1992 and 1996, can draw votes away from the major-party nominees but stands almost no chance of defeating them. A major-party nominee has the critical advantage of support from the party faithful. Although party loyalty has declined in recent decades (see Chapters 6 and 8), two-thirds of the nation's voters still identify themselves as Democrats or Republicans, and most of them support their party's presidential candidate.[32] Even Democrat George McGovern, who had the lowest level of party support among recent nominees, was backed in 1972 by nearly 60 percent of his party's voters.

Republican nominees normally find it easier to keep their party's loyalists in line.[33] The GOP is the more homogeneous party, and campaign appeals to traditional social values, restrained government spending, lower taxes, and a strong defense have usually maintained the Republican vote.

Election Strategy

Presidential candidates act strategically. In deciding on a course of action, they try to estimate its likely impact on the voters. For incumbents and challengers alike, some of these issues will be questions of past performance. During the 1992 campaign, a sign on the wall of Clinton's headquarters read, "The Economy, Stupid." The slogan was the idea of James Carville, Clinton's chief strategist, and was meant as a reminder to keep the campaign focused on the nation's sluggish economy, which ultimately was the issue that defeated Bush. As in 1980, when incumbent Jimmy Carter lost to Ronald Reagan during tough economic times, the voters were motivated largely by a desire for change.

Other issues will be questions of future performance. In 1996, Dole based his campaign on a proposed 15-percent cut in personal income taxes. The proposal did not boost Dole's candidacy as much as he had hoped, perhaps because it appeared to contradict his earlier pledge to give priority to balancing the federal budget.

Candidates try to project a strong leadership image. Whether voters accept this image, however, depends more on external factors than on a candidate's personal characteristics. In 1991, after the Persian Gulf war, Bush's approval rating reached 91 percent, the highest level recorded since polling began in the 1930s. A year later, with the Gulf war a receding memory and the nation's economy in trouble, Bush's approval rating dropped below 40 percent. Bush

Republican nominee Robert Dole (l) and Democratic nominee Bill Clinton (r) face moderator Jim Lehrer (c) at the first presidential debate of the 1996 general election campaign. (Reuters/Brian Snyder/Archive Photos)

tried to stir images of his strong leadership of the war, but voters remained preoccupied with the economy.

The candidates' strategies are shaped by many considerations, including the constitutional provision that each state shall have electoral votes equal in number to its representation in Congress. Each state thus gets two electoral votes for its Senate representation and a varying number of electoral votes depending on its House representation. Altogether, there are 538 electoral votes (including three for the District of Columbia, even though it has no voting representatives in Congress). To win the presidency, a candidate must receive at least 270 votes, an electoral majority.

The importance of the electoral votes is magnified by the existence of the *unit rule;* all the states except Maine and Nebraska grant all their electoral votes as a unit to the candidate who wins the state's popular vote. For this reason, candidates are particularly concerned with winning the most populous states, such as California (with 54 electoral votes), New York (33), Texas (32), Florida (25), Pennsylvania (23), Illinois (22), and Ohio (21). Victory in the eleven largest states alone would provide an electoral majority, and presidential candidates therefore spend most of their time campaigning in those states.[34] Because of the unit rule, the electoral vote margin is almost always much greater than the popular vote margin. Clinton received 49 percent of the popular vote in 1996, compared with Dole's 41 percent and Perot's 9 percent, but Clinton won in states that gave him an overwhelming 379 electoral votes (70 percent of the total), compared with 159 electoral votes (30 percent) for Dole and none for Perot (see Figure 14–1).

The electoral vote system creates the possibility that the winner of the pop-

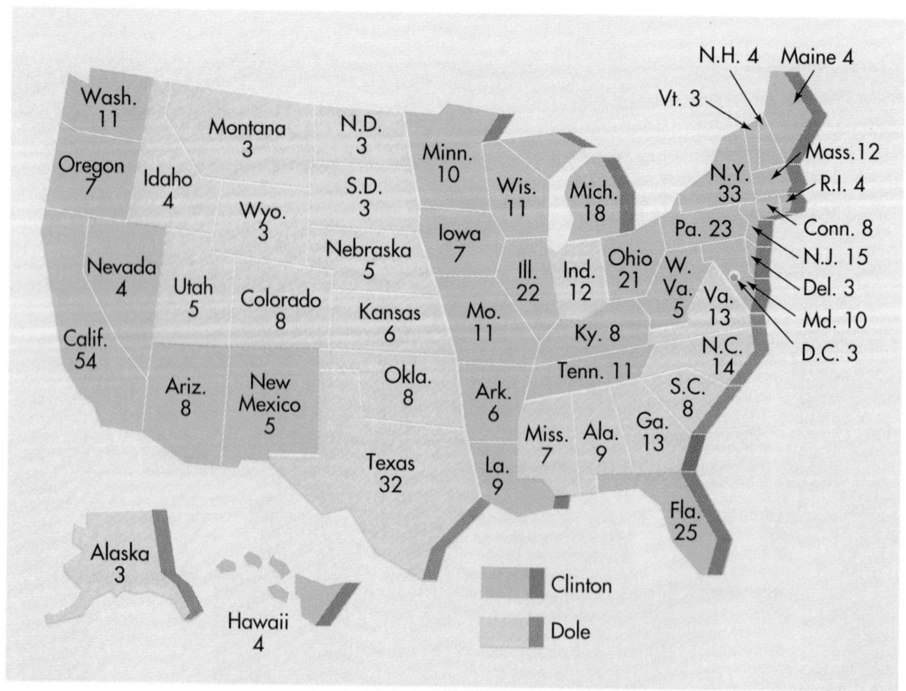

FIGURE 14–1
Electoral Votes in the Fifty States, and States Carried by the Presidential Candidates in the 1996 Election
The larger the population of a state, the more electoral votes it has—and the more important it is to presidential candidates. Each state's electoral votes are shown here, along with the states carried by candidates Bill Clinton and Bob Dole in the 1996 election. To win the presidency, a candidate must receive 270 of the national total of 538 electoral votes. Clinton won thirty-one states and the District of Columbia for 379 electoral votes, while Dole took nineteen states and 159 electoral votes. Ross Perot did not finish first in any state and thus received no electoral votes.

ular vote may lose the election. This is a significant, though unlikely, limit to the democratic election of a president. In 1976, a shift of less than 10,000 votes in Hawaii and Ohio would have given Gerald Ford an electoral vote victory, even though he trailed Jimmy Carter by 1.7 million votes nationally.

Media and Money

The modern presidential campaign is a media campaign. At one time, candidates relied heavily on party organization and rallies to carry their messages to the voters, but now they rely on the media, particularly television. Candidates strive to produce the pithy ten-second "sound bites" that the television networks prefer to highlight on the evening newscasts. In 1992, they also discovered the power of the "new media," making frequent appearances on such programs as *Larry King Live* and *The Phil Donahue Show.*

THE MEDIA AND THE PEOPLE

CAMPAIGN MESSAGES: BARRIER OR BRIDGE?

The Framers of the Constitution feared that the people would be exploited by demagogues. Americans would flock to the polls and deal self-government a deathblow by electing a leader who had aroused their worst instincts. What the Framers could not have foreseen was that the people would be confronted by election messages that are more discouraging than persuasive. Yet the story of the modern media campaign is a story of messages that do as much to alienate the voters as to inform and motivate them.

Presidential election news emphasizes the strategic game played by the candidates rather than their policy positions or leadership capabilities. Election news also has a negative bent. Bad news about the candidates takes precedence over good news. Soon after Arkansas Governor Bill Clinton broke to the front of the Democratic pack of presidential contenders in early 1992, he became the subject of news stories about his alleged marital infidelity. Unfavorable gossip about the private lives of candidates, it seems, has more news value than does information about their policy stands or political experience.

Televised political advertising also tends to be negative in tone. Media consultants have perfected what is called the "attack ad"—a blistering, negative assault on the opponent. A classic example is a 1988 Bush campaign ad which showed a revolving door that was meant to represent the Massachusetts prison furlough program; the suggestion was that Democratic nominee Michael Dukakis, as the state's governor, was personally responsible for the actions of furloughed prisoners.

Election polls suggest that such negative messages undermine the public's confidence not only in candidates but also in the electoral process itself. The messages that flow from the mass media of communication during a presidential campaign do not give people much reason to believe that they are participating in the noble process of democratic governance. The messages also do not give the public the kind of information that would ordinarily be most useful in making an educated choice between the contenders.

The presidential debates are an exception to the general pattern. The candidates' statements in debates tend to be positive and constructive, and the voters' response to the exchange is favorable. Postelection surveys by Times-Mirror in 1988 and 1992 indicate that of all forms of election communication, the public ranked the debates highest (the news ranked lowest). In 1992, the voters' opinions of Bush, Clinton, and Perot improved sharply when the debates gave people an opportunity to view the candidates through something other than the lens of daily journalism and televised advertising.

SOURCE: Thomas E. Patterson, *Out of Order* (New York: Vintage, 1994), 1–27, 150.

FORMAL AND INFORMAL REQUIREMENTS FOR BECOMING PRESIDENT

Formal Requirements. Article II of the U.S. Constitution requires a president to be:

- At least thirty-five years old
- A natural-born U.S. citizen
- A resident in the United States for at least fourteen years

Informal Requirements. In the nation's history, presidents have been:

- Male, without exception
- White, without exception
- Protestant, with the exception of John F. Kennedy
- Married, with the exceptions of James Buchanan and Grover Cleveland (who married in the White House)
- Career public servants—four were army generals, thirteen were vice-presidents (seven succeeded upon a president's death, one upon a president's resignation), eight were federal administrators, and the remainder were U.S. senators, U.S. representatives (only one), or state governors.

Television is the forum for the major confrontation of the fall campaign—the presidential debates. The first televised debate took place in 1960 between Kennedy and Nixon, and an estimated 100 million people saw at least one of their four debates.[35] Televised debates resumed in 1976 and have become an apparently permanent fixture of presidential campaigns. Studies indicate that presidential debates influence the votes of only a small percentage of the electorate. However, presidential elections are sometimes decided by a few percentage points, and the televised debates offer a candidate who is lagging in the race an opportunity to develop momentum. In 1992 Ross Perot capitalized on his opportunity. He was disarmingly direct, folksy, and iconoclastic during the debates, and half the 19 percent who voted for Perot in 1992 said that his performance had played an important role in their decision.[36] Perot was excluded from the debates in 1996 in part because Dole objected to his participation. However, Dole failed to take advantage of his one-on-one debates with Clinton: After both of their debates, viewers judged Clinton the winner and Dole failed to gain significant ground in the polls.

The television campaign includes political advertising. Televised commercials are by far the most expensive part of presidential campaign politics. Since 1976, political commercials on television have accounted for about half the candidates' expenditures in the general election campaign. Kathleen Hall Jamieson describes the role of advertising in the modern campaign as "packaging the presidency."[37] In 1996 Clinton and Dole each spent more than $30 million on advertising in the general election, and Perot spent more than $20 million.

Perot's advertising was financed by a federal grant of $29 million that he received for getting 19 percent of the vote in 1992 (see Chapter 8). Clinton and Dole each received a federal grant of $62 million for their general election campaigns. The only string attached to this funding is that candidates who accept it can spend no additional funds on their campaigns (though their party can spend additional money on their behalf). Presidential candidates can choose not to accept public funding, in which case the amount they spend is limited only by their ability to raise money privately. However, all major-party nominees since 1976 have accepted public funding. Other candidates for the presidency qualify for federal funding if they receive at least 5 percent of the vote and do not spend more than $50,000 of their own money on the campaign. Since Perot spent over $60 million of his own money on his 1992 campaign, he was ineligible for federal funding.

The Winners

The winners of all recent presidential elections, as it has been throughout the nation's history, have been white males. The great majority of presidents have been well-to-do Anglo-Saxon Protestants. Except for four Army generals, no man has won the presidency who has not first held high public office (see Table 14-2). Nearly a third of the nation's presidents had previously been vice-

TABLE 14-2 The Path to the White House for Twentieth-Century Presidents

President	*Years in Office*	*Highest Previous Office*	*Second-Highest Office*
William McKinley	1897–1901	Governor	U.S. Representative
Theodore Roosevelt	1901–1908	Vice-president*	Governor
William Howard Taft	1909–1912	Secretary of war	Federal judge
Woodrow Wilson	1913–1920	Governor	None
Warren G. Harding	1921–1924	U.S. senator	Lieutenant governor
Calvin Coolidge	1925–1928	Vice-president*	Governor
Herbert Hoover	1929–1932	Secretary of commerce	War relief administrator
Franklin D. Roosevelt	1933–1945	Governor	Assistant secretary of Navy
Harry S Truman	1945–1952	Vice-president*	U.S. senator
Dwight D. Eisenhower	1953–1960	None (Army general)	None
John F. Kennedy	1961–1963	U.S. senator	U.S. representative
Lyndon Johnson	1963–1968	Vice-president*	U.S. senator
Richard Nixon	1969–1974	Vice-president	U.S. senator
Gerald Ford	1974–1976	Vice-president*	U.S. representative
Jimmy Carter	1977–1980	Governor	State senator
Ronald Reagan	1981–1988	Governor	None
George Bush	1989–1992	Vice-president	Director, CIA
Bill Clinton	1993–	Governor	State attorney general

*Became president on death or resignation of incumbent.

presidents, and most of the rest were former U.S. senators, state governors, or top federal executives. In recent times, the vice-presidency has been the inside track to the presidency. Five of the nine presidents between 1948 and 1992 were former vice-presidents (Truman, Nixon, Johnson, Ford, and Bush), and two other vice-presidents (Humphrey and Mondale) were presidential nominees.

Staffing the Presidency

When Americans go to the polls on election day, they have in mind the choice between two individuals, the Democratic presidential nominee and the Republican nominee. In effect, however, they are choosing a lot more than a single executive leader. They are also picking a secretary of state, the director of the FBI, the chair of the Federal Reserve Board, and a host of other executives, all of whom are presidential appointees.

PRESIDENTIAL APPOINTEES

Newly elected presidents gain important advantages from their appointment power. First, their appointees are a source of policy information. Modern policymaking depends on detailed information, and control of information is a source of considerable power. Second, these appointees extend the president's reach into the huge federal bureaucracy, exerting influence on the day-to-day workings of government.

Not surprisingly, presidents have tended to appoint individuals who share their beliefs. In his initial appointments, President Clinton sought persons

The White House contains, on the first floor, the president's Oval Office, other offices, and ceremonial rooms. The First Family's living quarters are on the second floor. (Bruce Hoertel/Gamma Liaison)

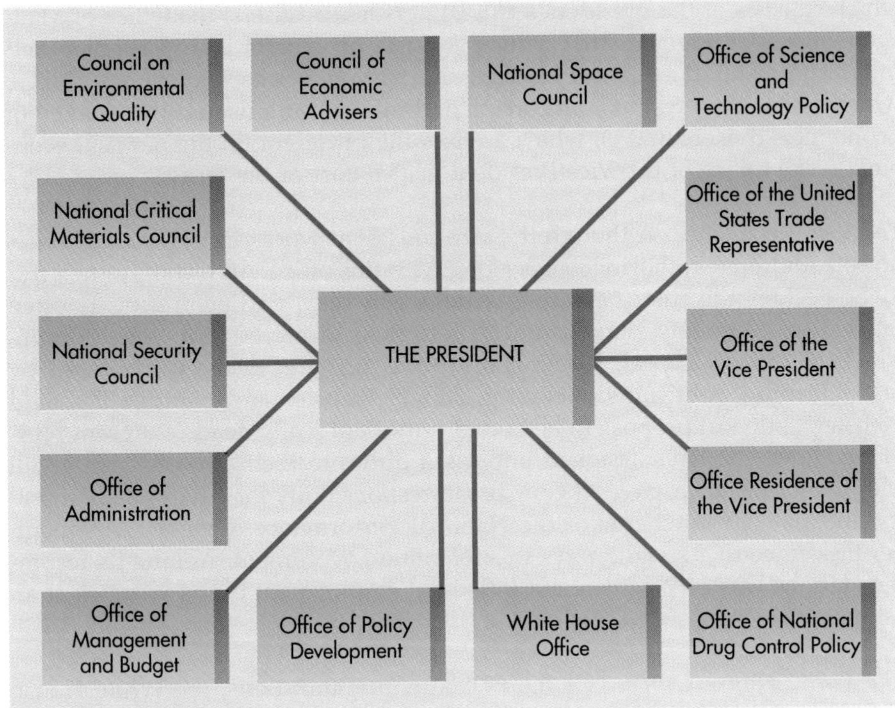

FIGURE 14-2 Executive Office of the President (EOP)
The EOP helps the president to manage the rest of the executive branch and promotes the president's policy and political goals. *Source: U.S. Government Manual.*

whose policy views were consistent with the programs he had proposed during his election campaign. He also used diversity as a criterion, seeking to appoint a significant number of women and minorities to executive positions. President Bush in his appointments sought to balance partisan considerations with his desire to build a team of skilled and personally loyal managers.[38] Among recent presidents, Ronald Reagan was the most adamant about ideological agreement as a criterion for appointment; he perceived career bureaucrats as being hostile to his ideas and believed that he needed Republicans who shared his philosophy in top positions.[39] Of Reagan's first-term appointees, only 18 percent were independents or from the opposing party; by comparison, 42 percent of President Jimmy Carter's appointees were in this category.[40] Reagan also rejected many Republicans who had worked in the Nixon and Ford administrations because he thought they were not conservative enough.

The Executive Office of the President

The key staff organization is the Executive Office of the President (EOP), which Congress created in 1939 to provide the president with the staff necessary to coordinate the activities of the executive branch.[41] The EOP has since become the command center of the presidency.[42] It currently consists of ten organizations (see Figure 14-2). They include the White House Office (WHO), which consists of the president's closest personal advisers; the Office of Management and Budget (OMB), which consists of experts who formulate and then administer the federal budget; the National Security Council (NSC), which assists the president on foreign and military affairs; and the Council of Economic Advisers (CEA), which advises the president on the national economy.[43] The Office of the Vice-President is also part of the EOP.

The Vice-President. Although the vice-president works in the White House, no constitutional authority comes along with this office. Accordingly, the president decides the role the vice-president will play. Earlier presidents often refused to assign any significant duties to their vice-president, which diminished the office's appeal. Nomination to the vice-presidency was refused by many leading politicians, including Daniel Webster and Henry Clay. Said Webster, "I do not propose to be buried until I am really dead."[44] Recent presidents, however, have assigned important duties to their vice-presidents. Bill Clinton, for instance, gave Al Gore broad responsibility for environmental policy and put him in charge of the National Performance Review, a 200-member task force that sought ways to streamline government. Among its recommendations was a 12 percent cut in federal employment over five years at an estimated savings of $108 billion.

The White House Office. Of the EOP's ten organizations, the White House Office serves the president most directly and personally. The WHO consists of the president's personal assistants, including close personal advisers, press agents, legislative and group liaison aides, and special assistants for domestic and international policy. They work in the White House, and the president can hire and fire them at will. The personal assistants do much of the legwork for the president and serve as a main source of advice. Because of their closeness and loyalty to the president, they are among the most powerful individuals in Washington.

The Constitution assigns no policy authority to the vice-president, whose role is determined by the president. Recent vice-presidents, including Al Gore, pictured here with President Clinton, have been assigned major policy responsibilities. Earlier vice-presidents played smaller roles. (C. Johnson/Gamma Liaison)

First Lady Hillary Rodham Clinton was given unprecedented policy responsibilities in the Clinton administration. She is shown here holding up a pamphlet on coronary bypass surgery while testifying on health reform before the House Energy Committee. (Wide World Photos)

President Clinton took the unprecedented step of assigning Hillary Rodham Clinton, his wife, the duties of an unofficial presidential assistant. She was placed in charge of health care reform, which was a centerpiece of Clinton's election campaign. As head of the policy task force, she put forth sweeping health care proposals, including universal access to medical coverage. Her assignment was controversial, but her handling of the health care issue initially brought considerable praise. When the proposed reform was defeated, there was the predictable criticism of her performance, although most analysts attributed the defeat primarily to opposition within and outside Congress to any comprehensive overhaul of the nation's medical system. Polls indicated that Americans were about evenly divided in their opinion of whether Hillary Clinton had too much or about the right amount of influence on administration policy.

Policy Experts. The president is also served by the policy experts in the EOP's other organizations, who include economists, legal analysts, national security specialists, and others. The president is advised on economic issues, for example, by the Council of Economic Advisers, headed by three economists who are appointed by the president and assisted by an expert staff. The CEA gathers information to develop indicators of the economy's strength and applies economic theories to various policy alternatives. Modern policymaking cannot be conducted in the absence of such expert advice and knowledge.

cabinet A group consisting of the heads of the (cabinet) executive departments, who are appointed by the president, subject to confirmation by the Senate. The cabinet was once the main advisory body to the president but no longer plays this role.

The President's Cabinet

The heads of the executive departments, such as the Department of Defense and the Department of Agriculture, constitute the president's **cabinet.** They are appointed by the president, subject to confirmation by Congress.

The cabinet is a tradition but has no formal authority, because the Constitution says nothing about it. When Abraham Lincoln was once unanimously opposed by his cabinet, he said, "Seven nays and one aye—the ayes have it." Although the cabinet once served as the president's main advisory group, it has not played this role since Herbert Hoover's administration. Dwight D. Eisenhower tried in the 1950s to restore the cabinet to its former prominence, but he eventually gave up. As national issues have become increasingly complex, the cabinet has become outmoded as a policymaking forum: department heads are likely to understand issues only in their respective policy areas.[45] Cabinet meetings have been largely reduced to gatherings at which only the most general matters are discussed.

Although the cabinet as a collective decision-making body is a thing of the past, the cabinet members, as individuals who head major departments, are important figures in any administration. They understand that their first responsibility is to carry out the president's instructions. Nevertheless, the president chooses most of them for their prominence in politics, business, government, or the professions. They may also bring to their office a high level of policy expertise and a group commitment.[46] Their stature and ideas can sometimes lead them to pursue their own agendas. President Carter believed that he had no choice in 1978 but to fire Joseph Califano, his secretary of health, education, and welfare, for disloyalty after Califano had repeatedly expressed disagreement with Carter's policies in statements to reporters and members of Congress. Carter also pressured four other cabinet secretaries to resign when he fired Califano.

Other Presidential Appointees

In addition to cabinet secretaries, the president appoints the directors and top deputies of federal agencies, members of federal commissions, and heads of regulatory agencies. Altogether, the president appoints more than 5,000 executive officials. However, most of these appointees are selected at the agency level or are part-time workers. This still leaves nearly 700 appointees who serve the president more or less directly, which is a much larger number than any other democracy's chief executive appoints.[47]

The Problem of Control

Although the president's appointees are a valuable asset, they also pose a problem: because they are so numerous, the president has difficulty controlling them. Most appointees are not under the president's direct supervision and have considerable freedom to act on their own initiative—not necessarily in accord with the president's wishes. President Truman had a wall chart in the Oval Office listing more than 100 officials who reported directly to him and often told visitors, "I cannot even see all of these men, let alone actually study what they are doing."[48] Since Truman's time the number of bureaucratic agencies has more than doubled, compounding the problem of presidential control over subordinates.[49]

The nature of the control problem varies with the type of appointee. The advantages of having the advice of policy experts, for example, is offset somewhat by the fact that many of them have a narrow view of the nation's priorities. Proposing "the best policy solution" means little if Congress finds it politically unacceptable. On the other hand, top political appointees, while adept at politics, have a tendency to act too independently. WHO assistants tend naturally to skew information in ways that favor their preferred policies.[50] At times they have even presumed to undertake important initiatives without first obtaining the president's approval, leading others to question whether the president is actually in charge.[51] The loyalty of agency heads and cabinet secretaries is often split between their commitment to the president and their commitment to the agency's interests or their own beliefs.[52] President Clinton in 1994 dismissed Surgeon General Jocyelyn Elders after she said she might consider teaching children about masturbation as part of sex education. Elder's independence and blunt talk had brought the administration unfavorable publicity several times previously, and this time Clinton fired her.

The problem of control is most severe in the case of lower-level appointees whom the president rarely if ever sees. Although they work for the president, these appointees do not always serve the president's interests as fully as might be expected. Most presidential appointees have two years or less of federal government experience and accordingly depend heavily on the expertise of career bureaucrats.[53] These appointees are sometimes "captured" by the agency in which they work because they spend nearly all their time on its activities and lack the policy expertise and managerial skills to control the careerists' activities. (Chapter 16 examines more closely the relationship between presidential appointees and career bureaucrats.)

ORGANIZING THE EXTENDED PRESIDENCY

Effective use of appointees by the president requires two-way communication. The president cannot possibly meet regularly with all appointees or personally oversee their activities. Yet to be in control, the president must receive essential advice from these subordinates and must have means of communicating with them.

The Pyramid Approach

Presidents have relied on a variety of techniques to regulate the flow of information to and from the Oval Office. One arrangement, used by Eisenhower, Nixon, Reagan, and Bush, resembles the way the military and most corporations are organized. It places the president at the top of an organizational pyramid and the personal assistants, each of whom is assigned specific responsibilities, at the next levels (see Figure 14-3). All information and recommendations from lower levels must be submitted to these top aides, who decide whether the reports should be forwarded to the president. This hierarchical arrangement, with its multiple levels of supervision, permits more effective control of subordinates. The pyramid form of organization also has the advantage of freeing the president from the need to deal with the many minor issues that reach the White House.

A major disadvantage of the pyramid form is the danger that presidential advisers will make decisions themselves that should be passed along for the president to make. Another disadvantage is that the pyramid form can result in misdirected or blocked information.[54] The president may be denied access to opinions that close advisers decide are wrong or unimportant. The risk is that the president will not be able to take important views and facts into account in making policy decisions.[55]

The Hub-of-the-Wheel Approach

A second approach to staff organization was developed by Franklin D. Roosevelt and adapted by presidents Kennedy, Johnson, Ford, Carter, and Clinton. Each placed himself at the center of the organization, accessible to a fairly large number of advisers (see Figure 14-4). This "hub-of-the-wheel" (or circular) form allows more information to reach the president, providing a greater range of options and opinions. Roosevelt and Kennedy were particularly adept at operating within this organizational framework; each surrounded himself with talented advisers and knew how to make them work together as a team even while they generated competing ideas.

Unfortunately, this system encourages personal rivalries. As assistants vie for the president's attention and for control of policy areas, their competition can undermine the team effort the president is looking for. Moreover, the pres-

FIGURE 14-3 Managing the Presidency: The Pyramid (Hierarchical) Form of Organization
In the pyramid form that some presidents have used to organize their staffs, information and recommendations that lower-level advisers wish to communicate to the president must be transmitted through—and thus "filtered" by—first top-level aides and then the White House chief of staff.

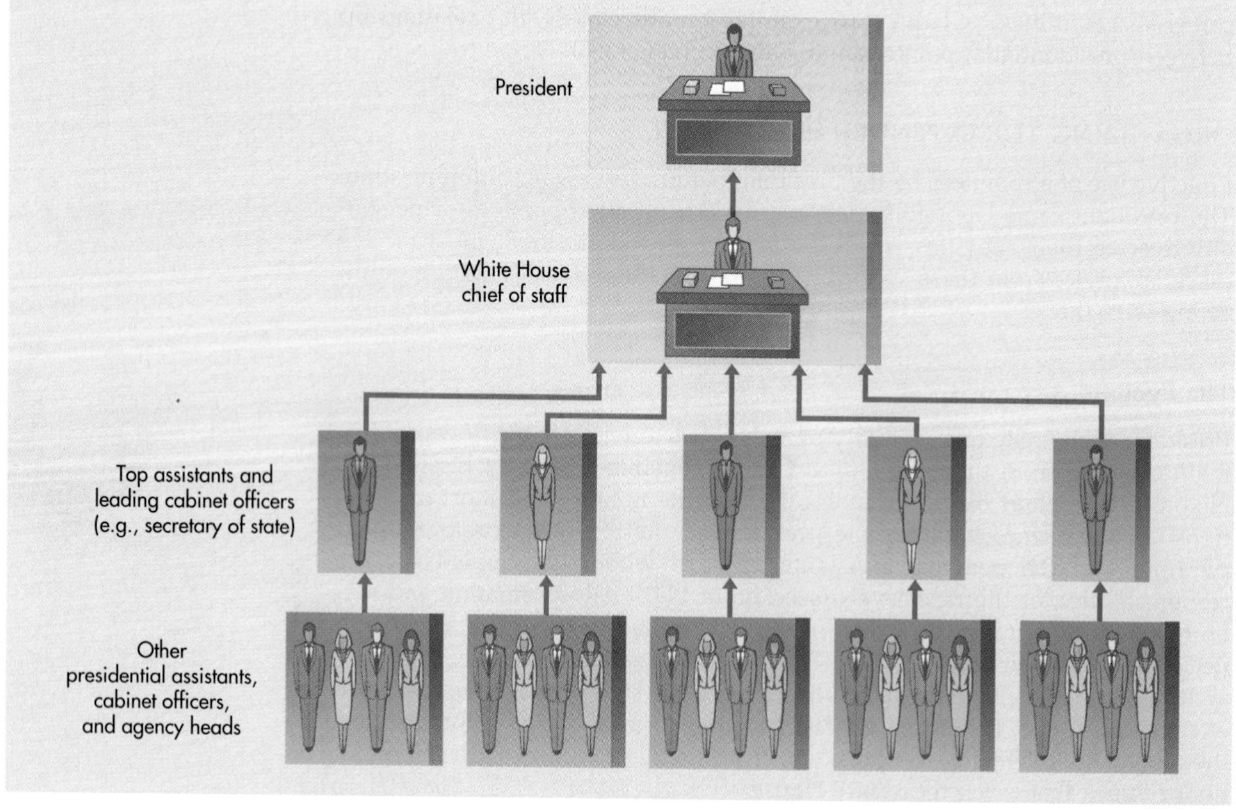

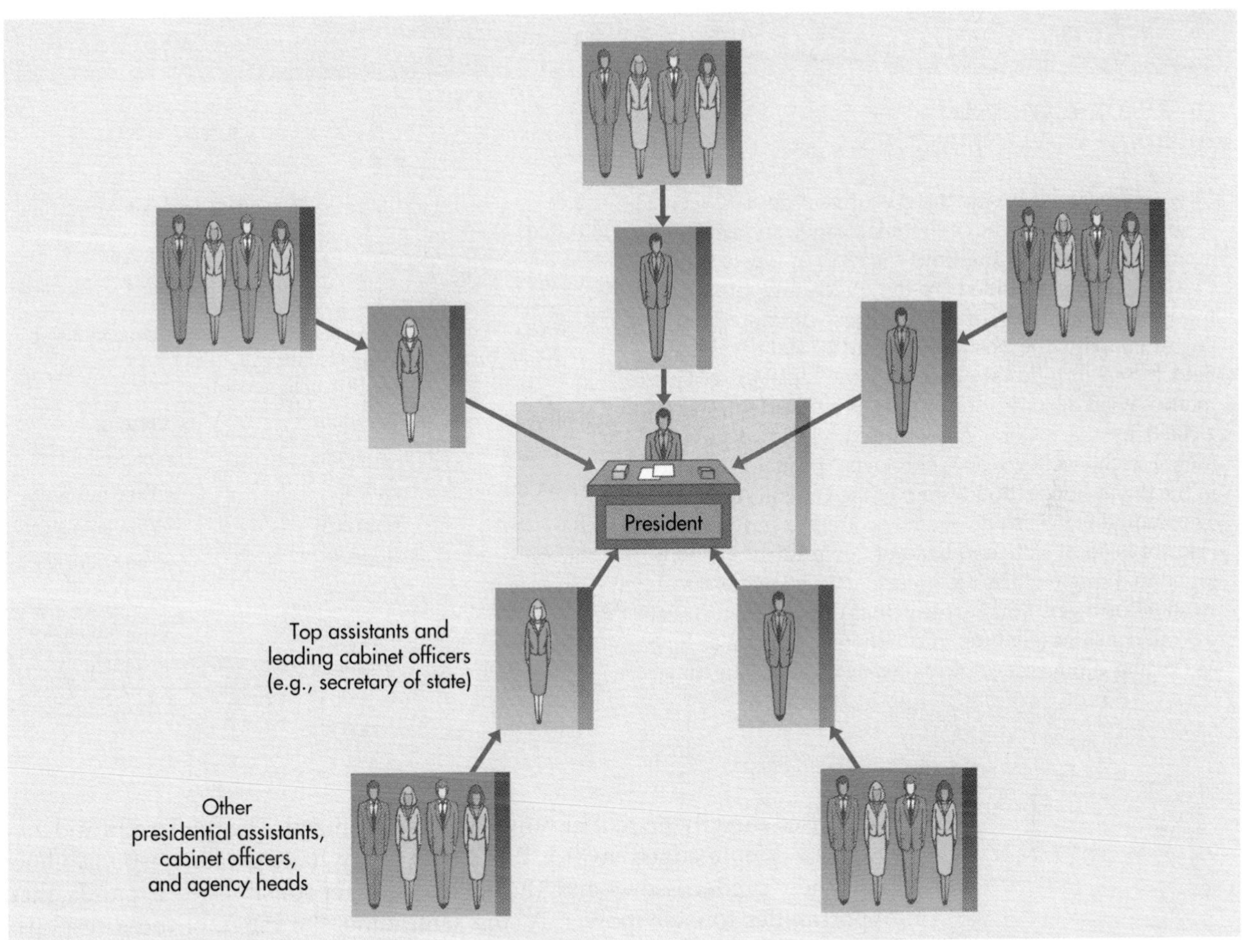

FIGURE 14-4 Managing the Presidency: The Hub-of-the-Wheel (Circular) Form of Organization
In the hub-of-the-wheel form of organization, the president is at the center of a circle composed of a fairly large number of top-level aides, each of whom has direct access to the president. Lower-level advisers have correspondingly closer access to the president than they do in the pyramidal form.

ident may become so overloaded with staff opinions that larger issues do not get the proper attention. This criticism was often leveled at President Carter; it was said that Carter knew the details of every policy issue but had difficulty establishing priorities and placing policies in the broad context that leads to effective action. Carter himself came to recognize that his hub-of-the-wheel organization was overloading him with detail, and he changed to a more hierarchically organized staff; the results, however, were not notably different. Ford and Clinton also replaced their collegial staff systems with a more hierarchical one. They faced criticisms that their presidencies lacked direction, and each turned to a strong chief of staff for help (former member of Congress and OMB director Leon Panetta was Clinton's choice).

THE INSOLUBLE PROBLEM

Ultimately the problem of presidential control is beyond an organizational solution.[56] The responsibilities of the Oval Office are so broad that presidents cannot do the job without hundreds of assistants who cannot possibly be

 HOW THE UNITED STATES COMPARES

HEADS OF STATE AND HEADS OF GOVERNMENT

Most democracies divide the executive office between a head of state, who is the ceremonial leader, and a head of government, who is the policy leader. In Great Britain these positions are filled by the queen and the prime minister, respectively. In democracies without a hereditary monarchy, the position of head of state is usually held by an individual chosen by the legislature. Germany's head of state, for example, is a president, who is elected by the Federal Assembly; the head of government is a chancellor, who is chosen by the majority party in the lower house (Bundestag) of the Federal Assembly. The United States is one of a few countries in which the roles of head of state and head of government are combined in a single office, the presidency. The major disadvantage of this arrangement is that the president must devote considerable time to ceremonial functions, such as hosting dinners for visiting heads of state. The major advantage is that the president alone is the center of national attention.

Country	*Head of State*	*Head of Government*
Canada	Governor general (representative of the British monarch)	Prime minister
France	President	Premier
Germany	President	Chancellor
Great Britain	Queen	Prime minister
Italy	President	Prime minister
Japan	Emperor	Prime minister
Mexico	President	President
Sweden	King	Prime minister
United States	President	President

supervised directly no matter how they are organized. The modern presidency is thus a double-edged sword. Presidents today have greater responsibilities than their predecessors, and the increase in responsibilities expands their opportunities to exert power. At the same time, the range of these responsibilities is so broad that they must rely on staffers who may or may not act in the best interests of the president. The modern president's recurring problem is to find some way of making sure that aides serve the interests of the presidency above all others. The subject of presidential control of the executive branch will be discussed further in Chapter 16.

Summary

The presidency has become a much stronger office than the Framers envisioned. The Constitution grants the president substantial military, diplomatic, legislative, and executive powers, and in each case the president's authority has increased measurably. Underlying this change is the president's position as the one leader chosen by the whole nation. The public's support and expectations underlie presidential claims of broad authority.

National crises have contributed to the growth of presidential power. The public looks to the president during national emergencies, in part because Congress is poorly suited to the decisive and continuous action that emergencies require. Changing world and national conditions have also enhanced the presidency. These changes have placed new and greater demands on the federal government, demands that the president is in some ways better able than Congress to meet.

The nation has had four systems of presidential selection. The first centered on Congress and the Electoral College, the second on party conventions, the third on a convention system with some state primaries, and the current one on state primaries and open caucuses as the dominant method of choosing presidential nominees. Each succeeding system has been more "democratic" in that it was designed to give the public greater influence in the choice of the president and thus to make the selection more legitimate.

To gain nomination, a strong showing in the early primaries is necessary because news coverage and other resources flow toward winning candidates. This momentum is a critical factor in nominating races but normally benefits a candidate who by virtue of past record, stands on issues, ideology, or other factors already is in the strongest position to win nomination. Once nominated, the major-party candidates receive federal funds for the general election campaign; much of this money is spent on televised political advertising. The candidates themselves spend their time traveling around the nation, concentrating on the states with large numbers of electoral votes and trying to get favorable coverage from the journalists who follow their every move.

Although the campaign tends to personalize the presidency, the responsibilities of the modern presidency far exceed any president's personal capacities. To meet their obligations, presidents have surrounded themselves with large staffs of advisers, policy experts, and managers. These staff members enable the president to extend control over the executive branch while providing the information necessary for policymaking. All recent presidents have discovered, however, that their control of staff resources is incomplete and that some things that others do on their behalf actually work against what they are trying to accomplish.

Major Concepts

cabinet
legitimacy (of election)
momentum
open party caucuses
stewardship theory
Whig theory

Suggested Readings

Arnold, Peri E. *Making the Managerial Presidency: Comprehensive Reorganization Planning.* Princeton, N.J.: Princeton University Press, 1986. Suggests that the very notion of a managerial presidency creates expectations of the office that cannot be met.

Burke, John P. *The Institutional Presidency.* Baltimore, Md.: Johns Hopkins University Press, 1992. A synthesis of what is known about the formal operations of White House personnel.

Ceaser, James W. *Presidential Selection: Theory and Development.* Princeton, N.J.: Princeton University Press, 1979. A historical review of the philosophy and practice of presidential selection.

Crabb, Cecil V., Jr., and Kevin V. Mulcahy. *Presidents and Foreign Policy Making.* Baton Rouge: Louisiana State University Press, 1986. An analysis of the impact of bureaucratic growth on policymaking, focusing on the foreign policy area during the years from Roosevelt to Reagan.

Kerbel, Mathew R. *Edited for Television: CNN, ABC, and the 1992 Presidential Campaign.* Boulder, Colo.: Westview Press, 1994. A careful analysis of presidential election coverage.

Natoli, Marie D. *American Prince, American Pauper: The Contemporary Vice Presidency in Perspective.* Westport, Conn.: Greenwood Press, 1985. A look at the modern vice-presidency.

Patterson, Thomas E. *Out of Order.* New York: Vintage, 1994. A study of the news media's coverage of presidential campaigns.

Pfiffner, James P. *The Strategic Presidency: Hitting the Ground Running.* Chicago: Dorsey Press, 1988. An analysis of the way a newly elected president can convert electoral support into power in office.

Wood, Robert C. *Whatever Possessed the President? Academic Experts and Presidential Policy, 1960–1988.* Amherst: University of Massachusetts Press, 1993. An analysis which suggests that academic experts make important contributions to presidential decision making.

CHAPTER 15

PRESIDENTIAL POLICYMAKING: ELICITING SUPPORT

The president's job in the constitutional system is not to lead a followership; it is to elicit leadership from the other institutions of self-government and help make that leadership effective.

—*Hugh Heclo*[1]

Bill Clinton was riding high when he took the oath of office in 1993. He would be the first president in more than a decade to have congressional majorities of the same party with which to work. Clinton's mood was also buoyed by the public's attitudes. The economic recession that had soured people on the Bush presidency was fading rapidly, and polls indicated that a majority of Americans thought Clinton's ideas for governing the country were right for the time.

Two years later, Newt Gingrich sat in the Speaker's chair behind Clinton as the president delivered his State of the Union address. The speech was upbeat in tone but offered very little that was new. It echoed Republican themes about tax cuts and smaller government and expressed the need for executive-legislative cooperation. The reality was that Clinton was in no position to offer bold leadership. His party had lost control of Congress and his popularity had dropped into the 40 percent range.

The Clinton story is but one in the saga of the ups and downs of the modern presidency. Lyndon Johnson's and Richard Nixon's dogged pursuit of the Vietnam war led to talk of "the imperial presidency," an office so powerful that constitutional checks and balances were no longer an effective constraint on it.[2] Within a few years, because of the undermining effects of Watergate and of changing international conditions during the Ford and Carter presidencies, the watchword was "the imperiled presidency," an office too weak to meet the nation's demands for executive leadership.[3] Reagan's policy successes before 1986 renewed talk heard in the Roosevelt and Kennedy years of "a heroic presidency," an office that is an inspirational center of American politics.[4] After the Iran-Contra scandal in 1986, Reagan was more often called a lame duck. George Bush's handling of the Gulf crisis—leading the nation into a major war and emerging from it with the highest public approval rating ever recorded for a president—bolstered the heroic conception of the office. A year later, Bush was on his way to being removed from office by the voters.

No other political institution has been subject to such varying characterizations as the modern presidency. One reason is that the formal powers of the office are somewhat limited, and thus presidential power changes with national conditions, political circumstances, and the office's occupant.[5] The American presidency is always a *central* office in that the president is constantly a focus of national attention. Yet the presidency is not an inherently powerful office in the sense that presidents always get what they want. Presidential power is conditional. It depends on the president's personal capacity but even more on the circumstances—on whether the situation demands strong leadership and whether the political support for that leadership exists. When conditions are favorable, the president will appear to be almost invincible. When conditions are adverse, the president will seem vulnerable. This chapter examines the correlates of presidential success and failure in policymaking, focusing on the following main points:

★ *Presidential influence on national policy is highly variable.* Whether presidents succeed or fail in getting their policies enacted depends heavily on the force of circumstance, the stage of their presidency, partisan support in Congress, and the foreign or domestic nature of the policy issue.

★ *The president's election by national vote and position as sole chief executive ensure that others will listen to his ideas; but, to lead effectively, the president must have the help of other officials and, to get their help, must respond to their interests as they respond to his.*

★ *The president often finds it difficult to maintain the high level of public support that gives force to his leadership.* The American people have unreasonably high expectations of their presidents and tend to blame them for national problems.

Factors in Presidential Leadership

At times presidents can make critical decisions on their own authority.[6] In December 1989 George Bush met secretly with his top advisers to plan a military action that would topple the Panamanian dictator Manuel Noriega. Bush decided on an invasion by U.S. Army and Marine units, supported by helicopter gunships and armored vehicles. After he gave the final orders for the invasion, he headed off to a Christmas party. Not until the party was over, and the troops had started to deploy, did Bush inform congressional leaders that the United States would invade Panama within hours. Such dramatic initiatives as Bush's invasion of Panama suggest that presidents regularly have the power of command. In fact, however, such unilateral policymaking is

U.S. troops move into Haiti in 1994 on the orders of President Bill Clinton, acting as commander in chief of the armed forces. Undertaking such short-term military actions without the formal consent of Congress is legal under the War Powers Act. (Stephen Ferry/Gamma Liaison)

uncommon. The president operates within a system of separate institutions that share power. Thus significant presidential action normally depends on the approval of Congress, the cooperation of the bureaucracy, and sometimes the acceptance of the judiciary. Since other officials also have priorities, presidents do not always get their way. The responsibility to initiate and coordinate policy places the president at the center of attention, but other institutions have the authority that can make presidential leadership effective. Congress in particular—more than the courts or the bureaucracy—holds the key to presidential success. Without congressional authorization and funding, most presidential proposals are nothing but ideas, empty of substance.

Given that presidents must elicit support from others if they are to succeed, what is the record of presidential success? One way to judge is to measure the extent to which Congress backs legislation on which a president has taken a stand. By this indicator, presidents have been reasonably successful (see Figure 15-1). Congress has agreed with the president in more than 50 percent of its votes in most years of recent decades. The low year was 1987, when only 45 percent of the proposals backed by Reagan won congressional approval. Another low point was 1990, when Congress agreed with George Bush on only 47 percent of legislative issues.[7] The high point of presidential-congressional agreement was 1965, when Lyndon Johnson's positions coincided with Congress's votes in 93 percent of cases.[8]

A tougher test of presidential success is the proportion of White House initiatives that are enacted by Congress. It is one thing for a president to take a stand on a bill that is already before the Congress, but quite another thing for the president to develop a legislative proposal and then see Congress enact it into law. In 1993, Bill Clinton had an 88 percent congressional success rate on legislation he endorsed, the highest level since Johnson's 93 percent in 1965. Clinton also had several important proposals enacted into law, including a comprehensive budget-deficit reduction package. Yet Clinton failed to get

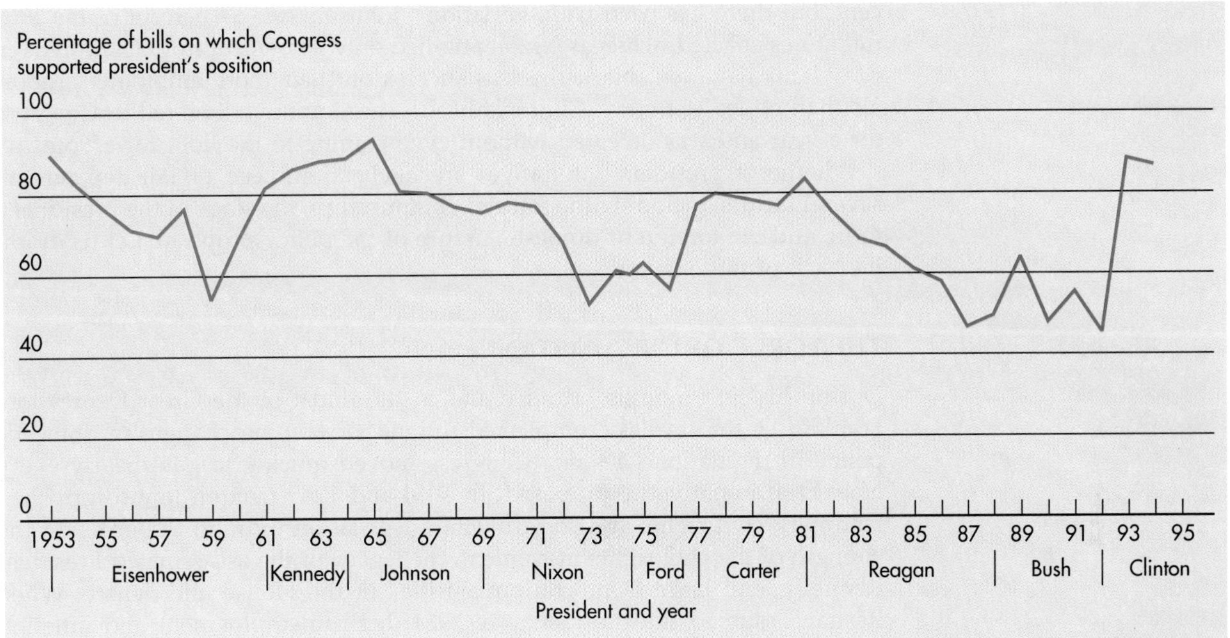

FIGURE 15-1 Percentage of Bills Passed by Congress on Which the President Announced a Position, 1953–1994
In most years presidents have been supported by Congress on a majority of policy issues on which they have taken a stand.
Source: Congressional Quarterly Weekly Report, December 31, 1994, 3620.

Congress to respond affirmatively to several initiatives, including a proposal to allow gays to serve in the military, and he delayed action on his health care reform bill in order to work it into a form that he thought Congress would accept. No president has come close to getting enactment of all the programs that he placed before Congress. The average success rate is just below 50 per-

President Lyndon Johnson addresses a joint session of Congress in 1965. Johnson had an extraordinary record of success with Congress, which adopted the great majority of his legislative proposals. (René Burri/Magnum) cent, but there has been wide variation.[9] Johnson saw 69 percent of his 1965 initiatives enacted, whereas Nixon attained only 20 percent in 1973. Moreover, presidents have had markedly less success on their more ambitious proposals than on lesser ones.[10] Clinton's health care initiative lingered in Congress for a year and was defeated without even coming to the floor for a vote.

Whether a president's initiatives are likely to succeed or fail depends on several factors, including the force of circumstance, the stage of the president's term, and the foreign or domestic nature of the policy proposal. Let us examine each of these factors.

THE FORCE OF CIRCUMSTANCE

During his first months in office and in the midst of the Great Depression, Franklin D. Roosevelt accomplished the most sweeping changes in domestic policy in the nation's history. Congress moved quickly to pass nearly every New Deal initiative he proposed. In 1964 and 1965 Lyndon Johnson pushed landmark civil rights and social welfare legislation through Congress on the strength of the civil rights movement, the legacy of the assassinated President Kennedy, and large Democratic majorities in the House and Senate. When Reagan assumed the presidency in 1981, high unemployment and inflation had greatly weakened the national economy and created a mood for significant change, which enabled Reagan to persuade Congress to enact some of the most substantial taxing and spending laws in history.

From presidencies such as these has come the popular impression that presidents single-handedly decide national policy. However, each of these periods of presidential dominance was marked by a special set of circumstances: a decisive election victory that gave added force to the president's leadership, a compelling national problem that convinced Congress and the public that bold presidential action was needed, and a president who was mindful of what was expected and who vigorously advocated policies consistent with those expectations.

When conditions are favorable, the power of the presidency appears awesome. The problem for most presidents is that conditions are not normally conducive to strong leadership. The political scientist Erwin Hargrove suggests that presidential influence depends largely on circumstance.[11] Some presidents serve in periods when important problems are surfacing in American society but have not yet become critical. Such a situation, Hargrove contends, works against a president's efforts to accomplish significant policy change. Kennedy was one such president; he recognized that federal intervention would be necessary to bring social justice to black Americans, but because conditions were unfavorable, he could not get Congress to act. The legislation was passed after his death, when Lyndon Johnson was president.

Of course, presidents have some control over their fate. Through effective leadership they can sometimes rally the public and Congress behind goals that they believe are important. In general, however, presidential achievement is heavily dependent on circumstance. Had Franklin Roosevelt been elected in 1960 rather than 1932, his place in American history would be very different and probably much less conspicuous. Roosevelt's genius lay in the devising

HOW THE UNITED STATES COMPARES

SYSTEMS OF EXECUTIVE POLICY LEADERSHIP

The United States instituted a presidential system in 1789 as part of its constitutional checks and balances. This form of executive leadership was copied in Latin America but not in Europe. European democracies adopted parliamentary systems, in which executive leadership is provided by a prime minister, who is a member of the legislature. In recent years some European prime ministers have campaigned and governed as if they were a singular authority rather than the head of a collective institution. France in the 1960s created a separate chief executive office but retained its parliamentary form of legislature.

The policy leadership of a president can differ substantially from that of a prime minister. As a singular head of an independent branch of government, a president does not have to share executive authority but nevertheless depends on the legislative branch for support. By comparison, a prime minister shares executive leadership with a cabinet, but once agreement within the cabinet is reached, he or she is almost assured of the legislative support necessary to carry out policy initiatives.

Presidential System	*Presidential/Parliamentary System*	*Parliamentary System*
Mexico	Finland	Australia
United States	France	Belgium
Venezuela		Canada
		Germany
		Great Britain
		Israel
		Italy
		Japan
		Netherlands
		Sweden

of extraordinary policies, not in the creation of conditions that led to their acceptance. In 1994, reflecting on the constraints of budget deficits and other factors beyond his control, Clinton said he had no choice but "to play the hand that history had dealt him."

THE STAGE OF THE PRESIDENT'S TERM

If conditions conducive to great accomplishments occur infrequently, it is nonetheless the case that nearly every president has favorable moments. Such moments tend to come during the first months in office. Most newly elected presidents enjoy a **honeymoon period** during which Congress, the press, and the public anticipate initiatives from the Oval Office and are more predisposed than usual to support these initiatives. The honeymoon is never an entirely smooth one. While Congress expects a flurry of legislative programs from new presidents, it does not always treat these proposals kindly.[12] And the media can be downright quick to turn on a president. During his first 100 days in office, Clinton's coverage on network television was more than 60 percent negative.[13] Nevertheless, presidents can normally expect a more unqualified form of support during their inaugural period than later.

honeymoon period The president's first months in office, a time when Congress, the press, and the public are more inclined than usual to support presidential initiatives.

Not surprisingly, presidents have put forth more new programs in their first year in office than in any subsequent year.[14] James Pfiffner uses the term "strategic presidency" to refer to a president's need to move quickly on priority items to take advantage of the policy momentum that is gained from the election.[15] Later in their terms, presidents tend to do less well in presenting initiatives and getting them enacted.[16] They may run out of good ideas or, more likely, deplete their political resources—the momentum of their election is gone and sources of opposition have emerged. Furthermore, if they blunder or if conditions turn sour—and it is hard for any president to serve for any length of time without a serious setback of one kind or another—they will lose some of their credibility and public support. Even highly successful presidents like Johnson and Reagan tend to have weak records in their final years. Franklin Roosevelt began his presidency with a remarkable period of achievement—the celebrated "Hundred Days"—but during his last six years in office, few of his major domestic proposals were enacted.

An irony of the presidency, then, is that presidents are most powerful when they are least knowledgeable—during their first months in office. These months can, as a result, be times of risk as well as times of opportunity. An example is the Bay of Pigs fiasco during the first year of John Kennedy's presidency, in which a U.S.-backed invasion force of anticommunist Cubans was easily defeated by Fidel Castro's army.

THE FOREIGN OR DOMESTIC NATURE OF THE POLICY PROPOSAL

In the 1960s the political scientist Aaron Wildavsky wrote that, while the nation has only one president, it has two presidencies: one domestic and one foreign.[17] Wildavsky was referring to Congress's differential responses to presidential initiatives in the areas of foreign and domestic policy. He found that since World War II, only 40 percent of presidential proposals in the domestic policy area had been enacted by Congress, compared with 70 percent of foreign policy initiatives. It must be noted that Wildavsky was looking back on a period when there was general agreement on U.S. foreign policy objectives. After World War II, Republican and Democratic leaders alike were largely united on the desirability of containing Soviet communism and establishing U.S. diplomatic, military, and economic influence around the world (see Chapter 20). Accordingly, presidents had strong backing for their foreign policy leadership. In 1964, for example, Lyndon Johnson urged Congress to ratify the Gulf of Tonkin resolution, which he then used as a mandate to escalate the Vietnam war. The resolution was passed unanimously in the House and with only two dissenting votes in the Senate.

By the late 1960s, however, the Vietnam war had gone sour, and the bipartisan consensus on foreign policy was disrupted. Those deep divisions have endured. The January 1991 authorization of the use of military force in the Gulf war was the first time Congress had voted directly for offensive military action since the Gulf of Tonkin resolution. Bush had asked for the vote (even though he said he would pursue the war regardless of what Congress decided) in order to strengthen his threat to use military force if Iraq did not withdraw from Kuwait. This time Congress was divided in its response to the president's request. The approval of military action in the Gulf was passed by margins of 52 to 47 in the Senate and 250 to 183 in the House.

Wildavsky's two-presidencies thesis is now regarded as a time-bound conception of presidential influence. Today, many of the same factors, such as the party composition of Congress, that affect a president's success on foreign policy also affect success on domestic policy.[18] Nevertheless, presidents are somewhat more likely to get what they want when the issue is foreign policy because they get more support from the opposite party in Congress.[19] Bush's foreign policy success rate was half again as high as his domestic policy success rate largely because congressional Democrats were more supportive of his foreign policy initiatives.[20] Similarly, Republican votes were crucial to Clinton's ability to get the North American Free Trade Agreement (NAFTA) and the General Agreement on Tariffs and Trade (GATT) through Congress.

The Supreme Court has recognized the special requirements of foreign policy, conceding to the president the power to take actions not expressly forbidden by law. As a result, presidents are able to make some major policy decisions—including those on deployments of military forces and the granting of diplomatic recognition—on their own authority. Thus, for example, Nixon's 1972 agreement with China's premier, Chou En-lai, to renew diplomatic relations between their countries was worked out in secret and presented to Congress after the fact. A more dramatic example of unilateral presidential action is Kennedy's 1962 decision to respond to the Soviet Union's deployment of nuclear missiles in Cuba by imposing an air and sea blockade and ordering U.S. Navy ships into position around Cuba. Congressional leaders were told of the plan only minutes before Kennedy announced it on television to the American people. On his own, Kennedy had committed the country to a course of action that could have led to a war between the superpowers.

Presidents owe their advantage in foreign and defense policy in part to their commanding position with the defense, diplomatic, and intelligence agencies. These are sometimes labeled "presidential agencies." As chief executive, the president is in charge of all federal agencies, but in practice the president's influence is strongest in those agencies which connect with his constitutional

★ CRITICAL THINKING

Foreign Policy: The President vs. Congress

In his first State of the Union address, President Bush said that Congress should stop trying to "micro-manage" foreign policy. Presidents Clinton, Reagan, Carter, and Ford had the same complaint, holding that the president should have broad discretion in carrying out foreign policy. Should Congress take an active role in setting precise limits on foreign policy, or should the president have this responsibility? What are the advantages and disadvantages of each arrangement?

Presidents rely heavily on their top-ranking cabinet officers and personal assistants in making major policy decisions. During the Cuban missle crisis in 1962, this group of advisers to President John F. Kennedy met regularly to help him decide upon a naval blockade as a means of forcing the Soviet Union to withdraw its missles from Cuba. (UPI/Bettmann Newsphotos)

authority as chief diplomat and commander in chief, such as the Departments of State and Defense and the CIA. These agencies have a tradition of deference to presidential authority that is not found in agencies that deal primarily with domestic policy. The Department of Agriculture, for example, responds to presidential direction but is also responsive (perhaps even more responsive) to farm-state senators and representatives. As Chapter 16 describes, bureaucratic support is important to a president's success with Congress, and that support is more likely to be forthcoming when the agency in question is part of the defense, diplomatic, or intelligence bureaucracy.

Although the two-presidencies thesis is an oversimplified notion, it is instructive to note that the presidency has declined in power since the end of the cold war. Tensions between the United States and the Soviet Union enabled presidents to take actions that were difficult for Congress to oppose because it might suggest a lack of national resolve. The secrecy and patriotic rigidity surrounding the cold war also had a chilling effect on congressional opposition. Now, since the fall of the Soviet Union, these aspects of foreign policy have diminished and the focus has shifted more to domestic issues. In the process, Congress has played a larger policy role. The political scientist Richard Rose concludes that changing world conditions have diminished the president's influence both at home and abroad.[21]

Presidential Leadership

Although the presidency is not nearly as powerful as most Americans assume, the capacity of presidents to influence the agenda of national debate is unrivaled, reflecting their unique claim to represent the whole country. Whenever the president directs attention to a particular issue or program, the attention of others usually follows. But will those others follow the president's lead? As we have noted, a president's support varies with conditions, some of which clearly cannot be controlled. Yet presidents are not entirely at the mercy of circumstance. As sole chief executive, a president is an active participant in his fate and can increase the chance of success by striving to build support in Congress and with the American people.

CONGRESSIONAL SUPPORT

Presidents cannot assume that support for their policies will automatically materialize. They have to build a following by taking into consideration the interests of other policymakers, who have their own jobs to do and their own interests to satisfy. Bill Clinton had this point in mind when, shortly after his election in 1992, he invited the top Democratic leaders in Congress—Senate majority leader George Mitchell, Speaker of the House Tom Foley, and House majority leader Richard Gephardt—to meet with him. He sought their agreement on a policy agenda that would break the gridlock between the executive and legislative branches. "We've got a big job to do and we've got to do it together," said Clinton.

As obvious as this type of thinking might seem, presidents sometimes think otherwise. Presidents can easily start to believe that their ideas ought to prevail because they were elected by all of the people, a claim no member of Congress can make. This line of reasoning invariably gets any president into trouble. Jimmy Carter had not held national office before he was elected in 1976, so he had no deep understanding of how Washington operates. In his memoirs, House Speaker Thomas P. "Tip" O'Neill, a fellow Democrat, said of Carter:

> Jimmy Carter was the smartest public officer I've ever known. . . . His mind was exceptionally well developed, and it was open, too. He was always willing to listen and to learn. *With one exception.* When it came to the politics of Washington, D.C., *he never really understood how the system worked.*[22]

Soon after taking office, for example, Carter eliminated from his budget nineteen public works projects that he believed were a waste of taxpayers' money, ignoring the importance that members of Congress attach to obtaining federally funded projects for their constituents. Carter's actions set the tone for a conflict-ridden relationship with Congress.

In order to get the help of members of Congress, the president must respond to their interests as they respond to his. The presidential scholar Fred Greenstein concludes that "whatever else his qualities, the president needs to be a working politician who can work with or otherwise win over the Washington community."[23]

The use of the presidential veto illustrates the point. Presidents can sometimes force Congress to accommodate their views through the use or threatened use of the veto. Congress can seldom muster the two-thirds majority in each chamber required to override a presidential veto (see Table 15-1), and so the threat of a veto can make Congress more responsive to the president's

TABLE 15-1 Number and Override of Presidential Vetoes

President	*Years in Office*	*Number of Vetoes*	*Number of Vetoes Overridden by Congress*
Franklin Roosevelt	1933–1945	635	9
Harry Truman	1945–1952	250	12
Dwight Eisenhower	1953–1960	181	2
John Kennedy	1961–1963	21	0
Lyndon Johnson	1963–1968	30	0
Richard Nixon	1969–1974	43	7
Gerald Ford	1974–1976	66	12
Jimmy Carter	1977–1980	31	2
Ronald Reagan	1981–1988	78	9
George Bush	1989–1992	46	1

SOURCE: *Congressional Quarterly Weekly Report,* January 7, 1989. Bush figures were provided by the White House Office of Legislative Affairs and include vetoes, pocket vetoes, and bills returned unsigned to Congress.

★ CRITICAL THINKING

Presidential "Character"
In a widely discussed book, *The Presidential Character* (1985), the political scientist James David Barber suggests that a president's orientation toward power ("active" or "passive," in Barber's terms) and politics ("positive" or "negative") affects the capacity to lead.

In Barber's view, "active" presidents are more effective than "passive" presidents. Active presidents have a drive to lead and succeed. Passive presidents are more willing to accept the direction of others and do not make full use of the office's resources. Barber also regards "positive" presidents as more effective than "negative" presidents. Positive presidents thrive on the give-and-take of politics. Negative presidents are driven by a compulsive sense of duty.

In fact, the presidents that Barber classifies as active-positive have tended to be more successful than most others. Franklin D. Roosevelt and Harry Truman are examples. As for Barber's other categories, he regards active-negative presidents as potentially the most dangerous. Although they are active in their drive to succeed, their negative traits of compulsiveness and distaste for the routines of politics can result in confrontation, stalemate, or deviousness. Woodrow Wilson and Richard Nixon are presidents in this category.

Do you accept Barber's conclusions that active-positive presidents are the most likely to succeed? Why or why not?

demands.[24] When a major civil rights bill was being debated in Congress in 1991, George Bush said flatly that he would veto any bill that imposed hiring "quotas" on employers; his ultimatum forced Congress to alter provisions of the bill. Yet the veto is more effective as a presidential restraint on Congress than as a device by which Congress can be forced to take positive action on the president's proposals. The presidential scholar Richard Neustadt argues that the veto is more a sign of presidential weakness than strength, because it usually comes into play when Congress has refused to go along with the president's ideas.[25] Clinton rarely even threatened a veto when the Democrats controlled Congress but resorted to the threat after the Republicans took control in 1995.

The Power to Persuade

According to Neustadt, the most basic fact about presidential leadership is that it takes place in the context of a system of divided powers. Although the president gets most of the attention, Congress has most of the constitutional authority in the American system. The powers of the presidential office are insufficient by themselves to keep the president in a strong position. Congress is a constituency that all presidents must serve if they expect to get its support.[26]

Neustadt's classic illustration of what presidents can do to help themselves with Congress is the Marshall Plan, a program to aid European countries devastated by World War II. The plan was enacted by Congress in 1948 at the request of Harry S Truman. Truman had become president upon the death of Franklin Roosevelt and was widely regarded in Washington as just a caretaker president who would be replaced by a Republican. (The Republicans had made substantial gains in the 1946 congressional elections.) Truman knew he could not simply demand that Congress make a commitment to the postwar rebuilding of Europe, in view of the cost of such a program (roughly $100 billion in today's dollars) and of its novelty (historically, the United States had stayed free of permanent European entanglements). Truman succeeded in getting congressional approval by subordinating his position to that of others.

First, rather than announce the program himself, Truman gave the task to General George C. Marshall, who had been chief of staff of the armed forces during World War II and was one of America's most widely admired leaders. Second, Truman made a special effort to gain the support of Arthur Vandenberg, a leading Republican senator and chairman of the Senate Foreign Relations Committee. Truman accepted Vandenberg's request that "politics" not be allowed to bog down the plan; he followed Vandenberg's advice on changes in financial and administrative aspects of the plan; and he allowed Vandenberg to choose a Republican, Paul Hoffman, to head the U.S. agency responsible for administering the plan. Through Vandenberg's backing, Truman gained the Republican congressional support that made the Marshall Plan possible.

From cases such as the Marshall Plan, Neustadt concluded that presidential power, at base, is "the power to persuade."[27] Like any singular notion of presidential power, Neustadt's has limitations. Presidents at times have the power to command and to threaten. But Congress can never be taken for granted. Theodore Roosevelt expressed the wish that he could "be the president and Congress, too," if only for a day, so that he would have the power to enact as well as propose laws.

Partisan Support in Congress

For most presidents, the next-best-thing to being "Congress, too" is to have a Congress filled with members of their own party. The sources of division within Congress are many. Legislators from urban and rural areas, wealthier and poorer constituencies, and different regions of the country often have very different views of the national interest. To obtain majority support in Congress, the president must find ways to overcome these differences.

No source of unity is more important to presidential success than partisanship. Presidents are more likely to succeed when their own party controls Congress. Between 1954 and 1992, each Republican president—Eisenhower, Nixon, Ford, Reagan, and Bush—had to contend with a Democratic majority in one or both houses of Congress. Congress passed a smaller percentage of the initiatives proposed by each of these presidents than by any Democratic president of the period—Kennedy, Johnson, or Carter.[28]

Democratic presidents have not always had an easy time with Congress, either. A chief obstacle has been southern Democrats, who tend to be more conservative than congressional Democrats from other regions and thus more likely to break party ranks and vote with their Republican colleagues. On such issues as social welfare and individual rights, southern Democrats have sometimes combined with Republicans (in the "conservative coalition") to block the legislative initiatives of Democratic presidents.[29] Nevertheless, Democratic majorities in Congress provided Democratic presidents an advantage. In his first year in office, Bill Clinton was able to persuade Congress to pass a deficit reduction bill, a feat which George Bush was unable to accomplish in his four years as president. As a Democrat, Clinton had more support in Congress with which to work. His deficit reduction bill was supported by 85 percent of congressional Democrats, which was all the help he needed. No Republican voted for the bill. After Republicans took control of Congress, however, Clinton's ability to achieve new programs was severely restricted.

Colliding with Congress

On rare occasions, presidents have pursued their goals so zealously that Congress has felt that it had no choice but to take steps to curb their use of power.

The ultimate sanction of Congress is its constitutional power to impeach and remove the president from office. The House of Representatives decides whether the president should be impeached (placed on trial), and the Senate conducts the trial and then votes on the president's guilt, with a two-thirds vote required for removal from office. In 1868 Andrew Johnson was impeached and came within one Senate vote of being removed from office for his opposition to Congress's harsh Reconstruction policies in the wake of the Civil War. In 1974 Richard Nixon's resignation halted congressional proceed-

★ STATES IN THE NATION

Presidential Support in Congress: Members of the president's party are the basis of his support in Congress.

	CLINTON SUPPORT SCORE, 1994	
STATE	DEMOCRATS	REPUBLICANS
Ala.	79%	42%
Alaska	–	44
Ariz.	80	42
Ark.	88	40
Calif.	80	45
Colo.	83	34
Conn.	89	65
Del.	89	64
Fla.	84	49
Ga.	81	41
Hawaii	85	–
Idaho	78	34
Ill.	77	47
Ind.	81	42
Iowa	89	51
Kan.	79	38
Ky.	85	39
La.	76	49
Maine	87	62
Md.	84	53
Mass.	79	68
Mich.	79	46
Minn.	74	52
Miss.	76	43
Mo.	77	48
Mont.	82	43
Neb.	87	51
Nev.	84	53
N.H.	71	37
N.J.	78	58
N.Mex.	89	53
N.Y.	80	57
N.C.	79	34
N.Dak.	80	–
Ohio	79	51
Okla.	80	39
Oreg.	81	62
Pa.	78	54
R.I.	95	76
S.C.	86	45
S.Dak.	88	34
Tenn.	82	42
Texas	77	38
Utah	70	37
Vt.	80	–
Va.	82	51
Wash.	84	52
W.Va.	79	–
Wis.	75	40
Wyo.	–	35

SOURCE: *Congressional Quarterly Weekly Report*, December 31, 1994, 3655–3657. The Clinton support score is based on the percent of recorded votes on which Clinton took a position and on which a legislator voted in agreement with it. The scores for each state are the average percentages for its Democratic and Republican senators and representatives.

ings on the Watergate affair that would almost certainly have ended in his impeachment and removal from office.

The gravity of impeachment action makes it an unsuitable basis for curbing presidential power except in rare instances. More often, Congress has responded to abuses of power with hearings or legislation designed to curb the practice. In 1974, for example, Congress passed a law forbidding the president to withhold appropriated funds. President Nixon had refused to release funds for programs he opposed, which meant in effect that the programs were nullified, even though they had been authorized and funded by act of Congress. The new legislation prohibited such action in the future.

The Nixon presidency also contributed to the War Powers Act, which is perhaps Congress's most significant effort in history to curb presidential power. During the Vietnam war, presidents Johnson and Nixon repeatedly told Congress that victory was near, providing intelligence estimates of enemy casualties and capabilities to support their argument. This information contributed to the continued willingness of Congress to appropriate the funds necessary for the conduct of the war. However, congressional support changed abruptly in 1971 with the publication in *The New York Times* of secret government documents (the so-called Pentagon Papers) which revealed that Johnson and Nixon had systematically lied to Congress in order to pursue the war as they saw fit. To prevent future presidential wars, Congress in 1973 passed the War Powers Act. Nixon vetoed the measure, but Congress overrode his veto. The act stipulates that:

- Within 48 hours of committing combat troops, the president must inform Congress in writing of the reasons for doing so.
- Unless Congress acts to extend the period, hostilities involving American troops must end in sixty days, although the troops can remain for an additional thirty days if the president declares that extra time is needed for their safe withdrawal.
- Within the extra thirty days, Congress can demand the immediate withdrawal of the troops by passing a concurrent resolution, which is not subject to presidential veto.
- In every possible instance, the president must consult with Congress before dispatching troops into hostile situations or into areas where such situations are likely to arise.

Every president from Nixon to Clinton has claimed that the act infringes on his constitutional power as commander in chief, and each has refused to accept it fully. For example, Congress was not formally consulted before Bush's intervention in Panama in 1989, Reagan's invasion of Grenada in 1983, Carter's military mission to rescue hostages in Iran in 1979, or Ford's action to free the crew of the *Mayaguez,* seized by Cambodia, in 1975. In each case the president obeyed the requirement to report the military commitment to Congress within forty-eight hours but at the same time refused to acknowledge limits on his authority. Clinton met with congressional leaders about preparations for the Haitian intervention in 1994 but declared that neither the timetable for an invasion nor the invasion itself would be determined by congressional action.

Nevertheless, the lessons of Vietnam have been a significant curb on presidential war making. Congress has shown no willingness to give the president

In a televised speech to the nation, President Richard Nixon points to a map of Cambodia as he announces that thousands of U.S. troops from Vietnam have entered Cambodia to attack communist base camps. The unilateral decisions of Presidents Nixon and Johnson to expand the Vietnam war led Congress to adopt the War Powers Act as a means of preventing future presidential wars. (UPI/Bettmann Newsphotos)

anything approaching a free hand in the use of military force. This posture was plainly evident when it became known in late 1986 that officials in the Reagan administration had attempted illegally and covertly to trade weapons for hostages held by the fundamentalist regime in Iran and had then used profits from the weapons sales to sneak arms to the Contra rebels fighting against the Sandanista government in Nicaragua. These policies violated a legislative prohibition on any form of military aid to the Contras, and Congress launched an immediate investigation that brought the unlawful practices to an abrupt halt, produced administrative changes designed to prevent such abuses of executive authority, and subjected President Reagan to sharp criticism and a loss of public support.

Thus the effect of executive efforts to circumvent congressional authority is heightened congressional opposition. Even if presidents gain in the short run by acting on their own, they undermine their capacity to lead in the long run by failing to keep in mind that Congress is a coequal branch of the American governing system.

PUBLIC SUPPORT

Harry Truman kept a sign on his desk that read, "The buck stops here"—a reference not only to the president's ultimate responsibility for the decisions of his administration but also to the public's tendency to hold the president responsible for national success or failure. Therein lies an axiom of presidential power. As much as from any constitutional grant, legislative statute, or precedent, the president's authority derives from his position as the sole official who can claim to represent the whole American public. As long as the public is behind him, the president's leadership cannot easily be dismissed by other Washington officials. If public support sinks, the public is less inclined to accept presidential leadership.[30]

Every recent president has had the public's confidence at the very start of the term of office. When asked in polls whether they "approve or disapprove of how the president is doing his job," a majority have expressed approval during the first months of the term. Sooner or later, however, all **presidential approval ratings** have slipped below this high point, and only Eisenhower, Kennedy, and Reagan left office with a final-year average higher than 50 percent.

presidential approval rating A measure of the degree to which the public approves or disapproves of the president's performance in office.

The president's personal character plays some part in the public's response. Charges of draft dodging, adultery, and financial misconduct weakened public confidence in Clinton's leadership. His approval rating averaged only 50 percent the first year; other presidents have averaged about 60 percent or higher during this period (see Table 15-2). Nevertheless, personal traits have only a small influence when compared with major national events. The same George Bush who had an approval rating of 91 percent at one point in his presidency had a 41 percent rating the next year. Bush's support peaked with the successful Gulf war in 1991 and then declined steadily as the nation's economy swooned.

Prosperity and Popularity

The economy is the factor that has the biggest impact on presidential approval. Studies have found that economic downswings sharply reduce the public's confidence in the president.[31] Ford, Carter, Reagan, and Bush experi-

TABLE 15-2 Percentage of Public Expressing Approval of President's Performance Presidential approval ratings are typically higher at the beginning of the term than at the end.

President	*Years in Office*	*Average during Presidency*	*First-Year Average*	*Final-Year Average*
Harry Truman	1945–1952	41%	63%	35%
Dwight Eisenhower	1953–1960	64	74	62
John Kennedy	1961–1963	70	76	62
Lyndon Johnson	1963–1968	55	78	40
Richard Nixon	1969–1974	49	63	24
Gerald Ford	1974–1976	46	75	48
Jimmy Carter	1977–1980	47	68	46
Ronald Reagan	1981–1989	53	58	57
George Bush	1989–1992	61	65	40
Bill Clinton	1993–	—	50	—

SOURCE: Averages compiled from Gallup polls.

Americans gather outside the White House to congratulate President Bush after the announcement of victory over Iraq in the Persian Gulf war. As the placard at right indicates, the president's approval rating had soared to a record high of 91 percent. (Brad Markel/Gamma Liaison)

enced precipitous declines in popularity in conjunction with deepening economic problems. A poor economy probably cost Ford a second term and was clearly the key factor in the failed bids for reelection of both presidents Carter and Bush. Apparently the best thing that a president can do to ensure his political success is to preside over a healthy economy.

An economic upswing helps a president, but only to the degree that people feel it in their pocketbooks. The economy moved steadily upward during Clinton's first years in office, but his approval rating did not. One reason is that a lot of people were being left behind economically. The annual income of the average middle-class family, adjusted for inflation, had not increased since the 1970s. If Clinton could hardly be blamed for this persistent problem, his popularity was nevertheless affected by it.

YOUR TURN

PRESIDENTIAL APPROVAL

The Question:

1. Do you approve or disapprove of the way the president is handling his job?

Approve | Disapprove | Not Sure

What Others Think: A form of this question has been asked in Gallup Polls since the 1930s. Presidential approval has become a standard survey item; in a three-month period in 1993, for example, there were more than thirty polls by major news organizations that included the question. Presidential approval ratings have been in the 40 to 60 percent range most of the time in recent decades.

Comment: Public approval is a vital component of presidential power. The president derives authority from his position as a nationally chosen official; as a result, his ability to get others in Washington to follow his lead depends partly on whether his public support is strong or weak. When a president's approval rating drops below 50 percent, resistance to his leadership usually intensifies.

The Public's Response to Crises

International crises nearly always have the effect of increasing the president's public standing, at least in the short run.[32] Threats from abroad tend to produce a patriotic "rally 'round the flag" reaction that initially creates widespread support for the president. Nearly every foreign policy crisis in the past four decades has conformed to this pattern. Even foreign policy disasters increase public support for the president. Reagan's popularity rose by several percentage points in 1983 after a terrorist bomb killed 241 U.S. Marines whom he had ordered into Lebanon in the midst of its civil war.

Yet ongoing crises can eventually erode a president's support. Within a month after Iranian extremists invaded the U.S. embassy in Teheran in November 1979 and took fifty-nine Americans hostage, Carter's public approval rating jumped from 32 to 51 percent.[33] The change revived Carter's prospects for reelection. Before the crisis began, he had trailed Senator Edward Kennedy as the choice of rank-and-file Democrats for the party's 1980 nomination. Kennedy held a 54 to 31 percent edge in a Gallup Poll taken only days before the crisis began; within a few weeks, Carter led, 63 to 24 percent. As months passed without a resolution of the hostage situation, however, Carter's popularity began to sink and his hold on the presidency again looked shaky. In April, Carter ordered a secret mission into Iran to rescue the American hostages. The mission had to be aborted when two of the U.S. rescue helicopters collided. Nonetheless, Carter's public approval rating rose by several points: Americans gave him credit for trying. Had Carter's rescue plan succeeded, it is possible that he would have won reelection. As it was, he nearly did pull off a victory when the Iranians seemed to be close to accepting a negotiated settlement on the eve of the November balloting.

Carter's problem stemmed from the public's high expectations of the president—the widespread belief that the president is the one who gets things

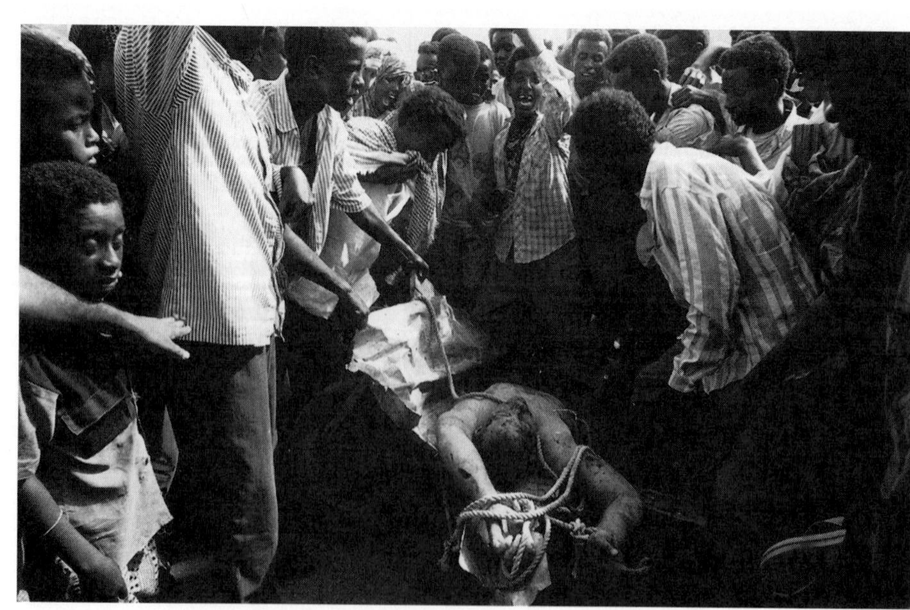

Somali clansmen celebrate the killing of an American soldier whose body was dragged through the streets of Mogadishu. Presidents Bush and Clinton had sent U.S. troops to Somalia as part of a UN operation that was intended to end the starvation and civil war plaguing the African nation. When fighting between a Somali clan and UN peacekeepers resulted in the deaths of more than a score of American soldiers, public and congressional opposition forced Clinton to withdraw U.S. forces. (Keith Bernstein/FSP/Gamma Liaison)

Ronald Reagan became known as the "Great Communicator" because of his skillful televised appeals to the public for support of his policies. (Dennis Brack/Black Star)

done. As Godfrey Hodgson puts it, the president is expected to "conduct the diplomacy of a superpower . . . , manage the economy, command the armed forces, serve as a spiritual example . . . [and] respond to every emergency."[34]

The Televised Presidency and the Illusion of Presidential Government

A major advantage that presidents enjoy in their efforts to nurture public support is their guaranteed access to the media, particularly television.[35] The television medium exalts personality, and the president is ordinarily the most compelling and familiar figure in the American political system. Only the president can expect the television networks to provide free air time on demand, and in terms of the amount of news coverage received, the president towers over all members of Congress combined (see box on next page).

The political scientist Samuel Kernell calls it "going public" when the president bypasses inside bargaining with Congress and promotes "himself and his policies by appealing to the American public for support."[36] Such appeals are at least as old as Theodore Roosevelt's use of the presidency as a "bully pulpit" but have increased substantially in recent years.[37] As the president has moved from an administrative leader to a policy advocate and agenda setter, public support has become increasingly important to presidential success.[38] Television has made it easier for presidents to go public with their programs. Ronald Reagan was called the "Great Communicator" in part because of his ability to use television to generate public support for his initiatives. Reagan's strength was the delivery of prepared speeches. Because he lacked a command of policy details, he did not perform well in informal settings, particularly

THE MEDIA AND THE PEOPLE

THE TELEVISED PRESIDENCY

The president's news coverage is a critical factor in his leadership role. The public looks to the president for leadership in part because the news media portray him as the driving force in the American constitutional system. The presidency receives an extraordinary amount of news attention compared with the Congress. The president and his top appointees receive more than half again as much coverage as all members of Congress combined (see Chapter 13). The president is the only top U.S. official who is guaranteed news coverage whenever he claims to have an important statement to make. The president's newsworthiness is such that he is trailed by a large entourage of reporters even when he goes on vacation.

Although the president is assured of heavy news coverage by the national media, he cannot be sure that the coverage will be favorable. Presidents have become very adept at managing the news, but the press has a somewhat critical view of all politicians, and no president can expect to serve out his term without running into policy problems of one kind or another. Robert Lichter and Linda Lichter are the editors of *Media Monitor,* a publication based on their ongoing content analysis of television news coverage. They have found that critical evaluations of the president often outpace positive ones. For example, Bill Clinton's coverage on the network evening newscasts during the first six months of his presidency was more negative (66 percent) than positive (34 percent). The low point was June when, after a series of personal controversies (including news stories reporting that he had his hair cut for $200), his news coverage dropped to 20 percent positive. "Amateur hour" was how CBS's Susan Spencer described his presidency.

Television in particular is a presidential medium. Television reports its news with pictures and through the actions of persons, which gives the president an advantage over Congress. When the national networks have been criticized for their preoccupation with the president, they have replied that members of Congress get more attention from local media. The Republican takeover in the 1994 elections placed Congress more squarely in the spotlight, and it is likely to stay there in the near future. However, coverage is normally heavily weighted toward the presidency, as indicated by the distribution of network news time in the first eighteen months of the Clinton administration:

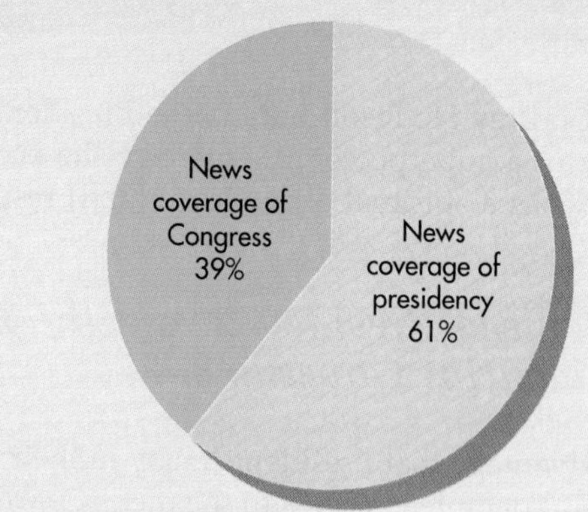

SOURCES: "The Honeymoon That Wasn't," *Media Monitor* 7, no. 7 (September/October 1993): 2–3; "They're No Friends of Bill," *Media Monitor* 8, no. 4 (July/August 1994): 1.

when he had to respond to questioning. In one form or another, however, the president must find ways to communicate effectively with the public.[39]

The "going public" strategy does not always work. In the selling of its health care reform proposal, the Clinton administration launched a campaign not unlike that of a candidate for office. President Clinton, Hillary Rodham Clinton, and cabinet secretaries traveled extensively to generate public support for the initiative. Although the public response was enthusiastic, it came so early that when Congress finally got down to serious business on the health care bill, it had been diluted by time and by the negative advertising campaigns of the insurance and medical lobbies.

Critics have charged that presidents are sometimes more concerned with speaking out about problems than with working to solve them.[40] During the second half of his presidency, for example, Reagan sent budgets to Congress that he knew had no chance of approval and then "went public" to make his point that the national government had become too large and expensive. Reagan's budgets were a statement about big government rather than a blueprint for spending in the next fiscal year.

A good public relations effort on television—and the short memory of the public and the press—can sometimes deflect criticism of the president.[41] Presidents have become adept at putting their preferred "spin" on the news. When it was reported that the performance of U.S. students on standardized achievement exams had declined yet again in 1991, the Bush administration came under attack for its failure to undertake major new initiatives in the education area despite the president's claim to be "the education president." Bush responded immediately with a public appearance at a school in Maine. Pictures of Bush "teaching" a group of students flashed across the news wires and on television news.

However, the press is also adept at putting its own spin on events, and this spin is typically a negative one. The press is often very critical of politicians and of the process within which they operate. During Clinton's first year, for example, the press roundly criticized him for reneging on his campaign promises. This for a president who according to a Knight-Ridder summary had kept or was actively pursuing in Congress 75 percent of the promises he had made during his election campaign; included were major legislative battles already won, such as a tax increase on upper incomes, gun control, an end to the ban on abortion counseling in federally funded clinics, and budget-deficit reduction. The press's version of reality was based on broken promises on a couple of problems that would not go away. Clinton had backed away from a pledge to open the nation's shores to the Haitian boat people, and each tide of immigrants produced additional stories on his broken promise. In contrast, the promises he kept were in the news only a day or two and then not mentioned again. Kept promises are not nearly as newsworthy as broken ones. The media's interpretation of Clinton's presidency has a substantial impact. Every rise in the press criticism of Clinton was followed soon thereafter by a drop in his public approval rating (see Figure 15-2).

Presidents have no choice but to try to counter this type of press coverage with their own version of their accomplishments. A public relations effort can carry a president only so far, however. National conditions ultimately determine the level of public confidence in the president. Indeed, presidents run a risk by trying to build up their images through public relations. Through their frequent television appearances and claims of success, presidents contribute to the public's belief that the president is in charge of the national government, a perception that the political scientist Hugh Heclo calls "the illusion of presidential government."[42]

Because the public expects so much from its presidents, they get too much credit when things go well and too much blame when things go badly. Therein lies an irony of the presidential office. More than from any constitutional grant, more than from any statute, and more than from any crisis, presidential power derives from the president's position as the sole official who can

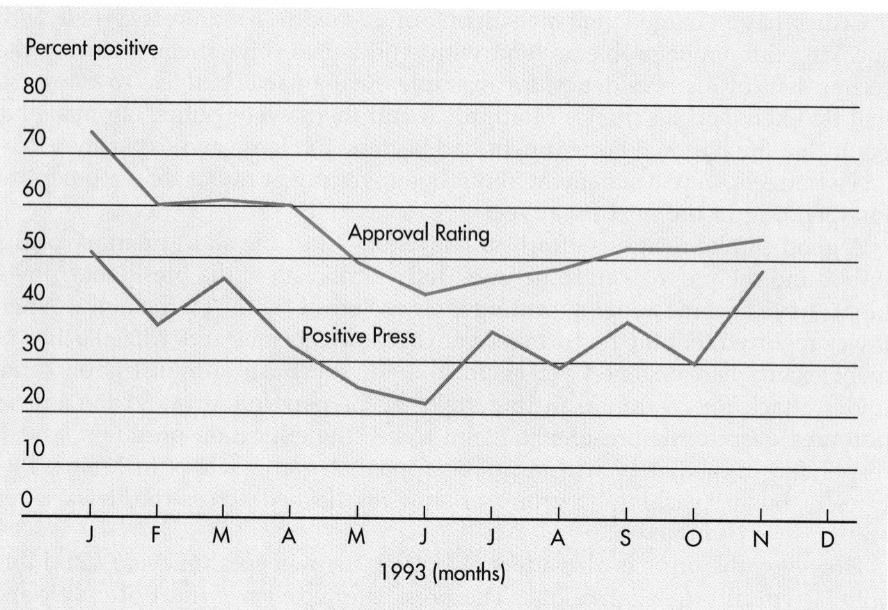

FIGURE 15-2 Relationship of President Clinton's Press Coverage and Public Approval Rating, 1993
Increases in the media's criticism of Clinton were followed by declines in his public approval.
Source: "They're No Friends of Bill," Media Monitor, 8, no. 4 (July/August 1994): 5.

claim to represent the whole American public. Yet because presidential power rests on a popular base, it erodes when public support declines. The irony is that the presidential office grows weaker as problems mount: just when the country could most use effective leadership, that leadership is often hardest to achieve.[43]

Summary

Presidents' records of success in getting their initiatives through Congress have varied considerably. The factors in a president's success include the presence or absence of national conditions that require strong leadership from the White House; the stage of the president's term (success usually comes early); the strength of the president's party in Congress; and the focus on the policy issue (presidents do somewhat better in the area of foreign policy than in domestic policy).

As sole chief executive and the nation's top elected leader, the president can always expect that his policy and leadership efforts will receive attention. However, other institutions, particularly Congress, have the authority to make this leadership effective. If the president is to succeed over the long run, he must have a proper conception of the presidency. Even more important, the president must have the help of other officials, and to get their cooperation he must respond to their concerns. The president operates within a system of divided powers and is almost sure to fail if he tries to go it alone.

To retain an effective leadership position, the president also depends on the strong backing of the American people. Recent presidents have made extensive use of the media to build public support for their programs. Yet they have had difficulty maintaining that support throughout their terms of office. A major reason is that the public expects far more from its presidents than they can deliver.

Major Concepts

honeymoon period
presidential approval rating

Suggested Ratings

Barber, James David. *The Presidential Character: Predicting Performance in the White House,* 3d ed. Englewood Cliffs, N.J.: Prentice-Hall, 1985. An analysis of presidential performance based on the incumbent's personal traits.

Edwards, George C., III. *At the Margins: Presidential Leadership of Congress.* New Haven, Conn.: Yale University Press, 1989. An assessment of the president's influence on Congress, which concludes that the president has a limited ability to lead Congress in directions that it would not otherwise go.

Jones, Charles. *The Presidency in a Separated System.* Washington, D.C.: Brookings Institution, 1994. An insightful analysis of presidential power in a system of divided powers.

Kernell, Samuel. *Going Public: New Strategies of Presidential Leadership.* Washington, D.C.: Congressional Quarterly Press, 1986. A careful analysis of how presidents use the media to build public support for their goals.

Light, Paul. *The President's Agenda: Domestic Policy Choice from Kennedy to Reagan,* rev. ed. Baltimore, Md.: Johns Hopkins University Press, 1991. An assessment of the process of presidential agenda-setting, based on interviews with presidential staff members from Kennedy to Reagan.

Neustadt, Richard E. *Presidential Power: The Politics of Leadership from FDR to Carter.* New York: Wiley, 1980. The classic analysis of the limitations on presidential power.

Rose, Richard. *The Postmodern President,* 2d ed. Chatham, N.J.: Chatham House, 1991. An incisive analysis of the challenges that changing international conditions pose to the president.

Smith, Craig Allen. *The White House Speaks: Presidential Leadership as Persuasion.* Westport, Conn.: Greenwood, 1994. A set of case studies of the role of discourse in presidential leadership.

Stuckey, Mary E. *The President as Interpreter-in-Chief.* Chatham, N.J.: Chatham House, 1991. A careful look at the president's power of communication.

Tulis, Jeffrey K. *The Rhetorical Presidency.* Princeton, N.J.: Princeton University Press, 1987. Argues that the modern presidency is split between its institutional and rhetorical aspects and that this division limits the president's effectiveness.

CHAPTER 16

THE FEDERAL BUREAUCRACY: ADMINISTERING THE GOVERNMENT

[No] industrial society could manage the daily operations of its public affairs without bureaucratic organizations in which officials play a major policymaking role.

—Norman Thomas[1]

Early on the morning of September 7, 1993, a truck pulled up to the south lawn of the White House and unloaded pallets stacked with federal rules and regulations. The display was the backdrop for a presidential speech announcing the completion of the National Performance Review or, as it is commonly called, NPR. The federal regulations piled atop the pallets symbolized bureaucratic red tape, and NPR was a statement of the Clinton administration's effort to make government more responsive. "Our goal," said Clinton, "is to make the entire federal government both less expensive and more efficient, and to change the culture of our national bureaucracy away from complacency and entitlement toward initiative and empowerment. We intend to redesign, to reinvent, to reinvigorate the entire national government."[2]

The origins of the National Performance Review were plain enough. For years, the federal bureaucracy had been derided as too big, too expensive, and too intrusive. These charges gained weight as federal budget deficits increased and the public became increasingly dissatisfied with the performance of the government in Washington. Reform attempts in the 1970s and 1980s had some success but did not stem the tide of federal deficits or markedly improve the bureaucracy's performance. Clinton campaigned on the issue of "reinventing government" and acted swiftly on the promise. During the transition phase, Vice-President–elect Al Gore was placed in charge of the National Performance Review. Once in office, Gore assembled more than 200 career bureaucrats who knew firsthand how the bureaucracy operated and organized them into "reinventing teams" that would recommend ways of improving government administration. The NPR's report included 384 specific recommendations, which were grouped into four broad imperatives: reducing red tape, putting customers first, empowering administrators, and cutting government back to basic services.[3]

NPR is the latest in a lengthy list of twentieth-century efforts to remake the federal bureaucracy. NPR is different in its particulars, but its claim to improve administration while saving money is consistent with the claims of earlier reform panels, including the Brownlow, Hoover, and Volcker commissions.[4] Whether NPR will actually achieve its goals in a major way is yet to be seen; most reform efforts have not lived up to their promise. Nevertheless, NPR addresses an enduring issue of American politics: the bureaucracy's efficiency, responsiveness, and accountability.

Modern government would be impossible without a bureaucracy. It is the government's enormous administrative capacity that makes it possible for the United States to have such ambitious programs as space exploration, social security, environmental protection, interstate highways, and universal postal service. Yet the bureaucracy is also a problem. Even those who work in federal agencies agree that current bureaucratic systems are not working all that well. Both these elements, the need for bureaucracy and the problems associated with it, must be taken into account in any effort to understand the bureaucracy's place in modern American politics.

This chapter describes the nature of the federal bureaucracy and the politics that surrounds it. The discussion initially aims to clarify the bureaucracy's

YOUR TURN

VIEWS OF THE BUREAUCRACY

The Questions:

1. Do you think the federal bureaucracy is doing a good job, fair job, or poor job of carrying out its responsibilities?

   Good job | Fair job | Poor job

2. Think back to the last time you had contact with a federal employee, perhaps while being assisted at the post office or at a national park or while seeking a summer job. What kind of service did you receive—good, fair, or poor service?

   Good service | Fair service | Poor service

What Others Think: According to polls, only a small percentage of Americans think the federal bureaucracy is doing a good job. In a Harris poll that asked respondents to rank order twenty-five institutions and organizations in terms of their effectiveness, the federal bureaucracy finished last. Yet surveys also indicate that most Americans believe they have been personally well-treated when in contact with federal administrators.

Comment: The federal bureaucracy's poor image is only partly deserved. Most Americans have no personal experience that would justify a poor opinion of the bureaucracy, and yet they believe it is remote and unresponsive. In *The Case for Bureaucracy* (1994), Charles Goodsell, a public administration scholar, concludes that the U.S. federal bureaucracy is actually among the world's best. "Some national bureaucracies," he writes, "may be roughly the same in quality of overall performance [as the U.S. bureaucracy], but they are few in number." In some countries, the bureaucracy is thoroughly inefficient and corrupt. Tasks are completed slowly and sometimes not at all unless a bribe has been paid. In other countries, the bureaucracy is overly rigid, centralized, and remote. Neither of these extreme tendencies is characteristic of the U.S. bureaucracy. Nevertheless, most analysts believe that federal agencies are less effective than they could and should be.

responsibilities, organizational structure, and management practices. But the chapter also shows that the bureaucracy is very much a part of the play of politics. Bureaucrats necessarily and naturally take an "agency point of view," seeking to promote their agency's objectives. The three constitutional branches of government impose a degree of accountability on the bureaucracy, but the sheer size and fragmented nature of the U.S. government confound the problem of control and make efforts to reform the bureaucracy a high priority. The main points discussed in this chapter are the following:

★ *Bureaucracy is an inevitable consequence of complexity and scale.* Modern government could not function without a large bureaucracy. Through authority, specialization, and rules, bureaucracy provides a means of managing thousands of tasks and employees.

★ *The bureaucracy is expected simultaneously to respond to the direction of partisan officials and to administer programs fairly and competently.* These conflicting demands are addressed through a combination of personnel management systems—the patronage, merit, and executive leadership systems.

★ *Bureaucrats naturally take an "agency point of view," which they promote through their expert knowledge, support from clientele groups, and backing by Congress or the president.*

★ *Although agencies are subject to scrutiny by the president, Congress, and the judiciary, bureaucrats are able to achieve power in their own right.* The issue of bureaucratic power and responsiveness is a basis of current efforts at "reinventing" government.

The executive bureaucracy tends to make news primarily for its blunders. Here President Clinton names outgoing Kansas Congressman Dan Glickman (center) as his choice to replace outgoing Agriculture secretary Mike Espy (right), who was forced to resign because of alleged ethical violations. (Wide World Photos)

Federal Administration: Form, Personnel, and Activities

For many Americans, the word "bureaucracy" brings to mind waste, mindless rules, and rigidity. This image is not unfounded, but it is one-sided. Bureaucracy is also an efficient and effective method of organization. Although Americans tend to equate bureaucracy with government, bureaucracy is found wherever there is a need to manage large numbers of people and tasks. All large-scale, task-oriented organizations—public and private—are bureaucratic in form.[5] General Motors is a bureaucracy. So, too, is the Catholic church and every large medical complex and educational institution. Bureaucracy alone facilitates the coordination of a large work force.

bureaucracy A system of organization and control based on the principles of hierarchical authority, job specialization, and formalized rules.

hierarchical authority A basic principle of bureaucracy that refers to the chain of command within an organization, whereby officials and units have control over those below them.

job specialization A basic principle of bureaucracy which holds that the responsibilities of each job position should be explicitly defined and that a precise division of labor within the organization should be maintained.

formalized rules A basic principle of bureaucracy that refers to the standardized procedures and established regulations by which a bureaucracy conducts its operations.

In formal terms, **bureaucracy** is a system of organization and control that is based on three principles: hierarchical authority, job specialization, and formalized rules. **Hierarchical authority** refers to a chain of command, whereby the officials and units at the top of a bureaucracy have authority over those in the middle, who in turn control those at the bottom. In a system of **job specialization,** the responsibilities of each job position are explicitly defined, and there is a precise division of labor within the organization. **Formalized rules** are the standardized procedures and established regulations by which a bureaucracy conducts its operations.

These features are the reason that bureaucracy, as a form of organization, is the most efficient means of getting people to work together on tasks of great magnitude and complexity. Hierarchy speeds action by reducing conflict over the power to make decisions: the higher an individual's position in the organization, the more decision-making power he or she has. Specialization yields efficiency because each individual is required to concentrate on a particular job: workers acquire specialized skills and knowledge. Formalized rules enable workers to act quickly and precisely because decisions are made on the basis of established organizational standards rather than their personal inclinations.[6]

These organizational characteristics are also the cause of bureaucracy's pathologies. Administrators perform not as whole persons but as parts of an organizational entity. Their behavior is governed by position, specialty, and rule. At its worst, bureaucracy grinds on, heedless of the feelings and needs of its members or their clients. Fixed rules come to dominate everything.[7]

If bureaucracy is an indispensable condition of large-scale organization, gross bureaucratic inefficiency and unresponsiveness are not, or at least that is the assumption underlying current efforts to reform the administration of government, a topic that will be examined later in this chapter.

THE FEDERAL BUREAUCRACY IN AMERICANS' DAILY LIVES

The U.S. federal bureaucracy has more than 2.5 million employees, who have responsibility for administering thousands of programs. The president and Congress may get far more attention in the news, but it is the bureaucracy that has the more immediate impact on the daily lives of Americans. The federal bureaucracy performs a wide range of functions: for example, it delivers the daily mail, maintains the national forests and parks, administers social security, builds dams and generates hydroelectric power, enforces environmental protection laws, develops the country's defense systems, provides foodstuffs for school lunch programs, and regulates the stock markets.

TYPES OF ADMINISTRATIVE ORGANIZATIONS

The chief organizational feature of the U.S. federal bureaucracy is its division into areas of specialization. One agency handles veterans' affairs, another specializes in education, a third is responsible for agriculture, and so on. No two units are exactly alike. Nevertheless, most of them take one of five general forms: cabinet department, independent agency, regulatory agency, government corporation, or presidential commission.

Cabinet Departments.

The major administrative units are the fourteen **cabinet** (or **executive**) **departments** (see Table 16-1). Each is headed by a secretary, who serves as a member of the president's cabinet and is responsible for establishing the department's general policy and overseeing its operations.

cabinet (executive) departments The major administrative organizations within the federal executive bureaucracy, each of which is headed by a secretary (cabinet officer) and has responsibility for a major function of the federal government, such as defense, agriculture, or justice.

Cabinet departments vary greatly in their visibility, size, and importance. The Department of State is one of the oldest and most prestigious departments, but it is also one of the smallest, with approximately 25,000 employees. The Department of Defense is the largest, with more than 750,000 civilian employees (apart from the more than 1.5 million uniformed members of the armed services). The Department of Health and Human Services has the largest budget; its activities account for about a third of all federal spending, much of it for social security benefits. The Department of Veterans Affairs is the newest department, having been formed in 1988.

Each cabinet department has responsibility for a general policy area. But executive departments are not monoliths: each department has a number of semiautonomous operating units that typically carry the label of "bureau," "agency," "division," or "service." The Department of Justice, for example, has thirteen such operating units, including the Federal Bureau of Investigation (FBI), Immigration and Naturalization Service (INS), and Drug Enforcement Administration (DEA). In short, the Department of Justice is itself a large, complex bureaucracy, as Figure 16-1 indicates.

Independent Agencies

Independent agencies resemble the cabinet departments, but most of them have a narrower area of responsibility. They include such organizations as the Central Intelligence Agency (CIA) and the National Aeronautics and Space Administration (NASA). The heads of these agencies are appointed by and report to the president but are not members of the cabinet. Like the executive departments, each of the independent agencies is divided into smaller operating units. In general, the independent agencies exist apart from cabinet departments because their placement within a department would pose symbolic or practical policy problems. NASA, for example, could conceivably be located in the Department of Defense, but this positioning would suggest that

independent agencies Bureaucratic agencies that are similar to cabinet departments but usually have a narrower area of responsibility. Each such agency is headed by a presidential appointee who is not a cabinet member. An example is the National Aeronautics and Space Administration (NASA).

TABLE 16-1 Budgets and Number of Employees of Cabinet Departments The executive departments vary greatly in size and budget.

Department	*Year Created*	*Budget (Billions of Dollars)*	*Number of Full-Time Civilian Employees*
State	1789	$ 5.2	25.0
Treasury	1789	328.7	157.6
Defense[a]	1789	252.2[b]	854.9[c]
Interior	1849	7.1	74.6
Justice[d]	1870	12.8	101.9
Agriculture	1889	61.7	108.5
Commerce[e]	1903	4.2	35.8
Labor	1913	36.0	19.5
Health and Human Services[f]	1953	667.0[g]	127.2
Housing and Urban Development	1965	27.5	13.4
Transportation	1966	40.8	67.5
Energy	1977	15.9	20.6
Education	1979	31.7	5.2
Veterans Affairs	1988	37.8	229.7

[a]Originally the Department of War. In 1947 the departments of the Army, Navy, and Air Force were combined into the Department of Defense.
[b]Military and civilian.
[c]Civilian only.
[d]The attorney general was earlier a member of the president's cabinet, but the Department of Justice was not created until 1870.
[e]Originally the Department of Commerce and Labor. A separate Department of Labor was created in 1913.
[f]Originally the Department of Health, Education, and Welfare. A separate Department of Education was formed in 1979.
[g]Including social security.

SOURCE: *Budget of the United States Government, 1995* (Washington, D.C.: U.S. Government Printing Office, 1994).

The bureaucracy's responsibilities include programs designed to reduce work-related accidents and illnesses. (Robert Fox/Impact Visuals)

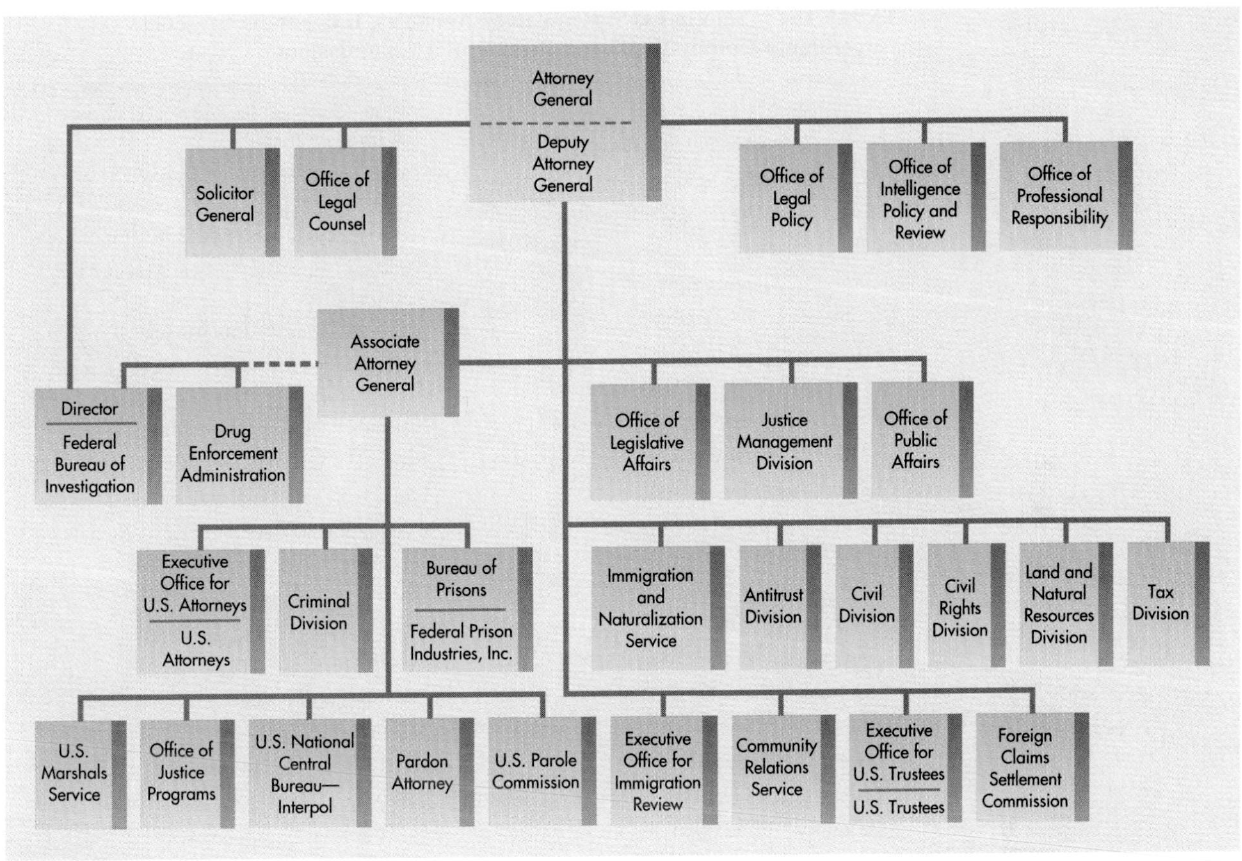

FIGURE 16-1 The U.S. Department of Justice
The major divisions of the U.S. Department of Justice are shown in this organization chart.
Source: The U.S. Government Manual.

the space program is intended for military purposes and not also for civilian purposes, such as space exploration and satellite communication.

Regulatory Agencies

regulatory agencies Administrative units, such as the Federal Communications Commission and the Environmental Protection Agency, that have responsibility for the monitoring and regulation of ongoing economic activities.

Regulatory agencies are created when Congress recognizes the importance of close and continuous regulation of an economic activity. Because such regulation requires more time and expertise than Congress can provide, the responsibility is delegated to a regulatory agency. The Securities and Exchange Commission (SEC), which oversees the stock and bond markets, is a regulatory agency. So is the Environmental Protection Agency (EPA), which works to monitor and prevent industrial pollution. Table 16-2 lists some of the regulatory agencies and other noncabinet units of the federal bureaucracy.

Beyond their executive functions, regulatory agencies have certain legislative and judicial functions. They issue regulations, implement them, and then judge whether individuals or organizations have followed them. Some regulatory agencies, particularly the older ones, are "independent" by virtue of their relative freedom from ongoing political control. They are headed by a

TABLE 16-2 Selected U.S. Regulatory Agencies, Independent Agencies, Government Corporations, and Presidential Commissions

Administrative Conference of the U.S.	National Aeronautics and Space Administration
African Development Foundation	National Archives and Records Administration
American Battle Monuments Commission	National Credit Union Administration
Appalachian Regional Commission	National Foundation on the Arts and the Humanities
Board for International Broadcasting	National Labor Relations Board
Central Intelligence Agency	National Railroad Passenger Corporation (Amtrak)
Commission on Civil Rights	National Science Foundation
Commission on Fine Arts	National Transportation Safety Board
Commodity Futures Trading Commission	Nuclear Regulatory Commission
Consumer Product Safety Commission	Occupational Safety and Health Review Commission
Environmental Protection Agency	Office of Personnel Management
Equal Employment Opportunity Commission	Peace Corps
Export-Import Bank of the U.S.	Postal Rate Commission
Farm Credit Administration	Securities and Exchange Commission
Federal Communications Commission	Selective Service System
Federal Deposit Insurance Corporation	Small Business Administration
Federal Election Commission	U.S. Arms Control and Disarmament Agency
Federal Emergency Management Agency	U.S. Information Agency
Federal Home Loan Bank Board	U.S. International Development Cooperation Agency
Federal Labor Relations Authority	U.S. International Trade Commission
Federal Maritime Commission	U.S. Postal Service
Federal Mediation and Conciliation Service	
Federal Reserve System, Board of Governors of the	
Federal Trade Commission	
General Services Administration	
Merit Systems Protection Board	

SOURCE: *The U.S. Government Manual*

commission of several members who are appointed by the president and confirmed by Congress but are not subject to removal by the president. Commissioners serve a fixed term, a legal stipulation intended to free their agencies from political interference. The newer regulatory agencies lack such autonomy; most are headed by a presidential appointee who can be removed at the president's discretion. (Regulatory agencies are discussed more fully in Chapter 18.)

government corporations Bodies, such as the U.S. Postal Service and Amtrak, that are similar to private corporations in that they charge for their services, but different in that they receive federal funding to help defray expenses. Their directors are appointed by the president with Senate approval.

Government Corporations

Government corporations are similar to private corporations in that they charge clients for their services and are governed by a board of directors. However, government corporations receive federal funding to help defray operating expenses, and their directors are appointed by the president with

Senate approval. The largest government corporation is the U.S. Postal Service, with roughly 800,000 employees. Other government corporations include the Federal Deposit Insurance Corporation (FDIC), which insures savings accounts against bank failures, and the National Railroad Passenger Corporation (Amtrak), which provides passenger rail service.

Presidential Commissions

Some **presidential commissions** are permanent commissions that provide ongoing recommendations to the president in particular areas of responsibility. Two such commissions are the Commission on Civil Rights and the Commission on Fine Arts. Other presidential commissions are temporary and disband after making recommendations on specific issues. An example is the President's Private Sector Survey on Cost Control, commonly known as the Grace Commission, which was created in the 1980s to propose ways of reducing waste in the administration of federal programs.

presidential commissions These organizations within the bureaucracy are headed by commissioners appointed by the president. An example of such a commission is the Commission on Civil Rights.

FEDERAL EMPLOYMENT

The more than 2.5 million civilian employees of the federal government include professionals who bring their expertise to the problems of governing

HOW THE UNITED STATES COMPARES

EDUCATIONAL BACKGROUNDS OF BUREAUCRATS

To staff its bureaucracy, the U.S. government tends to hire persons with specialized educations to hold specialized jobs; this approach heightens the tendency of bureaucrats to take the agency point of view. By comparison, Great Britain tends to recruit its bureaucrats from the arts and humanities, on the assumption that general ability and intelligence are the best qualifications for detached professionalism. The continental European democracies also emphasize detached professionalism, but in the context of the supposedly impartial application of rules. As a consequence, high-ranking civil servants in Europe tend to have legal educations. The college majors of senior civil servants in the United States and other democracies reflect these tendencies.

SOURCE: B. Guy Peters, *The Politics of Bureaucracy*, 3d ed. (New York: Longman, 1989), ch.3. Table adapted from table 3.7, 102–103.

College Major of Senior Civil Servants	*Denmark*	*Germany*	*Great Britain*	*Italy*	*Netherlands*	*United States*
Natural science/engineering	16%	11%	11%	27%	25%	43%
Social science/humanities	20	8	87	24	28	27
Law	60	65	—	49	45	24
Other	4	16	2	—	2	6
	100%	100%	100%	100%	100%	100%

The U.S. Postal Service, the largest government corporation, moves more mail, and does so more cheaply and reliably, than do the postal bureaucracies of most other industrialized nations. Yet the U.S. Postal Service, like most other federal agencies, has a poor public image. (Bob Daemmrich/Stock, Boston)

a large and complex society, service workers who perform such tasks as the typing of correspondence and the delivery of mail, and middle and top managers who supervise the work of the various federal agencies.

More than 90 percent of federal employees are hired by merit criteria, which include educational attainment, employment experience, and performance on competitive tests (such as the civil service and foreign service examinations). The merit system is intended to protect the public from the inept or discriminatory administrative practices that can result if partisanship is the employment criterion. A 1990 Supreme Court ruling prohibits patronage in all personnel operations (hiring, firing, transfers, promotions, training, and so on) unless the government can convincingly show that party affiliation is *positively* related to effective performance in a particular position.[8] This can be demonstrated in some cases, but not in the large majority of personnel operations, which are thereby off limits to partisan politics.

Although federal employees were once greatly underpaid in comparison with their counterparts in the private sector, they now receive somewhat competitive salaries, except at the top levels. The large majority of federal employees have a GS (Graded Service) job ranking. The rankings range from GS-1 (the lowest rank) to GS-18 (the highest). College graduates who enter the federal service usually start at the GS-5 level, which provides a salary of about $20,000 for a beginning employee. With a master's degree, the level is GS-9 at a $30,000 salary. Federal employees' salaries increase with rank and length of service. Public employees receive substantial fringe benefits, including full health insurance, liberal retirement plans, and generous vacation time and sick leave.

Public service has its drawbacks. Federal employees have few rights of collective action.[9] They can join labor unions, but their unions by law have limited authority: the government maintains full control of job assignments, compensation, and promotion. Moreover, the Taft-Hartley Act of 1947 prohibits strikes by federal employees and permits the firing of workers who do go on strike.[10] There are also some limits on the partisan activities of civil servants. The Hatch Act of 1939 prohibited them from holding key positions in election campaigns. In 1993, Congress relaxed this prohibition but retained it for certain high-ranking career bureaucrats (including those in the Senior Executive Service, which is discussed later in the chapter).

THE FEDERAL BUREAUCRACY'S POLICY RESPONSIBILITIES

The Constitution mentions executive departments but does not grant them any powers. Their authority derives from grants of power to the three constitutional branches: Congress, the president, and the courts. Nevertheless, the bureaucracy is far more than an administrative extension of the three branches. It never merely follows orders. The primary function of administrative agencies is **policy implementation,** which is to say that they carry out the authoritative decisions of Congress, the president, and the courts. Although implementation is sometimes described as "mere administration," it is a highly significant and creative function.

policy implementation The primary function of the bureaucracy is policy implementation, which refers to the process of carrying out the authoritative decisions of Congress, the president, and the courts.

Many ideas for legislative programs are initiated by the bureaucracy. In the course of their work, administrators come up with policy ideas that are then brought to the attention of the president or members of Congress. Adminis-

Unlike union members in the private sector, federal employees are prohibited by law from going on strike and can be fired if they do so. President Reagan summarily fired members of the air traffic controllers union (PATCO) who went on strike in 1981. President Clinton offered reinstatement in 1993, but by then most of them had retired or started other careers. (Charles Steiner/Sygma)

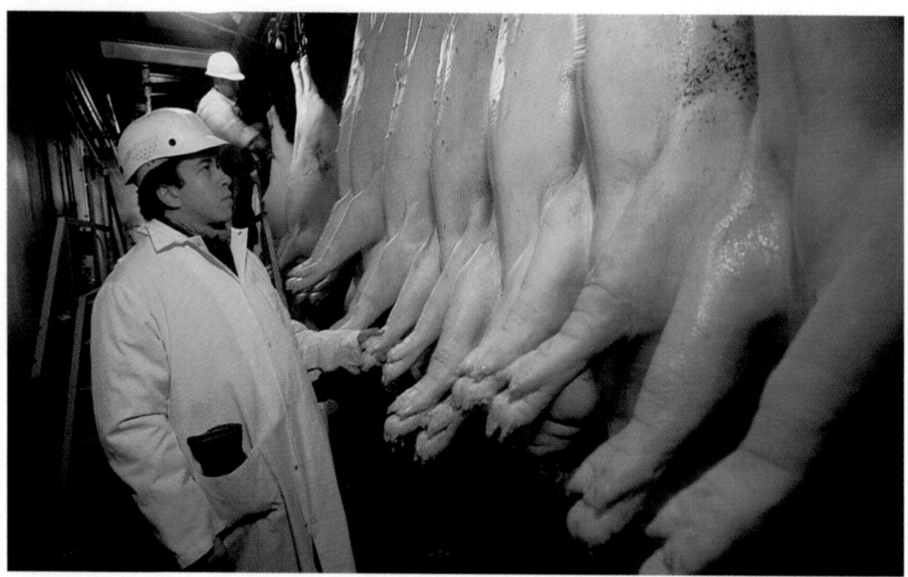

As one of thousands of services provided by the federal bureaucracy, the Department of Agriculture sets standards for the quality of meat and poultry sold to the public and conducts periodic inspections of processing plants to ensure compliance with those standards. (Paul S. Howell/Gamma Liaison)

trative agencies also develop public policy in the process of implementing it. The decisions of Congress, the president, and the courts typically need to be fleshed out by the bureaucracy.[11] Most legislative acts specify general goals, which bureaucrats then develop into specific programs. Consider the Drug-Free Workplace Act of 1988, which directs all organizations that receive grants from a federal agency to take steps to keep drugs out of the workplace or risk losing federal funding. The legislation provides that grantees will not lose their funds if drugs enter the workplace, if they have made "good-faith efforts" to keep drugs out. But what constitutes a "good-faith effort"? In large part, Congress left it to the administrators to devise the criteria for judging enforcement efforts, which in effect meant that they created the rules by which the Drug-Free Workplace Act would be applied. This development of policy—often through *rule making*—is perhaps the chief way that administrative agencies exercise real power. To an important degree, they decide how the law will operate in practice.

Agencies are also charged with the delivery of services—carrying the mail, processing welfare applications, approving government loans, and the like. Such activities are governed by rules, and in most instances the rules decide what gets done. But some services allow agency employees enough discretion that laws end up being applied arbitrarily, a situation that Michael Lipsky describes as "street-level bureaucracy."[12] For example, FBI agents more diligently pursue organized crime than white-collar crime.

The bureaucracy's policy role is perhaps clearest in its regulatory activities.[13] Lacking the necessary expertise and time, Congress has delegated regulatory responsibilities to specialized agencies. The Environmental Protection Agency (EPA), for example, can fine a company that is not complying with antipollution standards and can refer serious cases to the Justice Department for further action. Agencies possess considerable discretion in their regulatory function. Consider the difference in the performance of the EPA during the presidencies of Democrat Jimmy Carter and Republican Ronald Reagan. The number of cases of industrial pollution referred by the EPA to the Justice Department for prosecution declined from 252 in 1980, Carter's last year in office, to 78 in 1981, Reagan's first year.[14] The change reflected Reagan's pro-business philosophy.

In sum, administrators necessarily exercise discretion in carrying out their policy responsibilities. They initiate policy, develop it, evaluate it, apply it, and determine whether others are complying with it. The bureaucracy does not simply administer policy; it also *makes* policy.

Development of the Federal Bureaucracy: Politics and Administration

The organization and staffing of the bureaucracy have been administrative and political issues throughout the country's history. Agencies are responsible for carrying out programs that serve the society, and yet each agency was created and is maintained in response to partisan interests. Each agency thus confronts two simultaneous but incompatible demands: that it administer programs fairly and competently and that it respond to partisan claims.

Historically, this conflict has worked itself out in ways that have made the organization of the modern bureaucracy a blend of the political and the administrative. This dual line of development is clearly reflected in the mix of management systems that characterizes the bureaucracy today—the *patronage, merit,* and *executive leadership* systems (see Table 16-3).

SMALL GOVERNMENT AND THE PATRONAGE SYSTEM

The federal bureaucracy was originally small (3,000 employees in 1800, for instance). Under the U.S. Constitution, the states retained responsibility for nearly all domestic policy areas. The federal government's role was confined

TABLE 16-3 Justifications for Major Systems for Managing the Bureaucracy

System	*Justification*
Patronage	Makes the bureaucracy more responsive to election outcomes by allowing the president to appoint the top officials of executive agencies.
Merit	Provides for *competent* administration in that employees are hired on the basis of ability and allowed to remain on the job and thereby become proficient at their work, and provides for *neutral* administration in the sense that civil servants are not partisan appointees and thus are expected to do their work in an evenhanded way.
Executive leadership	Provides for presidential leadership of the bureaucracy in order to make it more responsive and to give it greater coordination and direction (left alone, the bureaucracy tends toward fragmentation).

mainly to defense and foreign affairs, currency and interstate commerce, and the delivery of the mail. The nation's first six presidents, from George Washington through John Quincy Adams, believed that only distinguished men should be entrusted with the management of the national government. Nearly all top presidential appointees were men of education and political experience, and many of them were members of socially prominent families. They often remained in their jobs year after year.

The nation's seventh president, Andrew Jackson, did not share his predecessors' admiration for the wellborn.[15] In Jackson's view, government would be more responsive to the people if it were administered by common men of good sense.[16] Jackson also believed that top administrators should remain in office for short periods, so that there would be a steady influx of fresh ideas.

patronage system An approach to managing the bureaucracy whereby people are appointed to important government positions as a reward for political services they have rendered and because of their partisan loyalty.

spoils system The practice of granting public office to individuals in return for political favors they have rendered.

Jackson's version of the **patronage system** was popular with the public, but critics labeled it a **spoils system**—a device for placing political cronies in government office as a reward for partisan service. Although Jackson was motivated as much by a concern for democratic government as by his desire to reward partisan supporters, later presidents were often more interested in distributing the spoils of victory. Jackson's successors extended patronage to all levels of administration.[17]

GROWTH IN GOVERNMENT AND THE MERIT SYSTEM

Because the government of the early nineteenth century was relatively small and limited in scope, it could be managed by employees who had little or no administrative training or experience. As the century advanced, however, the nature of the bureaucracy changed rapidly, as did the bureaucracy's personnel needs.

An impetus for change was the Industrial Revolution, which was creating a truly national economy and prompting economic groups to pressure Con-

The assassination of President James A. Garfield in 1881 by Charles Guiteau, a disappointed office seeker, did much to end the spoils system of distributing government jobs. (The Bettmann Archive)

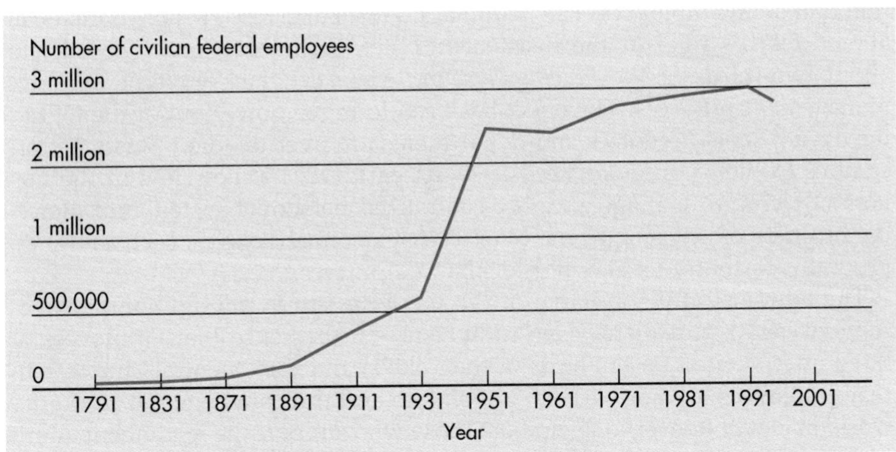

FIGURE 16-2 Number of Persons Employed by the Federal Government, 1791–1995 The federal bureaucracy grew slowly until the 1930s, when an explosive growth began in the number of programs that required ongoing administration by the federal government. *Source: Historical Statistics of the United States and Statistical Abstract of the United States, 1986, 322; 1991 and 1995 figures from U.S. Office of Personnel Management.*

gress to protect and promote their interests. Farmers were one of the groups that looked to the federal government for market and price assistance; in response, Congress created the Department of Agriculture in 1889. Business and labor interests also pressed their claims, and in 1903 Congress established the Department of Commerce and Labor to "promote the mutual interest" of the nation's firms and workers. (The separate interests of business and labor proved stronger than their shared concerns, and so in 1913 Labor became a separate department.)[18]

Because of the increased need for continuous administration of government, an ever-larger bureaucracy was required (see Figure 16-2). By 1930 federal employment had reached 600,000, a sixfold increase over the level of the 1880s.[19] During the 1930s, as a result of President Franklin Roosevelt's New Deal, the federal work force increased enormously, to 1.2 million. Roosevelt's programs were generated in response to public demands for relief from the economic hardship and uncertainty of the Great Depression. Administration of these programs necessitated the formation of economic and social welfare agencies such as the Securities and Exchange Commission and the Social Security Board. The effect was to give the federal government an ongoing role in promoting Americans' economic well-being.

A large and active government requires skilled and experienced personnel. In 1883 Congress passed the Pendleton Act, which established a **merit system** (or **civil service system**) whereby certain federal employees were hired through competitive examinations or by virtue of having special qualifications, such as an advanced degree in a particular field. The transition to a career civil service was gradual. Only 10 percent of federal positions in 1885 were filled on the basis of merit; by 1920, however, more than 70 percent were merit-based; and since 1950 the proportion of merit employees has not dipped below 80 percent.[20]

merit (civil service) system An approach to managing the bureaucracy whereby people are appointed to government positions on the basis of either competitive examinations or special qualifications, such as professional training.

The Pendleton Act created a Civil Service Commission to establish job classifications, administer competitive examinations, and oversee merit employees. The commission was replaced by two independent agencies in 1978. The Merit Service Protection Board handles appeals of personnel actions, and the Office of Personnel Management (OPM) supervises the hiring and classification of federal employees. The National Performance Review has dramatically altered OPM's role. At the insistence of Vice-President Gore, OPM deleted about two-thirds of the *Federal Personnel Manual,* which governs employee management practices. The effect has been to move power out of the OPM to the agency level. Agencies and departments are freer to adapt personnel procedures to their particular needs. For its part, OPM is now less in the business of trying to manage a highly centralized personnel system and more in the business of advising agencies on their personnel policies, such as training programs for entry-level and midcareer employees.[21]

neutral competence The administrative objective of merit-based bureaucracy. Such a bureaucracy should be "competent" in the sense that its employees are hired and retained on the basis of their expertise and "neutral" in the sense that it operates by objective standards rather than partisan ones.

The administrative objective of the merit system is **neutral competence.**[22] A merit-based bureaucracy is "competent" in the sense that employees are hired and retained on the basis of their skills, and it is "neutral" in the sense that employees are not partisan appointees and thus are expected to do their work on behalf of everyone, not just those who support the incumbent administration.

Although the merit system has wide acceptance, it does not guarantee impartial administration. Programs are not self-executing; they must be developed and applied by bureaucrats—a fact that both enables and requires them to play a policy role. Each agency naturally gives higher priority to its concerns than to those of other agencies and to those of Congress or the president. The consequences, as will be explained later in the chapter, include a more fragmented government and a weakening of political accountability because bureaucrats are not subject to election.[23]

BIG GOVERNMENT AND THE EXECUTIVE LEADERSHIP SYSTEM

executive leadership system An approach to managing the bureaucracy that is based on presidential leadership and presidential management tools, such as the president's annual budget proposal.

As problems with the merit system surfaced after the early years of this century, reformers looked to a strengthened presidency—an **executive leadership system**—as a means of coordinating the bureaucracy's activities to increase its efficiency and responsiveness.[24] The president was to provide the general leadership that would overcome agency fragmentation and provide a common direction. As we saw in Chapter 15, Congress in 1939 provided the president with some of the tools needed for improved coordination of the bureaucracy. The Office of Management and Budget (OMB) was created to allow the president to examine and adjust the annual budget proposal of each executive agency. The president was also empowered to reorganize the bureaucracy, subject to congressional approval, in order to reduce duplication of activities and strengthen the chain of command from the president to the agencies. Finally, the president was authorized to develop the Executive Office of the President, which oversees the agencies' activities on the president's behalf, assisting in the development of policy programs.

Like the merit and patronage systems, the executive leadership system has brought problems as well as improvements to the administration of government. The executive leadership concept, if carried too far, can threaten the balance between executive power and legislative power on which the U.S. constitutional system is based, and it can make the president's priorities, not fairness, the criterion by which provision of services is determined. Richard Nixon abused the system, for example, by ordering the OMB to impound (that is, fail to spend) more than $40 billion in appropriated funds of programs he disliked. (The courts ruled that Nixon's action was an unlawful infringement on Congress's constitutional authority over spending. To prevent a recurrence of the problem, Congress in 1974 passed legislation that gives the president the authority to withhold funds for only 45 days unless Congress passes legislation to rescind the appropriation.)

Nevertheless, executive leadership through the president is a vital part of the effort to bring greater accountability and direction to the administration of government. The executive leadership principle was the basis for the creation of the Senior Executive Service (SES). Established by Congress at the urging of President Carter, the SES represents a compromise between two traditions: a president-led bureaucracy and an expert one.[25] The SES consists of roughly 8,000 top-level career civil servants who receive higher salaries than their peers but who can be assigned, dismissed, or transferred by order of the president. Unlike regular presidential appointees, SES bureaucrats cannot be fired; if the president relieves them of their jobs, they have "fallback" rights to their former rank in the regular civil service. The SES gives the president greater access to and control over individuals who are already expert in the bureaucracy's work. However, the SES has at least one drawback: after years of work in the bureaucracy, some top-level bureaucrats have difficulty transferring their loyalty from an agency to the president.

The executive leadership system is not a panacea but, along with the patronage and merit systems, is a necessary component of any effective strategy for managing the modern federal bureaucracy.[26] The federal bureaucracy today embodies aspects of all three systems, a situation that reflects the tensions inherent in governmental administration. The bureaucracy is expected to carry out programs fairly, but it is also expected to respond to political forces and to principles of effective management. The first of these requirements is addressed primarily through the merit system, the second through the patronage system, and the third through the executive leadership system.

★ CRITICAL THINKING

The Proper Balance between the Merit and Executive Leadership Systems

An argument for the executive leadership model is that there is a democratic justification—the will of the people as expressed in a presidential election—for the bias it introduces into the administration of government. No advocate of the executive leadership model would hold that administration in all respects should be overtly partisan (imagine if monthly social security checks were sent only to Republicans or only to Democrats). However, proponents of executive leadership do argue that the driving force in bureaucratic politics (which includes, for example, the struggle over budgetary priorities) should be partisanship as expressed through elections and not partisanship as expressed through an entrenched civil service.

In contrast, supporters of the merit system say that neutral competence—impartial and expert administration—should be the primary goal of a governmental bureaucracy and that the merit system is the only realistic way of approaching the goal. They argue that career civil servants have a commendable record of impartial public service, which has served the country well.

What balance would you strike between the merit and executive leadership systems? Would you have the same opinion about the balance if control of the White House were to shift to the other major party?

The Bureaucracy's Power Imperative

A common misperception is that the president, as the chief executive, has the sole claim on the bureaucracy's loyalty. In fact, each of the elected institutions has reason to claim proprietorship: the president as chief executive and Congress as the source of the authorization and funding of the bureaucracy's programs. Faced with a threat from either Congress or the presidency, agencies often find an ally in the other institution. One presidential appointee asked a congressional committee whether it had any problem with his plans to reduce one of his agency's programs. The committee chairman replied, "No, you have the problem, because if you touch that bureau I'll cut your job out of the budget."[27]

The U.S. system of separate institutions sharing power results in a natural tendency for each institution to guard its turf. In addition, the president and members of Congress differ in their constituencies and thus in the interests to which they are most responsive. For example, although the agricultural sector is just one of many concerns of the president, it is of vital interest to senators and representatives from farm states. Finally, because the president and

Congress are elected separately, the White House and one or both houses of Congress may be in the hands of opposing parties. Since 1968, this source of executive-legislative conflict has been more often the rule than the exception.

If agencies are to operate successfully in this system, they must seek support where they can find it—if not from the president, then from Congress; if not today, then tomorrow. In other words, agencies must play politics.[28] Any agency that is content to sit idly by while new priorities for money and policy are determined is virtually certain to lose out to other agencies that are willing to fight for power.

THE AGENCY POINT OF VIEW

agency point of view The tendency of bureaucrats to place the interests of their agency ahead of other interests and ahead of the priorities sought by the president or Congress.

Administrators have little choice but to look out for their agency's interests, a perspective that is called the **agency point of view.**[29] This perspective comes naturally to most high-ranking civil servants. Their careers within the bureaucracy have taught them to do their part in making the organization effective. Many bureaucrats are also personally committed to their agency's objectives as a result of having spent years working on its programs. More than 80 percent of all top careerists reach their high-level positions by rising through the ranks of the same agency.[30] As one top administrator said when testifying before the House Appropriations Committee, "Mr. Chairman, you would not think it proper for me to be in charge of this work and not be enthusiastic about it . . . , would you? I have been in it for thirty years, and I believe in it."[31]

Professionalism also cements agency loyalties.[32] As public policymaking has become more complex, high-level administrative positions have increasingly been filled by scientists, engineers, lawyers, educators, physicians, and other professionals. Most of them take jobs in an agency whose programs are consistent with their professional values.

Studies confirm that bureaucrats believe in the importance of their agency's work.[33] One study found that social welfare administrators are three times as likely as other civil servants to believe that social welfare programs should be given a high budget priority.[34]

SOURCES OF BUREAUCRATIC POWER

In promoting their agency's interests, bureaucrats rely on their specialized knowledge, the support of interests that benefit from the programs they run, and the backing of the president and Congress.

The Power of Expertise

Most of the policy problems that the federal government confronts do not lend themselves to simple solutions. Whether the issue is space travel or hunger in America, expert knowledge is essential to the development of effective public policy. Much of this expertise is held by bureaucrats. They spend their careers working in a particular policy area, and many of them have had scientific, technical, or other specialized training.[35]

By comparison, elected officials are generalists. To some degree, members

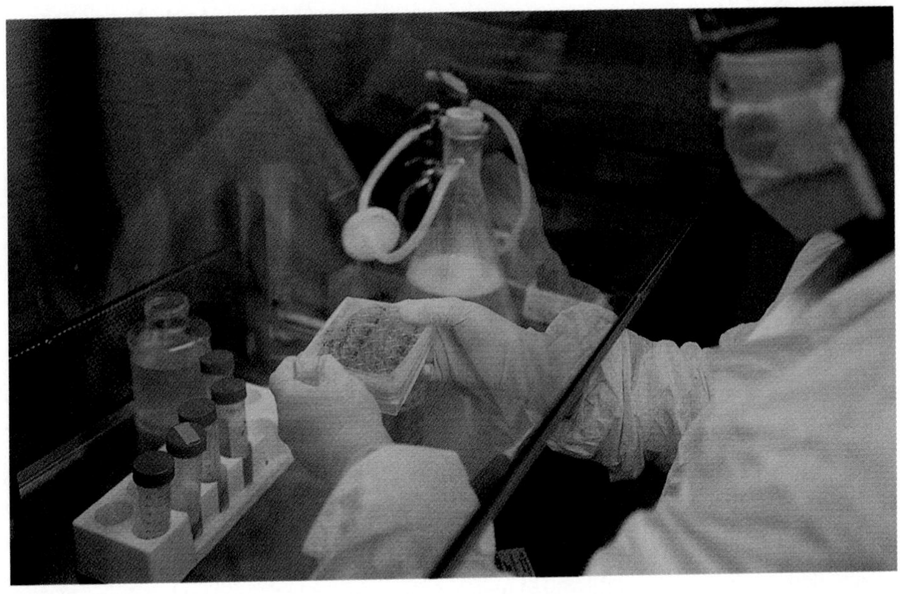

Research on AIDS conducted at the National Institutes of Health provided the expert knowledge that helped the agency to convince elected officials that AIDS-related policy measures were needed. (Steve Lehman/SABA)

of Congress do specialize through their committee work, but they rarely have the time or inclination to acquire a commanding knowledge of a particular issue. The president's understanding of policy issues is even more general. Not surprisingly, bureaucrats are a major source of policy ideas. They are more likely than either the president or members of Congress to be aware of particular problems and to have policy solutions in mind. According to Richard Rose, the president's influence on policy is felt primarily through decisions about which bureaucratic initiatives to embrace and which to ignore.[36] Congress is in somewhat the same situation; many bills proposed by members of Congress are conceived by careerists in the bureaucracy.

Not all agencies acquire a great amount of leverage from their staffs' expert knowledge. Those which do have an edge have highly specialized, professional staffs. For example, the expert judgments of the health scientists and physicians in the National Institutes of Health (NIH) are rarely challenged by elected officials. They may question the political assessments of these health professionals but are unlikely to question their scientific evaluations, which are sometimes decisive. For example, as much as some elected officials may have wanted to avoid the issues surrounding the emerging AIDS epidemic during the 1980s, they were eventually forced into action by the warnings of health scientists about the dire consequences of a do-nothing policy.

The power of expertise is conditioned by the extent to which an agency's employees share the same goals. In many agencies, such as the NIH, careerists with different professional backgrounds have similar values. In other agencies professional infighting breaks down this cohesiveness and gives outsiders an opportunity to support the faction whose aims agree with their own. An example is the Federal Trade Commission (FTC), which is divided between its lawyers, who tend to emphasize issues that can be quickly and successfully litigated, and its economists, who tend to stress larger and more complicated issues that have broad implications for national commerce.[37]

Nevertheless, all agencies acquire some power through their careerists' expertise.[38] No matter how simple a policy issue may appear at first, it invariably involves more than meets the eye. A recognition that the United States has a trade deficit with Japan, for example, can be the premise for policy change, but this recognition does not begin to address such basic issues as the form that the new policy might take, its probable cost and effectiveness, and its connection to other trade issues. Among the officials most likely to understand these issues are the bureaucrats in the Commerce Department and the Federal Trade Commission.

The Power of Clientele Groups

clientele groups Special-interest groups that benefit directly from the activities of a particular bureaucratic agency and are therefore strong advocates of the agency.

Most agencies have **clientele groups,** which are special interests that benefit directly from an agency's programs. Clientele groups place pressure on Congress and the president to retain the programs from which they benefit.[39] A result is that agency programs, once started, are difficult to terminate. "Government activities," as public administration expert Herbert Kaufman says, "tend to go on indefinitely."[40]

The importance of clientele groups was evident in 1995 when House Speaker Newt Gingrich threatened to "zero out" funding for the Corporation for Public Broadcasting. The threat produced an immediate response (some of it orchestrated by public broadcasting stations) from audience members and from groups such as the Childrens Television Workshop. They wrote, called, faxed, and cajoled members of Congress, saying that programs like *Sesame Street* and *All Things Considered* were irreplaceable by anything available from commercial broadcasting. Within a few weeks, Gingrich had relented somewhat, saying that a phase-out plan for ending the funding would be preferable to an abrupt cessation and that it might be prudent to retain funding for some activities, such as support of stations in rural areas not adequately served by commercial broadcasters.

In general, agencies lead and are led by the clientele groups that depend on the programs they administer.[41] Many agencies were created for the purpose of promoting particular interests in society. For example, the Department of Agriculture's career bureaucrats are dependable allies of farm interests year after year. The same cannot be said of the president, Congress as a whole, or either political party; they must balance farmers' demands against those of other interests.

The Power of Friends in High Places

Although members of Congress and the president sometimes appear to be at war with the bureaucracy, they need it as much as it needs them. An agency's resources—its programs, expertise, and group support—can assist elected officials in their efforts to achieve their goals. When George Bush came to the White House, he made the problem of drug-related crime a top priority, and he needed the help of Justice Department careerists to make his efforts successful. At a time when other agencies were feeling the pinch of a tight federal budget, the Justice Department's personnel increased by 20 percent during Bush's term of office.

Bureaucrats also seek favorable relations with members of Congress. Con-

THE MEDIA AND THE PEOPLE

BUREAUCRATIC IMAGES IN THE NEWS

The career bureaucracy is an institution, pure and simple. The presidency is personified by the president; the Congress by its elected members; and the Supreme Court by its justices. The bureaucracy, in contrast, is faceless. It can be represented by the titles and the symbols of its agencies, but it cannot be represented in any meaningful way through the person of a career bureaucrat or set of career bureaucrats.

As a result, the bureaucracy is the most difficult of all governing institutions for the news media to cover. The media have a tendency to personify the news. Stories of government are typically told through the actions of a leader. The more compelling the leader's role, the more frequent the coverage, which is why the president—the nation's most visible and individually powerful official—receives so much attention from the press. But there is no bureaucratic leadership to whom reporters can turn on a regular basis. Consequently, the bureaucracy is largely ignored by the media except when its activities intersect with those of the president and Congress.

Stories of bureaucratic bungling are an exception. The bureaucracy rarely makes the front page on its own except when it fouls up. The tone of such stories is often that of "what else could you expect—after all, it is the bureaucracy." However, instances of administrative misconduct are hardly a cause for disdain. No other collection of two-and-a-half million people is expected to behave flawlessly. The media do not portray a city as a den of iniquity every time a crime is committed there, so why does it generalize when the bureaucracy is the subject? Yet it does, as indicated by a Center for Media and Public Affairs' study of television coverage of federal agencies in 1993. Every agency that was the subject of heavy news coverage was targeted for criticism. Overall, this coverage was nearly 3 to 1 negative (see figure).

News coverage of the bureaucracy makes it everyone's favorite whipping boy. If George Wallace's attacks on "pointy-head" bureaucrats are more memorable than most, there is no institution that has been an easier target for politicians than the bureaucracy. The irony is that it is the politicians themselves who created and funded the programs that administrative agencies run. Hammered by the press and the politicians, it is hardly surprising that the bureaucracy is the public's least admired institution.

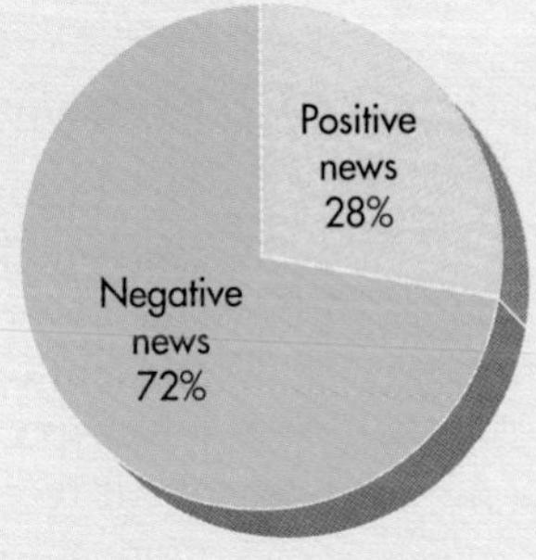

SOURCE: "The Honeymoon That Wasn't," *Media Monitor* 7, no. 7 (September/October 1993):5.

gressional support is vital because agencies' funding and programs are established through legislation. Agencies that offer benefits to major constituency interests are particularly likely to have close ties to Congress. In some policy areas, more or less permanent alliances—"iron triangles"—form among agencies, clientele groups, and congressional subcommittees.[42] In other policy areas, temporary "issue networks" form among bureaucrats, lobbyists, and members of Congress.[43] As we saw in Chapters 10 and 14, these alliances enable agencies and interest groups to promote the programs they want and provide members of Congress with electoral support.[44]

Bureaucratic Accountability

Bureaucratic politics raises the specter of a huge, permanent, and uncontrollable organizations run by entrenched unelected officials. Adapting the requirements of the bureaucracy to those of democracy has been a persistent

accountability The ability of the public to hold government officials responsible for their actions.

challenge for public administration.[45] The issue is **accountability:** the capacity of the public to hold officials responsible for their actions. In the case of the bureaucracy, accountability works primarily through other institutions: the presidency, Congress, and the courts.

ACCOUNTABILITY THROUGH THE PRESIDENCY

The president can only broadly influence, not directly control, the bureaucracy.[46] "We can outlast any president" is a maxim of bureaucratic politics. In recent years, with the emphasis on scaling down the bureaucracy, the saying seems more wishful than truthful. Nevertheless, each agency has its clientele and its congressional supporters, as well as statutory authority for its existence and activities. No president can unilaterally eliminate an agency or its funding and programs. Nor can the president be indifferent to the opinions of career civil servants—not without losing their support and expertise in developing and implementing his own policy objectives.

To encourage the bureaucracy to follow his lead, the president has important management tools that have developed out of the "executive leadership" concept discussed previously. These tools include reorganization, presidential appointees, and the executive budget.

Reorganization

The bureaucracy's extreme fragmentation—its hundreds of separate agencies—makes presidential coordination of its activities difficult. Agencies pursue independent, even contradictory paths, resulting in an undetermined amount of waste and duplication of effort. For example, more than 100 units are responsible for different pieces of education policy.

All recent presidents have tried to streamline the bureaucracy and make it more accountable.[47] The most ambitious reorganization plan was Nixon's proposal to combine fifty domestic agencies into four large departments, which would have given him tighter control over domestic policy. Existing agencies fought Nixon's plan because it threatened their independence. Their clientele groups joined the opposition since they feared the loss of programs. Members of Congress rejected Nixon's plan due to the objections raised by various interests and also because they recognized that centralization would reduce their influence on the bureaucracy.

Presidents have frequently been able to make less sweeping changes in the bureaucracy's organization, such as reducing the autonomy or number of employees of particular agencies.[48] These changes serve to upgrade or downgrade programs but ordinarily have not greatly improved presidential control of the bureaucracy.[49]

Presidential Appointments

Although there is almost no direct confrontation with a bureaucrat that a president cannot win, the president does not have time to deal personally with every troublesome careerist or make sure that the bureaucracy has complied with every presidential order. The president relies on political appointees in the agencies to ensure that directives are followed.

Regulatory agencies are the clearest illustration of the power of presidential appointments. Because these agencies have broad discretion over regulatory policy, a change in their leadership can have substantial effects. For example, President Reagan's appointee to head the Federal Trade Commission, James Miller III, was a strong-willed economist who shared Reagan's belief that consumer protection policy had gone too far and was adversely affecting business interests. In Miller's first year as head of the FTC, the commission dropped one-fourth of its pending cases against business firms.[50] Overall, enforcement actions declined by about 50 percent during Miller's tenure compared with the previous period (see Figure 16-3).

A determined president can use political appointees to alter the pattern of relationships between the bureaucracy and its other constituencies, including Congress and clientele groups. The Reagan administration relied on top bureaucrats to carry out programs but tried to keep them out of overall policy decisions and strategy, which were handled, as far as possible, by political appointees. The result, as the political scientist Joel Aberbach's research indicates, was a significant change in the groups with whom top civil servants had contact. Compared with a sample of bureaucrats surveyed in 1970, the bureaucrats questioned in 1986–1987 reported more contacts with White House officials and fewer contacts with members of Congress, interest-group representatives, and the general public (see Table 16-4). The 1986–1987 respondents' perception of their political influence was also substantially lower than that of the 1970 group.[51]

However, as we noted in Chapter 14, there are limits to what a president can accomplish through appointments.[52] High-level presidential appointees number in the hundreds, and their turnover rate is high: the average appointee remains in the administration for less than two years before moving on to other employment.[53] No president can keep track of all appointees, much less instruct them in detail on his intended policies. In addition, some presidential appointees will have a vested interest in the agencies they head.

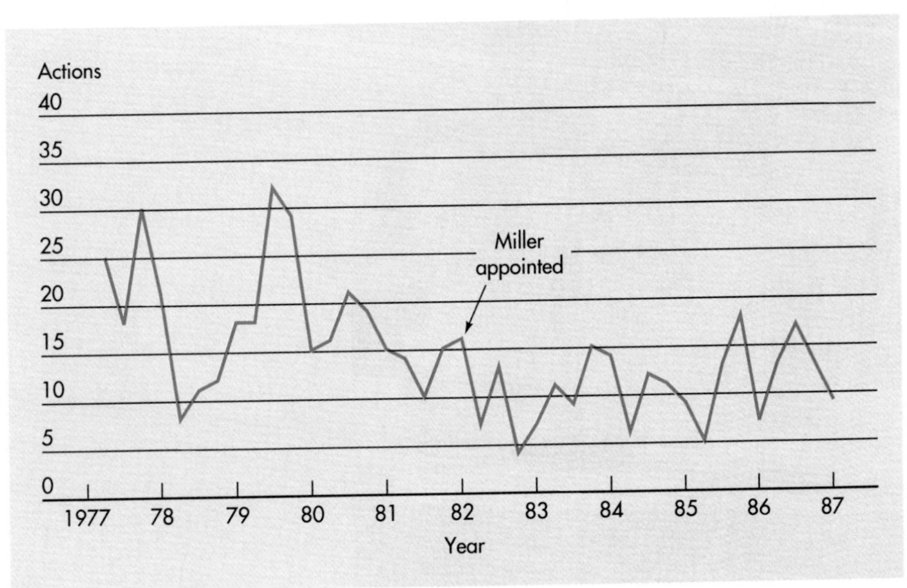

FIGURE 16-3 The Impact of a Presidential Appointee
President Reagan's appointment of James Miller III to head the Federal Trade Commission was followed by a sharp decline in its enforcement activities. *Source: Adapted from B. Dan Wood and Richard W. Waterman, "Political Control of the Bureaucracy," American Political Science Review 85 (September 1991):810, figure 2.*

TABLE 16-4 Contacts Reported by Top Federal Executives, 1970 and 1986–1987. Bureaucrats in 1986–1987 reported having more contacts with White House officials than were reported in 1970.

	POLITICAL APPOINTEES		CIVIL SERVANTS	
Contacts with . . .	*1970*	*1986–1987*	*1970*	*1986–1987*
White House	25%	41%	5%	20%
Own department head (cabinet member)	61	48	31	22
Other department head	19	6	18	2
Officials at your level in other departments	57	43	42	30
Members of Congress	42	48	43	20
Political party leaders	8	6	0	0
Interest-group representatives	69	67	69	46
General public	55	67	55	41

SOURCE: Joel D. Aberbach, "The President and the Executive Branch," in Colin Campbell and Bert A. Rockman, *The Bush Presidency: First Appraisals* (Chatham, N.J.: Chatham House, 1991), 234.

Donna Shalala, secretary of Health and Human Services, responding to questions during a news conference at which a new AIDS-prevention campaign was announced. Federal executives derive their program authority from acts of Congress but have leeway to decide how that authority will be applied in specific instances. (Wide World Photos)

In choosing political appointees, the president is lobbied by groups that depend on agency programs. Rather than antagonize these groups, the president will accept their recommendations in some cases.

The Executive Budget

Faced with the difficulty of controlling the bureaucracy, presidents have come to rely heavily on their personal bureaucracy, the Executive Office of the President (EOP).

In terms of presidential management, the key unit within the EOP is the Office of Management and Budget (OMB). Funding, programs, and regulations are the mainstays of every agency, and the OMB has substantial influence on each of these areas. No agency can issue a major regulation without the OMB's verification that the regulation's benefits outweigh its costs, and no agency can propose legislation to Congress without the OMB's approval. However, the OMB's greatest influence over agencies derives from its budgetary role. At the start of the annual budget cycle the OMB assigns each agency a budget limit in accord with the president's directives. The agency's tentative allocation requests are sent back to the OMB, which then conducts a final review of all requests before sending the full budget to Congress in the president's name.

In most cases, an agency's overall budget does not change much from year to year.[54] This fact indicates that a significant portion of the bureaucracy's activities persist regardless of who sits in the White House or Congress.[55]

ACCOUNTABILITY THROUGH CONGRESS

Congress has powerful means of influencing the bureaucracy. All agencies depend on Congress for their existence, authority, programs, and funding.

The most extreme action that Congress can take is to eliminate an agency's budget or programs. Congress can also pass legislation that reduces an agency's discretion or voids administrative action. However, Congress lacks the institutional capacity to work out complex policies down to the last detail.[56] The government would grind to a halt waiting for Congress to write legislation that covered every conceivable application. Congress has no option in most cases but to give administrators a general heading and let them proceed along that course. In its efforts to resolve the savings and loan crisis, for example, Congress in 1989 created the Resolution Trust Corporation (RTC), which, according to its authorizing statute, was required to oversee the recovery of assets from troubled thrifts in a manner that

> maximizes the net present value sale or other disposition of institutions;
>
> minimizes the impact of such transactions on local real estate and financial markets;
>
> makes efficient use of funds obtained from the Funding Corporation or the Treasury;
>
> minimizes the amount of any loss realized in the resolution of cases; and
>
> maximizes the preservation of the availability and affordability of residential real property for low- and moderate-income individuals.

★ STATES IN THE NATION

Federal Employees: Contrary to popular belief, the great majority of federal employees work in the states and not in Washington, D.C.

	FEDERAL WORKERS	
STATE	NUMBER	RANK
Ala.	58,000	17
Alaska	16,000	41
Ariz.	40,000	23
Ark.	21,000	36
Calif.	312,000	1
Colo.	57,000	18
Conn.	24,000	35
Del.	5,000	51
D.C.	223,000	2
Fla.	114,000	8
Ga.	93,000	11
Hawaii	25,000	34
Idaho	11,000	44
Ill.	106,000	9
Ind.	43,000	22
Iowa	20,000	37
Kan.	26,000	33
Ky.	38,000	24
La.	35,000	25
Maine	16,000	41
Md.	136,000	6
Mass.	62,000	15
Mich.	59,000	16
Minn.	34,000	27
Miss.	26,000	33
Mo.	66,000	14
Mont.	12,000	43
Neb.	16,000	41
Nev.	12,000	43
N.H.	8,000	48
N.J.	74,000	12
N.Mex.	28,000	31
N.Y.	149,000	5
N.C.	51,000	20
N.Dak.	8,000	48
Ohio	94,000	10
Okla.	46,000	21
Oreg.	31,000	29
Pa.	132,000	7
R.I.	10,000	46
S.C.	33,000	28
S.Dak.	10,000	46
Tenn.	54,000	19
Texas	179,000	3
Utah	35,000	25
Vt.	6,000	50
Va.	168,000	4
Wash.	69,000	13
W.Va.	17,000	38
Wis.	30,000	30
Wyo.	7,000	49

SOURCE: U.S. Office of Personnel Management, 1992. Figures exclude seasonal and other temporary workers.

Obviously, the language of the law gave the RTC broad discretion in deciding how to carry out its lawful responsibilities.

Correcting Administrative Error: Legislative Oversight

Congress exerts some control through its oversight function, which involves monitoring the bureaucracy's work to ensure compliance with legislative intent.[57] As we noted in Chapter 13, however, oversight is a difficult and relatively unrewarding task, and members of Congress ordinarily place less emphasis on oversight than on their other major duties. Only when an agency has clearly stepped out of line is Congress likely to take decisive corrective action by holding hearings to ask tough questions and to warn of legislative punishment.

A dramatic example is environmental regulation during Reagan's presidency. Regulatory activity, as was noted earlier in the chapter, dropped sharply when Reagan took office. Then in 1983, the news media disclosed that the Environmental Protection Agency (EPA) had privately arranged lenient settlements for firms that had committed serious violations of toxic-waste disposal regulations. The ensuing congressional investigation resulted in the resignation, dismissal, or conviction in court of more than a half-dozen top EPA officials. EPA director Anne Burford was cited for contempt of Congress for her refusal to cooperate with the investigation. The EPA's toxic-waste inspection level more than tripled soon thereafter, and when Congress restored EPA's budget, it rose again (see Figure 16-4). Within two years, EPA's inspection was nearly six times higher (from about 325 inspections a year to 2,000). In their study of this case, B. Dan Wood and Richard W. Waterman concluded: "Thus, for the EPA policy in which Congress was most directly involved, legislative influence was clearly manifest through the powers of oversight and appropriations."[58]

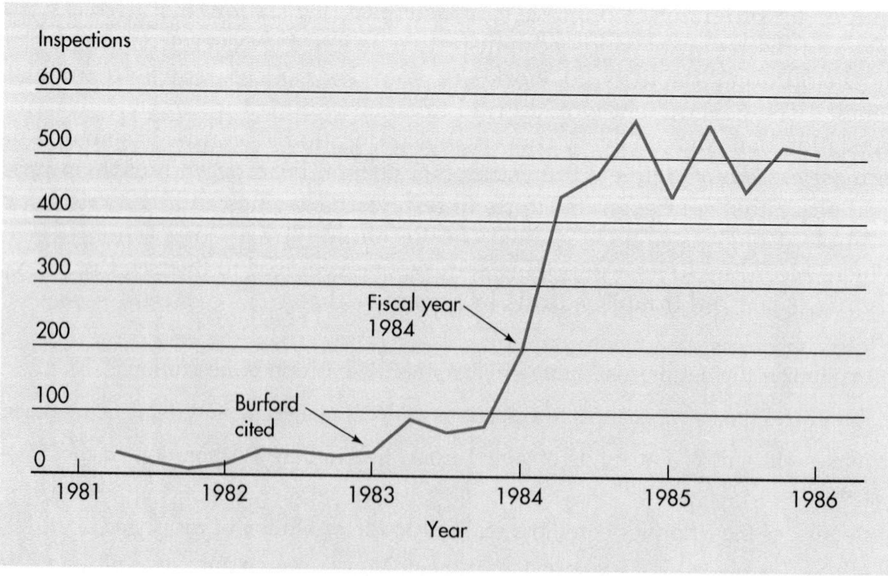

FIGURE 16-4 The Impact of a Congressional Investigation
A congressional investigation led to a contempt citation for EPA Director Anne Burford and an increase in the agency's toxic-waste inspections.
Source: Adapted from B. Dan Wood and Richard W. Waterman, "Political Control of the Bureaucracy," American Political Science Review 85 (September 1991): 821, figure 7.

In authorizing construction of the Alaska pipeline, Congress retained authority to veto the bureaucracy's decisions about the pipeline's route. The Supreme Court has since ruled that such legislative vetoes are unconstitutional in some forms and situations. (Michael G. Edrington / The Image Works)

Congress has sometimes legislated its own authority to void bureaucratic decisions—a device called the *legislative veto.* When Congress authorized the Alaska oil pipeline, for example, it retained the authority to veto bureaucratic decisions about the pipeline's route. In 1983, however, the Supreme Court voided the use of a legislative veto as interference with the president's constitutional authority to execute the laws but limited its ruling to the law in question. During the same year, the Court affirmed two lower-court rulings that the legislative veto was unconstitutional. Whether the Supreme Court in some situations will rule differently remains to be tested by future cases, but Congress has from time to time continued to include the legislative veto in bills that presidents have signed into law.[59]

Because oversight is so difficult and unrewarding, Congress has shifted much of its oversight responsibility to the Government Accounting Office (GAO). The GAO's primary function once was to keep track of the funds spent within the bureaucracy; now it also monitors the implementation of policies. The Congressional Budget Office (CBO) also does oversight studies. When the GAO or CBO uncovers a major problem with an agency's handling of a program, it notifies Congress, which can then take remedial action.

Restricting the Bureaucracy in Advance

Of course, an awareness by bureaucrats that misbehavior can trigger a response from Congress helps to keep them in line. Nevertheless, oversight cannot correct mistakes or abuses that have already occurred. Recognizing this limit on oversight, Congress has devised ways to constrain the bureaucracy *before* it acts. The simplest method is to draft laws that contain very specific provisions which limit bureaucrats' options when they implement policy. Another restrictive device is the "sunset law," which establishes a specific date when a law will expire unless it is reenacted by Congress. Advocates of sunset laws see them as a means to counter the bureaucracy's reluctance to give up programs that have outlived their usefulness.[60] Since members of Congress usually want their policies to last far into the future, however, most legislation does not include a sunset provision.

ACCOUNTABILITY THROUGH THE COURTS

The judiciary's influence on agencies is less direct than that of the elected branches, but the courts, too, can and do act to ensure the bureaucracy's compliance with Congress's requirements. Legally, the bureaucracy derives its authority from acts of Congress, and an injured party can bring suit against an agency on the grounds that it has failed to carry out the law properly. Judges can then order an agency to change its application of the law.[61]

However, the courts have tended to support administrators if their actions seem at all consistent with the laws they are administering. The Supreme Court has held that agencies can choose rule-making procedures that meet the minimal threshold set down by Congress, that agencies can apply any reasonable interpretation of statutes unless Congress has specifically stated something to the contrary, and that agencies in many instances have wide discretion in deciding whether to enforce statutes.[62] These positions reflect the need for flexibility in administration; the bureaucracy and the courts would both grind to a halt if judges routinely chose to substitute their interpretations of the law for those of administrators. The judiciary cannot conduct a decision-by-decision oversight of the bureaucracy. Judges recognize that constraints on the bureaucracy must work mainly through the Congress and the president. The judiciary has promoted bureaucratic accountability primarily by encouraging administrators to act responsibly in their dealings with the public and by protecting individuals and groups from the bureaucracy's worst abuses.

ACCOUNTABILITY WITHIN THE BUREAUCRACY ITSELF

A recognition of the difficulty of ensuring adequate accountability of the bureaucracy through the presidency, Congress, and the courts has led to the development of mechanisms of accountability within the bureaucracy itself. Two measures, whistle-blowing and demographic representativeness, are particularly noteworthy.

Whistle-Blowing

whistle-blowing An internal check on the bureaucracy whereby employees report instances of mismanagement that they observe.

Although the bureaucratic corruption that is rampant in some countries is relatively uncommon in the United States, a certain amount of waste, fraud, and abuse is inevitable in a bureaucracy as big as that of the federal government. **Whistle-blowing,** the act of reporting instances of corruption or mismanagement by one's fellow bureaucrats, is a potentially effective internal check.[63] Whistle-blowing, however, has not been highly successful. A survey con-

Karen Pitts (left) and Jacqueline Brever have sued the Rocky Flats plutonium plant near Denver, claiming that they were threatened and forced out of their jobs because managers feared that the two technicians would "blow the whistle" to the FBI about improper handling of toxic and nuclear materials at the facility. (Matthew Wald/New York Times)

ducted by a Senate subcommittee indicated that most federal employees will not report instances of mismanagement because they fear reprisals. In 1988, when Felix Smith, a biologist in the Department of the Interior, reported that the waters of California's San Joaquin Valley were being contaminated by poisonous selenium, his superiors tried to transfer him out of the region.[64]

To encourage federal employees to come forward when they see instances of mismanagement, Congress enacted the Whistle Blower Protection Act to protect them from retaliation. Federal law also provides whistle-blowers with financial rewards in some cases.

Demographic Representativeness

Although the bureaucracy is an unrepresentative institution in the sense that its officials are not elected by the people, it can be representative in the demographic sense. If bureaucrats were a demographic microcosm of the general public, they presumably would treat the various groups and interests in society more fairly.[65] "A public service . . . which is broadly representative of all categories of the population," public administration scholar Frederick Mosher concludes, "may be thought of as satisfying Lincoln's prescription of government 'by the people' in the limited sense."[66]

At present the bureaucracy is not demographically representative at its top levels (see Table 16-5). About 75 percent of managerial and professional positions are held by white males.[67] Women and minorities hold proportionally few high-ranking posts. However, the employment status of women and minorities has improved somewhat in recent years, and top officials in the bureaucracy include a greater proportion of women and minorities than is found in Congress, the judiciary, the diplomatic corps, or among high-rank-

TABLE 16-5 Federal Job Rankings (GS) of Various Demographic Groups
Women and minority group members are underrepresented in the top jobs of the federal bureaucracy.

	WOMEN'S SHARE		BLACKS' SHARE		HISPANICS' SHARE	
*Grade Level**	*1976*	*1990*	*1982*	*1990*	*1982*	*1990*
GS 1–4 (lowest ranks)	78%	75%	23%	29%	5%	7%
GS 5–8	60	70	19	23	4	6
GS 9–12	20	39	10	12	4	5
GS 13–15 (highest ranks)	5	19	5	6	2	3

*In general, the higher-numbered grades are managerial and professional positions, and the lower-numbered grades are clerical and manual labor positions.

SOURCE: Office of Personnel Management, 1992.

ing military officers.[68] Moreover, if all levels of the federal bureaucracy are considered, it comes reasonably close to being representative of the nation's population.[69]

demographic representativeness The idea that the bureaucracy will be more responsive to the public if its employees at all levels are demographically representative of the population as a whole.

Demographic representativeness is only a partial answer to the problem of bureaucratic accountability. A fully representative civil service would still be required to play agency politics. The careerists in, say, defense agencies and welfare agencies are not very different in their demographic backgrounds, but they differ markedly in their opinions about policy. Each group believes that the goals of its agency should take priority. The inevitability of agency politics is the most significant of all political facts about the U.S. federal bureaucracy.[70]

Reinventing Government

There have been numerous attempts during the twentieth century to enhance the bureaucracy's efficiency, responsiveness, and accountability. Another wave of this reform effort is under way, and it seeks to improve the administration of government by the reduction of its size, cost, and lines of authority.

This effort is based in part on the notion that the bureaucracy would be more effective and responsive if made smaller. In *Reinventing Government*, David Osborne and Ted Gaebler argue that the bureaucracy of today was created in response to earlier problems, particularly those spawned by the Industrial Revolution and a rampant spoils system. They claim that the information age requires a different kind of administrative structure, one that is more flexible and less hierarchical. Instead of the provision of goods and services, the bureaucracy ought to be in the business of creating incentives that will encourage individuals to make their own way and ought to foster competition among and between agencies and private firms. This requires a more decentralized form of administration that is oriented toward consumers and results. Osborne and Gaebler would empower lower-level employees to make decisions that previously were made at the top of the bureaucracy.[71]

This concept informed the Clinton administration's National Performance Review and is embedded in some laws and administrative practices. OPM's relationship to federal agencies, described earlier in the chapter, is a case in point. Another example is the practice of making extensive use of private contractors rather than government employees for certain tasks. Yet another example is a recent law that requires agencies to monitor their performance by standards such as efficiency, responsiveness, and outcomes. These standards have long been considered gauges of administrative effectiveness but have often been overlooked as bureaucrats went about their customary ways of doing business. The law seeks to overcome this inertia by requiring agencies to actively monitor their performance.

The downsizing of the federal bureaucracy is also being driven by political forces. Budget deficits and the public's dissatisfaction with Washington have helped create political momentum to reduce the scope of the federal government. The momentum intensified with the Republican takeover of Congress in 1995, but some results were already apparent. Federal employment, for example, had declined by 100,000 from its level when Clinton took office.[72] It is likely that some federal agencies, and perhaps even a few executive departments, will be eliminated in the near future. If a balanced-budget amendment should become part of the Constitution, the change will be even more dramatic.

The new era will be one of smaller government, not small government. There are limits to how far the federal government can be trimmed. Some activities can be delegated to states and localities, and others can be privatized, but many, if not most, of Washington's programs cannot be reassigned. National defense, social security, and Medicare are but three examples, and they alone account for the bulk of federal spending (see Chapters 19 and 20).

Some analysts question the logic and presumed consequences of the changes that are taking place. They have asked, for example, whether the principles of decentralized management and market-oriented programs are as sound as their advocates claim. The delegation of control to lower-level administrators weakens the hierarchical connection between elected and administrative officials. A reason for hierarchy was to ensure that decisions made at the bottom of the bureaucracy were faithful to the laws made by Congress. Free to act on their own, lower-level administrators, as they did under the spoils system, might favor certain people and interests over others.[73] There is also the issue of the identity of the "customers" in a market-oriented administration.[74] Who are the Security and Exchange Commission's customers—firms, brokerage houses, or shareholders? Will not some agencies inevitably favor their more powerful customers at the expense of the less powerful ones?

A second objection to the changes taking place is that government may be "hollowed out" in the sense that it may not have the financial and human resources to adequately perform the missions it retains.[75] Even many of those who are the strongest advocates of scaling down the federal government worry about this possibility in particular areas. For example, the House Republicans' Contract with America, which otherwise called for deep cuts in federal programs, proposed an increase in defense spending out of a belief that earlier cutbacks had reduced military readiness to an unacceptable level.

Thus, although the current wave of administrative reform is unique in its

★ CRITICAL THINKING

Reinventing Government

In *Reinventing Government* (1992), David Osborne and Ted Gaebler argue that the bureaucracy should be less hierarchical. They would delegate power downward, allowing working-level federal employees to make decisions that were previously made at the top. This change would make the bureaucracy more flexible and more responsive; it would be more market-oriented than in the past.

Other analysts contend that this idea rests on a faulty conception of government. They argue that lower-level employees should operate in a line-of-authority flowing from the top. Without this, the "faithful execution of the laws" is jeopardized. Working-level employees will make decisions that are inconsistent or at odds with the acts of Congress they are charged with implementing. Accountability is therefore diminished. The appropriateness of a market-centered government is also questioned. Are citizens equivalent to consumers, and if so, which consumers should be served when their interests conflict?

What is your view on this dispute? Are there particular activities of the federal government where Osborne and Gaebler's view is more appropriate? What criteria would you apply in determining whether an activity should be governed by the decentralized or the hierarchical model? How appropriate is the market-centered notion of government?

specific elements, it involves long-standing questions about the bureaucracy. How can it be made more responsive, and yet act fairly? How can it be made more efficient, and yet accomplish what Americans require of it? How can it be made more creative, and yet be held accountable? There are, as history makes clear, no easy or final answers to these questions.

Summary

Bureaucracy is a method of organizing people and work; it is based on the principles of hierarchical authority, job specialization, and formalized rules. As a form of organization, bureaucracy is the most efficient means of getting people to work together on tasks of great magnitude and complexity. It is also a form of organization that is prone to waste and rigidity, which is why efforts are being made to "reinvent" it.

The United States could not be governed without a large federal bureaucracy. The day-to-day work of the federal government, from mail delivery to provision of social security to international diplomacy, is done by the bureaucracy. Federal employees work in roughly 400 major agencies, including cabinet departments, independent agencies, regulatory agencies, government corporations, and presidential commissions. Yet the bureaucracy is more than simply an administrative giant. Administrators exercise considerable discretion in their policy decisions. In the process of implementing policy, they make important policy and political choices.

Each agency of the federal government was created in response to political demands on national officials. Because of its origins in political demands, the administration of government is necessarily political. An inherent conflict results from two simultaneous but incompatible demands on the bureaucracy: that it respond to the demands of partisan officials but also that it administer programs fairly and competently. These tensions are evident in the three concurrent personnel management systems under which the bureaucracy operates: patronage, merit, and executive leadership.

Administrators are actively engaged in politics and policymaking. The fragmentation of power and the pluralism of the American political system result in a policy process that is continually subject to conflict and contention. There is no clear policy or leadership mandate in the American system, and hence government agencies must compete for the power required to administer their programs effectively. Accordingly, civil servants tend to have an agency point of view: they seek to advance their agency's programs and to repel attempts by others to weaken their position. In promoting their agency, civil servants rely on their policy expertise, the backing of their clientele groups, and support from the president and Congress.

Because administrators are not elected by the people they serve yet wield substantial independent power, the bureaucracy's accountability is a major issue. The major checks on the bureaucracy are provided by the president, Congress, and the courts. The president has some power to reorganize the bureaucracy and the authority to appoint the political head of each agency. The president also has management tools (such as the executive budget) that can be used to limit administrators' discretion. Congress has influence on bureaucratic agencies through its authorization and funding powers and through various devices (including sunset laws and oversight hearings) that hold administrators accountable for their actions. The judiciary's role in ensuring the bureaucracy's accountability is smaller than that of the elected branches, but the courts do have the authority to force agencies to act in accordance with legislative intent, established procedures, and constitutionally guaranteed rights. Nevertheless, administrators are not fully accountable. They exercise substantial independent power, a situation that is not easily reconciled with democratic values.

Efforts are currently under way to scale down the federal bureaucracy. This reduction includes cuts in budgets, staff, and organizational units, and also involves changes in the way the bureaucracy does its work. This process is a response to political forces and also new management theories.

Major Concepts

accountability
agency point of view
bureaucracy
cabinet (executive) departments
clientele groups
demographic representativeness
executive leadership system
formalized rules
government corporations
hierarchical authority
independent agencies
job specialization
merit (civil service) system
neutral competence
patronage system
policy implementation
presidential commissions
regulatory agencies
spoils system
whistle-blowing

Suggested Readings

Aberbach, Joel D. *Keeping a Watchful Eye.* Washington, D.C.: Brookings Institution, 1990. A careful assessment of congressional oversight of the bureaucracy.

Barzlay, Michael. *Breaking through Bureaucracy: A New Vision for Managing in Government.* Berkeley: University of California Press, 1992. A provocative critique which argues that government must become more customer-centered.

Bryner, Gary C. *Bureaucratic Discretion: Law and Policy in Federal Regulatory Agencies.* Elmsford, N.Y.: Pergamon Press, 1987. An exploration of the relationship of bureaucratic policies to the laws that authorize them.

Goodsell, Charles T. *The Case for Bureaucracy,* 3d ed. Chatham, N.J.: Chatham House, 1994. A defense of the bureaucracy against many of the common complaints (e.g., red tape, wastefulness) about it.

Gore, Albert. *Creating a Government That Works Better and Costs Less: The Report of the National Performance Review.* Washington, D.C.: U.S. Superintendent of Documents, 1993. The report of Vice-President Gore's task force on streamlining government.

Ingraham, Patricia, and David Rosenbloom. *The Promise and Paradox of Civil Service Reform.* Pittsburgh, Pa.: University of Pittsburgh Press, 1992. An insightful analysis of the civil service reform issue.

Johnson, Cathy Marie. *The Dynamics of Conflict between Bureaucrats and Legislators.* Armonk, N.Y.: M.E. Sharpe, 1992. An analysis that indicates policy differences are an important source of conflict between bureaucrats and Congress.

Light, Paul C. *Thickening Government: Federal Hierarchy and the Diffusion of Accountability.* Washington, D.C.: Brookings Institution, 1995. An illuminating study of the impact of bureaucratic hierarchy on accountability.

Osborne, David, and Ted Gaebler. *Reinventing Government: How the Entrepreneurial Spirit Is Transforming the Public Sector.* New York: Addison-Wesley, 1992. The book that Washington policymakers regard as the guide to transforming the bureaucracy.

Wilson, James Q. *Bureaucracy.* New York: Basic Books, 1989. An insightful analysis of what government agencies do and why they do it.

CHAPTER 17

THE FEDERAL JUDICIAL SYSTEM: APPLYING THE LAW

It is emphatically the province and duty of the judicial department to say what the law is. Those who apply the rule to particular cases, must of necessity expound and interpret that rule. If two laws conflict with each other, the courts must decide on the operation of each.
—John Marshall[1]

For two weeks in the fall of 1991, the focus of the national news was not the president or a member of Congress, but a federal judge—Clarence Thomas. Thomas had been head of the Equal Employment Opportunity Commission (EEOC) during the Reagan administration and was serving on the U.S. Court of Appeals for the District of Columbia when President Bush nominated him to the nation's highest court. Thomas, an African American, was chosen to fill the vacancy created by the retirement of Justice Thurgood Marshall, who was the first black person ever to serve on the Supreme Court.

The appointment of Thomas to the Supreme Court was opposed by several major civil rights groups, including the NAACP. The AFL-CIO also formally opposed his confirmation. Thomas had worked against most affirmative action plans while head of the EEOC, and civil rights leaders accused him of turning his back on the needs of minority group members less fortunate than himself. They also pointed out the irony of Thomas's appointment: he and Bush were both avowed opponents of "quotas," yet Thomas seemed to have been picked to fill the "African American seat" on the Supreme Court. He was a relatively inexperienced jurist who had not developed a reputation as a leading theorist of the law. When the Thomas hearings were turned topsy-turvy by Anita Hill's allegations that Judge Thomas had sexually harassed her when he headed the EEOC, which was established to protect women and minority group members from discrimination, the irony was compounded.

The fight over Thomas's nomination reflected a deep division over the direction of the Supreme Court. In his final opinion before resigning from the Court, Justice Marshall accused its conservative majority of a "far-reaching assault" on the Bill of Rights. In recent decisions the Court had restricted the rights of the criminally accused and had ruled that physicians have no free speech right to counsel patients on abortion. The Court also appeared ready to reconsider several important precedents, including minority participation in government contracts and the abortion right itself. At stake in the Thomas appointment was the ideological position of the Court. How far to the right would it go?

The Senate hearings gave Americans an opportunity to learn about the workings of the government's judicial branch, which is by far the least publicized and least understood of the three branches of the U.S. government. Yet, as the fight over the Thomas nomination suggested, the judicial branch, from the Supreme Court on down, is a consequential part of the American political system. Although law and politics are sometimes portrayed as separate activities, they are inseparable parts of the governing process. Once a law is established, it is expected to be administered in an evenhanded way. But the law itself is a product of contending political forces; it is developed through a political process and has political content.

The nomination of Clarence Thomas, a conservative, to the Supreme Court was controversial from the outset because it was widely believed that he would tilt the Court further toward the right. Anita Hill's allegation that Thomas had sexually harassed her caused a nationwide uproar but did not prevent Thomas's confirmation. (Top: Markel / Gamma Liaison; bottom: David Longstreath / AP / Wide World)

This chapter describes the federal judiciary and the work of its judges and justices. The focus then shifts to the influence of legal and political factors on judicial decisions. The chapter concludes with a discussion of the controversy surrounding the judiciary's policy role; a critical question is how far judges, who are not elected, ought to go in substituting their policy judgments for those of officials who are chosen by the people. The main points made in this chapter are the following:

★ *The federal judiciary includes the Supreme Court of the United States, which functions mainly as an appellate court; courts of appeals, which hear appeals; and district courts, which hold trials.* Each state has a court system of its own, which for the most part is independent of supervision by the federal courts.

★ *Judicial decisions are constrained by applicable constitutional law, statutory law, and precedent.* Nevertheless, political factors have a major influence on judicial appointments and decisions; judges are political officials as well as legal ones.

★ *The judiciary has become an increasingly powerful policymaking body in recent decades, which has raised the question of the judiciary's proper role in a democracy.* The philosophies of judicial restraint and judicial activism provide different answers to this question.

The Federal Judicial System

The writers of the Constitution were determined that the judiciary would be a separate branch of the federal government but, for practical reasons, did not spell out the full structure of the federal court system. The Constitution simply establishes the Supreme Court of the United States and grants Congress the authority to establish lower federal courts of its choosing.

Federal judges are nominated by the president, and if confirmed by the U.S. Senate, they are appointed by the president to the office. The Constitution states that judges "shall hold their offices during good behavior." However, the Constitution does not contain a precise definition of "good behavior," and no Supreme Court justice and only a very small number of lower-court judges have been removed from office through impeachment and conviction by Congress. In practice, federal judges and justices serve until they retire or die.

Unlike the offices of president, senator, and representative, the Constitution places no age, residency, or citizenship qualifications on federal judicial office. Nor does the Constitution require a judge to have legal training. Tradition alone dictates that federal judges have an educational or professional background in the law.

THE SUPREME COURT OF THE UNITED STATES

The Supreme Court of the United States is the nation's highest court. The chief justice of the United States presides over the Supreme Court and, like the eight associate justices, is selected by the president and is subject to Senate confirmation. The chief justice has the same voting power as the other justices but has usually exercised additional influence because of the position's leadership role.

jurisdiction (of a court) A given court's authority to hear cases of a particular kind. Jurisdiction may be original or appellate.

original jurisdiction The authority of a given court to be the first court to hear a case.

appellate jurisdiction The authority of a given court to review cases that have already been tried in lower courts and are appealed to it by the losing party; such a court is called an appeals court or appellate court.

The Constitution grants the Supreme Court both original and appellate jurisdiction. A court's **jurisdiction** is its authority to hear cases of a particular type. **Original jurisdiction** is the authority to be the first court to hear a case. The Supreme Court's original jurisdiction embraces legal disputes involving foreign diplomats or two or more states. The Court in its entire history has convened as a court of original jurisdiction only a few hundred times and has rarely done so in recent years.

The Supreme Court does its most significant work as an appellate court. **Appellate jurisdiction** is the authority to review cases that have already been heard in lower courts and are appealed to the higher court by the losing party; such courts are called appeals courts or appellate courts. The Supreme Court's appellate jurisdiction extends to cases arising under the Constitution, federal law and regulations, and treaties. The Court also hears appeals involving admiralty or maritime issues and legal controversies that cross state or national boundaries. Appellate courts, including the Supreme Court, do not retry cases; rather, they determine whether a trial court acted in accord with applicable law.

Selecting Cases

The primary function of the judiciary is to interpret the law in such a way that rules made in the past (for example, the Constitution or legislation) can be applied reasonably in the present. This function gives the courts—all courts—a role in policymaking. Antitrust legislation, for example, is designed to prevent uncompetitive business practices, but like all such legislation, it is not self-enforcing. It is up to the courts to decide whether and how these laws apply to the case at hand.

As the nation's highest court, the Supreme Court is particularly important in establishing legal precedents that guide lower courts. A *precedent* is a judicial decision that serves as a rule for settling subsequent cases of a similar

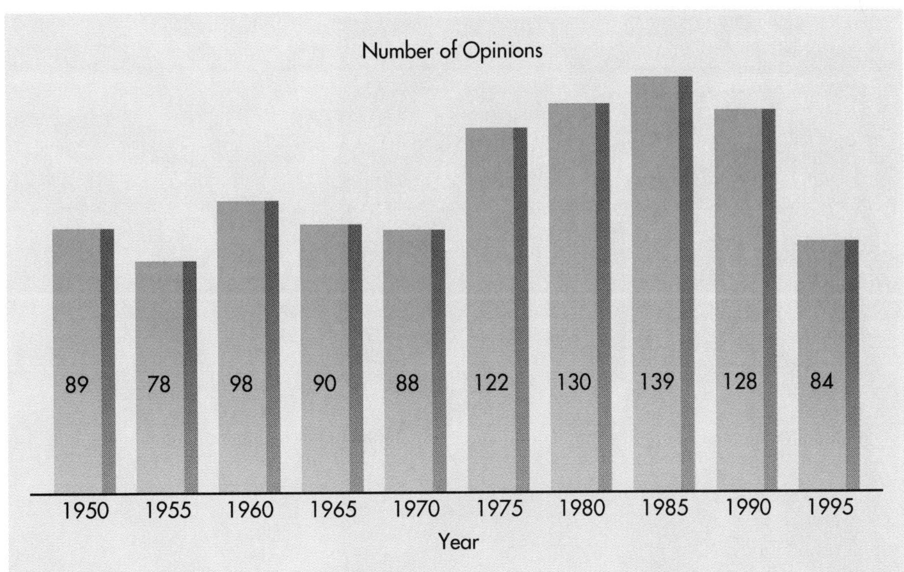

FIGURE 17-1 Supreme Court Opinions, 1950–1994
The number of signed Supreme Court opinions each term has generally been in the 100 to 125 range, although it has declined in the past few years. *Source: Supreme Court of the United States. The Court's term runs from October 1 to June 30; the year indicated is the closing year of the term.*

nature. Lower courts are expected to follow precedent—that is, to resolve cases of a like nature in ways consistent with upper-court rulings. However, for reasons that will be explained later, they do not always do so.

The Supreme Court's ability to set legal precedent is strengthened by its nearly complete discretion in choosing the cases it will hear. The large majority of cases reach the Supreme Court through a **writ of *certiorari*** in which the losing party in a lower-court case explains in writing why its case should be ruled upon by the Court. Four of the nine justices must agree to accept a particular case before it is granted a writ. Each year roughly 7,000 parties apply for *certiorari,* but the Court accepts only about 100 cases for a full hearing and signed ruling (see Figure 17-1). The Court issues another 100 to 200 *per curiam* (unsigned) decisions, which are made summarily without a hearing and simply state the facts of the case and the Court's decision. The Court is most likely to grant *certiorari* when the U.S. government through the solicitor general (the high-ranking Justice Department official who serves as the government's lawyer in Supreme Court cases) requests it.[2]

writ of *certiorari* Permission granted by a higher court to allow a losing party in a legal case to bring the case before it for a ruling; when such a writ is requested of the U.S. Supreme Court, four of the Court's nine justices must agree to accept the case before it is granted *certiorari.*

Case selection is a vital part of the Supreme Court's work. Through its review of applications for *certiorari,* the Court keeps abreast of legal controversies. Justice William Brennan noted that the *certiorari* process enables the Court to acquire a general idea of the compelling legal issues arising in lower courts and to address those that are most in need of immediate attention.[3] When the Court does accept a case, chances are that most of the justices disagree with the lower court's ruling. In recent years about three-fourths of the Supreme Court's decisions have reversed the judgments of lower courts.[4]

The Court seldom accepts a routine case, even if the justices believe that a lower court has erred. The Supreme Court's job is not to correct every mistake of other courts, but to resolve broad legal questions. As a result, the justices usually choose cases that involve substantial legal issues. This criterion is vague but essentially means that a case must center on an issue of signifi-

The Supreme Court building is located across from the Capitol in Washington, D.C. The courtroom, the justices' offices, and the conference room are on the first floor. Administrative staff offices and the Court's records and reference materials occupy the other floors. (Dennis Brack/Black Star)

cance not merely to the parties involved but to the nation. As a result, most of the cases heard by the Court raise major constitutional issues, or affect the lives of many Americans, or address issues that are being decided inconsistently by the lower courts, or are in conflict with a previous Supreme Court ruling.[5] The last of these situations is particularly likely to propel a case to the Supreme Court, which naturally takes a keen interest in lower-court judgments that depart from its rulings.

Deciding Cases

Once the Supreme Court accepts a case, it sets a date on which the attorneys for the two sides will present their oral arguments. Strict time limits, usually thirty minutes per side, are placed on these arguments, because each side has already submitted written arguments to the justices.

judicial conference A closed meeting of the justices of the U.S. Supreme Court to discuss and vote upon the cases before them; the justices are not supposed to discuss conference proceedings with outsiders.

The open hearing is far less important than the **judicial conference** that follows, which is attended only by the nine justices. The conference's proceedings are kept strictly confidential. This secrecy allows the justices to speak freely and tentatively about a case. The chief justice presides over the conference and ordinarily speaks first.[6] The other justices then speak in order of their seniority (length of service on the Court); this arrangement enhances the senior members' ability to influence the discussion. After the discussion, the justices vote on the case; the least senior justice usually votes first and the Chief Justice votes last.

The chief justice is expected to provide leadership but has no power to compel the other justices to respond. Consequently, the chief justice's intellectual capacities, knowledge of the law, political awareness, and persuasiveness are significant aspects of his leadership. Charles Evans Hughes is reputed to have been the most effective leader in the Court's history, although John Marshall is generally regarded as the greatest chief justice. The current chief justice, William Rehnquist, is widely viewed as a personally aloof but intellectually assertive leader.

Issuing Decisions and Opinions

After a case has been discussed and decided upon in conference, the Court prepares and issues its ruling, which consists of a decision and one or more opinions. The **decision** indicates which party the Court supports and by how large a margin. The **opinion** explains the reasons behind the decision. The opinion is the most important part of a Supreme Court ruling because it informs others of the justices' interpretations of laws. When a majority of the justices agree on the legal basis of a decision, the result is a **majority opinion.** For example, in the landmark *Brown* v. *Board of Education of Topeka* (1954) opinion, the Court held that government-sponsored school segregation was unconstitutional because it violated the Fourteenth Amendment's guarantee that all Americans are entitled to equal protection under the laws. Enforced segregation of the public schools was therefore constitutionally impermissible. This opinion became the legal basis by which communities throughout the southern states were ordered by lower courts to end their policy of segregating students in their public schools by race.[7]

decision A vote of the Supreme Court in a particular case that indicates which party the justices side with and by how large a margin.

opinion (of a court) A court's written explanation of its decision which serves to inform others of the legal basis for the decision. Supreme Court opinions are expected to guide the decisions of other courts.

majority opinion A Supreme Court opinion that results when a majority of the justices are in agreement on the legal basis of the decision.

When part of the majority, the chief justice decides which of the justices will write the majority opinion. Otherwise, the senior justice in the majority determines the author. Chief justices have often given themselves the influential task of writing the majority opinion in important cases. John Marshall did so often: *Marbury* v. *Madison* (1802) and *McCulloch* v. *Maryland* (1819) were among the opinions he wrote.

The justice who writes the Court's majority opinion has an important and difficult job, since the other justices who voted with the majority must agree with the written opinion. Because the vote on a case is not considered final until the decision is made public, plenty of compromising and old-fashioned horse trading can take place during the writing stage. The majority opinion often goes through a series of drafts and is circulated among all nine justices. In *Brown* v. *Board of Education,* Justice Felix Frankfurter, the lone initial holdout, was persuaded to make the decision unanimous by the continued urgings of his colleagues and by their willingness to incorporate some of his concerns into the majority opinion.

In some cases there is no majority opinion because a majority of the justices agree on the decision but cannot agree on the legal basis for it. The result is a **plurality opinion,** which presents the view held by most of the justices who side with the winning party. Another type of opinion is a **concurring opinion,** which is a separate view written by a justice who votes with the majority but disagrees with their reasoning.

Justices on the losing side can write a **dissenting opinion** to explain their reasons for disagreeing with the majority position. Sometimes these dissent-

plurality opinion A court opinion that results when a majority of justices agree on a decision in a case but do not agree on the legal basis for the decision. In this instance, the legal position held by most of the justices on the winning side is called a plurality opinion.

concurring opinion A separate opinion written by a Supreme Court justice who votes with the majority in the decision on a case but who disagrees with their reasoning.

dissenting opinion The opinion of a justice in a Supreme Court case that explains the reasons for disagreeing with the majority's decision.

ing views become a later Court's majority position. In a 1942 dissenting opinion, Justice Hugo Black wrote that defendants in state felony trials should have legal counsel, even if they could not afford to pay for it. Two decades later, in *Gideon* v. *Wainwright* (1963), the Court adopted this position.[8]

OTHER FEDERAL COURTS

There are more than 100 federal courts but there is only one Supreme Court, and its position at the top of the country's judicial system gives the Supreme Court unparalleled importance. It is a mistake, however, to conclude that the Supreme Court is the only court of consequence. Judge Jerome Frank once wrote of the "upper-court myth," which is the view that appellate courts and in particular the Supreme Court make up the only truly significant judicial arena and that lower courts just dutifully follow the rulings handed down by the appellate level.[9] The reality is very different, as the following discussion will explain.

U.S. District Courts

The lowest federal courts are the district courts (see Figure 17-2). There are more than ninety federal district courts altogether—at least one in every state and as many as four in some states. District court judges, who number about 800 in all, are appointed by the president with the consent of the Senate. Federal cases usually originate in district courts, which are trial courts, where the parties argue their sides. District courts are the only courts in the federal system in which juries hear testimony. Most cases at this level are presented before a single judge.

Lower federal courts unquestionably rely on and follow Supreme Court decisions in their own rulings. This requirement was reiterated in a 1982 case, *Hutto* v. *Davis:* "Unless we wish anarchy to prevail within the federal judicial system, a precedent of this Court must be followed by the lower federal courts no matter how misguided the judges of those courts may think it to be."[10]

However, the idea that lower courts are guided strictly by Supreme Court

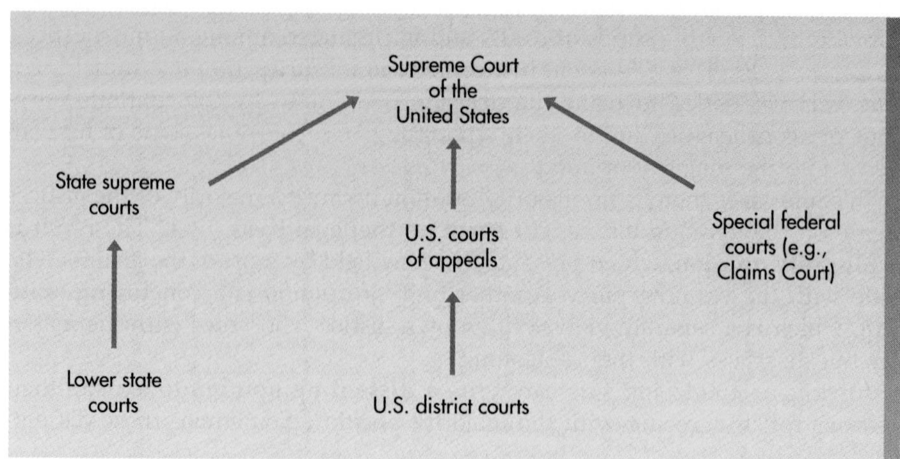

FIGURE 17-2 The Federal Judicial System
This simplified diagram shows the relationships among the various levels of federal courts and between state and federal courts. The losing party in a case can appeal a lower-court decision to the court at the next-highest level, as the arrows indicate. Decisions can be removed from state courts to federal courts only if they raise a federal question.

The Supreme Court is not the only federal court that "matters" in the American judicial system. Most federal cases originate in U.S. district courts, and most appealed cases are settled in U.S. courts of appeals, never reaching the Supreme Court. Shown here is testimony at a trial in district court, the only level in the federal system in which juries decide the outcome of cases. (Billy E. Barnes/Stock, Boston)

rulings is part of the "upper-court myth." District court judges may misunderstand the Supreme Court's position and deviate from it for that reason. In addition, the facts of a case before a district court are seldom identical to those of a case settled by the Supreme Court. The lower-court judge must decide whether a different legal principle must be invoked. In some cases, district court judges have willfully disregarded Supreme Court precedent, finding a basis for decision that allows them to reach a judgment they prefer. For example, after the Supreme Court declared in *Brown* v. *Board of Education* that racial segregation of public schools violated the Fourteenth Amendment's guarantee of equal protection under the law, many southern district court judges who opposed the principle of racial equality concluded that the issue in the school desegregation cases before them was not equal protection but the maintenance of public order and that school desegregation could not be allowed because it would disrupt public order. Finally, it is not unusual for the Supreme Court to take a very broad legal position that is general and ambiguous enough to allow lower courts to decide its exact meaning in practice. Trial-court judges then have a creative role in judicial decision making which rivals that of appellate court judges.

Most federal cases end with the district court's decision; the losing party does not appeal the decision to a higher court. This is another indication of the highly significant role of district court judges.

U.S. Courts of Appeals

When cases are appealed from district courts, they go to a federal court of appeals. These appellate courts make up the second level of the federal court system. Courts of appeals do not use juries. No new evidence is submitted in an appealed case; appellate courts base their decisions on a review of lower-court records. Appellate judges act as supervisors in the legal system, reviewing trial-court decisions and correcting what they consider to be legal errors. Facts (i.e., the circumstances of a case) found by district courts are presumed to be correct.

The United States has twelve general appeals courts, each of which serves a "circuit" that is comprised of between three and nine states, except the one that serves the District of Columbia only. There is also the U.S. Court of Appeals for the Federal Circuit, which specializes in appeals of cases involving patents and international trade. Between four and twenty-six judges sit on each court of appeals, but each case is usually heard by a panel of three judges. On rare occasions, all the judges of a court of appeals sit as a body (*en banc*) in order to resolve difficult controversies, typically ones that have resulted in conflicting decisions within the same circuit.

Courts of appeals offer the only real hope of reversal for many appellants, since the Supreme Court hears so few cases. Fewer than 1 percent of the cases heard by federal appeals courts are later reviewed by the Supreme Court.[11] "Because the Supreme Court only handles several hundred cases a year," Sheldon Goldman points out, "the influence of lower courts is considerable. For most intents and purposes, the courts of appeals function as regional supreme courts for the nation. As a result, we're talking about some major policy makers."[12]

Special U.S. Courts

In addition to the Supreme Court, the courts of appeals, and the district courts, the federal judiciary includes a few specialty courts. Among them are the U.S. Claims Court, which hears cases in which the U.S. government has been sued for damages; the U.S. Court of International Trade, which handles cases involving appeals of U.S. Customs Office rulings; and the U.S. Court of Military Appeals, which hears appeals of military courts-martial. Some federal agencies and commissions also have adjudicative powers, and their decisions can be appealed to a federal court of appeals.

THE STATE COURTS IN THE FEDERAL SYSTEM

The American states are separate governments within the United States' federal system. Each state is protected in its sovereignty by the Tenth Amendment, and each state has its own court system. Like the federal courts, state court systems have trial courts at the bottom level and appellate courts at the top.

Each state decides for itself the structure of its courts and the method of judicial appointment. In some states, judges are appointed by the governor, but judgeships are *elective offices* in most states. The common form involves competitive elections of either a partisan or nonpartisan nature, although some states use a system called the *merit plan* (also called the "Missouri Plan" because Missouri was the first state to use it) under which the governor selects a judge from a short list of acceptable candidates provided by a judicial selection commission. After a year or more on the bench, the judge selected must be approved by the voters in order to serve a longer term. Thereafter, the judge must face a periodic (usually every six years) "retention election" in which voters decide whether he or she will continue in the office (see box: States in the Nation).

Besides the upper-court myth, there exists a "federal court myth," which holds that the federal judiciary is the most significant part of the judicial system and that state courts play a subordinate role. This view is inaccurate as well. More than 95 percent of the nation's legal cases are decided in state courts. Most crimes (from shoplifting to murder) and most civil controversies (such as divorces and corporate disputes) are defined by state or local law. Moreover, nearly all cases that originate in state courts also end there; the federal courts never come into the picture since the case does not involve a federal issue.

In state criminal cases, after a person has been convicted and after all avenues of appeal in the state court system have been exhausted, the defendant can seek a writ of habeas corpus from a federal district court (see Chapter 4). The federal court often confines itself to the federal aspects of the matter, such as whether the defendant in a criminal case received the protections guaranteed by the U.S. Constitution. In addition, the federal court must accept the facts determined by the state court unless such findings are clearly in error. In short, legal and factual determinations of state courts can bind the federal courts—a clear contradiction of the federal court myth.

However, cases traditionally within the jurisdiction of the states can become federal cases through rulings of federal courts. In *Roe* v. *Wade* (1973), for example, the Supreme Court concluded that women had the right under the Constitution to choose an abortion, thus making abortion rights, which had been a state issue, also a federal one.[13] (This situation is called "diversity of citizenship" jurisdiction, meaning that both state and federal courts have some jurisdiction over the issue.)

★ STATES IN THE NATION

Principal Methods of Selecting State Judges

STATE	METHOD
Ala.	Election (P)
Alaska	Merit plan
Ariz.	Merit plan
Ark.	Election (P)
Calif.	Governor
Colo.	Merit plan
Conn.	Legislature
Del.	Governor
D.C.	Merit plan
Fla.	Merit plan
Ga.	Election (N)
Hawaii	Merit plan
Idaho	Election (N)
Ill.	Election (P)
Ind.	Merit plan
Iowa	Merit plan
Kan.	Merit plan
Ky.	Election (N)
La.	Election (N)
Maine	Governor
Md.	Merit plan
Mass.	Governor
Mich.	Election (N)
Minn.	Election (N)
Miss.	Election (P)
Mo.	Merit plan
Mont.	Election (N)
Neb.	Merit plan
Nev.	Election (N)
N.H.	Governor
N.J.	Governor
N.Mex.	Election (P)
N.Y.	Governor
N.C.	Election (P)
N. Da.	Election (N)
Ohio	Election (N)
Okla.	Merit plan
Oreg.	Election (P)
Pa.	Election (P)
R.I.	Merit plan
S.C.	Legislature
S.Dak.	Merit plan
Tenn.	Election (P)
Texas	Election (P)
Utah	Merit plan
Vt.	Merit plan
Va.	Legislature
Washington	Election (P)
W.Va.	Election (P)
Wis.	Election (P)
Wyo.	Merit plan

SOURCE: Council of State Governments. (For the election method, P designates partisan election and N designates nonpartisan election.)

Federal Court Appointees

The quiet setting of the courtroom, the dignity of its proceedings, and the lack of fanfare with which a court delivers its decisions give the impression that the judiciary is about as far removed from the world of politics as a governmental institution can possibly be. The reality, however, is different. Federal judges and justices are political officials who exercise the authority of a separate and powerful branch of government. All federal jurists bring their political views with them to the courtroom and have regular opportunities to promote their political beliefs through the cases they decide. Accordingly, the process by which federal judges are appointed is a partisan one.

SELECTING SUPREME COURT JUSTICES AND FEDERAL JUDGES

The formal mechanism for appointments to the Supreme Court and the lower federal courts is the same: the president nominates and the Senate confirms or rejects. Beyond that basic similarity, however, there are significant differences.

THE MEDIA AND THE PEOPLE

THE SUPREME COURT: IN AND OUT OF THE LIMELIGHT

The Supreme Court has become more conservative in recent years. Its decisions, for example, have substantially weakened the exclusionary rule in criminal trials and have given states more authority to regulate abortions. These Court decisions brought expressions of opposition and, in some cases, cries of outrage from liberal groups and Democratic officeholders. The opposite situation had prevailed during the 1960s, when the Court had moved to the left in a series of decisions that, for example, broadened the rights of minorities and extended the fair-trial protections of the accused to include action by state governments. At that time, conservative groups and some Republican leaders were vocal opponents of the rulings.

During each of these eras, the Supreme Court received extraordinary attention from the media. It is relatively rare, for example, for the Supreme Court to be the basis for the cover story of a weekly newsmagazine. Yet in the 1960s and again in the early 1990s the Court was the subject of several cover stores in *Time, Newsweek*, and *U.S. News & World Report*. The media's coverage and the Court's actions had an effect on public opinion. When asked in a 1991 Gallup poll whether the Court was too conservative or too liberal, the larger proportion of respondents said it was too conservative. Comparable polls in the 1960s indicated that a plurality then thought it was too liberal.

The Supreme Court is not ordinarily an issue in political campaigns, but the 1960s and early 1990s were exceptions. Law and order, for example, was a strong issue for Republicans in the presidential election of 1968. Richard Nixon relied on the issue, which he linked to the Supreme Court's decisions on the rights of the accused, to appeal to working-class voters in urban areas. By comparison, the abortion issue appeared to benefit the Democrats in the 1990 elections. Douglas Wilder was helped in the governor's race in Virginia, for example, by his pro-choice position on abortion, which appealed most strongly to middle-class voters in the Virginia suburbs of Washington, D.C.

Controversial decisions on busing and affirmative action (see Chapter 5) thrust the Supreme Court into the limelight again in 1995.

Supreme Court Nominees

A Supreme Court appointment is a critical choice for a president. The cases that come before the Court tend to be controversial and have far-reaching implications. And since the Court is a small body, each justice's vote can be crucial to the decisions it makes. As most justices retain their positions for many years, presidents can influence judicial policy through their appointments long after they have left office. The careers of some Supreme Court justices provide dramatic testimony to the enduring effects of judicial appointments. Franklin D. Roosevelt appointed William O. Douglas to the Supreme Court in 1939, and for thirty years after Roosevelt's death in 1945, Douglas remained a strong liberal influence on the Court. John Marshall was appointed chief justice in 1801 by the second president, John Adams, and served until 1835, when the seventh president, Andrew Jackson, was in his second term.

Presidents have employed a variety of approaches in their efforts to select a Supreme Court nominee who will reflect their political philosophy. A president may choose to depend chiefly on his own counsel, ask the Justice Department for advice, or seek the views of interested parties who share his general philosophy. Nominees must also be acceptable to others. Every nominee is closely scrutinized by the legal community, interested groups, and the media, and must also undergo an extensive background check by the FBI.[14]

Within the Senate, a key body is the Judiciary Committee, whose members have responsibility for conducting hearings on judicial nominees and recommending their confirmation or rejection by the full Senate. Nearly 20 percent of presidential nominees have been rejected by the Senate on grounds of judicial qualification, political views, personal ethics, or partisanship. Most of these rejections in the country's history occurred before 1900, and partisan politics was the main reason. Today a nominee with strong professional and ethical credentials is less likely to be blocked for partisan reasons alone. An exception was Robert Bork, whose 1987 nomination by President Reagan was rejected primarily because of strong opposition from Senate Democrats who disagreed with his judicial philosophy. Middle-of-the-road, noncontroversial nominees almost always are approved by the Senate. One such nominee, Ruth Bader Ginsberg, was confirmed by a 96–3 Senate vote in 1993.

Presidents often take into account the Senate's probable reaction when choosing a nominee. In selecting Ginsberg and Stephen Breyer as his first nominees, President Clinton eschewed the choice of more controversial judges who might have been closer to his own views on issues before the Court. In general, though, the burden of proof rests with the Senate. To avoid the charge of unprincipled partisanship, the Senate has unofficially accepted the premise that it must build an overwhelming case against confirmation before denying the president's nominee a seat on the nation's highest court. This approach was evident in 1991 during confirmation hearings on Republican President George Bush's nomination of Clarence Thomas. Lacking confirming evidence of Anita Hill's charges of sexual harassment, the Democratic-controlled Senate voted to seat Thomas on the Supreme Court.

The justices of the Supreme Court pose in 1995 for a photo. Front row, from left, are Antonin Scalia, John Paul Stevens, Chief Justice William Rehnquist, Sandra Day O'Connor, and Anthony Kennedy. Back row, from left, are Ruth Bader Ginsburg, David Souter, Clarence Thomas, and Stephen Breyer. (Wide World Photos)

Lower-Court Nominees

senatorial courtesy The tradition that a U.S. senator from the state in which a federal judicial vacancy has arisen should have a say in the president's nomination of the new judge if the senator is of the same party as the president.

The president normally gives the deputy attorney general the task of screening potential nominees for lower-court judgeships.[15] **Senatorial courtesy** is also a consideration in these appointments: this tradition, which dates back to the 1840s, holds that a senator from the state in which a vacancy has arisen should be given a say in the nomination if the senator is of the same party as the president.[16] If not consulted, the senator involved can request that confirmation be denied, and other senators will normally grant the request as a "courtesy" to a fellow senator.[17] Not surprisingly, presidents have preferred to give senators a voice in judicial appointments.

Although the president does not become as personally involved in selecting lower-court nominees as in naming potential Supreme Court justices, lower-court appointments are collectively a significant factor in the impact of a president's administration. Recent presidents have appointed about 200 judges each term.

JUSTICES AND JUDGES AS POLITICAL OFFICIALS

By the time President Ronald Reagan left office in January 1989, he had appointed almost half of all federal judges, filling vacancies that had resulted from resignations, retirements, and deaths. Reagan selected his appointees with care; the new judges were expected to alter liberal principles that had been laid down by federal courts in the previous three decades. Among the areas in which Reagan hoped for significant change were abortion, affirmative action, and the rights of the accused.

The Role of Partisanship

Presidents generally manage to appoint jurists who have a similar political philosophy. Although Supreme Court justices are free to make their own decisions, their legal positions can usually be inferred from their prior activities. A study by the judicial scholar Robert Scigliano found that about three of every four appointees have behaved on the Supreme Court approximately as presidents could have expected.[18] Of course, a president has no guarantee that a nominee will fulfill his hopes. Justices Earl Warren and William Brennan proved more liberal than President Dwight D. Eisenhower would have liked. When he was asked whether he had made any mistakes as president, Eisenhower replied, "Yes, two, and they are both sitting on the Supreme Court."[19]

In nearly every instance, presidents have chosen members of their own party as Supreme Court nominees. Partisanship is also decisive in nominations to lower-court judgeships. All recent presidents except Gerald Ford have selected more than 90 percent of their district and appeals court nominees from among members of their own party.[20]

The fact that judges and justices are chosen through a partisan political process should not be interpreted to mean that they engage in blatant partisanship while on the bench. Judges and justices are officers of a separate branch and prize their judicial independence. All Republican appointees do not vote the same way on cases, nor do all Democrats. Nevertheless, the partisan backgrounds of judges are a significant influence on their decisions. A study of the voting records of appellate court judges, for example, found that Republican appointees tend to be more conservative than Democratic appointees in their civil rights and civil liberties decisions.[21] In Supreme Court cases, Democratic and Republican appointees have often been on opposite sides, although other divisions also occur.

Other Characteristics of Judicial Appointees

In recent years, increasing numbers of federal justices and judges have had prior judicial experience; the assumption is that such individuals are best qualified for appointment to the federal bench. Most recent appellate court appointees have been district or state judges or have worked in the office of the attorney general.[22] Elective office (particularly a seat in the U.S. Senate) was once the typical route to the Supreme Court,[23] but now most justices have held an appellate court judgeship or high administrative office in the Justice Department before their appointment (see Table 17-1).

White male Protestants are greatly overrepresented in the federal courts, just as they dominate in Congress and at the top levels of the executive branch.[24] Women and minorities make up less than 25 percent of federal judges.[25] Partisanship has been a significant factor in the appointment of women and minorities to the bench (see Table 17-2). Republican presidents Reagan and Bush were less likely than Democratic presidents Carter and Clinton to appoint such individuals, a reflection of the differences in the parties' coalitions (see Chapter 9).

The Supreme Court itself is also demographically unrepresentative. Until 1916, when Louis D. Brandeis was appointed to the Court, no Jewish justice had ever served. At least one Catholic, but at most times only one, has been on the Court almost continuously for nearly a century. Thurgood Marshall in 1967 became the first black justice, and Sandra Day O'Connor in 1981 became

TABLE 17-1 Justices of the Supreme Court, 1995 Most recent appointees held an appellate court position before being nominated to the Supreme Court.

Justice	*Year of Appointment*	*Nominating President*	*Position before Appointment*
William Rehnquist*	1971	Nixon	Assistant attorney general
John Paul Stevens	1975	Ford	Judge, U.S. Court of Appeals
Sandra Day O'Connor	1981	Reagan	Judge, Arizona Court of Appeals
Antonin Scalia	1986	Reagan	Judge, U.S. Court of Appeals
Anthony Kennedy	1988	Reagan	Judge, U.S. Court of Appeals
David Souter	1990	Bush	Judge, U.S. Court of Appeals
Clarence Thomas	1991	Bush	Judge, U.S. Court of Appeals
Ruth Bader Ginsberg	1993	Clinton	Judge, U.S. Court of Appeals
Stephen Breyer	1994	Clinton	Judge, U.S. Court of Appeals

*Appointed chief justice in 1986.

★ CRITICAL THINKING

Should Merit Play a Larger Role in Judicial Selection?

Over the years the partisanship evident in court appointments has occasionally come under attack. In the early twentieth century, Progressive reformers persuaded some states to exclude their judgeships from party patronage positions. The Missouri Plan (described in the section of this chapter on "The State Courts in the Federal System") is a more recent reflection of the belief that partisan loyalty should not play a deciding role in the filling of judicial offices. No such thoroughgoing reform has taken place at the federal level, although Jimmy Carter used selection panels to compile lists of five candidates to fill appellate court vacancies on the basis of merit.

The issue of merit in the case of judges and justices is a complicated one because there is no consensus even on the issue of whether prior judicial experience is desirable for appointees. Justice Felix Frankfurter claimed that "the correlation between prior judicial experience and fitness for the Supreme Court is zero" and felt that the greatest jurists—Oliver Wendell Holmes, Jr., and Benjamin Cardozo among them—were essentially "legal philosophers."

What is your view? Should merit play a larger role in judicial appointments, or is it more important that judges be chosen on the basis of their policy views? What are the relative advantages of appointing "politicians" and "judges" to the Supreme Court?

TABLE 17-2 Background Characteristics of Presidents' Judicial Appointees The judicial appointees of recent presidents have differed in their gender and racial characteristics.

	JUDICIAL APPOINTEES OF:			
	Carter	*Reagan*	*Bush*	*Clinton*
Men	84.5%	91.8%	82.8%	62.5%
Women	15.5	8.2	17.2	37.5
Whites	78.7%	93.9%	88.7%	70.8%
African Americans	14.3	2.1	6.3	22.9
Hispanics	6.2	3.4	4.6	6.3
Asians	0.8	0.5	0.4	—

SOURCE: People for the American Way. Clinton appointees for 1993 only.

the first woman. Antonin Scalia in 1986 became the Court's first justice of Italian descent. No person of Hispanic or Asian descent has ever been a member of the Court.

Judicial scholars disagree on the importance of the Court's demographic makeup. Henry J. Abraham dismisses concerns about it, claiming that the Court was never meant to be a representative body. In contrast, Sheldon Goldman asserts that the judiciary's sensitivity to society's diverse interests depends to a degree on the social backgrounds that the justices bring with them to the Court.[26]

The Nature of Judicial Decision Making

Federal judges and justices are political officials: they constitute one of three coequal branches of the national government. Yet, unlike members of Congress or the president, judges serve in a legal institution and make their decisions in a legal context. As a consequence, their discretionary power is less than that of elected officials. Article III of the Constitution bars the federal judiciary from issuing decisions except on actual cases before it. This restriction prevents the courts from developing legal positions outside the context of the judicial process. As federal judge David Bazelon noted, a judge "can't wake up one morning and simply decide to give a helpful little push to a school system, a mental hospital, or the local housing agency."[27]

THE LEGAL CONTEXT OF JUDICIAL DECISIONS

The most substantial restriction on the courts is the law itself. Although a president or Congress can make almost any decision that is politically acceptable, the judiciary must justify its decision in terms of existing provisions of the law.[28] When asked by a friend to "do justice," Oliver Wendell Holmes, Jr., replied, "That is not my job. My job is to play the game according to the rules."[29] In playing according to the rules, judges engage in a creative legal process that requires them to identify the facts of the case, determine and sometimes formulate the relevant legal principles or rules, and then apply them to the case at hand.

The Constraints of the Facts

A basic distinction in any legal case is between "the facts" and "the laws." The **facts** of a case, as determined by trial courts, are the relevant circumstances of a legal dispute or offense. In the case of a person accused of murder, for example, key facts would include evidence about the murder and whether the rights of the accused were respected by police in the course of their investigation. The facts of a case are crucial because they determine which law or laws are applicable to the case. The courts must respond to the facts of a dispute. This restriction is a very substantial one. A case that centers on a defendant's right to a fair trial cannot be used as an occasion to pronounce judgment on freedom of religion.

facts (of a court case) The relevant circumstances of a legal dispute or offense as determined by a trial court. The facts of a case are crucial because they help to determine which law or laws are applicable in the case.

The Constraints of the Law

In deciding cases, the judiciary is also constrained by existing laws. As distinct from the facts of a case, the **laws** of a case are the constitutional provisions, legislative statutes, or judicial precedents that apply to the situation. To use an obvious comparison, the laws governing a case of alleged murder differ from the laws that apply to an antitrust suit. When addressing a case, a court must determine which laws are relevant.

laws (of a court case) The constitutional provisions, legislative statutes, or judicial precedents that apply to a court case.

Interpretation of the Constitution. The Constitution is the nation's highest law, but it is a sparsely worded document and for that reason is open to interpretation. For example, the Fourth Amendment of the Constitution protects individuals against "unreasonable searches and seizures," but the meaning of "unreasonable" is not spelled out. Nevertheless, judges respect the Constitution's purpose and intent. The question for a judge is what the Framers had in mind by a particular provision. For example, in deciding whether wiretapping and other electronic means of surveillance are covered by the prohibition against unreasonable searches and seizures, the issue is what rights the amendment was designed to protect. Electronic surveillance was not invented until 150 years after the Fourth Amendment was ratified. But the Fourth Amendment was intended to protect individuals against the government's intrusion into their private lives; for this reason, the courts have concluded that government cannot indiscriminately tap a person's telephone.

Interpretation of Statutes. The power of the courts to decide whether a governmental institution has acted within its constitutional powers is called *judicial review* (see Chapter 3). Without this power, the judiciary would be unable to restrain a Congress or presidency that has gone out of control. Yet the process of judicial review pits a court's judgment against that of another institution and invokes the nation's highest law—the Constitution. The imposing nature of judicial review has led the judiciary, when possible, to prefer statutory rulings to constitutional ones.

As a practical matter, it is also true that most cases arising in the courts involve issues of statutory law rather than constitutional law. Statutory law includes legislation that has been enacted by Congress and administrative regulations that have been developed by the bureaucracy on the basis of statutory provisions. All federal courts are bound by federal statutes and administrative regulations, as well as treaties. When a statute is challenged in a case, the judiciary will initially see whether its meaning can be determined by common sense (the "plain-meaning rule").

Congress occasionally structures its debate to ensure that courts will later be readily able to understand its intent. For example, the Civil Rights Act of 1964 was designed in part to prohibit racial discrimination in public accommodations, such as restaurants, hotels, and movie theaters. In the congressional debate, the legislation's supporters stressed the adverse effects of racial discrimination on the free flow of commerce. As its supporters in Congress had anticipated, the Civil Rights Act's ban on racial discrimination in public accommodations was later challenged in court. The Supreme Court upheld the law, noting that "the legislative history of the Act is replete with evidence

YOUR TURN

CONFIDENCE IN THE JUDICIARY

The Question:

Do you approve or disapprove of the way in which the Supreme Court of the United States is handling its responsibilities?

Approve   Disapprove

What Others Think: Whenever they have been asked this question in opinion polls, Americans express more confidence in the Supreme Court than they do in the presidency, Congress, or the federal bureaucracy. Federal judges and justices also rank ahead of members of Congress and bureaucrats in public esteem. In fact, members of the federal bench typically rank higher in opinion polls than nearly any other job category. Moreover, public opinion is more consistently favorable toward the judiciary than toward other institutions. In the 1950s and 1960s, the public expressed a great deal of confidence in *all* federal institutions; but this confidence was undermined in the late 1960s and early 1970s by the Vietnam war, racial riots in the cities, and Watergate. Only about a fifth of the American people expressed confidence in Congress and the presidency by the end of this period. Confidence in all institutions, public and private, including the Supreme Court, also declined during the period, but, in relative terms, the Court's reputation remained strong.

Comment: The reasons for the public's confidence in the Supreme Court are many. A deep-seated belief in rule by law—and trust in the leading instrument of this justice—is certainly one reason. Another is the way in which the Supreme Court is handled by the press. Unlike its coverage of Congress and the presidency, the press's coverage of the Court does not go behind the scenes to the bargaining process by which decisions are made. Although compromise and negotiation are a part of Supreme Court decision making, news reports seem almost to imply that justices make choices based on only legal interpretations. The justices are shown to differ in their legal views, but they are not portrayed as political actors in the same way that elected officials are routinely portrayed. Moreover, the press does not probe deeply into the personal and professional lives of the justices. For instance, any difficulties an elderly justice may have in keeping up with the work load or with the intellectual demands of the position are seldom publicized.

SOURCES OF LAW THAT CONSTRAIN THE DECISIONS OF THE FEDERAL JUDICIARY

U.S. Constitution: The federal courts are bound by the provisions of the U.S. Constitution. The sparseness of its wording, however, requires the Constitution to be applied in the light of present circumstances. Thus judges are accorded some degree of discretion in their constitutional judgments.

Statutory law: The federal courts are constrained by statutes and by administrative regulations derived from the provisions of statutes. Most laws, however, are somewhat vague in their provisions and often have unanticipated applications. As a result, judges have some freedom in deciding cases based on statutes.

Precedent: Federal courts tend to follow precedent (or *stare decisis*), which is a legal principle developed in earlier court decisions. Because times change and not all cases have a clear precedent, judges have some discretion in their evaluation of the way earlier cases apply to a current case.

of the burdens that discrimination by race or color places upon interstate commerce."[30]

Interpretation of Precedent. The U.S. legal system developed from the English common-law tradition, which includes the principle that a court's decision on a case should be consistent with previous rulings. This principle is known as **precedent** and reflects the philosophy of *stare decisis* (Latin for "to stand by things that have been settled")—the doctrine that principles of law, once established, should be accepted as authoritative in all subsequent similar cases. Precedent is an important constraint on the courts. To persist in ignoring precedent would be to direct the law onto an unpredictable course, creating confusion and uncertainty among those who must make choices on the basis of their understanding of the law.

precedent A judicial decision in a given case that serves as a rule of thumb for settling subsequent cases of a similar nature; courts are generally expected to follow precedent.

Political Influences on Judicial Decisions

Although judicial rulings are justified by reference to laws, judges nearly always have some degree of discretion in their decisions.[31] The Constitution is a sparsely worded document and must be adapted to new and changing situations; as a result, federal judges must interpret the Constitution in the context of the issue at hand. The judiciary also has no choice at times but to apply its own judgment to statutory law. Congress often cannot anticipate or reach agreement on all the specific applications of a legislative act and therefore uses general language to state the act's purpose. The judiciary must decide what this language means in the context of a specific case arising under the act. Precedent is even less precise as a guide to decision. Precedent is more a rule of thumb than a strict command; it must constantly be weighed against what Justice Oliver Wendell Holmes, Jr., described as the "felt necessities of the time."

In sum, judges have leeway in their decisions. As a consequence, their rulings reflect not only legal influences but political ones, which come from both outside and inside the judicial system.

"OUTSIDE" INFLUENCES ON COURT DECISIONS

The courts can make unpopular choices, but, in the long run, their decisions must be seen as fair if they are to be obeyed. In other words, the judiciary cannot ignore the expectations of the general public, interest groups, and elected officials, particularly the president and members of Congress. The precise impact of these outside pressures cannot be measured, but judicial experts agree that the courts are affected by them.

The Force of Public Opinion

Judges are responsive to public opinion, although much less so than are elected officials. In some cases, the Court has tailored its rulings in an effort to gain public support or dampen public resistance. In the *Brown* case, for example, the justices, recognizing that school desegregation would be an explosive issue in the South, attempted to defuse the reaction by requiring only that desegregation take place "with all deliberate speed" rather than immediately or on a fixed timetable. The Supreme Court's apparent strategy has been to stay close enough to popular opinion to avoid seriously eroding public support for its decisions.[32]

The judiciary does not have to follow public opinion slavishly in order to keep its authoritative position. Only a few judicial decisions affect a large por-

To some extent, judges take public opinion into account in weighing their decisions. Recently the Supreme Court, perhaps partly in response to the public's concern with crime, has made it harder for state prisoners in death penalty cases to appeal to the federal judiciary. (Shepard Sherbell/SABA)

The judicial branch is increasingly an arena in which interest groups contend for influence. Many of these disputes have pitted environmental groups against business firms. Shown here are demonstrators on both sides of the issue of whether protection of the spotted owl, an endangered species, should take precedence over the interests of the timber industry. (Joe Cempa / Black Star)

tion of the public directly, and most Americans do not want to endure the legal difficulties that might attend violation of the law. Moreover, the fact that public opinion on controversial issues is always divided means that the courts will not stand alone no matter which side of such an issue their rulings favor. As an example, opinion polls indicate that Americans are sharply divided on the issue of a woman's right to obtain an abortion in the early months of pregnancy.

Lobbying the Courts

Interest groups use the courts to advance their policy goals. Although litigation is expensive (the cost of carrying a case all the way to the Supreme Court can run as high as $500,000), it often costs less than lobbying Congress or the executive on a major issue. And obviously some interests, particularly those represented by persons who are in an unpopular or underprivileged minority, may have a better chance of success in a legal suit than with an elected institution.

The array of interests that use lawsuits as a policy tactic include traditional advocacy groups such as the American Civil Liberties Union (ACLU), which concentrates on human rights issues, and the National Association for the Advancement of Colored People (NAACP), which focuses on racial equality disputes. Newer controversies have also spawned their groups; the Alliance Defense Fund, the American Center for Law and Justice, the Becket Fund for Religious Liberty, the Christian Legal Society's Center for Law and Religious Freedom, the Rutherford Institute, and the Western Center for Law and Religious Freedom are a few of the litigant groups involved just in the area of religious rights and practices.

Lawsuits are only one way in which interest groups make their views

Thurgood Marshall (*center*) was the special counsel for the NAACP lawyers who argued the *Brown* school desegregation case before the Supreme Court in 1954. Other members of the team were George E. C. Hayes (left) and James Nabret, Jr. (right). In 1967 Marshall was appointed to the Supreme Court (and retired in 1991). (UPI/Bettmann Newsphotos)

known to the courts. They also participate in cases brought by others through *amicus curiae* ("friend of the court") briefs, which they file in support of one of the parties to the case.[33] Traditionally *amicus* briefs were brought primarily by liberal groups, but today conservative groups also use them heavily because of a recognition that the courts are today more conservative than before. Overall, the number of *amicus* briefs has risen dramatically, both in the number of cases in which such briefs are filed and in the number of briefs filed in individual cases.

The Leverage of Public Officials

The influence of groups and the general public on the judiciary is also registered indirectly, through the elected branches of government. In response to public and group pressure, elected officials try to persuade the judiciary to hand down rulings favored by their constituents. Both Congress and the president have powerful means of influencing the federal judiciary.

Congress is constitutionally empowered to establish the Supreme Court's size and appellate jurisdiction, and Congress can rewrite legislation that it feels the Court has misinterpreted. Although Congress has seldom confronted the Court directly, it has often demonstrated displeasure with Supreme Court rulings, in the hope that the justices would respond favorably. For example, when the Court handed down its *Swann* decision permitting busing for the purposes of achieving racial integration in the schools, members of Congress threatened to pass legislation that would prevent the Court from hearing appeals of busing cases. Busing was never used to its full potential in part because of its unpopularity with many members of Congress.

The executive branch is responsible for implementing court decisions and also affects the judiciary by pursuing or overlooking possible legal controversies, thereby influencing the cases that come before the courts. Under President Ronald Reagan, for instance, the Justice Department vigorously backed several suits challenging affirmative action programs and made no great attempt to push cases that would have expanded the application of such programs.

Presidents can also influence the federal courts through their judicial appointments. When Democrat Bill Clinton took office in 1992, more than a hundred federal judgeships were vacant. President Bush had expected to win reelection and had not moved quickly to fill vacancies as they arose. By the time it was apparent that Bush might lose the election, the Democratic-controlled Congress was able to delay action on the nominations. This enabled Clinton to fill the positions with loyal Democrats who could be expected to partially offset the influence of the Republican judges appointed during the previous twelve years by presidents Reagan and Bush.

Although subject to the influence of elected institutions, the judiciary views certain positions as basic to individual rights rather than as matters of majority opinion. In such instances the judiciary seldom lets the public or elected officials dictate its course of action. Despite continuing criticism of its 1960s ban on school prayer, for instance, the Supreme Court has not backed down from its basic position. The Court prizes its independence and its position as a coequal branch of government. The fact that judges are not popularly elected and that they hold their appointments indefinitely makes it possible for them to resist pressures from Congress and the president.

"INSIDE" INFLUENCES: THE JUSTICES' OWN POLITICAL BELIEFS

The judiciary symbolizes John Adams's characterization of the U.S. political system as "a government of laws, and not of men." The characterization has value as myth, but as the judicial scholar John Schmidhauser notes, "laws are made, enforced, and interpreted by men."[34] As an inevitable result, the decisions of the courts bear the indelible imprint of judges' political beliefs.[35]

This influence is most evident in the case of the Supreme Court. The jus-

The Supreme Court resists pressure from the public and from elected officials on some issues, such as school prayer, that it considers to be questions of individual rights rather than of majority opinion. (Bruce Flynn / Picture Group)

tices are frequently divided in their opinions, and the nature of this division is often based on the justices' political backgrounds. On fair-trial cases in the 1970s, for example, justices William Brennan and Thurgood Marshall, both Democrats when they were appointed to the Court, were "liberals," that is, they were highly protective of the rights of the accused. They were opposed most often by justices Warren Burger and William Rehnquist, both of whom were Republicans when they were appointed to the Court and were "conservative" in the sense that they usually supported police practices when these conflicted with the rights of the accused. In one four-year period Burger and Rehnquist agreed with each other on 80 percent of the Court's decisions and voted with Brennan and Marshall on less than 50 percent of the cases.[36]

The relationship between justices' personal beliefs and their decisions is not a simple one. Liberalism and conservatism are not the same among justices as among elected officials. Because justices are constrained by legal principles, their political differences, though not small or inconsequential, are seldom total. For example, today's conservative-leaning Rehnquist Court has modified substantially the criminal justice rulings of the more liberal Warren Court of the 1960s but has not repudiated what is arguably the Warren Court's most important legacy in this area: the broad principle that the Constitution provides substantial protections for the accused in state trial proceedings. Moreover, the position of some justices depends on the type of issue in question.[37] For example, Justice Byron White, who was appointed by the Democratic president John F. Kennedy, proved to be fairly conservative on civil liberties issues, particularly the rights of the accused, but moderate on questions of governmental regulation of the economy.

Most Supreme Court justices hold relatively stable political views during their tenure. As a result, major shifts in the Supreme Court's position usually occur in conjunction with changes in its membership. When the Court in the 1980s moved away from the criminal justice rulings of the 1960s, it was because the more recently appointed justices believed that government should have more leeway in its efforts to fight crime. Shifts in the Court's direction are related to political trends. Justices are political appointees who are nominated in part because their legal positions seem to be compatible with those of the president.

Nevertheless, the Court's membership has its unpredictable aspects. The turnover of justices depends on retirement and death, which occur irregularly. Whether a president will be able to appoint several, one, or no justices is never certain. The Republican president Richard Nixon made four Supreme Court appointments during his six years in office, whereas the Democratic president Jimmy Carter made none during his four-year term.

Judicial Power and Democratic Government

The issue of judicial power is heightened by the fact that the courts are not a majoritarian institution. Federal judges are not elected and cannot be held directly accountable by the public for their decisions. The principle of self-government asserts that lawmaking majorities have the power to decide society's policies. Because the United States has a constitutional system that places checks on the will of the majority, however, there is obviously an important role in the system for a countermajoritarian institution such as the judiciary. Yet court decisions often reflect the political philosophy of the judges, who constitute a tiny political elite that wields significant power.[38] A critical question is how far judges, who are not elected, ought to go in substituting their policy judgments for those of officials who are elected by the people.

This power is most dramatically evident when a court declares unconstitutional a law enacted by Congress. Such acts of judicial review place the judgment of unelected judges over the decision of the people's elected representatives. The difficult process of amending the Constitution (needing two-thirds majorities in the House and Senate and approval by three-fourths of the states) makes such amendments an impracticable means of reversing the Supreme Court. In the nation's history only four constitutional amendments (for example, the Sixteenth, which permits a federal income tax) have reversed Supreme Court decisions.

THE DEBATE OVER THE PROPER ROLE OF THE JUDICIARY

legitimacy (of judicial power) The issue of the proper limits of judicial authority in a political system based in part on the principle of majority rule.

The question of judicial power centers on the basic isssue of **legitimacy**—the proper authority of the judiciary in a political system based in part on the principle of majority rule. The judiciary's policymaking significance and discretion have been sources of controversy throughout the country's history, but the controversies have perhaps never been livelier than during recent decades. The judiciary at times has acted almost legislatively by ordering broad social policies, such as busing and prison reform. In a recent year, for example, the prison systems in 42 states were operating under court orders that mandated improvements in health care or overcrowding. Through such actions the judiciary has restricted the policymaking authority of the states, has narrowed legislative discretion, and has made judicial action an effective alternative to election victory for certain interests.[39]

The judiciary has become more extensively involved in policymaking for many of the same reasons that Congress and the president have been thrust into new policy areas and become more deeply involved in old ones. Social and economic changes have required government to play a larger role in society, and this development has generated a seemingly endless series of new legal controversies.

Of course, the structure of the U.S. political system requires a relatively assertive judiciary. When the U.S. Constitution established the judiciary as a coequal branch of government, it broke from the English tradition whereby courts had an active role in defining private relationships (*private law*) but were not allowed to define governmental relationships or the relationship of individuals to government (*public law*). Under the U.S. constitutional system, the judiciary in general and the Supreme Court in particular were granted a major role in the sphere of public-law policymaking. The Supreme Court has the responsibility of interpreting the Constitution, overseeing federalism and the separation of powers, and defining individual rights.

Nevertheless, the scope of judicial action raises an important question. How

HOW THE UNITED STATES COMPARES

JUDICIAL POWER

U.S. courts are highly political by comparison with the courts of most other democracies. First, U.S. courts operate within a common-law tradition, which makes judge-made law (through precedent) a part of the legal code. Many democracies have a civil-law tradition, in which nearly all law is defined by legislative statutes. Second, because U.S. courts operate in a constitutional system of divided power, they are required to rule on conflicts between state and nation or between the executive and legislative branches, which thrusts the judiciary into the middle of political conflicts. It should not be surprising, then, that federal judges and justices are appointed through an overtly political process in which partisan views and activities are major considerations. Many federal judges, particularly at the district level, have no significant prior judicial experience. In fact, the United States is one of the few countries that does not mandate formal training for judges.

The pattern is different in most European democracies. Judgeships there tend to be career positions. Individuals are appointed to the judiciary at an early age and then work their way up the judicial ladder largely on the basis of seniority. Partisan politics does not play a large role in appointment and promotion. By tradition, European judges see their job as the strict interpretation of statutes, not the creative application of them.

The power of U.S. courts is nowhere more evident than in the exercise of judicial review—the voiding of a legislative or executive action on the grounds that it violates the Constitution. Judicial review had its origins in European experience and thought, but it was first formally applied in the United States when, in *Marbury* v. *Madison* (1803), the Supreme Court declared an act of Congress unconstitutional. Some democracies, including Great Britain, still do not allow broadscale judicial review, but most democracies now provide for it.

In the so-called American system of judicial review, all judges can evaluate the applicability of constitutional law to particular cases and can declare ordinary law invalid when it conflicts with constitutional law. By comparison, the so-called Austrian system restricts judicial review to a special constitutional court. Judges in other courts cannot declare a law void on the grounds that it is unconstitutional: they must apply ordinary law as it is written. In the Austrian system, moreover, constitutional decisions are made mainly in response to requests for judicial review by political officials (such as the chief executive).

	Austria	Canada
Belgium	Germany	Japan
France	Italy	Mexico*
Great Britain	Turkey	United States
No judicial review	*Austrian system*	*American system*
Least judicial authority	⟵⟶	Most judicial authority

*Mexico is included under the American system even though its judiciary has elements of the Austrian system.

SOURCE: Mauro Cappelletti and William Cohen, *Comparative Constitutional Law* (Indianapolis: Bobbs-Merrill, 1979), chap. 4.

far should the judiciary go in asserting its authority when that authority collides with or goes beyond the action of elected institutions? There are two general schools of thought on this question: those of judicial restraint and judicial activism. Although these terms are somewhat imprecise and often misused, they are helpful in efforts to clarify opposing philosophical positions on the Court's proper role.[40]

judicial restraint The doctrine that the judiciary should be highly respectful of precedent and should defer to the judgment of legislatures. The doctrine claims that the job of judges is to work within the confines of laws set down by tradition and lawmaking majorities.

The Doctrine of Judicial Restraint

The doctrine of **judicial restraint** holds that the judiciary should be highly respectful of precedent and should defer to the judgment of legislatures. The restraint doctrine emphasizes the consistency of law and rule through elected institutions. It holds that broad issues of the public good should be decided in nearly all cases by the majority through legislation enacted by elected officials. The judges' role is to discover the application of legislation and precedent to specific cases rather than to search for new principles that essentially change the meaning of the law.

Advocates of judicial restraint support their position with two major arguments. First, they contend that when the judiciary assumes policy functions that traditionally belong to elected institutions, it undermines the fundamental premise of self-government: the right of the majority to choose society's policies.[41] Second, judicial self-restraint is admired because it preserves the public support that is essential to the long-term authority of the courts.[42] The judiciary must be concerned with **compliance**—with whether its decisions will be respected and obeyed. If the judiciary thwarts the majority's desires, public confidence in its legitimacy can be endangered, and other officials may act to undermine judicial decisions.[43]

compliance The issue of whether judicial decisions will be respected and obeyed.

Advocates of judicial restraint acknowledge that established law is never so precise as to provide exact answers to every question raised by every case and requires some degree of judicial discretion. And in rare circumstances, decisive judicial action may be both appropriate and necessary, as in the historic *Brown* v. *Board of Education* decision (1954). Although the Constitution does not provide an explicit basis for school desegregation, government-supported racial discrimination violates the principle of equal justice under the law.[44] Louis Lusky is among the advocates of judicial restraint who argue that the broad moral language of the Fourteenth Amendment, which says that no state shall deny to any person the equal protection of its laws, was adequate justification for the Supreme Court to require state governments to end their policy of segregated public schools.[45]

Yet many advocates of judicial restraint see no constitutional justification for the Supreme Court's busing and abortion decisions. In *Roe* v. *Wade* (1973),

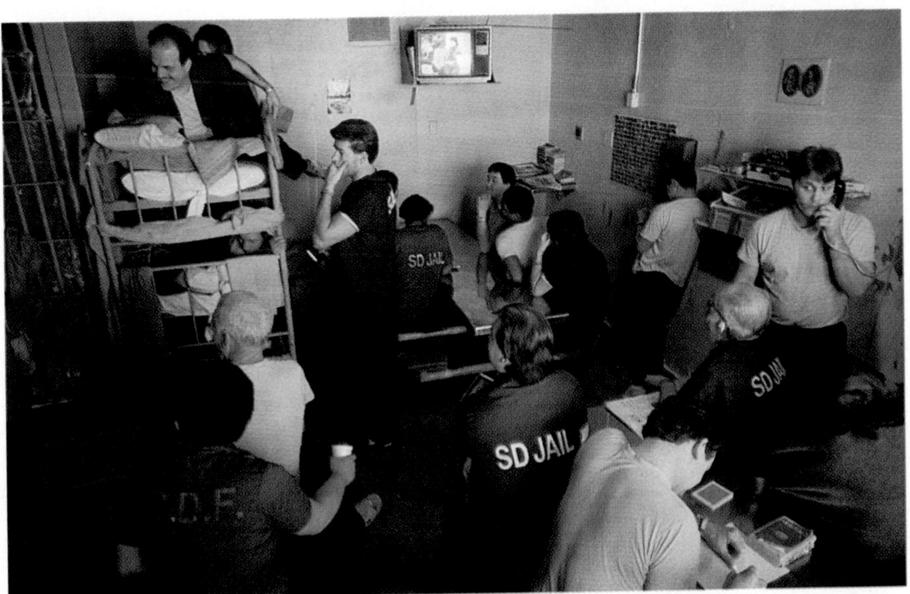

The question of how far the courts should go in placing their judgments ahead of those of elected officials is an ongoing controversy. For example, should the courts be allowed to order state and local officials to relieve overcrowding in jails? (Alon Reininger/Woodfin Camp)

for example, the Court struck down state laws restricting a woman's right to choose an abortion, which it held violated the right to privacy first established in 1965 in *Griswold* v. *Connecticut*.[46] To advocates of judicial restraint, *Roe* v. *Wade* is an example of judicial interference in the exercise of powers that belong rightfully to the majority through its elected representatives. As Justice John Harlan argued in a 1964 opinion: "The Constitution is not a panacea for every blot upon the public welfare; nor should this Court, ordained as a legal body, be thought of as a general haven for reform movements."[47]

The Doctrine of Judicial Activism

judicial activism The doctrine that the courts should develop new legal principles when judges see a compelling need, even if this action places them in conflict with the policy decisions of elected officials.

In contrast to the judicial restraint position is the idea that the courts should take a generous view of judicial power and involve themselves extensively in interpreting and enlarging upon the law. Although advocates of this doctrine, which is known as **judicial activism,** acknowledge the principles of precedent and majority rule, they claim that the courts should not be overly deferential to existing legal principles or to the judgments of elected officials.

Until recently, the doctrine of judicial activism was associated almost entirely with liberal activists who contend that courts should resort to general principles of fairness when existing law is insufficient. Liberal judicial activists argue, for example, that fairness for African American children requires that in some circumstances children should be bused to achieve school integration. In areas where social justice depends substantially on protection of the rights of the individual, the judiciary is said to have a responsibility to act positively and decisively.[48]

Activists who emphasize the Court's obligation to protect civil rights and liberties find justification for their position in the U.S. Constitution's strong

Criminal defendants await their day in court in a holding cell in Philadelphia. Judicial activists gained a major victory in the 1960s when the Supreme Court ruled that defendants in felony cases who cannot afford a lawyer must be provided with legal counsel at public expense. (Chris Gardner/AP/Wide World Photos)

moral language and several of its provisions.[49] They view the Constitution as designed chiefly to protect people from unreasonable governmental interference in their lives—a goal that can be accomplished only by a judiciary that is willing to stand up to the lawmaking majority whenever the latter tries to restrict individual choice. They see the Constitution as a charter for liberties, not as a set of narrow rules. An activist interprets the Sixth Amendment's right to counsel, for example, not just as the right of a defendant to hire counsel but as the right to have a competent lawyer even if the defendant cannot afford one. When the Sixth Amendment was enacted in the late eighteenth century, criminal trials were short and straightforward, and it was at least possible in some instances for poor people to defend themselves competently. But criminal law and procedures today are so complex that a defendant without legal counsel would be at a serious disadvantage. Moreover, society today can afford to provide poor defendants with legal assistance. By such reasoning, the judicial activist school would argue that the Supreme Court was acting properly when it ruled in *Gideon* v. *Wainwright* (1963) that state governments had to provide indigent defendants with counsel at public expense.[50]

Judicial activism is not, however, confined to liberals. In the 1930s conservative activists on the Supreme Court struck down many of the early New Deal programs (see Chapter 2). Judicial activism from the right recently became an issue again when the Court overturned several precedents in the area of the rights of the accused. In 1990 Chief Justice William Rehnquist, in a rare action, asked Congress to restrict the right of people convicted in state courts to file habeas corpus appeals in federal courts. Congress rejected the proposal, and in 1991 a majority on the Rehnquist Court took action on its own to achieve the goal. In one ruling, the Court held that an inmate could not obtain a federal appeal simply because his or her lawyer had made a procedural mistake during the trial in a state court. Chief Justice William Rehnquist wrote that precedent is not "an inexorable command."[51]

These examples illustrate the difficulty of applying the terms "judicial activism" and "judicial restraint" in consistent ways. In fact, some observers argue that all judges—conservatives, moderates, and liberals—are activists in the sense that their decisions are necessarily creative ones.

THE JUDICIARY'S PROPER ROLE: A QUESTION OF COMPETING VALUES

The dispute between advocates of judicial activism and advocates of judicial restraint is a philosophical one that involves opposing values. The debate is important because it addresses the normative question of what role the judiciary ought to play in American democracy. Should unelected judges involve themselves deeply in policy by adopting a broad conception of their power, or should they give wide discretion to elective institutions? Should judges defer to precedent, or should they be willing to change course, even at the risk of sending the law down uncharted paths? These questions cannot be answered simply on the basis of whether one personally agrees or disagrees with a particular judicial decision. The answer necessarily depends on a value judgment about the role of the judiciary in a governing system based on the often-conflicting concepts of majority rule and individual rights.

★ CRITICAL THINKING

Is The Supreme Court Suited to the Making of Broad Social Policy?

As the Supreme Court has extended its reach into areas that were once dominated by Congress and the president, some analysts have questioned whether the Court has the capacity (as distinct from the right) to devise workable policies in all these areas. The way in which the Supreme Court gathers information and formulates decisions bears little resemblance to the way in which Congress or the White House carries out its tasks. These differences, Donald Horowitz argues in *The Courts and Social Policy* (1977), prevent the Supreme Court from being a fully effective policymaking body when it comes to social issues.

Horowitz notes that, unlike members of Congress or executive officials, who usually start their policy deliberations from a general perspective, justices of the Supreme Court start with a particular case, which often involves unusual or extreme circumstances.

Horowitz also notes that the Court acts on the basis of less complete information than Congress, which often holds hearings, conducts research, and by other means considers a wide range of facts before deciding on policy. The basic function of courts is to resolve specific disputes, and admissible evidence is generally limited to material directly relevant to the case at hand.

How important do you judge these limits on the Court's policymaking capacity to be? Why?

The United States is a constitutional democracy that recognizes both the power of the majority to rule and the claim of the minority to protection of its rights. The judiciary was not established as the nation's moral conscience and does not have a monopoly on the issue of minority interests and rights. Yet the judiciary was established as a coequal branch of government and was charged with the responsibility for protecting individual rights and minority interests. In short, the constitutional question of how far the courts should be allowed to go in substituting their judgment for that of elected institutions and established law is open to interpretation. The trade-off is significant on all issues: minority rights vs. majority rule, states' rights vs. federal power, legislative authority vs. judicial authority. The question of whether judicial restraint or judicial activism is more desirable is one that every student of American government should ponder.

Summary

At the lowest level of the federal judicial system are the district courts, where most federal cases begin. Above them are the federal courts of appeals, which review cases appealed from the lower courts. The U.S. Supreme Court is the nation's highest court. Each state has its own court system, consisting of trial courts at the bottom and one or two appellate levels at the top. Cases originating in state courts ordinarily cannot be appealed to the federal courts unless a federal issue is involved, and then the federal courts can choose to rule only on the federal aspects of the case. Federal judges at all levels are nominated by the president, and if confirmed by the Senate, they are appointed by the president to the office. Once on the federal bench, they serve until they die, retire, or are removed by impeachment and conviction.

The Supreme Court is unquestionably the most important court in the country. The legal principles it establishes are binding on lower courts, and its capacity to define the law is enhanced by the control it exercises over the cases it hears. However, it is inaccurate to assume that lower courts are inconsequential (the upper-court myth). Lower courts have considerable discretion, and the great majority of their decisions are not reviewed by a higher court. It is also inaccurate to assume that federal courts are far more significant than state courts (the federal court myth).

The courts have less discretionary authority than elected institutions. The judiciary's positions are constrained by the facts of a case and by the laws as defined through the Constitution, statutes and government regulations, and legal precedent. Yet existing legal guidelines are seldom so precise that judges have no choice in their decisions. As a result, political influences have a strong impact on the judiciary. It responds to national conditions, public opinion, interest groups, and elected officials, particularly the president and members of Congress. Another political influence on the judiciary is the personal beliefs of judges, who have individual preferences that are evident in the way they decide on issues that come before the courts. Not surprisingly, partisan politics plays a significant role in judicial appointments.

In recent decades the Supreme Court has issued broad rulings on individual rights, some of which have required governments to take positive action on behalf of minority interests. As the Court has crossed into areas traditionally left to lawmaking majorities, the legitimacy of its policies has been questioned. Advocates of judicial restraint claim that the justices' personal values are inadequate justification for exceeding the proper judicial role. They argue that the Constitution entrusts broad issues of the public good to elective institutions and that judicial activism ultimately undermines public respect for the judiciary. Judicial activists counter that the courts were established as an independent branch and should not hesitate to promote new principles when they see a need, even if this action puts them into conflict with elected officials.

Major Concepts

appellate jurisdiction
compliance
concurring opinion
decision
dissenting opinion
facts (of a court case)
judicial activism
judicial conference
judicial restraint
jurisdiction (of a court)
laws (of a court case)
legitimacy (of judicial power)
majority opinion
opinion (of a court)
original jurisdiction
plurality opinion
precedent
senatorial courtesy
writ of *certiorari*

Suggested Readings

Abraham, Henry J. *The Judicial Process,* 6th ed. New York: Oxford University Press, 1993. An explanation of how state and federal courts form the judicial system of the United States.

Baum, Lawrence. *The Supreme Court,* 5th ed. Washington, D.C.: Congressional Quarterly Press, 1994. A survey of the personnel, procedures, and policymaking function of the Supreme Court.

Bickel, Alexander M. *The Supreme Court and the Idea of Progress.* New Haven, Conn.: Yale University Press, 1978. A critical assessment of the policy rulings of the Warren Court from the perspective of an advocate of judicial restraint.

Carp, Robert A., and Ronald Stidham. *The Federal Courts,* 2d ed. Washington, D.C.: Congressional Quarterly Press, 1990. An analysis of the federal court system.

Maltz, Earl M. *Rethinking Constitutional Law: Originalism, Interventionism, and the Politics of Judicial Review.* Lawrence: University of Kansas Press, 1994. A critical and timely analysis of constitutional interpretation in the modern age.

O'Brien, David M. *Storm Center,* 3d ed. New York: Norton, 1993. An analysis of the Supreme Court in the context of the controversy surrounding the role of the judiciary in the U.S. political system.

Perry, Michael J. *The Constitution and the Courts: Law or Politics?* New York: Oxford University Press, 1994. A sweeping assessment of the constitutional role of the Supreme Court by a proponent of judicial activism.

Provine, D. Marie. *Case Selection in the United States Supreme Court.* Chicago: University of Chicago Press, 1980. An analysis of the process by which the Supreme Court chooses the cases it reviews.

Salokar, Rebecca Mae. *The Solicitor General: The Politics of Law.* Philadelphia, Pa.: Temple University Press, 1992. A study of the important and increasingly political role of the nation's top trial lawyer.

Segal, Jeffrey A. and Harold J. Spaeth. *The Supreme Court and the Attitudinal Model.* New York: Cambridge University Press, 1993. A provocative analysis which claims that justices' personal beliefs are the main determinant of Supreme Court decisions.

WOODLANDS
SCHOOL

PART FOUR

PUBLIC POLICY

The term "public policy" refers to action (or inaction) by government which is directed toward a goal or purpose. Busing to achieve racial integration in the public schools is an example of public policy—a goal-oriented governmental action.

In a sense, all the preceding sections of this book have led up to this one. Public policy is the major consequence of political activity. National policy is established directly by public officials (discussed in Part Three), but these officials operate within a constitutionally established framework of governmental institutions and individual rights (Part One), and they make decisions in the context of public opinion and political organizations (Part Two). Any realistic assessment of public policy requires that all these factors be taken into account. This fact is evident in the discussion in this section's four chapters: fiscal, monetary, and regulatory policy (Chapter 18); welfare, education, and health policy (Chapter 19), foreign and military policy (Chapter 20); and the challenge of governance (Chapter 21).

The dynamic aspects of government come into play in any discussion of public policy because it is inherently dynamic in nature. Policy questions are rarely settled once and for all. As changes occur in society or in the balance of power between contending interests, public policy changes, sometimes substantially. In the past decade, for example, U.S. policy on international trade has changed greatly as a result of a transformation of the global economy and the dissolution of the Soviet bloc.

The policy process is also the point where politics is most evident. Politics, said Harold Lasswell, is the struggle over "who gets what, when, and how." Americans differ in many of their interests, and accordingly they disagree over policy. Some of their differences—over abortion policy, for example—are so fundamental as to be irreconcilable. If abortion policy is an extreme case, there is hardly a public policy that does not in one way or another create winners and losers. Yet competing interests are often able to find common ground on policy issues. The typical impulse when a policy problem arises is not only to resolve it, but to do so in a way that accommodates as many of society's divergent interests as possible. This philosophy speaks volumes about the nature of governance is a truly democratic society.

The four chapters in this section are designed mainly to address discrete subjects, but during the discussion, a common pattern emerges. U.S. policy tends to be piecemeal and reactive. The nation's fragmented governing structure, diverse interests, and cultural bias against intrusive government make it difficult for policymakers to deal with major issues except in small parts and until they have reached a problematic stage.

Analysts are divided as to whether the piecemeal and reactive nature of U.S. public policy is a strength or weakness. Incrementalists such as Charles Lindbloom have argued that a piecemeal approach reduces the calculation demands on policymakers and minimizes the chance of a dreadful mistake of the kind that resulted when Soviet central planners imposed a radically new economic system on their country in the 1920s. Other analysts, while not embracing the concept of radical policy change, argue that a piecemeal approach is sometimes inferior because it does not entail a full analysis of a policy's costs and benefits. They have cited Europe's government-run health care systems, which are half as costly and more equitable than America's, as an example.

Whatever one's view on this issue, there is no question that a nation's policies are fundamentally important. They are the instrument by which people pursue solutions to the complex problems of collective life.

★ ★ ★

CHAPTER 18

ECONOMIC POLICY: CONTRIBUTING TO PROSPERITY

We the people of the United States, in order to . . . insure domestic tranquility . . .
—Preamble, U.S. Constitution

The public's confidence in the economy was thoroughly shaken as 1992 began. The University of Michigan's Index of Consumer Confidence had declined to 50 percent, matching the lowest level in the forty years that the index had been compiled. General Motors announced that over the next three years it would close several plants and permanently eliminate 70,000 jobs. IBM planned to cut 20,000 employees. Zales, the jewelry retailer, said it would close 400 stores. An estimated 25 million Americans, a fifth of the work force, had been out of a job at some time in 1991, and the future looked worse. A loss of 100,000 jobs in the banking industry alone was projected for 1992. The country's economic woes awakened memories of another severe downturn sixty years earlier—the Great Depression. Would history repeat itself? Was the United States on the verge of another economic collapse in which millions of Americans would find themselves without work and without hope?

There was at least one major difference between the 1930s and the early 1990s. When the Great Depression struck, no substantial government programs were in place to stabilize and stimulate the U.S. economy. Moreover, the response to the 1930s crash guaranteed that the economic disaster would worsen. Businesses cut back on production, depositors withdrew their savings, and consumers slowed their spending; all these actions accelerated the downward spiral. In the early 1990s, however, government was there to assure depositors that their savings were insured, to encourage consumers to keep spending, and to inform business that government would not allow interest rates to soar.

This chapter examines the economic role of the government, focusing on its promotion and regulation of economic interests and its fiscal and monetary policies, which affect economic growth. Directly or indirectly, the federal government is a party to almost every economic transaction in which Americans engage. Although the private decisions of firms and individuals are the main force in the American economic system, these decisions are influenced by government policy. Washington seeks to maintain high productivity, employment, and purchasing power; regulates business practices that would otherwise result in economic inefficiencies and inequities; and promotes economic interests. To an important extent, the condition of the U.S. economy depends on how well the government in Washington performs these roles. And certainly no issue is more politically significant than the state of the economy. Americans have high expectations about their financial well-being and, to a large degree, judge their national leaders by whether the economy is doing well or poorly. The main ideas presented in the chapter are the following:

- ★ *Through regulation, the U.S. government imposes restraints on business activity that are designed to promote economic efficiency and equity.* This regulation is often the cause of political conflict, which is both ideological and group-centered.
- ★ *Through promotion, the U.S. government helps private interests to achieve their economic goals.* Business in particular benefits from the government's promotional efforts, which take place largely in the context of group politics.
- ★ *Through fiscal and monetary policy, the U.S. government seeks to maintain a stable and prosperous general economy.* The overall condition of the U.S. economy is generally the leading issue in American electoral politics and has a major influence on each party's success.

Regulating the Economy

economy A system of production and consumption of goods and services, which are allocated through exchange among producers and consumers.

laissez-faire doctrine A classic economic philosophy which holds that owners of business should be allowed to make their own production and distribution decisions without government regulation or control.

An **economy** is a system of production and consumption of goods and services, which are allocated through exchange. When a shopper chooses groceries at a store and pays money for them, that transaction is one of the million economic exchanges that make up the economy. In *The Wealth of Nations* (1776), Adam Smith presented the case for the **laissez-faire doctrine,** which holds that private individuals and firms should be left alone to make their own production and distribution decisions. Smith reasoned that when there is a demand for a good (that is, when people are willing and able to buy a good), private entrepreneurs will respond by producing the good and distributing it to places where demand exists. Smith argued that the desire for profit is the "invisible hand" that guides the system of demand and supply toward the greatest benefit for all.

Smith acknowledged that the doctrine of laissez-faire capitalism had a few limits. Certain areas of the economy, such as roadways and postal services, were natural monopolies and were better run by government than by private firms. In addition, by regulating banking, currency, and contracts, government could give stability to private transactions. Otherwise, Smith argued, the economy was best left in private hands.

In contrast, Karl Marx proposed a worker-controlled economy. In *Das Kapital* (*Capital*, 1867) Marx argued that a free market system is exploitative because producers, through their control of production and markets, can compel workers to labor at a wage below the value they add to production and can force consumers to pay higher prices for goods than are justified by the cost of production. To end the exploitation of labor, Marx proposed a collective economy. When the workers owned the means of production, the economy would operate in the interest of all people.

In *The Wealth of Nations* (1776), Adam Smith provided a philosophical justification for a free market economy. (National Portrait Gallery, London)

Marx and Smith represent the extremes of economic theory. No country in the world has an economy that conforms fully to either the laissez-faire or the collectivist model. All national economies today are of "mixed" form in that they contain elements of both private and public control. However, the world's economies vary greatly in their mix. The United States tends toward private ownership, whereas China tends toward collective ownership. In between, but closer to the American type of economy, are certain European countries whose governments, on behalf of their people, own and operate a number of key industries, including steel, airlines, banking, and oil.

Although the U.S. government itself owns only a few businesses (such as Amtrak), it plays a substantial economic role through the **regulation** of privately owned businesses. U.S. firms are not free to act as they please but must operate within production and distribution rules set by federal regulations. Regulatory policy is generally intended to promote either economic *efficiency* or *equity* (see Table 18-1).

regulation A term that refers to government restrictions on the economic practices of private firms.

PROMOTING EFFICIENCY

Economic efficiency requires firms to fulfill as many of society's needs as possible while using as few of its resources as possible. **Efficiency** refers to production processes and the relationship of inputs to outputs; the greater the output for a given input, the more efficient the economy. Efficiency is often

efficiency An economic principle which holds that firms should fulfill as many of society's needs as possible while using as few of its resources as possible. The greater the output (production) for a given input (for example, an hour of labor), the more efficient the process.

TABLE 18-1 The Main Objectives of Regulatory Policy The government intervenes in the economy to promote efficiency and equity.

Objective	*Definition*	*Representative Actions by Government*
Efficiency	Fulfillment of as many of society's needs as possible at the cost of as few of its resources as possible. The greater the output for a given input, the more efficient is the process.	Preventing restraint of trade; requiring producers to pay the costs of damage to the environment; reducing restrictions on business that cannot be justified on a cost-benefit basis.
Equity	When the outcome of an economic transaction is fair to each party.	Requiring firms to bargain in good faith with labor; protecting consumers in their purchases; protecting workers' safety and health.

In *Das Kapital* (1867), Karl Marx argued that a collective economy would end the exploitation of labor by those who controlled the means of production. (German Information Center)

measured in terms of worker productivity—the output of the average worker for each hour on the job. In the past two decades, the productivity of U.S. workers has risen about 50 percent as a result of changes in technology, management techniques, and labor practices. Stated differently, the U.S. economy has become increasingly efficient in recent years.

Adam Smith and other classical economists believed that the free market was the optimal means of achieving efficiency. Competition among producers would compel the producers to use as few resources as possible in producing goods and to charge consumers the lowest possible prices. This idea remains a central tenant of free market economics. The notion that government through its decisions can somehow achieve the same result was thoroughly discredited by the collapse of Soviet-style communism. Soviet central planners found it impossible to handle the computational complexity of demand, supply, and price decisions for a national economy. A marketplace system does not depend on such a mechanism: the uncoordinated decisions of individual firms and consumers serve to bring demand, supply, and price into line.

Preventing Restraint of Trade

Nevertheless, the assumption that the market *always* determines price is flawed. The same incentive—the profit motive—that drives producers to respond to demand can drive them to try to corner the market on a good. If a producer gains a monopoly on a good or colludes with other producers to fix its price, consumers are forced to pay an artificially high price. This possibility is a justification for government regulation for purposes of efficiency. By intervening to prevent restraint of trade, government can restore competition to the marketplace.

Restraint of trade was prevalent in the United States in the late nineteenth century when large trusts came to dominate many areas of the economy, including the oil, steel, railroad, and sugar markets. Railroad companies, for example, had no competition on short routes and gouged their customers, who had no choice but to pay the asking price if they wanted to get their goods to market.[1] In 1887, Congress took its first step toward regulating the trusts by enacting the Interstate Commerce Act. The legislation created the Interstate Commerce Commission (ICC), which was charged with regulating railroad practices and fares. Three years later, the Sherman Antitrust Act declared that any business combination or practice in restraint of trade was illegal. A pro-business Supreme Court made these legislative acts less effective than anticipated, and so the Mann-Elkins Act (1911) and the Clayton Act (1914) were passed to broaden the government's regulatory authority. The Federal Trade Commission (FTC) was established in 1914 to regulate trade practices.

Today the FTC is one of many federal agencies charged with regulating business competition. In a few cases, the government has prohibited mergers or required divestments in order to increase competition. The largest antitrust suit in the country's history was settled in 1984 when AT&T was forced to sell its regional Bell Telephone companies, which had enabled it to monopolize access to long-distance telephone service. AT&T must now compete for long-distance customers with MCI, Sprint, and other carriers.

In general, however, the U.S. government tolerates business concentration. Corporate takeovers and mergers are common, although most of them involve the joining of corporations that are not direct competitors. An example is the acquisition of Carrier, a manufacturer of air conditioners, and Otis, an elevator manufacturer, by United Technologies Corporation (UTC). UTC is a conglomerate—a business organization that consists of a number of noncompeting corporations. The government has concluded that conglomerates do not substantially threaten competitive trade practices. But the government has also permitted some mergers of competing firms, such as Chrysler's acquisition of AMC and Pennzoil's takeover of Getty Oil. Although such mergers reduce competition, the government tolerates concentrated ownership in the oil, automobile, and other industries in which high capital costs make it difficult for smaller firms to compete successfully. Government acceptance of corporate giants also reflects a realization that market competition no longer involves just domestic firms. For example, the "Big Three" U.S. automakers (General Motors, Ford, and Chrysler) face stiff competition from imports, particularly those from Japan and Germany. The U.S. government's general policy toward corporate giants that act in restraint of trade has been to penalize them financially. In 1993, a number of air carriers (including American, Delta, United, Northwest, and US Air) were found to have engaged in price fixing and were ordered to award hundreds of millions of dollars in certificates to travelers who could prove they had flown on these carriers during the period in question. More than 4 million individuals, organizations, and businesses filed claims.

The government has shifted some of the cost of cleaning up toxic waste dumps and other kinds of pollution from the general public to the firms that discharge the pollutants. (Fred Ward/Black Star)

Making Business Pay for Indirect Costs

Economic inefficiencies can result not only from restraint of trade but from the failure of businesses or consumers to pay the full costs of resources used in production. Classical economics assumed that market prices reflect all the costs of production, but this assumption is rarely warranted. Consider the case of persons who become disabled on the job. A large part of the cost of maintaining these now less productive persons is borne, not by their former employers, but by society through public welfare programs. Or consider companies that dump their industrial wastes in a nearby river. The price of these companies' products does not reflect the water pollution, and hence customers do not pay all the costs that society has incurred in the making of the products. Economists label such unpaid costs **externalities.**

externalities Burdens that society incurs when firms fail to pay the full costs of production. An example of an externality is the pollution that results when corporations dump industrial wastes into lakes and rivers.

Until the 1960s, the federal government did not require firms to help pay for such costs. The impetus to begin doing so came not only from lawmakers but also from the scientific community and environmental groups. The Clean Air Act of 1963 and the Water Pollution Control Act of 1964 required industry to install antipollution devices to keep the discharge of air and water pollutants within specified limits. In 1970 Congress created the Environmental Protection Agency (EPA) to monitor compliance with federal regulations governing air and water quality and the disposal of toxic wastes.

Regulatory activity has had a dramatic impact on the quality of the environment. Pollution levels today are far below their levels of the 1960s when yellowish-gray fog hung over cities like Los Angeles and when rivers like the Potomac were open sewers. Environmental protection has gained broad public support. Although Americans are divided over the issue of whether government has gone too far in regulating business, they oppose the lifting of existing regulations in a wide range of areas, from automobile emission standards to industrial waste–water standards (see box: Your Turn).

Curbing Overregulation

Although government intervention is intended to increase economic efficiency, the effect can be the opposite. If government places needless or excessive regulatory burdens on firms, they waste resources in the process of complying. The result is higher-priced goods that are more expensive for consumers and less competitive in the domestic and global markets.

Federal regulation substantially raises the cost of doing business. Firms have to expend work hours to monitor and implement government regulations, which in some instances (for example, pollution control) also require companies to buy and install expensive equipment.[2] State and local governments are also affected, since they operate many of the sewer, water, and other systems covered by the regulations. Some critics have estimated that federal regulation costs as much as $500 billion annually, although the actual figure would seem much lower. The Environmental Protection Agency itself estimated that compliance with its rules cost $140 billion in 1994, which is more money than was spent on any federal program except defense and social security.

The costs of compliance are efficient to the degree that they produce com-

YOUR TURN

REGULATION AND THE ENVIRONMENT

The Questions:

1. In general, do you think there is too much, too little, or about the right amount of government regulation of business and industry?

[Too much] [Too little] [About the right amount]

2. Here's a list of steps that could be taken to lift regulations on business. For each one indicate whether you would be in favor of such a step or opposed to it.
   a. End government requirements that electrical appliances have a specific level of energy efficiency [Favor] [Oppose]
   b. Change or put off new and stricter standards on things such as asbestos, scaffolding, and chemical exposure [Favor] [Oppose]
   c. Postpone stronger exhaust emission standards for cars and trucks [Favor] [Oppose]
   d. Eliminate the requirement that future model cars have air bags that inflate automatically in the event of a collision [Favor] [Oppose]
   e. Postpone stronger requirements for industry to clean up its wastewater before it dumps it [Favor] [Oppose]
   f. Postpone stronger air pollution standards for factories and utilities [Favor] [Oppose]

What Others Think: The first question was asked in a 1993 USA Today/CNN survey conducted by the Gallup Organization. Of the respondents, 37 percent said there was too much regulation, 30 percent said the amount was about right, and 28 percent said there was too little regulation. The second question was asked in a 1991 Roper Organization survey and produced sharply different results. A majority of respondents opposed each of the proposed regulatory cutbacks, usually by a margin of more than 3 to 1. For example, 70 percent of respondents opposed the postponement of stronger exhaust emission standards for cars and trucks while only 20 percent favored this action.

Comment: Although Americans want to reduce government intervention in the economy, regulatory cutbacks are not a simple issue, as the second question illustrates. There are important trade-offs involved in either reducing or increasing regulatory levels. The ongoing challenge for policymakers is to strike a proper balance between regulatory and free market mechanisms.

Environmental regulations restricting the level of automobile pollution have greatly improved air quality in America's cities. (Jim Pickerell/Stock, Boston)

mensurate benefits. As a result of regulation, for example, worker safety has improved greatly (in the 1980s alone, for example, workplace deaths decreased by 23 percent).

Yet numerous regulations result in inefficiency; the costs they impose are not offset by corresponding benefits. In fact, some federal regulations do not permit costs to be a consideration at all. Key provisions of the Clean Air Act and Safe Drinking Water Act, for instance, impose strict minimum standards on all communities. Absurd remedies have resulted. The city of Anchorage, Alaska, had to ask local fish-processing plants to dump their waste into the sewer system so that it would have pollutants to remove from the water supply. Without the fish entrails, Anchorage's water was so clean already that the city would have had to build a $135 million sewage treatment plant to comply with a mandate requiring it to reduce contaminants from the current level, whatever that level happened to be.[3]

The problem of rigid regulations was addressed in the Regulatory Flexibility Act of 1980. The legislation has limited scope but does require cost-benefit analysis and risk assessment (the severity of the problem) to be taken into account in certain regulatory decisions. The act also gives administrators some leeway in determining appropriate remedies. In 1995, Congress enacted legislation to tighten the regulatory process by extending cost-benefit calculations to a broader set of applications. Other policy innovations of recent years include the EPA's negotiated regulation process, in which interested parties (for example, policymakers, firms, communities, and environmental groups) are brought together in advance of the issuing of a regulation in order to negotiate its content.

Implementing Deregulation

deregulation The rescinding of excessive government regulations for the purpose of improving economic efficiency.

Another response to regulatory excess is the policy of **deregulation**—the rescinding of regulations then in force for the purpose of improving efficiency. This process began in 1977 with passage of the Airline Deregulation Act, which eliminated government-set air fares and, in some instances, government-mandated air routes. Airline regulation had begun in the 1930s to guarantee service to smaller cities and ensure that fledgling air carriers could accumulate the capital to build large fleets of up-to-date aircraft. By the 1970s, the airline industry had changed so completely that deregulation was justified. Since deregulation, air travelers have had more flights to choose from and have paid lower fares, although the airline industry itself has struggled to make a profit. Some analysts suggest that the economic pressures associated with deregulation have also made air travel less safe, although the evidence for this claim is inconclusive.

Congress followed airline deregulation with partial deregulation of the trucking, banking, energy, and communications industries, among others. These industries had operated under federal regulations that substantially restricted their activities, including what they could charge for services. The free market would govern a wider range of their activities.

The free market principle has its limits, however, just as the regulatory principle can be carried too far. Deregulation has not been an unqualified success.[4]

In an effort to recover their money, depositors line up outside a failed savings and loan institution in Paterson, New Jersey. The S&L crisis illustrates that the real issue of business regulation is the proper balance of regulatory and free market mechanisms. The crisis was precipitated by deregulation of the S&Ls and exacerbated by the presence of a remaining regulatory device—federally insured savings accounts. (Norman R. Rowan/Stock, Boston)

The savings and loan (S&L) industry is a prime example.[5] S&Ls had been hit hard by the high inflation of the 1970s, and they hoped to restore their financial base through high-yield investments. Since existing regulations prevented them from pursuing riskier investments, the S&L industry successfully lobbied Congress for a change. When deregulation lifted restrictions on how S&Ls could invest depositors' savings, many of them began to engage in highly speculative ventures, such as commercial real estate.

Ironically, the ability of S&Ls to speculate was enhanced by a remaining regulatory device—the Federal Savings and Loan Insurance Corporation (FSLIC). Like the Federal Deposit Insurance Corporation (FDIC), which insures the savings deposits of bank customers, the FSLIC insured S&L savings accounts for a maximum of $100,000 each. The insurance meant that savers were not risking their money when they placed it in S&Ls that were offering extraordinary interest rates in order to attract the funds they needed to pursue their speculative ventures. Financially sound S&Ls were forced to match these high rates in order to keep their customers.

By 1989 the S&L industry was in crisis. Bad management, poor investments, and outright fraud had resulted in an industrywide loss of billions of dollars. In order to save what was left of the industry, President Bush and Congress developed a bailout plan that will eventually cost the taxpayers more than $100 billion.

The savings and loan crisis demonstrates that the issue of business regulation is not a simple question of whether or not to regulate. On the one hand, too much regulation can burden firms with bureaucratic red tape, costly implementation procedures, and limited options. On the other hand, too little regulation can give firms the leeway to exploit the public unfairly or recklessly. As the S&L crisis illustrates, either too little or too much regulation can result in economic inefficiency. The challenge for policymakers is to strike the proper balance between regulatory measures and free market mechanisms.

PROMOTING EQUITY

equity (in relation to economic policy) The situation in which the outcome of an economic transaction is fair to each party. An outcome can usually be considered fair if each party enters into a transaction freely and is not knowingly at a disadvantage.

As we noted earlier, the government intervenes in the economy to bring equity as well as efficiency to the marketplace. **Equity** occurs when an economic transaction is fair to each party. In contrast to efficiency, which refers to the relationship of inputs to outputs, equity refers to *outcomes:* whether they are reasonable and mutually acceptable. An outcome can usually be considered fair if each party enters into a transaction freely and is not unknowingly at a disadvantage. If a seller knows a product is defective, for example, the buyer must also know of the defect.

An early equity measure was the creation of the Food and Drug Administration (FDA) in 1907. Because consumers are often unable to tell whether foods and drugs are safe to use, the FDA works to keep adulterated foods and dangerous or ineffective drugs off the market. In the 1930s, financial reforms were among the equity measures enacted under the New Deal. The Securities and Exchange Act of 1934 and the Banking Act of 1934 were designed in part to protect investors and savers from dishonest or imprudent brokers and bankers. The New Deal also provided greater equity for organized labor, which previously had been in a weak position in its dealings with management. Under the terms of the 1935 National Labor Relations Act (also called the Wagner Act), employers could no longer refuse to negotiate pay and working conditions with employees' unions. The Fair Labor Standards Act of 1938 established minimum wages, maximum working hours, and constraints on the use of child labor.[6]

The 1960s and 1970s produced the greatest number of equity reforms. From 1965 to 1977, ten federal agencies, such as the Consumer Product Safety Commission, were established to protect the public from harmful effects of business activity. Among the products declared to be unsafe in the 1960s and 1970s were the insecticide DDT, cigarettes, the Chevrolet Corvair, phosphates, Firestone radial tires, and leaded gasoline.[7] The rule eliminating lead in gasoline, for example, has given society a major benefit; the average level of lead in children's blood has decreased by 75 percent since the measure went into effect.[8]

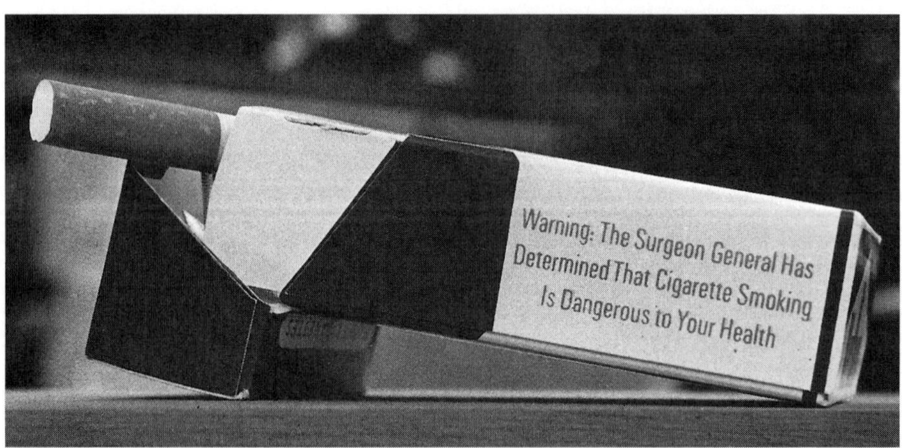

Health warnings on cigarette packages are an example of government regulation aimed at achieving equity by providing consumers with relevant product information. (George W. Gardner/Stock, Boston)

THE POLITICS OF REGULATORY POLICY

Economic regulation has come in waves, as changes in national conditions have produced intermittent bursts of social consciousness.

The Reforms of the Progressive and New Deal Eras

The first wave of regulation came during the Progressive era, when reformers sought to break the power of the trusts by placing constraints on unfair business practices. The second wave came in the New Deal era, when reformers sought to stimulate economic recovery by regulatory policies that they designed as much to save business as to reform it. For example, 1930s banking regulations were meant not only to protect depositors but also to save the banking system, which was threatened by bank closings arising from financial institutions' unsound investments and from mass withdrawals of funds by panicked depositors.

Although business fought Progressive and New Deal reforms, long-term opposition was lessened by the fact that most of the resulting regulation applied to a particular industry rather than to firms of all types. This pattern made it possible for an affected industry to gain influence with those officials who were responsible for regulating its activities. By cultivating close ties to the Federal Communications Commission (FCC), for example, the networks managed to gain policies that protected their near monopoly on broadcasting and gave them high and sustained profits. Although not all industries have had as much leverage with their regulators as broadcasting, it is generally true that industries have not been greatly hampered by the older form of regulation and in many cases have substantially benefited from it.

Most of the regulatory functions that were established during the Progressive and New Deal periods are organized in ways that facilitate group access and influence. Some regulatory functions are located within departments, such as the Department of Commerce, that are oriented toward the promotion of particular economic interests. Other functions are carried out by regulatory commissions (including, as we saw in Chapter 16, the FTC, FCC, SEC, and CAB), whose sole responsibility is the regulation of a given activity or industry. The members of these commissions are appointed by the president with Senate approval but serve fixed terms and are not subject to removal by the president. In other words, regulatory commissioners are relatively independent officials who have broad authority in their policy areas. A regulated interest that acquires influence with commissioners is positioned to obtain favorable policies.

The Era of New Social Regulation

The third wave of regulatory reform, in the 1960s and 1970s, differed from the Progressive and New Deal waves in both its policies and its politics. The third wave has been called the era of "new social regulation" by some economists because of the social goals it addressed in its three major policy areas: environmental protection, consumer protection, and worker safety.[9]

Most of the regulatory agencies established during the third wave have much broader policy mandates than those created earlier. They have responsibility not for a single industry but for firms of all types, and their policy scope covers a wide range of activities. The Environmental Protection Agency (EPA), for example, is charged with regulating environmental pollution of almost any kind by almost any firm. Unlike the older agencies that are run by a commission whose members serve for fixed terms, some of the newer agencies, including the EPA, are headed by a single director, who is appointed by the president with Senate approval.

Because newer agencies such as the EPA have a wide-ranging clientele, no one firm or industry can easily influence agency policy to a great extent. There is also strong group competition in some of the newer regulatory spheres; for example, business lobbies must compete with environmental groups such as the Sierra Club and Greenpeace for influence with the EPA.[10] The firms regulated by the older agencies, in contrast, face no powerful competition in their lobbying activities; broadcasters, for example, are largely unopposed in their efforts to influence the Federal Communications Commission. In both cases,

HOW THE UNITED STATES COMPARES

NATIONAL ECONOMIES

All western democracies have a market economy, but they differ in the degree to which key industries are run by government. In many democracies, the government owns and operates a number of leading industries, such as steel, oil, banking, and the airlines. The U.S. government has traditionally owned and operated very little in the way of industry, a model that is gaining strength elsewhere. In western Europe, there is a trend toward privatization of public industries to increase economic efficiency and reduce taxation levels. Although most Americans feel that their taxes are too high, they are actually taxed at a substantially lower rate than citizens of most western democracies.

The U.S. economy is the world's largest and in some respects the strongest. In the past decade, U.S. firms have substantially modernized and streamlined their economic operations, which has improved their competitiveness in the domestic and world markets. Yet the country has a substantial trade imbalance. Americans are heavy consumers, and the United States consequently imports far more goods than it exports. Another consequence of the nation's consumer-oriented economy is a national rate of savings that is substantially lower than that of most other industrialized democracies. (The importance of the global economy to the United States is discussed further in Chapter 20.)

	Gross Domestic Product (GDP) (Billions of Dollars)	*Total Tax Receipts (Percent of GDP)*	*Trade: Exports Minus Imports (Billions of Dollars)*	*Savings (as Percent Disposable Income)*
Canada	$562	37%	$ −6	10.6%
Germany	$1,763	38	+31	12.1
Great Britain	$1,039	37	−9	11.5
Japan	$3,699	31	+62	14.6
United States	$5,881	30	−101	4.6

SOURCE: Organization for Economic Cooperation and Development (OECD), 1993.

a form of *pluralist* politics prevails, but the range of influential groups is broader in the case of the newer agencies.

The newer agencies are more affected by partisan politics. With their stronger commitment to business interests, Republican leaders have been less supportive of environmental, consumer, and worker interests than have Democratic leaders and have thus been less supportive of regulatory activity in these areas. When Republicans took control of Congress in 1995, for example, they wrote legislation restricting the scope of environmental regulation.

How the Government Promotes Various Economic Interests

The U.S. government has always made important contributions to the nation's economy. The Constitution was written in part to provide for a national government strong enough to promote a sound economy. The Constitution stipulated that the government was to regulate commerce, create a strong currency, develop uniform commercial standards, and provide a stable credit system. The fledgling government also immediately demonstrated its concern for economic interests. Congress in 1789 gave a boost to the nation's shipping industry by placing a tariff on imported goods carried by foreign ships. Since that first favor, the U.S. government has provided thousands of direct benefits to economic interests.

In Chapters 13 and 16 we described how congressional and bureaucratic politics results in the promotion of group interests. Here we will briefly examine a few illustrations of the scope of government's contribution to the *pluralistic* interests of business, labor, and agriculture.

PROMOTING BUSINESS

American business is not opposed to government regulation as such. It objects only to regulatory policies that are adverse to its interests. We have noted that, at various times and in differing ways, many federal regulatory agencies have served primarily the interests of the industries they are intended to regulate.

Tax breaks are another way that government promotes business. Firms receive tax credits for capital investments and get tax deductions for capital depreciation. At times, these tax breaks have literally been giveaways. Provisions of the 1981 tax legislation that the Reagan administration engineered through Congress were so generous to business that many corporations got money back from government. Tax loopholes enabled 128 corporations to cut their tax bills to less than zero in at least one of the years between 1981 and 1983. General Electric had profits of $6.5 billion in the 1981–1983 period, but instead of paying taxes, it received $283 million in tax rebates from the federal government.[11]

Over the past forty years the burden of federal taxation has shifted dramatically, from corporations to individuals. A few decades ago, the revenues raised from taxes on corporate income were roughly the same as the revenues raised from taxes on individual income. Today, individual taxpayers carry the heavier burden by a more than 5-to-1 ratio. Some analysts do not regard the change as overly significant, arguing that higher corporate taxes would be passed along to the public anyway in the form of higher prices for goods and services.

Government also promotes business through loans and loan guarantees. In 1979 the Chrysler Corporation was about to go bankrupt. The doctrine of laissez-faire economics would have dictated that any unprofitable and poorly managed company be allowed to fail. Instead, Washington guaranteed $1.5 billion in loans for Chrysler: the federal government would repay the lenders if Chrysler defaulted. Although this loan guarantee came under criticism, it was remarkable only in the amount of money involved. The federal government has guaranteed thousands of business loans and also makes direct loans to businesses. Many firms have received grants and loans from federal, state, or local government for construction and equipment costs. Often, public funding is the price that a community pays to keep or lure a firm. For example, Detroit gave General Motors a $200 million aid package in order to persuade it to build a new assembly plant in the city rather than elsewhere.[12]

The most significant contribution that government makes to business is the traditional services it provides, such as education, transportation, and defense. Colleges and universities, which are funded primarily by governments, furnish business with most of its professional and technical work force and with much of the basic research that goes into product development. The nation's roadways, waterways, and airports are other public sector contributions without which business could not operate. There is an entire industry—defense contracting—that exists almost entirely on government money. In short, America's business has no better booster than government.

Although corporate mergers decrease competition, the government has generally tolerated mergers in business sectors in which high capital costs occur. Here, Ted Turner (l) and Gerald Levin (r) shake hands to mark the merger of the Turner Broadcasting System and Time-Warner, which created one of the world's largest news and entertainment conglomerates. (A. Tannenbaum/Sigma)

PROMOTING LABOR

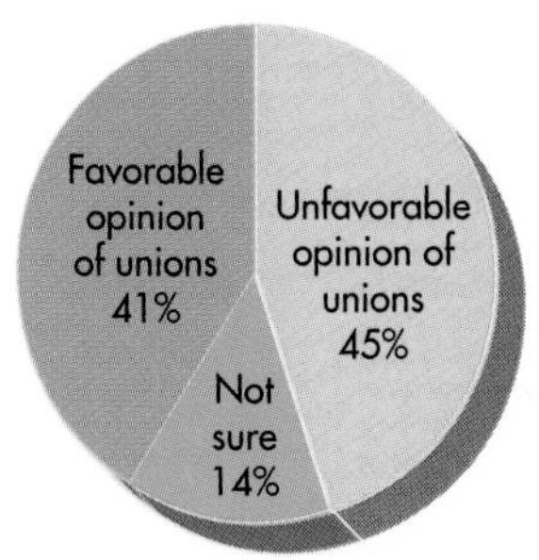

FIGURE 18-1 Opinions on Labor Unions
Americans are not strongly supportive of labor unions.
Source: Time/CNN survey by Yankelovich Partners, June 2, 1994.

Laissez-faire thinking dominated government's approach to labor well into the twentieth century. The governing principle, developed by the courts in the early nineteenth century, was that workers had limited rights of collective action. Union activity was regarded as interference with the natural supply of labor and the free setting of wages. The extent of hostility toward labor can be seen in the use of federal troops to break up strikes.

The 1930s brought significant changes. The key legislation was the National Labor Relations Act of 1935, which guaranteed workers the right to bargain collectively and prohibited business from discriminating against union employees and from unreasonably interfering with union activities. The Taft-Hartley Act of 1947 took away some of labor's gains, including compulsory union membership for workers whose workplace is unionized. Under the provisions of Taft-Hartley, each state can decide for itself whether all workers in work units that are unionized must become union members (union shop) or whether a worker can choose not to join the union (open shop). Despite these modifications, the National Labor Relations Act has remained a cornerstone of labor's power. The legislation not only required that business bargain with organized labor but also established the National Labor Relations Board (NLRB), an independent regulatory commission that is empowered to enforce compliance with labor law by both business and labor. Government has also aided labor by legislating minimum wages and maximum hours, unemployment benefits, safer and more healthful working conditions, and nondiscriminatory hiring practices.

Although government support for labor extends beyond these examples, it is not nearly so extensive as its assistance to business. America's individualistic culture has worked against efforts to establish labor policies as strong as those of western European democracies. Even today, Americans are split in their opinion of unions (see Figure 18-1).

Labor has not fared well in recent years. Firms have forced wage and benefit concessions from unions, which have failed to convince the courts to side with them in labor-management disputes. In a 1984 case, for example, the Supreme Court ruled in favor of a company that had filed for bankruptcy for the purpose of voiding its union contracts.[13] After filing, the corporation resumed its operations with new workers hired at much lower wage and benefit levels. U.S. labor unions were also rebuffed in a 1992 Supreme Court ruling which declared that they almost never have a right to go onto a company's property to distribute union recruitment materials.[14]

At their peak, unions represented a third of America's work force; they now represent less than a sixth. Their decline has been paralleled by a decline in the purchasing power of nonsalaried workers. Job growth has been concentrated in the nonunion retail trade and service sectors, which, according to Department of Commerce data, provide an average wage of slightly more than $200 weekly. Unionized workers, who earn an average of $450 a week, have been declining in number. Some analysts claim that cheap labor, while advantageous to the individual firm, is disadvantageous to the overall economy because lower-income persons do not have the money to buy new cars,

Members of the United Auto Workers (UAW) rally in support of striking workers at the Caterpillar corporation's headquarters in Peoria, Illinois. Although government provides support for labor through a wide range of policies, U.S. workers have less power and fewer rights than their European counterparts, a reflection of America's individualistic culture. (Jim West / Impact Visuals)

homes, and durable goods.[15] Other analysts contend that labor costs are a major factor in the ability of firms to compete in global markets and that additional high-paying jobs will be lost if U.S. firms are uncompetitive.

PROMOTING AGRICULTURE

Until well into the twentieth century, most Americans still lived on farms and in small rural communities. Agriculture was America's dominant business and was assisted by government's land policies. The Homestead Act of 1862, for example, opened government-owned lands to settlement, creating spectacular "land rushes" by offering 160 free acres of government land to each family that staked a claim, built a house, and farmed the land for five years.

Farm programs today provide assistance to small farmers and large commercial enterprises (agribusinesses) and cost the federal government billions of dollars annually (see Figure 18-2). One goal of this spending is to stabilize farmers' income, which can fluctuate greatly from one year to the next, depending on market and growing conditions. Midwestern floods in 1993, for example, caused extensive crop damage to farms along the Mississippi and Missouri rivers. The federal government responded with several billion dollars in emergency assistance to the afflicted farmers. Income stabilization policy, however, is not limited to emergency aid. There are a variety of federal programs in place that aim to stabilize farmers' incomes. Price support programs, for example, are designed to keep the prices of farm products relatively high even when the market is weak.

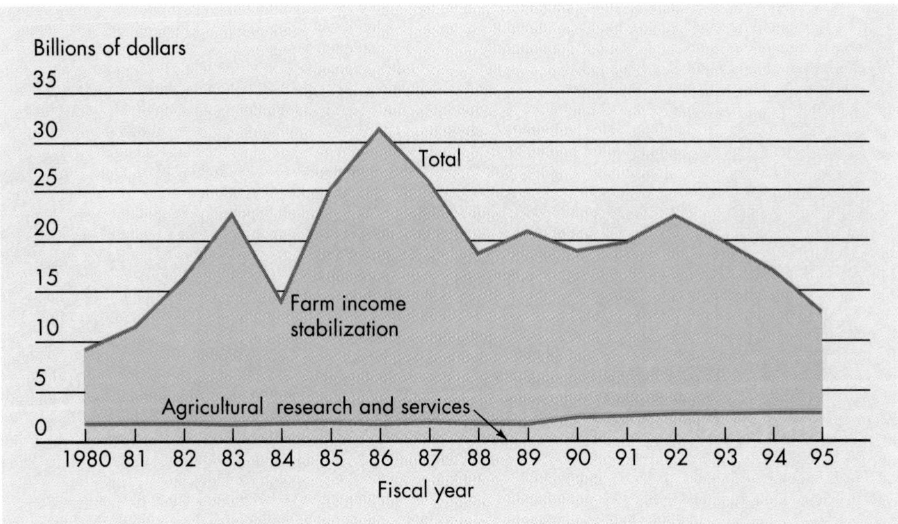

FIGURE 18-2 Federal Expenditures for Agriculture, 1980–1995
Federal assistance to farmers is substantial and is aimed chiefly at stabilizing their yearly income. *Source: Office of Management and Budget.*

A second goal of U.S. agricultural policy is to control production. U.S. farmland is so fertile that it produces more crops than can be marketed. Surpluses keep market prices low because supply exceeds demand. In a program designed to reduce farm surpluses, the government offered payments to dairy farmers who voluntarily destroyed their dairy herds. Another program gave surplus wheat and other commodities to farmers who had agreed to take their land out of production.

Farm programs face an uncertain future. Agricultural interests have strong support in Congress, but reductions in price support and other federal agricultural programs are a virtual certainty as part of future budget-deficit reduction efforts.

A Missouri farmer rescues pigs stranded by the 1993 flood that inundated millions of acres of midwestern farmland. Through its disaster relief and loan programs, the federal government assisted farmers who lost crops and livestock to the flooding. (Steve Mellon/Impact Visuals)

During the Great Depression of the 1930s, the federal government intervened on a massive scale to stabilize the economy and reduce unemployment. In the Works Progress Administration (WPA), a New Deal program, jobless men were given work on public improvement projects, such as this Arkansas flood control project. (UPI/Bettmann Newsphotos)

Maintaining a Stable Economy

Until the 1930s, the federal government adhered to the prevailing free market theory and made no attempt to maintain the stability of the economy as a whole. The economy was regarded as largely self-regulating. The U.S. economy was fairly prosperous, but it periodically experienced economic depression that resulted in widespread joblessness and financial loss.

The greatest economic catastrophe in the nation's history—the Great Depression of the 1930s—finally brought an end to traditional economics. Franklin D. Roosevelt's emergency spending and job programs, designed to stimulate the economy and put Americans back to work, heralded the change. Roosevelt's efforts to stimulate the economy were controversial at the time, but today government is expected to have ongoing policies that will maintain high economic production, employment, and growth and will control prices and interest rates.

Fiscal policy and *monetary policy* are the economic instruments which the government utilizes most heavily to promote these goals. Each mechanism is complex and is based on several schools of thought. Accordingly, the following discussion attempts merely to outline some of the basic components of fiscal and monetary policy.

FISCAL POLICY

fiscal policy A tool of economic management by which government attempts to maintain a stable economy through its taxing and spending decisions.

The government's efforts to maintain a stable economy are made mainly through its taxing and spending decisions, which together are referred to as its **fiscal policy** (see Table 18-2).

The annual federal budget is the foundation of fiscal policy. George Washington wrote his budget on a single sheet of paper, but the federal budget today is thousands of pages long and takes eighteen months to prepare and

TABLE 18-2 Fiscal Policy: A Summary Taxing and spending levels can be adjusted in order to affect economic conditions.

Problem	*Fiscal Policy Actions*
Low productiviity and high unemployment	Demand side: increase spending Supply side: cut business taxes
Excess production and high inflation	Decrease spending Increase taxes

enact. The budget is a massive policy statement that allocates federal expenditures among thousands of government programs and provides for the revenues—taxes, social insurance receipts, and borrowed funds—to pay for these expenditures (see Figure 18-3). From one perspective, the budget is the national government's allocation of costs and benefits. Every federal program benefits some interest, whether it be farmers who get price supports, defense firms that obtain military contracts, or retirees who receive monthly social security checks. Not surprisingly, the process of enacting the annual federal budget is a highly political one. Agencies and groups have an obvious stake in promoting their interests.

From another standpoint, that of fiscal policy, the budget is a device for stimulating or dampening economic growth. Changes in overall levels of spending and taxing are means of keeping the economy's normal ups and downs from becoming extreme.

Fiscal policy has its origins in the economic theories of John Maynard Keynes. In *The General Theory of Employment, Interest, and Money* (1936), Keynes noted that employers become overly cautious during a depression and will not expand production, even as wages drop. Challenging the traditional idea that government should draw back during depressions, Keynes claimed that severe economic downturns can be shortened only by increased government

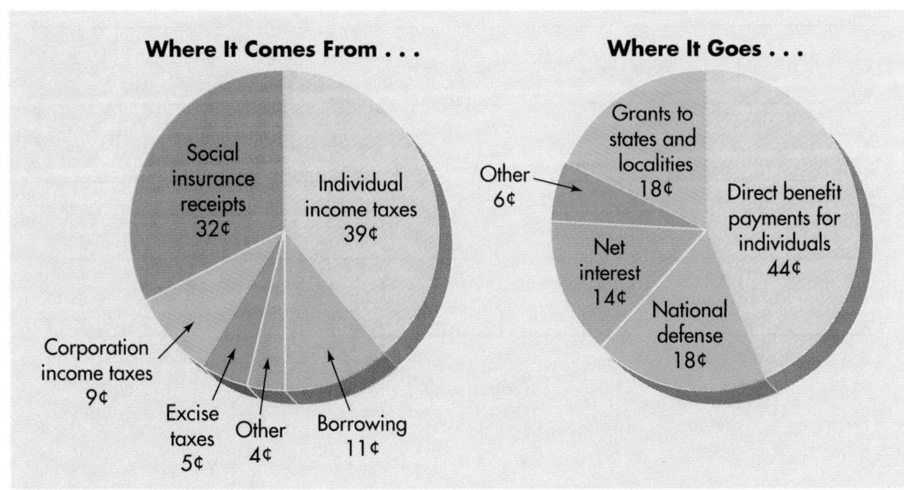

FIGURE 18-3 The Federal Budget Dollar, Fiscal Year 1995
Source: Office of Management and Budget.

spending. By placing additional money in the hands of consumers and investors, government can stimulate production, employment, and spending and thus promote recovery.[16]

Demand-Side Stimulation and the Deficit Problem

demand-side economics A form of fiscal policy that emphasizes "demand" (consumer spending). Government can use increased spending or tax cuts to place more money in consumers' hands and thereby increase demand.

Keynes's theory focused on government's efforts to stimulate consumer spending. This **demand-side economics** emphasizes the consumer "demand" component of the supply-demand equation. When the economy is sluggish, the government can increase its spending, thus placing more money in consumers' hands. With additional money to spend, consumers buy more goods and services. This increased demand, in turn, fosters production and employment. In this way, government spending contributes to economic recovery.

The use of fiscal policy as a means of economic stimulation has been greatly diminished by the unprecedented size of the national debt. By 1995 it was approaching $5 trillion, up from less than $1 trillion in 1980 (see Figure 18-4). As a consequence, an enormous amount of money is required each year to pay the interest on the national debt. The interest payments today are larger than the entire federal budget as recently as 1969. They are now the third largest item in the federal budget; the only costlier programs are defense and social security. The interest payments each year are roughly equal to all federal domestic spending—for roads, education, prison, food stamps, and the rest—except for social security. The payments exceed by two times the federal taxes paid by corporations and are about the total of federal income taxes paid by Americans who live west of the Mississippi River.

This growing drain on the government's resources has made it very difficult for policymakers to increase the level of spending in order to boost the economy. In the early 1990s, the U.S. economy was in its longest downturn

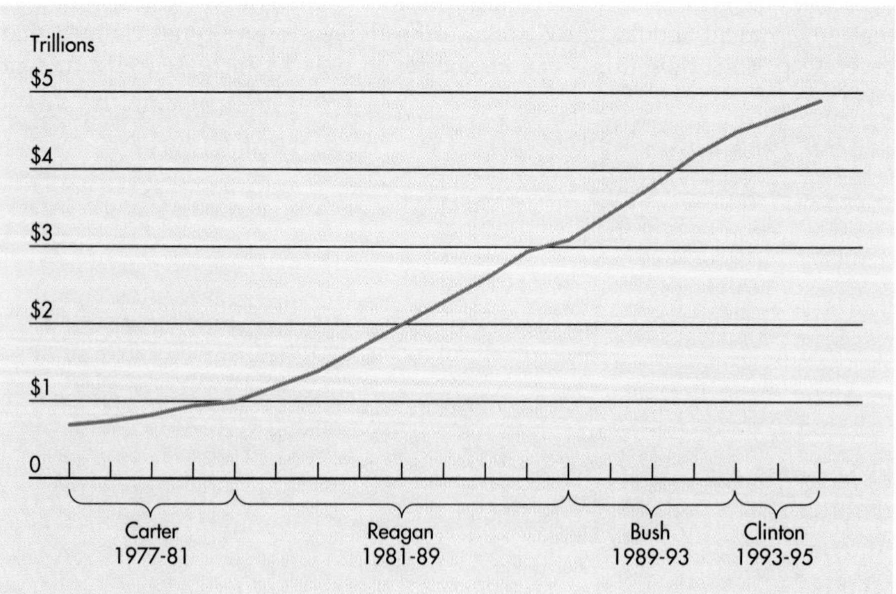

FIGURE 18-4 The National Debt, 1977–1995
The national debt was relatively small until the 1980s, when it increased rapidly. *Source: Office of Management and Budget.*

Senate Budget Committee Chairman Pete Domenici (R-N.M.) points to a chart during a 1995 hearing. The massive federal debt has restricted the use of government spending as a tool of fiscal policy. (Wide World Photos)

since World War II, but the government's fiscal condition ruled out any significant new spending programs.

If the balanced-budget amendment should become part of the Constitution, demand-side economics might become a thing of the past. The proposed amendment was part of the Republicans' Contract With America and would require federal expenditures not to exceed revenues. During an economic slowdown, government revenues decrease, firms make less profit, and people work less and pay fewer taxes as a result. Under the amendment any such decrease in revenues would have to be offset by corresponding reductions in government spending, which would result in further job and sales losses. In other words, government might someday be forced into fiscal decisions that would actually intensify economic downturns. *The Wall Street Journal,* which is a long-standing critic of federal deficits, expressed doubt in an editorial that the balanced-budget amendment was the proper solution to the problem: "While politically appealing, [the amendment] makes no particular sense economically."[17]

Supply-Side Stimulation

A fiscal policy alternative to demand-side stimulation is **supply-side economics,** which emphasizes the business (supply) component of the supply-demand equation.[18] Supply-side theory was a cornerstone of President Reagan's economic program. He believed that economic growth would flow as easily from stimulation of the business sector as from stimulation of consumer demand. "Reaganomics" included substantial tax breaks for businesses and upper-income individuals.

supply-side economics A form of fiscal policy that emphasizes "supply" (production). An example of supply-side economics would be a tax cut for business.

Reagan contended that increased prosperity for wealthy Americans would "trickle down" to those at the bottom as production increased and more jobs were created. However, the benefits of the economic growth of the 1980s were

Economic prosperity is a key factor in determining a president's chances of being returned to office. One reason that Bill Clinton, shown here campaigning in West Virginia, was reelected by a comfortable margin in 1996 was that many voters perceived themselves as being better off economically than they had been before he came to office. (Dirck Halstead/Gamma)

confined largely to higher-income Americans. The real income of the poorest 20 percent of families dropped by more than 10 percent during the decade, while the real income of the richest 20 percent rose by roughly 30 percent. Meanwhile, taxes for the poorest 20 percent increased by 3 percent, while taxes for the highest 20 percent decreased by 5 percent.[19]

The analyst Kevin Phillips argues that "trickle-down" theory failed because of a fundamental change in the U.S. economy. In the past, money at the top made its way to the bottom through the jobs created when factories were built with the money. According to Phillips, money at the top today goes primarily into the international financial markets; most of it never makes its way into the pockets of the domestic work force.[20]

Despite the discouragements of recent years, supply-side economics has its applications. Under some conditions, business tax cuts and incentives encourage firms to expand production, thus creating jobs and enlarging supply, each of which can stimulate consumer demand.

Controlling Inflation

High unemployment and low production are only two of the economic problems that government is called upon to solve. Another is inflation, which is an increase in the average level of prices of goods and services. Before the late 1960s, inflation was a minor irritant: prices rose by less than 4 percent annu-

★ CRITICAL THINKING

Is a $5 Trillion Debt a National Disaster?
The size of the federal debt poses several problems for the nation. One is that the rising interest payments on the federal debt have inhibited spending on existing and new programs. Another problem is that when the government is forced to borrow large sums of money to pay the interest on its debt and to cover its annual deficit, interest rates go up. Faced with higher rates, other sectors borrow less, which means that there is less business investment and less consumer spending.

Some economists, however, argue that the negative effects of the national debt are exaggerated. They point out that it often makes sense to borrow. Families borrow in order to buy a home or car. Businesses borrow in order to grow. Government should also borrow when the economy requires the stimulus of federal spending. Most economists would caution against too much debt, but some have concluded that, so far, the advantages have outweighed the disadvantages. For one thing, the borrowed dollars are worth more than the inflated dollars with which the debt will someday be repaid. In addition, many of the dollars that the government has borrowed have come from foreign lenders. The Japanese, the Germans, and others have provided revenues that Americans have used for their own purposes.

Which of these positions is the more compelling? Are there other arguments for and against the claim that the size of the federal debt is a threat to America's future?

ally. But inflation rose sharply during the last years of the Vietnam war and remained high throughout the 1970s, reaching a postwar record rate of 13 percent in 1979. Since then, inflation has moderated (see Figure 18-5) and concern about it has lessened.

To fight inflation, government can apply remedies opposite to those used to fight unemployment and low productivity. Inflation normally occurs when jobs are plentiful and people have extra money to spend. Demand is high in such periods, and prices are pulled up in what is known as "demand-pull" inflation. By reducing its spending or by raising personal income taxes, government takes money from consumers, thus reducing demand and dampening prices. (The main policy tool for addressing inflation is monetary policy, which is discussed later in the chapter.)

The Fiscal Policy Structure

The president and Congress determine fiscal policy. The Constitution grants Congress the power to tax and spend, but the president normally initiates major policies in these areas and directs most of the fiscal policy structure.

The Employment Act of 1946 created the Council of Economic Advisers (CEA) and placed it within the Executive Office of the President (see Chapter 14). The CEA advises the president on economic policy and assists in preparing the annual economic report to Congress. The president also has the services of economic and revenue experts in the Treasury, Labor, and Commerce departments. The Office of Management and Budget (OMB), another presidential staff agency, is the chief instrument of fiscal policy; it prepares the annual budget that the president submits to Congress. The budget contains the president's recommendations on overall government spending and on the allocation of these expenditures among various programs. The combination of taxes and government borrowing necessary to finance this spending is also part of the president's annual budget message.

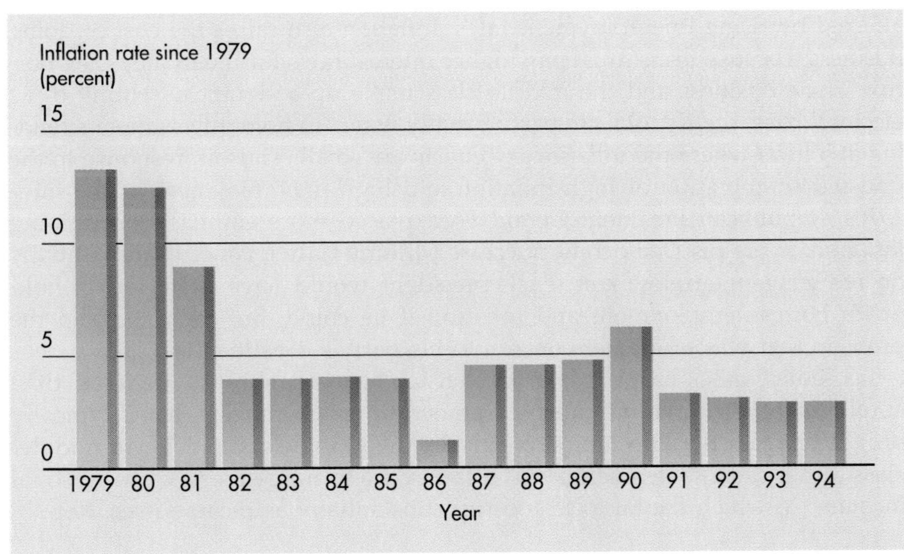

FIGURE 18-5 The Annual Rate of Inflation
Price increases have declined in the last decade in comparison with the late 1970s. *Source: U.S. Department of Labor.*

★ STATES IN THE NATION

Individual Income Taxes: Tax rates on taxable income are within the 2 to 8 percent range in most states.

STATE	PERSONAL INCOME TAX RATE RANGE LOW	HIGH
Ala.	2.0%	5.0%
Alaska	No tax	
Ariz.	3.8	7.0
Ark.	1.0	7.0
Calif.	1.0	11.0
Colo.	5.0	5.0
Conn.	4.5	4.5
Del.	3.2	7.7
D.C.	6.0	9.5
Fla.	No tax	
Ga.	1.0	6.0
Hawaii	2.0	10.0
Idaho	2.0	8.2
Ill.	3.0	3.0
Ind.	3.4	3.4
Iowa	0.4	10.0
Kan.	4.4	7.8
Ky.	2.0	6.0
La.	2.0	6.0
Maine	2.0	8.5
Md.	2.0	6.0
Mass.	5.9	5.9
Mich.	4.6	4.6
Minn.	6.0	8.5
Miss.	3.0	5.0
Mo.	1.5	6.0
Mont.	2.0	11.0
Neb.	2.6	7.0
Nev.	No tax	
N.H.	No tax	
N. J.	2.0	7.0
N. Mex.	1.8	8.5
N.Y.	4.0	7.9
N.C.	6.0	7.8
N.Dak.	2.7	12.0
Ohio	0.7	7.5
Okla.	0.5	7.0
Oreg.	5.0	9.0
Pa.	2.8	2.8
R.I.	*	*
S.C.	2.5	7.0
S.Dak.	No tax	
Tenn.	No tax	
Texas	No tax	
Utah	2.6	7.2
Vt.	*	*
Va.	2.0	5.8
Wash.	No tax	
W.Va.	3.0	6.5
Wis.	4.9	6.9
Wyo.	No Tax	

SOURCE: U.S. Advisory Commission on Intergovernmental Relations, 1994. Asterisk (*) indicates that tax rate is tied to individual's federal income tax liability.

Until the creation of the Congressional Budget Office (CBO) in 1974, Congress was at a disadvantage in budget deliberations because it was dependent on OMB's assessments. OMB's estimates of revenues and program costs tend to favor the president's proposals. Often, presidential initiatives have cost more than OMB predicted. Since cost is a factor in congressional deliberations on new programs, the CBO gives Congress a firmer basis for judging the accuracy of the president's estimates. (See Chapters 12 and 13 for a discussion of Congress's budgetary role.)

The CBO was established by the Congressional Budget and Impoundment Control Act of 1974 (see Chapter 12), which also created the House and Senate budget committees, which are responsible for proposing spending ceilings for various budget categories. Before 1974, areas of the budget were divided among congressional committees, whose actions were not coordinated so as to stay within specific budgetary limits. Finally, the act restricts the president's ability to impound, or freeze, funds that Congress has appropriated. Congress must approve any impoundments that last more than a short period.

The Politics of Fiscal Policy

Politics plays a significant part in the making of fiscal policy because Democrats and Republicans often disagree over its direction.[21] The Democratic coalition has traditionally included the majority of lower-income and working-class Americans. Accordingly, the party's leaders are sensitive to rising unemployment because blue-collar workers are usually the first and most deeply affected. Democrats in Washington have usually responded to a sluggish economy with increased government spending, which offers direct help to the unemployed and stimulates demand. Virtually every increase in federal unemployment benefits during the past fifty years, for example, has been initiated by Democratic officeholders.

Republican leaders are more likely than Democrats to be concerned about inflation. It attacks the purchasing power of all Americans, including higher-income individuals who are less likely than lower-income persons to be affected by rising unemployment rates. Inflation also raises the cost of doing business, because firms must pay higher interest rates for the money they borrow. Since business and the middle class make up a significant chunk of its electoral base, the Republican party usually wants to hold government spending at a level where the inflationary effects are small. Thus, in response to the unusual combination of high inflation and high unemployment in the mid-1970s, Republican President Gerald Ford placed more emphasis on fighting inflation, while his Democratic successor, Jimmy Carter, concentrated initially on reducing unemployment. Each president would have preferred to hold down both unemployment and inflation if he could, but each attacked the problem that was of greater concern to his party's constituents.

Tax policy also has partisan dimensions, even more so perhaps than employment or inflation policy. Democratic policymakers have typically sought tax cuts that are more beneficial to working-class and lower-middle-class Americans.[22] Democrats have favored a progressive tax on personal incomes, in which the tax rate goes up substantially as income rises. Republicans have preferred to keep taxes on upper incomes at a relatively low level, contending that this policy encourages the savings and investment that foster economic growth. The Republicans' Contract With America, for example, called for a steep cut in the capital gains tax (the tax on profits from the sale of stock, real estate, and other assets). About 70 percent of the tax savings would go to the richest 1 percent of Americans. Republicans argued that the tax cut would stimulate the economy and create jobs for lower-income persons. Democrats claimed the cut would be a boon for the rich and provide very few benefits to those of lower income.

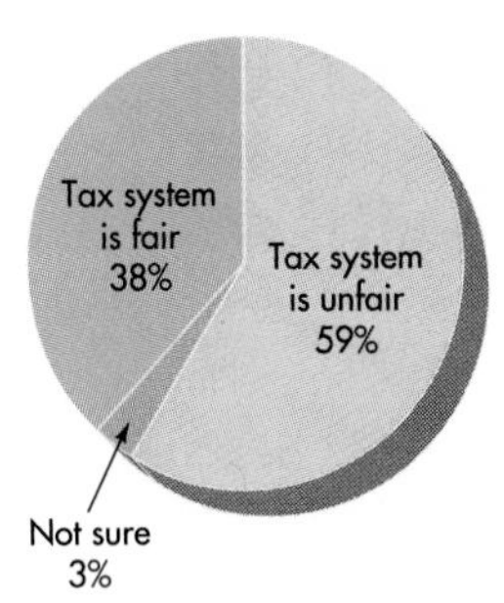

FIGURE 18-6 Opinions about the Tax System's Fairness
A majority of Americans claim the tax system is unfair; the main complaint is that the tax burden falls too heavily on middle-income families. *Source: NBC News/Walls Street Journal poll by Hart and Teeter, July 1994.*

Partisan differences were also evident in the tax increase enacted by Congress in 1993 at the urging of President Clinton, who proposed it as part of a deficit reduction package. The congressional vote divided sharply along party lines; no Republicans supported the tax bill while 89 percent of Senate Democrats and 84 percent of House Democrats did so. The legislation raised the tax rate on family incomes above $140,000 from 31 to 36 percent, with a 10 percent surtax added to incomes above $250,000. The tax rate on incomes below the $140,000 level was unchanged.

The American tax system does impose higher rates on higher income levels but also contains loopholes (such as tax deductions for interest paid on home mortgages) that benefit mostly higher-income taxpayers. The net effect is that Americans of modest and high incomes have traditionally paid taxes at about the same rate.

Middle-class taxpayers have become the political battlefield of the 1990s. Their federal taxes rose in the 1980s mainly as a result of an increase in social security taxes. This and other financial pressures fostered a belief among many middle-class Americans that the tax system was unfair (see Figure 18-6), a sentiment that made taxes a major issue of the 1992 and 1994 elections. The Republican's Contract With America called for a tax cut for everyone making $200,000 or less. President Clinton countered with proposed tax benefits for families with incomes under $75,000. Many economists took a dim view of both proposals, saying that the tax saving to the individual (about $20 a week in many cases) was negligible compared to the adverse effect the tax cuts would have on budget deficits.

The Electoral Connection

We noted in Chapter 14 that the issues that affect Americans' pocketbooks have the most influence on their presidential voting decisions, which makes fiscal policy largely an issue of *majoritarian* politics. As Seymour Martin Lipset writes, "Voters are disposed to credit or blame incumbent administrations for the state of the economy."[23]

An economic slowdown is a main concern of officials at election time.[24] Officeholders get less credit when the economy is healthy than blame when it goes bad.[25] A stagnant economy can result in a drop of several percentage points in the vote obtained by the party holding the presidency.[26] Like other presidents before him, George Bush faced the political consequences of poor economic conditions. The unemployment level rose steadily during 1991 and passed 7 percent at the beginning of 1992. The rise was accompanied by a steady decline in Bush's public support and contributed to his defeat in the November election.

It is difficult for incumbents to get the economy to respond to their efforts. If government could easily control the economy, it would always be strong. In reality, however, the economy has natural ups and downs that so far have defied the mastery of economists and politicians.

MONETARY POLICY

monetary policy A tool of economic management, available to government, based on manipulation of the amount of money in circulation.

We noted earlier that fiscal policy is not the only instrument of economic management available to government; another is **monetary policy,** which is based on manipulation of the amount of money in circulation (see Table 18-3). Monetarists such as the economist Milton Friedman hold that control of the money supply is the key to sustaining a healthy economy. Too much money in circulation contributes to inflation because too many dollars are chasing too few goods, which drives up prices. Too little money in circulation results in a slackening economy and rising unemployment, because consumers lack the ready cash and easy credit required to push spending levels up. Monetarists believe in tightening or loosening the money supply as a way of slowing or invigorating the economy.

The Federal Reserve System

Control over the money supply rests not with the president or Congress but with the Federal Reserve System (known as "the Fed"), which was created by the Federal Reserve Act of 1913. The Fed is directed by a board of governors whose seven members serve for fourteen years, except for the chair and vice-chair, who serve for four years. All members are appointed by the president with the approval of the Senate. The Fed regulates the activities of all national banks and those state banks which choose to become members of the Federal Reserve System—about 6,000 banks in all.

TABLE 18-3 Monetary Policy: A Summary The money supply can be adjusted in order to affect economic conditions.

Problem	*Monetary Policy Action by Federal Reserve*
Low productiviity and high unemployment (require an increase in the money supply)	Buys securities Lowers interest rate on loans to member banks Loweres cash reserve that member banks must deposit in Federal Reserve System
Excess productivity and high inflation (require a decrease in the money supply)	Sells securities Raises interest rate on loans to member banks Raises cash reserve that member banks must deposit in Federal Reserve System

THE MEDIA AND THE PEOPLE

THE ECONOMY AND AGENDA SETTING BY THE PRESS

Studies of the media's effects have concluded that the press helps set the country's political agenda by influencing what is uppermost in the minds of policymakers and the American people. The media may not have a powerful influence on people's attitudes, but they do have a powerful influence on people's attention. The press, as Bernard Cohen once said, "may not be successful much of the time in telling people what to think but it is stunningly successful in telling them what to think about." The economy is a prime example. Persons who have lost their jobs do not have to be told that unemployment is a problem. But jobs are lost every day, year in and year out. There are also new job openings every day. How then do people find out about broader economic tendencies? The news media are a prime source of information about whether the national economy is headed upward or downward.

Economic conditions are always an important news item, and the economy becomes truly big news when a recession hits. During 1991, when the nation was undergoing the longest economic downturn since World War II, the American economy generated more news stories than any other domestic topic. The media also helped convince the American people that their country was in a recession and not simply in a mild economic slump. During the six months from October 1990 through March 1991, according to *Media Monitor,* more than 90 percent of the descriptive terms used by reporters in connection with the economy were negative. On network television, the word "recession" accounted for three-fifths of the descriptive terms. The Bush administration, trying to evade the political repercussions, had been reluctant to say that the economy was in a recession. It is probably fair to say that the news media forced the administration to start using the word. On January 2, 1991, the president's chief economic adviser, Michael Boskin, grudgingly admitted, "The country has probably entered a recession."

Although the agenda-setting power of the news media does not affect people's attitudes directly, it has an important indirect influence. When people are paying attention to one issue rather than another, different attitudes come into play. Early in 1991, when the Persian Gulf conflict was uppermost in people's minds, George Bush's approval rating, 91 percent, was the highest ever recorded by the Gallup Poll. Late in 1991, when the economy had moved to the forefront in people's thinking, Bush's approval rating dropped below 50 percent.

A strong economy has less impact on a president's approval rating than a weak economy, and news practices may be a reason. The media are less interested in good news than bad news, and economic growth gets less coverage than economic stagnation. The economy's steady growth during President Clinton's first years in office was not accompanied by correspondingly high approval ratings.

SOURCE: Bernard C. Cohen, *The Press and Foreign Policy* (Princeton, N.J.: Princeton University Press, 1963), 13; "Reporting on Recession," *Media Monitor* 5 (May 1991): 1–6; "1991—The Year in Review," *Media Monitor* 6 (January 1992): 2.

Essentially, the Fed decides how much money to add to or subtract from the economy, estimating the amount that will permit the most economic growth without leading to an unacceptable level of inflation. The Fed controls the money supply primarily through three activities. First, it buys and sells securities on the open market. When it buys securities from the public, the Fed puts money into private hands to be spent or invested, thus stimulating the economy. When it sells securities to the public, the Fed takes money out of circulation, thereby slowing spending and investment.

Second, the Fed can raise or lower the cash reserve that member banks are required to deposit with the regional Federal Reserve banks. This reserve is a proportion of each member bank's total deposits. By increasing the reserve rate, the Fed takes money from member banks and thus takes it out of circulation; when the Fed lowers the reserve rate, banks keep more of their money and can make more loans to consumers and investors.

★ CRITICAL THINKING

How Powerful Should the Fed Be?

The Federal Reserve Board has had trouble keeping its hands off the nation's economy. It has repeatedly raised or lowered interest rates in anticipation of an overly strong or weak economy.

In the minds of some observers, the Fed is the preferred vehicle for economic management. They argue that the Fed can help manage growth and inflation by manipulating interest rates and should make effective use of this power. They note that the Federal Reserve Board carefully monitors the economy and ought to use this knowledge base to promote economic goals. They claim that Congress and the president base decisions on political factors rather than sound economic principles.

Other analysts contend that the Fed has gotten carried away with its power. They argue that economic theories are not as precise as the Fed assumes. The Fed's assumption that an unemployment rate below 6 percent is inflationary, for example, is regarded by some economists as mere guesswork. The argument against the Fed's role also stems from a belief that it is too beholden to the bankers and thus too willing to trade employment goals for inflationary objectives. Finally, there is the argument that macroeconomic decisions properly belong in the hands of the people's representatives, since these decisions affect everyone.

What is your position in this debate? Is the Fed too powerful?

Demonstrators picket the Federal Reserve Board's decision to raise interest rates a fifth time in 1994 as a means of controlling inflation. As interest rates rise, firms and consumers reduce their spending, which slows the growth of jobs and wages. (Jerome Friar/Impact Visuals)

Third, the Fed affects the money supply by lowering or raising the interest charged on money borrowed by member banks from their regional Federal Reserve bank. When the Fed raises the interest rate for banks, they are discouraged from borrowing from the Federal Reserve, and hence they have less money available to lend. Conversely, by lowering the interest rate, the Fed encourages its member banks to borrow, thus increasing their loan funds. When more credit is available, consumers and investors can obtain loans at lower rates and are thereby encouraged to borrow and spend.

The last of these activities, the lowering and raising of interest rates, is the one that receives the most public attention. Any such decision is a sign to the financial markets that the Fed has concluded that the economy is growing too fast or too slowly, and the decision nearly always affects these markets to some degree. A raise in interest rates, for example, usually causes a dip in the stock market because higher rates encourage investors to place their money in Treasury bonds and money markets rather than stocks. Rising interest rates also mean less consumer and business spending, and thus a reduction in firms' profits and dividends.

Economists debate the relative effectiveness of monetary policy and fiscal policy, but monetary (money-supply) policy has one obvious advantage: it can be implemented more quickly. The Fed can adjust interest and reserve rates on short notice, thus providing a psychological boost to go along with the financial effect. In contrast, changes in fiscal (taxing and spending) policy normally take time to implement because Congress is a slow-acting institution.

The Issue of the Fed's Accountability

The Fed's policies are not always popular with elected officials. In 1994, the Fed embarked on a series of interest rate hikes to contain economic growth. In defending the action, the Fed's chairman Alan Greenspan argued that it was designed to head off an upward spiral of wages and prices. Yet the Fed acted before signs of inflation were clearly present in the economy, bringing criticism from congressional Democrats and Clinton administration officials, who complained that the Fed was blunting the nation's economic recovery. Unemployment exceeded the 6 percent level, and the Fed's critics said that unseen inflationary pressures should not drive economic policy when millions of Americans were still looking for work. House Democratic leader Richard Gephardt complained that the Fed was placing the interests of bankers and financiers ahead of those of ordinary Americans. If this is true, the obvious question is why the Fed, an unelected body, should have such power. "The Man Who Really Runs America" is how a *Washington Post* economic correspondent described Alan Greenspan.[27]

The issue of the Fed's accountability remains unsettled. Because the Fed has nearly unrestricted powers to set interest rates and affect the money supply, it is unrealistic to expect it to watch idly while the economy shrinks or grows. But should the Fed routinely place its judgment ahead of that of elected officials? The Fed is a very powerful institution, yet it operates behind closed doors and its decisions are not subject to review.

The Fed is a preeminent example of *elitist* politics at work. Congress at some future point may decide that an independent Fed can no longer be tolerated and may bring monetary policy more directly under the control of elected institutions. Whether this happens may hinge on the Fed's willingness to exercise power sparingly. The economist Milton Friedman argues that economic models are not precise enough to warrant the Fed's tendency to surgically manipulate the marketplace or act in advance of clear signs that the action is needed. Paul Volker, who was Greenspan's predecessor at the Fed, had an even harsher assessment. Central bankers, he wrote in 1994, should remind "themselves of what they are wont to warn others about: excess of zeal and confidence."[28]

Summary

Although private enterprise is the main force in the American economic system, the federal government plays a significant role through its policies to regulate, promote, and stimulate the economy.

Regulatory policy is designed to achieve efficiency and equity, which require government to intervene, for example, to maintain competitive trade practices (an efficiency goal) and to protect vulnerable parties in economic transactions (an equity goal). Many of the regulatory decisions of the federal government, particularly those of older agencies, are made largely in the context of group politics; business lobbies have an especially strong influence on the regulatory policies that affect them. In general, newer regulatory agencies have policy responsibilities that are broader in scope and apply to a larger number of firms than those of the older agencies. As a result, the policy decisions of newer agencies are more often made in the context of party politics. Republican administrations are less vigorous in their regulation of business than are Democratic administrations.

Business is the major beneficiary of the federal government's efforts to promote economic interests. A large number of programs, including those to provide loans and research grants, are designed to assist businesses, which are also protected from failure through such measures as tariffs and favorable tax laws. Labor, for its part, gets government assistance through laws concerning such matters as worker safety, the minimum wage, and collective bargaining; yet America's individualistic culture tends to put labor at a disadvantage, keeping it less powerful than business in its dealings with the government. Agriculture is another economic sector that depends substantially on government's help, particularly in the form of income stabilization programs, such as those that provide subsidies and price supports.

Through its fiscal and monetary policies, Washington attempts to maintain a strong and stable economy—one that is characterized by high productivity, high employment, and low inflation. Fiscal policy is based on government decisions in regard to spending and taxing, which are aimed at either stimulating a weak economy or dampening an overheated (inflationary) economy. Fiscal policy is worked out through Congress and the president and is consequently responsive to political pressures. However, since it is difficult to raise taxes or cut programs, the government's ability to apply fiscal policy as an economic remedy is limited. Monetary policy is based on the money supply and works through the Federal Reserve System, which is headed by a board whose members hold office for fixed terms. The Fed is a relatively independent body, a fact that has given rise to questions as to whether it should have such a large role in national economic policy.

Major Concepts

demand-side economics
deregulation
economy
efficiency
equity (in relation to economic policy)
externalities
fiscal policy
laissez-faire doctrine
monetary policy
regulation
supply-side economics

Suggested Readings

Eisner, Marc Allen. *Regulatory Politics in Transition.* Baltimore, Md.: Johns Hopkins University Press, 1993. A thorough assessment of the changing nature of regulatory policy.

Friedman, Milton, and Walter Heller. *Monetary vs. Fiscal Policy.* New York: Norton, 1969. Opposing arguments by a leading monetarist and a leading Keynesian.

Gerston, Larry N., Cynthia Fraleigh, and Robert Schwab. *The Deregulated Society.* Pacific Grove, Calif.: Brooks/Cole, 1988. An assessment of deregulation and its effects.

Heilman, John G., and Gerald W. Johnson. *The Politics and Economics of Privatization: The Case of Wastewater Treatment.* Tuscaloosa: University of Alabama Press, 1992. A careful assessment of the effects of substituting private sector mechanisms for those of the public sector.

John, Dewitt. *Civic Environmentalism: Alternatives to Regulation in States and Communities.* Washington, D.C.: Congressional Quarterly Press, 1994. A set of careful case studies of environmental policymaking.

Kettl, Donald F. *Deficit Politics: Public Budgeting in Its Institutional and Historical Context.* New York: Macmillan, 1992. Analysis of budgetary politics that aims to explain why the United States suffers repeated annual deficits.

Kiewiet, D. Roderick. *Macro-Economics and Micro-Politics.* Chicago: University of Chicago Press, 1983. An analysis of the relationship between general economic conditions and election outcomes.

Peterson, Peter G. *Facing Up: How to Rescue the Economy from Crushing Debt and Restore the American Dream.* New York: Simon & Schuster, 1993. A blueprint for economic revitalization by a former Commerce Department official.

Wildavsky, Aaron. *The New Politics of the Budgetary Process,* 2d ed. New York: HarperCollins, 1992. An overview of the federal budgetary process, including new developments related to the deficit.

Zieger, Robert H. *American Workers, American Unions,* 2d ed. Baltimore, Md.: Johns Hopkins University Press, 1994. An overview of labor history and industrial relations.

CHAPTER 19

SOCIAL WELFARE POLICY: PROVIDING FOR PERSONAL SECURITY AND NEED

We the people of the United States, in order to . . . promote the general welfare . . .
—Preamble, U.S. Constitution

The new Republican Congress had been in session only a few weeks when hearings began on a restructuring of the nation's welfare system. Republicans vowed not only to cut costs but to establish policies that would discourage welfare dependency. Congress thought it had tackled this tough issue in 1988 when it enacted the Family Support Act, which in theory required able-bodied welfare recipients to work as a condition of their support. The policy had not worked as planned. "We ended welfare as we know it in 1988, but six to seven years later it is clear that we did not really change the system," said Republican Bill Archer, chairman of the House Ways and Means Committee.[1]

Democrats agreed that the welfare system required a thorough overhaul. "We should require work and responsibility," President Clinton said.[2] But the shared rhetoric masked deep differences in party philosophy. Conservative Republicans proposed unrestricted cash payments to states to spend as they deemed best and floated the idea of forcing unwed mothers and legal immigrants off the welfare rolls. Liberal Democrats expressed dismay that anyone would even consider denying benefits to children and taxpaying immigrants. The differences suggested the likelihood of a drawn-out fight that in the end might not produce the type of major change that all agreed was necessary. "I think we might be in for the same kind of gut-wrenching debate on welfare that we had on health care and come out producing a mouse," the economist Robert Haveman observed.[3]

The public was located somewhere in the middle on this controversy. A Time/CNN poll indicated that 78 percent of Americans favored welfare reform and 52 percent wanted cuts in welfare spending. Yet a solid majority was against denying payments to unwed teenage mothers.[4]

If the debate over social welfare was precipitated by rising costs and the

★ STATES IN THE NATION

Below the Poverty Line: Poverty levels vary widely, but tend to be highest in southern states.

STATE	PERCENT OF RESIDENTS IN POVERTY	RANK
Ala.	17.1%	12
Alaska	10.0	46
Ariz.	15.1	20
Ark.	17.4	11
Calif.	15.8	14
Colo.	10.6	40
Conn.	9.4	48
Del.	7.6	51
D.C.	20.3	5
Fla.	15.3	19
Ga.	17.8	10
Hawaii	11.0	38
Idaho	15.0	21
Ill.	15.3	19
Ind.	11.7	32
Iowa	11.3	35
Kan.	11.0	38
Ky.	19.7	6
La.	24.2	2
Maine	13.4	26
Md.	11.6	33
Mass.	10.0	46
Mich.	13.5	25
Minn.	12.8	27
Miss.	24.5	1
Mo.	15.6	16
Mont.	13.7	24
Neb.	10.3	43
Nev.	14.4	23
N.H.	8.6	50
N.J.	10.0	46
N.Mex.	21.0	4
N.Y.	15.3	19
N.C.	15.7	15
N.Dak.	11.9	30
Ohio	12.4	28
Okla.	18.4	8
Oreg.	11.3	35
Pa.	11.7	32
R.I.	12.0	29
S.C.	18.9	7
S.Dak.	14.8	22
Tenn.	17.0	13
Texas	17.8	10
Utah	9.3	49
Vt.	10.4	41
Va.	9.4	48
Wash.	11.0	38
W.Va.	22.3	3
Wis.	10.8	39
Wy.	10.3	43
National average	14.5	

SOURCE: U.S. Bureau of the Census, 1992.

growing number of recipients, the opposing views on what should be done were rooted in the conflict between America's individualistic and egalitarian values. Unlike Europeans, who accept the idea that citizens are more or less entitled to a minimum standard of living at government expense if necessary, Americans expect individuals to care for themselves and believe that welfare payments to able-bodied individuals discourage personal effort and create welfare dependency. Yet Americans also believe in helping those who are demonstrably unable to work or who need assistance while training for work.

Another influence on Americans' thoughts about welfare is the country's federal system of government. Welfare was traditionally a responsibility of state and local governments; only since the 1930s has the federal government also played a significant role. Some welfare programs are jointly run by the federal and state governments; they are funded at different levels from one state to the next but operate within guidelines set down by the national government. These programs are often controversial, as in the case of Aid for Families with Dependent Children (AFDC), which was established in 1935 to assist children whose fathers had died. AFDC lost public support as it grew gradually to assist nearly 5 million families, half headed by single mothers who were never married. Blamed for encouraging welfare dependency and personal irresponsibility, AFDC was terminated in 1996 and replaced with a program that provides welfare assistance only for limited periods, after which recipients are expected to work.

This chapter examines the social problems that federal welfare programs are designed to alleviate and describes how these programs operate. Some of the programs will change in the near future, but the problems they address will not disappear. A goal of this chapter is to provide an informed basis for understanding issues of social welfare and to show why disagreements in this area are so substantial. Social welfare policy involves hard choices that almost inevitably require trade-offs between federal and state power and between the values of individual self-reliance and egalitarian compassion. The main points of the chapter are these:

★ *Poverty is a large and persistent problem in America, deeply affecting about one in seven Americans, including many of the country's most vulnerable individuals—children, female-headed families, and minority group members.* Social welfare programs have been a major factor in reducing the extent of poverty in the United States.

★ *Welfare policy has been a partisan issue, with Democrats taking the lead on government programs to alleviate economic insecurity and Republicans acting to slow down or reverse these initiatives.* Major changes in social welfare have usually occurred in the context of majority support for the change.

★ *Social welfare programs are designed to reward and foster self-reliance or, when this is not possible, to provide benefits only to those individuals who are truly in need.* U.S. welfare policy is *not* based on the assumption that every citizen has a right to material security.

★ *Americans favor social insurance programs (such as social security) over public assistance programs (such as AFDC).* As a result, most social welfare expenditures are not targeted toward the nation's neediest citizens.

★ *A prevailing principle in the United States is equality of opportunity, which in terms of public policy is most evident in the area of education.*

Poverty in America: The Nature of the Problem

In the broadest sense, social welfare policy encompasses all efforts by government to improve the social conditions of any and all citizens. In a narrower sense, which is the way the term will be used in most of this chapter, social welfare policy refers to those efforts by government to help individuals avoid becoming burdens to society or, when that is not possible, to help individuals who cannot fully help themselves to meet their basic human needs, including food, clothing, and shelter.

THE POOR: WHO AND HOW MANY?

America's social welfare needs are substantial. Although Americans are far better off economically than most of the world's peoples, poverty is a significant and persistent problem in the United States. The government defines the **poverty line** as the annual cost of a thrifty food budget for an urban family of four, multiplied by three to include the cost of housing, clothing, and other expenses. Families whose incomes fall below that line are officially considered poor. In 1994 the poverty line was set at an annual income of roughly $14,000 for a family of four. About one in seven Americans, more than 35 million people, including nearly 15 million children, live at or below the poverty line. If they could join hands, they would form a line that stretched from New York to Tokyo and back again.

poverty line As defined by the federal government, the poverty line is the annual cost of a thrifty food budget for an urban family of four, multiplied by three to allow also for the cost of housing, clothes, and other expenses. Families below the poverty line are considered poor and are eligible for certain forms of public assistance.

Of the millions of Americans who live below the poverty line, nearly half are female heads of household and their children, a situation referred to as "the feminization of poverty." (Alan Weiner/Gamma Liaison)

in-kind benefits Government benefits that are cash equivalents, such as food stamps or rent vouchers. This form of benefit ensures that recipients will use public assistance in a specified way.

Observers disagree on whether the official poverty line is a valid indicator of the true extent of poverty in the United States. Some benefit programs, such as social security for retirees, provide cash payments to recipients. Other programs provide **in-kind benefits,** which are cash equivalents such as food stamps. The purpose of in-kind benefits is to ensure that recipients use the support as government intends—on groceries rather than on luxuries. In-kind government benefits are not included in the calculation of family income, which has led some observers to say that the official poverty line overestimates the number of poor people. If in-kind benefits were included, the proportion of the population living below the poverty line would drop about two percentage points.[5]

Other analysts say that the income level set by the government, regardless of how it is calculated, is set too low, that a family of four cannot live adequately on $14,000 a year. They would place the poverty line higher, perhaps in the $15,000 to $20,000 range. Arguments about the poverty line are not mere verbal battles. The U.S. government's official poverty line is used to determine eligibility for a number of welfare programs, including food stamps and health care.

Sheer hard work does not guarantee that a family will rise above the poverty line. A family of four with one employed adult who works forty hours a week at the minimum wage level (about $5 an hour) has an annual income of $10,000, which is well below the poverty line. Many Americans—mostly household workers, service workers, unskilled laborers, and farm workers—are in this position. A high proportion of newly created jobs are in fast-food restaurants and other service businesses, many of which pay their employees relatively low wages. The U.S. Bureau of the Census estimates that nearly one in five Americans who work full time do not earn enough to lift their family above the poverty line.

America's poor include individuals of all ages, races, religions, and regions, but poverty is not randomly distributed across the population. Children are one of the largest groups of poor Americans. They constitute nearly 40 percent of the total, and one in every five children lives in poverty. Most poor children live in single-parent families, usually with the mother. In fact, as can be seen from Table 19.1, almost half of all Americans residing in families headed by divorced, separated, or unmarried women live below the poverty line. These families are at a disadvantage because most women earn less than men for comparable work, especially in nonprofessional fields. Women without higher education or a special skill often cannot find a job that pays enough to justify the child care expenses they incur due to their work. In recent years single-parent, female-headed families have been three times as likely as single-parent, male-headed families and seven times as likely as two-income families to fall below the poverty line. Poverty in America has increasingly become a women's problem, a situation referred to as "the feminization of poverty."

Poverty is also widespread among minority group members. About 10 percent of whites live below the official poverty line, compared with about 30 percent of African Americans and Hispanics.

Poverty is geographically concentrated. Although it is often portrayed as an urban problem, it is somewhat more prevalent in rural areas. About one in six

TABLE 19-1 Percent of Persons in Poverty, by Selected Characteristics Poverty is more prevalent among some groups than others.

Characteristic	*Percent Who Are Poor*
AGE:	
Under 15	21.9%
65 years and over	12.9
MARITAL STATUS:	
Married-couple families	11.7
Married-couple families, with children	7.0
Female householder	34.9
Female householder, with children	46.0
PLACE OF RESIDENCE:	
Metropolitan residents, outside central city	12.9
Metropolitan residents, inside central city	20.5
Nonmetropolitan residents	16.8
RACE:	
White persons	11.6
African Americans	33.3
Hispanics	29.3
Asians	12.5
EDUCATION:	
Less than high school	24.1
High school graduate	11.0
Some college	7.2
College graduate	2.2

SOURCE: U.S. Bureau of the Census, 1994.

rural residents—as compared with one in eight urban residents—live in families with incomes below the poverty line. The urban figure is misleading, however, in that the poverty rate is very high in inner-city areas, where minority group members are concentrated.[6] Suburbs are the safe haven from poverty. Because suburbanites are removed from it, many of them have no sense of the impoverished condition of what Michael Harrington called "the other America."[7] Edwin Meese, when he was serving as President Reagan's domestic policy adviser, claimed there were no homeless people in the United States except for the bums who preferred to live on the streets. There are, in fact, hundreds of thousands of homeless people in America, some of whom are women and children. One estimate is that, of every 1,000 homeless people, 120 are adults with children, 100 are single women, and 100 are children without an accompanying adult.[8]

WELFARE: DEPENDENCY OR MISFORTUNE?

Many Americans hold to the idea that welfare support creates a vicious circle of dependency. In his book *Losing Ground,* Charles Murray argued that welfare programs are the foundation for a permanent underclass of unproductive

THE MEDIA AND THE PEOPLE

THE VISIBILITY OF POVERTY

America is often described as a society in which economic class is not important. Most people are not particularly class conscious; the vast majority label themselves "middle class" and let it go at that. Thus, in a 1992 Roper poll, 92 percent of the respondents described themselves as "middle class" (of which 14 percent and 21 percent called themselves "upper middle class" and "lower middle class," respectively). Only 1 percent said that they were "upper class," and 5 percent described themselves as "lower class."

This lack of class consciousness might be taken as evidence that Americans from all walks of life interact freely and regularly. However, particularly in cities, there is not a great deal of contact between people at the top and bottom of the income ladder. The lifestyle of middle- and upper-income Americans is more suburban than urban, and the automobile rather than public transporation is their major form of conveyance. As a result, they typically have little direct contact with poor people, who rely heavily on public transporation and tend to live within the city proper.

Nor is there much contact through the media. The news is about the powerful, not the poor. Perhaps it is not surprising, then, that the problems of poverty and homelessness are not very high on Americans' list of priorities. Polltakers have routinely asked Americans what they regard as "the most important problem facing the country today." In the 1981–1994 period, when poverty and homelessness were on the increase, there was only one year (1991) in which poverty was mentioned as the top problem by as many as 10 percent of respondents.

Americans, who prefer to live on welfare and whose children receive little educational encouragement at home and grow up in environments where crime, delinquency, drug abuse, and teenage pregnancy are commonplace.[9]

Many Americans are caught in the vicious circle described by Murray, and their numbers increase yearly. They are the toughest challenge for policymakers because almost nothing about their lives equips them to escape from poverty and its attendant ills. Their chances of committing a violent crime before reaching adulthood, for example, are nearly 20 times greater than that of others their age.[10]

Yet most people are poor as a result of transitory circumstances rather than chronic dependency.[11] A ten-year study of American families by researchers at the University of Michigan found that the poor are usually only poor for a while, staying on the welfare rolls for three years or less, and that they are poor for temporary reasons—loss of a job, birth of a child, desertion by the father, and so on.[12] When the U.S. economy goes into a long tailspin, the impact devastates many families. In the recessionary period of 1990–1992, more than 4 million Americans fell into poverty as a result of job loss or unemployment.

The percentage of the population living in poverty is higher now than when President Lyndon Johnson left office in 1969 (see Figure 19-1). Johnson's antipoverty programs helped cut poverty by more than 80 percent in the decade of the 1960s, but poverty has edged up by 20 percent since then.[13] Stagnant wages are a reason. Some Americans who were above the poverty line two decades ago are now below it, even though they have held a job throughout this period.[14] Median family income, when adjusted for inflation, has declined since the mid-1970s.

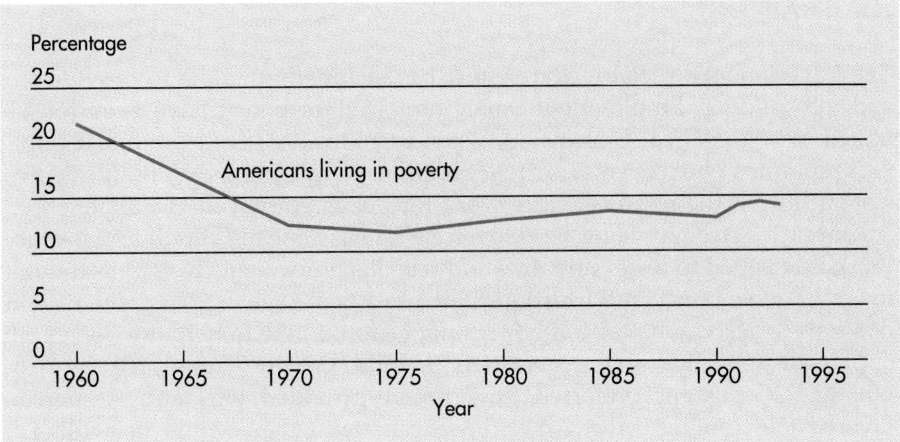

FIGURE 19-1 Percentage of Americans Living in Poverty The War on Poverty during the 1960s helped bring about a significant reduction in the percentage of Americans living in poverty, but the figure leveled off as funding for antipoverty programs was cut back beginning in the 1970s. *Source: U.S. Bureau of the Census.*

The Politics and Policies of Social Welfare

Welfare policy has generally been debated along partisan lines, a reflection of differences in the coalitions and philosophies of the Republican and Democratic parties. With its ties to labor, the poor, and minorities, the Democratic party has initiated nearly all major federal welfare programs. The key House of Representatives vote on the Social Security Act of 1935, for example, found 85 percent of Democrats supporting it and 99 percent of Republicans against it.[15]

Republicans gradually came to accept the idea that the federal government has a role in social welfare but argued that the role should be kept as small as practicable. Thus, during the 1960s, Republican opposition to President Lyndon Johnson's Great Society was substantial. His programs included federal initiatives in health care, education, public housing, nutrition, and other areas traditionally dominated by state and local government.[16] The Great Society programs were enacted largely because they were supported by Johnson's fellow Democrats. More than 70 percent of congressional Republicans voted against the 1965 Medicare and Medicaid programs, which provide government-paid medical assistance for the elderly and the poor. In the 1980s, in the face of opposition from congressional Democrats, Republican President Reagan made social welfare spending the prime target of his effort to cut the domestic budget. Compared with the decade beginning in the late 1960s, when welfare spending per poor person nearly tripled, the 1980s saw a 20 percent decline in actual dollars spent on each welfare recipient. The welfare reforms initiated by the Republican Congress elected in 1994 have reduced spending even further.

Although the Republican and Democratic parties have been at odds on the issue of social welfare, they have also had reason to work together. Social welfare is an ongoing issue because it is a pressing problem that requires action; there are millions of Americans who need help from government if they are to meet their basic subsistence needs. This help has taken various forms—job training efforts, special education programs, income redistribution measures, and individual-benefit policies.

JOB TRAINING

The government's social welfare effort has included attempts to provide jobs and job training. Employment policy and welfare policy have been loosely linked since the Great Depression, when Franklin Roosevelt combined public jobs programs with social security legislation. At one point during the Depression, a fifth of the nation's entire work force was employed in public jobs.

Americans strongly favor work over welfare as a means of public assistance. Work is believed to foster initiative and responsibility, while welfare is thought to create dependency and irresponsibility. In a Los Angeles *Times* poll, respondents were asked what action government should take to help the poor. Only 6 percent said that the government should provide money or services, whereas 20 percent preferred government-provided jobs and 72 percent favored job training. Most Americans even claim they would be willing to delay savings from welfare cutbacks to fund job training programs for welfare recipients (see Figure 19-2).

The history of work and job training programs, however, is an uneven one. For example, an ambitious program that began in the early 1970s under Republican President Richard Nixon, and which at its peak provided employment for 4 million people, was terminated a decade later amid charges that it was too costly and had failed to place people in permanent jobs, as opposed to subsidized temporary positions. The 1988 Family Support Act was even less effective. It required welfare recipients to accept education, training, or work as a condition of retaining their welfare eligibility. However, the program did not give the states, which administered the program, enough money or incentives to establish viable welfare-to-work programs. Eight years after the Family Support Act was passed, less than 10 percent of welfare families were getting earnings from full-time or part-time jobs.[17]

FIGURE 19-2 Opinions on Job Training for Welfare Recipients Most Americans favor job training as the solution to the nation's welfare problem. *Source: Time/CNN survey by Yankelovich Partners, December 7–8, 1994.*

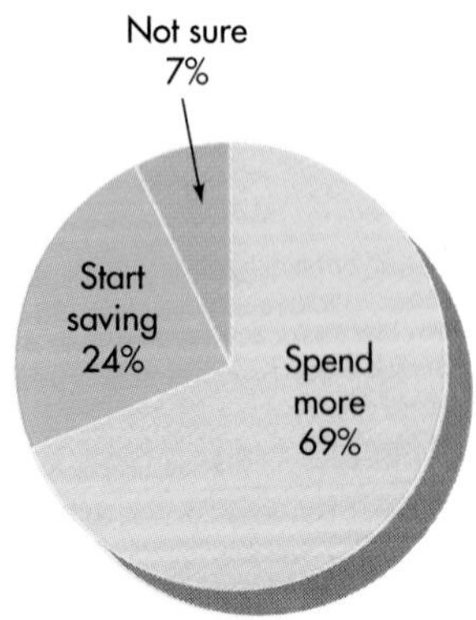

Should welfare reform start saving taxpayers money immediately, or is it more important to train welfare recipients for jobs, which means the government would spend more money in the short run?

In his 1992 presidential campaign, Bill Clinton promised "to end welfare as we know it," claiming that a work-based welfare system alone could break the cycle of poverty in which increasing numbers of welfare recipients were trapped. It was not until the Republicans gained control of Congress, however, that welfare reform became a reality. In 1996, the Republican-controlled Congress passed a sweeping welfare reform act known as the Personal Responsibility and Work Opportunity Reconciliation Act.

The historic bill ended a six-decades federal guarantee of cash assistance to needy families, replacing it with a system of cash grants to the states, which have responsibility for caring for welfare recipients and getting them into jobs. The legislation's goal is to reduce long-term welfare dependency by limiting the time that recipients can receive welfare and by providing the states with incentives to prepare recipients for work. States may not let recipients receive federal welfare assistance for more than five years (although a fifth of recipients can be exempted from this requirement), and within two years on welfare, a recipient must find work or face the loss of benefits. States receive federal funds with which to provide benefits, community service jobs, and job training, but unless they meet the program's goals (for example, half of their welfare recipients must be moved from welfare to work by the year 2002), they will have their federal assistance reduced. In other words, the welfare reform act includes incentives to encourage both states and welfare recipients to create situations that will lead to employment.

The welfare reform act of 1996 has been described as a "great experiment" because, in truth, no one knows whether it is possible to provide gainful employment to large numbers of long-term welfare recipients. Many of them have little education, few practical skills, and no substantial job experience. Many of them also have young children and, unless they receive child care and medical assistance, they will not be able to subsist on the low-paying jobs they are likely to get. In signing the legislation, President Clinton described it as "a historic opportunity to make welfare what it was meant to be: a second chance, not a way of life." Senator Daniel Patrick Moynihan, a critic of the legislation, called it "the most brutal act of social policy since Reconstruction." Only time will tell whether the Personal Responsibility and Work Opportunity Reconciliation Act of 1996 will improve America's welfare problem or push America's poor further into poverty. (The 1996 welfare reform act is discussed further later in the chapter.)

SPECIAL EDUCATION: HEAD START

The social welfare effort also includes special education programs, most notably Head Start. It provides preschool education for poor children in order to give them a better chance to succeed when they begin school. Head Start was established in the 1960s as part of President Lyndon Johnson's War on Poverty, which was designed to alleviate the problems of America's poor, such as malnutrition, job training, health care, and housing. Funding in some of

President Clinton signs into law the 1996 welfare reform bill that ended the 61-year-old federal guarantee of aid to the poor. The new legislation limits federal welfare assistance to a period of five years. (Reuters/Stephen Jaffe/Archive Photos)

these areas was cut sharply in the 1980s. Head Start's budget dropped to a level which allowed only 10 percent of eligible children to participate. As evidence mounted of poverty's devastating impact on children's development, President Bush and the Democratic Congress concluded that Head Start was the kind of social investment that the country could hardly afford not to make, and it became one of the few domestic programs to receive a substantial funding increase during the Bush administration. Additional funding was provided when Bill Clinton took office. Nevertheless, less than half of the eligible children are enrolled in Head Start, and many who complete the program do not sustain their advantage because their home situation provides no support for educational achievement.

INCOME AND TAX MEASURES

The income of the average American family exceeds $35,000, which, although below the average of several other countries, is substantial enough to provide a reasonable standard of living. Of course, the average income is just that—an average. It hides other averages—for example, the average white family has an income that is more than $15,000 higher than the average black family's income—and it hides wide disparities in the income of those individuals at the top and the bottom of the income ladder. The top fifth of Americans in terms of income get nearly half of the total, while the other four-fifths share the other half. The bottom fifth get slightly less than 5 percent.

Income taxes in the United States have not been the instrument of redistribution that they are in European democracies. The top tax rate in the United States is 39.5 percent and does not apply until income reaches the $250,000 level. An upper tax rate of 50 percent is common in Europe, and there are fewer loopholes, such as the deduction of home mortgage interest, that provide tax breaks for the more well-to-do. In terms of actual rate of taxes paid, moderate- and higher-income Americans are not greatly different. The higher marginal tax rate on upper-income people is offset substantially by their additional deductions and the existence of nonprogressive taxes such as the social security tax. The net effect is that the U.S. tax system is only marginally redistributive.

Although well-to-do Americans pay relatively low taxes, the fact that they make a lot of money means, in absolute terms, that they contribute a sizable share of tax revenues. The top 10 percent of taxpayers in terms of income pay about half of the personal income taxes received by the federal government. Some of this tax revenue is redistributed downward to lower-income groups through social welfare programs.

The United States also has a policy designed to reallocate income directly to lower-income persons. This policy is the Earned Income Tax Credit (EITC). Low-income families with at least one child are eligible for EITC. In 1995, 11 million American families received EITC payments; the maximum payment to any one family was $2,528. Eligibility for payment is determined when persons file their personal income taxes. Those with family incomes below a specified level receive the payment, which phases out as income rises. Increased funding for EITC was a major component of President Clinton's first budget.

A high proportion of newly created jobs are in fast-food restaurants and other service businesses, many of which do not pay well enough to provide individuals with long-term economic security. (Hazel Hankin)

EITC involves what is called a **transfer payment,** or a government benefit that is given directly to an individual. All spending to promote the general welfare is designed to help individuals, but much of it—such as federal funds for public school construction and hospital equipment—is not in the form of transfer payments. Many federal programs, however, do transfer benefits directly to individuals, such as social security payments to retired people. These individual-benefit programs are what most people have in mind when they speak of "social welfare."

transfer payment A government benefit that is given directly to an individual, as in the case of social security payments to a retiree.

Individual-Benefit Programs

Individual-benefit programs are designed to alleviate the personal hardships associated with such conditions as joblessness, poverty, and old age. Any individual who meets the established criteria of eligibility is entitled to the benefits afforded by these programs. For this reason, each of these programs is termed an **entitlement program.** In this sense, they have the same force in law as taxes. Just as individuals are required by law to pay taxes to government on the income they earn, individuals are entitled by law to receive government benefits for which they qualify. Because of this feature, spending on entitlement programs is difficult to control. Unlike programs which have a fixed budget, entitlement spending is determined by the number of eligible recipients. As they increase in number, entitlement spending increases, whether the money has been budgeted or not. The Republican blueprint for welfare reform developed in 1995 calls for replacing the entitlement provision of some welfare programs with a fixed level of spending. Once the spending limit is reached, otherwise eligible individuals would not receive payments. They would also be unable, as they can with an entitlement, to seek a court order requiring government to pay them the benefit.

entitlement program Any of a number of individual benefit programs, such as social security, that require government to provide a designated benefit to any person who meets the legally defined criteria for eligibility.

All told, individual-benefit programs are the major thrust of U.S. social wel-

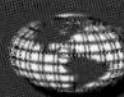

HOW THE UNITED STATES COMPARES

PERSONS LIVING IN POVERTY

Poverty is more prevalent in the United States than in many other industrialized countries, including Canada, Germany, and Sweden. Although the overall standard of living in the United States is relatively high, poor American families earn less than the poor families in comparable countries for which poverty-level data are available. The reasons are several. Income in the United States is less evenly distributed than in these other countries, and the U.S. government does not spend as much on social welfare assistance to the poor. If government spending on health care is included (the figures below do not include health care spending), the difference in welfare spending between the United States and other countries is even more substantial. Many low-income families in the United States receive no help from government; in the other countries, virtually all low-income families receive public assistance in one form or another. Poverty in the United States is also made worse by the relatively large number of single-parent families, although Sweden, which has a similarly large number, has the lowest percentage of persons living in poverty.

Country	*Percent below U.S. Poverty Line*	*Government Expenditures on Social Security and Welfare (Percent of Gross Domestic Product)*
Australia	15.0%	0.9%
Canada	9.0	not available
Germany	9.5	2.1
Great Britain	13.5	1.5
Sweden	6.5	4.9
United States	14.5	0.4

SOURCE: Organization for Economic Cooperation and Development (1993) for welfare data; poverty figures estimated from OECD and U.S. Bureau of Census data.

fare policy. The federal budget for such programs exceeds $600 billion, which is more money than is spent on all other government activity, including national defense.

At an earlier time in the nation's history, the federal government spent almost nothing on social welfare. Welfare policy was deemed to fall within the powers reserved to the states by the Tenth Amendment and to be adequately addressed by them, even though they did not offer substantial welfare services. Individuals were expected to fend for themselves, and when they were unable to do so, they were usually supported by relatives and friends. This approach reflected the idea of **negative government,** which holds that government governs best by staying out of people's lives, thus giving them as much freedom as possible to determine their own pursuits and encouraging them to become self-reliant.

negative government The philosophical belief that government governs best by staying out of people's lives, thus giving individuals as much freedom as possible to determine their own pursuits.

The situation changed dramatically with the Great Depression. The unemployment level reached 25 percent, which prompted demands for help from the federal government. Franklin D. Roosevelt's New Deal brought economic relief in the form of public works jobs and welfare programs, and helped change public attitudes about the federal government's welfare role.[18] Americans came to look favorably upon Washington's help. This attitude reflected a faith in **positive government**—the idea that government intervention is necessary in order to enhance personal liberty and security when individuals are buffeted by economic and social forces beyond their control.

positive government The philosophical belief that government intervention is necessary in order to enhance personal liberty when individuals are buffeted by economic and social forces beyond their control.

Since the 1930s the federal government's welfare role has increased immeasurably, and individuals now expect the federal government to provide benefits to ease the loss of income caused by retirement, disability, unemployment, and the like. Not all individual-benefit programs are alike, however, in their philosophy or level of public support. Individual-benefit programs fall into two general categories: *social insurance* and *public assistance.* Programs in the first category enjoy widespread public support and receive a higher level of funding; programs in the second category encounter substantial public opposition and receive a lower level of funding.

SOCIAL INSURANCE PROGRAMS

More than 40 million Americans receive benefits from social insurance programs—including social security, Medicare, unemployment insurance, and workers' compensation. The two major programs, social security and Medicare, cost the federal government more than $400 billion per year. Individuals who paid special payroll taxes when they were employed are eligible for benefits. This is why such programs are labeled **social insurance:** recipients get an insurance benefit under a program that they have helped fund. This self-financing feature of social insurance programs accounts for their strong public support.

social insurance Social welfare programs based on the "insurance" concept, so that individuals must pay into the program in order to be eligible to receive funds from it. An example is social security for retired people.

Social Security

The leading social insurance program is social security for retirees.[19] The program began with passage of the Social Security Act of 1935 and is funded through payroll taxes on employees and employers (currently set at 6.2 percent). Franklin D. Roosevelt emphasized that retiring workers would receive an insurance benefit that they had earned through their payroll taxes, not a handout from the government. Today social security has Americans' full support. Social security is also one of the few welfare programs run entirely by the federal government. Washington collects the payroll taxes that fund the program and sends monthly checks directly to the more than 35 million social security recipients, who, on average, receive more than $600 a month.

Although many people believe that an individual's social security benefits are financed by his or her past contributions, they are actually funded largely through payroll taxes on the current work force. The typical social security recipient gets far more money from the government than he or she has paid into the fund; thus it is necessary to use contributions from the current work force to finance the program. The average recipient takes less than eight years to recover his or her lifetime contributions plus interest and receives "free" benefits from that time forward. In the 1970s expenditures for social security began to exceed contributions as the number of retirees and the size of benefit payments increased. The program would have gone bankrupt in the late 1970s had the social security tax rate not been raised.[20]

For many elderly Americans, social security benefits make it possible to maintain a secure, independent retirement. (William Johnson/Stock, Boston)

Social security is likely to remain a lively political issue for years to come. Because of medical and other advances, Americans live longer than they once did, and this trend could create a social security crisis during the next century. Roughly 20 percent of the U.S. population—55 million people—will be over age sixty-five in the year 2030, and there may not be enough workers by then to fund the payout to retirees.

Unemployment Insurance

The 1935 Social Security Act provides for unemployment benefits for workers who have lost their jobs involuntarily. Unemployment insurance is a joint federal-state program. The federal government collects the payroll taxes that fund unemployment benefits, but states have the option of deciding whether the taxes will be paid by employers only or by both employees and employers (most states use the first option). Individual states also set the tax rate, conditions of eligibility, and benefit level, subject to minimum standards established by the federal government. Although unemployment benefits vary widely among states, they average about a third ($150 a week) of what an average worker makes while employed, and in most cases the benefits are terminated after 26 to 39 weeks.

The unemployment program does not have the same high level of public support as social security. The situation reflects in part a common belief that the loss of a job, or the failure to find a new one right away, is somehow a personal failing. Unemployment statistics, however, suggest otherwise. For example, U.S. Bureau of Labor statistics indicate that, of those who lost their jobs in 1990, only 23 percent had made the decision to quit working. The others became unemployed because of either a temporary layoff (22 percent) or the permanent elimination of a job position (55 percent).

Medicare

After World War II, most European democracies instituted systems of government-paid health care, and President Harry Truman, a Democrat, proposed a similar program for Americans. The American Medical Association (AMA) called Truman's plan "un-American," lobbied hard against it, and threatened to mobilize local physicians to campaign against members of Congress who supported "socialized medicine." Truman's proposal never came to a vote in Congress. In 1961 President John F. Kennedy, also a Democrat, proposed a health care program restricted to social security recipients, but the AMA, the insurance industry, and conservative members of Congress succeeded in blocking the plan.[21]

The 1964 elections swept a tide of liberal Democrats into Congress, and the result was Medicare. Enacted in 1965, the program provides medical assistance to retirees and is funded primarily through payroll taxes (the current tax rate is 2.9 percent). Medicare, too, is based on the insurance principle, and therefore it has gained nearly the same high level of public support as social security.

Medicare provides for care in a hospital or nursing home, but the recipient pays part of the initial cost and pays most of the expenses after 100 days. Medicare does not cover all physicians' fees, but enrollees in the program have the option of paying an insurance premium for fuller coverage of these fees. Enrollees who cannot afford the additional premium can apply to have the government pay it.

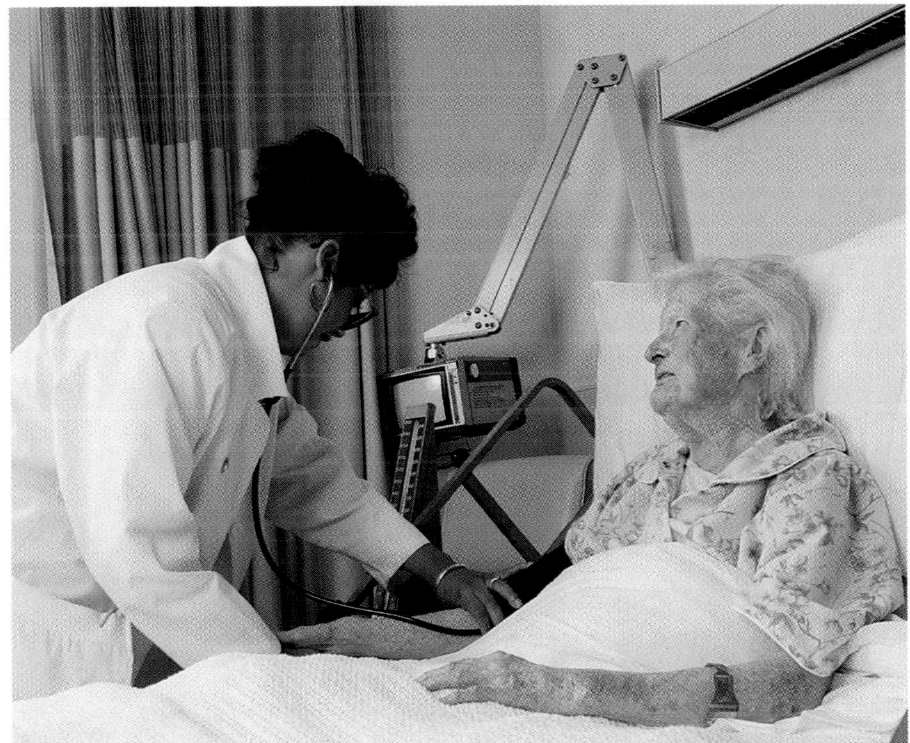

Medicare pays part of the hospitalization and other medical expenses of millions of elderly Americans. Rising medical costs threaten the solvency and scope of this popular federal program. (Larry Mulvehill/Photo Researchers)

PUBLIC ASSISTANCE PROGRAMS

public assistance A term that refers to social welfare programs funded through general tax revenues and available only to the financially needy. Eligibility for such a program is established by a means test.

means test The requirement that applicants for public assistance must demonstrate they are poor in order to be eligible for the assistance.

Unlike social insurance programs, **public assistance** programs are funded through general tax revenues and are available only to the financially needy. Eligibility for such entitlement programs is established by a **means test,** a demonstration that the applicant is poor enough to qualify for the benefit. In other words, applicants for public assistance must prove that they are poor. Public assistance programs are commonly referred to as "welfare" and the recipients as "welfare cases." Opinion polls show that public assistance programs have less public support than do social insurance programs.

About 30 million Americans receive public assistance, typically through programs established by the federal government, administered mainly by the states, and funded jointly by the state and federal governments. Most Americans have the mistaken impression that public assistance programs account for the lion's share of federal welfare spending. A 1994 poll found that Americans believe welfare programs are the second-largest federal program (foreign aid ranked first).[22] In fact, the federal government spends roughly three times as much on its two major social insurance programs, social security and Medicare, as it does on all public assistance programs combined.

Supplemental Security Income (SSI)

A major public assistance program is Supplemental Security Income (SSI), which originated as federal assistance to the blind and elderly poor as part of

Supplemental Security Income (SSI) is a combined federal–state program that provides public assistance to blind and disabled people. (Spencer Grant/Gamma Liaison)

the Social Security Act of 1935. By the 1930s most states had begun or were considering such programs. Although the federal legislation was designed to replace their efforts, the states have retained a measure of control over benefits and eligibility and are required to provide some of the funding. Because SSI recipients (who now include the disabled in addition to the blind and elderly poor) have obvious reasons for their inability to provide for themselves, this public assistance program is not widely criticized. In 1996, however, Congress tightened the rules for SSI so that "maladaptive behavior," which is difficult to define and was manipulated in some instances to give aid to undeserving recipients, no longer qualifies children for disability assistance. The 1996 change also limits SSI benefits to U.S. citizens, thereby disqualifying legal immigrants.

Aid to Needy Families

Perhaps the most controversial of the major public assistance programs was Aid for Families with Dependent Children (AFDC). Partly funded by the federal government but administered by the states, the AFDC program was created in the 1930s as survivors' insurance to assist children whose fathers had died prematurely. Relatively small and noncontroversial at inception, AFDC was the target of severe criticism by the 1970s. Although some attacks on it were based on false claims (for example, that most of the recipients were unwed teenage mothers when, in fact, less than 10 percent were in this category),[23] AFDC was widely unpopular because it was linked in people's minds to welfare dependency and irresponsibility. It was an entitlement program, which meant that any single parent (or, in some states, two parents) living in poverty could claim the benefit and keep it for as long as a dependent child was in the household. Some AFDC recipients were content to live indefinitely on this assistance, and, in some cases, their children also grew to become AFDC recipients, thereby creating what was called "a vicious cycle of poverty." By 1995, AFDC was supporting 14 million Americans at an annual cost of more than $15 billion.

In 1996, AFDC was terminated as part of the Personal Responsibility and Work Opportunity Reconciliation Act. Funding for AFDC was replaced by the Temporary Assistance for Needy Families block grant (TANF), which gives each state an annual cash grant that is to be used to design its own program for assisting needy families and getting welfare recipients into jobs. These programs must operate within tight federal guidelines, including:

- Americans' eligibility for federal cash assistance is limited to no more than five years in their lifetime.
- Within two years, the head of most families on welfare will have to find work or risk the loss of benefits.
- Unmarried teenage mothers are qualified for welfare benefits only if they remain in school and live with a parent or legal guardian.
- Single mothers will lose a portion of their benefits if they refuse to cooperate in identifying the father of their children.

Although states are allowed to make some exceptions to some of the rules (for example, an unmarried teenage mother who faces sexual abuse at home can be allowed to live elsewhere), there are restrictions on these exceptions such that the rules will govern in most cases. States are also empowered in some areas to impose more restrictive rules. For example, a state can deny additional assistance to a mother who is already receiving benefits and has another child.

Within the limits, states can design a program of their choosing, and wide differences are expected. Even AFDC benefits varied widely, ranging from less than $300 in most southern and southwestern states to more than $450 in most northeastern and some midwestern states. Since the TANF grants that states will initially receive are roughly proportional to the amounts they were spending on AFDC, these regional differences are certain to persist. Perhaps the biggest challenge facing the states, in addition to ensuring that the poor do not wind up in the streets, is the development of welfare-to-work programs that actually do free families from welfare dependency.

As we discussed earlier in the chapter, the new welfare program is such a radical departure from the past that its consequences are difficult to predict. Some observers believe it will be a disaster. The Urban Institute estimates that within a decade the bill will push more than 1 million children into poverty as their family's eligibility for assistance expires. Other observers see it as the long awaited answer to welfare dependency. They point, for example, to a pilot program in Wisconsin that was reasonably successful in moving people off welfare without throwing them into poverty. The safest prediction, however, was offered by President Clinton. In signing the bill, he conceded that nobody knows for sure what will happen: "we all need a certain level of humility today." He called the bill a first step in a new era of social welfare and said the bill would "need some fixing" once its effects are known.

Food Stamps

The food stamp program, which took its present form in 1961, is fully funded by the federal government. The program provides an in-kind benefit—not cash, but food stamps that can be spent only on grocery items.

Food stamps are available only to people who qualify on the basis of low income. The program is intended to improve the nutrition of poor families by enabling them to purchase qualified items, mainly foodstuffs, with food stamps. Some critics say that food stamps stigmatize their users by making it obvious to onlookers in the checkout line that they are "welfare cases." More prevalent criticisms are that the program is too costly and that too many undeserving people receive food stamps.

The 1996 welfare reform bill eliminated food stamp eligibility for legal immigrants and also restricts to three months in any three-year period the eligibility of able-bodied adults with no dependent children.

Subsidized Housing

Low-income persons are also eligible for subsidized housing. Most of the federal spending in this area is on housing vouchers rather than the construction of low-income housing units. Under the voucher system, the individual receives a monthly rent-payment voucher, which is given in lieu of cash to the landlord, who then hands the voucher over to the government in exchange for cash. The welfare recipient is given a voucher (an in-kind benefit) rather than cash in order to ensure that the funds are actually used to obtain housing. About 6 million households annually receive a federal housing subsidy.

The U.S. government spends much less on public housing than on tax breaks for homeowners, most of whom are middle- and upper-income Americans. Homeowners are allowed a tax deduction for their mortgage interest payments and for local property taxes, which in fiscal year 1994, for example, resulted in a $70 billion tax break. This was three times as much as was spent by the federal government in 1994 on housing for low-income families.

Medicaid

When it enacted Medicare in 1965, Congress also established Medicaid, which provides health care for poor people who are already on welfare. It is considered a public assistance program, rather than a social insurance program like Medicare, because it is based on need and funded by general tax revenues. Half of Medicaid funding is provided by the federal government and half by the states. More than 30 million Americans receive Medicaid assistance.

Medicaid is controversial because of its costs. As health care costs have spiraled, far ahead of the inflation rate, so have the costs of Medicaid. It absorbs more than half of all public assistance dollars spent by the U.S. government

YOUR TURN

SPENDING ON WELFARE ENTITLEMENTS

The Questions:

Please indicate whether you favor or oppose *reducing* government spending on each of the following entitlement programs:

Food stamps?	Favor	Oppose
Welfare?	Favor	Oppose
Farm subsidies?	Favor	Oppose
Housing subsidies for poor?	Favor	Oppose
Medicaid?	Favor	Oppose
Social security?	Favor	Oppose
Medicare?	Favor	Oppose

What Others Think: These questions were asked in a December 1994 Time/CNN survey by Yankelovich Partners. Support for reducing government spending ranged from 53 percent for food stamps to 43 percent for social security and Medicare. Only in the case of social security and Medicare did a majority of respondents express opposition to reductions in government spending.

Comment: Americans have always been less supportive of welfare programs for the poor than of social security. Nevertheless, the level of public support for all forms of entitlement spending, including social security, has declined in recent years. The escalating costs of social welfare appear to underlie the change in attitude.

and has forced state and local governments to cut other services to meet the costs of their share. "It's killing us," was how one local official described the impact of Medicaid on his community's budget.[24]

As is true of other public assistance programs, Medicaid has been criticized for supposedly serving too many people who could take care of themselves if they tried harder. The idea is contradicted, ironically, by the situation faced by many working Americans. There are nearly 40 million Americans who make too much money to qualify for Medicaid but who cannot afford health insurance. This situation encouraged President Clinton in 1993 to propose a comprehensive program that would entitle nearly all Americans to health care, at government expense if necessary. The proposal was defeated without coming to a vote in either the House or Senate (see Chapters 10 and 15).

★ CRITICAL THINKING

What System of Health Care Should America Have?

There are two broad approaches to medical care. One, which exists throughout Europe and in Canada, is a national (government-based) health system. The alternative approach, which exists in the United States, is based on the private sector but also includes public aspects.

The United States has the most expensive health care system in the world; it absorbs 14 percent of the gross national product (GNP). The national health care systems of western Europe account for less than 10 percent of GNP. A national health care system also provides broader coverage; everyone has access. In contrast, more than 35 million Americans are too poor to buy their own health insurance but are not poor enough to qualify for public insurance (Medicaid). The U.S. health system performs worse than those of western Europe on many indicators (for example, infant mortality rates).

The advantages of a private-centered health system are its responsiveness to eligible persons and its level of services. In a national health care system, there is often a long wait to obtain certain services, such as elective surgery, and some services are denied to particular categories of patients (for example, kidney dialysis is not available to all elderly patients who might benefit from it). The private-centered system in the United States is widely regarded as the most advanced in the world.

Which type of medical system do you favor? Why?

Equality of Opportunity through Education: The American Way

All democratic societies promote economic security, but they do so to different degrees. Economic security has a higher priority in European democracies than in the United States. European democracies have instituted such programs as government-paid health care for all citizens, compensation for all unemployed workers, and retirement benefits for all elderly citizens. As we have seen, the United States provides these benefits only to some citizens in each category. For example, not all elderly Americans are entitled to social security benefits. If they paid social security taxes for a long enough period when they were employed, they (including their spouses) receive benefits. Otherwise, they do not, even if they are in dire economic need.

Such policy differences between Europe and the United States stem from cultural and historical differences. Democracy developed in Europe in reaction to centuries of aristocratic rule, the inequities of which brought the issue of human equality to the forefront. When strong labor and socialist parties then emerged as a consequence of industrialization, European democracies initiated sweeping social welfare programs that brought about greater economic equality. In contrast, American democracy emerged out of a tradition of limited government that emphasized personal freedom. Equality was a lesser issue, and class consciousness was weak. No major labor or socialist party emerged in America during industrialization to represent the working class, and there was no persistent and strong demand for welfare policies that would bring about an economic leveling.

INDIVIDUALISM AND PUBLIC OPINION

These differing legacies are evident today in the opinions of Americans and Europeans toward liberty and equality. When asked in a Gallup study whether they placed a higher value on freedom or on equality, Americans chose freedom by 72 percent to 20 percent. Among Europeans, the margin was only 49 percent to 35 percent.[25] On the basis of his study of political values,

Karl Lamb concluded that most Americans "cannot really imagine a society that would provide substantial material equality."[26]

Instead, Americans place their trust in the economic marketplace. They look upon jobs and the personal income that comes from work as the proper basis of economic security. Americans are disinclined to help the poor through welfare payments; they prefer that the poor be given training and education so that they can learn to help themselves. This attitude is consistent with Americans' preference for **equality of opportunity,** which is the idea that individuals should have an equal chance to succeed on their own. The concept embodies equality in its emphasis on giving everyone a fair chance to get ahead. Yet equality of opportunity also embodies liberty because it allows people to succeed or fail on their own as a result of what they do with their opportunities. The presumption is that people will end up differently—some rich, some poor. It is sometimes said that equality of opportunity offers individuals an equal chance to become unequal.

equality of opportunity The idea that all individuals should be given an equal chance to succeed on their own.

In practice, equality of opportunity works itself out primarily in the private sector, where Americans compete for jobs, promotions, and other advantages. However, a few public policies have the purpose of enhancing equality of opportunity. The most significant of these policies is public education.

PUBLIC EDUCATION: LEVELING THROUGH THE SCHOOLS

In the nation's first century of existence, the question of whether government should provide free education to all children divided the landed wealthy from the advocates of broad-based democracy. The wealthy feared that an educated public would challenge their entrenched power. The democrats wanted to provide more people with the foundation for economic advantage. The democrats won out. Public schools sprang up in nearly every community and were open free of charge to children who could attend.

Today, as was discussed in Chapter 1, the United States invests more heavily in public education at all levels than any other country. The curriculum in American schools is also relatively standardized; unlike those countries that divide children even at the grade school level into different tracks that lead ultimately to different occupations, the United States aims to educate children in much the same way. Of course, public education is not a uniform experience for American children. The quality of education depends significantly on the wealth of the community in which a child resides. The federal program that provides aid to poorer school districts does not appreciably alter the situation; in creating the program, members of Congress wrote the legislation broadly enough to enable schools in their constituencies to get some of the money. To receive federal assistance, a school district needs only ten poor students, which means that 93 percent of school districts qualify. Less than half of the roughly $6 billion in the education aid program for poor children goes to schools in areas where poverty is widespread.[27]

Nevertheless, the United States through its public schools educates a broad segment of the population. Arguably, no country in the world has made an equivalent effort to give children, whatever their parents' background, an equal opportunity in life through education. This effort extends to college; the

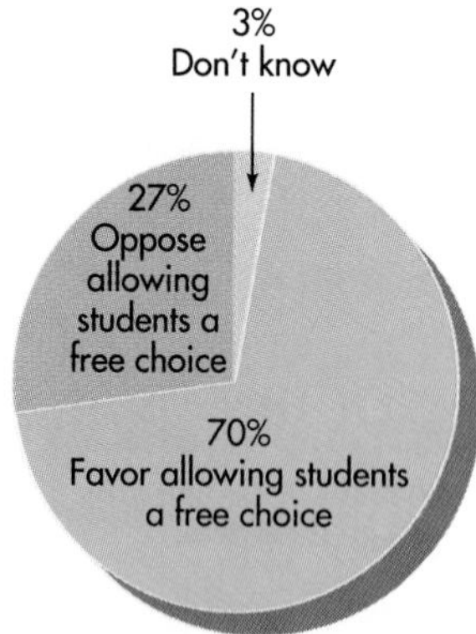

FIGURE 19-3 Opinions on Freedom of Choice for Public School Students
Most Americans favor allowing students and parents to choose which public school in the community a student will attend.
Source: Gallup Poll for the Christian Science Monitor, September 21, 1992.

United States is far and away the world leader in terms of the proportion of adults receiving a college education.[28]

The nation's education system preserves both the myth and reality of the American dream. The belief that success can be had by anyone who works for it could not be sustained if the education system were tailored for a privileged elite. And educational attainment is related to personal success, at least as measured by annual incomes. In fact, the gap in income between those with and without a college education is now greater than at any time in the country's history.

In part because the public schools have such a large role in creating an equal opportunity society, they have been heavily criticized in recent years. Violence in the schools is a major parental concern. So, too, is the decline in student performance on standardized tests, such as the Scholastic Aptitude Test (SAT).[29] American students are not even in the top ten internationally by their test scores in science or math.[30]

Disgruntled parents have demanded changes,[31] and these demands have led some communities to allow parents to choose the public school their children will attend. Under this policy, the schools compete for students, and those which attract the most students are rewarded with the largest budgets. A Gallup Poll indicated that Americans favor such a policy by more than a 2-to-1 margin (see Figure 19-3). Advocates of the policy contend that it compels school administrators and teachers to do a better job and gives students the option of rejecting a school that is performing poorly. Opponents of the policy say that it creates a few well-funded schools and a lot of poorly funded ones, yielding no net gain in educational quality. Critics also claim that the policy discriminates against poor and minority group children, whose parents are less likely to be in a position to steer them toward the better schools.

The issue of school choice goes to the heart of the issue of equal opportunity. On the one hand, an elite-centered school system widens the gap between the country's richer and poorer groups. On the other hand, making students compete with one another for the best education can be justified in terms of the country's individualistic tradition.

Culture, Politics, and Social Welfare

Surveys have repeatedly indicated that a majority of Americans are convinced that most people on welfare could get along without it if they tried. Because public assistance programs have limited public support, there are constant political pressures to reduce welfare expenditures and to weed out undeserving recipients. The unwritten principle of social welfare in America, reflecting the country's individualistic culture, is that the individual must somehow earn any social welfare benefit or, barring that, demonstrate a convincing need for the benefit. The result is a welfare system that is both *inefficient,* in that much of the money spent on welfare never reaches the recipients, and *inequitable,* in that most of the money spent on social welfare never gets to the people who are most in need of help.

INEFFICIENCY: THE WELFARE WEB

The United States has by far the most intricate system of social welfare in the world. Scores of separate programs have been established to address different, often overlapping needs. A single individual in need of public assistance may qualify for many, none, or one of these programs, and the eligibility criteria are sometimes bizarre. Consider the case of Gary Myers of Springfield, Missouri, who declared bankruptcy because he could not afford to pay $1,400 in hospital bills that his family had incurred. Had Myers made exactly $4 less than his $509 monthly wage as a security guard, he would have qualified for government payment of his medical expenses. Because of the extra $4, however, Myers received nothing.[32]

Beyond the question of the equity of such rules is the question of their efficiency. The unwritten principle that the individual must somehow earn or deserve a particular benefit makes the U.S. welfare system highly labor-intensive. Consider, for example, the 1996 welfare reform bill, which limits eligibility to families with incomes below a certain level and, in most instances, to families with a single parent living in the home. Because of this requirement, the eligibility of each applicant must be periodically checked by a caseworker (see Figure 19-4). This procedure makes such programs doubly expensive; in addition to payments to the recipients, there are the costs of paying caseworkers, supervisors, and support staffs, as well as processing the extensive paperwork involved.

The administrative costs of welfare are substantially lower in Europe since eligibility is either universal, as in the case of health care, or less stringently defined. There have been proposals to adopt a European-like system in the Unites States; President Nixon's attempt to establish a guaranteed annual income for every American family is an example.[33] All of these proposals have failed to win broad support, mainly because they run counter to Americans' belief in individualism. Thus, it is not surprising that the 1996 welfare bill will create additional layers of welfare administration. Recipients' lifetime welfare histories will have to be maintained, and states will have to establish job placement and training programs that can move millions of people from welfare to work. Whether the change will be cost-effective will be determined by whether large numbers of welfare recipients actually find long-term employment. Whether the change fits the American way of welfare is more easily judged: it clearly does. The reform gives the poor an incentive to fend for themselves.

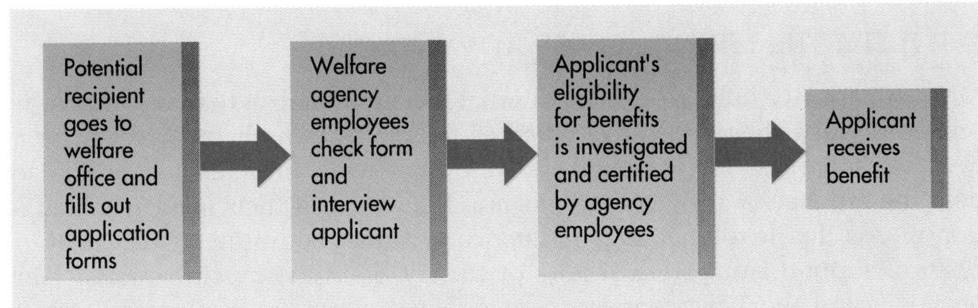

FIGURE 19-4 The Cumbersome Administrative Process by Which Welfare Recipients Get Their Benefits

One of the many ironies of U.S. social welfare policy is that tax deductions on home mortgages for the middle and upper classes are government subsidies, just as are rent vouchers for the poor, but only the latter are stigmatized as "welfare handouts." (Top, Sally Weigand/The Picture Cube; bottom, Glenn Kulbako/Picture Cube)

INEQUITY: THE MIDDLE-CLASS ADVANTAGE

Most Americans hold to the traditional belief in individualism and self-reliance, which they generalize to other people. Although they recognize a need for programs for the poor and disadvantaged, they tend to minimize both the number of such individuals and the extent of their need. The situation means that less advantaged Americans cannot count on a great deal of political support from other sectors of society. Even the much-heralded War on Poverty of the 1960s was less a war than a skirmish. Weak middle-class support for the effort, reports that the programs were poorly administered and were not reaching the target audience, and the fiscal pressures of the Vietnam conflict combined to undermine the antipoverty effort. Congressional appropriations for the War on Poverty programs never totaled as much as $2 billion in a given year.

Social security and Medicare are another story entirely. These two social insurance programs have broad public support even though together they cost the federal government nearly three times what is spent on the major public assistance programs (see Table 19-2). One major reason for the difference in public funding and approval for social security is that it benefits the majority. Most Americans are either actual or potential social security recipients. It is good politics for elected officials to appeal to the 40 million retired Americans who get a monthly social security check.[34]

Social security recipients feel entitled to their benefits by virtue of their payroll tax contributions. As indicated earlier, however, they receive far greater benefits than they have "earned" through their payroll taxes. So they are, in a sense, getting public assistance.

It is important to note, however, that the existence of social security substantially lessens the demand for other forms of public assistance. Social security keeps millions of Americans, mostly widows, out of poverty. About a fourth of social security recipients have no other significant source of income. Without social security, they would be completely dependent on public assistance programs.

Nevertheless, many social security recipients, while legally entitled to the benefits they receive, have no actual financial need for them. Only a third of social security recipients are in the lowest fifth of the population in income.

TABLE 19-2 Federal Spending for Major Social Insurance and Public Assistance Programs, 1995 Social insurance spending far exceeds public assistance spending.

Program	*Number of Recipients (in Millions)*	*Expenditures (in Billions)*
Social insurance		
Social security	40	$339
Medicare	32	158
		Total $497
Public assistance		
SSI	6	$ 27
AFDC	6*	17
Food stamps	27	28
Housing subsidies	7*	21
Medicaid	34	89
		Total $182

*Families.

SOURCE: Data are based on estimates contained in *The United States Budget, Fiscal Year 1995.*

TABLE 19-3 Transfer Payments to American Families Half of all families receive federal benefits.

Benefit	*Families Receiving Benefit*
Social security	26%
Medicare	24
Medicaid	12
Food stamps	9
Unemployment compensation	9
Subsidized school lunch	8
Government retirement	5
Aid to Families with Dependent Children	4
Supplemental Security Income	4
Public housing	3
Veterans benefits	2
At least one benefit	52%

SOURCE: Congressional Research Service. Figures based on 1992 payments.

Families in the top fifth of the income population receive more in federal social insurance benefits than is spent on family assistance, food stamps, and housing subsidies combined.

The contradictions and difficulties of social welfare in America come together in the contrasting cases of social insurance and public assistance. Although the latter is targeted toward the truly needy, it is less acceptable politically and culturally and receives much less funding. The situation testifies to the strength of traditional American values of individualism and self-reliance and to the power of money and votes. The social security program is a preeminent example of *majoritarian* politics at work.

A more complete picture of the distribution of government transfer benefits is provided by Table 19-3. Half of all families get one kind of transfer payment or another. The most common benefits are social security (26 percent of families) and Medicare (24 percent). Public assistance programs reach a smaller proportion of Americans: Medicaid (12 percent of families) tops this list while housing (3 percent) is at the bottom. The percentage of families who receive government benefits declines as income rises, but the benefits are nonetheless widely distributed: for example, 30 percent of the richest fifth of families and 37 percent of the next-richest fifth receive federal benefits.[35]

WHAT DOES THE FUTURE OF WELFARE REFORM LOOK LIKE?

Few analysts believe that the overhaul of the welfare system ended with passage of the 1996 welfare reform bill. Indeed, during negotiations with the White House and in Congress, the bill's sponsors dropped provisions that would have substantially revised the Medicaid and food stamp programs.

Social security is the one program that is not likely to be touched. Congressional Republicans and Democrats alike say no effort will be made to reduce spending on this entitlement. Small steps might be taken to slow the increase in social security spending, but even this would be politically difficult.

Medicare will also be around for decades to come. However, the program will run out of money in a few years, requiring changes in its funding. The political sensitivity of this issue was evident in late 1995 when congressional Republicans proposed to increase the share of Medicare costs to be paid by recipients, which President Clinton opposed. Senior-citizen groups sided with Clinton, forcing congressional Republicans into a showdown that strengthened Clinton's public support and led GOP lawmakers to withdraw their proposal. Given the political clout of the elderly, lawmakers may have to resolve the Medicare funding problem in the same way they handled the threatened insolvency of social security some years ago. Then, a nonpartisan commission was formed to develop a proposal that Congress could accept or reject in its entirety, thus reducing the direct pressure that the seniors' lobby could place on lawmakers.

Little else about the future of social welfare is clear. Social welfare, as we have seen, is the arena in which many of the conflicts of the American political system come together: individualism versus equality, Congress versus the president, national authority versus local authority, public sector versus private sector, Republicans versus Democrats, poorer versus richer, social insurance versus public assistance. The politics of welfare is a politics of contradictory values and competing interests, which ensures that it will be a contentious issue for years to come.

Summary

The United States has a complex social welfare system of multiple programs addressing specific welfare needs. Each program applies only to those individuals who qualify for benefits by meeting the specific eligibility criteria. In general, these criteria are designed to reward and promote self-reliance or, when help is necessary, to ensure that laziness is not rewarded or fostered—in short, to limit benefits to those individuals who truly cannot help themselves. This approach to social welfare reflects Americans' traditional belief in individualism.

Poverty is a large and persistent problem in America. About one in seven people fall below the government-defined poverty line, and they include a disproportionate number of children, female-headed families, minority group members, and rural and inner-city dwellers. The ranks of the poor are increased by economic recessions and reduced through government welfare programs.

Welfare policy has been a partisan issue, with Democrats taking the lead on government programs to alleviate economic insecurity. Changes in social welfare have usually occurred in the context of majority support for the change. Welfare policy has been worked out through programs to provide jobs and job training, education programs, income measures, and, especially, transfer payments through individual-benefit programs.

Individual-benefit programs fall into two broad categories: social insurance and public assistance. The former includes such programs as social security for retired workers and Medicare for the elderly. Social insurance programs are funded by payroll taxes on potential recipients, who thus, in a sense, earn the benefits they later receive. Because of this arrangement, social insurance programs have broad public support. Public assistance programs, in contrast, are funded by general tax revenues and are targeted toward needy individuals and families. These programs are not controversial in principle: most Americans believe that government should assist the truly needy. However, because of a widespread belief that most welfare recipients could get along without assistance if they tried, these programs do not have universal public support, are only modestly funded, and are politically vulnerable.

The balance between economic equality and individualism tilts more heavily toward individualism in the United States than in other advanced industrialized democracies. Entitlement to social security, for example, is not a universal right of the elderly in the United States, whereas it is elsewhere. Compared to other democracies, however, the United States attempts to more equally educate its children, a policy consistent with its cultural emphasis on equality of opportunity.

The social welfare system in the United States is criticized in all quarters, but reform is controversial. A major reason is that opposing sides disagree fundamentally on the nature of the problem. In one view, social welfare is too costly and assists too many people who could help themselves; another view holds that too many disadvantaged Americans live in poverty.

Major Concepts

entitlement program
equality of opportunity
in-kind benefits
means test
negative government
positive government
poverty line
public assistance
social insurance
transfer payment

Suggested Readings

Chubb, John E., and Terry M. Moe. *Politics, Markets, and America's Schools.* Washington, D.C.: Brookings Institution, 1990. The authors recommend a new system of public education designed around parent-student choice and school competition.

Cook, Fay Lomax, and Edith J. Barrett. *Support for the American Welfare State: The Views of Congress and the Public.* New York: Columbia University Press, 1992. A thorough study of the views underlying welfare policy.

Danziger, Sheldon H., Gary D. Sandefur, and Daniel H. Weinberg (eds.). *Confronting Poverty: Prescriptions for Change.* Cambridge, Mass.: Harvard University Press, 1994. A set of forward-looking studies on the nature of poverty and poverty policy in America.

Hochschild, Jennifer. *What's Fair?* Cambridge, Mass.: Harvard University Press, 1981. A careful study of Americans' conceptions of fairness, with an emphasis on economic issues.

Levitan, Sar. *Programs in Aid of the Poor,* 6th ed. Baltimore: Johns Hopkins University Press, 1990. A thorough overview of poverty and poverty programs in America.

Murray, Charles. *Losing Ground: American Social Policy, 1950–1980.* New York: Basic Books, 1984. An unfavorable assessment of the U.S. welfare system.

Quadagno, Jill. *The Transformation of Old Age Security.* Chicago: University of Chicago Press, 1988. A study that traces the development of old-age security and the rise of the American welfare state.

Rich, Michael J. *Federal Policymaking and the Poor: National Goals, Local Choices, and Distributional Outcomes.* Princeton, N.J.: Princeton University Press, 1993. An insightful study of the impact of a federal poverty program.

Schwarz, John E. *America's Hidden Success,* rev. ed. New York: Norton, 1988. A favorable assessment of the U.S. welfare system.

Wilson, William Julius. *The Truly Disadvantaged: The Inner City, the Underclass, and Public Policy.* Chicago: University of Chicago Press, 1987. An important analysis of poverty in the inner city.

CHAPTER 20

FOREIGN AND DEFENSE POLICY: PROTECTING THE AMERICAN WAY

We the people of the United States, in order to . . . provide for the common defense . . .
—Preamble, U.S. Constitution

The leaders of the world's seven most powerful industrial nations met in Naples, Italy, in 1994 for their first annual G-7 summit meeting. The 1994 meeting was designed to solidify historic changes in international free trade, which were expected to contribute billions of dollars to global wealth within the decade. The summit also addressed issues of mutual interest to the G-7 nations, including the question of how to integrate Russia more fully into the global economy.[1] Russian President Boris Yeltsin was invited to participate in the summit's final day of discussion, a signal that the G-7 might soon become the G-8. President Clinton had pressed for Yeltsin's participation, which the Italian Prime Minister Silvio Berlusconi called a "historic" development and which German Chancellor Helmut Kohl said was by far the most important aspect of the meeting.[2]

The G-7 summit meeting sharply dramatized the changing nature of world politics and the role of the United States in it. America's once bitter enemy, Russia, was no longer a main adversary. In a one-on-one meeting with Yeltsin, President Clinton talked of the bonds of friendship and common interest that now connected the two countries. In fact, the other countries at the summit, particularly Germany and Japan, were closer to the position of rivals of the United States than was Russia. Germany and Japan had trade surpluses with the United States and were strong competitors in the global marketplace. Yet, at the same time, the focus of the summit was cooperation rather than competition. The underlying assumption of the summit was that the world's most powerful nations could all gain by setting aside their differences and working together to promote economic growth and to contain regional conflicts, such as those involving Bosnia, Korea, and Rwanda.

As the G-7 summit illustrates, national security is an issue of economic vitality as well as of military strength. The primary goal of U.S. foreign policy is the preservation of the American state. This objective requires military readiness in order to protect the territorial integrity and international interests of the United States. But the American state also represents a society of more than 250 million people, whose livelihood depends in significant part upon the nation's position in the international economy. Through participation in global policies that foster economic growth, the United States can secure the jobs and trade that contribute to the maintenance of a high standard of living.

The national security policies of the United States embrace an extraordinary array of activities—so many, in fact, that they could not possibly be addressed adequately in an entire book, much less a single chapter. There are some 160 countries in the world, and the United States has relations of one kind or another—military, diplomatic, economic—with all of them. This chapter narrows the subject of national security policy by focusing on a few main ideas:

★ *Since World War II, the United States has acted in the role of world leader, which has substantially affected its military, diplomatic, and economic policies.*

★ *The policy machinery for foreign and defense affairs is dominated by the president and includes military, intelligence, diplomatic, and economic agencies and organizations.*

★ *The United States maintains a high degree of defense preparedness.* This readiness mandates a substantial level of defense spending and a worldwide deployment of U.S. conventional and strategic forces. A consequence of these requirements is a military-industrial complex that benefits from and is a cause of high levels of military spending.

★ *Changes in the international marketplace have led to increased economic interdependence among nations, which has had a marked influence on the United States' economy and on its security planning.* Increasingly, national security policy has been defined in economic terms rather than military terms.

The Roots of U.S. Foreign and Defense Policy

For nearly half a century, U.S. defense policy was defined by conflict with the Soviet Union. From the Berlin airlift in 1948 to the Vietnam escalation in 1965 to the Star Wars initiative in 1983, the United States seemed willing to pay any price to halt the spread of communism. Then in the late 1980s, the Soviet empire suddenly and dramatically began to fall apart. In December 1991, the Soviet Union itself ceased to exist. For decades, there had been two superpowers, the Soviet Union and the United States. Now there is only one.

With the end of the cold war, the United States is positioned to redefine its foreign and defense policies. The country is still at the center of world politics, but its challenges have changed: they are less military and more economic.[3] A strong domestic base, more than a mighty military arsenal, has become the key to global success.

Great Britain's Winston Churchill, America's Franklin D. Roosevelt, and the Soviet Union's Josef Stalin meet at Yalta in 1945 to discuss the order of the postwar world. (Courtesy of the US Army)

Although the age of superpower conflict is over, the changes in foreign and defense policy that lie ahead will take shape within a context defined by that era. Decisions made in the past carry into the future, both informing and channeling new ones.

THE UNITED STATES AS GLOBAL SUPERPOWER

Before World War II, the United States was an **isolationist** country, deliberately avoiding a large role in world affairs. A different America emerged from the war. It had more land, sea, and air power than any other country in the world, a huge military-industrial base, and several hundred overseas military bases. The United States had become an **internationalist** country, deeply involved in the affairs of other nations.

isolationism The view that the country should deliberately avoid a large role in world affairs and, instead, concentrate on domestic concerns.

internationalism The view that the country should involve itself deeply in world affairs.

U.S. national security policy after World War II was built upon a concern with the power and intentions of the Soviet Union.[4] At the Yalta Conference in 1945, U.S. President Franklin Roosevelt and Soviet leader Josef Stalin had agreed that east European nations were entitled to self-determination within a Soviet zone of influence, but Stalin breached the agreement. After the war, Soviet occupation forces assisted the communist parties in eastern Europe in capturing state power, usually by coercive means. In the words of Britain's wartime prime minister, Winston Churchill, an "iron curtain" had fallen across Europe.

The Doctrine of Containment

The Soviet Union's aggressive action led U.S. policymakers to assess Soviet aims.[5] Particularly noteworthy was the evaluation of George Kennan, a U.S. diplomat and expert on Soviet affairs. Kennan concluded that invasions from the west in World Wars I and II had made the Soviet Union (which had lost

25 million lives in World War II, compared with U.S. losses of 500,000) almost paranoid in its concern for regional security. Although Kennan believed that the USSR would someday mature into a responsible world power, he contended that it was an immediate threat to neighboring countries and that the United States, although not directly endangered, would have to take the lead in discouraging Soviet aggression. He counseled a policy of "long-term, patient but firm, and vigilant containment."[6]

containment A doctrine developed after World War II, based on the assumptions that the Soviet Union was an aggressor nation and that only a determined United States could block Soviet territorial ambitions.

Kennan's analysis contributed to the formulation of the doctrine of **containment,** which was based on the idea that the Soviet Union was an aggressor nation that had to be stopped from achieving its territorial ambitions.

Harry S Truman, who became president after Roosevelt's death in 1945, rejected Kennan's view that the USSR was motivated by a concern for *regional* security. Truman saw the Soviet Union as an aggressive ideological foe that was bent on *global* domination and that could be stopped only by the forceful use of U.S. power. Truman's view was based on assumptions derived from territorial concessions made to Germany's Adolf Hitler by Britain and France at a conference in Munich in 1938; rather than appeasing Hitler, these concessions convinced him that Germany could bully its way to further gains. The idea that appeasement only encourages further aggression was the *lesson of Munich,* and it became the dominant view of U.S. policymakers in the postwar period.

The Cold War

cold war The lengthy period after World War II when the United States and the USSR were not engaged in actual combat (a "hot war") but were nonetheless locked in a state of deep-seated hostility.

Developments in the late 1940s embroiled the United States in a **cold war** with the Soviet Union. The term refers to the fact that the two countries were not directly engaged in actual combat (a "hot war") but were locked into a deep-seated hostility, which lasted forty-five years. From the United States' perspective, the cold war was an extension of containment policy and included support for governments threatened by communist takeovers. In China the Nationalist government had the support of the United States, but it was defeated in 1949 by the Soviet-supplied communist forces of Mao Zedong. In June 1950, when the Soviet-backed North Koreans invaded South Korea, President Truman immediately committed U.S. troops to the conflict, which ended in stalemate and the loss of 35,000 American lives.

In order to contain the Soviet Union itself, the United States encircled it with a ring of military bases and built up its nuclear arsenal. In 1962 President John F. Kennedy took the country to the brink of war with the Soviet Union. U.S. intelligence sources had discovered that the Soviet Union was constructing nuclear missile sites in Cuba, which lies only 90 miles from Key West, Florida. Kennedy responded with a naval blockade of Cuba, threatening to attack any Soviet ship that tried to pass through the blockade. At the last moment, Soviet ships heading for Cuba turned around, and Premier Nikita Khrushchev ordered the dismantling of the missile sites. The Cuban missile crisis, however, provoked an arms race. The Soviets backed down over Cuba partly because they had a weak navy and an inferior nuclear force. Pledging not to be humiliated again, the Soviets began a twenty-year buildup of their naval and nuclear forces.

Cold war propaganda, like this poster warning Americans of the danger of Soviet-backed communist encroachment in the Philippines in the late 1940s, contributed to a climate of opinion in the United States that led to public support of efforts to contain Soviet power. (Library of Congress)

THE LIMITS OF AMERICAN POWER: THE VIETNAM WAR

For the United States, a major turning point in foreign policy was the Vietnam war. It was the most costly application of the containment doctrine: 58,000 American soldiers lost their lives.

Vietnam was part of France's colonial empire until the French army was defeated in 1954 by guerrilla forces, which were led by Ho Chi Minh, a nationalist with communist sympathies. The Geneva conference that ended the war resulted in a partitioning of Vietnam: the northern region was placed under Ho Chi Minh's leadership and the southern region under anticommunist leaders. The United States provided economic assistance to South Vietnam, anticipating that its government would quickly develop the public support that would enable it to prevail in a Vietnam unification election that was scheduled for 1956. When it became apparent that Ho Chi Minh would easily win the election, the United States helped to get it canceled and began to increase its military assistance to the South Vietnamese army. By the time of President Kennedy's assassination in 1963, the United States had about 17,000 military advisers in South Vietnam. Lyndon Johnson sharply escalated the war in 1965 by committing U.S. combat units to the conflict. By the late 1960s, 550,000 Americans were fighting in South Vietnam.

U.S. forces in Vietnam were technically superior in combat to the communist fighters, but they were fighting an enemy they could not easily identify in a society they did not fully understand.[7] Vietnam was a guerrilla war, with no front lines and few set battles. As the conflict dragged on, American pub-

In the jungle warfare of Vietnam, American soldiers had difficulty finding the enemy and adapting to guerrilla tactics. (James Pickerill/Black Star)

lic opinion, most visibly among the young, turned against the war, which contributed to President Johnson's decision not to run for reelection in 1968. Public opinion forced Richard Nixon, who became president in 1969, to aim not for victory but for a gradual disengagement that he called "peace with honor."

Détente

America's defeat in Vietnam forced U.S. policymakers to reconsider the country's international role. The *lesson of Vietnam* was that there were limits to the country's ability to assert its will in the world. Nixon claimed that the United States could no longer act as the "Lone Ranger" for the free world and sought to reduce tensions with communist countries.[8] The new philosophy was reflected by the Helsinki Accords of 1971, in which the United States accepted the territorial boundaries of eastern Europe. Then Nixon took a historic journey to the People's Republic of China in 1972, the first official contact with that country since the communists took power in 1949.

Another indication of a change in policy was the Strategic Arms Limitation Talks (SALT), which began in 1969. The SALT talks presumed that the United States and the Soviet Union each had an interest in retaining enough nuclear weapons to deter the other from an attack but that neither side had an interest in mutual destruction. Along with the lowering of east-west trade barriers, these efforts marked the start of a new era of communication and cooperation, or **détente** (a French word meaning "a relaxing"), between the United States and the Soviet Union.[9]

détente A French word meaning "a relaxing" and used to refer to an era of improved relations between the United States and the Soviet Union that began in the early 1970s.

Disintegration of the "Evil Empire"

Although the period of détente during the 1970s marked a major shift in U.S.-Soviet relations, it did not last.[10] The Soviet invasion of Afghanistan in 1979 convinced U.S. leaders that the USSR was still bent on expansion and threatened western interests in the oil-rich Middle East. Ronald Reagan, elected president in 1980, called for a renewed hard line toward the Soviet Union, which he described as the "evil empire."[11]

Reagan's proposal for a doubling of defense expenditures during the next five years marked the beginning of the largest peacetime military buildup in the nation's history. Reagan pushed for deployment of new nuclear weapons systems, including MX missiles, cruise missiles, and Pershing missiles. During Reagan's presidency, 4,500 tanks and 300 attack helicopters were added to the Army, the Navy got 80 new ships, and the Air Force acquired 1,300 additional fighter jets. The Soviet Union, for its part, had been building up its conventional and nuclear forces since the Cuban missile crisis of 1962.[12]

U.S. policymakers did not fully realize it at the time, but the Soviet Union was collapsing under its heavy defense expenditures, isolation from western technology and markets, and inefficient centralized command economy. In March 1985 Mikhail Gorbachev became the Soviet leader and proclaimed a need to restructure the Soviet economy and society, an initiative known as *per-*

THE MEDIA AND THE PEOPLE

THE GLOBAL VILLAGE

In his classic book, *Understanding Media,* Marshall McLuhan described the modern world as "a global village" because communication technology had brought people everywhere into close and instantaneous contact. However, it took the American press a long time to start bringing the rest of the world to its audience. Only a few newspapers, such as *The New York Times,* made a substantial effort at in-depth international coverage. This pattern began to change after World War II, when the United States took on the role of world leader. As the world became more important to America, the press brought more news of the world to the American people.

The introduction of television accelerated the process: the networks have a national audience and concentrate on national and international affairs. They devote proportionally more of their news-gathering efforts to international affairs than do newspapers. The most recently established major network, CNN, even has a world edition of its news that is transmitted daily in countries around the globe.

In recent years, the top news story in the U.S. media has often been an international story rather than a domestic one. Between 1989 and 1991, for example, the news story that received the most attention during each of these years was an international one. The breakup of the Soviet bloc was the leading story in 1989 and the Persian Gulf crisis received the most attention in 1990 and 1991. In 1992 a domestic story, the presidential election and the country's economic problems, took center stage.

Opinion polls reflect this pattern. In the past half century, there has been a gradual increase in the proportion of Americans who claim that international affairs is the level of politics that is of greatest interest to them. The size of this proportion is affected, however, by the issues of the moment. Opinion polls in 1992 showed that Americans' attention had shifted from events in Europe and the Middle East to the domestic economy. Nevertheless, in a way that would have been unimaginable earlier in the century, Americans have truly become part of McLuhan's global village.

SOURCES: Marshall McLuhan, *Understanding Media: The Extensions of Man* (New York: McGraw-Hill, 1964); *Media Monitor,* various issues, 1989–1992.

estroika. He also ordered the withdrawal of Soviet troops from Afghanistan (which had become his country's Vietnam) and sought to reduce tensions with the United States.

Gorbachev's efforts came too late to save the Soviet Union. In 1989, the withdrawal of Soviet troops from eastern Europe accelerated a pro-democracy movement that was already under way in the region. Poland initiated major reforms. Hungary dismantled the "iron curtain" that had blocked free travel to Austria. Then, in November, the Berlin Wall between East and West Germany—the most visible symbol of the separation of east and west—came down. On December 8, 1991, the leaders of the Russian, Belarus, and Ukrainian republics declared that the Soviet Union no longer existed.

A NEW WORLD ORDER

The end of the cold war prompted President George Bush to call for a "new world order." His formulation abandoned the assumption that world affairs are a zero-sum game, in which for one nation to gain something, another nation has to lose. Bush contended that nations can move forward together. The concept emphasized **multilateralism**—the idea that major nations should act together in response to problems and crises.[13]

multilateralism The situation in which nations act together in response to problems and crises.

Multilateralism characterized the U.S. response to Iraq's invasion of Kuwait in August 1990. President Bush worked through the United Nations, which demanded the unconditional withdrawal of Iraqi forces and imposed a trade embargo on Iraqi oil. The military force arrayed against Iraq was also nomi-

U.S. soldiers were deployed to Bosnia in early 1996 as part of a multinational force. Their mission was to promote peace by acting as a buffer between the warring sides and by helping to restore civilian authority through elections, disarmament, and a rebuilding of transportation, communication, and other public systems. (Stoddart/Katz/SABA)

nally a UN force, although it was led by a U.S. commander and consisted mostly of U.S. troops. Several countries, including Germany and Japan, supported the effort with money instead of troops. The Soviet Union cooperated by sharing intelligence information and by putting diplomatic pressure on the Iraqi government, which had been its close ally in the past.

The Gulf operation was militarily successful but did not resolve the regional conflicts or misguided leadership that prompted Iraq's aggression. The termination of the UN operation was followed by ethnic and religious repression within Iraq and a renewal of Iraqi threats to Kuwait's sovereignty (in response to Iraqi aggression against the Kurds in 1996, the U.S. twice launched bombing raids against Iraqi military targets).

In 1992, as another application of multilateralism, U.S. troops were deployed as part of a UN force to Somalia, where thousands of people had died and thousands more had become refugees as a result of civil war and famine. The humanitarian mission prevented additional deaths from starvation but turned sour when warring Somali clans turned against soldiers of the UN force. Thirty-six American soldiers were killed before U.S. troops were withdrawn, and a year later the UN mission was itself terminated. The anarchy and famine that had led to the UN mission still plagued Somalia when the last of the UN troops exited the country.

The war in Bosnia also prompted multilateral action. At first, the United Nations placed an arms embargo on Bosnia in an attempt to bring the fighting to a halt. However, the Bosnian Serbs continued their military attacks and used forced evacuations and mass executions to rid conquered areas of Bosnian Muslims and Croats. The UN then authorized limited air strikes against Serb positions by planes from the NATO countries (North Atlantic Treaty Organization, discussed below). When this strategy also failed, NATO planes, mainly from the United States, undertook a bombing campaign against the Serbs in September 1995. This action led directly to U.S.-negotiated peace talks in Dayton, Ohio, which brought the 39-month war finally to a halt. As part of the Dayton peace agreement, 60,000 troops from 32 countries, including 20,000 from the United States, were sent to Bosnia to maintain the peace (see Table 20-1). Whether the Dayton accord will result in lasting peace and stability in Bosnia is yet to be determined, although many analysts are pessimistic about the prospects.

As these examples suggest, multilateralism has been only somewhat successful as a strategy for resolving international conflicts. With the deployment of enough resources, the world's major powers can intervene with some success in many parts of the developing world. However, these interventions are not always popular at home; public opinion in the United States, for example, turned strongly against the relief operation in Somalia after U.S. soldiers were killed there. Multilateral intervention also does not guarantee long-term success. Regional and internal conflicts typically stem from enduring ethnic, factional, or national hatreds, or from chronic problems such as famine and overcrowding. Even if these hatreds or problems can be momentarily eased, they are often too deep-seated to be permanently resolved. The preference of major nations for peaceful and low-cost solutions to regional and internal conflicts will continue to be tested by the hardship and enmity faced daily by many of the world's people.

TABLE 20-1 The Peacekeeping Force in Bosnia As part of the Dayton accord, a peacekeeping force of 60,000 troops, a third of whom were Americans, was sent to Bosnia.

Total Troops by Country	
United States	20,000
Britain	13,000
France	10,000
Netherlands	2,000
Russia	1,800
Others	13,200
Total	60,000

The Process of Foreign and Military Policymaking

National security is unlike other areas of government policy because it rests on relations with powers outside rather than within a country. Nations have sovereignty within their recognized territory; each nation is the ultimate governing authority over this territory and the people within it. In reality, of course, the world is not composed of equal sovereign states. Some are more powerful than others, and the strong sometimes bully the weak. Nevertheless, there is no international body that is recognized by all nations as the final (sovereign) authority on disputes between them.

As a result, the chief instruments of national security policy—diplomacy, military force, economic exchange, and intelligence gathering—differ from those of domestic policy.

THE POLICYMAKING INSTRUMENTS

Diplomacy is the process of negotiation between countries. In most cases, nations prefer to settle their differences by talking rather than by fighting. By definition, acts of diplomacy involve two (*bilateral*) or more (*multilateral*) nations.

Military power is a second instrument of foreign policy, and it can be used *unilaterally*—that is, by a single nation acting alone. Most countries use military power as a defensive measure; they maintain forces, or enter into military alliances with other countries, in order to protect themselves from potential aggressors. Throughout the history of nations, however, there have always been a few countries that use military force more actively. The United States is such a nation. In the nineteenth century, it used force to take territory from the Indian tribes and from Mexico and Spain. Although the United States has not pursued territorial goals since then, it has otherwise made frequent use of its military power. Recent examples include the unilateral invasions of Grenada in 1983, Panama in 1989, Haiti in 1994, and the multilateral war against Iraq in 1991.

Economic exchange is a third instrument of world politics. This form of international relations usually takes one of two forms—trade or assistance. Trade among nations is the more important form. Nearly all countries aspire to a strong trading position so as to have access to outside products and markets for their products. Some countries, however, are so weak economically that they require assistance from more prosperous countries. This assistance is typically designed to help both the weaker and stronger partners.

A fourth instrument of world politics is intelligence gathering, which is the process of monitoring other countries' activities. For many reasons, but primarily because all nations pursue their individual self-interest, each nation keeps a watchful eye on the others.

THE POLICYMAKING MACHINERY

In the case of the United States, the lead actor in the application of these instruments of foreign policy is the president. As we indicated in Chapters 14 and

In a ceremony symbolizing America's role as world leader, President Clinton brings Israeli Prime Minister Yitzhak Rabin (left) and PLO Chairman Yasser Arafat together for a historic handshake after the signing of the Israeli-PLO peace accord in 1993. (Reuters/Bettmann)

15 and will discuss later in this chapter, the president shares power and responsibility for foreign and military policy with Congress, but the president has the stronger claim to leadership because of his constitutional roles as commander in chief, chief diplomat, and chief executive. For example, although President Clinton discussed his plans for invading Haiti with congressional leaders, he said the military operation would proceed even if they opposed it.

The president has an executive agency, the National Security Council (NSC), that provides advice on foreign and military issues. The NSC is chaired by the president and includes the vice-president and the secretaries of state and defense as full members, and the director of the Central Intelligence Agency (CIA) and the chairman of the Joint Chiefs of Staff as advisory members. Since State, Defense, and the CIA often have conflicting and self-centered views of national security, the NSC acts to keep the president in charge by providing a broader perspective. The NSC's staff of experts is directed by the president's national security adviser, who, with an office in the White House and access to defense, diplomatic, and intelligence sources, has become influential in the formulation of U.S. policy.

The complexity of international politics makes it impossible for any individual or government agency to direct U.S. policy single-handedly. Moreover, as a world power, the United States relies upon outside institutions, such as the United Nations, to pursue some of its policy objectives. The key organizational units in the foreign policy area can be categorized according to their primary functions—defense, intelligence, diplomacy, and trade.

Defense Organizations

The Department of Defense (DOD), which has more than 1.5 million uniformed personnel and 750,000 civilian employees, is in charge of the military

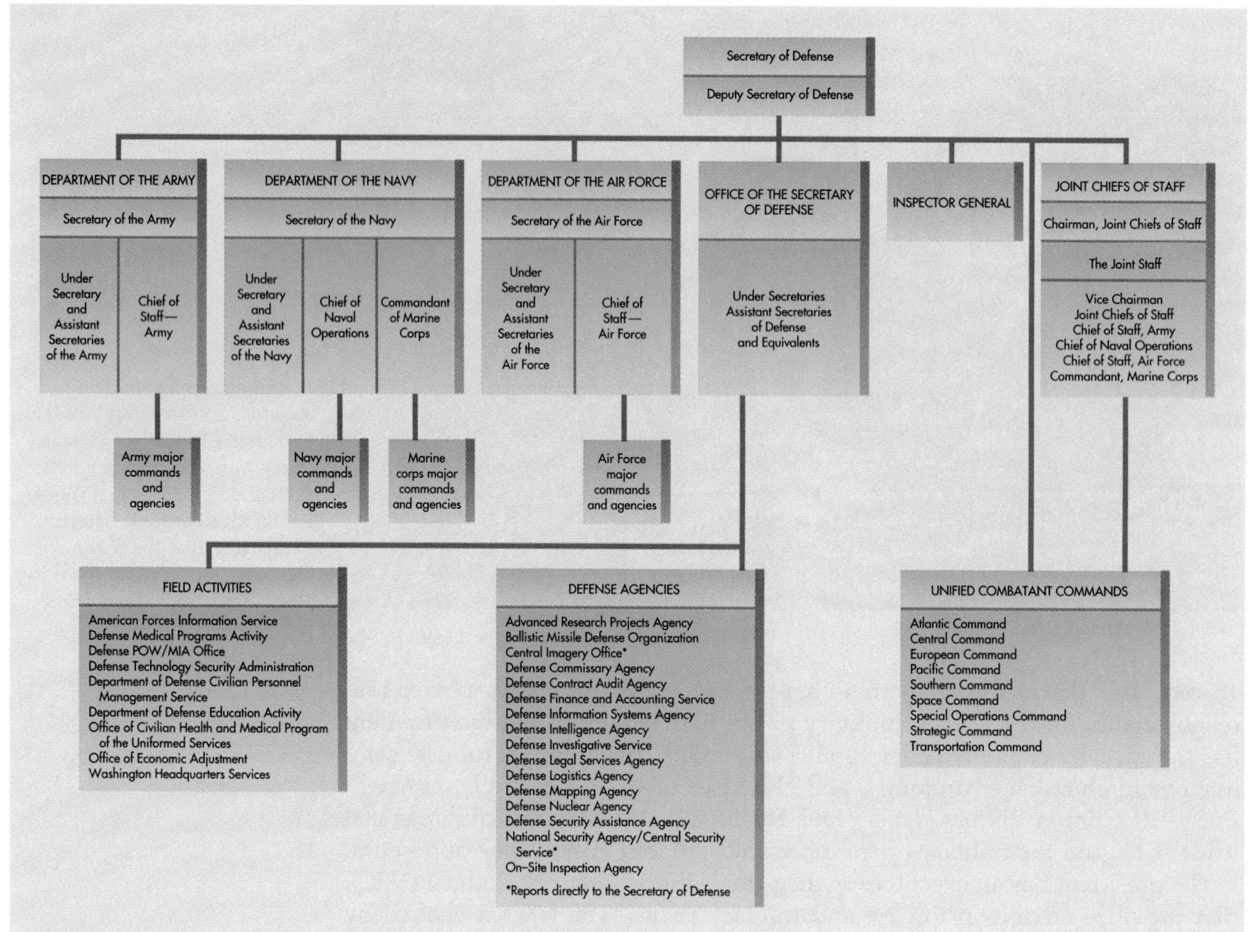

FIGURE 20-1 Department of Defense (DOD)
The DOD consists of the three uniformed services (Army, Navy, Air Force), the Joint Chiefs of Staff, and various commands and agencies. *Source: U.S. Government Manual.*

security of the United States (see Figure 20-1). DOD was created in 1947 when the three military services—the Army, Navy, and Air Force—were placed under the secretary of defense. Each service has its own secretary, but they report to the defense secretary, who represents all the services in relations with Congress and the president. Each service naturally regards its mission and budget as more important than those of the other services. The defense secretary helps reduce the adverse effects of these interservice rivalries.

The secretary of defense is always an important policymaker, but the influence of recent secretaries has varied widely, depending on the secretary's personality and the president's inclinations. Bush's defense secretary, Dick Cheney, played a major and highly visible role, for example, in the planning of the Persian Gulf conflict.

The president also receives military advice from the Joint Chiefs of Staff (JCS). The JCS includes a chairman, a vice-chairman, and a member from each of the uniformed services—the Army, Navy, Air Force, and Marine Corps. The JCS helps to shape military strategy and evaluates the military's personnel and weapons needs. Whenever the members of the JCS disagree, the chairman's view prevails. During the Persian Gulf war, General Colin Powell, the first African American to serve as JCS chair, was deeply involved in strategic decision making, including a controversial recommendation that President Bush halt the fighting before all major Iraqi combat units were destroyed.

Of the country's military alliances, the North Atlantic Treaty Organization (NATO) is the most important. NATO was created as a "forward defense" against the possibility of a Soviet invasion of western Europe. NATO countries conduct joint military exercises and engage in joint strategic and tactical military planning. The NATO forces, which include troops of the United States, Canada, and most western European countries, are under an integrated command.

Since NATO's charter prohibits it from acting "out of area," it had no authority to act in the Persian Gulf war. Moreover, the demise of the Soviet Union threatened NATO's survival. In 1991 NATO was restructured as a smaller, more flexible force that might deal with new risks, such as international terrorism and ethnic rivalries.

The Bosnian war initially created a rift within NATO over the use of force in the European theater. Europe's NATO members, particularly France, were opposed at first to a U.S. proposal to use massive airpower against Bosnian Serb forces. The Europeans thought a diplomatic solution would work and accepted the U.S. plan only after it became abundantly clear that force alone would halt Serb attacks on the Muslim population. During the interim, the United States refrained from intense criticism of its allies for fear of splitting the NATO alliance. "We've been trying and struggling to get NATO air power to be used more aggressively," a Clinton administration official said,

General Colin Powell, chairman of the Joint Chiefs of Staff, briefs reporters at the Pentagon during the Persian Gulf war. (Martin Simon/SABA)

"[but we] couldn't keep asking for things that weren't going to happen. The strain on the alliance, the credibility question, the futility of it all—it is better to be realistic."[14]

NATO's latest plans include expanding its membership to include countries of eastern Europe, a move Russia opposes. Poland, Hungary, the Czech Republic, and other eastern European countries were once part of the Soviet military alliance (the Warsaw Pact countries), and Russia has said it would view any NATO expansion as a threat to its interests. NATO leaders see a European-wide alliance as the best guarantee of lasting peace on the continent.

Intelligence Organizations

Foreign and military policy requires a high state of knowledge about what is happening in the world and what other countries are planning to do. A large part of the responsibility for the gathering of such information falls on specialized federal agencies, including the Central Intelligence Agency (CIA); the National Security Agency, which specializes in electronic communications analysis; and separate intelligence agencies within the departments of State and Defense. Although the exact amount that the federal government spends annually on intelligence activities is not easily determined, the figure apparently exceeds $20 billion.[15]

Of the various intelligence agencies, the CIA is the most prominent.[16] The agency gathers and assesses information on foreign affairs. Much of this effort consists of the routine monitoring of international developments. With the decline of the Soviet threat, which had occupied the agency's attention since its formation in 1947, the CIA is giving more attention to drug trafficking, industrial espionage, and terrorism.

Diplomatic Organizations

The U.S. Department of State conducts most of the country's day-to-day business with foreign countries through its embassies, headed by U.S. ambassadors. The department's traditional duties include negotiating political agreements with other nations, protecting U.S. citizens and interests abroad, promoting U.S. economic interests, gathering foreign intelligence, and representing the United States abroad. For all of its activities and prominence, the State Department is relatively small. Only about 25,000 people—foreign service officers, policy analysts, administrators, and others—work in State. Some observers regard the State Department as tradition-bound and less central to foreign policy decision making than its reputation seems to suggest.[17]

The secretary of state is often described as second in importance only to the president within the executive branch in the determination of national security policy. Whether the secretary, in fact, has this level of influence depends on the president's willingness to rely heavily on the secretary. Dean Rusk, secretary of state under Presidents Kennedy and Johnson, had less influence than top presidential assistants or Secretary of Defense Robert McNamara. In con-

Since the end of the cold war, the United Nations has played an increasingly large role in international politics. Shown here is a court session at The Hague, Netherlands, where a UN war crimes tribunal is holding the trials of those accused of genocide, murder, torture, and rape during the war in Bosnia. (Raphael Gaillarde/Gamma)

trast, George Bush chose James Baker as his secretary of state precisely because he wanted Baker to take the lead role in foreign policy.

American's diplomatic efforts also take place through international organizations, such as the Organization of American States (OAS) and the United Nations. The UN was established after the Second World War by the victorious allies.[18] Its security council, which included the United States, France, Britain, the Soviet Union, and the Republic of China, was to be an instrument of multilateral policymaking; the world's strongest powers would work together for global harmony and prosperity. When the United States and Soviet Union entered into the cold war, all hope of such cooperation vanished.

The breakdown of the Soviet bloc in 1989 renewed the possibility that the world's great powers could work together to achieve common goals. The first major opportunity came in the Persian Gulf conflict of 1990–1991, when the United States led a UN force that first blocked Iraqi forces and then attacked them. Some analysts believe that the UN may finally be able to play the large role in international affairs that was envisioned for it when it was chartered. International terrorism, ethnic conflict, and drug trafficking are among the problems that the UN has recently addressed.

Other analysts believe the United Nations is basically unsuited to the role of global arbiter on a large scale. UN operations are normally effective only to the degree that member nations are in agreement on a course of action and have the resolve to implement it fully. This agreement and resolve are often lacking because nations have conflicting objectives. Moreover, the realities of politics require national leaders to be more responsive to domestic public opinion than to the views of the international community. The killing of U.S. troops in Somalia turned American public opinion against the country's par-

YOUR TURN

UN PEACEKEEPING OPERATIONS

The Question:

Generally speaking, do you think the United States should or should not send U.S. troops to participate in UN peacekeeping forces around the world?

Should send troops	Should not send troops

What Others Think: This question was asked in a November 1993 ABC News/Washington Post survey. By the substantial margin of 60 to 35 percent, most respondents said the United States should participate in UN peacekeeping operations.

Comment: Americans are generally willing to support UN operations, particularly when they see unilateral action on the part of the United States as the alternative. Nevertheless, Americans do not always maintain this attitude when a peacekeeping operation goes sour. There was broad public support for U.S. participation in UN operations in Somalia until American soldiers lost their lives. A CBS News poll taken shortly after the killings indicated that Americans by a 2-to-1 margin now wanted the troops withdrawn as quickly as possible.

ticipation in the UN operation there, and President Clinton responded by withdrawing U.S. forces.

Although the United States was a leader in the formation of the United Nations and has been its principal financial backer, U.S. politicians have had divided opinions of the organization. Critics say the United States pays an unfair share of the UN's costs and argue that the country's foreign policy should not be subordinate to the goals of the UN's member nations. The Republicans' Contract with America, for example, called for a severe cut in U.S. financial support for UN peacekeeping operations and a ban on the placement of U.S. troops in peacekeeping roles under foreign commanders.

Economic Organizations

The shift in emphasis in global affairs from military forces to economic markets has brought to the fore a new set of government agencies, those representing economic sectors. The Agriculture, Commerce, Labor, and Treasury departments are playing increasingly important roles in foreign affairs. In addition, some specialty agencies, such as the Federal Trade Commission and the Export-Import Bank of the United States, are involved in international trade and finance.

The United States also works through international institutions, such as the International Monetary Fund (IMF), the World Bank, and the General Agreement on Tariffs and Trade (GATT). These agencies tend to promote goals, such as economic development and free trade, that are consistent with U.S. policy goals. The IMF and the World Bank were established through the efforts of the United States for the purpose of assisting developing countries. The IMF provides short-term loans so that countries experiencing temporary trade deficits do not have to take drastic measures, such as the imposition of high tariffs, that would hurt them and the world economy in the long run. The World Bank makes long-term loans to poorer countries for capital investment projects, such as the construction of factories. The GATT is the organization through which nations hold multilateral talks to establish the general rules governing international trade. (GATT is discussed further later in the chapter.)

The Military Dimension of National Security Policy

The dissolution of the Soviet Union brought about the first significant scaling back of U.S. defense spending since the end of the Vietnam war (see Figure 20-2). Nevertheless, the United States spends far more on defense, in both relative and absolute terms, than its allies. On a per capita basis, U.S. military spending is more than twice that of other members of the NATO alliance (see box: How the United States Compares). The U.S. defense budget is second to none in the world, but so is the military power it buys. During the Gulf war, the world's fourth largest army, the Iraqi army, was no match for the United States' superior military equipment and technology. The war lasted about six weeks, with fewer than 200 U.S. casualties, but left an estimated 50,000 to 100,000 Iraqi dead.

DEFENSE CAPABILITY

The United States owes its status as the world's only superpower in part to the strength of its conventional forces. The United States Navy has a dozen aircraft carriers, nearly 100 attack submarines, and hundreds of other fighting and supply ships. The U.S. Air Force has thousands of high-performance aircraft. The U.S. Army has more than 500,000 troops on active duty, and they are amply supported by tanks, artillery pieces, armored personnel carriers, and attack helicopters.

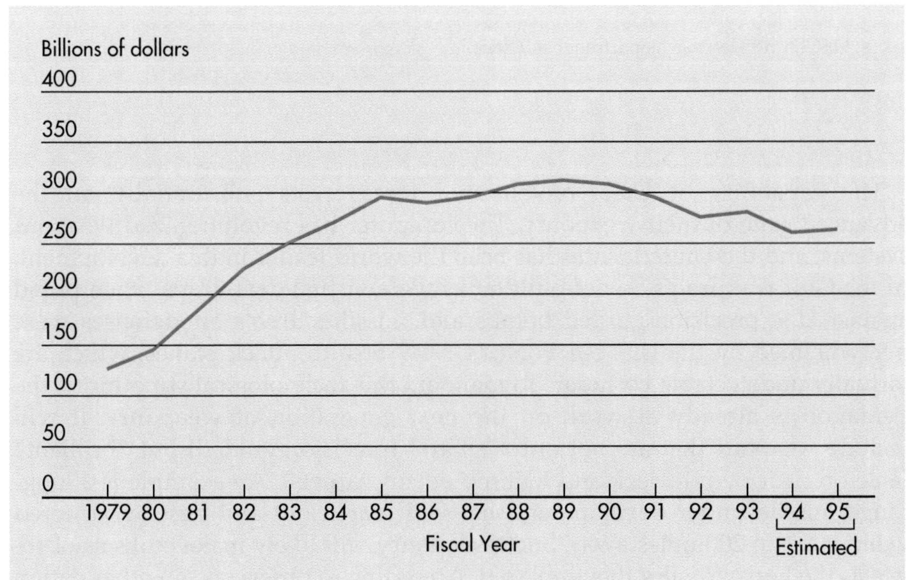

FIGURE 20-2 Defense Spending Spending on national defense, which more than doubled during the 1980s, has begun to decline because of the end of the cold war. *Source: Office of Management and Budget, 1995.*

HOW THE UNITED STATES COMPARES

THE BURDEN OF MILITARY SPENDING

The United States bears a disproportionate share of the defense costs of the NATO alliance. The U.S. military establishment is huge and is deployed all over the world, and the taxpayers spend more than $250 billion per year to maintain it. These expenditures directly account for roughly 5 percent of the U.S. gross national product (GNP). By comparison, defense spending by Germany, Italy, and Canada accounts for 3 percent or less of their GNPs. The percentages for Britain and France are higher but not as high as for the United States. Japan, which is not part of NATO, spends only 1 percent of its GNP on defense. Japan's small military force is confined by World War II peace agreements to the country's islands and the adjoining waters.

The United States has pressured its allies to carry a larger share of the defense burden, but these countries have resisted, contending that the cost would be too high and that their security would not be substantially improved. A partial exception to this situation was the Persian Gulf war. U.S. troops and equipment accounted for the bulk of the military strength arrayed against Iraq, but the financial cost of the war effort was borne by other countries. Germany, Japan, Saudi Arabia, and Kuwait were among the countries that helped fund the war. In fact, other countries gave the United States $20 billion more than it spent on the war.

The chart below indicates the approximate per capita level of defense spending in the United States and countries with which it is closely aligned.

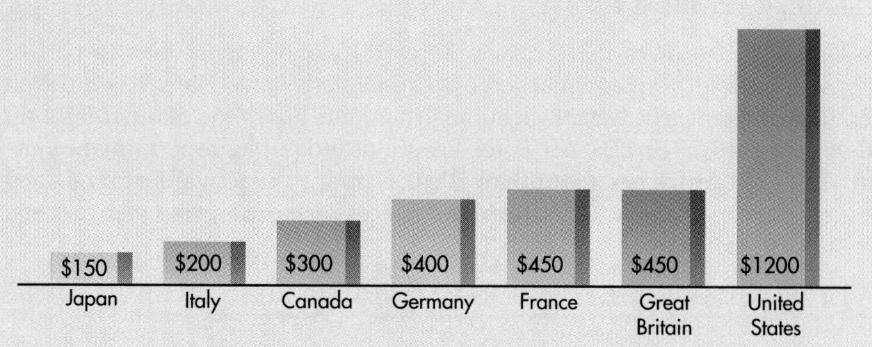

SOURCE: OECD and Defense Department statistics.

The capability of U.S. conventional forces rests substantially on the advanced state of their weaponry. The computer has revolutionized weapons systems, and the United States has been the world leader in this development. In the Gulf war, Iraq's Soviet-built tanks were virtual deathtraps when pitted against U.S. precision-guided bombs and missiles. Iraq's air defenses were overwhelmed by the U.S. Air Forces's F-117 Stealth attack planes, which are virtually undetectable by radar. To maintain this technological superiority, the Pentagon is already at work on the next generation of weaponry. It will include weapons that are not only "smart" (precision-guided) but "brilliant" (able on their own to seek and identify enemy targets). An example is a long-range missile under development that will search out and destroy armored vehicles up to 200 miles away. Such weaponry will likely make tanks as obsolete as the horse cavalry they replaced. According to observers, no other nation is anywhere close to the United States in the testing and production of advanced weapon systems.[19]

The U.S. military also possesses the nuclear weapons that starkly defined the nation's cold war with the Soviet Union. The United States followed a policy of **deterrence,** which included a nuclear arsenal capable of destroying the Soviet Union many times over. Deterrence was based on the notion that the Soviet Union would be deterred from launching a nuclear attack by the knowledge that, even if it destroyed the United States, it too would be obliterated.[20]

deterrence The idea that nuclear war can be discouraged if each side in a conflict has the capacity to destroy the other with nuclear weapons.

America's nuclear weapons are deployed in what is called the "nuclear triad," which refers to the three ways in which these weapons can be launched—by land-based missiles, submarine-based missiles, and bombers. The triad provides a "second-strike capability"—the ability to absorb a first-strike nuclear attack and survive with enough nuclear power for massive retaliation (second strike). The United States also has tactical (battlefield) nuclear weapons in its arsenal. These are short-range, low-yield nuclear weapons that can be used against battlefield targets, such as enemy troop concentrations or artillery installations.

THE USES OF MILITARY POWER

U.S. military forces have been trained for or called upon for six types of military action.

Unlimited Nuclear Warfare

The idea of an all-out nuclear war was always too horrible to imagine, but the fear of nuclear holocaust has diminished greatly since the cold war ended. Following the lead of the United States, the president of the Russian republic, Boris Yeltsin, initiated deep, unilateral cuts in his country's nuclear arsenal. In the past, nuclear arms limitation had required protracted bilateral negotiations between the United States and the Soviet Union.

Limited Nuclear Warfare

Some experts believe that, while the risk of an all-out nuclear attack on the United States has diminished, the possibility that a single nuclear weapon might be used against the United States may have increased. A major concern arising from the breakup of the Soviet Union has been control of its nuclear weapons, strategic and tactical. In addition, terrorist groups or "outlaw" regimes, such as Iraq, pose a serious threat because the technology and materials that are required to build nuclear weapons are more widely accessible than ever before. Accordingly, the United States, Russia, and other nuclear powers are cooperating to reduce the spread of nuclear weapons. One goal of the Persian Gulf conflict was the destruction of Iraq's nuclear program.

Unlimited Conventional Warfare

The end of the cold war has also reduced the prospect of an unlimited conventional war. A great part of U.S. military preparedness and strategy in the past half century was based on the scenario of an invasion of western Europe by the Soviet Union and its allies. Even if the cold war should begin anew, Russia or any other part of the former Soviet Union would require years to build its military capacity to the point where it could pose a credible threat to the west.

Limited Conventional Warfare

The Persian Gulf war demonstrated that the United States possesses the might to win a limited conventional war against a well-organized and well-armed foe. Despite the size of Iraq's army and the combat readiness of its forces, the war turned out to be no contest, prompting George Bush to claim the United States had "kicked the Vietnam syndrome once and for all."

A problem of limited conventional wars is that they do not always produce satisfactory results. The military action is likely to be quick and decisive, but the political aspect tends to be troublesome. The Bush administration's decision to stop the Gulf war short of a march on Baghdad was a calculated one. Said one analyst: "The President was not prepared to pay the political price that increased American casualties would have involved or to take responsibility for putting Iraq back together after an unconditional surrender or to figure out how to contain the power of Iran and Syria once the Iraqi regime was destroyed."[21]

Counterinsurgency

insurgency A type of military conflict in which irregular soldiers rise up against an established regime.

The Vietnam conflict was an **insurgency,** an uprising by irregular forces against an established government. In most third world countries, insurgencies originate in the grievances of people who are struggling against the monopoly of economic and political power by a ruling elite. In the past, the

An American soldier checks a roster of Haitian detainees at a Guantanamo Bay refugee camp. Since the end of the Cold War, U.S. troops have been increasingly used to support police-type action, including immigration control. (Feanny/SABA)

insurgents often received support in the form of military equipment from the Soviet Union. Most insurgencies were therefore seen by the United States as a threat to its political and economic interests.

U.S. attempts to quell third world insurgencies have diminished since the Vietnam war, which reduced public support for U.S. military involvement in the internal affairs of other countries. Throughout the 1980s, polls showed that a large majority of Americans were steadfastly opposed to sending U.S. troops to quell insurgencies in Central America.

Police-Type Action

With the end of the cold war, U.S. policymakers have begun to pay closer attention to other global problems, including drug trafficking, terrorism, political instability, and population movement. The U.S. military has become increasingly involved with these problems. U.S. military facilities and personnel were deployed in 1992 to detain and return hundreds of "boat people" from Haiti who were seeking asylum in the United States. In 1994, Haiti became the target of a U.S. military mission that was planned as a combat operation but became a police-type action, thanks to a last-minute agreement negotiated by former President Jimmy Carter that resulted in the departure of Haiti's ruling generals from the island. The mission restored elected President Jean-Bertrand Aristide to power and, six months after it began, U.S. forces turned control over to UN peacekeepers.

Police-type actions are not regarded favorably by military commanders, who have expressed opposition to suggestions, for example, that U.S. troops be used to stop the flow of illegal aliens from Mexico and to help keep the peace in drug-ridden inner-city neighborhoods. But given the high cost of keeping a large defense force, and the absence of a highly visible and dangerous enemy like the former Soviet Union, it is likely that new proposals and new pressures to use the troops in unconventional ways will develop.

THE POLITICS OF NATIONAL DEFENSE

All Americans would agree that the physical security of the United States is a paramount concern. The consensus breaks down, however, on specific issues. The Vietnam conflict created deep and lasting divisions of opinion over the proper uses of America's military capacity. In contrast, U.S. policy in the Persian Gulf crisis had majority support from start to end.

Majoritarianism and Elitism in Defense Policy

Defense policy is a mix of *majoritarian* and *elite* politics. On critical international issues of broad national concern, majority opinion is a vital component. It was the public that ultimately forced U.S. policymakers to withdraw American troops from Vietnam and Somalia, and public support that enabled President Bush to move from economic sanctions to combat operations in the Persian Gulf crisis.

Most conflicts over defense policy, however, take place between political elites.[22] Since Vietnam, liberal Democratic elites have been more reluctant than conservative Republicans to support increases in military spending and to use military force abroad. Institutional perspective is also significant: presidents, functioning as commander in chief, have generally been stronger advocates of military spending and power than has Congress. (See Chapters 13 and 15 for a more detailed discussion of congressional-presidential interaction on policy issues.)

The Military-Industrial Complex

Political disputes over defense policy are more than honest differences of opinion among people. They also involve billions of dollars in jobs and contracts.[23] In fiscal year 1994, the U.S. defense budget exceeded $250 billion, or roughly 5 percent of the gross national product. A high level of defense spending has been justified by reference to the nation's security needs. However, an alternative explanation for high defense spending points to the insatiable demands of the U.S. armed services and defense firms. In his 1961 farewell address, President Dwight D. Eisenhower warned against the "unwarranted influence" and "misplaced power" of what he termed "the military-industrial complex."[24]

military-industrial complex The three components (the military establishment, the industries that manufacture weapons, and the members of Congress from states and districts that depend heavily on the arms industry) that mutually benefit from a high level of defense spending.

The **military-industrial complex** has three components: the military establishment, the industries that manufacture weapons, and the members of Congress from states and districts that depend heavily on the arms industry. The military-industrial complex is not, as is sometimes suggested, a well-coordinated, unified network of interests engaged in a conspiracy to keep the United States on a wartime footing. Rather, it is an aggregation of interests that benefit from a high level of defense spending, regardless of whether these expenditures can be justified from the standpoint of national security.

Many U.S. firms could not flourish without military contracts, and some could not survive at all, for they produce only military equipment. These firms

A B-2 "Stealth" bomber sits on the runway of Whiteman Air Force Base in Missouri. The B-2 is one of the newest and most expensive weapons in America's arsenal. (P. Shambroom/Photo Researchers)

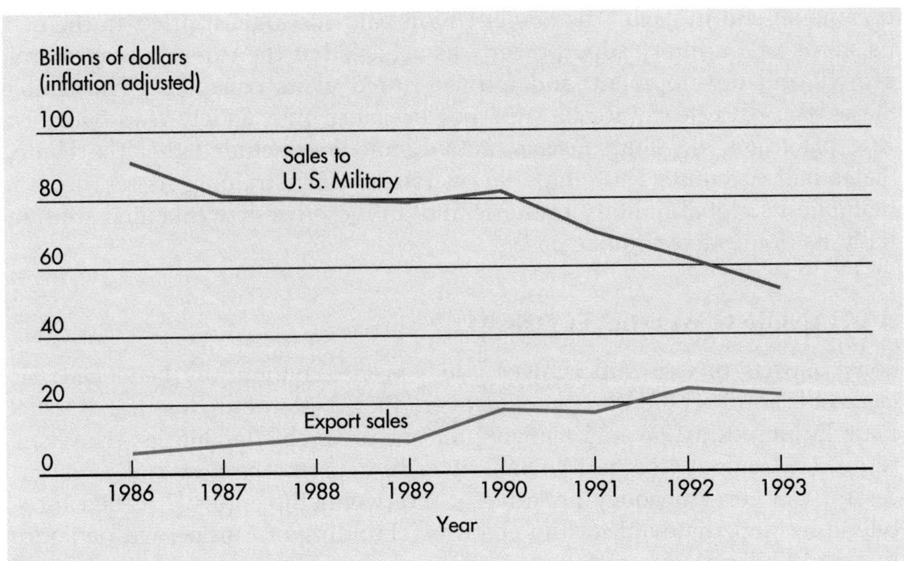

FIGURE 20-3 Arms Sales The U.S. defense industry's weapons sales to the U.S. military have decreased while sales abroad have increased. *Source: Congressional Research Service and Defense Budget Project.*

obviously do not act only out of patriotism; they are profit-making organizations whose business includes the aggressive marketing of weapons. They often get a receptive response from members of Congress from states and districts that depend heavily on defense contracts. The economic impact of even a single weapon system can be substantial. The B-1 bomber, for example, was built with the help of 5,200 subcontractors located in forty-eight states and in all but a handful of congressional districts. "This geographic spread gives all sections of the country an important stake in the airplane," one assessment of the B-1 concluded.[25] Without doubt, some proportion of U.S. defense spending reflects the workings of the military-industrial complex rather than the requirements of national security.[26] The problem is that no one knows exactly what this proportion is, and the estimates vary widely.

Defense firms have been hurt by recent cutbacks in U.S. military spending, and they have turned increasingly to export sales (see Figure 20-3). Nine of the world's ten largest arms-making companies are American firms, and they currently control two-thirds of the world's arms sales.[27] The demand for U.S. arms stems from the decline in Russia's arms-building capacity and from the superior performance of U.S. military equipment in the Persian Gulf war.[28]

The Economic Dimension of National Security Policy

Economic considerations are a vital component of national security policy. In the simplest sense, economic strength is a prerequisite of military strength: a powerful defense establishment can only be maintained by a country that is economically well off. In a broader and more important sense, economic prosperity enables a people to "secure" their way of life. As President Eisenhower said, it is folly to weaken at home what one is trying to strengthen abroad.

The cold war sometimes hid the essential truth of this observation. Global power, in addition to being a means by which nations achieved other goals, became an end in itself. The Soviet Union paid the highest price. In the end, its status as a military superpower was achieved at the expense of economic growth and development, and ultimately led to its collapse.[29] The United States also paid dearly for its superpower status. In a widely read book, *The Rise and Fall of the Great Powers,* Paul Kennedy concluded that the United States had succumbed to "imperial overstretch" by straining its resources to maintain its global military presence and, in the process, weakening substantially its domestic economic base.[30]

A CHANGING WORLD ECONOMY

Some aspects of U.S. superpower policy were economically beneficial. The clearest example is the European Recovery Plan, better known as the Marshall Plan. Proposed in 1947 and named after one of its chief architects, the widely respected General George Marshall, it is perhaps the boldest and most successful U.S. foreign policy initiative of the twentieth century. It called for $3 billion in immediate aid for the postwar rebuilding of Europe, with an additional $10 billion or so to follow. The Marshall Plan was unprecedented both in its scope (today, the equivalent cost would be more than $100 billion) and in its implications—for the first time, the United States had committed itself to a continuing major role in European affairs. Through the Marshall Plan, the countries of western European regained economic and political stability in a relatively short time.

Apart from enabling the countries of western Europe to better confront the perceived Soviet military and political threat, the Marshall Plan was also designed to meet the economic needs of the United States. Wartime production had lifted the country out of the Great Depression, but the end of the war in 1945 brought a recession and renewed fears of hard times. A rejuvenated western Europe furnished a market for U.S. goods. In effect, western Europe became a junior partner within a system of global trade that worked to the advantage of the United States.

A high level of military spending in conjunction with several other factors, however, gradually weakened the position of the United States in the world economy.[31] Whereas the United States at one time could almost define international economic conditions, it is now also defined by them.[32] Germany and Japan have become powerful economic rivals of the United States. Today Japan, not the United States, is the world's leading exporter, and trade between the two countries results in a huge surplus for Japan. The United States has also experienced a trade deficit with Germany. Japan particularly, but also Germany, benefited economically by spending less on the military than the United States. The Japanese yen and German deutschemark have at times been stronger currencies than the American dollar. In addition, western Europe as a whole has become a less receptive market for U.S. goods; European countries are now one another's best customers, trading among themselves through the European Union (EU).

In economic terms, the world can best be described as tripolar—in other words, economic power is concentrated in three centers. One center is the United States, which produces nearly 20 percent of the world's goods and services. Another center is Japan, which accounts for 10 to 15 percent of the world's economy. The third and largest economy, with 25 to 30 percent of the world's gross product, is the EU, which includes the countries of Belgium, Denmark, France, Germany, Great Britain, Greece, Ireland, Italy, Luxembourg, the Netherlands, Portugal, Spain, Sweden, Finland, and Austria.

The three centers, although they have less than 15 percent of the world's population, account for 60 percent of its economic output. In many respects, the United States is the strongest of the three centers. Although it has economic weaknesses, including a trade imbalance,[33] the United States is the world leader in technological innovation and foreign investment. The U.S. economy is also more well-rounded than those of Japan and the EU. Like them, the United States has a strong corporate sector, but, unlike Japan, it also has a strong agricultural sector, and, unlike both Japan and the EU, it is rich in natural resources.

AMERICAN GOALS IN THE GLOBAL ECONOMY

The United States depends on other countries for raw materials, finished goods, and capital to meet Americans' production and consumption demands. Meeting this objective requires the United States to have influence on world markets. The broad goals of the United States in the world economy include:

- Sustaining an open system of trade that will promote prosperity at home
- Maintaining access to energy and other resources that are vital to the regular functioning of the U.S. economy
- Keeping the widening gap between the rich and poor countries from destabilizing the world's economy[34]

President Clinton meets with other G-7 leaders during a working session at their 1996 summit meeting in Lyon, France. The G-7 is a group of seven of the world's most economically powerful countries: the United States, Japan, Italy, Germany, France, Great Britain, and Canada. (Apesteguy-Benainous/Gamma)

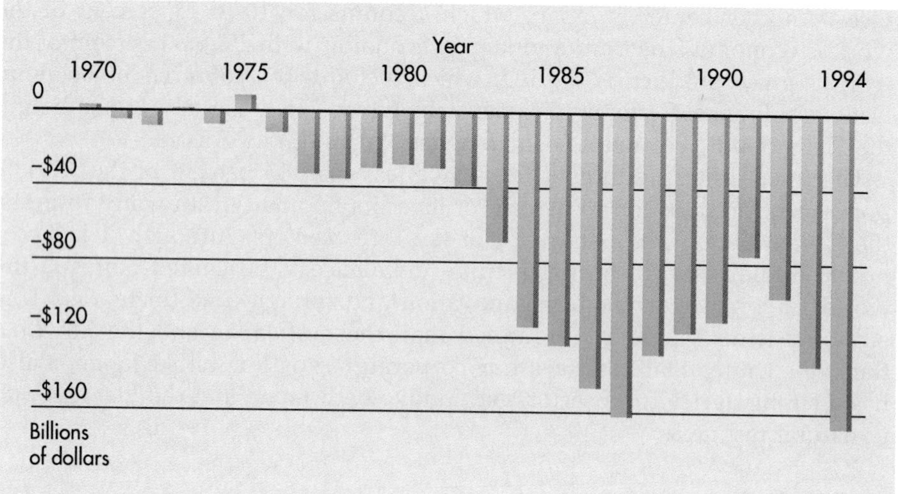

FIGURE 20-4 The Trade Deficit Not since 1975 has the United States had a trade surplus; the deficit reached a record $166 billion in 1994. *Source: Department of Commerce.*

Global Trade

The United States was most able to sustain domestic prosperity through global trade in the period after World War II. Industrialized Europe had been devastated by the war, but U.S. factories and farmlands emerged untouched by its effects and were producing more than two-fifths of the world's goods, triggering an unprecedented period of domestic prosperity. The fabled American middle class was essentially forged on the strength of this economic boom. High-paying factory jobs were particularly important in the broadening of the middle class.

The situation today is markedly different. The postwar U.S. trade surplus lasted into the 1970s but has since become a trade deficit (see Figure 20-4). The United States has the world's largest trade deficit, and in 1994 it reached a record high. Exports were a record $503 billion in 1994, but they paled alongside a record $669 billion imports, for a trade deficit of $166 billion. An imbalance of trade with China and Japan accounted for more than half the deficit. The trade imbalance of recent years has meant that many of the goods Americans buy are produced by foreign workers; there has been a net loss of manufacturing jobs in the United States and wage stagnation is a consequence (see Chapter 18).

Not surprisingly, global trade has become an increasingly important domestic issue in the United States. Trade issues are a mixture of economics and politics. Protective tariffs and import restrictions, for example, are political responses to foreign economic competition. By placing a tariff or other restrictions on a product from abroad, and thereby increasing its price or limiting its availability, government can protect domestic producers of that product.

protectionism The view that the immediate interests of domestic producers should have a higher priority (through, for example, protective tariffs) than free trade between nations.

To oversimplify, the opposing sides on trade issues reflect the protectionism and the free trade positions. **Protectionism** emphasizes the immediate interests of domestic producers and includes measures necessary to give them an advantage in the domestic market over foreign competitors. The center of protectionist sentiment in the United States has been Congress. Many of its members are determined to protect locally operating firms that are adversely affected by foreign competitors. The **free trade** position assumes that the long-term economic interests of all countries are advanced when tariffs and other trade barriers are kept to a minimum. The leadership on free trade has usually come from the White House, although it is fair to say that most members of Congress, except on vital interests affecting their constituencies, support the principle of global free trade.

These opposing positions clashed in 1993 over the issue of the North American Free Trade Agreement (NAFTA), which aims to create an EU-type market among the United States, Canada, and Mexico. Opponents of the agreement, who included organized labor, most environmental groups, and a majority of the Democrats in Congress, argued that it would result in the loss of countless jobs to Mexico. Its proponents, who included President Clinton, most large U.S. corporations, and most congressional Republicans, contended that the agreement would boost the economies of all three counties and was necessary if the United States was to maintain a leading position in global trade. The measure obtained majority support in Congress, but only after side agreements were worked out to protect some American workers from the adverse effects of open trade in North America.

In its first year, NAFTA was a boon to all three countries involved. U.S. exports to Mexico rose sharply, while Mexico received an inflow of capital and Canada increased its exports to both the United States and Mexico. In late 1994, though, the value of the Mexican peso dropped sharply, slowing U.S. exports and requiring the United States to provide Mexico with billions of dollars to stabilize its currency (see Chapter 13). The long-term benefits of NAFTA apparently will depend mainly on the ability of Mexico to stabilize its economy.

The new rules expanding the General Agreement on Tariffs and Trade (GATT) may have an even greater impact than NAFTA on America's economy in the years to come. The GATT rules received congressional approval in 1994 and aim at creating nearly a global free market: the rules lower worldwide tariffs by a third, strengthen protections for intellectual property (such as patents and copyrights), and create panels that will arbitrate trade disputes and establish standards in areas such as the environment, securities, and worker safety. The GATT's 124 member nations have basically committed themselves to an open trade policy buttressed by regulations that are designed to ensure fair play among the participants.[35]

The debate over GATT resembled that over NAFTA. GATT was backed by business and free trade advocates and faced opposition from labor and those who favored protectionist policy. In the final analysis, the debate on GATT, as with NAFTA, will be settled by whether its costs outweigh its benefits. Proponents foresee a global economic expansion, with the United States a major winner on the strength of its technological know-how. Opponents project a further shrinking of the domestic industrial base, as capital and jobs flow to countries with low labor costs.

★ STATES IN THE NATION

Foreign Trade: Exported goods constitute about 5 percent of most states' economies.

STATE	EXPORTS AS PERCENT OF ECONOMY	RANK
Ala.	4.0%	30
Alaska	11.0	3
Ariz.	5.6	13
Ark.	2.4	42
Calif.	5.6	13
Colo.	3.2	37
Conn.	4.6	26
Del.	6.7	8
D.C.	0.9	49
Fla.	4.7	21
Ga.	4.2	27
Hawaii	0.6	51
Idaho	4.7	21
Ill.	4.8	20
Ind.	4.7	21
Iowa	3.9	32
Kan.	4.1	28
Ky.	4.7	21
La.	15.6	2
Maine	3.8	34
Md.	2.4	42
Mass.	6.2	10
Mich.	9.8	5
Minn.	5.1	16
Miss.	4.0	30
Mo.	3.0	38
Mont.	1.8	46
Neb.	2.1	44
Nev.	1.3	48
N.H.	4.1	28
N.J.	3.7	35
N.Mex.	0.9	49
N.Y.	4.7	21
N.C.	5.7	12
N.Dak.	3.0	38
Ohio	6.0	11
Okla.	2.9	40
Oreg.	7.4	7
Pa.	3.5	36
R.I.	2.8	41
S.C.	4.9	19
S.Dak.	1.6	47
Tenn.	3.9	32
Texas	8.8	6
Utah	5.1	16
Vt.	10.5	4
Va.	6.6	9
Wash.	22.4	1
W.Va.	5.5	15
Wis.	5.1	16
Wyo.	2.0	45

SOURCE: U.S. Bureau of the Census, 1993.

★ CRITICAL THINKING

Free Trade: Good or Bad? Two of the most heated congressional debates in recent years were those on NAFTA and GATT. The debates pitted proponents of free trade against advocates of protectionism.

The free trade faction argued that protectionism is ultimately self-defeating, that other nations will simply respond in kind. The free traders cautioned against the notion that the global economy is a zero-sum game, saying that the economic interests of all countries are furthered by an open trading system. They also argued that the United States has a competitive advantage because of its technological know-how and will be one of the big winners in a global free trade system.

The protectionist faction argued that the United States is already a big loser in the international market, that its trade deficit far exceeds that of other countries. They also noted the loss of jobs and factories to overseas locations. They contended that U.S. firms should be protected from foreign competitors who gain an unfair advantage from their access to cheap labor and that the United States should first secure its own market, which would generate new jobs and income for Americans.

What is your position on the free trade versus protectionist issue? What arguments, other than those above, would you make in support of your position?

Access to Natural Resources

Although the United States is rich in natural resources, it is not self-sufficient. The major deficiency is oil; domestic production provides for only about half the nation's use.

Outside the United States, most of the world's oil is found in the Middle East, Latin America, and Russia. Access to this oil has occurred mainly through the marketplace, but U.S. military force has also been instrumental. In the Middle East, for example, U.S. oil companies controlled one-tenth of Middle Eastern oil reserves before World War II began; just twenty years later, they controlled six-tenths.[36] This change was in part the result of the ability of U.S. firms after the war to furnish the capital to reopen oil fields damaged by the conflict and to open new fields. The United States also gained leverage through its support of reactionary regimes in Iran and other Middle Eastern countries, which responded by giving U.S. firms a larger role in their oil production.

The 1990–1991 war in the Persian Gulf is a more recent example of how U.S. military force has served the nation's resource needs. Iraq's invasion of oil-rich Kuwait threatened western supplies, and its defeat quelled the threat.

In general, however, military power has increasingly become a less effective means of preserving economic leverage.[37] Economic interdependence has made military intervention mostly counterproductive. For example, when Iranian fundamentalists took over the U.S. embassy in Teheran in 1979, one of the reasons the United States refrained from attacking Iran's oil fields was that the action would have substantially reduced the Middle East's oil-producing capacity.

Relations with the Developing World

Political instability in the less developed countries, as in the case of Iraq's invasion of Kuwait, is disruptive to world markets. Less developed countries also offer marketplace opportunities. In order to progress, they need to acquire the goods and services that more industrialized countries can provide. To foster this demand, the United States and the other industrialized countries provide developmental assistance to poorer countries. These contributions include direct foreign aid and also indirect assistance through international organizations such as the IMF and the World Bank. Since World War II, the United States has been far and away the leading source of aid to the developing countries of the world. The United States is still near the top in terms of its total annual contributions but is now far down the list in terms of its per capita annual contributions (see Table 20-2). The primary recipient of U.S. foreign aid is Israel, which, at $3 billion annually, gets more than a fourth of the total.

Foreign aid is a favorite target of politicians. Upon being named chair of the Senate Foreign Relations Committee, Jesse Helms (R-N.C.) said he would trim millions in aid "going down foreign ratholes."[38] Many Americans share the view that the United States ought not to be funding discretionary programs abroad when there are pressing needs at home. The unpopularity of foreign aid is also a consequence of the public's exaggerated notion of how

TABLE 20-2 U.S. Assistance to Developing Countries The United States ranks high in terms of total amount spent on development assistance but ranks low in terms of per capita expenditure.

	DEVELOPMENT ASSISTANCE	
	Total (Billion)	*Per Capita*
Canada	$ 2.6	$ 96
France	7.4	129
Germany	6.9	108
Great Britain	3.2	56
Italy	3.4	59
Japan	11.0	88
Sweden	2.1	245
United States	11.3	44

SOURCE: *OECD in Figures* (Paris: Organization for Economic Cooperation and Development, 1993).

much the United States spends in this area. In a 1994 poll that asked respondents to name the largest federal programs, foreign aid was at the top of the list (27 percent said it was the most expensive federal program). In fact, foreign aid is near the bottom, accounting for less than 1 percent of the total federal budget.[39]

Foreign assistance is only one source of the funds that flow from the United States to developing countries: private investment is the other major source. After trailing Japan for much of the 1980s, the United States has again emerged as the country whose firms invest most heavily abroad. In 1993, U.S. *multinational corporations* (firms that have major operations in more than one country) invested $50 billion abroad, double that of Japanese, French, German, or British firms. Foreign investment by U.S.-based multinationals works to America's advantage in at least two important ways. First, it sends a flow of overseas profits back to the United States, which strengthens the country's financial base. Second, it makes other nations dependent on the prosperity of the United States; their economies are linked to the condition of U.S. business.

★ CRITICAL THINKING

Trade and Human Rights
Under pressure from business, the Clinton administration decided in 1994 to renew China's favored-nation trade status despite earlier threats to rescind it because of the country's human rights abuses. With the renewal, U.S. firms could continue to invest heavily in China.

After the China decision, the Clinton administration tried to get business leaders to formulate a set of principles for the treatment of foreign workers by U.S. multinationals. The principles were to be a model for all U.S. firms doing business abroad, in China and elsewhere. The effort failed; business leaders could not agree on a set of principles of any consequence.

What is the obligation of U.S. multinationals, if any, to develop high labor standards in their foreign operations? For example, if a local economy permits the unrestricted use of child labor, should U.S. firms hire such workers?

THE POLITICS OF GLOBAL ECONOMIC POLICY

The global economy has changed a great deal since America's halcyon days in the period immediately following World War II. It is greatly more competitive and less responsive to military power. Of course, the United States still derives economic advantages from its superpower status. Many countries prefer a militarily strong United States to the alternatives. China, for example, does not fear that the United States will use military power against it but is unsure whether a remilitarized Japan would hesitate to do so. Such situations provide the United States with special opportunities for favorable economic relationships.

U.S. trade representative Mickey Kantor, left, and China's Liu Jiyuan shake hands to mark the signing of a memorandum of understanding regarding commercial satellite launches. China agreed not to undercut the international market for such launches. Trade disputes and opportunities have become an increasingly important issue of U.S. foreign policy. (AP/Wide World Photos)

Nevertheless, the United States necessarily depends more heavily than in the past on the strength of its own economy to forge a favorable position in world trade. This situation has caused U.S. corporations in recent years to launch cost-cutting measures in order to make their products more competitive in the global market. The changes have also led U.S. policymakers to alter their approaches to business regulation, public education, and many other policies that affect the country's competitive position. Another indicator of a new approach is the emphasis that the United States has placed on lowering trade barriers so as to promote the type of world trading system that can benefit all participating countries.

Public opinion in recent years has consistently supported the idea that the United States should turn its attention away from military priorities toward economic ones. A 1991 ATI survey indicated that more than three-fourths of Americans believed that the United States "can't afford to defend so many nations." This opinion seems to reflect the lesson that American elites and officials have drawn from international experiences during the last half century, particularly during the past decade or so. The consensus is broad enough to suggest that American politics in the 1990s will focus on reinvigorating the U.S. economy.

Summary

From 1945 to 1990, U.S. foreign and defense policies were dominated by a concern with the Soviet Union. During most of this period the United States pursued a policy of containment based on the premise that the Soviet Union was an aggressor nation bent on global conquest. Containment policy led the United States into wars in Korea and Vietnam and to maintain a large defense establishment. U.S. military forces were deployed around the globe, and the nation built a large nuclear arsenal. The end of the cold war, however, made some of this weaponry and much of the traditional military strategy less relevant to maintaining America's security. Cutbacks in military spending and a redefinition of the military's role are under way.

With the end of the cold war, the United States has taken a new approach to foreign affairs, which President

George Bush labeled as a "new world order." It proposes that nations work together toward common goals and includes efforts to address global problems, such as drug trafficking and environmental pollution. Although multilateralism succeeded in the Persian Gulf war, its failure in Bosnia and Somalia has raised questions about its usefulness as a general strategy for resolving international problems.

Increasingly, national security is being defined in economic terms. After World War II, the United States helped establish a global trading system within which it was the leading partner. The nation's international economic position, however, has gradually weakened, owing to domestic problems and to the emergence of strong competitors, particularly Japan and Germany. Many analysts believe that a revitalized economic sector rather than military power holds the key to America's future position in international affairs.

The chief instruments of national security policy are diplomacy, military force, economic exchange, and intelligence gathering. These are exercised through specialized agencies of the U.S. government, such as the departments of State and Defense, which are largely responsive to presidential leadership. Increasingly, national security policy has also relied on international organizations, such as the UN and GATT, which are responsive to the global concerns of major nations.

Major Concepts

cold war
containment
détente
deterrence
free trade
insurgency
internationalism
isolationism
military-industrial complex
multilateralism
protectionism

Suggested Readings

Dallek, Robert. *The American Style of Foreign Policy: Cultural Politics and Foreign Affairs.* New York: Oxford University Press, 1990. A critical assessment of the forces that have shaped American foreign policy in the twentieth century.

Franck, Thomas M. *Political Questions/Judicial Questions: Does the Rule of Law Apply to Foreign Affairs?* Princeton, N.J.: Princeton University Press, 1992. An accounting of the judiciary's abdication of a role in foreign policy.

Jervis, Robert. *The Illogic of American Nuclear Strategy.* Ithaca, N.Y.: Cornell University Press, 1984. A critical view of U.S. nuclear policy.

Karnow, Stanley. *Vietnam: A History.* New York: Penguin, 1983. A thorough history of American involvement in Vietnam.

Kennedy, Paul. *The Rise and Fall of the Great Powers.* New York: Random House, 1988. A provocative history which claims that great nations, including the United States, have weakened themselves by failing to restrain the use of their power.

Koistinen, Paul A. *The Military-Industrial Complex.* New York: Praeger, 1980. An analysis of the military-industrial complex and its effect on defense spending and policy.

Lindsay, James M. *Congress and the Politics of U.S. Foreign Policy.* Baltimore, Md.: Johns Hopkins University Press, 1994. An analysis of Congress's increasingly assertive role in foreign policy.

Nye, Joseph. *Bound to Lead: The Changing Nature of United States Power.* New York: Basic Books, 1990. An analysis of the U.S. role in world affairs in the aftermath of the cold war.

Oye, Kenneth A., Robert J. Lieber, and Donald Rothchild. *Eagle in a New World: American Grand Strategy in the Post–Cold War Era.* New York: HarperCollins, 1992. A collection of essays on the choices the United States faces now that the cold war has ended.

Quester, George H. *The Future of Nuclear Deterrence.* Lexington, Mass.: Lexington Books, 1986. A forward look at nuclear strategy.

CHAPTER 21

CONCLUSION: RENEWING AMERICA'S IDEALS

Out of the experiences and ideas of many people in many places in the course of centuries, there has come a great deal of agreement about what democracy is, but nobody has a monopoly of it and the last word has not been spoken.

—*E. E. Schattschneider*[1]

For nearly sixty years, the Gallup Poll has regularly asked Americans about their country and its government. For the first few decades, Americans had an optimistic outlook. They were worried about the global threat of totalitarianism, but they felt good about their own country, its future, and the strength of its political institutions. By the late 1960s, however, the Gallup Poll was indicating that Americans were growing somewhat disillusioned with their government. During the 1970s, this dissatisfaction with government intensified. Americans' outlook brightened for a few years in the mid-1980s but then headed downward again. By 1995, only a third of the Gallup respondents said they were satisfied with the direction their country was taking.

This decline of confidence has roots in many aspects of American life, but government is the chief culprit in many people's minds. Government is expected to provide peace abroad, a healthy economy, strong systems of health and education, security for the elderly, a clean environment, progress in race relations, safe streets. In the late 1960s, people began to question whether government was fulfilling its responsibilities adequately. The scope of government kept increasing, but the performance of government was not keeping pace. More was becoming less.

The roots of this situation are found in the nature of modern government. One feature of government today is its complexity. Social, economic, and technological changes have increased and complicated the relationships between people, organizations, and the natural world in which they operate. The complexity of government has risen proportionally. Public policy issues today can have so many dimensions and so many consequences, some of which are not recognized until years after the fact, that they almost defy resolution. Policymakers often have to struggle just to understand the nature of a problem, let alone develop a sensible policy response. Scores of communities have spent a decade or more trying to find environmentally and financially acceptable ways to dispose of their garbage but have not yet been able to do so. And waste management is probably one of the simpler problems of modern life. Consider poverty in the inner city or competitiveness in the global marketplace. Who has the final answers to problems such as these?

A second characteristic of modern government is its bigness. The scope of public policy is almost beyond imagination. To one degree or another, government has its hand in nearly every aspect of Americans' lives. There are thousands of public policies, nearly all of which contribute positively to society. The sad fact, however, is that no nation, no matter how rich or efficient, has enough resources to do all that is required of it. Hard choices are everywhere. For example, although everyone would like to stop acid rain and the greenhouse effect, which are creating environmental havoc, no one wants to shut down the industries and scrap the automobiles that are the main causes of the problem.

Complexity and bigness have made the work of government exceedingly difficult. Complexity increases both the cost of the search for policy solutions and the probability that policy actions will not turn out as expected. For its part, bigness dilutes the resources of society, forcing trade-offs among goals that all agree are worthwhile. A result is that government does not perform to the level of the public's expectations. Americans often complain that their leaders are not trying hard enough or are not competent enough when, in fact, their leaders are confronted by bewildering and costly choices. Nearly everyone agrees, for example, that the nation's schools must be revitalized if the United States is to compete effectively in the global economy of today; but there is no agreement on what changes must be made, how long the reforms will take, or whether the United States can afford to remake its schools.

In a word, a problem of modern government is "overload." As more and more is expected of government, it becomes less and less capable of performing as expected. This situation poses extraordinary challenges for America's leaders, its people, and its political ideals.

The Challenge of Leadership

Modern leaders need help, lots of it, if they are to govern effectively. Help is available, particularly from the bureaucrats who staff executive agencies and the groups that lobby government. They are storehouses of the information and expertise that are essential components of effective policymaking in the modern age. Government simply could not do its work properly without the specialized contributions of groups and bureaucratic agencies. Yet their help comes at a stiff price: their overriding goal is to further their own narrow interests, not the broad public interest (see Chapters 10 and 16).

Of course, special interests and the general interest have always been somewhat at odds. The U.S. Constitution's elaborate system of checks and balances was designed to prevent a factional interest from gaining all power and using it to the detriment of other interests and the community as a whole. In *Federalist* No. 51, James Madison explained the necessity of constitutional safeguards against the selfish and potentially tyrannical tendencies of special interests: "In framing a government to be administered by men over men, the great difficulty lies in this: you must first enable the government to control the governed; and in the next place oblige it to control itself." The Framers' system has served its purpose well (see Chapters 2 to 5). In fact, for a long period in U.S. history, constitutional checks and balances were nearly an unqualified benefit. They kept government at bay during the nation's early years, thereby simultaneously preserving individual liberty and promoting social and economic progress and stability.

The nation's system of checks and balances is more problematic today. Madison's solution to the problem of factions has itself become a problem. There is a severe tension between the extreme pluralism of contemporary society and a constitutional framework designed primarily to protect against majority tyranny. The growing complexity of society is reflected in the growing number of interest groups, which, as they have multiplied, have also narrowed. The same system of checks and balances that was designed to frustrate a majority faction has made it relatively easy for these narrow interests to achieve their specialized goals. The support of a relatively few well-placed policymakers is often all the help that they need (see Chapters 10, 13, and 16). The political consultant Eddie Mahe has described the situation as "the tribalization of politics," saying that it represents the triumph of "the special interest over the general interest."[2]

The nation's system of checks and balances is also a cause of policy deadlock since agreement among the president, the House, and the Senate is normally necessary before significant action is possible. Often, particularly when control of the institutions of government is divided between the parties, problems linger because agreement on a policy response cannot be reached. Rarely are problems addressed in their early stages. The separation of power within the system makes it difficult in most instances for any leader or set of leaders to muster widespread support for a major policy until a general sense of urgency exists. Separate interests and institutions are not inclined to give up their individual agendas until nearly forced by circumstances to do so. Even then, there is no guarantee that decisive leadership will emerge.

The shape of America's future will depend substantially on the ability of its leaders to confront the difficult policy issues facing the country. Of all the marks of genuine leadership, none is more crucial than the courage to build public support for burdensome policies—those which require people to sacrifice their short-term and special interests to the long-term and general interest. Such leadership is usually in short supply, and recent years have been no exception. No national emergency, such as a catastrophic war or great depression, forced America's leaders to overspend federal revenues by thousands of billions of dollars in recent years. They did so willfully, bending to immediate pressures and passing on to future generations the burden of the debt.

Such actions are fostered by an ascendant form of candidate-centered politics that serves the personal power and reelection needs of public officials at the expense of their collective accountability and the effectiveness of the institutions within which they operate (see Chapters 9, 12, and 14). The writers of the Constitution warned that leadership wrenched from an institutional context cannot serve the public's true interest, and the axiom is as valid today as it was 200 years ago.

With their individualistic tradition, Americans have difficulty thinking of institutions rather than a single person exercising leadership. This perspective is the reason that Americans assign the president too much credit when things go well and too much blame when things go badly. This view may be understandable, but it cannot be allowed to determine institutional arrangements. The problem of modern government is not one of electing a president big enough for the job but of forging effective instruments of collective leadership and purpose.

Historically, political parties have been the best of these instruments. It is no coincidence that the legislative effort to greatly reduce the federal deficit came in the form of a partisan initiative, the Republicans' Contract with America. Whether Republican unity can be maintained in the face of the fragmenting tendencies within the American political system is an open question. Yet if there were any doubt about the importance of parties in collective action, the Contract with America should have settled the question. Party ideology is the foundation of majoritarian politics; it is the binding agent that enables diverse interests to stay together in the pursuit of common goals. Competitive, disciplined, and programmatic parties are the strongest system of leadership that democracies have yet devised.

The Challenge of Citizenship

The scope and complexity of modern government are as much a challenge to the public as they are to leaders. Since the time of Aristotle, the principal objection to democracy has been that the people are prone to rash judgments, that self-government devolves inexorably into majority tyranny. The more appropriate objection today may be that the people are not capable of any public judgment at all—that democracy devolves into formlessness. The complex nature of contemporary issues and their great number combine with the sheer size of the public and the relative insignificance of any one of its members to discourage civic involvement. The problem is not that Americans are indifferent to how they are governed. The problem is that they are too diverse in their ways of life and too pressed for time to recognize easily their common interests and act upon them (see Chapters 6 and 7).

They also live in a world that is not easily scaled down to the level of their daily lives. Proposals for the decentralization of government have come from both the right and the left, but decentralization is neither easily nor fully attainable. Not all problems can be solved by city councils or neighborhood groups. As the political scientist Benjamin Barber recently observed, "There's no question that at the local level democracy works naturally and works well, but it is also the case that we live in a world of institutions and problems that are not only national but also international and interdependent."[3]

A great deal of misplaced romanticism surrounds the concept of democracy. It is not realistic to think that democracy requires individuals to take an active role in all decisions that affect them. Any society of substantial size requires the delegation of broad power and responsibility to a small set of leaders. Yet democracy requires that individuals be something more than subjects of government and followers of leaders.

True citizenship is "public" rather than "private" in nature. The community, not the individual, is the realm of citizenry. Although individualism can heighten self-esteem and personal security, and in this way strengthen the basis of community, individualism can also—as Tocqueville recognized as early as the 1830s—undermine people's sense of community by degenerating into outright selfishness. In addition to its ability to drive people ever deeper into their private affairs, individualism can foster a form of politics in which the chief goal is narrow gain, the public is seen merely in terms of the special interests within it, and the relative strength of the contending interests is regarded as a just basis for public policy (see Chapters 7 and 10).

Thus the sharp rise in interest-group activity since the 1960s is not necessarily an indication of deepening democracy. Although many lobbying groups seek policies that can serve the general interest and actively engage their members in the pursuit of these goals, many others do not. Group membership today is often of the mail-order variety: participation consists of sending money in response to a letter prepared by computer. Moreover, most groups are self-seeking: they aim to promote the narrow interests of their member individuals or firms. Participation in lobbying groups is an essential part of the representational process, but it is not the same thing as active citizenship. There is no genuine sense of "the public" in political participation that is dedicated to the furthering of special interests (see Chapter 10).

Lobbying groups also highlight the gap in the participation rates of rich and poor. Interest-group activity has traditionally been dominated by persons of higher economic status. In recent years there has been a relative decline in the number of groups, such as labor unions, that enroll significant numbers of working-class people, and a relative as well as an absolute increase in the number of groups with a middle-class membership (see Chapter 10). Increasingly, the vote is also dominated by persons with higher levels of income and education; the decline in turnout in recent decades is attributable largely to a sharp drop in participation by those Americans who are in the lowest categories of income and education (see Chapter 7).

Participation differences are part of a widening gap between the poor and the rest of America (see Chapter 19). Although critics of American society with a Marxist or elitist perspective have usually concentrated their attention on the richest 1 or 2 percent of the U.S. population, Karl Marx's collaborator, Friedrich Engels, chose to focus on those at the low end. A century ago, Engels claimed that the most remarkable feature of American society was the optimism and progress of its lower-middle and working classes; unlike their counterparts in other industrialized societies, they were not mired in poverty or trapped in their position. As a result, he concluded, they had no reason for a high degree of class antagonism.

However, in recent years, the position of less affluent Americans has deteriorated in relation to the position of those who are better off. The 1980s saw a widening of the gap between the richest and the poorest Americans. The rate of inflation in the 1980s exceeded the average wage increase among Americans in the bottom fifth income bracket and was only slightly less than the average wage increase among middle-income persons. The Americans who made real progress were those who were already at the top of the income ladder; moreover, the richer they were, the more their income increased during the 1980s.[4]

These disparities are attributable in part to public policy. Changes in the tax laws in the 1980s encouraged American business to engage in a leveraged buyout spree that resulted in the flow of capital into mergers and takeovers rather than new plants and equipment. One aspect of this trend was a decrease in the number of manufacturing jobs and an increase in service jobs, which generally pay much less. The pattern was a historical first; always in the past, newer jobs had paid more than older ones. To make matters worse, the tax codes were changed to shift the tax burden downward. The writer Studs Terkel remarked that the politics of the 1980s taught Americans that "it is good to have sharp elbows."[5]

Public policy is not the only, or even the most important, reason for the declining fortunes of many Americans. Technological and scientific changes threaten to make a permanent underclass of those who cannot meet society's new educational, social, and economic demands (see Chapters 1 and 19). There can be no effective citizenship for individuals who have lost the ability to direct their own lives.

Richard Harwood's study for the Kettering Foundation found that Americans feel politically powerless rather than apathetic. They believe that public policy is important, but they feel that the issues have become so intricate that they cannot understand them and so dominated by special interests that they cannot influence them. They are at a loss to know how to exert influence on the political process, which seems to them to take little notice of their concerns.[6]

The challenge of democracy today, as always, is a matter not of a spontaneous outpouring of civic energy by the masses, but of conditions conducive to civic interest and involvement (see Chapters 3–11). When politics takes on the appearance of a game played among entrepreneurial leaders and the policy process seems designed for the benefit of special interests, democracy will not flourish at any level of society. Indeed, democracy will take on a false character: it will appear to be an issue of what is good for the individual rather than the larger community. A strengthening of democracy can come through attention to those things that, 200 years ago, Thomas Jefferson identified as the proper foundation of public life: sound education, a general prosperity, meaningful work, personal liberty, exemplary leadership, a free and vigorous press, strong face-to-face institutions, a broad sharing of political power, and social tolerance. These are demanding requirements, but democracy is not a trivial pursuit. As the ancient Greeks first recognized, democracy is nothing less than a way of life.

The Challenge of Ideals

For more than 200 years, Americans have been guided by the same set of ideals: liberty, equality, self-government, individualism, diversity, and unity (see Chapter 1). These ideals have challenged each generation, but today, as a result of the complexity and scale of modern government, the challenge has new dimensions.

A crucial difference is that it is no longer so obvious what can be done to achieve a fuller realization of America's traditional ideals. In the past, the question in many cases was not so much what could be done as when and at what cost it would be accomplished. Thus the ink was barely dry on the Constitution before advocates of popular government began their efforts to extend suffrage and to broaden the range of offices filled by popular election (see Chapters 3, 7, and 14). This campaign took 175 years; not until 1965, with the passage of the Voting Rights Act, was it truthful to say that the vote belonged to all Americans (see Chapter 5). Like other developments, such as judicial protection of civil liberties from infringement by the state governments (see Chapter 4), the struggle to extend suffrage met strong resistance but could always claim moral superiority: How could it truly be proclaimed that Americans were a self-governing people when whole groups of them were not allowed to participate in the election of their leaders?

Today it is less clear what might be done to advance America's principles. Consider, for example, the question of self-government. At present the United States holds more public elections than any other country; it is the only country in which the voters regularly choose party nominees through primary elections; and it has laws and procedures that safeguard the right to vote of those who want to exercise it. In view of all this, the question of self-government in America might be thought to be more or less settled. The reality, however, is that self-government is an increasingly difficult challenge, because modern America is more than a representative democracy: it is also a bureaucratic society, a corporate society, a mass-communication society, a scientific-technological society, and more.[7]

Each of these dimensions of contemporary America poses special problems for the practice of self-government. More elections and more voters are not the answer, for example, to the problem of popular control of bureaucratic agencies. What, then, is the answer? The fact is, no one is quite sure. There is agreement on the need to make the bureaucracy more accountable to the people it serves, but there is no agreement on the best way to accomplish this (see Chapter 16).

The complexity and large scale of modern government have also challenged America's ideals by intensifying the conflicts between them. America's principles have never been fully reconcilable with one another. There are, for example, inherent tensions between the ideal of self-government, which implies that the view of the many should prevail over the opinion of the few, and the ideal of liberty, which implies that individuals have rights and interests that must be preserved. Such tensions were formerly eased by the simplicity of society and government. Thus, during the whole of the nineteenth century there was no reason to abridge personal liberty because of threats from foreign powers (see Chapter 4). However, as society has become increasingly interdependent and government increasingly intrusive, conflicts among America's ideals have grown exponentially. For example, each of the many extensions of individual rights in recent years has narrowed the realm of self-government. It is impossible today to set aside an area of individual discretion—that is, to grant or extend a right—without taking power away from the majority. This fact does not necessarily diminish a claim to a particular right, but it does put the claim in perspective: no right is granted without cost to other values. The axiom applies generally to each and all of America's traditional values.

The current challenges to the fuller realization of America's ideals will have to be met under conditions that, in historical perspective, are unfavorable. The advancement of principles such as liberty, equality, and self-government requires that people look beyond their selfish and immediate concerns to the universal and enduring benefits of a society in which power and opportunity are shared by all, not hoarded by those who already possess most of it (see Chapters 1, 3, and 5). This outlook is fostered when people believe that their progress will not be greatly retarded by the progress of others.

In the past, Americans had special advantages that made it easier for them to believe that collective progress was possible. The first of these advantages was the country's open frontier—what the nineteenth-century historian Frederick Jackson Turner called the "Great West."[8] As long as there was abundant cheap land and a shortage of labor in America, there was unbridled opportunity. The second advantage was a result of the timing of America's Industrial Revolution. The industrial age began in the late 1700s in England and spread to western Europe before its major impact was felt in the United States. The delay did not substantially affect prosperity in the United States, because the country was still in the process of westward expansion. However, because of its later start and abundant natural resources, the United States, once industrialization did take firm hold, soon had the most modern and productive industrial sector in the world. The final advantage was provided by the Second World War, which left the industrial capacity of Europe and Japan in ruins. In 1946 the United States, which had emerged from the war with its industrial base intact, was producing more than a third of all goods and services in the world. The result was a level of affluence that no previous society in history had enjoyed.

Since the 1970s, the United States has had to compete on a more nearly equal basis with other highly developed countries. It no longer enjoys an extraordinary advantage, and Americans have struggled economically as they have attempted to adjust to the change (see Chapters 1, 18, and 20). The median family income rose by 89 percent in the twenty years between 1950 and 1970 but by only 13 percent in the twenty-year period from 1970 to 1990.[9]

Widening prosperity lets society avoid making agonizing choices. With the end of the era of fast economic growth in America, however, the future looks less promising than it used to. People now seem more ready to blame others for their problems. Sexual, racial, ethnic, generational, and income conflicts are getting stronger.

This situation is a severe challenge to America's ideals, but also a time when ideals are most needed. It has always been a formidable job to frame society's problems in ways that people can understand and for which they will sacrifice. But societies need ideals. Theodore White said it as well as anyone: "Nations need dreams, goals they seek in common, within which the smaller dreams of individuals can guide their personal lives."[10] Without a governing vision people will lapse, as they have in recent years, into a narrow selfishness. Confronting a similar challenge 200 years ago, the writers of the Constitution plumbed America's ideals in search of a lasting and prosperous union. Today's Americans can do nothing less.

STATE AND LOCAL POLITICS

Before there was an American union, there were the American states. When the Framers of the Constitution gathered in Philadelphia in the summer of 1787, they invented a new form of government—federalism—because the states would not consent to a union that required their elimination (see Chapter 2).

The establishment of the Union meant that the states would have to give up some of their independence. The states did not always do so willingly, as the Civil War and countless lesser disputes over federalism indicate. The cumulative effect of two centuries of federalism, however, has been a gradual diminution of state-to-state differences. In the twentieth century particularly, a "nationalization" of American politics has taken place. Extensions of national power have narrowed the limits within which states can operate (see Chapters 2, 4, 5, 18, and 19).

Despite this development, the state political systems differ in many significant ways. Although Americans, as was indicated in Chapter 1, share a common political heritage that is built around principles such as liberty, equality, and self-government, distinctive regional subcultures persist. These subcultures reflect differences in ethnic settlement patterns, historical episodes, economic conditions, partisan competition, and other influences.

The states in the northern tier of the nation have what the political scientist Daniel Elazar describes as a **moralistic subculture.**[1] This subculture is characterized by an emphasis on "good government" (the public interest), "clean government" (honesty), and "civic government" (public participation). The states that share this subculture were populated primarily by northern Europeans, including the English, Germans, and Scandinavians. Minnesota is an example of a moralistic state; Minnesota has one of the highest rates of voter turnout in the country, one of the lowest rates of political corruption, and a high level of public services, including some of the nation's best public schools.

The middle part of the United States, from Massachusetts to Maryland and then westward through Illinois and Missouri to southwestern states such as Arizona, has an **individualistic subculture.** This subculture is oriented toward private life and economic gain, and politics is largely an extension of this perspective. Political conflict is rough and tumble, political power is closely guarded, and public policy is often narrowly applied. Illinois is an example of an individualistic state and is renowned for the battles between the city of Chicago and the downstate area for political control and policy advantage.

A **traditionalistic subculture,** in Elazar's terms, typifies the states of the old Confederacy and a few states bordering on it, such as West Virginia. This subculture reflects the stratified, plantation society out of which it grew: it is conservative in its focus and elitist in its leadership. The politics of a traditionalistic state is likely to be dominated by a small number of prominent leaders, many of whom have gained power through family ties. Government is likely to be a topic of considerable interest in a traditionalistic state, but not because government is activist. In fact, traditionalists prefer a government that reinforces the existing power structure. Until recent decades, when the influence of suburban Washington brought political change to Virginia, it epitomized the traditionalistic subculture. For years, Virginia politics was controlled by elite families, such as the Byrds, who aimed to preserve the racial, social, and economic hierarchy that had defined Virginia society since the colonial period.

The purpose of this appendix is to describe more fully the American states and the localities that constitute them. The great number of state and local governments, and the variety they exhibit, make difficult an easy summary of what they are all about. Yet there are some general patterns; it is these patterns on which this appendix concentrates. It concludes with a comparison of the states, which will indicate major factors behind differences in their politics and policies. The main points of discussion in this appendix are the following:

- ★ *All states apply the constitutional principle of separation of powers, but the states otherwise differ from one another, and from the federal government, in the way in which they structure their governments.* The use of elections as a means of choosing officials of all types, including judges and lesser executives (for example, state treasurer), is particularly widespread.

- ★ *Local governments are not sovereign; they are chartered by their state government, which sets the limits of their power.* Of the units of local government (county, municipality, school district, and special district), the basic unit is the municipality. A municipality may be governed in one of four ways—the strong mayor–council, weak mayor–council, commission, or city manager system.

- ★ *States and localities have primary responsibility for most of the policies, such as public education, that directly touch Americans' daily lives.* The nature of these policies is affected by the wealth of the state and locality, and also by their political culture, party system, and group system.

States and Localities in the Constitutional System

The Constitution of the United States contains provisions that forbid the states from interfering with the lawful exercise of national authority, and the states are required by the Constitution to provide their citizens with a "republican" form of government. The Constitution also guarantees that each state will have equal representation in the U.S. Senate. Nevertheless, the Constitution was intended primarily to define national power and national institutions and does not say very much about the states or their powers.

In fact, the Framers of the Constitution did not believe it was necessary to define the powers of the states. They held that the Constitution implied that the states held all legitimate governing powers not granted to the national government. This situation was unsettling to states'-rights advocates, who insisted upon a constitutional amendment—the Tenth—which reserves for the states those powers not delegated to the national government (see Chapter 2).

The states have their own constitutions, which vary greatly in length. On average, they are roughly four times the length of the U.S. Constitution. Vermont is the only state whose constitution is shorter than the nation's. Until it was replaced in 1974, Louisiana's constitution was by far the longest and most detailed. At 250,000 words, it was nearly thirty times the length of the U.S. Constitution. The longest state constitution still in effect today is Alabama's, which has approximately 175,000 words and more than 500 amendments.

State constitutions contain many provisions that more properly belong in statutes than in a constitution. Enterprising state legislators have often preferred to embed their favorite policies in constitutional amendments, which are harder to change than ordinary laws. For example, many of the state constitutions include benefits for special-interest groups, such as veterans, farmers, and businesses. Minnesota's constitution was amended in the early 1970s to permit the state to give each Vietnam veteran from the state a $600 bonus. California's constitution is filled with all sorts of tax provisions, which, among other things, limit the types and amount of taxation.

Most constitutional scholars would agree that the length of state constitutions is a drawback. As we indicated in Chapter 2, the U.S. Constitution is a sparsely worded document, which has enabled succeeding generations to adapt it to their changing needs. Not so with many of the state constitutions. They are so loaded down with narrow and detailed provisions that they deny policymakers the flexibility to respond effectively to change. The constitutional provisions that bestow benefits on interest groups, for example, do more than confer a special status on a particular group; they also bind the subsequent decisions of policymakers.[2]

Each state's constitution is its supreme law, except where valid national law applies. By the same token, local laws (called ordinances) cannot legitimately conflict with a state's constitution. Local governments are not sovereign. Their authority derives from the state's. The century-old general principle that describes the relationship between state power and localities is called **Dillon's rule.**[3] It holds that local governments are creatures of their state, which in theory even has the power to abolish them. The forced consolidation of school districts and the forced merger of a smaller town with a larger adjoining one are dramatic examples of a state's power over its local units. The most important aspect of Dillon's rule is that local governments must act within constraints placed on them by the state. The state's reach extends even to the issue of whether a local unit of government will provide a particular service. The state of Wisconsin, for example, requires each of its cities to have a solid-waste disposal facility.

States differ markedly in the degree of freedom they grant their local units. The states that grant the highest degree of autonomy to local units, and those which grant the least, are found in all regions of the country. For example, Oregon, North Carolina, and Connecticut rank high on local autonomy, while Idaho, Mississippi, and Massachusetts rank low.

The chief instrument by which a state governs its local units is the **charter.** No local government can exist without a charter, which is issued by the state and defines the limits within which a local unit must operate. By tradition, local charters are restrictive; they spell out in considerable detail what a local government can and cannot do. A typical charter, for example, specifies the types and limits of taxation that a local government may impose on its residents.

There are limits, however, to a state's ability to control its local units. A state government does not have the time, the money, or the staff to make all the decisions concerning its many local units. Nor can a state expect the same restrictions to work equally well for all local units. A charter that is suited to a city of a million inhabitants would probably not be suited to a village of several hundred people. Accordingly, all states give their local units some discretionary authority and make allowance for differences among them. In most cases, the charters for cities are different from those for towns, which in turn differ from those for villages.

Home rule is a device that is designed to give local governments more leeway in their policies. Home rule was first tried in 1875 in Missouri, and it allows a local government to design its own charter, subject to the laws and constitution of the state and also subject to veto by the state. The long-term trend in the states has been toward home rule and other means of granting localities a larger measure of independence.

State Political Structures

All states make use of the principle of checks and balances that underpins the national government (see Chapter 3). There is nothing in the Constitution of the United States that would prohibit a state from adopting a parliamentary form of government, but no state has tried it. The executive, legislative, and judiciary in each state are separate branches that share power. Each branch thus serves as a check on the power of the others.

THE EXECUTIVE BRANCH

Most states wrote their first constitutions during periods when mistrust of executive authority was high; consequently, they provided for relatively weak governors. The model still applies in some states, especially in the South and in New England. In these states, governors are limited in their powers or in the length of their term. North Carolina's governor, for example, does not have the power to veto legislation. The governor of Vermont is elected for a term of only two years. Kentucky's 1891 constitution limits its governor to a single four-year term.

The organization of the executive branch in many states reflects the influence of the Progressives and other popularly based movements. In a number of states, the voters choose one or more of the following executive officials: education commissioner, agriculture commissioner, and public utilities commissioner. Moreover, more than half the states hold separate elections for the offices of secretary of state, attorney general, and treasurer. In other words, the executive office in most states, unlike the presidency, is not unified. The governor is the chief executive but shares executive power with other officials, who have separate electoral bases and who, in some cases, are of the opposite party. In only two states, Maine and New Jersey, is the governor, like the president at the national level, the sole chief executive.

Although the governorship is not a very powerful office in most states, governors have gained power in recent decades.[4] Just as the complexity of modern government has led to an increase in presidential authority (see Chapter 14), it has contributed to an increase in the authority of governors. The initiation of the state budget now resides with the legislature or an independent board rather than the governor in only a handful of states. In forty-three states, the governor even has a line-item veto, which allows the option of rejecting a part of an appropriations bill without voiding the whole act.

Of the executive officials other than governor, the most powerful is the attorney general, who is elected to the post in forty-three states. The attorney general is the state's chief legal officer and sets priorities for legal action. An attorney general might decide, for example, to concentrate the state's legal resources on environmental protection or investigations of alleged political corruption. The office of attorney general has often been a stepping stone to a governorship or a seat in the U.S. Senate.

THE LEGISLATIVE BRANCH

Like the U.S. Congress, state legislatures are bicameral except in the case of Nebraska's, which is unicameral. In the large majority of states, the two chambers are called the house and the senate.

Like Congress, state legislatures have within their authority the most impressive array of constitutional powers that a democracy can bestow. The legislatures make the laws, appropriate the money, define the structure of the executive and the judiciary, oversee the operations of the other branches, and represent the people. These powers are typically carried out within an organizational structure similar to that of Congress (see Chapter 12). The top leadership in state legislatures are the party leaders, but most of the work is carried out in committees.

For a long period, state legislatures were synonymous with malapportionment. Cities were grossly underrepresented because rural legislators, who had controlled the state legislatures since the days when the United States was a farming nation, refused to reapportion them. Vermont was the extreme case. From 1793 to the 1960s, its legislative distribution did not change. In the state's lower house, each village, town, or city had one representative, regardless of population. Thus, the city of Burlington had exactly the same voting power as the smallest village in the state. Not surprisingly, the policy needs of America's cities were neglected by state legislatures, while the interests of farmers and rural communities were quite well served.

The situation changed abruptly in the early 1960s when the Supreme Court of the United States declared that state legislatures must represent people rather than communities or areas.[5] The "one person, one vote" method of apportioning state legislatures immediately gave a larger share of legislative seats to populated urban areas—although, ironically, the cities never got their full due. By the time the Supreme Court outlawed malapportionment in the 1960s, so many people had moved out of the central cities that the suburbs gained the most advantage from reapportionment. The suburbs, like the rural areas, are more conservative and more Republican than the cities; thus, there has never been a time when the concerns of cities have dominated the actions of state legislatures.

Until recently, most of the state legislatures were relatively unimposing institutions. They were in session only for short periods each year, were deficient in staff and information resources, and were vulnerable to powerful lobbying groups. Beginning in the 1960s, however, they began to meet for longer periods and to expand their staffs. Legislators' pay also increased significantly at this time. The increase was substantial enough in a few states, such as New York and California, to create professional legislators—individuals whose chief occupation is an elective position within a state legislature. New York provides the highest level of compensation; its legislators are paid nearly $60,000 a year in salary. Many of them also hold party or committee leadership positions, for which they receive supplementary allowances (nicknamed "lulus" because they are fixed amounts paid "in lieu of" reimbursement for actual expenses).

Most analysts have welcomed the change toward more professional state legislatures. The Advisory Commission on Intergovernmental Relations, an agency established by Congress, noted in one of its reports: "Today's state legislatures are more functional, accountable, independent, and representative, and are equipped with greater information handling capacity than their predecessors."[6]

Some states, however, have resisted the tendency toward longer sessions, larger staffs, and higher salaries. New Hampshire, Rhode Island, Alabama, Nebraska, and West Virginia are among the states that pay their legislators $10,000 a year or less. The term-limitation movement that is currently under way (see Chapter 3) could restore the "citizen legislature." California, Oklahoma, and Colorado led the move when their voters decided in 1990 to restrict the number of terms that state legislators could serve. Additional states adopted the policy in 1992 and 1994. Supporters of term limitation argue that "amateur" legislators are more responsive to the public they serve than are long-term incumbents.

THE JUDICIAL BRANCH

As a consequence of America's federal system, as we indicated in Chapter 17, each state has its separate court system. Like the federal system, the state systems have trial courts at the bottom level and appellate courts at the top. About two-thirds of the states have two appellate levels, and the other third have only a single appellate court. Most of the less populated states have determined that they do not need a second appellate level.

The states vary in the way they organize and label their courts. Most of the states have district courts and a supreme court, but the states tend also to give some lower courts specialized titles and jurisdictions. Family courts, for example, settle such issues as divorce and child-custody disputes, and probate courts handle the disposition of the estates of people who have died. Below such specialized trial courts are less formal trial courts, such as magistrate courts and justice of the peace courts. They handle a variety of minor cases, such as traffic infractions, and usually do not use a jury. Jury trial is not a constitutional requirement of the states, nor do they have to follow the federal tradition of a twelve-member jury or require a unanimous verdict when a jury is used.

States also vary in their methods of selecting judges. In about a fourth of the states, judges are appointed by the governor, but in most states, judgeships are elective offices. Several states use the Missouri Plan (so called because Missouri was the first state to use it), under which a judicial selection commission provides a short list of acceptable candidates from which the governor selects one; after a trial period of a year or more, the judge selected must be approved by the electorate in a yes-no vote in order to serve a longer term.

State courts are undeniably important. As we indicated in Chapter 17, there is a "federal court myth" which holds that the federal courts are the more significant component of the American judicial system. In fact, the state judiciary is the locus of most court action. Upward of 95 percent of the nation's legal cases are decided in state courts (or local courts, which are agents of the states). Moreover, nearly all cases that originate in state courts also end there; the federal courts never enter the picture. Of course, one federal court—the Supreme Court—is a silent partner of the state and local courts, requiring them to act within minimum standards of justice (for example, the prohibition of forced confessions).

Most states have made efforts in recent decades to raise the performance level of their court systems. Administrative and legal procedures have been changed, for example, to expedite the handling of cases. In the past, the pursuit of justice in many state courts was slow and procedurally arbitrary. There are still delays and procedural injustices, but they are less prevalent today as a result of federally imposed standards and state-initiated reforms, such as those which require law enforcement officials to dismiss a case unless it is presented to a judge or grand jury within a specified period of time.

THE STATE ELECTORAL PROCESS

When the Framers wrote the U.S. Constitution, they allowed for only minimal popular participation. The House of Representatives was the only popularly elected institution and the only one with a short term of office, two years. The democratic spirit of the Revolution of 1776 was more apparent at the state level. Every state but South Carolina held an annual legislative election, and several states chose their governors through annual election by the people.

Today, the states hold elections less frequently, but they have stayed ahead of the federal government in their emphasis on elections as a means of popular influence and control. As was noted previously, most states elect their treasurer, attorney general, and secretary of state by popular ballot. Many states also choose their judges by direct election. No federal judges are chosen by this means.

Citizens as Legislators

State voters also get the opportunity to vote directly on issues of policy. In all states except Delaware, amendments to the state constitution require the approval of the electorate. In addition, more than a third of the states give popular majorities the power of the **initiative,** which allows citizens through signature petitions to place legislative measures on the ballot. If such a measure receives a majority vote, it becomes law, just as if it had been enacted by the state's legislature. A related measure is the **referendum,** which permits the legislature to submit proposals to the voters for approval or rejection. The initiative and referendum were introduced around 1900 as Progressive reforms. The Progressives also sought to protect the public from wayward state and local officials through the **recall,** in which citizens can petition for the removal from office of an elected official before the scheduled completion of his or her term. The state of Arizona would probably have recalled its governor, Evan Mecham, in 1987 had he not been impeached by the state legislature before the recall process could be completed.

Voter Registration and Turnout

Although the states have been electoral innovators, their history also includes attempts to restrict access to the ballot. The clearest example is that of southern states after the Civil War. The Fifteenth Amendment was ratified in 1870, prohibiting states from using race as the basis for denial of suffrage. Southern states responded with a number of devices that were designed to keep African Americans from voting. Through poll taxes, the grandfather clause, whites-only primary elections, and rigged literacy tests as a qualification for registration to vote, blacks in many areas of the South were effectively disenfranchised.[7]

Action by the national government was necessary to bring a halt to state efforts to disenfranchise large groups of voters (see Chapter 5). Major steps included a Supreme Court decision outlawing whites-only primaries, a constitutional amendment barring poll taxes, and the Voting Rights Act of 1965, which forbids discrimination in voting and registration. However, the legacy of a century of state-supported efforts to keep blacks and poor whites from voting in the South is still evident. The region has the lowest voter turnout rate in the country. By comparison, states such as Minnesota, Wisconsin, and Idaho, which have pioneered methods designed to encourage voting, such as election-day registration, are among the leaders in voter turnout.

The decline in voter turnout in presidential and congressional elections in recent decades (see Chapter 7) has also been characteristic of state elections. The average turnout in gubernatorial elections that do not coincide with a presidential election, for example, is less than 40 percent—a drop of several percentage points since the early 1960s.[8]

Local Political Structures

If the significance of a level of government was determined strictly on the basis of numbers, the local level would win handily. The United States has one national government and fifty state governments, but it has more than 80,000 local governments, which include counties, municipalities, school districts, and special districts, such as water, sewage, and conservation districts.

Local government is the source of most public employment. Compared with fewer than 3 million federal workers and 4 million state employees, more than 8 million people work in local government. They are one of the most heavily unionized groups in the country. Schoolteachers are represented through the American Federation of Teachers (AFT) and the National Education Association (NEA), and other local public employees are represented through such unions as the International Association of Fire Fighters (IAFF) and the American Federation of State, County, and Municipal Employees (AFSCME). These unions have more than 3 million members, and they have been quite successful in obtaining better working conditions and job benefits for their members.

COUNTY GOVERNMENT

The oldest form of local government in the United States is the county, and it remains a top local governing unit in rural areas and in those few states, such as New York, where the county has broad responsibility for providing government services. The county is governed through an elected county commission (which, in some states, is called a county legislature or board of supervisors). In most states, there are also elected county sheriffs and county attorneys, and a few states have elected chief county executives.

In most states, the county functions as an administrative subdivision of the state. The county's responsibility is to carry out programs, such as highway maintenance or welfare services, that are established by the state. Some analysts believe that the county will increase in importance in upcoming years because of the prominence of issues, such as waste disposal, that cannot be addressed adequately at the municipal level but require a regional response.

MUNICIPAL GOVERNMENT

In most parts of the United States, the major unit of local government is the municipality, which can be a city, town, or village. Municipalities exist partly to carry out activities of the state government, but they also serve their residents directly: most Americans depend on their municipal governments for law enforcement, water, and sanitation services.

The traditional and most common form of municipal government is the mayor-council system, which includes the mayor as the chief executive and the local council as the legislative body. The mayor–council system takes two forms. The more common form is the **strong mayor–council system,** in which the mayor has the veto power and a prescribed responsibility for budgetary and other policy actions. The mayor, rather than the council, is the more powerful policymaker. The alternative is the **weak mayor–council system,** in which the mayor's policymaking powers are less substantial than the council's. The mayor has no power to veto the council's actions and often has no formal role in such activities as budget making.

A different type of municipal government entirely is the **commission system.** This form invests executive and legislative authority in a commission, with each commissioner serving as a member of the local council but also having a specified executive role, such as police commissioner or public works commissioner. The commission system has lost favor in recent decades. Its major weakness is that it has no chief executive with the power and responsibility to set the local government's overall direction.

A final type of municipal government is the **city manager system,** which was pioneered in Ohio during the Progressive era as a reaction against inefficiency and partisan corruption in many of the nation's cities. The system entrusts the executive role to a professionally trained manager, who is chosen, and can be fired, by the city council. This arrangement ensures that the manager will be at least somewhat responsive to political and popular pressures.

Most city managers have specialized university training in the operation of municipal government, so they bring expertise to their position. However, the city manager may be an outsider who does not have the political support that is required for major undertakings. Most of the larger cities that installed the city manager system have since reverted to the mayor-council system, but the city manager form is the most common type of government in smaller cities.

A local chief executive, whether a mayor or city manager, is, above all, an administrator whose main responsibility is to oversee the work of the component units of local government—the police, fire, sanitation, and other departments. Increasingly, local chief executives are also expected to provide economic leadership by fostering a business climate that will keep old firms in the community and attract new ones. In many cities, including Baltimore, San Antonio, and Minneapolis, mayors have played key roles in the revitalization of downtown areas. Of course, not all chief executives accomplish much, or even get the opportunity. In smaller towns and villages particularly, the position of mayor is often more honorary than active; it is a part-time position held by a trusted member of the community.

SCHOOL DISTRICTS

The tradition of local public schools is deeply embedded in the American political experience. Unlike Europe, where private schools and national educational standards have historically been more important, the United States has emphasized public education and local control. This control is exercised through local school boards. In a few places the school board is subordinate to the municipal government, but elsewhere it is an independent body. School policy is established by the local board rather than by the local mayor or council. The chief executive of the local public school system is a specially trained professional, the superintendent of schools.

SPECIAL DISTRICTS

A final form of municipal government, and one of increasing importance, is the special district. As society has become more complex and interdependent, a need has arisen for local governing institutions that are responsive to the resulting policy needs. Special districts that deal with such policy areas as water supply, soil conservation, and waste disposal are an answer. These districts also provide an answer to the problem of coordinating the efforts of independent municipal governments. Issues such as pollution control are not easily addressed within a single community. Special districts bring municipalities together; the typical form of governance of these district is a board that includes a member from each municipality within the district's boundaries.

LOCAL ELECTIONS

The principle of elective office dominates local government. In addition to an elected mayor, most communities have an elected town or city council. The office of county commissioner is also an elective office throughout the country. Except in a few eastern states, local officials are chosen in nonpartisan elections; no party labels appear on the ballot.

Perhaps no local institution symbolizes the nature of American democracy better than the public schools. School board members are elected and, in many communities, the voters even have the opportunity to approve or reject school budgets and bonding proposals. In contrast, school officials in European countries are typically appointed to their positions, and school budgets are set primarily by national governments.

Voting in local elections is subject to state registration laws. However, as we saw in Chapter 7, many local governments have tried to weaken the link between their level of government and the state and national levels by scheduling local elections for odd-numbered years rather than the even-numbered ones during which all federal and most state elections are held. A predictable effect of this scheduling is that voter turnout is somewhat lower at each level than would be the case if national, state, and local elections were held simultaneously. The average turnout in local elections in most states is very low—30 percent or less. Turnout figures can be deceptive, however. There are countless instances of extraordinary turnout in local elections when a contentious issue is on the ballot. School bonding proposals, for example, often produce a high turnout.

State and Local Policy

Through the Tenth Amendment the states possess what is sometimes called the **police power,** a term that refers to the broad power of government to regulate the health, safety, and morals of the citizenry. Possession of this power has meant that the American states carry out many of the policy responsibilities that in other countries are dealt with at the national level. Law enforcement, public education, public health, and roads are among the policy areas that are defined largely by the state and local governments.

Although the policies enacted by Congress get more attention from the press, the acts of state legislatures have more influence on the day-to-day lives of most Americans. For example, most crimes are defined by state law, most criminal acts are investigated by authorities operating under state law, most trials take place under state law, and most prisoners are held in penitentiaries and jails that operate under laws enacted by state legislatures.

One way to see how the states use their power is to rank policy areas by level of spending. The top spending category for the states is public welfare, followed by public education, health and hospitals, and highways. These four areas are by far the most significant components of state spending. There is a large dropoff in spending between the fourth category, highways, and the fifth one, police.

The policy priorities of local governments are less easily described. Some local units, such as school boards, operate in only one policy area. Municipalities vary in size from the largest cities to the smallest villages, and their policies differ accordingly. Despite such differences, a few patterns to local spending are discernible. Far and away the biggest expense for local governments is public education; it accounts for more than 40 percent of all spending at the local level. Health and hospital spending ranks second at roughly 10 percent. Welfare, roads, and law enforcement follow, in that order.

A brief description of some of the policy activities of state and local governments, and where they get the money to pay for these activities, will provide a broader perspective on the role of states and localities in the American system.

STATE AND LOCAL POLICY PRIORITIES

Education

Public education, including primary schools, secondary schools, and colleges and universities, accounts for the largest share of combined state and local spending, about a third of the total. Education spending by state and local governments dwarfs that of the federal government—more than 90 percent to less than 10 percent. Even higher education is mainly a state and local responsibility, which means that the greatest share of the country's investment in the technical research and personnel that underpin the economy is provided by subnational governments. They also make the key substantive policy decisions in the education area, from curriculum to performance standards to length of schooling.

Of the many issues affecting public education in the states, two have stood out in recent years. One is the disparity in spending among school districts, which, in most instances, reflects differences in communities' wealth. Suburban schools, for example, are typically better funded and have better facilities than the inner-city schools in the same metropolitan area. Should such differences be allowed? In a 1976 Texas case, the Supreme Court concluded that a state has no obligation to provide students with an equal education: its obligation is "to provide an 'adequate' education for all children."[9] Nevertheless, state financial contributions to local schools are typically designed to help poorer districts more than wealthier ones. This tendency, however, does not begin to offset the disparity in the quality of schools between a state's poorest communities and its richest ones.

The other conspicuous education issue is the quality of American schools (see Chapter 19). The performance of U.S. students on standardized tests such as the SATs has declined in recent decades, and some analysts claim that American public schools are not providing the quality of education that is found in Japan and western Europe. The situation has provoked ongoing heated disputes over merit pay for teachers, national tests for all students, and parent-student choice of schools.

Welfare Assistance

The most expensive social welfare program in the United States is entirely a national one—social security for retirees. However, the states are vitally involved in the provision of most welfare services, particularly public assistance programs for the needy (see Chapter 19). Programs such as AFDC, Medicaid, and food stamps operate within federal guidelines, but the states have discretionary authority over benefit and eligibility levels. These programs are funded jointly by the state and national governments and are administered primarily by the state governments. They have the local offices that are necessary for administering need-based welfare programs, which, as we noted in Chapter 19, require regular contacts between caseworkers and welfare recipients.

Welfare programs account for about 15 percent of all state and local spending. This spending and the American tradition of self-reliance make welfare an ongoing political issue. The states have devised various ways of holding down spending. In response to the rapid increase in Medicaid costs, for example, the state of Oregon conducted a systematic study of medical procedures in order to identify, and make ineligible for Medicaid reimbursement, those procedures which physicians apply electively.

Health and Hospitals

About 10 percent of state and local expenditures are in the health and hospitals policy area. All states and many localities operate public hospitals, and most of the laws and regulations affecting medical practices are established by state governments. In addition, states and localities have public health programs such as immunization campaigns, mobile x-ray units, and health inspections of motels and restaurants.

Highways

Until the 1950s the roadways of America were built almost entirely with state and local funds. The interstate highway system was begun in the 1950s and was funded largely by the national government. Today, Washington provides about a third of the total spending on highways, and states and localities contribute the rest. State and local governments set most policies governing use of highways, including traffic infractions and shipping methods. Highway spending accounts for about 8 percent of state and local expenditures.

Police

Some democracies have a national police force, but the United States does not. It has local and state police forces. They enforce state laws and local ordinances, which collectively govern most aspects of crime and punishment. The state police include the highway patrol, game wardens, prison guards, and liquor control officers, and they are generally well trained and highly professional. Local police are less specialized, are more uneven in their training and professionalism, and are required to do most of the "dirty" work of law enforcement—crime control and the maintenance of public order. Roughly 5 percent of state and local spending is for police-related activities.

THE ECONOMICS OF STATE AND LOCAL POLICY

The federal government raises more tax revenues than do all fifty states and the thousands of local governments combined. Although states and localities have a substantial tax base, they are in an inherently competitive situation. People and businesses faced with state or local tax increases can move to another state or locality where taxes are lower. Between the 1960s and 1980s, there was a substantial movement of business firms from the Northeast and Midwest to the South and Southwest. These firms were lured by the cheaper labor and lower energy costs of the sunbelt, and also by the lower tax rates of southern states.

Local governments are also in a relatively weak tax position. They compete with one another for the jobs and income that business firms represent. Every city of any size in the United States offers tax breaks or other incentives to companies that might relocate there. The predatory nature of the competition makes it difficult for any locality to raise its tax rate substantially and virtually forces them to give tax breaks to firms that could well afford to pay.

The major sources of state revenue are sales taxes, corporate income taxes, personal income taxes, and user fees, such as motor vehicle licenses and hunting and fishing licenses. There are, however, substantial variations in the taxing policies of the states. A few states have no personal income tax. South Dakota is one of these states. It also has no corporate income tax. Not surprisingly, South Dakota has one of the lowest levels of public services in the nation. Its neighboring state of Minnesota, for example, spends substantially more per capita on public education than does South Dakota.

The sales tax is the chief source of revenue for the states, accounting for about half of all taxes they raise. The sales tax is a flat-rate tax on consumer goods and thereby places a relatively heavy burden on lower-income persons, who spend a higher proportion of their income on such goods than do upper-income persons. The regressive nature of the sales tax has been a source of criticism, and some states exempt food and medicine from the sales tax in order to relieve somewhat the burden it places on lower-income people. Nevertheless, the sales tax is a reliable method of raising large sums of money, and the states have increasingly used it to obtain their revenues.

Local governments rely primarily on the property tax for their revenues. This form of taxation accounts for nearly half of all revenues raised directly by local government, but it has drawbacks. It is paid, for example, in a lump sum, which heightens taxpayers' awareness of its cost and leads them to resist any increase. Accordingly, localities have turned increasingly to sales taxes (shared with the state and collected with the state's permission) and local income taxes (collected with the state's permission). The revenues from these sources increase automatically when the economy expands, thus providing localities with increased revenues without a raise in the tax rate.

States and localities also depend on revenues provided by other governments. About 15 percent of state revenues are provided by federal grant-in-aid programs, while local governments get about 30 percent of their revenues from the state and 5 percent from Washington. The states and localities also benefit from federal spending. The states of the South and West, particularly, owe many of their jobs to federal programs. In Hawaii, for example, 30,000 active U.S. military personnel are stationed at bases that include Pearl Harbor (navy), Schofield Barracks (army), and Hickam Field (air force.)

Federal grants-in-aid and other federal policies tend to reduce the importance of state-to-state differences in wealth as a factor in state and local policies. Federal assistance is targeted disproportionately for less affluent states and communities. In addition, many federal programs require matching grants and uniform standards of participating states. However, the leveling effect of this federal policy is not very great, and states differ enormously in their economic wealth. The level of public services in all areas—education, welfare, health, and so on—is higher in wealthier states. In comparison with the five poorest states (Mississippi, West Virginia, Utah, Arkansas, and South Carolina), the five wealthiest states (Connecticut, New Jersey, Alaska, Massachusetts, and New York) spend about $400 more per capita on public education each year.[10]

Some analysts have concluded that economics, not politics, is the chief determinant of a state's public policies. Whether that observation is literally true, there is no question that the wealth of a state has a great influence on its policies. In the early 1980s, the states were beneficiaries of a sharp upturn in the national economy. As corporate and personal incomes rose, so did the tax revenues flowing into the state treasuries. Policy initiatives flowed from the states, which seemed especially adept at combining programs designed to stimulate economic development with programs designed to tighten fiscal responsibility.

Innovative governors were leaders of the change. Their experimental economic and social programs, from technological development to welfare reform, were widely publicized.[11] An example was the so-called Massachusetts Miracle. In Boston and the surrounding area, dozens of high-technology firms sprang up almost overnight, creating unprecedented prosperity for the state. Its governor, Michael Dukakis, was given much of the credit for the economic boom. He was voted the nation's most effective governor by the other governors, which contributed to the political reputation that helped him gain the Democratic party's 1988 presidential nomination.

By 1990, however, many of the states were in trouble. More than half had budget deficits and faced the prospect of service cuts and tax increases. Many states faced serious long-term economic problems in the form of declining industries and strong foreign competitors. All the states had no choice but to cut back on either their plans or their programs; they had no money for significant new initiatives.

This situation also encouraged states to develop new approaches in areas such as health and welfare policy. Led once again by innovative governors, such as Wisconsin's Tommy Thompson, the states devised programs that were more efficient and in many instances more effective than the previous ones. By 1995, the state capitals had clearly eclipsed Washington as a source of policy ideas. This realization encouraged Congress to shift additional policy responsibilities to the states through, for example, the expanded use of block grants (see Chapter 2).

THE POLITICS OF STATE AND LOCAL POLICY

If general economic conditions and the wealth of a state have a powerful impact on policy, so does the nature of a state's politics. The states vary significantly in their support for one major party or the other. Where the Republicans are stronger, as in the Mountain states, taxes and the quality of public services tend to be lower. Where Democrats are stronger, as in the Northeast, the reverse situation tends to predominate.

The intensity of party competition has a somewhat less obvious, but no less important, relationship to public policy. In states where party competition is weak, politics tends to be somewhat exclusive: a sizable share of the population, usually the poorest groups, will be more or less ignored by government. The dominant party has gained control without the help of these groups, and the minority party could not gain control even with their help. In other words, neither party has a strong incentive to seek their vote. The classic case of a neglected public was the black community in the South in the period before the modern civil rights movement of the 1950s and 1960s. African Americans were politically powerless. Neither the white Democrats who ran the South nor the white Republicans who offered token opposition had a real interest in bringing black people into their coalition.

Where party competition is more intense, any sizable group in a state is likely to receive the attention of one party or the other and thus to be in a position to influence public policy. In the modern South, which is increasingly competitive between the parties, black voters are a growing force and have tipped the balance in some elections. They are also more likely than at any time in the past to have policy influence.

Interest-group systems can be looked at in a similar way. In those states where interest groups are many in number and somewhat evenly balanced in their political resources, public policy tends to serve a broad range of interests. An example is the state of New York, which has many competing factions, including, for example, business and labor, the upstate and downstate areas, and environmentalists and developers. Almost any legislation that makes it through the New York state legislature requires negotiation among numerous groups.

In states where a particular group or interest is dominant, however, government tends to serve that group or interest above all others. A classic example was the Anaconda Copper Company in Montana, which, during the period that it accounted for nearly all the state's mining and manufacturing, nearly ran the state. A more recent example is the influence of the Church of Latter-Day Saints in Utah. The large share of the state's residents are Mormons, and a policy alternative that is actively opposed by the church has almost no chance of becoming law. Thus, the church for years opposed the sale of hard liquor in Utah, and such sales were prohibited by law. The law was changed recently, but only after Mormon leaders agreed not to oppose the change, which was prompted by the state's desire to improve its ability to attract conventions and perhaps a future Winter Olympics.

Utah with its Mormon population is one of the most distinctive states in the union, but every state has its special characteristics. California is no more like Mississippi than Mississippi is like Rhode Island. Yet, as we have seen, the American states also have many things in common. The differences and similarities among the states are testimony to the enduring nature of the American governing experiment. The states are different enough to provide their residents with a special identity and a special political experience; yet they are alike enough to allow the triumph of the national union that the Framers so keenly envisioned 200 years ago.

Summary

Although developments in the twentieth century have narrowed the differences among the American states, they, and the localities that govern under their authority, remain distinctive and vital systems of government.

All states apply the constitutional principle of separate branches sharing power, but the structure of the state governments differs in some respects from that of the federal government. An example is the more widespread use of elections at the state level. Most states elect by popular vote their judges and a number of executives, including an attorney general and treasurer in addition to a governor. Through the initiative and the referendum, nearly all states also allow their residents to vote directly on issues of policy.

Local governments are chartered by the state. They are not sovereign governments, but most states have chosen to grant local units a considerable level of policymaking discretion. Local governments include counties, municipalities, school districts, and special districts. Of these, the independent school district is the most distinctively American institution, but the municipality is the primary governing unit. Municipalities are governed by one of four types of systems: the strong mayor–council system, the weak mayor–council system, the commission system, or the city manager system.

The states and localities have primary responsibility for most of the public policies that directly touch Americans' daily lives. For example, the major share of legislation devoted to public education and about 90 percent of the funding for it are provided by the states and localities. Public welfare, public health, roads, and police are other policy areas dominated by these subnational governments. They do not, however, have the amount of revenue that is available to the federal government; competition between them holds down their taxing capacity. Their policies are also conditioned by the wealth of the state or locality, and by the structure of its party and interest group systems.

Major Concepts

charter
city manager system
commission system
Dillon's rule
home rule
individualistic subculture
initiative
moralistic subculture
police power
recall
referendum
strong mayor–council system
traditionalistic subculture
weak mayor–council system

THE DECLARATION OF INDEPENDENCE

In Congress, July 4, 1776,

THE UNANIMOUS DECLARATION
OF THE THIRTEEN UNITED
STATES OF AMERICA

When, in the course of human events, it becomes necessary for one people to dissolve the political bands which have connected them with another, and to assume, among the powers of the earth, the separate and equal station to which the laws of nature and of nature's God entitle them, a decent respect to the opinions of mankind requires that they should declare the causes which impel them to the separation.

We hold these truths to be self-evident, that all men are created equal; that they are endowed by their Creator with certain unalienable rights; that among these, are life, liberty, and the pursuit of happiness. That, to secure these rights, governments are instituted among men, deriving their just powers from the consent of the governed; that, whenever any form of government becomes destructive of these ends, it is the right of the people to alter or to abolish it, and to institute a new government, laying its foundation on such principles, and organizing its powers in such form, as to them shall seem most likely to effect their safety and happiness. Prudence, indeed, will dictate that governments long established, should not be changed for light and transient causes; and, accordingly, all experience hath shown, that mankind are more disposed to suffer, while evils are sufferable, than to right themselves by abolishing the forms to which they are accustomed. But, when a long train of abuses and usurpations, pursuing invariably the same object, evinces a design to reduce them under absolute despotism, it is their right, it is their duty, to throw off such government and to provide new guards for their future security. Such has been the patient sufferance of these colonies, and such is now the necessity which constrains them to alter their former systems of government. The history of the present King of Great Britain is a history of repeated injuries and usurpations, all having, in direct object, the establishment of an absolute tyranny over these States. To prove this, let facts be submitted to a candid world:

He has refused his assent to laws the most wholesome and necessary for the public good.

He has forbidden his governors to pass laws of immediate and pressing importance, unless suspended in their operation till his assent should be obtained; and, when so suspended, he has utterly neglected to attend to them.

He has refused to pass other laws for the accommodation of large districts of people, unless those people would relinquish the right of representation in the legislature; a right inestimable to them, and formidable to tyrants only.

He has called together legislative bodies at places unusual, uncomfortable, and distant from the depository of their public records, for the sole purpose of fatiguing them into compliance with his measures.

He has dissolved representative houses repeatedly for opposing, with manly firmness, his invasions on the rights of the people.

He has refused, for a long time after such dissolutions, to cause others to be elected; whereby the legislative powers, incapable of annihilation, have returned to the people at large for their exercise; the state remaining, in the meantime, exposed to all the danger of invasion from without, and convulsions within.

He has endeavored to prevent the population of these States; for that purpose, obstructing the laws for naturalization of foreigners, refusing to pass others to encourage their migration hither, and raising the conditions of new appropriations of lands.

He has obstructed the administration of justice, by refusing his assent to laws for establishing judiciary powers.

He has made judges dependent on his will alone, for the tenure of their offices, and the amount and payment of their salaries.

He has erected a multitude of new offices, and sent hither swarms of officers to harass our people, and eat out their substance.

He has kept among us, in time of peace, standing armies, without the consent of our legislatures.

He has affected to render the military independent of, and superior to, the civil power.

He has combined, with others, to subject us to a jurisdiction foreign to our Constitution, and unacknowledged by our laws; giving his assent to their acts of pretended legislation:

For quartering large bodies of armed troops among us:

For protecting them by a mock trial, from punishment, for any murders which they should commit on the inhabitants of these States:

For cutting off our trade with all parts of the world:

For imposing taxes on us without our consent:

For depriving us, in many cases, of the benefit of trial by jury:

For transporting us beyond seas to be tried for pretended offences:

For abolishing the free system of English laws in a neighboring province, establishing therein an arbitrary government, and enlarging its boundaries, so as to render it at once an example and fit instrument for introducing the same absolute rule into these colonies:

For taking away our charters, abolishing our most valuable laws, and altering, fundamentally, the powers of our governments:

For suspending our own legislatures, and declaring themselves invested with power to legislate for us in all cases whatsoever.

He has abdicated government here, by declaring us out of his protection, and waging war against us.

He has plundered our seas, ravaged our coasts, burnt our towns, and destroyed the lives of our people.

He is, at this time, transporting large armies of foreign mercenaries to complete the works of death, desolation, and tyranny, already begun, with circumstances of cruelty and perfidy scarcely paralleled in the most barbarous ages, and totally unworthy of the head of a civilized nation.

He has constrained our fellow citizens, taken captive on the high seas, to bear arms against their country, to become the executioners of their friends, and brethren, or to fall themselves by their hands.

He has excited domestic insurrections amongst us, and has endeavored to bring on the inhabitants of our frontiers, the merciless Indian savages, whose known rule of warfare is an undistinguished destruction of all ages, sexes, and conditions.

In every stage of these oppressions, we have petitioned for redress, in the most humble terms; our repeated petitions have been answered only by repeated injury. A prince, whose character is thus marked by every act which may define a tyrant, is unfit to be the ruler of a free people.

Nor have we been wanting in attention to our British brethren. We have warned them, from time to time, of attempts made by their legislature to extend an unwarrantable jurisdiction over us. We have reminded them of the circumstances of our emigration and settlement here. We have appealed to their native justice and magnanimity, and we have conjured them, by the ties of our common kindred, to disavow these usurpations, which would inevitably interrupt our connections and correspondence. They, too, have been deaf to the voice of justice and of consanguinity. We must, therefore, acquiesce in the necessity which denounces our separation, and hold them as we hold the rest of mankind, enemies in war, in peace, friends.

We, therefore, the representatives of the United States of America, in general Congress assembled, appealing to the Supreme Judge of the world for the rectitude of our intentions, do, in the name, and by the authority of the good people of these colonies, solemnly publish and declare, that these united colonies are, and of right ought to be, free and independent states: that they are absolved from all allegiance to the British Crown, and that all political connection between them and the state of Great Britain is, and ought to be, totally dissolved; and that, as free and independent states, they have full power to levy war, conclude peace, contract alliances, establish commerce, and to do all other acts and things which independent states may of right do. And, for the support of this declaration, with a firm reliance on the protection of Divine Providence, we mutually pledge to each other our lives, our fortunes, and our sacred honor.

The foregoing Declaration was, by order of Congress, engrossed, and signed by the following members:

JOHN HANCOCK

New Hampshire
Josiah Bartlett
William Whipple
Matthew Thornton

Massachusetts Bay
Samuel Adams
John Adams
Robert Treat Paine
Elbridge Gerry

Rhode Island
Stephen Hopkins
William Ellery

Connecticut
Roger Sherman
Samuel Huntington
William Williams
Oliver Wolcott

New York
William Floyd
Philip Livingston
Francis Lewis
Lewis Morris

New Jersey
Richard Stockton
John Witherspoon
Francis Hopkinson
John Hart
Abraham Clark

Pennsylvania
Robert Morris
Benjamin Rush
Benjamin Franklin
John Morton
George Clymer
James Smith
George Taylor
James Wilson
George Ross

Delaware
Caesar Rodney
George Reed
Thomas M'Kean

Maryland
Samuel Chase
William Paca
Thomas Stone
Charles Carroll, of Carrollton

Virginia
George Wythe
Richard Henry Lee
Thomas Jefferson
Benjamin Harrison
Thomas Nelson, Jr.
Francis Lightfoot Lee
Carter Braxton

North Carolina
William Hooper
Joseph Hewes
John Penn

South Carolina
Edward Rutledge
Thomas Heyward, Jr.
Thomas Lynch, Jr.
Arthur Middleton

Georgia
Button Gwinnett
Lyman Hall
George Walton

Resolved, That copies of the Declaration be sent to the several assemblies, conventions, and committees, or councils of safety, and to the several commanding officers of the continental troops; that it be proclaimed in each of the United States, at the head of the army.

THE CONSTITUTION OF THE UNITED STATES OF AMERICA[1]

We the People of the United States, in Order to form a more perfect Union, establish Justice, insure domestic Tranquility, provide for the common defence, promote the general Welfare, and secure the Blessings of Liberty to ourselves and our Posterity, do ordain and establish this CONSTITUTION for the United States of America.

Article 1

SECTION 1

All legislative Powers herein granted shall be vested in a Congress of the United States, which shall consist of a Senate and House of Representatives.

SECTION 2

The House of Representatives shall be composed of Members chosen every second Year by the People of the several States, and the Electors in each State shall have the Qualifications requisite for Electors of the most numerous Branch of the State Legislature.

[1]This version, which follows the original Constitution in capitalization and spelling, was published by the United States Department of the Interior, Office of Education, in 1935.

No Person shall be a Representative who shall not have attained to the Age of twenty-five Years, and been seven Years a Citizen of the United States, and who shall not, when elected, be an Inhabitant of that State in which he shall be chosen.

[Representatives and direct Taxes[2] shall be apportioned among the several States which may be included within this Union, according to their respective Numbers, which shall be determined by adding to the whole Number of free Persons, including those bound to Service for a Term of Years, and excluding Indians not taxed, three fifths of all other Persons.][3] The actual Enumeration shall be made within three Years after the first Meeting of the Congress of the United States, and within every subsequent Term of ten Years, in such Manner as they shall by Law direct. The Number of Representatives shall not exceed one for every thirty Thousand, but each State shall have at Least one Representative; and until such enumeration shall be made, the State of New Hampshire shall be entitled to chuse three, Massachusetts eight, Rhode-Island and Providence Plantations one, Connecticut five, New York six, New Jersey four, Pennsylvania eight, Delaware one, Maryland six, Virginia ten, North Carolina five, South Carolina five, and Georgia three.

[2]Altered by the Sixteenth Amendment.
[3]Negated by the Fourteenth Amendment.

When vacancies happen in the Representation from any State, the Executive Authority thereof shall issue Writs of Election to fill such Vacancies.

The House of Representatives shall chuse their Speaker and other Officers; and shall have the sole Power of Impeachment.

SECTION 3

The Senate of the United States shall be composed of two Senators from each State, chosen by the Legislature thereof, for six Years; and each Senator shall have one Vote.

Immediately after they shall be assembled in Consequence of the first Election, they shall be divided as equally as may be into three Classes. The Seats of the Senators of the first Class shall be vacated at the Expiration of the second Year, of the second Class at the Expiration of the fourth Year, and of the third Class at the Expiration of the sixth Year, so that one-third may be chosen every second Year; and if Vacancies happen by Resignation, or otherwise, during the Recess of the Legislature of any State, the Executive thereof may make temporary Appointments until the next Meeting of the Legislature, which shall then fill such Vacancies.

No Person shall be a Senator who shall not have attained to the Age of thirty Years, and been nine Years a Citizen of the United States, and who shall not, when elected, be an Inhabitant of that State for which he shall be chosen.

The Vice President of the United States shall be President of the Senate, but shall have no vote, unless they be equally divided.

The Senate shall chuse their other Officers, and also a President pro tempore, in the absence of the Vice President, or when he shall exercise the Office of President of the United States.

The Senate shall have the sole Power to try all Impeachments. When sitting for that purpose they shall be on Oath or Affirmation. When the President of the United States is tried, the Chief Justice shall preside: And no person shall be convicted without the Concurrence of two thirds of the Members present.

Judgment in Cases of Impeachment shall not extend further than to removal from Office, and disqualification to hold and enjoy any Office of honor, Trust, or Profit under the United States: but the Party convicted shall nevertheless be liable and subject to Indictment, Trial, Judgment and Punishment, according to Law.

SECTION 4

The Times, Place and Manner of holding Elections for Senators and Representatives, shall be prescribed in each State by the Legislature thereof; but the Congress may at any time by Law make or alter such Regulations, except as to the Places of Chusing Senators.

The Congress shall assemble at least once in every Year, and such Meeting shall be on the first Monday in December, unless they shall by Law appoint a different Day.

SECTION 5

Each House shall be the Judge of the Elections, Returns and Qualifications of its own Members, and a Majority of each shall constitute a Quorum to do Business; but a smaller number may adjourn from day to day, and may be authorized to compel the Attendance of absent Members, in such Manner, and under such Penalties, as each House may provide.

Each House may determine the Rules of its Proceedings, punish its Members for disorderly Behaviour, and, with the Concurrence of two thirds, expel a Member.

Each House shall keep a Journal of its Proceedings, and from time to time publish the same, excepting such Parts as may in their Judgment require Secrecy; and the Yeas and Nays of the Members of either House on any question shall, at the Desire of one fifth of those Present, be entered on the Journal.

Neither House, during the Session of Congress, shall, without the Consent of the other, adjourn for more than three days, nor to any other Place than that in which the two Houses shall be sitting.

SECTION 6

The Senators and Representatives shall receive a Compensation for their Services, to be ascertained by Law, and paid out of the Treasury of the United States. They shall in all Cases, except Treason, Felony, and Breach of the Peace, be privileged from Arrest during their Attendance at the Session of their respective Houses, and in going to and returning from the same; and for any Speech or Debate in either House, they shall not be questioned in any other Place.

No Senator or Representative shall, during the Time for which he was elected, be appointed to any civil Office under the Authority of the United States, which shall have been created, or the Emoluments whereof shall have been increased, during such time; and no Person holding any Office under the United States shall be a Member of either House during his continuance in Office.

SECTION 7

All Bills for raising Revenue shall originate in the House of Representatives; but the Senate may propose or concur with Amendments as on other bills.

Every Bill which shall have passed the House of Representatives and the Senate, shall, before it becomes a Law, be presented to the President of the United States; if he approve he shall sign it, but if not he shall return it, with his Objections, to that House in which it shall have originated, who shall enter the Objections at large on their Journal, and proceed to reconsider it. If after such Reconsideration two thirds of that House shall agree to pass the bill, it shall be sent, together with the objections, to the other House, by which it shall likewise be reconsidered, and if approved by two thirds of that House, it shall become a Law. But in all such Cases the Votes of both Houses shall be determined by Yeas and Nays, and the Names of the Persons voting for and against the Bill shall be entered on the Journal of each House respectively. If any Bill shall not be returned by the President within ten Days (Sundays excepted) after it shall have been presented to him, the Same shall be a Law, in like Manner as if he had signed it, unless the Congress by their Adjournment prevent its Return, in which Case it shall not be a Law.

Every Order, Resolution, or Vote to which the Concurrence of the Senate and House of Representatives may be necessary (except on a question of Adjournment) shall be presented to the President of the United States; and before the Same shall take Effect, shall be approved by him, or being disapproved by him, shall be repassed by two thirds of the Senate and House of Representatives, according to the Rules and Limitations prescribed in the Case of a Bill.

SECTION 8

The Congress shall have Power To lay and collect Taxes, Duties, Imposts and Excises, to pay the Debts and provide for the common Defence and general Welfare of the United States; but all Duties, Imposts and Excises shall be uniform throughout the United States;

To borrow money on the credit of the United States;

To regulate Commerce with foreign Nations, and among the several States, and with the Indian Tribes;

To establish a uniform rule of Naturalization, and uniform Laws on the subject of Bankruptcies throughout the United States;

To coin Money, regulate the Value thereof, and of foreign Coin, and fix the Standard of Weights and Measures;

To provide for the Punishment of counterfeiting the Securities and current Coin of the United States;

To establish Post Offices and post Roads;

To promote the Progress of Science and useful Arts, by securing for limited Times to Authors and Inventors the exclusive Right to their respective Writings and Discoveries;

To constitute Tribunals inferior to the Supreme Court;

To define and punish Piracies and Felonies committed on the high Seas, and Offenses against the Law of Nations;

To declare War, grant Letters of Marque and Reprisal, and make Rules concerning Captures on Land and Water;

To raise and support Armies, but no Appropriation of Money to that Use shall be for a longer Term than two Years;

To provide and maintain a Navy;

To make Rules for the Government and Regulation of the land and naval forces;

To provide for calling forth the Militia to execute the Laws of the Union, suppress Insurrections and repel Invasions;

To provide for organizing, arming, and disciplining the Militia, and for governing such Part of them as may be employed in the Service of the United States, reserving to the States respectively, the Appointment of the Officers, and the Authority of training the Militia according to the discipline prescribed by Congress;

To exercise exclusive Legislation in all Cases whatsoever, over such District (not exceeding ten Miles square) as may, by Cession of particular States, and the acceptance of Congress, become the Seat of the Government of the United States, and to exercise like Authority over all Places purchased by the Consent of the Legislature of the State in which the Same shall be, for the Erection of Forts, Magazines, Arsenals, Dock-yards, and other needful Buildings;—And

To make all Laws which shall be necessary and proper for carrying into Execution the foregoing Powers, and all other Powers vested by this Constitution in the Government of the United States, or in any Department or Officer thereof.

SECTION 9

The Migration or Importation of such Persons as any of the States now existing shall think proper to admit, shall not be prohibited by the Congress prior to the Year one thousand eight hundred and eight, but a tax or duty may be imposed on such Importation, not exceeding ten dollars for each Person.

The privilege of the Writ of Habeas Corpus shall not be suspended, unless when in Cases of Rebellion or Invasion the public Safety may require it.

No bill of Attainder or ex post facto Law shall be passed.

No capitation, or other direct, Tax shall be laid unless in Proportion to the Census or Enumeration herein before directed to be taken.

No Tax or Duty shall be laid on Articles exported from any State.

No Preference shall be given by any Regulation of Commerce or Revenue to the Ports of one State over those of another: nor shall Vessels bound to, or from, one State, be obliged to enter, clear, or pay Duties in another.

No Money shall be drawn from the Treasury, but in Consequence of Appropriations made by Law; and a regular Statement and Account of the Receipts and Expenditures of all public Money shall be published from time to time.

No Title of Nobility shall be granted by the United States: And no Person holding any Office of Profit or Trust under them, shall, without the Consent of the Congress, accept of any present, Emolument, Office, or Title, of any kind whatever, from any King, Prince, or foreign State.

SECTION 10

No State shall enter into any Treaty, Alliance, or Confederation; grant Letters of Marque and Reprisal; coin Money; emit Bills of Credit; make any Thing but gold and silver Coin a Tender in Payment of Debts; pass any Bill of Attainder, ex post facto Law, or Law impairing the Obligation of Contracts, or grant any Title of Nobility.

No State shall, without the Consent of the Congress, lay any Imposts or Duties on Imports or Exports, except what may be absolutely necessary for executing its inspection Laws; and the net Produce of all Duties and Imposts, laid by any State on Imports or Exports, shall be for the use of the Treasury of the United States; and all such Laws shall be subject to the Revision and Control of the Congress.

No state shall, without the Consent of Congress, lay any duty of Tonnage, keep Troops, or Ships of War in time of Peace, enter into any Agreement or Compact with another State, or with a foreign Power, or engage in War, unless actually invaded, or in such imminent Danger as will not admit of delay.

Article II

SECTION 1

The executive Power shall be vested in a President of the United States of America. He shall hold his Office during the Term of four years, and, together with the Vice President, chosen for the same Term, be elected, as follows:

Each State shall appoint, in such Manner as the Legislature thereof may direct, a Number of Electors, equal to the whole Number of Senators and Representatives to which the State may be entitled in the Congress: but no Senator or Representative, or Person holding an Office of Trust or Profit under the United States, shall be appointed an Elector.

[The Electors shall meet in their respective States, and vote by Ballot for two persons, of whom one at least shall not be an Inhabitant of the same State with themselves. And they shall make a List of all the Persons voted for, and of the Number of Votes for each; which List they shall sign and certify, and transmit sealed to the Seat of the Government of the United States, directed to the President of the Senate. The President of the Senate shall, in the Presence of the Senate and House of Representatives, open all the Certificates, and the Votes shall then be counted. The Person having the greatest Number of Votes shall be the President, if such Number be a Majority of the whole Number of Electors appointed; and if there be more than one who have such Majority, and have an equal Number of Votes, then the House of Representatives shall immediately chuse by Ballot one of them for President; and if no Person have a Majority, then from the five highest on the List the said House shall in like Manner chuse the President. But in chusing the President, the Votes shall be taken by States, the Representation from each State having one Vote; a quorum for this Purpose shall consist of a Member or Members from two-thirds of the States, and a Majority of all the States shall be necessary to a Choice. In every Case, after the Choice of the President, the Person having the greatest Number of Votes of the Electors shall be the Vice President. But if there should remain two or more who have equal votes, the Senate shall chuse from them by Ballot the Vice President.][4]

The Congress may determine the Time of chusing the Electors, and the Day on which they shall give their Votes; which Day shall be the same throughout the United States.

No person except a natural-born Citizen, or a Citizen of the United States, at the time of the Adoption of this Constitution, shall be eligible to the Office of President; neither shall any Person be eligible to that Office who shall not have attained to the Age of thirty-five years, and been fourteen Years a Resident within the United States.

[4]Revised by the Twelfth Amendment.

In Case of the Removal of the President from Office, or of his Death, Resignation, or Inability to discharge the Powers and Duties of the said Office, the same shall devolve on the Vice President, and the Congress may by Law provide for the Case of Removal, Death, Resignation, or Inability, both of the President and Vice President, declaring what Officer shall then act as President, and such Officer shall act accordingly, until the disability be removed, or a President shall be elected.

The President shall, at stated Times, receive for his Services a Compensation, which shall neither be increased nor diminished during the Period for which he shall have been elected, and he shall not receive within that Period any other Emolument from the United States, or any of them.

Before he enter on the execution of his Office, he shall take the following Oath or Affirmation:—"I do solemnly swear (or affirm) that I will faithfully execute the Office of President of the United States, and will, to the best of my Ability, preserve, protect, and defend the Constitution of the United States."

SECTION 2

The President shall be Commander in Chief of the Army and Navy of the United States, and of the Militia of the several States, when called into the actual Service of the United States; he may require the Opinion, in writing, of the principal Officer in each of the executive Departments, upon any subject relating to the Duties of their respective Offices, and he shall have Power to Grant Reprieves and Pardons for Offenses against the United States, except in Cases of Impeachment.

He shall have Power, by and with the Advice and Consent of the Senate, to make Treaties, provided two-thirds of the Senators present concur; and he shall nominate, and by and with the Advice and Consent of the Senate, shall appoint Ambassadors, other public Ministers and Consuls, Judges of the supreme Court, and all other Officers of the United States, whose Appointments are not herein otherwise provided for, and which shall be established by Law: but the Congress may by Law vest the Appointment of such inferior Officers, as they think proper, in the President alone, in the Courts of Law, or in the Heads of Departments.

The President shall have Power to fill up all Vacancies that may happen during the Recess of the Senate, by granting Commissions which shall expire at the End of their next Session.

SECTION 3

He shall from time to time give to the Congress Information of the State of the Union, and recommend to their Consideration such Measures as he shall judge necessary and expedient; he may, on extraordinary occasions, convene both Houses, or either of them, and in Case of Disagreement between them, with respect to the Time of Adjournment, he may adjourn them to such Time as he shall think proper; he shall receive Ambassadors and other public Ministers; he shall take care that the Laws be faithfully executed, and shall Commission all the Officers of the United States.

SECTION 4

The President, Vice President and all civil Officers of the United States, shall be removed from Office on Impeachment for, and Conviction of, Treason, Bribery, or other high Crimes and Misdemeanors.

Article III

SECTION 1

The judicial Power of the United States, shall be vested in one supreme Court, and in such inferior Courts as the Congress may from time to time ordain and establish. The Judges, both of the supreme and inferior Courts, shall hold their Offices during good Behaviour, and shall, at stated Times, receive for their Services, a Compensation, which shall not be diminished during their Continuance in Office.

SECTION 2

The judicial Power shall extend to all Cases, in Law and Equity, arising under this Constitution, the Laws of the United States, and Treaties made, or which shall be made, under their Authority;—to all Cases affecting ambassadors, other public ministers and consuls;—to all cases of admiralty and maritime Jurisdiction;—to Controversies to which the United States shall be a Party;—to Controversies between two or more states;—between a State and Citizens of another State;[5]—between Citizens of different States—between Citizens of the same State claiming Lands under Grants of different States, and between a State, or the Citizens thereof, and foreign States, Citizens, or Subjects.

In all Cases affecting Ambassadors, other public Ministers and Consuls, and those in which a State shall be Party, the supreme Court shall have original Jurisdiction.

[5]Qualified by the Eleventh Amendment.

In all the other Cases before mentioned, the supreme Court shall have appellate Jurisdiction, both as to Law and Fact, with such Exceptions, and under such Regulations as the Congress shall make.

The trial of all Crimes, except in Cases of Impeachment, shall be by Jury; and such Trial shall be held in the State where the said Crimes shall have been committed; but when not committed within any State, the Trial shall be at such Place or Places as the Congress may by Law have directed.

SECTION 3

Treason against the United States, shall consist only in levying War against them, or in adhering to their Enemies, giving them Aid and Comfort. No Person shall be convicted of Treason unless on the Testimony of two Witnesses to the same overt Act, or on Confession in open Court.

The Congress shall have power to declare the Punishment of Treason, but no Attainder of Treason shall work Corruption of Blood, or Forfeiture except during the Life of the Person attainted.

Article IV

SECTION 1

Full Faith and Credit shall be given in each State to the public Acts, Records, and judicial Proceedings of every other State. And the Congress may by general Laws prescribe the Manner in which such Acts, Records and Proceedings shall be proved, and the Effect thereof.

SECTION 2

The Citizens of each State shall be entitled to all Privileges and Immunities of Citizens in the several States.

A Person charged in any State with Treason, Felony, or other Crime, who shall flee from Justice, and be found in another State, shall on demand of the executive Authority of the State from which he fled, be delivered up, to be removed to the State having Jurisdiction of the crime.

No Person held to Service or Labour in one State, under the Laws thereof, escaping into another, shall, in Consequence of any Law or Regulation therein, be discharged from such Service or Labour, but shall be delivered up on Claim of the Party to whom such Service or Labour may be due.

SECTION 3

New States may be admitted by the Congress into this Union; but no new State shall be formed or erected within the Jurisdiction of any other State; nor any State be formed by the Junction of two or more States, or parts of States, without the Consent of the Legislatures of the States concerned as well as of the Congress.

The Congress shall have Power to dispose of and make all needful Rules and Regulations respecting the Territory or other Property belonging to the United States; and nothing in this Constitution shall be so construed as to Prejudice any Claims of the United States, or of any particular State.

SECTION 4

The United States shall guarantee to every State in this Union a Republican Form of Government, and shall protect each of them against Invasion; and on Application of the Legislature, or of the Executive (when the Legislature cannot be convened) against domestic Violence.

Article V

The Congress, whenever two-thirds of both Houses shall deem it necessary, shall propose Amendments to this Constitution, or, on the Application of the Legislatures of two-thirds of the several States, shall call a Convention for proposing Amendments, which, in either Case, shall be valid to all Intents and Purposes, as part of this Constitution, when ratified by the Legislatures of three-fourths of the several States, or by Conventions in three-fourths thereof, as the one or the other Mode of Ratification may be proposed by the Congress; Provided that no Amendment which may be made prior to the Year One thousand eight hundred and eight shall in any Manner affect the first and fourth Clauses in the Ninth Section of the first Article; and that no State, without its Consent, shall be deprived of its equal Suffrage in the Senate.

Article VI

All Debts contracted and Engagements entered into, before the Adoption of this Constitution, shall be as valid against the United States under this Constitution, as under the Confederation.

This Constitution, and the Laws of the United States which shall be made in Pursuance thereof; and all Treaties made, or which shall be made, under the Authority of the United States, shall be the supreme Law of the Land; and the Judges in every State shall be bound thereby, any Thing in the Constitution or Laws of any State to the Contrary notwithstanding.

The Senators and Representatives before mentioned, and the Members of the several State Legislatures, and all executive and judicial Officers, both of the United States and of the several States, shall be bound by Oath or Affirmation to support this Constitution; but no religious Tests shall ever be required as a qualification to any Office or public Trust under the United States.

Article VII

The Ratification of the Conventions of nine States shall be sufficient for the Establishment of this Constitution between the States so ratifying the same.

Done in Convention by the Unanimous Consent of the States present the Seventeenth Day of September in the Year of our Lord one thousand seven hundred and Eighty seven, and of the Independence of the United States of America the Twelfth. In Witness whereof We have hereunto subscribed our Names.[6]

[6]These are the full names of the signers, which in some cases are not the signatures on the document.

George Washington
President and deputy from Virginia

New Hampshire
John Langdon
Nicholas Gilman

Massachusetts
Nathaniel Gorham
Rufus King

Connecticut
William Samuel Johnson
Roger Sherman

New York
Alexander Hamilton

New Jersey
William Livingston
David Brearley
William Paterson
Jonathan Dayton

Pennsylvania
Benjamin Franklin
Thomas Mifflin
Robert Morris
George Clymer
Thomas FitzSimmons
Jared Ingersoll
James Wilson
Gouverneur Morris

Delaware
George Read
Gunning Bedford, Jr.
John Dickinson
Richard Bassett
Jacob Broom

Maryland
James McHenry
Daniel of St. Thomas Jenifer
Daniel Carroll

Virginia
John Blair
James Madison, Jr.

North Carolina
William Blount
Richard Dobbs Spaight
Hugh Williamson

South Carolina
John Rutledge
Charles Cotesworth Pinckney
Charles Pinckney
Pierce Butler

Georgia
William Few
Abraham Baldwin

Articles in Addition to, and Amendment of, the Constitution of the United States of America, Proposed by Congress, and Ratified by the Legislatures of the Several States, Pursuant to the Fifth Article of the Original Constitution[7]

[7]This heading appears only in the joint resolution submitting the first ten amendments, which are collectively known as the Bill of Rights. They were ratified on December 15, 1791.

Amendment I

Congress shall make no law respecting an establishment of religion, or prohibiting the free exercise thereof; or abridging the freedom of speech, or of the press; or the right of the people peaceably to assemble, and to petition the Government for a redress of grievances.

Amendment II

A well regulated Militia, being necessary to the security of a free State, the right of the people to keep and bear Arms shall not be infringed.

Amendment III

No Soldier shall, in time of peace, be quartered in any house, without the consent of the Owner, nor in time of war, but in a manner to be prescribed by law.

Amendment IV

The right of the people to be secure in their persons, houses, papers, and effects, against unreasonable searches and seizures, shall not be violated, and no Warrants shall issue, but upon probable cause, supported by Oath or affirmation, and particularly describing the place to be searched, and the persons or things to be seized.

Amendment V

No person shall be held to answer for a capital or otherwise infamous crime, unless on a presentment or indictment of a Grand Jury, except in cases arising in the land or naval forces, or in the Militia, when in actual service in time of War or public danger; nor shall any person be subject for the same offence to be twice put in jeopardy of life or limb; nor shall be compelled in any criminal case to be a witness against himself, nor be deprived of life, liberty, or property, without due process of law; nor shall private property be taken for public use, without just compensation.

Amendment VI

In all criminal prosecutions, the accused shall enjoy the right to a speedy and public trial, by an impartial jury of the State and district wherein the crime shall have been committed, which district shall have been previously ascertained by law, and to be informed of the nature and cause of the accusation; to be confronted with the witnesses against him; to have compulsory process for obtaining witnesses in his favour, and to have the Assistance of Counsel for his defence.

Amendment VII

In suits at common law, where the value in controversy shall exceed twenty dollars, the right of trial by jury shall be preserved, and no fact tried by a jury, shall be otherwise reexamined in any Court of the United States, than according to the rules of the common law.

Amendment VIII

Excessive bail shall not be required, nor excessive fines imposed, nor cruel and unusual punishments inflicted.

Amendment IX

The enumeration of the Constitution, of certain rights, shall not be construed to deny or disparage others retained by the people.

Amendment X

The powers not delegated to the United States by the Constitution, nor prohibited by it to the States, are reserved to the States respectively, or to the people.

Amendment XI [1798]

The Judicial power of the United States shall not be construed to extend to any suit in law or equity, commenced or prosecuted against one of the United States by Citizens of another State, or by Citizens or Subjects of any Foreign State.

Amendment XII [1804]

The Electors shall meet in their respective States and vote by ballot for President and Vice-President, one of whom, at least, shall not be an inhabitant of the same State with themselves; they shall name in their ballots the person voted for as President, and in distinct ballots the person voted for as Vice-President, and they shall make distinct lists of all persons voted for as President, and of all persons voted for as Vice-President, and of the number of votes for each, which lists they shall sign and certify, and transmit sealed to the seat of the government of the United States, directed to the President of the Senate;—

The President of the Senate shall, in the presence of the Senate and House of Representatives, open all the certificates and the votes shall then be counted;—The person having the greatest number of votes for President, shall be the President, if such number be a majority of the whole number of Electors appointed; and if no person have such majority, then from the persons having the highest numbers not exceeding three on the list of those voted for as President, the House of Representatives shall choose immediately, by ballot, the President. But in choosing the President, the votes shall be taken by states, the representation from each state having one vote; a quorum for this purpose shall consist of a member or members from two-thirds of the states, and a majority of all the states shall be necessary to a choice. And if the House of Representatives shall not choose a President whenever the right of choice shall devolve upon them, before the fourth day of March next following, then the Vice-President shall act as President, as in the case of the death or other constitutional disability of the President.—The person having the greatest number of votes as Vice-President, shall be the Vice-President, if such number be a majority of the whole number of Electors appointed, and if no person have a majority, then from the two highest numbers on the list, the Senate shall choose the Vice-President; a quorum for the purpose shall consist of two-thirds of the whole number of Senators, and majority of the whole number shall be necessary to a choice. But no person constitutionally ineligible to the office of President shall be eligible to that of Vice-President of the United States.

Amendment XIII [1865]

SECTION 1

Neither slavery nor involuntary servitude, except as a punishment for crime whereof the party shall have been duly convicted, shall exist within the United States, or any place subject to their jurisdiction.

SECTION 2

Congress shall have power to enforce this article by appropriate legislation.

Amendment XIV [1868]

SECTION 1

All persons born or naturalized in the United States, and subject to the jurisdiction thereof, are citizens of the United States and of the State wherein they reside. No State shall abridge the privileges or immunities of citizens of the United States; nor shall any State deprive any person of life, liberty, or property, without due process of law; nor deny to any person within its jurisdiction the equal protection of the laws.

SECTION 2

Representatives shall be apportioned among the several States according to their respective numbers, counting the whole number of persons in each State, excluding Indians not taxed. But when the right to vote at any election for the choice of electors for President and Vice-President of the United States, Representatives in Congress, the Executive and Judicial officers of a State, or the members of the Legislature thereof, is denied to any of the male inhabitants of such State, being twenty-one years of age, and citizens of the United States, or in any way abridged, except for participation in rebellion, or other crime, the basis of representation therein shall be reduced in the proportion which the number of such male citizens shall bear to the whole number of male citizens twenty-one years of age in such State.

SECTION 3

No person shall be a Senator or Representative in Congress, or elector of President and Vice-President, or hold any office, civil or military, under the United States, or under any State, who, having previously taken an oath, as a member of Congress, or as an officer of the United States, or as a member of any State legislature, or as an executive or judicial officer of any State, to support the Constitution of the United States, shall have engaged in insurrection or rebellion against the same, or given aid or comfort to the enemies thereof. But Congress may by a vote of two-thirds of each House, remove such disability.

SECTION 4

The validity of the public debt of the United States, authorized by law, including debts incurred for payment of pensions and bounties for services in suppressing insurrection or rebellion, shall not be questioned. But neither the United States nor any State shall assume or pay any debts or obligation incurred in aid of insurrection or rebellion against the United States, or any claim for the loss or emancipation of any slave; but all such debts, obligations, and claims shall be held illegal and void.

SECTION 5

The Congress shall have the power to enforce, by appropriate legislation, the provisions of this article.

Amendment XV [1870]

SECTION 1

The right of citizens of the United States to vote shall not be denied or abridged by the United States or by any State on account of race, color, or previous condition of servitude—

SECTION 2

The Congress shall have power to enforce this article by appropriate legislation.

Amendment XVI [1913]

The Congress shall have power to lay and collect taxes on incomes, from whatever source derived, without apportionment among the several States, and without regard to any census or enumeration.

Amendment XVII [1913]

The Senate of the United States shall be composed of two Senators from each State, elected by the people thereof, for six years; and each Senator shall have one vote. The electors in each State shall have the qualifications requisite for electors of the most numerous branch of the State legislatures.

When vacancies happen in the representation of any State in the Senate, the executive authority of such State shall issue writs of election to fill such vacancies: *Provided,* That the legislature of any State may empower the executive thereof to make temporary appointments until the people fill the vacancies by election as the legislature may direct.

This amendment shall not be so construed as to affect the election or term of any Senator chosen before it becomes valid as part of the Constitution.

Amendment XVIII [1919]

SECTION 1

After one year from the ratification of this article the manufacture, sale, or transportation of intoxicating liquors within, the importation thereof into, or the exportation thereof from the United States and all territory subject to the jurisdiction thereof for beverage purposes is hereby prohibited.

SECTION 2

The Congress and the several States shall have concurrent power to enforce this article by appropriate legislation.

SECTION 3

This article shall be inoperative unless it shall have been ratified as an amendment to the Constitution by the legislatures of the several States, as provided in the Constitution, within seven years from the date of the submission hereof to the States by the Congress.

Amendment XIX [1920]

The right of citizens of the United States to vote shall not be denied or abridged by the United States or by any State on account of sex.

Congress shall have power to enforce this article by appropriate legislation.

Amendment XX [1933]

SECTION 1

The terms of the President and Vice-President shall end at noon on the 20th day of January, and the terms of Senators and Representatives at noon on the 3d day of January, of the years in which such terms would have ended if this article had not been ratified; and the terms of their successors shall then begin.

SECTION 2

The Congress shall assemble at least once in every year, and such meeting shall begin at noon on the 3d day of January, unless they shall by law appoint a different day.

SECTION 3

If, at the time fixed for the beginning of the term of the President, the President elect shall have died, the Vice-President elect shall become President. If a President shall not have been chosen before the time fixed for the beginning of his term or if the President elect shall have failed to qualify, then the Vice-President elect shall act as

President until a President shall have qualified; and the Congress may by law provide for the case wherein neither a President elect nor a Vice-President elect shall have qualified, declaring who shall then act as President, or the manner in which one who is to act shall be selected, and such person shall act accordingly until a President or Vice-President shall have qualified.

SECTION 4

The Congress may by law provide for the case of the death of any of the persons from whom the House of Representatives may choose a President whenever the right of choice shall have devolved upon them, and for the case of the death of any of the persons from whom the Senate may choose a Vice-President whenever the right of choice shall have devolved upon them.

SECTION 5

Sections 1 and 2 shall take effect on the 15th day of October following the ratification of this article.

SECTION 6

This article shall be inoperative unless it shall have been ratified as an amendment to the Constitution by the legislatures of three-fourths of the several States within seven years from the date of its submission.

Amendment XXI [1933]

SECTION 1

The eighteenth article of amendment to the Constitution of the United States is hereby repealed.

SECTION 2

The transportation or importation into any State, Territory, or possession of the United States for delivery or use therein of intoxicating liquors, in violation of the laws thereof, is hereby prohibited.

SECTION 3

This article shall be inoperative unless it shall have been ratified as an amendment to the Constitution by conventions in the several States, as provided in the Constitution, within seven years from the date of the submission hereof to the States by the Congress.

Amendment XXII [1951]

No person shall be elected to the office of the President more than twice, and no person who has held the office of President, or acted as President, for more than two years of a term to which some other person was elected President shall be elected to the office of the President more than once.

But this Article shall not apply to any person holding the office of President when this Article was proposed by the Congress, and shall not prevent any person who may be holding the office of President, or acting as President, during the term within which this Article becomes operative from holding the office of President or acting as President during the remainder of such term.

This article shall be inoperative unless it shall have been ratified as an amendment to the Constitution by the legislatures of three-fourths of the several states within seven years from the date of its submission to the states by the Congress.

Amendment XXIII [1961]

SECTION 1

The District constituting the seat of Government of the United States shall appoint in such manner as the Congress may direct:

A number of electors of President and Vice-President equal to the whole number of Senators and Representatives in Congress to which the District would be entitled if it were a State, but in no event more than the least populous State; they shall be in addition to those appointed by the States, but they shall be considered, for the purposes of the election of President and Vice-President, to be electors appointed by a State; and they shall meet in the District and perform such duties as provided by the twelfth article of amendment.

SECTION 2

The Congress shall have power to enforce this article by appropriate legislation.

Amendment XXIV [1964]

SECTION 1

The right of citizens of the United States to vote in any primary or other election for President or Vice President, for electors for President or Vice President, or for Senator or Representative in Congress, shall not be denied or abridged by the United States or any state by reason of failure to pay any poll tax or other tax.

SECTION 2

The Congress shall have the power to enforce this article by appropriate legislation.

Amendment XXV [1967]

SECTION 1

In case of the removal of the President from office or of his death or resignation, the Vice President shall become President.

SECTION 2

Whenever there is a vacancy in the office of the Vice President, the President shall nominate a Vice President who shall take office upon confirmation by a majority vote of both Houses of Congress.

SECTION 3

Whenever the President transmits to the President Pro Tempore of the Senate and the Speaker of the House of Representatives his written declaration that he is unable to discharge the powers and duties of his office, and until he transmits to them a written declaration to the contrary, such powers and duties shall be discharged by the Vice President as Acting President.

SECTION 4

Whenever the Vice President and a majority of either the principal officers of the executive departments or of such other body as Congress may by law provide, transmit to the President Pro Tempore of the Senate and the Speaker of the House of Representatives their written declaration that the President is unable to discharge the powers and duties of his office, the Vice President shall immediately assume the powers and duties of the office as Acting President.

Thereafter, when the President transmits to the President Pro Tempore of the Senate and the Speaker of the House of Representatives his written declaration that no inability exists, he shall resume the powers and duties of his office unless the Vice President and a majority of either the principal officers of the executive departments or of such other body as Congress may by law provide, transmit within four days to the President Pro Tempore of the Senate and the Speaker of the House of Representatives their written declaration that the President is unable to discharge the powers and duties of his office. Thereupon Congress shall decide the issue, assembling within forty-eight hours for that purpose if not in session. If the Congress, within twenty-one days after receipt of the latter written declaration, or, if Congress is not in session, within twenty-one days after Congress is required to assemble, determines by two-thirds vote of both Houses that the President is unable to discharge the powers and duties of his office, the Vice President shall continue to discharge the same as Acting President; otherwise, the President shall resume the powers and duties of his office.

Amendment XXVI [1971]

SECTION 1

The right of citizens of the United States, who are eighteen years of age or older, to vote shall not be denied or abridged by the United States or by any State on account of age.

SECTION 2

The Congress shall have the power to enforce this article by appropriate legislation.

Amendment XXVII [1992]

No law varying the compensation for the service of Senators and Representatives shall take effect until an election of Representatives shall have intervened.

FEDERALIST NO. 10 (JAMES MADISON)

Among the numerous advantages promised by a well-constructed Union, none deserves to be more accurately developed than its tendency to break and control the violence of faction. The friend of popular governments never finds himself so much alarmed for their character and fate as when he contemplates their propensity to this dangerous vice. He will not fail, therefore, to set a due value on any plan which, without violating the principles to which he is attached, provides a proper cure for it. The instability, injustice, and confusion introduced into the public councils have, in truth, been the mortal diseases under which popular governments have everywhere perished, as they continue to be the favorite and fruitful topics from which the adversaries to liberty derive their most specious declamations. The valuable improvements made by the American constitutions on the popular models, both ancient and modern, cannot certainly be too much admired; but it would be an unwarrantable partiality to contend that they have as effectually obviated the danger on this side, as was wished and expected. Complaints are everywhere heard from our most considerate and virtuous citizens, equally the friends of public and private faith and of public and personal liberty, that our governments are too unstable, that the public good is disregarded in the conflicts of rival parties, and that measures are too often decided, not according to the rules of justice and the rights of the minor party, but by the superior force of an interested and overbearing majority. However anxiously we may wish that these complaints had no foundation, the evidence of known facts will not permit us to deny that they are in some degree true. It will be found, indeed, on a candid review of our situation, that some of the distresses under which we labor have been erroneously charged on the operation of our governments; but it will be found, at the same time, that other causes will not alone account for many of our heaviest misfortunes; and, particularly, for that prevailing and increasing distrust of public engagements and alarm for private rights which are echoed from one end of the continent to the other. There must be chiefly, if not wholly, effects of the unsteadiness and injustice with which a factious spirit has tainted our public administration.

By a faction I understand a number of citizens, whether amounting to a majority or minority of the whole, who are united and actuated by some common impulse of passion, or of interest, adverse to the rights of other citizens, or to the permanent and aggregate interests of the community.

There are two methods of curing the mischiefs of faction: the one, by removing its causes; the other, by controlling its effects.

There are again two methods of removing the causes of faction: the one, by destroying the liberty which is essential to its existence; the other, by giving to every citizen the same opinions, the same passions, and the same interests.

It could never be more truly said than of the first remedy that it was worse than the disease. Liberty is to faction what air is to fire, an ailment without which it instantly expires. But it could not be a less folly to abolish liberty, which is essential to political life, because it nourishes faction than it would be to wish the annihilation of air, which is essential to animal life, because it imparts to fire its destructive agency.

The second expedient is as impracticable as the first would be unwise. As long as the reason of man continues fallible, and he is at liberty to exercise it, different opinions will be formed. As long as the connection subsists between his reason and his self-love, his opinions and his passions will have a reciprocal influence on each other; and the former will be objects to which the latter will attach themselves. The diversity in the faculties of men, from which the rights of property originate, is not less an insuperable obstacle to a uniformity of interest. The protection of these faculties is the first object of government. From the protection of different and unequal faculties of acquiring property, the possession of different degrees and kinds of property immediately results; and from the influence of these on the sentiments and views of the respective proprietors ensues a division of the society into different interests and parties.

The latent causes of faction are thus sown in the nature of man; and we see them everywhere brought into different degrees of activity, according to the different circumstances of civil society. A zeal for different opinions concerning religion, concerning government, and many other points, as well of speculation as of practice; an attachment to different leaders ambitiously contending for pre-eminence and power; or to persons of other descriptions whose fortunes have been interesting to the human passions, have, in turn, divided mankind into parties, inflamed them with mutual animosity, and rendered them much more disposed to vex and oppress each other than to co-operate for their common good. So strong is this propensity of mankind to fall into mutual animosities that where no substantial occasion presents itself the most frivolous and fanciful distinctions have been sufficient to kindle their unfriendly passions and excite their most violent conflicts. But the most common and durable source of factions has been the various and unequal distribution of property. Those who hold and those who are without property have ever formed distinct interests in society. Those who are creditors, and those who are debtors, fall under a like discrimination. A landed interest, a manufacturing interest, a mercantile interest, a moneyed interest, with many lesser interests, grow up of necessity in civilized nations, and divide them into different classes, actuated by different sentiments and views. The regulation of these various and interfering interests forms the principal task of modern legislation and involves the spirit of party and faction in the necessary and ordinary operations of government.

No man is allowed to be a judge in his own cause, because his interest would certainly bias his judgment, and, not improbably, corrupt his integrity. With equal, nay with greater reason, a body of men are unfit to be both judges and parties at the same time; yet what are many of the most important acts of legislation but so many judicial determinations, not indeed concerning the rights of single persons, but concerning the rights of large bodies of citizens? And what are the different classes of legislators but advocates and parties to the causes which they determine? Is a law proposed concerning private debts? It is a question to which the creditors are parties on one side and the debtors on the other. Justice ought to hold the balance between them. Yet the parties are, and must be, themselves the judges; and the most numerous party, or in other words, the most powerful faction must be expected to prevail. Shall domestic manufacturers be encouraged, and in what degree, by restrictions on foreign manufacturers? [These] are questions which would be differently decided by the landed and the manufacturing classes, and probably by neither with a sole regard to justice and the public good. The apportionment of taxes on the various descriptions of property is an act which seems to require the most exact impartiality; yet there is, perhaps, no legislative act in which greater opportunity and temptation are given to a predominant party to trample on the rules of justice. Every shilling with which they overburden the inferior number is a shilling saved to their own pockets.

It is in vain to say that enlightened statesmen will be able to adjust these clashing interests and render them all subservient to the public good. Enlightened statesmen will not always be at the helm. Nor, in many cases, can such an adjustment be made at all without taking into view indirect and remote considerations, which will rarely prevail over the immediate interest which one party may find in disregarding the rights of another or the good of the whole.

The inference to which we are brought is that the *causes* of faction cannot be removed and that relief is only to be sought in the means of controlling its *effects*.

If a faction consists of less than a majority, relief is supplied by the republican principle, which enables the majority to defeat its sinister views by regular vote. It may clog the administration, it may convulse the society; but it will be unable to execute and mask its violence under the forms of the Constitution. When a majority is included in a faction, the form of popular government, on the other hand, enables it to sacrifice to its ruling passion or interest both the public good and the rights of other citizens. To secure the public good and private rights against the danger of such a faction, and at the same time to preserve the spirit and the form of popular government, is then the great object to which our inquiries are directed. Let me add that it is the great desideratum by which alone this form of government can be rescued from the opprobrium under which it has so long labored and be recommended to the esteem and adoption of mankind.

By what means is this object attainable? Evidently by one of two only. Either the existence of the same passion or interest in a majority at the same time must be prevented, or the majority, having such coexistent passion or interest, must be rendered, by their number and local situation, unable to concert and carry into effect schemes of oppression. If the impulse and the opportunity be suffered to coincide, we well know that neither moral nor religious motives can be relied on as an adequate control. They are not found to be such on the injustice and violence of individuals, and lose their efficacy in proportion to the number combined together, that is, in proportion as their efficacy becomes needful.

From this view of the subject it may be concluded that a pure democracy, by which I mean a society consisting of a small number of citizens, who assemble and administer the government in person, can admit of no cure for the mischiefs of faction. A common passion or interest will, in almost every case, be felt by a majority of the whole, a communication and concert results from the form of government itself; and there is nothing to check the inducements to sacrifice the weaker party or an obnoxious individual. Hence it is that such democracies have ever been spectacles of turbulence and contention; have ever been found incompatible with personal security or the rights of property; and have in general been as short in their lives as they have been violent in their deaths. Theoretic politicians, who have patronized this species of government, have erroneously supposed that by reducing mankind to a perfect equality in their political rights, they would at the same time be perfectly equalized and assimilated in their possessions, their opinions, and their passions.

A republic, by which I mean a government in which the scheme of representation takes place, opens a different prospect and promises the cure for which we are seeking. Let us examine the points in which it varies from pure democracy, and we shall comprehend both the nature of the cure and the efficacy which it must derive from the Union.

The two great points of difference between a democracy and a republic are: first, the delegation of the government, in the latter, to a small number of citizens elected by the rest; secondly, the greater number of citizens and greater sphere of country over which the latter may be extended.

The effect of the first difference is, on the one hand, to refine and enlarge the public views by passing them through the medium of a chosen body of citizens, whose wisdom may best discern the true interest of their country and whose patriotism and love of justice will be least likely to sacrifice it to temporary or partial considerations. Under such a regulation it may well happen that the public voice, pronounced by the representatives of the people, will be more consonant to the public good than if pronounced by the people themselves, convened for the purpose. On the other hand, the effect may be inverted. Men of factious tempers, of local prejudices, or of sinister designs, may, by intrigue, by corruption, or by other means, first obtain the suffrages, and then betray the interests of the people. The question resulting is, whether small or extensive republics are most favorable to the election of proper guardians of the public weal; and it is clearly decided in favor of the latter by two obvious considerations.

In the first place it is to be remarked that however small the republic may be the representatives must be raised to a certain number in order to guard against the cabals of a few; and that however large it may be they must be limited to a certain number in order to guard against the confusion of a multitude. Hence, the number of representatives in the two cases not being in proportion to that of the constituents, and being proportionally greatest in the small republic, it follows that if the proportion of fit characters be not less in the large than in the small republic, the former will present a greater option, and consequently a greater probability of a fit choice.

In the next place, as each representative will be chosen by a greater number of citizens in the large than in the small republic, it will be more difficult for unworthy candidates to practice with success the vicious arts by which elections are too often carried; and the suffrages of the people being more free, will be more likely to center on men who possess the most attractive merit and the most diffusive and established characters.

It must be confessed that in this, as in most other cases, there is a mean, on both sides of which inconveniencies will be found to lie. By enlarging too much the number of electors, you render the representative too little acquainted with all their local circumstances and lesser interests; as by reducing it too much, you render him unduly attached to these, and too little fit to comprehend and pursue great and national objects. The federal Constitution forms a happy combination in this respect; the great and aggregate interests being referred to the national, the local and particular to the State legislatures.

The other point of difference is the greater number of citizens and extent of territory which may be brought within the compass of republican than of democratic government; and it is this circumstance principally which renders factious combinations less to be dreaded in the former than in the latter. The smaller the society, the fewer probably will be the distinct parties and interests composing it; the fewer the distinct parties and interests, the more frequently will a majority be found of the same party; and the smaller the number of individuals composing a majority, and the smaller the compass within which they are placed, the more easily will they concert and execute their plans of oppression. Extend the sphere and you take in a greater variety of parties and interests; you make it less probable that a majority of the whole will have a common motive to invade the rights of other citizens; or if such a common motive exists, it will be more difficult for all who feel it to discover their own strength and to act in unison with each other. Besides other impediments, it may be remarked that, where there is a consciousness of unjust or dishonorable purposes, communication is always checked by distrust in proportion to the number whose concurrence is necessary.

Hence, it clearly appears that the same advantage which a republic has over a democracy in controlling the effects of faction is enjoyed by a large over a small republic—is enjoyed by the Union over the States composing it. Does this advantage consist in the substitution of representatives whose enlightened views and virtuous sentiments render them superior to local prejudices and to schemes of injustice? It will not be denied that the representation of the Union will be most likely to possess these requisite endowments. Does it consist in the greater security afforded by a greater variety of parties, against the event of any one party being able to outnumber and oppress the rest? In an equal degree does the increased variety of parties comprised within the Union increase this security. Does it, in fine, consist in the greater obstacles opposed to the concert and accomplishment of the secret wishes of an unjust and interested majority? Here again the extent of the Union gives it the most palpable advantage.

The influence of factious leaders may kindle a flame within their particular States but will be unable to spread a general conflagration through the other States. A religious sect may degenerate into a political faction in a part of the Confederacy; but the variety of sects dispersed over the entire face of it must secure the national councils against any danger from that source. A rage for paper money, for an abolition of debts, for an equal division of property, or for any other improper or wicked project, will be less apt to pervade the whole body of the Union than a particular member of it, in the same proportion as such as malady is more likely to taint a particular county or district than an entire State.

In the extent and proper structure of the Union, therefore, we behold a republican remedy for the diseases most incident to republican government. And according to the degree of pleasure and pride we feel in being republicans ought to be our zeal in cherishing the spirit and supporting the character of federalists.

FEDERALIST NO. 51 (JAMES MADISON)

To what expedient, then, shall we finally resort, for maintaining in practice the necessary partition of power among the several departments as laid down in the Constitution? The only answer that can be given is that as all these exterior provisions are found to be inadequate, the defect must be supplied, by so contriving the interior structure of the government as that its several constituent parts may, by their mutual relations, be the means of keeping each other in their proper places. Without presuming to undertake a full development of this important idea I will hazard few general observations which may perhaps place it in a clearer light, and enable us to form a more correct judgment of the principles and structure of the government planned by the convention.

In order to lay a due foundation for that separate and distinct exercise of the different powers of government, which to a certain extent is admitted on all hands to be essential to the preservation of liberty, it is evident that each department should have a will of its own; and consequently should be so constituted that the members of each should have as little agency as possible in the appointment of the members of the others. Were this principle rigorously adhered to, it would require that all the appointments for the supreme executive, legislative, and judiciary magistracies should be drawn from the same fountain of authority, the people, through channels having no communication whatever with one another. Perhaps such a plan of constructing the several departments would be less difficult in practice than it may be in contemplation appear. Some difficulties, however, and some additional expense would attend the execution of it. Some deviations, therefore, from the principle must be admitted. In the constitution of the judiciary department in particular, it might be inexpedient to insist rigorously on the principle: first, because peculiar qualifications being essential in the members, the primary consideration ought to be to select that mode of choice which best secures these qualifications; second, because the permanent tenure by which the appointments are held in that department must soon destroy all sense of dependence on the authority conferring them.

It is equally evident that the members of each department should be as little dependent as possible on those of the others for the emoluments annexed to their offices. Were the executive magistrate, or the judges, not independent of the legislature in this particular, their independence in every other would be merely nominal.

But the great security against a gradual concentration of the several powers in the same department consists in giving to those who administer each department the necessary constitutional means and personal motives to resist encroachments of the others. The provision for defense must in this, as in all other cases, be made commensurate to the danger of attack. Ambition must be made to counteract ambition. The interest of the man must be connected with the constitutional rights of the place. It may be a reflection on human nature that such devices should be necessary to control the abuses of government. But what is government itself but the greatest of all reflections on human nature? If men were angels no government would be necessary. If angels were to govern men, neither external nor internal controls on government would be necessary. In framing a government which is to be administered by men over men, the great difficulty lies in this: you must first enable the government to control the governed; and in the next place oblige it to control itself. A dependence on the people is, no doubt, the primary control on the government; but experience has taught mankind the necessity of auxiliary precautions.

This policy of supplying, by opposite and rival interests, the defect of better motives, might be traced through the whole system of human affairs, private as well as public. We see it particularly displayed in all the subordinate distributions of power, where the constant aim is to divide and arrange the several offices in such a manner as that each may be a check on the other—that the private interest of every individual may be a sentinel over the public rights. These inventions of prudence cannot be less requisite in the distribution of the supreme powers of the State.

But it is not possible to give to each department an equal power of self-defense. In republican government, the legislative authority necessarily predominates. The remedy for this inconveniency is to divide the legislature into different branches; and to render them, by different modes of election and different principles of action, as little connected with each other as the nature of their common functions and their common dependence on the society will admit. It may even be necessary to guard against dangerous encroachments by still further precautions. As the weight of the legislative authority requires that it should be thus divided, the weakness of the executive may require, on the other hand, that it should be fortified. An absolute negative on the legislature appears, at first view, to be the natural defense with which the executive magistrate should be armed. But perhaps it would be neither altogether safe nor alone sufficient. On ordinary occasions it might not be exerted with the requisite firmness, and on extraordinary occasions it might be perfidiously abused. May not this defect of an absolute negative be supplied by some qualified connection between this weaker department and the weaker branch of the stronger department, by which the latter may be led to support the constitutional rights of the former, without being too much detached from the rights of its own department?

If the principles on which these observations are founded be just, as I persuade myself they are, and they be applied as a criterion to the several State constitutions, and to the federal Constitution, it will be found that if the latter does not perfectly correspond with them, the former are infinitely less able to bear such a test.

There are, moreover, two considerations particularly applicable to the federal system of America, which place that system in a very interesting point of view.

First. In a single republic, all the power surrendered by the people is submitted to the administration of a single government; and the usurpations are guarded against by a division of the government into distinct and separate departments. In the compound republic of America, the power surrendered by the people is first divided between two distinct governments, and then the portion allotted to each subdivided among distinct and separate departments. Hence a double security arises to the rights of the people. The different governments will control each other, at the same time that each will be controlled by itself.

Second. It is of great importance in a republic not only to guard the society against the oppression of its rulers, but to guard one part of the society against the injustice of the other part. Different interests necessarily exist in different classes of citizens. If a majority be united by a common interest, the rights of the minority will be insecure. There are but two methods of providing against this evil: the one by creating a will in the community independent of the majority—that is, of the society itself; the other, by comprehending in the society so many separate descriptions of citizens as will render an unjust combination of a majority of the whole very improbable, if not impracticable. The first method prevails in all governments possessing an hereditary or self-appointed authority. This, at best, is but a precarious security; because a power independent of the society may as well espouse the unjust views of the major as the rightful interests of the minor party, and may possibly be turned against both parties. The second method will be exemplified in the federal republic of the United States. Whilst all authority in it will be derived from and dependent on the society, the society itself will be broken into so many parts, interests and classes of citizens, that the rights of individuals, or of the minority, will be in little danger from interested combinations of the majority. In a free government the security for civil rights must be the same as that for religious rights. It consists in the one case in the multiplicity of interests, and in the other in the multiplicity of sects. The degree of security in both cases will depend on the number of interests and sects; and this may be presumed to depend on the extent of country and number of people comprehended under the same government. This view of the subject must particularly recommend a proper federal system to all the sincere and considerate friends of republican government, since it shows that in exact proportion as the territory of the Union may be formed into more circumscribed Confederacies, or States, oppressive combinations of a majority will be facilitated; the best security, under the republican forms, for the rights of every class of citizen, will be diminished; and consequently the stability and independence of some member of the government, the only other security, must be proportionally increased. Justice is the end of government. It is the end of civil society. It ever has been and ever will be pursued until it be obtained, or until liberty be lost in the pursuit. In a society under the forms of which the stronger faction can readily unite and oppress the weaker, anarchy may as truly be said to reign as in a state of nature, where the weaker individual is not secured against the violence of the stronger; and as, in the latter state, even the stronger individuals are prompted, by the uncertainty of their condition, to submit to a government which may protect the weak as well as themselves; so, in the former state, will the more powerful factions or parties be gradually induced, by a like motive, to wish for a government which will protect all parties, the weaker as well as the more powerful. It can be little doubted that if the State of Rhode Island was separated from the Confederacy and left to itself, the insecurity of rights under the popular form of government within such narrow limits would be displayed by such reiterated oppressions of factious majorities that some power altogether independent of the people would soon be called for by the voice of the very factions whose misrule had proved the necessity of it. In the extended republic of the United States, and among the great variety of interests, parties, and sects which it embraces, a coalition of a majority of the whole society could seldom take place on any other principles than those of justice and the general good; whilst there being thus less danger to a minor from the will of a major party, there must be less pretext, also, to provide for the security of the former, by introducing into the government a will not dependent on the latter, or, in other words, a will independent of the society itself. It is no less certain than it is important, notwithstanding the contrary opinions which have been entertained, that the larger the society, provided it lie within a practicable sphere, the more duly capable it will be of self-government. And happily for the *republican cause,* the practicable sphere may be carried to a very great extent by a judicious modification and mixture of the federal principle.

Notes

Chapter 1

[1]Alexis de Tocqueville, *Democracy in America* (1835–1840), ed. J. P. Mayer and A. P. Kerr (Garden City, N.Y.: Doubleday/Anchor, 1969), 640.
[2]See Jay Fliegelman, *Declaring Independence: Jefferson, Natural Language and the Culture of Performance* (Stanford, Calif.: Stanford University Press, 1993).
[3]See Peter Lawler and Robert Schaefer, *American Political Rhetoric*, 2d ed. (Totowa, N.J.: Rowman and Littlefield, 1990).
[4]See Rogers M. Smith, "The American Creed and American Identity: The Limits of Liberal Citizenship in the United States," *Western Political Quarterly* 41 (1988): 225–252; Robert S. Erikson, John P. McIver, and Gerald C. Wright, Jr., "State Political Culture and Public Opinion," *American Political Science Review* 81 (September 1987): 797–813.
[5]Clinton Rossiter, *Conservatism in America* (New York: Vintage Books, 1962), 67.
[6]James Bryce, *The American Commonwealth*, vol. 2 (New York: Macmillan, 1960), 247–254. First published in 1900.
[7]Theodore H. White, "The American Idea," *New York Times Magazine*, July 6, 1986, 12.
[8]Ralph Barton Perry, *Puritanism and Democracy* (New York: Vanguard Press, 1944), 124–125; see also Seymour Martin Lipset, *The First New Nation* (New York: Basic Books, 1963); Louis Hartz, *The Liberal Tradition in America* (New York: Harcourt, Brace, 1955).
[9]See Gabriel Almond and Sidney Verba, *The Civic Culture* (Boston: Little, Brown, 1963); Richard Merelman, *Making Something of Ourselves: On Culture and Politics in the United States* (Berkeley: University of California Press, 1984); Richard J. Ellis, *American Political Cultures* (New York: Oxford University Press, 1993).
[10]Tocqueville, *Democracy in America*, 310.
[11]William James, *The Principles of Psychology* (New York: Dover Publications, 1950), 638. First published in 1918.
[12]See Douglas Muzzio and Richard Behn, "Thinking about Welfare," *The Public Perspective*, February/March 1995, 35–38; Stanley Feldman and John Zaller, "The Political Culture of Ambivalence: Ideological Responses to the Welfare State," *American Journal of Political Science*, 36 (1992): 268–307.
[13]See Claude Lévi-Strauss, *Structural Anthropology* (Chicago: University of Chicago Press, 1983); Clifford Geertz, *Myth, Symbol, and Culture* (New York: Norton, 1974); Anne Norton, *Republic of Signs* (Chicago: University of Chicago Press, 1993).
[14]U.S. Census Bureau figures, except for the data on sentencing in interracial murders: *The New York Times*, April 23, 1987.
[15]Quoted in Ralph Volney Harlow, *The Growth of the United States*, vol. 2 (New York: Henry Holt, 1943), 497.
[16]Paul Gagnon, "Why Study History?" *Atlantic Monthly*, November 1988, 47.
[17]White, "The American Idea," 12.
[18]George Thomas Kurian, *The New Book of World Rankings*, 3d ed. (New York: Facts on File, 1991), 479–480.
[19]See Kevin Phillips, *Boiling Point* (New York: Random House, 1993); Kevin Phillips, *The Politics of Rich and Poor* (New York: Random House, 1990).
[20]Everett Carll Ladd, "An Ideology Regnant," *The Public Perspective*, September/October 1994, 15–16.
[21]Harold D. Lasswell, *Politics: Who Gets What, When, How* (New York: McGraw-Hill, 1938).
[22]Theodore Lowi, *Incomplete Conquest: Governing America* (New York: Holt, Rinehart & Winston, 1981), ch. 1.
[23]Quoted in Michael Harrington, *Socialism* (New York: Bantam, 1973), 142.
[24]*San Antonio Independent School District* v. *Rodriguez*, 411 U.S. 1 (1973).
[25]Harold D. Lasswell and Abraham Kaplan, *Power and Society* (New Haven, Conn.: Yale University Press, 1950), 75–77.
[26]*Federalist* No. 47.
[27]See Charles H. McIlwain, *Constitutionalism: Ancient and Modern* (Ithaca, N.Y.: Cornell University Press, 1983).
[28]Alan S. Rosenbaum, ed., *Constitutionalism: The Philosophical Dimension* (Westport, Conn.: Greenwood Press, 1988), 4.
[29]Tocqueville, *Democracy in America*, ch. 6.
[30]Benjamin I. Page and Robert Shapiro, "Effects of Public Opinion on Policy," *American Political Science Review* 77 (March 1983): 178.
[31]See Robert Dahl, *Democracy and Its Critics* (New Haven, Conn.: Yale University Press, 1989).
[32]C. Wright Mills, *The Power Elite* (New York: Oxford University Press, 1965).
[33]See William Domhoff, *The Power Elite and the State: How Policy Is Made in America* (New York: Aldine de Gruyter, 1990).
[34]David Easton, *The Political System* (New York: Knopf, 1965), 97.
[35]E. E. Schattschneider, *Two Hundred Million Americans in Search of a Government* (New York: Holt, Rinehart & Winston, 1969), 42.

Chapter 2

[1]Woodrow Wilson, *Constitutional Government in the United States* (New York: Columbia University Press, 1908), 173.
[2]See Vincent Ostrom, *The Meaning of American Federalism* (San Francisco: Institute for Contemporary Studies, 1991).
[3]George Bancroft, *History of the Formation of the Constitution of the United States of America*, 3d ed., vol. 1 (New York: D. Appleton, 1883), 166.
[4]Catherine Drinker Bowen, *Miracle at Philadelphia* (Boston: Little, Brown, 1986), 10.
[5]William Wirt Henry, *Patrick Henry: Life, Correspondence, and Speeches*, vol. 3 (New York: Scribner's, 1891), 431.
[6]Alfred H. Kelly, Winifred A. Harbison, and Herman Belz, *The American Constitution*, 7th ed. (New York: Norton, 1991), 122.
[7]*Federalist* No. 2.
[8]*Federalist* No. 45.
[9]*McCulloch* v. *Maryland*, 4 Wheaton 316 (1819).
[10]See also *Martin* v. *Hunter's Lessee*, 1 Wheaton 304 (1816); Stanley Elkins and Eric McKitrick, *The Age of Federalism: The Early American Republic, 1788–1800* (New York: Oxford University Press, 1993).
[11]Oliver Wendell Holmes, Jr., *Collected Legal Papers* (New York: Harcourt, Brace, 1920), 295–296.
[12]John C. Calhoun, *The Works of John C. Calhoun* (New York: Russell & Russell, 1968).

[13]See *Cooley* v. *Board of Wardens of the Port of Philadelphia*, 53 Howard 299 (1851).
[14]*Dred Scott* v. *Sanford*, 19 Howard 393 (1857).
[15]*U.S.* v. *Cruikshank*, 92 U.S. 452 (1876).
[16]*Santa Clara County* v. *Southern Pacific Railroad Co.*, 118 U.S. 394 (1886).
[17]Edward S. Corwin, *The Constitution and What It Means Today*, 12th ed. (Princeton, N.J.: Princeton University Press, 1958), 248.
[18]*U.S.* v. *E. C. Knight Co.*, 156 U.S. 1 (1895).
[19]*Hammer* v. *Dagenhart*, 247 U.S. 251 (1918).
[20]*Lochner* v. *New York*, 198 U.S. 25 (1905).
[21]Kelly, Harbison, and Belz, *The American Constitution*, 529.
[22]James E. Anderson, *The Emergence of the Modern Regulatory State* (Washington, D.C.: Public Affairs Press, 1962), 2–3.
[23]*Schechter Poultry Co.* v. *United States*, 295 U.S. 495 (1935).
[24]*NLRB* v. *Jones and Laughlin Steel*, 301 U.S. 1 (1937).
[25]*American Power and Light* v. *Securities and Exchange Commission*, 329 U.S. 90 (1946); see also Richard A. Maidment, *The Judicial Response to the New Deal* (New York: Manchester University Press, 1992).
[26]See *Heart of Atlanta Motel* v. *United States*, 379 U.S. 241 (1964).
[27]Louis Fisher, *American Constitutional Law* (New York: McGraw-Hill, 1990), 384.
[28]*Brown* v. *Board of Education of Topeka*, 347 U.S. 483 (1954).
[29]*Miranda* v. *Arizona*, 384 U.S. 436 (1966).
[30]For an interesting assessment of change in what has traditionally been America's most distinctive region, see Robert P. Steed, Laurence W. Moreland, and Tod A. Baker, eds., *The Disappearing South?* (Tuscaloosa: University of Alabama Press, 1990).
[31]*Garcia* v. *San Antonio Transit Authority*, 469 U.S. 528 (1985).
[32]See Thomas Anton, *American Federalism and Public Policy* (Philadelphia: Temple University Press, 1989).
[33]Morton Grodzins, *The American System: A New View of Government in the United States* (Chicago: Rand McNally, 1966).
[34]John E. Chubb, "The Political Economy of Federalism," *American Political Science Review* 79 (December 1985): 994–1015.
[35]See Wallace Oates, *Fiscal Federalism* (New York: Harcourt Brace Jovanovich, 1972); Rosella Levaggi, *Fiscal Federalism and Grants-in-Aid* (Brookfield, Vt.: Avebury, 1991).
[36]See David L. Shapiro, *Federalism: A Dialogue* (Evanston, Ill.: Northwestern University Press, 1995); David B. Walker, *Toward a Functioning Federalism* (Cambridge, Mass.: Winthrop, 1981), 102. See also Douglas D. Rose, "National and Local Forces in State Politics," *American Political Science Review* 67 (December 1973): 1162–1173; Morton Grodzins, "Centralization and Decentralization in the American Federal System," in Robert A. Goldwin, ed., *A Nation of States* (Chicago: Rand McNally, 1963), 1–4.
[37]Michael A. Pagano and Ann O'M. Bowman, "The State of American Federalism 1988–1989," *Publius* 19 (Summer 1989): 1.
[38]Charles Schultze, "Federal Spending: Past, Present and Future," in Henry Owen and Charles Schultze, eds., *Setting National Priorities: The Next Ten Years* (Washington, D.C.: Brookings Institution, 1976), 323–369.
[39]Richard Nathan and Fred Doolittle, *Reagan and the States* (Princeton, N.J.: Princeton University Press, 1987); Timothy J. Conlan, *New Federalism* (Washington, D.C.: Brookings Institution, 1988).
[40]Richard Lacayo, "They Can Multiply without Dividing," *Time*, November 21, 1994, 66.
[41]Andrew W. Dobelstein, *Politics, Economics, and Public Welfare* (Englewood Cliffs, N.J.: Prentice-Hall, 1980), 5.
[42]Lloyd A. Free and Hadley Cantril, *The Political Beliefs of Americans* (New York: Simon & Schuster, 1968), 21; see also William Lunch, *The Nationalization of American Politics* (Berkeley: University of California Press, 1987).
[43]Survey for the Times Mirror Center for the People and the Press by Princeton Survey Research Associates, July 12–27, 1994.
[44]Wilson, *Constitutional Government*, 173.

Chapter 3

[1]Quoted in Charles S. Hyneman, "Republican Government in America," in George J. Graham, Jr., and Scarlett G. Graham, eds., *Founding Principles of American Government*, rev. ed. (Chatham, N.J.: Chatham House, 1984), 19.
[2]Thomas Jefferson to John Trumball, February 15, 1789, quoted in Dumas Malone, *Jefferson and the Rights of Man* (Boston: Little, Brown, 1951), 211.
[3]John Locke, *The Two Treatises of Government*, ed. Thomas I. Cook (New York: Hafner, 1947), 159–186, 228–247.
[4]Winthrop D. Jordon and Leon F. Litwack, *The United States*, 6th ed. (Englewood Cliffs, N.J.: Prentice-Hall, 1987), 72–74.
[5]Max Weber, "Politics as a Vocation," in Hans H. Gerth and C. Wright Mills, eds., *From Max Weber: Essays in Sociology* (New York: Oxford University Press, 1958), 78.
[6]Gaillard Hunt, ed., *The Writings of James Madison* (New York: Putnam, 1904), 274.
[7]*Federalist* No. 47.
[8]See *Federalist* Nos. 47 and 48.
[9]Richard Neustadt, *Presidential Power* (New York: Macmillan, 1986), 33.
[10]Henry J. Abraham, *The Judicial Process*, 6th ed. (New York: Oxford University Press, 1993), 320–322.
[11]*Marbury* v. *Madison*, 1 Cranch 137 (1803).
[12]Robert A. Dahl, *Pluralist Democracy in the United States* (Chicago: Rand McNally, 1967), 30.
[13]Quoted in Thomas J. Maroney, "Supreme Law Checks Powers of Government," *Syracuse Herald American*, May 24, 1987, T5.
[14]Daniel Bell, *The End of Ideology* (New York: Collier, 1961), 67.
[15]Quoted in Richard M. Johnson, *The Dynamics of Compliance* (Evanston, Ill.: Northwestern University Press, 1967), 10, 11.
[16]See Hyneman, "Republican Government in America," 19.
[17]Martin Diamond, *The Founding of the Democratic Republic* (Itasca, Ill.: Peacock, 1981), 62–71.
[18]*Federalist* No. 10.
[19]Ibid.
[20]Leslie F. Goldstein, "Judicial Review and Democratic Theory: Guardian Democracy vs. Representative Democracy," *Western Political Quarterly* 40 (1987): 391–412.
[21]Rosemarie Zagarri, "Two Revolutions," *The New Republic*, May 28, 1984, 10.
[22]Richard Henry Lee, "Letters from the Federal Farmer," in Forrest McDonald, ed., *Empire and Nation* (Englewood Cliffs, N.J.: Prentice-Hall, 1962), 103–117.
[23]Ibid.
[24]Hannah Arendt, *On Revolution* (New York: Viking, 1963), ch. 6.
[25]Benjamin Ginsberg, *The Consequences of Consent* (New York: Random House, 1982), 22.

[26]Dahl, *Pluralist Democracy*, 92.
[27]This interpretation is taken from Walter Lippmann, *Public Opinion* (New York: Free Press, 1965), 178–179; for a general discussion of the uncertain meaning of the Constitution, see Lawrence H. Tribe and Michael C. Dorf, *On Reading the Constitution* (Cambridge, Mass.: Harvard University Press, 1991).
[28]James MacGregor Burns, *The Vineyard of Liberty* (New York: Knopf, 1982), 368.
[29]See William Allen White, "The Boss System," in Richard Hofstadter, ed., *The Progressive Movement, 1900–1915* (Englewood Cliffs, N.J.: Prentice-Hall, 1963), 104–107; for a discussion of the modern issue of popular government, see Thomas Cronin, *Direct Democracy* (Cambridge, Mass.: Harvard University Press, 1989).
[30]Woodrow Wilson, *Constitutional Government in the United States* (New York: Columbia University Press, 1908), 67.
[31]Charles S. Beard, *An Economic Interpretation of the Constitution* (New York: Macmillan, 1941). First published in 1913.

Chapter 4

[1]Julian P. Boyd, ed., *The Papers of Thomas Jefferson*, vol. 12 (Princeton, N.J.: Princeton University Press, 1955), 440.
[2]*Anderson* v. *Creighton*, 483 U.S. 635 (1987).
[3]*Bose Corp.* v. *Consumers Union of the United States*, 466 U.S. 485 (1984).
[4]*Schenck* v. *United States*, 249 U.S. 47 (1919).
[5]*Dennis* v. *United States*, 341 U.S. 494 (1951).
[6]See, for example, *Yates* v. *United States*, 354 U.S. 298 (1957); *Noto* v. *United States*, 367 U.S. 290 (1961); *Scales* v. *United States*, 367 U.S. 203 (1961).
[7]*United States* v. *Carolene Products Co.*, 304 U.S. 144 (1938).
[8]*United States* v. *O'Brien*, 391 U.S. 367 (1968).
[9]*United States* v. *Eichman*, 496 U.S. 310 (1990).
[10]*Texas* v. *Johnson*, 491 U.S. 397 (1989).
[11]*New York Times Co.* v. *United States*, 403 U.S. 713 (1971).
[12]*Nebraska Press Assn.* v. *Stuart*, 427 U.S. 539 (1976).
[13]*Barron* v. *Baltimore*, 7 Peters 243 (1833).
[14]*Gitlow* v. *New York*, 268 U.S. 652 (1925).
[15]*Fiske* v. *Kansas*, 274 U.S. 30 (1927) (speech); *Near* v. *Minnesota*, 283 U.S. 697 (1931) (press); *Cantwell* v. *Connecticut*, 310 U.S. 296 (1940) (religion); and *DeJonge* v. *Oregon*, 299 U.S. 253 (1937) (assembly and petition).
[16]*Near* v. *Minnesota*, 283 U.S. 697 (1931).
[17]*Brandenburg* v. *Ohio*, 395 U.S. 444 (1969).
[18]*National Socialist Party* v. *Skokie*, 432 U.S. 43 (1977).
[19]*R.A.V.* v. *St. Paul*, No. 90–7675 (1992).
[20]*Wisconsin* v. *Mitchell*, No. 92–515 (1993).
[21]*Forsyth County* v. *Nationalist Movement*, No. 91–538 (1992).
[22]*New York Times Co.* v. *Sullivan*, 376 U.S. 254 (1964).
[23]*Milkovich* v. *Lorain Journal*, 497 U.S. 1 (1990); see also *Masson* v. *The New Yorker*, No. 89–1799 (1991).
[24]*Miller* v. *California*, 413 U.S. 15 (1973).
[25]*Pope* v. *Illinois*, 85–1973 (1987).
[26]*Barnes* v. *Glen Theatre*, No. 90–26 (1991).
[27]*Stanley* v. *Georgia*, 394 U.S. 557 (1969).
[28]*Osborne* v. *Ohio*, 495 U.S. 103 (1990).
[29]See Frank J. Sorauf, *Wall of Separation: The Constitutional Politics of Church and State* (Princeton, N.J.: Princeton University Press, 1976).
[30]*Board of Regents* v. *Allen*, 392 U.S. 236 (1968).
[31]*Lemon* v. *Kurtzman*, 403 U.S. 602 (1971).
[32]Ibid.
[33]Ibid.
[34]*Engel* v. *Vitale*, 370 U.S. 421 (1962).
[35]*Abington School District* v. *Schempp*, 374 U.S. 203 (1963).
[36]*Wallace* v. *Jaffree*, 472 U.S. 38 (1985).
[37]*Lee* v. *Weisman*, No. 90–1014 (1992); *Rosenberger* v. *Rector (and Visitors*, University of Virginia, 94–329, (1995).
[38]*Goldman* v. *Weinberger*, 475 U.S. 503 (1986).
[39]*Wisconsin* v. *Yoder*, 406 U.S. 295 (1972); see also *Church of the Lukumi Babalu Aye* v. *City of Hialeah*, No. 91–948 (1993).
[40]*McNabb* v. *United States*, 318 U.S. 332 (1943).
[41]*Powell* v. *Alabama*, 287 U.S. 45 (1932).
[42]*Palko* v. *Connecticut*, 302 U.S. 319 (1937).
[43]*Mapp* v. *Ohio*, 367 U.S. 643 (1961).
[44]*Gideon* v. *Wainwright*, 372 U.S. 335 (1963).
[45]*Malloy* v. *Hogan*, 378 U.S. 1 (1964).
[46]*Miranda* v. *Arizona*, 384 U.S. 436 (1966); see also *Escobedo* v. *Illinois*, 378 U.S. 478 (1964).
[47]*Pointer* v. *Texas*, 380 U.S. 400 (1965).
[48]*Klopfer* v. *North Carolina*, 386 U.S. 213 (1967).
[49]*Duncan* v. *Louisiana*, 391 U.S. 145 (1968).
[50]*Benton* v. *Maryland*, 395 U.S. 784 (1969).
[51]See Richard L. Medalic, Leonard Zeitz, and Paul Alexander, "Custodial Police Interrogation in Our Nation's Capital: The Attempt to Implement *Miranda*," *Michigan Law Review* 66 (1968): 1347; David M. O'Brien, *Storm Center: The Supreme Court in American Politics*, 2d ed. (New York: Norton, 1990), 354–358.
[52]*Weeks* v. *United States*, 232 U.S. 383 (1914).
[53]*Nix* v. *Williams*, 467 U.S. 431 (1984); see also *United States* v. *Leon*, 468 U.S. 897 (1984).
[54]*Michigan* v. *Sitz*, No. 88-1897 (1990).
[55]*Whren* v. *United States*, No. 95-5841 (1996).
[56]*Townsend* v. *Sain*, 372 U.S. 293 (1963).
[57]*Keeney* v. *Tamaya-Reyes*, No. 90–1859 (1992); see also *Coleman* v. *Thompson*, No. 89–7662 (1991).
[58]*Brecht* v. *Abrahamson*, No. 91–7358 (1993); see also *McCleskey* v. *Zant*, No. 89–7024 (1991).
[59]*Felker* v. *Turpin*, No. 95-8836 (1996).
[60]See *Batson* v. *Kentucky*, 476 U.S. 79 (1986); *Edmonson* v. *Leesville Concrete Company*, No. 89–7743 (1991); *Powers* v. *Ohio*, 499 U.S. 400 (1991).
[61]*Minnick* v. *Mississippi*, 498 U.S. 146 (1991).
[62]Kurt Heine, "Philadelphia Cops Beat One of Their Own," *Syracuse Herald-American*, January 15, 1995, A13.
[63]*Wilson* v. *Seiter*, No. 89–7376 (1991).
[64]*Harmelin* v. *Michigan*, No. 89–7272 (1991).
[65]*Griswold* v. *Connecticut*, 381 U.S. 479 (1965).
[66]*Roe v. Wade*, 401 U.S. 113 (1973).
[67]*Webster* v. *Reproductive Health Services*, 492 U.S. 490 (1989); see also *Rust* v. *Sullivan*, 500 U.S. 173 (1991).
[68]*Planned Parenthood* v. *Casey*, No. 91–744 (1992).
[69]Charles H. Franklin and Liane C. Kosacki, "Republican Schoolmaster: The U.S. Supreme Court, Public Opinion, and Abortion," *American Political Science Review* 83 (1989): 751–772; see also Barbara Hinkson Craig and David M. O'Brien, *Abortion and American Politics* (Chatham, N.J.: Chatham House, 1993).

Chapter 5

[1]Speech of Martin Luther King, Jr., in Washington, D.C., August 2, 1963.
[2]*Washington Post* wire story, May 14, 1991.
[3]Reported on *CBS Evening News,* January 16, 1989.
[4]Robert Nisbet, "Public Opinion versus Popular Opinion," *Public Interest* 41 (1975): 171.
[5]See Jennifer Hochschild, *The New American Dilemma* (New Haven, Conn.: Yale University Press), 1984.
[6]The classic analysis of this system of legalized segregation is C. Vann Woodward, *The Strange Career of Jim Crow,* 3d rev. ed. (New York: Oxford University Press, 1974).
[7]*Plessy* v. *Ferguson,* 163 U.S. 537 (1896).
[8]See, for example, *Missouri ex rel. Gaines* v. *Canada,* 305 U.S. 57 (1938).
[9]See Richard Kugler, *Simple Justice: The History of* Brown *v.* Board of Education *and Black America's Struggle for Equality* (New York: Knopf, 1977).
[10]*Brown* v. *Board of Education of Topeka,* 347 U.S. 483 (1954).
[11]See Francis M. Wilhoit, *The Politics of Massive Resistance* (New York: Braziller, 1973).
[12]See David J. Garrow, *Protest at Selma: Martin Luther King and the Voting Rights Act of 1965* (New Haven, Conn.: Yale University Press, 1978).
[13]See Steven A. Shull, *The President and Civil Rights Policy: Leadership and Change* (Westport, Conn.: Greenwood Press, 1989).
[14]See Sar Levitan, William Johnson, and Robert Taggert, *Still a Dream* (Cambridge, Mass.: Harvard University Press, 1975).
[15]See Derrick Bell, *And We Are Not Saved: The Elusive Quest for Racial Justice* (New York: Basic Books, 1987).
[16]See Robert C. Smith and Richard S. Hzer, *Race, Class, and Culture* (Albany: State University of New York Press, 1992).
[17]See Michael B. Preston, Lenneal J. Henderson, Jr., and Paul Puryear, eds., *The New Black Politics* (New York: Longman, 1982).
[18]See Glenna Matthews, *The Rise of Public Women* (New York: Oxford University Press, 1994).
[19]*Tinker* v. *Colwell,* 193 U.S. 473 (1904).
[20]For a history of the women's rights movement, see Eleanor Flexner, *Century of Struggle,* rev. ed. (Cambridge, Mass.: Harvard University Press, 1975).
[21]See Ellen Carol DuBois, *Feminism and Suffrage: The Emergence of an Independent Women's Movement in America, 1848–1869* (Ithaca, N.Y.: Cornell University Press, 1978); Susan Cary Nicholas, *Rights and Wrongs* (Old Westbury, N.Y.: Feminist Press, 1979).
[22]See Jane Mansbridge, *Why We Lost the ERA* (Chicago: University of Chicago Press, 1986).
[23]See Joyce Gelb and Marian Lief Paley, *Women and Public Policies* (Princeton, N.J.: Princeton University Press, 1982).
[24]M. Margaret Conway, David W. Ahern, and Gertrude A. Steuernagel, *Women and Public Policy: A Revolution in Progress* (Washington, D.C.: Congressional Quarterly Press, 1994).
[25]Susan J. Carroll, *Women as Candidates in American Politics* (Bloomington: Indiana University Press, 1985).
[26]See Linda Witt, Karen M. Paget, and Glenna Matthews, *Running as a Woman* (New York: Free Press, 1994).
[27]Mary Lou Kendrigan, *Political Equality in a Democratic Society: Women in the United States* (Westport, Conn.: Greenwood Press, 1984).
[28]Timothy Bledsoe and Mary Herring, "Victims of Circumstance: Women in Pursuit of Political Office," *American Political Science Review* 84 (1990): 213–224.
[29]"The Gender Gap at the State Level," *The Public Perspective,* January/February 1993, 100.
[30]See, however, Sara M. Evans and Barbara Nelson, *Wage Justice* (Chicago: University of Chicago Press, 1989).
[31]See Ellen Frankel Paul, *Equity and Gender* (New Brunswick, N.J.: Transaction Books, 1989).
[32]"Confusion Exists on Issue of Harassment," *Minneapolis Star Tribune,* October 13, 1991, 1A, 4A, 5A.
[33]Ibid.
[34]See Rudulfo O. de la Garza, Louis DeSipio, F. Chris Garcia, John Garcia, and Angelo Falcon, *Latino Voices* (Boulder, Colo.: Westview Press, 1992).
[35]*De Canas* v. *Bica,* 424 U.S. 351 (1976).
[36]Nancy Gibbs, "Keep Out, You Tired, You Poor . . .," *Time,* October 3, 1994, 46–47.
[37]James Truslow Adams, *The March of Democracy,* vol. 4 (New York: Scribner's, 1933), 284–285.
[38]*Lau* v. *Nichols,* 414 U.S. 563 (1974).
[39]See, for example, *Plyler* v. *Doe,* 457 U.S. 202 (1982).
[40]See *Reed* v. *Reed,* 404 U.S. 71 (1971).
[41]*Craig* v. *Boren,* 429 U.S. 190 (1976).
[42]*Rostker* v. *Goldberg,* 453 U.S. 57 (1980).
[43]*United States* v. *Virginia,* No. 94-1941 (1996).
[44]Federal Reserve Bank data, 1991.
[45]See J. Morgan Kousser, *The Shaping of Southern Politics: Suffrage Restriction and the Establishment of the One-Party South, 1880–1910* (New Haven, Conn.: Yale University Press, 1974).
[46]V. O. Key, Jr., *Southern Politics* (New York: Knopf, 1949), 495.
[47]*Smith* v. *Allwright,* 321 U.S. 649 (1944).
[48]See Bernard Grofman, Lisa Handley, and Richard Niemi, *Minority Representation and the Quest for Voting Equality* (New York: Cambridge University Press, 1992).
[49]*Bush* v. *Verg,* No. 94-805 (1996); *Shaw* v. *Hunt,* No. 94-923 (1996); *Muller* v. *Johnson,* 94-631 (1995).
[50]*University of California Regents* v. *Bakke,* 438 U.S. 265 (1978).
[51]*Steelworkers* v. *Weber,* 443 U.S. 193 (1979); *Fullilove* v. *Klutznick,* 448 U.S. 448 (1980).
[52]*Local No. 28, Sheet Metal Workers* v. *Equal Employment Opportunity Commission,* 478 U.S. 421 (1986); see also *Local No. 93, International Association of Firefighters* v. *Cleveland,* 478 U.S. 501 (1986).
[53]*Firefighters* v. *Stotts,* 459 U.S. 969 (1984); see also *Wygant* v. *Jackson,* 476 U.S. 238 (1986).
[54]*Martin* v. *Wilks,* 490 U.S. 755 (1989).
[55]*Wards Cove Packing* v. *Antonio,* 490 U.S. 642 (1989).
[56]*Adarand* v. *Pena,* 94-310 (1995).
[57]See Robert M. O'Neill, *Discrimination against Discrimination* (Bloomington: Indiana University Press, 1975).
[58]Herbert McClosky and John Zaller, *American Ethos: Public Attitudes toward Capitalism and Democracy* (Cambridge, Mass.: Harvard University Press, 1985), 93.
[59]Richard Morin and Barbara Vobejda, "It Was the Year of the Angry (White) Man," *The Washington Post National Weekly Edition,* November 14–20, 1994, 37.
[60]Gunnar Myrdal, *An American Dilemma: The Negro Problem and Modern Democracy* (New York: Harper, 1944).

[61]*Swann* v. *Charlotte-Mecklenburg County Board of Education*, 402 U.S. 1 (1971).
[62]See Hochschild, *The New American Dilemma;* Michael W. Giles and Thomas G. Walker, "Judicial Policy-Making and Southern School Segregation," *Journal of Politics* 37 (1975); 936.
[63]*Washington* v. *Seattle School District*, 458 U.S. 457 (1982).
[64]*Milliken* v. *Bradley*, 418 U.S. 717 (1974).
[65]*Missouri* v. *Jenkins* (1995); see also *Board of Education (Oklahoma City)* v. *Dowell*, 498 U.S. 237 (1991).
[66]Hochschild, *The New American Dilemma.*

Chapter 6

[1]V. O. Key, Jr., *Public Opinion and American Democracy* (New York: Knopf, 1961), 8.
[2]Elisabeth Noelle-Neumann, *The Spiral of Silence*, 2d ed. (Chicago: University of Chicago Press, 1993), ch. 1.
[3]See Benjamin I. Page and Robert Shapiro, *The Rational Public* (Chicago: University of Chicago Press, 1992), 285–288.
[4]Jerry L. Yeric and John R. Todd, *Public Opinion*, 2d ed. (Itasca, Ill.: Peacock, 1989), 3.
[5]Noelle-Neumann, *The Spiral of Silence*, ch. 1.
[6]Robert Nisbet, "Public Opinion versus Popular Opinion," *Public Interest* 41 (1975): 167.
[7]Ibid.
[8]*Federalist* No. 10.
[9]George Gallup, "Polls and the Political Process—Past, Present, and Future," *Public Opinion Quarterly* 40 (Winter 1965): 547–548.
[10]Warren E. Leary, "Two Superpowers' Citizens Do Badly in Geography," *The New York Times*, November 9, 1989, A6.
[11]Survey of students of the eight Ivy League schools by Luntz & Weber Research and Strategic Services, for the University of Pennsylvania's Ivy League Study, November 13–December 1, 1992.
[12]Sidney Verba and Norman H. Nie, *Participation in America: Political Democracy and Social Equality* (New York: Harper & Row, 1972), 281–284.
[13]Debra J. Saunders, "Poll Shows America in Deep Dumbo," *The San Francisco Chronicle*, April 23, 1993, A30.
[14]David W. Moore and Frank Newport, "Misreading the Public: The Case of the Holocaust Poll," *The Public Perspective*, March/April 1994, 28–29.
[15]James Bryce, *The American Commonwealth*, vol. 2 (New York: Macmillan, 1900), 247–254.
[16]Steven A. Peterson, *Political Behavior: Patterns in Everyday Life* (Newbury Park, Calif.: Sage Publications, 1990), 28–29.
[17]Ibid.
[18]See James E. Combs, *Polpop 2: Politics and Popular Culture in America* (Bowling Green, Ohio: Bowling Green University Press, 1991).
[19]See Murray Edelman, *Politics as Symbolic Action* (Chicago: Markham, 1971).
[20]See M. Kent Jennings and Richard Niemi, "The Transmission of Political Values from Parent to Child," *American Political Science Review* 62 (March 1968): 169–184.
[21]M. Kent Jennings and Richard G. Niemi, *Generations and Politics* (Princeton, N.J.: Princeton University Press, 1981), 91.
[22]See David Easton and Jack Dennis, *Children in the Political System* (New York: McGraw-Hill, 1969); Gabriel Almond and Sidney Verba, *The Civic Culture* (Boston: Little, Brown, 1965), 276.
[23]Kent Tedin, "The Influence of Parents on the Political Attitudes of Adolescents," *American Political Science Review* 68 (December 1974): 1579–1592; M. Kent Jennings and Richard G. Niemi, *The Political Character of Adolescence* (Princeton, N.J.: Princeton University Press, 1974).
[24]See Robert D. Hess and Judith V. Torney, *The Development of Political Attitudes in Children* (Chicago: Aldine, 1967), 219; Orit Ichilov, *Political Socialization, Citizenship Education, and Democracy* (New York: Teachers College Press, 1990).
[25]Noelle-Neumann, *The Spiral of Silence.*
[26]See Shanto Iyengar, *Is Anyone Responsible? How Television Frames Political Issues* (Chicago: University of Chicago Press, 1991); Shanto Iyengar and Donald Kinder, *News That Matters: Television and American Opinion* (Chicago: University of Chicago Press, 1987).
[27]See David Green, *Shaping Political Consciousness: The Language of Politics in America from McKinley to Reagan* (Ithaca, N.Y.: Cornell University Press, 1988).
[28]See Paul Brace and Barbara Hinckley, *Follow the Leader: Opinion Polls and Modern Presidents* (New York: Basic Books, 1992).
[29]See Richard Merelman, *Making Something of Ourselves* (Berkeley: University of California Press, 1984); John White, *The New Politics of Old Values* (Hanover, N.H.: University Press of New England, 1988); Richard J. Ellis, *American Political Cultures* (New York: Oxford University Press, 1993).
[30]Surveys by Princeton Survey Research Associates for Times-Mirror, conducted throughout 1990 and 1991.
[31]Alternative conceptualizations that are potentially useful have not been widely explored. See, for example, Pamela Johnston Conover and Stanley Feldman, "Belief System Organization in the American Electorate: An Alternative Approach," in John C. Pierce and John L. Sullivan, eds., *The Electorate Reconsidered* (Beverly Hills, Calif.: Sage, 1980); Shawn Rosenberg, Dana Ward, and Stephen Chilton, *Political Reasoning and Cognition* (Durham, N.C.: Duke University Press, 1988).
[32]CBS News/New York Times surveys, 1988 and 1992.
[33]Philip Converse, "The Nature of Belief Systems in Mass Publics," in David Apter, ed., *Ideology and Discontent* (New York: Free Press, 1965), 206.
[34]John L. Sullivan, James E. Pierson, and George E. Marcus, "Ideological Constraint in the Mass Public," *American Journal of Political Science* 22 (May 1978): 233–249; Eric R. A. N. Smith, *The Unchanging American Voter* (Berkeley: University of California Press, 1989).
[35]Yeric and Todd, *Public Opinion*, 103–105.
[36]See E. J. Dionne, *Why Americans Hate Politics* (New York: Simon & Schuster, 1992).
[37]Gallup poll for CNN/USA Today, 1994; see also William S. Maddox and Stuart A. Little, *Beyond Liberal and Conservative* (Washington, D.C.: Cato Institute, 1984).
[38]Converse, "The Nature of Belief Systems."
[39]Survey by Louis Harris and Associates for the NAACP Legal Defense and Educational Fund, June 3–September 12, 1988.
[40]See Angus Campbell, Philip Converse, Warren Miller, and Donald Stokes, *The American Voter* (New York: Wiley, 1960), chs. 3–4.
[41]Martin P. Wattenberg, *The Decline of American Political Parties, 1952–1984* (Cambridge, Mass.: Harvard University Press, 1990).
[42]See E. E. Schattschneider, *The Semisovereign People* (New York: Holt, Rinehart & Winston, 1980), ch. 8.

[43]See William Domhoff, *The Power Elite and the State* (New York: Aldine de Gruyter, 1990).
[44]Benjamin I. Page and Robert Y. Shapiro, "Effects of Public Opinion on Policy," *American Political Science Review* 77 (March 1983): 178.
[45]See Benjamin Ginsberg, *The Consequences of Consent* (New York: Random House, 1982).

Chapter 7

[1]Walter Lippmann, *Public Opinion* (New York: Free Press, 1965), 36. First published in 1922.
[2]"Congress's Sour Finish," *The New York Times*, October 8, 1994, 22.
[3]Sidney Verba and Norman H. Nie, *Participation in America: Political Democracy and Social Equality* (New York: Harper & Row, 1972), 1; see also Steven J. Rosenstone and John Mark Hansen, *Mobilization, Participation and Democracy in America* (New York: Macmillan, 1993).
[4]Quoted in Ralph Volney Harlow, *The Growth of the United States* (New York: Henry Holt, 1943), 312.
[5]See William H. Flanigan and Nancy Zingale, *The Political Behavior of the American Electorate*, 8th ed. (Washington, D.C.: Congressional Quarterly Press, 1994), 24–26.
[6]Example from Gus Tyler, "One Cheer for the Democrats," *New Leader*, November 3, 1986, 6.
[7]Turnout figures provided by Washington, D.C., embassies of the respective countries, 1995.
[8]Philip E. Converse, "Change in the American Electorate," in Philip E. Converse and Angus Campbell, eds., *The Human Meaning of Social Change* (New York: Russell Sage Foundation, 1972), 281; see also Stanley Kelley, Jr., Richard E. Ayres, and William G. Bowen, "Registration and Voting: Putting First Things First," *American Political Science Review* 61 (June 1967): 359–379. For insights into the impact on electoral behavior of another reform, the Australian ballot, see Jerrold D. Rusk, "The Effect of the Australian Ballot Reform on Split Ticket Voting: 1876–1908," *American Political Science Review* 64 (December 1970): 1220–1238.
[9]Ivor Crewe, "Electoral Participation," in David Butler, Howard R. Penniman, and Austin Ranney, eds., *Democracy at the Polls* (Washington, D.C.: American Enterprise Institute, 1981), 249.
[10]Philip E. Converse with Richard Niemi, "Non-Voting among Young Adults in the United States," in William J. Crotty et al., eds., *Political Parties and Political Behavior* (Boston: Allyn & Bacon, 1971), 456.
[11]Benjamin Ginsberg, *The Consequences of Consent* (New York: Random House, 1982), 49.
[12]Richard Scammon, "Senate Kills Filibuster Threat, Clears 'Motor Voter' Bill," *Congressional Quarterly Weekly Report*, May 15, 1993, 1221.
[13]Crewe, "Electoral Participation," 230.
[14]Malcom Jewell and David Olson, *American State Politics and Elections* (Homewood, Ill.: Irwin Press, 1978), 50.
[15]A. Karnig and B. Walter, "Municipal Elections," in *Municipal Yearbook, 1977* (Washington, D.C.: International City Management Assn., 1977).
[16]Richard Boyd, "Decline of U.S. Voter Turnout," *American Politics Quarterly* 9 (April 1981), 142.
[17]Austin Ranney, "Candidate Selection," in Butler, Penniman, and Ranney, *Democracy at the Polls*, 88.
[18]See Ruy A. Teixeira, *The Disappearing American Voter* (Washington, D.C.: Brookings Institution, 1992).
[19]Crewe, "Electoral Participation," 251–253.
[20]See G. Bingham Powell, "Voting Turnout in Thirty Democracies," in Richard Rose, ed., *Electoral Participation: A Comparative Analysis* (Beverly Hills, Calif.: Sage, 1980).
[21]Warren E. Miller, Arthur H. Miller, and Edward J. Schneider, *American National Election Studies Sourcebook* (Cambridge, Mass.: Harvard University Press, 1980), table 5.23.
[22]Jerry L. Yeric and John R. Todd, *Public Opinion*, 2d ed. (Itasca, Ill.: Peacock, 1989), 226.
[23]See, for example, Norman H. Nie, G. Bingham Powell, and Kenneth Prewitt, "Social Structure and Political Participation," *American Political Science Review* 63 (September 1969).
[24]Yeric and Todd, *Public Opinion*, 226.
[25]Verba and Nie, *Participation in America*, 139; John M. Strate, Charles J. Parrish, Charles D. Elder, and Coit Ford III, "Life Span Civic Development and Voting Participation," *American Political Science Review* 83 (June 1989): 443–465.
[26]Boyd, "Decline of U.S. Voter Turnout," 136. The trend toward increased turnout between 1920 and 1960 supports Boyd's explanation. The period was marked by a decline in the birthrate, particularly during the Depression of the 1930s.
[27]M. Margaret Conway, *Political Participation in the United States*, 2d ed. (Washington, D.C.: Congressional Quarterly Press, 1991), 23–25.
[28]Ibid., 122–123.
[29]Raymond E. Wolfinger and Steven J. Rosenstone, *Who Votes?* (New Haven, Conn.: Yale University Press, 1980), 17–21.
[30]Nelson W. Polsby, *Consequences of Party Reform* (New York: Oxford University Press, 1983), 158.
[31]Verba and Nie, *Participation in America*, 340.
[32]Mark Kesselman and Joel Kreiger, *European Politics in Transition* (Lexington, Mass.: Heath, 1987), 87.
[33]Arthur T. Hadley, *The Empty Polling Booth* (Englewood Cliffs, N.J.: Prentice-Hall, 1978), 40.
[34]Seymour Martin Lipset, *Political Man* (Garden City, N.Y.: Doubleday/Anchor, 1963), 194.
[35]Walter Dean Burnham, "The Class Gap," *The New Republic*, May 9, 1988, 30, 32.
[36]Edie N. Goldenberg and Michael W. Traugott, *Campaigning for Congress* (Washington, D.C.: Congressional Quarterly Press, 1984), ch. 9.
[37]Thomas E. Patterson, *The Mass Media Election* (New York: Praeger, 1980), chs. 7–10.
[38]V. O. Key, Jr., *The Responsible Electorate* (Cambridge, Mass.: Belknap Press of Harvard University Press, 1966), ch. 1.
[39]Seymour Martin Lipset, "The Economy, Elections, and Public Opinion," *Tocqueville Review* 5 (Fall 1983): 431.
[40]D. Roderick Kiewiet, *Macro-Economics and Micro-Politics* (Chicago: University of Chicago Press, 1983), 154–158.
[41]Gallup Reports, 1936–1994.
[42]Richard Rose and Harve Mossawir, "Voting and Elections: A Functional Analysis," *Political Studies Quarterly* 15 (1967): 173.
[43]Joseph Schumpeter, *Capitalism, Socialism, and Democracy* (New York: Harper Torchbooks, 1950), 269.
[44]W. Russell Neuman, *The Paradox of Mass Politics* (Cambridge, Mass.: Harvard University Press, 1986), 176.
[45]Samuel H. Barnes et al., eds., *Political Action* (Beverly Hills, Calif.: Sage, 1979), 541–542.

[46]Russell J. Dalton, *Citizen Politics in Western Democracies* (Chatham, N.J.: Chatham House, 1988), 43.
[47]Barnes et al., *Political Action*, 541–542.
[48]Marshall McLuhan, *Understanding Media: The Extensions of Man* (New York: McGraw-Hill, 1964).
[49]Robert Entman, *Democracy without Citizens* (New York: Oxford University Press, 1989).
[50]Verba and Nie, *Participation in America*, 131.
[51]Ibid., 80.
[52]Ibid., 131.
[53]Neuman, *The Paradox of Mass Politics*, 99.
[54]See Ginsberg, *The Consequences of Consent*, ch. 2.
[55]Conway, *Political Participation*, 76–78; see also Laura R. Woliver, *From Outrage to Action* (Urbana: University of Illinois Press, 1993).
[56]J. Craig Jenkins, *The Politics of Insurgency: The Farm Workers Movement in the 1960s* (New York: Columbia University Press, 1985).
[57]See Jerome K. Skolnick, *The Politics of Protest* (New York: Ballantine, 1969).
[58]Dalton, *Citizen Politics in Western Democracies*, 59–61; see also Katherine Tate, *From Protest to Politics* (Cambridge, Mass.: Harvard University Press, 1994).
[59]Ibid., 68.
[60]Ronald Inglehart, "Post-Materialism in an Environment of Insecurity," *American Political Science Review* 75 (1981): 880–900; Edward N. Mueller and Mitchell A. Seligson, "Inequality and Insurgency," *American Political Science Review* 81 (1987): 425–451.
[61]William Watts and Lloyd A. Free, eds., *The State of the Nation* (New York: University Books, Potomac Associates, 1967), 97.
[62]Harry Holloway with John George, *Public Opinion*, 2d ed. (New York: St. Martin's Press, 1986), 157.
[63]Robert E. Lane, "Market Justice, Political Justice," *American Political Science Review* 80 (1986): 383; see also Jennifer Nedelsky, *Private Property and the Limits of American Constitutionalism* (New York: Oxford University Press, 1990).
[64]Wolfinger and Rosenstone, *Who Votes?* 110.
[65]See Frances Fox Piven and Richard A. Cloward, *Why Americans Don't Vote* (New York: Pantheon, 1988).
[66]Burnham, "The Class Gap," 30; see also Stephen Earl Bennett and David Resnick, "The Implications of Nonvoting for Democracy in the United States," *American Journal of Political Science* 34 (August 1990); 771–802.
[67]See Verba and Nie, *Participation in America*, 332; V. O. Key, Jr., *Southern Politics* (New York: Vintage Books, 1949), 527.

Chapter 8

[1]E. E. Schattschneider, *Party Government* (New York: Rinehart, 1942), 1.
[2]Leon D. Epstein, *Political Parties in Western Democracies* (New York: Praeger, 1967), 9.
[3]Paul J. Best, Kul B. Rai, and David F. Walsh, *Politics in Three Worlds* (New York: Wiley, 1986), 324.
[4]E. E. Schattschneider, *The Semisovereign People: A Realist's View of Democracy in America* (New York: Holt, Rinehart & Winston, 1961), 86–96.
[5]L. Sandy Maisel, *Parties and Elections in America*, 2d ed. (New York: McGraw-Hill, 1993), 27.
[6]Walter Dean Burnham, "The End of American Party Politics," in Walter Dean Burnham, ed., *Politics/America: The Cutting Edge of Change* (New York: Van Nostrand, 1973), 132.
[7]See Richard P. McCormick, *The Second American Party System: Party Formation in the Jacksonian Era* (Chapel Hill: University of North Carolina Press, 1966).
[8]Alexis de Tocqueville, *Democracy in America* (1835–1840), ed. J. P. Mayer and A. P. Kerr (Garden City, N.Y.: Doubleday/Anchor, 1969), 60.
[9]Glyndon G. Van Deusen, "The Whig Party," in Arthur M. Schlesinger, Jr., ed., *History of the U.S. Political Parties*, vol. 1 (New York: Chelsea House, 1973), 344.
[10]Ibid.
[11]William Crotty, "The Party Symbol and Its Changing Meaning," in William Crotty, ed., *The Party Symbol* (San Francisco: Freeman, 1980), 6.
[12]See Kristi Andersen, *The Creation of a Democratic Majority, 1928–1936* (Chicago: University of Chicago Press, 1979).
[13]See Kevin Phillips, *The Emerging Republican Majority* (New Rochelle, N.Y.: Arlington House, 1969).
[14]See Harold W. Stanley, "Southern Partisan Changes: Dealignment, Realignment or Both?" *Journal of Politics* 50 (1988): 64–88; Earl Black and Merle Black, *Politics and Society in the South* (Cambridge, Mass.: Harvard University Press, 1987); Robert H. Swansbrough and David M. Brodsky, eds., *The South's New Politics: Realignment and Dealignment* (Columbia: University of South Carolina Press, 1988); Dewey L. Grantham, *The Life and Death of the Solid South* (Lexington: University of Kentucky Press, 1988); Alexander P. Lamis, ed., *The Two-Party South* (New York: Oxford University Press, 1988).
[15]William H. Flanigan and Nancy Zingale, *Political Behavior of the American Electorate*, 8th ed. (Washington, D.C.: Congressional Quarterly Press, 1994), 58–63.
[16]See Bernard Berelson, Paul Lazarsfeld, and William McPhee, *Voting* (Chicago: University of Chicago Press, 1954), 18.
[17]See Phillips, *The Emerging Republican Majority.*
[18]The classic account of the relationship of electoral and party systems is Maurice Duverger, *Political Parties* (New York: Wiley, 1954), bk. II, ch. 1; see also Giovanni Sartori, *Parties and Party Systems* (Cambridge, England: Cambridge University Press, 1976); Arend Lijphardt, *Electoral Systems and Party Systems* (New York: Oxford University Press, 1994).
[19]See Frank Smallwood, *The Other Candidates: Third Parties in Presidential Elections* (Dartmouth, N.H.: University Press of New England, 1983); Steven J. Rosenstone, Roy L. Behr, and Edward H. Lazarus, *Third Parties in America* (Princeton, N.J.: Princeton University Press, 1984).
[20]Daniel A. Mazmanian, *Third Parties in Presidential Elections* (Washington, D.C.: Brookings Institution, 1984), 143–144.
[21]Walter Dean Burnham, *Critical Elections and the Mainsprings of American Politics* (New York: Norton, 1970), 27.
[22]James L. Sundquist, *Dynamics of the Party System* (Washington, D.C.: Brookings Institution, 1973), 140.
[23]See Lawrence Goodwyn, *The Populist Movement* (New York: Oxford University Press, 1978).
[24]Clinton Rossiter, *Parties and Politics in America* (Ithaca, N.Y.: Cornell University Press, 1960), 11.
[25]See G. William Domhoff, *Who Rules America Now?* (Englewood Cliffs, N.J.: Prentice-Hall, 1983), 117–129.
[26]See Anthony Downs, *An Economic Theory of Democracy* (New York: Harper & Row, 1957), chs. 7 and 8.

[27]Data from network exit polls, November 1992.
[28]Gerald M. Pomper, *Passions and Interests: Political Party Concepts of American Democracy* (Lawrence: University of Kansas Press, 1992), ch. 1.
[29]John F. Bibby, *Politics, Parties, and Elections in America,* 2d ed. (Chicago: Nelson-Hall, 1992), 275–283.
[30]See John R. Petrocik, *Party Coalitions: Realignments and the Decline of the New Deal System* (Chicago: University of Chicago Press, 1981).
[31]Schattschneider, *The Semisovereign People,* 140.
[32]See Domhoff, *Who Rules America Now?* 117–129.
[33]Pomper, *Passions and Interests,* ch. 6.

Chapter 9

[1]Frank J. Sorauf, *Party Politics in America,* 5th ed. (Boston: Little, Brown, 1984), 61.
[2]"The Clean-Slate Club,"*Newsweek,* October 17, 1994, p. 35.
[3]See Alan Ehrenhalt, *The United States of Ambition* (New York: Times Books, 1991).
[4]See Xander Kayden and Eddie Mahe, *The Party Goes On* (New York: Basic Books, 1985).
[5]William Crotty, "The Party Symbol and Its Changing Meaning," in William Crotty, ed., *The Party Symbol* (San Francisco: Freeman, 1980), 13.
[6]James W. Davis, *National Conventions in an Age of Party Reform* (Westport, Conn.: Greenwood Press, 1983), 4.
[7]William L. Riordon, *Plunkitt of Tammany Hall* (New York: Dutton, 1963), xvi.
[8]Lyle W. Dorsett, *The Pendergast Machine* (New York: Oxford University Press, 1968), 42.
[9]Robert M. La Follette, Sr., *La Follette's Autobiography* (Madison, Wis.: R. M. La Follette, 1913), 197–198; quoted in Sorauf, *Party Politics in America,* 210.
[10]V. O. Key, Jr., *American State Politics* (New York: Knopf, 1956), 88, 117.
[11]Sarah McCally Morehouse, "The Effect of Pre-Primary Endorsements on State Party Strength," paper delivered at the 1980 meeting of the American Political Science Association, August 1980, 17.
[12]See Malcolm Jewell, *Parties and Primaries* (New York: Praeger, 1984), 67.
[13]Samuel J. Eldersveld, *Political Parties in American Society* (New York: Basic Books, 1982), 96–97.
[14]Leon Epstein, *Political Parties in the American Mold* (Madison: University of Wisconsin Press, 1986), 244–245.
[15]See James Q. Wilson, *The Amateur Democrat* (Chicago: University of Chicago Press, 1962); Robert S. Hirschfield, Bert E. Swanson, and Blanche D. Blank, "A Profile of Political Activists in Manhattan," *Western Political Quarterly* 15 (1962): 489–506.
[16]Joseph Schlesinger, *Ambition and Politics* (Chicago: Rand McNally, 1966), 125–133.
[17]See Edie N. Goldenberg and Michael W. Traugott, *Campaigning for Congress* (Washington, D.C.: Congressional Quarterly Press, 1984), 86.
[18]David B. Magleby and Candice J. Nelson, *The Money Chase: Congressional Campaign Finance Reform* (Washington, D.C.: Brookings Institution, 1990).
[19]Michael Wines, "Who? Us? Washington Really Is in Touch. We're the Problem," *The New York Times,* October 16, 1994, sec. 4, p. 1.
[20]See Paul S. Herrnson, *Party Campaigning in the '80s* (Cambridge, Mass.: Harvard University Press, 1988).
[21]See James L. Gibson, John P. Frendreis, and Laura L. Vertz, "Party Dynamics in the 1980s: Change in County Party Organizational Strength, 1980–1984," *American Journal of Political Science* 33 (1989): 67–90.
[22]Richard J. Tobin and Edward Keynes, "Institutional Differences in the Recruitment Process," *American Journal of Political Science* 19 (November 1975): 674.
[23]Paul S. Herrnson, "Do Parties Make a Difference? The Role of Party Organizations in Congressional Elections," *Journal of Politics* 48 (1986): 589–615.
[24]See Milton Rakove, *Don't Make No Waves, Don't Back No Losers* (Bloomington: Indiana University Press, 1975); see also John Allswang, *Bosses, Machines, and Urban Voters* (Baltimore, Md.: Johns Hopkins University Press, 1986).
[25]John F. Bibby, *Politics, Parties, and Elections in America,* 2d ed. (Chicago: Nelson-Hall, 1992), 97.
[26]See John P. Frendreis, James L. Gibson, and Laura L. Vertz, "The Electoral Relevance of Local Party Organizations," *American Political Science Review* 84 (1990): 226–235.
[27]Quoted in Malcolm Jewell and David Olson, *American State Political Parties and Elections,* 2d ed. (Homewood, Ill.: Dorsey Press, 1982), 185.
[28]Gibson, Frendreis, and Vertz, "Party Dynamics in the 1980s," 67–90.
[29]Bibby, *Politics, Parties, and Elections in America,* 97.
[30]Jewell and Olson, *American State Political Parties,* 67–70.
[31]James L. Gibson, Cornelius P. Cotter, John F. Bibby, and Robert J. Huckshorn, "Assessing Party Organizational Strength," *American Journal of Political Science* 27 (May 1983): 200; John F. Bibby, Cornelius P. Cotter, James L. Gibson, and Robert L. Huckshorn, "Parties in State Politics," in Virginia Gray, Herbert Jacob, and Kenneth N. Vines, eds., *Politics in the American States* (Boston: Little, Brown, 1983), 77.
[32]See, for example, Sarah McCally Morehouse, "Money versus Party Effort: Nominating for Governor," *American Journal of Political Science* 34 (1990): 706–724.
[33]See Denis G. Sullivan, Jeffrey L. Pressman, Benjamin I. Page, and John J. Lyons, *The Politics of Representation: The Democratic Convention, 1972* (New York: St. Martin's Press, 1974).
[34]Bibby, *Politics, Parties, and Elections in America,* 86.
[35]William Crotty, "National Committees as Grass-Roots Vehicles of Representation," in Crotty, *The Party Symbol,* 33–49.
[36]*Cousins* v. *Wigoda,* 419 U.S. 477 (1975); *Democratic Party of the United States* v. *La Follette,* 450 U.S. 107 (1975).
[37]Quoted in Bibby, *Politics, Parties, and Elections in America,* 88.
[38]Frank J. Sorauf, *Money in American Elections* (Glenview, Ill.: Scott, Foresman, 1988), 132.
[39]Observation based on unpublished Ph.D. dissertation research, Diana Dwyer, Syracuse University, Syracuse, New York, 1994.
[40]Ibid.
[41]See Peter Byrne Edsall, *The New Politics of Inequality* (New York: Norton, 1984).
[42]David Adamany, "Political Parties in the 1980s," in Michael J. Malbin, ed., *Money and Politics in the United States* (Chatham, N.J.: Chatham House, 1984), 114.

[43]Gibson et al., "Assessing Party Organizational Strength," 206; Charles H. Longley, "National Party Renewal," in Gerald M. Pomper, ed., *Party Renewal in America* (New York: Praeger, 1980), 69–86.
[44]See James P. Pfiffner, *The Modern Presidency* (New York: St. Martin's Press, 1994), ch. 6.
[45]See Sidney Milkus, *The President and the Parties* (New York: Oxford University Press, 1993).
[46]Harris poll, July 17–19, 1992.

Chapter 10

[1]Jeffrey M. Berry, *The Interest Group Society* (Boston: Little, Brown, 1984), 1.
[2]Robin Toner, "Making Sausage: The Art of Reprocessing the Democratic Process," *The New York Times*, September 4, 1994, sec. 4, p. 1.
[3]Quoted in Norman J. Ornstein and Shirley Elder, *Interest Groups, Lobbying, and Policymaking* (Washington, D.C.: Congressional Quarterly Press, 1978), 11.
[4]Alexis de Tocqueville, *Democracy in America* (1835–1840), ed. J. P. Mayer and A. P. Kerr (Garden City, N.Y.: Doubleday/Anchor, 1969), bk. II, ch. 4.
[5]E. Pendleton Herring, *Group Representation before Congress* (Washington, D.C.: Brookings Institution, 1929), 78.
[6]Kay Lehman Schlozman and John T. Tierney, *Organized Interests and American Democracy* (New York: Harper & Row, 1986), 24, 41.
[7]Ibid, 41; see also Graham Wooton, *Interest Groups, Policy, and Politics in America* (Englewood Cliffs, N.J.: Prentice-Hall, 1985), 103.
[8]See Robert H. Salisbury, John P. Heinz, Edward O. Leumann, and Robert L. Nelson, "Who Works with Whom? Interest Group Alliances and Opposition," *American Political Science Review* 81 (December 1987): 1217–1234.
[9]Mancur Olson, *The Logic of Collective Action*, rev. ed. (Cambridge, Mass.: Harvard University Press, 1971), 147.
[10]Peter Clarke and James Q. Wilson, "Incentive Systems: A Theory of Organizations," *Administrative Science Quarterly* (1961): 135; Terry Moe, "A Calculus of Group Membership," *American Journal of Political Science* 24 (November 1980): 593–632.
[11]See Lawrence Rothenberg, *Linking Citizens to Government: Interest Group Politics at Common Cause* (New York: Cambridge University Press, 1992).
[12]Olson, *The Logic of Collective Action*, 64.
[13]Ronald G. Shaiko, "Greenpeace U.S.A.: Something Old, New, Borrowed," *ANNALS* 528 (July 1993): 93.
[14]Robert H. Salisbury, "An Exchange Theory of Interest Groups," *Midwest Journal of Political Science* 13 (February 1969): 1–32; see also Jack L. Walker, Jr., *Mobilizing Interest Groups: Patrons, Professions, and Social Movements* (Ann Arbor: University of Michigan Press, 1991).
[15]E. J. Dionne, Jr., *Why Americans Hate Politics* (New York: Touchstone Books, 1991), 231.
[16]Christopher J. Bosso, "The Color of Money: Environmental Groups and the Pathologies of Fund Raising," in Allan J. Cigler and Burdett Loomis, *Interest Group Politics*, 4th ed. (Washington, D.C.: Congressional Quarterly Press, 1995), 101–103.
[17]See Steve Bruce, *The Rise and Fall of the New Christian Right* (New York: Oxford University Press, 1988); Allen D. Hertzke, *Representing God in Washington* (Knoxville: University of Tennessee Press, 1988); Matthew Moen, *The Christian Right and Congress* (Tuscaloosa: University of Alabama Press, 1989).
[18]Schlozman and Tierney, *Organized Interests*, 54; see also Ronald J. Hrebenar and Ruth K. Scott, *Interest Group Politics in America* (Englewood Cliffs, N.J.: Prentice-Hall, 1990), 167.
[19]See Beverly A. Cigler, "Not Just Another Special Interest: Intergovernmental Representation," in Cigler and Loomis, *Interest Group Politics*, 4th ed., 131–153.
[20]E. E. Schattschneider, *The Semisovereign People: A Realist's View of Democracy in America* (New York: Holt, Rinehart & Winston, 1960), 20–46.
[21]Jeffrey Berry, *Lobbying for the People* (Princeton, N.J.: Princeton University Press, 1977), 62.
[22]Ornstein and Elder, *Interest Groups, Lobbying, and Policymaking*, 82–86.
[23]Robert H. Salisbury and Paul Johnson, "Who You Know versus What You Know," *American Journal of Political Science* 33 (February 1989): 175–195.
[24]Quoted in Schlozman and Tierney, *Organized Interests*, 24.
[25]See Joseph Goulden, *The Superlawyers* (New York: Dell, 1973).
[26]Bill Keller, "Former House Members Ichord, Wilson Sign Up with Top Defense Contractors," *Congressional Quarterly*, June 13, 1984, 1052.
[27]Ornstein and Elder, *Interest Groups, Lobbying, and Policymaking*, 70.
[28]Quoted in Schlozman and Tierney, *Organized Interests*, 85.
[29]For the classic study of this process, see Raymond A. Bauer, Ithiel de Sola Pool, and Lewis Anthony Dexter, *American Business and Public Policy* (New York: Atherton, 1963).
[30]Jeffrey M. Berry, *The Interest Group Society* (Boston: Little, Brown, 1984), 121–122.
[31]Quoted in Ornstein and Elder, *Interest Groups, Lobbying, and Policymaking*, 77.
[32]See Elizabeth Drew, "Charlie," in Allan J. Cigler and Burdett A. Loomis, eds., *Interest Group Politics* (Washington, D.C.: Congressional Quarterly Press, 1986), 217–250; for an alternative view, see William P. Browne, "Organized Interests, Confidants, and Congress," in Cigler and Loomis, 4th ed., 284–287.
[33]See Marver Bernstein, *Regulating Business by Independent Commission* (Princeton, N.J.: Princeton University Press, 1955).
[34]Paul J. Quirk, *Industry Influence in Federal Regulatory Agencies* (Princeton, N.J.: Princeton University Press, 1981); James Q. Wilson, ed., *The Politics of Regulation* (New York: Basic Books, 1980).
[35]John E. Chubb, *Interest Groups and the Bureaucracy: The Politics of Energy* (Stanford, Calif.: Stanford University Press, 1983), 200–201.
[36]Charles T. Goodsell, *The Case for Bureaucracy*, 3rd ed. (Chatham, N.J.: Chatham House, 1994), 55–60.
[37]Joseph Stewart, Jr., and James F. Sheffield, Jr., "Does Interest Group Litigation Matter? The Case of Black Political Mobilization in Mississippi," *Journal of Politics* 49 (August 1987): 780–798; Joseph F. Kobylka, "A Court-Related Context for Group Litigation," *Journal of Politics* 49 (November 1987): 1061–1078; Lee Epstein and C. K. Rowland, "Interest Groups in the Courts," *American Political Science Review*, 85 (1991): 205–217.
[38]See J. Leiper Freeman, *The Political Process* (New York: Random House, 1965); John Mark Hansen, *Gaining Access* (Chicago: University of Chicago Press, 1991).

[39]Hugh Heclo, "Issue Networks and the Executive Establishment," in Anthony King, ed., *The New American Political System* (Washington, D.C.: American Enterprise Institute, 1978), 87–124; Thomas L. Gais, Mark A. Peterson, and Jack L. Webb, "Interest Groups, Iron Triangles, and Representative Institutions in American National Government," *British Journal of Political Science* 14 (1984): 161–185.
[40]Ornstein and Elder, *Interest Groups, Lobbying, and Policymaking,* 88–93; Berry, *The Interest Group Society,* 151.
[41]Kay Lehman Schlozman and John T. Tierney, "More of the Same: Washington Pressure Group Activity in a Decade of Change," *Journal of Politics* 45 (May 1983): 363–364.
[42]Richard E. Cohen, "Controlling the Lobbyists," *National Journal,* December 31, 1983, 2591; Linda L. Fowler and Ronald G. Shaiko, "The Grass Roots Connection," *American Journal of Political Science* 31 (August 1987): 484.
[43]Quoted in Mark Green, "Political PAC-Man," *The New Republic,* December 13, 1982, 20; see also Frank J. Sorauf, *Inside Campaign Finance* (New Haven, Conn.: Yale University Press, 1992).
[44]Quoted in Larry Sabato, *PAC Power: Inside the World of Political Action Committees* (New York: Norton, 1984), 72.
[45]Alissa J. Rubin, "With Health Overhaul on Stage, PACs Want Front Row Seat," *Congressional Quarterly,* July 31, 1993, 2048–2049.
[46]Frank J. Sorauf, *Money in American Politics* (Glenview, Ill.: Scott, Foresman, 1988), 103; Federal Elections Commission (FEC) Report, April 29, 1993.
[47]See Michael J. Malbin, "Of Mountains and Molehills," in Michael J. Malbin, *Parties, Interest Groups, and Campaign Finance Laws* (Washington, D.C.: American Enterprise Institute, 1981), 157–177.
[48]See Dan Clawson, Alan Neustadtl, and Denise Scott, *Money Talks* (New York: Basic Books, 1992).
[49]V. O. Key, Jr., *Public Opinion and American Democracy* (New York: Knopf, 1961), 428.
[50]Ernest Wittenberg and Elisabeth Wittenberg, *How to Win in Washington* (Cambridge, Mass.: Blackwell, 1989), 81.
[51]See Robert Dahl, *Who Governs?* (New Haven, Conn.: Yale University Press, 1961); Robert Dahl, *Dilemmas of Pluralist Democracy* (New Haven, Conn.: Yale University Press, 1982).
[52]Theodore J. Lowi, *The End of Liberalism: The Second Republic of the United States* (New York: Norton, 1979).
[53]Berry, *The Interest Group Society,* 172.
[54]See William Domhoff, *The Power Elite and the State* (New York: Aldine de Gruyter, 1990).
[55]See Andrew McFarland, *Public Interest Lobbies* (Washington, D.C.: American Enterprise Institute, 1976).
[56]Benjamin Ginsberg, *The Consequences of Consent* (New York: Random House, 1982), 214; see also Frances Fox Piven and Richard A. Cloward, *Poor People's Movements* (New York: Random House, 1979), ch. 5.
[57]See, for example, Andrew S. McFarland, *Common Cause* (Chatham, N.J.: Chatham House, 1984), 48–49.

Chapter 11

[1]Theodore H. White, *The Making of the President, 1972* (New York: Bantam Books, 1973), 327.
[2]See Richard Davis, *The Press and American Politics* (New York: Longman, 1992), 24–27.
[3]Comment at the annual meeting of the American Association of Political Consultants, Washington, D.C., 1977.
[4]Thomas Jefferson to Colonel Edward Carrington, January 16, 1787.
[5]Frank Luther Mott, *American Journalism, a History: 1690–1960* (New York: Macmillan, 1962), 114–115.
[6]Culver H. Smith, *The Press, Politics, and Patronage* (Athens: University of Georgia Press, 1977), 163–168.
[7]Doris A. Graber, *Mass Media and American Politics,* 4th ed. (Washington, D.C.: Congressional Quarterly Press, 1993), 36; Mark Wahlgren Summers, *The Press Gang* (Chapel Hill: University of North Carolina Press, 1994).
[8]See Michael Schudson, *Discovering the News* (New York: Basic Books, 1978).
[9]Mott, *American Journalism,* 122–123, 220–227.
[10]Quoted in Smith, *The Press, Politics, and Patronage,* 241.
[11]Commission on Freedom of the Press, *A Free and Responsible Press* (Chicago: University of Chicago Press, 1974), 62–63.
[12]Mott, *American Journalism,* 220–227, 241, 243.
[13]Edwin Emery, *The Press and America: An Interpretive History of the Mass Media* (Englewood Cliffs, N.J.: Prentice-Hall, 1977), 350.
[14]Quoted in Mott, *American Journalism,* 529.
[15]See Theodore Peterson, "The Social Responsibility Theory of the Press," in Fred Siebert, Theodore Peterson, and Wilbur Schramm, eds., *Four Theories of the Press* (Urbana: University of Illinois Press, 1956).
[16]Quoted in David Halberstam, *The Powers That Be* (New York: Knopf, 1979), 208–209.
[17]Roger Gafke and David Leathold, "A Caveat on E & P Poll on Newspaper Endorsements," *Journalism Quarterly* 56 (Summer 1979): 384; Joseph E. Pillegge, Jr., "Two-Party Endorsements in a One-Party State," *Journalism Quarterly* 58 (Autumn 1981): 449–453.
[18]Leo Bogart, *The Age of Television* (New York: Unger, 1956), 213.
[19]Theodore H. White, *America in Search of Itself: The Making of the President, 1956–1980* (New York: Harper & Row, 1982), 172–173.
[20]Quoted in Michael Robinson and Margaret Sheehan, *Over the Wire and on TV* (New York: Russell Sage Foundation, 1983), 226.
[21]Ernest C. Hynds, *American Newspapers in the 1980s* (New York: Hastings House, 1980); Annual Report, Federal Communications Commission, fiscal year 1985.
[22]Figures from *Standard Rate and Data Service* and *Electronic Media,* various dates.
[23]Graber, *Mass Media and American Politics,* 36.
[24]Maxwell E. McCombs and Donald L. Shaw, "Structuring the 'Unseen Environment'" *Journal of Communication,* Spring 1976, 18–22.
[25]Edward J. Epstein, *News from Nowhere: Television and the News* (New York: Random House, 1973), 37.
[26]Timothy Crouse, *The Boys on the Bus* (New York: Ballantine, 1973), 20.
[27]White, *The Making of the President, 1972,* 346–348.
[28]Quoted in Kathleen Hall Jamieson and Karlyn Kohrs Campbell, *The Interplay of Influence* (Belmont, Calif.: Wadsworth, 1983), 9–10.
[29]See David Manning White, "The Gatekeeper," *Journalism Quarterly* 27 (Fall 1950): 383–388; John Chancellor and Walter R. Mears, *The News Business* (New York: Harper & Row, 1983).

[30]David L. Paletz and Robert M. Entman, *Media Power Politics* (New York: Free Press, 1981), 16.
[31]James David Barber, "Characters in the Campaign: The Literary Problem," in James David Barber, ed., *Race for the Presidency* (Englewood Cliffs: N.J.: Prentice-Hall, 1978), 114–115.
[32]Bernard Rushko, *Newsmaking* (Chicago: University of Chicago Press, 1975), 105.
[33]Walter Lippman, *Public Opinion* (New York: Macmillan, 1922), 214. First published in 1922.
[34]See Allen Barton, "Consensus and Conflict among American Leaders," *Public Opinion Quarterly* 38 (Winter, 1974–1975): 507–530; Stephen Hess, "A Washington Perspective," paper presented at the Donald S. McNaughton Symposium, sponsored by Syracuse University, New York City, April 1985.
[35]See Bernard C. Cohen, *The Press and Foreign Policy* (Princeton, N.J.: Princeton University Press, 1963), 13.
[36]See, for example, F. Cook, T. Tyler, E. Goetz, M. Gordon, D. Protess, D. Leff, and H. Molotch, "Media and Agenda Setting: Effects on the Public, Interest Group Leaders, Policy Makers, and Policy," *Public Opinion Quarterly* 47 (1983): 16–35.
[37]"1993—The Year in Review," *Media Monitor,* January/February 1994, 2.
[38]David P. Fan, "Predicting Public Opinion from Press Coverage," *The Public Perspective,* July/August 1994, 22–23.
[39]Quoted in Richard Davis, "News Media Coverage of National Political Institutions," unpublished Ph.D. dissertation, Syracuse University, 1986.
[40]Michael Baruch Grossman and Martha Joynt Kumar, *Portraying the President* (Baltimore: Johns Hopkins University Press, 1981), 83.
[41]Timothy E. Cook, *Making Laws and Making News* (Washington, D.C.: Brookings Institution, 1989), 31.
[42]B. H. Winfield, "Franklin D. Roosevelt's Efforts to Influence the News during His First-Term Press Conferences," *Presidential Studies Quarterly* 9 (Spring 1981): 189–199. See also George Juergens, *News from the White House* (Chicago: University of Chicago Press, 1981), 65.
[43]Quoted in Robinson and Sheehan, *Over the Wire and on TV,* 206.
[44]"Clinton's the One," *Media Monitor,* Center for Media and Public Affairs, Washington, D.C., December 1992, 2.
[45]Ibid.
[46]Thomas E. Patterson, *Out of Order* (New York: Vintage, 1994), 76.
[47]See John Anthony Maltese, *Spin Control* (Chapel Hill: University of North Carolina Press, 1994).
[48]Williams Rivers, *The Other Government: Power and the Washington Media* (New York: Universe Books, 1982), Ch. 1; Douglass Cater, *The Fourth Branch of Government* (Boston: Houghton Mifflin, 1955).
[49]Patterson, *Out of Order,* 243.
[50]Ibid., 19–27.
[51]See *Lessons for Campaign '92,* (Cambridge, Mass.: Joan Shorenstein Center, John F. Kennedy School of Government, Harvard University 1991).
[52]Times-Mirror surveys, April and July, 1994.
[53]Quoted in Max Kampelman, "The Power of the Press," *Policy Review* 6 (1978): 19.
[54]Ibid.
[55]James Reston, "End of the Tunnel," *The New York Times,* April 30, 1975, 41.
[56]See Peter Braestrup, *The Big Story,* 2 vols. (Boulder, Colo.: Westview Press, 1977).
[57]Quoted in Epstein, *News from Nowhere,* ix; see also Paul Weaver, *News and the Culture of Lying* (New York: Free Press, 1994).
[58]Barber, "Characters in the Campaign," 114–117.
[59]Quoted in Howard Kurtz, "Media Circus," *Washington Post Magazine,* July 12, 1992, 36.
[60]Patterson, *Out of Order,* chs. 2–4.
[61]Ibid., 148.
[62]Dan Balz, "Clinton Hits Both GOP, Democrats on Economy," *The Washington Post,* November 21, 1991, A4.
[63]Patterson, *Out of Order,* 148.
[64]Diana Owen, *Media Messages in American Presidential Campaigns* (Westport, Conn.: Greenwood Publishing, 1991).
[65]Shanto Iyengar and Donald Kinder, *News That Matters* (Chicago: University of Chicago Press, 1987), 4.
[66]Michael Levy, "Disdaining the News," *Journal of Communication* 3 (1981): 24–31.
[67]Quoted in Jeffrey Katz, "Tilt?" *Washington Journalism Review,* January–February 1993, 24.
[68]Lippmann, *Public Opinion,* 221.

Chapter 12

[1]David R. Mayhew, *Congress: The Electoral Connection* (New Haven, Conn.: Yale University Press, 1974), 49.
[2]Kevin Merida, "The Voters' Ax Fells Foley," *The Washington Post National Weekly Edition,* November 14–20, 1994, 12–13.
[3]Mayhew, *Congress: The Electoral Connection,* 16.
[4]Lawrence C. Dodd, "A Theory of Congressional Cycles," in Gerald Wright, Leroy Rieselbach, and Lawrence C. Dodd, *Congress and Policy Change* (New York: Agathon, 1986).
[5]See Morris P. Fiorina, *Congress: Keystone of the Washington Establishment,* 2d ed. (New Haven, Conn.: Yale University Press, 1989).
[6]Richard Fenno, Jr., *Home Style: House Members in Their District* (Boston: Little, Brown, 1970), 101.
[7]For the opposing views, see Fiorina, *Congress: Keystone of the Washington Establishment,* ch. 7; John R. Johannes, *To Serve the People* (Lincoln: University of Nebraska Press, 1984), ch. 8.
[8]See Diana Evans Yiannakis, "House Members' Communication Styles," *Journal of Politics* 44 (November 1982): 1049–1073.
[9]"Congressional Facts and Figures," *The National Journal,* September 3, 1994, 2038.
[10]Paul S. Herrnson, *Congressional Elections: Campaigning at Home and in Washington* (Washington, D.C.: Congressional Quarterly Press, 1995).
[11]Jennifer Babson and Kelly St. John, "Momentum Helps GOP Collect Record Amounts from PACs," *Congressional Quarterly Weekly Report,* December 3, 1994, 3456.
[12]See Gary C. Jacobson, *Money in Congressional Elections* (New Haven, Conn.: Yale University Press, 1980); Gary C. Jacobson, *The Politics of Congressional Elections,* 3d ed. (New York: HarperCollins, 1992).
[13]*Congressional Quarterly Guide to Congress,* 3d ed. (Washington, D.C.: Congressional Quarterly Press, 1982), 666; see also Frank J.

Sorauf, *Inside Campaign Finance* (New Haven, Conn.: Yale University Press, 1992), 67, 86.

[14]Barbara Hinckley, *Congressional Elections* (Washington, D.C.: Congressional Quarterly Press, 1981), 29.

[15]Edie N. Goldenberg and Michael W. Traugott, *Campaigning for Congress* (Washington, D.C.: Congressional Quarterly Press, 1984), 81; Sorauf, *Inside Campaign Finance*, 67, 86.

[16]Babson and St. John, "Momentum Helps GOP Collect Record Amounts from PACs," 3456.

[17]*Wesberry* v. *Sanders*, 376 U.S. 1 (1964).

[18]*Davis* v. *Bandemer*, 478 U.S. 109 (1986). See Bernard Grofman, ed., *Political Gerrymandering and the Courts* (New York: Agathon Press, 1991).

[19]See Thomas E. Mann, *Unsafe at Any Margin: Interpreting Congressional Elections* (Washington, D.C.: American Enterprise Institute, 1978); see also Gary C. Jacobson, *The Electoral Origins of Divided Government* (Boulder, Colo.: Westview Press, 1990).

[20]Quoted in "A Tale of Myths and Measures: Who Is Truly Vulnerable?" *Congressional Quarterly Weekly Report*, December 4, 1993, 7.

[21]See Alan I. Abramowitz, "A Comparison of Voting for U.S. Senator and Representative in 1978," *American Political Science Review* 74 (September 1980): 633.

[22]Linda L. Fowler and Robert D. McClure, *Political Ambition* (New Haven, Conn.: Yale University Press, 1989); see also Jonathan S. Krasno and Donald Philip Green, "Preempting Quality Challengers in House Elections," *Journal of Politics* 50 (November 1988), 878.

[23]Thomas Kazee, "Recruiting Challengers in U.S. House Elections," *Legislative Studies Quarterly* (August 1983): 469–480.

[24]Keith R. Poole and Howard Rosenthal, "Patterns of Congressional Voting," *American Journal of Political Science*, 35 (February 1991): 228.

[25]See Linda L. Fowler, *Candidates, Congress, and the American Democracy* (Ann Arbor: University of Michigan Press, 1994).

[26]Compiled from "Characteristics of Congress," *Congressional Quarterly Weekly Report*, vol. 49, January 12, 1991, 118–127.

[27]Barbara Sinclair, *Majority Leadership in the U.S. House* (Baltimore: Johns Hopkins University Press, 1983), 34–41; Ronald M. Peters, Jr., *The American Speakership* (Baltimore: Johns Hopkins University Press, 1990).

[28]See Bruce Oppenheimer, "The Rules Committee: New Arm of Leadership in a Decentralized House," in Lawrence C. Dodd and Bruce I. Oppenheimer, eds., *Congress Reconsidered* (New York: Praeger, 1977), 96–116; Spark M. Matsunga and Ping Chen, *Rulemakers of the House* (Urbana: University of Illinois Press, 1976).

[29]Sidney Waldman, "Majority Leadership in the House of Representatives," *Political Science Quarterly*, Fall 1980, 377.

[30]See David W. Rhode, *Parties and Leaders in the Postreform House* (Chicago: University of Chicago Press, 1991).

[31]Fred R. Harris, *Deadlock or Decision: The U.S. Senate and the Rise of National Politics* (New York: Oxford University Press, 1993), 182.

[32]CBS News, February 27, 1987.

[33]Roger H. Davidson and Walter J. Oleszek, *Congress and Its Members* (Washington, D.C.: Congressional Quarterly Press, 1981), 185.

[34]Harris, *Deadlock or Decision*, ch. 4.

[35]Quoted in Frank H. Mackamar, *Understanding Congressional Leadership: The State of the Art* (Pekin, Ill.: Dickson Center, 1981), 9.

[36]Steven S. Smith, *The American Congress* (Boston: Houghton Mifflin, 1995), 152.

[37]Quoted in Randall B. Ripley, *Party Leaders in the House of Representatives* (Washington, D.C.: Brookings Institution, 1967), 185.

[38]See Nelson W. Polsby, Miriam Gallagher, and Barry S. Rundquist, "The Growth of the Seniority System in the U.S. House of Representatives," *American Political Science Review* 63 (September 1969): 787–807.

[39]See Barbara Hinckley, *The Seniority System in Congress* (Bloomington: Indiana University Press, 1971), 111.

[40]Kenneth Shepsle, "Representation and Governance: The Great Legislative Tradeoff," paper presented at the Constitutional Bicentennial Conference, Nelson A. Rockefeller Center, Dartmouth College, Hanover, N.H., May 5, 1987, 19–20.

[41]Jonathan D. Salant, "New Chairmen Swing to Right; Freshmen Get Choice Posts," *Congressional Quarterly Weekly Report*, December 10, 1994, 3493.

[42]See Steven H. Haeberle, "The Institutionalization of the Subcommittee in the United States House of Representatives," *Journal of Politics* 40 (November 1978): 1054–1065.

[43]See Richard L. Hall and C. Lawrence Evans, "The Power of Subcommittees," *Journal of Politics* (May 1990): 335–355.

[44]Ibid.

[45]See Gerald S. Strom, *The Logic of Lawmaking* (Baltimore: Johns Hopkins University Press, 1990); Steven S. Smith and Christopher J. Deering, *Committees in Congress*, 2d ed. (Washington, D.C.: Congressional Quarterly Press, 1990).

[46]Hall and Evans, "The Power of Subcommittees."

[47]Dodd and Oppenheimer, "The House in Transition," in Dodd and Oppenheimer, *Congress Reconsidered*, 2d ed., 41.

[48]See Smith and Deering, *Committees in Congress*, 125–165.

[49]Harris, *Deadlock or Decision*, 143–144.

[50]David W. Rhode and Kenneth A. Shepsle, "Domestic Committee Assignments in the House of Representatives," *American Political Science Review*, September 1973, 889–905; see also Kenneth A. Shepsle, *The Giant Jigsaw Puzzle: Democratic Committee Assignments in the Modern House* (Chicago: University of Chicago Press, 1978).

[51]Smith, *The American Congress*, 189–198.

[52]See Stephen E. Frantzich and Steven E. Schier, *Congress: Games and Strategies* (Dubuque, Iowa: Brown & Benchmark, 1995), 127.

[53]See Frederick C. Mosher, *The GAO* (Boulder, Colo.: Westview Press, 1979).

[54]See Lance T. LeLoup, "Fiscal Policy and Congressional Politics," in Christopher J. Deering, ed., *Congressional Politics* (Chicago: Dorsey Press, 1989), 277.

Chapter 13

[1]Roger H. Davidson and Walter J. Oleszek, *Congress and Its Members*, 2d ed. (Washington, D.C.: Congressional Quarterly Press, 1985), 7.

[2]Ibid.

[3]Randall B. Ripley, *Congress: Process and Policy*, 4th ed. (New York: Norton, 1988), 76.

[4]See Ernest Griffith and Francis Valeo, *Congress: Its Contemporary Role*, 5th ed. (New York: New York University Press, 1975), ch. 1.

[5]James L. Sundquist, "Congress and the President: Enemies or Partners?" in Lawrence C. Dodd and Bruce I. Oppenheimer, eds., *Congress Reconsidered* (New York: Praeger, 1977), 240.
[6]Steven S. Smith, *The American Congress* (Boston: Houghton Mifflin, 1995), 218–220.
[7]Bruce I. Oppenheimer, "Congress and the New Obstructionism: Developing an Energy Program," in Lawrence C. Dodd and Bruce I. Oppenheimer, *Congress Reconsidered,* 2d ed. (Washington, D.C.: Congressional Quarterly Press, 1981), 275–295.
[8]See George C. Edwards, *At the Margins: Presidential Leadership of Congress* (New Haven, Conn.: Yale University Press, 1989).
[9]See Charles O. Jones, *Clean Air: The Policies and Politics of Pollution Control* (Pittsburgh: University of Pittsburgh Press, 1975).
[10]See Timothy J. Conlan, Margaret T. Wrightson, and David R. Beam, *Taxing Choices: The Politics of Tax Reform* (Washington, D.C.: Congressional Quarterly Press, 1990).
[11]Arthur Maass, *Congress and the Common Good* (New York: Basic Books, 1983), 14.
[12]See Paul C. Light, *The President's Agenda* (Baltimore: Johns Hopkins University Press, 1982).
[13]Hugh Heclo, "Introduction: The Presidential Illusion," in Hugh Heclo and Lester M. Salamon, *The Illusion of Presidential Government* (Boulder, Colo.: Westview Press, 1981), 1–2.
[14]Quoted in Ripley, *Congress: Process and Policy,* 326.
[15]See Allen Schick, *Congress and Money* (Washington, D.C.: Urban Institute, 1980); Lance T. LeLoup, *The Fiscal Congress* (Westport, Conn.: Greenwood Press, 1980).
[16]Light, *The President's Agenda,* 90–91.
[17]See, for example, Stanley Bach and Steven S. Smith, *Managing Uncertainty in the House of Representatives* (Washington, D.C.: Brookings Institution, 1989).
[18]Benjamin Page, "Cooling the Legislative Tea," in Walter Dean Burnham and Martha Wagner Weinberg, *American Politics and Public Policy* (Cambridge, Mass.: MIT Press, 1978), 171–187; Stephen E. Frantzich and Steven E. Schier, *Congress: Games and Strategies* (Dubuque, Iowa: Brown & Benchmark, 1995), 28–30.
[19]Quoted in Martin Tolchin, "How Senators View the Senate," *The New York Times,* November 25, 1984, 40.
[20]See Gerald S. Strom, *The Logic of Lawmaking* (Baltimore: Johns Hopkins University Press, 1990).
[21]Smith, *The American Congress,* 210–212.
[22]See Susan Webb Hammond, "Congressional Caucuses and Party Leaders in the U.S. House of Representatives," *Political Science Quarterly* 106 (Summer 1991): 277–294.
[23]See Kenneth Shepsle, "Representation and Governance: The Great Legislative Tradeoff," paper presented at the Constitutional Bicentennial Conference, Nelson A. Rockefeller Center, Dartmouth College, Hanover, N.H., May 5, 1987.
[24]Morris P. Fiorina, "The Decline of Collective Responsibility in American Politics," *Daedalus* 109 (1980): 40.
[25]See Herbert Storing, *What the Anti-Federalists Were For* (Chicago: University of Chicago Press, 1981).
[26]See David J. Vogler and Sidney R. Waldman, *Congress and Democracy* (Washington, D.C.: Congressional Quarterly Press, 1985); David C. Kozak, *Contexts of Congressional Decision Behavior* (Lanham, Md.: University Press of America, 1984).
[27]See Richard F. Fenno, Jr., *Home Style: House Members in Their Districts* (Boston: Little, Brown, 1978).
[28]See Bruce Cain, John Ferejohn, and Morris Fiorina, *The Personal Vote* (Cambridge, Mass.: Harvard University Press, 1987).
[29]Thomas E. Cavanaugh, "The Calculus of Representation," *Western Political Quarterly,* March 1982, 120–129.
[30]Steven S. Smith and Christopher J. Deering, *Committees in Congress* (Washington, D.C.: Congressional Quarterly Press, 1990), 74.
[31]Keith Krehbiel, "Are Congressional Committees Composed of Preference Outliers?" *American Political Science Review* 84 (1990): 149–164; Richard L. Hall and Bernard Grofman, "The Committee Assignment Process and the Conditional Nature of Committee Bias," *American Political Science Review* 84 (1990): 1149–1166.
[32]See Aage R. Clausen, *How Congressmen Decide* (New York: St. Martin's Press, 1973).
[33]See John R. Wright, "Contributions, Lobbying, and Committee Voting in the U.S. House of Representatives," *American Political Science Review* 84 (1990): 417–438.
[34]Richard L. Hall and Frank W. Wayman, "Buying Time: Moneyed Interests and the Mobilization of Bias in Congressional Committees," *American Political Science Review* 84 (1990): 797–820.
[35]See Gary W. Cox and Mathew D. McCubbins, *Legislative Leviathan* (Berkeley: University of California Press, 1993).
[36]"With Democrat in White House, Partisanship Hits New High," *1993 Congressional Quarterly Almanac* (Washington, D.C.: Congressional Quarterly Press, 1984): 14-C; Donna Cassata, "Political Heat Puts a Chill on Partisan-Vote Rate," *Congressional Quarterly Weekly,* December 31, 1994, 3624.
[37]Richard E. Cohen and William Schneider, "Epitaph for an Era," *National Journal,* January 14, 1995, 83.
[38]Mathew D. McCubbins and Thomas Schwartz, "Congressional Oversight Overlooked," *American Journal of Political Science* 2 (February 1984): 165–179.
[39]Joel A. Aberbach, *Keeping a Watchful Eye* (Washington, D.C.: Brookings Institution, 1990); William T. Gormley, *Taming the Bureaucracy* (Princeton, N.J.: Princeton University Press, 1989).
[40]See Allen Schick, "The Battle of the Budget," in Harvey C. Mansfield, Sr., *Congress against the President* (New York: Praeger, 1975).
[41]McCubbins and Schwartz, "Congressional Oversight Overlooked."
[42]See Aberbach, *Keeping a Watchful Eye.*
[43]See Barbara H. Craig, *Chadha: The Story of an Epic Constitutional Struggle* (New York: Oxford University Press, 1988).

Chapter 14

[1]Woodrow Wilson, *Constitutional Government in the United States* (New York: Columbia University Press, 1908), 67.
[2]Robert Hirschfield, ed., *The Power of the Presidency,* 3d ed. (New York: Aldine, 1982), 3.
[3]James W. Davis, *The American Presidency,* 2d ed. (Westport, Conn.: Praeger, 1995), 13.
[4]See Barry M. Blechman and Stephen S. Kaplan, *Force without War* (Washington, D.C.: Brookings Institution, 1978).
[5]Edward S. Corwin, *The President: Office and Powers, 1787–1957* (New York: New York University Press, 1959), 180–181.
[6]*United States* v. *Belmont,* 57 U.S. 758 (1937).
[7]Robert DiClerico, *The American President,* 4th ed. (Englewood Cliffs, N.J.: Prentice-Hall, 1995), 47.

[8]Quoted in Wilfred E. Binkley, *President and Congress*, 3d ed. (New York: Vintage, 1962), 142.
[9]Theodore Roosevelt, *An Autobiography* (New York: Scribner's, 1931), 383.
[10]George C. Edwards and Stephen J. Wayne, *Presidential Leadership* (New York: St. Martin's Press, 1985), 6–7.
[11]See Richard M. Pious, *The American Presidency* (New York: Basic Books, 1979), 83.
[12]Robert J. Spitzer, *President and Congress* (New York: McGraw-Hill, 1993), 35–37.
[13]Raymond Tatalovich and Byron W. Daynes, *Presidential Power in the United States* (Monterey, Calif.: Brooks/Cole, 1984), 322–323.
[14]*Korematsu* v. *United States*, 323 U.S. 214 (1944); *Ex parte Endo*, 323 U.S. 283 (1944).
[15]Harry S Truman, *1946–1952: Years of Trial and Hope* (New York: Signet, 1956), 535.
[16]Davis, *The American Presidency*, 25–26.
[17]James Bryce, *The American Commonwealth* (New York: Commonwealth Edition, 1908), 230.
[18]Davis, *The American Presidency*, 20.
[19]See Richard Rose, *The Postmodern President*, 2d ed. (Chatham, N.J.: Chatham House, 1991).
[20]Quoted in Arthur M. Schlesinger, Jr., *The Coming of the New Deal* (Boston: Houghton Mifflin, 1958), 13.
[21]Hugh Heclo, "Introduction: The Presidential Illusion," in Hugh Heclo and Lester M. Salamon, eds., *The Illusion of Presidential Government* (Boulder, Colo.: Westview Press, 1981), 6.
[22]James Sundquist, *The Decline and Resurgence of Congress* (Washington, D.C.: Brookings Institution, 1981), 150.
[23]James Pfiffner, *The Modern Presidency* (New York: St. Martin's Press, 1994), 141–150.
[24]Ibid.
[25]Thomas R. Marshall, *Presidential Nominations in a Reform Age* (New York: Praeger, 1981); James W. Ceaser, *Reforming the Reforms: A Critical Analysis of the Presidential Selection Process* (Cambridge, Mass.: Ballinger, 1982), 81; James W. Ceaser, *Presidential Selection: Theory and Development* (Princeton, N.J.: Princeton University Press, 1979).
[26]Ceaser, *Presidential Selection*, 19.
[27]See Noble E. Cunningham, Jr., "Presidential Leadership, Political Parties, and the Congressional Caucus, 1800–1824," in Patricia Bonami, James MacGregor Burns, and Austin Ranney, eds., *The American Constitutional System under Strong and Weak Parties* (New York: Praeger, 1981), 1–20.
[28]See Michael Nelson, ed., *The Elections of 1992* (Washington, D.C.: Congressional Quarterly Press, 1993), 2–4.
[29]See Hugh Winebrenner, *The Iowa Precinct Caucuses* (Ames: Iowa State University Press, 1987); Gary R. Orren and Nelson W. Polsby, eds., *Media and Momentum: The New Hampshire Primary and Nomination Politics* (Chatham, N.J.: Chatham House, 1987).
[30]Thomas E. Patterson, *The Mass Media Election* (New York: Praeger, 1980), chs. 5–11.
[31]William Flanigan and Nancy Zingale, *Political Behavior of the American Electorate*, 8th ed. (Washington, D.C.: Congressional Quarterly Press, 1994), 163–164.
[32]Ibid., 189.
[33]See John Kenneth White, *The New Politics of Old Values*, 2d ed. (Hanover, N.H.: University Press of New England, 1991).
[34]Myron A. Levine, *Presidential Campaigns and Elections* (Itasca, Ill.: Peacock, 1995), 30.
[35]Sidney Kraus, ed., *The Great Debates* (Bloomington: Indiana University Press, 1962), 190.
[36]"Perot: Eccentric Perhaps, but No Joke," *The New York Times*, November 5, 1992, B4.
[37]Kathleen Hall Jamieson, *Packaging the Presidency*, 2d ed. (New York: Oxford University Press, 1992).
[38]Joel D. Aberbach, "The President and the Executive Branch," in Colin Campbell and Bert A. Rockman, eds., *The Bush Presidency: First Appraisals* (Chatham, N.J.: Chatham House, 1991), 238–240.
[39]See James P. Pfiffner, *The Strategic Presidency: Hitting the Ground Running* (Chicago: Dorsey Press, 1988).
[40]Davis, *The American Presidency*, 296.
[41]Richard P. Nathan, *The Administrative Presidency* (New York: Wiley, 1983), 36.
[42]Davis, *The American Presidency*, 240; see also Bradley Patterson, *The Ring of Power* (New York: Basic Books, 1988), 90–91.
[43]Pfiffner, *The Modern Presidency*, 91–96.
[44]Quoted in Stephen J. Wayne, *Road to the White House, 1992* (New York: St. Martin's Press, 1992), 143.
[45]R. Gordon Hoxie, "The Cabinet in the American Presidency, 1789–1984," *Presidential Studies Quarterly*, Spring 1984, 226–228.
[46]See Jeffrey E. Cohen, *The Politics of the United States Cabinet* (Pittsburgh: University of Pittsburgh Press, 1988).
[47]Pfiffner, *The Modern Presidency*, 123.
[48]Quoted in James MacGregor Burns, "Our Super-Government—Can We Control It?" *The New York Times*, April 24, 1949, 32.
[49]See Peri E. Arnold, *Making the Managerial Presidency: Comprehensive Reorganization Planning* (Princeton, N.J.: Princeton University Press, 1986); Paul C. Light, *Thickening Government: Federal Hierarchy and the Diffusion of Accountability* (Washington, D.C.: Brookings Institution, 1995).
[50]James Pfiffner, "The President's Chief of Staff: Lessons Learned," *Presidential Studies Quarterly* 22 (Winter 1993): 77–102.
[51]Rose, *The Postmodern President*, 142.
[52]Pfiffner, *The Modern Presidency*, 117–122.
[53]Joel D. Aberbach and Bert A. Rockman, "Clashing Beliefs within the Executive Branch," *American Political Science Review* 70 (June 1976): 461; see also G. Calvin Mackenzie, "Partisan Presidential Leadership: The President's Appointees," in Sandy Maisel, ed., *The Parties Respond* (Boulder, Colo.: Westview Press, 1990), 283–284.
[54]Richard T. Johnson, *Managing the White House* (New York: Harper & Row, 1974), 238; Stephen Hess, *Organizing the Presidency* (Washington, D.C.: Brookings Institution, 1988), 118.
[55]See Pfiffner, *The Modern Presidency*, 65–68.
[56]See Arnold, *Making the Managerial Presidency*.

Chapter 15

[1]Hugh Heclo, "Introduction: The Presidential Illusion," in Hugh Heclo and Lester M. Salamon, ed. *The Illusion of Presidential Government* (Boulder, Colo.: Westview Press, 1981), 2.
[2]Arthur M. Schlesinger, Jr., *The Imperial Presidency* (Boston: Houghton Mifflin, 1989).

[3]See Thomas Franck, ed., *The Tethered Presidency* (New York: New York University Press, 1981); Richard M. Pious, *The American Presidency* (New York: Basic Books, 1979); Harold M. Barger, *The Impossible Presidency* (Glenview, Ill.: Scott, Foresman, 1984); George Reedy, *The Twilight of the Presidency* (New York: New American Library, 1970); Aaron Wildavsky, *The Beleaguered Presidency* (New Brunswick, N.J.: Transaction Books, 1991).
[4]See Grant McConnell, *The Modern Presidency* (New York: St. Martin's Press, 1967); Clinton Rossiter, *The American Presidency* (New York: Harcourt, Brace & World, 1960).
[5]Charles O. Jones, *The Presidency in a Separated System* (Washington, D.C.: Brookings Institution, 1994).
[6]James P. Pfiffner, *The Modern Presidency* (New York: St. Martin's Press, 1994), 176.
[7]George Hager, "Bush's Success Rate Sinks to Near-Record Low," *Congressional Quarterly Weekly Report*, December 22, 1990, 1484.
[8]*Congressional Quarterly Weekly Reports*, December 19, 1992, 3896.
[9]Michael Mezey, *Congress, the President, and Public Policy* (Boulder, Colo.: Westview Press, 1989), 110–115.
[10]George Edwards III, *At the Margins* (New Haven, Conn.: Yale University Press, 1989), 39–46.
[11]Erwin Hargrove, *The Power of the Modern Presidency* (New York: Knopf, 1974).
[12]Richard E. Neustadt and Ernest R. May, *Thinking in Time* (New York: Free Press, 1986), 72.
[13]"The Honeymoon That Wasn't," *Media Monitor*, September/October 1993, 2.
[14]Paul C. Light, *The President's Agenda* (Baltimore: Johns Hopkins University Press, 1982), 41–45.
[15]James P. Pfiffner, *The Strategic Presidency: Hitting the Ground Running* (Chicago: Dorsey Press, 1988).
[16]Ibid., 45.
[17]Aaron Wildavsky, "The Two Presidencies," *Trans-action*, December 1966, 7.
[18]Lance T. LeLoup and Steven A. Shull, "Congress versus the Executive: The Two Presidencies Reconsidered," *Social Science Quarterly*, March 1979, 707 (for 1965–1975); Harvey G. Zeidenstein, "The Two Presidencies Thesis Is Alive and Well and Has Been Living in the U.S. Senate Since 1973," *Presidential Studies Quarterly* 2 (1981): 511–525; see also Michael Mumper, "The President and Domestic Policy-Making," *Congress and the Presidency*, Spring 1985, 75–80.
[19]Pfiffner, *The Modern Presidency*, ch. 6.
[20]Hager, "Bush's Success Rate Sinks to Near-Record Low," 1485.
[21]Richard Rose, *The Postmodern President*, 2d ed. (Chatham, N.J.: Chatham House, 1991).
[22]Thomas P. (Tip) O'Neill, with William Novak, *Man of the House: The Life and Political Memoirs of Speaker Tip O'Neill* (New York: Random House, 1987), 297 (emphasis added).
[23]Fred I. Greenstein, ed., *Leadership in the Modern Presidency* (Cambridge, Mass.: Harvard University Press, 1988), ch. 10.
[24]Robert J. Spitzer, *The Presidential Veto: Touchstone of the American Presidency* (Albany: State University of New York Press, 1988).
[25]Richard E. Neustadt, *Presidential Power: The Politics of Leadership from FDR to Carter* (New York: Wiley, 1980), 67.
[26]Ibid., 33.
[27]Ibid.
[28]*Congressional Quarterly Weekly Reports*, December 19, 1992, 3896.
[29]See Mark C. Shelley, *The Permanent Majority: The Conservative Coalition in the United States Congress* (University: University of Alabama Press, 1983).
[30]Harvey G. Zeidenstein, "Presidents' Popularity and Their Wins and Losses on Major Issues: Does One Have a Greater Influence over the Other?" *Presidential Studies Quarterly*, Spring 1985, 287–300; see also Richard Brody, *Assessing the President* (Stanford, Calif.: Stanford University Press, 1991).
[31]John E. Mueller, "Presidential Popularity from Truman to Johnson," *American Political Science Review* 64 (March 1970): 18–34; Kathleen Frankovic, "Public Opinion in the 1992 Campaign," in Gerald M. Pomper, ed., *The Election of 1992* (Chatham, N.J.: Chatham House, 1993).
[32]Paul Brace and Barbara Hinckley, *Follow the Leader* (New York: Basic Books, 1992).
[33]Gallup Polls, November 2–5, 1979, and November 30–December 3, 1979.
[34]Godfrey Hodgson, *All Things to All Men* (New York: Simon & Schuster, 1980), 239.
[35]See John Anthony Maltese, *Spin Control* (Chapel Hill: University of North Carolina Press, 1994); Michael Baruch Grossman and Martha Joynt Kumar, *Portraying the President* (Baltimore: Johns Hopkins University Press, 1981); Robert E. Denton, Jr., and Dan F. Hahn, *Presidential Communication* (New York: Praeger, 1986).
[36]Samuel Kernell, *Going Public: New Strategies of Presidential Leadership* (Washington, D.C.: Congressional Quarterly Press, 1986), 1.
[37]Jeffrey Tulis, *The Rhetorical Presidency* (Princeton, N.J.: Princeton University Press, 1987); see also Craig Allen Smith, *The White House Speaks* (Westport, Conn.: Greenwood, 1994).
[38]Mary E. Stuckey, *The President as Interpreter-in-Chief* (Chatham, N.J.: Chatham House, 1991).
[39]Lyn Ragsdale, "Presidential Speechmaking and the Public Audience," *Journal of Politics* 49 (August 1987): 704–736.
[40]See Roderick Hart, *The Sound of Leadership* (Chicago: University of Chicago Press, 1987).
[41]Bruce Miroff, "Monopolizing the Public Space," in Thomas E. Cronin, ed., *Rethinking the Presidency* (Boston: Little, Brown, 1982), 218–232; see also Lyn Ragsdale, "The Politics of Presidential Speechmaking, 1949–1980," *American Political Science Review* 78 (December 1984): 971–984.
[42]Heclo, "Introduction: The Presidential Illusion," 2.
[43]Theodore J. Lowi, *The "Personal" Presidency: Power Invested, Promise Unfulfilled* (Ithaca, N.Y.: Cornell University Press, 1985).

Chapter 16

[1]Norman Thomas, *Rule 9: Politics, Administration, and Civil Rights* (New York: Random House, 1966), 6.
[2]Albert Gore, Jr., *From Red Tape to Results: Creating a Government That Works Better and Costs Less* (Washington, D.C.: U.S. Superintendent of Documents, 1993), 1.
[3]James P. Pfiffner, "The National Performance Review in Perspective," working paper, 94–4, The Institute of Public Policy, George Mason University, 1994, p. 2.
[4]Ibid., p. 12.
[5]Max Weber, *Economy and Society*, trans. Guenther Roth and Claus Wittich (New York: Bedminster Press, 1968), 23.

[6]Hans H. Gerth and C. Wright Mills, eds., *From Max Weber: Essays in Sociology* (New York: Oxford University Press, 1946).
[7]See John J. DiIulio, ed., *Deregulating the Public Service* (Washington, D.C.: Brookings Institution, 1994).
[8]*Rutan* v. *Republican Party of Illinois*, 497 U.S. 62 (1990).
[9]Sar A. Levitan and Alexandra B. Noden, *Working for the Sovereign* (Baltimore: Johns Hopkins University Press, 1983), 28–29, 39.
[10]See Wilson R. Hart, *Collective Bargaining in the Federal Civil Service* (New York: Harper & Row, 1961), ch. 3.
[11]For a different perspective, see James Q. Wilson, *Bureaucracy* (New York: Basic Books, 1989).
[12]Michael Lipsky, *Street-Level Bureaucracy* (New York: Russell Sage Foundation, 1980).
[13]See Gary C. Bryner, *Bureaucratic Discretion: Law and Policy in Federal Regulatory Agencies* (Elmsford, N.Y.: Pergamon, 1987).
[14]Kenneth J. Meier, *Regulation* (New York: St. Martin's Press, 1985), 164.
[15]Fredrick C. Mosher, *Democracy and the Public Service*, 2d ed. (New York: Oxford University Press, 1982), 64–66.
[16]Paul Van Riper's *History of the United States Civil Service* (Evanston, Ill.: Peterson, 1958), 36.
[17]Jay M. Shafritz, *Personnel Management in Government* (New York: Marcel Dekker, 1981), 9–13; Herbert Kaufman, "Emerging Conflicts in the Doctrine of Public Administration," *American Political Science Review* 50 (December 1956): 1060.
[18]James Q. Wilson, "The Rise of the Bureaucratic State," *Public Interest* 41 (Fall 1975): 77–103.
[19]David Nachmias and David H. Rosenbloom, *Bureaucratic Government: U.S.A.* (New York: St. Martin's Press, 1980), 39; U.S. Bureau of the Census, *Historical Statistics of the United States: Colonial Times to 1970*, pt. 2 (Washington, D.C.: U.S. Government Printing Office, 1975), 1102.
[20]David H. Rosenbloom, *Federal Service and the Constitution* (Ithaca, N.Y.: Cornell University Press, 1971), 83.
[21]For insights on this and other civil service reforms, see Patricia Ingraham and David Rosenbloom, *The Promise and Paradox of Civil Service Reform* (Pittsburgh: University of Pittsburgh Press, 1992); Pfiffner, "The National Performance Review in Perspective."
[22]Herbert Kaufman, "Emerging Conflicts in the Doctrine of Public Administration," *American Political Science Review* 50 (December 1956): 1060.
[23]Ibid., 1063.
[24]Ibid., 1062.
[25]See Mark W. Huddleston, "The Carter Civil Service Reforms," *Political Science Quarterly*, Winter 1981–82, 607–622.
[26]See Richard W. Waterman, *Presidential Influence and the Administrative State* (Knoxville: University of Tennessee Press, 1989).
[27]Quoted in Hugh Heclo, *A Government of Strangers* (Washington, D.C.: Brookings Institution, 1977), 225.
[28]Norton E. Long, "Power and Administration," *Public Administration Review* 10 (Autumn 1949), 269; Joel D. Aberbach, Robert A. Putnam, and Bert A. Rockman, *Bureaucrats and Politicians in Western Democracies* (Cambridge, Mass.: Harvard University Press, 1980).
[29]See William A. Niskanen, Jr., *Bureaucracy and Representation* (Chicago: Aldine-Atherton, 1971), 38; Morton H. Halperin, *Bureaucratic Politics and Foreign Policy* (Washington, D.C.: Brookings Institution, 1974), 39–40; Herbert Kaufman, *The Administrative Behavior of Federal Bureaucrats* (Washington, D.C.: Brookings Institution, 1981), 4.
[30]Heclo, *A Government of Strangers*, 117–118.
[31]Quoted in Aaron Wildavsky, *The Politics of the Budgetary Process*, 4th ed. (Boston: Little, Brown, 1984), 19.
[32]Mosher, *Democracy and the Public Service*, ch. 2.
[33]See Kenneth J. Meier and Lloyd Nigro, "Representative Bureaucracy and Policy Preferences," *Public Administrative Review* 36 (July/August 1976): 44.
[34]Joel D. Aberbach and Bert A. Rockman, "Clashing Beliefs within the Executive Branch," *American Political Science Review* 70 (June 1976): 461.
[35]Aberbach, Putnam, and Rockman, *Bureaucrats and Politicians in Western Democracies*, 52.
[36]Richard Rose, *Managing Presidential Objectives* (New York: Free Press, 1976), 149.
[37]Meier, *Regulation*, 16.
[38]Jonathan Bendor, Serge Taylor, and Roland Van Gaalen, "Stacking the Deck: Bureaucratic Missions and Policy Design," *American Political Science Review* 81 (September 1987): 873–896.
[39]See Peter Woll, *American Bureaucracy*, 2d ed. (New York: Norton, 1977), ch. 1.
[40]Herbert Kaufman, *Are Government Organizations Immortal?* (Washington, D.C.: Brookings Institution, 1976), 76.
[41]Long, "Power and Administration," 269.
[42]See Harold Seidman, *Politics, Position, and Power: The Dynamics of Federal Organization*, 2d ed. (New York: Oxford University Press, 1975), 150.
[43]Hugh Heclo, "Issue Networks and the Executive Establishment," in Anthony King, ed., *The New American Political System* (Washington, D.C.: American Enterprise Institute, 1978), 102.
[44]Joel D. Aberbach and Bert A. Rockman, "Bureaucrats and Client Groups: A View from Capital Hill," *American Journal of Political Science* 22 (November 1978): 821.
[45]See Bernard Rosen, *Holding Government Bureaucrats Accountable* (New York: Praeger, 1982); Martin Laffin, "Reinventing the Federal Government," in Christopher Peele, Christopher J. Bailey, Bruce Cain, and B. Guy Peters, eds., *Developments in American Politics 2* (Chatham, N.J.: Chatham House, 1995), 172–176.
[46]Phillip B. Heymann, *The Politics of Public Management* (New Haven, Conn.: Yale University Press, 1988); James G. Benze, Jr., *Presidential Power and Management Techniques* (New York: Greenwood Press, 1987).
[47]See Woll, *American Bureaucracy*, 207–229; Peter Szanton, *Federal Reorganization* (Chatham, N.J.: Chatham House, 1981).
[48]See Waterman, *Presidential Influence and the Administrative State.*
[49]James G. March and Johan P. Olson, "Organizing Political Life: What Administrative Reorganization Tells Us about Government," *American Political Science Review* 77 (June 1983): 281–296.
[50]Meier, *Regulation*, 110–111.
[51]Joel D. Aberbach, "The President and the Executive Branch," in Colin Campbell and Bert Rockman, eds., *The Bush Presidency: First Appraisals* (Chatham, N.J.: Chatham House, 1991), 232–235.
[52]See Richard P. Nathan, *The Plot That Failed: Nixon and the Administrative Presidency* (New York: Wiley, 1975); Paul C. Light, *Thickening Government: Federal Hierarchy and the Diffusion of Accountability* (Washington, D.C.: Brookings Institution, 1995).
[53]See Heclo, *A Government of Strangers.*
[54]See Wildavsky, *The Politics of the Budgetary Process.*
[55]Benjamin Ginsberg, *The Consequence of Consent* (New York: Random House, 1982), 207.

[56]See Ronald E. Kettl, *Deficit Politics* (New York: Macmillan, 1992).
[57]See Joel D. Aberbach, *Keeping a Watchful Eye* (Washington, D.C.: Brookings Institution, 1990).
[58]B. Dan Wood and Richard W. Waterman, "Political Control of the Bureaucracy," *American Political Science Review* 85 (September 1991): 820–821; see also Cathy Marie Johnson, *The Dynamics of Conflict between Bureaucrats and Legislators* (Armonk, N.Y.: Sharpe, 1992).
[59]Louis Fisher, *American Constitutional Law* (New York: McGraw-Hill, 1990), 280–281.
[60]See Theodore Lowi, *The End of Liberalism* (New York: Norton, 1979), 309–310.
[61]David Rosenbloom, "The Evolution of the Administrative State, and Transformations of Administrative Law," in David Rosenbloom and Richard Schwartz, eds., *Handbook of Regulation and Administrative Law* (New York: Dekker, 1994), 3–36.
[62]See *Vermont Yankee Nuclear Power Corp.* v. *National Resources Defense Council, Inc.*, 435 U.S. 519 (1978); *Chevron* v. *National Resources Defense Council*, 467 U.S. 837 (1984); *Heckler* v. *Chaney*, 470 U.S. 821 (1985).
[63]Roberta Ann Johnson and Michael E. Kraft, "Bureaucratic Whistleblowing and Policy Change," *Western Political Quarterly* 43 (December 1990): 849–874.
[64]Bob Cohn, "New Help for Whistle Blowers," *Newsweek*, June 27, 1988, 43.
[65]See Kathleen Staudt, *Women, Foreign Assistance, and Advocacy Administration* (New York: Praeger, 1985).
[66]Mosher, *Democracy and the Public Service*, 13.
[67]Levitan and Noden, *Working for the Sovereign*, 116.
[68]Meier and Nigro, "Representative Bureaucracy," 538.
[69]Ibid., 532.
[70]For a broad discussion of the issue of representativeness, see Samuel Krislov and David H. Rosenbloom, *Representative Bureaucracy and the American Political System* (New York: Praeger, 1981).
[71]David Osborne and Ted Gaebler, *Reinventing Government: How the Entrepreneurial Spirit Is Transforming the Public Sector* (New York: Addison-Wesley, 1992); see also Michael Barzelay and Babak J. Armajani, *Breaking through Bureaucracy* (Berkeley: University of California Press, 1992); Robert D. Behn, *Leadership Counts* (Cambridge, Mass.: Harvard University Press, 1991).
[72]Pfiffner, "The National Performance Review in Perspective," 7.
[73]Ronald C. Moe, "The 'Reinventing Government' Exercise: Misinterpreting the Problem, Misjudging the Results," *Public Administration Review* (March/April, 1994): 125–136.
[74]Tom Shoop, "From Citizens to Customers," *Government Executive* (May 1994): 27–30.
[75]See Mark Goldstein, *America's Hollow Government: How Washington Has Failed the People* (Homewood, Ill.: Business One Irwin, 1992).

Chapter 17

[1]*Marbury* v. *Madison*, 1 Cranch 137 (1803).
[2]Rebecca Mae Salokar, *The Solicitor General: The Politics of Law* (Philadelphia: Temple University Press, 1992); see also Cornell W. Clayton, *The Politics of Justice: The Attorney General and the Making of Legal Policy* (Armonk, N.Y.: Sharpe, 1992).
[3]D. Marie Provine, *Case Selection in the United States Supreme Court* (Chicago: University of Chicago Press, 1980), 62–63; see also H. W. Perry, *Deciding to Decide* (Cambridge, Mass.: Harvard University Press, 1991).
[4]Henry Glick, *Courts, Politics, and Justice*, 3d ed. (New York: McGraw-Hill, 1993), 214.
[5]See Saul Brenner, "The New Certiorari Game," *Journal of Politics* 41 (1979): 649–655; Donald R. Songer, "Concern for Policy Outputs as a Cue for Supreme Court Decisions on Certiorari," *Journal of Politics* 41 (1979): 1185–1194; S. Sidney Ulmer, "The Supreme Court's Certiorari Decisions: Conflict as a Predictive Variable," *American Political Science Review* 78 (1984): 901–911.
[6]Lawrence Baum, *The Supreme Court*, 5th ed. (Washington, D.C.: Congressional Quarterly Press, 1994), 117.
[7]*Brown* v. *Board of Education of Topeka*, 347 U.S. 483 (1954).
[8]*Gideon* v. *Wainwright*, 372 U.S. 335 (1963).
[9]From a letter to the author by Frank Schwartz of Beaver College, 1986. This section reflects substantially Professor Schwartz's recommendations to the author, as does the later section that addresses the "federal court myth."
[10]*Hutto* v. *Davis*, 370 U.S. 256 (1982).
[11]Howard Brownstein, "With or without Supreme Court Changes, Reagan Will Reshape the Federal Court," *National Journal*, December 8, 1984, 2238.
[12]Ibid.
[13]*Roe* v. *Wade*, 410 U.S. 113 (1973).
[14]David M. O'Brien, *Storm Center: The Supreme Court in American Politics*, 3d ed. (New York: Norton, 1993), 69–76.
[15]For a study of lower-court appointments, see Sheldon Goldman, "Reagan's Second-Term Judicial Appointments: The Battle at Midway," *Judicature* 70 (April-May 1987).
[16]Stephen L. Wasby, *The Supreme Court in the Federal Judicial System*, 4th ed. (Chicago: Nelson-Hall, 1993), 75.
[17]Henry J. Abraham, *The Judicial Process*, 6th ed. (New York: Oxford University Press, 1993), 24–26.
[18]Robert Scigliano, *The Supreme Court and the Presidency* (New York: Free Press, 1971), 146; see also David Savage, *Turning Right: The Making of the Rehnquist Supreme Court* (New York: Wiley, 1992).
[19]Quoted in Baum, *The Supreme Court*, 37.
[20]Herbert Jacob, *Justice in America: Courts, Lawyers, and the Judicial Process*, 4th ed. (Glenview, Ill.: Scott, Foresman, 1984), 122; Herman Schwartz, *Packing the Courts* (New York: Scribner's, 1988).
[21]John Gottschall, "Reagan's Appointments to the U.S. Courts of Appeals," 70 *Judicature* 48 (1986): 54.
[22]John Schmidhauser, *Judges and Justices: The Federal Appellate Judiciary* (Boston: Little, Brown, 1979), 84–85.
[23]Joseph B. Harris, *The Advice and Consent of the Senate* (Berkeley: University of California Press, 1953), 313.
[24]Goldman, "Reagan's Second-Term Judicial Appointments," 328, 331.
[25]Ibid.
[26]Henry J. Abraham, "The Judicial Function under the Constitution," *News for Teachers of Political Science* 41 (Spring 1984): 14; Sheldon Goldman, "Should There Be Affirmative Action for the Judiciary?" *Judicature* 62 (May 1979): 494.
[27]Quoted in Louis Fisher, *American Constitutional Law* (New York: McGraw-Hill, 1990), 5.
[28]Baum, *The Supreme Court*, 117.
[29]Quoted in Charles P. Curtis, *Law and Large as Life* (New York: Simon & Schuster, 1959), 156–157.

[30]See, for example, *Heart of Atlanta Motel* v. *United States*, 371 U.S. 241 (1964).
[31]Martin Shapiro, *The Supreme Court and Administrative Agencies* (New York: Free Press, 1968), 71.
[32]Wasby, *The Supreme Court in the Federal Judicial System*, 53.
[33]See Lee Epstein, *Conservatives in Court* (Knoxville: University of Tennessee Press, 1985), 80–88.
[34]John Schmidhauser, *The Supreme Court* (New York: Holt, Rinehart & Winston, 1964), 6.
[35]Jeffrey A. Segal and Harold J. Spaeth, *The Supreme Court and the Attitudinal Model* (New York: Cambridge University Press, 1993).
[36]David Rhode and Harold Spaeth, *Supreme Court Decision Making* (San Francisco: Freeman, 1976), 138.
[37]See Glendon Schubert, *The Judicial Mind* (Evanston, Ill.: Northwestern University Press, 1965); Glendon Schubert, *The Judicial Mind Revisited* (New York: Oxford University Press, 1974).
[38]O'Brien, *Storm Center*, 14–15.
[39]Ibid., 59–61.
[40]The references cited in the following sections are taken substantially from Abraham, "The Judicial Function," 12–14; see also Stephen C. Halpern and Charles M. Lamb, eds., *Supreme Court Activism and Restraint* (Lexington, Mass.: Lexington Books, 1982); Harry H. Wellington, *Interpreting the Constitution* (New Haven, Conn.: Yale University Press, 1990).
[41]Abraham, "The Judicial Function," 14.
[42]Alexander M. Bickel, *The Supreme Court and the Idea of Progress* (New Haven, Conn.: Yale University Press, 1978), 173–181.
[43]Ibid.
[44]Louis Lusky, *By What Right? A Commentary on the Supreme Court's Power to Revise the Constitution* (Charlottesville, Va.: Michie, 1975), 214–216.
[45]Ibid.
[46]*Griswold* v. *Connecticut*, 381 U.S. 479 (1965).
[47]*Reynolds* v. *Sims*, 377 U.S. 533 (1964).
[48]Abraham, "The Judicial Function," 13.
[49]See Michael J. Perry, *The Constitution and the Courts* (New York: Oxford University Press, 1994); Arthur Selwyn Miller, *Toward Increased Judicial Activism* (Westport, Conn.: Greenwood Press, 1982).
[50]*Gideon* v. *Wainwright*, 372 U.S. 335 (1963). Example and argument are from Richard A. Posner, "What Am I? A Potted Plant?" *The New Republic*, September 28, 1987, 25.
[51]"Good for the Left, Now Good for the Right," *Newsweek*, July 8, 1991, 22.

Chapter 18

[1]James E. Anderson, *The Emergence of the Modern Regulatory State* (Washington, D.C.: Public Affairs Press, 1962), 408.
[2]Murray Weidenbaum, "An Overview of Government Regulation," *Journal of Commercial Lending*, January 1981, 29; see also Marc Allen Eisner, *Regulatory Politics in Transition* (Baltimore: Johns Hopkins University Press, 1993).
[3]Paul Portney, "Beware of the Killer Clauses inside the GOP's 'Contract,'" *The Washington Post National Weekly Edition*, January 23–29, 1995, 21.
[4]See Larry N. Gerston, Cynthia Fraleigh, and Robert Schwab, *The Deregulated Society* (Pacific Grove, Calif.: Brooks/Cole, 1988).
[5]See Donald F. Kettl, "The Savings and Loan Bailout: The Mismatch between the Headlines and the Issues," *PS: Political Science and Politics* 23 (September 1991): 441–447.
[6]Henry C. Dethluff, *Americans and Free Enterprise* (Englewood Cliffs, N.J.: Prentice-Hall, 1971), 257.
[7]David E. Vogel, "The 'New' Social Regulation in Historical and Comparative Perspective," in Thomas McGraw, ed., *Regulation in Perspective* (Cambridge, Mass.: Harvard University Press, 1981), 173.
[8]Molly Ivins, "GOP Job Bill Is Truly Bad," *Syracuse Post-Standard*, February 15, 1995, A10.
[9]William Cilley III and James Miller III, "The New Social Regulation," in Ellen F. Paul and Phillip A. Russo, Jr., *Public Policy* (Chatham, N.J.: Chatham House, 1982), 216.
[10]Vogel, "'The New' Social Regulation," 173.
[11]"Tax Reform Means End of the Line for Many Corporations' Free Ride," *Syracuse Post-Standard*, April 29, 1988, A7.
[12]Bryan D. Jones and Lynn W. Bachelor with Carter Wilson, *The Sustaining Hand* (Lawrence: University of Kansas Press, 1986).
[13]*National Labor Relations Board* v. *Bildisco and Bildisco*, 465 U.S. 513 (1984).
[14]*Lechmere* v. *National Labor Relations Board*, 502 U.S. 527 (1992).
[15]See Kevin Phillips, *Boiling Point* (New York: Random House, 1993).
[16]See Robert Lekachman, *The Age of Keynes* (New York: Random House, 1966).
[17]"Balance by Amendment?" *The Wall Street Journal*, November 18, 1994, A18; see also Peter G. Peterson, *Facing Up* (New York: Simon & Schuster, 1993).
[18]See Bruce Bartlett, *Reaganomics: Supply-Side Economics* (Westport, Conn.: Arlington House, 1981); Kenneth Hoover and Raymond Plant, *Conservative Capitalism in Britain and the United States* (New York: Routledge, 1989).
[19]House Ways and Means Committee data, 1991.
[20]Phillips, *Boiling Point*.
[21]See Douglas Hibbs, "Political Parties and Macroeconomic Policy" *American Political Science Review* 77 (December 1977): 1467–1487; David Lowery, "The Keynesian and Political Determinants of Unbalanced Budgets: U.S. Fiscal Policy from Eisenhower to Reagan," *American Journal of Political Science* 29 (1985): 426.
[22]See Richard E. Cohen, "Rating Congress—A Guide Separating the Liberals from the Conservatives," *National Journal*, May 8, 1982, 800–810.
[23]Seymour Martin Lipset, "The Economy, Elections, and Public Opinions, "*Tocqueville Review* 5 (Fall 1983): 431.
[24]D. Roderick Kiewiet, *Macro-Economics and Micro-Politics* (Chicago: University of Chicago Press, 1983), 154–158; Donald R. Kinder and D. Roderick Kiewiet, "Economic Discontent and Political Behavior," *American Journal of Political Science* 23 (1979): 495–527.
[25]Howard S. Bloom and H. Douglas Price, "Voter Response to Short-Run Economic Conditions: The Asymmetric Effect of Prosperity and Recession," *American Political Science Review* 69 (1976): 1240–1254.
[26]Edward R. Tufte, *Political Control of the Economy* (Princeton, N.J.: Princeton University Press, 1978), ch. 5; Francisco Arcelus and Allen H. Meltzer, "The Effect of Aggregate Economic Variables on Congressional Elections," *American Political Science Review* 69 (1975): 1232–1239.

[27]Steven Pearlstein, "The Man Who Really Runs America," *The Washington Post National Weekly Edition*, February 6–12, 1995, 23.

Chapter 19

[1]Barbara Vobejda and Judith Havemann, "Let the Welfare Debate Begin," *The Washington Post National Weekly Edition*, January 23–27, 1995, 26.
[2]Robert Pear, "Meeting Narrows Discord on Change in Welfare Policy," *The New York Times*, January 29, 1995, 20.
[3]Vobejda and Havemann, "Let the Welfare Debate Begin," 26.
[4]Time/CNN survey by Yankelovich partners, December 7–8, 1994; for a broader view of public attitudes, see Fay Cook Lomax and Edith J. Barrett, *Support for the American Welfare State* (New York: Columbia University Press, 1992).
[5]Sar Levitan, *Programs in Aid of the Poor*, 6th ed. (Baltimore: Johns Hopkins University Press, 1990), 36–37; Michael J. Rich, *Federal Policymaking and the Poor* (Princeton, N.J.: Princeton University Press, 1993).
[6]William Julius Wilson, *The Truly Disadvantaged: The Inner City, the Underclass, and Public Policy* (Chicago: University of Chicago Press, 1987).
[7]Michael Harrington, *The Other America: Poverty in the United States* (New York: Macmillan, 1962); see also Sheldon H. Danziger, Gary D. Sandefur, and Daniel H. Weinberg, eds., *Confronting Poverty* (Cambridge, Mass.: Harvard University Press, 1994).
[8]James D. Wright, *Address Unknown: The Homeless in America* (New York: Aldine De Gruyter, 1989).
[9]Charles Murray, *Losing Ground: American Social Policy, 1950–1980* (New York: Basic Books, 1984).
[10]John J. DiIulio, "True Welfare Reform," *The Washington Post National Weekly Edition*, January 23–29, 1995, 20.
[11]See David T. Ellwood and Lawrence H. Summers, "Is Welfare Really the Problem?" *Public Interest* 83 (Spring 1986): 57–78.
[12]*Five Thousand American Families* (Ann Arbor: University of Michigan Institute for Social Research, 1977).
[13]Michael Kramer, "A Poverty of Compassion," *Time*, January 16, 1995, 32.
[14]See John E. Schwarz, *America's Hidden Success*, rev. ed. (New York: Norton, 1988).
[15]Everett Carll Ladd, *American Political Parties* (New York: Norton, 1970), 205.
[16]David B. Walker, *Toward a Functioning Federalism* (Cambridge, Mass.: Winthrop, 1981), 102.
[17]Pear, "Meeting Narrows Discord on Change in Welfare Policy," 20.
[18]V. O. Key, Jr., *The Responsible Electorate* (Cambridge, Mass.: Belknap Press of Harvard University, 1966), 43.
[19]See Jill Quadrangle, *The Transformation of Old Age Security* (Chicago: University of Chicago Press, 1988); Martha Derthick, *Policy Making for Social Security* (Washington, D.C.: Congressional Quarterly Press, 1979).
[20]Paul Light, *Artful Work: The Politics of Social Security* (New York: Random House, 1985), ch. 9.
[21]For a general overview of 1950s and 1960s policy disputes, see James Sundquist, *Politics and Policy* (Washington, D.C.: Brookings Institution, 1968).
[22]Hobart Rowan, "The Budget: Fact and Fiction," *The Washington Post National Weekly Edition*, January 16–22, 1995, 5.
[23]"Welfare: Myths, Reality," Knight-Ridder News Service story, *Syracuse Post-Standard*, December 5, 1994, A1, A6.
[24]Quoted in Malcolm Gladwell, "The Medicaid Muddle," *The Washington Post National Weekly Edition*, January 16–22, 1995, 31.
[25]Herbert McClosky and John Zaller, *The American Ethos* (Cambridge, Mass.: Harvard University Press, 1984), 18.
[26]Karl A. Lamb, *As Orange Goes: Twelve California Families and the Future of American Politics* (New York: Norton, 1974), 178.
[27]Constance Johnson and Penny Loeb, "Stupid Spending Tricks,"*U.S. News & World Report*, July 18, 1994, 26.
[28]Based on Organization for Economic Co-Operation and Development (OECD) data, 1993.
[29]Jonathan Kozol, *Illiterate America* (Garden City, N.Y.: Anchor Press/Doubleday, 1985).
[30]Laurel Shaper Walters, "World Educators Compare Notes," *Christian Science Monitor*, September 7, 1994, 8.
[31]See John E. Chubb and Terry M. Moe, *Politics, Markets, and America's Schools* (Washington, D.C.: Brookings Institution, 1990).
[32]Matt Clark, "Forgotten Patients," *Newsweek*, August 22, 1988, 52.
[33]See Daniel Patrick Moynihan, *The Politics of a Guaranteed Income* (New York: Random House, 1973), 446.
[34]See William Mitchell, *The Popularity of Social Security: A Political Paradox* (Washington, D.C.: American Enterprise Institute, 1977).
[35]Robert J. Samuelson, "Sowing More Cynicism," *Newsweek*, October 24, 1994, 45.
[36]Pear, "Meeting Narrows Discord on Change in Welfare Policy," 20.

Chapter 20

[1]"Pageantry Aside, Summits Do Work," *Syracuse Post-Standard*, July 11, 1994, A4.
[2]"Yeltsin Joins Fold at Summit," *Syracuse Post-Standard*, July 11, 1994, A1.
[3]American Assembly Report (cosponsored by the Council on Foreign Relations), *Rethinking America's Security*, (New York: Harriman, 1991), 8.
[4]For an overview of Soviet policy, see Alvin Z. Rubenstein, *Soviet Foreign Policy since World War II*, 4th ed. (New York: HarperCollins, 1992); for an assessment of U.S. policy, see Robert Dallek, *The American Style of Foreign Policy* (New York: Oxford University Press, 1990).
[5]See John Lewis Gaddis, *Strategies of Containment* (New York: Oxford University Press, 1982).
[6]Mr. X. (George Kennan), "The Sources of Soviet Conduct," *Foreign Affairs* 25 (July 1947): 566–582.
[7]See David Halberstam, *The Making of a Quagmire: America and Vietnam during the Kennedy Era*, 2d ed. (New York: Random House, 1988); Stanley Karnow, *Vietnam: A History* (New York: Penguin, 1983); Guenter Lewy, *America in Vietnam* (New York: Oxford University Press, 1980); David M. Barrett, *Uncertain Warriors: Lyndon Johnson and His Vietnam Advisors* (Lawrence: University of Kansas Press, 1993).
[8]Charles Kegley and Eugene Wittkopf, *American Foreign Policy*, 2d ed. (New York: St. Martin's Press, 1982), 48.
[9]See Keith L. Nelson, *The Making of Détente* (Baltimore: Johns Hopkins University Press, 1995).
[10]Robert G. Kaiser, "U.S.-Soviet Relations: Goodbye to Détente," *Foreign Affairs* 59 (Winter 1979/1980): 500–521.

[11]See Russell J. Ling, "R eagan and the Russians," *American Political Science Review* 78 (June 1984): 338–355; Seweryn Bialer and Joan Afferica, "Reagan and Russia," *Foreign Affairs* 61 (Winter 1982/1983): 249–271.

[12]See William Zimmerman and Glenn Palmer, "Words and Deeds in Soviet Foreign Policy: The Case of Soviet Military Expenditures," *American Political Science Review* 77 (June 1983): 358–367.

[13]For a general view of America's new world role, see Kenneth A. Oye, Robert J. Lieber, and Donald Rothchild, *Eagle in a New World: American Grand Strategy in the Post-Cold War Era* (New York: HarperCollins, 1992).

[14]Ruth Marcus and John F. Harris, "Ditching Bosnia to Keep NATO," *The Washington Post National Weekly Edition,* December 12–18, 1994, 16.

[15]"The CIA's Next Generation," *Newsweek,* February 17, 1992, 27.

[16]See Rhodri Jeffreys-Jones, *The CIA and American Democracy* (New Haven, Conn.: Yale University Press, 1989); Loch K. Johnson, *America's Secret Power* (New York: Oxford University Press, 1989).

[17]See Barry Rubin, *Secrets of State: The State Department and the Struggle over U.S. Foreign Policy* (New York: Oxford University Press, 1985).

[18]Adam Roberts and Benedict Kingsbury, *United Nations, Divided World,* 2d ed. (New York: Oxford University Press, 1993).

[19]John Barry, "The Battle over Warfare," *Newsweek,* December 5, 1994, 27–28.

[20]See Jerome H. Kahan, *Security in the Nuclear Age* (Washington, D.C.: Brookings Institution, 1975); Glenn Snyder, *Deterrence and Defense* (Princeton, N.J.: Princeton University Press, 1961); Spurgeon M. Keeny, Jr., and Wolfgang K. H. Panofsky, "MAD vs. NUTS: The Mutual Hostage Relationship of the Superpowers," *Foreign Affairs* 60 (Winter 1981/1982): 287–304; Robert Jervis, *The Illogic of American Nuclear Strategy* (Ithaca, N.Y.: Cornell University Press, 1984).

[21]Richard J. Barnet, "Reflections: The Disorders of Peace," *The New Yorker,* January 20, 1992, 61; see also George H. Quester, *The Future of Nuclear Deterrence* (Lexington, Mass.: Lexington Books, 1986).

[22]See James M. Lindsay, *Congress and the Politics of U.S. Foreign Policy* (Baltimore: Johns Hopkins University Press, 1994); William Conrad Gibbons, *The U.S. Government and the Vietnam War* (Washington, D.C.: U.S. Government Printing Office, 1994).

[23]Murray L. Weidenbaum, *Small Wars, Big Defense* (New York: Oxford University Press, 1992).

[24]See Steve Rosen, *Testing Theories of the Military-Industrial Complex* (Lexington, Mass.: Lexington Books, 1973), 1.

[25]"The B-1: A Flight through Adversity," *Los Angeles Times,* reprinted in *Syracuse Post-Standard,* July 29, 1983, A7.

[26]Seymour Melman, *Pentagon Capitalism* (New York: McGraw-Hill, 1970), 175; Paul A. Koistinen, *The Military-Industrial Complex* (New York: Praeger, 1980).

[27]"Merchants Go Great Guns after Cold War," *The Wall Street Journal,* January 28, 1994, A6.

[28]Mark Thompson, "Going Up in Arms," *Time,* December 12, 1994, 48.

[29]See Elie Abel, *The Shattered Bloc: Beyond the Upheaval in Eastern Europe* (Boston: Houghton Mifflin, 1990).

[30]Paul Kennedy, *The Rise and Decline of the Great Powers* (New York: Random House, 1988); for an alternative view, see Joseph Nye, *Bound to Lead: The Changing Nature of American Power* (New York: Basic Books, 1990).

[31]William Diebold, Jr., "The United States in the World Economy: A Fifty-Year Perspective," *Foreign Affairs* 62 (Fall 1983): 81–104; see also Walter Russell Mead, *Mortal Splendor: The American Empire in Transition* (Boston: Houghton Mifflin, 1987).

[32]See Robert W. Tucker, "America in Decline: The Foreign Policy Maturity," *Foreign Affairs* 58 (Winter 1979/1980): 449–484.

[33]Peter G. Peterson, "The Morning After," *Atlantic Monthly,* October 1987, 46.

[34]American Assembly, *Rethinking America's Security,* 9; see also Robert O. Keohane, Joseph S. Nye, and Stanley Hoffmann, eds., *After the Cold War* (Cambridge, Mass.: Harvard University Press, 1993).

[35]Peter Behr, "What We Gave and What We GATT," *The Washington Post National Weekly Edition,* December 12–18, 1994, 220.

[36]Harry Magdoff, *The Age of Imperialism: The Economics of U.S. Foreign Policy* (New York: Monthly Review Press, 1969), 43.

[37]See Robert O. Keohane and Joseph S. Nye, *Power and Interdependence: World Politics in Transition,* 2d ed. (Boston: Little, Brown, 1989).

[38]Tom Masland, "Going Down the Aid 'Rathole'?" *Newsweek,* December 5, 1994, 39.

[39]Hobart Rowen, "The Budget: Fact and Fiction," *The Washington Post National Weekly Edition,* January 16–22, 1995, 5.

Chapter 21

[1]E. E. Schattschneider *Two Hundred Million Americans in Search of a Government,* (New York: Holt, Rinehart & Winston, 1969), 42.

[2]Quoted in "Problems of Governance,"A Report to the Ford Foundation, The Maxwell School of Citizenship, Syracuse University, Syracuse, New York, December, 1991, 25.

[3]Ibid., 27.

[4]Internal Revenue Sevice figures, cited in Donald L. Barlett and James B. Steel, "Rules of the Gamed Rigged to Favor Rich and Influential," *Syracuse Herald American,,* January 5, 1992, E4.

[5]Quoted in "Problems of Governance," 16.

[6]Ibid., 26.

[7]David Mathews, "We, the People . . . ," *National Forum* 50 (Fall 1983): 65.

[8]Cited in Ralph Volney Harlow, *The Growth of the United States,* vol. 2 (New York: 1943), 134.

[9]U.S. Bureau of the Census data, 1992.

[10]Quoted in "Problems of Governance," 15.

Appendix: State and Local Politics

[1]Daniel Elazar, *American Federalism: A View from the States,* 2d ed. (New York: Crowell, 1972).

[2]Kim Quaile Hill and Kenneth R. Mladenka, *Democratic Governance in American States and Cities* (Pacific Grove, Calif.: Brooks/Cole, 1992), 39–44.

[3]John F. Dillon, *Commentaries on the Law of Municipal Corporations* (Boston: Little, Brown, 1881).

[4]Thad L. Beyle, "Governors," in Virginia Gray, Herbert Jacob,

and Kenneth N. Vines, eds., *Politics in the American States: A Comparative Analysis*, 4th ed. (Boston: Little, Brown, 1983), 202.

[5]*Baker* v. *Carr,* 369 U.S. 186 (1962); *Gray* v. *Sanders,* 372 U.S. 368 (1963); *Reynolds* v. *Sims,* 377 U.S. 533 (1964).

[6]Advisory Commission on Intergovernmental Relations (ACIR), *The Question of State Government Capability* (Washington, D.C.: ACIR, 1985), 123.

[7]V. O. Key, Jr., *Southern Politics* (New York: Knopf, 1949), 495.

[8]Michael M. Gant and Norman R. Luttbeg, *American Electoral Behavior* (Itasca, Ill.: Peacock, 1991), 110.

[9]*San Antonio Independent School District* v. *Rodriguez,* 411 U.S. 1 (1973).

[10]Advisory Commission on Intergovernmental Relations, *Significant Features of Fiscal Federalism* (Washington, D.C.: U.S. Government Printing Office, 1994): 120–121.

[11]David Osborne, *Laboratories of Democracy: A New Breed of Governor Creates Models for National Growth* (Cambridge, Mass.: Harvard Business School Press, 1988).

AUTHOR INDEX*

*Note: The single entries (e.g., 455) refer to text pages. The double entries refer to notes (e.g., 20-29 is a reference to note 29 in Chapter 20). The notes follow the appendixes (pages A-35 through A-53).

SUBJECT INDEX*

Note: **Bold** pages indicate glossary terms.

CREDITS

Chapter 1, Figure: From Times-Mirror Center for The People & The Press Survey, 1990–1991. Copyright, 1990–1991, *Los Angeles Times.* Reprinted with permission.

Chapter 1, Figure: From *The Civic Culture* by Gabriel Almond and Sidney Verba, Little, Brown and Company, 1965, p. 64.

Figure 1-1: From Times-Mirror Center for The People & The Press Surveys, 1990–1991. Copyright, 1990–1991, *Los Angeles Times.* Reprinted with permission.

Figure 1-4: From August 1994 Survey. Reprinted by permission of Frank Luntz Research Companies.

Figure 1-6: Adapted from *The American Ethos: Public Attitudes Toward Capitalism and Democracy* by Herbert McClosky and John Zaller, Harvard University Press, 1994, pp. 133 and 140, Tables 5-1 and 5-3.

Chapter 2, Table: From National Education Association. *1993–1994 Estimates of School Statistics.* Washington, D.C.: NEA. 1944. Reprinted with permission.

Figure 3-2: From CBS News/New York Times poll, September 8–11, 1994.

Chapter 4, Figure: From "Locking People Up Around the World," *U.S. News and World Report,* September 19, 1994, p. 17. Reprinted by permission of U.S. News and World Report.

Figure 4-3: From NBC/Wall Street Journal poll, April 17–20, 1993. Reprinted by permission of *The Wall Street Journal,* © 1993 Dow Jones & Company, Inc. All Rights Reserved Worldwide.

Figure 4-4: From Time/CNN Survey, January 17–18, 1994. Reprinted with permission of Yankelovich Partners Inc.

Table 5-2: From Latino National Political Survey, reported in R. O. de la Garza, A. Falcon, F. C. Garcia, and J. A. Garcia, "Hispanic Americans in the Mainstream of U.S. Politics," *The Public Perspective,* July/August 1992, p. 19. © *The Public Perspective,* a publication of the Roper Center for Public Opinion Research, University of Connecticut, Storrs. Reprinted by permission.

Table 5-4: From *The Wall Street Journal,* February 15, 1994. Reprinted by permission of *The Wall Street Journal,* © 1994 Dow Jones & Company, Inc. All Rights Reserved Worldwide.

Chapter 5, Box: From "The News in Black and White," *Media Monitor,* 4, February 1990, pp. 1–6; and from "The Rodney King Case, Part II," *Media Monitor,* 7, April 1993., pp 1–6. *Media Monitor* is the Center for Media & Public Affair's regular newsletter. CMPA is a nonprofit and nonpartisan research organization that uses scientific content analysis to study how networks cover major news stories.

Chapter 6, Figure: Adapted from Wright, Gerald C., Robert S. Erikson, and John P. McIver. "Public Opinion and Policy Liberalism in the American States." *American Journal of Political Science,* Volume 31 (November, 1987): 989. Reprinted by permission of The University of Wisconsin Press.

Figure 7-6: From National Opinion Research Center Survey, 1990. Reprinted by permission.

Figure 7-6: From Roper Surveys, 1993. Reprinted by permission of Roper Starch Worldwide.

Figure 7-7: From H. I. Anheier, L. M. Salamon, and E. Archambault, "Participating Citizens: U.S.-Europe Comparisons in Volunteer Action," *The Public Perspective,* March/April 1994, p. 17. © *The Public Perspective,* a publication of the Roper Center for Public Opinion Research, University of Connecticut, Storrs. Reprinted by permission.

Chapter 7, Table: From "Mixed Message about Press Freedom on Both Sides of the Atlantic," Times-Mirror Center for The People & The Press, March 16, 1994, pp. 30–31. Copyright, 1994, *Los Angeles Times.* Reprinted with permission.

Table 8-2: From CBS News/New York Times surveys, 1992.

Table 9-1: Adapted from Gibson, James L., John P. Frendreis, and Laura Vertz. "Party Dynamics in the 1980's. *American Journal of Political Science,* Volume 33 (February, 1989): 73–74. Reprinted by permission of The University of Wisconsin Press.

Figure 9-4: From CBS News/New York Times poll, September 8–11, 1994.

Chapter 10, Box: From "Diagnosing Health Care Reform," *Media Monitor,* May/June 1994, p. 2. *Media Monitor* is the Center for Media & Public Affair's regular newsletter. CMPA is a nonprofit and nonpartisan research organization that uses scientific content analysis to study how networks cover major news stories.

Figure 11-1: From *Out of Order* by Thomas E. Patterson. Copyright © 1993 by Thomas E. Patterson. Reprinted by permission of Alfred A. Knopf, Inc.

Figure 11-3: Adapted from Daniel C. Hallin, "Sound Bite News: Television Coverage of Elections 1968–1988," *Journal of Communication,* Spring 1992, p. 6. Reprinted with permission of Oxford University Press.

Figure 11-3: Data from "Clinton's the One," *Media Monitor,* November 1992, p. 2. *Media Monitor* is the Center for Media & Public Affair's regular newsletter. CMPA is a nonprofit and nonpartisan research organization that uses scientific content analysis to study how networks cover major news stories.

Chapter 11, Table: From *Editor & Publisher International Yearbook, 1992, Annual.* Reprinted by permission.

Figure 11-4: From *Out of Order* by Thomas E. Patterson. Copyright © 1993 by Thomas E. Patterson. Reprinted by permission of Alfred A. Knopf. Inc.

Figure 11-5: From Times-Mirror Center for The People & The Press Surveys, April and July 1994. Copyright, 1994, *Los Angeles Times.* Reprinted with permission.

Table 12-1: From *Congressional Quarterly Weekly Report,* various dates. Reprinted by permission of Congressional Quarterly, Inc.

Figure 12-1: From *Congressional Quarterly Weekly Report,* various dates. Reprinted by permission of Congressional Quarterly, Inc.

Figure 13-5: Adapted from Richard E. Cohen and William Schneider, "Epitaph for an Era," *National Journal,* January 14, 1995, p. 83. Copyright 1995 by National Journal, Inc. All rights reserved. Reprinted by permission.

Chapter 13, Figure: From "Mixed Message about Press Freedom on Both Sides of the Atlantic," Times-Mirror Center for The People & The Press, March 16, 1994, p. 55. Copyright, 1994, *Los Angeles Times.* Reprinted with permission.

Chapter 14, quote: From *Out of Order* by Thomas E. Patterson. Copyright © 1933 by Thomas E. Patterson. Reprinted by permission of Alfred A. Knopf, Inc.

Figure 15-1: From *Congressional Quarterly Weekly Report,* December 31, 1994, p. 3620. Reprinted by permission of Congressional Quarterly, Inc.

Table 15-1: From *Congressional Quarterly Weekly Report,* January 7, 1989. Reprinted by permission of Congressional Quarterly, Inc.

Chapter 15, Table: From *Congressional Quarterly Weekly Report,* December 31, 1994, pp. 3655–3657. Reprinted by permission of Congressional Quarterly, Inc.

Chapter 15, Box: From "The Honeymoon that Wasn't ," *Media Monitor,* 7, no. 7, September/October 1993, pp 2–3; and from "They're No Friends of Bill," *Media Monitor,* 8, no. 4, July/August, 1994, p. 1. *Media Monitor* is the Center for Media & Public Affair's regular newsletter. CMPA is a nonprofit and nonpartisan research organization that uses scientific content analysis to study how networks cover major news stories.

Figure 15-2: From "They're No Friends of Bill," *Media Monitor,* July/August, 1994, p. 5. *Media Monitor* is the Center for Media & Public Affair's regular newsletter. CMPA is a nonprofit and nonpartisan research organization that uses scientific content analysis to study how networks cover major news stories.

Chapter 16, Figure: From "The Honeymoon that Wasn't," *Media Monitor,* September/October 1993, pp. 5. *Media Monitor* is the Center for Media & Public Affair's regular newsletter. CMPA is a nonprofit and nonpartisan research organization that uses scientific content analysis to study how networks cover major news stories.

Figures 16-3, 16-4: Adapted from B. Dan Wood and Richard W. Waterman, "Political Control of the Bureaucracy," *American Political Science Review,* 85, September 1991, pp. 810 and 821. Reprinted by permission of American Political Science Association.

Table 16-4: From Joel D. Aberbach, "The President and the Executive Branch," in *The Bush Presidency: First Appraisals,* edited by Colin Campbell and Bert A. Rockman, 1991, p. 234. © 1991 by Chatham House Publishers, Inc.

Table 17-2: "Judicial Appointees of: Carter, Reagan, Bush, Clinton." Reprinted by permission of People for the American Way.

Chapter 17, Table: From *Comparative Constitutional Law* by Mauro Cappelletti and William Cohen, 1979, Chapter 4. Reprinted by permission of The Michie Company. All rights reserved.

Figure 18-1: From Time/CNN Survey by Yankelovich Partners, June 2, 1994. Reprinted with permission of Yankelovich Partners Inc.

Figure 18-6: From NBC News/Wall Street Journal poll, July 1994. Reprinted by permission of *The Wall Street Journal,* © 1994 Dow Jones & Company, Inc. All Rights Reserved Worldwide.

Figure 19-2: From Time/CNN Survey, December 7–8, 1994. Reprinted with permission of Yankelovich Partners Inc.

Chapter 19 Figure: From Time/CNN Survey, December, 1994. Reprinted with permission of Yankelovich Partners Inc.

Figure 19-6: From CBS News Survey, November 27–28, 1994. Reprinted by permission of CBS News Polls.